GENDER AND LAW

ASPEN CASEBOOK SERIES

GENDER AND LAW

THEORY, DOCTRINE, COMMENTARY

NINTH EDITION

KATHARINE T. BARTLETT
A. KENNETH PYE PROFESSOR EMERITA OF LAW
DUKE UNIVERSITY SCHOOL OF LAW

DEBORAH L. RHODE
LATE ERNEST W. MCFARLAND PROFESSOR OF LAW
STANFORD UNIVERSITY LAW SCHOOL

JOANNA L. GROSSMAN
ELLEN K. SOLENDER ENDOWED CHAIR IN WOMEN
AND THE LAW AND PROFESSOR OF LAW
SMU DEDMAN SCHOOL OF LAW

DEBORAH L. BRAKE
JOHN E. MURRAY FACULTY SCHOLAR AND PROFESSOR OF LAW
ASSOCIATE DEAN FOR RESEARCH AND FACULTY DEVELOPMENT
UNIVERSITY OF PITTSBURGH SCHOOL OF LAW

FRANK RUDY COOPER
WILLIAM S. BOYD PROFESSOR OF LAW
DIRECTOR, PROGRAM ON RACE, GENDER & POLICING
WILLIAM S. BOYD SCHOOL OF LAW AT THE
UNIVERSITY OF NEVADA, LAS VEGAS

ASPEN PUBLISHING

To contact Customer Service, e-mail customer.service@aspenpublishing.com, call 1-800-950-5259, or mail correspondence to:

Aspen Publishing
Attn: Order Department
PO Box 990
Frederick, MD 21705

Printed in the United States of America.

1 2 3 4 5 6 7 8 9 0

ISBN 979-8-8861-4346-1

Library of Congress Cataloging-in-Publication Data
Names: Bartlett, Katharine T., author. | Rhode, Deborah L., author. | Grossman, Joanna L., author. | Brake, Deborah L., author. | Cooper, Frank Rudy, author.
Title: Gender and law : theory, doctrine, commentary / Katharine T. Bartlett, A. Kenneth Pye Professor Emerita of Law, Duke University School of Law; Deborah L. Rhode, Late Ernest W. McFarland Professor of Law, Stanford University Law School; Joanna L. Grossman, Ellen K. Solender Endowed Chair in Women and the Law and Professor of Law, SMU Dedman School of Law; Deborah L. Brake, John E. Murray Faculty Scholar and Professor of Law, Associate Dean for Research and Faculty Development, University of Pittsburgh School of Law; Frank Rudy Cooper, William S. Boyd Professor of Law Director, Program on Race, Gender & Policing, William S. Boyd School of Law at the University of Nevada, Las Vegas.
Description: Ninth edition. | Frederick, MD : Aspen Publishing, [2023] | Series: Aspen casebook series | Includes bibliographical references and index. | Summary: "Casebook to be used as a text in law school courses on Gender and Law, Women and Law, and Sexual Discrimination"— Provided by publisher.
Identifiers: LCCN 2022042762 | ISBN 9798886143461 (hardcover) | ISBN 9798886143478 (ebook)
Subjects: LCSH: Women—Legal status, laws, etc.—United States. | Sex and law—United States. | Sex discrimination against women—Law and legislation—United States. | Feminist jurisprudence—United States. | LCGFT: Casebooks (Law)
Classification: LCC KF478 .B37 2023 | DDC 342.7308/78—dc23/eng/20220924

About Aspen Publishing

Aspen Publishing is a leading provider of educational content and digital learning solutions to law schools in the U.S. and around the world. Aspen provides best-in-class solutions for legal education through authoritative textbooks, written by renowned authors, and breakthrough products such as Connected eBooks, Connected Quizzing, and PracticePerfect.

The Aspen Casebook Series (famously known among law faculty and students as the "red and black" casebooks) encompasses hundreds of highly regarded textbooks in more than eighty disciplines, from large enrollment courses, such as Torts and Contracts to emerging electives such as Sustainability and the Law of Policing. Study aids such as the *Examples & Explanations* and the *Emanuel Law Outlines* series, both highly popular collections, help law students master complex subject matter.

Major products, programs, and initiatives include:

- **Connected eBooks** are enhanced digital textbooks and study aids that come with a suite of online content and learning tools designed to maximize student success. Designed in collaboration with hundreds of faculty and students, the Connected eBook is a significant leap forward in the legal education learning tools available to students.
- **Connected Quizzing** is an easy-to-use formative assessment tool that tests law students' understanding and provides timely feedback to improve learning outcomes. Delivered through CasebookConnect.com, the learning platform already used by students to access their Aspen casebooks, Connected Quizzing is simple to implement and integrates seamlessly with law school course curricula.
- **PracticePerfect** is a visually engaging, interactive study aid to explain commonly encountered legal doctrines through easy-to-understand animated videos, illustrative examples, and numerous practice questions. Developed by a team of experts, PracticePerfect is the ideal study companion for today's law students.
- The **Aspen Learning Library** enables law schools to provide their students with access to the most popular study aids on the market across all of their courses. Available through an annual subscription, the online library consists of study aids in e-book, audio, and video formats with full text search, note-taking, and highlighting capabilities.
- Aspen's **Digital Bookshelf** is an institutional-level online education bookshelf, consolidating everything students and professors need to ensure success. This program ensures that every student has access to affordable course materials from day one.
- **Leading Edge** is a community centered on thinking differently about legal education and putting those thoughts into actionable strategies. At the core of the program is the Leading Edge Conference, an annual gathering of legal education thought leaders looking to pool ideas and identify promising directions of exploration.

To the late Deborah Rhode, a foremother of gender law.

Summary of Contents

CONTENTS

True to its initial vision thirty years ago, this ninth edition organizes the field of gender and law into five theoretical perspectives: formal equality, substantive equality, difference theory, nonsubordination, and autonomy. These perspectives are not mutually exclusive, nor are they "total" theories intended to answer every doctrinal and policy question that may arise concerning the relationship between gender and law. Rather, they represent alternative diagnostic and normative lenses through which the relationship between law and gender can be understood and improved. We believe that each theoretical framework has significant value and limitations. The approach of this book works best if readers attempt to be both open to, and critical of, each perspective. An introduction provides students with an overview of each of the five theoretical models and then introduces three critical perspectives that complicate, challenge, and enrich these theories: the contested nature of the male-female binary and the issues that arise from classification by sex, gender, gender identity, and sexual orientation; intersectionality analysis; and masculinities theory. These adjacent theories are then explored throughout the book.

As the field of gender law has grown, it now touches virtually every area of law and policy. It is also a field that is in flux, as political and ideological battles play out in legislatures and courts across the country. The updates in this edition include coverage of the elimination of constitutional protection for abortion, the recognition of protection against sexual orientation and identity discrimination, bans on participation by transgender athletes, and numerous other developments. As with earlier editions, this edition provides comprehensive coverage of gender issues as they relate to work, education, intimate relationships, and sexual violence; it also draws out connections to less obvious contexts—insurance and public benefits law, for example, as well as legal ethics, contract law, property law, public health, and criminal justice reforms addressing mass incarceration.

This edition retains the integration of theory and practice for which the book is known. We have added dozens more problems, almost all of them from actual cases or disputes. If anyone believes that the gender problem in this society has been solved, we can report that the easiest part of keeping this book up to date remains finding fresh examples of gender controversy with the potential to challenge ordinary understandings of gender justice and gender progress.

We feel it once more necessary to say that, with respect to edited materials in this book, additions to, deletions from, and other alterations to quoted material are indicated by brackets and ellipses, except for footnotes and citations, which are typically deleted without notice. Where retained, original footnote numbering is used. Paragraph breaks and the order of paragraphs are occasionally modified without notice to make edited excerpts easier to follow.

We appreciate your use of this book and welcome your feedback, including feedback by students, to make it better. The book is committed to helping all audiences think more critically, broadly, and deeply in their analysis of gender and law. But, like gender law more generally, the book is an ongoing work in progress. Thanks for being part of the process of keeping the field responsive to social and legal realities.

Katharine T. Bartlett
Duke University School of Law

Joanna L. Grossman
SMU Dedman School of Law

Deborah L. Brake
University of Pittsburgh School of Law

Frank Rudy Cooper
*William S. Boyd School of Law at the
University of Nevada, Law Vegas*

November 2022

This book has been a truly collaborative effort. While each section had a lead author, it went through numerous drafts as we discussed, refined, expanded, shortened, reorganized, and edited the material. In addition, the book benefited from feedback from an expanding circle of faculty who use the book in their teaching, students enrolled in their courses, and practitioners who have used the book as a source. We are saddened to have lost our friend and co-author Deborah L. Rhode, to whom we dedicate this edition. Deborah passed away in January 2021, but her significant and invaluable contributions to the book carry on in this edition, as do her monumental insights that helped shape the field of gender law more broadly. We are excited to welcome Frank Rudy Cooper as a co-author on this edition. Thank you to Samara Taper and Christa Bunce, law students at SMU; and to Justin Iverson, Research Librarian and Assistant Professor, and Carressa Browder, Administrative Assistant, of the Boyd School of Law at UNLV.

American Law Institute, Model Penal Code § 213(e). Copyright © by the American the American Law Institute. Reprinted with permission.

Leslie Bender, A Lawyer's Primer on Feminist Theory and Tort, 38 J. Legal Educ. 3 (1988). Copyright © 1988 by the Association of American Law Schools. Reprinted with permission of the author and publisher.

Kingsley R. Browne, Sex and Temperament in Modern Society: A Darwinian View of the Glass Ceiling and the Gender Gap, 37 Ariz. L. Rev. 971 (1995). Copyright © 1995 by Arizona Board of Regents and Kingsley R. Browne. Reprinted with permission of the author and publisher.

Erin Buzuvis, Sarah Litwin & Warren K. Zola, Sport Is for Everyone: A Legal Roadmap for Transgender Participation in Sport, 31 J. Legal Aspects of Sport 212, 232-36 (2021).

Naomi R. Cahn & Linda C. McClain, Gendered Complications of Covid-19: Towards a Feminist Recovery Plan, 22 Geo. J. Gender & L. 1 (2020). Reprinted with permission of the authors.

Devon W. Carbado & Mitu Gulati, The Fifth Black Woman, 11 J. Contemp. Legal Issues 701 (2001). Copyright © 2001 The Journal of Contemporary Legal Issues. Reprinted with permission of the authors and publisher.

Martha Chamallas, Listening to Dr. Fiske: The Easy Case of *Price Waterhouse v. Hopkins*, 15 Vt. L. Rev. 89 (1999). Reprinted with permission of the author and publisher.

Donna K. Coker, Heat of Passion and Wife Killing: Men Who Batter/Men Who Kill, 2 S. Cal. Rev. L. & Women's Stud. 71 (1992). Reprinted with permission of the author and publisher.

Frank Rudy Cooper, "Who's the Man?" Masculinities Studies, Terry Stops, and Police Training, 18 Colum. J. Gender & L. 671 (2009). Reprinted with permission of the author.

Nancy E. Dowd, Asking the Man Question: Masculinities Analysis and Feminist Theory, 33 Harv. J. L. & Gender 415. Reprinted with permission.

Elizabeth Emens, *Life Admin: How I Learned to Do Less, Do Better, and Live More* (2019). New York, NY: Houghton Mifflin Harcourt Trade & Reference Publishers.

Martha Albertson Fineman, Cracking the Foundational Myths: Independence, Autonomy, and Self- Sufficiency, 8 Am. U. J. Gender Soc. Pol'y & L. 13 (2000). Reprinted with permission of the author and publisher.

Karla Fischer, Neil Vidmar, & René Ellis, The Culture of Battering and the Role of Mediation in Domestic Violence Cases, 46 SMU L. Rev. 2117 (1993). Reprinted by permission of the authors, the SMU Law Review, and the Southern Methodist University Dedman School of Law.

Katharine Francke, The Central Mistake of Sex Discrimination Law: The Disaggregation of Sex from Gender, 144 U. Pa. L. Rev. 1, 1-4 (1995). Reprinted with permission.

Katharine Francke, Theorizing Yes: An Essay on Feminism, Law, and Desire, 101 Colum. L. Rev. 181, 186-87 (2001). Reprinted with permission.

Sara Sternberg Greene, The Bootstrap Trap, 67 Duke L.J. 233, 235-41 (2017). Reprinted with permission.

Joanna L. Grossman, Pregnancy, Work, and the Promise of Equal Citizenship, 98 Geo. L. Rev. 567 (2010). Reprinted with permission of the author.

L. Camille Hébert, The Economic Implications of Sexual Harassment for Women, 3 Kan. J.L. & Pub. Pol'y 41 (Spring 1994). Reprinted with permission of the author and publisher.

Herma Hill Kay, Equality and Difference: The Case of Pregnancy, 1 Berkeley Women's L.J. 1 (1985). Reprinted from 1 Berkeley Women's L.J. Copyright © 1985 by the Regents of the University of California. Reprinted with permission of the author and of the Regents of the University of California.

Jerry Kang et al., Implicit Bias in the Courtroom, 59 UCLA L. Rev. 1124 (2012). Reprinted with permission.

Dorchen Leidholdt, Prostitution: A Violation of Women's Human Rights, 1 Cardozo Women's L.J. 133 (1993). This article originally appeared in 1 Cardozo Women's L.J. 133 (1993). Reprinted with permission of the author and publisher.

Catharine A. MacKinnon, Feminism Unmodified: Discourses on Life and Law (1987). Copyright ©1987 by the President and Fellows of Harvard College. Reprinted with permission of the author.

Martha R. Mahoney, Legal Images of Battered Women: Redefining the Issue of Separation, 90 Mich. L. Rev. 1 (1991). Reprinted with permission of the author and publisher.

L. Amede Obiora, Bridges and Barricades: Rethinking Polemics and Intransience in the Campaign Against Female Circumcision, 47 Case W. Res. L. Rev. 275 (1997). Reprinted with permission of the author and publisher.

Richard A. Posner, Conservative Feminism, 1989 U. Chi. Legal F. 191 (1989). Originally appeared in the University of Chicago Legal Forum, Vol. 1989. Reprinted with permission of the author and from the University of Chicago Legal Forum and the University of Chicago Law School.

Rachel Rebouché, Reproducing Rights: The Intersection of Reproductive Justice and Human Rights, 7 UC Irvine L. Rev. 579, 591-95 (2017). Reprinted with permission.

Darren Rosenblum, Unsex Mothering: Toward a New Culture of Parenting, 35 Harv. J.L. & Gender 57, 58 (2012). Reprinted with permission of the author and publisher.

Andrea Kupfer Schneider, What's Sex Got To Do With It? Questioning Research on Gender & Negotiation 19 Nev. L. J. 919 (2019). Reprinted with permission of the author.

Vicki Schultz, "Life's Work." This article originally appeared in Colum. L. Rev. 1881 (2000). Reprinted with permission.

Reva Siegel, Reasoning from the Body: A Historical Perspective on Abortion Regulation and Questions of Equal Protection, 44 Stan. L. Rev. 261, 267, 361-63, 370 (1992). Reprinted with permission of the author.

Jeannie Suk, Criminal Law Comes Home, 116 Yale L.J. 2 (2006). Reprinted with permission of the author and The Yale Law Journal Company, Inc.

Deborah Tuerkheimer, Incredible Women: Sexual Violence and the Credibility Discount, 166 U. Pa. L. Rev. 3, 16-17, 20, 32-33, 35, 40 (2017). Reprinted with permission of the author.

Robin West, The Supreme Court 1989 Term, Foreword: Taking Freedom Seriously, 104 Harv. L. Rev. 43 (1990). Reprinted with permission of the author and publisher.

Jamillah Bowman Williams, Maximixing #MeToo: Intersectionality & The Movement, 62 B.C. L. Rev. 1797 (2021). Reprinted with permission of the author.

Joan Williams, Do Wives Own Half? Winning for Wives After Wendt, 32 Conn. L. Rev. 249 (1999). Reprinted with the permission of the author and publisher.

GENDER AND LAW

INTRODUCTION*

Many of the subjects studied in a course on gender and law are derived from conventional legal fields, such as employment law, family law, criminal law, and constitutional law. What makes gender law a subject in its own right, however, are the different theoretical frameworks that cut across traditional subject matter lines, often in a way that challenges how those subjects are typically understood and taught. These different frameworks are defined by their own particular, albeit overlapping, combination of factual assumptions, theoretical understandings, and normative aspirations. Although the components of the theories sometimes overlap, each perspective offers a different lens through which a gender law issue may be examined. The organization of this book emphasizes the significance of each theoretical lens.

The categories used in this book are formal equality, substantive equality, nonsubordination theory, difference, and autonomy. There is nothing authoritative in the terminology. As feminist theory has evolved and ideas have proliferated, the meaning of these terms has shifted, not always in an agreed direction. Even within the structure used in this book, the boundaries blur. However, we find them helpful as organizing principles to identify core themes. The purpose of this introduction is to briefly explain the meaning of these theoretical categories. It also anticipates and reviews a number of challenges and qualifications, especially those raised by instability over the meaning and classifications of gender, by intersectionality analysis, and by a revival of interest in masculinities studies. The five chapters in the book develop these ideas more fully.

A. THE BASIC THEORETICAL FRAMEWORKS

1. Formal Equality

Formal equality, explored in Chapter 1, is the familiar principle that individuals who are alike should be treated alike, according to their actual characteristics, rather than stereotypes about them. The principle of formal equality can be applied either to single individuals, whose right to be treated on the individual's own merits can be viewed as a right of individual autonomy, or to groups, whose members seek the same treatment as members of other, similarly situated groups. What makes an issue one of formal equality is that the claim is limited to treatment in relation to

---

* Section A of this Introduction borrows heavily, without citation, from Katharine T. Bartlett, Gender Law, 1 Duke J. Gender L. Pol'y 1 (1994).

a similarly situated individual or group and does not extend to demands for any particular substantive treatment.

Feminist litigators and academics advocated legal reform in the 1970s using primarily a formal equality model that emphasized the similarities between men and women and the desirability of treating them the same.[1] The commitment to formal equality was typically combined with a belief in the importance of autonomy and the desirability that both women and men be free to make their own choices, unconstrained by artificial barriers and prohibitions; in this book, autonomy is also explored (in Chapter 5) as a separate analytical framework, with its own assumptions, goals, and challenges.

The success of the formal equality approach is evidenced by the fact that most Supreme Court cases striking down sex-based classifications and practices have been grounded within a formal equality framework, as have most federal anti-discrimination statutes. Under this framework, the emphasis is on examining the factual assumptions of sex-based constraints, exposing the stereotypes underlying those constraints, and removing the barriers to free choice.

Formal equality has met the most resistance when confronted with rules and practices that distinguish between men and women on the basis of sex-linked characteristics, especially pregnancy and childbearing. As explained in the next section, some critics of formal equality urge special measures to overcome the disadvantages of these characteristics, such as mandatory job security for women who leave work for pregnancy or childbirth. Formal equality advocates oppose such "special" measures when comparable benefits are not provided to workers who leave work for other disabilities. While acknowledging that pregnancy and childbearing are biologically unique, these advocates contend that the differences are less significant and less relevant to employee benefit policies than the similarities. They point out that the arguments used to justify special accommodations for pregnant women are the same as those used to impose undesirable "protections" or limitations on women, such as maximum hour restrictions not imposed on men, mandatory maternity leave, and the exclusion of pregnancy from disability insurance plans. Given the dangers of special treatment, formal equality advocates prefer to view pregnancy as similar to other disabilities that men also experience, and thus entitled to treatment no worse, and no better, than those conditions. Formal equality advocates are also hesitant to support affirmative measures that might reinforce stereotypes about women's abilities, job preferences, and commitment to the work force, or that might suggest that they need special treatment to succeed.

2. *Substantive Equality*

While formal equality judges the form of a rule and requires that it treat women and men on the same terms without special barriers or benefits due to their

---

1. A well-known example is Justice Ruth Bader Ginsburg, who, as a litigator, challenged sex-based classifications that discriminated against men as well as those that discriminated against women. See, e.g., Ruth Bader Ginsburg, Sex and Unequal Protection: Men and Women as Victims, 11 J. Fam. L. 347 (1971).

sex, a substantive equality approach looks to a rule's results or effects. It points out that equal treatment leads to outcomes that are unequal because of differences between men and women. Advocates of substantive equality demand that rules take account of these differences in order to eliminate the disadvantages they bring to women.

Just what differences should be recognized and how they should be taken into account is not, of course, self-evident. The different possibilities have resulted in several models of substantive equality, each responding to different circumstances and conditions.

One focus of substantive equality has been the lingering effects of past discrimination. For example, women historically have been excluded from certain jobs, and they have been paid less than men for comparable jobs. Affirmative action plans that boost women into occupational fields historically dominated by men and comparable worth measures that restructure wage scales to eliminate the effects of past gender-based job segregation exemplify remedial measures designed to reverse the effects of past discrimination.

Another emphasis of substantive equality has been the biological differences between women and men. To counteract the disadvantages women experience as a result of their capacity to bear children and to breastfeed, many feminist theorists advocate special accommodations for women to eliminate these disadvantages, such as job security for women who leave the workplace to bear children.[2] Legislation mandating this accommodation was upheld by the United States Supreme Court even in the absence of mandatory leave for workers who leave work for other reasons.[3]

Others have focused on the social norms and practices that disadvantage women. Various social pressures, for example, steer women into lower paying occupational categories, encourage their economic dependence on men, and lead them to be the primary caretakers of children. In response to these pressures, some advocates have favored affirmative measures such as policies that encourage men to take parenting leave and better public support for families.

Substantive equality theory focuses on outcomes but does not necessarily require identical or mirror-image outcomes. Some substantive equality advocates favor equal treatment in some situations and special accommodation in others, insisting, for example, on equal access for women to men's athletic teams, private clubs, and colleges, but on separate teams, clubs, and colleges for women to meet their special needs. In family law, substantive equality theorists have urged the elimination of rules favoring men while arguing for the adoption of child custody standards that take special account of women's disproportionate investment in childbearing and standards for property division and alimony at divorce that are more likely to eliminate society-wide disadvantages faced by women than are current standards. In each instance, the argument is not that women should be entitled to whatever is most favorable to them, but that, depending on the circumstances,

---

2. We recognize that transmen and some non-binary individuals can also become pregnant or breastfeed.

3. See Cal. Fed. Sav. & Loan Ass'n v. Guerra, 479 U.S. 272 (1987) (withstanding challenge under Pregnancy Discrimination Act).

equality sometimes requires equal treatment and sometimes requires special measures to counteract men's advantages over women.

3. *Nonsubordination*

The nonsubordination perspective shifts the focus of attention away from gender-based differences to the imbalance of power between women and men. This perspective, also known as dominance theory (or, in Catharine MacKinnon's words, feminism "unmodified"), focuses not on the significance of similarities or differences between men and women, but on the imbalance of power between them.[4] Under this theory, the sex differences perceived to exist between women and men are not inevitable givens, but rather social constructs that make one set of social arrangements seem more natural, and thus more legitimate, than another. These social constructs serve, systematically, to subordinate women to men. For example, under nonsubordination theory, the focus of sexual harassment is not on equal treatment, as such, but on how the ordinary ways men treat women define women as inferior and subservient to men and create expectations that limit women's ability to succeed. Similarly, the harm of pornography is what it defines sex to be — i.e., a demeaning activity through which women serve as objects of men's sexual pleasure.

Nonsubordination theory offers a neo-Marxist account of how law reflects the interests of those with power, invisibly protecting those interests in the name of neutrality and freedom. For example, the law gives the highest status to freedom of speech under the First Amendment and touts it as a universal and neutral principle, for the benefit of all. Yet its effect is to protect the right of the powerful to demean women through, say, pornography, constructing women in ways that render them unable to effectively rebut their construction as inferior objects. Similarly, in demarcating a space between the private sphere, into which the law should not intrude, and the public sphere, where the law operates to create order and facilitate commerce, the law, in a seemingly neutral way, legitimizes a legal system that protects men from the harms they experience, but leaves women to fend for themselves behind closed doors.

The emphasis of nonsubordination theory on the social construction of sex and women leads it to make a strong claim about how all women are harmed by norms and practices that subordinate women, not simply individual victims. For example, in degrading some workers in the workplace in particular ways, the assertion of nonsubordination theory is that sexual harassment degrades all women. Likewise, insofar as sexual violence enacts the power of men over women, it reinforces men's higher status and authority. Important to this dynamic is the extent to which women fail to understand that the system is stacked against them and thus adopt the prevailing social norms as legitimate. Methodologically, nonsubordination is committed to the power of women sharing accounts of their own

---

4. Catharine A. MacKinnon, Feminism Unmodified: Discourses on Life and Law 32-34 (1987).

experiences so that they can come to understand the commonality of those experiences. The #MeToo movement is a contemporary example of that method in action.

Nonsubordination theory bears a complex relationship to equality theory. Its basic critique is that both formal and substantive equality maintain men as the reference point — i.e., the basic norm — to which women are compared. As such, all that the principle of equality could achieve for women is to extend to women that which men have already defined as important.[5] At the same time, to have legal weight, advocates have had to articulate the insights of nonsubordination theory within an equality framework. As a result, one could fairly say that advocates have smuggled nonsubordination theory into equality principles, even as it remains a significant challenge to those principles.

Nonsubordination theory, increasingly, has spread beyond women to other groups who have historically been disadvantaged by social norms that reflect the interests of those in power. For example, nonsubordination theory has been useful in understanding discrimination against lesbian, gay, bisexual, transgender, and queer (LGBTQ+)[6] populations as a form of sex discrimination, insofar as this discrimination is a form of gender policing, intended to keep intact the existing system of gender privilege. Again, for these claims to have legal salience, advocates have had to articulate these insights within an equality framework, which has led to a blended version of equality and nonsubordination exemplified in many of the cases in this book.

4. Difference

Equality and nonsubordination theories of gender view women's differences as factually insignificant, or as problems to be solved through remedial accommodations, or as excuses to subordinate women. In contrast, difference theory, also referred to as connection theory or different voice theory, views women's differences from men as potentially valuable resources that might serve as a better model of social organization and law than existing "male" characteristics and values. Within difference theory, women are said to have a greater sense of interconnectedness than men; to value relationships more than individual rights; to favor an "ethic of care" over "justice" or "rights" models of morality; and to use less abstract, more contextual forms of reasoning than men that focus on the unique context of a dilemma and the on-going relationships and interdependencies of the parties. Different voice theorists argue that as to each of these distinctions, women's values have the potential to improve existing law.

Scholarship that uses difference theory to promote legal reform has extended to so many conventional fields of law — from tort law, tax law, and corporate law

---

5. Id. at 34-36.

6. Except where a more specific term is warranted by context, this book uses "LGBTQ+" to refer to lesbians, gay men, bisexuals, transgender people, queer people, and other sexual and gender identity minorities. See Human Rights Campaign (HRC) Foundation, Glossary of Terms, https://www.hrc.org/resources/glossary-of-terms.

to mandatory workplace policies that allow workers to better integrate responsibilities to their families and employers — that it is possible to speak in terms of mainstreaming difference theory. Difference theory has infiltrated proposals challenging the adversarial models of adjudication. It has also influenced calls for more contextualized methods of legal reasoning and decisionmaking, not only because these methods better correspond to women's "different voice," but also because they illuminate the "maleness" of abstract legal principles, encourage a greater respect for difference, and foster a more critical awareness of the importance of the reasoner's own particular perspective. Some proponents of difference theory have also called for methods of judging that emphasize not only greater contextualization, but also collaborative decisionmaking and empathy.

The biggest challenge for difference theory, and an objection raised by non-subordination theorists, is the danger that it may reinforce the subordination historically associated with the assertion of women's differences and ignore equally important differences among women based on race, ethnicity, class, gender identity, and sexual orientation. Formal equality theorists might also resist difference theory insofar as it posits meaningful differences between the sexes, differences that formal equality theorists tend to view as stereotypes. At the same time, the values associated with difference theory are reflected in many contemporary policy recommendations, including such things as workplace models for better work-life balance, more public support for families, and better representation of women on corporate boards or in job categories historically reserved for men.

5.   *Autonomy*

While equality requires that likes be treated alike, autonomy is a value that does not rest on comparison. An autonomy right is based on the importance of the right, not the importance of being treated like others. For example, one might have an autonomy right to marry a person of one's own choosing, not because others have that right, but because it is important enough that all people should have it.

Autonomy can be viewed in terms of both negative and positive rights — sometimes phrased as freedom from regulation or coercion by the state, on the one hand, and freedom to pursue one's own life goals, on the other. With respect to reproductive rights and justice, the autonomy to be free from government restrictions on obtaining an abortion would be an example of a negative, "freedom from" right; having the resources and facilities that would enable one to obtain an abortion would be an example of a positive, "freedom to" autonomy right. There are many other examples in this book — e.g., domestic abuse and sexual assault — where advocates claim that it is not enough for the state to leave people alone. Rather, the state should have an affirmative obligation to enable vulnerable people to be free from control by others and exercise meaningful choices.

One question is what it means to make one's own choices. The law generally assumes that individuals are capable of having "intent," of exercising "choice" or "consent," and of acting and thinking like "reasonable" people. A central tenet of nonsubordination theory is that individuals are "constructed" by social norms, including gender norms, such that their choices are not really their "own." In its emphasis on the power of stereotypes, formal equality also assumes that people are often shaped by the expectations that others have of them. An important challenge to the autonomy perspective is the extent to which individuals are capable of making "free" choices with respect to such things as their career choices, whether they want to have sex or become pregnant, or whether to stay in an abusive relationship.

PUTTING THEORY INTO PRACTICE

I-1. Read United States v. Virginia,[7] excerpted in Chapter 2, Section C. Examine each of the positions taken by the advocates on each side, and each of the court decisions described in the case. Which proposed resolution of the case best exemplifies a formal equality approach? What would substantive equality require? How about nonsubordination theory, or difference theory? Would any of these theories suggest that VMI should be shut down altogether?

I-2. Read Stevenson v. Stevenson,[8] excerpted in Chapter 3, Section C. Should a court be able to keep a domestic restraining order in effect over the objection of the victim of domestic abuse? Which theoretical perspective would be most helpful in support of the court's approach, and which one would be most supportive of the victim's perspective?

B. CHALLENGES AND COMPLICATIONS TO THE BASIC THEORETICAL FRAMEWORKS

Throughout this book, there are a number of important, cross-cutting sub-themes: definitional questions about the categories of sex and gender and the interrelation of sex, gender, sexuality, and gender identity; an intersectionality critique that looks at which women are centered in the study of gender equality and which women are marginalized; and connections between men, masculinities, and gender equality. These constitute, in part, an extension of the theoretical frameworks described above and, in part, a challenge to these frameworks.

1. Who Is a "Woman"? Deconstructing Sex, Gender, and Sexual Orientation

The traditional view of "sex" as a biologically stable category, easily discernible at birth, posits a sharp distinction between men and women, male and female. The term "the opposite sex" itself reflects a polarized view of male and female as nonintersecting categories. In this view, gender is understood as the cultural component of being a man or a woman, while sex is understood as a fixed biological marker for

---

7. 518 U.S. 515 (1996).
8. 714 A.2d 986 (N.J. Super. Ct. Ch. Div. 1998).

being male or female. Finally, sexual orientation, an aspect of sexuality, traditionally refers to an individual's sexual preference in relation to the sex or gender of a sexual partner.

However, these terms and their interrelationships turn out to be much more complex. Advances in science, medicine, and the social sciences, along with critical cultural analysis, have destabilized this traditional understanding. Sex is more fluid and much less determinate than the traditional understanding allows. Gender, too, is fluid, and is not determined by sex. Sexuality is still another component of identity that has historically been linked to gendered expectations (e.g., assumptions, embedded in law and culture, that men are sexually attracted to women and vice versa). This set of traditional definitions has been contested in science, culture, and law, spawning lines of inquiry into the nature and stability of the categories of sex and gender and the emergence of queer theory. The following foundational readings introduce some of the most important themes and debates.

a. Framing the Sex/Gender/Sexuality Divide

Katherine M. Franke

The Central Mistake of Sex Discrimination Law: The Disaggregation of Sex from Gender

144 U. Pa. L. Rev. 1, 1-4 (1995)

Contemporary sex discrimination jurisprudence accepts as one of its foundational premises the notion that sex and gender are two distinct aspects of human identity. That is, it assumes that the identities male and female are different from the characteristics masculine and feminine. Sex is regarded as a product of nature, while gender is understood as a function of culture. This disaggregation of sex from gender represents a central mistake of equality jurisprudence.

Antidiscrimination law is founded upon the idea that sex, conceived as biological difference, is prior to, less normative than, and more real than gender. Yet in every way that matters, sex bears an epiphenomenal relationship to gender; that is, under close examination, almost every claim with regard to sexual identity or sex discrimination can be shown to be grounded in normative gender rules and roles. Herein lies the mistake. In the name of avoiding "the grossest discrimination," that is, "treating things that are different as though they were exactly alike," sexual equality jurisprudence has uncritically accepted the validity of biological sexual differences. By accepting these biological differences, equality jurisprudence reifies as foundational fact that which is really an effect of normative gender ideology. This jurisprudential error not only produces obvious absurdities at the margin of gendered identity, but it also explains why sex discrimination laws have been relatively ineffective in dismantling profound sex segregation in the wage-labor market, in shattering "glass ceilings" that obstruct women's entrance into the upper echelons of corporate management, and in increasing women's wages, which remain a fraction of those paid men.

The targets of antidiscrimination law, therefore, should not be limited to the "gross, stereotyped distinctions between the sexes" but should also include the social processes that construct and make coherent the categories male and female.

In many cases, biology operates as the excuse or cover for social practices that hierarchize individual members of the social category "man" over individual members of the social category "woman." In the end, biology or anatomy serve as metaphors for a kind of inferiority that characterizes society's view of women.

The authority to define particular categories or types of people and to decide to which category a particular person belongs is a profoundly powerful social function. . . . Rather than accepting sexual differences as the starting point of equality discourse, sex discrimination jurisprudence should consider the role that the ideology of sexual differences plays in perpetuating and ensuring sexual hierarchy.

A reconceptualization of the two most fundamental elements of sexual equality jurisprudence is necessary to correct this foundational error. First, sexual identity — that is, what it means to be a woman and what it means to be a man — must be understood not in deterministic, biological terms, but according to a set of behavioral, performative norms that at once enable and constrain a degree of human agency and create the background conditions for a person to assert, I am a woman. . . .

Second, what it means to be discriminated against because of one's sex must be reconceived beyond biological sex as well. To the extent that the wrong of sex discrimination is limited to conduct or treatment which would not have occurred but for the plaintiff's biological sex, antidiscrimination law strives for too little. Notwithstanding an occasional gesture to the contrary, courts have not interpreted the wrong of sex discrimination to reach rules and policies that reinforce masculinity as the authentic and natural exercise of male agency and femininity as the authentic and natural exercise of female agency.

In order to explore these fundamental issues of equality, difference, and identity, I will ask a seemingly simple question: What is the wrong of sex discrimination? Is it the unfair consideration of biological differences between males and females? The resort to archaic notions about the skills, abilities, or desires of men and women? The perpetuation of stereotypical notions of masculinity and femininity? Or the unwelcome instigation of sexual behavior in inappropriate settings, such as the workplace? Close examination reveals that both the case law and the theory of sex discrimination draw in kaleidoscopic fashion from each of these formulations to determine what it means to be discriminated against because of one's sex. The result is an unstable conception of both who it is that deserves equal protection of the laws and what it would mean to treat her fairly. While instability is not an intrinsic flaw in the doctrine, the theory's surface chaos masks a deeper reality within sexual equality jurisprudence — that the wrong of sex discrimination is premised upon a right of sexual differentiation, that is, a fundamental belief in the truth of biological sexual difference. This belief in the truth of sexual identity inevitably reifies masculinity as the natural expression of male subjectivity and femininity as the natural expression of female subjectivity. In accepting this belief, the law has played a significant role in perpetuating, rather than dismantling, sexual inequality. . . .

Defining sex in biological or anatomical terms represents a serious error that fails to account for the complex behavioral aspects of sexual identity. In so doing, this definition elides the degree to which most, if not all, differences between men and women are grounded not in biology, but in gender normativity. Ultimately, there is no principled way to distinguish sex from gender, and concomitantly, sexual differentiation from sexual discrimination.

Mary Anne Case

Disaggregating Gender from Sex and Sexual Orientation: The Effeminate Man in the Law and Feminist Jurisprudence

105 Yale L.J. 1, 10-18 (1995)

[Justice Ruth Bader Ginsburg] was in large part responsible for the fact that the words "sex" and "gender" are now used interchangeably in the law, creating what I shall argue is an unfortunate terminological gap. According to Ginsburg, "[f]or impressionable minds the word 'sex' may conjure up improper images" of what occurs in porno theaters. Therefore, she

> stopped talking about sex discrimination years ago. . . . [S]he explained that a secretary once told her, "I'm typing all these briefs and articles for you and the word sex, sex, sex, is on every page. Don't you know those nine men [on the Supreme Court], they hear that word and their first association is not the way you want them to be thinking? Why don't you use the word 'gender'? It is a grammatical term and it will ward off distracting associations."

Whatever advantages it may have in warding off embarrassment or salacious thoughts in the minds of judges, this interchangeability of the words "sex" and "gender" has contributed to some analytic confusion between the categories of male and female, on the one hand, and masculine and feminine, on the other. To help clear this up, I would urge a return to the distinction between the concepts of sex and gender as commonly defined by scholars in women's studies. As most feminist theorists use the terminology, "sex" refers to the anatomical and physiological distinctions between men and women; "gender," by contrast, is used to refer to the cultural overlay on those anatomical and physical distinctions. While it is a sex distinction that men can grow beards and women typically cannot, it is a gender distinction that women wear dresses in this society and men typically do not.

[Professor Case notes that Justice Scalia and scholar Richard Epstein also urge a distinction between sex and gender. She differs from Epstein, however, in the reason for the distinction.] According to Epstein:

> Gender, when used as applied to nouns, carries with a somewhat arbitrary appearance. . . . The clear implication, therefore, is that once we shift from sex, which is not arbitrary, to gender, which may be, we have strengthened the case for thinking gender differences irrelevant in all social contexts. From there it is a shorter step to Title VII's prohibition against discrimination on the ground of sex. [Citing Richard A. Epstein, Gender Is for Nouns, 41 DePaul L. Rev. 981, 982 (1992).]

It seems that Epstein objects to the terminological substitution in large part because, as a fan of sociobiology, he assumes that sex and gender are necessarily closely related. I object because I assume the opposite: There can be, I would contend, a world of difference between being female and being feminine. . . .

It is in part because gender differences, unlike sex differences, may not be irrelevant in the employment context that I want to keep the terminology clear. One might reasonably, for example, want a nurse or a flight attendant to display characteristics conventionally gendered feminine, such as being "understanding," "warm," "able to devote oneself completely to others," "gentle," "helpful to others," "kind," and "aware of others' feelings." This does not mean, however, that [an employer can hire only female nurses].

[There is also the question of sexual orientation.] In this society, sexual orientation is measured chiefly by the relationship the sex of the object(s) of one's sexual desire bears to one's own sex. . . . [H]owever, for much of Western history an important axis of sexual orientation was instead that of active/passive or penetrative/receptive. With this as the axis, women together with males who allowed themselves to be penetrated orally or anally were opposed and seen as subordinate to "active" penetrative males. To the extent "passivity" in a male was itself seen as effeminate or associated with other effeminate behaviors, and to the further extent that the sex of the person penetrated was seen as a matter of some indifference in defining the orientation of the "active" male, sexual orientation can thus be said to have once been constructed . . . on gender rather than on sex.

One simple vision of sex, gender and orientation sees them as coming packaged together such that once one is identified, all the rest are determined. So closely linked can the three be seen to be that some transsexuals seem to have felt it necessary to cut off their penises and construct vaginas in order to be gendered feminine — e.g., to wear dresses. Determining which is the easiest of the three to identify has always been more complicated. Studies show that young children have an easier time telling a boy from a girl when each is fully dressed in gender-stereotypical attire than when each is naked, but for us grown-ups today sex is the least problematized of these categories. . . . We have come to realize that the categories of sex, gender, and orientation do not always come together in neat packages. Not only are they not as binary as we might once have thought, they can in fact be disaggregated. . . .

[An interdisciplinary examination of gender theory reveals the following themes:] that gendered characteristics are often bundled; that what is seen as masculine is more highly valued than what is seen as feminine, at least in part because the latter is associated with women; that, in addition to being generally devalued, the feminine is viewed as completely unacceptable in males; and that a woman exhibiting masculine characteristics is today viewed, both descriptively and normatively, quite differently from a man who exhibits feminine ones.

[Among the conclusions reached by Professor Case is that unless sex, gender, and sexual orientation are disaggregated, some forms of discrimination, such as discrimination against men exhibiting female characteristics, will not be recognized.]

Francisco Valdes

Queers, Sissies, Dykes, and Tomboys: Deconstructing the Conflation of "Sex," "Gender," and "Sexual Orientation" in Euro-American Law and Society

83 Calif. L. Rev. 1, 5-10 (1995)

Queer. Sissy. Dyke. Tomboy. What do these vulgar terms have in common? Why do they sting? And, perhaps most curiously, why do they carry a common sting?

Our childhood memories confirm that these epithets, and the stereotypes that they invoke, travel through American society as synonyms. For many, these words resonate in memories harkening back to days in the school yard. They conjure remembered peers, or perhaps youthful selves, who were chosen to sustain and survive the common ridicule of their perceived transgressions against a sex-ordered world. Clearly, the synonymity of these terms, and others like them, informed the social order into which we were inducted as children. . . .

[T]his synonymity is created and sustained by a phenomenon named here: the "conflation" of "sex," "gender," and "sexual orientation." . . . [E]ven though sex, gender, and sexual orientation popularly refer to putatively distinctive constructs, they formally and frequently conflate to forcibly homogenize human personalities, including sexualities. Through conflation, this triad of constructs regulates the social and sexual lives of everyone.

This conflation, moreover, is both a formal, intellectual belief system that was codified through various clinical theories and a pervasive normative standard that shapes and governs human life more generally. This conflation, in other words, reflects, and simultaneously projects, the dominant Euro-American social and sexual order. This conflation was and is encoded in the heritage and life of the United States — our children invoke terms signifying sex, gender, and sexual orientation interchangeably precisely because our society and its antecedents continually conceived and categorized the three as mutually dependent constructs. . . .

[T]he conflation's impact on life and law is neither natural, nor neutral, nor benign. On the contrary, this conflation is a highly problematic contrivance that exerts a divisive force on society and a destabilizing influence in law: this conflation embodies, exudes, and extends androsexist and heterosexist biases, which engender and accentuate social and sexual rankings and acrimonies in both law and society. In other words, this conflation constitutes and validates hetero-patriarchy. As such, it creates and reinforces artificial and oppressive dictates and distinctions that affect all of us, but that specifically impede social and legal equality for (heterosexual) women and for sexual minorities. . . .

[T]he legal system simply cannot fulfill the nation's existing, formal anti-discrimination mandate regarding sex and gender unless and until we recognize how sex, gender, and sexual orientation are mutually-related constructs that animate mutually-reinforcing strains of conflationary biases. . . .

Dean Spade

Resisting Medicine, Re/Modeling Gender

18 Berkeley Women's L.J. 15, 29 (2003)

Informed by my own experiences navigating the medical model of transsexuality, and those of my friends and clients, my goal for trans law and policy remains demedicalization and an end to practices that coerce people into expressing gender identity through a narrowly defined binary. I would like to see the end of gender designation on government documents, the end of gender segregation of bathroom and locker room facilities, and the end of involuntary "corrective" surgeries for babies with intersex conditions. I would like people to have the freedom to determine their own gender identity and expression and not be forced to declare such an identity involuntarily or pick between a narrow set of choices. And I would want no person to be required to show medical or psychiatric evidence to document that they are who and what they say they are. I would like self-identification to be the determining factor for a person's membership in a gender category to the extent that knowledge of the person's membership in such a category is necessary.

I certainly believe that we can move toward de-regulating gender and still engage in important corrective practices like gender-based affirmative action. I am not arguing for a gender-blind society in which all people are similarly androgynous, but instead for a world in which diverse gender expressions and identities occur, but none are punished and membership in these categories is used less and less to distribute rights and privileges.

Similarly, I would want various groups of similarly-identified people to be able to seek spaces to meet together and for the inevitable conflicts that emerge regarding the identity borders erected by those groups to be determined by negotiation and cultural work, not by legal or medical determinations of gender category membership. These are my goals for gender and law, but in my work as an advocate for low-income gender transgressive people I am often forced to recognize how far we are from attaining those goals. Consequently, I engage in compromises that I hope will be steps toward the deregulation of gender, compromises which provide access to vitally needed services and entitlements for gender transgressive people who are in crisis now.

b. Implications of the Sex/Gender/Sexuality Divide

The complex categories of sex, gender, and sexual orientation intersect with law in numerous ways throughout this book. One significant example, addressed in Chapters 1 and 3, relates to whether discrimination based on sexual orientation or gender identity constitutes discrimination "because of sex," prohibited under Title VII of the Civil Rights Act of 1964 (and its successor enactments). Discrimination against persons who identify as LGBTQ+ is pervasive and affects virtually all aspects of life.[9] Legal scholars have long wrestled with the relationship between sexual orientation discrimination and sex discrimination, and this book continues to explore the law's evolving approach to this interrelation.[10] Discrimination

---

9. See Segal Singh & Laura E. Durso, Ctr. for Am. Progress, Widespread Discrimination Continues to Shape LGBT People's Lives in Both Subtle and Significant Ways (May 2, 2017). A 2021 U.S. Census report says that 7.7 to 11.7 percent of adults over 18 are LGBTQ+. Lydia Anderson et al., U.S. Census Bureau, New Household Pulse Survey Data Reveals Differences between LGBT and Non-LGBT Respondents During COVID-19 Pandemic (Nov. 4, 2021). As of 2019, the Williams Institute estimated that approximately 4.5 percent of the U.S. population identifies as LGBT. Williams Institute, Adult LGBT Population in the United States (March 2019).

10. For classic works analogizing sexual orientation to sex discrimination, see Sylvia A. Law, Homosexuality and the Social Meaning of Gender, 1988 Wis. L. Rev. 187; Andrew Koppelman, Why Discrimination Against Lesbians and Gay Men Is Sex Discrimination, 69 N.Y.U. L. Rev. 197 (1994).

specifically targeting transgender individuals[11] is increasingly the subject of legal challenges. The sex discrimination in gender identity discrimination is particularly apparent in this context, where the essence of unfair treatment is based on a person's rejection of their assigned sex at birth. The transgender issues addressed in this book include sex-specific bathroom designations, employer and student dress codes, and the treatment of transgender athletes.

The question of how to refer to a person whose gender identity is deemed ambiguous in some way is a significant issue at the intersection of gender and LGBTQ+ rights. Many people are asking to be referred to as "he" or "she" when traditional social norms would dictate otherwise. A person might also want to be referred to as "they" or some other gender-nonspecific pronoun. In short, people want to be referred to by the gendered, or non-gendered, terms through which they see themselves. Chan Tov McNamarah has recently challenged the assertion of a right to misgender people. They write,

> Today, the vast majority of Americans can easily see the indignity imposed by referring to a Black man as "boy." And yet, they remain oblivious to the harm of referring to a transgender girl or a nonbinary person as the same. Reintroducing historical context, therefore, is promising. Framed with such perspective, opposition to misgendering can be understood, not as demands for new "special rights" or "radical grammatical modifications," but as a link in an ongoing fight against verbal violence inflicted upon minority social groups. . . .
>
> [T]he rights of gender minorities have sharply come into focus. In rapid succession, the spread of bathroom bills, the rolling back of trans-protective Title VII and IX positions, the Trump Administration's ban on transgender military service, and most recently, the *Bostock v. Clayton County* holding, have bombarded the societal consciousness. In their wake, now so more than ever, Americans have begun to acknowledge and address the second-class citizenship imposed upon persons who are transgender, genderqueer, gender nonbinary, agender, and otherwise gender diverse.[12]

Another example of how the law constructs the categories of sex and gender is in the treatment of persons who are intersex, born without singularly defining markers for male or female. Estimates vary as to the percentage of the world's population who are born intersex, in part because definitions of the this status also vary widely. With a broad definition, including anyone born with sex chromosomes, gonads, or internal or external sexual anatomy that does not neatly correspond

---

11. "Transgender" is "[a]n adjective to describe people whose gender identity differs from the sex they were assigned at birth," irrespective of appearance or medical procedures. See GLAAD Media Reference Guide, https://www.glaad.org/reference/trans-terms (11th ed. 2022). One study estimates that over 1.6 million people aged 13 and above identify as transgender. Jody Herman et al., Williams Inst., How Many Adults and Youth Identify as Transgender in the U.S. 1 (June 2022).

12. Chan Tov McNamarah, Misgendering, 109 Cal. L. Rev. 2227, 2231–32 (2021).

with "male" or "female," the estimated intersex rate is 1 to 2 percent of the population.[13] A narrower definition focusing only on those with significant atypicalities, perhaps unusual enough to spark discussion with sex differentiation specialists and consideration of surgical alteration, produces estimates closer to 1 in 4,500 births.[14]

A controversial response to the reality of intersexuality is the use of surgery to "correct" intersexed conditions, sometimes called gender reassignment or gender confirmation surgery. Surgery on infants with such a condition has been a standard protocol since the late 1950s. Clinicians have advised parents over the years that the surgical potential for "normal"-looking genitalia should dictate the child's gender and that any innate gender propensity of the child can be changed by careful upbringing. They have also counseled parents that children who do not have the surgery as infants become confused and distressed by their sexual ambiguity, are often teased and rejected by other children, and are not as successful in adapting to gender reassignment if they later undergo surgery. For more than two decades, intersex advocacy groups have strongly opposed infant surgery, preferring to have parents raise their intersex children as social males or females, and then let the children decide for themselves at puberty whether they would like to change their social sex, with or without surgery.[15] The delay prevents some "mistakes" from being made, although, as a practical matter, lack of financial resources, support networks, and safe educational environments often prevent exercise of free choice by the children.[16] Why isn't intersex surgery on infants and children as resoundingly condemned as female genital cutting, which has been attributed to patriarchal "culture" and condemned by the United Nations and by many Western feminists?[17] Should it be?

A broader question is why the medical community and the legal system insist on identifying persons as male or female at all. As more people have come of age with a fluid understanding of gender, gender nonconformity activists have increasingly mobilized to resist a binary, government-assigned system of gender. A growing number of U.S. states and localities have responded by adding an X option to government documents such as driver's licenses and allowing changes to birth certificates.[18] Is a three-gender option still too constraining? In 2014, Facebook began

---

13. See Melanie Blackless et al., How Sexually Dimorphic Are We? Review and Synthesis, 12 Am. J. Hum. Biology 151, 161 (2000); see also Nancy Ehrenreich & Mark Barr, Intersex Surgery, Female Genital Cutting, and the Selective Condemnation of "Cultural Practices," 40 Harv. C.R.-C.L. L. Rev. 71, 73 (2005).

14. See Julie A. Greenberg, Intersexuality and the Law: Why Sex Matters 1-2 (2012). Prevalence and other issues relating to intersex conditions are tracked by the Intersex Society of North America. See Intersex Society of North America, http://www.isna.org.

15. See Jessica A. Clarke, They, Them, and Theirs, 132 Harv. L. Rev. 894, 930 (2019). The lead advocacy group today is Advocates for Informed Choice; information about this group is available at https://aiclegal.org.

16. See Amanda Kennedy, Because We Say So: The Unfortunate Denial of Rights to Transgender Minors Regarding Transition, 19 Hastings Women's L.J. 281 (2008).

17. Ehrenreich & Barr, supra note 13.

18. Amy Harmon, M, F or X? Added Option Makes States Rethink Nature of Gender, N.Y. Times, May 29, 2019, at A1.

offering more than fifty gender options for users who do not identity as simply male or female, including intersex, agender, gender-questioning, and two-spirit.

More subversive to the dichotomy of sex/gender than adding an X or other gender-neutral alternative is the case for rejecting gender designations altogether. Should gender be abolished, relegated to other outmoded cultural practices? A recent survey found that 5.1 percent of young adults aged 18 to 29 in the United States now identify as nonbinary or transgender individuals, and there is a growing call for recognition of gender-fluid and nonbinary identities among the young.[19] This movement is forcing some institutions to rethink how and why they insist on ascribing gender. In a recent shift, most major airlines now allow passengers to fly without disclosing their gender.

But for now, at least, such changes have done little to dislodge the overarching force of gender as an organizing principle of society. This book discusses many issues relating to women's lives and women's equality. But it is important to acknowledge at the outset that the categories of women, men, female, male, feminine, masculine, gay, and straight, are contested, and that there is controversy and judgment in deciding who fits these categories, and about the legitimacy of the categories themselves. Does it reinforce biologically reductionist and exclusionary understandings of sex to talk about "women"? Is it possible to recognize that sex and gender are still culturally and socially relevant categories, and that women are, in many respects, a socially and economically subordinated group, while arguing that these categories should be understood expansively?

PUTTING THEORY INTO PRACTICE

I-3. Government requirements for changing a person's designated gender on official documents vary widely. The U.S. State Department, for example, no longer requires medical documentation to change an individual's gender identification on their passport; it is also the first federal agency to offer an X option, in addition to M and F.[20] Other agencies and organizations have required some form of medical documentation or intervention to change an official gender designation. For example, the NCAA has required hormone suppression treatment for transgender women to compete on women's teams in NCAA championships. (The NCAA's evolving approach to transgender athletes is discussed in Chapter 2.) How should concerns about privacy and "outing" transgender individuals who might otherwise conceal that their gender had changed since birth be taken into account in designing policies on gender documentation?[21] What framework would you design for defining and/or changing gender designations on government records?

---

19. See Anna Brown, Pew Rsch. Ctr. About 5% of Young Adults in the U.S. Say Their Gender Is Different From Their Sex Assigned at Birth,, June 7, 2022; Bianca D. M. Wilson & Ilan H. Meyer, Williams Inst., Nonbinary LGBTQ Adults in the United States (June 2021); Daniel Bergner, Neither/Nor, N.Y. Times Mag., June 8, 2019, at 36.

20. See Anthony J. Blinken, State Dep't, Press Statement: X Gender Marker Available on U.S. Passports Starting April 11 (Mar. 31, 2022).

21. See, e.g., Elliot S. Rozenberg, The NCAA's Transgender Student-Athlete Policy: How Attempting to Be More Inclusive Has Led to Gender and Gender-Identity Discrimination, 22 Sports L.J. 193 (2015).

I-4. Traditionally, law school professors have "called on" students using their last names, identifying them by Mr. or Ms. What objections would you foresee to a law professor following this practice today? If you were advocating on behalf of your law school's LGBTQ+ student group, what arguments might you make to try to convince the professor to change this practice?

I-5. The leader of a group calling itself the Women's Liberation Front (WLF) recently testified in opposition to a state legislative bill that would recognize gender-neutral designations on driver's licenses. The group's position is that "bolstering the nonbinary category will harm people who face discrimination and violence precisely because they are born with female anatomy." As the leader of the WLF explained the group's position: "To deny the reality of sex means we're not able to name, address, and fix systemic sex-based oppression and exploitation."[22] How would you respond? By that theory, should a person's sexual orientation also be noted on the person's driver's license?

I-6. Sam doesn't identify as either male or female. Sam objects to the label "non-binary," out of a belief that the prefix "non" implies a negative, or an absence — an aberration from the norm. It would be like referring to women as "non-men," Sam argues, or gay men as "non-heterosexual." Do you agree? If so, what language should be adopted to address Sam's concern?

I-7. The preferred terminology to refer to sexual and gender minorities (persons other than cisgender heterosexuals) has been in flux in recent years. One way this has been expressed is through the expansion of letters in the preferred acronym, from LGBT to LGBTQIA+, with many variations in between. Definitions and descriptions are also fraught, as exemplified in a controversy over how the Netflix show "Big Mouth" stumbled in an episode purporting to explain the difference between bisexuality and pansexuality.[23] Is it possible to focus too much on gender labels and their meanings? Are there costs to the growing interest and controversy over such labeling, and are they worth paying?

2. *Which Women?*

In 1989, Kimberlé Crenshaw introduced the concept of "intersectionality" to explain how race and sex often work together to aggravate, or even transform, the experience of discrimination.[24] Crenshaw highlighted how courts would typically miss cases of intersectional discrimination against Black women by concluding that as long as an employer hired some women and some Black employees, neither sex nor race discrimination had occurred.[25]

---

22. See Amy Harmon, Which Box Do You Check? Some States Are Offering a Nonbinary Option, N.Y. Times, May 29, 2019, at A1.

23. See LaToya Ferguson, "Big Mouth" Co-Creators Apologize for Inaccurate Pansexuality Scene, IndieWire (Oct. 8, 2019).

24. Kimberlé Crenshaw, Demarginalizing the Intersection of Race and Sex: A Black Feminist Critique of Antidiscrimination Doctrine, Feminist Theory, and Antiracist Politics, 1989 U. Chi. Legal F. 139, 140-143.

25. Id.

Crenshaw's insight began a broader conversation about how "individuals differentially positioned 'within intersecting systems of power' develop 'different points of view on their own and others' experiences,' "[26] as well as a debate within feminist legal theory about whether, in speaking about women and women's interests, feminists too often presuppose a particular privileged norm — that of white, middle-class women — and thereby deny or ignore differences based on race and class. This work has been extended in a number of directions. Scholars have shown how white suffragettes exploited the civil rights claims of racial minorities, often strengthening their own arguments at the expense of slaves and free Blacks.[27] They have also demonstrated how women of color often view rape and domestic violence differently because of the racism that permeates the criminal legal system within which these crimes are prosecuted.[28] They have further shown how minority women are penalized by seemingly neutral policies relating to child welfare and poverty,[29] as well as how legal reforms widely viewed to have improved circumstances for women have, in fact, disproportionately helped white, middle-class women, often to the detriment of minority women.[30] They have revealed how overlapping subordinated identities can lead to tricky questions about how to perform one's identity in discrimination-avoiding ways at work.[31] These and other questions have been expanded well beyond the original terms of the intersectionality critique to include intersections involving Asian, Latinx, and other minority women; LGBTQ+ populations; age; disability; class; and women from religious or cultural traditions not fully aligned with mainstream Western liberal norms and values.

As the intersectionality critique has matured, so have the responses to it — responses that have both highlighted the importance of the critique, and the difficulties of escaping it. As you study the materials in this book, be aware of the race-laden assumptions made by various arguments and policies. For example, does welfare policy make any specific assumptions about its intended recipients?[32] Do proposals for more publicly supported day care make assumptions about who is to

---

26. Patricia Hill Collins, Intersectionality's Definitional Dilemmas, 41 Ann. Rev. Socio. 1, 14 (2015).

27. See, e.g., Serena Mayeri, Reasoning From Race: Feminism, Law, and the Civil Rights Revolution (2011). See also bell hooks, Ain't I a Woman: Black Women and Feminism 127-39 (1981) (describing historical tensions over race within the women's movement). The relationship between the women's suffrage movement and abolitionism is explored in Chapter 1.

28. See Angela P. Harris, Race and Essentialism in Feminist Legal Theory, 42 Stan. L. Rev. 581, 601 (1990). For a discussion of intersectionality in rape law, see Chapter 5, Section A.

29. See, e.g., Camille Gear Rich, Reclaiming the Welfare Queen: Feminist and Critical Race Theory Alternatives to Existing Anti-Poverty Discourse, 25 S. Cal. Interdisc. L.J. 257, excerpted in Chapter 5, Section C; Dorothy E. Roberts, Race and the New Reproduction, 47 Hastings L.J. 935, 953-54 (1996); see also materials considered in Chapter 5.

30. See Dorothy Roberts, Spiritual and Menial Housework, 9 Yale J.L. & Feminism 51, 55-59 (1997), excerpted in Chapter 4, Section B.

31. See Devon W. Carbado & Mitu Gulati, The Fifth Black Woman, 11 J. Contemp. Legal Issues 701, 710-15, 717-20 (2001), excerpted in Chapter 1, Section C.

32. See Chapter 5, Section C.

care for children?[33] Do employer dress and appearance regulations police certain people's racial identities?[34] Ask yourself also how intersectionality concerns should be addressed. To what extent is it possible to avoid categories that include some and exclude others? Is it possible to avoid making assumptions about individuals within a category based on the dominant cultural frame associated with that group?

Kimberlé Crenshaw

Demarginalizing the Intersection of Race and Sex: A Black Feminist Critique of Antidiscrimination Doctrine, Feminist Theory, and Antiracist Politics

1989 U. Chi. Legal F. 139, 140-43

With black women as the starting point, it becomes more apparent how dominant conceptions of discrimination condition us to think about subordination as disadvantage occurring along a single categorical axis. . . . [T]his single-axis framework erases Black women in the conceptualization, identification and remediation of race and sex discrimination by limiting inquiry to the experiences of otherwise-privileged members of the group. In other words, in race discrimination cases, discrimination tends to be viewed in terms of sex- or class-privileged Blacks; in sex discrimination cases, the focus is on race- and class-privileged women.

This focus on the most privileged group members marginalizes those who are multiple-burdened and obscures claims that cannot be understood as resulting from discrete sources of discrimination. [T]his focus on otherwise-privileged group members creates a distorted analysis of racism and sexism because the operative conceptions of race and sex become grounded in experiences that actually represent only a subset of a much more complex phenomenon.

Th[e] problems of exclusion cannot be solved simply by including Black women within an already established analytical structure. Because the intersectional experience is greater than the sum of racism and sexism, any analysis that does not take intersectionality into account cannot sufficiently address the particular manner in which Black women are subordinated.

Angela P. Harris

Race and Essentialism in Feminist Legal Theory

42 Stan. L. Rev. 581, 588-89, 595 (1990)

[T]he story [feminists] tell about "women," despite its claim to universality, seems to black women to be peculiar to women who are white, straight, and

---

33. See Chapter 4, Section B.
34. See Chapter 1, Section B; see also Angela Onwuachi-Willig, Another Hair Piece: Exploring New Strands of Analysis Under Title VII, 98 Geo. L.J. 1079, 1131 (2010).

socioeconomically privileged — a phenomenon Adrienne Rich terms "white solipsism." . . .

The notion that there is a monolithic "women's experience" that can be described independent of other facts of experience like race, class, and sexual orientation is one I refer to . . . as "gender essentialism." A corollary to gender essentialism is "racial essentialism" — the belief that there is a monolithic "Black Experience," or "Chicano Experience." The source of gender and racial essentialism (and all other essentialisms, for the list of categories could be infinitely multiplied) is the . . . voice that claims to speak for all. The result of essentialism is to reduce the lives of people who experience multiple forms of oppression to addition problems: "racism + sexism = straight black women's experience," or "racism + sexism + homophobia = black lesbian experience." Thus, in an essentialist world, black women's experience will always be forcibly fragmented before being subjected to analysis, as those who are "only interested in race" and those who are "only interested in gender" take their separate slices of our lives. . . .

[T]he "nuance theory" approach to the problem of essentialism . . . [is to offer generalization] about "all women" while qualifying statements, often in footnotes, supplement the general account with the subtle nuances of experience that "different" women add to the mix. Nuance theory thus assumes the commonality of all women — differences are a matter of "context" or "magnitude"; that is, nuance.

The problem with nuance theory is that by defining black women as "different," white women quietly become the norm, or pure, essential woman.

✳✳✳

Is it possible for Black women to take feminism to task for ignoring the particularity of Black women's experience, without overgeneralizing about that experience?[35] Insofar as categories cause us to overgeneralize and leave people out, is it possible to leave them out? How much parsing of social divisions is necessary to address the intersectionality critique?

> Every person, and perhaps even every object that we encounter in the world, is unique, but to treat each as such would be disastrous. Were we to perceive each object *sui generis*, we would rapidly be inundated by an unmanageable complexity that would quickly overwhelm our cognitive processing and storage capabilities. Similarly, if our species were "programmed" to refrain from drawing inferences or taking action until we had complete, situation-specific data about each person or object we encountered, we would have died out long ago. To function at all, we must design strategies for simplifying the perceptual environment and acting on less-than-perfect information. A major way we accomplish both goals is by creating categories. . . .
>
> What happens when we group objects into categories? First, we tend to perceive members of the same category as being more similar to each other, and members of different categories as more dissimilar to each

---

35. Richard T. Ford raises this issue in Richard T. Ford, Racial Culture: A Critique: 24-26 (2005), excerpted in Chapter 1, Section C.

other, than when all the objects are viewed in aggregate. The same results adhere when the "objects" we categorize are other human beings. . . .

Second, although some debate exists on this issue, it appears that we create a mental prototype, often visual, of the "typical" category member. To determine whether an item is a member of a particular category, we match the object perceived with the category prototype and determine the "distance" between the two. We experience an object first as a member of its "basic" category — the category most accessible at the moment. Only with additional mental processing do we identify it as a member of its superordinate or subordinate categories. . . .

But the price of this cognitive economy is that categorical structures . . . bias what we see, how we interpret it, how we encode and store it in memory, and what we remember about it later. In intergroup relations, these biases, mediated through perception, inference, and judgment, can result in discrimination, whether we intend it or not, whether we know it or not.[36]

With so many possible categories and ways of thinking about them in play, is it even possible for a category such as gender to retain meaning, or does intersectionality mean that everything matters all the time?

PUTTING THEORY INTO PRACTICE

I-8. Judith Butler observes that scholars resort to using "etc." after race, class, and gender to denote the limitless nature of social divisions, or even out of exhaustion, attempting to be inclusive of so many differences.[37] Is this a nod to the diversity of systems of discrimination that is a helpful reminder of our limitations? Or a cop-out?

I-9. What do you make of the fact that identities may be simultaneously privileged and subordinated? Should white women be less protected by antidiscrimination law than women of color because of their racial privilege?

3. What About Men?

The emphasis of this book is on women, but there is little doubt that understandings of men and masculinities are important to this subject because of their impact not only on men's interests, but on women's interests as well, and on the prospects for gender equality more broadly. By the late 1970s, the study of masculinities became a topic in its own right. As two theorists have put it, "[m]asculinities theorists would agree with feminists that men as a group have power over women as a group, but they tend to complicate the situation . . . by examin[ing] the effects

---

36. Linda Hamilton Krieger, The Content of Our Categories, 47 Stan. L. Rev. 1161, 1188-90 (1995).

37. Judith Butler, Gender Trouble: Feminism and the Subversion of Identity 18-22 (1990).

of the social construction of men."[38] According to masculinities scholars, the study of masculinities is necessary to understand and effectively address issues relating to gender and inequality for everyone.

a.   Introducing Masculinities

Nancy E. Dowd

Asking the Man Question: Masculinities Analysis and Feminist Theory

33 Harv. J. Law & Gender 415, 416-419 (2010)

Masculinities work can be used to understand more clearly how male privilege and dominance are constructed. It can make us see harms suffered by boys and men that we have largely ignored. It may also reinforce and strengthen the commitment to anti-essentialism in feminist theory. Exposing the complexities and multiplicity of masculinities leads toward understanding intersection and multiple forms of discrimination more clearly. . . .

Masculinities analysis may also remind us to be attentive to different patterns of inequality and to our interpretation of those patterns. Where one sex is sole or dominant, dominance should be something that triggers scrutiny. This should matter both when the dominant sex benefits (as in occupying high paid jobs) or is harmed (as in occupying more prison cells). We should question not only why one sex fills or dominates the pattern, but also the gendered meaning of both who is present and who is absent. Oddly, when one sex is dominant, sometimes gender issues are rendered invisible. Examples of this are male predominance in the juvenile and adult criminal justice systems, and women's predominance in the welfare system. Invisibility is fostered by gender-neutral language that covers the predominance of gender patterns, but also by the acceptance of the pattern as usual, normal, and taken for granted.

On the other hand, where both sexes are present, one or both may claim bias. We tend to frame competing claims of bias as requiring prioritization or hierarchy rather than seeing how they interconnect. We tend to argue over who has the more important issues to address or the most pressing "crisis." Resisting this "either/or" approach of a hierarchy of inequalities is critical. For example, in education there are inequality issues for both girls and boys, women and men. Rather than exclusively focusing on the issues of one sex to the exclusion of the other, as if only one can claim our focus or deserve our attention, we should see and insist on addressing both. Inequalities often interlock. A battle of the sexes, moreover, may only divert attention from more serious issues of race and class. Examining subordination in isolation undermines our understanding and our attack upon the interacting dynamic, even if gender-specific problem solving is needed. . . .

---

38. Ann C. McGinley & Frank Rudy Cooper, Introduction: Masculinities, Multidimensionality, and Law: Why They Need One Another, in Masculinities and the Law: A Multidimensional Approach 1, 3 (Frank Rudy Cooper & Ann C. McGinley, eds., 2012).

Raising issues about men when so many issues about women remain generates resistance and distrust. . . . Masculinities analysis needs to continually challenge itself to challenge the hegemony of men and male power. The project of imagining positive, affirming, egalitarian masculinities is ongoing, but it is absolutely essential. . . .

The implications of these teachings . . . are that feminists should "ask the man question."

Frank Rudy Cooper

"Who's the Man?": Masculinities Studies, Terry Stops, and Police Training

18 Colum. J. Gender & Law 671, 671-72, 674-76, 741 (2009)

We men have some strange rituals. One occurs on the basketball court. A player will make a move around a defender and score a basket. Then he'll shout, "Who's the man?" He wants his opponent to say, "*You* are the man." This episode is a paradigmatic description of how masculinities work. Men often act with the goal of impressing other men. We gain our masculine esteem and relative masculine stature from other men's acknowledgements of our masculinity. Sociologist Michael Kimmel puts it best: "[w]e are under the constant careful scrutiny of other men. Other men watch us, rank us, grant our acceptance into the realm of manhood. Manhood is demonstrated for other men's approval. . . ."

How does masculinity affect policing?. . . .

The short answer is that officers may get "macho" with civilians. Specifically, they may enact a command presence in situations where it only serves to boost the officer's masculine esteem. To enact command presence is to take charge of a situation. It involves projecting an aura of confidence and decisiveness. It is justified by the need to control dangerous suspects. A situation that does not justify enacting command presence is what I call a "masculinity contest." A masculinity contest is a face-off between men where one party is able to bolster his masculine esteem by dominating the other. A prototypical masculinity contest is a bar fight. Men will glare at each other and ratchet up their challenges until one party backs down or is subdued. Male police officers may sometimes be tempted to turn encounters with male civilians into masculinity contests.

The insight that policemen may sometimes enact command presence in order to stage masculinity contests and boost their masculine esteem is important because it helps explain patterns of law enforcement. . . . [S]cholars have long noted that officers sometimes use their Terry v. Ohio stop-and-frisk powers to racially profile. The usual explanation for that practice is racial animus. However, concentrating solely on race as an explanation for police behaviors ignores the fact that the overwhelming majority of police officers are men and the overwhelming majority of those they stop are men. As David Sklansky says, "One train may hide another." I contend that the desire to boost one's masculine esteem is a train traveling behind, and obscured by, the desire to boost one's racial esteem in some officers' decision to disproportionately stop and frisk men belonging to racial minorities. . . .

[A]side from the question of whether policemen should bully civilians, we might ask whether such actions can ever actually sate the desire to prove one's masculinity. According to Kimmel, they cannot:

[T]he bully is the *least* secure about his manhood, and so he is constantly trying to prove it. But he proves it by choosing opponents he is absolutely certain he can defeat; thus the standard taunt to a bully is to "pick one someone your own size." He can't, though, and after defeating a smaller and weaker opponent, which he was sure would prove his manhood, he is left with the empty gnawing feeling that he has not proved it after all, and he must find another opponent, again one smaller and weaker, that he can again defeat to prove it to himself. . . . When does it end? Never.

So bullying is a counter-productive activity for the bully himself. . . .

The bully's conundrum demonstrates that no one really benefits from the current structure of masculinity. Ultimately, hegemonic masculinity is the source of the problem of police harassment of men.

b.   Relating Men and Masculinities to the Study of Women and Gender

In exhorting feminists to "ask the man question," Dowd suggests that any study of gender is incomplete without considering what role masculinity plays in supporting the status quo or might play in subverting it. Feminists might focus on men to analyze how masculinity norms might interfere with gender equality. Alternatively, the goal might be to unearth ways in which men themselves are harmed by gender norms and gender inequality. Keep the difference in mind as you study the materials in this book. For each subject matter, what does it mean to "ask the man question," and how does it affect your understanding of the law's approach to issues relating to gender?

One important principle in masculinities studies is that the field of "masculinities" is plural because there is no singular, inherent masculinity that men exhibit. There are many ways of "being" a man, and normative masculinity (the preferred masculinity to which men are exhorted to conform) varies by context and by other dimensions of men's identities besides gender. Dowd observes that a singular masculinity may be dominant over other masculinities (she calls this "hegemonic" masculinity), but masculinities scholars tend to agree that even hegemonic masculinity may shift over time and become less "toxic" or harmful in response to the elevation of alternative, more inclusive masculinities. Importantly, what becomes defined as the dominant masculinity in a particular setting is shaped by context, including race and class.

The excerpt from Frank Rudy Cooper illustrates how a particular dominant masculinity takes hold in one setting: encounters between police and civilians. As with Cooper's discussion of masculinity in policing, the dominant masculinity in many settings frequently emphasizes strength and toughness, which are established by exerting dominance over others. One study of the construction industry documented working conditions producing hypermasculinized behaviors of "manning up," risk-taking, aggressiveness, and denigrating women.[39] Along similar lines, Ann McGinley's analysis of Ricci v. DeStefano, a U.S. Supreme Court case ruling that a city's failure to certify the results of promotional exams for firefighters because of their disparate impact on Blacks and Hispanics unlawfully discriminated based on race, argues that the case embraced a white, heterosexual, breadwinning masculinity to valorize the white firefighters who lost out on promotions.[40] As McGinley describes the reactions of some U.S. Senators in hearings about the case:

> The explicit message was that the nearly all-white plaintiffs were "real men" and "real firefighters" who worked hard and cared for their families. The implicit message was that female firefighters of all races were not qualified to do the job and that African American and Hispanic firefighters who complained about the disparate impact were lazy and could not measure up.[41]

Because masculinities are contextual, the dominant form of masculinity in a given setting need not be based on physical strength and power over others. A large national survey by the Center for Work-Life Policy on the female "brain drain" in science, engineering, and technology documents very different macho cultures that prevail in these fields.[42] Sociologist Marianne Cooper, who has analyzed the Silicon Valley culture, explains that men in this culture express their masculinity by working lots of hours. As one man explains: "Guys constantly try to out-macho each other, but in engineering it's really perverted because out-machoing someone means being more of a nerd than the other person. . . . It's not like being a brave firefighter and going up one more flight than your friend. There's a lot of see how many hours I can work. . . . He's a real man, he works ninety-hour weeks; he's a slacker, he works fifty hours a week."[43] She summarizes: "The successful enactment of this masculinity involves displaying one's exhaustion, physically and verbally, in order to convey the depth of one's commitment, stamina, and virility."[44]

Hegemonic masculinity, as in Frank Rudy Cooper's discussion of the effects of bullying on the bully, can be harmful, even to the men who exhibit it. For example, some commentators argue that many men, including those in blue-collar occupations, are caught in a "daddy double-bind": they are expected to be both

---

39. See Letitia M. Saucedo & Maria Christina Morales, Masculinities Narratives and Latino Immigrant Workers: A Case Study of the Las Vegas Residential Construction Trades, 33 Harv. J. Law & Gender 625 (2010).

40. Ann C. McGinley, *Ricci v. DeStefano*: A Masculinities Theory Analysis, 33 Harv. J. Law & Gender 581, 584 (2010); see also Ricci v. DeStefano, 557 U.S. 557 (2009).

41. McGinley, supra note 40, at 584. See generally Ann C. McGinley, Through a Different Lens: Multidimensional Masculinities and Employment Discrimination Law (2013).

42. Sylvia Ann Hewlett, The Athena Factor: Reversing the Brain Drain in Science, Engineering, and Technology, Harv. Bus. Rev. Rsch. Rep. (May 2008).

43. Marianne Cooper, Being the "Go-To Guy": Fatherhood, Masculinity, and the Organization of Work in Silicon Valley, 23 Qualitative Socio. 379, 382 (2000).

44. Id. at 383.

breadwinners and involved fathers in settings that provide inadequate support for that dual role.[45] Others, like Darren Rosenblum, emphasize the ways in which men, as parents, suffer from interlocking gender stereotypes.[46]

Increasingly, masculinities scholars have called for attention to other forms of masculinity that are not hegemonic but are instead inclusive and egalitarian. Many of these visions would enlist men in the same struggles against male violence, homophobia, and gender inequality in which feminists have engaged.[47] This effort builds on a long tradition that has included historic leaders such John Stuart Mill, Frederick Douglass, and W. E. B. Dubois.[48]

It is clear that "gender for men and boys does not operate uniformly and is strongly influenced by intersections with race, class, and sexual orientation."[49] For example, as many scholars have pointed out, Black men have vastly disproportionate rates of unemployment, police stops, incarceration, and substance abuse convictions and lower rates of college attendance and marriage.[50] In his groundbreaking work about Black disembodiment, and the unique threats faced by Black males in America, Ta-Nehisi Coates considers the experience in the form of a letter to his son:

> "If you're black, you were born in jail," Malcolm [X] said. And I felt the truth of this in the blocks I had to avoid, in the times of day when I must not be caught walking home from school, in my lack of control over my body. . . . [Y]ou are a black boy, and you must be responsible for your body in a way that other boys cannot know. . . . Disembodiment is a kind of terrorism . . . [t]he dragon that compelled the boys I knew, way back, into extravagant theater of ownership. . . . The demon that pushed the middle-class black survivors into aggressive passivity, our conversation restrained in public quarters, our best manners on display, our hands never out of pockets, our whole manner ordered as if to say, "I make no sudden moves." . . . The serpent of school years, demanding I be twice as good, though I was but a boy.[51]

---

45. Kari Palazzari, The Daddy Double-Bind: How the Family and Medical Leave Act Perpetuates Sex Inequality Across All Class Levels, 16 Colum. J. Gender & L. 429 (2008).

46. Darren Rosenblum, Unsex Mothering: Toward a New Culture of Parenting, 35 Harv. J. Law & Gender 57 (2012).

47. For examples, see Handbook of Studies on Men & Masculinities (Michael S. Kimmel et al., eds., 2005); The Black Male Handbook (Kevin Powell, ed., 2007); Michael Kimmel, Guyland (2008); R. W. Connell, The Men and the Boys (2000).

48. Shira Tarrent, Men and Feminism 28-39 (2009).

49. Nancy E. Dowd et al., Feminist Legal Theory Meets Masculinities Theory, in Masculinities and the Law, supra note 38, at 25.

50. See, e.g., Ta-Nehisi Coates, Between the World and Me 36, 71, 114 (2015); Olatunde C. A. Johnson, Disparity Rules, 107 Colum. L. Rev. 374 (2007). See also Khiara M. Bridges, TANF and the End (Maybe?) of Poor Men, 93 B.U. L. Rev. 1141, 1143 (2013) ("if we are witnessing the end of men . . . then we are witnessing the end of non-white men, not the end of men generally"); Nancy E. Dowd, What Men?: The Essentialism Error of the "End of Men," 93 B.U. L. Rev. 1205, 1208 (2013) ("Male hierarchy is raced, classed, and gendered on the basis of sexual orientation.").

51. Coates, supra note 50, at 114.

Finally, the diversity of views about masculinity includes those that celebrate traditional masculine values. Prominent advocates for traditional masculine values often appeal to biological understandings of masculinity. Harvard Professor Harvey Mansfield, for example, argues that men are by nature dominant, aggressive, self-confident risk-takers. This view of manliness, at its best, encourages men to defend higher ends, but has often merged with the view that men's distinctive role has become threatened by "feminist nihilism." Although in the public sphere, the sexes should have equal rights, in the private sphere, Mansfield argues for respect for men's differences and wants society to stop trying to "feminize boys." "Men should be expected, not merely free to be manly."[52] This view resonates with that of poet Robert Bly, an active proponent of the "men's movement," who urged men in the 1990s to "retreat from the world of women to temporary male sanctuaries in order to recapture some 'deep' or 'wild' masculinity that has become dormant in today's modern technological society in which women actively participate."[53]

Other commentators, although not necessarily supporting the movement to celebrate traditional male values, seek to put men's anxiety about their manhood in a sympathetic light. Susan Faludi, for example, argues that hypermasculine behavior is often a response to men's feeling of being "downsized," economically and emotionally, both by the erosion of traditional male jobs and the rise in women's rights.[54] Christina Hoff Sommers takes it a step further, specifically blaming feminists for men's sense of disempowerment and disadvantage.[55] The theme of men and boys falling behind has been augmented by more recent claims that women have overtaken men in work, in education, and in love and marriage.[56]

In the chapters that follow, consider whether the theories explored understate the distinctive burdens faced by men in a gendered society. As women have made advances in the name of equality, is it possible to think of men, for some purposes at least, and for some men, as now being the subordinated sex?

PUTTING THEORY INTO PRACTICE

I-10. A survey in the 1990s asked women and men what they were most afraid of. "Women responded that they were most afraid of being raped and murdered. Men responded that they were most afraid of being laughed at."[57] Do you suppose

---

52. Harvey C. Mansfield, Manliness 244 (2006).

53. Michael S. Kimmel, Issues for Men in the 1990s, 46 U. Miami L. R. 671, 672, (1992), citing Robert Bly, Iron John: A Book About Men 6, 222-37, 244-49 (1990).

54. Susan Faludi, Stiffed: The Betrayal of the American Man (2000).

55. Christina Hoff Sommers, The War Against Boys: How Misguided Feminism Is Harming Our Young (2000).

56. See, e.g., Hanna Rosin, The End of Men (2012). For a law review symposium responding to Rosin's book, see Symposium: Evaluating Claims About the "End of Men": Legal and Other Perspectives, 93 B.U. L. Rev. 663 (2013).

57. Michael S. Kimmel, Masculinity as Homophobia: Fear, Same, and Silence in the Construction of Gender Identity, in Theorizing Masculinities 119, 133 (Harry Brod & Michael Kaufman eds., 1994).

this is still true? Does the asserted difference have potential legal and policy implications?

I-11. One of President Obama's signature initiatives, My Brother's Keeper, sought to remove barriers to education and employment for Black boys and men.[58] A nonprofit spinoff, My Brother's Keeper Alliance, has raised more than $80 million from major corporations for specialized programs for young Black and Latino men.[59] The Black Lives Matter movement initially called attention to the tragedy of Black men being shot and killed by police (though it was formed by Black women and has always focused on the whole community). In response, the #WhyWeCan'tWait movement, led by women of color and various activist groups, advocates for the inclusion of women in initiatives now focused on Black boys and men. Representing this voice, Kimberlé Crenshaw argues that the My Brother's Keeper Alliance and Black Lives Matter movements create a false impression that Black girls do not need the same kind of emphasis. "The gender-exclusive focus on boys (of color) as ground zero . . . continues to undermine the well-being of our entire community."[60] In a TED Talk, she calls attention to female victims of police shootings, who have failed to receive the attention given to male victims.[61] Do the problems of Black boys and men warrant a distinct, separate set of initiatives? Can their issues be addressed without marginalizing the experience of women of color?

---

58. See My Brother's Keeper, https://www.whitehouse.gov/my-brothers-keeper.
59. See Brandon Robinson, President Obama Announces Launch of My Brother's Keeper Alliance, Ebony (May 6, 2015).
60. See Melinda D. Anderson, Black Girls Should Matter, Too, Atlantic (May 11, 2015).
61. Kimberlé Crenshaw, The Urgency of Intersectionality, Ted.com (Oct. 2016).

CHAPTER 1

FORMAL EQUALITY

Formal equality is the principle of treating like people alike. In determining whether people are alike, and thus deserve the same treatment, formal equality demands that people be judged according to their actual characteristics rather than on the basis of assumptions or stereotypes about who they are or who they ought to be. In the context of sex, formal equality requires the state to provide men and women the same opportunity to exercise civic responsibility, such as by voting and serving on juries. It requires that public benefits such as Social Security and unemployment compensation be available to men and women on the same terms, and that property rules, tax liabilities, and alimony rules be sex neutral. Formal equality also dictates that employers apply the same hiring and promotion criteria to men and women.

Chapter 1 begins with several cases illustrating traditional legal restrictions against women. It then explores the constitutional and statutory doctrines that evolved to dismantle these restrictions. These doctrines emerged from a series of decisions by the U.S. Supreme Court beginning in the early 1970s and drew heavily from earlier civil rights cases brought under the Fourteenth Amendment of the United States Constitution and from the formal equality model that undergirded these cases.

One central issue for sex discrimination law involves the appropriate standard of judicial review. Muller v. Oregon and Goesart v. Cleary, set forth in Section A, illustrate the application of the rational basis test. Starting with Reed v. Reed in 1971,[1] the Supreme Court gradually moved to a more stringent "intermediate" standard. Craig v. Boren, decided in 1976, held that a classification based on sex "must serve important governmental objectives and . . . be substantially related to achievement of those objectives."[2] In 1994, the U.S. Supreme Court held in J.E.B. v. Alabama that a sex-based classification be supported by "an exceedingly persuasive justification."[3] Although many sex-based classifications have been invalidated under this standard, a number of sex-based rules have survived as well.

In reviewing the legitimacy of sex-based classifications, a chief concern under both the U.S. Constitution and various civil rights statutes has been the accuracy of the underlying assumptions. Many of the laws and practices challenged in

---

1. 404 U.S. 71 (1971).
2. 429 U.S. 190 (1976).
3. 511 U.S. 127 (1994).

courts are based on stereotypes about women. Some are descriptive stereotypes, meaning they are based upon generalizations about women that are overbroad or factually unsupported, such as that women do not have the strength or ability to work in certain jobs. Others are prescriptive, meaning they are based on expectations about what characteristics a woman *should* possess or what role she should assume, such as that a woman's place is in the home, not the workplace.[4] Courts have invalidated many laws and practices that were based on stereotypes, and those that remain are usually difficult to justify under the formal equality principle.

Some assumptions about women have some factual basis; nonetheless, statutes or practices based on these assumptions are impermissible under the formal equality principle because they are not drawn narrowly enough to support sufficiently important state objectives. Women *on average* may be less strong than men, but not *all women* are less strong than *all men*; thus, ordinarily, formal equality requires that individual women have the opportunity to prove that they have the strength required for a particular job. Not only fairness concerns demand this opportunity, but also the danger that limiting women's opportunities will reinforce and perpetuate the stereotypes on which the limitations were based.

Sometimes job requirements that appear neutral may in fact rest on traditional stereotypes. For example, a workplace may use equipment designed with the heights and weights of men in mind, as the work in question traditionally has been "men's work." Similarly, an employer may require all of its employees to work from 8 a.m. to 5 p.m., or attend evening events, even though these hours may be relatively disadvantageous to women because of the greater family obligations they tend to assume. A continuing dilemma within the formal equality framework is what to do about rules and practices that are "formally" equal to men and women but have a disparate impact on women. Chapter 1 focuses on claims for identical treatment. Chapter 2 focuses on claims for a broader equality that takes into account the practical realities of men's and women's lives.

Formal equality applies to sex-based classifications that discriminate against men, as well as those that discriminate against women. As women's rights advocates who have supported male litigants in their challenges to sex-based rules and practices note, equality for men is not only as a matter of fair treatment for men, but also a means of reducing stereotypes that restrict opportunities for women. For example, a policy that gives parental leaves only to women deprives men of a benefit and also reinforces a domestic division of labor that penalizes women in the world outside of work.

The formal equality framework has facilitated substantial progress for women, but are there problems that it does not adequately address? What additional theoretical tools would be necessary to support an appropriate remedy in those cases?

---

4. For research on the different types of stereotypes, see Diana Burgess & Eugene Borgida, Who Women Are, Who Women Should Be: Descriptive and Prescriptive Gender Stereotyping in Sex Discrimination, 5 Psych., Pub. Pol'y, & L. 665 (1999).

A.   HISTORICAL FOUNDATIONS FOR WOMEN'S CLAIM TO FORMAL EQUALITY

1.   The Historical Legacy: Women as Different and in Need of Protection

a.   Economic and Social Legislation to Protect Women

Historically, the traditional view was that women are unfit for many occupations, and that their biological characteristics and reproductive role make it necessary to limit their employment. This section includes two cases illustrating this traditional view. Muller v. Oregon was decided during a period between 1905 and 1937, referred to as the *Lochner* era,[5] when the U.S. Supreme Court routinely invalidated statutes that interfered with the ability of individuals and businesses to make contracts controlling their own commercial relationships. In upholding economic legislation that limited the number of hours women could work in a factory, the *Muller* case represented a strong message about women's need for protection, since it was an exception to the *Lochner*-era emphasis on freedom of contract. The *Lochner* era ended in 1937 with West Coast Hotel Co. v. Parrish,[6] in which the Court upheld a state's Minimum Wage for Women Act and established the modern principle that courts should defer to legislatures when they enact economic and social legislation unless that the legislation has no rational basis. In Goesart v. Cleary, decided in 1948, the Supreme Court upheld a Michigan law that prevented the licensing of women as bartenders unless the woman was the wife or daughter of a male who owned the bar where she worked, stressing the moral dangers for women who are without the protection of their fathers or husbands. *Goesart* was decided after the *Lochner* period, and although its deference to legislatures was typical of that period, the decision is also striking for what it assumed about women's "difference." Note that the laws in both *Muller* and *Goesart* were challenged by employers, not by the women negatively affected by the law.

Muller v. Oregon
208 U.S. 412 (1908)

Mr. Justice BREWER delivered the opinion of the Court.

On February 19, 1903, the legislature of the State of Oregon passed an act, [providing that it would be a misdemeanor to employ any female in any mechanical establishment, or factory, or laundry more than ten hours in any one day. Defendant was charged with violation of the statute for ordering Mrs. E. Gotcher to work more than ten hours per day in defendant's laundry]. . . .

---

5. The era began with the Supreme Court's decision in Lochner v. New York, 198 U.S. 45 (1905).

6. 300 U.S. 379 (1937).

A trial resulted in a verdict against the defendant, who was sentenced to pay a fine of $10. The Supreme Court of the State affirmed the conviction . . . whereupon the case was brought here on writ of error.

The single question is the constitutionality of the statute under which the defendant was convicted so far as it affects the work of a female in a laundry. . . .

It is the law of Oregon that women, whether married or single, have equal contractual and personal rights with men. . . .

[Yet the] legislation and opinions referred to [above, including a brief by Mr. Louis D. Brandeis,] are significant of a widespread belief that woman's physical structure, and the functions she performs in consequence thereof, justify special legislation restricting or qualifying the conditions under which she should be permitted to toil. Constitutional questions, it is true, are not settled by even a consensus of present public opinion, for it is the peculiar value of a written constitution that it places in unchanging form limitations upon legislative action, and thus gives a permanence and stability to popular government which otherwise would be lacking. At the same time, when a question of fact is debated and debatable, and the extent to which a special constitutional limitation goes is affected by the truth in respect to that fact, a widespread and long continued belief concerning it is worthy of consideration. We take judicial cognizance of all matters of general knowledge.

That woman's physical structure and the performance of maternal functions place her at a disadvantage in the struggle for subsistence is obvious. This is especially true when the burdens of motherhood are upon her. Even when they are not, by abundant testimony of the medical fraternity continuance for a long time on her feet at work, repeating this from day to day, tends to injurious effects upon the body, and as healthy mothers are essential to vigorous offspring, the physical well-being of woman becomes an object of public interest and care in order to preserve the strength and vigor of the race.

Still again, history discloses the fact that woman has always been dependent upon man. He established his control at the outset by superior physical strength, and this control in various forms, with diminishing intensity, has continued to the present. As minors, though not to the same extent, she has been looked upon in the courts as needing especial care that her rights may be preserved. Education was long denied her, and while now the doors of the schoolroom are opened and her opportunities for acquiring knowledge are great, yet even with that and the consequent increase of capacity for business affairs it is still true that in the struggle for subsistence she is not an equal competitor with her brother. Though limitations upon personal and contractual rights may be removed by legislation, there is that in her disposition and habits of life which will operate against a full assertion of those rights. She will still be where some legislation to protect her seems necessary to secure a real equality of right. Doubtless there are individual exceptions, and there are many respects in which she has an advantage over him; but looking at it from the viewpoint of the effort to maintain an independent position in life, she is not upon an equality. Differentiated by these matters from the other sex, she is properly placed in a class by herself, and legislation designed for her protection may be sustained, even when like legislation is not necessary for men and could not be sustained. It is impossible to close one's eyes to the fact that she still looks to her brother and depends upon him. Even though all restrictions on political, personal and contractual rights were taken away, and she stood, so far as statutes are concerned, upon an absolutely equal plane with him, it would still be true that she is so constituted that she will rest upon and look to him for protection; that her physical structure and a proper discharge of her maternal functions—having in view not merely her own health, but the well-being of the race—justify legislation to protect her from the greed as well as the passion of man. The limitations which this statute places upon her contractual powers, upon her right to agree with her employer as to the time she shall labor, are not imposed solely for her benefit, but also largely for the benefit of all. Many words cannot make this plainer. The two sexes differ in structure of body, in the functions to be performed by each, in the amount of physical strength, in the capacity for long-continued labor, particularly when done standing, the influence of vigorous health upon the future well-being of the race, the self-reliance which enables one to assert full rights, and in the capacity to maintain the struggle for subsistence. This difference justifies a difference in legislation and upholds that which is designed to compensate for some of the burdens which rest upon her.

We have not referred in this discussion to the denial of the elective franchise in the State of Oregon, for while it may disclose a lack of political equality in all things with her brother, that is not of itself decisive. The reason runs deeper, and rests in the inherent difference between the two sexes, and in the different functions in life which they perform.

For these reasons, and without questioning in any respect the decision in Lochner v. New York, we are of the opinion that it cannot be adjudged that the act in question is in conflict with the Federal Constitution, so far as it respects the work of a female in a laundry, and the judgment of the Supreme Court of Oregon is affirmed.

Goesart v. Cleary

335 U.S. 464 (1948)

Mr. Justice FRANKFURTER delivered the opinion of the Court.

As part of the Michigan system for controlling the sale of liquor, bartenders are required to be licensed in all cities having a population of 50,000 or more, but no female may be so licensed unless she be "the wife or daughter of the male owner" of a licensed liquor establishment. The case is here on direct appeal from an order of the District Court of three judges, . . . denying an injunction to restrain the enforcement of the Michigan law. The claim, denied below, one judge dissenting, and renewed here, is that Michigan cannot forbid females generally from being barmaids and at the same time make an exception in favor of the wives and daughters of the owners of liquor establishments. Beguiling as the subject is, it need not detain us long. To ask whether or not the Equal Protection of the Laws Clause of the Fourteenth Amendment barred Michigan from making the classification the State has made between wives and daughters of owners of liquor places and wives and daughters of non-owners, is one of those rare instances where to state the question is in effect to answer it.

We are, to be sure, dealing with a historic calling. We meet the alewife, sprightly and ribald, in Shakespeare, but centuries before him she played a role in the social life of England. The Fourteenth Amendment did not tear history up by the roots, and the regulation of the liquor traffic is one of the oldest and most untrammeled of legislative powers. Michigan could, beyond question, forbid all women from working behind a bar. This is so despite the vast changes in the social and legal position of women. The fact that women may now have achieved the virtues that men have long claimed as their prerogatives and now indulge in vices that men have long practiced, does not preclude the States from drawing a sharp line between the sexes, certainly in such matters as the regulation of the liquor traffic. The Constitution does not require legislatures to reflect sociological insight, or shifting social standards, any more than it requires them to keep abreast of the latest scientific standards.

While Michigan may deny to all women opportunities for bartending, Michigan cannot play favorites among women without rhyme or reason. The Constitution in enjoining the equal protection of the laws upon States precludes irrational discrimination as between persons or groups of persons in the incidence of a law. But the Constitution does not require situations "which are different in fact or opinion to be treated in law as though they were the same." . . . Since bartending by women may, in the allowable legislative judgment, give rise to moral and social problems against which it may devise preventive measures, the legislature need not go to the full length of prohibition if it believes that as to a defined group of females other factors are operating which either eliminate or reduce the moral and social problems otherwise calling for prohibition. Michigan evidently believes that the oversight assured through ownership of a bar by a barmaid's husband or father minimizes hazards that may confront a barmaid without such protecting oversight. This Court is certainly not in a position to gainsay such belief by the Michigan legislature. If it is entertainable, as we think it is, Michigan has not violated its duty to afford equal protection of its laws. We cannot cross-examine either actually or argumentatively the mind of Michigan legislators nor question their motives. Since the line they have drawn is not without a basis in reason, we cannot give ear to the suggestion that the real impulse behind this legislation was an unchivalrous desire of male bartenders to try to monopolize the calling . . . .

Nor is it unconstitutional for Michigan to withdraw from women the occupation of bartending because it allows women to serve as waitresses where liquor is dispensed. The District Court has sufficiently indicated the reasons that may have influenced the legislature in allowing women to be waitresses in a liquor establishment over which a man's ownership provides control. Nothing need be added to what was said below as to the other grounds on which the Michigan law was assailed.

Judgment affirmed.

Mr. Justice RUTLEDGE, with whom Mr. Justice DOUGLAS and Mr. Justice MURPHY join, dissenting.

While the equal protection clause does not require a legislature to achieve "abstract symmetry" or to classify with "mathematical nicety," that clause does require lawmakers to refrain from invidious distinctions of the sort drawn by the statute challenged in this case.

The statute arbitrarily discriminates between male and female owners of liquor establishments. A male owner, although he himself is always absent from his bar, may employ his wife and daughter as barmaids. A female owner may neither work as a barmaid herself nor employ her daughter in that position, even if a man is always present in the establishment to keep order. This inevitable result of the classification belies the assumption that the statute was motivated by a legislative solicitude for the moral and physical well-being of women who, but for the law, would be employed as barmaids. Since there could be no other conceivable justification for such discrimination against women owners of liquor establishments, the statute should be held invalid as a denial of equal protection.

PUTTING THEORY INTO PRACTICE

1-1. An Oregon statute in the mid-1950s makes it a crime for women to "participat[e] in wrestling competition and exhibition." A woman is charged under the statute and offers as a defense that the statute violates her equal protection rights. Defend the statute, and her prosecution, based on the arguments presented in *Muller* and *Goesart*.

1-2. In evaluating the constitutionality of the statute described in Problem 1-1 above, a court found that

> [the Oregon legislature] intended that there should be at least one island on the sea of life reserved for man that would be impregnable to the assault of woman. It had watched her emerge from long tresses and demure ways to bobbed hair and almost complete sophistication; from a creature needing and depending upon the protection and chivalry of man to one asserting complete independence. She had already invaded practically every activity formerly considered suitable and appropriate for men only. In the field of sports she had taken up, among other games, baseball, basketball, golf, bowling, hockey, long distance swimming, and racing, in all of which she had become more or less proficient, and in some had excelled. In the business and industrial fields as an employe[e] or as an executive, in the professions, in politics, as well as in almost every other line of human endeavor, she had matched her wits and prowess with those of mere man, and . . . in many instances had outdone him.[7]

Does this rationale have any continuing resonance in U.S. society? Does it apply to all women alike, or is it—at least implicitly—reserved for a particular group of women? Assuming the rationale would no longer be constitutionally sufficient, is there another purpose that might justify the statute?

b. Women's Differences and the Practice of Law

For most of this nation's history, the conventional view was that women's "difference" made women unfit for law and made law unfit for women. In the colonial

---

7. State v. Hunter, 300 P.2d 455, 458 (Or. 1956).

era, when labor was scarce and relatively few occupations required formal licenses, a few women did manage to participate in legal transactions either by acting as their husband's representative or by obtaining special authorization to proceed independently. During the late eighteenth century, however, the gradual formalization of bar admission criteria made it increasingly difficult for women to act as lawyers. The inability of married women to make contracts reinforced the barriers to any independent career. And, of course, African-American women under slavery had no capacity to assert even their own legal rights, let alone represent others.

After the Civil War, the rise in women's educational and political activism contributed to a growing stream of female applicants to the bar. In 1867, Iowa became the first state to license a woman attorney, Belle Babb Mansfield, and the following decades witnessed a gradual increase in female candidates from largely white middle- and upper-middle-class backgrounds. Women's initial reception as lawyers in most jurisdictions was less than enthusiastic. Many nineteenth-century lawmakers invested the sexes' "separate spheres" with both spiritual and constitutional significance. The following excerpt from Justice Bradley's concurring opinion in Bradwell v. Illinois was typical in rooting women's domesticity in "the divine ordinance." In addition to raising concerns over women's proper role and "peculiar sensibilities," commentators linked female professional careers to infertility, frigidity, and "race suicide." According to Deborah Rhode, "[t]heories about the deadly 'brain–womb' conflict warned that women who diverted their scarce energies to cognitive rather than reproductive pursuits risked permanent physical and psychological damage."[8]

Myra Bradwell based her claim for entrance to the bar on the Privileges and Immunities clause of the Fourteenth Amendment of the U.S. Constitution. This clause provides: "No State shall make or enforce any law which shall abridge the privileges or immunities of citizens of the United States." Her claim arose before other provisions of the Fourteenth Amendment, notably the Equal Protection Clause and the Due Process Clause, became the more important legal foundations for women's rights in the twentieth century.

Bradwell v. Illinois

83 U.S. (16 Wall.) 130 (1872)

Mrs. Myra Bradwell, residing in the State of Illinois, made application to the judges of the Supreme Court of that State for a license to practice law. . . .

[The Supreme Court of Illinois denied the application because she was a married woman. Mrs. Bradwell challenged the denial under the Privileges and Immunities clause of the Fourteenth Amendment of the U.S. Constitution, but the decision of the Illinois Supreme Court was upheld. The opinion of the Court is omitted here; what follows is the concurring opinion of Justice Bradley.]

---

8. Deborah L. Rhode, Midcourse Corrections: Women in Legal Education, 53 J. Legal Educ. 475, 477 (2003).

Mr. Justice BRADLEY, concurring: . . .

The claim of the plaintiff, who is a married woman, to be admitted to practice as an attorney and counsellor-at-law, is based upon the supposed right of every person, man or woman, to engage in any lawful employment for a livelihood. The Supreme Court of Illinois denied the application on the ground that, by the common law, which is the basis of the laws of Illinois, only men were admitted to the bar, and the legislature had not made any change in this respect. . . .

The claim that, under the fourteenth amendment of the Constitution, which declares that no State shall make or enforce any law which shall abridge the privileges and immunities of citizens of the United States, the statute law of Illinois, or the common law prevailing in that State, can no longer be set up as a barrier against the right of females to pursue any lawful employment for a livelihood (the practice of law included), assumes that it is one of the privileges and immunities of women as citizens to engage in any and every profession, occupation, or employment in civil life.

It certainly cannot be affirmed, as an historical fact, that this has ever been established as one of the fundamental privileges and immunities of the sex. On the contrary, the civil law, as well as nature herself, has always recognized a wide difference in the respective spheres and destinies of man and woman. Man is, or should be, woman's protector and defender. The natural and proper timidity and delicacy which belongs to the female sex evidently unfits it for many of the occupations of civil life. The constitution of the family organization, which is founded in the divine ordinance, as well as in the nature of things, indicates the domestic sphere as that which properly belongs to the domain and functions of womanhood. The harmony, not to say identity, of interests and views which belong, or should belong, to the family institution is repugnant to the idea of a woman adopting a distinct and independent career from that of her husband. So firmly fixed was this sentiment in the founders of the common law that it became a maxim of that system of jurisprudence that a woman had no legal existence separate from her husband, who was regarded as her head and representative in the social state; and, notwithstanding some recent modifications of this civil status, many of the special rules of law flowing from and dependent upon this cardinal principle still exist in full force in most States. One of these is, that a married woman is incapable, without her husband's consent, of making contracts which shall be binding on her or him. This very incapacity was one circumstance which the Supreme Court of Illinois deemed important in rendering a married woman incompetent fully to perform the duties and trusts that belong to the office of an attorney and counsellor.

It is true that many women are unmarried and not affected by any of the duties, complications, and incapacities arising out of the married state, but these are exceptions to the general rule. The paramount destiny and mission of woman are to fulfil the noble and benign offices of wife and mother. This is the law of the Creator. And the rules of civil society must be adapted to the general constitution of things, and cannot be based upon exceptional cases.

The humane movements of modern society, which have for their object the multiplication of avenues for woman's advancement, and of occupations adapted to her condition and sex, have my heartiest concurrence. But I am not prepared to say that it is one of her fundamental rights and privileges to be admitted into every office and position, including those which require highly special qualifications and demanding special responsibilities. In the nature of things it is not every citizen of every age, sex, and condition that is qualified for every calling and position. It is the prerogative of the legislator to prescribe regulations founded on nature, reason, and experience for the due admission of qualified persons to professions and callings demanding special skill and confidence. This fairly belongs to the police power of the State; and, in my opinion, in view of the peculiar characteristics, destiny, and mission of woman, it is within the province of the legislature to ordain what offices, positions, and callings shall be filled and discharged by men, and shall receive the benefit of those energies and responsibilities, and that decision and firmness which are presumed to predominate in the sterner sex.

For these reasons I think that the laws of Illinois now complained of are not obnoxious to the charge of abridging any of the privileges and immunities of citizens of the United States.

2. *The Case for Women's Suffrage*

Modern feminism has its roots in the nineteenth-century movement for women's suffrage. Although several states briefly allowed women to cast ballots in state and local elections, women did not achieve the vote until the passage of the Nineteenth Amendment in 1920. Efforts to include women in the Civil Rights Amendments that enfranchised former slaves were unsuccessful.

Declaration of Sentiments

Seneca Falls Convention, Seneca Falls, New York (July 1848)

When, in the course of human events, it becomes necessary for one portion of the family of man to assume among the people of the earth a position different from that which they have hitherto occupied, but one to which the laws of nature and of nature's God entitle them, a decent respect to the opinions of mankind requires that they should declare the causes that impel them to such a course.

We hold these truths to be self-evident: that all men and women are created equal; that they are endowed by their Creator with certain inalienable rights; that among these are life, liberty, and the pursuit of happiness; that to secure these rights governments are instituted, deriving their just powers from the consent of the governed. Whenever any form of government becomes destructive of these ends, it is the right of those who suffer from it to refuse allegiance to it, and to insist upon the institution of a new government, laying its foundation on such principles, and organizing its powers in such form, as to them shall seem most likely to affect their safety and happiness. Prudence, indeed, will dictate that governments long established should not be changed for light and transient causes; and accordingly, all experience hath shown that mankind is more disposed to suffer, while evils are sufferable, than to right themselves by abolishing the forms to which they were accustomed. But when a long train of abuses and usurpations, pursuing invariably the same object evinces a design to reduce them under absolute despotism, it is their duty to throw off such government, and to provide new guards for their future security. Such has been the patient sufferance of the women under this government, and such is now the necessity which constrains them to demand the equal station to which they are entitled.

The history of mankind is a history of repeated injuries and usurpations on the part of man toward woman, having in direct object the establishment of an absolute tyranny over her. To prove this, let facts be submitted to a candid world.

He has never permitted her to exercise her inalienable right to the elective franchise.

He has compelled her to submit to laws, in the formation of which she had no voice.

He has withheld from her rights which are given to the most ignorant and degraded men—both natives and foreigners.

Having deprived her of this first right of a citizen, the elective franchise, thereby leaving her without representation in the halls of legislation, he has oppressed her on all sides.

He has made her, if married, in the eye of the law, civilly dead.

He has taken from her all right in property, even to the wages she earns.

He has made her, morally, an irresponsible being, as she can commit many crimes with impunity, provided they be done in the presence of her husband. In the covenant of marriage, she is compelled to promise obedience to her husband, he becoming, to all intents and purposes, her master—the law giving him power to deprive her of her liberty, and to administer chastisement.

He has so framed the laws of divorce, as to what shall be the proper causes, and in case of separation, to whom the guardianship of the children shall be given, as to be wholly regardless of the happiness of women—the law, in all cases, going upon a false supposition of the supremacy of man, and giving all power into his hands.

After depriving her of all rights as a married woman, if single, and the owner of property, he has taxed her to support a government which recognizes her only when her property can be made profitable to it.

He has monopolized nearly all the profitable employments, and from those she is permitted to follow, she receives but a scanty remuneration. He closes against her all the avenues to wealth and distinction which he considers most honorable to himself. As a teacher of theology, medicine, or law, she is not known.

He has denied her the facilities for obtaining a thorough education, all colleges being closed against her.

He allows her in Church, as well as State, but a subordinate position, claiming Apostolic authority for her exclusion from the ministry, and with some exceptions, from any public participation in the affairs of the Church.

He has created a false public sentiment by giving to the world a different code of morals for men and women, by which moral delinquencies which exclude women from society, are not only tolerated, but deemed of little account in man.

He has usurped the prerogative of Jehovah himself, claiming it as his right to assign for her a sphere of action, when that belongs to her conscience and to her God.

He has endeavored, in every way that he could, to destroy her confidence in her own powers, to lessen her self-respect, and to make her willing to lead a dependent and abject life.

Now, in view of this entire disfranchisement of one-half the people of this country, their social and religious degradation—in view of the unjust laws above mentioned, and because women do feel themselves aggrieved, oppressed, and fraudulently deprived of their most sacred rights, we insist that they have immediate admission to all the rights and privileges which belong to them as citizens of the United States.

In entering upon the great work before us, we anticipate no small amount of misconception, misrepresentation, and ridicule; but we shall use every instrumentality within our power to effect our object. We shall employ agents, circulate tracts, petition the State and National legislatures, and endeavor to enlist the pulpit and the press in our behalf. We hope this Convention will be followed by a series of Conventions embracing every part of the country.

United States v. Anthony

1873

Miss ANTHONY: All my prosecutors, from the 8th Ward corner grocery politician, who entered the complaint, to the United States Marshal, Commissioner, District Attorney, District Judge, your honor on the bench, not one is my peer, but each and all are my political sovereigns; and had your honor submitted my case to the jury, as was clearly your duty, even then I should have had just cause of protest, for not one of those men was my peer; but, native or foreign, white or black, rich or poor, educated or ignorant, awake or asleep, sober or drunk, each and every man of them was my political superior; hence, in no sense, my peer. Even, under such circumstances, a commoner of England, tried before a jury of lords, would have far less cause to complain than should I, a woman, tried before a jury of men. Even my counsel, the Hon. Henry R. Selden, who has argued my cause so ably, so earnestly, so unanswerably before your honor, is my political sovereign. Precisely as no disfranchised person is entitled to sit upon a jury, and no woman is entitled to the franchise, so, none but a regularly admitted lawyer is allowed to practice in the courts, and no woman can gain admission to the bar—hence, jury, judge, counsel, must all be of the superior class.

Judge HUNT: The Court must insist—the prisoner has been tried according to the established forms of law.

Miss ANTHONY: Yes, your honor, but by forms of law all made by men, interpreted by men, administered by men, in favor of men, and against women; and hence, your honor's ordered verdict of guilty, against a United States citizen for the exercise of "that citizen's right to vote," simply because that citizen was a woman and not a man. But, yesterday, the same man-made forms of law declared it a crime punishable with $1,000 fine and six months' imprisonment, for you, or me, or any of us, to give a cup of cold water, a crust of bread, or a night's shelter to a panting fugitive as he was tracking his way to Canada. And every man or woman in whose veins coursed a drop of human sympathy violated that wicked law, reckless of consequences, and was justified in so doing. As then the slaves who got their freedom must take it over, or under, or through the unjust forms of law, precisely so now must women, to get their right to a voice in this Government, take it; and I have taken mine, and mean to take it at every possible opportunity.

Judge HUNT: The Court orders the prisoner to sit down. It will not allow another word.

Miss ANTHONY: When I was brought before your honor for trial, I hoped for a broad and liberal interpretation of the Constitution and its recent amendments, that should declare all United States citizens under its protecting aegis — that should declare equality of rights the national guarantee to all persons born or naturalized in the United States. But failing to get this justice — failing, even, to get a trial by a jury not of my peers — I ask not leniency at your hands — but rather the full rigors of the law.

Judge HUNT: The Court must insist — (Here the prisoner sat down.)

Judge HUNT: The prisoner will stand up. (Here Miss Anthony arose again.) The sentence of the Court is that you pay a fine of one hundred dollars and the costs of the prosecution.

Miss ANTHONY: May it please your honor, I shall never pay a dollar of your unjust penalty. All the stock in trade I possess is a $10,000 debt, incurred by publishing my paper — *The Revolution* — four years ago, the sole object of which was to educate all women to do precisely as I have done, rebel against your man-made, unjust unconstitutional forms of law, that tax, fine, imprison, and hang women, while they deny them the right of representation in the Government; and I shall work on with might and main to pay every dollar of that honest debt, but not a penny shall go to this unjust claim. And I shall earnestly and persistently continue to urge all women to practical recognition of the old revolutionary maxim, that "Resistance to tyranny is obedience to God."

Elizabeth Cady Stanton

Address to the Legislature of the State of New York

(February 14, 1854)

The tyrant, Custom, has been summoned before the bar of Common-Sense. His majesty no longer awes his multitude — his sceptre is broken — his crown is trampled in the dust — the sentence of death is pronounced upon him. . . . [A]nd now, that the monster is chained and caged, timid woman, on tiptoe, comes to look him in the face, and to demand of her brave sires and sons, who have struck stout blows for liberty, if, in this change of dynasty, she, too, shall find relief. Yes, gentlemen, in republican America, in the nineteenth century, we, the daughters of the revolutionary heroes of '76, demand at your hands the redress of our grievances — a revision of your State Constitution — a new code of laws. Permit us then, as briefly as possible, to call your attention to the legal disabilities under which we labor.

1st. Look at the position of woman as woman. . . . We are persons; native, free-born citizens; property-holders, tax-payers; yet we are denied the exercise of our right to the elective franchise. We support ourselves, and, in part, your schools, colleges, churches, your poor-houses, jails, prisons, the army, the navy, the whole machinery of government, and yet we have no voice in your councils. . . . We are moral, virtuous, and intelligent, and in all respects quite equal to the proud white man himself and yet by your laws we are classed with idiots, lunatics, and negroes; and though we do not feel honored by the place assigned us in fact, our legal position is lower than that of either; for the negro can be raised to the dignity of a voter if he possess himself of $250; the lunatic can vote in his moments of sanity, and the idiot, too, if he be a made one, and not more than nine-tenths a fool; but we, who have guided great movements of charity, established missions, edited journals, published works on history, economy, and statistics; who have governed nations, led armies, filled the professor's chair, taught philosophy and mathematics to the savants of our age, discovered planets, piloted ships across the sea, are denied the most sacred rights of citizens, because, forsooth, we came not into this republic crowned with the dignity of manhood! . . .

Now, gentlemen, who would fain know by what authority you have disfranchised one-half the people of this State? You who have so boldly taken possession of the bulwarks of this republic, show us your credentials, and thus prove your exclusive right to govern, not only yourselves, but us. . . . Can it be that here, where we acknowledge no royal blood, no apostolic descent, that you, who have declared that all men were created equal—that governments derive their just powers from the consent of the governed, would willingly build up an aristocracy that places the ignorant and vulgar above the educated and refined—the alien and the ditch-digger above the authors and poets of the day—an aristocracy that would raise the sons above the mothers that bore them? Would that the men who can sanction a Constitution so opposed to the genius of this government, who can enact and execute laws so degrading to womankind, had sprung, Minerva-like, from the brains of their fathers, that the matrons of this republic need not blush to own their sons!. . .

[Y]ou place the negro, so unjustly degraded by you, in a superior position to your own wives and mothers; for colored males, if possessed of a certain amount of property and certain other qualifications, can vote, but if they do not have these qualifications they are not subject to direct taxation; wherein they have the advantage of woman, she being subject to taxation for whatever amount she may possess. . . .

[W]e demand in criminal cases that most sacred of all rights, trial by a jury of our own peers. . . .

Shall an erring woman be dragged before a bar of grim-visaged judges, lawyers, and jurors, there to be grossly questioned in public on subjects which women scarce breathe in secret to one another? Shall the most sacred relations of life be called up and rudely scanned by men who, by their own admission, are so coarse that woman could not meet them even at the polls without contamination? [A]nd yet shall she find there no woman's face or voice to pity and defend? Shall the frenzied mother, who, to save herself and child from exposure and disgrace, ended the life that had but just begun, be dragged before such a tribunal to answer for her crime? How can man enter into the feelings of that mother? How can he judge of the agonies of soul that impelled her to such an outrage of maternal instincts? How can he weigh the mountain of sorrow that crushed that mother's heart when she wildly tossed her helpless babe into the cold waters of the midnight sea? Where is he who by false vows thus blasted this trusting woman? Had that helpless child no claims on his protection? Ah, he is freely abroad in the dignity of manhood, in the pulpit, on the bench, in the professor's chair. The imprisonment of his victim and the death of his child, detract not a tithe from his standing and complacency. His peers made the law, and shall law-makers lay nets for those of their own rank? Shall laws which come from the logical brain of man take cognizance of violence done to the moral and affectional nature which predominates, as is said, in woman?

Statesmen of New York, whose daughters guarded by your affection, and lapped amidst luxuries which your indulgence spreads, care more for their nodding plumes and velvet trains than for the statute laws by which their persons and properties are held — who, blinded by custom and prejudice to the degraded position which they and their sisters occupy in the civil scale, haughtily claim that they already have all the rights they want, how, think ye, you would feel to see a daughter summoned for such a crime — and remember these daughters are but human — before such a tribunal? Would it not, in that hour, be some consolation to see that she was surrounded by the wise and virtuous of her own sex; by those who had known the depth of a mother's love and the misery of a lover's falsehood; to know that to these she could make her confession, and from them receive her sentence? . . .

2d. Look at the position of woman as wife. Your laws relating to marriage — founded as they are on the old common law of England, a compound of barbarous usages, but partially modified by progressive civilization — are in open violation of our enlightened ideas of justice, and of the holiest feelings of our nature. If you take the highest view of marriage, as a Divine relation, which love alone can constitute and sanctify, then of course human legislation can only recognize it. Men can neither bind nor loose its ties, for that prerogative belongs to God alone, who makes man and woman, and the laws of attraction by which they are united. But if you regard marriage as a civil contract, then let it be subject to the same laws which control all other contracts. Do not make it a kind of half-human, half-divine institution, which you may build up, but can not regulate. Do not, by your special legislation for this one kind of contract, involve yourselves in the grossest absurdities and contradictions. . . .

The wife who inherits no property holds about the same legal position that does the slave on the Southern plantation. She can own nothing, sell nothing. She has no right even to the wages she earns; her person, her time, her services are the property of another. She can not testify, in many cases, against her husband. She can get no redress for wrongs in her own name in any court of justice. She can neither sue nor be sued. She is not held morally responsible for any crime committed in the presence of her husband so completely is her very existence supposed by the law to be merged in that of another. Think of it; your wives may be thieves, libelers, burglars, incendiaries, and for crimes like these they are not held amenable to the laws of the land, if they but commit them in your dread presence. For them, alas! there is no higher law than the will of man. . . .

4th. Look at the position of woman as mother. There is no human love so strong and steadfast as that of the mother for her child; yet behold how ruthless are your laws touching this most sacred relation. Nature has clearly made the mother the guardian of the child; but man, in his inordinate love of power, does continually set nature and nature's laws at open defiance. The father may apprentice his child, bind him out to a trade, without the mother's consent — yea, in direct opposition to her most earnest entreaties, prayers and tears.

He may apprentice his son to a gamester or rum-seller, and thus cancel his debts of honor. By the abuse of this absolute power, he may bind his daughter to the owner of a brothel, and, by the degradation of his child, supply his daily wants; and such things, gentlemen, have been done in our very midst. Moreover, the father, about to die, may bond out all his children wherever and to whomsoever he may see fit, and thus, in fact, will away the guardianship of all his children from the mother. . . . [B]y your laws, the child is the absolute property of the father, wholly at his disposal in life or at death.

In case of separation, the law gives the children to the father; no matter what his character or condition. At this very time we can point you to noble, virtuous, well-educated mothers in this State, who have abandoned their husbands for their profligacy and confirmed drunkenness. All these have been robbed of their children, who are in the custody of the husband, under the care of his relatives, whilst the mothers are permitted to see them but at stated intervals. . . .

Many times and oft it has been asked us, with unaffected seriousness, "What do you women want? What are you aiming at?" Many have manifested a laudable curiosity to know what the wives and daughters could complain of in republican America, where their sires and sons have so bravely fought for freedom and gloriously secured their independence, trampling all tyranny, bigotry, and caste in the dust, and declaring to a waiting world the divine truth that all men are created equal. What can woman want under such a government? Admit a radical difference in sex, and you demand different spheres—water for fish, and air for birds. . . .

When we plead our cause before the law-makers and savants of the republic, they can not take in the idea that men and women are alike; and so long as the mass rest in this delusion, the public mind will not be so much startled by the revelations made of the injustice and degradation of woman's position as by the fact that she should at length wake up to a sense of it.

If you, too, are thus deluded, what avails it that we show by your statute books that your laws are unjust—that woman is the victim of avarice and power? . . .

Would to God you could know the burning indignation that fills woman's soul when she turns over the pages of your statute books, and sees there how like feudal barons you freemen hold your women. Would that you could know the humiliation she feels for sex, when she thinks of all the beardless boys in your law offices, learning these ideas of one-sided justice—taking their first lessons in contempt for all womankind—being indoctrinated into the incapacities of their mothers, and the lordly, absolute rights of man over all women, children, and property, and to know that these are to be our future presidents, judges, husbands, and fathers; in sorrow we exclaim, alas! for that nation whose sons bow not in loyalty to woman. . . .

But if, gentlemen, you take the ground that the sexes are alike, and, therefore, you are our faithful representatives—then why all these special laws for woman? Would not one code answer for all of like needs and wants? Christ's golden rule is better than all the special legislation that the ingenuity of man can devise: "Do unto others as you would have others do unto you." This, men and brethren, is all we ask at your hands. We ask no better laws than those you have made for yourselves. We need no other protection than that which your present laws secure to you.

In conclusion, then, let us say, in behalf of the women of this State, we ask for all that you have asked for yourselves in the progress of your development, since the Mayflower cast anchor beside Plymouth rock; and simply on the ground that the rights of every human being are the same and identical. You may say that the mass of the women of this State do not make the demand; it comes from a few sour, disappointed old maids and childless women.

You are mistaken; the mass speak through us. A very large majority of the women of this State support themselves and their children, and many their husbands too. . . .

Now, do you candidly think these wives do not wish to control the wages they earn—to own the land they buy—the houses they build? To have at their disposal their own children, without being subject to the constant interference and tyranny of an idle, worthless profligate? Do you suppose that any woman is such a pattern of devotion and submission that she willingly stitches all day for the small sum of fifty cents, that she may enjoy the unspeakable privilege, in obedience to your laws, of paying for her husband's tobacco and rum? Think you the wife of the confirmed, beastly drunkard would consent to share with him her home and bed, if law and public sentiment would release her from such gross companionship? Verily, no! Think you the wife with whom endurance has ceased to be a virtue, who, through much suffering, has lost all faith in the justice of both heaven and earth, takes the law in her own hand, severs the unholy bond, and turns her back forever upon him whom she once called husband, consents to the law that in such an hour tears her child from her—all that she has left on earth to love and cherish? The drunkards' wives speak through us, and they number 50,000. Think you that the woman who has worked hard all her days in helping her husband to accumulate a large property, consents to the law that places this wholly at his disposal? Would not the mother whose only child is bound out for a term of years against her expressed wish, deprive the father of this absolute power if she could?

For all these, then, we speak. If to this long list you add the laboring women who are loudly demanding remuneration for their unending toil; those women who teach in our seminaries, academies, and public schools for a miserable pittance; the widows who are taxed without mercy; the unfortunate ones in our workhouses, poor-houses, and prisons; who are they that we do not now represent? But a small class of the fashionable butterflies, who, through the short summer days, seek the sunshine and the flowers; but the cool breezes of autumn and the hoary frosts of winter will soon chase all these away; then they, too, will need and seek protection, and through other lips demand in their turn justice and equity at your hands.

Sojourner Truth: Reminiscences by Frances D. Gage

Akron Convention (May 28-29, 1851)

The leaders of the movement trembled on seeing a tall, gaunt black woman in a gray dress and white turban, surmounted with an uncouth sun-bonnet, march deliberately into the church, walk with the air of a queen up the aisle, and take her seat upon the pulpit steps. A buzz of disapprobation was heard all over the house, and there fell on the listening ear, "An abolition affair!" "Go it, darkey!"

I chanced on that occasion to wear my first laurels in public life as president of the meeting. At my request order was restored, and the business of the convention went on. Morning, afternoon, and evening exercises came and went. Through all these sessions old Sojourner, quiet and reticent as the "Lybian Statue," sat crouched against the wall on the corner of the pulpit stairs, her sun-bonnet shading her eyes, her elbows on her knees, her chin resting upon her broad, hard palms. At intermission she was busy selling the "life of Sojourner Truth," a narrative of her own strange and adventurous life. Again and again, timorous and trembling ones came to me and said, with earnestness, "Don't let her speak, Mrs. Gage, it will ruin us. Every newspaper in the land will have our cause mixed up with abolition and niggers, and we shall be utterly denounced." My only answer was, "We shall see when the time comes."

The second day the work waxed warm, Methodist, Baptist, Episcopal, Presbyterian, and Universalist ministers came in to hear and discuss the resolutions presented. One claimed superior rights and privileges for man, on the ground of "superior intellect"; another, because of the "manhood of Christ; if God had desired the equality of woman, He would have given some token of His will through the birth, life, and death of the Saviour." Another gave us a theological view of the "sin of our first mother."

There were very few women in those days who dared to "speak in meeting"; and the august teachers of the people were seemingly getting the better of us, while the boys in the galleries, and the sneerers among the pews, were hugely enjoying the discomfiture, as they supposed, of the "strong-minded." Some of the tender-skinned friends were on the point of losing dignity, and the atmosphere betokened a storm. When, slowly from her seat in the corner rose Sojourner Truth, who, till now, had scarcely lifted her head. "Don't let her speak?" gasped half a dozen in my ear. She moved slowly and solemnly to the front, laid her old bonnet at her feet, and turned her great speaking eyes to me. There was a hissing sound of disapprobation above and below. I rose and announced "Sojourner Truth," and begged the audience to keep silence for a few moments.

The tumult subsided at once, and every eye was fixed on this almost Amazon form, which stood nearly six feet high, head erect, and eyes piercing the upper air like one in a dream. At her first word there was a profound hush. She spoke in deep tones, which, though not loud, reached every ear in the house, and away through the throngs at the doors and windows.

"Wall, chilern, whar dar is so much racket dar must be somethin' out o' kilter. I think dat 'twixt de niggers of de Souf and de womin at de Norf, all talk' 'bout right, de white men will be in a fix pretty soon. But what's all this here talkin' 'bout?

"Dat man over dar say dat womin needs to be helped into carriages, and lifted ober ditches, and to hab de best place everwhar. Nobody evber helps me into carriages, or ober mud puddles, or gibs me any best place!" And raising herself to her full height, and her voice to a pitch to like rolling thunder, she asked, "And a'n't I a woman? Look at me! Look at my arm! (and she bared her right arm to the shoulder, showing her tremendous muscular power). I have ploughed, and planted, and gathered into barns, and no man could head me! And a'n't I a woman? I could work as much and eat as much as a man—when I could get it—and bear de lash as well! And a'n't I a woman? I have borne thirteen chilern, and seen 'em mos' all sold off to slavery, and when I cried out with my mother's grief, none but Jesus heard me! And a'n't I a woman?

"Den dey talks 'bout dis ting in de head; what dis dey call it?" ("Intellect," whispered some one near.) "Dat's it, honey. What's dat got to do wid womin's rights or nigger's rights? If my cup won't hold but a pint and yourn holds a quart, wouldn't ye be mean now to let me have my little half-measure full?" And she pointed her significant finger, and sent a keen glance at the ministers who had made the argument. The cheering was long and loud.

"Den dat little man in black dar, he say women can't have as much rights as men, 'cause Christ wan't a woman! Whar did your Christ come from?" Rolling thunder couldn't have stilled that crowd, as did those deep wonderful tones, as she stood there with outstretched arms and eyes of fire. Raising her voice still louder, she repeated, "Whar did your Christ come from? From God and a woman! Man had nothin' to do wid Him." Oh, what rebuke that was to that little man.

Turning again to another objector, she took up the defense of Mother Eve. I can not follow her through it all. It was pointed, and witty, and solemn; eliciting at almost every sentence deafening applause; and she ended by asserting: "If de fust woman God ever made was strong enough to turn de world upside down all alone, dese women togedder (and she glanced her eye over the platform) ought to be able to turn it back, and get it right side up again! And now dey is asking to do it, de men better let 'em." Long continued cheering greeted this. "Bleeged to ye for hearin' on me, and now ole Sojourner han't got nothin' more to say."

Amid roars of applause, she returned to her corner, leaving more than one of us with streaming eyes, and hearts beating with gratitude. She had taken us up in her strong arms and carried us safely over the slough of difficulty turning the whole tide in our favor. I have never in my life seen anything like the magical influence that subdued the mobbish spirit of the day, and turned the sneers and jeers of an excited crowd into notes of respect and admiration. Hundreds rushed up to shake hands with her, and congratulate the glorious old mother, and bid her God-speed on her mission of "testifyin' agin concerning the wickedness of this 'ere people."

Nell Painter

Sojourner Truth: A Life, A Symbol

125-26, 170-71, 174 (1996)

A much later report would attribute a dominant role to Sojourner Truth. In fact she was only one of several self-possessed, competent, and experienced anti-slavery feminists who conducted this meeting so boldly—and with the support of the men who were there. Her remarks did not bring the meeting to a halt or even change its course, but they engrossed the audience. Her friend and host, Marius Robinson, was used to her way of speaking and was also serving as secretary of the convention. He printed his report of her whole address:

> One of the most unique and interesting speeches of the Convention was made by Sojourner Truth, an emancipated slave. It is impossible to transfer it to paper, or convey any adequate idea of the effect it produced upon the audience. Those only can appreciate it who saw her powerful forms, her whole souled, earnest gestures, and listened to her strong and truthful tones. She came forward to the platform and addressing the President said with great simplicity:
>
> May I say a few words?

Receiving an affirmative answer, she proceeded:

I want to say a few words about this matter. I am a woman's rights. I have as much muscle as any man, and can do as much work as any man. I have plowed and reaped and husked and chopped and mowed, and can any man do more than that? I have heard much about the sexes being equal; I can carry as much as any man, and can eat as much too, if I can get it. I am as strong as any man that is now. As for intellect, all I can say is, if a woman have a pint and man a quart—for fear we will take too much—for we cant take more than our pint'll hold. The poor men seem to be all in confusion, and don't know what to do. Why children, if you have woman's rights give it to her and you will feel better. You will have your own rights, and they wont be so much trouble. I cant read, but I can hear. I have heard the bible and have learned that Eve caused man to sin. Well if woman upset the world, do give her a chance to set it right side up again. The lady has spoken about Jesus, how he never spurned woman from him, and she was right. When Lazarus died, Mary and Martha came to him with faith and love and besought him to raise their brother. And Jesus wept—and Lazarus came forth. And how came Jesus into the world? Through God who created him and woman who bore him. Man, where is your part? But the woman are coming up blessed by God and few of the men are coming up with them. But man is in a tight place, the poor slave is on him, woman is coming on him, and he is surely between a hawk and a buzzard.

In Gage's scenario, Truth addresses male critics and antiblack women, not a meeting full of people who agreed with and supported her. Gage does two things with her set-up: She reiterates a familiar Christian narrative in which a lone preacher—like Sojourner Truth against the rowdies at Northhampton—subdues and converts a body of unruly non-believers. And she plays on the irony of white women advocating women's rights while ignoring women who are black. White feminists' hostility is the bedrock of the emblematic Sojourner Truth who emerges from Gage's narrative. Their antagonism proves the power of Truth, the preacher able to convert them. . . .

Gage's Truth speaks in an inconsistent dialect that may have been inspired by the South Carolinians around Gage in 1863 . . . [T]he dialect serves primarily to measure the distance between Truth and her white audience. . .

"Ar'n't I a woman?" was Gage's invention. Had Truth said it several times in 1851, as in Gage's article, Marius Robinson, who was familiar with Truth's diction, most certainly would have noted it. . . .

One of only a few black women regulars on the feminist and antislavery circuit, Truth was . . . in Gage's report . . . the pivot that linked two causes—of women (presumed to be white) and of blacks (presumed to be men)—through one black female body. One phrase sums up the emblematic Sojourner Truth today: "ar'n't I a woman?"

We cannot know exactly what Truth said at Akron in 1851, an unusually well reported appearance. . . . [S]eekers after Truth are now at the mercy of what other people said she said. . . .

Unlike professional historians, whose eyes are fixed on accuracy, Truth's modern admirers almost universally prefer the account that Gage presented twelve years after the fact. It fits far better with what we believe Truth to have been like. But this is testimony to the role of symbol in our public life and to our need for this symbol. To Robinson's contemporaneous report in standard English, we prefer the Sojourner Truth in the dialect of a skilled feminist writer.

NOTES

1. **The Nineteenth Amendment.** The Declaration of Sentiments was adopted at the Seneca Falls Convention in Seneca Falls, New York, in July 1848.[9] As historian Gerda Lerner notes, this Convention was the "first forum in which women gathered together to publicly air their own grievances, not those of the needy, the enslaved, orphans, or widows." The Declaration quite clearly uses the Declaration of Independence as the template. Lerner suggests that the naming of "man" as the culprit, which anticipated the subsequent, radical feminist critique of patriarchy detailed in Chapter 3 of this casebook, was probably intended more as part of the Declaration's "rhetorical flourishes" than an "actual analysis of women's situation."[10]

Elizabeth Cady Stanton's address to the New York legislature in 1854 reflects the prevailing views about women at the time. To what extent does this address assume men and women are the same, and to what extent does it assume important differences between them?

Susan B. Anthony's statement occurred during her successful prosecution for violation of an 1870 federal civil rights statute intended to prohibit multiple voting by white voters in order to dilute Black votes. After dedicating much of her life to the suffrage struggle, Anthony died in 1906, fourteen years before the Nineteenth Amendment was passed in 1920.

Passage of the Nineteenth Amendment reflected women's increasing role in public life and gratitude for their service during World War I, and followed a mass movement of women's rights supporters who pursued tactics of escalating pressure, including parades, White House pickets, and hunger strikes. After that victory, the women's movement dissolved. Although many women remained active in progressive causes, and a few continued to struggle for a constitutional equal rights amendment, an organized feminist campaign did not reemerge until the 1960s.

2. **Suffrage and Abolitionism.** The women's suffrage movement was intertwined with the campaign to abolish slavery. Indeed, the idea for the Seneca Falls Convention was inspired by a London Anti-Slavery Convention a few years earlier at which two American participants, Lucretia Mott, a Quaker minister, and Elizabeth Cady Stanton, were barred from participation and required to sit behind a

---

9. The Declaration of Sentiments, as well as all of the other documents excerpted in this section, can be found in a multivolume collection of women's suffrage documents, History of Woman Suffrage, edited by Elizabeth Cady Stanton, Susan B. Anthony, and Matilda Joslyn Gage (reprint ed. 1985).

10. Gerda Lerner, The Meaning of Seneca Falls, 1848-1998, Dissent 35, 37-39 (Fall 1998).

curtain.[11] Some suffragettes also had close ties to other social movements, such as campaigns to protect children from abuse, to criminalize the sale and consumption of liquor, to combat "vices" such as prostitution and obscenity, and to improve the conditions of the working poor.

Nineteenth-century suffragettes exploited both the civil rights principles underlying abolition and the racism that persisted after the Civil War. Elizabeth Cady Stanton in the passage above, for example, claimed both affinity with Negro slaves and superiority over them, reminding white political leaders of the obvious injustice that Black men could vote while white women could not: "[Y]ou place the [N]egro, so unjustly degraded by you, in a superior position to your own wives and mothers," she complained.[12] Later suffragettes used even more explicitly racist arguments, asserting the desirability of diluting the Negro vote as a rationale for supporting women's suffrage. For example, one Southern suffragist at a 1903 convention of the National American Women Suffrage Association claimed that "[t]he enfranchisement of women would insure immediate and durable white supremacy, honestly attained."[13]

Does any of this sound familiar today? Does white women's equality continue to depend on the inequality of minority women? Do majority women feel entitled, at least subconsciously, to status and income at least as high as that of minority women? What, if anything, does the Black Lives Matter movement suggest about the relationship of racism to sexism?

Sojourner Truth was a former slave and abolitionist missionary. What do you make of the debate over what she said at the Akron Convention? If historian Nell Painter is right that white women suffragettes were not as hostile to Truth as Frances Gage suggests, why do you suppose Gage portrays the situation the way she does? Is she trying to express solidarity with Truth, burnish her own credentials, or something else? If she exaggerates Truth's dialect, as Painter suggests, why might she have done so?

3. **The Birth and Rebirth of Modern Feminism.** The women's movement resurfaced in the 1960s in response to a variety of social, economic, and political trends. One was demographic: the increase in women's life expectancy and control over reproduction and the rise in divorce rates meant that domesticity was a less stable basis for an entire life. At the turn of the twentieth century, women's average life expectancy was forty-eight, and women could contemplate living only ten to fifteen years after the last child left home. By the 1960s, the average woman could contemplate living two-thirds of her adult life with no children under eighteen.[14]

---

11. See Sara M. Evans, Born for Liberty: A History of Women in America 81 (1989).

12. Elizabeth Cady Stanton, Address to the Legislature of the State of New York (Feb. 14, 1854) (excerpted above).

13. Evans, supra note 11, at 155. For a discussion of how feminist advocates, often in collaboration with African-American women, used the race analogy in complex ways, to help secure women's rights and also disaggregate race from sex when it became a liability, see Serena Mayeri, Reasoning from Race: Feminism, Law, and the Civil Rights Revolution (2011); see also bell hooks, Ain't I a Woman: Black Women and Feminism 127-39 (1981).

14. Alice Rossi, Family Development in a Changing World, 128 Am. J. Psychiatry 1057, 1058 (1972).

So, too, women's increasing education and employment experience, particularly during World War II, made them less content with full-time domesticity. Rising economic expectations also propelled more women into the paid labor force and led to frustration with the discrimination they encountered there. Women's discontent was the subject of Betty Friedan's widely read publication, The Feminine Mystique (1963). The book, which became an instant best-seller, reported the results of Friedan's interviews with affluent fellow graduates of Smith College, then suburban housewives like Friedan herself. Despite their material privilege, these women were bored and deeply unhappy, often seeking fulfillment in sexual affairs, shopping, and tranquilizers. Friedan labeled their disaffection "the problem that has no name."[15]

As was true of the first wave of feminism, the contemporary women's rights movement drew inspiration and supporters from the civil rights struggle and other progressive social movements. Female activists who encountered gender discrimination in those movements began increasingly to turn their energy to the emerging struggle for "women's liberation," based on a fundamental equality between the sexes. Materials in this chapter represent many of the key legal outcomes of these efforts, while subsequent chapters reflect theories that developed once the basic civil rights framework for gender equality was in place.

4. **The Future Promise of the Nineteenth Amendment?** When the Nineteenth Amendment was ratified, many women's rights advocates believed it would lead to recognition of a broad spectrum of civil and political rights. But, as Reva Siegel explains, "[s]oon after ratification, the judiciary moved to repress the structural significance of women's enfranchisement, by reading the Nineteenth Amendment as a rule concerning voting that had no normative significance for matters other than the franchise."[16] The year 2020 marked the centennial of the Nineteenth Amendment, prompting fresh reflections on the Amendment's legacy and efforts to extend its reach. Paula Monopoli, for example, argues that both the text and history of the Amendment are capacious enough to invite an intersectional analysis of how modern voting restrictions burden women of color.[17] To date, however, efforts to use the Nineteenth Amendment to challenge various types of voting restrictions have not succeeded, and in 2020, a federal court construed the Amendment as limited to intentional discrimination.[18] New feminist legal scholarship criticizes such a narrow view of the Amendment and explains the basis for embracing a more "thick" understanding of the sex equality principles embodied in it.[19]

---

15. Betty Friedan, The Feminine Mystique 57-78 (1963).

16. Reva Siegel, She the People: The Nineteenth Amendment, Sex Equality, Federalism, and the Family, 115 Harv. L. Rev. 947, 1012 (2002).

17. See Paula A. Monopoli, Gender, Voting Rights, and the Nineteenth Amendment, 20 Geo. J. Gender L. & Pub. Pol'y 91 (2022); Paula A. Monopoli, Constitutional Orphan: Gender Equality and the Nineteenth Amendment (2020).

18. See Jones v. DeSantis, 426 F. Supp. 3d 1196 (N.D. Fla. 2020).

19. See, e.g., Symposium: Commemorating the 100th Anniversary of the Nineteenth Amendment, 20 Geo. J. Gender L. & Pub. Pol'y 1 (2022).

B. FORMAL EQUALITY AND THE CONSTITUTIONAL RIGHT TO EQUAL PROTECTION

1. The Right to Equal, Individualized Treatment

Equality claims often arise in a context in which a person asks to be treated as an individual, and without regard to membership in a particular category. The state cannot avoid all categories when it makes laws. For example, the state sets age limits concerning rights to vote, to drink alcoholic beverages, and to marry, even though maturity levels vary, because it would be too difficult to make an individual determination of maturity in every case. So, too, employers' hiring decisions may depend on applicants' educational levels, years of experience, or test scores, even though these are not perfect measures of job fitness.

The state is not allowed to rely on some categories, however, regardless of administrative convenience. Classifications based on race and national origin are subject to strict scrutiny, meaning they must be based on a compelling state interest that cannot be achieved through other, more tailored means. The Supreme Court has never held that strict scrutiny is required for sex-based classifications. Instead, the Court has opted for the "intermediate standard of review," which evolved in the cases that follow.

Reed v. Reed

404 U.S. 71 (1971)

Mr. CHIEF JUSTICE BURGER delivered the opinion of the Court.

[This case challenges an Idaho statute that designates an order of priority for courts to designate the administrator of an estate of a person who dies intestate (without a will). Parents are one priority group, and for all priority groups, Idaho law provides that males are preferred to females. The case is brought by the mother of a child who died intestate, after the probate court issued an order naming the child's father as the administrator of the child's estate.]

In issuing its order, the probate court implicitly recognized the equality of entitlement of the two [parent] applicants; . . . the court ruled, however, that appellee, being a male, was to be preferred to the female appellant [under Idaho law]. In stating this conclusion, the probate judge gave no indication that he had attempted to determine the relative capabilities of the competing applicants to perform the functions incident to the administration of an estate. It seems clear the probate judge considered himself bound by statute to give preference to the male candidate over the female, each being otherwise "equally entitled." . . .

[W]e have concluded that the arbitrary preference established in favor of males . . . cannot stand in the face of the Fourteenth Amendment's command that no State deny the equal protection of the laws to any person within its jurisdiction.

In applying that clause, this Court has consistently recognized that the Fourteenth Amendment does not deny to States the power to treat different classes of persons in different ways. . . . The Equal Protection Clause of that amendment does, however, deny to States the power to legislate that different treatment be accorded to persons placed by a statute into different classes on the basis of criteria wholly unrelated to the objective of that statute. A classification "must be reasonable, not arbitrary, and must rest upon some ground of difference having a fair and substantial relation to the object of the legislation, so that all persons similarly circumstanced shall be treated alike. . . ." . . .

In upholding the [Idaho statute], the Idaho Supreme Court concluded that its objective was to eliminate one area of controversy when two or more persons, equally entitled under [Idaho law], seek letters of administration and thereby present the probate court "with the issue of which one should be named." The court also concluded that where such persons are not of the same sex, the elimination of females from consideration "is neither an illogical nor arbitrary method devised by the legislature to resolve an issue that would otherwise require a hearing as to the relative merits . . . of the two or more petitioning relatives. . . ." . . .

Clearly the objective of reducing the workload on probate courts by eliminating one class of contests is not without some legitimacy. The crucial question, however, is whether [Idaho law] advances that objective in a manner consistent with the command of the Equal Protection Clause. We hold that it does not. To give a mandatory preference to members of either sex over members of the other, merely to accomplish the elimination of hearings on the merits, is to make the very kind of arbitrary legislative choice forbidden by the Equal Protection Clause of the Fourteenth Amendment; and whatever may be said as to the positive values of avoiding intrafamily controversy, the choice in this context may not lawfully be mandated solely on the basis of sex. . . .

Reversed and remanded.

Frontiero v. Richardson

411 U.S. 677 (1973)

Mr. Justice BRENNAN announced the judgment of the Court in an opinion in which Mr. Justice DOUGLAS, Mr. Justice WHITE, and Mr. Justice MARSHALL join.

The question before us concerns the right of a female member of the uniformed services to claim her spouse as a "dependent" for the purposes of obtaining increased quarters allowances and medical and dental benefits under [federal law] on an equal footing with male members. Under the [federal statutes at issue], a serviceman may claim his wife as a "dependent" without regard to whether she is in fact dependent upon him for any part of her support. . . . A servicewoman, on the other hand, may not claim her husband as a "dependent" under these programs unless he is in fact dependent upon her for over one-half of his support. . . . [T]he question for decision is whether this difference in treatment constitutes an unconstitutional discrimination against servicewomen in violation of the Due Process Clause of the Fifth Amendment.

In an effort to attract career personnel through reenlistment, Congress established . . . a scheme for the provision of fringe benefits to members of the uniformed services on a competitive basis with business and industry. [Under this scheme] a member of the uniformed services with dependents is entitled to an increased "basic allowance for quarters" and . . . a member's dependents are provided comprehensive medical and dental care.

Appellant Sharron Frontiero, a lieutenant in the United States Air Force, sought increased quarters allowances, and housing and medical benefits for her husband, appellant Joseph Frontiero, on the ground that he was her "dependent." Although such benefits would automatically have been granted with respect to the wife of a male member of the uniformed services, appellant's application was denied because she failed to demonstrate that her husband was dependent on her for more than one-half of his support. [Joseph Frontiero, a student who received veterans' benefits, was not dependent upon Sharron Frontiero.] Appellants then commenced this suit, contending that, by making this distinction, the statutes unreasonably discriminate on the basis of sex in violation of the Due Process Clause of the Fifth Amendment. In essence, appellants asserted that the discriminatory impact of the statutes is twofold: first, as a procedural matter, a female member is required to demonstrate her spouse's dependency, while no such burden is imposed upon male members; and, second, as a substantive matter, a male member who does not provide more than one-half of his wife's support receives benefits, while a similarly situated female member is denied such benefits. Appellants therefore sought a permanent injunction against the continued enforcement of these statutes and an order directing the appellees to provide Lieutenant Frontiero with the same housing and medical benefits that a similarly situated male member would receive.

Although the legislative history of these statutes sheds virtually no light on the purposes underlying the differential treatment accorded male and female members, a majority of the three-judge District Court [which voted to uphold the statutes] surmised that Congress might reasonably have concluded that, since the husband in our society is generally the "breadwinner" in the family — and the wife typically the "dependent" partner — "it would be more economical to require married female members claiming husbands to prove actual dependency than to extend the presumption of dependency to such members." Indeed, given the fact that approximately 99% of all members of the uniformed services are male, the District Court speculated that such differential treatment might conceivably lead to a "considerable saving of administrative expense and manpower."

At the outset, appellants contend that classifications based upon sex, like classifications based upon race, alienage, and national origin, are inherently suspect and must therefore be subjected to close judicial scrutiny. We agree and, indeed, find at least implicit support for such an approach in our unanimous decision only last Term in Reed v. Reed. . . .

[The Court reviews the attitude of "romantic paternalism" discussed in *Reed*.] As a result of notions such as these, our statute books gradually became laden with gross, stereotyped distinctions between the sexes and, indeed, throughout much of the 19th century the position of women in our society was, in many respects, comparable to that of blacks under the pre-Civil War slaves codes. Neither slaves nor women could hold office, serve on juries, or bring suit in their own names, and married women traditionally were denied the legal capacity to hold or convey property or to serve as legal guardians of their own children. . . . And although blacks were guaranteed the right to vote in 1870, women were denied even that right . . . until adoption of the Nineteenth Amendment half a century later.

It is true, of course, that the position of women in America has improved markedly in recent decades. Nevertheless, it can hardly be doubted that, in part because of the high visibility of the sex characteristic, women still face pervasive, although at times more subtle, discrimination in our educational institutions, in the job market and, perhaps most conspicuously, in the political arena. . . .

Moreover, since sex, like race and national origin, is an immutable characteristic determined solely by the accident of birth, the imposition of special disabilities upon the members of a particular sex because of their sex would seem to violate "the basic concept of our system that legal burdens should bear some relationship to individual responsibility." . . . And what differentiates sex from such non-suspect statuses as intelligence or physical disability, and aligns it with the recognized suspect criteria, is that the sex characteristic frequently bears no relation to ability to perform or contribute to society. As a result, statutory distinctions between the sexes often have the effect of invidiously relegating the entire class of females to inferior legal status without regard to the actual capabilities of its individual members.

We might also note that, over the past decade, Congress has itself manifested an increasing sensitivity to sex-based classifications. In [Title VII] of the Civil Rights Act of 1964, for example, Congress expressly declared that no employer, labor union, or other organization subject to the provisions of the Act shall discriminate against any individual on the basis of "race, color, religion, sex, or national origin." Similarly, the Equal Pay Act of 1963 provides that no employer covered by the Act "shall discriminate . . . between employees on the basis of sex." And §1 of the Equal Rights Amendment, passed by Congress on March 22, 1972, and submitted to the legislatures of the States for ratification, declares that "(e)quality of rights under the law shall not be denied or abridged by the United States or by any State on account of sex." Thus, Congress itself has concluded that classifications based upon sex are inherently invidious, and this conclusion of a coequal branch of Government is not without significance to the question presently under consideration. . . .

With these considerations in mind, we can only conclude that classifications based upon sex, like classifications based upon race, alienage, or national origin, are inherently suspect, and must therefore be subjected to strict judicial scrutiny. Applying the analysis mandated by that stricter standard of review, it is clear that the statutory scheme now before us is constitutionally invalid.

The sole basis of the classification established in the challenged statutes is the sex of the individuals involved. . . .

[T]he Government concedes that the differential treatment accorded men and women under these statutes serves no purpose other than mere "administrative convenience." In essence, the Government maintains that, as an empirical matter, wives in our society frequently are dependent upon their husbands, while husbands rarely are dependent upon their wives. Thus, the Government argues that Congress might reasonably have concluded that it would be both cheaper and easier simply conclusively to presume that wives of male members are financially dependent upon their husbands, while burdening female members with the task of establishing dependency in fact.[22]

---

22. It should be noted that these statutes are not in any sense designed to rectify the effects of past discrimination against women. . . . On the contrary, these statutes seize upon a group—women—who have historically suffered discrimination in employment and rely on the effects of this past discrimination as a justification for heaping on additional economic disadvantages.

The Government offers no concrete evidence, however, tending to support its view that such differential treatment in fact saves the Government any money. In order to satisfy the demands of strict judicial scrutiny, the Government must demonstrate, for example, that it is actually cheaper to grant increased benefits with respect to all male members, than it is to determine which male members are in fact entitled to such benefits and to grant increased benefits only to those members whose wives actually meet the dependency requirement. Here, however, there is substantial evidence that, if put to the test, many of the wives of male members would fail to qualify for benefits. And in light of the fact that the dependency determination with respect to the husbands of female members is presently made solely on the basis of affidavits rather than through the more costly hearing process, the Government's explanation of the statutory scheme is, to say the least, questionable.

In any case, our prior decisions make clear that, although efficacious administration of governmental programs is not without some importance, "the Constitution recognizes higher values than speed and efficiency. . . ." And when we enter the realm of "strict judicial scrutiny," there can be no doubt that "administrative convenience" is not a shibboleth, the mere recitation of which dictates constitutionality. . . . We therefore conclude that, by according differential treatment to male and female members of the uniformed services for the sole purpose of achieving administrative convenience, the challenged statutes violate the Due Process Clause of the Fifth Amendment insofar as they require a female member to prove the dependency of her husband. Reversed.

Mr. Justice POWELL, with whom THE CHIEF JUSTICE and Mr. Justice BLACKMUN join, concurring in the judgment. . . .

It is unnecessary for the Court in this case to characterize sex as a suspect classification, with all of the far-reaching implications of such a holding. Reed v. Reed, [1971], which abundantly supports our decision today, did not add sex to the narrowly limited group of classifications which are inherently suspect. . . . In my view, we can and should decide this case on the authority of *Reed* and reserve for the future any expansion of its rationale.

There is another, and I find compelling, reason for deferring a general categorizing of sex classifications as invoking the strictest test of judicial scrutiny. The Equal Rights Amendment, which if adopted will resolve the substance of this precise question, has been approved by the Congress and submitted for ratification by the States. If this Amendment is duly adopted, it will represent the will of the people accomplished in the manner prescribed by the Constitution. . . . It seems to me that this reaching out to pre-empt by judicial action a major political decision which is currently in process of resolution does not reflect appropriate respect for duly prescribed legislative processes. . . .

Orr v. Orr

440 U.S. 268 (1979)

Mr. Justice BRENNAN delivered the opinion of the Court.

The question presented is the constitutionality of Alabama alimony statutes which provide that husbands, but not wives, may be required to pay alimony upon divorce.

The fact that the classification expressly discriminates against men rather than women does not protect it from scrutiny. . . . "To withstand scrutiny" under the Equal Protection Clause, "classifications by gender must serve important governmental objectives and must be substantially related to achievement of those objectives." . . .

Appellant [husband, who was ordered to pay alimony and challenges the Alabama alimony statutes as a violation of the Equal Protection Clause in a contempt action brought against him for being in arrears on his alimony obligations] views the Alabama alimony statutes as effectively announcing the State's preference for an allocation of family responsibilities under which the wife plays a dependent role, and as seeking for their objective the reinforcement of that model among the State's citizens. . . .

The opinion of the Alabama Court of Civil Appeals suggests other purposes that the statute may serve. Its opinion states that the Alabama statutes were "designed" for "the wife of a broken marriage who needs financial assistance." This may be read as asserting either of two legislative objectives. One is a legislative purpose to provide help for needy spouses, using sex as a proxy for need. The other is a goal of compensating women for past discrimination during marriage, which assertedly has left them unprepared to fend for themselves in the working world following divorce. We concede, of course, that assisting needy spouses is a legitimate and important governmental objective. We have also recognized "[r]eduction of the disparity in economic condition between men and women caused by the long history of discrimination against women . . . as . . . an important governmental objective." It only remains, therefore, to determine whether the classification at issue here is "substantially related to achievement of those objectives."

Ordinarily, we would begin the analysis of the "needy spouse" objective by considering whether sex is a sufficiently "accurate proxy" . . . for dependency to establish that the gender classification rests "upon some ground of difference having a fair and substantial relation to the object of the legislation." [Reed v. Reed (1971).] . . . Similarly, we would initially approach the "compensation" rationale by asking whether women had in fact been significantly discriminated against in the sphere to which the statute applied a sex-based classification, leaving the sexes "not similarly situated with respect to opportunities" in that sphere. . . .

But in this case, even if sex were a reliable proxy for need, and even if the institution of marriage did discriminate against women, these factors still would "not adequately justify the salient features of" Alabama's statutory scheme. . . . Under the statute, individualized hearings at which the parties' relative financial circumstances are considered already occur. . . . There is no reason, therefore, to use sex as a proxy for need. Needy males could be helped along with needy females with little if any additional burden on the State. In such circumstances, not even an administrative-convenience rationale exists to justify operating by generalization or proxy. Similarly, since individualized hearings can determine which women were in fact discriminated against vis-à-vis their husbands, as well as which family units defied the stereotype and left the husband dependent on the wife, Alabama's alleged compensatory purpose may be effectuated without placing burdens solely on husbands. Progress toward fulfilling such a purpose would not be hampered, and it would cost the State nothing more, if it were to treat men and women equally by making alimony burdens independent of sex. "Thus, the gender-based distinction is gratuitous; without it, the statutory scheme would only provide benefits to those men who are in fact similarly situated to the women the statute aids," . . . and the effort to help those women would not in any way be compromised.

Moreover, use of a gender classification actually produces perverse results in this case. As compared to a gender-neutral law placing alimony obligations on the spouse able to pay, the present Alabama statutes give an advantage only to the financially secure wife whose husband is in need. Although such a wife might have to pay alimony under a gender-neutral statute, the present statutes exempt her from that obligation. Thus, "[t]he [wives] who benefit from the disparate treatment are those who were . . . nondependent on their husbands" . . . . They are precisely those who are not "needy spouses" and who are "least likely to have been victims of . . . discrimination," . . . by the institution of marriage. A gender-based classification, which, as compared to a gender-neutral one, generates additional benefits only for those it has no reason to prefer cannot survive equal protection scrutiny.

Legislative classifications which distribute benefits and burdens on the basis of gender carry the inherent risk of reinforcing the stereotypes about the "proper place" of women and their need for special protection. . . . Thus, even statutes purportedly designed to compensate for and ameliorate the effects of past discrimination must be carefully tailored. Where, as here, the State's compensatory and ameliorative purposes are as well served by a gender-neutral classification as one that gender classifies and therefore carries with it the baggage of sexual stereotypes, the State cannot be permitted to classify on the basis of sex. And this is doubly so where the choice made by the State appears to redound—if only indirectly—to the benefit of those without need for special solicitude. Reversed and remanded.

PUTTING THEORY INTO PRACTICE

1-3. The following exchange is reported as part of a voir dire examination conducted by a judge in a criminal case in a municipal court in California:

The Court: Miss Bobb, what is your occupation?
Miss Bobb: I'm an attorney.
The Court: And in your practice do you practice criminal law as well as civil law?
Miss Bobb: No, I practice entirely bankruptcy law.
The Court: All right. Is there a Mr. Bobb?
Miss Bobb: I have some difficulty with that question because I've noticed only the women have been asked to answer that.
The Court: Yes, I know. Do you have a Mr. Bobb—is there a Mr. Bobb?
Miss Bobb: Are you going to [poll] the men to see if they care to disclose—
The Court: No, I'm just going to ask you if you have a husband or not. Do you have a husband?
Miss Bobb: I don't care to answer it then. What's relative to women is relative to men.
The Court: Yes, I know. What is your husband's occupation?
Miss Bobb: I don't care to answer that.
The Court: I instruct you to answer.
Miss Bobb: I don't think I should.

The Court: I've got — you understand that you'll be in contempt of Court—jury—you're an attorney, you understand these rules, don't you?

Miss Bobb: No, I do not understand why only the women are asked certain questions and the men aren't asked the same questions.

The Court: The question to you, Mrs. Bobb — you're an attorney at law, you understand the rules and regulations of—of—of being an attorney. And the question to you now simply is: What is your husband's occupation?

Miss Bobb: I refuse to answer.

The Court: You're held in contempt of Court, Mrs. Bobb.[20]

Is Mrs. Bobb's resistance reasonable? To what extent will formal equality principles provide relief to Mrs. Bobb?

Upon appeal, the Court of Appeals of California decided that Carolyn Bobb was improperly held in contempt of court. The reviewing court found no compelling state interest for posing questions to female jurors that were not posed to male jurors, and thereby held that requiring Mrs. Bobb to answer the question denied her equal protection of the law. Is this ruling good for women? Does it prevent the court from learning the information, or is there another way to get an answer that is consistent with formal equality principles?

2. The Right to Equal Group Treatment

In *Reed, Frontiero,* and *Orr,* the state had in place a system of individualized fact-finding; the only question was whether part of that fact-finding could be abbreviated by using sex as a proxy—in *Reed,* a proxy for ability and interest in administering an estate, and in *Frontiero* and *Orr,* a proxy for financial dependency. In each of these contexts, eliminating sex as a proxy (as the Supreme Court did) does not impose a great administrative burden and is likely to produce more accurate results in terms of the goals of the statutes.

In many contexts, however, the state needs to draw lines to decide questions that do not lend themselves to individualized fact-finding. Common examples include the right to vote, to marry, to drive, to serve in the military, and to attend public schools. This section examines two other examples.

Stanton v. Stanton

421 U.S. 7 (1975)

Mr. Justice BLACKMUN delivered the opinion of the Court.

This case presents the issue whether a state statute specifying for males a greater age of majority than it specifies for females denies, in the context of a parent's obligation for support payments for his children, the equal protection of the laws . . . .

---

20. Bobb v. Municipal Court, 192 Cal. Rptr. 270, 270-71 (Cal. Ct. App. 1983).

[The case is an appeal arising from divorce proceedings, following a judgment requiring the father to pay child support to the mother for a daughter and a son. The father discontinued support payments for the daughter when she turned 18, pursuant to Utah law, which set the age of majority for girls at 18 and the age of majority for boys at 21. The trial court denied the mother's motion for further support, which the Supreme Court of Utah affirmed.]

We find it unnecessary in this case to decide whether a classification based on sex is inherently suspect. . . . [Reed v. Reed (1971)] we feel, is controlling here. . . . "A classification 'must be reasonable, not arbitrary, and must rest upon some ground of difference having a fair and substantial relation to the object of the legislation, so that all persons similarly circumstanced shall be treated alike.'" . . . The test here, then, is whether the difference in sex between children warrants the distinction in the appellee's obligation to support that is drawn by the Utah statute. We conclude that it does not. It may be true, as the Utah court observed and as is argued here, that it is the man's primary responsibility to provide a home and that it is salutary for him to have education and training before he assumes that responsibility; that girls tend to mature earlier than boys; and that females tend to marry earlier than males. The last mentioned factor, however, under the Utah statute loses whatever weight it otherwise might have, for the statute states that "all minors obtain their majority by marriage"; thus minority, and all that goes with it, is abruptly lost by marriage of a person of either sex at whatever tender age the marriage occurs.

Notwithstanding the "old notions" to which the Utah court referred, we perceive nothing rational in the distinction drawn by [the statute] which, when related to the divorce decree, results in the appellee's liability for support for Sherri only to age 18 but for Rick to age 21. This imposes "criteria wholly unrelated to the objective of that statute." A child, male or female, is still a child. No longer is the female destined solely for the home and the rearing of the family, and only the male for the marketplace and the world of ideas. . . . Women's activities and responsibilities are increasing and expanding. Coeducation is a fact, not a rarity. The presence of women in business, in the professions, in government and, indeed, in all walks of life where education is a desirable, if not always a necessary, antecedent is apparent and a proper subject of judicial notice. If a specified age of minority is required for the boy in order to assure him parental support while he attains his education and training, so, too, is it for the girl. To distinguish between the two on educational grounds is to be self-serving: if the female is not to be supported so long as the male, she hardly can be expected to attend school as long as he does, and bringing her education to an end earlier coincides with the role-typing society has long imposed. And if any weight remains in this day to the claim of earlier maturity of the female, with a concomitant inference of absence of need for support beyond 18, we fail to perceive its unquestioned truth or its significance, particularly when marriage, as the statute provides, terminates minority for a person of either sex. . . .

[Whether the common law age of 21 applies to both children or the remedy for the unconstitutional inequality is to treat males as adults at age 18] is an issue of state law to be resolved by the Utah courts on remand. . . .

Craig v. Boren

429 U.S. 190 (1976)

Mr. Justice BRENNAN delivered the opinion of the Court, with whom Mr. Justice POWELL, Mr. Justice STEVENS, Mr. Justice BLACKMUN (in part), and Mr. Justice STEWART concurred.

The interaction of two sections of an Oklahoma statute . . . prohibits the sale of "nonintoxicating" 3.2% beer to males under the age of 21 and to females under the age of 18. The question to be decided is whether such a gender-based differential constitutes a denial to males 18-20 years of age of the equal protection of the laws in violation of the Fourteenth Amendment.

This action was brought in the District Court for the Western District of Oklahoma on December 20, 1972, by appellant Craig, a male then between 18 and 21 years of age, and by appellant Whitener, a licensed vendor of 3.2% beer. The complaint [alleged] that [the law] constituted invidious discrimination against males 18-20 years of age. A three-judge court . . . sustained the constitutionality of the statutory differential and dismissed the action. . . . We reverse. . . .

To withstand constitutional challenge . . . classifications by gender must serve important governmental objectives and must be substantially related to achievement of those objectives. . . . We accept for purposes of discussion the District Court's identification of the objective underlying [the statutes in question] as the enhancement of traffic safety. Clearly, the protection of public health and safety represents an important function of state and local governments. However, appellees' statistics in our view cannot support the conclusion that the gender-based distinction closely serves to achieve that objective and therefore the distinction cannot under [Reed v. Reed (1971)] withstand equal protection challenge.

The appellees introduced a variety of statistical surveys. First, an analysis of arrest statistics for 1973 demonstrated that 18-20-year-old male arrests for "driving under the influence" and "drunkenness" substantially exceeded female arrests for that same age period. Similarly, youths aged 17-21 were found to be overrepresented among those killed or injured in traffic accidents, with males again numerically exceeding females in this regard. Third, a random roadside survey in Oklahoma City revealed that young males were more inclined to drive and drink beer than were their female counterparts. Fourth, Federal Bureau of Investigation nationwide statistics exhibited a notable increase in arrests for "driving under the influence." Finally, statistical evidence gathered in other jurisdictions, particularly Minnesota and Michigan, was offered to corroborate Oklahoma's experience by indicating the pervasiveness of youthful participation in motor vehicle accidents following the imbibing of alcohol. Conceding that "the case is not free from doubt" . . . , the District Court nonetheless concluded that this statistical showing substantiated "a rational basis for the legislative judgment underlying the challenged classification." . . .

Even were this statistical evidence accepted as accurate, it nevertheless offers only a weak answer to the equal protection question presented here. The most focused and relevant of the statistical surveys, arrests of 18-20-year-olds for alcohol-related driving offenses, exemplifies the ultimate unpersuasiveness of this evidentiary record. Viewed in terms of the correlation between sex and the actual activity that Oklahoma seeks to regulate — driving while under the influence of alcohol — the statistics broadly establish that .18% of females and 2% of males in that age group were arrested for that offense. While such a disparity is not trivial in a statistical sense, it hardly can form the basis for employment of a gender line as a classifying device. Certainly if maleness is to serve as a proxy for drinking and driving, a correlation of 2% must be considered an unduly tenuous "fit." Indeed, prior cases have consistently rejected the use of sex as a decisionmaking factor even though the statutes in question certainly rested on far more predictive empirical relationships than this.

Moreover, the statistics exhibit a variety of other shortcomings that seriously impugn their value to equal protection analysis. Setting aside the obvious methodological problems,[14] the surveys do not adequately justify the salient features of Oklahoma's gender-based traffic-safety law. None purports to measure the use and dangerousness of 3.2% beer as opposed to alcohol generally, a detail that is of particular importance since, in light of its low alcohol level, Oklahoma apparently considers the 3.2% beverage to be "nonintoxicating." . . . Moreover, many of the studies, while graphically documenting the unfortunate increase in driving while under the influence of alcohol, make no effort to relate their findings to age-sex differentials as involved here. Indeed, the only survey that explicitly centered its attention upon young drivers and their use of beer — albeit apparently not of the diluted 3.2% variety — reached results that hardly can be viewed as impressive in justifying either a gender or age classification.[16]

---

14. The very social stereotypes that find reflection in age-differential laws, see Stanton, are likely substantially to distort the accuracy of these comparative statistics. Hence, "reckless" young men who drink and drive are transformed into arrest statistics, whereas their female counterparts are chivalrously escorted home. . . . Moreover, the Oklahoma surveys, gathered under a regime where the age-differential law in question has been in effect, are lacking in controls necessary for appraisal of the actual effectiveness of the male 3.2% beer prohibition. In this regard, the disproportionately high arrest statistics for young males — and, indeed, the growing alcohol-related arrest figures for all ages and sexes — simply may be taken to document the relative futility of controlling driving behavior by the 3.2% beer statute and like legislation, although we obviously have no means of estimating how many individuals, if any, actually were prevented from drinking by these laws.

16. The random roadside survey of drivers conducted in Oklahoma City during August 1972 found that 78% of drivers under 20 were male. Turning to an evaluation of their drinking habits and factoring out nondrinkers, 84% of the males versus 77% of the females expressed a preference for beer. Further 16.5% of the men and 11.4% of the women had consumed some alcoholic beverage within two hours of the interview. Finally, a blood alcohol concentration greater than .01% was discovered in 14.6% of the males compared to 11.5% of the females. "The 1973 figures, although they contain some variations, reflect essentially the same pattern." . . . Plainly these statistical disparities between the sexes are not substantial. Moreover, when the 18-20 age boundaries are lifted and all drivers analyzed, the 1972 roadside survey indicates that male drinking rose slightly whereas female exposure to alcohol remained relatively constant. Again, in 1973, the survey established that "compared to all drivers interviewed, . . . the under-20 age group generally showed a lower involvement

There is no reason to belabor this line of analysis. It is unrealistic to expect either members of the judiciary or state officials to be well versed in the rigors of experimental or statistical technique. But this merely illustrates that proving broad sociological propositions by statistics is a dubious business, and one that inevitably is in tension with the normative philosophy that underlies the Equal Protection Clause. Suffice to say that the showing offered by the appellees does not satisfy us that sex represents a legitimate, accurate proxy for the regulation of drinking and driving. In fact, when it is further recognized that Oklahoma's statute prohibits only the selling of 3.2% beer to young males and not their drinking the beverage once acquired (even after purchase by their 18-20-year-old female companions), the relationship between gender and traffic safety becomes far too tenuous to satisfy *Reed*'s requirement that the gender-based difference be substantially related to achievement of the statutory objective.

We hold, therefore, that under *Reed*, Oklahoma's 3.2% beer statute invidiously discriminates against males 18-20 years of age. . . .

Mr. Justice STEVENS, concurring.

There is only one Equal Protection Clause. It requires every State to govern impartially. It does not direct the courts to apply one standard of review in some cases and a different standard in other cases. Whatever criticism may be leveled at a judicial opinion implying that there are at least three such standards applies with the same force to a double standard. . . .

In this case, the classification is not as obnoxious as some the Court has condemned, nor as inoffensive as some the Court has accepted. It is objectionable because it is based on an accident of birth, because it is a mere remnant of the now almost universally rejected tradition of discriminating against males in this age bracket, and because, to the extent it reflects any physical difference between males and females, it is actually perverse [because males are on average heavier than females and thus have a greater capacity to consume alcohol without impairing their ability to drive]. The question then is whether the traffic safety justification put forward by the State is sufficient to make an otherwise offensive classification acceptable.

The classification is not totally irrational. For the evidence does indicate that there are more males than females in this age bracket who drive and also more who drink. Nevertheless, there are several reasons why I regard the justification as unacceptable. It is difficult to believe that the statute was actually intended to cope with the problem of traffic safety, since it has only a minimal effect on access to a not very intoxicating beverage and does not prohibit its consumption. Moreover, the empirical data submitted by the State accentuate the unfairness of treating all 18-20-year-old males as inferior to their female counterparts. The legislation imposes a restraint on 100% of the males in the class allegedly because about 2% of them have probably violated one or more laws relating to the consumption of alcoholic

---

with alcohol in terms of having drunk within the past two hours or having a significant BAC (blood alcohol content)." [Id.] In sum, this survey provides little support for a gender line among teenagers and actually runs counter to the imposition of drinking restrictions based upon age.

beverages. It is unlikely that this law will have a significant deterrent effect either on that 2% or on the law-abiding 98%. But even assuming some such slight benefit, it does not seem to me that an insult to all of the young men of the State can be justified by visiting the sins of the 2% on the 98%. . . .

Mr. Justice REHNQUIST, dissenting. . . .

I think the Oklahoma statute challenged here need pass only the "rational basis" equal protection analysis . . . and I believe that it is constitutional under that analysis.

Most obviously unavailable to support any kind of special scrutiny in this case, is a history or pattern of past discrimination, such as was relied on by the plurality in [Frontiero v. Richardson (1973)] to support its invocation of strict scrutiny. There is no suggestion in the Court's opinion that males in this age group are in any way peculiarly disadvantaged, subject to systematic discriminatory treatment, or otherwise in need of special solicitude from the courts.

The Court does not discuss the nature of the right involved, and there is no reason to believe that it sees the purchase of 3.2% beer as implicating any important interest, let alone one that is "fundamental" in the constitutional sense of invoking strict scrutiny. . . .

It is true that a number of our opinions contain broadly phrased dicta implying that the same test should be applied to all classifications based on sex, whether affecting females or males. . . . However, before today, no decision of this Court has applied an elevated level of scrutiny to invalidate a statutory discrimination harmful to males, except where the statute impaired an important personal interest protected by the Constitution. There being no such interest here, and there being no plausible argument that this is a discrimination against females,[2] the Court's reliance on our previous sex-discrimination cases is ill-founded. It treats gender classification as a talisman which — without regard to the rights involved or the persons affected — calls into effect a heavier burden of judicial review.

The Court's conclusion that a law which treats males less favorably than females "must serve important governmental objectives and must be substantially related to achievement of those objectives" apparently comes out of thin air. The Equal Protection Clause contains no such language, and none of our previous cases adopt that standard. I would think we have had enough difficulty with the two standards of review which our cases have recognized — the norm of "rational basis," and the "compelling state interest" required where a "suspect classification" is involved — so as to counsel weightily against the insertion of still another "standard" between those two. How is this Court to divine what objectives

---

2. I am not unaware of the argument from time to time advanced, that all discriminations between the sexes ultimately redound to the detriment of females, because they tend to reinforce "old notions" restricting the roles and opportunities of women. As a general proposition applying equally to all sex categorizations, I believe that this argument was implicitly found to carry little weight in our decisions upholding gender-based differences. . . . Seeing no assertion that it has special applicability to the situation at hand, I believe it can be dismissed as an insubstantial consideration.

are important? How is it to determine whether a particular law is "substantially" related to the achievement of such objective, rather than related in some other way to its achievement? Both of the phrases used are so diaphanous and elastic as to invite subjective judicial preferences or prejudices relating to particular types of legislation, masquerading as judgments whether such legislation is directed at "important" objectives or, whether the relationship to those objectives is "substantial" enough. I would have thought that if this Court were to leave anything to decision by the popularly elected branches of the Government, where no constitutional claim other than that of equal protection is invoked, it would be the decision as to what governmental objectives to be achieved by law are "important," and which are not. As for the second part of the Court's new test, the Judicial Branch is probably in no worse position than the Legislative or Executive Branches to determine if there is any rational relationship between a classification and the purpose which it might be thought to serve. But the introduction of the adverb "substantially" requires courts to make subjective judgments as to operational effects, for which neither their expertise nor their access to data fits them. And even if we manage to avoid both confusion and the mirroring of our own preferences in the development of this new doctrine, the thousands of judges in other courts who must interpret the Equal Protection Clause may not be so fortunate. . . .

NOTES

1. **"Simple Little Case"?**   At a distance of three decades, the cases in this section do not seem difficult, but at the time they were decided, most members of the all-male Court did not perceive them as straightforward. Justice Blackmun's papers offer a window into how one of those who voted ultimately to overturn the gender preference in *Reed* viewed the case and the arguments underlying it. The brief in *Reed*, on which Justice Ruth Bader Ginsburg had collaborated as an advocate, argued that the probate code compounded the "subordination of women." It claimed that "American women have been stigmatized historically as an inferior class and are today subject to pervasive discrimination. . . . A person born female continues to be branded inferior for this congenital and unalterable condition of birth." Justice Blackmun found the brief "mildly offensive and arrogant" and out of proportion to what he considered "a very simple little case." It was "much ado about nothing" since the estate in dispute amounted to less than $1,000 — clothes, a clarinet, and less than $500 in savings of an adolescent who had committed suicide. However, Justice Blackmun also recognized that it was meant as a "test case," and he was prepared to join the majority because "there can be no question that women have been held down in the past in almost every area." He advised the Court to write a "brief and simple opinion" and hoped that "we do not get into a long and emotional discussion about women's rights."[21]

Was the Court's decision to write a "brief and simple" opinion in *Reed* the right choice? How much guidance does it provide about which kinds of classifications do

---

21. For the full story, see Linda Greenhouse, Becoming Justice Blackmun: Harry Blackmun's Supreme Court Journey 209-11 (2005).

not pass constitutional scrutiny? Does Justice Blackmun's reference to "emotional" arguments about women's rights reflect the very same stereotypes that underpinned the classifications in *Reed, Orr,* and the cases that followed? Is it relevant that Sally Reed alleged her husband was abusive and abandoned the family when their son was young? Or that the son shot himself with one of his father's rifles during a visit, after the family court shifted the custody arrangement to allow more visitation after the boy, as an adolescent, had troubles with the law?[22]

As in *Reed,* an irony of Craig v. Boren is that one of the nation's most important sex discrimination cases arose in one of the least important factual contexts. Ruth Bader Ginsburg, then director of the Women's Rights Project of the American Civil Liberties Union, filed an amicus curiae brief in the case and noted later: "It was a petty law, mercifully terminated. One might wish the Court had chosen a less frothy case" for announcing a crucial principle.[23] Even in *Craig,* do the stereotypes underlying the Oklahoma law have broader repercussions for women?

2. **The Role of Stereotyping in Formal Equality Analysis.**   The articulated standard in these cases, at least from Craig v. Boren forward, is that the challenged classification must bear a substantial relationship to important governmental objectives. Note the frequency with which the Supreme Court's analysis focuses on the fact of stereotyping by the legislature. What did the Court mean in *Craig* by saying that "proving broad sociological propositions by statistics . . . inevitably is in tension with the normative philosophy" of the Equal Protection Clause? Was the Supreme Court concerned that the legislature was misdescribing the behavior of boys versus girls—or that stereotypes, even when they are accurate, perpetuate the inequalities that they reflect?

3. **Sexual Orientation Discrimination and Transgender Discrimination as Forms of Gender Discrimination.**   LGBT rights advocates have long attempted to establish that sexual orientation and gender identity warrant special constitutional protection under the Equal Protection Clause. The two major lines of argument are (1) that sexual orientation discrimination constitutes sex discrimination, and (2) that sexual orientation has the characteristics that warrant heightened constitutional protection in its own right.

Is discrimination because of a person's sexual orientation a form of sex discrimination? After all, anti-gay bias depends on a judgment that an individual man or woman should be attracted to people of the "opposite" sex. It is impossible to carry out that bias independent of the sex of the person targeted. Another argument for finding sexual orientation discrimination a form of sex discrimination is that anti-gay bias depends on normative sex stereotypes about how "real" men and "real" women should carry out their sexual and romantic lives.[24] Do these judgments

22. Rosalind Rosenberg, Jane Crow: The Life of Pauli Murray 341 (2017); Natalie Wexler, Sally Reed, in 100 Americans Making Constitutional History: A Biographical History 169-71 (Melvin Urofsky ed., 2004).

23. Ruth Bader Ginsburg, Remarks for the Celebration of 75 Years of Women's Enrollment at Columbia Law School, 102 Colum. L. Rev. 1441, 1445 (2002).

24. See Andrew Koppelman, Why Discrimination Against Lesbians and Gay Men Is Sex Discrimination, 69 N.Y.U. L. Rev. 197 (1994); Sylvia A. Law, Homosexuality and the Social Meaning of Gender, 1988 Wis. L. Rev. 187.

rest on assumptions about the nature of men and women that are incompatible with the formal equality model embraced by the Court's equal protection cases?

How about whether sexual orientation should be recognized as a suspect class in its own right, without having to be folded into constitutional protection for sex discrimination. The Supreme Court has never recognized sexual orientation as a suspect class, despite having invalidated restrictions burdening some LGBT individuals in the exercise of other fundamental rights,[25] and having construed Title VII's ban on sex discrimination to encompass discrimination on the basis of sexual orientation or gender identity.[26] In Romer v. Evans, the Court invalidated a Colorado constitutional amendment (Proposition 2) repealing and prohibiting all state and local anti-discrimination policies with respect to homosexuals.[27] In the majority's view, this amendment failed to meet the rational relationship standard under the Equal Protection Clause because it arbitrarily prevented a group from protecting its interests through the normal political process. This discrimination, the Court stated, could not be justified by a "bare desire to harm a politically unpopular group."[28] The Court then drew on *Romer* when invalidating the federal Defense of Marriage Act (explored in Chapter 2D), which prohibited a valid same-sex marriage from being given effect for any federal-law purpose. Congress' departure from a longstanding history of deference to state marriage rules was a "discrimination of unusual character" (in *Romer's* words) and thus invalid under the Equal Protection Clause. But in neither of these cases did the Court expressly consider or hold that sexual orientation classifications merit heightened scrutiny.

Do gays and lesbians, as a group, meet the following criteria that are often used to identify a protected class: (1) a history of discrimination; (2) exhibition of obvious, immutable, or distinguishing characteristics that define them as members of a discrete group; and (3) political powerlessness? Or, apart from the characteristics of gays and lesbians as a class, should anti-gay discrimination be strictly scrutinized because it burdens a fundamental right?

Gay and lesbian individuals have, of course, faced a history of discrimination, but it is not clear that they face special burdens in the political process, and legislative wins in the modern era arguably show that gays and lesbians are not politically powerless. The issue of "immutability" also poses a dilemma for gays and lesbians. On the one hand, part of the harm of discrimination is the pressure it creates to suppress, and thereby alter, same-sex orientation. On the other hand, if sexual orientation is alterable, gays and lesbians have the ability to avoid discrimination. The costs of such alteration might be clearer to heterosexuals if they imagined the tables turned:

> Would heterosexuals living in a city that passed an ordinance banning those who engaged in or desired to engage in sex with persons of the

---

25. United States v. Windsor, 570 U.S. 744 (2013); Romer v. Evans, 517 U.S. 620 (1996); cf. Lawrence v. Texas, 539 U.S. 558 (2003) (O'Connor, J., concurring). These cases are considered in Chapter 2, Section D1.

26. Bostock v. Clayton Cty., 140 S. Ct. 1731 (2020). This case appears in Section C of this Chapter.

27. 517 U.S. 620 (1996).

28. Dep't of Agric. v. Moreno, 413 U.S. 528, 534 (1973).

opposite sex find it easy not only to abstain from heterosexual activity but also to shift the object of their sexual desires to persons of the same sex?[29]

Should the immutability requirement be redefined? Judge Norris argued that "the Court has never meant strict immutability in the sense that members of the class must be physically unable to change or mask the trait defining their class. People can have operations to change their sex. . . . Reading the case law in a more capacious manner, 'immutability' may describe those traits that are so central to a person's identity that it would be abhorrent for government to penalize a person for refusing to change them, regardless of how easy that change might be physically."[30] Janet Halley has argued that a focus on immutability is inappropriate because it misrepresents the complex and changing way that sexual orientation evolves and misperceives the harm of discrimination. Rather, she explains, "[such] discrimination encourages people to manipulate the identity they attach to themselves, both in the secrecy of their own minds and on the public stage, in . . . their subjective and their public identities. It ensures that personal desires, sexual behavior, subjective identity and public identity will frequently get out of sync with each other."[31] Is there a plausible constitutional theory there? Or should full protection from sexual orientation discrimination be left to the legislative process?

The arguments for extending constitutional protection to transgender persons share some similarities with those for sexual orientation. One main difference is how the sex discrimination argument would apply to transgender discrimination. If the trigger for discrimination is that an individual is transitioning (or has transitioned) from male to female, or vice versa, the resulting discrimination appears to be quite literally because of sex. Does the logic of the Court's sex discrimination cases encompass discrimination against transgender persons? Or is it a stronger argument to advocate for constitutional protection for transgender persons as a distinct suspect class?[32] More in-depth treatment of issues relating to LGBTQ+ individuals can be found throughout this book.[33]

4. **Remedying Inequality in Formal Treatment.** Problems of formal equality often can be eliminated in more than one way. Formal gender neutrality could be achieved in *Orr* either by eliminating alimony for both husbands and wives (leveling

---

29. Watkins v. United States Army, 847 F.2d 1329, 1347-48 (9th Cir. 1988), after reh'g, 875 F.2d 699 (9th Cir. 1990) (en banc).

30. *Watkins*, 875 F.2d at 1347 (Norris, J., concurring).

31. Janet E. Halley, The Politics of the Closet: Towards Equal Protection for Gay, Lesbian, and Bisexual Identity, 36 UCLA L. Rev. 915, 933 (1989); see also Gary Mucciaroni & Mary Lou Killian, Immutability, Science, and Legislative Debate over Gay, Lesbian, and Bisexual Rights, 47 J. Homosexuality 53 (2004); Qazi Rahman & Glenn D. Wilson, Born Gay? The Psychobiology of Human Sexual Orientation, 34 Personality & Individual Differences 1337 (2003).

32. For an extensive discussion of constitutional protections from discrimination against transgender persons, see Jennifer L. Levi & Kevin M. Barry, Transgender Tropes and Constitutional Review, 37 Yale L. & Pol'y Rev. 589 (2019).

33. As recommended by GLAAD, we use LGBTQ+ to encompass all non-heterosexual, non-cisgender identities. See https://www.glaad.org/reference/terms. Where necessary for legal or doctrinal accuracy, we sometimes use more targeted or limited terms.

down) or by leaving the state's system of individualized alimony determinations in place and extending eligibility to husbands who can prove their dependency (leveling up). The latter alternative, which Alabama chose, presents the classic "won the battle but lost the war" scenario for Mr. Orr: He prevails on the constitutional point, but remains liable for alimony under a different, gender-neutral regime. The formal equality principle applied in *Craig* and *Stanton* also did not compel any particular resolution: The state could use the higher age or the lower age or some other age altogether, just so long as it used the same age for both males and females. Just such a remedy was imposed by the Court, with Justice Ginsburg writing the majority opinion, in Sessions v. Morales-Santana,[34] striking down a sex-based immigration law preference for nonmarital children born overseas to citizen mothers but refusing to extend the favorable citizenship treatment to the plaintiff, the child of a citizen father.[35]

The inequality in Frontiero v. Richardson could have been remedied by requiring all employees to demonstrate dependency or extending dependency benefits to all spouses. The first option would have the same effect as the ultimate result in *Orr*: all spouses would have to show dependency to receive the benefits, which Mr. Orr could not do. Instead, the court extended the presumption of dependency to all spouses, putting the burden on Congress to eliminate the presumption if it so chose, which had the effect of giving a windfall to some employees—female as well as male. It seems clear enough why Mr. Orr should not have relief—escape from alimony obligations—simply because other husbands (dependent ones) were victims of unconstitutional discrimination: Mr. Orr was not like those other, dependent husbands. But should Sharron Frontiero and her husband have received dependency benefits when her husband was not a dependent, simply because some other potential claimants, who also were not dependent, were receiving them? Another way of looking at this issue is that while in *Reed, Orr, Craig*, and *Stanton* the Court forces the state to abandon gender-based stereotypes and adopt an approach that is *more* accurate, in *Frontiero*, extension of the presumption actually renders the fringe-benefit scheme *less* accurate. Should this be a problem, constitutionally speaking? Alternatively, does it reflect legitimate differences in the administrative burdens associated with individualized determinations of eligibility? Are there other interests at stake, besides accuracy and efficiency, when inequality is remedied by imposing equal disadvantages, rather than extending the more favorable treatment to persons previously denied it?[36]

5. **Who Is the Protected Victim?**   One question in some of these cases is who the victim of discrimination is. In *Frontiero*, for example, is it the female wage-earner whose benefits are lower because her husband is not presumed to be a dependent, or the male dependent himself?

What are the consequences of the answer to this question? None, if you think that discrimination against men should be analyzed in the same way as

---

34. 137 S. Ct. 1678 (2017).

35. See Tracy A. Thomas, Leveling Down Gender Equality, 42 Harv. Women's L. J. 177 (2019) (critiquing the case).

36. See Deborah L. Brake, When Equality Leaves Everyone Worse Off: The Problem of Leveling Down in Equality Law, 46 Wm. & Mary L. Rev. 513 (2004).

discrimination against women. But Justice Rehnquist's view in his dissenting opinion in *Craig* (and other early cases) was that when the "victim" of the discrimination is male, the constitutional standard of review appropriate to other forms of "social welfare legislation"—i.e., the rational basis test—is all that is required (and that administrative convenience satisfies this standard). Consider this position, in light of the Court's view, shared by Chief Justice Rehnquist and explored in Chapter 2, that affirmative action plans designed to eliminate the effects of past discrimination against racial minorities be subject to the same strict standard as rules and practices that exclude or disadvantage those minorities. Even apart from any inconsistencies in judicial philosophy, Justice Rehnquist's assessment that men are not disadvantaged by their gender is worth interrogating. Scholars of masculinities studies (discussed in the Introduction) argue that not all men are situated similarly when it comes to male privilege; for some men, particularly when other aspects of identity are considered, such as race, gender may well be one basis of disadvantage. Even men who benefit from gender privilege in certain areas of their lives may experience costs and disadvantages in others.

Another approach to the "victim" problem is reflected in such cases as *Orr* and *Craig*, but found frivolous by Justice Rehnquist in footnote 2 to his dissent in *Craig*. That approach assumes that women are harmed not only by discrimination against them, but also by discrimination that favors them, when this "benign" discrimination reflects, and thus perpetuates, traditional stereotypes. How would you evaluate this claim? Are women harmed by preventing men from buying 3.2 percent beer? Are women potentially harmed in other areas of social or economic life by the stereotypes underlying the Oklahoma law? Does it matter what the legislative history of the statute suggests about the role of stereotypes? In *Craig*, the sparse information available on the state legislature's 1972 retention of different ages for alcohol purchases suggests the influence of religious fundamentalist concerns. The principal testimony opposing equalization of ages came from a minister who wanted to protect young men from the "pool, beer, and girls syndrome."[37]

Finally, footnote 22 of Justice Brennan's opinion in *Frontiero* notes that the statutes at issue in that case were not designed to rectify the effects of past discrimination against women. If they had been so designed, should the result in the case be different?

6. **Women in the Military.**   Throughout the nation's history, cultural expectations and legal restrictions expressly limited female involvement in the armed forces. Until the early 1970s, women constituted less than 2 percent of the U.S. military and discrimination in placement and promotion was widespread, particularly for women of color. Enrollment was limited through quotas on female applicants; exclusion from combat positions, military academies, and training programs; and disqualification of women who became pregnant or had minor children. The prevailing view was apparent in one 1968 federal district court opinion: "In providing for involuntary service for men and voluntary service for women, Congress followed the teachings of history that if a nation is to survive, men must provide the first line of defense while women keep the home fires burning."[38]

---

37. Brief of Appellants at 11, Craig v. Boren, 429 U.S. 190 (1976) (No. 75-628).
38. United States v. St. Clair, 291 F. Supp. 122, 125 (S.D.N.Y. 1968).

In the mid-1970s, many of these restrictions were modified or withdrawn, without judicial intervention. As a result, female participation in the armed forces substantially increased, reaching 10 percent by the late 1980s, 13 percent by the turn of the twentieth century, and 15 percent by 2009.[39] Despite this gradual integration, the combat exclusion would last several more decades before being lifted, piecemeal, by the Department of Defense. Finally, in December 2015, Secretary of Defense Ash Carter announced that all remaining barriers to women's service in combat would be lifted. This meant, he explained, "They'll be allowed to drive tanks, fire mortars and lead infantry soldiers into combat. They'll be able to serve as Army Rangers and Green Berets, Navy SEALs, Marine Corps infantry, Air Force parajumpers, and everything else that was previously open only to men."[40] Data from 2019 show that women now comprise about 17 percent of active-duty military personnel.[41]

What changes and challenges might you expect from more gender integration in the military, especially in combat roles? According to a Pew Research survey, the female force is more racially diverse than the male force, just as likely to experience the "struggles and benefits of service upon discharge," and more likely than their male counterparts to be critical of the wars in Iraq and Afghanistan.[42] But opponents of women in combat also raise a host of concerns about pregnancy, promiscuity, and "gender-norming" — the practice of adjusting strength and fitness standards to reflect sex-based differences. According to these commentators, the military's effort to accommodate women is fostering resentment, diluting performance requirements, creating double standards, inspiring inappropriate chivalry, compromising morale, impairing recruitment, and diverting attention from more central goals of combat preparedness. Underlying these concerns has been a host of symbolic issues about masculinity, manhood, and dominance. The view that General William Westmoreland expressed might not be that unusual: "No man with any gumption wants a woman to fight his nation's battles."[43] Proponents of equal treatment point out that the most comprehensive studies conclude that with appropriate training, the vast majority of women can meet the physical demands of combat, and that their presence does not cause declines in unit cohesiveness.[44] As in civilian contexts, military positions requiring particular levels of strength, endurance, or agility can be allocated under gender-neutral guidelines that match individual capabilities with job requirements. Moreover, as many experts have noted,

---

39. See Service Women's Action Network, Women in the Military: Where They Stand (10th ed. 2019).

40. Cheryl Pelleran, Dept. Def., Carter Opens All Military Occupations, Positions to Women (Dec. 3, 2015).

41. See Katharina Buchholz, Military Women Remain in the Minority, Statista (Sept. 23, 2021).

42. See Pelleran, supra note 40.

43. William Westmoreland, quoted in Judith Wagner Decrew, The Combat Exclusion and the Role of Women in the Military, 10 Hypatia 56, 62 (Winter 1995).

44. See, e.g., Martha McSally, Women in Combat: Is the Current Policy Obsolete?, 14 Duke J. Gender L. & Pol'y 1011, 1029-40 (2007); Blythe Leszkay, Feminism on the Front Lines, 14 Hastings Women's L.J. 133, 161 (2003).

technological changes in warfare have reduced the relevance of physical strength in combat and eroded the distinctions between combat and combat-related positions. Judge Richard Posner puts it this way: "We live in an age of push-button warfare. Women can push buttons as well as men."[45] The Marine Corps, which has a lower proportion of women than the other services, separates men and women for basic training.[46] Is this likely to facilitate or impede the full integration of women into the service?

Does the military reinforce stereotypes about men and masculinity? As John Kang asks, "What is the role of law, in the context of the military, in reinforcing stereotypes about men as courageous? Theoretically, female soldiers can be punished for cowardice, but, so far, none have, as though martial courage was expected only of men. Compare two of the most highly publicized disciplinary cases in the military involving the first woman B-52 bomber pilot, Kelly Flinn, and Lt. Colonel Karen Tew. Both officers were court martialed, not for lacking the male virtue of courage, but for having sexual relations with male soldiers.[47] What stereotypes do these cases reinforce?

If service in the military is a responsibility of citizenship, should women feel obligated to serve? Men but not women are required to register with the Selective Service at age eighteen. This policy, which was upheld by the U.S. Supreme Court in Rostker v. Goldberg,[48] when women could not serve in combat roles, has faced several recent challenges.[49] In one case, a federal district court in Texas found the policy unconstitutional,[50] but the Fifth Circuit Court of Appeals reversed the decision,[51] and the United States Supreme Court declined to review that reversal.[52] None of the Congressional efforts to extend the Selective Service requirement to women have succeeded. Should women, nonetheless, feel a moral obligation to register?

7. **LGBT Inclusion in (and Exclusion from) the Military.**   For most of American military history, gays and lesbians were excluded from service. Former President Bill Clinton attempted to ease the exclusion in 1993 with the Don't Ask Don't Tell (DADT) policy, which allowed gay and lesbian individuals to serve as long as they did not admit their sexual orientation or engage in homosexual conduct.[53] However, this supposed compromise resulted in the firing of 14,500 service

---

45. Richard Posner, Overcoming Law 55 (1995).

46. Daniel Villarreal, Marines Only Military Branch to Avoid Gender Integration Requirements, Newsweek (Feb. 8, 2022).

47. John M. Kang, The Burdens of Manliness, 33 Harv. J. Law & Gender 477, 495 (2010).

48. Rostker v. Goldberg, 453 U.S. 57 (1981). The case is discussed in the note following the next section.

49. Kristy Kamarch, Women and the Selective Service, CRS Insight (Dec. 15, 2015).

50. See Nat'l Coalition for Men v. Selective Serv. Sys., 355 F. Supp. 3d 568 (S.D. Tex. 2019).

51. Nat'l Coalition for Men v. Selective Serv. Sys., 969 F.3d 546 (5th Cir. 2020).

52. Nat'l Coalition for Men v. Selective Serv. Sys., 141 S. Ct. 1815 (2021).

53. National Defense Authorization Act of 1994, Pub. L. No. 103-60, 107 Stat. 1547 § 571, codified as amended at 10 U.S.C. § 654 (2006).

members across all branches, and a disproportionate number of those discharged were female. Repeal efforts were catalyzed during the Obama administration by a federal district court's ruling that DADT violated the Fifth Amendment's guarantee of due process and the First Amendment's guarantee of freedom of speech.[54] While the case was pending on appeal, Congress repealed DADT during a lame-duck session in December 2010.[55] The repeal became effective in September 2011, replacing DADT with a policy of nondiscrimination under which the military may not take administrative action against any personnel, or persons seeking to become personnel, on the basis of sexual orientation. While this policy has remained largely in effect, in March 2018, the Trump administration enacted a new policy under which service members can identify as transgender, but must use the uniforms, pronouns, and sleeping and bathroom facilities associated with their biological sex. The policy banned individuals from military service who had a diagnosis of gender dysphoria, and would not permit individuals to initiate the process of transitioning to conform to their gender identity while they were in military service.[56] The policy was initially enjoined, but the Supreme Court voted 5-4 to allow the ban to take effect while lower courts consider its constitutionality.[57] The issue became moot when, on the first day of his administration, President Biden issued an executive order reversing the Trump policy.[58] Is a ban on military service by transgender individuals a form of sex discrimination? Why or why not?

8. **The Equal Rights Amendment.** The Equal Rights Amendment (ERA) was initially proposed in 1923. It reads: "Equality of rights under the law shall not be denied or abridged by the United States or by any state on account of sex." The ERA failed by three states to gain the support of two-thirds (thirty-eight) of the states by the 1982 congressional deadline (a date extended three years beyond the original 1979 deadline). It has been reintroduced in every congressional session since 1982 but never emerged from committee. On January 27, 2020, Virginia became the thirty-eighth state, after Nevada (2017) and Illinois (2018), to ratify the ERA. That same month, the Department of Justice's Office of Legal Counsel issued an opinion saying that, despite its ratification by thirty-eight states, the ERA was dead because not all of those ratifications occurred within the time limit set by Congress. Subsequently, the House of Representatives passed a resolution declaring the time limits to its passage inoperative, but Senate Republicans prevented the issue from coming to a vote in the Senate. Advocates for the ERA continue to exert pressure on the political process to clear the hurdles for its approval.[59]

---

54. Log Cabin Republicans v. United States, 716 F. Supp. 2d 884 (C.D. Cal. 2010).

55. Don't Ask, Don't Tell Repeal Act of 2010, Pub. L. No. 111-321, § 2(a)(2)(C), 124 Stat. 3515 (2010).

56. Presidential Memorandum for the Secretary of Defense and the Secretary of Homeland Security Regarding Military Service by Transgender Individuals (Mar. 23, 2018).

57. Trump v. Karnoski, 139 S. Ct. 950 (2019).

58. Joseph R. Biden, Executive Order on Enabling All Qualified Americans to Serve Their Country in Uniform, Jan. 25, 2021.

59. For continuing updates on the status of the ERA, as well as arguments that the ERA would help protect women's reproductive rights and other areas in which women's rights are still vulnerable, see Alice Paul Inst., Frequently Asked Questions, https://www.equalrightsamendment.org/faq.

Complicating the issue is the fact that five states that ratified the ERA in the 1970s—Idaho, Kentucky, Nebraska, South Dakota, and Tennessee—subsequently rescinded their votes.[60]

The United States is one of a small number of nations that does not have an explicit guarantee of women's rights in its Constitution. Julie Suk draws on global constitutionalism to argue for a broader ERA that goes beyond traditional nondiscrimination norms and embraces a "constitutional guarantee of sex equality" that can "significantly disrupt the remaining manifestations of gender inequality, such as pay inequity; women's economic disadvantages related to pregnancy, maternity, and caregiving; women's underrepresentation in positions of economic and political power; and violence against women."[61] Is it important to have an express commitment to sex equality in the Constitution?

Debate over the Amendment generally assumed that it would require "strict scrutiny" of sex-based classifications, along the lines favored by four Justices in *Frontiero*. If so, what are the implications? As explored further in Chapter 2, Section A2, race-based measures designed to eliminate the effects of past discrimination against African Americans are subject to the same strict scrutiny that is applied to race-based discrimination against African Americans. Gender-based measures designed to overcome the effects of past discrimination or biological differences between men and women are not.

Kim Forde-Mazrui argues that the ERA would, as in the case of race, require strict scrutiny both for discrimination against women, and for accommodations that take into account the past discrimination against them and their biological differences.[62] He argues that the ERA would unnecessarily jeopardize single-sex schools and camps, and laws directed specifically at such things as violence against women, sexual harassment, and pay equity.[63] Is this a reasonable concern? The ERA website responds that the Amendment would not make all single-sex institutions unconstitutional, only those that "perpetuate the historic dominance of one sex over the other."[64] Is this limitation found in the language of the ERA? Is it supported by the formal equality principle?

At least twenty-six states have enacted versions of an equal rights amendment in their own constitutions, with either partial or full guarantees of equal rights on the basis of sex. The exact language of the amendments varies, as have judicial interpretations of the provisions. Three states with state constitutional provisions—Florida, Louisiana, and Utah—have not yet ratified the federal ERA.[65]

---

60. See The Equal Rights Amendment May Be Only One State Away from Enactment, at https://govtrackinsider.com/the-equal-rights-amendment-may-be-only-one-state-away-from-enactment-f04f4a628cf5.

61. Julie C. Suk, An Equal Rights Amendment for the Twenty-First Century: Bringing Global Constitutionalism Home, 28 Yale J. L. & Feminism 381, 384-85 (2017); see also Julie C. Suk, We the Women: The Unstoppable Mothers of the Equal Rights Amendment (2022).

62. See Kim Forde-Mazrui, Why the Equal Rights Amendment Would Endanger Women's Equality: Lessons from Colorblind Constitutionalism, 16 Duke J. Const. L. & Pol'y 1 (2021).

63. Id.

64. Alice Paul Inst., supra note 59.

65. Id.

PUTTING THEORY INTO PRACTICE

1-4. Should the tradition of having boys and girls dress differently for graduation be allowed in a public high school? One Connecticut school, for example, required boys to wear blue robes, while girls wore white robes and carried flowers.[66] Does this practice violate the Equal Protection Clause? If so, what remedy would best satisfy formal equality? Further materials relating to dress and appearance standards may be found in Section C2b of this chapter (employment) and in Chapter 2, Section C3 (education).

1-5. Does formal equality require that if men are required to register for the Selective Service, so should women?

1-6. Justice Ruth Bader Ginsburg gave a speech in 2017 in which she expressed strong support for the ERA: "I would like to be able to take out my pocket Constitution and say the equal citizenship stature of men and women is a fundamental tenet of our society like free speech."[67] Would this offer practical as well as symbolic benefits? In what ways? How important is symbolism in this context?

3. Indirect Discrimination

The cases examined so far are examples of "facial" or "direct discrimination," which means that the classifications are explicitly based on sex. When an employer fires or fails to promote someone because of her sex, this is also a case of direct discrimination. Examples of direct discrimination under employment discrimination law are explored later in this chapter.

Discrimination can also be indirect, such as when a state acts on a basis other than sex, but the impact of its laws or practices disproportionately affects members of one sex. Personnel Administrator of Massachusetts v. Feeney, excerpted below, concerns the disproportionate effect of a veterans' preference system on women's opportunities for state civil service positions.

Personnel Administrator of Massachusetts v. Feeney

442 U.S. 256 (1979)

Mr. Justice STEWART delivered the opinion of the Court.

This case presents a challenge to the constitutionality of the Massachusetts veterans' preference statute . . . on the ground that it discriminates against women in violation of the Equal Protection Clause of the Fourteenth Amendment. Under [this statute], all veterans who qualify for state civil service positions must be

---

66. See Joanna L. Grossman & Katharine T. Bartlett, Blue for Boys, White with Flowers for Girls: When Commencement Is an Exercise in Discrimination, Justia's Verdict (May 3, 2016).

67. Susan Chira, Do American Women Still Need an Equal Rights Amendment?, N.Y. Times, Feb. 16, 2019, at SR3.

considered for appointment ahead of any qualifying nonveterans. The preference operates overwhelmingly to the advantage of males.

The appellee Helen B. Feeney is not a veteran. She brought this action pursuant to 42 U.S.C. §1983, alleging that the absolute preference formula established in [the Massachusetts statute] inevitably operates to exclude women from consideration for the best Massachusetts civil service jobs and thus unconstitutionally denies them the equal protection of the laws. The three-judge District Court agreed, one judge dissenting. . . .

The Federal Government and virtually all of the States grant some sort of hiring preference to veterans. The Massachusetts preference, which is loosely termed an "absolute lifetime" preference, is among the most generous. It applies to all positions in the State's classified civil service, which constitute approximately 60% of the public jobs in the State. It is available to "any person, male or female, including a nurse," who was honorably discharged from the United States Armed Forces after at least 90 days of active service, at least one day of which was during "wartime." Persons who are deemed veterans and who are otherwise qualified for a particular civil service job may exercise the preference at any time and as many times as they wish. . . .

[The record shows that Ms. Feeney, who entered the state civil service system in 1963, did quite well in the competitive civil service examinations she took in order to obtain a promotion, but was "consistently eclipsed by veterans."]

The sole question for decision on this appeal is whether Massachusetts, in granting an absolute lifetime preference to veterans, has discriminated against women in violation of the Equal Protection Clause of the Fourteenth Amendment. . . .

The cases of Washington v. Davis, [1976], and Arlington Heights v. Metropolitan Housing Dev. Corp., [1977], recognize that when a neutral law has a disparate impact upon a group that has historically been the victim of discrimination, an unconstitutional purpose may still be at work. But those cases signaled no departure from the settled rule that the Fourteenth Amendment guarantees equal laws, not equal results. *Davis* upheld a job-related employment test that white people passed in proportionately greater numbers than Negroes, for there had been no showing that racial discrimination entered into the establishment or formulation of the test. *Arlington Heights* upheld a zoning board decision that tended to perpetuate racially segregated housing patterns, since, apart from its effect, the board's decision was shown to be nothing more than an application of a constitutionally neutral zoning policy. Those principles apply with equal force to a case involving alleged gender discrimination.

When a statute, gender-neutral on its face, is challenged on the ground that its effects upon women are disproportionably adverse, a twofold inquiry is thus appropriate. The first question is whether the statutory classification is indeed neutral in the sense that it is not gender-based. If the classification itself, covert or overt, is not based upon gender, the second question is whether the adverse effect reflects invidious gender-based discrimination. . . . In this second inquiry, impact provides an "important starting point," but purposeful discrimination is "the condition that offends the Constitution." . . .

Veteran status is not uniquely male. Although few women benefit from the preference the nonveteran class is not substantially all female. To the contrary, significant numbers of nonveterans are men, and all nonveterans—male as well as female—are placed at a disadvantage. Too many men are affected by [the statute] to permit the inference that the statute is but a pretext for preferring men over women. . . .

Discriminatory intent is . . . either . . . a factor that has influenced the legislative choice or it is not. The District Court's conclusion that the absolute veterans' preference was not originally enacted or subsequently reaffirmed for the purpose of giving an advantage to males as such necessarily compels the conclusion that the State . . . intended nothing more than to prefer "veterans." Given this finding, simple logic suggests that an intent to exclude women from significant public jobs was not at work in this law. To reason that it was, by describing the preference as "inherently nonneutral" or "gender-biased," is merely to restate the fact of impact, not to answer the question of intent. . . .

The basic distinction between veterans and nonveterans, having been found not gender-based, and the goals of the preference having been found worthy, [the statute] must be analyzed as is any other neutral law that casts a greater burden upon women as a group than upon men as a group. The enlistment policies of the Armed Services may well have discriminated on the basis of sex. . . . But the history of discrimination against women in the military is not on trial in this case. . . .

"Discriminatory purpose" . . . implies more than intent as volition or intent as awareness of consequences. . . . It implies that the decisionmaker, in this case a state legislature, selected or reaffirmed a particular course of action at least in part "because of," not merely "in spite of," its adverse effects upon an identifiable group. Yet, nothing in the record demonstrates that this preference for veterans was originally devised or subsequently re-enacted because it would accomplish the collateral goal of keeping women in a stereotypic and predefined place in the Massachusetts Civil Service. . . .

Veterans' hiring preferences represent an awkward—and, many argue, unfair—exception to the widely shared view that merit and merit alone should prevail in the employment policies of government. After a war, such laws have been enacted virtually without opposition. During peacetime, they inevitably have come to be viewed in many quarters as undemocratic and unwise. Absolute and permanent preferences, as the troubled history of this law demonstrates, have always been subject to the objection that they give the veteran more than a square deal. But the Fourteenth Amendment "cannot be made a refuge from ill-advised . . . laws." . . . The substantial edge granted to veterans by [the Massachusetts statute] may reflect unwise policy. The appellee, however, has simply failed to demonstrate that the law in any way reflects a purpose to discriminate on the basis of sex.

The judgment is reversed, and the case is remanded for further proceedings consistent with this opinion. . . .

Mr. Justice MARSHALL, with whom Mr. Justice BRENNAN joins, dissenting. . . .

In the instant case, the impact of the Massachusetts statute on women is undisputed. Any veteran with a passing grade on the civil service exam must be placed ahead of a nonveteran, regardless of their respective scores. The District Court found that, as a practical matter, this preference supplants test results as the determinant of upper level civil service appointments. . . . Because less than 2% of the women in Massachusetts are veterans, the absolute-preference formula has rendered desirable state civil service employment an almost exclusively male prerogative. . . .

As the District Court recognized, this consequence follows foreseeably, indeed inexorably, from the long history of policies severely limiting women's participation in the military. . . .

The legislative history of the statute reflects the Commonwealth's patent appreciation of the impact the preference system would have on women, and an equally evident desire to mitigate that impact only with respect to certain traditionally female occupations. Until 1971, the statute and implementing civil service regulations exempted from operation of the preference any job requisitions "especially calling for women." . . . In practice, this exemption, coupled with the absolute preference for veterans, has created a gender-based civil service hierarchy, with women occupying low-grade clerical and secretarial jobs and men holding more responsible and remunerative positions. . . .

Thus, for over 70 years, the Commonwealth has maintained, as an integral part of its veterans' preference system, an exemption relegating female civil service applicants to occupations traditionally filled by women. Such a statutory scheme both reflects and perpetuates precisely the kind of archaic assumptions about women's roles which we have previously held invalid. . . . The Court's conclusion to the contrary—that "nothing in the record" evinces a "collateral goal of keeping women in a stereotypic and predefined place in the Massachusetts Civil Service"—displays a singularly myopic view of the facts established below.

To survive challenge under the Equal Protection Clause, statutes reflecting gender-based discrimination must be substantially related to the achievement of important governmental objectives. . . . Appellants here advance three interests in support of the absolute-preference system: (1) assisting veterans in their readjustment to civilian life; (2) encouraging military enlistment; and (3) rewarding those who have served their country. . . . Although each of those goals is unquestionably legitimate, the "mere recitation of a benign, compensatory purpose" cannot of itself insulate legislative classifications from constitutional scrutiny. . . . And in this case, the Commonwealth has failed to establish a sufficient relationship between its objectives and the means chosen to effectuate them. . . .

I would affirm the judgment of the court below.

NOTE ON NONDISCRIMINATORY AND DISCRIMINATORY INTENT

Did the Idaho and Alabama legislatures in *Reed* and *Orr* "intend" to disadvantage people because of their sex? Probably not, but the point of these cases is that laws based on stereotyped thinking about women are unacceptable, even if—perhaps *especially* if—they are unintentional.

Why, then, in *Feeney*, does the Court allow to stand a system that has a substantially disproportionate impact against women—a much greater practical impact, indeed, than the statutes in *Reed* and *Orr*? One explanation is that an explicit sex-based distinction is, by definition, discriminatory (whether or not it is justified is a separate question), while it is less clear that a rule or practice with a disproportionate impact on women has discriminated based on sex.

Does it follow that intent should be required when the challenged statute is neutral on its face? On the one hand, as noted above, the requirement reflects the fact that it is harder to know if a facially neutral classification was the result of discrimination or some more benign explanation. On the other hand, rules and practices that are not explicitly sex-based but that have a disproportionate, negative impact against women may be even more dangerous than cases of explicit sex-based discrimination, in that the stereotypes that guide decisionmaking in such cases may be more hidden and thus easier to perpetuate. In fact, Title VII of the Civil Rights Act of 1964, explored later in this chapter, requires that rules and practices in the employment context that have a disparate impact on women and minorities must be job-related and justified by business necessity, regardless of the "intent" of the employer.

Ironically, some direct or explicit sex-based classifications are actually "saved" by the intention to discriminate. When the Supreme Court upheld the male-only draft registration system in Rostker v. Goldberg (discussed above), for example, it did so on the theory that, since females could not serve in combat, they were not likely to be subjected to future drafts.[68] Because reasons for the exclusion of women were well-reviewed in the legislative history, the Court reasoned, the statute was not an "accidental by-product" of narrow, outmoded stereotypes about women, but a deliberate, reasoned choice. Conversely, in Mississippi University for Women (MUW) v. Hogan, discussed in Chapter 2, the Court's conclusion that an all-female, state-supported nursing school was a violation of the Equal Protection Clause turned in part on the origins of the school and stereotyped notions about what it was appropriate to train women to do.[69] Justice O'Connor suggests in her opinion for the Court that if the intent had been to compensate women for the disadvantage they experienced in their educational or employment opportunities, another result might have followed. An example in the affirmative action context is Contractors Ass'n of Eastern Pennsylvania v. City of Philadelphia, which held that an affirmative action plan favoring women will pass intermediate scrutiny if it is shown to be "a product of analysis rather than a stereotyped reaction based on habit."[70]

To the extent that a showing of discriminatory intent seems desirable, how should it be demonstrated? In *Feeney*, the fact that a few women qualified as veterans is taken as a neutral fact that disproves discriminatory intent. Is this analysis sound?

PUTTING THEORY INTO PRACTICE

1-7. A Veterans Administration (VA) rule requires that all chaplains at VA hospitals be "ordained" clergy members. The requirement is shown to have a disparate impact on women because the Roman Catholic Church, among others, will not ordain women as priests. Does the rule offend formal equality principles? Is this an example of direct discrimination, indirect discrimination, or neither?

1-8. Although women make up about 50 percent of medical school graduates, less than one-quarter of surgeons are women and in some sub-specialties, like orthopedic surgery, women comprise only about 5 percent.[71] A significant part of

---

68. 453 U.S. 57 (1981).
69. 458 U.S. 718 (1982).
70. 6 F.3d 990, 1010 (3d Cir. 1993).
71. See Julia Haskins, Where Are All the Women in Surgery?, AAMC News, July 15, 2019.

the gender gap is thought to be attributable to the high stress and irregular hours involved in the surgical profession.[72] Is this a problem that needs fixing? If so, who has responsibility for it, and what should be done?

1-9. Customer evaluations of marketers show that female marketers are undervalued by customers, as against objective criteria, by about 20 percent.[73] Student evaluations of teachers also show a systematic bias against women.[74] Are companies that use customer evaluations to help evaluate their employees or schools that use students' evaluations to help evaluate their teachers engaged in sex discrimination? If so, what should be done?[75]

1-10. Although organ donation policies in the United States are gender-neutral on their face, the data show that 62 percent of kidney donors are women, while only 19 percent of kidney transplant recipients are women.[76] Is this a problem? What kind of problem? How would you fix it?

C. FORMAL EQUALITY IN EMPLOYMENT

The preceding cases involve constitutional challenges to classifications by Congress or state legislatures. The U.S. Constitution, of course, is but one legal tool to address sex-based discrimination. State and federal anti-discrimination laws also play a critical role. Important federal statutes include the Equal Pay Act of 1963,[77] which requires employers to give women and men equal pay for equal work, and Title VII of the Civil Rights Act of 1964 (Title VII),[78] which prohibits employers from discriminating with respect to the compensation, terms, conditions, or privileges of employment based on the individual's race, color, religion, sex, or national origin. Both of these statutes track formal equality principles in ways that are illustrated in the discussion that follows.

1. The Equal Pay Act: Formal Equality Paradigm

The Equal Pay Act requires that men and women receive "equal pay" for "equal work." Equal work is defined as "jobs the performance of which requires

---

72. See Suvarna Bhatt, Is There a Glass Ceiling for Female Surgeons?, Health Careers Network (Nov. 2, 2010).

73. See Bryce Covert, Female Client Service Reps Get Lower Scores Despite Better Performance and Experience, Think Progress (May 22, 2014).

74. David A. M. Peterson, Mitigating Gender Bias in Student Evaluations of Teaching, PLoS ONE (May 15, 2019).

75. See Katharine T. Bartlett & Mitu Gulati, Discrimination by Customers, 102 Iowa L. Rev. 223 (2016).

76. See Sohini Chattopadhyay, Organ Donation's Burden on Women, N.Y. Times, Dec. 16, 2018, at SR9.

77. 29 U.S.C. § 206 (2018).

78. 42 U.S.C. § 2000 et seq. (2018).

equal skills, effort, and responsibility, and which are performed under similar working conditions." The Act also includes some exceptions, such as a seniority or merit system, and a catch-all exception for "a differential based on any other factor other than sex."[79]

EEOC v. Madison Community Unit School District No. 12

818 F.2d 577 (7th Cir. 1987)

POSNER, Circuit Judge.

The Equal Employment Opportunity Commission brought this suit against the school district of Madison, Illinois, charging that the district was paying female athletic coaches in its high school and junior high school less than male coaches, in violation of the Equal Pay Act of 1963. . . .

[Luvenia] Long was paid substantially less for coaching girls' track than Steptoe, a man, was paid for coaching boys' track. Although the boys' track program included more students and had more meets than the girls', Steptoe had two assistant coaches compared to Long's one, and as a result Long and Steptoe devoted approximately equal time to their coaching jobs. Long also coached the girls' tennis team, and Jakich, a man, the boys' tennis team; and Jakich was paid more than Long even though there were no significant differences between the teams in number of students, length of season, or number of practice sessions; however, the boys' team played almost twice as many matches as the girls' team. Long was also assistant coach of the girls' basketball team one year and received lower pay than Tyus, the male assistant coach of the boys' track team. The district judge found that the work of the two assistant coaches was substantially equal and required the same skill, effort, and responsibility—except that Long worked longer hours than Tyus. [Carol] Cole, who coached the girls' volleyball, girls' basketball, and girls' softball teams, was paid less for coaching volleyball than the male coach of the boys' soccer team, less for coaching basketball than the male coach of the boys' soccer team, and less for coaching softball than the male coach of the boys' baseball team. Also, as assistant coach of the girls' track team she was paid less than the assistant coach of the boys' track team. In all of these cases the judge found that the work of the female coach and her male counterpart was the same in skill, effort (including time), and responsibility. Any potential differences in effort and responsibility stemming from the fact that the boys' teams were sometimes larger and played longer seasons were, he found, offset by the fact that the head coaches of the boys' teams had more assistants than their female counterparts. . . .

The first question we must decide is whether the pairs of jobs that the district judge compared in finding unequal pay are sufficiently similar to be "equal work" within the meaning of the Equal Pay Act. The Act is not a general mandate of sex-neutral compensation. It does not enact "comparable worth"—the principle that wages should be based on "objective" factors, rather than on market conditions of demand and supply which may depress wages in jobs held mainly by women

---

79. 29 U.S.C. §206(d)(iv) (2018).

relative to wages in jobs held mainly by men. . . . A female secretary paid less than a male janitor cannot complain under the Equal Pay Act that the disparity in their wages is not justified by "objective" factors such as differences in skill, responsibility, and effort. . . . The Act requires equal pay only when men and women are performing "equal work on jobs the performance of which requires equal skill, effort, and responsibility, and which are performed under similar working conditions." The working conditions of a janitor are different from those of a secretary, and so are the skills and responsibilities of the two jobs. The Act does not prohibit paying different wages even if the result is to pay a woman less than a man and by doing so "underpay" her because the difference in the wage rate is greater than necessary to compensate the male for any greater skill, effort, or responsibility required by, or any inferior working conditions encountered in, his job.

Thus the jobs that are compared must be in some sense the same to count as "equal work" under the Equal Pay Act; and here we come to the main difficulty in applying the Act: whether two jobs are the same depends on how fine a system of job classifications the courts will accept. If coaching an athletic team in the Madison, Illinois school system is considered a single job rather than a congeries of jobs, the school district violated the Equal Pay Act prima facie by paying female holders of this job less than male holders, and the only question is whether the district carried its burden of proving that the lower wages which the four female coaches received were lower than the wages of their male counterparts because of a factor other than sex. If on the other hand coaching the girls' tennis team is considered a different job from coaching the boys' tennis team, and a fortiori if coaching the girls' volleyball or basketball team is considered a different job (or jobs) from coaching the boys' soccer team, there is no prima facie violation. So the question is how narrow a definition of job the courts should be using in deciding whether the Equal Pay Act is applicable. . . .

The Act requires that the jobs compared have "similar working conditions," not the same working conditions. This implies that some comparison of different jobs is possible. It is true that similarity of working conditions between the jobs being compared is not enough to bring the Act into play — the work must be "equal" and the jobs must require "equal" skill, effort, and responsibility, as well as similar working conditions. But since the working conditions need not be "equal," the jobs need not be completely identical.

Estimating and comparing the skill, effort, responsibility, and working conditions in two jobs are factual determinations. . . . We can overturn them, therefore, only if they are clearly erroneous. . . . The district judge found (among other things) that coaching a girls' tennis team is sufficiently like coaching a boys' tennis team, coaching a girls' softball team is sufficiently like coaching a boys' hardball team, and, indeed, coaching a girls' volleyball or basketball team is sufficiently like coaching a boys' soccer team, to allow each pair of jobs to be described as involving equal work, as requiring equal skill, effort, and responsibility, and as being performed under similar working conditions. . . .

There are pitfalls in allowing any comparisons between different jobs, and they are illustrated by this case. One is a tendency to focus entirely on the measurable differences and ignore the equally or more important but less readily measurable ones. The witnesses in this case concentrated on the amount of skill and time required for coaching girls' and boys' teams and paid little attention to responsibility. It may be true that because the boys' teams tend to have more assistant coaches than the girls' teams, the head coaches of the boys' teams put in no more time than the head coaches of the girls' teams even when the boys' teams are larger and play more matches. But normally there is greater responsibility (one of the dimensions in which the statute requires equality between the jobs compared) if you have a staff than if you don't. That is one reason why the president of a company is paid more than a junior executive who, lacking staff assistance, may work longer hours. . . .

Another difference tends to be ignored when effort, which is hard to measure, is equated to time, which is easy to measure. Boys and girls differ on average in strength, speed, and perhaps other dimensions of athletic ability; there may also be important differences in their attitudes toward athletic competition. The differences between boys and girls in athletic aptitude and interest may make coaching a boys' team harder—or easier—than coaching a girls' team; there can be no confidence that the two jobs require equal effort. The district judge set aside this consideration by ruling that a difference in the sex of students, customers, etc., can't be used to justify a pay difference under the Equal Pay Act. But this is wrong. The reference to "factor other than sex" refers to the sex of the employee, not the sex of the employer's customers, clients, or suppliers. . . . Suppose that the school district happened to have just male, or just female, coaches and paid coaches more for coaching boys' teams than girls' teams. Men paid less than other men for coaching, or women paid less than other women, could not complain of a violation of the Equal Pay Act. . . . The Act did not seek to eliminate whatever differences between the sexes might make it harder to coach a boys' team than a girls' team. If it is harder (we are not saying it is harder—we are just discussing possibilities), the statutory requirement of equal effort is not met and the differential in pay is outside the scope of the Act.

Nevertheless, we are unwilling to hold that coaches of girls' and boys' teams can never be found to be doing equal work requiring equal skill, effort, and responsibility and performed under similar working conditions. Above the lowest rank of employee, every employee has a somewhat different job from every other one, even if the two employees being compared are in the same department. So if "equal work" and "equal skill, effort, and responsibility" were taken literally, the Act would have a minute domain. . . .

But the words "very much alike," "closely related," or, as the cases sometimes say, "substantially equal"—even the words "virtually identical"—are not synonymous with "identical." . . . There is a gray area, which we must be vigilant to police, between "very much alike," which is within the scope of the Act, and "comparable," which is outside; for it is plain that Congress did not want to enact comparable worth as part of the Equal Pay Act of 1964. . . .

Whatever answer we might give, if we were the finders of fact, to the question whether coaching a girls' tennis team and coaching a boys' tennis team are sufficiently alike to be equal work within the meaning of the Act, we cannot, on the record compiled in this case (a potentially important qualification), deem the district court's determination clearly erroneous. . . .

Although we conclude that there is no objection in principle to comparing different coaching jobs, the record of the present case does require us to distinguish between coaching boys' and girls' teams of the same sport and coaching boys' and girls' teams of different sports. [The court sets aside as arbitrary the judge's equation of girls' basketball and girls' volleyball with boys' track.] . . .

With this exception we conclude that the plaintiffs did establish a prima facie case of violation of the Equal Pay Act, and we move on to consider defenses, of which only one ("factor other than sex") is relevant. Madison argues that the sex of the teams is a factor other than sex. . . . If Madison, having decided for reasons unrelated to the sex of the coaches that coaches of male teams should be paid more than coaches of female teams, neither prohibited nor even discouraged women from coaching male teams, the difference in pay between male coaches of boys' teams and female coaches of girls' teams would be due to a decision unrelated to the sex of the coaches. But Madison discouraged women, including Cole and Long, from applying to coach boys' teams, which not only adds a reason related to the sex of the coaches for a difference in pay between men and women to a reason related solely to the sex of the team members, but also casts doubt on the bona fides of the school district's claim to have based the difference in the pay of coaches of male and of female teams solely on the sex of the team members. . . .

The reason for discouraging women from coaching boys' teams was that the school authorities were concerned about the "locker room problem." This may or may not be a good reason . . . but it does suggest that women receive less pay than men for doing what the district court found was equal work within the meaning of the Equal Pay Act because they are women; their sex makes them ineligible to receive the higher wage that men receive for equal work. Even if the school district is entitled to insist that coaches and coached be of the same sex, if the work of each coach is the same and the reason for the difference in pay is the difference in sex of the coach, the Equal Pay Act is violated. An employer cannot divide equal work into two job classifications that carry unequal pay, forbid women to compete for one of the classifications, and defend the resulting inequality in pay between men and women by reference to a "factor other than [the] sex" of the employees. . . . It would not be the sexual segregation that had caused the inequality in pay, but a decision to pay men more for doing the same work as women (albeit with a "clientele" of a different sex from the women's "clientele").

Rizo v. Yovino

950 F.3d 1217 (9th Cir. 2020) (en banc)

CHRISTEN, Circuit Judge:

In 1963, Congress enacted the Equal Pay Act with a mandate as simple as it was profound: equal pay for equal work. The question we consider today is whether Aileen Rizo's prior rate of pay is a "factor other than sex" that allows Fresno County's Office of Education to pay her less than male employees who perform the same work. We conclude it is not. . . .

The express purpose of the Equal Pay Act (EPA) was to eradicate the practice of paying women less simply because they are women. Allowing employers to escape liability by relying on employees' prior pay would defeat the purpose of the Act and perpetuate the very discrimination the EPA aims to eliminate. Accordingly, we hold that an employee's prior pay cannot serve as an affirmative defense to a prima facie showing of an EPA violation.

I. BACKGROUND

The Fresno County Office of Education hired Aileen Rizo as a math consultant in October 2009. She held two master's degrees when she was hired: one in educational technology and one in mathematics education. She began teaching middle and high school math in 1996. Her employment experience included three years as head of the math department for an online school and designer of the school's math curriculum. Rizo worked at this position while earning her first master's degree. She taught middle school math for six more years, and then she was hired by Fresno County.

The County set its new employees' salaries according to a pay schedule governed by Standard Operating Procedure 1440 (SOP 1440). The schedule designated 12 salary levels. Each level corresponded to different job classifications and had up to 10 steps. To calculate a new employee's pay, the County started with the employee's prior wages, increased the wages by 5%, and placed the employee at the corresponding step on its pay schedule. Rizo's prior employer paid her $50,630 for 206 days of work, plus an additional $1,200 because she had a master's degree. Based on her prior wages, the County placed Rizo at Step 1, Level 1 on its pay schedule. Her starting wage at Fresno County was $62,133 for 196 days of work, plus an additional $600 for holding a master's degree.

While having lunch with colleagues in 2012, Rizo learned that a newly hired male math consultant had been placed at Level 1, Step 9. That put the new consultant's starting pay at $79,088, significantly more than Rizo was paid after working three years for the County. Rizo realized that she was the only female math consultant at Fresno County, and that all of her male colleagues were paid more than she was, even though she had more education and experience. She expressed concern about this pay disparity to the Human Resources department, and an administrator gave her a copy of SOP 1440. The administrator assured Rizo that the policy was applied across the board, regardless of the employee's sex.

In February 2014, Rizo filed a complaint [that] alleged that the County violated the Equal Pay Act and included claims for sex discrimination under Title VII. . . . In the district court, both parties argued that Kouba v. Allstate Insurance Co., 691 F.2d 873 (9th Cir. 1982), supported their positions. *Kouba* considered whether an employee's prior pay, in combination with other factors, justified a pay differential between two workers of the opposite sex. We held that the EPA "does not impose a strict prohibition against the use of prior salary," so long as employers consider prior pay "reasonably" to advance "an acceptable business reason." . . . The district court concluded that *Kouba* did not resolve whether the pay disparity in Rizo's case violated the EPA because the differential resulted solely from Rizo's prior rate of pay, not from her prior pay in combination with other factors. . . .

We affirm. . . .

III. DISCUSSION

We took this case en banc to reconsider *Kouba*'s rule that prior pay can qualify as an affirmative defense to an EPA claim if the employer considers prior pay in combination with other factors and uses it reasonably to effectuate a business policy. . . .

The EPA's four exceptions operate as affirmative defenses. . . . If the plaintiff puts forth a prima facie case of an EPA violation, "the burden shifts to the employer to show that the differential is justified under one of the Act's four exceptions." To counter a prima facie case, an employer must prove "not simply that the employer's proffered reasons *could* explain the wage disparity, but that the proffered reasons *do in fact* explain the wage disparity."

A wage differential arose in *Corning Glass* because male employees were not willing to work for the low wages paid to women. *Corning Glass* rejected what was later called the "market force theory," holding that the EPA did not permit Corning Glass to pay women less simply because they were willing to work for less. The Court explained that although it may have been "understandable as a matter of economics" that the company took advantage of these market conditions, "its [wage] differential nevertheless became illegal once Congress enacted into law the principle of equal pay for equal work."

Unlike Title VII, the EPA does not require proof of discriminatory intent. For that reason, the familiar three-step *McDonnell Douglas* framework that applies to Title VII claims is not used in EPA cases. . . . EPA claims have just two steps: (1) the plaintiff bears the burden to establish a prima facie showing of a sex-based wage differential; (2) if the plaintiff is successful, the burden shifts to the employer to show an affirmative defense. No showing of pretext is required.

This appeal requires that we consider the scope of the EPA's fourth exception. . . . Based on the text and purpose of the Act, we conclude that the fourth affirmative defense comprises only job-related factors, not sex. To define the scope of the EPA's fourth exception, we begin with the language of the statute and apply familiar principles of statutory construction. Congress first defined the protection afforded by the statute in job-related terms — equal pay for "equal work on jobs the performance of which requires equal skill, effort, and responsibility, and which are performed under similar working conditions." It then specifically enumerated three exceptions to the prohibition of sex-based distinctions for such work, but described the fourth generally as "any other factor other than sex." The fourth exception is often shortened to "any factor other than sex," but here we are called upon to define its precise contours and we examine every word: "any *other* factor other than sex." Giving meaning to each word by its context, the phrase "any other factor other than sex" requires that the fourth exception be read in relation to the three exceptions that precede it, as well as in relation to the "equal work" principle to which it is an exception. If *any* factor other than sex could defeat an EPA claim, the first "other" in the phrase "any other factor other than sex" would be rendered meaningless, as would the three enumerated exceptions. Because the three enumerated exceptions are all job-related, and the elements of the "equal work" principle are job-related, Congress' use of the phrase "any *other* factor other than sex" (emphasis added) signals that the fourth exception is also limited to job-related factors. . . .

As the Supreme Court did in *Corning Glass*, we also look to the EPA's history and purpose. Both confirm the scope of the Act's fourth exception. The Supreme Court emphasized in *Corning Glass* that the EPA was intended to address "the fact that the wage structure of 'many segments of American industry [had] been based on an ancient but outmoded belief that a man, because of his role in society, should be paid more than a woman even though his duties are the same.'" The problem of wage discrimination was "overwhelmingly apparent" to Congress when it passed the EPA in 1963. . . .

The County's suggestion that the EPA's legislative history supports an expansive reading of the fourth exception is unavailing. The House Report provided several examples that it anticipated would qualify as exceptions to the equal pay mandate, and all were job related: shift differentials, differences based on time of day worked, hours of work, lifting or moving heavy objects, and differences based on experience, training, or ability. The equal-pay-for-equal-work mandate would mean little if employers were free to justify paying an employee of one sex less than an employee of the opposite sex for reasons unrelated to their jobs.

Other circuits agree that only job-related factors provide affirmative defenses to EPA claims. . . . Only the Seventh Circuit has held that the scope of the fourth exception "embraces an almost limitless number of factors, so long as they do not involve sex." The Seventh Circuit has not required that those factors be related "to the requirements of the particular position in question." The Seventh Circuit's opinion is an outlier, and we cannot reconcile it with either well-settled rules of statutory construction or the "broadly remedial" purpose of the EPA. . . .

[W]e next consider whether prior pay qualifies as a job-related factor that can defeat a prima facie EPA claim. The answer to this question is compelled by the EPA's narrow focus on the purest form of sex-based wage discrimination and the statute's two-step framework. Prior pay — pay received for a different job — is necessarily not a factor related to the job for which an EPA plaintiff must demonstrate unequal pay for equal work.

In 1963, Congress not only knew that wages earned by America's workforce were infused with the legacy of sex discrimination, that legacy motivated Congress to act. The Assistant Secretary of Labor testified that women on average earned only about 59% of what their male colleagues earned, but Congress recognized that America's pay gap was not entirely attributable to sex-based wage discrimination. The gap was also due to circumstances that caused women to be less prepared to enter the workforce, such as fewer opportunities for training, education, skills development, and experience. Though Congress knew the cause of America's earnings gap was multi-factorial, it kept its solution simple. The EPA did not raise women's wages nor create remedial education or training opportunities. The Act's limited goal was to eliminate only the purest form of sex-based wage discrimination: paying women less *because* they are women.

The precise and focused goal of the EPA is evidenced by the exceptions built into it that expressly allow employers to pay different wages to employees of the opposite sex if the differences are caused by job-related factors other than sex. As the Supreme Court explained in County of Washington v. Gunther, the EPA's fourth exception was intended "to confine the application of the Act to wage differentials attributable to sex discrimination." The EPA's limited aim at just one of the many causes of the wage gap reinforces our conclusion that allowing prior pay to serve as an affirmative defense would undermine the Act's promise of equal pay for equal work. . . .

The County argues that Rizo presumes the use of past wages perpetuates historical pay discrimination, and that Rizo impermissibly shifts the burden to the County to disprove the influence of wage discrimination on her prior pay. . . . We agree the EPA does not require employers to prove that the wages paid to their employees at prior jobs were unaffected by wage discrimination. But if called upon to defend against a prima facie showing, the EPA requires employers to demonstrate that only job-related factors, not sex, caused any wage disparities that exist between employees of the opposite sex who perform equal work. Accordingly, what the County considers to be an impermissible shift is actually the burden-shift *required* by the EPA's two-step framework. After Rizo established a prima facie showing, the County had the burden of proving that "sex provide[d] *no* part of the basis for the wage differential."

We do not presume that any particular employee's prior wages were depressed as a result of sex discrimination. But the history of pervasive wage discrimination in the American workforce prevents prior pay from satisfying the employer's burden to show that sex played no role in wage disparities between employees of the opposite sex. And allowing prior pay to serve as an affirmative defense would frustrate the EPA's purpose as well as its language and structure by perpetuating sex-based wage disparities.

We acknowledge that prior pay could be viewed as a *proxy* for job-related factors such as education, skills, or experience related to an employee's prior job, and that prior pay can be a *function* of factors related to an employee's prior job. But prior pay itself is not a factor related to the work an employee is currently performing, nor is it probative of whether sex played any role in establishing an employee's pay. Here, the County has not explained why or how prior pay is indicative of Rizo's ability to perform the job she was hired to do. An employer may counter a prima facie EPA claim by pointing to legitimate job-related factors, if they exist. Accordingly, using the heuristic of an employee's prior pay, rather than relying on job-related factors actually associated with an employee's present position, does not suffice to defeat an EPA claim.

We agree with Rizo and the EEOC that setting wages based on prior pay risks perpetuating the history of sex-based wage discrimination. . . . Hopefully, we have moved past the days when employers maintained separate pay scales that explicitly condoned paying women less than men for comparable work, but the wage gap that so concerned Congress in 1963 has only narrowed, not closed. The wage gap persists across nearly all occupations and industries, regardless of education, experience, or job title. . . .

To the extent the present-day pay gap is the product of historical wage discrimination based on sex — rather than different pay due to unequal qualifications, effort, productivity, regional cost of living, or other factors other than sex — the gap is a continuation of the very discrimination Congress sought to end. . . .

The EPA's fourth exception allows employers to justify wage disparities between employees of the opposite sex based on any job-related factor other than sex. Because prior pay may carry with it the effects of sex-based pay discrimination, and because sex-based pay discrimination was the precise target of the EPA, an employer may not rely on prior pay to meet its burden of showing that sex played no part in its pay decision. For purposes of the fourth exception, we conclude that the wage associated with an employee's prior job does not qualify as a factor other than sex that can defeat a prima facie EPA claim. Having reconsidered *Kouba*, we are persuaded that it must be overruled. . . .

Kouba's consideration of whether the employer used prior pay reasonably is also in tension with the EPA's strict liability framework, in which intent to discriminate plays no role. . . .

Some case law from other circuits suggests that prior pay may serve as an affirmative defense if it is considered in combination with other factors, but these cases uniformly rely on those other factors to excuse wage differentials. None of these cases suggests that the use of prior pay is acceptable, so long as it is sufficiently diluted by other considerations. . . .

Our holding prevents employers from relying on prior pay to defeat EPA claims, but the EPA does not prevent employers from considering prior pay for other purposes. For example, it is not unusual for employers and prospective employees to discuss prior pay in the course of negotiating job offers, and the EPA does not prohibit this practice. Certainly, our opinion does not prohibit this practice. But whatever factors an employer considers, if called upon to defend against a prima facie showing of sex-based wage discrimination, the employer must demonstrate that any wage differential was in fact justified by job-related factors other than sex. Prior pay, alone or in combination with other factors, cannot serve as a defense. . . . To meet this burden, employers may rely on any bona fide job-related factor other than sex. But relying on the heuristic of prior pay, rather than the actual factors associated with employees' current work, risks perpetuating historical sex discrimination.

Applying the rule that only job-related factors qualify under the EPA's fourth affirmative defense and that prior pay is not one of them, resolution of Rizo's case is straightforward. . . . The County cites no other reason for paying Rizo less. We therefore affirm the district court's order denying Fresno County's motion for summary judgment. . . .

McKEOWN, Circuit Judge, with whom Judge TALLMAN and Judge MURGUIA, Circuit Judges, join, concurring:

The majority embraces a rule not adopted by any other circuit—prior salary may never be used, even in combination with other factors, as a defense under the Equal Pay Act. The circuits that have considered this important issue have either outright rejected the majority's approach or declined to adopt it. I see no reason to deepen the circuit split. What's more, the majority's position is at odds with the view of the Equal Employment Opportunity Commission ("EEOC"), the agency charged with administering the Act. And, perhaps most troubling, the majority fails to account for the realities of today's dynamic workforce, choosing instead to view the workplace in a vacuum. In doing so, it betrays the promise of equal pay for equal work and disadvantages workers regardless of gender identity.

I agree with much of the majority opinion—particularly the observation that past salary can reflect historical sex discrimination. For decade after decade, gender discrimination has been baked into our pay scales, with the result that women still earn only 80 percent of what men make. As the majority notes, this pay gap is "even more pronounced among women of color." Unfortunately, women employed in certain sectors face an even larger gap. This disparity is exacerbated when a woman is paid less than a man for a comparable job solely because she earned less at her last job. The Equal Pay Act prohibits precisely this kind of "piling on," whereby women can never overcome the historical inequality.

I welcome the day when this would no longer be so because women have achieved parity in the workplace. But the majority goes too far in holding that any consideration of prior pay is "inconsistent" with the Equal Pay Act, even when it is assessed alongside other job-related factors such as experience, education, past performance, and training. This declaration may in fact disadvantage job applicants, whether female, male, or non-binary. For this reason, I concur in the result but not in the majority's rationale. In my view, prior salary alone is not a defense to unequal pay for equal work. If an employer's only justification for paying men and women unequally is that the men had higher prior salaries, odds are that the one-and-only "factor" causing the difference is sex. However, employers do not necessarily violate the Equal Pay Act when they consider prior salary among other factors when setting initial wages. As always, the employer has the burden to show that any pay differential is based on a valid factor other than sex. . . .

NOTES

1. **The Wage Gap.**   Although the wage gap between women's and men's earnings has been slowly eroding, it remains significant. Adjusting for hours worked (but not for differences in education, experience, or time in the work force), women's median weekly earnings are between 83 and 84 percent of those of men, as compared to 62 percent in 1979.[80] When white men's wages are used for comparison, women of color fare even more poorly than white women. African-American women earn only 64 cents for every dollar earned by white men, and the number falls to 57 cents for Latinas.[81] The disparity in men's and women's wages grows over time; full-time working women in the 20-24 age bracket earn on average 93.4 percent of what men earn, while women in the 55-64 age range earn only 77.8 percent.[82] Over the course of a worker's lifetime, the gender wage gap adds up. One

---

80. Bureau of Labor Stats., Dept. of Labor, BLS Reports (Jan. 24, 2022). According to the U.S. Census Bureau, women earn 83 cents for every dollar earned by men. U.S. Census Bureau, Current Population Survey, 1961 to 2021 Annual Social and Economic Supplements (CPS ASEC), at fig. 5. The Pew Research Center puts the gap at 84 percent. Amanda Barroso & Anna Brown, Gender Pay Gap in U.S. Held Steady in 2020, Pew Research Center: Fact Tank (May 25, 2021). Different data sets explain the variation, but the results are largely consistent throughout the literature. See Francine D. Blau & Lawrence M. Kahn, The Gender Wage Gap: Extent, Trends, and Explanations, 55 J. Econ. Literature 789, 797-800 (2017); see also Elise Gould et al., Econ. Pol'y Inst., What Is the Gender Pay Gap and Is It Real?, at 1 (Oct. 20, 2016) ("In simple terms, no matter how you measure it, there is a gap").

81. Bureau of Labor Stats., Dept. of Labor, BLS Reports (Jan. 24, 2022); Bureau of Labor Stats., Dept. of Labor, BLS Reports, at tbl. 2 (Jan. 19, 2022); Census Bureau, Current Population Survey (CPS) Annual Social and Economic (ASEC), at Table PINC-05; Robin Bleiweis et al., Ctr. for Am. Progress, Women of Color and the Wage Gap (Nov. 17, 2021).

82. Women's Bureau, Dept. of Labor, Data and Statistics—Earnings, Gender Earnings Ratios and Wage Gaps by Age (Annual).

estimate puts the average lifetime disparity between men's and women's wages at more than $590,000, and the amount rises to nearly $800,000 for college-educated workers.[83] According to the Institute for Women's Policy Research, closing the gender wage gap would reduce the rate of poverty among women by more than 40 percent.[84]

No one factor can explain the gender wage gap. Part of the explanation is the occupational distribution of male and female workers.[85] As compared to men, women are much less likely to work in construction (10.3 percent female) or in repair and maintenance services (13.3 percent female), which are relatively well paid, and they are more likely to work in lower-paid job categories such as human resources (73.5 percent female) and personal care and service occupations (76.9 percent female). However, women earn less than men even within the same occupational field. Within industry groups, women are overrepresented in the lower-paying job categories. In the legal profession, for example, women are over 89.6 percent of paralegals and legal assistants, but only 36.4 percent of lawyers. Women also earn less than men within the same job category. Female financial managers, for example, earn only 63.6 percent of what their male counterparts make, female physicians make only 75.1 percent, and women in sales earn only 68.9 percent. Even after accounting for every identifiable variable (including occupation, industry, job, skill, education, experience, hours worked, and performance), a significant portion of the gender wage gap remains unexplained.

Although the gender wage gap has narrowed significantly since the 1960s, progress in recent decades has slowed. If the pace of progress since 2001 is used in projecting future progress, the wage gap will not close until the year 2152. The Equal Pay Act was passed in 1963. What changes in the law would you propose to close the gap? What costs and challenges would you anticipate?

Is progress in this area hindered by a lack of public understanding about the pay gap? Recent polls find that just 62 percent of Americans believe there is a gap (53 percent of men and 71 percent of women), and fully half of male millennials think that men and women are paid equally. Sixty-seven percent of women but only 41 percent of men think that the government should do more to address gender-based pay disparities.[86] Almost four in ten Americans (and 46 percent of men) believe that the gender pay gap is made up to serve a political purpose. What fuels this gender gap in perception?

2. **The Formal Equality Paradigm.**   The Equal Pay Act of 1963 is a paradigmatic application of formal equality principles. The main interpretative task is defining what work is equal. It obviously would be unfair to allow employers to circumvent the Act by minor variations in job titles or job descriptions. Thus, the Act

---

83. Gould et al., supra note 80, at 7; Chris Wilson, Just How Bad Is the Gender Pay Gap? Brutal, When You Look at a Lifetime of Work, Time.com (Apr. 2, 2019).

84. Elyse Shaw & Halie Mariano, Women's Pol'y Res., Narrow the Gender Pay Gap, Reduce Poverty for Families: The Economic Impact of Equal Pay by State (May 11, 2021).

85. U.S. Bureau of Labor Statistics, Women in the Labor Force: A Databook, tbl. 11, 14, 18 (Apr. 2021).

86. Kerri A. Renzulli, 46% of American Men Think the Gender Pay Gap Is "Made Up to Serve a Political Purpose," CNBC.com (Apr. 4, 2019).

has been applied to require the same wages for different job classifications entailing substantially equal duties and involving comparable skill, responsibility, and effort, such as female "cleaners" and male "janitors," "beauticians" and "barbers," and "seamstresses" and "tailors."[87]

Equal Pay Act cases can be difficult to win, particularly in cases involving upper-level employees.[88] The main problem with administrative and executive positions is finding a close enough comparator. Courts generally require the plaintiff in an Equal Pay Act suit to identify a particular employee, working for the same employer, who is earning more for the same work, and it is more difficult to compare the substance of white-collar jobs than lower-level positions.[89] A representative example is Georgen-Saad v. Texas Mutual Insurance Co.[90] There, the plaintiff, a Senior Vice President of Finance, alleged underpayment in comparison with other senior vice presidents in the company. The court dismissed that claim on the ground that "the assertion that any one of these jobs requires 'equal skill, effort, and responsibility' . . . cannot be taken seriously. . . . These are Senior Vice Presidents in charge of different aspects of Defendant's operation; these are not assembly-line workers or customer-service representatives." In the court's view, the Equal Pay Act could deal with "commodity-like" work, not the functions of high-level executives.[91]

Judge Posner's opinion in EEOC v. Madison Community Unit School District No. 12 strikes a compromise position, allowing the comparison between boys' and girls' coaches of the same sport, but not for coaches of different sports, such as volleyball and track. Is this a defensible compromise?

The Equal Pay Act addresses unjustified wage differentials based on sex but does not deal with gender biases that underlie the disparities. For example, the Act would not encompass discriminatory behavior that may have prevented women from becoming coaches of boys' sports teams at Madison Community Unit School. Such claims would need to proceed under Title VII, discussed below.

Should pay discrimination on the basis of sexual orientation or gender identity be actionable given that the Supreme Court has now held that discrimination "because of sex" under Title VII includes those characteristics?[92] What should courts do if a plaintiff has an intersectional claim based on discrimination because of both sex and sexual orientation, or sex and race?

---

87. See, e.g., Aldrich v. Randolph Central Sch. Dist., 963 F.2d 520 (2d Cir. 1992).

88. See Deborah Thompson Eisenberg, Shattering the Equal Pay Act's Glass Ceiling, 63 SMU L. Rev. 17 (2010).

89. See, e.g., Juliene James, The Equal Pay Act in the Courts: A De Facto White-Collar Exemption, 79 N.Y.U. L. Rev. (2004); Mary E. Graham & Julie L. Hotchkiss, A Systematic Assessment of Employer Equal Employment Opportunity Efforts as a Means of Reducing the Gender Earnings Gap, 12 Cornell J.L. & Pub. Pol'y 169 (2002).

90. 195 F. Supp. 2d 853 (W.D. Tex. 2002).

91. See also Chairamonte v. Animal Med. Ctr., 667 Fed. App'x 689 (2d Cir. 2017); EEOC v. Port Authority, 768 F.3d 247 (2d Cir. 2014). But see Lawin-McEleney v. Marist College, 239 F.3d 476 (2d Cir. 2001).

92. See Bostock v. Clayton Cty, 140 S. Ct. 1731 (2020), excerpted in Section 2C of this chapter; Adam P. Romero, Does the Equal Pay Act Prohibit Discrimination on the Basis of Sexual Orientation or Gender Identity?, 10 Ala C.R. & C.L. L. Rev. 35 (2019).

3. **Factors "Other than Sex" Justifying Differences in Pay.**   As the court notes in *Rizo*, an employer may successfully defend a proven pay disparity if it can prove that it was based on a factor "other than sex." This is one of four statutory affirmative defenses available to equal pay claims under both the Equal Pay Act and, by incorporation, Title VII. Some of the factors offered by employers arguably reinstate the very gender bias that the Equal Pay Act is intended to eliminate. For example, what if the man negotiated for a higher salary while the woman did not? An illustrative study found that male Carnegie Mellon University graduates were eight times more likely to negotiate a starting salary than their female classmates.[93] Why do you suppose this is? One reason is that stereotypes make assertive behavior more costly for women than men: women who act assertively are deemed less likable and are less likely to be hired and viewed as good colleagues than men.[94] Some researchers advise women to be "relentlessly pleasant" and to stress benefits for others, including employers and family members.[95]

Whatever the reason, research shows that women, when negotiating for themselves, are less likely than men to initiate bargaining and to ask for what they need, that women set lower goals, and that they feel less confident than men even when there are no objective differences in outcome.[96] In the context of compensation, where research consistently finds gender differences, women tend to have lower expectations than men, feel less entitled to higher salaries, and place less value on pay than on other aspects of their jobs. The result is that women demand and accept less in negotiations and are less confident and satisfied with their negotiation performance.[97] Is there a fix? Some commentators have recommended that organizations devise compensation systems that rely more on objective performance

---

93. See Linda Babcock & Sara Laschever, Women Don't Ask: Negotiations and the Gender Divide (2003).

94. Emily T. Amanatullah & Catherine H. Tinsely, Punishing Female Negotiators for Asserting Too Much . . . Or Not Enough: Exploring Advocacy as a Moderator of Backlash Against Assertive Female Negotiators, 120 Org. Behav. & Hum. Decision Processes 110 (2013); Jessica A. Kennedy & Laura J. Kray, A Pawn in Someone Else's Game? The Cognitive, Motivational, and Paradigmatic Barriers to Women's Excelling in Negotiation, 35 Res. Organizational Behav, 3, 6 (2015).

95. See Kennedy & Kray, supra note 94, at 21; Hannah Riley Bowles & Linda Babcock, How Can Women Escape the Compensation Negotiation Dilemma? Relational Accounts Are One Answer, 37 Psych. Women Q. 80 (2013).

96. Jens Mazei et al., A Meta-Analysis on Gender Differences in Negotiation Outcomes and Their Moderators, 141 Psych. Bull. 85 (2015). For factors that moderate this finding, see Kennedy & Kray, supra note 94. For reviews of multiple studies, see Deborah M. Kolb, Negotiating in the Shadow of Organizations: Gender Negotiation, and Change, 28 Ohio St. J. Disp. Res. 241, 243 (2013). When there is no explicit statement that wages are negotiable, men are likely to negotiate for a higher wage and women more likely to signal their willingness to work for a lower wage. Andrew Leibbrandt & John A. List, Do Women Avoid Salary Negotiations? Evidence from a Large-Scale Natural Field Experiment, 61 Mgmt. Sci. 2016 (2015). On gender and negotiation styles, see Rebecca Hollander-Blumoff, It's Complicated: Reflections on Teaching Negotiation for Women, 62 Wash. U. J.L. & Pol'y 77 (2020).

97. Kolb, supra note 96, at 243-44; Kennedy & Kray, supra note 94, at 7.

criteria and peer review and less on individual ability to self-promote.[98] Would this be moving in the right direction?

This disparity in negotiation behavior is especially crucial with respect to starting salaries, where the difference between a $25,000 and a $30,000 starting job salary, assuming 3 percent wage increases, would amount to over $350,000 over the next twenty-eight years.[99] In light of this disparity, should negotiation be a "factor other than sex" under the Equal Pay Act?[100] Is it relevant that women are more likely to be penalized by employers when they do attempt to negotiate pay?[101]

As a general proposition, market conditions that reflect discriminatory practices by the employer cannot justify a pay disparity. In Corning Glass Works v. Brennan, cited in *Rizo*, the Supreme Court rejected the employer's claim that market forces justified paying night workers more than day workers given that women had previously been excluded from such positions.[102] As is evident from the divisions among the judges in *Rizo*, the issue of whether employers may rely on more diffuse market conditions not traceable to the employer, such as prior salary, to justify a pay disparity has divided the courts.[103] Under the majority's reasoning in *Rizo*, the Equal Pay Act does not permit employers to defend a pay disparity based on an employee's pay history. Formal equality would have less bite if it required only prospectively equal treatment and allowed employers to rely on facially neutral practices, such as reliance on prior salary, that perpetuate what the majority called "baked-in sex discrimination." On the other hand, the concurring judges object that this approach is too constraining, tying employers' hands in responding to "today's dynamic workforce." By restricting employer considerations to only bona fide, job-related criteria to justify a pay disparity, has *Rizo* pushed the formal equality envelope too far? Or is this a necessary move to keep formal equality from becoming a rubber stamp on lingering inequities?

Several states have moved to ban employers from asking job candidates about their salary history. In 2016, Massachusetts passed the first such law, prohibiting employers from asking about prior salary until after an offer with compensation is made.[104] A handful of other states and cities have followed suit, sparking a reaction in the opposite direction by some jurisdictions, including Michigan and Wisconsin, to ban interference with employer discussion of applicants' salary histories. Are laws prohibiting employers from inquiring into prior salary an effective way to stop the perpetuation of pervasive pay discrimination in the labor market? Or will

---

98. Amanatullah & Tinsely, supra note 94, at 119-20.

99. See Shankar Bedantam, Salary, Gender and the Social Cost of Haggling, Wash. Post, July 30, 2007.

100. See Christine Elzer, Wheeling, Dealing, and the Glass Ceiling: Why the Gender Difference in Salary Negotiation Is Not a "Factor Other than Sex" Under the Equal Pay Act, 10 Geo. J. Gender & L. 1 (2009).

101. See Hannah Riley Bowles et al., Social Incentives for Gender Differences in the Propensity to Initiate Negotiation: Sometimes It Does Hurt to Ask, 103 Org. Behav. & Hum. Decision Processes 84 (2007).

102. 417 U.S. 188, 205-07 (1974).

103. Compare, e.g., Wernsing v. Illinois Dep't of Hum. Servs., 427 F.3d 466 (7th Cir. 2005), with Glenn v. Gen. Motors Corp., 841 F.2d 1567 (11th Cir. 1988).

104. See Mass. Gen. Laws ch. 149 § 105A (2022).

employers unconsciously presume women draw lower pay and are worth less in the labor market anyway?[105]

A case study in the difficulties of applying equal pay principles involves athletic coaches, the subject of the *Madison* case. In intercollegiate sports, women hold fewer than 3.5 percent of the coaching jobs in men's sports in all divisions, and the coaches for men's teams are paid more than twice the amount paid to coaches for women's teams. The percentage of women who are head coaches of women's teams has declined from 90 percent to 43 percent since enactment of Title IX, largely due to the increase in resources and status of women's sports.[106] What factors might justify pay disparities in male and female coaches' salaries? Judge Posner in *Madison* reasoned that the sex of the athletes coached might be "a factor other than sex" as long as women have equal access to the higher-paid jobs coaching male athletes. Is he right? Are differences in the revenue generated by sports teams a legitimate basis for a pay differential? Where does the difference in revenue capacity come from? If it is from greater spectator interest in men's sports, do universities bear any responsibility for creating or contributing to this state of affairs?[107] At the high school level, sports rarely generate a significant amount of revenue, but this is a common justification for paying intercollegiate coaches of women's teams less than coaches of men's teams. Does the challenge of coaching a team that produces revenues, and the corresponding stress and media demands, justify the large gap in coaching salaries between men's and women's intercollegiate teams? One court thought so, siding with the University of Southern California in celebrated women's basketball coach Marianne Stanley's Equal Pay Act claim.[108]

In an effort to address sex-based pay disparities in coaches' pay, the federal Equal Employment Opportunity Commission (EEOC) promulgated guidelines in 1997 clarifying that factors justifying pay differences must not themselves stem from sex-based differences in treatment. If the university provided discriminatorily reduced support to the women's team, higher revenue produced by the men's team would not be a factor other than sex, the EEOC cautioned. To justify unequal salaries based on differential revenues, the institution must demonstrate that the female coach received the same opportunities as the male coach to be a revenue producer, and that the differences in revenue did not trace back to lower resources for female athletic programs. The EEOC guidelines also make clear that that

---

105. See Orly Lobel, Knowledge Pays: Reversing Information Flows & The Future of Pay Equity, 120 Colum. L. Rev. 547 (2020).

106. Linda Jean Carpenter & R. Vivian Acosta, Women in Intercollegiate Sport: A Longitudinal, National Study—Thirty-Five Year Update 1977-2014, at 17-18 (2014). Some evidence suggests that if football, basketball, and ice hockey were excluded, the salaries for male and female head coaches would be nearly equal. Robert Drago et al., CAGE: The Coaching and Gender Equity Report 11 (2005); Nicole LaVoi et al., Women in College Coaching Report Card 4, 13 (2021-22).

107. See Katharine T. Bartlett & Mitu Gulati, Discrimination by Customers, 102 Iowa L. Rev. 223 (2016) (arguing that colleges and universities could use tools, like ticket-bundling, to help build demand for women's sports and thus even out current inequities attributable to differences in fan preference for men's over women's sports).

108. Stanley v. U.S.C., 13 F.3d 1313 (9th Cir. 1994).

"[s]ex discrimination in the marketplace which results in lower pay for jobs done by women will not support the marketplace value defense."[109] However, this EEOC guidance has not been noticeably influential in the courts.

   4. **Lilly Ledbetter and Pay Discrimination Claims Under Title VII.**   Plaintiffs can bring wage discrimination claims under Title VII as well as the Equal Pay Act. The Equal Pay Act has some advantages, including a longer statute of limitations and the lack of an intent requirement, but under Title VII, a plaintiff can prove wage discrimination without necessarily proving that a particular man was being paid more than the plaintiff for doing the same job.

   In 2006, the Supreme Court considered a Title VII wage discrimination claim in Ledbetter v. Goodyear Tire & Rubber Co., a case that captured the public attention and led to congressional action.[110] The lawsuit was brought by Lilly Ledbetter, the only female production supervisor at a Goodyear plant in Gadsen, Alabama. She proved to a jury that she suffered illegal pay discrimination on the basis of sex—her salary was as much as 40 percent lower than that of the lowest paid male supervisor—and was awarded the maximum available damages under Title VII.[111] On appeal, Goodyear successfully argued before the Eleventh Circuit that her claim was time-barred because every discriminatory pay decision occurred more than 180 days prior to when she first filed a charge with the EEOC.[112] Title VII provides that an EEOC charge must be brought within 180 or 300 days (depending on the jurisdiction) "after the alleged unlawful employment practice occurred." There are three possible dates from which the 180-/300-day clock could run: (1) from the date of the pay decision that sets a discriminatory wage, (2) from the date an employee learns her pay is discriminatory (a "discovery" rule), or (3) from the date any paycheck that contains an amount affected by a prior discriminatory pay decision is issued (the "paycheck accrual" rule). The Supreme Court opted for the first approach, holding that a plaintiff has 180/300 days after the pay decision that sets the discriminatory wage to file her charge with the EEOC in compliance with Title VII's statute of limitations. The majority flatly rejected the paycheck accrual rule, reasoning that a paycheck containing a discriminatory amount of money is not a present violation, but, instead, is merely the present effect of a prior act of discrimination. "[C]urrent effects alone cannot breathe life into prior, charged discrimination," the Court wrote; "such effects have no present legal consequences."[113] Although *Ledbetter* dealt with a rather technical rule, it promised

---

   109. U.S. Equal Emp. Opportunity Comm'n, Enforcement Guidance on Sex Discrimination in the Compensation of Sports Coaches in Educational Institutions (1997). For discussion, see Deborah L. Rhode & Christopher J. Walker, Gender Equity in College Athletics, 4 Stan. J. C.R. & C.L. 101, 117-19 (2008).

   110. 550 U.S. 618 (2007).

   111. Id. Ledbetter also alleged an Equal Pay Act violation, but lost on that claim because her job, supervising one aspect of production, was not similar enough to that of the higher-paid male supervisors who supervised different aspects of production at the plant. Ledbetter did not appeal the Equal Pay Act ruling.

   112. 421 F.3d 1169 (11th Cir. 2005).

   113. *Ledbetter*, 550 U.S. at 628.

significantly adverse effects for victims of pay discrimination who were not able to quickly identify and complain about pay disparities. The ruling provoked public outcry and became a hot-button issue in the 2008 presidential campaign. After President Barack Obama was elected, Congress passed the Lilly Ledbetter Fair Pay Act of 2009, and it became the first bill signed into law during his presidency.[114] The new law provides that an

> unlawful employment practice occurs, with respect to discrimination in compensation in violation of this title, when a discriminatory compensation decision or other practice is adopted, when an individual becomes subject to a discriminatory compensation decision or other practice, or when an individual is affected by application of a discriminatory compensation decision or other practice, including each time wages, benefits, or other compensation is paid, resulting in whole or in part from such a decision or other practice.[115]

In effect, the Act adopts the "paycheck accrual" rule that the Supreme Court rejected in *Ledbetter*.

The Ledbetter Act does not address obstacles to successful proof of pay discrimination other than the limitations period. One major obstacle to suing for pay discrimination is the well-documented phenomenon of pay secrecy, which some employers enforce by penalizing employees who discuss their pay with other employees.[116] The Paycheck Fairness Act (PFA), which has been introduced in several sessions of Congress to make it easier to prove wage discrimination, would make it illegal for employers to penalize employees who discuss their salaries.[117] The PFA would also expand damages under the EPA and narrow the "factor other than sex" defense to Equal Pay Act claims by requiring the employer to prove that the factor is job related and justified by business necessity. Is this stricter than or effectively the same as the standard adopted in *Rizo*? It would certainly change the standard in jurisdictions that have interpreted the defense to impose no constraints apart from sex-neutrality.[118] So far, the proposed PFA has been repeatedly defeated in Congress.[119]

Perhaps because of the lack of success on the federal level, states have begun to enact more demanding equal pay laws. Mississippi became the last state to

---

114. See Lilly Ledbetter Fair Pay Act of 2009, Pub. L. No. 111-2, 123 Stat. 5 (codified as amended at 42 U.S.C. § 2000e-5(e)(3)(A) (2018)).

115. Id.

116. Leonard Bierman & Rafael Gely, "Love, Sex and Politics? Sure. Salary? No Way": Workplace Social Norms and the Law, 25 Berkeley J. Emp. & Lab. L. 167, 168, 171 (2004).

117. See Paycheck Fairness Act, H.R.7, 117th Congress (1st sess. 2021).

118. See Deborah L. Brake, Reviving Paycheck Fairness: Why and How the Factor-Other-Than-Sex Defense Matters, 52 Idaho L. Rev. 889, 893-901 (2016); see also Deborah L. Brake, The Shifting Sands of Employment Discrimination: From Unjustified Impact to Disparate Treatment in Pregnancy and Pay, 105 Geo. L. J. 559, 603-13 (2017).

119. David S. Joachim, Senate Republicans Block Bill on Equal Pay, N.Y. Times, Apr. 9, 2014, at A14.

enact an equal pay law in 2022, and most state laws track the federal Equal Pay Act.[120] Some states have gone further in the last few years with laws that loosen the standard for comparing jobs from "equal work" to "substantially similar work"; restrict reliance on prior salary; require transparency around salary ranges; require employers to collect and report pay data; and protect employees who discuss their pay.[121] In 2018, Massachusetts revised and strengthened its Equal Pay Act to impose many of these changes but also to add an affirmative defense if the employer voluntarily undertakes a good faith, reasonable audit of its pay practices and demonstrates reasonable progress toward closing its pay gap.[122] Might employers still be reluctant to undertake pay equity studies? What provisions would you include if you were drafting a state equal pay law?

5. **"Comparable Worth" or "Pay Equity."**   Should teachers and secretaries be paid less than sanitation workers, maintenance staff, and mechanics? Should child care workers be paid less than gas station attendants and pet sitters? What do you suppose explains the differences? Can they be successfully challenged through the principle of formal equality?

The Equal Pay Act requires that women and men be paid the same for the same work, but it does not require pay equity between job categories. In other words, it demands that male and female nurses be paid the same, but not that the wage structures for traditionally female occupations like nurses, teachers, and secretaries be fair in relation to wage structures for traditionally male occupations like sanitation workers, mechanics, and appliance repair workers.

A principle that goes beyond the Equal Pay Act and Title VII to address these kinds of arguable inequities *between* job categories is referred to as comparable worth or pay equity. Pay equity seeks not only to ensure equal pay for equal work, but also to achieve salary comparability for workers in different, sex-segregated job classifications requiring equivalent degrees of training, experience, and effort. In the *Madison* case, Justice Posner concludes the Equal Pay Act does not mandate comparable worth. Other courts have agreed that federal law does not encompass comparable worth.[123] Should it? Does the principle of pay equity fit within formal equality?

Arguments for and against pay equity turn on assumptions about the causes of occupational segregation, and on the form of equality to which one is committed. If occupational segregation follows from the different priorities and lifestyle choices of men and women, there is arguably no problem to solve. Human capital theorists posit that women anticipate working fewer years than men with more interruptions, and so "self-select" into occupations requiring lower levels of skill and less educational investment. They may also choose jobs that offer lower pay in exchange for more pleasant and less hazardous working conditions, and more

120. Thomas Akpan & Maureen H. Lavery, Soc'y Hum. Res. Mgmt., Mississippi Becomes the Last State to Enact an Equal Pay Law (May 19, 2022).

121. Nat'l Women's L. Ctr., Progress in the States for Equal Pay (Nov. 2020).

122. Mass. Gen. Laws ch. 149 § 105A (2022).

123. See AFSCME v. Washington, 770 F.2d 1401 (9th Cir. 1985); Spaulding v. Univ. of Wash., 740 F.2d 686 (9th Cir. 1984); American Nurses Ass'n v. Illinois, 606 F. Supp. 1313 (N.D. Ill. 1985).

flexible schedules.[124] Some argue that these choices are, at least in part, hard-wired into women's biology.[125] Opponents of pay equity argue also that free markets will operate to eliminate pay structures that are unequal: If men are overpaid, women will move into those fields, creating surpluses in those occupations and shortages in traditionally female occupations. The result will be to eliminate pay discrepancies that are not justified by the nature and demands of the work. Under this market view, women not satisfied to be teachers at existing salary levels should seek higher pay as sanitation workers or mechanics.

But do jobs have a market value that is objective, apart from societal and organizational biases tied to the gender of the people performing the work?[126] Female-dominated occupations pay less than male-dominated occupations even when they require similar levels of skill, education, and experience.[127] And when women do move into a field, changing its gender composition from male-dominated to female-dominated, median wages (adjusted for inflation) decline precipitously.[128] Does this cast doubt on women's choice and market explanations for paying female-dominated occupations less than male-dominated ones?

Even if sex-segregated job categories help to explain why women's earnings are only 83 percent of men's,[129] they do not explain why, within the same occupational category, significant salary disparities exist.[130] Does this phenomenon demonstrate the fundamental failure of the Equal Pay Act to eliminate discrimination in wages? Or does it show that women are making trade-offs not only between occupational categories, but within them? One expert, Claudia Goldin, suggests that occupations that most value long hours, face time at the office, and being on call—like business, law, and surgery—tend to have the widest pay gaps, whereas professions like pharmacy, where employees can easily substitute for one another and are paid in proportion to the hours they work, have the narrowest pay gaps.[131] What implications do you draw from this?

To what extent do women's "choices" in the paid labor market simply reflect the same broader patterns of societal discrimination that affirmative action in the hiring context are designed to overcome—i.e., gendered definitions of work and past discrimination? Or workplace policies that steer employees in gendered

[handwritten margin note: women more likely to require flexibility]

---

124. See Warren Farrell, Why Men Earn More: The Startling Truth About the Pay Gap—and What Women Can Do About It (2005).

125. See Kingsley Browne, Sex and Temperament in Modern Society: A Darwinian View of the Glass Ceiling and the Gender Gap, 37 Ariz. L. Rev. 971 (1995).

126. For a critique of "the market" as a justification for pay inequity in arguments opposing comparable worth, see Martha Chamallas, The Market Excuse, 68 U. Chi. L. Rev. 579 (2001).

127. Stephanie Bornstein, Equal Work, 77 Md. L. Rev. 581, 595-96 (2018).

128. Id. at 582-83, 596-97.

129. Jody Feder & Benjamin Collins, Pay Equity: Legislative and Legal Developments 1 (CRS Report RL31867) (2016).

130. See Claudia Goldin, A Grand Gender Convergence: Its Last Chapter, 104 Am. Econ. Rev. 1091, 1098 (2014); see also Bornstein, supra note 127, at 597.

131. See Claire Cain Miller, Pay Gap Is Because of Gender, Not Jobs, N.Y. Times, Apr. 23, 2014, at B3.

directions?[132] Will supply and demand take care of job segregation and low pay in traditionally female occupations? Some say no, especially given the social reasons why men tend to invest more heavily in their human capital and do not participate as much in the family responsibilities that constrain the job choices of many women.

If affirmative action is justified to overcome these factors on the hiring side, should wage structures be proactively examined with the goal of recalibrating the wage scales for job categories that have been historically dominated by women? A number of states have done so, undertaking pay equity studies and making adjustments in various pay categories in state employment where bias was identified. In addition, Minnesota and Iowa have passed legislation requiring pay equity in state employment, and Maine requires it for private sector jobs as well. Other countries, including Sweden, England, Australia, and Canada (specifically, Ontario), also have pay equity requirements. European Council Directive 75.117, Article I, provides that the principle of equal pay under Article 119 of the EEC Treaty requires equal pay for "work to which equal value is attributed." The Fair Pay Act (not to be confused with the Paycheck Fairness Act, discussed in Note 4, above) has been introduced in consecutive Congresses for over a decade. It would require employers to provide equal pay for "equivalent" jobs, but the bill has never made it out of committee.[133] Why has comparable worth, at least at the federal level, been a non-starter in the United States?

6. **Women and Contingent Work.**   More than 40 percent of the U.S. work force is made up of "contingent workers"—i.e., those employed other than on a full-time, permanent basis.[134] This group includes part-time workers, on-call workers, temporary workers, independent contractors, gig workers, day laborers, and home-based workers. Part-time workers have lower wages, fewer benefits, and less job stability than full-time workers.[135] According to data from the Bureau of Labor Statistics, almost 18 percent of the U.S. work force work part time, with women making up 64 percent of the part-time work force.[136] In 2016, 25 percent of employed women worked part time, compared with about 12 percent of employed men.[137] Contingent work has been growing, and some researchers argue that it is increasingly necessary to provide flexibility in a global environment characterized by cheap overseas labor and "just in time" production methods. Platform-facilitated labor in the "gig" economy also comprises an increasing share of contingent work and poses special challenges for equal pay. One case study found that despite working more hours on the platform, women earned about two-thirds of men's hourly

---

132. For examples and analysis, see Vicki Schultz, Telling Stories About Women and Work: Judicial Interpretations of Sex Segregation in the Workplace in Title VII Cases Raising the Lack of Interest Argument, 103 Harv. L. Rev. 1749, 1808 (1990).

133. Feder & Collins, supra note 129, at 7-9.

134. U.S. Gov't Accountability Office, Contingent Workforce: Size, Characteristics, Earnings, and Benefits 4 (Apr. 20, 2015).

135. Id.

136. U.S. Bureau of Labor Stats., Household Data Annual Averages, Table 8, https://www.bls.gov/cps/cpsaat08.pdf.

137. Women's Bureau, U.S. Dept. of Labor, Full-Time/Part-Time, https://www.dol.gov/wb/stats/NEWSTATS/latest/parttime.htm#ftpt-sex.

rates, and a gender wage gap persisted even after controlling for customer feed-back score, experience, occupational category, hours worked, and education.[138] Does women's role in the contingent work force raise gender equity concerns?[139] If so, does formal equality provide adequate tools for addressing them?

PUTTING THEORY INTO PRACTICE

1-11. Pay inequality in Hollywood made news in 2015 when a hack at Sony Pictures revealed stark inequalities in what actors and actresses were paid to star in the same film. Jennifer Lawrence, an Oscar-winning actress, wrote an open let-ter asking, "Why Do I Make Less Than My Male Co-Stars?"[140] Concerns escalated when pay inequality intersected with #MeToo: *All the Money in the World*, an Oscar contender, was overhauled to exclude scenes with Kevin Spacey, who was accused by numerous men of sexual misconduct. It was later revealed that in reshooting the excluded scenes, actor Mark Wahlberg earned $1.5 million, while his co-lead Michele Williams was paid less than $1,000. Other examples in the industry include the revelation that Netflix paid lead actress Claire Foy, who played the Queen in *The Crown*, less than the actor playing the supporting role of Prince Philip.[141]

Why do you suppose pay inequality is so entrenched in the entertainment industry? What justifications might there be for paying actors more than actresses to star in equally significant roles in the same production? If "the market" is offered as the reason, what does "the market" mean when actors and actresses are starring in the same film?

1-12. In 2016, five members of the U.S. Women's National Team in soccer filed a complaint with the EEOC alleging that the U.S. Soccer Federation (USSF), the national governing body for the sport, paid them as little as 40 percent of what it pays members of the U.S. Men's National Team. After many years of litigation, the U.S. Soccer Federation settled the lawsuit in 2022 by agreeing to new collective bar-gaining agreements that pay the two teams equally and provide the women's team with $24 million in back pay.[142] The settlement also provides that the two teams will pool prize money from their respective World Cup appearances and split the total

---

138. Arianne Renan Barzilay & Anat Ben-David, Platform Inequality: Gender in the Gig-Economy, 47 Seton Hall L. Rev. 393 (2017).

139. See Nantiya Ruan & Nancy Reichman, Hours Equity Is the New Pay Equity, 59 Vill. L. Rev. 35 (2014) (discussing the vulnerabilities of women working part time, including inflexible scheduling and disparities in hours offered to male and female workers); see also Martha T. McCluskey, Precarity, Productivity and Gender, 49 U. Tol. L. Rev. 631, 648 (2018) (arguing that "the new economy runs on old gender practices").

140. Jennifer Lawrence, Why Do I Make Less Than My Male Co-Stars?, Lenny (Oct. 13, 2015); see also Madeline Berg, Everything You Need to Know About the Hollywood Pay Gap, Forbes, Nov. 12, 2015.

141. Alicia Adamczyk, Why You Should Care About the Hollywood Wage Gap, Time. com (Feb. 26, 2016) (noting, also, that earnings for female actresses peak around age 34, while those for male actors do not peak until age 51).

142. Andrew Das, U.S. Soccer and Women's Players Agree to Settle Equal Pay Lawsuit, N.Y. Times, Feb. 22, 2022, at A1.

proceeds. Given that the women's team has won four World Cup championships, while the men sometimes don't even qualify to participate, is this a victory? Are there any relevant differences between the two teams that might justify a different pay contract? The women's team had suffered a significant setback when a court in 2020 dismissed their equal pay claims.[143] Why might USSF have nonetheless settled a case it was unlikely to lose in court?

1-13. Does the pay equality analysis for athletes change when the rules of the game are different for men and women? Since 2007, all of the Grand Slam tennis events have paid men and women winners the same prize money, but this is not the case with all tournaments. In the 2022 Italian Open, for example, the winner of the women's event earned less than 40 percent than the winner of the men's event.[144] Under Equal Pay Act principles, what might justify this discrepancy? The fact that men play best-of-five-set matches, while women play best-of-three? What if men's tennis is more competitive than women's in the top ranks and thus more physically demanding? What if fans and sports commentators believe it to be more entertaining?

1-14. Under pressure to be more transparent about its costs, the BBC released a list of its highest paid stars, revealing few women made the cut. BBC's China editor, Carrie Grace, one of the BBC's four foreign editors, was not on the list. The other three included a woman who covered Europe and earned about the same as Grace, a more highly paid man who covered the Middle East, and an even higher paid man who covered North America. The two women earned about 50 percent less than their male counterparts. Grace filed a grievance with the BBC seeking to be paid equally to the North America correspondent. The BBC initially offered Grace a modest raise but resisted paying her the same as the North America correspondent, whose job was more "relentless" in "scope and scale." Grace countered that if anything, the China job was more demanding, requiring mastery of a different culture and language, distant travel, and dealing with government surveillance. How would Grace's claim be analyzed under U.S. law?[145]

1-15. The Boston Symphony Orchestra was sued by its top flute player, Elizabeth Rowe, for paying her just 75 percent of the salary paid to the orchestra's lead oboe player, a man. Both musicians are leaders of their respective woodwind sections and have similar leadership roles in the orchestra. Since joining the orchestra, Rowe has been selected to perform as a special soloist more than any other principal player. Rowe claims that the salary criteria used by the orchestra suppresses the pay of musicians who play instruments traditionally played by women. The oboe player publicly supported the flutist's claim, stating, "I consider Elizabeth to be my peer and equal, at least as worthy of the compensation that I receive as I am." How

---

143. Morgan v. U.S. Soccer Fed., Inc., 445 F. Supp.3d 635 (C.D. Cal. 2020).

144. Matthew Johns, Why is There Still a Gender Pay Gap in Tennis in 2022?, Last Word on Sports (May 22, 2022).

145. Santiago-Ramos v. Centennial P.R. Wireless Corp., 217 F.3d 46 (1st Cir. 2000); see also Lauren Collins, What Women Want, New Yorker (July 23, 2018).

would you expect the orchestra to defend the claim? How do you think a court would rule?[146]

1-16. The EEOC filed a lawsuit against the University of Denver Sturm College of Law on behalf of its tenured women faculty. The EEOC alleged that the mean annual salary of the law school's sixteen tenured male professors was $159,721, compared to a mean of $139,940 for the law school's nine tenured women professors. Each female tenured professor earned a lower salary than the mean salary for the tenured men. In 2018, the University settled the case, agreeing to pay nearly $2.7 million and to allow monitoring of its compensation practices by an independent consultant for a six-year period.[147] Assume that many faculties have gendered pay disparities similar to the University of Denver's. What factors should an independent consultant consider in evaluating salary disparities between male and female faculty? If the law school bases annual raises on a combination of teaching, scholarship, and service, how should performance in these areas be fairly measured? In addition to differences in raises, it is common for law faculty salary disparities to reflect differences in negotiated starting pay, competitive offers from other schools, and lingering effects from holding prior administrative positions (e.g., former deans or associate deans). How should these factors be evaluated?

1-17. Suppose a recently hired first-woman-of-color CEO has made an offer to another woman of color for a senior position. If the CEO is motivated to be a tough negotiator because she doesn't want to be seen as "soft" given her "first" status, is that sex discrimination? If the woman of color offeree negotiates strenuously and is then bad-mouthed by the CEO for being "difficult," is that sex discrimination? How does the women's racial or ethnic identity affect your analysis? Can Title VII take that into account? Should it?

1-18. With the heightened attention to equal pay issues in recent years, a number of proposed law reform measures and government policies have pursued a different path than a nondiscrimination, formal equality approach. Such measures include protecting employees who share pay information, prohibiting employers from seeking prior salary information, incentivizing employers to conduct voluntary pay audits, and publicizing employee salaries in a publicly available database. Are any of these measures likely to be more effective than stronger sex discrimination laws prohibiting pay discrimination? What is their relationship to formal equality?[148]

1-19. One study by Stanford business faculty found that a 7 percent pay gap between male and female Uber drivers could be explained by three factors: (1) experience on the platform (learned strategies for strategically accepting and canceling trips); (2) geographic preferences for where to drive (male drivers tend to live and drive in more lucrative areas and are more willing to drive in high-crime areas and to and from drinking establishments); and (3) preferences for driving speed (men tend to driver faster and increasing speed increases driver

146. Jeremy Eichler, The BSO's Principal Flutist Says She Is Paid Far Less than the Man Who Is the Principal Oboist, Bos. Globe, July 2, 2018.

147. Michael Roberts, DU Won't Apologize for Underpaying Female Law Profs, But It Will Pay Millions, Westword (May 18, 2018).

148. See Lobel, supra note 105.

earnings).[149] If this analysis is correct, is the pay disparity justifiable under the factor other than sex defense to the Equal Pay Act?

1-20. In 2011, two women employed at the University of Tennessee sued, claiming that they were paid less to serve as the Director and Associate Director for Women's Strength and Conditioning than were the male employees who worked for Men's Strength and Conditioning. The University's "Office of Equity and Diversity" denied their claims, with this reasoning:

> Football overwhelmingly is the top revenue-generating sport in Athletics and the sport that generates the most fan interest. If the University's football team is successful, then the entire Athletics program reaps the monetary benefits. If the University's football team is unsuccessful even partly because football injuries are not being prevented, diagnosed, treated and rehabilitated successfully, then the entire Athletics program suffers. With no disrespect being intended to [the claimants], the Director of Men's Strength and Conditioning is more important to athletics because of its football-related responsibilities.[150]

In bringing a claim in court, how would you respond to the internal ruling?

2. *Title VII: Finding the Limits of Formal Equality*

The linchpin of federal employment discrimination law is Title VII of the Civil Rights Act of 1964. Two theories of employment discrimination have emerged under Title VII. The *disparate treatment* theory addresses employment rules or decisions that intentionally treat an employee less favorably than others because of the employee's race, sex, religion, or national origin. When plaintiffs challenge a formal policy that discriminates on the basis of sex, the employer's only statutory defense is to prove that a sex-based requirement or restriction is a bona fide occupational qualification (BFOQ). While a number of different tests for the BFOQ defense exist, the standard basically requires the employer to show that "the essence of the business operation would be undermined" by hiring employees without the qualification in question and that either virtually all members of the excluded sex lack the qualification, or it is impossible to test for it individually. When plaintiffs challenge adverse employment actions that are not rooted in a formal policy, they must prove that the decisions were made "because of sex." In systemic cases, they do so through a combination of statistical evidence and individual anecdotes that reveal the underlying discriminatory motive;[151] in individual cases, they utilize the proof structures laid out below.

---

149. See Cody Cook et al., The Gender Earnings Gap in the Gig Economy: Evidence from Over a Million Rideshare Drivers, NBER Working Paper 24732 (June 2018).

150. Erin Buzuvis, Tennessee Rejects Equal Pay for Women's Athletics Officials, Title IX Blog (Nov. 17, 2011); see also Steve Megargee, Settlement Reached in Tennessee Discrimination Lawsuit, Wash. Post., Jan. 4, 2016.

151. Most systemic disparate treatment claims are litigated as class actions. Obtaining class certification in an employment discrimination case is less likely after the Supreme Court's ruling in Wal-Mart Stores, Inc. v. Dukes, 564 U.S. 338 (2011), discussed in Note 8 below.

The second theory under Title VII is *disparate impact* discrimination. Under this theory, the plaintiff must show that a facially neutral job requirement or policy disproportionately affects women. Unlike discrimination cases brought under the U.S. Constitution, like Massachusetts v. Feeney (excerpted earlier), the plaintiff in a Title VII disparate impact case need not show discriminatory intent. Once the plaintiff introduces facts showing disparate impact, the employer must either refute those facts, or demonstrate that the facially neutral job requirement is both job-related and consistent with business necessity. Even then, the plaintiff has the opportunity to show that the employer's goals could be met in a less restrictive manner. To the extent that the discriminatory impact approach focuses on the *effects* of a rule rather than its *form*, it more closely fits the model of substantive, rather than formal, equality—a model examined more closely in Chapter 2.

Title VII has been a significant tool in helping women gain access to areas of employment previously closed to them—although proving discrimination, absent a facially discriminatory policy, can be difficult. The statute has had greater difficulty, however, with rules that are based on women's actual differences from men. Such questions tend to divide into two separate phases of Title VII analysis: (1) whether the claimed discrimination constitutes "discrimination on the basis of sex"; and (2) whether, if a classification constitutes sex discrimination, it is nonetheless justified because of its relationship to legitimate business concerns.

a. What Is Discrimination "Because of Sex"?

When an employer discriminates "because of sex," the only remaining question is whether or not the sex-based discrimination is justified (see next section). But the meaning of that phrase took many years to take shape. In Phillips v. Martin Marietta Corp., the Supreme Court first considered this question when asked to determine whether a policy against hiring women with preschool-age children constituted sex discrimination.[152] Although the Court ruled that it did—adopting the so-called sex-plus doctrine that treats discrimination against a subclass of one gender as unlawful—questions during oral argument showed the lack of consensus on the meaning of the phrase. As Gillian Thomas writes, the Justices displayed a "skeptical, even bemused tenor to several of their questions about the scope of Title VII's sex provision."[153] Justice Hugo Black asked the plaintiff's lawyer whether Title VII required an employer to "give the woman a job of digging ditches and things of that kind," while Justice Blackmun asked whether a hospital that hired only female nurses for a long time and "like[d] them and got along well" would now have to hire male nurses?[154] Justice Burger, meanwhile, asked whether "if a federal judge as a matter of policy would decline to hire a law clerk who had an infant child, a lady law clerk, but was willing to hire a man whose wife had infant children, they would be in violation of the statute, if the statute applied to them?"[155] After this plodding start, the Supreme Court would gradually hammer out a more robust definition of

---

152. 400 U.S. 542 (1971).

153. Gillian Thomas, Because of Sex: One Law, Ten Cases, and Fifty Years That Changed American Women's Lives at Work 24 (2016).

154. Id.

155. Id.

sex discrimination, but it is still not always easy for courts to determine whether an action was taken "because of sex."

Courts have recognized two proof structures for individual disparate treatment claims: pretext and mixed-motive. In pretext claims, the plaintiff bears the burden of proving that the discrimination complained of was based on sex. The first step (the "prima facie case") requires the plaintiff to establish several factors that eliminate some of the obvious nondiscriminatory explanations for the adverse decision (e.g., that the applicant was not qualified for the position). The defendant then has the burden to articulate a legitimate, nondiscriminatory reason for the decision. Finally, the plaintiff has the ultimate burden of proving that the reason given is a pretext for sex discrimination. Ezold v. Wolf, Block, Schorr & Solis-Cohen, excerpted below, is an example.

In mixed-motive cases, both discriminatory and nondiscriminatory reasons are present. Price Waterhouse v. Hopkins, also excerpted below, is an example of this model.

For either model of disparate treatment, an important question is what discrimination because of "sex" encompasses. The Supreme Court's most recent interpretation of that requirement addresses the relationship between discrimination based on sex, sexual orientation, and gender identity. That case, Bostock v. Clayton County, is also excerpted below.

Ezold v. Wolf, Block, Schorr & Solis-Cohen

983 F.2d 509 (3d Cir. 1992)

HUTCHINSON, Circuit Judge.

Wolf, Block, Schorr and Solis-Cohen (Wolf) appeals from a judgment of the United States District Court for the Eastern District of Pennsylvania granting relief in favor of Nancy O'Mara Ezold (Ezold) on her claim that Wolf intentionally discriminated against her on the basis of her sex in violation of Title VII . . . when it decided not to admit her to the firm's partnership effective February 1, 1989. . . .

The district court held that the nondiscriminatory reason articulated by Wolf for its rejection of Ezold's candidacy—that her legal analytical ability failed to meet the firm's partnership standard—was a pretext. . . .

Ezold was hired by Wolf as an associate on a partnership track in July 1983. She had graduated in the top third of her class from the Villanova University School of Law in 1980 and then worked at two small law firms in Philadelphia. . . . Ezold was hired at Wolf by Seymour Kurland, then chairman of the litigation department. The district court found that Kurland told Ezold during an interview that it would not be easy for her at Wolf because "she was a woman, had not attended an Ivy League law school, and had not been on law review." . . . [She] was assigned to the firm's litigation department. From 1983-87, Kurland was responsible for the assignment of work to associates in the department. He often delegated this responsibility to partner Steven Arbittier. . . . The district court found that Arbittier assigned Ezold to actions that were "small" by Wolf standards. . . .

Senior associates within two years of partnership consideration are evaluated annually; non-senior associates are evaluated semi-annually. The firm's partners are asked to submit written evaluations on standardized forms. . . . Ten criteria of legal performance are listed on the forms in the following order: legal analysis, legal writing and drafting, research skills, formal speech, informal speech, judgment, creativity, negotiating and advocacy, promptness and efficiency. Ten personal characteristics are also listed: reliability, taking and managing responsibility, flexibility, growth potential, attitude, client relationship, client servicing and development, ability under pressure, ability to work independently, and dedication. As stated by Ian Strogatz, Chairman of the Associates Committee: "The normal standards for partnership include as factors for consideration all of the ones . . . that are contained [on] our evaluation forms." . . .

The firm's partners evaluated Ezold twice a year as an associate and once a year as a senior associate from October 1983 until the Associates Committee determined that it would not recommend her for partnership in September 1988. The district court found that "in the period up to and including 1988, Ms. Ezold received strongly positive evaluations from almost all of the partners for whom she had done any substantial work." . . . Ezold's overall score in legal skills in the 1988 bottom line memorandum before the Associates Committee was a "G" for good [the second highest rating on a 5-part scale ranging from exceptional to unacceptable]. . . .

Evaluations in Ezold's file not mentioned by the district court show that concerns over Ezold's legal analytical ability arose early during her tenure at the firm. In an evaluation covering the period from November 1984 through April 1985, Arbittier wrote:

> I have discussed legal issues with Nancy in connection with [two cases]. I found her analysis to be rather superficial and unfocused. I am beginning to doubt that she has sufficient legal analytical ability to make it with the firm. . . . She makes a good impression with people, has common sense, and can handle routine matters well. However these traits will take you just so far in our firm. I think that due to the nature of our practice Nancy's future here is limited. . . .

That same year Schwartz wrote:

> I have worked a great deal with Nancy since my last evaluation. . . . Both cases are complex, multifaceted matters that have presented novel issues to us. While her enthusiasm never wanes and she keeps plugging away—I'm often left with a product that demonstrates uncertainty in the analysis of a problem. After extensive discussions with me, the analysis becomes a little more focused, although sometimes I get the sense that Nancy feels adrift and is just marching as best she can to my analytical tune. . . . In my view her energy, enthusiasm and fearlessness make her a valuable asset to us. While she may not be as bright as some of our best associates, her talents will continue to serve us well.

[A]lso in 1985, partner Donald Joseph rated Ezold's legal analytical ability as marginal and wrote "its [sic] too early to tell but I have been disappointed on her grasp of the problem, let alone performance." . . .

During her next evaluation period from April through November 1985, Ezold received similar negative evaluations. Arbittier, Robert Fiebach and Joseph rated her legal analytical abilities as marginal. Arbittier wrote:

> She took a long time getting [a summary judgment brief] done and I found it to be stilted and unimaginative. One of the main issues—dealing with the issue of notice—she missed completely and did not grasp our position. . . . Also, in considering whether to file a defensive motion . . . she failed to cite me to a clause in the agreement that was highly relevant leaving me with the impression that the motion could not succeed. I think Nancy tries hard and can handle relatively straight-forward matters with a degree of maturity and judgment, but when she gets into more complicated areas she lacks real analytical skill and just does what she is told in a mechanical way. She is not up to our minimal Wolf, Block standards. . . .

Boote made the following report on his performance review with Ezold after this evaluation period:

> Nancy appeared to accept the judgment, albeit a little grudgingly, that her analytical, research and writing ability was not up to our standards and that she should focus on the types of matters that she can handle effectively. . . . We made it very clear to Nancy that if she pursues general civil litigation work she is not on track toward partnership and that her only realistic chance for partnership in our opinion is to develop a good reputation for herself in one of the specialized areas of practice. . . .

In the evaluation period covering November 1985 to April 1986, Boote wrote the following to the Associates Committee:

> Nancy continues to get mixed reviews. Her pluses are that she is mature, courageous, pretty good on her feet and has the capacity to inspire confidence in clients. Her minuses are that there is doubt about her analytic and writing ability. . . . In considering Nancy's prospects for the long range, I think we should bear in mind that we have made mistakes in the past in letting people go to other firms who really could have filled a valuable niche here. Whether Nancy is such a person, of course, remains to be seen. . . .

A summary of Ezold's performance review from October 1986 prepared by Schwartz stated:

> Nancy was advised that several of the lawyers feel she has made very positive progress as a lawyer, Sy [Kurland] being one of them. However, he told her that other lawyers had strong negative sentiments about her capabilities and they feel she has a number of shortcomings in the way of complicated analysis of legal problems and in being able to handle the big complicated corporate litigation, and therefore, does not meet the standard for partnership at Wolf, Block. . . . Both Sy and I urged Nancy to seriously consider looking for employment elsewhere as she may not be able to turn the tide. . . .

Although several partners saw improvement in Ezold's work, negative comments about her analytical ability continued up until, and through, her 1988 senior associate evaluation, the year she was considered for partnership. . . . [In the 1988 review,] the Associates Committee voted 9-1 not to recommend Ezold for . . . partnership. . . .

Out of a total of eight candidates in Ezold's class, five male associates and one female associate were recommended for regular partnership. One male associate, Associate X, was not recommended for either regular or special partnership. . . . Ezold resigned from the firm on June 7, 1989. . . .

Ezold claims Wolf intentionally discriminated against her because of her sex. Intentional discrimination in employment cases falls within one of two categories: "pretext" cases and "mixed-motives" cases. See Price Waterhouse v. Hopkins, 490 U.S. 228, 247 n.12 (1989) (plurality). . . . [She] litigated this case as a pretext case. . . . The plaintiff must first establish by a preponderance of the evidence a prima facie case of discrimination. . . . The plaintiff can establish a prima facie case by showing that she is a member of a protected class; that she was qualified for and rejected for the position; and that non-members of the protected class were treated more favorably. . . . The parties do not dispute the district court's conclusion of law that Ezold demonstrated a prima facie case. . . .

The defendant may rebut the presumption of discrimination arising out of the plaintiff's prima facie case by producing evidence that there was a "legitimate, nondiscriminatory reason" why the plaintiff was rejected. . . . The burden then shifts to the plaintiff to show that the defendant's articulated reasons are pretextual. This burden merges into the plaintiff's ultimate burden of persuading the court that she has been the victim of intentional discrimination. The plaintiff must demonstrate "by competent evidence that the presumptively valid reason[] for [the alleged unlawful employment action was] in fact a coverup for a . . . discriminatory decision." . . . Explicit evidence of discrimination—i.e., the "smoking gun"—is not required. . . . A plaintiff can establish pretext in one of two ways: "either directly by persuading the court that a discriminatory reason more likely motivated the employer or indirectly by showing that the employer's proffered reason is unworthy of credence." . . .

In proving that the employer's motive was more likely than not the product of a discriminatory reason instead of the articulated legitimate reason, sufficiently strong evidence of an employer's past treatment of the plaintiff may suffice. . . . The employer's "general policy and practice with respect to minority employment" may also be relevant. . . . Alternately, if a plaintiff produces credible evidence that it is more likely than not that "the employer did not act for its proffered reason, then the employer's decision remains unexplained and the inferences from the evidence produced by the plaintiff may be sufficient to prove the ultimate fact of discriminatory intent." . . .

Wolf's articulated nondiscriminatory reason for denying Ezold's admission to the partnership was that she did not possess sufficient legal analytical skills to handle the responsibilities of partner in the firm's complex litigation practice. Ezold attempted to prove that Wolf's proffered explanation was "unworthy of credence" by showing she was at least equal to, if not more qualified than, similarly situated males promoted to partnership. She also contended that her past treatment at the firm showed Wolf's decision was based on a discriminatory motive rather than the legitimate reason of deficiency in legal analytical ability that the firm had articulated.

The district court compared Ezold to eight successful male partnership candidates. . . . It found:

> The test that was put to the plaintiff by the Associates Committee that she have outstanding academic credentials and that before she could be admitted to the most junior of partnerships, she must demonstrate that she had the analytical ability to handle the most complex litigation was not the test required of male associates. . . .

The district court then concluded:

> Ms. Ezold has established that the defendant's purported reasons for its conduct are pretextual. The defendant promoted to partnership men having evaluations substantially the same or inferior to the plaintiff's, and indeed promoted male associates who the defendant claimed had precisely the lack of analytical or writing ability upon which Wolf, Block purportedly based its decision concerning the plaintiff. The defendant is not entitled to apply its standards in a more "severe" fashion to female associates. . . . Such differential treatment establishes that the defendant's reasons were a pretext for discrimination. . . .

[The district court was wrong.]

The record does not show that anyone was taken into the partnership without serious consideration of their strength in the category of legal analytic ability. . . . Wolf reserves for itself the power to decide, by consensus, whether an associate possesses sufficient analytical ability to handle complex matters independently after becoming a partner. It is Wolf's prerogative to utilize such a standard. . . . The partnership evaluation process at Wolf, though formalized, is based on judgment, like most decisions in human institutions. A consensus as to that judgment is the end result of Wolf's formal process. In that process, the Associates Committee has the role of collecting and weighing hundreds of evaluations by partners with diverse views before reaching its consensus as to a particular associate's abilities. . . . The differing evaluations the partners first submit to the Associates Committee are often based on hearsay or reputation. No precise theorem or specific objective criterion is employed. . . .

Were the factors Wolf considered in deciding which associates should be admitted to the partnership objective, as opposed to subjective, the conflicts in various partners' views about Ezold's legal analytical ability that this record shows might amount to no more than a conflict in the evidence that the district court as factfinder had full power to resolve. . . . [The difficulty in this case] is the lack of an objective qualification or factor that a plaintiff can use as a yardstick to compare herself with similarly situated employees. . . .

When an employer relies on its subjective evaluation of the plaintiff's qualifications as the reason for denying promotion, the plaintiff can prove the articulated reason is unworthy of credence by presenting persuasive comparative evidence that non-members of the protected class were evaluated more favorably, i.e., their deficiencies in the same qualification category as the plaintiff's were overlooked for no apparent reason when they were promoted to partner.

A plaintiff does not establish pretext, however, by pointing to criticisms of members of the non-protected class, or commendation of the plaintiff, in categories the defendant says it did not rely upon in denying promotion to a member of the protected class. . . .

The district court's failure to consider the negative evaluations of Ezold's legal analytic ability because the partners making them had little contact with Ezold cannot be excused in the face of the credence the district court gave to positive comments about Ezold's ability from those who likewise had little or no contact with her. While a factfinder can accept some evidence and reject other evidence on the basis of credibility, it should not base its credibility determination on a conflicting double standard.

Moreover, . . . [t]here is no evidence that Wolf's practice of giving weight to negative votes and comments of partners who had little contact and perhaps knew nothing about an associate beyond the associate's general reputation was not applied equally to female and male associates. . . .

This Court has recognized that when an employer discriminatorily denies training and support, the employer may not then disfavor the plaintiff because her performance is affected by the lack of opportunity. . . . Even if we assume that Ezold received "small" cases at the beginning of her tenure at Wolf, however, there is no evidence this was the result of sex discrimination. Her evaluations indicate, rather, that it may have been her academic credentials that contributed to her receipt of less complex assignments. For example, Davis stated that "the Home Unity case was the first really fair test for Nancy. I believe that her background relegated her to . . . matters (where she got virtually no testing by Wolf, Block standards) and small matters." . . . It is undisputed that Arbittier opposed hiring Ezold because of her academic history and lack of law review experience. In one of Ezold's early evaluations, Kurland wrote: "She has not, in my view, been getting sufficiently difficult matters to handle because she is not the Harvard Law Review type. . . . We must make an effort to give her more difficult matters to handle." . . . He also stated: "I envisioned . . . her when I hired her as a 'good, stand-up, effective courtroom lawyer.'" . . . In urging the Executive Committee to reconsider Ezold's candidacy one partner wrote:

> [The] perception [that she is not able to handle complex cases] appears to be a product of how Sy Kurland viewed Nancy's role when she was initially hired. For the first few years Sy would only assign Nancy to non-complex matters, yet, at evaluation time, Sy, and some other partners, would qualify their evaluations by saying that Nancy does not work on complex matters. . . .

Nancy was literally trapped in a Catch-22. The Chairman of the Litigation Department would not assign her to complex cases, yet she received negative evaluations for not working on complex matters. . . . While it would be unfortunate if these academic and intellectual biases were perpetuated after the decision was made to hire Ezold, academic or intellectual bias is not evidence of sex discrimination. The district court made no finding that Ezold was given small assignments because of her sex. . . .

The district court found that when Ezold suggested to Schwartz in her early years at Wolf that an unfairness in case assignments may have occurred because she was a woman, Schwartz replied: "Nancy, don't say that around here. They don't want to hear it. Just do your job and do well." . . . This statement, made years before the 1988 decision to deny Ezold partnership, does not show that Wolf's evaluation of her legal ability was pretextual. . . .

Finally, the district court found that by allowing partners to bypass the formal assignment system, Kurland and Arbittier "prevented the plaintiff from securing improved assignments . . . [and] impaired her opportunity to be fairly evaluated for partnership." . . . The fact that Wolf's formal assignment process was often bypassed does not support the district court's finding of pretext. Title VII requires employers to avoid certain prohibited types of invidious discrimination, including sex discrimination. It does not require employers to treat all employees fairly, closely monitor their progress and insure them every opportunity for advancement. "Our task is not to assess the overall fairness of [Wolf's] actions." . . . It is a sad fact of life in the working world that employees of ability are sometimes overlooked for promotion. Large law firms are not immune from unfairness in this imperfect world. The law limits its protection against that unfairness to cases of invidious illegal discrimination. This record contains no evidence that Wolf's assignment process was tainted by a discriminatory motive. . . .

The district court found that Ezold was "evaluated negatively for being 'very demanding,' while several male associates who were made partners were evaluated negatively for lacking sufficient assertiveness in their demeanors." . . . The criticisms of Ezold's assertiveness related to the way in which she handled administrative matters such as office and secretarial space, and not legal matters. . . . In particular, David Hofstein's evaluation of Ezold in 1984 stated:

> My one negative experience did not involve legal work. When my group moved to the south end of the 21st floor, Nancy had a fit because she had to move. As I. Strogatz and our [Office Manager] know, Nancy's behavior was inappropriate and I think affected everyone's perception of her. Dealing with administrative matters professionally is almost as important as dealing with legal matters competently, and at least in that instance, Nancy blew it. . . .

The district court refers to criticisms of male associates for lacking assertiveness, but in connection with their handling of legal matters. The district court was comparing apples and oranges. The record shows that male associates were also criticized for their improper handling of administrative problems. . . . The district court also quotes an evaluation of Ezold as a "prima donna" on administrative matters, but leaves out the full context of the statement which compares her to a male associate: "Reminds me of [a male associate] — very demanding, prima donna-ish, not a team player." . . .

The district court's finding that this evidence supports its conclusion that Ezold was treated differently because of her gender is clearly erroneous. An "unfortunate and destructive conflict of personalities does not establish sexual discrimination." . . . Further, by the time of Ezold's final evaluation in 1988, there was no mention of her attitude on administrative matters. Rosoff testified that in independently reviewing the Associate Committee's decision not to recommend Ezold for partnership, he disregarded the criticisms of her handling of administrative matters from earlier years as "ancient history." . . .

We have reviewed the evidence carefully and hold that it is insufficient to show pretext. Despite Ezold's disagreement with the firm's evaluations of her abilities, and her perception that she was treated unfairly, there is no evidence of sex discrimination here. . . .

Accordingly, we will reverse the judgment of the district court in favor of Ezold and remand for entry of judgment in favor of Wolf.

Price Waterhouse v. Hopkins

490 U.S. 228 (1989)

Justice BRENNAN announced the judgment of the Court and delivered an opinion, in which Justice MARSHALL, Justice BLACKMUN, and Justice STEVENS join.

Ann Hopkins was a senior manager in an office of Price Waterhouse when she was proposed for partnership in 1982. . . . When the partners in her office later refused to repropose her for partnership, she sued Price Waterhouse under Title VII . . . charging that the firm had discriminated against her on the basis of sex in its decisions regarding partnership. Judge Gesell in the Federal District Court for the District of Columbia ruled in her favor on the question of liability . . . and the Court of Appeals for the District of Columbia Circuit affirmed. . . . We granted certiorari to resolve a conflict among the Courts of Appeals concerning the respective burdens of proof of a defendant and plaintiff in a suit under Title VII when it has been shown that an employment decision resulted from a mixture of legitimate and illegitimate motives. . . .

Ann Hopkins had worked at Price Waterhouse's Office of Government Services in Washington, D.C., for five years when the partners in that office proposed her as a candidate for partnership. Of the 662 partners at the firm at that time, 7 were women. Of the 88 persons proposed for partnership that year, only 1 — Hopkins — was a woman. Forty-seven of these candidates were admitted to the partnership, 21 were rejected, and 20 — including Hopkins — were "held" for reconsideration the following year. Thirteen of the 32 partners who had submitted comments on Hopkins supported her bid for partnership. Three partners recommended that her candidacy be placed on hold, eight stated that they did not have an informed opinion about her, and eight recommended that she be denied partnership.

In a jointly prepared statement supporting her candidacy, the partners in Hopkins' office showcased her successful 2-year effort to secure a $25 million contract with the Department of State, labeling it "an outstanding performance" and one that Hopkins carried out "virtually at the partner level." Despite Price Waterhouse's attempt at trial to minimize her contribution to this project, Judge Gesell specifically found that Hopkins had "played a key role in Price Waterhouse's successful effort to win a multi-million dollar contract with the Department of State." Indeed, he went on, "[n]one of the other partnership candidates at Price Waterhouse that year had a comparable record in terms of successfully securing major contracts for the partnership."

The partners in Hopkins' office praised her character as well as her accomplishments, describing her in their joint statement as "an outstanding professional" who had a "deft touch," a "strong character, independence and integrity." Clients appear to have agreed with these assessments. At trial, one official from the State Department described her as "extremely competent, intelligent," "strong and forthright, very productive, energetic and creative." Another high-ranking official praised Hopkins' decisiveness, broadmindedness, and "intellectual clarity"; she was, in his words, "a stimulating conversationalist." Evaluations such as these led Judge Gesell to conclude that Hopkins "had no difficulty dealing with clients and her clients appear to have been very pleased with her work" and that she "was generally viewed as a highly competent project leader who worked long hours, pushed vigorously to meet deadlines and demanded much from the multidisciplinary staffs with which she worked."

On too many occasions, however, Hopkins' aggressiveness apparently spilled over into abrasiveness. Staff members seem to have borne the brunt of Hopkins' brusqueness. Long before her bid for partnership, partners evaluating her work had counseled her to improve her relations with staff members. Although later evaluations indicate an improvement, Hopkins' perceived shortcomings in this important area eventually doomed her bid for partnership. Virtually all of the partners' negative remarks about Hopkins — even those of partners supporting her — had to do with her "interpersonal skills." Both "[s]upporters and opponents of her candidacy," stressed Judge Gesell, "indicated that she was sometimes overly aggressive, unduly harsh, difficult to work with and impatient with staff."

There were clear signs, though, that some of the partners reacted negatively to Hopkins' personality because she was a woman. One partner described her as "macho"; another suggested that she "overcompensated for being a woman"; a third advised her to take "a course at charm school." Several partners criticized her use of profanity; in response, one partner suggested that those partners objected to her swearing only "because it's a lady using foul language." Another supporter explained that Hopkins "ha[d] matured from a tough-talking somewhat masculine hard-nosed mgr to an authoritative, formidable, but much more appealing lady ptr candidate." But it was the man who, as Judge Gesell found, bore responsibility for explaining to Hopkins the reasons for the Policy Board's decision to place her candidacy on hold who delivered the coup de grace: in order to improve her chances for partnership, Thomas Beyer advised, Hopkins should "walk more femininely, talk more femininely, dress more femininely, wear make-up, have her hair styled, and wear jewelry."

Dr. Susan Fiske, a social psychologist and Associate Professor of Psychology at Carnegie-Mellon University, testified at trial that the partnership selection process at Price Waterhouse was likely influenced by sex stereotyping. Her testimony focused not only on the overtly sex-based comments of partners but also on gender-neutral remarks, made by partners who knew Hopkins only slightly, that were intensely critical of her. One partner, for example, baldly stated that Hopkins was "universally disliked" by staff, and another described her as "consistently annoying and irritating"; yet these were people who had had very little contact with Hopkins. According to Fiske, Hopkins' uniqueness (as the only woman in the pool of candidates) and the subjectivity of the evaluations made it likely that sharply critical remarks such as these were the product of sex stereotyping—although Fiske admitted that she could not say with certainty whether any particular comment was the result of stereotyping. Fiske based her opinion on a review of the submitted comments, explaining that it was commonly accepted practice for social psychologists to reach this kind of conclusion without having met any of the people involved in the decisionmaking process.

In previous years, other female candidates for partnership also had been evaluated in sex-based terms. As a general matter, Judge Gesell concluded, "[c]andidates were viewed favorably if partners believed they maintained their femin[in]ity while becoming effective professional managers"; in this environment, "[t]o be identified as a women's lib[b]er" was regarded as [a] negative comment. In fact, the judge found that in previous years "[o]ne partner repeatedly commented that he could not consider any woman seriously as a partnership candidate and believed that women were not even capable of functioning as senior managers—yet the firm took no action to discourage his comments and recorded his vote in the overall summary of the evaluations."

Judge Gesell found that Price Waterhouse legitimately emphasized interpersonal skills in its partnership decisions, and also found that the firm had not fabricated its complaints about Hopkins' interpersonal skills as a pretext for discrimination. Moreover, he concluded, the firm did not give decisive emphasis to such traits only because Hopkins was a woman; although there were male candidates who lacked these skills but who were admitted to partnership, the judge found that these candidates possessed other, positive traits that Hopkins lacked.

The judge went on to decide, however, that some of the partners' remarks about Hopkins stemmed from an impermissibly cabined view of the proper behavior of women, and that Price Waterhouse had done nothing to disavow reliance on such comments. He held that Price Waterhouse had unlawfully discriminated against Hopkins on the basis of sex by consciously giving credence and effect to partners' comments that resulted from sex stereotyping. Noting that Price Waterhouse could avoid equitable relief by proving by clear and convincing evidence that it would have placed Hopkins' candidacy on hold even absent this discrimination, the judge decided that the firm had not carried this heavy burden.

The Court of Appeals affirmed the District Court's ultimate conclusion, but departed from its analysis in one particular: it held that even if a plaintiff proves that discrimination played a role in an employment decision, the defendant will not be found liable if it proves, by clear and convincing evidence, that it would have made the same decision in the absence of discrimination. Under this approach, an employer is not deemed to have violated Title VII if it proves that it would have made the same decision in the absence of an impermissible motive, whereas under the District Court's approach, the employer's proof in that respect only avoids equitable relief. We decide today that the Court of Appeals had the better approach, but that both courts erred in requiring the employer to make its proof by clear and convincing evidence. . . .

Justice O'CONNOR, concurring. . . .

Thus, stray remarks in the workplace, while perhaps probative of sexual harassment, *see Meritor Savings Bank v. Vinson* (1986), cannot justify requiring the employer to prove that its hiring or promotion decisions were based on legitimate criteria. Nor can statements by nondecisionmakers, or statements by decisionmakers unrelated to the decisional process itself, suffice to satisfy the plaintiff's burden in this regard. In addition, in my view testimony such as Dr. Fiske's in this case, standing alone, would not justify shifting the burden of persuasion to the employer. Race and gender always "play a role" in an employment decision in the benign sense that these are human characteristics of which decisionmakers are aware and about which they may comment in a perfectly neutral and nondiscriminatory fashion. For example, in the context of this case, a mere reference to "a lady candidate" might show that gender "played a role" in the decision, but by no means could support a rational factfinder's inference that the decision was made "because of" sex. What is required is what Ann Hopkins showed here: direct evidence that decisionmakers placed substantial negative reliance on an illegitimate criterion in reaching their decision.

Justice KENNEDY, with whom THE CHIEF JUSTICE and Justice SCALIA join, dissenting. . . .

The ultimate question in every individual disparate-treatment case is whether discrimination caused the particular decision at issue. Some of the plurality's comments with respect to the District Court's findings in this case, however, are potentially misleading. As the plurality notes, the District Court based its liability determination on expert evidence that some evaluations of respondent Hopkins were based on unconscious sex stereotypes,[5] and on the fact that Price Waterhouse failed to disclaim reliance on these comments when it conducted the partnership review. The District Court also based liability on Price Waterhouse's failure to "make partners sensitive to the dangers [of stereotyping], to discourage comments tainted by sexism, or to investigate comments to determine whether they were influenced by stereotypes."

Although the District Court's version of Title VII liability is improper under any of today's opinions, I think it important to stress that Title VII creates no independent cause of action for sex stereotyping. Evidence of use by decisionmakers of sex stereotypes is, of course, quite relevant to the question of discriminatory intent.

---

5. The plaintiff who engages the services of Dr. Susan Fiske should have no trouble showing that sex discrimination played a part in any decision. Price Waterhouse chose not to object to Fiske's testimony, and at this late stage we are constrained to accept it, but I think the plurality's enthusiasm for Fiske's conclusions unwarranted. Fiske purported to discern stereotyping in comments that were gender neutral — e.g., "overbearing and abrasive" — without any knowledge of the comments' basis in reality and without having met the speaker or subject. "To an expert of Dr. Fiske's qualifications, it seems plain that no woman could be overbearing, arrogant, or abrasive: any observations to that effect would necessarily be discounted as the product of stereotyping. If analysis like this is to prevail in federal courts, no employer can base any adverse action as to a woman on such attributes." . . . Today's opinions cannot be read as requiring factfinders to credit testimony based on this type of analysis. . . .

The ultimate question, however, is whether discrimination caused the plaintiff's harm. Our cases do not support the suggestion that failure to "disclaim reliance" on stereotypical comments itself violates Title VII. Neither do they support creation of a "duty to sensitize." As the dissenting judge in the Court of Appeals observed, acceptance of such theories would turn Title VII "from a prohibition of discriminatory conduct into an engine for rooting out sexist thoughts."

Bostock v. Clayton County, Georgia

140 S. Ct. 1731 (2020)

Justice GORSUCH delivered the opinion of the Court.

Sometimes small gestures can have unexpected consequences. Major initiatives practically guarantee them. In our time, few pieces of federal legislation rank in significance with the Civil Rights Act of 1964. There, in Title VII, Congress outlawed discrimination in the workplace on the basis of race, color, religion, sex, or national origin. Today, we must decide whether an employer can fire someone simply for being homosexual or transgender. The answer is clear. An employer who fires an individual for being homosexual or transgender fires that person for traits or actions it would not have questioned in members of a different sex. Sex plays a necessary and undisguisable role in the decision, exactly what Title VII forbids.

Those who adopted the Civil Rights Act might not have anticipated their work would lead to this particular result. Likely, they weren't thinking about many of the Act's consequences that have become apparent over the years, including its prohibition against discrimination on the basis of motherhood or its ban on the sexual harassment of male employees. But the limits of the drafters' imagination supply no reason to ignore the law's demands. When the express terms of a statute give us one answer and extratextual considerations suggest another, it's no contest. Only the written word is the law, and all persons are entitled to its benefit.

I. . .

Each of the three cases before us started the same way: An employer fired a long-time employee shortly after the employee revealed that he or she is homosexual or transgender—and allegedly for no reason other than the employee's homosexuality or transgender status.

Gerald Bostock worked for Clayton County, Georgia, as a child welfare advocate. Under his leadership, the county won national awards for its work. After a decade with the county, Mr. Bostock began participating in a gay recreational softball league. Not long after that, influential members of the community allegedly made disparaging comments about Mr. Bostock's sexual orientation and participation in the league. Soon, he was fired for conduct "unbecoming" a county employee.

Donald Zarda worked as a skydiving instructor at Altitude Express in New York. After several seasons with the company, Mr. Zarda mentioned that he was gay and, days later, was fired.

Aimee Stephens worked at R.G. & G.R. Harris Funeral Homes in Garden City, Michigan. When she got the job, Ms. Stephens presented as a male. But two years into her service with the company, she began treatment for despair and loneliness. Ultimately, clinicians diagnosed her with gender dysphoria and recommended that she begin living as a woman. In her sixth year with the company, Ms. Stephens wrote a letter to her employer explaining that she planned to "live and work full-time as a woman" after she returned from an upcoming vacation. The funeral home fired her before she left, telling her "this is not going to work out."

While these cases began the same way, they ended differently. Each employee brought suit under Title VII alleging unlawful discrimination on the basis of sex. In Mr. Bostock's case, the Eleventh Circuit held that the law does not prohibit employers from firing employees for being gay and so his suit could be dismissed as a matter of law. Meanwhile, in Mr. Zarda's case, the Second Circuit concluded that sexual orientation discrimination does violate Title VII and allowed his case to proceed. . . . [In Ms. Stephens's case] the Sixth Circuit [held] that Title VII bars employers from firing employees because of their transgender status. . . . [W]e granted certiorari in these matters to resolve at last the disagreement among the courts of appeals over the scope of Title VII's protections for homosexual and transgender persons.

II

This Court normally interprets a statute in accord with the ordinary public meaning of its terms at the time of its enactment. . . . With this in mind, our task is clear. We must determine the ordinary public meaning of Title VII's command that it is "unlawful . . . for an employer to fail or refuse to hire or to discharge any individual, or otherwise to discriminate against any individual with respect to his compensation, terms, conditions, or privileges of employment, because of such individual's race, color, religion, sex, or national origin." To do so, we orient ourselves to the time of the statute's adoption, here 1964. . . .

The only statutorily protected characteristic at issue in today's cases is "sex"—and that is also the primary term in Title VII whose meaning the parties dispute. Appealing to roughly contemporaneous dictionaries, the employers say that, as used here, the term "sex" in 1964 referred to "status as either male or female [as] determined by reproductive biology." The employees counter by submitting that, even in 1964, the term bore a broader scope, capturing more than anatomy and reaching at least some norms concerning sex identity and sexual orientation. But because nothing in our approach to these cases turns on the outcome of the parties' debate, and because the employees concede the point for argument's sake, we proceed on the assumption that "sex" signified what the employers suggest, referring only to biological distinctions between male and female.

Still, that's just a starting point. The question isn't just what "sex" meant, but what Title VII says about it. Most notably, the statute prohibits employers from taking certain actions "because of" sex. . . . This can be a sweeping standard. Often, events have multiple but-for causes. So, for example, if a car accident occurred *both* because the defendant ran a red light *and* because the plaintiff failed to signal his turn at the intersection, we might call each a but-for cause of the collision. When it comes to Title VII, the adoption of the traditional but-for causation standard means a defendant cannot avoid liability just by citing some *other* factor that contributed to its challenged employment decision. So long as the plaintiff's sex was one but-for cause of that decision, that is enough to trigger the law.

No doubt, Congress could have taken a more parsimonious approach. As it has in other statutes, it could have added "solely" to indicate that actions taken "because of" the confluence of multiple factors do not violate the. Or it could have written "primarily because of" to indicate that the prohibited factor had to be the main cause of the defendant's challenged employment decision. But none of this is the law we have. If anything, Congress has moved in the opposite direction, supplementing Title VII in 1991 to allow a plaintiff to prevail merely by showing that a protected trait like sex was a "motivating factor" in a defendant's challenged employment practice. . . .

[T]he question becomes: What did "discriminate" mean in 1964? As it turns out, it meant then roughly what it means today: "To make a difference in treatment or favor (of one as compared with others)." Webster's New International Dictionary 745 (2d ed. 1954). To "discriminate against" a person, then, would seem to mean treating that individual worse than others who are similarly situated. . . .

The consequences of the law's focus on individuals rather than groups are anything but academic. Suppose an employer fires a woman for refusing his sexual advances. It's no defense for the employer to note that, while he treated that individual woman worse than he would have treated a man, he gives preferential treatment to female employees overall. The employer is liable for treating *this* woman worse in part because of her sex. Nor is it a defense for an employer to say it discriminates against both men and women because of sex. This statute works to protect individuals of both sexes from discrimination, and does so equally. So an employer who fires a woman, Hannah, because she is insufficiently feminine and also fires a man, Bob, for being insufficiently masculine may treat men and women as groups more or less equally. But in *both* cases the employer fires an individual in part because of sex. Instead of avoiding Title VII exposure, this employer doubles it.

From the ordinary public meaning of the statute's language at the time of the law's adoption, a straightforward rule emerges: An employer violates Title VII when it intentionally fires an individual employee based in part on sex. It doesn't matter if other factors besides the plaintiff's sex contributed to the decision. And it doesn't matter if the employer treated women as a group the same when compared to men as a group. If the employer intentionally relies in part on an individual employee's sex when deciding to discharge the employee — put differently, if changing the employee's sex would have yielded a different choice by the employer — a statutory violation has occurred. Title VII's message is "simple but momentous": An individual employee's sex is "not relevant to the selection, evaluation, or compensation of employees."

The statute's message for our cases is equally simple and momentous: An individual's homosexuality or transgender status is not relevant to employment decisions. That's because it is impossible to discriminate against a person for being homosexual or transgender without discriminating against that individual based on sex. Consider, for example, an employer with two employees, both of whom are attracted to men. The two individuals are, to the employer's mind, materially identical in all respects, except that one is a man and the other a woman. If the employer fires the male employee for no reason other than the fact he is attracted to men, the employer discriminates against him for traits or actions it tolerates in his female colleague. . . . If the employer retains an otherwise identical employee who was identified as female at birth, the employer intentionally penalizes a person identified as male at birth for traits or actions that it tolerates in an employee identified as female at birth. Again, the individual employee's sex plays an unmistakable and impermissible role in the discharge decision. . . .

Nor does it matter that, when an employer treats one employee worse because of that individual's sex, other factors may contribute to the decision. Consider an employer with a policy of firing any woman he discovers to be a Yankees fan. Carrying out that rule because an employee is a woman *and* a fan of the Yankees is a firing "because of sex" if the employer would have tolerated the same allegiance in a male employee. Likewise here. When an employer fires an employee because she is homosexual or transgender, two causal factors may be in play—*both* the individual's sex *and* something else (the sex to which the individual is attracted or with which the individual identifies). . . .

Reframing the additional causes in today's cases as additional intentions can do no more to insulate the employers from liability. Intentionally burning down a neighbor's house is arson, even if the perpetrator's ultimate intention (or motivation) is only to improve the view. No less, intentional discrimination based on sex violates Title VII, even if it is intended only as a means to achieving the employer's ultimate goal of discriminating against homosexual or transgender employees. There is simply no escaping the role intent plays here: Just as sex is necessarily a but-for *cause* when an employer discriminates against homosexual or transgender employees, an employer who discriminates on these grounds inescapably *intends* to rely on sex in its decisionmaking. . . .

If more support for our conclusion were required, there's no need to look far. All that the statute's plain terms suggest, this Court's cases have already confirmed. Consider three of our leading precedents.

In *Phillips v. Martin Marietta Corp.*, 400 U.S. 542 (1971) (*per curiam*), a company allegedly refused to hire women with young children, but did hire men with children the same age. Because its discrimination depended not only on the employee's sex as a female but also on the presence of another criterion—namely, being a parent of young children—the company contended it hadn't engaged in discrimination "because of" sex. The company maintained, too, that it hadn't violated the law because, as a whole, it tended to favor hiring women over men. Unsurprisingly by now, these submissions did not sway the Court. That an employer discriminates intentionally against an individual only in part because of sex supplies no defense to Title VII. Nor does the fact an employer may happen to favor women as a class.

In *Los Angeles Dept. of Water and Power v. Manhart* (1978), an employer required women to make larger pension fund contributions than men. The employer sought to justify its disparate treatment on the ground that women tend to live longer than men, and thus are likely to receive more from the pension fund over time. . . . [T]he Court dismissed as irrelevant the employer's insistence that its actions were motivated by a wish to achieve classwide equality between the sexes. . . . The employer violated Title VII because, when its policy worked exactly as planned, it could not "pass the simple test" asking whether an individual female employee would have been treated the same regardless of her sex.

In *Oncale v. Sundowner Offshore Services, Inc.* (1998), a male plaintiff alleged that he was singled out by his male co-workers for sexual harassment. The Court held it was immaterial that members of the same sex as the victim committed the alleged discrimination. Nor did the Court concern itself with whether men as a group were subject to discrimination or whether something in addition to sex contributed to the discrimination, like the plaintiff's conduct or personal attributes. "[A]ssuredly," the case didn't involve "the principal evil Congress was concerned with when it enacted Title VII." But, the Court unanimously explained, it is "the provisions of our laws rather than the principal concerns of our legislators by which we are governed." Because the plaintiff alleged that the harassment would not have taken place but for his sex—that is, the plaintiff would not have suffered similar treatment if he were female—a triable Title VII claim existed.

The lessons these cases hold for ours are by now familiar.

First, it's irrelevant what an employer might call its discriminatory practice, how others might label it, or what else might motivate it. In *Manhart*, the employer called its rule requiring women to pay more into the pension fund a "life expectancy" adjustment necessary to achieve sex equality. In *Phillips*, the employer could have accurately spoken of its policy as one based on "motherhood." In much the same way, today's employers might describe their actions as motivated by their employees' homosexuality or transgender status. But just as labels and additional intentions or motivations didn't make a difference in *Manhart* or *Phillips*, they cannot make a difference here. When an employer fires an employee for being homosexual or transgender, it necessarily and intentionally discriminates against that individual in part because of sex. And that is all Title VII has ever demanded to establish liability.

Second, the plaintiff's sex need not be the sole or primary cause of the employer's adverse action. In *Phillips*, *Manhart*, and *Oncale*, the defendant easily could have pointed to some other, nonprotected trait and insisted it was the more important factor in the adverse employment outcome. So, too, it has no significance here if another factor—such as the sex the plaintiff is attracted to or presents as—might also be at work, or even play a more important role in the employer's decision.

Finally, an employer cannot escape liability by demonstrating that it treats males and females comparably as groups. As *Manhart* teaches, an employer is liable for intentionally requiring an individual female employee to pay more into a pension plan than a male counterpart even if the scheme promotes equality at the group level. Likewise, an employer who intentionally fires an individual homosexual or transgender employee in part because of that individual's sex violates the law even if the employer is willing to subject all male and female homosexual or transgender employees to the same rule.

III

[T]he employers assert that discrimination on the basis of homosexuality and transgender status aren't referred to as sex discrimination in ordinary conversation. . . . But this submission rests on a mistaken understanding of what kind of cause the law is looking for in a Title VII case. In conversation, a speaker is likely to focus on what seems most relevant or informative to the listener. . . . But these conversational conventions do not control Title VII's legal analysis, which asks simply whether sex was a but-for cause. . . .

Trying another angle, the defendants before us suggest that an employer who discriminates based on homosexuality or transgender status doesn't *intentionally* discriminate based on sex, as a disparate treatment claim requires. But, as we've seen, an employer who discriminates against homosexual or transgender employees necessarily and intentionally applies sex-based rules. . . .

What, then, do the employers mean when they insist intentional discrimination based on homosexuality or transgender status isn't intentional discrimination based on sex? Maybe the employers mean they don't intend to harm one sex or the other as a class. But as should be clear by now, the statute focuses on discrimination against individuals, not groups. Alternatively, the employers may mean that they don't perceive themselves as motivated by a desire to discriminate based on sex. But nothing in Title VII turns on the employer's labels or any further intentions (or motivations) for its conduct beyond sex discrimination. . . .

Next, the employers turn to Title VII's list of protected characteristics—race, color, religion, sex, and national origin. Because homosexuality and transgender status can't be found on that list and because they are conceptually distinct from sex, the employers reason, they are implicitly excluded from Title VII's reach. Put another way, if Congress had wanted to address these matters in Title VII, it would have referenced them specifically.

But that much does not follow. We agree that homosexuality and transgender status are distinct concepts from sex. But, as we've seen, discrimination based on homosexuality or transgender status necessarily entails discrimination based on sex; the first cannot happen without the second. . . .

The employers try the same point another way. Since 1964, they observe, Congress has considered several proposals to add sexual orientation to Title VII's list of protected characteristics, but no such amendment has become law. Meanwhile, Congress has enacted other statutes addressing other topics that do discuss sexual orientation. This postenactment legislative history, they urge, should tell us something.

But what? There's no authoritative evidence explaining why later Congresses adopted other laws referencing sexual orientation but didn't amend this one. Maybe some in the later legislatures understood the impact Title VII's broad language already promised for cases like ours and didn't think a revision needed. Maybe others knew about its impact but hoped no one else would notice. Maybe still others, occupied by other concerns, didn't consider the issue at all. All we can know for certain is that speculation about why a later Congress declined to adopt new legislation offers a "particularly dangerous" basis on which to rest an interpretation of an existing law a different and earlier Congress did adopt. . . .

Ultimately, the employers are forced to abandon the statutory text and precedent altogether and appeal to assumptions and policy. Most pointedly, they contend that few in 1964 would have expected Title VII to apply to discrimination against homosexual and transgender persons. And whatever the text and our precedent indicate, they say, shouldn't this fact cause us to pause before recognizing liability? . . .

That is exactly the sort of reasoning this Court has long rejected. . . . As one Equal Employment Opportunity Commission (EEOC) Commissioner observed shortly after the law's passage, the words of " 'the sex provision of Title VII [are] difficult to . . . control.' " Franklin, Inventing the "Traditional Concept" of Sex

Discrimination, 125 Harv. L. Rev. 1307, 1338 (2012). The "difficult[y]" may owe something to the initial proponent of the sex discrimination rule in Title VII, Representative Howard Smith. On some accounts, the congressman may have wanted (or at least was indifferent to the possibility of) broad language with wide-ranging effect. Not necessarily because he was interested in rooting out sex discrimination in all its forms, but because he may have hoped to scuttle the whole Civil Rights Act and thought that adding language covering sex discrimination would serve as a poison pill. Certainly nothing in the meager legislative history of this provision suggests it was meant to be read narrowly.

Whatever his reasons, thanks to the broad language Representative Smith introduced, many, maybe most, applications of Title VII's sex provision were "unanticipated" at the time of the law's adoption. . . .

Title VII's prohibition of sex discrimination in employment is a major piece of federal civil rights legislation. It is written in starkly broad terms. It has repeatedly produced unexpected applications, at least in the view of those on the receiving end of them. Congress's key drafting choices — to focus on discrimination against individuals and not merely between groups and to hold employers liable whenever sex is a but-for cause of the plaintiff's injuries — virtually guaranteed that unexpected applications would emerge over time. This elephant has never hidden in a mousehole; it has been standing before us all along. . . .

Separately, the employers fear that complying with Title VII's requirement in cases like ours may require some employers to violate their religious convictions. We are also deeply concerned with preserving the promise of the free exercise of religion enshrined in our Constitution; that guarantee lies at the heart of our pluralistic society. But worries about how Title VII may intersect with religious liberties are nothing new; they even predate the statute's passage. As a result of its deliberations in adopting the law, Congress included an express statutory exception for religious organizations. . . . And Congress has gone a step further yet in the Religious Freedom Restoration Act of 1993 (RFRA). . . . Because RFRA operates as a kind of super statute, displacing the normal operation of other federal laws, it might supersede Title VII's commands in appropriate cases. . . .

Some of those who supported adding language to Title VII to ban sex discrimination may have hoped it would derail the entire Civil Rights Act. Yet, contrary to those intentions, the bill became law. Since then, Title VII's effects have unfolded with far-reaching consequences, some likely beyond what many in Congress or elsewhere expected.

But none of this helps decide today's cases. Ours is a society of written laws. Judges are not free to overlook plain statutory commands on the strength of nothing more than suppositions about intentions or guesswork about expectations. In Title VII, Congress adopted broad language making it illegal for an employer to rely on an employee's sex when deciding to fire that employee. We do not hesitate to recognize today a necessary consequence of that legislative choice: An employer who fires an individual merely for being gay or transgender defies the law.

Justice ALITO, with whom Justice THOMAS joins, dissenting.

There is only one word for what the Court has done today: legislation. The document that the Court releases is in the form of a judicial opinion interpreting a statute, but that is deceptive.

Title VII of the Civil Rights Act of 1964 prohibits employment discrimination on any of five specified grounds: "race, color, religion, sex, [and] national origin." Neither "sexual orientation" nor "gender identity" appears on that list. For the past 45 years, bills have been introduced in Congress to add "sexual orientation" to the list, and in recent years, bills have included "gender identity" as well. But to date, none has passed both Houses. . . .

Because no such amendment of Title VII has been enacted in accordance with the requirements in the Constitution (passage in both Houses and present-ment to the President, Art. I, § 7, cl. 2), Title VII's prohibition of discrimina-tion because of "sex" still means what it has always meant. But the Court is not deterred by these constitutional niceties. Usurping the constitutional authority of the other branches, the Court has essentially taken H.R. 5's provision on employment discrimination and issued it under the guise of statutory interpre-tation. A more brazen abuse of our authority to interpret statutes is hard to recall.

The Court tries to convince readers that it is merely enforcing the terms of the statute, but that is preposterous. Even as understood today, the concept of discrimi-nation because of "sex" is different from discrimination because of "sexual orienta-tion" or "gender identity." And in any event, our duty is to interpret statutory terms to "mean what they conveyed to reasonable people *at the time they were written*." If every single living American had been surveyed in 1964, it would have been hard to find any who thought that discrimination because of sex meant discrimination because of sexual orientation—not to mention gender identity, a concept that was essentially unknown at the time.

The Court attempts to pass off its decision as the inevitable product of the textualist school of statutory interpretation championed by our late colleague Jus-tice Scalia [*Oncale*], but no one should be fooled. The Court's opinion is like a pirate ship. It sails under a textualist flag, but what it actually represents is a theory of statutory interpretation that Justice Scalia excoriated—the theory that courts should "update" old statutes so that they better reflect the current values of soci-ety. If the Court finds it appropriate to adopt this theory, it should own up to what it is doing.

Many will applaud today's decision because they agree on policy grounds with the Court's updating of Title VII. But the question in these cases is not whether discrimination because of sexual orientation or gender identity *should be* outlawed. The question is *whether Congress did that in 1964.* . . .

It indisputably did not. . . .

I respectfully dissent.

Justice KAVANAUGH, dissenting.

Like many cases in this Court, this case boils down to one fundamental ques-tion: Who decides? Title VII of the Civil Rights Act of 1964 prohibits employment discrimination "because of" an individual's "race, color, religion, sex, or national origin." The question here is whether Title VII should be expanded to prohibit employment discrimination because of sexual orientation. Under the Constitu-tion's separation of powers, the responsibility to amend Title VII belongs to Con-gress and the President in the legislative process, not to this Court. . . .

NOTES

1. **Assessing the Facts in *Ezold*.** The evidence showed that only one of fifty-five litigation partners in the law firm in *Ezold* was a woman, that most of the law firm partners had gone to a more prestigious law school than the plaintiff, that some male associates with less favorable evaluations than the plaintiff had made partner, and that the plaintiff was involved with women's issues at the firm, especially concerning the firm's treatment of paralegals. Although the trial court ruled in the plaintiff's favor, the appellate court reversed because it was persuaded that two-thirds of the partners voted against the plaintiff primarily because she lacked the analytic ability to handle complex litigation. The only woman litigation partner voted against her, no women testified in her favor, and several gave evidence concerning the firm's fairness toward women. How would you assess such evidence? Which factors seem the most important?[156]

What do you make of the different views in the district court and appellate court about Ezold's involvement with women's issues at the firm? One partner wrote in his evaluation that Ezold's "[j]udgment is better, although it still can be clouded by over-sensitivity to what she misperceives as 'womens' [sic] issues." The district court found that Ezold "was evaluated negatively for being too involved with women's issues . . . specifically her concern about the [firm's] treatment of paralegals." However, the appellate court concluded that the criticism was for her misperception that the firm's treatment of paralegals was a women's issue and was not evidence of sex discrimination against her. Which court has the better view?

2. **Recognizing "Mixed-Motive" Discrimination.** The model for proving discrimination in *Ezold* asks the judge (or jury) to decide a fairly straightforward question: was the challenged employment decision because of the plaintiff's sex or because of the legitimate reason put forward by the employer? But what if both the discriminatory reason and the legitimate reason entered into the decision? The plaintiff in *Price Waterhouse*, Ann Hopkins, presented evidence of the partners' discriminatory motivation. The firm presented evidence of a nondiscriminatory reason for denying her partnership. The district court found both reasons played a role. Who should win? The Supreme Court ruled that if a plaintiff could show that sex was a substantial motivating factor for the employment action at issue, the burden would shift to the employer, who must then prove by a preponderance of the evidence that it would have made the same decision even in the absence of a discriminatory motive to avoid liability. After the decision, Congress enacted the Civil Rights Act of 1991, which codified a more pro-plaintiff version of the mixed-motive model. After the 1991 Act, Title VII now provides that if sex or any other protected characteristic is "a motivating factor for any employment practice, even though other factors also motivated the practice," the employer is liable for committing an unlawful employment practice. The Supreme Court further clarified that proof of the "motivating factor" model under the 1991 Act does not require "direct

---

156. For a case history of the litigation, see Deborah L. Rhode, What's Sex Got to Do with It: The Challenge of Diversity in the Legal Profession, in Legal Ethics: Law Stories 233 (Deborah L. Rhode & David Luban eds., 2005); see also Thomas, supra note 153, at 127-47.

evidence" of bias (contrary to Justice O'Connor's concurring opinion, which would have required direct evidence).[157] Once liability is established, the employer can avoid monetary damages and certain other remedies by proving it "would have taken the same action in the absence of the impermissible motivating factor."[158] In such cases, remedies are limited to declaratory relief, injunctive relief, and attorney fees. Financial damages, reinstatement, hiring, and promotion are not available. A plaintiff bringing a disparate treatment case may proceed under either the "pretext" model applied in *Ezold* or the mixed-motive model as codified by the 1991 Act.

3. **Sex Stereotyping.**   Both Ezold and Hopkins claimed that they were subjected to sex stereotyping in their evaluation for partnership. As mentioned earlier in Section B.1 of this chapter, stereotypes can be *descriptive*, generalizations about "how people with certain characteristics behave, what they prefer and where their competencies lie," or *prescriptive*, normative judgments about "how members of a certain group should think, feel or behave."[159] What kind of stereotyping was at play in Ezold's and Hopkins's cases? How might those stereotypes affect other women at those firms, if left unchecked? Ezold and Hopkins both brought individual disparate treatment cases; should it help prove their cases if they can show other women at their firms were also subjected to sex stereotyping?[160] If so, should it hurt their cases if their female colleagues testify that they themselves were treated fairly and did not experience any such stereotyping?[161] Stephanie Bornstein argues that understanding how stereotypes operate holds great potential to "frame disparate treatment that can reach second generation discrimination by exposing how workplace structures rely on stereotypes associated with protected class status to disadvantage members of that class."[162] For further discussion of stereotyping in the legal profession, see the Note on Discrimination in the Legal Profession, at the end of this section.

4. **Discerning and Proving Discriminatory Intent.**   Individual disparate treatment cases are said to require proof of discriminatory intent, a matter about which there is often disagreement.[163] In *Price Waterhouse*, the trial court found that the firm discriminated against Hopkins on the basis of sex "by consciously giving credence

---

157. Desert Palace, Inc. v. Costa, 539 U.S. 90 (2003).

158. 42 U.S.C. §§ 2000e-2(m), 2000e-5(g)(2)(B) (2018).

159. Martha Chamallas, Of Glass Ceilings, Sex Stereotypes, and Mixed Motives: The Story of *Price Waterhouse v. Hopkins*, in Women and Law Stories 307, 315 (Elizabeth M. Schneider & Stephanie M. Wildman eds., 2011).

160. See Tristin Green, Insular Individualism: Employment Discrimination Law after Ledbetter v. Goodyear, 43 Harv. C.R.-C.L. L. Rev. 353 (2008).

161. See Emma Pelkey, Comment, The "Not Me Too" Evidence Doctrine in Employment Discrimination Law: Courts' Disparate Treatment of "Me Too" Versus "Not Me Too" Evidence in Employment Discrimination Cases, 92 Or. L. Rev. 545 (2014).

162. Stephanie Bornstein, Unifying Antidiscrimination Law Through Stereotype Theory, 20 Lewis & Clark L. Rev. 919, 938 (2016).

163. As scholars have explained, the case law on discriminatory intent should not be understood to require a subjective state of mind; the issue is whether the plaintiff was treated worse because of sex. See, e.g., Katherine T. Bartlett, Making Good on Good Intentions: The Critical Role of Motivation in Reducing Implicit Workplace Discrimination, 95 Va. L. Rev. 1893, 1920-26 (2009).

and effect to partners' comments that resulted from sex stereotyping." Note that the partners' statements do not necessarily reveal conscious bias against women. Indeed, some of the comments about Hopkins that reflected stereotypes, such as the "walk more femininely" comment, came from her strongest mentor at the firm, who testified he thought he was providing helpful advice. Must stereotypes be consciously held for biased decisionmaking to violate Title VII?

Such "smoking gun" comments like the charm school comment are increasingly rare. Human resources personnel advise managers to ensure that written performance reviews include concrete examples of employee weaknesses and avoid stereotypical characterizations. Many researchers believe that implicit bias in evaluations is now more of a problem than deliberate discrimination.[164]

Perhaps an even bigger problem than individual biased decisionmakers is the structure of the workplace and decisionmaking processes.[165] Employee search processes, for example, may not access the best sources of female or minority candidates, or they may use selection criteria or algorithms that disfavor candidates who are not already well represented in the work force.[166] Workplaces may lack strong mentoring for workers who feel isolated by reason of their sex or minority status. The process of making assignments, along with inflexible workplace structures, may particularly disadvantage women. Work groups may be organized to reinforce rather than reduce status differentials and exacerbate stereotyping. "Diversity" programs are often mere window dressing that obscures institutional bias. Should employment structures and decisionmaking processes that facilitate and exacerbate biased employment decisions be found to violate Title VII? Without blatantly sexist comments, how would such discrimination be proven? The Center for Worklife Law, founded by Joan Williams, proposes the use of "bias interrupters"—an evidence-based approach to changing workplace systems to reduce the transmission of bias.[167] What decision points might an employer focus on?

---

164. See Susan Sturm, Second Generation Employment Discrimination: A Structural Approach, 101 Colum. L. Rev. 458, 460 (2001). For more on unconscious bias, see Jerry Kang, Trojan Horses of Race, 118 Harv. L. Rev. 1489 (2005); Linda Hamilton Krieger, The Content of Our Categories: A Cognitive Bias Approach to Discrimination and Equal Employment Opportunity, 47 Stan. L. Rev. 1161 (1995). Other scholars caution against taking the focus off of explicit bias, which remains rampant. See Jessica A. Clarke, Explicit Bias, 113 Nw. U. L. Rev. 505 (2018); Michael Selmi, The Paradox of Implicit Bias and a Plea for a New Narrative, 50 Ariz. St. L. J. 193 (2017).

165. See Naomi Cahn et al., Gender and the Tournament: Reinventing Antidiscrimination Law in the Age of Inequality, 96 Tex. L. Rev. 849 (2007). See, e.g., Sturm, supra note 164; Tristin K. Green, Insular Individualism: Employment Discrimination Law After Ledbetter v. Goodyear, 43 Harv. C.R.-C.L. L. Rev. 353 (2008); Tristin K. Green, A Structural Approach as Antidiscrimination Mandate: Locating Employer Wrong, 60 Vand. L. Rev. 353, 354 (2008); see also discussion of unconscious bias in Notes 2 & 4, above, and 8, below.

166. See Stephanie Bornstein, Antidiscriminatory Algorithms, 70 Ala. L. Rev. 519 (2018).

167. Bias Interrupters, Center for Worklife Law (Aug. 24, 2019), https://biasinterrupters.org/about.

Might the low numbers of women in high-level positions be probative of discriminatory intent? As one commentator notes about the significance of the partnership numbers in *Hopkins*:

> Glass ceiling cases are rarely stronger than this. At the time when Price Waterhouse withheld her promotion, all but 7 of the firm's 662 partners were male. Hopkins billed more hours and brought in more business than any other person nominated for partnership in the year of her rejection, and clients generally had given her high ratings. . . . Several men who obtained partnerships [in the year that Hopkins did not] were characterized as "abrasive," "overbearing," or "cocky." No one mentioned charm school for them.[168]

A substantial body of research indicates that the likelihood of bias in performance evaluations is greater in settings where women constitute a minority of the work force, the applicant pool, and the senior management.[169] The expert testimony of Professor Susan Fiske in the *Price Waterhouse* case, introduced to explain the influence of gender stereotypes, drew on the influential work of Rosabeth Moss Kanter. Kanter's research on tokenism established that groups constituting 15 percent or less of an organization are particularly vulnerable to stereotyping. As Martha Chamallas explains:

> Fiske stated that when there is dramatic underrepresentation of a group, the token individuals are much more likely to be thought about in terms of their social category. People expect token individuals to fit preconceived views about the traits of the group. . . . When a token person behaves in a way that is counter stereotypical—for example, when a woman acts in an aggressive, competitive, ambitious, independent, or active way—she is more likely to be regarded as uncaring or lacking in understanding. This does not mean that women can play safe by conforming to conventional stereotypes. The Catch-22 or double bind of the powerless group is that stereotypes associated with nondominant groups are also traits that are not highly valued in the organization. A woman who acts womanly acts in a way that may cast doubt on her competence and effectiveness; a woman who is thought to be too masculine may be regarded as deviant.
>
> In describing how persons respond to an individual whose behavior is incongruent with prevailing stereotypes, Fiske referred to Kanter's four "role traps." Under this scheme, the dominant male group perceives token women as mothers, seductresses, iron maidens, or pets. . . . The role trap most applicable to Hopkins was that of the "iron maiden." . . . Under Fiske's theory, the explicitly sex-based comments describing Hopkins were a predictable response to her status as a token woman who did not fit the conventional feminine mold. . . .
>
> An additional cue Fiske found which indicated that stereotyping was influencing decision-making was the intensity of the negative reaction

---

168. Deborah Rhode, Speaking of Sex: The Denial of Gender Equality 161 (1997).
169. Virginia Valian, Why So Slow?, in The Advancement of Women 139, 139-41 (1998).

toward Hopkins. . . . Claims were made, for example, that Hopkins was universally disliked, potentially dangerous, and likely to abuse authority. Fiske contrasted these extremely negative comments with positive comments by others in the organization who seemed to describe the same behavior. Supporters found Hopkins as "outspoken, sells her own ability, independent, [has] the courage of her convictions." Detractors found her "overbearing, arrogant, abrasive, runs over people, implies she knows more than anyone in the world about anything and is not afraid to let anybody know it." Fiske's testimony on this phenomenon of "selective perception" suggested that the differing reactions to Hopkins were not simply a function of the slice of Hopkins' behavior that each individual evaluator had witnessed. Instead, when all the evidence was in, the "real" Ann Hopkins might still not clearly emerge from putting all the pieces together. Fiske's use of Kanter's role traps also demonstrated how other people can contribute to the social construction of the personality of an individual. This made it more difficult to separate Hopkins' "real" personality from the environment in which she worked.[170]

Is this testimony persuasive? What accounts for the unimpressed, even scathing, reaction to it from the Justices in the dissent? If Fiske's testimony is accepted, does that mean that gender discrimination presumptively is unlikely to occur in workplaces with high numbers of women?[171]

5. **The Significance of Stray Remarks.** Justice O'Connor's opinion in *Hopkins* contrasted the partner's sexist comments from "stray remarks" in the workplace that are not indicative of discrimination. In *Ezold*, the hiring partner's comment suggesting that Ezold's gender was a strike against her did not prove sex discrimination in the partnership decision. What explains the different treatment of these comments in the cases?

Even after the Supreme Court clarified that direct evidence is not required to prove discrimination under the 1991 Act's "motivating factor" model, lower courts continue to parse Justice O'Connor's distinction between direct evidence and "stray remarks." Sexist comments that are labeled "stray" may be ruled insufficient to permit a jury to find that discrimination occurred or even inadmissible because it is not relevant to show discrimination against the plaintiff.[172] Lower courts have discounted blatantly biased remarks by upper level employees in the workplace because they deem them too remote in time or not sufficiently tied to the challenged decision to provide evidence of discrimination.[173] In one recent

---

170. Martha Chamallas, Listening to Dr. Fiske: The Easy Case of *Price Waterhouse v. Hopkins*, 15 Vt. L. Rev. 89, 96-99 (1990).

171. Compare Jackson v. VHS Detroit Receiving Hosp., Inc., 814 F.3d 769 (6th Cir. 2016) with McMichael v. Transocean Offshore Deepwater Drilling, Inc., 934 F.3d 447 (5th Cir. 2019). See also Joan C. Williams & Rachel Dempsey, What Works for Women at Work 179-204.

172. Clarke, supra note 164, at 542.

173. Id. at 543 (discussing one case in which women were called "Barbie dolls" and another in which plaintiff's supervisor called women "bitch, cunt, whore, slut, and tart," and the courts disregarded the comments as insufficiently probative of sex discrimination against the plaintiff).

case affirming summary judgment for the employer, the court found no evidence the decisionmaker acted with bias in not promoting the plaintiff, even though he stated in his deposition that he did not believe a woman would return to work after giving birth based on his experience with other female employees.[174] Other courts have accepted similarly gendered, derisive comments as sufficient evidence of discrimination to support a plausible discrimination claim.[175] The cases tend to be highly fact-specific and can be difficult to reconcile.

In a highly publicized sex discrimination case in Silicon Valley, Ellen Pao presented several pieces of evidence suggesting that the venture capital firm where she had worked, Kleiner Perkins, bore animosity toward women, yet the jury voted against her claim. The facts included that Ellen's boss and most prominent partner, John Doerr, told "an investigator that Ms. Pao had a 'female chip on her shoulder.' Chi-Hua Chien, a partner, said women should not be invited to a dinner with former Vice President Al Gore because they 'kill the buzz.' A senior partner at the time, Ray Lane, joked to a junior partner that she should be 'flattered' that a colleague showed up at her hotel room door wearing only a bathrobe."[176] Are these comments "stray remarks" or evidence of discrimination?

6. **Implicit Bias.** Much of the insistence by courts on "intentional" discrimination — to the extent that courts use that term to require conscious bias — ignores the social psychology of bias, which has identified a host of cognitive mechanisms that hide harmful discrimination even from the individual who is engaged in it. For example, confirmation biases lead individuals to notice and recall information that confirms their prior assumptions or stereotypes they may hold and filter out information that contradicts those assumptions.[177] Those who assume that women, particularly women of color, are beneficiaries of preferential treatment, rather than merit-based selection, will recall these women's errors more readily than their insights. Similar distortions stem from what psychologists label a "just world" bias.[178] People want to believe that individuals generally get what they deserve and deserve what they get. To sustain this belief, people will adjust their evaluations of performance to match observed outcomes. If women are underrepresented in leadership, the most psychologically convenient explanation is that they lack the necessary qualifications or commitment.

In-group favoritism reinforces these tendencies. Extensive research documents the preferences that individuals feel for members of their own groups.

---

174. Pribyl v. County of Wright, 964 F.3d 793 (8th Cir. 2020).

175. See, e.g., Plotke v. White, 405 F.3d 1092 (10th Cir. 2005) (evidence that male supervisors referred to a woman physician as "Jane" instead of "Dr." and called her a "femi-Nazi" were relevant and precluded summary judgment, even though not directly related to the termination decision).

176. David Streitfeld, Ellen Pao Loses Silicon Valley Bias Case Against Kleiner Perkins, N.Y. Times, Mar. 27, 2015, at A1.

177. Cecilia L. Ridgeway, Gender as an Organizing Force in Social Relations: Implications for the Future of Inequality, in The Declining Significance of Gender 279 (Francine D. Blau et al., eds., 2006).

178. Melvin J. Lerner, The Belief in a Just World: A Fundamental Delusion vi-vii (1980); Virginia Valian, The Cognitive Bases of Gender Bias, 65 Brook. L. Rev. 1037 (2017).

Without realizing it, this preference may cause them to understand the success of ingroup members as something earned, while the success of others may be viewed as a matter of luck, or favoritism. Conversely, they may understand misconduct by a group member as a rare and forgivable exception, even as the same act is viewed as par for the course if committed by someone who is not a member of the group.[179]

What is the potential legal significance of these documented cognitive distortions? Dr. Susan Fiske, the expert witness for Ann Hopkins, has been a leading researcher in the field of implicit bias.[180] To what extent does *Price Waterhouse* recognize their reality? Does *Ezold?*

7. **Upper-Level Employees.**   A threshold question in *Price Waterhouse* and *Ezold* is the extent to which Title VII regulates employment practices by partnerships. The U.S. Supreme Court, in Hishon v. King & Spalding, held that the decision by a private law firm whether to offer partnership to a law associate falls under Title VII because opportunities for partnership constituted a term or privilege "linked directly with an [associate's] status as an employee."[181] It is not clear, however, whether Title VII covers an employment package that, from the outset, decouples partnership consideration from performance as an associate. Justice Powell, in a concurring opinion in *Hishon*, stated his view that absent a claim based on the law firm's promise of partnership consideration, Title VII would not apply to such decisions.[182] Subsequent developments confirm that even if Title VII covers the partnership decision, it does not necessarily cover treatment of partners by the partnership, at least when the partner has equity in the partnership, has a significant degree of control over the partnership, and is subject to liability.[183]

Apart from complications related to partnership, cases such as *Ezold* and *Price Waterhouse* demonstrate the difficulties for plaintiffs in proving discrimination in professional and upper-level employment positions. At high-level positions, it can be challenging to find a similarly situated comparator.[184] In both *Ezold* and *Hopkins*, male colleagues were identified who were similar in some respects, but too different in others to establish discriminatory treatment. High-level positions also tend to depend on subjective employer judgments that can be difficult to rebut, such as analytical ability in *Ezold* and interpersonal skills in *Hopkins*.

8. **Systemic Bias.**   Title VII recognizes a claim for systemic disparate treatment where "intentional" discrimination against persons in the protected class is

---

179. See Katharine T. Bartlett, Making Good Out of Good Intentions: The Critical Role of Motivation in Reducing Implicit Workplace Discrimination, 95 Va. L. Rev. 1893, 1912-13 (2009) (citing sources).

180. See, e.g., Susan T. Fiske, Stereotyping, Prejudice, and Discrimination, in 2 Handbook of Social Psychology, 357, 362 (Daniel T. Gilbert et al., eds. 1998); Susan T. Fiske, Intent and Ordinary Bias, Unintended Thought and Social Motivation Create Casual Prejudice, 17 Soc. Just. Rsch. 117, 123-24 (2004).

181. 467 U.S. 69, 76 (1984).

182. Id. at 79-80, n.3 (Powell, J., concurring).

183. See, e.g., EEOC v. Sidley Austin Brown & Wood, 315 F.3d 696, 703-07 (7th Cir. 2002) (partners may still be employees when they lack equity in the partnership, receive regular salary, and lack meaningful management over the partnership); EEOC Compliance Manual, ¶ 7110, §2-III-A.1.d (2000).

184. Suzanne Goldberg, Discrimination by Comparison, 120 Yale L.J. 728 (2011).

standard operating procedure throughout the workplace. The claim is largely based on statistical evidence showing a disparity between the qualified labor pool and the at-issue jobs, often supplemented by anecdotal, individual evidence of discrimination. The theory of the claim is that, over time, a nondiscriminatory employer will hire women and minorities roughly proportionate to their representation in the labor pool from which the employer draws. Based on this assumption, unexplained disparities raise an inference of intentional discrimination.[185] Title VII allows systemic disparate treatment claims to be brought by the federal Equal Employment Opportunity Commission (EEOC) or as a class action under Rule 23 of the Federal Rules of Civil Procedure if the requirements of the rule are met (numerosity, typicality, common question of law or fact, and adequacy of representation). Even when a systemic disparity is proven, however, the evidence must convince the court that the reason is discrimination, and not something else, such as lesser interest on the part of women in obtaining competitive, stressful jobs.[186]

The difficulties of framing a case of systemic discrimination are apparent in, and exacerbated by, the Supreme Court's 2011 ruling in Wal-Mart Stores, Inc. v. Dukes.[187] Plaintiffs in *Wal-Mart* alleged in 2001 that Wal-Mart's personnel system was plagued by several factors that set the stage for biased and stereotyped decision-making, including a highly subjective and discretionary system that allowed mostly male supervisors to make biased pay and promotion decisions. Their evidence included statistical analysis showing that women's pay averaged $1,100 less annually for hourly workers and $14,500 less for salaried management positions, despite having greater seniority and higher average performance ratings. With respect to promotion, while women comprised 67 percent of hourly workers and 78 percent of hourly department managers, only 35.7 percent of assistant managers, 14.3 percent of store managers, and 9.8 percent of district managers were women. Plaintiffs showed that women were significantly less likely to be promoted than men and had to wait longer for promotions. They also showed that competitor big-box stores had significantly higher percentages of women in upper-level management positions than Wal-Mart. Plaintiffs sought certification of a class of approximately 1.5 million women who were employed at any Wal-Mart domestic retail store at any time since December 26, 1998, and who had been or may have been subjected to Wal-Mart's challenged pay and promotion policies and practices.

In a 5-4 ruling, the Supreme Court held that the class failed to satisfy the Rule 23 requirement that the class action lawsuit present common questions of law or

---

185. Teamsters v. United States, 431 U.S. 324 (1977).

186. See EEOC v. Sears, Roebuck & Co., 839 F.2d 302 (7th Cir. 1988) (accepting Sears's argument that the disparity between men and women in higher-paying commission sales jobs was traceable to women's lower level of interest in working in such jobs and not intentional discrimination by Sears); Vicki Schultz, Telling Stories About Women and Work: Judicial Interpretation of Sex Segregation in the Workplace in Title VII Cases Raising the Lack of Interest Argument, 103 Harv. L. Rev. 1749 (1990).

187. 564 U.S. 338 (2011); see also generally Roger W. Reinsch & Sonia Goltz, You Can't Get There from Here: Implications of the *Walmart v. Dukes* Decision for Addressing Second-Generation Discrimination, 9 N.W. J.L. & Soc. Pol'y 264 (2014).

fact.[188] The opinion leaves individuals free to make their own discrimination claims against Wal-Mart but unable to sue as a nationwide class for Wal-Mart's allegedly discriminatory personnel practices.[189] The majority opinion by Justice Scalia reasoned that the commonality requirement was not met because plaintiffs failed to establish a company-wide policy of discrimination against women or a common source of discrimination. Instead, the only companywide policies the Court could discern were a policy of allowing discretion by individual managers—"a very common and presumptively reasonable way of doing business"—and an official company policy of nondiscrimination.[190] In a revealing passage, the Court opined, "left to their own devices, most managers in any corporation—and surely most managers in a corporation that forbids sex discrimination—would select sex-neutral, performance-based criteria for hiring and promotion and that produce no actionable disparity at all."[191] Why didn't the statistical disparities cited above establish a common practice of discrimination? Does the Court's reasoning cast doubt on the very theory of the systemic disparate treatment claim (that left unexplained, a disparity between the qualified labor pool and the composition of the work force gives rise to an inference of intentional discrimination)?

The Court's opinion heavily criticized the social framework evidence offered by the plaintiffs.[192] Plaintiffs offered the testimony of an expert in organizational sociology who opined that Wal-Mart's "strong corporate culture" and organizational structure made it vulnerable to pervasive gender bias. The Court dismissed the testimony as unhelpful because the expert himself admitted that he could not determine how many of the company's thousands upon thousands of employment decisions were biased.[193] Many systemic disparate treatment cases have relied on similar kinds of expert evidence, drawing on social science research about the types of structures and conditions that give rise to biased or stereotyped decisionmaking, as a way of bolstering the inference that a statistical disparity reflects discriminatory treatment. The testimony in *Price Waterhouse* by Susan Fiske, drawing on the work of Rosabeth Moss Kanter, discussed above, is an example of such evidence. Does the

---

188. In a second holding, the Justices unanimously agreed that the class was improvidently certified under Rule 23(b)(2), which authorizes class actions seeking injunctive and declaratory relief, because the monetary relief sought by plaintiffs was not incidental to the injunctive and declaratory remedies. This ruling complicates all future (b)(2) class actions seeking monetary relief.

189. The *Wal-Mart* decision does not restrict the ability of the EEOC to sue an employer for a "pattern and practice" of discrimination using the systemic disparate treatment claim. However, the EEOC has limited resources, and its enforcement priorities are set by the president. More conservative administrations tend to de-emphasize systemic claims in the agency's docket.

190. 564 U.S. at 355.

191. Id.

192. For opposing views on the admissibility and usefulness of social framework evidence, compare Melissa Hart & Paul M. Secunda, A Matter of Context: Social Framework Evidence in Employment Discrimination Class Actions, 78 Fordham L. Rev. 37 (2009) (supportive) with John Monahan et al., Contextual Evidence of Gender Discrimination: The Ascendance of "Social Frameworks," 94 Va. L. Rev. 1715 (2008) (critical).

193. 564 U.S. at 353-54.

Court's expressed disdain for such evidence in *Wal-Mart* reflect a skepticism about systemic disparate treatment claims overall?

In theory, the disparate impact claim might fill in the gaps left by systemic disparate treatment claims where women fare badly in a particular workplace in a systematic way but cannot attribute the disparities to discriminatory intent. Indeed, the plaintiffs in *Wal-Mart* also brought a class claim for disparate impact. Here too, though, the Court ruled that the plaintiffs failed to establish a common policy that would satisfy Rule 23. Although the Court's prior case law permits disparate impact challenges to discretionary decisionmaking, the Court in *Wal-Mart* ruled that it is not enough for plaintiffs to prove that a sex-based disparity resulted from a discretionary decisionmaking system; plaintiffs must identify and challenge the specific employment practice that disproportionately disadvantages women.[194]

The limits of both systemic disparate treatment and disparate impact claims are apparent in a case like *Wal-Mart*. An employer's failure to undertake measures to curtail the exercise of unconscious bias or otherwise eliminate disparities in the workplace generally does not violate Title VII. The law imposes a duty on employers not to discriminate, but it does not require them to address disparities that cannot be traced to an employer policy or that arise from broader, society-wide dynamics.

Some commentators suggest reformulating the disparate treatment and disparate impact theories to more fully recognize discrimination when employers fail to take steps to restructure a workplace that they should realize does not promote gender equity and inclusiveness.[195] Yet there is an understandable reluctance to treat employers who do not mean to discriminate the same as those who do.[196] Is it reasonable to expect employers affirmatively to identify potential sources of discrimination in the workplace and take steps to eliminate them? Or for Title VII to require them to structure decisionmaking in a way that reduces the chance that bias will infect it?

9. **Strategies for Countering Bias in the Workplace.** Approaches to dealing with employment bias involve both individual and institutional initiatives. Commonly recommended individual strategies include being clear about one's values and goals, seeking mentors, improving negotiation skills, and adopting a style that makes others comfortable. However, individual strategies may come at a cost. Members of groups who perceive themselves as subject to negative stereotypes often feel the need to engage in what Devon Carbado and Mitu Gulati label "identity work to counter those stereotypes."[197] Examples include acting harried and tired to overcome the impression that they are not busy or sending emails late at night to indicate that they have worked late. Some strategies may compromise

---

194. Id. at 355-57.

195. See, e.g., Stephanie Bornstein, Reckless Discrimination, 105 Cal. L. Rev. 1055 (2017); Ann McGinley, Masculinity at Work 158-71 (2016); Deborah M. Weiss, A Grudging Defense of *Wal-Mart v. Dukes*, 24 Yale J. Law & Feminism 119 (2012); David Benjamin Oppenheimer, Negligent Discrimination, 141 U. Pa. L. Rev. 899 (1993).

196. See Samuel R. Bagenstos, The Structural Turn and the Limits of Antidiscrimination Law, 94 Cal. L. Rev. 1 (2006).

197. See Devon W. Carbado & Mitu Gulati, Working Identity, 85 Cornell L. Rev. 1259 (2000).

individuals' identities or have other psychic costs: heterosexual "performances" to counter suspicions of homosexuality; avoidance of social events that might suggest racial "cliquishness"; and laughing at racist or sexist jokes to demonstrate a sense of humor, prevent discomfort, and indicate a lack of obsession with "outsider status."[198] Even when individual strategies succeed in boosting some members of subordinate groups up the career ladder, evidence suggests these efforts are unlikely to produce systemic change. Incentives exist for high-achieving women and minorities to differentiate themselves from less successful members of these groups and to conform with existing workplace landscapes instead of trying to change them.[199]

If individual strategies are not enough, what structural changes need to occur to reduce systemic bias? Some commentators believe that the most promising approach to reducing gender inequality in the work force is to shift emphasis away from after-the-fact enforcement of anti-discrimination prohibitions and to rely more on improving an employer's capacities to identify, prevent, and redress unconscious bias and exclusionary practices. Consider Susan Sturm's analysis:

> [Take the example of a large law firm that] aggressively recruits women at the entry level and [yet] fails to track patterns in work assignment and promotion so [that] the firm's management [was] largely unaware of any problem until [the following] complaints arose: . . . differences in patterns of work assignment and training opportunities among men and women; tolerance of a sexualized work environment by partners who are otherwise significant "rainmakers"; routine comments by male lawyers, particularly in the predominantly male departments, on the appearance, sexuality, and competence of women; harsh assessments of women's capacities and work styles based on gender stereotypes; avoidance of work-related contact with women by members of particular departments; and hyper-scrutiny of women's performance by some, and the invisibility of women's contributions to others. These complaints coincide with a concern about low morale and productivity among diverse work teams. Upon examination, the firm discovers dramatic differences in the retention and promotion rates of men and women in the firm. . . .
>
> [These] second generation problems cannot be reduced to a fixed code of specific rules or commands that establishes clear boundaries governing conduct. Instead, their resolution requires a different process, namely problem solving. That process identifies the legal and organizational dimensions of the problem, encourages organizations to gather and share relevant information, builds individual and institutional capacity to respond, and helps design and evaluate solutions that involve employees who participate in the day-to-day patterns that produce bias and exclusion. An effective system of external accountability, including judicial involvement as a catalyst, would encourage organizations to identify and correct these problems without creating increased exposure to liability, and to learn from other organizations that have engaged in similar efforts.

198. Id. at 1262.
199. See Devon W. Carbado & Mitu Gulati, Race to the Top of the Corporate Ladder: What Minorities Do When They Get There, 61 Wash. & Lee L. Rev. 1645 (2004).

A rule-enforcement approach . . . discourages this type of proactive problem solving. That approach treats regulation as punishing violations of predefined legal rules and compliance as the absence of identifiable conduct violating those rules. . . .

In a rule-enforcement process, problems tend to be redefined as discrete legal violations with sanctions attached. Fear of liability for violation of ambiguous legal norms induces firms to adopt strategies that reduce the short-term risk of legal exposure rather than strategies that address the underlying problem. They accomplish this in significant part by discouraging the production of information that will reveal problems, except in the context of preparation for litigation. Under the current system, employers producing information that reveals problems or patterns of exclusion increase the likelihood that they will be sued. Thus, lawyers counsel clients not to collect data that could reveal racial or gender problems or to engage in self-evaluation, because that information could be used to establish a plaintiff's case. . . .

Fundamentally, the rule-enforcement model encourages lawyers to see issues as potential legal claims, rather than as problems in need of systemic resolution. This narrow focus on avoiding liability diverts attention from the structural dimensions underlying the legal violations, as well as the organizational patterns revealed through aggregating claims. . . .[200]

Professor Sturm, along with other experts, proposes that the law should incentivize employers to establish systems to collect information on recruitment, hiring, promotion, retention, and quality of life issues; monitor evaluation, assignment, and mentoring practices; provide adequate diversity training, family leave, and alternative schedule policies; and hold managers accountable for their performance in achieving diversity-related goals.[201]

However, many commentators are skeptical of employer-controlled initiatives and instead urge more expansive liability for implicit bias or "unconscious" discrimination.[202] Tristin Green warns that judges place too much emphasis on employer "diversity" initiatives that turn out to be largely symbolic, a phenomenon she calls "discrimination laundering."[203] Will stronger legal standards produce more egalitarian behavior by employers? Katharine Bartlett suggests it may not, drawing on

---

200. Sturm, supra note 164, at 468, 470-71, 475-76.

201. Id.; see also Deborah L. Rhode & Barbara Kellerman, Gender Differences and Gender Stereotypes — Crossing the Bridge: Reflections on Women and Leadership, in Women and Leadership: The State of Play and Strategies for Change 29-31 (Barbara Kellerman & Deborah L. Rhode, eds., 2007).

202. See, e.g., Linda Hamilton Krieger, Rachel Kahn Best & Lauren B. Edelman, When "Best Practices" Win, Employees Lose: Symbolic Compliance and Judicial Inference in Federal Equal Employment Opportunity Cases, 40 Law & Soc. Inquiry 843 (2015); Russell K. Robinson, Perceptual Segregation, 108 Colum. L. Rev. 1093 (2008); Tristin K. Green, A Structural Approach as Antidiscrimination Mandate: Locating Employer Wrong, 60 Van. L. Rev. 849 (2007).

203. Tristin K. Green, Discrimination Laundering: The Rise of Organizational Innocence and the Crisis of Equal Opportunity Law (2016).

social science research indicating that measures that affirm people's intentions to act in nondiscriminatory ways are more effective in reducing discrimination than legal coercion that assumes the worst in people. She argues:

> [t]hreat and confrontation about race and gender bias, which people do not want to possess or exhibit, may inadvertently provoke shame, guilt, and resentment, which lead to avoidance and resistance, and ultimately to more stereotyping. In other words, pressure and threat will often deepen bias rather than correct it. Positive strategies that affirm people's good intentions, in contrast, engage people constructively in defining their better, nondiscriminatory selves and aligning their conduct accordingly. While coercion and threat make people defensive, opportunity and engagement leverage people's good intentions into a deeper commitment to a more inclusive, nondiscriminatory workplace. It is this type of commitment—not legal coercion—that will best address the implicit bias that is most characteristic of today's workplace . . . . [A]ttention needs to be given to the means by which internal commitment to those standards, or what I refer to as good intentions, is generated . . . . [P]eople who have an internal commitment to nondiscrimination norms will combat implicit discrimination more effectively than those motivated by traditional legal sanctions.[204]

Is she right? What are the implications for law? Studies by Frank Dobbin and Alexandra Kalev have found that companies that require their managers to attend diversity training often end up with less diversity in their workforce five years later, while companies that offer voluntary diversity training seem to end up with better representation of women and people of color. Why might that be?[205] Might "white fragility," or sensitivity to being asked to acknowledge bias, cause hostility?[206]

10. **Transgender and Sexual Orientation Bias as "Sex" Discrimination Under Title VII.** Lower courts struggled for decades to discern whether sex discrimination encompasses discrimination because of sexual orientation and gender identity under Title VII. Early cases viewed such claims as a thinly veiled effort to bootstrap new protected classes into the statute. Discerning a legislative intent to codify a traditional, biological definition of sex, the first courts to hear such claims ruled that Title VII does not protect any individual, male or female, from being disadvantaged for their sexual orientation or gender identity.[207] It was not

---

204. Katharine T. Bartlett, Making Good on Good Intentions: The Critical Role of Motivation in Reducing Implicit Workplace Discrimination, 95 Va. L. Rev. 1893, 1901-02 (2009).

205. See Frank Dobbin and Alexandra Kalev, Why Diversity Programs Fail, 94 Harv. Bus. Rev. 14 (2016)

206. Robin D'Angelo, White Fragility: Why It's So Hard for White People to Talk About Racism (2018).

207. See Ulane v. E. Airlines, Inc., 742 F.2d 1081 (7th Cir. 1984) (Title VII does not proscribe discrimination against transgender persons); DeSantis v. Pacific Telephone & Telegraph Co., 608 F.2d 327 (9th Cir. 1979) (Title VII does not cover sexual orientation discrimination).

until after the Court decided *Hopkins*, that some — though far from all — lower courts began to view sexual orientation and transgender discrimination as a form of sex stereotyping at odds with Title VII.[208] As recently as 2019, one federal appellate court found it per se unreasonable to believe that Title VII's ban on sex discrimination encompasses discrimination based on sexual orientation.[209] Why did lower courts struggle for so long to see what this (conservative) Court in *Bostock* describes as a "clear" answer in Title VII's plain language?[210]

Prior to *Bostock*, lower courts recognizing claims for anti-gay or anti-transgender bias relied on a gender stereotyping theory to find that Title VII covers such discrimination, on the theory that such bias is based on prescriptive gender roles about how men and women should conduct themselves, in their relationships and in their gender presentations.[211] But the Court in *Bostock* did not go there; instead it embraced a textualist approach relying on formal logic about the necessary role of sex as a but-for cause of such discrimination. Why didn't the Court rely on the gender stereotyping theory? Would the *Bostock* opinion have a broader scope or be more persuasive if it had?[212]

How broad a scope of protection does the Court's decision provide for LGBTQ+ employees? The Court stopped short of saying whether transgender employees have a Title VII right to access bathrooms and other sex-segregated facilities in the workplace according to their gender identity. What rights do transgender employees have under Title VII to a workplace that does not merely refrain from punishing an employee's transgender status, but recognizes and respects their gender identity? Consider the implications of the *Bostock* decision for bisexual employees. Does an employer that accepts gay and lesbian employees, but discriminates against bisexual employees discriminate in violation of Title VII? What are the implications for non-binary individuals who do not identify as either male or female, but embrace a gender-fluid identity or reject gender altogether? Does discrimination against any of these individuals violate Title VII under the logic of *Bostock*?[213]

The Court's decision flags, but stops short of deciding, possible religious conflicts with the statute's coverage of anti-gay and anti-trans bias.[214] How should such

---

208. Compare Rene v. MGM Grand Hotel, Inc., 305 F.3d 1061 (9th Cir. 2002) (en banc) with Vickers v. Fairfield Med. Ctr., 453 F.3d 757 (6th Cir. 2006). See also Etsitty v. Utah Transit Auth., 502 F.3d 1215 (10th Cir. 2007).

209. O'Daniel v. Indus. Serv. Sols., 922 F.3d 299 (5th Cir. 2019) (rejecting plaintiff's retaliation claim on this basis).

210. See Jessica A. Clarke, How the First Forty Years of Circuit Precedent Got Title VII's Sex Discrimination Provision Wrong, 98 Tex. L. Rev. Online 83 (2019).

211. See, e.g., EEOC v. Bohs Bros. Constr. Co., LLC, 731 F.3d 444 (5th Cir. 2013) (en banc).

212. For a range of views, see Deborah A. Widiss, Proving Discrimination by the Text, 106 Minn. L. Rev. 354 (2021); Anthony Michael Kreis, Unlawful Genders, 85 Law & Contemp. Probs. 103 (2022); Mitchell N. Berman & Guha Krishnamurthi, *Bostock* was Bogus, 97 Notre Dame L. Rev. 67 (2021).

213. See Jeremiah A. Ho, Queering *Bostock*, 29 Am. U. J. Gender Soc. Pol'y & L. 283 (2021); Ann C. McGinley et al., Feminist Perspectives on Bostock v. Clay County, Georgia, 53 Conn. L. Rev. CONNtemplations 1 (2020).

214. See Susan Bisom-Rapp, The Landmark *Bostock* Decision, 43 T. Jefferson L. Rev. 1 (2021).

conflicts be resolved? Should an employer's asserted religious conflict with the Title VII rights of LGBTQ+ employees be treated any differently than religious conflicts with other forms of discrimination covered by the statute, such as pregnancy discrimination against unmarried women? Religiously motivated resistance to gender equality mandates in public accommodations laws is taken up in the next section.

Until the Court's decision in *Bostock*, the lack of clarity about whether Title VII encompassed discrimination based on sexual orientation and gender identity meant that such protections depended on state and local legislatures adding these protected classes to their antidiscrimination laws. Many states have enacted laws prohibiting discrimination based on sexual orientation and gender identity in various settings, including employment.[215] As the Court's opinion acknowledges, Congress has repeatedly considered amending Title VII to add sexual orientation and gender identity as protected classes, but never marshalled the votes to do so. More recently, LGBTQ+ advocates abandoned the longstanding legislative vehicle for doing this, the proposed Employment Nondiscrimination Act (ENDA) in favor of a broader anti-discrimination bill, the Equality Act. This bill, which was first introduced in the House in 2015, would ban sexual orientation and gender identity discrimination in employment, housing, public accommodations, and any other context in which federal law bans discrimination.[216] The argument that sexual orientation and gender identity are best viewed as forms of sex discrimination has both adherents and critics in the LGBTQ+ rights community. Some in that community have pressed for recognizing the role of gender ideology and the traditional binary understanding of sex as central to such discrimination, while others would prefer to gain such protections through laws, like the Equality Act, that expressly prohibit discrimination based on a person's sexual orientation or gender identity. Which is the better path?

11. **Race, Sex, and Intersectional Bias Under Title VII.** Ida Phillips, Nancy Ezold, and Ann Hopkins were all white women. Were their experiences of sex discrimination and gender stereotyping shaped by their race? Are the sex stereotypes that penalize white women in the workplace the same as the sex stereotypes that disadvantage Black women at work? How does race intersect with sex discrimination in employment and how do courts understand multidimensional accounts of discrimination? Consider these questions as you read the following excerpt.

Devon W. Carbado & Mitu Gulati

The Fifth Black Woman

11 J. Contemp. Legal Issues 701, 710-715, 717-720 (2001)

Consider the following hypothetical. Mary, a black woman, works in an elite corporate firm. There are eighty attorneys at the firm, twenty of whom are partners.

215. For a frequently updated listing, see Human Rights Campaign, State Maps of Laws & Policies, https://www.hrc.org/state-maps/employment.

216. H.R. 3186, Equality Act, 114th Cong., 1st Sess. (2015-16); see also Lisa Bornstein & Megan Bench, Married on Sunday, Fired on Monday: Approaches to Federal LGBT Civil Rights Protections, 22 Wm. & Mary J. Women & L. 31 (2015).

Only two of the partners are black, and both are men. The firm has three female partners, and all three are white. There are no Asian American, Native American, or Latina/o partners. The firm is slightly more diverse at the associate rank. There are fifteen female associates: three, including Mary, are black, two are Asian American, and one is Latina. The remaining female associates are white. Of the forty-five male associates, two are black, two are Latino, three are Asian American, and the rest are white.

Mary is a seventh-year associate at the firm. She, along with five other associates, is up for partnership this year. Her annual reviews have been consistently strong. The partners for whom she has worked praise her intellectual creativity, her ability to perform well under pressure, her strong work ethic, her client-serving skills, and her commitment to the firm. She has not brought in many new clients, but, as one of the senior partners puts it, "that is not unusual for a person on the cusp of partnership."

For the past three years, the Chair of the Associate's Committee, the committee charged with making partnership recommendations to the entire partnership, has indicated to Mary that she is "on track." Being "on track" was important to Mary because, were she not on track, she would have seriously explored the option of moving either to another firm with better partnership prospects for her or in-house to an investment bank that provided greater job security. It was generally understood, however, and the Chair made sure to make it clear that "being on track is not a guarantee that you will ultimately make partner." . . .

The Associate Committee recommends that the firm promote all six. However, the partners vote only four into the partnership: one black man, one Asian American male, one white man, and one white woman. They deny partnership to Mary and a white male associate. The partnership's decision to depart from the Associate Committee's recommendation is not unusual. . . . [I]t accepts the committee's positive recommendation only half of the time.

Subsequently, Mary brings a disparate treatment discrimination suit under Title VII. She advances three separate theories: race discrimination, sex discrimination, and race and sex discrimination. She does not, however, have any direct evidence of animus against her on the part of the employer. In other words, Mary can point to no explicit statements such as "We don't like you because you are a woman," or "We think that you are incompetent; all blacks are." The evidence is all circumstantial: Mary was highly qualified, but was rejected for a position that was arguably open.

The court, ruling in favor of the firm's summary judgment motion, rejects all three of Mary's claims. With respect to the race discrimination claim, the court reasons that it is not supported by evidence of intentional or animus-based discrimination. According to the court, there is no evidence that the firm dislikes (or has a taste for discrimination against) blacks. In fact, argues the court, the evidence points in the other direction. The very year the firm denied partnership to Mary, it extended partnership to another African-American. Further, within the past five years, the firm had promoted two other African-Americans to the partnership. The court notes that both of these partners participated in the deliberations as to whether Mary would be granted partnership, and neither has suggested that the firm's decision to deny Mary partnership was discriminatorily motivated. The court concludes that the simple act of denying one black person a promotion is, especially when other blacks have been promoted, insufficient to establish discrimination.

The court disposes of Mary's gender discrimination claim in a similar way. That is, it concludes that the fact that the firm has in the past promoted women to the partnership, that the partners who voted to deny partnership to Mary extended partnership to another woman, and that women participated in the firm's deliberations as to whether Mary would be promoted, and none of these women have claimed that Mary was treated unfairly because she is a woman, suggests that the firm did not engage in sex-based discrimination against Mary.

The court concludes its dismissal of Mary's compound discrimination claim (the allegation of discrimination based on her race and sex) with an argument about cognizability. . . . According to the court, there is no indication in the legislative history of Title VII that the statute intended "to create a new classification of 'black women' who would have greater standing than, for example, a black male." According to the court, "the prospect of the creation of new classes of protected minorities, governed only by mathematical principles of permutation and combination, clearly raises the prospect of opening the hackneyed Pandora's box."

The foregoing hypothetical articulates the classic intersectionality problem wherein black women fall through an anti-discrimination gap constituted by black male and white female experiences. The problem can be framed in terms of essentialism. Consider first the court's response to Mary's race discrimination claim. In determining whether Mary experienced race discrimination, the court assumes that there is an essential black experience that is unmodified by gender. The court's adjudication of Mary's race discrimination claim conveys the idea that racism is necessarily total. It is a particular kind of animus that reaches across gender, and affects men and women in the same way. It is about race—a hostility against all black people. . . .

Consider now the court's adjudication of Mary's sex discrimination. Here, too, the court's analysis reflects essentialism. The essentialism in this context conveys the idea that women's experiences are unmodified by race. The court assumes that if a firm engages in sex discrimination, such discrimination will negatively affect all women—and in the same way. . . .

Finally, consider the court's rejection of Mary's compound discrimination claim. Here, the court doctrinally erases black women's status identity as black women. Its conclusion that this identity status is not cognizable means that, for purposes of Title VII, black women exist only to the extent that their experiences comport with the experiences of black men or white women. Under the court's view, and in the absence of explicit race/gender animus, black women's discriminatory experiences as black women are beyond the remedial reach of Title VII. . . .

To appreciate the identity performance problem, assume again that Mary is an African American female in a predominantly white elite corporate law firm. As before, Mary is up for partnership and her evaluations have been consistently strong. Stipulate now that four other black women are up for partnership, as are two white women and two white men. The Associate's Committee recommends that the firm extends partnership to all nine associates. The members of the partnership, however, decide to depart from this recommendation. They grant partnership to four of the black women. The fifth black woman, Mary, does not make partner.

Of the four white associates, the firm extends partnership to one of the men and one of the women.

The partnership's decision creates a buzz around the firm. The firm had never before granted partnership to so many non-white attorneys. Moreover, in the firm's fifty-year history, it had only ever promoted two black people to partnership. Both of these partners are men, and the firm promoted both of them in the mid-1980s, a period during which the firm, along with many others, had enjoyed a high level of prosperity.

Prior to 1980, the firm had never hired a black female associate. Furthermore, most of those who were hired after that date left within two to three years of their arrival. Given the history of black women at the firm — low hiring rate, high attrition rate, low promotion rate — associates at the firm dubbed this year the "year of the black woman."

Mary, however, does not agree. Subsequent to the partnership decision, she files a Title VII discrimination suit, alleging (1) race and sex compound discrimination, i.e., discrimination against her on account of her being a black woman, and (2) discrimination based on identity performance. The firm moves for summary judgment on two theories. First, it argues that Mary may not ground her discrimination claim on her race and sex. According to the firm, Mary may separately assert a race discrimination claim and/or a sex discrimination claim; however, she may not, under Title VII, advance a discrimination claim combining race and sex. Second, the firm contends that whatever identity Mary invokes to ground her claim, there is simply no evidence of intentional discrimination.

With respect to the first issue, the court agrees with Mary that a discrimination claim combining race and sex is, under Title VII, legally cognizable. The court has read, and understood, and it agrees with the literature on intersectionality. Under the court's view, black women should be permitted to ground their discrimination claims on their specific status identity as black women. According to the court, failing to do so would be to ignore the complex ways in which race and gender interact to create social disadvantage: a result that would be inconsistent with the goals of Title VII.

With respect to the second issue, the court agrees with the firm. The court reasons that recognizing Mary's status identity does not prove that the firm discriminated against her because of that identity. It explains that the firm promoted four associates with Mary's precise status identity — that is, four black women. Why, the court rhetorically asks, would a racist/sexist firm extend partnership to these women? The court suggests that when there is clear evidence of nondiscrimination against the identity group within which the plaintiff is situated, that produces an inference that the plaintiff was not the victim of discrimination.

The court rejects the plaintiff's arguments that Title VII itself and the Supreme Court's interpretation of Title VII focuses on protecting individuals, not groups, from discrimination. . . .

The problem with the court's approach is that it fails to consider whether Mary was the victim of an intra-racial (or intra-gender) distinction based not simply on her identity status as a black woman but on her performance of that identity. In effect, the court's approach essentializes the identity status "black female." More specifically, the court assumes that Mary and the other four black women are similarly situated with respect to their vulnerability to discrimination. However, this might not be the case. The social meaning of being a black woman is not monolithic and static but contextual and dynamic. An important way in which it is shaped is by performance. In other words, how black women present their identity can (and often does) affect whether and how they are discriminated against.

Consider, for example, the extent to which the following performance issues might help to explain why Mary was not promoted, but the other black women were.

Dress. While Mary wears her hair in dreadlocks, the other black women relax their hair. On Casual Fridays, Mary sometimes wears West African influenced attire. The other black women typically wear khaki trousers or blue jeans with white cotton blouses.

Institutional Identity. Mary was the driving force behind two controversial committees: the committee for the Recruitment and Retention of Women and Minorities and the committee on Staff/Attorney Relations. She has been critical of the firm's hiring and work allocation practices. Finally, she has repeatedly raised concerns about the number of hours the firm allocates to pro bono work. None of the other four black women have ever participated on identity-related or employee relations-related committees. Nor have any of them commented on either the racial/gender demographics of the firm or the number of hours the firm allocates for pro bono work.

Social Identity. Mary rarely attends the firm's happy hours. Typically, the other four black women do. Unlike Mary, the four black women each have hosted at least one firm event at their home. All four play tennis, and two of them play golf. Mary plays neither. Finally, while all four black women are members of the country club to which many of the partners belong, Mary is not.

Educational Affiliations. Two of the other four black women graduated from Harvard Law School, one graduated from Yale, and the other graduated from Stanford. Mary attended a large local state law school at the bottom of the second tier of schools.

Marital Status. All four of the other black women are married. Two are married to white men and each of them is married to a professional. Mary is a single mother.

Residence. Each of the other four black women lives in predominantly white neighborhoods. Mary lives in the inner city, which is predominantly black.

Professional Affiliation. Mary is an active member of the local black bar association, the Legal Society Against Taxation, and the Women's Legal Caucus. None of the four black women belongs to any of these organizations. One of them is on the advisory board of the Federalist Society. One of the four black women is a Catholic, two are Episcopalian, and the other does not attend church. Mary is a member of the Nation of Islam. . . .

Intersectionality does not capture this form of preferential treatment. While intersectionality recognizes that institutions make intra-group distinctions, that understanding is situated in an anti-discrimination context that is buttressed by a status conception of identity.

Assuming the foregoing performance issues obtain in Mary's case, do they reflect impermissible discrimination? The answer is not obviously yes. Perhaps the partners simply do not like Mary. Based on the description of how Mary performs her identity, could one not reasonably conclude the following: She does not attend happy hours, she creates trouble, she is not a team player, she does not dress or act professionally. Redescribing Mary's performance in this way makes the employer's decision to deny her partnership appear non-discriminatory (and even legitimate). After all, working and succeeding in an organization is not only about doing work. It is also about getting along with people and getting them to like you. An argument can be made that Mary simply did not do much work in the direction of getting the people who mattered to like her. The other four black women did; and they got promoted. On its face some—perhaps—will see this as fair. Those who do the extra work of making people like them should get promoted. Given our claim that this line of reasoning is flawed, the question is: What exactly is the relationship between identity performance and workplace discrimination? . . .

Broadly speaking, there are two ways to make the point that intra-group distinctions based on identity performance implicate workplace discrimination. The first is to focus on the preferred group members. In our hypothetical, they are the four black women. The second way is to focus on the disfavored group members. Mary, the fifth black woman, falls into this category. . . .

In a prior article, *Working Identity* [85 Cornell L. Rev. 1259 (2000)], we argued that an employee's awareness that identity-based assumptions about her are at odds with the institutional norms and criteria of a firm creates an incentive for that employee to work her identity. There are a number of ways an employee might do this. The employee might laugh in response to, or engage in racist humor (signaling collegiality). She might socialize with her colleagues after work (signaling that she can fit in; is one of the boys). She might avoid contact with other employees with negative workplace standing (signaling that she is not really "one of them"). The list goes on. The point is that whatever particular strategy the employee deploys, her aim will likely be to comfort her supervisors/colleagues about her negative workplace standing. Specifically, the employee will attempt to signal that she can fit in, that she is not going to make her supervisors/colleagues uncomfortable about her identity—or theirs—and, at bottom, that the negative stereotypes that exist about her status identity are inapplicable to her. *Working Identity* refers to these strategies collectively as "comfort strategies." These strategies are constituted by identity performances.

Stipulate that the four black women in the hypothetical performed comfort strategies. The claim that the performance of such strategies constitutes discrimination is based on the idea that people with negative workplace standing (e.g., people of color) have a greater incentive to perform comfort strategies than people with positive workplace standing. This means that identity performances burden some employees (e.g., blacks) more than others (e.g., whites). Without more, this racial distribution of identity performances is problematic. The problem is compounded by the fact that identity performances constitute work, a kind of "shadow work." This work is simultaneously expected and unacknowledged. Plus, it is work that is often risky. Finally, this work can be at odds with the employee's sense of her identity. That is, the employee may perceive that she has to disassociate from or disidentify with her identity in order to fit in. To the extent the employee's continued existence and success in the workplace is contingent upon her behaving in ways that operate as a denial of self, there is a continual harm to that employee's dignity.

Recall that the claim is that the firm's discrimination against Mary derives from an intra-group distinction based on Mary's dress, institutional identity, marital status, professional and educational affiliations, and residence. The question becomes, why is this discrimination impermissible? The short answer is that the distinction creates an intra-racial and an inter-racial problem. The problem is that the firm draws a line between black people who do (or whom the firm perceives as performing) identity work to fit in at the firm and black people who do not perform (or whom the firm perceives as not performing) such work. The interracial problem is that white people are not subject to this subcategorization.

* * *

Early courts had difficulty understanding intersectional claims, where race and sex combine to trigger discrimination against women of color, as a violation of Title VII.[217] More recently, courts have recognized that discrimination specifically targeting Black women does violate the statute.[218] Yet there are still a range of approaches courts take to intersectional bias, and a richer analytical framework is needed.[219] Some courts have accepted intersectional theories of discrimination even when the claim asserts violations of two different statutes, such as Title VII and the Age Discrimination in Employment Act in the case of discrimination targeting older women.[220] Disability is another axis of bias that can intersect with gender, even though covered under a separate statute (the Americans with Disabilities Act).[221] Although courts are becoming more receptive to intersectional theories of discrimination, empirical research has found that claiming more than one type of discrimination, such as sex or race, and/or having a plaintiff who belongs to more than one historically discriminated-against protected class, reduces a plaintiff's chances of victory under Title VII.[222]

In the case of Mary, above, the problem goes beyond a difficulty recognizing that discrimination specifically targeting women of color can violate Title VII. The issue for Mary is that Black women who "perform" their identity in a way that is acceptable to the firm succeed, while Black women (like Mary) who do not are penalized. Does Mary have a winnable claim for sex and race discrimination under Title VII? How should Title VII apply to Mary's situation?

---

217. Logan v. St. Luke's Hosp. Ctr., 428 F. Supp. 2d 127 (S.D.N.Y. 1977); DeGraffenreid v. Gen. Motors Assembly Div., 413 F. Supp. 2d 142 (E.D. Mo. 1976); Jewel C. Rich v. Martin Marietta, 522 F.2d 333 (10th Cir. 1975).

218. Shazor v. Prof'l Transit Mgt., 744 F.3d 948 (6th Cir. 2014); Lam v. Univ. of Hawaii, 40 F.3d 1551 (9th Cir. 1994).

219. See Jamillah Bowman Williams, Beyond Sex+: Acknowledging Black Women in Employment Law and Policy, 25 Emp. Rts. & Emp. Pol'y J. (2021).

220. Frappied v. Affinity Gaming Black Hawk LLC, 966 F.3d 1038 (10th Cir. 2020).

221. Michelle A. Travis, Gendering Disability to Enable Disability Rights Law, 105 Cal. L. Rev. 837 (2017); Jennifer Bennett Shinall, The Substantially Impaired Sex: Uncovering the Gendered Nature of Disability Discrimination, 101 Minn. L. Rev. 1099 (2017).

222. Rachel Kahn Best et al., Multiple Disadvantages: An Empirical Test of Intersectionality Theory in EEO Litigation, 45 Law & Soc'y Rev. 991 (2011); Minna Kotkin, Diversity and Discrimination: A Look at Complex Bias, 50 Wm. & Mary L. Rev. 1439 (2009).

PUTTING THEORY INTO PRACTICE

1-21. Susie, the newest consultant hired in a management consulting firm, was told at her six-month review by her male supervisor that she was "too girly" to succeed at the company long-term. He added that he had "no problem with women" and pointed out that half of the company's new hires for similar jobs in the past five years had been women, and that the rate of retention for men and women in consultant positions at the firm was about the same. When Susie asked what he meant by being too girly, he said that clients would not take her seriously unless she toned down her style, lowered her voice, and presented in a more hard-hitting, forceful manner. Susie was fired six months later. If Susie sued for sex discrimination, should she win? Does she have a harder or easier case than the plaintiff in *Hopkins*? How about *Ezold*?[223]

1-22. A female professor denied tenure at an elite university was described by her evaluation committee as "gentle and caring," "nice," "a pushover" and "nurturing," all of which were used in the committee's report describing her as a teacher. The university's stated reason for denying her tenure, however, was not her teaching, but her research. In evaluating her research, the evaluation committee faulted her for not being a "driven, scientifically-minded, competitive academic researcher." Does she have a winnable Title VII case?[224]

1-23. In September 2014, three women filed a class action lawsuit against Microsoft alleging that the company's "stack ranking" (otherwise known as "rank and yank") system of grading technical and engineering employees on a forced curve disadvantaged women in the company. The system forces managers to identity a top of group of employees in line for raises and promotions, a middle tier of satisfactory but non-exceptional employees, and a bottom group of employees who are encouraged to leave. Employees are ranked on a 1 to 5 scale, using a distributional curve (so that a certain percentage of employees must be in each rank). Eighty percent of the managers assigning rankings are male, while only 17 percent of the tech employees whose performance is being rated are female. The practice results in a highly competitive culture in which individualism, competition, risk-taking, and short-term goals are rewarded. How should their Title VII claim be decided? If you were counseling Microsoft, would you advise any changes to this system?[225]

1-24. Ellen Pao's lawsuit brought attention to the treatment of women in Silicon Valley, but there have been many other lawsuits as well. A survey called Elephant in the Valley focused on women with at least ten years of experience who had reached positions of power and influence in tech firms. An overwhelming majority had been told they were too aggressive, were asked to do low-level tasks not asked of their male counterparts, were subjected to demeaning comments from male colleagues, and were asked during interviews about their marital and parental status, as well as their political views on abortion and religion.[226] If you were at the helm of

---

223. Adapted from Kerri Lynn Stone, Teaching the Post-Sex Generation, 58 St. Louis U. L. J. 223 (2013).

224. See Weinstock v. Colum. Univ., 224 F.3d 33 (2d Cir. 2000).

225. Moussouris v. Microsoft Corp., 2016 WL 5870010 (N.D. Cal. Oct. 7, 2016).

226. Women in Tech, Elephant in the Valley (2015).

a tech start-up, what measures might you take to prevent this type of culture from developing? Would the strategies be the same in law firms?

1-25. After retiring from the federal bench, Judge Nancy Gertner began to write about her views of law and justice. She has this to say about the challenges facing employment discrimination plaintiffs:

> Just as the social-psychological literature is exploding with studies about implicit race and gender bias—in organizational settings, in apparently neutral evaluative processes, and among decisionmakers of different races or genders—federal discrimination law lurches in the opposite direction, often ignoring or trivializing evidence of explicit bias. And just as empirical studies highlight the stubborn persistence of discrimination at all levels of jobs and in salaries, federal discrimination law assumes the opposite. In summary judgment decisions, judges search for explicitly discriminatory policies and rogue actors; failing to find them, they dismiss the cases. It is as if the bench is saying: "Discrimination is over. The market is bias-free. The law's task is to find the aberrant individual who just did not get the memo." The complex phenomenon that is discrimination can be reduced to a simple paradigm of the errant discriminator or the explicitly biased policy, a paradigm that rarely matches the reality of twenty-first-century life. . . .
>
> When the defendant successfully moves for summary judgment in a discrimination case, the case is over. Under Rule 56 of the Federal Rules of Civil Procedure, the judge must "state on the record the reasons for granting or denying the motion," which means writing a decision. But when the plaintiff wins, the judge typically writes a single word of endorsement—"denied"—and the case moves on to trial. Plaintiffs rarely move for summary judgment. They bear the burden of proving all elements of the claim, particularly intent, and must do so based on undisputed facts. Defendants need only show contested facts in their favor on one element of a plaintiff's claim. The result of this practice—written decisions only when plaintiffs lose—is the evolution of a one-sided body of law.[227]

If you were given the opportunity to speak to judges about the substance and procedure of discrimination law, what might you say? Would the perspectives in this book help frame your remarks?

1-26. Anna, who is Latina, was fired from her job at a nonprofit organization with the explanation from her supervisor, a white man, that her "style of communication" was perceived by her co-workers as "aggressive and inflammatory" and that she had a "hot" temper and seemed "angry and defensive all the time." When asked for examples, he did not provide any. When Anna noted that she was one of only two Latina employees and suggested that perhaps this perception was based more on stereotype than reality, he responded, "If being angry all the time is a cultural thing, then maybe we should tell the staff it's a cultural thing and they should buck up and take it. But I don't think it's a cultural thing." He also pointed out that the

---

227. Nancy Gertner, Losers' Rules, 122 Yale L.J. Online 109, 110-15 (2012).

other Latina employee was soft-spoken, well-liked, and had worked there for fifteen years. If Anna brought a Title VII claim, what challenges would she encounter? What arguments would you make on her behalf?[228]

1-27. John, who is gay, was fired from a job he has held for ten years with no complaints until a new manager took the helm. John believes that his sexual orientation played a role in the decision. John overheard a conversation during Gay Pride week during which the new manager made derisive comments about gay men who "flaunt" their sexuality. Also, shortly before he was fired, John was talking in the breakroom about several men he had dated, when the manager walked in and overheard him. One of John's co-workers, Rob, is also gay, but Rob does not talk about his private life at work. When the manager learned from a colleague that Rob is gay, the manager was overheard saying, "Well, at least Rob doesn't flaunt it." Rob was not fired. Does John have a winnable Title VII case against the company?

NOTE ON DISCRIMINATION IN THE LEGAL PROFESSION

After a long history of discrimination against women by both law schools and the legal profession, women now make up about half of law school attendees and 37 percent of the legal profession.[229] Yet female practitioners remain underrepresented at the top and overrepresented at the bottom in terms of status, power, and financial reward. For example, women account for only 21 percent of equity law firm partners, and the average pay of these partners is 85 percent of the average compensation for their male counterparts.[230]

The gap widens for women of color and LGBTQ+ lawyers. Women of color, for example, account for only 3 percent of law firm partners, and in a 2019 survey, 70 percent of female lawyers of color reported leaving or considering leaving the legal profession.[231] Openly LGBTQ+ lawyers account for just 2 percent of partners, although by 2019, the percentage of LGBTQ+ associates had grown to almost 7 percent.[232]

What accounts for these disparities? It appears that men bring in more high-paying matters, or at least are better at getting credit for doing so.[233] Some say that they also pass down their clients to other men without formal succession planning, pressure women into remaining as service partners who do the work but don't receive the financial recognition, and use women as "eye candy" to show diversity

---

228. Adapted from Valles-Hall v. Ctr. for Nonprofit Advancement, 481 F. Supp. 2d 118 (D.D.C. 2007).

229. ABA, Profile of the Legal Profession, Women in the Legal Profession, https://www.abalegalprofile.com/women.

230. Id.

231. Id.

232. Nat'l Ass'n for Law Placement, LGBT Representation Among Lawyers 2019 (Jan. 2020).

233. Elizabeth Olson, A 44% Pay Divide for Female and Male Law Partners, Survey Says, N.Y. Times, Oct. 12, 2016, at B3; Jeffrey Low, Major, Lindsey & Africa, 2016 Partner Compensation Survey (2016).

at pitches without receiving origination credit if the pitches are successful.[234] Many lawyers complain about the system for allocating credit for originating business on the grounds that the process lacks transparency, clear metrics for decision, and a way to challenge decisions.[235]

A 2008 report by the American Bar Association on women in the legal profession identified a range of operative stereotypes that interfere with women's success and happiness as lawyers.[236] After having children, women's competence is evaluated more negatively. Mothers' and fathers' requests for time off or reduced hours are subject to a double standard, with fathers viewed favorably and mothers pegged as lacking commitment to clients. Even well-intentioned efforts toward new mothers, such as sending them home early or assigning less challenging work, can harm women's career tracks and reinforce the belief that women cannot be both good mothers and good lawyers. Shifting to part-time work or a reduced schedule can exacerbate these biases, ending the default benefit of the doubt that presumes work is being completed promptly, and replacing it with a presumption that work output would be higher if only she worked more hours. Double standards abound: women are presumed less competent than men and must provide more evidence of job effectiveness for a positive performance review; men's success is attributed to skill, women's to luck (as in, lucky to draw a friendly judge, for example); men's failures are seen as situational, while women's are attributed to their own inadequacies; and certain criteria are given more weight when they favor men (e.g., education or job experience might be reprioritized, depending on who they favor). The report also confirmed longstanding findings that qualities praised in men (assertive, hard-driving, tough, confident) are found grating in women (abrasive, cold, unlikeable, self-promoting). A decade later, a new ABA report found that women continue to receive less access than men to opportunities for advancement and encounter more negative work experiences, such as being mistaken for a lower-level employee, subjected to demeaning comments or "jokes," and being perceived as less committed to legal practice.[237]

The types and extent of gender bias in the legal profession are even more pronounced for women of color. A 2018 report cosponsored by the ABA Commission on Women, The Minority Corporate Counsel Association, and the Center on Worklife Law at the University of California Hastings College of Law found that

---

234. Joan C. Williams & Marina Multhaup, What the Partner Pay Gap Tells Us About Bias, Nat'l L. J., Oct. 24, 2016. See also Heidi Gardner, Harv. Ctr. on the Legal Pro., Harvard Study: On Gender and Origination in the Legal Profession (2016) (finding that gender was a strong factor in explaining the origination gap, largely because male partners passed clients down to other partners who looked "just like me").

235. Kathryn Rubino, Biglaw Firm Battling a Gender Discrimination Lawsuit Will Have to Fight on a New Front, Above the Law (Jan. 24, 2019); Joan C. Williams & Veta Richardson, New Millenium, Same Glass Ceiling—The Impact of Law Firm Compensation Systems on Women, 62 Hastings L. J. 597 (2011).

236. American Bar Association Commission on Women in the Profession, Fair Measure: Toward Effective Attorney Evaluations 17-23 (2d ed. 2008).

237. Roberta D. Liebenberg & Stephanie A. Scharf, Walking Out the Door: The Facts, Figures, and Future of Experienced Women Lawyers in Private Practice (2019).

women, particularly women of color, were persistently excluded from challenging work assignments and informal networks of support, sponsorship, mentoring, and business development. The same report stated that many lawyers of color reported substantially less satisfaction than their white male counterparts concerning assignments, mentoring, and business development.[238] As one woman of color noted,

> There are subtle forms of "discrimination" that are difficult to truly pinpoint or detail. . . . [H]ow is one to know whether missed opportunities are a result of a racial or gender bias. . .? However, it is very apparent that being of the same race, ethnicity or gender as a "powerful partner" can be an advantage when it makes the partner "fee[l] comfortable with the associate."[239]

Minority lawyers also reported feeling like "tokens" when they were subject to "race matching": receiving certain work because of their identity, not their interests, to create the right "look" in courtrooms, client presentations, recruiting, and marketing. Although this strategy can sometimes open opportunities, it also can place lawyers in what they describe as "mascot" roles in which they are not developing professional skills.[240] Women of color are particularly likely to have their competence questioned and their authority resisted, resented, undermined, or ignored, leading to a climate of toxic disrespect.[241] One African-American woman reported that she had a junior associate question whether "I was smart enough to manage him."[242] Another noted that "you can't have an honest conversation about these issues."[243]

With respect to the problems of double standards and double binds, race has a compounding effect. Donna Edwards, the first African-American congresswoman from Maryland, recalled being told she was " 'aggressive' not in a positive way," and noted that women of color are punished "if they do not stay in their lanes."[244] One Asian-American woman similarly explained, "I am frequently perceived as being very demure and passive and quiet, even though I rarely fit any of those categories. When I successfully overcome those misperceptions, I am often thrown into the 'dragon lady' category. It is almost impossible to be perceived as a balanced and appropriately aggressive lawyer."[245]

Even judges face race and gender bias. One study found that the American Bar Association gives lower ratings to women and people of color than to white,

---

238. See Minority Corporate Counsel Association (MCCA), Sustaining Pathways to Diversity: Comprehensive Examination of Diversity Demographics, Initiatives, and Policies in Corporate Legal Departments 13, 23-30 (2018).

239. Id. at 20.

240. Id. at 14.

241. Catalyst, Advancing African-American Women in the Workplace: What Managers Need to Know (2004); Marilyn Y. Byrd, Telling Our Stories of Leadership: If We Don't Tell Them They Won't Be Told, 11 Advances in Developing Hum. Rsch. 582, 587, 598 (2009).

242. Id.

243. Id. (quoting Alanna Rutherford).

244. Interview with Donna Edwards, NPR Takeaway (Apr. 16, 2019).

245. ABA Comm'n on Women in the Pro., Visible Invisibility: Women of Color in Law Firms 25.

male nominees.[246] Another study concluded that female nominees to the Supreme Court have faced substantively different questioning, with race and gender playing a role in questions relating to their competence.[247] Even when they reach the high court, bias may continue. Studies show that female Justices on the Supreme Court are interrupted more often than their male counterparts, both by other Justices, and by male attorneys. Justice Sotomayor is the most interrupted Supreme Court justice.[248] What's the problem—that men interrupt too much, or that women don't interrupt enough?

In 2016, the American Bar Association adopted a new subsection to Rule 8.4 of the Model Rules of Professional Conduct. As amended, Rule 8.4 provides that:

> It is professional misconduct for a lawyer to . . . (g) engage in conduct that the lawyer knows or reasonably should know is harassment or discrimination on the basis of race, sex, religion, national origin, ethnicity, disability, age, sexual orientation, gender identity, marital status, or socio-economic status in conduct related to the practice of law. This paragraph does not limit the ability of a lawyer to accept, decline or withdraw from a representation.

Soon after it was adopted in Pennsylvania, a federal judge struck down the rule as in violation of the First Amendment.[249] The Pennsylvania Supreme Court then adopted a revised version of the rule excluding speeches and other actions outside of litigation, and confining the prohibition to conduct the lawyer knows manifests an intention to discriminate; however, controversy over the rule's constitutionality remains.[250] So far, only seven jurisdictions have adopted some version of the rule, although many already had some anti-discrimination language in their rules or comments.[251] Even if Model Rule 8.4 is more widely adopted, and assuming it is constitutional, commentators remain skeptical that it will have much of an effect on the legal profession, when so many of the problems involve structural discrimination, unconscious bias, in-group favoritism and work-life balance conflicts.[252]

---

246. See Maya Sen, How Judicial Qualification Ratings May Disadvantage Minority and Female Candidates, 2 J. L & Cts. 63 (2014).

247. See Christina L. Boyd et al., The Role of Nominee Gender and Race at U.S. Supreme Court Confirmation Hearings, 52 Law & Soc'y Rev. 871, 895 (2018); Tonja Jacobi & Dylan Schweers, Justice, Interrupted: The Effect of Gender, Ideology and Seniority at Supreme Court Oral Arguments, 103 Va. L. Rev. 1379 (2017).

248. Boyd et al., supra note 247, at 876, 893.

249. Greenberg v. Haggery, 491 F. Supp.3d 12 (2020).

250. In re Amendment of Rule 8.4 of the Pennsylvania Rules of Professional Conduct, No. 123 Disciplinary Rules Docket, Order (July 26, 2021); id. (Mundy, J., dissenting); Eugene Volokh, Letter to the Arizona Supreme Court, In the Matter of Petition to Amend ER 8.4, Rule 42, May 15, 2018.

251. Fed Bar Ass'n, Blog, Efforts Toward Improved Diversity and Inclusion Through the Anti-Bias Rule (Dec. 15, 2021); see also Veronica Root, Combating Silence in the Profession, 105 Va. L. Rev. 805, 824-25 (2019).

252. Alex B. Long, Employment Discrimination in the Legal Profession: A Question of Ethics?, 2016 U. Ill. L. Rev. 445, 449, 458; Root, supra note 251, at 824-33.

Non-legal strategies for addressing the obstacles described above fall into two categories. One is to assist women, particularly women of color, in competing on a playing field that is not yet equal. Many bar associations and women's organizations are active in providing research, educational materials, training, and programs seeking to improve formal mentoring programs so that women do not lose opportunities as a result of implicit bias, low expectations, or structural barriers.[253]

A second set of strategies aims at reforming institutional structures to create fairer evaluation, assignment, and reward systems, as well as more effective work/family policies. The Minority Corporate Counsel Association's report echoes many of these recommendations and proposes that law firms implement "360-degree feedback loops" to provide bottom-up evaluations and gather information from all lawyers concerning their experiences and opportunities.[254] Other commentators have encouraged clients to direct business only to firms with demonstrable commitments to diversity, and that law students pressure legal employers to improve their diversity and family-friendly policies.[255] Which, if any, of these strategies do you think are most likely to be effective in addressing the disparities discussed in this note?

PUTTING THEORY INTO PRACTICE

1-28. A study by McKinsey & Company concluded that only 58 percent of women, compared with 73 percent of men, expressed a desire to become a partner. The major reason for women was the inability to balance family and work commitments.[256] Is this a reasonable explanation—that women simply choose, in higher numbers than men, not to sacrifice their families for their jobs? Or is it a problem to be solved? This issue is further examined in Chapter 2, Section B, and in Chapter 4, Section B.

1-29. Women law professors are concentrated in relatively less prestigious fields such as legal research and writing or family law, while the more prestigious fields of constitutional and commercial law are dominated by men.[257] Do you think

---

253. Deborah L. Rhode, Balanced Lives: Changing the Culture of Legal Practice 16 (A.B.A. Comm'n on Women in the Prof. 2002); Linda Krieger, The Content of Our Categories: A Cognitive Bias Approach to Discrimination and Equal Employment Opportunity, 47 Stan. L. Rev. 1161 (1994).

254. MCCA, Sustaining Pathways to Diversity, supra note 238, at 38-39.

255. Judith S. Kaye & Ann C. Reddy, The Progress of Women Lawyers at Big Firms: Steadied or Simply Studied?, 76 Fordham L. Rev. 1941, 1969-70 (2008).

256. Vivia Chen, Women Take a Pass on the Big Law Brass Ring, Am. Law., Feb. 27, 2018.

257. See generally Ann McGinley, Reproducing Gender on Law School Faculties, 2009 B.Y.U. L. Rev. 99, 136-38; Marjorie E. Kornhauser, Rooms of Their Own: An Empirical Study of Occupational Segregation by Gender Among Law Professors, 73 UMKC L. Rev. 293 (2004). The Association of American Law Schools no longer tracks the distribution of professors by field and gender, but the gender breakdown in types of law faculty jobs is reported. See Kristen K. Tiscione, Gender Inequity Throughout the Legal Academy: A Quick Look at the (Surprisingly Limited) Data, 69 J. Legal Educ. 116 (2019) (72 percent of legal writing faculty are women).

this is a problem that needs a solution, or that women simply prefer these fields? In commenting on women's overrepresentation in less prestigious fields, Dan Subotnik notes, "[i]t is said that if there is no problem there is no solution . . . . Do we want deans to ram courses down faculty throats to right gender imbalances?"[258] But might students respond poorly to the rare female and racial minority professors in more prestigious fields until those faculty reach a critical mass? How would you respond?

1-30. In her memoir, former litigator, legal commentator, and talk show host Megyn Kelly writes:

> Oprah is my role model. In her years coming up, she never made a "thing" of her gender or her race. She just wowed us all. That's my goal: do the absolute best I can, and don't waste time complaining. The less time talking about our gender the better. . . . Most of my own power has come from excellence, not advocacy. My approach is to say to myself, "Just *do* better. *Be* better." That is not to say there's no bias, no sexism. There is, and it's not good. It's just that for me, the solution of *doing better* is far more empowering than lamenting on ones' circumstances. . . . It's not that I reject the idea of demanding a place at the table—quite the contrary. But in my own experience the most effective way to get opportunities is with performance, not persistence.[259]

Similarly, at a cocktail party for minority law students in New York, Preet Bharara, the former U.S. Attorney for the Southern District of New York, gave this response to a question about what lawyers of color can do to overcome discrimination in the legal profession: "The best way to overcome anything is to work really, really hard. You can overcome prejudice by sheer excellence of work."[260]

How would you respond to Kelly and Bharara?

1-31. In an article in The Atlantic, attorney Lara Bazelon explored the experiences of female trial lawyers.[261] One trial lawyer told her that 90 percent of her courtroom opponents file a "no-crying motion" when they begin trial against her. Though she has never cried in court, and though the motions are always denied, the lawyer complained that she finds the practice sexist and demeaning. Bazelon explores other ways in which "sexism infects every kind of courtroom encounter, from pretrial motions to closing arguments—a glum ubiquity that makes clear how difficult it will be to eradicate gender bias not just from the practice of law, but from society as a whole." Women, she claims, are scrutinized for their clothes, resting facial expressions, tone of voice, hand gestures, and expressions of emotion, and often held to different standards than their male counterparts in the courtroom. How should female trial lawyers navigate these experiences? Should courts try to intervene or change their practices to minimize this type of sexism? How?

---

258. Dan Subotnik, Do Law Schools Mistreat Women Faculty? Or, Who's Afraid of Virginia Woolf?, 44 Akron L. Rev. 867, 875 (2011).

259. Megyn Kelly, Settle for More 211 (2016).

260. Vivia Chen, It's Not Just About the Work, Am. Law., Aug. 7, 2017.

261. Lara Bazelon, What It Takes to Be a Trial Lawyer if You're Not a Man, Atlantic (Sept. 2018).

1-32. In 2016, in a wrongful death action, Claypole v. County of Monterey,[262] a federal magistrate found that Peter Bertling, counsel for the defendant, engaged in various forms of discovery abuse. At a contentious deposition, when plaintiff's counsel, Lori Rifkin, asked Bertling not to interrupt her, Bertling responded, "[D]on't raise your voice at me. It's not becoming of [sic] a woman. . . ." In a brief declaration filed in response to the motion for sanctions, Bertling wrote, "In retrospect, the proper term for me to have used in this context would have been 'attorney.' I apologize to Ms. Rifkin if I offended her by referring to her as a 'woman' instead of as an 'attorney.'" Bertling claimed that his remarks were made "in the context of Ms. Rifkin literally yelling at my client and creating a hostile environment during the deposition." The magistrate characterized this response as "only a halfhearted politician's apology," and noted that Bertling had failed to apologize at a hearing on the matter. The magistrate found that Bertling had acted in "bad faith" and in violation of a lawyer's duty of professionalism. In the magistrate's view, "A sexist remark is not just a professional discourtesy. . . . The bigger issue is that comments like Bertling's reflect and reinforce the male-dominated attitude of our profession." Because the magistrate had already awarded fees and costs for Bertling's other discovery abuse, the magistrate added the additional sanction that Bertling donate $250 to the Women Lawyers Association of Los Angeles Foundation. Do you agree that Bertling's conduct should have been sanctioned? If this was a jurisdiction that had adopted new Model Rule 8.4, was it also a violation of the rule, in addition to the more general duty of professionalism? If properly sanctionable, was the magistrate's sanction an appropriate response?

1-33. A study by Catalyst, an organization dedicated to advancing professional women, catalogs "unwritten rules" that are critical in career development. The most important rules cited by survey participants were to

- network and build relationships within and outside the organization (71 percent);
- find ways to become visible (51 percent);
- communicate effectively and ask for frequent feedback (43 percent);
- perform well and produce results (35 percent);
- find a mentor, coach, or sponsor (32 percent);
- work long hours (29 percent); and
- develop a good career plan (20 percent).[263]

Other advocacy groups have proposed institutional strategies for changing the profession, including securing the commitment of leaders to diversity and inclusion; ensuring representation in leadership positions; using metrics to identify and correct hidden biases; improving outreach to diverse applicant pools; curating

---

262. Claypole v. Monterey, No. 14-CV-02730-BLF, 2016 WL 145557 (N.D. Cal., Jan. 12, 2016).

263. Laura Sabattini, Unwritten Rules: What You Don't Know Can Hurt Your Career, Catalyst 5 (2008).

mentoring and networking channels; fostering workplace flexibility; and enforcing anti-discrimination policies.[264]

Which of the above strategies do you think are most likely to change the lingering inequalities discussed above? Which do you think are the least likely? If you were hired as a consultant to a law firm seeking to improve its track record on diversity and inclusion, what you recommend?

b. What Is Discrimination? The Special Case of Appearance Regulation

Many workplaces require their employers to meet certain appearance standards, which are often sex-specific. For example, employers may require women to wear skirts or high heels, and men to wear ties or have short hair. These cases often present difficult issues about what constitutes sex discrimination. On the one hand, a rule that allows (or requires) only women to wear skirts explicitly discriminates on the basis of sex. On the other hand, it may seem reasonable to give employers some latitude in regulating appearance and to absolve courts from having to spend scarce resources micromanaging dress codes. Complicating the analysis is the extent to which standards of appearance are racialized and linked to perceptions of an individual's ability status or gender identity.

Courts have avoided finding that sex-specific grooming regulations constitute unlawful sex discrimination through various approaches. The first federal appellate case on the subject upheld a hair-length requirement imposed only on male employees on the grounds that the "discrimination" was based not on the "immutable characteristics" of sex, but rather on a characteristic — e.g., hair length — over which the individual had control.[265] Other courts have determined that appearance regulations discriminate not on the basis of sex but rather on "neutral" generally accepted community grooming standards (that happen to be sex-specific).[266] The notes below explore such reasoning. The following case, Jespersen v. Harrah's Operating Company, took a still different approach.

Jespersen v. Harrah's Operating Company, Inc.

444 F.3d 1104 (9th Cir. 2006) (en banc)

SCHROEDER, Chief Judge:

We took this sex discrimination case en banc in order to reaffirm our circuit law concerning appearance and grooming standards, and to clarify our evolving law of sex stereotyping claims.

---

264. Nat'l Ass'n Women Laws., Actions for Advancing Women into Law Firm Leadership (2008); Rhode & Kellerman, Women and Leadership, supra note 201, at 90-92; Joan C. Williams et al., You Can't Change What You Can't See: Interrupting Racial & Gender Bias in the Legal Profession 14-15 (2018).

265. See Baker v. Cal. Land Title Co., 507 F.2d 895 (9th Cir. 1974).

266. See, e.g., Willingham v. Macon Tel. Publ'g Co., 507 F.2d 1084 (5th Cir. 1975).

The plaintiff, Darlene Jespersen, was terminated from her position as a bartender at the sports bar in Harrah's Reno casino not long after Harrah's began to enforce its comprehensive uniform, appearance and grooming standards for all bartenders. The standards required all bartenders, men and women, to wear the same uniform of black pants and white shirts, a bow tie, and comfortable black shoes. The standards also included grooming requirements that differed to some extent for men and women, requiring women to wear some facial makeup and not permitting men to wear any. Jespersen refused to comply with the makeup requirement and was effectively terminated for that reason.

The district court granted summary judgment to Harrah's on the ground that the appearance and grooming policies imposed equal burdens on both men and women bartenders because, while women were required to use makeup and men were forbidden to wear makeup, women were allowed to have long hair and men were required to have their hair cut to a length above the collar. The district court also held that the policy could not run afoul of Title VII because it did not discriminate against Jespersen on the basis of the "immutable characteristics" of her sex. The district court further observed that the Supreme Court's decision in Price Waterhouse v. Hopkins, prohibiting discrimination on the basis of sex stereotyping, did not apply to this case because in the district court's view, the Ninth Circuit had excluded grooming standards from the reach of *Price Waterhouse*. The district court granted summary judgment to Harrah's on all claims. [The en banc court affirmed.]

I. BACKGROUND

Plaintiff Darlene Jespersen worked successfully as a bartender at Harrah's for twenty years and compiled what by all accounts was an exemplary record. During Jespersen's entire tenure with Harrah's, the company maintained a policy encouraging female beverage servers to wear makeup. The parties agree, however, that the policy was not enforced until 2000. In February 2000, Harrah's implemented a "Beverage Department Image Transformation" program at twenty Harrah's locations, including its casino in Reno. Part of the program consisted of new grooming and appearance standards, called the "Personal Best" program. The program contained certain appearance standards that applied equally to both sexes, including a standard uniform of black pants, white shirt, black vest, and black bow tie. Jespersen has never objected to any of these policies. The program also contained some sex-differentiated appearance requirements as to hair, nails, and makeup.

In April 2000, Harrah's amended that policy to require that women wear makeup. Jespersen's only objection here is to the makeup requirement. The amended policy provided in relevant part (emphasis added):

> All Beverage Service Personnel, in addition to being friendly, polite, courteous and responsive to our customer's needs, must possess the ability to physically perform the essential factors of the job as set forth in the standard job descriptions. They must be well groomed, appealing to the eye, be firm and body toned, and be comfortable with maintaining this look while wearing the specified uniform. Additional factors to be considered include, but are not limited to, hair styles, overall body contour, and degree of comfort the employee projects while wearing the uniform. . . .

Beverage Bartenders and Barbacks will adhere to these additional guidelines:

Overall Guidelines (applied equally to male/female):

Appearance: Must maintain Personal Best image portrayed at time of hire.

Jewelry, if issued, must be worn. Otherwise, tasteful and simple jewelry is permitted; no large chokers, chains or bracelets.

No faddish hairstyles or unnatural colors are permitted.

Males:

Hair must not extend below top of shirt collar. Ponytails are prohibited.

Hands and fingernails must be clean and nails neatly trimmed at all times. No colored polish is permitted.

Eye and facial makeup is not permitted. . . .

Shoes will be solid black leather or leather type with rubber (non skid) soles.

Females:

Hair must be teased, curled, or styled every day you work. Hair must be worn down at all times, no exceptions.

Stockings are to be of nude or natural color consistent with employee's skin tone. No runs.

Nail polish can be clear, white, pink or red color only. No exotic nail art or length. . . .

Shoes will be solid black leather or leather type with rubber (non skid) soles.

Make up (face powder, blush and mascara) must be worn and applied neatly in complimentary colors. Lip color must be worn at all times.

Jespersen did not wear makeup on or off the job, and in her deposition stated that wearing it would conflict with her self-image. It is not disputed that she found the makeup requirement offensive, and felt so uncomfortable wearing makeup that she found it interfered with her ability to perform as a bartender. Unwilling to wear the makeup, and not qualifying for any open positions at the casino with a similar compensation scale, Jespersen left her employment with Harrah's.

. . . In her complaint, Jespersen sought damages as well as declaratory and injunctive relief for discrimination and retaliation for opposition to discrimination, alleging that the "Personal Best" policy discriminated against women by "(1) subjecting them to terms and conditions of employment to which men are not similarly subjected, and (2) requiring that women conform to sex-based stereotypes as a term and condition of employment."

Harrah's moved for summary judgment, supporting its motion with documents giving the history and purpose of the appearance and grooming policies. Harrah's argued that the policy created similar standards for both men and women, and that where the standards differentiated on the basis of sex, as with the face and hair standards, any burdens imposed fell equally on both male and female bartenders.

In her deposition testimony, attached as a response to the motion for summary judgment, Jespersen described the personal indignity she felt as a result of attempting to comply with the makeup policy. Jespersen testified that when she wore the makeup she "felt very degraded and very demeaned." In addition, Jespersen testified that "it prohibited [her] from doing [her] job" because "it affected [her] self-dignity . . . [and] took away [her] credibility as an individual and as a person." . . .

The record therefore does not contain any affidavit or other evidence to establish that complying with the "Personal Best" standards caused burdens to fall unequally on men or women, and there is no evidence to suggest Harrah's motivation was to stereotype the women bartenders. Jespersen relied solely on evidence that she had been a good bartender, and that she had personal objections to complying with the policy, in order to support her argument that Harrah's "'sells' and exploits its women employees." Jespersen contended that as a matter of law she had made a prima facie showing of gender discrimination, sufficient to survive summary judgment on both of her claims.

II. UNEQUAL BURDENS

. . . [T]his case involves an appearance policy that applied to both male and female bartenders, and was aimed at creating a professional and very similar look for all of them. All bartenders wore the same uniform. The policy only differentiated as to grooming standards.

In *Frank v. United Airlines, Inc.* [2000], we dealt with a weight policy that applied different standards to men and women in a facially unequal way. The women were forced to meet the requirements of a medium body frame standard while men were required to meet only the more generous requirements of a large body frame standard. In that case, we recognized that "an appearance standard that imposes different but essentially equal burdens on men and women is not disparate treatment." The *United* weight policy, however, did not impose equal burdens. On its face, the policy embodied a requirement that categorically "'applied less favorably to one gender[,]'" and the burdens imposed upon that gender were obvious from the policy itself.

This case stands in marked contrast, for here we deal with requirements that, on their face, are not more onerous for one gender than the other. Rather, Harrah's "Personal Best" policy contains sex-differentiated requirements regarding each employee's hair, hands, and face. While those individual requirements differ according to gender, none on its face places a greater burden on one gender than the other. Grooming standards that appropriately differentiate between the genders are not facially discriminatory. . . .

Not every differentiation between the sexes in a grooming and appearance policy creates a "significantly greater burden of compliance." For example, . . . this court upheld Safeway's enforcement of its sex-differentiated appearance standard, including its requirement that male employees wear ties, because the company's actions in enforcing the regulations were not "overly burdensome to its employees." Similarly, as the Eighth Circuit has recognized, "where, as here, such [grooming and appearance] policies are reasonable and are imposed in an evenhanded manner on all employees, slight differences in the appearance requirements for males and females have only a negligible effect on employment opportunities." . . .

Jespersen asks us to take judicial notice of the fact that it costs more money and takes more time for a woman to comply with the makeup requirement than it takes for a man to comply with the requirement that he keep his hair short, but these are not matters appropriate for judicial notice. . . .

. . . Jespersen did not submit any documentation or any evidence of the relative cost and time required to comply with the grooming requirements by men and women. As a result, we would have to speculate about those issues in order to then guess whether the policy creates unequal burdens for women. This would not be appropriate.

III. SEX STEREOTYPING

In *Price Waterhouse*, the Supreme Court considered a mixed-motive discrimination case. There, the plaintiff, Ann Hopkins, was denied partnership in the national accounting firm of Price Waterhouse because some of the partners found her to be too aggressive. While some partners praised Hopkins's "'strong character, independence and integrity,'" others commented that she needed to take "a course at charm school" . . . .

The stereotyping in *Price Waterhouse* interfered with Hopkins' ability to perform her work; the advice that she should take "a course at charm school" was intended to discourage her use of the forceful and aggressive techniques that made her successful in the first place. Impermissible sex stereotyping was clear because the very traits that she was asked to hide were the same traits considered praiseworthy in men.

Harrah's "Personal Best" policy is very different. The policy does not single out Jespersen. It applies to all of the bartenders, male and female. It requires all of the bartenders to wear exactly the same uniforms while interacting with the public in the context of the entertainment industry. It is for the most part unisex, from the black tie to the non-skid shoes. There is no evidence in this record to indicate that the policy was adopted to make women bartenders conform to a commonly accepted stereotypical image of what women should wear. The record contains nothing to suggest the grooming standards would objectively inhibit a woman's ability to do the job. The only evidence in the record to support the stereotyping claim is Jespersen's own subjective reaction to the makeup requirement.

Judge Pregerson's dissent improperly divides the grooming policy into separate categories of hair, hands, and face, and then focuses exclusively on the makeup requirement to conclude that the policy constitutes sex stereotyping. This parsing, however, conflicts with established grooming standards analysis. . . . The requirements must be viewed in the context of the overall policy. The dissent's conclusion that the unequal burdens analysis allows impermissible sex stereotyping to persist if imposed equally on both sexes . . . is wrong because it ignores the protections of *Price Waterhouse* our decision preserves. If a grooming standard imposed on either sex amounts to impermissible stereotyping, something this record does not establish, a plaintiff of either sex may challenge that requirement under *Price Waterhouse*.

We respect Jespersen's resolve to be true to herself and to the image that she wishes to project to the world. We cannot agree, however, that her objection to the makeup requirement, without more, can give rise to a claim of sex stereotyping under Title VII. If we were to do so, we would come perilously close to holding that every grooming, apparel, or appearance requirement that an individual finds personally offensive, or in conflict with his or her own self-image, can create a triable issue of sex discrimination.

This is not a case where the dress or appearance requirement is intended to be sexually provocative, and tending to stereotype women as sex objects. The "Personal Best" policy does not, on its face, indicate any discriminatory or sexually stereotypical intent on the part of Harrah's. . . . Jespersen's claim here materially differs from Hopkins' claim in *Price Waterhouse* because Harrah's grooming standards do not require Jespersen to conform to a stereotypical image that would objectively impede her ability to perform her job requirements as a bartender.

We emphasize that we do not preclude, as a matter of law, a claim of sex stereotyping on the basis of dress or appearance codes. Others may well be filed, and any bases for such claims refined as law in this area evolves. This record, however, is devoid of any basis for permitting this particular claim to go forward, as it is limited to the subjective reaction of a single employee, and there is no evidence of a stereotypical motivation on the part of the employer. This case is essentially a challenge to one small part of what is an overall apparel, appearance, and grooming policy that applies largely the same requirements to both men and women. . . . [T]he touchstone is reasonableness. A makeup requirement must be seen in the context of the overall standards imposed on employees in a given workplace.

PREGERSON, Circuit Judge, with whom Judges KOZINSKI, GRABER, and W. FLETCHER join, dissenting:

. . . I believe that the "Personal Best" program was part of a policy motivated by sex stereotyping and that Jespersen's termination for failing to comply with the program's requirements was "because of" her sex. Accordingly, I dissent from Part III of the majority opinion and from the judgment of the court.

The majority contends that it is bound to reject Jespersen's sex stereotyping claim because she presented too little evidence—only her "own subjective reaction to the makeup requirement." I disagree. Jespersen's evidence showed that Harrah's fired her because she did not comply with a grooming policy that imposed a facial uniform (full makeup) on only female bartenders. Harrah's stringent "Personal Best" policy required female beverage servers to wear foundation, blush, mascara, and lip color, and to ensure that lip color was on at all times. Jespersen and her female colleagues were required to meet with professional image consultants who in turn created a facial template for each woman. Jespersen was required not simply to wear makeup; in addition, the consultants dictated where and how the makeup had to be applied. . . .

This policy did not, as the majority suggests, impose a "grooming, apparel, or appearance requirement that an individual finds personally offensive," but rather one that treated Jespersen differently from male bartenders "because of" her sex. I believe that the fact that Harrah's designed and promoted a policy that required women to conform to a sex stereotype by wearing full makeup is sufficient "direct evidence" of discrimination.

The majority contends that Harrah's "Personal Best" appearance policy is very different from the policy at issue in *Price Waterhouse* in that it applies to both men and women. . . . The fact that a policy contains sex-differentiated requirements that affect people of both genders cannot excuse a particular requirement from scrutiny. By refusing to consider the makeup requirement separately, and instead stressing that the policy contained some gender-neutral requirements, such as color of clothing, as well as a variety of gender-differentiated requirements for "hair, hands, and face," the majority's approach would permit otherwise impermissible gender stereotypes to be neutralized by the presence of a stereotype or burden that affects people of the opposite gender, or by some separate non-discriminatory requirement that applies to both men and women. . . . But the fact that employees of both genders are subjected to gender-specific requirements does not necessarily mean that particular requirements are not motivated by gender stereotyping.

Because I believe that we should be careful not to insulate appearance requirements by viewing them in broad categories, such as "hair, hands, and face," I would consider the makeup requirement on its own terms. Viewed in isolation — or, at the very least, as part of a narrower category of requirements affecting employees' faces — the makeup or facial uniform requirement becomes closely analogous to the uniform policy held to constitute impermissible sex stereotyping in *Carroll v. Talman Federal Savings & Loan Ass'n of Chicago*, [1979]. In *Carroll*, the defendant bank required women to wear employer-issued uniforms, but permitted men to wear business attire of their own choosing. The Seventh Circuit found this rule discriminatory because it suggested to the public that the uniformed women held a "lesser professional status" and that women could not be trusted to choose appropriate business attire.

Just as the bank in *Carroll* deemed female employees incapable of achieving a professional appearance without assigned uniforms, Harrah's regarded women as unable to achieve a neat, attractive, and professional appearance without the facial uniform designed by a consultant and required by Harrah's. The inescapable message is that women's undoctored faces compare unfavorably to men's, not because of a physical difference between men's and women's faces, but because of a cultural assumption — and gender-based stereotype — that women's faces are incomplete, unattractive, or unprofessional without full makeup. We need not denounce all makeup as inherently offensive, just as there was no need to denounce all uniforms as inherently offensive in *Carroll*, to conclude that *requiring* female bartenders to wear full makeup is an impermissible sex stereotype and is evidence of discrimination because of sex. Therefore, I strongly disagree with the majority's conclusion that there "is no evidence in this record to indicate that the policy was adopted to make women bartenders conform to a commonly-accepted stereotypical image of what women should wear."

I believe that Jespersen articulated a classic case of *Price Waterhouse* discrimination and presented undisputed, material facts sufficient to avoid summary judgment. Accordingly, Jespersen should be allowed to present her case to a jury.

KOZINSKI, Circuit Judge, with whom Judges GRABER and W. FLETCHER join, dissenting:

I agree with Judge Pregerson and join his dissent — subject to one caveat: I believe that Jespersen also presented a triable issue of fact on the question of disparate burden.

The majority is right that "the [makeup] requirements must be viewed in the context of the overall policy." But I find it perfectly clear that Harrah's overall grooming policy is substantially more burdensome for women than for men. Every requirement that forces men to spend time or money on their appearance has a corresponding requirement that is as, or more, burdensome for women: short hair v. "teased, curled, or styled" hair; clean trimmed nails v. nail length and color requirements; black leather shoes v. black leather shoes. The requirement that women spend time and money applying full facial makeup has no corresponding requirement for men, making the "overall policy" more burdensome for the former than for the latter. The only question is how much.

It is true that Jespersen failed to present evidence about what it costs to buy makeup and how long it takes to apply it. But is there any doubt that putting on makeup costs money and takes time? Harrah's policy requires women to apply face powder, blush, mascara and lipstick. You don't need an expert witness to figure out that such items don't grow on trees.

Nor is there any rational doubt that application of makeup is an intricate and painstaking process that requires considerable time and care. Even those of us who don't wear makeup know how long it can take from the hundreds of hours we've spent over the years frantically tapping our toes and pointing to our wrists. It's hard to imagine that a woman could "put on her face," as they say, in the time it would take a man to shave—certainly not if she were to do the careful and thorough job Harrah's expects. Makeup, moreover, must be applied and removed every day; the policy burdens men with no such daily ritual. While a man could jog to the casino, slip into his uniform, and get right to work, a woman must travel to work so as to avoid smearing her makeup, or arrive early to put on her makeup there.

It might have been tidier if Jespersen had introduced evidence as to the time and cost associated with complying with the makeup requirement, but I can understand her failure to do so, as these hardly seem like questions reasonably subject to dispute. We could—and should—take judicial notice of these incontrovertible facts.

Alternatively, Jespersen did introduce evidence that she finds it burdensome to *wear* makeup because doing so is inconsistent with her self-image and interferes with her job performance. My colleagues dismiss this evidence, apparently on the ground that wearing makeup does not, as a matter of law, constitute a substantial burden. This presupposes that Jespersen is unreasonable or idiosyncratic in her discomfort. Why so? Whether to wear cosmetics—literally, the face one presents to the world—is an intensely personal choice. Makeup, moreover, touches delicate parts of the anatomy—the lips, the eyes, the cheeks—and can cause serious discomfort, sometimes even allergic reactions, for someone unaccustomed to wearing it. If you are used to wearing makeup—as most American women are—this may seem like no big deal. But those of us not used to wearing makeup would find a requirement that we do so highly intrusive. Imagine, for example, a rule that all judges wear face powder, blush, mascara and lipstick while on the bench. Like Jespersen, I would find such a regime burdensome and demeaning; it would interfere with my job performance. I suspect many of my colleagues would feel the same way.

Everyone accepts this as a reasonable reaction from a man, but why should it be different for a woman? It is not because of anatomical differences, such as a requirement that women wear bathing suits that cover their breasts. Women's faces, just like those of men, can be perfectly presentable without makeup; it is a cultural artifact that most women raised in the United States learn to put on — and presumably enjoy wearing — cosmetics. But cultural norms change; . . . a large (and perhaps growing) number of women choose to present themselves to the world without makeup. I see no justification for forcing them to conform to Harrah's quaint notion of what a "real woman" looks like.

Nor do I think it appropriate for a court to dismiss a woman's testimony that she finds wearing makeup degrading and intrusive, as Jespersen clearly does. Not only do we have her sworn statement to that effect, but there can be no doubt about her sincerity or the intensity of her feelings: She quit her job — a job she performed well for two decades — rather than put on the makeup. That is a choice her male colleagues were not forced to make. To me, this states a case of disparate burden, and I would let a jury decide whether an employer can force a woman to make this choice.

Finally, I note with dismay the employer's decision to let go a valued, experienced employee who had gained accolades from her customers, over what, in the end, is a trivial matter. Quality employees are difficult to find in any industry and I would think an employer would long hesitate before forcing a loyal, longtime employee to quit over an honest and heart-felt difference of opinion about a matter of personal significance to her. Having won the legal battle, I hope that Harrah's will now do the generous and decent thing by offering Jespersen her job back, and letting her give it her personal best — without the makeup.

D. Wendy Greene

A Multidimensionality Analysis of What Not to Wear in the Workplace: Hijabs and Natural Hair

8 Fla. Int'l U. L. Rev. 333, 335-36 (2013)

Though courts often view . . . grooming codes as harmless acts of employer prerogative, multidimensional and intersectional analyses of workplace grooming codes banning and regulating natural hairstyles and hijabs delineate that employers' implementation and enforcement of these mandates arbitrarily deprive or tend to deprive Black women and Muslim women acquisition and maintenance of employment for which they are qualified in violation of Title VII's plain language. In order to obtain or maintain employment, Black and Muslim women's conformity with such exclusionary workplace grooming mandates may in effect require their compliance with express and implicit forms of gender-based subordination and differential treatment in the workplace to which other women and men are not subject. . . .

Viewing these grooming codes cases through a multidimensional lens illuminates the individual and collective harm of employers' seemingly innocuous implementation and enforcement of grooming codes implicating Black and Muslim women's hair. Uniquely, Black and Muslim women experience economic and stigmatic injury due to employment conditions that moderate and exclude their presence — via their hair — from private workplaces, regardless of the industry or organization type. Indeed, workplace regulations banning hijabs and naturally textured hairstyles may doubly affect women of color who are both Muslim and Black and don hijabs and natural hair. Consequently, granting indefinite power to private employers to specifically regulate the hair of women of color may not simply reify but also amplify their exclusion from the workplace and corresponding social, economic, political and legal disadvantage at the intersection of race, religion, and sex.

NOTES

1. **The Importance of Appearance and Appearance Discrimination.** In the nineteenth century, cities such as Chicago, Denver, Omaha, and San Francisco banned appearances in public by people deemed "unsightly." An 1867 San Francisco law, for example, prohibited "any person, who is diseased, maimed, mutilated or in any way deformed, so as to be an unsightly or disgusting object . . . [from] exposing himself or herself to public view."[267] While no such laws exist today, there is little doubt that there is a premium for good looks, especially in the workplace. Beauty may be only "skin deep," but that is deep enough to confer significant advantages.[268] Attractive applicants receive more callbacks, making good looks even more important than experience.[269] They are more likely to be hired and promoted, and it is estimated that they make 14 percent more per hour than their less attractive counterparts.[270] One study found that attractive attorneys, regardless of qualification and experience, earned significantly more than their less attractive counterparts, and that the disparity increases over time.[271] Another study showed that NFL quarterbacks who are considered attractive are paid more than their less good-looking counterparts, even accounting for such other factors as passing yards, years of experience, draft position, and Pro Bowl experiences.[272] In a national poll, about 16 percent of individuals believed that they had been subject to appearance-related

---

267. See Susan M. Schweik, The Ugly Laws: Disability in Public 24 (2009).

268. See Deborah L. Rhode, The Beauty Bias 23-44 (2010); Daniel S. Hamermesh, Beauty Pays (2011).

269. See Emily A. Beam et al., The Relative Returns to Education, Experience, and Attractiveness for Young Workers, Econ. Dev. & Cultural Change (Jan. 2020) (23%).

270. See Hamermesh, supra note 268. See also the studies reviewed in Deborah L. Rhode, The Injustice of Appearance, 61 Stan. L. Rev. 1033, 1038-1039 (2009); Megumi Hosoda et al., The Effects of Physical Attractiveness on Job Related Outcomes: A Meta-Analysis of Experimental Studies, 56 Personnel Psych. 431 (2003); Kristie M. Engemann & Michael T. Owyang, So Much for That Merit Raise: The Link Between Wages and Appearance, Q. Rev. Bus. & Econ. Conditions 10 (Apr. 2005).

271. The classic study is Jeff E. Biddle & Daniel S. Hamermesh, Beauty, Productivity and Discrimination: Lawyers' Looks and Lucre, 16 J. Lab. Econ. 172, 185-90 (1998). For a general account of the importance of appearance for women lawyers, see Peggy Li, Physical Attractiveness and Femininity: Helpful or Hurtful for Female Attorneys, 47 Akron L. Rev. 997 (2015).

272. See David J. Berri et al., What Does It Mean to Find the Face of the Franchise? Physical Attractiveness and the Evaluation of Athletic Performance, 111 Econ. Letters 200 (June 2011).

discrimination, a higher percentage than those in other polls reporting gender or racial discrimination (12 percent).[273]

Appearance bias is not only a problem for individuals considered unattractive. Very attractive or "sexy" women can also be subject to bias, particularly for upper-level jobs traditionally viewed as masculine. These women can be subject to prejudices labeled the "beauty to beastly" effect, the "femme fatale" effect, or the "Boopsy effect" (named after a cartoon character).[274] These women's appearance seems to suggest to others less competence, intellectual ability, truthfulness, and trustworthiness. It may also cause other women to envy or otherwise resent them.[275] Looking as if they care too much about their looks can also subject women to criticisms that they are vain, narcissistic, and shallow.

Another critical layer of the problem of dress and appearance standards is how they may interact with an individual's race, disability, or non-conforming gender identity. Gay men may be told not to wear earrings, and lesbians may be told to avoid pantsuits or flat shoes. A Black Congressional candidate running in 2018 was told that her hairstyle, Senegalese twists, was "too ethnic," and insufficiently "polished."[276] Such individuals must often choose mask or "cover" important aspects of their identity, or be excluded from the workplace.[277] For a fuller discussion of the issue of hair regulation, particularly as it relates to Black women, see Note 4, below.

Even when subject to the same rules, those rules may be applied differently to individuals whose identity does not conform to a white, able-bodied, heterosexual ideal. One woman of color, for example, describes how as a summer law firm associate, she was asked to go home and change because the "cut" of her dress was "not professional," even though it was knee-length, worn beneath a conservative blazer, and neither low-cut nor otherwise revealing.[278]

Are the costs of appearance-related bias inevitable? One way to view the matter is that a person's appearance is something like intelligence, which contributes to different opportunities that we must simply accept. Should the law view it this way? Would your answer be affected by research showing that some appearance preferences such as facial symmetry and unblemished skin appear to be innate?[279] If so, what if "in-group" preferences underlying racial and ethnic discrimination also appear to be hard-wired?

273. See polls cited in Rhode, The Injustice of Appearance, supra note 270, at 1068-69.

274. See Leah D. Sheppard & Stefanie K. Johnson, The Femme Fatale Effect: Attractiveness is a Liability for Businesswomen's Perceived Truthfulness, Trust and Deservingness of Termination, Sex Roles 1 (2019).

275. Id.

276. Caitlin Moscatello, See Jane Win: The Inspiring Story of the Women Changing American Politics 160 (2019).

277. See Devon W. Carbado & Mitu Gulati, Acting White? Rethinking Race in "Post-Racial" America (2013); Kenji Yoshino, Covering: The Hidden Assault on Our Civil Rights (2007). See also Devon W. Carbado & Mitu Gulati, The Fifth Black Woman, 11 J. Contemp. Legal Issues 701 (2001), excerpted in Section C of this chapter.

278. See Priya-Alika Elias, What Does Dressing "Professionally" Mean for Women of Color, Racked on Vox (Mar. 8, 2018).

279. See Nancy Etcoff, Survival of the Prettiest: The Science of Beauty 31-32 (1999) (describing study of babies).

2. **Legal Standards.** The unequal burden test endorsed in the *Jespersen* decision marks an advance over prior law, which saw grooming codes as neutral and acceptable as long as they merely reflected "community standards." Commentators often had pointed out that reliance on community standards, discussed further below, only served to reinforce the very stereotypes that Title VII was intended to eliminate.[280] Does the unequal burden test do much better? What would Jespersen have needed to show in order to demonstrate that the makeup requirement imposed an unequal burden on women? Couldn't a court take judicial notice of the fact that cosmetics don't grow on trees and that it takes time to style hair? Does the equal burden test capture all that is objectionable in Harrah's policy? Consider Rhode's claim:

> The problem with this prevailing approach to appearance regulation is not only that judges often seem clueless about the disproportionate demands that many codes impose on women. The difficulty is also that a framework comparing male and female burdens fails to capture all of what makes these regulations objectionable. Darlene Jespersen resisted Harrah's makeup requirement not because it took more time and money for her to be presentable than her male counterparts, but because she felt that being "dolled up" was degrading and undermined her credibility with unruly customers. Dress codes that require women to wear skirts and high heels are problematic for similar reasons, regardless of what the codes demand of men.[281]

In Rhode's view,

> [j]ustifications for banning appearance discrimination rest on three basic claims. The first is that such discrimination offends principles of equal opportunity; individuals should be judged on merit and performance, not irrelevant physical characteristics. A second rationale is that appearance-related bias reinforces group subordination; it exacerbates disadvantages based on gender, race, ethnicity, class, age, and sexual orientation. A third justification is that some decisions based on appearance unduly restrict self-expression and cultural identity. Although opponents of prohibiting appearance discrimination raise some legitimate concerns, these can be met through well-designed statutory schemes. The excessive liability and business backlash that critics have predicted have not in fact materialized in the few jurisdictions that have prohibited appearance-related bias.[282]

Which of these three grounds provides the strongest basis for challenging sex-specific dress and appearance requirements? In general, courts have upheld sex-specific requirements even when the standards are stricter or more burdensome for one sex. This is the case whether the standards are alleged to weed out women

---

280. See, e.g., Katharine T. Bartlett, Only Girls Wear Barrettes: Dress and Appearance Standards, Community Norms, and Workplace Equality, 92 Mich. L. Rev. 2541 (1994).

281. Rhode, Beauty Bias, supra note 268, at 121.

282. Id. at 93.

who are not attractive enough,[283] or women who are deemed too attractive or who dress too sexily.[284] Only a few courts, in a few circumstances, have been willing to see standards of attractiveness as a form of sex stereotyping. In Lewis v. Heartland Inns of America, the Eighth Circuit Court of Appeals found that the plaintiff had established a prima facie case of sex discrimination based on allegations that she had lost her position as a front desk hotel clerk because she was not "pretty," and lacked the "Midwestern girl look."[285]

Why do organizations want to control the appearance of their employees? Ordinarily, a business cannot discriminate on the basis of race, sex, or other prohibited factors just because customers may prefer it. The reasons are obvious, and explored more fully in Wilson v. Southwest Airlines, discussed below. Often, these preferences reflect precisely the biases that anti-discrimination laws seek to address. Yet dress and appearance standards are typically upheld even though they rely on customer preferences. One highly publicized example is the 1983 case of Craft v. Metromedia, Inc.[286] There, a local television station anchorwoman, Christine Craft, filed suit against her employer after she was moved to an off-camera position because producers found her hair and makeup to be inappropriate. Craft claimed that she was judged by harsher standards than male anchors. The station responded with audience research including focus groups and a telephone survey, which showed that the plaintiff's appearance had an adverse impact on her acceptance among viewers. The court determined that she was properly reassigned due to the demonstrated negative viewer response.[287] By that logic, could television stations require that female but not male anchors look young and attractive? Customer preference is generally not a defense to discrimination claims. Is viewer preference any different? On the other hand, should we expect employers to avoid using attractiveness as a job criteria when it makes a demonstrable difference to their bottom line?

One problem with imposing a double standard for appearance based on market factors like customer preference is that it can become self-perpetuating. Viewers may expect youth and beauty in female newscasters partly because they lack exposure to the obvious alternative—women who gained their position through merit-related qualifications. Reconsider how to approach this question after reading Wilson v. Southwest Airlines, below.

Guidelines from the New York City Commission on Human Rights expressly prohibit "enforcing dress codes, uniforms, and grooming standards that impose

283. See, e.g., Schiavo v. Marina Dist. Dev. Co., 123 A.3d 272 (N.J. Super. Ct. App. Div. 2015) (under New Jersey state law, "as informed by Title VII"); Jordan D. Bello, Attractiveness as a Hiring Criteria: Savvy Business Practice or Racial Discrimination, 8 J. Gender, Race & Just. 483, 483 (2004).

284. See Goodwin v. Harvard Coll., JVR No. 806230, 2005 WL 4256570 (D. Mass. May 17, 2005).

285. 591 F.3d 1033, 1036 (2010).

286. 572 F. Supp. 868 (W.D. Mo. 1983), rev'd in part, 766 F.2d 1205 (8th Cir. 1985).

287. For Craft's own account of her experience, see Christine Craft, Too Old, Too Ugly, and Not Deferential to Men (1988).

different requirements based on sex and gender."[288] Is this blanket prohibition the right approach? What would happen in most workplaces if sex-specific dress and grooming codes were considered to be unlawful discrimination? Would it have a major effect on employee appearance? Would there be any significant negative consequences?

Notably, without much law to rely upon, some employees have succeeded in pressuring employers to drop their dress and appearance requirements. Some airlines, for example, have dropped requirements of skirts and makeup for female crew members in response to staff feedback.[289]

3. **Weight.**   One of the most common forms of appearance discrimination concerns weight. A wide array of research finds that fat or overweight people[290] are more likely to be judged as unsuitable for a wide variety of occupations,[291] and that overweight females are judged even more harshly than overweight males.[292] Studies have found a significant correlation between an individual's BMI (body mass index), and whether they have a job and how much they are paid.[293] Because being above average weight is more common among African-American and low-income women compared to white women and middle- to upper-class women, weight stigma has a disproportionate impact based on race and class.

At one time, weight limits were common for flight attendants and in some other occupations. Courts initially upheld strict restrictions even when the standards for men took into account large frame sizes while the standards for women presupposed small or medium builds. One court relied on the "fact" that the weight restrictions for women did not concern an "immutable characteristic": weight, unlike height, was thought to be subject to the "reasonable control" of most individuals.[294] Frank v. United Airlines, Inc.,[295] cited approvingly in *Jespersen*, reversed such rulings. There, the Ninth Circuit Court of Appeals found that a policy permitting

---

288. Vanessa Friedman, The End of the Office Dress Code, N.Y. Times, May 25, 2016, at D2.

289. Ceylabn Yeginsu, Virgin Atlantic Won't Make Female Flight Attendants Wear Makeup or Skirts Anymore, N.Y. Times, Mar. 5, 2019, at B3.

290. The term is contested. Some activists prefer the term "fat" because "overweight" conveys a normative judgment about weight norms. Many women, however, find the term "fat" more stigmatizing.

291. See, e.g., Stuart W. Flint et al., Obesity Discrimination in the Recruitment Process: "You're *Not* Hired!", 7 Frontiers in Psych. 647 (2016) (reporting study demonstrating systematic ratings of obese candidates as less suitable for a variety of sedentary, standing, manual, and heavy manual occupations, as compared with normal weight candidates).

292. Id.; J. Spahlhoz et al., Obesity and Discrimination—A Systematic Review and Meta-Analysis of Observational Studies, 17 Obesity Revs. 43 (2016).

293. Hyeain Lee et al., Impact of Obesity on Employment and Wages Among Young Adults: Observational Study with Panel Data, 16 Int'l J. Env't. Rsch. Pub. Health 139 (2019) (study reporting obese women are one-third as likely to have a permanent job compared to their normal weight counterparts, and showing, by a range of measures, that obesity affects compensation opportunities).

294. Jarrell v. E. Airlines, Inc., 430 F. Supp. 884, 892 (E.D. Va. 1977), aff'd mem., 577 F.2d 869 (4th Cir. 1978).

295. 216 F.3d 845 (9th Cir. 2000).

men's weight to vary within a broader range of frame sizes than was allowed for women's weight constituted unlawful sex discrimination.

The proposition that weight is a matter of personal choice and self-discipline is highly contested. Some studies show that weight is largely a product of genetic and environmental factors over which the individual has no control, and that most obese people are not able to lose much weight through dieting.[296] Others seem to show that obesity is primarily caused by voluntary overeating and a sedentary lifestyle.[297] To what extent should it matter which is right? Weight control also gets significantly more difficult with age. Should we thus consider weight requirements a form of age discrimination?

Discrimination based on weight contributes to eating disorders, which disproportionately affect women and girls.[298] About one in five females experience an eating disorder by the age of 40. By adolescence, an estimated half of female adolescents have engaged in extreme dieting (e.g., fasting, laxatives, and purging).[299] Over 90 percent of those suffering from anorexia or bulimia are female, although some recent research suggests that the problems are growing among men.[300] Should this disparity matter, from a legal standpoint?

Some plaintiffs have successfully sued for weight discrimination under the federal Americans with Disabilities Act (ADA) and analogous state provisions. However, governing regulations under the ADA interpret the Act to cover only extremely severe obesity (100 percent over average weight) caused by a physiological disorder.[301] Although a few state and local ordinances offer broader coverage, the vast majority of individuals remain unprotected.[302]

In a widely publicized lawsuit against an Atlantic City casino, a number of "Borgata Babes" claimed, among other things, that the defendant's Personal Appearance Standards were based on gender stereotypes and were not enforced as rigorously against men as against women.[303] The standards required that the plaintiff beverage servers not gain or lose more than 7 percent of their baseline

---

296. See Gina Kolata, Rethinking Thin: The New Science of Weight Loss — And the Myths and Realities of Dieting (2008) (describing studies).

297. See Francesco Rubino et al., Joint International Consensus Statement for Ending Stigma of Obesity, 26 Nature Med. 485 (2020) (consensus statement of thirty-six internationally recognized academics across a variety of disciplines, reviewing the evidence).

298. See Ruth H. Striegel-Moore et al., Gender Difference in the Prevalence of Eating Disorder Symptoms, 45 Int'l J. Eating Disorders 471 (2009).

299. Zachary J. Ward et al., Estimation of Eating Disorders Prevalence by Age and Associations with Mortality in a Simulated Nationally Representative US Cohort, 2 JAMA Network Open e191925 (2019); Rachel Simmons, Enough as She Is 53 (2018).

300. See Ward et al., supra note 299 (one in seven men experience eating disorder, as compared to one in five women); Simmons, supra note 299 (research shows that up to 25 percent of men are on diets at any given time).

301. 29 C.F.R. § 1630 (2022). See Richardson v. Chicago Transit Authority, No. 18-2199 926 F.3d 881 (7th Cir. 2019).

302. Rhode, The Injustice of Appearance, supra note 270, at 1078-79; Elizabeth E. Theran, Legal Theory of Weight Discrimination, in Weight Bias: Nature, Consequences and Remedies 195, 206 (Kelly D. Brownell et al. eds., 2005).

303. Schiavo v. Marina Dist. Dev. Co., 123 A.3d 272 (N.J. Super. Ct. App. Div. 2015).

weight—the weight at which they were hired. Undisputed evidence showed that more than twenty women and no men were suspended for noncompliance with the weight policy and that weight checks were much more common for women than men. While the courts have consistently upheld the weight requirement itself, a recent appellate decision in the case found that some plaintiffs stated a claim that they were subjected to a hostile work environment in the way in which the policy was enforced.[304] How relevant is it that many women are eager for jobs involving a sexualized appearance—4,000 women applied for the first 200 Borgata Babes jobs[305]—and that these jobs, counting tips, are very well paid?

4. **The Regulation of Hair.**   Dress and appearance standards often prohibit certain hairstyles, prohibitions that have a discriminatory impact on Black people. In Rogers v. American Airlines,[306] a Black woman challenged an airline grooming policy prohibiting employees from wearing an all-braided hairstyle. The court held that because the policy applied to all employees—women and men, Black and white—it was not discrimination on the basis of either race or gender.

Critics attacked the case for ignoring "intersectionality"—or the interrelationships between race and gender. According to law professor Paulette Caldwell:

> Wherever they exist in the world, black women braid their hair. They have done so in the United States for more than four centuries. African in origin, the practice of braiding is as American—black American—as sweet potato pie. A braided hairstyle was first worn in a nationally-televised media event in the United States—and in that sense "popularized"—by a black actress, Cicely Tyson, nearly a decade before the movie "10." More importantly Cicely Tyson's choice to popularize (i.e., to "go public" with) braids, like her choice of acting roles, was a political act made on her own behalf and on behalf of all black women.
>
> The very use of the term "popularized" to describe Bo Derek's wearing of braids—in the sense of rendering suitable to the majority—specifically subordinates and makes invisible all of the black women who for centuries have worn braids in places where they and their hair were not overt threats to the American aesthetic.[307]

How compelling is this critique?

How would you have decided the *Rogers* case? What evidence would have been relevant to your decision? In 2016, the Eleventh Circuit rejected a discrimination claim based on a dreadlocks ban, concluding that "Title VII protects persons in protected categories with respect to their immutable characteristics, but not their cultural

---

304. For a brief summary of the numerous stages of this decade-long litigation, see Jim Walsh, Borgata Babe Servers Can Take Weight-Gain Lawsuit to Jury, Courier-Post, May 20, 2019.

305. Joanna L. Grossman, Hit the Gym, Borgata Babes, Justia's Verdict (Sept. 29, 2015).

306. 527 F. Supp. 229 (S.D.N.Y. 1981).

307. Paulette M. Caldwell, A Hair Piece: Perspectives on the Intersection of Race and Gender, 1991 Duke L.J. 365, 379.

practices."[308] Does that sort of reasoning limit Title VII's ability to address intersectional discrimination?

Angela Onwuachi Willig points out that Harrah's policy requiring women to wear their hair down and teased, curled, and styled at all times is not just gendered but also racially biased, based on an invisibly white gender norm—a norm that would require straightening with a flat iron and/or chemical relaxants.[309] Do you agree?

Federal legislation aimed at prohibiting discrimination based on hair texture and hairstyle, referred to as the Crown ("Creating a Respectful and Open World for Natural Hair") Act, was introduced in the U.S. Congress in the 2019-2020 session, and reintroduced on March 25, 2021. While it has not passed at the federal level, in 2019, California became the first state to enact its version of the Crown Act.[310] As of January 2022, eleven additional states had passed some version of the Crown Act.[311] Is this law likely to solve the problem?

5. **Veiling.**   The practice of veiling, or hijab, involves many different types of coverings of the female body, all of which can be source of discrimination against Muslim women. A meta-analysis of seven studies published between 2010 and 2020 suggests that Muslim women wearing the hijab are 40 percent less likely to be hired,[312] which may help to explain why Muslim women report more discrimination than Muslim men. In one survey, 62.4 percent of Muslim women thought discrimination against Muslims in the United States was a major problem, while only 37.6 percent of men did.[313]

Muslim women identify many reasons for covering. Some engage in the practice out of loyalty to the Muslim communities with whom they identify. Other women may see it as a form of resistance, although what they are resisting may vary. One writer explains that, "[c]ontrary to what outsiders generally suppose, the typical Muslim women in a Muslim city doesn't wear the veil because her grandmother did, but because her grandmother did *not*."[314] Some Muslim women—who tend to be "young, urban, and typically the daughters of migrants from rural areas—deliberately embrace[] the choice to cover, challenging . . . both the secular construction of the headscarf as a means of Islamic male oppression [and] the Islamic

---

308. EEOC v. Catastrophe Mgmt. Sols., 837 F.3d 1156, 1167 (2016).

309. Angela Onwuachi-Willig, Another Hair Piece: Exploring New Strands of Analysis under Title VII, 98 Geo. L. J. 1079 (2010).

310. Cal. S.B. 188 (signed July 3, 2019) (enacted in response to evidence of bias that forced Black women to conform their hair to a "Eurocentric image of professionalism" or lose their jobs).

311. See Discrimination Based on Hair Texture in the United States, Wikipedia, https://en.wikipedia.org/wiki/Discrimination_based_on_hair_texture_in_the_United_States.

312. Sophia Ahmed & Kevin M. Gorey, Employment Discrimination Faced by Muslim Women Wearing the Hijab: Exploratory Meta-Analysis, J. Ethnic & Cultural Diversity in Soc. Work (online Jan. 31, 2021).

313. Nura Sideqe, Muslim Women in Hijab Get the Brunt of Discrimination. I Asked Them What That's Like, Wash. Post, Mar. 28, 2022.

314. Pnina Werbner, Veiled Interventions in Pure Space: Honour, Shame, and Embodied Struggles Among Muslims in Britain and France, 24 Theory, Culture & Soc'y 173 (2007).

masculinist construction of the veil as a protector of women's modesty and place in . . . the domestic sphere."[315] Some Muslim women also embrace covering as a protection from sexual assault and harassment, as well as a challenge to Western imperialism and objectification of women's bodies. "Why is a veil more oppressive than a miniskirt?" asks one woman.[316] Islamic veiling is not just a religious practice," one scholar writes, but "a highly contested political symbol within Muslim societies and the global political arena."[317]

Bans on covering in both Germany and France have been upheld by European Union courts. The German rule, challenged in separate cases by a special needs carer and a sales assistant/cashier, respectively, allows employers to prohibit "any visible form of expression of political, philosophical or religious beliefs in the workplace," so long as it is justified by the employer's "need to present a neutral image before customers and to avoid social disputes." The Court of Justice of the European Union upheld the rule, emphasizing that the need must be "genuine." In addition, the Court stated that a national court may take into account the "specific context" of its member state, and "in particular, more favourable national provisions on the protection of the freedom of religion."[318]

The French case challenged a ban enacted in 2010, making it illegal for anyone to cover their face in a public place.[319] The challenger, a French citizen of Pakistani origin, claimed that the ban was "inhumane and degrading, against the right of respect for family and private life, freedom of thought, conscience and religion, freedom of speech and discriminatory."[320] The French government claimed that the law was not aimed at the veil or the burqa, but at any head covering, including hoods and helmets when not worn on a motor vehicle. The ban was defended on the grounds that it served the purpose of social integration and "the right to interact with someone by looking them in the face and about not disappearing under a piece of clothing." The European Court of Human Rights held that a certain idea of "living together" was a "legitimate aim" of France.[321] The Court had previously upheld bans on headscarves in educational establishments, public buildings, and for purposes of security checks.[322]

In the United States, Title VII requires employers to accommodate the religious practices of their employees, as long as it does not constitute an "undue hardship." Cases applying the undue hardship standard are split. A 1990 Title VII case, for example, upheld the right of a school board to refuse to allow a teacher to wear a hijab on the grounds that accommodating the teacher's religious practice would

---

315. Valorie K. Vojdik, Politics of the Headscarf in Turkey: Masculinities, Feminism, and the Construction of Collective Identities, 33 Harv. J. Law & Gender 664-65 (2010).

316. Estelle Freedman, No Turning Back 223-24 (2002); see Joan Scott, The Politics of the Veil (2007).

317. Vojdik, supra note 315, at 661.

318. Ct. Justice Eur. Union, Press Release (July 15, 2021), https://curia.europa.eu/jcms/upload/docs/application/pdf/2021-07/cp210128en.pdf.

319. See France's Burqa Ban Upheld by Human Rights Court, Guardian (July 1, 2014).

320. Id.

321. Id.

322. See, e.g., Sahin v. Turk., App. 44774/98, Eur. Ct. H.R. (Nov. 11, 2005).

be an undue hardship on the school.[323] In a case against Alamo Rent-A-Car, on the other hand, the rental car agency was found to have violated Title VII when it fired a woman for not removing her headscarf during the holy month of Ramadan. In 1999 and 2000, Alamo had allowed the wearing of headscarves, but it changed its policy after 9/11.[324] More recently Disney Corporation discharged a Muslim woman as a restaurant hostess after she began wearing a hijab and would not accept proposed accommodations that would have moved her to the back of the restaurant or required her to wear a large hat to mitigate the conspicuous nature of the head covering.[325]

Should employees wearing visible signs of their religion be required to move to the back office in such circumstances? How broad an expansion of Title VII should there be to accommodate persons practicing the Muslim faith?[326]

6. **Sex and Age.** Sex and age can be a devastating combination, particularly for women. Even in jobs where appearance is considered less important, older women earn lower salaries than men and younger women, and they may lack opportunities to obtain higher-paying and more prestigious jobs.[327] Older women's concerns about the economic and social consequences of "letting themselves go" is part of what has fueled the dramatic increase in cosmetic procedures, which have more than doubled since the turn of the twenty-first century.[328] The silver hair and furrowed brows that make aging men look distinguished carry a different meaning for aging women, yet those who attempt to camouflage the problem risk ridicule for efforts to pass as young.[329]

In the case involving Christine Craft, discussed in Note 2, above, the network determined, based in part on focus group input, that Craft was "too old, too unattractive and wouldn't defer to men." Two separate juries awarded her $500,000 in damages, but her awards were overturned by the Eighth Circuit Court of Appeals and the United States Supreme Court denied review.[330] With the increase in the numbers of female news anchors, discrimination based on age and sex may seem

323. U.S. v. Bd. of Educ. for Sch. Dist. of Phila., 911 F.2d 882 (3d Cir. 1990).
324. See EEOC v. Alamo Rent-A-Car, 432 F. Supp. 2d 1006 (D. Ariz. 2006); see also, EEOC, Alamo Car Rental Guilty of Religious Bias Federal Court Rules in EEOC Lawsuit, Press Release, May 30, 2006 (described as example of post-9/11 backlash bias).
325. This case is described in Nida Alvi, Dressed to Oppress? An Analysis of the Legal Treatment of the First Amendment and Its Effect on Muslim Women Who Wear Hijabs, 21 Cardozo J.L. & Gender 785, 796-98 (2015). The case eventually settled.
326. See Sahar F. Aziz, Coercive Assimilationism, The Perils of Muslim Women's Identity Performance in the Workplace, Mich. J. Race & L. 1 (2014) (arguing for a broad expansion to alleviate the many stereotypes and identity performance challenges and contradictions faced by Muslim women).
327. See Nicole Buonocore Porter, Sex Plus Age Discrimination: Protecting Older Women Workers, 81 Denv. U. L. Rev. 79, 94-99 (2003).
328. Joel Stein, Nip. Tuck. Or Else: Why You'll Be Getting Cosmetic Procedures Even if You Don't Really Want To, Time, June 29, 2015, at 45. According to one researcher, cosmetic surgery has become the "new makeup." Id. (quoting Abigail Brooks).
329. Jessica Bennett, I Am (an Older) Woman. Hear Me Roar, N.Y. Times, Jan. 8, 2019, at A1 (quoting Rhode's Beauty Bias).
330. See Craft, supra note 287.

like less of a problem today. Yet the age-gender gap remains, with male broadcast journalists, on average, being seven years older than their female counterparts.[331]

The Borgata Babes lawsuit, discussed above, also included an age component. In that case, cocktail servers, including women aged 54, 57, and 66, claimed that they had been dismissed after having to audition in "skimpy flapper" costumes. Gloria Allred, who represented the women, maintained that maybe owners believed that "they can profit by using young women as bait to hook in young men to buy drinks, but it's wrong. Women are not just sex objects."[332] One commentator responded, "The whole point of being a cocktail waitress in a casino is to be a sex object. . . . And eventually, grandma needs to take off the cocktail underwear."[333] Who is right?

7. **Laws Against Discrimination Based on Appearance.**   A few jurisdictions have specific prohibitions against appearance discrimination. Michigan and San Francisco ban discrimination based on height and weight. Local ordinances in the District of Columbia; Madison, Wisconsin; Urbana, Illinois; Santa Cruz, California; and several counties in Maryland ban appearance discrimination more generally, although often with certain exceptions such as for grooming requirements or for characteristics within an individual's control.[334]

Should more jurisdictions enact such prohibitions? In one opinion poll, 39 percent of Americans believed that employers should be allowed to discriminate based on appearance, and 33 percent thought they should not.[335] Scholars are also divided. Some worry that extending civil rights acts to such claims will erode support for such legislation and trivialize what they view as more serious forms of bias. Law professor Richard Ford frames a common objection:

> [T]here are practical limits of human attention and sympathy. The good-natured humanitarian who listens attentively to the first claim of social injustice will become an impatient curmudgeon after multiple similar admonishments. . . . And a business community united in frustration at a bloated civil rights regime could become a powerful political force for reform or even repeal. . . . The growing number of social groups making claims to civil rights protection threatens the political and practical viability of civil rights for those who need them most.
>
> The law can identify a small set of social prejudices — race, sex, religion, national origin, age and disability — that are so unjustified and

---

331. Broadcast Journalist Demographics and Statistics in the US, Zippia (Dec. 14, 2021).

332. Elie Mystal, Women Are Not Sex Objects; Cocktail Waitresses, on the Other Hand . . . , Above the Law (May 31, 2011) (quoting Allred).

333. Id.

334. See, e.g., District of Columbia Code § 2-1401.01 (2022); Prince George's County, MD, Code §§ 2-186 (14) and 2-185 (2022); Howard County, MD, Code §§ 12.200 and 12.201 (xy) (2022); Harford County, MD, Code §§ 95-3 and 95-5 (2022); Urbana, Ill., Municipal Code § 12-37 (amended version enacted Nov. 19, 2018 (Supp. No 42)).

335. Press Release, Employment Law Alliance, National Poll Shows Public Opinion Sharply Divided on Regulating Appearance — From Weight to Tattoos — in the Workplace (Mar. 22, 2005).

so socially destructive that we're confident that the benefits of prohibiting them outweigh the costs. . . . But there are limits. . . . It's a mistake
to turn civil rights against truly invidious discrimination into an omnibus
requirement that we reward intrinsic merit. . . . The fantastic aspiration
to somehow make society perfectly "fair" through force of law reflects a
dangerous combination of gauzy idealism, narcissistic entitlement and
reckless hubris.[336]

Is this a fair point? One survey of appearance discrimination laws concluded
that they remedied some of the worst abuses and attracted public attention to the
problem without evidence of such backlash. It also found, however, that there was
limited enforcement activity surrounding these laws, partly due to the costs and
difficulties of proof and the limited remedies available.[337] This raises the question
whether these laws are worth the trouble. What other policy strategies might be
useful?

8. **Feminism and Appearance.**   Issues of appearance have long been divisive
issues for feminists. While some leaders of the women's movement have denounced
makeup, high heels, and cosmetic surgery as forms of objectification and subordination, other feminists (sometimes referring to themselves as "sex-positive"[338]) see
them as sources of pleasure and agency. Where do you fall in this debate?

For example, what do you make of the choice by many powerful women,
including outspoken feminists, to wear stylish but uncomfortable shoes? One successful personal injury trial lawyer told an Atlantic reporter that she always wears
heels in front of a jury "unless I am in pain." In one case when her tendons were
inflamed and she had worn flats, a female juror told her afterwards that "she had
not cared for her shoes."[339] In her book *Becoming*, Michelle Obama describes an
occasion in which she exchanged pleasantries with the Queen of England and the
subject quickly turned to footwear:

"These shoes are unpleasant, are they not?" [the Queen] said. She ges-
tured with some frustration at her own black pumps. I confessed to the
Queen that my feet were hurting. She confessed that hers hurt too. For-
getting that she sometimes wore a diamond crown and that I'd flown to
London on the presidential jet, we were just two tired ladies oppressed by
their shoes.[340]

Some women claim to feel more confident, powerful, and attractive when
wearing high heels. What are the implications of that fact?

Is there a way to find common ground among feminists by focusing not on
individual practices but on social forces that shame and stigmatize non-conforming

---

336. Richard Ford, The Race Card 176-77 (2007).

337. Rhode, The Injustice of Appearance, supra note 270, at 1095-96.

338. See, e.g., Susan Frelich Appleton, Sex-Positive Feminism's Values in Search of the
Law of Pleasure, in the Oxford Handbook of Feminism & Law in the United States (Deborah L. Brake, Martha Chamallas & Verna L. Williams, eds., forthcoming 2022).

339. Lara Bazelon, Female Lawyers Still Face Sexism in the Courtroom, Atlantic, Sept.
2018 (quoting Kila Baldwin).

340. Michelle Obama, Becoming 318 (2018).

women, and that fail to provide sufficient safeguards against unsafe or fraudulent cosmetic practices? Consider Rhode's view:

> The overemphasis of attractiveness diminishes women's credibility and diverts attention from their capabilities and accomplishments. In the long run, these are more stable sources of self-esteem and social power than appearance. Prevailing beauty standards also place women in a double bind. They are expected to conform yet condemned as vain and narcissistic for attempts to do so. Neither should they "let themselves go," nor look as if they were trying too hard not to. Beauty must seem natural, even, or especially, when it can only be accomplished through considerable unnatural effort . . . . Feminists are in a particularly problematic situation. Those who defy conventional standards are ridiculed as homely harpies; those who comply are dismissed as hypocrites.
>
> Whatever their other disagreements on these issues, most individuals appear to share certain core values. Appearance should be a source of pleasure, not of shame. Individuals should be able to make decisions about whether to enhance their attractiveness without being judged politically incorrect or professionally unacceptable. Our ideals of appearance should reflect diversity across race, ethnicity, age, and body size. In this ideal world, the importance of appearance would not be overstated. Nor would it spill over to employment and educational contexts in which judgments should be based on competence, not cosmetics. Women would not be held to higher standards than men. Neither would they be subject to sexualized grooming requirements unless sex is the commodity being sold. Women's self-esteem would be tied to accomplishment, not appearance. In order for appearance to be a source of enjoyment rather than anxiety, it cannot dictate women's self-worth.[341]

Do you agree? Is a unifying agenda for feminists possible on this issue? How important is such unification? Is fighting appearance discrimination a fruitless diversion from more important battles? Comedian Joan Rivers advised women, "It's the way things are, accept it, or go live under a rock."[342] How would you respond?

9. *Jespersen* **and Its Aftermath.**   The lineup of votes in *Jespersen* was somewhat surprising. Judge Mary Schroeder, who wrote the majority decision, is widely viewed as liberal, while Judge Alex Kozinski, one of the nation's most prominent conservative judges at the time, dissented. Some have speculated that Schroeder was aware that Jespersen would lose and voted with the majority to assign herself the opinion and to minimize its negative impact on discrimination law. Others have suggested that she decided that the burdens involved were relatively trivial and wanted to discourage comparable litigation.

Follow-up research suggests that although Harrah's changed its policy, the decision has not significantly influenced practices in the casino industry and has

---

341. Rhode, Beauty Bias, supra note 268, at 76, 87.

342. Emily Nussbaum, Last Girl in Larchmont, New Yorker, Feb. 23 & Mar. 2, 2015, at 171 (quoting Rivers).

not triggered further lawsuits. Part of the reason is that female workers generally view makeup as a means of ensuring good tips, and lawyers do not believe these cases are sufficiently remunerative to file.[343] Do either of these factors strengthen, or weaken, the rationale in *Jespersen*?

Is there any reason to expect that challenges to dress and appearance regulations would fare any better in the educational context, under Title IX of the Education Amendments of 1972, than they have under Title VII? If anything, one might expect *more* deference to be given to the judgments of school administrators about what their students should wear. Yet a recent decision by the Fourth Circuit Court of Appeals, sitting en banc, explicitly rejects the reasoning of *Jespersen* in the context of a challenge to a charter school's "skirt-only" requirement for girls. The Court held that the requirement violated both the Equal Protection Clause and Title IX.[344] The case is excerpted in Chapter 2, SectionC3.

PUTTING THEORY INTO PRACTICE

1-34. Shortly before Brett Kavanaugh's confirmation as a Justice of the Supreme Court, stories broke in The Guardian and Slate reporting that Yale law students claimed that two law professors had coached women applying for clerkships that the Judge liked a "certain look" among his female clerks, and that it was "not an accident" that all of them "looked like models."[345] The professors denied the allegations, but the Dean announced that they were of "enormous concern" and would be fully investigated.[346] If the allegations had been substantiated, what action should the school have taken?

1-35. In 2019, Univia, a cosmetics company, polled 997 employed adults, 26 percent of whom reported appearance discrimination at work, and 70 percent of whom believed that appearance is the deciding factor in the hiring process. The authors of the study concluded that "it might be worth taking a second look at how you choose to wake up and present yourself to the world. Are you choosing behaviors, clothing, and self-care practices that best prepared you for a successful day at work?"[347] To what extent do you think commercial advertising affects appearance norms?

1-36. A retail sales manager for L'Oreal USA, a prominent cosmetics and fragrance company, complained about hostile adverse treatment after she refused to

---

343. Tracey E. George et al., The New Old Legal Realism, 105 Nw. L. Rev. 689, 715-16, 723, 727 (2011); Rhode, Beauty Bias, supra note 268, at 14.

344. See Peltier, 37 F.4th 102 (4th Cir. 2022) (en banc).

345. Stephanie Kirchgaessner & Jessica Glenza, "No Accident" Brett Kavanaugh's Female Law Clerks "looked like models," Yale Professor Told Students, Guardian, Sept. 20, 2018; Dahlia Lithwick & Susan Matthews, Investigation at Yale Law School, Slate (Oct. 5, 2018).

346. Adam Edelman & Kasie Hunt, Yale Law Dean: Reports That Professor Groomed Female Clerks for Kavanaugh of "Enormous Concern," NBC News (Sept. 20, 2018).

347. See C. W. Headley, Nearly 70% of Employees Believe That Appearance is the Deciding Factor in the Hiring Process, Ladders, Oct. 22, 2019.

fire a female sales associate who was not sufficiently sexually attractive or "hot." Should such adverse treatment be considered a form of sex discrimination, in violation of employment discrimination law?[348]

1-37. A temporary worker, Nicola Thorp, was sent home from at her receptionist job at PricewaterhouseCoopers in east London for wearing flat shoes, rather than the two-inch to four-inch high heels required by her agency, Portico. "If you can give me a reason as to why wearing flats would impair me to do my job today, then fair enough," she is reported as saying, "but they couldn't. I was expected to do a nine-hour shift on my feet escorting clients to meeting rooms. I said I just won't be able to do that in heels."[349]

Would Thorp prevail under U.S. law? Would it be relevant that 90 percent of all forefoot surgery is performed on women, and that "seventy-five percent of the problems eventuating in [the foot] corrections performed annually in the United States either result from or are greatly aggravated by the use of high-fashion footwear."[350] Or would it matter that, in addition to the adverse health consequences, high heels long served as a symbol of what sociologist Thorstein Veblen described as "the wearer's abstinence from productive employment"?[351]

1-38. At the Seventh Circuit Annual Judicial Conference, some judges complained of distracting attire—"blouses so short there's no way the judges wouldn't look" and a velour outfit that looked as if the lawyer was "on her way home from the gym."[352] Is it appropriate for firms to monitor what lawyers wear to court on the grounds that some judges have complained about overly sexy or informal attire? Is it appropriate for judges to comment publicly on women's attire? How about if the judges also regularly criticize male lawyers who fail to wear a tie, or come to court in crumpled trousers?

1-39. Jazzercise refused a franchise to Jennifer Portnick, a 245-pound aerobics instructor, on the ground that the company sold "fitness." According to its lawyer, "One of the keys to success is extending franchises to instructors with a fit, toned body. Being able to portray this image inspires students. The fit and toned body image is a necessary part of what students seek to achieve." Portnick was in fact fit. She worked out six days a week, taught back-to-back exercise classes, and had no history of performance problems or lack of students. Can she win a lawsuit against Jazzercise under San Francisco's ordinance banning discrimination based

---

348. Yanowitz v. L'Oreal U.S.A., 32 Cal. Rptr.3d 436 (Cal. 2005) (no, under state law, referencing Title VII, because supervisor did not sufficiently communicate reasonable concerns that the employer acted in an unlawful discriminatory manner).

349. Nadia Khomami, Receptionist "Sent Home from PwC for Not Wearing High Heels," Guardian, May 11, 2016. After Ms. Thorp started a petition drive for a parliamentary hearing on the subject, Portico changed its policy. Id.

350. See Marc Linder, Smart Women, Stupid Shoes, and Cynical Employers: The Unlawfulness and Adverse Health Consequences of Sexually Discriminatory Workplace Footwear Requirements for Female Employees, J. Corp. L. 295, 296 (Winter 1997).

351. Thorstein Veblen, The Theory of the Leisure Class: An Economic Study of Institutions 121 (1899).

352. John Schwartz, At a Symposium of Judges, a Debate on the Laws of Fashion, N.Y. Times, May 23, 2009, at A10.

on height or weight, or is the company legally justified in refusing to be associated with an instructor because of the stereotypes some students might have about being overweight?[353]

1-40. In 2013, at a public event with California's then-Attorney General Kamala Harris, President Barack Obama stated, "You have to be careful to, first of all, say she is brilliant and she is dedicated and she is tough, and she is exactly what you'd want in anybody who is administering the law, and making sure that everybody is getting a fair shake. She also happens to be by far the best-looking attorney general in the country." When the crowd began laughing, Obama added, "It's true! C'mon."[354] Public outcry was immediate. Within hours, the President called Harris to apologize. According to White House spokesperson Jay Carney, "They are old friends and good friends and he did not want in any way to diminish the attorney general's professional accomplishments and her capabilities."[355]

Media commentary was mixed. In an article headlined, "Obama in Need of Gender Sensitivity Training," Jonathan Chait of New York Magazine claimed that Obama's comment "was not a compliment," and that the example he set was "disgraceful."[356] By contrast, Jonathan Capehart of the Washington Post commented, "Lighten up, people. You'd swear the President was guilty of luridly cat-calling a woman he doesn't know."[357] Similarly, Liza Minnelli didn't see anything wrong with Obama's compliment. After all, she pointed out, Harris was applying makeup and styling her hair in order to "be thought of as attractive. She's not doing that for no reason."[358]

If you were commenting on the incident, what would you say? How would you respond to an Asian-American author who wrote an op-ed objecting to all the people who had commented favorably on her appearance at literary events? "Stop calling Asian women adorable," she suggested. In professional contexts, "don't comment on [their] appearance at all."[359]

1-41. Sarah Robles, who is 23 years old and weighs 275 pounds, is the highest-ranked weightlifter of either gender in the United States. Robles had trouble gaining a corporate sponsor, requiring her to live on a subsistence allowance from the U.S. Weightlifting Federation while she trained for the 2016 Olympics. Critics claimed that the lack of corporate support for Robles is due to her masculine appearance, pointing out that only female athletes who are feminine and attractive receive lucrative sponsorships (including two slimmer, though less accomplished,

---

353. Letter from C. Robert Sturm, Law Firm of Littler Mendelson, to the San Francisco Commission on Human Rights, Oct. 26, 2001, at 6. The case was mediated to a successful resolution and the complaint dismissed.

354. Eun Kyungh Kim, Obama Apologizes to Kamala Harris for "Best Looking Attorney General" Comment, Today (Apr. 5, 2013) (quoting Obama).

355. Id. (quoting Carney).

356. Jonathan Chait, Obama in Need of Gender-Sensitivity Training, N.Y. Mag., Apr. 4, 2013.

357. Kim, supra note 354 (quoting Capehart).

358. Id. (quoting Minnelli).

359. R. O. Kwon, Stop Calling Asian Women Adorable, N.Y. Times, Mar. 24, 2019, at SR3.

female weightlifters). Former professional basketball player Lisa Leslie appears in one Nike ad, stating, "I'm a fashion model who can dunk."

Is it sex discrimination for corporations to support only attractive female athletes and not more accomplished ones?

1-42. Employees at Twin Peaks, a Dallas-based "breastaurant," filed a charge with the EEOC alleging sex discrimination. According to the complaint, the managers engaged in several objectionable practices: (i) hiring women to wear one uniform but ordering them to wear bikinis and lingerie instead; (ii) insisting on uniforms that resulted in police citations for indecent exposure; (iii) requiring women to change into skimpy outfits in front of kitchen staff; (iv) requiring women to shop for revealing clothing and text photos from the dressing room to their bosses who could evaluate whether they were revealing enough for work; (v) subjecting women to weekly "tone grade" evaluations in which they were rated based on body, hair, and makeup; and (vi) allowing them to eat only from a special low-calorie "spa" menu at work.[360] Which, if any, of these practices constitute unlawful gender discrimination? Why? Does it matter whether all the employees are female?

c. When Is Sex a "Bona Fide Occupational Qualification"?

Once plaintiffs demonstrate that they have been treated differently on the basis of sex, employers are liable under Title VII unless they can meet the high burden of showing that sex is a bona fide occupational qualification (BFOQ).[361] For cases brought under the disparate impact theory of Title VII, the employer must meet the somewhat lower burden of "business necessity." Can you think of particular jobs where sex should be either a BFOQ or a business necessity?

Dothard v. Rawlinson

433 U.S. 321 (1977)

Mr. Justice STEWART delivered the opinion of the Court.

Appellee Dianne Rawlinson sought employment with the Alabama Board of Corrections as a prison guard, called in Alabama a "correctional counselor." After her application was rejected, she brought this class suit under Title VII of the Civil Rights Act of 1964 . . . .

At the time she applied for a position as correctional counselor trainee, Rawlinson was a 22-year-old college graduate whose major course of study had been correctional psychology. She was refused employment because she failed to meet the minimum 120-pound weight requirement established by an Alabama statute. The statute also establishes a height minimum of 5 feet 2 inches. [Rawlinson subsequently amended her complaint to challenge Alabama Administrative Regulation

---

360. Erica Demarest & Dana Rebik, Employees at Chicago-Area Twin Peaks Say They Were Graded on Looks, Forced to Wear Lingerie, WGN 9 (Apr. 26, 2018).

361. Under the terms of the statute, the BFOQ defense does not apply to discrimination on the basis of race or color; it is only a defense to discrimination based on the protected classes of sex, national origin, and religion.

204 that established a "gender criteria" for assigning correctional counselors to "contact positions" requiring close physical proximity to inmates.] . . .

Like most correctional facilities in the United States, Alabama's prisons are segregated on the basis of sex. . . . A correctional counselor's primary duty within these institutions is to maintain security and control of the inmates by continually supervising and observing their activities. . . .

At the time this litigation was in the District Court, the Board of Corrections employed a total of 435 people in various correctional counselor positions, 56 of whom were women. Of those 56 women, 21 were employed at the Julia Tutwiler Prison for Women, 13 were employed in noncontact positions at the four male maximum-security institutions, and the remaining 22 were employed at the other institutions operated by the Alabama Board of Corrections. Because most of Alabama's prisoners are held at the four maximum-security male penitentiaries, 336 of the 435 correctional counselor jobs were in those institutions, a majority of them concededly in the "contact" classification. Thus, even though meeting the statutory height and weight requirements, women applicants could under Regulation 204 compete equally with men for only about 25% of the correctional counselor jobs available in the Alabama prison system. . . .

It is asserted . . . that these facially neutral qualifications standards work . . . disproportionately to exclude women from eligibility for employment by the Alabama Board of Corrections. We dealt in Griggs v. Duke Power Co. [1971] [and other cases] with similar allegations that facially neutral employment standards disproportionately excluded Negroes from employment, and those cases guide our approach here.

Those cases make clear that to establish a prima facie case of discrimination, a plaintiff need only show that the facially neutral standards in question select applicants for hire in a significantly discriminatory pattern. Once it is thus shown that the employment standards are discriminatory in effect, the employer must meet "the burden of showing that any given requirement (has) . . . a manifest relationship to the employment in question [*Griggs*]." If the employer proves that the challenged requirements are job related, the plaintiff may then show that other selection devices without a similar discriminatory effect would also "serve the employer's legitimate interest in 'efficient and trustworthy workmanship.' " . . .

. . . In considering the effect of the minimum height and weight standards on this disparity in rate of hiring between the sexes, the District Court found that . . . [w]hen the height and weight restrictions are combined, Alabama's statutory standards would exclude 41.13% of the female population while excluding less than 1% of the male population. Accordingly, the District Court found that Rawlinson had made out a prima facie case of unlawful sex discrimination.

The appellants argue that a showing of disproportionate impact on women based on generalized national statistics should not suffice to establish a prima facie case. They point in particular to Rawlinson's failure to adduce comparative statistics concerning actual applicants for correctional counselor positions in Alabama. There is no requirement, however, that a statistical showing of disproportionate impact must always be based on analysis of the characteristics of actual applicants. . . . The application process might itself not adequately reflect the actual potential applicant pool, since otherwise qualified people might be discouraged from applying because of a self-recognized inability to meet the very standards challenged as being discriminatory. . . . A potential applicant could easily determine her height and weight and conclude that to make an application would be futile. Moreover, reliance on general population demographic data was not misplaced where there was no reason to suppose that physical height and weight characteristics of Alabama men and women differ markedly from those of the national population.

For these reasons, we cannot say that the District Court was wrong in holding that the statutory height and weight standards had a discriminatory impact on women applicants. . . .

We turn, therefore, to the appellants' argument that they have rebutted the prima facie case of discrimination by showing that the height and weight requirements are job related. These requirements, they say, have a relationship to strength, a sufficient but unspecified amount of which is essential to effective job performance as a correctional counselor. In the District Court, however, the appellants produced no evidence correlating the height and weight requirements with the requisite amount of strength thought essential to good job performance. Indeed, they failed to offer evidence of any kind in specific justification of the statutory standards. . . .

[T]he District Court was not in error in holding that Title VII . . . prohibits application of the statutory height and weight requirements to Rawlinson and the class she represents.

III

Unlike the statutory height and weight requirements, Regulation 204 [excluding women from maximum security "contact positions"] explicitly discriminates against women on the basis of their sex. In defense of this overt discrimination, the appellants rely on [Title VII's BFOQ defense], which permits sex-based discrimination "in those certain instances where . . . sex . . . is a bona fide occupational qualification reasonably necessary to the normal operation of that particular business or enterprise." . . .

We are persuaded by the restrictive language of [Title VII], the relevant legislative history, and the consistent interpretation of the Equal Employment Opportunity Commission that the BFOQ exception was in fact meant to be an extremely narrow exception to the general prohibition of discrimination on the basis of sex. In the particular factual circumstances of this case, however, we conclude that the District Court erred in rejecting the State's contention that Regulation 204 falls within the narrow ambit of the BFOQ exception.

The environment in Alabama's penitentiaries is a peculiarly inhospitable one for human beings of whatever sex. Indeed, a Federal District Court has held that the conditions of confinement in the prisons of the State, characterized by "rampant violence" and a "jungle atmosphere," are constitutionally intolerable. . . . The record in the present case shows that because of inadequate staff and facilities, no attempt is made in the four maximum-security male penitentiaries to classify or segregate inmates according to their offense or level of dangerousness — a procedure that, according to expert testimony, is essential to effective penological administration. Consequently, the estimated 20% of the male prisoners who are sex offenders are scattered throughout the penitentiaries' dormitory facilities.

In this environment of violence and disorganization, it would be an oversimplification to characterize Regulation 204 as an exercise in "romantic paternalism." [Frontiero v. Richardson.] In the usual case, the argument that a particular job is too dangerous for women may appropriately be met by the rejoinder that it is the purpose of Title VII to allow the individual woman to make that choice for herself. More is at stake in this case, however, than an individual woman's decision to weigh and accept the risks of employment in a "contact" position in a maximum-security male prison.

The essence of a correctional counselor's job is to maintain prison security. A woman's relative ability to maintain order in a male, maximum-security, unclassified penitentiary of the type Alabama now runs could be directly reduced by her womanhood. There is a basis in fact for expecting that sex offenders who have criminally assaulted women in the past would be moved to do so again if access to women were established within the prison. There would also be a real risk that other inmates, deprived of a normal heterosexual environment, would assault women guards because they were women.[22] In a prison system where violence is the order of the day, where inmate access to guards is facilitated by dormitory living arrangements, where every institution is understaffed, and where a substantial portion of the inmate population is composed of sex offenders mixed at random with other prisoners, there are few visible deterrents to inmate assaults on women custodians.

Appellee Rawlinson's own expert testified that dormitory housing for aggressive inmates poses a greater security problem than single-cell lockups, and further testified that it would be unwise to use women as guards in a prison where even 10% of the inmates had been convicted of sex crimes and were not segregated from the other prisoners. The likelihood that inmates would assault a woman because she was a woman would pose a real threat not only to the victim of the assault but also to the basic control of the penitentiary and protection of its inmates and the other security personnel. The employee's very womanhood would thus directly undermine her capacity to provide the security that is the essence of a correctional counselor's responsibility. . . .

The judgment is accordingly affirmed in part and reversed in part, and the case is remanded to the District Court for further proceedings consistent with this opinion. . . .

Mr. Justice MARSHALL, with whom Mr. Justice BRENNAN joins, concurring in part and dissenting in part. . . .

The Court properly rejects two proffered justifications for denying women jobs as prison guards. It is simply irrelevant here that a guard's occupation is dangerous and that some women might be unable to protect themselves adequately. Those themes permeate the testimony of the state officials below, but as the Court holds, "the argument that a particular job is too dangerous for women" is refuted

---

22. The record contains evidence of an attack on a female clerical worker in an Alabama prison, and of an incident involving a woman student who was taken hostage during a visit to one of the maximum-security institutions.

by the "purpose of Title VII to allow the individual woman to make that choice for herself." . . . Some women, like some men, undoubtedly are not qualified and do not wish to serve as prison guards, but that does not justify the exclusion of all women from this employment opportunity. . . .

What would otherwise be considered unlawful discrimination against women is justified by the Court, however, on the basis of the "barbaric and inhumane" conditions in Alabama prisons, conditions so bad that state officials have conceded that they violate the Constitution. . . . To me, this analysis sounds distressingly like saying two wrongs make a right. It is refuted by the plain words of [Title VII, which] requires that a BFOQ be "reasonably necessary to the normal operation of that particular business or enterprise." But no governmental "business" may operate "normally" in violation of the Constitution. . . .

The Court's error in statutory construction is less objectionable, however, than the attitude it displays toward women. Though the Court recognizes that possible harm to women guards is an unacceptable reason for disqualifying women, it relies instead on an equally speculative threat to prison discipline supposedly generated by the sexuality of female guards. There is simply no evidence in the record to show that women guards would create any danger to security in Alabama prisons significantly greater than that which already exists. All of the dangers with one exception discussed below are inherent in a prison setting, whatever the gender of the guards.

The Court first sees women guards as a threat to security because "there are few visible deterrents to inmate assaults on women custodians." . . . In fact, any prison guard is constantly subject to the threat of attack by inmates, and "invisible" deterrents are the guard's only real protection. No prison guard relies primarily on his or her ability to ward off an inmate attack to maintain order. Guards are typically unarmed and sheer numbers of inmates could overcome the normal complement. Rather, like all other law enforcement officers, prison guards must rely primarily on the moral authority of their office and the threat of future punishment for miscreants. As one expert testified below, common sense, fairness, and mental and emotional stability are the qualities a guard needs to cope with the dangers of the job. . . . Well qualified and properly trained women, no less than men, have these psychological weapons at their disposal.

The particular severity of discipline problems in the Alabama maximum-security prisons is also no justification for the discrimination sanctioned by the Court. . . . If male guards face an impossible situation, it is difficult to see how women could make the problem worse, unless one relies on precisely the type of generalized bias against women that the Court agrees Title VII was intended to outlaw. For example, much of the testimony of appellants' witnesses ignores individual differences among members of each sex and reads like "ancient canards about the proper role of women." . . . The witnesses claimed that women guards are not strict disciplinarians; that they are physically less capable of protecting themselves and subduing unruly inmates; that inmates take advantage of them as they did their mothers, while male guards are strong father figures who easily maintain discipline, and so on. Yet the record shows that the presence of women guards has not led to a single incident amounting to a serious breach of security in any Alabama institution.[3] And, in any event, "[g]uards rarely enter the cell blocks and dormitories" . . . where the danger of inmate attacks is the greatest.

It appears that the real disqualifying factor in the Court's view is "[t]he employee's very womanhood." . . . The Court refers to the large number of sex offenders in Alabama prisons, and to "[t]he likelihood that inmates would assault a woman because she was a woman." . . . In short, the fundamental justification for the decision is that women as guards will generate sexual assaults. With all respect, this rationale regrettably perpetuates one of the most insidious of the old myths about women that women, wittingly or not, are seductive sexual objects. The effect of the decision, made I am sure with the best of intentions, is to punish women because their very presence might provoke sexual assaults. It is women who are made to pay the price in lost job opportunities for the threat of depraved conduct by prison inmates. Once again, "[t]he pedestal upon which women have been placed has . . . , upon closer inspection, been revealed as a cage." . . . It is particularly ironic that the cage is erected here in response to feared misbehavior by imprisoned criminals.

The proper response to inevitable attacks on both female and male guards is not to limit the employment opportunities of law-abiding women who wish to contribute to their community, but to take swift and sure punitive action against the inmate offenders. Presumably, one of the goals of the Alabama prison system is the eradication of inmates' antisocial behavior patterns so that prisoners will be able to live one day in free society. Sex offenders can begin this process by learning to relate to women guards in a socially acceptable manner. To deprive women of job opportunities because of the threatened behavior of convicted criminals is to turn our social priorities upside down.[5] . . .

---

3. The Court refers to two incidents involving potentially dangerous attacks on women in prisons. . . . But these did not involve trained corrections officers; one victim was a clerical worker and the other a student visiting on a tour.

5. The appellants argue that restrictions on employment of women are also justified by consideration of inmates' privacy. It is strange indeed to hear state officials who have for years been violating the most basic principles of human decency in the operation of their prisons suddenly become concerned about inmate privacy. It is stranger still that these same officials allow women guards in contact positions in a number of non-maximum-security institutions, but strive to protect inmates' privacy in the prisons where personal freedom is most severely restricted. I have no doubt on this record that appellants' professed concern is nothing but a feeble excuse for discrimination. As the District Court suggested, it may well be possible, once a constitutionally adequate staff is available, to rearrange work assignments so that legitimate inmate privacy concerns are respected without denying jobs to women. Finally, if women guards behave in a professional manner at all times, they will engender reciprocal respect from inmates, who will recognize that their privacy is being invaded no more than if a woman doctor examines them. The suggestion implicit in the privacy argument that such behavior is unlikely on either side is an insult to the professionalism of guards and the dignity of inmates.

Wilson v. Southwest Airlines Co.

517 F. Supp. 292 (N.D. Tex. 1981)

HIGGINBOTHAM, District Judge.

This case presents the important question whether femininity, or more accurately female sex appeal, is a bona fide occupational qualification ("BFOQ") for the jobs of flight attendant and ticket agent with Southwest Airlines. Plaintiff Gregory Wilson and the class of over 100 male job applicants he represents have challenged Southwest's open refusal to hire males as a violation of Title VII. . . .

At the phase one trial on liability, Southwest conceded that its refusal to hire males was intentional. . . . Southwest contends, however, that the BFOQ exception to Title VII's ban on sex discrimination justifies its hiring only females for the public contact positions of flight attendant and ticket agent. The BFOQ window through which Southwest attempts to fly permits sex discrimination in situations where the employer can prove that sex is a "bona fide occupational qualification reasonably necessary to the normal operation of that particular business or enterprise." Southwest reasons it may discriminate against males because its attractive female flight attendants and ticket agents personify the airline's sexy image and fulfill its public promise to take passengers skyward with "love." Defendant claims maintenance of its females-only hiring policy is crucial to the airline's continued financial success. . . .

FACTUAL BACKGROUND . . .

Southwest was incorporated in March of 1967 and . . . as a result of the defensive tactics of Southwest's competitors . . . [i]n December of 1970, Southwest had $143 in the bank and was over $100,000 in debt, though no aircraft had ever left the ground.

Barely intact, Southwest, in early 1971, called upon a Dallas advertising agency, the Bloom Agency, to develop a winning marketing strategy. Planning to initiate service quickly, Southwest needed instant recognition and a "catchy" image to distinguish it from its competitors.

The Bloom Agency evaluated both the images of the incumbent competitor airlines as well as the characteristics of passengers to be served by a commuter airline. Bloom determined that the other carriers serving the Texas market tended to project an image of conservatism. The agency also determined that the relatively short haul commuter market which Southwest hoped to serve was comprised of predominantly male businessmen. Based on these factors, Bloom suggested that Southwest break away from the conservative image of other airlines and project to the traveling public an airline personification of feminine youth and vitality. A specific female personality description was recommended and adopted by Southwest for its corporate image: This lady is young and vital . . . she is charming and goes through life with great flair and exuberance . . . you notice first her exciting smile, friendly air, her wit . . . yet she is quite efficient and approaches all her tasks with care and attention. . . .

From the personality description suggested by The Bloom Agency, Southwest developed its now famous "Love" personality. Southwest projects an image of feminine spirit, fun, and sex appeal. Its ads promise to provide "tender loving care" to its predominantly male, business passengers. The first advertisements run by the airline featured the slogan, "AT LAST THERE IS SOMEBODY ELSE UP THERE WHO LOVES YOU." Variations on this theme have continued through newspaper, billboard, magazine and television advertisements during the past ten years.[4] . . .

Over the years, Southwest gained national and international attention as the "love airline." Southwest Airlines' stock is traded on the New York Stock Exchange under the ticker symbol "LUV." During 1977 when Southwest opened five additional markets in Texas, the love theme was expanded to "WE'RE SPREADING LOVE ALL OVER TEXAS."

As an integral part of its youthful, feminine image, Southwest has employed only females in the high customer contact positions of ticket agent and flight attendant. From the start, Southwest's attractive personnel, dressed in high boots and hot-pants, generated public interest and "free ink." Their sex appeal has been used to attract male customers to the airline. . . . The airline also encourages its attendants to entertain the passengers and maintain an atmosphere of informality and "fun" during flights. According to Southwest, its female flight attendants have come to "personify" Southwest's public image.

Southwest has enjoyed enormous success in recent years.[6] This is in no small part due to its marketing image. . . . The evidence was undisputed that Southwest's unique, feminized image played and continues to play an important role in the airline's success.

Less certain, however, is Southwest's assertion that its females-only hiring policy is necessary for the continued success of its image and its business. Based on two on-board surveys, one conducted in October, 1979, before this suit was filed, and another in August, 1980, when the suit was pending, Southwest contends its attractive flight attendants are the "largest single component" of its success. In the 1979 survey, however, of the attributes considered most important by passengers, the category "courteous and attentive hostesses" ranked fifth in importance behind (1) on time departures, (2) frequently scheduled departures, (3) friendly and helpful reservations and ground personnel, and (4) convenient departure times. . . . Apparently, one of the remaining eight alternative categories, "attractive hostesses," was not selected with sufficient frequency to warrant being included in the reported survey results. . . .

---

4. Unabashed allusions to love and sex pervade all aspects of Southwest's public image. Its T.V. commercials feature attractive attendants in fitted outfits, catering to male passengers while an alluring feminine voice promises in-flight love. On board, attendants in hot-pants (skirts are now optional) serve "love bites" (toasted almonds) and "love potions" (cocktails). Even Southwest's ticketing system features a "quickie machine" to provide "instant gratification."

6. From 1979 to 1980, the company's earnings rose from $17 million to $28 million when most other airlines suffered heavy losses. As a percentage of revenues, Southwest's return is considered to be one of the highest in the industry.

[R]ather than Southwest's female personnel being the "sole factor" distinguishing the airline from its competitors, as Defendant contends, the 1980 survey lists Southwest's "personnel" as only one among five characteristics contributing to Southwest's public image. . . . Accordingly, there is no persuasive proof that Southwest's passengers prefer female over male flight attendants and ticket agents, or, of greater importance, that they would be less likely to fly Southwest if males were hired.

In evaluating Southwest's BFOQ defense, therefore, the Court proceeds on the basis that "love," while important, is not everything in the relationship between Defendant and its passengers. Still, it is proper to infer from the airline's competitive successes that Southwest's overall "love image" has enhanced its ability to attract passengers. To the extent the airline has successfully feminized its image and made attractive females an integral part of its public face, it also follows that femininity and sex appeal are qualities related to successful job performance by Southwest's flight attendants and ticket agents. The strength of this relationship has not been proved. It is with this factual orientation that the Court turns to examine Southwest's BFOQ defense.

INTERPRETATIONS OF THE BONA FIDE OCCUPATIONAL QUALIFICATION . . .

Southwest concedes with respect to the *Weeks* test that males are able to perform safely and efficiently all the basic, mechanical functions required of flight attendants and ticket agents. . . . Southwest's position, however, is that females are required to fulfill certain non-mechanical aspects of these jobs: to attract those male customers who prefer female attendants and ticket agents, and to preserve the authenticity and genuineness of Southwest's unique, female corporate personality.

A similar, though not identical, argument that females could better perform certain non-mechanical functions required of flight attendants was rejected in Diaz v. Pan American World Airways, Inc., [1971]. There, the airline argued and the trial court found that being female was a BFOQ because women were superior in "providing reassurance to anxious passengers, giving courteous personalized service and, in general, making flights as pleasurable as possible within the limitations imposed by aircraft operations." . . . Although it accepted the trial court findings, the Court of Appeals reversed, holding that femininity was not a BFOQ, because catering to passengers' psychological needs was only "tangential" to what was "reasonably *necessary*" for the business involved (original emphasis). . . . Characterizing the "essence" or "primary function" of Pan American's business as the safe transportation of passengers from one point to another, the court explained:

> While a pleasant environment, enhanced by the obvious cosmetic effect that female stewardesses provide as well as, according to the findings of the trial court, their apparent ability to perform the non-mechanical functions of the job in a more effective manner than most men, may all be important, they are tangential to the essence of the business involved. No one has suggested that having male stewards will so seriously affect the operation of the airline as to jeopardize or even minimize its ability to provide safe transportation from one place to another. . . .

Similar reasoning underlay the appellate court's rejection of Pan American's claim that its customers' preference for female attendants justified its refusal to hire males. Because the non-mechanical functions that passengers preferred females to perform were tangential to the airline's business, the court held, "the fact that customers prefer (females) cannot justify sex discrimination." . . . The Fifth Circuit in *Diaz* did not hold that customer preference could never give rise to a sex BFOQ. Rather, consistent with the EEOC's exception for authenticity and genuineness, the Court allowed that customer preference could "be taken into account only when it is based on the company's inability to perform the primary function or service it offers," that is, where sex or sex appeal is itself the dominant service provided.

Diaz and its progeny establish that to recognize a BFOQ for jobs requiring multiple abilities, some sex-linked and some sex-neutral, the sex-linked aspects of the job must predominate. Only then will an employer have satisfied [the] requirement that sex be so essential to successful job performance that a member of the opposite sex could not perform the job. An illustration of such dominance in sex cases is the exception recognized by the EEOC (Equal Employment Opportunity Commission) for authenticity and genuineness. In the example given in [EEOC Regulations], that of an actor or actress, the primary function of the position, its essence, is to fulfill the audience's expectation and desire for a particular role, characterized by particular physical or emotional traits. Generally, a male could not supply the authenticity required to perform a female role. Similarly, in jobs where sex or vicarious sexual recreation is the primary service provided, e.g. a social escort or topless dancer, the job automatically calls for one sex exclusively; the employee's sex and the service provided are inseparable. Thus, being female has been deemed a BFOQ for the position of a Playboy Bunny, female sexuality being reasonably necessary to perform the dominant purpose of the job which is forthrightly to titillate and entice male customers. . . . One court has also suggested, without holding, that the authenticity exception would give rise to a BFOQ for Chinese nationality where necessary to maintain the authentic atmosphere of an ethnic Chinese restaurant. . . .

APPLICATION OF THE BONA FIDE OCCUPATIONAL QUALIFICATION TO SOUTHWEST AIRLINES

Applying the first level test for a BFOQ, with its legal gloss, to Southwest's particular operations results in the conclusion that being female is not a qualification required to perform successfully the jobs of flight attendant and ticket agent with Southwest. Like any other airline, Southwest's primary function is to transport passengers safely and quickly from one point to another.[25] To do this, Southwest employs ticket agents whose primary job duties are to ticket passengers and check

---

25. Southwest's argument that its primary function is "to make a profit," not to transport passengers, must be rejected. Without doubt the goal of every business is to make a profit. For purposes of BFOQ analysis, however, the business "essence" inquiry focuses on the particular service provided and the job tasks and functions involved, not the business goal. If an employer could justify employment discrimination merely on the grounds that it is necessary to make a profit, Title VII would be nullified in short order.

baggage, and flight attendants, whose primary duties are to assist passengers during boarding and deboarding, to instruct passengers in the location and use of aircraft safety equipment, and to serve passengers cocktails and snacks during the airline's short commuter flights. Mechanical, non-sex-linked duties dominate both these occupations. Indeed, on Southwest's short-haul commuter flights there is time for little else. That Southwest's female personnel may perform their mechanical duties "with love" does not change the result. "Love" is the manner of job performance, not the job performed.

While possession of female allure and sex appeal have been made qualifications for Southwest's contact personnel by virtue of the "love" campaign, the functions served by employee sexuality in Southwest's operations are not dominant ones. According to Southwest, female sex appeal serves two purposes: (1) attracting and entertaining male passengers and (2) fulfilling customer expectations for female service engendered by Southwest's advertising which features female personnel. As in *Diaz*, these non-mechanical, sex-linked job functions are only "tangential" to the essence of the occupations and business involved. Southwest is not a business where vicarious sex entertainment is the primary service provided. Accordingly, the ability of the airline to perform its primary business function, the transportation of passengers, would not be jeopardized by hiring males.

Southwest does not face the situation . . . where an established customer preference for one sex is so strong that the business would be undermined if employees of the opposite sex were hired. Southwest's claim that its customers prefer females rests primarily upon inferences drawn from the airline's success after adopting its female personality. But according to Southwest's own surveys, that success is attributable to many factors. There is no competent proof that Southwest's popularity derives directly from its females-only policy to the exclusion of other factors like dissatisfaction with rival airlines and Southwest's use of convenient Love and Hobby Fields. Nor is there competent proof that the customer preference for females is so strong that Defendant's male passengers would cease doing business with Southwest as was the case in [Fernandez v. Wynn Oil Co.]. In short, Southwest has failed in its proof to satisfy Diaz's business necessity requirement, without which customer preference may not give rise to a BFOQ for sex. . . .

It is also relevant that Southwest's female image was adopted at its discretion, to promote a business unrelated to sex. Contrary to the unyielding South American preference for males encountered by the Defendant company in *Fernandez*, Southwest exploited, indeed nurtured, the very customer preference for females it now cites to justify discriminating against males. . . . Moreover, the fact that a vibrant marketing campaign was necessary to distinguish Southwest in its early years does not lead to the conclusion that sex discrimination was then, or is now, a business necessity. Southwest's claim that its female image will be tarnished by hiring males is, in any case, speculative at best. . . .

[S]ex does not become a BFOQ merely because an employer chooses to exploit female sexuality as a marketing tool, or to better insure profitability. . . .

CONCLUSION . . .

Rejecting a wider BFOQ for sex does not eliminate the commercial exploitation of sex appeal. It only requires, consistent with the purposes of Title VII, that employers exploit the attractiveness and allure of a sexually integrated work force. Neither Southwest, nor the traveling public, will suffer from such a rule. More to the point, it is my judgment that this is what Congress intended.

NOTES

1. **Disparate Impact Doctrine and the Business Necessity Defense.** The Supreme Court reasoned in *Dothard* that the height and weight requirements were proxies for strength, which could have been measured more directly and without sex discrimination. (The state did not present any evidence to support the height and weight minimums it had imposed.)[362] How likely do you think it is that substantially more women could qualify under a strength test? Of course, if a disproportionate impact remained, that rule, too, would need to be justifiable under the business necessity test. What if the defendant had shown that the height and weight restrictions were necessary to create the *appearance* of strength, as vital to prison security as strength itself? (Justice Rehnquist, concurring in the opinion, raises this possibility.)

2. **BFOQ and Sexual Authenticity.** As facially discriminatory exclusions based on sex, the prison regulation excluding women as prison guards in maximum-security areas in *Dothard* and the exclusion of men as flight attendants in *Wilson* are examples of disparate treatment discrimination, which are justified under Title VII only if the sex of the employee in each case is shown to be a bona fide occupational qualification, or BFOQ. Sex is a BFOQ in the entertainment industry if an actor's or actress's plausibility depends on sexual identity with the character portrayed. Should sexual authenticity be determined by a person's sex, in the biological sense, or by their gender presentation, i.e., how they perform their gender? Where do transgender women fit into this analysis? In Shakespearian times, male actors often played female roles. Is a sexual authenticity BFOQ really necessary? Is it based on gender stereotypes?

It may also be a BFOQ, according to *Wilson*, when the "essence" of a business requires a certain kind of sex appeal. Thus, while a family restaurant cannot discriminate between men and women for waiter positions, it generally is assumed that a topless bar may hire only women dancers and may discharge an employee for failure to meet the employer's criteria relating to sexual image. Ironically, then, the more explicitly the employer's business exploits sex for money, the more easily sex will be viewed as a BFOQ. Is this perverse? Does it fail to protect women when they most need it? Kimberly Yuracko explains the BFOQ case law as permitting employers to hire women to sell sex, but not to sexualize the sale of other goods and services, such as the in-flight services in *Wilson*.[363] Yuracko argues that this line of cases at least puts the brakes on sexualizing employment settings that are not already "selling sex only," to the benefit of women's equality in the workplace.[364]

---

362. Thomas, supra note 153, at 44-45.

363. Kimberly A. Yuracko, Private Nurses and Playboy Bunnies: Explaining Permissible Sex Discrimination, 92 Cal. L. Rev. 147 (2004).

364. Id. at 175.

Does this argument adequately take account of arguments like those of Hooters, which—when the EEOC sued it under Title VII for excluding men from wait staff jobs—claimed: "A lot of places sell good burgers. Hooters Girls, with their charm and all-American sex appeal, are what our customers come for"?[365] The sexual subordination of women in the workplace is explored more fully in Chapter 3.

Even when an employer, like a topless club, is selling "only" sex, why should it be allowed to hire only women, when men, too, can sell sex appeal? Is it because sexual authenticity as a BFOQ depends on an assumption of heterosexuality in the sexualized workplace? Should businesses be allowed to cater only to heterosexual men? What if they had reason to believe that hiring men in an effort to appeal to a broader client base (i.e., bisexual men and women, gay men, straight women) would ultimately hurt, rather than help, their business? Should the legal analysis at least press employers to defend presumptions of heterosexual sex appeal in order to establish a BFOQ based on sex appeal?

A sexual authenticity BFOQ need not involve sex appeal per se. Some expensive New York French restaurants hire only male waiters, in line with the tradition of the "classiest" Continental establishments. Are they violating Title VII? What if they hire only French waiters, and thereby virtually exclude waiters of color? What is the "essence" of such a job?

3. **BFOQ and Customer Preferences.** Under what circumstances might customer preference justify discriminatory conduct? In the lower court decision in *Diaz*, the airline introduced evidence of a survey indicating that 79 percent of all passengers, male and female, preferred being served by female flight attendants. Expert psychological evidence was also introduced to explain the general preference of airline passengers for female attendants. It posited that the unique experience of being levitated off the ground and transported through the air at high speeds creates feelings of apprehension, boredom, and excitement; females were psychologically better equipped to cope with these conflicting states and especially adept at relieving passenger apprehension; and passengers of both sexes responded better to the presence of females. This and other evidence persuaded the district court that sex was a BFOQ for flight attendants. The Fifth Circuit Court of Appeals, held, however, that although the airline could take the interpersonal skills of flight attendant applicants into account, it could not do so by categorically excluding all men.

As noted in the previous section, the court in Craft v. Metromedia came to a different conclusion. There, the court determined that a television anchorwoman could be properly reassigned due to the demonstrated negative viewer response. Is the rejection of the survey evidence in *Diaz* and *Wilson* reconcilable with its use in *Craft*? Fernandez v. Wynn Oil Co., cited in *Wilson*, held that an oil company could not refuse to hire female executives because its South American clients would refuse to deal with them.[366] Is this the correct decision? Is it reconcilable with *Craft*?

---

365. Rhode, The Beauty Bias, supra note 268, at 13 (quoting Hooters' spokesperson). After launching a major media campaign defending its hiring practices, Hooters settled with the EEOC without admitting wrongdoing.

366. 653 F.2d 1273 (9th Cir. 1981).

When do you think negative viewer or customer response to an employee based on sex should justify discrimination?

Are *Jespersen*, which is excerpted in the previous section, and *Wilson* consistent? Aren't both cases about whether an employer can make employment decisions based on female sex appeal? The difference is that the question in *Jespersen* is framed in terms of whether the dress and appearance standards at issue in the case discriminate on the basis of sex. The *Jespersen* court found that there was no sex discrimination because both male and female bartenders had to satisfy appearance standards, which it determined were substantially equal. In *Wilson*, by contrast, the airline excluded men from certain jobs so there was no question but that it discriminated on the basis of sex. That made it necessary for the airline to prove that the exclusion was a BFOQ. Is this a viable distinction, or sleight of hand?

The ease with which most courts have found that sex-specific dress and appearance standards do not constitute sex discrimination is consistent with how Emily Gold Waldman has rated the degree of judicial deference afforded to employers raising a BFOQ defense based on customer preference. Waldman contends that despite categorical pronouncements by courts (as in *Weeks, Diaz,* and *Fernandez*) that customer preference is not a BFOQ, in fact, courts sometimes do allow customer preferences to justify discrimination.[367] Waldman identifies a hierarchy of customer preferences with diminishing judicial deference that includes, in the top three: (1) aesthetic appeal (including sex appeal); (2) physical privacy; and (3) psychological comfort.[368] If Waldman is correct, what explains this ranking? Is this hierarchy of preferences defensible under the purposes of sex discrimination law?

4. **BFOQ and Privacy Considerations.** Courts have also found the BFOQ defense to be satisfied in some cases in which sex-specific hiring accommodates privacy or related interests. In Fesel v. Masonic Home of Delaware, Inc., for example, nine of the nursing home's female residents signed an affidavit objecting "most strenuously" to male nurses or male nurses' aides, though apparently not to male physicians.[369] The court accepted the employer's defense that female sex was a BFOQ for the nursing positions. Quite a number of cases in the context of hospitals and nursing homes have reached the same conclusion. Does it seem reasonable to restrict hiring by sex when the employment at issue implicates sex-specific privacy or therapeutic interests?[370] UAW v. Johnson Controls, excerpted in Chapter 2, includes a suggestion that the Court was prepared to endorse a privacy application of the BFOQ defense. Does a privacy-based BFOQ rest on an assumption that only employees of the "opposite" sex present the risk of triggering sexual desire?[371] Or are there other interests in physical privacy vis-à-vis persons of the other sex that are unrelated to sexual attraction?

---

367. Emily Gold Waldman, The Preferred Preferences, 97 N.C. L. Rev. 91 (2018).

368. Id.

369. 447 F. Supp. 1346 (D. Del. 1978), aff'd mem., 591 F.2d 1334 (3d Cir. 1979).

370. See Emily Gold Waldman, The Case of the Male OB-GYN: A Proposal for the Expansion of the Privacy BFOQ in the Healthcare Context, 6 U. Pa. J. Lab. & Emp. L. 357, 366-92 (2004) (proposing that employers should be able to hire, for example, only female obstetricians and gynecologists).

371. See Noa Ben-Asher, The Two Laws of Sex Stereotyping, 57 B.C. L. Rev. 1187, 1225 (2016).

Does allowing the BFOQ exception in this context perpetuate age-old stereotypes that Title VII was meant to condemn—i.e., that women's role is washing and cleaning up after people, and men's role is that of the skilled professional?[372] One case suggests that the BFOQ privacy defense is narrow, and only comes into play when hiring members of one sex would undermine the institution's safety and effectiveness. In Slivka v. Camden-Clark Memorial Hospital, the West Virginia Supreme Court struck down a hospital policy to hire only female obstetrics nurses, despite evidence that 80 percent of patients demanded female nurses and female nurses were needed as chaperones for male physicians.[373] The *Slivka* court noted the importance of not deferring to personal preferences based on dated world views. Is there a stronger argument for a BFOQ defense to hiring female OB-GYN doctors than for hiring only female nurses based on patient preference?[374] Would such a distinction be consistent with formal equality? How should privacy-based BFOQs fare in prison, given the lower expectations of privacy?[375] Privacy-based BFOQs in women's prisons, which are also designed to reduce the risk of sexual assault, have tended to fare better than privacy-based BFOQs in men's prisons.[376] Is this defensible under the BFOQ analysis? Is it defensible under formal equality?

Some believe that privacy-based BFOQs are less objectionable than other discriminatory preferences because they tend to affect men's and women's employment in parallel, symmetrical ways. Should this symmetry be legally relevant?[377] Or does symmetry simply reinforce stereotypes about gender roles?

5. **BFOQs and Formal Equality Analysis.** Justice Stewart's opinion upholding the female ban on maximum security positions in *Dothard* articulates the most common defense to a formal equality claim: Women are different from men in ways that justify different treatment. Sex-based differential treatment need only be justified as a BFOQ if it meets a threshold of material adversity. Sometimes courts

---

372. See Amy Kapczynski, Same-Sex Privacy and the Limits of Antidiscrimination Law, 112 Yale L.J. 1257 (2003).

373. 594 S.E.2d 616 (W. Va. 2004). For a discussion of the ethical considerations hospitals face in deciding whether to accommodate discriminatory patient preferences for medical staff, see Kwame Anthony Appiah, Should Patients Be Allowed to Choose Doctors by Race or Gender?, N.Y. Times Mag., Aug. 11, 2019, at 14.

374. See Veleanu v. Beth Israel Medical Ctr., 2000 WL 1400965 (S.D.N.Y. 2000).

375. See, e.g., Oliver v. Scott, 276 F.3d 736 (5th Cir. 2002) (holding that constitutional privacy rights did not bar cross-sex surveillance of male prisoners or require shower partitions and that such conditions did not violate prisoners' Fourth Amendment or equal protection rights).

376. Compare, e.g., Gunther v. Iowa State Men's Reformatory, 612 F.2d 1079 (8th Cir. 1980) (rejecting BFOQ defense to prison policy of excluding women guards from men's prison because interest in inmate privacy could be protected by less restrictive alternative practices, such as male-only staffing to conduct strip searches and oversee showers) with Teamsters Local Union No. 117 v. Wash. Dept. of Corr., 789 F.3d 979 (9th Cir. 2015) (upholding sex as a BFOQ for certain positions in women's prison, including those involving pat-downs and strip searches and close proximity to inmates while showering or using the restroom, based on the interest in protecting inmate privacy and preventing sexual assault). For further discussion of the BFOQ defense in the context of prisons, see note 6, infra.

377. See Abby Ellin, When a Man Needs a Safe Space, N.Y. Times, Dec. 20, 2017, at D8.

dodge the BFOQ analysis by finding that sex-based job assignments have only a minimal impact on job opportunities.[378] In *Dothard*, however, sex was used to exclude women from prison guard jobs in men's maximum-security prisons altogether. The reasoning of the opinion leaves no room for a woman to become qualified for the position. Safety at the prison—safety of the woman and of the prison population more generally—would be compromised by "womanhood," referring to both women's relative weakness, and their vulnerability to sexual assault. Viewed this way, women's unsuitability for the position reflects inherent sex differences, not ones that the state has produced or perpetuated by excluding them from the position.

Justice Marshall's dissent challenges the majority's assumptions about women's differences on multiple grounds. It (1) disputes the factual premises of the rule—for example, that female guards would create a danger to the prison's basic security; (2) identifies the stereotypes about women as "seductive sexual objects" that are reinforced through the exclusion; (3) insists that some women will be able to protect themselves and should be given the chance to prove their individual ability despite the average characteristics of their sex; and (4) claims that improvements in staffing (as a prior case had already required) was essentially a less restrictive alternative to excluding women from the positions.

If you think *Dothard* is wrongly decided, is it because the Court failed to apply standard formal equality principles correctly? Or because formal equality does not provide the tools necessary to analyze an exclusion based on factors "unique" to women?

Is excluding women where they might present temptation for the prisoners comparable to giving in to "customer preference"? Might the rationale in *Dothard* justify excluding women from work opportunities based on men's fears of being tempted into a sexual relationship or accused of sexual harassment? Or is the concern for prison safety and security sufficiently distinguishable from the kinds of business justifications rejected in other cases? Isn't it just a question of economics? Why should Southwest Airlines be required to forgo the income attributable to being the "LUV" airline, while the state of Alabama may defend its exclusion of women based on inadequate protection of their safety under present staffing arrangements? Should courts be more sympathetic when taxpayers are footing the bill and underfunding causes chronic security problems?

Would the analysis in *Dothard* be less troubling if courts required a detailed "basis in fact" for assumptions about how men or women are likely to behave on the job? A number of courts in recent years have denied employer motions for summary judgment in BFOQ cases because the factual predicate was insufficient.[379] One court observed that "the BFOQ defense generally requires a 'case-by-case' analysis."[380] Are juries any more or less likely than judges to be convinced that a gender-based BFOQ is justified?

---

378. See Tharp v. Iowa Dept. of Corr., 68 F.3d 223 (8th Cir. 1995).

379. See, e.g., White v. Dep't of Corr. Servs., 814 F. Supp. 2d 374 (S.D.N.Y. 2011); Reese v. Michigan Dep't of Corr., No. 08-10261, 2009 WL 799173 (E.D. Mich. Mar. 24, 2009); Inscore v. Doty, No. 4:08 CV 00337 JLH, 2009 WL 2753049 (E.D. Ark. Aug. 27, 2009).

380. *Reese*, 2009 WL 799173, at *4.

6. **His Very Manhood?**   The majority in *Dothard* allowed the prison's BFOQ defense in part because a female correctional officer's "very womanhood" would "directly undermine her capacity to provide the security that is the essence of a correctional counselor's responsibility."[381] Can the "very manhood" of male correctional counselors undermine their ability to carry out the essence of a prison's business? In several cases over the last decade, prisons have been sued over policies that exclude men from certain positions in women's prisons as a means of curbing the sexual abuse of female prisoners, with different results.[382] If *Dothard* was correctly decided, does it follow that men can be excluded as guards from women's prisons? Does the protection of female inmates offset any harm from the possible perpetuation of gender stereotypes?

7. **The Ministerial Exception.**   In addition to the BFOQ exception, there is an exception to Title VII for employment discrimination in certain positions within religious organizations. In the unanimous 2012 decision of Hosanna-Tabor Evangelical Lutheran Church and School v. EEOC,[383] the United States Supreme Court held that both the Establishment Clause and the Free Exercise Clause bar employment discrimination lawsuits based on the termination of employees by a religious institution when that employee is a "minister" within the "ministerial exception" to nondiscrimination statutes. The Court determined that the complainant, a teacher at the Lutheran elementary school, who alleged she was fired in violation of the Americans with Disabilities Act, was a minister on the basis of her title ("Minister of Religion, Commissioned") and the fact that she taught religious as well as secular subjects. The Court's decision was highly fact-specific, noting a number of factors supporting the application of the ministerial exception in that case, including that teachers in the school accepted a "calling" based on their religious faith and were approved by the congregation. In 2020, the Supreme Court expanded the exception even further, holding in Our Lady of Guadalupe School v. Morrissey-Berru that the ministerial exception encompasses decisions involving any employee who performs an important religious function, even if not a religious leader, a definition that will include most if not all teachers at religious schools.[384]

There is some question whether the ministerial exception should apply even when the religious institution's discrimination has nothing to do with a religious belief or practice.[385] A decision of the Ninth Circuit Court of Appeals prior to *Hosanna-Tabor* had held that the ministerial exception did not extend to cases of sexual harassment, where the employer did not claim a religious purpose for the harassment.[386] But in *Hosanna-Tabor*, the Supreme Court stated that the claimed

---

381. *Dothard*, 433 U.S. at 336.

382. Compare Everson v. Michigan Dep't of Corrections, 391 F.3d 737 (6th Cir. 2004), with Breiner v. Nevada Dep't of Corrections, 610 F.3d 1202 (9th Cir. 2010).

383. 565 U.S. 171 (2012).

384. 140 S. Ct. 2049 (2020).

385. See Ira C. Lupu & Robert W. Tuttle, #MeToo Meets the Ministerial Exception: Sexual Harassment Claims by Clergy and the First Amendment's Religion Clauses, 25 Wm. & Mary J. Race, Gender & Soc. Justice 249 (2019).

386. Bollard v. California Province of the Soc'y of Jesus, 196 F.3d 940, 944 (9th Cir. 1999). *Bollard* was applied and reaffirmed in Elvig v. Calvin Presbyterian Church, 375 F.3d 941 (9th Cir. 2004).

discriminatory behavior need not be connected to a particular tenet of the religion: "The purpose of the exception is not to safeguard a church's decision to fire a minister only when it is made for a religious reason. The exception instead ensures that the authority to select and control who will minister to the faithful . . . is the church's alone."[387] At the same time, the Court limited the case to the church's decision to fire an employee and holds that the ministerial exception operates as an "affirmative defense to an otherwise cognizable claim, not a jurisdictional bar."[388] Is it appropriate to give religious institutions the right to discriminate on the basis of sex? Why or why not?

Other potential conflicts between women's equality interests and religion are explored in Section D of this chapter (public accommodations).

PUTTING THEORY INTO PRACTICE

1-43. A mid-sized law firm handles, among other things, insurance and employment discrimination defense. A number of the firm's oldest and best clients prefer to work with male attorneys. Most recently, an insurance client threatened to take his business elsewhere if a female lawyer, who was assigned to handle a personal injury trial for his company, was not replaced by one of the firm's "bright, new" (male) attorneys. The client claims that the man will be more effective in the small "redneck" Southern town where the case is scheduled for trial. The law firm makes the reassignment to please the client. Is this discrimination based on sex? Is the firm's use of sex valid as a BFOQ?[389]

1-44. The firm in Problem 1-43 also has a practice of assigning women attorneys to defend employment discrimination cases brought by women claiming sex discrimination and of assigning minority attorneys to defend employment discrimination cases in which race is an issue. A white male attorney with the firm believes that this policy reduces his opportunities to excel at the firm. Is this discrimination based on sex and race? Is it justified? Would the issue be different if a Black woman is assigned as defense counsel in a rape trial before a largely Black jury on the theory that she would have the most credibility in cross-examining the Black female complainant?

1-45. In 2017, Facebook announced that it would require at least one-third of the lawyers working as outside counsel on legal matters for the company to be women or ethnic minorities.[390] A law firm that performs a significant amount of client work for Facebook cannot meet that demand without diversifying its pool of associates. If a white male attorney seeking to work at the firm is rejected for diversity reasons, does he have a winning Title VII lawsuit? If the firm restricts its hiring to women for a period of time to meet its diversity goals, could it establish a BFOQ?

---

387. *Hosanna-Tabor*, 565 U.S. 171, 194-95 (2012).

388. Id. at 195 n. 4 (citing *Bollard* with approval).

389. This case is modeled on Karen Horowitz, a video vignette from Stephen Giller's Series, Adventures in Legal Ethics (1992).

390. Ellen Rosen, Facebook Pushes Outside Law Firms to Become More Diverse, N.Y. Times, Apr. 2, 2017, at B2.

1-46. A trucking company has a policy that new drivers must be accompanied by an experienced driver for six months. In response to a sexual harassment lawsuit, the company implemented a "same-sex trainer policy," under which female drivers could only be accompanied by other female drivers, to alleviate safety and privacy concerns. However, new female drivers were often placed on a "female waiting list" because there were no female drivers available to train. Is this policy legal?[391]

1-47. In the wake of highly publicized incidents of sexual violence by male Uber and Lyft drivers against female passengers, a new ride-sharing company establishes itself as a transportation service for women only, and with only women drivers picking up and transporting passengers. Is the company's exclusion of male drivers a BFOQ?[392]

1-48. The FBI requires male trainees to perform thirty push-ups and female trainees to do fourteen push-ups, in recognition of physiological differences between men and women and research showing that the differential standard corresponds to comparable levels of physical fitness in men and women. The FBI does not contend that a certain number of push-ups is necessary for successful performance in the FBI, but rather that physical fitness is necessary. A male cadet was flunked out of the FBI training academy for not meeting the male standard, even though he satisfied the standard females must meet. If he sues for sex discrimination, should the employer have to defend its sex-based different treatment under the BFOQ analysis? Could it?[393]

1-49. Transition House, New England's first battered women's shelter, caused controversy by hiring a man as its interim executive director. About Women, a collective of psychologists and social workers who were influential in creating shelters, including Transition House, wrote a public letter of protest. In their view, the decision constituted a "flagrant violation" of the organization's founding principle to establish a space where women could feel safe from male intrusion and could openly unburden themselves of the experiences of male violence they had undergone without fear of censure, criticism, or inhibition by male presence. The male interim director responded by noting that he spent his time in administrative offices in a separate location from the shelter and had limited contact with residents.[394] Who is right? If the male director is fired based on the rationale of About Women, would he have a sex discrimination claim under Title VII?

1-50. Defendant operates Pin-Ups, a live adult entertainment venue. The business has "numerous image-related requirements for its entertainers in order to make sure the entertainers present the image and service that the defendant sells." Plaintiff worked as a dancer at Pin-Ups but was terminated when she was far enough along in her pregnancy that she could no longer hide her condition (around four

---

391. See EEOC v. New Prime, Inc., 42 F. Supp. 3d 1201 (W.D. Mo. 2014).

392. See Elizabeth Brown, Fare Trade: Reconciling Public Safety and Gender Discrimination in Single-Sex Ridesharing, 35 Yale L. & Pol'y Rev. 367 (2017); Cristina Medina, Women-Only Ridesharing in America: Rising Sexual Assault Rates Demand an Exception to Anti-Discrimination Laws, 50 Loy. L.A. L. Rev. 691 (2017).

393. See Bauer v. Lynch, 812 F.3d 340 (4th Cir. 2016).

394. Courtney E. Martin, Violence Shelter Considers Hiring Male Director (Aug. 22, 2005), www.womensenews.org.

months). Defendant argued that the discharge was lawful because "sex appeal" is a job requirement that is an integral part of its business. Plaintiff countered that her pregnancy did not affect her ability to dance and that many people find pregnant women beautiful and sexy. Who should prevail?[395]

1-51. A rape counseling organization uses only female counselors and rejects a transgender woman who sought a counselor position. After *Bostock* (excerpted in Section C2), this is unlawful sex discrimination under Title VII unless justified by the BFOQ defense. The organization claims that it has a compelling interest in having women who are sexually assaulted helped by those who have "suffered oppression from birth."[396] Can the organization establish that being cisgender female is a BFOQ for this position?

1-52. Dissenting in *Bostock*, Justice Alito warned that the Court's holding means that a professional women's sports team that employs only women as players will now discriminate on the basis of sex in violation of Title VII unless the employer can establish that being a cisgender female is a BFOQ. What arguments could be raised for and against a BFOQ in this setting, and how do you think they should be resolved? (Issues related to sex separation and transgender participation in sports are also considered in Chapter 2.)

D. STATE PUBLIC ACCOMMODATIONS LAWS AND ASSOCIATIONAL FREEDOMS

In addition to federal and state laws prohibiting sex discrimination in employment, many states have passed civil rights acts prohibiting sex discrimination in public accommodations and in private clubs and organizations. These laws were largely passed in the 1960s and 1970s, as one outgrowth of the civil rights movement generally and targeted advocacy by the National Organization for Women specifically.[397] Against a landscape that included pervasive sex segregation by "law and custom," feminists fighting for equal access to public accommodations had to "dismantle the remnants of sex segregation, resist regulation of sexuality, and confront norms of masculinity and femininity."[398] Women's demand for access was directly at odds with men's insistence on being in a class, and sometimes a room, by themselves.

---

395. Problem modified from Berry v. Great Am. Dream, Inc., 88 F. Supp. 3d 1378 (N.D. Ga. 2015).

396. Nixon v. Vancouver Rape Relief Soc'y, 2002 C.L.L.C 230-009, 42 C.H.R.R. D/20.

397. On the history of these laws, see Elizabeth Sepper & Deborah Dinner, Sex in Public, 129 Yale L.J. 78 (2019). Forty-five states have public accommodations laws today, and all of them include sex as a protected characteristic. See also Nat'l Conf. State Legislatures, State Public Accommodation Laws (June 25, 2021); see Joseph William Singer, No Right to Exclude: Public Accommodations and Private Property, 90 Nw. U. L. Rev. 1283, 1478-1495 (1996)

398. Sepper & Dinner, supra note 397, at 86, 96.

Challenges to the application of these public accommodation statutes have claimed infringement of rights of expression, association, and privacy protected by the federal and state constitutions. Such rights have long served to protect the activities and privacy of politically unpopular groups, including those involved in the civil rights movement. The question is how far this protection extends, and to whom. In 1984, the United States Supreme Court faced this issue with respect to sex discrimination in the case of Roberts v. United States Jaycees. There, the Court rejected First Amendment challenges to a Minnesota anti-discrimination statute under which the Jaycees had been required to admit women as full voting members.[399] Three years later, the Court considered a challenge to California's Unruh Act, a broad public accommodations law that had been used to require Rotary Clubs in the state to admit women.

These materials also introduce the question of whether sex-based exclusion from public spaces can ever be consistent with gender equality—or even necessary sometimes to promote it. What justifications might be sufficient to support a policy of sex discrimination in public accommodations and in what contexts? When do other democratic values like liberty and freedom of association outweigh the commitment to formal gender equality?

Board of Directors of Rotary International v. Rotary Club of Duarte

481 U.S. 537 (1987)

Mr. Justice POWELL delivered the opinion of the Court.

We must decide whether a California statute that requires California Rotary Clubs to admit women members violates the First Amendment.

I

Rotary International (International) is a nonprofit corporation founded in 1905, with headquarters in Evanston, Illinois. It is "an organization of business and professional men united worldwide who provide humanitarian service, encourage high ethical standards in all vocations, and help build goodwill and peace in the world." . . . Individual members belong to a local Rotary Club rather than to International. In turn, each local Rotary Club is a member of International. . . . In August 1982, shortly before the trial in this case, International comprised 19,788 Rotary Clubs in 157 countries, with a total membership of about 907,750. . . .

Individuals are admitted to membership in a Rotary Club according to a "classification system." The purpose of this system is to ensure "that each Rotary Club includes a representative of every worthy and recognized business, professional, or institutional activity in the community." . . . Each active member must work in a leadership capacity in his business or profession. The general rule is that "one active member is admitted for each classification, but he, in turn, may propose an additional active member, who must be in the same business or professional

---

399. 468 U.S. 609 (1984).

classification." Thus, each classification may be represented by two active members. In addition, "senior active" and "past service" members may represent the same classifications as active members. . . . There is no limit to the number of clergymen, journalists, or diplomats who may be admitted to membership. . . . Subject to these requirements, each local Rotary Club is free to adopt its own rules and procedures for admitting new members. . . .

Membership in Rotary Clubs is open only to men. . . . Herbert A. Pigman, the General Secretary of Rotary International, testified that the exclusion of women results in an "aspect of fellowship . . . that is enjoyed by the present male membership," . . . and also allows Rotary to operate effectively in foreign countries with varied cultures and social mores. Although women are not admitted to membership, they are permitted to attend meetings, give speeches, and receive awards. Women relatives of Rotary members may form their own associations and are authorized to wear the Rotary lapel pin. Young women between 14 and 28 years of age may joint Interact or Rotaract, organizations sponsored by Rotary International . . . .

In 1977 the Rotary Club of Duarte, California, admitted Donna Bogart, Mary Lou Elliott, and Rosemary Freitag to active membership. International notified the Duarte Club that admitting women members is contrary to the Rotary constitution. After an internal hearing, International's board of directors revoked the charter of the Duarte Club and terminated its membership in Rotary International. The Duarte Club's appeal to the International Convention was unsuccessful.

The Duarte Club and two of its women members filed a complaint in the California Superior Court for the County of Los Angeles. The complaint alleged, inter alia, that appellants' actions violated the Unruh Civil Rights Act.[2] . . . [fn. 2: The Unruh Civil Rights Act provides, in part: "All persons within the jurisdiction of this state are free and equal, and no matter what their sex, race, color, religion, ancestry, or national origin are entitled to the full and equal accommodations, advantages, facilities, privileges, or services in all business establishments of every kind whatsoever." Cal. Civ. Code Ann. § 51 (West 1982).

II

In Roberts v. United States Jaycees, [468 U.S. 609 (1984),] we upheld against First Amendment challenge a Minnesota statute that required the Jaycees to admit women as full voting members. *Roberts* provides the framework for analyzing appellants' constitutional claims. As we observed in *Roberts*, our cases have afforded constitutional protection to freedom of association in two distinct senses. First, the Court has held that the Constitution protects against unjustified government interference with an individual's choice to enter into and maintain certain intimate or private relationships. Second, the Court has upheld the freedom of individuals to associate for the purpose of engaging in protected speech or religious activities. In many cases, government interference with one form of protected association will also burden the other form of association. In *Roberts* we determined the nature and degree of constitutional protection by considering separately the effect of the challenged state action on individuals' freedom of private association and their freedom of expressive association. We follow the same course in this case . . . .

A

The Court has recognized that the freedom to enter into and carry on certain intimate or private relationships is a fundamental element of liberty protected by the Bill of Rights. Such relationships may take various forms, including the most intimate . . . . We have not attempted to mark the precise boundaries of this type of constitutional protection. The intimate relationships to which we have accorded constitutional protection include marriage . . . the begetting and bearing of children . . . child rearing and education . . . and cohabitation with relatives . . . . In determining whether a particular association is sufficiently personal or private to warrant constitutional protection, we consider factors such as size, purpose, selectivity, and whether others are excluded from critical aspects of the relationship. [468 U.S. at 620.]

The evidence in this case indicates that the relationship among Rotary Club members is not the kind of intimate or private relation that warrants constitutional protection. The size of the local Rotary Clubs ranges from fewer than 20 to more than 900. . . . There is no upper limit on the membership of any local Rotary Club. About 10 percent of the membership of a typical club moves away or drops out during a typical year. . . . The clubs therefore are instructed to "keep a flow of prospects coming" to make up for the attrition and gradually to enlarge the membership . . . . The purpose of Rotary "is to produce an inclusive, not exclusive, membership, making possible the recognition of all useful local occupations, and enabling the club to be a true cross section of the business and professional life of the community." . . . The membership undertakes a variety of service projects designed to aid the community, to raise the standards of the members' businesses and professions, and to improve international relations. Such an inclusive "fellowship for service based on diversity of interest," . . . however beneficial to the members and to those they serve, does not suggest the kind of private or personal relationship to which we have accorded protection under the First Amendment. To be sure, membership in Rotary Clubs is not open to the general public. But each club is instructed to include in its membership "all fully qualified prospective members located within its territory," to avoid "arbitrary limits on the number of members in the club," and to "establish and maintain a membership growth pattern."

Many of the Rotary Clubs' central activities are carried on in the presence of strangers. Rotary Clubs are required to admit any member of any other Rotary Club to their meetings. Members are encouraged to invite business associates and competitors to meetings. At some Rotary Clubs, the visitors number "in the tens and twenties each week." . . . Joint meetings with the members of other organizations, and other joint activities, are permitted. The clubs are encouraged to seek coverage of their meetings and activities in local newspapers. In sum, Rotary Clubs, rather than carrying on their activities in an atmosphere of privacy, seek to keep their "windows and doors open to the whole world." . . . We therefore conclude that application of the Unruh Act to local Rotary Clubs does not interfere unduly with the members' freedom of private association.

B

The Court also has recognized that the right to engage in activities protected by the First Amendment implies "a corresponding right to associate with others in pursuit of a wide variety of political, social, economic, educational, religious, and cultural ends." Roberts v. United States Jaycees, [468 U.S. at 622] . . . . For this reason, "[i]mpediments to the exercise of one's right to choose one's associates can violate the right of association protected by the First Amendment . . . ." Hishon v. King & Spalding, [467 U.S. 69, 80 n.4 (1984)] (Powell, J., concurring) (citing NAACP v. Button, [371 U.S. 415 (1963)]; NAACP v. Alabama ex rel. Patterson, [357 U.S. 449 (1958)]). In this case, however, the evidence fails to demonstrate that admitting women to Rotary Clubs will affect in any significant way the existing members' ability to carry out their various purposes.

As a matter of policy, Rotary Clubs do not take positions on "public questions," including political or international issues . . . . To be sure, Rotary Clubs engage in a variety of commendable service activities that are protected by the First Amendment. But the Unruh Act does not require the clubs to abandon or alter any of these activities. It does not require them to abandon their basic goals of humanitarian service, high ethical standards in all vocations, good will, and peace. Nor does it require them to abandon their classification system or admit members who do not reflect a cross section of the community. Indeed, by opening membership to leading business and professional women in the community, Rotary Clubs are likely to obtain a more representative cross section of community leaders with a broadened capacity for service.

Even if the Unruh Act does work some slight infringement on Rotary members' right of expressive association, that infringement is justified because it serves the State's compelling interest in eliminating discrimination against women. See Buckley v. Valeo, [424 U.S. 1, 25 (1976)] (per curiam) (right of association may be limited by state regulations necessary to serve a compelling interest unrelated to the suppression of ideas). On its face the Unruh Act, like the Minnesota public accommodations law we considered in *Roberts*, makes no distinctions on the basis of the organization's viewpoint. Moreover, public accommodations laws "plainly serv[e] compelling state interests of the highest order." [468 U.S. at 624.] In *Roberts* we recognized that the State's compelling interest in assuring equal access to women extends to the acquisition of leadership skills and business contacts as well as tangible goods and services. [Id. at 626.] The Unruh Act plainly serves this interest. We therefore hold that application of the Unruh Act to California Rotary Clubs does not violate the right of expressive association afforded by the First Amendment . . . .

Justice SCALIA concurs in the judgment.

Justice BLACKMUN and Justice O'CONNOR took no part in the consideration or decision of this case.

Foster v. Back Bay Spas

1997 Mass. Super. LEXIS 194 (Sept. 29, 1997)

BURNS, Judge . . .

This motion for summary judgment arises out of plaintiff James Foster's action to require the defendant . . . to allow him to join the health club. The club does not admit men. Foster argues that this policy violates [the Massachusetts public accommodations statute that prohibits discrimination based on sex].

BACKGROUND

Plaintiff James Foster [lives] in Boston. Defendant Back Bay Spas, Inc. d/b/a Healthworks Fitness Center ("Healthworks") owns and operates a health club facility in the Back Bay area of Boston which accepts only women. Foster is a member of the Marriott Health Club at Copley Place, directly across the street from a Healthworks facility. There exist a large number of other, co-ed exercise facilities in the Boston area with similar resources as Healthworks. Nevertheless, Foster seeks membership at Healthworks Fitness Center, the one facility which caters only to women.

Healthworks was developed and designed for use by women, and thus its programs and facilities—including locker rooms and restrooms—cater to women. Healthworks, in addition to providing a full range of exercise equipment and facilities, offers various fitness and health classes, including classes tailored towards female concerns such as pre-natal programs and special nutrition counseling for women. Healthworks has also contracted with the YWCA Boston so that its members may use its facility. Healthworks promotes itself as an all women's facility, by its advertising and facility window displays.

Healthworks opened its Back Bay facility in February 1996 and its membership is now over 3,500. Foster inquired about membership at Healthworks in February 1996 and was turned away because he is a man.

Affidavits submitted by Healthworks reveal that many of the club's members based their decision to join and to remain members of the facility because it is only open to women. Moreover, Healthworks submitted an affidavit of a Robert Tanenbaum, Ph.D., an expert on areas that impact exercise behavior and fitness including knowledge of gender differences, human sexuality, and reduction of performance anxiety . . . . In his affidavit, Dr. Tanenbaum concludes that over 80% of the members he interviewed stated that the all female aspect of the club was the most important reason for joining Healthworks; that many of the members are of "post-childbearing age and have experienced bodily changes resulting from pregnancy and childbirth which alter their appearance . . . older members who have recently gone through menopause . . . feel intimidated exercising in a coed environment;" that many of the women expressed concern about being watched by members of the opposite sex while exercising; and, that several were recovering from past physical or sexual abuse, or had specific religious concerns about exercising in a coed facility. Most significantly, Dr. Tanenbaum concluded that "approximately 87% of the women . . . said that they would stop exercising at Healthworks if men were permitted to join. . . . Healthworks meets an existing need among the women described and minimizes the hurdles typically found in a coed setting, particularly for women who do not have a consistent fitness history."

DISCUSSION

No material facts are in dispute. The Court, therefore, is charged with determining whether Foster has proved, as a matter of law, that Healthworks' refusal to allow men membership in its facility is in violation of the Massachusetts Public

Accommodation Law, . . . and, if so, whether there is any exception to the anti-discrimination provisions in that law.

[Massachusetts law] provides [that]:

> No . . . place of public accommodation, resort or amusement shall, directly or indirectly . . . distribute or display . . . any . . . notice or sign, . . . intended to discriminate against or actually discriminating against persons of any . . . sex . . . in the full enjoyment of the accommodations, advantages, facilities or privileges offered to the general public by such places of public accommodation. . . .

The statute further defines a "place of public accommodation" [to include]:

> any place, . . . which is open to and accepts or solicits the patronage of the general public and . . . (8) a place of public amusement, recreation, sport, exercise or entertainment. . . .

[The law provides]:

> Whoever makes any distinction, discrimination or restriction on account of . . . sex . . . relative to the admission of any person to, or his treatment in any place of public accommodation, resort or amusement, as defined in Section ninety-two A, . . . shall be punished. . . . All persons shall have the right to the full and equal accommodations, advantages, facilities and privileges of any place of public accommodation, resort or amusement subject only to the conditions and limitations established by law and applicable to all persons.

Healthworks has stipulated that it is "a place of public accommodation." . . . On its face, therefore, there is no dispute that the exclusion of males from this place of public accommodation is in violation of the public accommodation law. Healthworks claims, however, that women have a privacy right to exercise in an all female environment.

The privacy statute grants a right to privacy. [The statute provides that] "a person shall have a right against unreasonable, substantial or serious interference with his privacy." The central issue in this case, therefore, is whether a privacy right exists, or can be read into the public accommodations statute, which would permit the exclusion of all men from an all women's exercise facility.

Healthworks claims that its customers' privacy rights are protected by [the law]; that there exists within the public accommodations statute an implied right of privacy for all women to exercise in an all women environment; and that the public accommodation statute was amended to protect women, not men. Specifically, Healthworks argues that a privacy right exists, based on the customer gender preferences of Healthworks's membership. [In a Pennsylvania case identical to this one,] the Commonwealth Court of Pennsylvania held that based on a "customer gender privacy" defense, an all women's health club would be permitted to exclude all men from its facility, stating that "this defense recognizes a pervasive public policy that certain conduct that relates to and between genders is inappropriate." . . . In determining that the membership had a privacy interest in exercising in a single sex club the court concluded that "they [the members] expose parts of the body about which they are most sensitive, assume awkward and compromising positions, and move themselves in a way which would embarrass them if men were present."

This Court recognizes the difficulty in defining what constitutes "privacy rights." Nevertheless, it is clear that the cases relied upon [in the Pennsylvania case] all involve the exposure or the touching of intimate body parts. This case, on the other hand, involves exercising—an activity—performed before numerous other people, in full exercise attire. Moreover, as Foster points out, at the Healthworks facility in Boston's Back Bay area, the exercisers can be seen from the street as there are two large windows at the front of the facility. Healthworks argues that although there is little nudity involved, and recognizes that any such nudity is voluntary, the compromising positions and contours the customers must invariably assume while exercising raises this clothed activity to a level of exposure akin to nudity or physical contact and thus requires the protection of a privacy right. Again, this Court disagrees. No exercise position, performed while dressed, would result in the sort of exposure of intimate body parts which has been protected by the privacy right. . . .

Here, the putative privacy right is only the right to exercise in a same-sex facility. No private information is being disclosed, and no highly personal or intimate facts are being revealed. The only basis for the claimed right is the exposure of one's clothed anatomy while exercising. Massachusetts case law supports no such right.

Healthworks' affidavits and personal statements describe the sense of intimidation certain women, including post-menopausal women, and women who have undergone mastectomies or who have suffered abuse, will feel in a coed exercise atmosphere, such that they would cease their exercise program. While the Court recognizes the impact that the admission of men into the club may have on these women, intimidation and the assumption that all male Healthworks members will harass and leer at their exercise compatriots is still an insufficient ground on which to create a privacy exception. Absent the unclothed exposure of intimate body parts, or the touching of body parts by members of the opposite sex, this Court can find no basis for overriding the public accommodations statute's mandate.

Further, an affidavit from a member of the Islamic faith stated that Islamic women, who are forbidden from revealing any part of their body (except for their face and hands) while in the presence of men, would no longer be able to use the Healthworks facility at all if men were allowed to join. Healthworks, however, is not a religious facility providing exercise facilities only to Islamic women. It is a public health club. And while this Court recognizes the disparate impact the inclusion of men will have on women of the Islamic faith, this Court cannot allow Healthworks to discriminate against men by allowing women of all faiths access to a single-sex exercise space on the basis of the religious beliefs of a portion of its members.

Because this Court concludes that there is no legitimate privacy interest to be recognized or protected which would excuse the discriminatory exclusion of males in violation of the public accommodations statute, the inquiry need not go further. Since the customers of Healthworks have no privacy right to be protected, the Court is not required, indeed cannot, consider whether Healthworks' policy is reasonable.

For the reasons set forth above, [Foster's motion for summary judgment is granted].

NOTES

1. **First Amendment Challenges.** Under *Roberts* and *Rotary Club*, the more personal and intimate the association in terms of its size, purpose, selectivity, and agenda, and the more engaged in a specific political, social, or religious agenda, the greater the protection the First Amendment affords. Is it appropriate that the more exclusive the association, the greater autonomy it will enjoy? Is it perverse that a neo-Nazi group but not a Little League may be able to exclude Jews?

Anti-discrimination statutes similar to the one applied in the Healthworks case also have faced First Amendment challenges. An important early case involved a successful challenge to the exclusion of girls by the Boys' Club of Santa Cruz. The Club's mission was to combat delinquency in boys, who were four times more likely than girls to get into trouble with the law. Club owners, and the principal donor, had determined that male juvenile delinquency could be more effectively addressed in an all-male setting.[400] But the court found that exclusion of girls constituted arbitrary discrimination in violation of the Unruh Act. The court rejected the club's First Amendment argument, finding that the club was a business establishment that was open to the public and that did not have any particular expressive purpose. A few years after the litigation, 30 percent of the members of the Boys' Club in Santa Cruz were girls, involved in all aspects of the club, including football and baseball. According to one report, there were "no signs of tension" as a result of the change in admission policy.[401]

A divided U.S. Supreme Court in Boy Scouts of America v. Dale upheld the right of the Boy Scouts to exclude members based on sexual orientation despite a state public accommodations law that prohibited exclusion on the basis of sexual orientation.[402] Writing for the majority, Chief Justice Rehnquist concluded that the New Jersey law violated the Boy Scouts' rights of speech and association. Under the Court's analysis, the presence of a gay rights activist "would, at the very least, force the organization to send a message . . . that the Boy Scouts accepts homosexual conduct as a legitimate form of behavior."[403] According to Scout leadership, such a message would be inconsistent with its oath and laws requiring Scouts to be "morally straight" and "clean" in body and mind.[404]

The *Dale* holding has been controversial among constitutional scholars, policymakers, and the general public. Some commentators have viewed the decision as inconsistent with prior cases involving discrimination by private associations. They are also troubled by granting First Amendment protection to an organization that discriminates on the basis of status, not conduct: heterosexual troop leaders who support gay rights were not dismissed.

Should the Jaycees and Rotary Club be required to admit women, while the Boy Scouts are entitled to exclude gays?

---

400. Isbister v. Boys Club of Santa Cruz, 707 P.2d 212 (Cal. 1985).

401. Jill Zuckman, Boys' Club Finds Sugar and Spice, San Jose Mercury News, Aug. 14, 1987, at 1B.

402. 530 U.S. 640 (2000).

403. Id. at 653.

404. Id. at 650.

In piecemeal fashion, Boy Scouts lifted their bans on participation by gay scouts, leaders, and employees, but still allow local chapters to continue excluding gay volunteer leaders at their discretion, permitting scouts and their parents to "select local units, chartered to organizations with similar beliefs, that best meet the needs of their families."[405] How would you evaluate this compromise? In 2017, Boy Scouts USA decided to permit transgender boys to participate. Should the organization's discriminatory legacy continue to influence the decision whether to join?

2. The Scope of State and Local Public Accommodations Laws.   Federal law prohibits discrimination in public accommodations on the basis of race, color, religion, national origin or disability, but not sex.[406] Federal constitutional guarantees of equal protection apply only to public entities. Thus, challenges to sex-based exclusions from private associations, as in *Rotary Club*, from private businesses, or from retail establishments have been brought under state civil rights acts, the scope of which varies. Some prohibit discrimination only as to places of public accommodation, construed to mean entities that exist at a particular place, such as hotels or restaurants, and thereby excluding organizations that may meet in different locations, such as the Jaycees, Rotary Clubs, and some scouting organizations. Others apply to private clubs only in areas or at functions where nonmembers are present. Some apply only to businesses, although business may be quite broadly construed. Some statutes specifically exempt "private" or "distinctly private" clubs.[407]

Although the plaintiff won his case against Healthworks, the Massachusetts legislature then passed legislation exempting fitness facilities from its general public accommodations law.[408] A handful of other states have also carved out narrow exemptions for health clubs, changing rooms, bath houses, and other places where privacy concerns might be relevant.[409] Are targeted exemptions a reasonable compromise? If Massachusetts wants to allow all-women's health clubs, is it also required to allow all-men's health clubs? Do the reasons given in support of single-sex fitness facilities also support single-sex bathrooms?

Professor Mary Anne Case has argued that the idea of a single-sex restroom as refuge from unwanted sexual attention or other annoyance only works if you ignore the possibility of attention from a person of the same sex and rely on stereotyped

405. Boy Scouts of Am., Membership Standards, https://www.scouting.org/about/membership-standards; see also Michelle Boorstein, Boy Scouts of America Votes to End Controversial Ban on Openly-Gay Scout Leaders, Wash. Post, July 27, 2015.

406. 42 U.S.C. § 2000a (2018); 42 U.S.C. § 12182 (2018). The Equality Act, discussed above, would add "sex" to the list of prohibited characteristics.

407. Examples of each of these types of statutes are discussed in Sally Frank, The Key to Unlocking the Clubhouse Door: The Application of Antidiscrimination Laws to Quasi-Private Clubs, 2 Mich. J. Gender & L. 27 (1994).

408. See Mass. Gen. Laws Ch. 272 § 92A (2022) ("this section shall not apply to a place of exercise for the exclusive use of persons of the same sex which is a bona fide fitness facility established for the sole purpose of promoting and maintaining physical and mental health through physical exercise and instruction").

409. See 775 Ill. Comp. Stat. 5/5-103 (West 2022); Tenn. Code Ann. § 4-21-503 (2022); see also David S. Cohen, The Stubborn Persistence of Sex Segregation, 20 Colum. J. Gender & L. 51 (2011).

assumptions about behavior. "A woman can escape her boss in the office women's room only if the bosses are men," as well as the suitors.[410] Does the embrace of single-sex restrooms, locker rooms, and fitness centers trade, as David Cruz argues, on "occupational sex stratification and on the privileging of different-sex dating and the interests of heterosexually-identified persons over same-sex dating or the interests of gay, lesbian, and bisexual persons"?[411] This question will arise again in Chapter 2, when we explore separation versus integration in the context of educational programs and athletics.

All-male golf and country clubs have been another site of controversy. Public pressure led the Augusta National Golf Club to integrate racially in the 1970s and caused the withdrawal of corporate sponsorships from the prestigious Masters tournament in 2003 and 2004 because of its sex discrimination.[412] As late as 2012, the club reaffirmed its all-male policy.[413] A handful of prestigious clubs continue to exclude women today.[414] Why do you suppose that it has been harder to get clubs and corporate sponsors to take sex discrimination as seriously as race discrimination?

3. **Gender-Based Pricing.**   In states with broad public accommodations laws, men and women have challenged pricing differentials that benefit the other sex.[415] Early cases upheld the differentials.[416] However, the law has begun to shift the other way. The California Supreme Court ruled in Koire v. Metro Car Wash that several car washes and a bar violated the public accommodations law by providing "ladies' day" discounts to women.[417] The legislature later adopted a law making clear that price differentials cannot be based on sex and requiring certain businesses, including dry cleaners and hair salons, to post a notice informing customers that state law prohibits discrimination "with respect to the price charged for services of similar or like kind, against a person because of the person's gender."[418] In 2004, the New

---

410. Mary Anne Case, Why Not Abolish Laws of Urinary Segregation?, *in* Toilet: Public Restrooms and the Politics of Sharing 211, 223 (Harvey Molotch & Lauren Norén eds., 2010).

411. David B. Cruz, Making Sex Matter: Common Restrooms as "Intimate" Spaces, 40 Minn. J. L. & Ineq. 99, 109 (2022).

412. See Frank J. Ferraro, Prerogative or Prejudice?: The Exclusion of Women from Augusta National, 1 DePaul J. Sports L. Contemp. Probs. 39 (2003); Martha Burk, Cult of Power: Sex Discrimination in Corporate America and What Can Be Done About It (2005).

413. Karen Crouse, Touchy Day at Augusta National Men's Club, N.Y. Times, Apr. 4, 2012, at B11; Elisabeth Bumiller, Avid Golfer Rice Jumps a Barrier Again, N.Y. Times, Aug. 20, 2012, at B9.

414. Michael McCann, Why Private Golf Clubs Are Legally Still Able to Discriminate Against Women, Sports Illustrated (July 1, 2019).

415. See Mark Allan Herzberg, "Girls Get in Free": A Legal Analysis of the Gender-Based Door Entry Policies, 19 S. Cal. Rev. L. & Soc. Just. 479 (2010).

416. See, e.g., Tucich v. Dearborn Indoor Racquet Club, 309 N.W.2d 615, 619 (Mich. Ct. App. 1981); Dock Club, Inc. v. Illinois Liquor Control Comm'n, 428 N.E.2d 735 (Ill. App. Ct. 1981); MacLean v. First Nw. Indus., 635 P.2d 683 (Wash. 1981).

417. 707 P.2d 195 (Cal. 1985); see also Ladd v. Iowa W. Racing Ass'n, 438 N.W.2d 600 (Iowa 1989) (racetrack's policy of giving free admission and discounted concessions to women constituted unlawful discrimination).

418. Cal. Civ. Code § 51.6 (2022).

Jersey Director of Civil Rights issued a ruling that a restaurant's "ladies' night"—a night each week when it admitted women free of charge and charged them less for drinks—violated the state's anti-discrimination law.[419] The restaurant argued that it had a legitimate purpose for the promotion—to increase patronage and revenue by bringing more women to the restaurant because of the reduced prices and more men because of the greater number of women. It also argued that this type of discrimination was too trivial to matter and, in any event, was canceled out by similar promotions, on different nights, for men. The director rejected all these arguments and held that the New Jersey law contained no exceptions.

Are some forms of discrimination too trivial to bother with, or is it important to pursue all instances of discrimination?

4. **Public Breastfeeding.**   As these materials make clear, private businesses have the right to exclude unless doing so violates a public accommodations law. Likewise, they have the right to set rules for customer behavior—"no shirt, no shoes, no service"—unless that power is circumscribed. Women who breastfeed in stores or restaurants, or on airplanes, have sometimes encountered hostility and, in some cases, been thrown out. Incidents of exclusion, in turn, sometimes provoke public protests, such as "nurse-ins," in which large numbers of women show up to the location of a controversy and simultaneously breastfeed.[420]

Why do people object to public breastfeeding? Meghan Boone argues that laws to protect the right to breastfeed in public "are necessary because in the United States the female breast is commonly sexualized, such that many Americans believe that breasts should not be exposed in public."[421] Every state now has such a law, which permits people to breastfeed in any public or private location where they otherwise have the right to be.[422] Yet, despite these protections, women are sometimes still ordered to leave public and private places when they breastfeed or required to cover a baby's head with a blanket.[423] Do laws that protect women inevitably perpetuate some gender stereotypes, such as that feeding infants is an essential female activity?[424]

---

419. Gillespie v. Coastline Rest., CRT 2579-03, Order, N.J. Dep't of Law & Public Safety (June 1, 2004).

420. See Lawrence M. Friedman & Joanna L. Grossman, The Walled Garden: Law and Privacy in Modern Society 59-64 (2022).

421. Meghan Boone, Lactation Law, 106 Cal. L. Rev. 1827, 1840 (2018).

422. For a current list of laws, see Nat'l Conf. of State Legis., State Breastfeeding Laws. Although the federal accommodations law does not cover sex-based exclusion, a 1999 amendment to a postal appropriations bill provides that women can breastfeed in any federal building or on federal property. See Treasury and General Government Appropriations Act, Pub. L. No. 106-58, § 647, 113 Stat. 478 (1999).

423. See, e.g., Martha Neil, Public Breastfeeding May Be Legal in Mich., But It's Not OK in My Court, Judge Told Mom, ABA J. (Nov. 11, 2011); Amy Graff, Pastor Calls Breast-feeding Mom a Stripper, SFGate (Feb. 28, 2012), http://blog.sfgate.com/sfmoms/2012/02/28/pastor-calls-breastfeeding-mom-a-stripper.

424. Boone, supra note 421, at 1831 (arguing that many lactation laws designed to help women are often conditioned on "a woman's adherence to traditionally feminine and appropriately maternal gender norms").

NOTE ON SEXUAL ORIENTATION AND PUBLIC ACCOMMODATIONS LAW

Public accommodations laws have also been used to challenge exclusions based on sexual orientation. A growing number of states ban discrimination by public accommodations on grounds of sexual orientation and, in a smaller number of states, gender identity.[425] The Supreme Court of California in North Coast Women's Care Medical Group, Inc. v. Superior Court held that California's Unruh Act, invoked in *Koire* and *Isbister*, was violated by a medical group's refusal to provide infertility treatment to lesbian women.[426] The statute at the time did not prohibit sexual orientation discrimination, although it was amended in 2005 to provide protection for sexual orientation and gender identity and expression.[427] But even before that amendment, the list of protected characteristics in the statute was treated as illustrative rather than exhaustive, and courts had repeatedly applied it to exclusions on the basis of sexual orientation. The court in *North Coast* rejected the argument that the doctors' religious objections to inseminating a lesbian, unmarried woman were sufficient to excuse the clear violation of the public accommodations law.[428] Medical practices, like other business establishments, must provide "full and equal" access to all patients. Physicians' organizations are not in complete agreement on the issue. The American Society for Reproductive Medicine opines that there is no ethical basis for physicians to deny access to fertility services on the basis of marital status or sexual orientation.[429] The American College of Obstetrics and Gynecology gives doctors more room to exercise conscientious objection by refusing to provide particular services or to treat particular patients.[430] Regardless of the ethics, however, surveys suggest that many fertility specialists do indeed discriminate on the basis of sexual orientation and marital status.[431]

The Supreme Court's ruling in Obergefell v. Hodges,[432] which held bans on same-sex marriage unconstitutional (discussed in Chapter 2), provoked a number

---

425. See also Nat'l Conf. of State Legis., State Public Accommodation Laws (June 25, 2021), http://www.ncsl.org/research/civil-and-criminal-justice/state-public-accommodation-laws.aspx.

426. 189 P.3d 959 (Cal. 2008).

427. Cal. Civ. Code § 51 (2022)

428. *North Coast Women's Care Medical Group*, 189 P.3d at 971.

429. ASRM-Ethics Committee, Access to Fertility Treatment Irrespective of Marital Status, Sexual Orientation, or Gender Identity, 116 Fertility & Sterility 326 (2021).

430. ACOG-Committee on Ethics, The Limits of Conscientious Refusal in Reproductive Medicine, 110 Obstetrics & Gynecology 1203 (2007) (reaffirmed 2016).

431. See Liza Mundy, Everything Conceivable: How the Science of Assisted Reproduction is Changing Men, Women, and the World 202 (2008) (citing 2005 study of doctors finding that half would refuse infertility services to a lesbian woman); Abirami Kirubarajan, Cultural Competence in Fertility Care for Lesbian, Gay, Bisexual, Transgender, and Queer People: A Systematic Review of Patient and Provider Perspectives, 115 Fertility & Sterility 1294 (2021) (analyzing studies that show barriers to access, including physician discrimination and gatekeeping behavior).

432. 576 U.S. 644 (2015). This case is excerpted in Chapter 3 of this book.

of new lawsuits about the denial of public accommodations to gay and lesbian individuals by bakers, photographers, and wedding venues. The individuals and businesses in these cases have argued that providing goods or services in connection with gay or lesbian weddings violates their religious freedom. The Supreme Court agreed to review a case in which a bakery owner refused to create a cake for a gay couple's wedding because of his religious opposition to same-sex marriage, and the couple sued under the state's public accommodations law. In Masterpiece Cakeshop v. Colorado Civil Rights Commission,[433] the Court did not rule on the merits whether the First Amendment protects such a refusal on free speech or religious freedom grounds; it held instead that the baker was entitled to reconsideration by the Colorado Civil Rights Commission because he had been subjected to anti-religious bias in the process.[434] But Justice Kennedy explored the tension between the civil rights protected by public accommodations laws and the rights protected by the First Amendment.

> The case presents difficult questions as to the proper reconciliation of at least two principles. The first is the authority of a State and its governmental entities to protect the rights and dignity of gay persons who are, or wish to be, married but who face discrimination when they seek goods or services. The second is the right of all persons to exercise fundamental freedoms under the First Amendment, as applied to the States through the Fourteenth Amendment. . . .
>
> One of the difficulties in this case is that the parties disagree as to the extent of the baker's refusal to provide service. If a baker refused to design a special cake with words or images celebrating the marriage—for instance, a cake showing words with religious meaning—that might be different from a refusal to sell any cake at all. In defining whether a baker's creation can be protected, these details might make a difference. . . .
>
> Our society has come to the recognition that gay persons and gay couples cannot be treated as social outcasts or as inferior in dignity and worth. For that reason the laws and the Constitution can, and in some instances must, protect them in the exercise of their civil rights. The exercise of their freedom on terms equal to others must be given great weight and respect by the courts. At the same time, the religious and philosophical objections to gay marriage are protected views and in some instances protected forms of expression. As this Court observed in *Obergefell v. Hodges* (2015), "[t]he First Amendment ensures that religious organizations and persons are given proper protection as they seek to teach the principles that are so fulfilling and so central to their lives and faiths." Nevertheless,

---

433. 138 S. Ct. 1719 (2018).

434. The claim of anti-religious hostility was contested. Justice Kennedy cited statements by members of the Commission that implied "that religious beliefs and persons are less than fully welcome in Colorado's business community," such as statements that religious freedom "has been used to justify all kinds of discrimination throughout history, whether it be slavery, whether it be the holocaust" and that a person can believe what he wants but cannot act on religious beliefs "if he decides to do business in this state." Id. at 1729.

while those religious and philosophical objections are protected, it is a general rule that such objections do not allow business owners and other actors in the economy and in society to deny protected persons equal access to goods and services under a neutral and generally applicable public accommodations law.

When it comes to weddings, it can be assumed that a member of the clergy who objects to gay marriage on moral and religious grounds could not be compelled to perform the ceremony without denial of his or her right to the free exercise of religion. This refusal would be well understood in our constitutional order as an exercise of religion, an exercise that gay persons could recognize and accept without serious diminishment to their own dignity and worth. Yet if that exception were not confined, then a long list of persons who provide goods and services for marriages and weddings might refuse to do so for gay persons, thus resulting in a community-wide stigma inconsistent with the history and dynamics of civil rights laws that ensure equal access to goods, services, and public accommodations.

It is unexceptional that Colorado law can protect gay persons, just as it can protect other classes of individuals, in acquiring whatever products and services they choose on the same terms and conditions as are offered to other members of the public. And there are no doubt innumerable goods and services that no one could argue implicate the First Amendment. . . .

Phillips claims, however, that a narrower issue is presented. He argues that he had to use his artistic skills to make an expressive statement, a wedding endorsement in his own voice and of his own creation. As Phillips would see the case, this contention has a significant First Amendment speech component and implicates his deep and sincere religious beliefs. . . .

Phillips' dilemma was particularly understandable given the background of legal principles and administration of the law in Colorado at that time. His decision and his actions leading to the refusal of service all occurred in the year 2012. At that point, Colorado did not recognize the validity of gay marriages performed in its own State. At the time of the events in question, this Court had not issued its decisions either in *United States v. Windsor* (2013), or *Obergefell*. . . . Since the State itself did not allow those marriages to be performed in Colorado, there is some force to the argument that the baker was not unreasonable in deeming it lawful to decline to take an action that he understood to be an expression of support for their validity when that expression was contrary to his sincerely held religious beliefs, at least insofar as his refusal was limited to refusing to create and express a message in support of gay marriage, even one planned to take place in another State. . . .

The neutral and respectful consideration to which Phillips was entitled was compromised here, however. The Civil Rights Commission's treatment of his case has some elements of a clear and impermissible hostility toward the sincere religious beliefs that motivated his objection.

The outcome of cases like this in other circumstances must await further elaboration in the courts, all in the context of recognizing that these disputes must be resolved with tolerance, without undue disrespect to sincere religious beliefs, and without subjecting gay persons to indignities when they seek goods and services in an open market.

Did Justice Kennedy dictate the result by framing the case as a conflict between two sets of rights: "the authority of a State and its governmental entities to protect the rights and dignity of *gay persons* who are, or wish to be, married but who face discrimination when they seek goods or services[]" and "the right of all persons to exercise fundamental freedoms under the First Amendment, as applied to the States through the Fourteenth Amendment[]?"[435] Should the conflict more properly be framed as "the rights of gay persons to be treated equally" versus "the right of religious people to discriminate?"

Before *Masterpiece Cake*, these types of challenges were largely unsuccessful. To what extent does that decision resolve future ones?[436] The baker in *Masterpiece Cake* later refused to bake a "gender-reveal" cake to celebrate the anniversary of a transgender person's transition. Does that refusal present identical issues? How might the ruling be applied in contexts other than cake? Could a hardware store simply refuse to sell anything to LGBTQ+ people? Why or why not? In 2019, the Supreme Court declined to consider one question left open in *Masterpiece Cakeshop*: whether individuals or organizations with sincerely held religious beliefs can demand an exemption from generally applicable neutral laws. However, it granted review and vacated a judgment in favor of a lesbian couple who had been refused services by a wedding designer, directing the lower court to reconsider the claim in light of the ruling in *Masterpiece Cakeshop*.[437]

Are courts reaching the correct results in these cases? Do straight women have a stake in the outcome? Consider Mary Anne Case's observations about the "live-and-let-live" solution that some have urged in the era of marriage equality:

> Although the claim of the proponents of living-and-letting-live is that "we can and should protect the liberty of both sides in the culture wars," every proposal I have seen provides far more protection to the religious objectors than to the proponents of sexual liberty and equality, among which latter group I unequivocally count myself. In particular, [W]hile it is clearly correct to say, as [Douglas] Laycock does, that, "[i]f we are to preserve liberty for both sides in the culture wars, then we have to preserve some space where each side can live its own values and where its rules control," no proposal I yet have seen offers my side in the culture wars anything like the "space . . .

---

435. *Masterpiece Cakeshop*, 138 S. Ct. at 1723.

436. See State v. Arlene's Flowers, Inc., 441 P.3d 1203 (Wash. 2019) (upholding finding that flower shop owner illegally discriminated by refusing to provide floral arrangements for a same-sex wedding against constitutional challenge); see also See Netta Barak-Corren, A License to Discriminate? The Market Response to Masterpiece Cakeshop, 56 Harv. C.R.-C.L. L. Rev. 315 (2021) (documenting an increase in service refusals to LGBT customers after the decision was issued).

437. Klein v. Bureau of Labor & Indus., 139 S. Ct. 2713 (2019).

[to] live its own values and where its rules control" such proposals insist our conservative religious opponents are entitled to. As a strong supporter of rights to sexual liberty and equality, I instead observe that many religiously motivated opponents of such rights seem to want to have their cake, eat it too, and shove it down my throat; and that most, if not all, religious liberty scholars who claim their goal is a live-and-let-live solution seem to support my religious opponents in their ongoing efforts to realize these desires at my expense.

Nor am I reassured by the insistence of proponents of live-and-let-live that while religious liberty may be in great peril, women's rights are secure, that there is of course no danger of retrogression on aspects of our current law crucial to women's legal and social equality. . . .[438]

PUTTING THEORY INTO PRACTICE

1-53. A law firm advertises on billboards with the tagline: "Divorce: Men Only" and describes its mission as "fighting for men's rights." The firm accepts only male clients and also provides fee discounts for all law enforcement officers and "firemen." Is this lawful in a state with a public accommodations law that protects against sex discrimination? Do any potential justifications for the focus on men's rights offset any harms to women?[439] What about a competitor to Uber called Chariot for Women, which operated briefly under the tagline "Driving Women Towards Empowerment and Safety" and accepted only female riders?[440] Is this lawful? Might it be even if the men-only divorce firm is not? Why or why not?

1-54. After the successful challenge to sex segregation by Boys' Club in California, there was similar litigation against the Boy Scouts of America.[441] But the plaintiffs were unsuccessful; the court concluded that Boy Scouts were operating a private, social club rather than a business establishment, at least in part because boys who sought membership had to "understand and agree to obey the Scout Oath, which requires that he commit to do his duty to God and country." Is that a persuasive distinction? Could the Girl Scouts claim that their case for sex segregation is stronger, as a strategy to remedy past discrimination against girls?[442] In 2019,

---

438. Mary Anne Case, Why "Live-and-Let-Live" Is Not a Viable Solution to the Difficult Problems of Religious Accommodation in the Age of Sexual Civil Rights, 88 S. Cal. L. Rev. 463, 471, 489 (2015).

439. This problem is modeled on one described in Michele N. Struffolino, For Men Only: A Gap in the Rules Allows Sex Discrimination to Avoid Ethical Challenge, 23 Am. U. J. Gender Soc. Pol'y & L. 487 (2014). In Nathanson v. Commonwealth, 16 Mass. L. Rep. 761 (Super. Ct. 2003), the court affirmed a ruling of the Massachusetts Commission Against Discrimination that fined a female matrimonial lawyer $5,000 for refusing to accept male clients. For discussion, see the symposium in 20 W. New Eng. L. Rev. 5 (1998).

440. Justin Wm. Moyer, A "Female-Only Uber" Called Chariot Is Coming to Boston Next Week. But Is It Legal?, Wash. Post, Apr. 11, 2016.

441. See Yeaw v. Boy Scouts of Am., 64 Cal. Rptr. 2d 85 (Ct. App. 1997).

442. These questions should be considered again in the context of the materials in Chapter 2, Section C.

Boy Scouts of America formally changed its name to Scouts BSA and opened all programs to girls as well as boys. If you were choosing a scouting organization for a young girl, would you choose the newly integrated Scouts BSA or the Girl Scouts? In response to BSA's announcement, Girl Scouts issued a press release claiming that "The need for female leadership has never been clearer or more urgent than it is today—and only Girl Scouts has the expertise to give girls and young women the tools they need for success."[443] Is this persuasive? Why? Would you expect similar effects of gender integration in both scouting organizations?

1-55. Consider the following club policies:

- A public golf course runs all-male tournaments and all-female tournaments, but no integrated tournaments.[444]
- An athletic club offers cheaper sign-up rates for women than for men, because it has more trouble attracting women as members and seeks to increase its female clientele.[445]
- An athletic club has male and female members but makes available a "women-only" workout room.
- An elite university sets aside six hours a week in one of its gyms solely for use by its female Muslim students. Critics viewed it as a concession to sexist cultural norms and invoked visions of women in veils and chadors on treadmills.[446]
- An athletic club offers sex-segregated topless swimming pools.[447]
- The Nevada Hard Rock Hotel and Casino promises that "ladies dressed in schoolgirl outfits drink free Champagne all night."[448]

Which of these are most likely to violate a public accommodations law? Which, if any, are objectionable from an equality standpoint? Why?

1-56. Harvard has a long tradition of all-male social clubs. In 1984, the university required these clubs to admit women. At that point, the clubs broke official ties with Harvard and were no longer recognized by the university. A spokesman for the 215-year-old all-male Porcellian Club justified the group's policy on the ground that admitting women could increase the chances of sexual misconduct.[449] The University claimed that the elite clubs foster a culture that invites sexual misconduct on campus. Which argument do you find more convincing? The University then announced a new policy prohibiting members of single-sex clubs from holding leadership positions on campus, including captains of athletic teams, and

---

443. Taylor Hosking, Why Do the Boy Scouts Want to Include Girls?, Atlantic, Oct. 12, 2017.

444. See Joyce v. Town of Dennis, 705 F. Supp. 2d 74 (D. Mass. 2010).

445. See Steve Friess, A Las Vegas Gym Faces a "Ladies' Night" Bias Case, N.Y. Times, Dec. 12, 2007, at A27.

446. Katha Pollitt, Sweatin' to the Koran?, Nation, Apr. 28, 2008, at 14.

447. See Phillips v. Las Vegas Athletic Club, Nev. Dep't Empl., Training and Rehab., Charge No. 0828-07-0563L (2008).

448. Friess, supra note 445 (describing Nevada litigation); Lauren Collins, Hey LA-A-A-Dies!, New Yorker, Aug. 6, 2007, at 22-23 (describing litigation against several nightclubs in New York that offer ladies' nights).

449. Jess Bidgood, Social Club at Harvard Rejects Calls to Admit Women, Citing Risk of Sexual Misconduct, N.Y. Times, Apr. 13, 2016, at A17.

barring them from receiving official recommendations required for prestigious fellowships. An estimated 30 percent of Harvard undergraduates belong to the six male "final clubs," five women's "final clubs," and nine sororities and fraternities. Harvard dropped the policy after a lawsuit was filed under Title IX.[450] How should Harvard balance its concerns about gender equality with the students' associational freedom?[451]

1-57. The Black Women's Health Imperative is a membership organization dedicated to "health policy, education, research, knowledge and leadership development and communications to save and extend the lives of Black women." The organization's services and programs are all geared toward Black women and girls. Should this organization be subject to state legislation banning race and sex discrimination? How would you respond to the view propounded in relation to the organization's predecessor organization, the National Black Women's Health Project?

> If African-American women do not exclude white women from their association, their sharing will be chilled by the presence of white women. African-American women will spend valuable time listening to white women defend their actions. In essence, African-American women will spend time concentrating on white women, instead of focusing on themselves. Their communications will become stilted until they are effectively silenced in their own associations.[452]

Do you agree with the statement? Does it satisfy any formal equality objections?

1-58. Nineteenth-century hotels used to have separate floors for women. These were abandoned by the 1980s, but they are returning, as customer research has indicated that many women prefer the privacy and special amenities of floors that cater particularly to women. Is this a positive development, or a throwback to a discriminatory era?

1-59. Good Eats is a restaurant that, in order to develop new markets to boost sagging sales, decides to offer a 20 percent discount to all groups of eight who are meeting during the lunch service for the purpose of a bridal shower, baby shower, birthday party, book club meeting, bridge club meeting, or sewing circle. As it turns out, groups that meet for these purposes during the lunch period are almost exclusively female. Public accommodation laws in the state prohibit discrimination on the basis of sex. Is the Good Eats discount unlawful?

1-60. In 2016, a group of powerful women founded The Wing, a private social club and co-working space for women who pay dues to access the "safe space." Men were excluded as members and guests. (A similar club called The Salon recently opened in Pittsburgh.) The company attracted more than $40 million in venture capital and a lot of publicity. The New York City Commission on Human Rights opened an investigation to explore possible violations of the city's law against

450. Kappa Alpha Theta Fraternity, Inc. v. Harvard Univ., 397 F. Supp. 3d 97 (D. Mass. 2019).

451. Laura Krantz, Sororities, Fraternities Sue Harvard over Social Club Crackdown, Bos. Globe, Dec. 3, 2018.

452. Pamela J. Smith, We Are Not Sisters: African-American Women and the Freedom to Associate and Disassociate, 66 Tul. L. Rev. 1467, 1511 (1992).

gender discrimination, which permits businesses to apply for an exemption based on "bona fide considerations of public policy."[453] Is this a good case for an exemption? Are the reasons women might seek refuge in an all-female club similar to those driving men to all-male clubs?[454] Might separate reasons be given for seeking an all-female workspace?

1-61.   How do the identity-based student organizations on your campus handle membership and leadership? Do you see any problem with their approaches? Are "safe spaces" on campus for particular groups a good idea? Why or why not?

1-62.   As a gift to her mother, Seandria purchased the Miracle Morning package from an Elizabeth Arden Red Door Salon and Spa in suburban Washington, D.C., which included a facial, massage, manicure, and lunch. While her mother, who is African American, was at the salon, she asked that the salon also color, cut, and style her hair. The receptionist refused, telling her that the salon "does not do black people's hair."[455] Should this refusal be legal? Why or why not?

---

453. See Joanna L. Grossman, Fly Away: The New York City Human Rights Commission to Investigate The Wing, a Private Club and Workspace That Is Just for Women, Justia's Verdict (Apr. 10, 2018).

454. Id.; J. K. Trotter, The New York Human Rights Commission Is Investigating The Wing, Jezebel (Mar. 26, 2018).

455. See Denny v. Elizabeth Arden Salons, 456 F.3d 427 (4th Cir. 2006).

CHAPTER 2

SUBSTANTIVE EQUALITY

When men and women are similarly situated, requiring that they be treated equally often opens up opportunities for women that were previously unavailable to them. To the extent that men and women are differently situated, however, applying the same rules to them may produce different, unequal outcomes. Theories of substantive equality seek to avoid these unequal outcomes by taking differences into account and eliminating their negative effects on women. Deciding which differences matter and what alternative approach will best accommodate them can involve complex, contested judgments.

One source of unequal outcomes for women is past discrimination. Women historically have been excluded, either by law or by gender roles and customs, from obtaining jobs equal to men in status and compensation. Examples of remedial measures intended to reverse the effects of past discrimination include "affirmative action" plans designed to increase female representation in traditionally male occupations and "pay equity" schemes designed to restructure wage scales that historically have developed job categories held disproportionately by women.

Biological differences are another potential target of substantive equality strategies. Only women and other persons with female reproductive organs[1] become pregnant, for example, and pregnancy can disadvantage workers with respect to hiring, promotion, and job security. Measures to make those environments more compatible with pregnancy and related conditions aim to neutralize this disadvantage.

Many differences between men and women are matters of averages, rather than definitional or categorical differences. Formal equality rules level the playing field for the exceptional or "non-average" woman who can compete successfully for an opportunity on the same basis as the average man. Other, more result-oriented approaches may be necessary, however, if the goal is to ensure that women and men have functionally equivalent opportunities. In the educational context, for example, some argue that all-female classrooms or sports teams are necessary to ensure that competition with boys does not deprive girls of equally valuable opportunities. In family law, similarly, some rules are better than others at recognizing tendencies toward women's economic vulnerability and the greater investment they make in their children.

In considering the examples of substantive equality in this chapter, it is important to note (1) which differences in circumstances or characteristics between men

---

1. Although we frequently refer to "women" when we address issues relating to pregnancy, we recognize that transgender men and some nonbinary persons who do not identify as "women" can also become pregnant.

and women are, or should be, significant, (2) what outcomes are just, and (3) what strategies are most likely to lead to those outcomes.

To what extent does a substantive equality approach differ from formal equality?

A.   REMEDYING THE EFFECTS OF PAST DISCRIMINATION

1.   Sex-Specific Public Benefits to Remedy Past Societal Discrimination

One of the circumstances that might justify different treatment for otherwise similarly situated people is past discrimination that has disadvantaged members of one group. This rationale has been at the heart of affirmative action programs for racial and ethnic minorities and is also used to justify some measures to remedy past discrimination against women. Kahn v. Shevin, excerpted below, would likely be decided differently today because the Court has since raised the level of scrutiny applied to sex-based classifications, but the opinion is an important historical marker for use of affirmative remedies to address gender inequalities.

Kahn v. Shevin

416 U.S. 351 (1974)

Mr. Justice DOUGLAS delivered the opinion of the Court.

Since at least 1885, Florida has provided for some form of property tax exemption for widows. The current law granting all widows an annual $500 exemption . . . has been essentially unchanged since 1941. Appellant Kahn is a widower who lives in Florida and applied for the exemption to the Dade County Tax Assessor's Office. It was denied because the statute offers no analogous benefit for widowers. [T]he Circuit Court for Dade County, Florida, held the statute violative of the Equal Protection Clause of the Fourteenth Amendment. . . . The Florida Supreme Court reversed. . . .

There can be no dispute that the financial difficulties confronting the lone woman in Florida or in any other State exceed those facing the man. Whether from overt discrimination or from the socialization process of a male-dominated culture, the job market is inhospitable to the woman seeking any but the lowest paid jobs. There are, of course, efforts under way to remedy this situation. . . . But firmly entrenched practices are resistant to such pressures, and, indeed, data compiled by the Women's Bureau of the United States Department of Labor show that in 1972 a woman working full time had a median income which was only 57.9% of the median for males—a figure actually six points lower than had been achieved in 1955. . . . The disparity is likely to be exacerbated for the widow. While the widower can usually continue in the occupation which preceded his spouse's death, in many cases the widow will find herself suddenly forced into a job market with which she is unfamiliar, and in which, because of her former economic dependency, she will have fewer skills to offer.

There can be no doubt, therefore, that Florida's differing treatment of widows and widowers "rest[s] upon some ground of difference having a fair and substantial relation to the object of the legislation." [Reed v. Reed (1971).] . . .

This is not a case like Frontiero v. Richardson . . . where the Government denied its female employees both substantive and procedural benefits granted males "solely . . . for administrative convenience." We deal here with a state tax law reasonably designed to further the state policy of cushioning the financial impact of spousal loss upon the sex for which that loss imposes a disproportionately heavy burden. . . .

Affirmed.

Mr. Justice BRENNAN, with whom Mr. Justice MARSHALL joins, dissenting . . . .

In my view . . . a legislative classification that distinguishes potential beneficiaries solely by reference to their gender-based status as widows or widowers, like classifications based upon race, alienage, and national origin, must be subjected to close judicial scrutiny, because it focuses upon generally immutable characteristics over which individuals have little or no control, and also because gender-based classifications too often have been inexcusably utilized to stereotype and stigmatize politically powerless segments of society. See Frontiero v. Richardson [1973] . . . .

I agree that, in providing special benefits for a needy segment of society long the victim of purposeful discrimination and neglect, the statute serves the compelling state interest of achieving equality for such groups. No one familiar with this country's history of pervasive sex discrimination against women can doubt the need for remedial measures to correct the resulting economic imbalances. . . . [T]he purpose and effect of the suspect classification are ameliorative; the statute neither stigmatizes nor denigrates widowers not also benefited by the legislation. Moreover, inclusion of needy widowers within the class of beneficiaries would not further the State's overriding interest in remedying the economic effects of past sex discrimination for needy victims of that discrimination. While doubtless some widowers are in financial need, no one suggests that such need results from sex discrimination as in the case of widows.

The statute nevertheless fails to satisfy the requirements of equal protection, since the State has not borne its burden of proving that its compelling interest could not be achieved by a more precisely tailored statute or by use of feasible, less drastic means. [The statute] is plainly overinclusive, for the $500 property tax exemption may be obtained by a financially independent heiress as well as by an unemployed widow with dependent children. The State has offered nothing to explain why inclusion of widows of substantial economic means was necessary to advance the State's interest in ameliorating the effects of past economic discrimination against women. . . .

By merely redrafting that form to exclude widows who earn annual incomes, or possess assets, in excess of specified amounts, the State could readily narrow the class of beneficiaries to those widows for whom the effects of past economic discrimination against women have been a practical reality.

Mr. Justice WHITE, dissenting.

The Florida tax exemption at issue here is available to all widows but not to widowers. The presumption is that all widows are financially more needy and less trained or less ready for the job market than men. It may be that most widows have been occupied as housewife, mother, and homemaker and are not immediately prepared for employment. But there are many rich widows who need no largess from the State; many others are highly trained and have held lucrative positions long before the death of their husbands. At the same time, there are many widowers who are needy and who are in more desperate financial straits and have less access to the job market than many widows. Yet none of them qualifies for the exemption. . . .

I find the discrimination invidious and violative of the Equal Protection Clause. There is merit in giving poor widows a tax break, but gender-based classifications are suspect and require more justification than the State has offered. . . .

It may be suggested that the State is entitled to prefer widows over widowers because their assumed need is rooted in past and present economic discrimination against women. But this is not a credible explanation of Florida's tax exemption; for if the State's purpose was to compensate for past discrimination against females, surely it would not have limited the exemption to women who are widows. Moreover, even if past discrimination is considered to be the criterion for current tax exemption, the State nevertheless ignores all those widowers who have felt the effects of economic discrimination, whether as a member of a racial group or as one of the many who cannot escape the cycle of poverty. It seems to me that the State in this case is merely conferring an economic benefit in the form of a tax exemption and has not adequately explained why women should be treated differently from men.

I dissent.

NOTE ON "BENIGN" CLASSIFICATIONS FAVORING WOMEN

As a result of the statute upheld in Kahn v. Shevin, a wealthy widow could receive a $500 property tax exemption while an impoverished widower could not. Can this result be justified under substantive equality principles?

Justice Douglas, one of the Court's most liberal members and strongest supporters of gender equality, was convinced that Florida's preference for women was justifiable. Some commentators have attributed this view to Douglas' own experience. At age six, his mother was left destitute by the death of his father, a rural preacher. Douglas and his older sister washed store windows and picked fruit to earn the nickels and dimes that, as he later recalled, "often meant the difference between dinner and no dinner." At oral argument, the lawyer for the widower, Ruth Bader Ginsburg, attempted to convince the Court that the preference was an inadequate way of responding to widows' plight: "if need is the concern, then sex should not substitute for an income test. And if widowed state is the concern, then it is irrational to distinguish between taxpayers based on their sex."[2] Does Justice Douglas' opinion respond to this argument?

---

2. Fred Strebeigh, Equal: Women Reshape American Law 63 (2009).

Kahn v. Shevin is one of a few public benefits decisions that have allowed group-based treatment more favorable to women than to men. The other principal case along this line is Califano v. Webster (1977), in which the Court upheld a Social Security provision applicable to retirements before 1972 and computed old-age benefits under a formula more favorable to women than to men. The benefits for both sexes were determined according to an average monthly wage earned during certain years, but women were given the opportunity of excluding three additional lower earning years than men. In a per curiam opinion, the Court concluded:

> The more favorable treatment of the female wage earner enacted here was not a result of "archaic and overbroad generalizations" about women . . . or of "the role typing society has long imposed" upon women . . . such as casual assumptions that women are "the weaker sex" or are more likely to be child-rearers or dependents. . . . Rather, "the only discernible purpose of [the statute's more favorable treatment is] the permissible one of redressing our society's longstanding disparate treatment of women."
>
> The challenged statute operated directly to compensate women for past economic discrimination. Retirement benefits under the Act are based on past earnings. But as we have recognized: "Whether from overt discrimination or from the socialization process of a male-dominated culture, the job market is inhospitable to the woman seeking any but the lowest paid jobs." [Kahn v. Shevin.] Thus, allowing women, who as such have been unfairly hindered from earning as much as men, to eliminate additional low-earning years from the calculation of their retirement benefits works directly to remedy some part of the effect of past discrimination.[3]

How "benign" is the classification that *Kahn* upheld? In an illuminating international study by Peter Glick and Susan Fiske, some 15,000 men and women were rated on attitudes of hostile sexism and benevolent sexism (an example of the latter would be "women should be cherished and protected by men"). They found that the two forms of sexism were related and together were better predictors of gender inequality than either alone.[4] What are the policy implications of this research?

A premise of many of the cases considered in Chapter 1, such as Orr v. Orr, is that sex-based classifications that appear to benefit women, in fact, may foster the kind of stereotypes that do more harm than good. Is there any other problem with "benign" classifications? Consider Catharine A. MacKinnon's observation about Kahn v. Shevin:

> The special benefits side of the difference approach has not compensated for the differential of being second class. . . . Under its double standard, women who stand to inherit something when their husbands die have gotten the exclusion of a small percentage of the inheritance tax to the tune of Justice Douglas waxing eloquent about the difficulties of all women's

---

3. 430 U.S. 313, 317-18 (1977).
4. Peter T. Glick et al., Beyond Gender Prejudice as Simple Antipathy: Hostile and Benevolent Sexism Across Cultures, 79 J. Personality & Soc. Psych. 763 (2000).

economic situation. If we're going to be stigmatized as different, it would be nice if the compensation would fit the disparity.[5]

Is MacKinnon's criticism fair to Justice Douglas? Aren't legislatures entitled to partially address an inequality? Is the complaint that Kahn v. Shevin is mere tokenism? Should we also be concerned about which women benefited?

PUTTING THEORY INTO PRACTICE

2-1. The U.S. Navy at one time had a policy under which male officers were terminated after they were passed over for promotion a second time after nine years, while female officers were discharged for non-promotion only after thirteen years. The rationale was that women could only be assigned to hospital ships and transports and not to vessels involved in combat, so they did not have the same opportunities as men to compile records warranting promotion.[6] Was this a reasonable policy? If so, are ameliorative measures for women in the military still justified now that the ban on women in combat has been lifted? How should the passage of time and changes in circumstances affect the evaluation of affirmative measures to remedy inequality? Chapter 1 addresses further issues relating to women in the military.

2-2. In the United States, women older than 65 are significantly more likely to live in poverty than men in this age group. Women on average receive lower Social Security benefits than men (about $1,200/month compared to a little over $1,500/month) and are more reliant on Social Security as their sole or primary source of income. Older women who are Black, Hispanic, or Native American are nearly twice as likely as older white women to live in poverty. Older women who are unmarried and older women who identify as LGBTQ are also significantly more likely to be impoverished. Higher health care costs and greater longevity mean that women on average have greater economic need than men in old age.[7] Should Congress reinstate a sex-based formula for calculating Social Security benefits to help offset older women's economic hardships? If so, should all women be eligible for an extra amount or just some women?

2.   "Affirmative Action" in Employment

Under certain circumstances, Title VII permits affirmative action to redress a significant gender imbalance in the workplace. An affirmative action plan might give preference to qualified women for a job they previously would not have

5. Catharine A. MacKinnon, Feminism Unmodified: Discourses on Life and Law 38 (1987).

6. See Schlesinger v. Ballard, 419 U.S. 498 (1975).

7. For a comprehensive review of the economic challenges older women face, see Amber Christ & Tracey Gronniger, Justice in Aging, Older Women & Poverty: Special Report (Dec. 2018).

obtained because of past discrimination, or because of historical patterns that channeled male and female workers into separate and unequal positions.

Litigation may force employers to implement an affirmative action plan to remedy past discrimination, but employers might also wish to voluntarily integrate their work force even in the absence of legal liability. The latter situation was at issue in the next case.

Johnson v. Transportation Agency

480 U.S. 616 (1987)

Justice BRENNAN delivered the opinion of the Court.

Respondent, Transportation Agency of Santa Clara County, California, unilaterally promulgated an Affirmative Action Plan . . . pursuant to which the Agency passed over petitioner Paul Johnson, a male employee [for promotion to road dispatcher], and promoted a female employee applicant, Diane Joyce. The question for decision is whether in making the promotion the Agency impermissibly took into account the sex of the applicants in violation of Title VII of the Civil Rights Act of 1964. The District Court for the Northern District of California . . . held that respondent had violated Title VII. The Court of Appeals for the Ninth Circuit reversed. . . . We affirm.[2]

I

In December 1978, the Santa Clara County Transit District Board of Supervisors adopted an Affirmative Action Plan (Plan) for the County Transportation Agency. The Plan implemented a County Affirmative Action Plan, which had been adopted, declared the County, because "mere prohibition of discriminatory practices is not enough to remedy the effects of past practices and to permit attainment of an equitable representation of minorities, women and handicapped persons." . . . Relevant to this case, the Agency Plan provides that, in making promotions to positions within a traditionally segregated job classification in which women have been significantly underrepresented, the Agency is authorized to consider as one factor the sex of a qualified applicant.

In reviewing the composition of its work force, the Agency noted in its Plan that women were represented in numbers far less than their proportion of the County labor force in both the Agency as a whole and in five of seven job categories. Specifically, while women constituted 36.4% of the area labor market, they composed only 22.4% of Agency employees. Furthermore, women working at the Agency were concentrated largely in EEOC job categories traditionally held by women: women made up 76% of Office and Clerical Workers, but only 7.1% of Agency Officials and Administrators. . . . As for the job classification relevant to this case, none of the 238 Skilled Craft Worker positions was held by a woman. . . . The Plan noted that this underrepresentation of women

---

2. No constitutional issue was either raised or addressed in the litigation below. . . . We therefore decide in this case only the issue of the prohibitory scope of Title VII. . . .

in part reflected the fact that women had not traditionally been employed in these positions, and that they had not been strongly motivated to seek training or employment in them "because of the limited opportunities that have existed in the past for them to work in such classifications." . . . The Plan also observed that, while the proportion of ethnic minorities in the Agency as a whole exceeded the proportion of such minorities in the County work force, a smaller percentage of minority employees held management, professional, and technical positions.

The Agency stated that its Plan was intended to achieve "a statistically measurable yearly improvement in hiring, training, and promotion of minorities and women throughout the Agency in all major job classifications where they are underrepresented." . . . As a benchmark by which to evaluate progress, the Agency stated that its long-term goal was to attain a work force whose composition reflected the proportion of minorities and women in the area labor force. . . . Thus, for the Skilled Craft category in which the road dispatcher position at issue here was classified, the Agency's aspiration was that eventually about 36% of the jobs would be occupied by women. . . .

The Agency's Plan . . . set aside no specific number of positions for minorities or women, but authorized the consideration of ethnicity or sex as a factor when evaluating qualified candidates for jobs in which members of such groups were poorly represented. . . .

On December 12, 1979, the Agency announced a vacancy for the promotional position of road dispatcher in the Agency's Roads Division. Dispatchers assign road crews, equipment, and materials, and maintain records pertaining to road maintenance jobs. . . .

Twelve County employees applied for the promotion, including Joyce and Johnson. Joyce had worked for the County since 1970, serving as an account clerk until 1975. She had applied for a road dispatcher position in 1974, but was deemed ineligible because she had not served as a road maintenance worker. In 1975, Joyce transferred from a senior account clerk position to a road maintenance worker position, becoming the first woman to fill such a job. . . . During her four years in that position, she occasionally worked out of class as a road dispatcher.

Petitioner Johnson began with the County in 1967 as a road yard clerk, after private employment that included working as a supervisor and dispatcher. He had also unsuccessfully applied for the road dispatcher opening in 1974. In 1977, his clerical position was downgraded, and he sought and received a transfer to the position of road maintenance worker. . . . He also occasionally worked out of class as a dispatcher while performing that job.

Nine of the applicants, including Joyce and Johnson, were deemed qualified for the job, and were interviewed by a two-person board. Seven of the applicants scored above 70 on this interview, which meant that they were certified as eligible for selection by the appointing authority. The scores awarded ranged from 70 to 80. Johnson was tied for second with a score of 75, while Joyce ranked next with a score of 73. A second interview was conducted by three Agency supervisors, who ultimately recommended that Johnson be promoted. Prior to the second interview, Joyce had contacted the County's Affirmative Action Office because she feared that her application might not receive disinterested review.[5] The Office in turn contacted the Agency's Affirmative Action Coordinator, whom the Agency's Plan makes responsible for, *inter alia*, keeping the Director informed of opportunities for the Agency to accomplish its objectives under the Plan. At the time, the Agency employed no women in any Skilled Craft position, and had never employed a woman as a road dispatcher. The Coordinator recommended to the Director of the Agency, James Graebner, that Joyce be promoted.

Graebner, authorized to choose any of the seven persons deemed eligible, thus had the benefit of suggestions by the second interview panel and by the Agency Coordinator in arriving at his decision. After deliberation, Graebner concluded that the promotion should be given to Joyce. As he testified: "I tried to look at the whole picture, the combination of her qualifications and Mr. Johnson's qualifications, their test scores, their expertise, their background, affirmative action matters, things like that. . . . I believe it was a combination of all those." . . .

The certification form naming Joyce as the person promoted to the dispatcher position stated that both she and Johnson were rated as well qualified for the job. . . . Graebner testified that he did not regard as significant the fact that Johnson scored 75 and Joyce 73 when interviewed by the two-person board. . . .

Petitioner Johnson filed a complaint with the EEOC alleging that he had been denied promotion on the basis of sex in violation of Title VII. . . .

II

As a preliminary matter, we note that petitioner bears the burden of establishing the invalidity of the Agency's Plan. . . .

The assessment of the legality of the Agency Plan must be guided by our decision in Steelworkers v. Weber, [1979]. In that case, the Court [held that] a voluntary affirmative action plan designed to "eliminate manifest racial imbalances in traditionally segregated job categories" [did not violate Title VII]. As we stated:

> It would be ironic indeed if a law triggered by a Nation's concern over centuries of racial injustice and intended to improve the lot of those who had

---

5. Joyce testified that she had had disagreements with two of the three members of the second interview panel. One had been her first supervisor when she began work as a road maintenance worker. In performing arduous work in this job, she had not been issued coveralls, although her male co-workers had received them. After ruining her pants, she complained to her supervisor, to no avail. After three other similar incidents, ruining clothes on each occasion, she filed a grievance, and was issued four pairs of overalls the next day. . . . Joyce had dealt with a second member of the panel for a year and a half in her capacity as chair of the Roads Operation Safety Committee, where she and he "had several differences of opinion on how safety should be implemented." . . . In addition, Joyce testified that she had informed the person responsible for arranging her second interview that she had a disaster preparedness class on a certain day the following week. By this time about 10 days had passed since she had notified the person of her availability, and no date had yet been set for the interview. Within a day or two after this conversation, however, she received a notice setting her interview at a time directly in the middle of her disaster preparedness class. . . . This same panel member had earlier described Joyce as a "rebel-rousing, skirt-wearing person." . . .

"been excluded from the American dream for so long" constituted the first legislative prohibition of all voluntary, private, race-conscious efforts to abolish traditional patterns of racial segregation and hierarchy. . . .

We noted that the plan did not "unnecessarily trammel the interests of the white employees," since it did not require "the discharge of white workers and their replacement with new black hirees." Nor did the plan create "an absolute bar to the advancement of white employees," since half of those trained in the new program were to be white. . . . Finally, we observed that the plan was a temporary measure, not designed to maintain racial balance, but to "eliminate a manifest racial imbalance." . . . As Justice Blackmun's concurrence made clear, *Weber* held that an employer seeking to justify the adoption of a plan need not point to its own prior discriminatory practices, nor even to evidence of an "arguable violation" on its part. Rather, it need point only to a "conspicuous . . . imbalance in traditionally segregated job categories." Our decision was grounded in the recognition that voluntary employer action can play a crucial role in furthering Title VII's purpose of eliminating the effects of discrimination in the workplace, and that Title VII should not be read to thwart such efforts.

The first issue [in this case] is therefore whether consideration of the sex of applicants for Skilled Craft jobs was justified by the existence of a "manifest imbalance" that reflected underrepresentation of women in "traditionally segregated job categories." In determining whether an imbalance exists that would justify taking sex or race into account, a comparison of the percentage of minorities or women in the employer's work force with the percentage in the area labor market or general population is appropriate in analyzing jobs that require no special expertise. . . . Where a job requires special training, however, the comparison should be with those in the labor force who possess the relevant qualifications. . . .

A manifest imbalance need not be such that it would support a prima facie case against the employer . . . since we do not regard as identical the constraints of Title VII and the Federal Constitution on voluntarily adopted affirmative action plans. Application of the "prima facie" standard in Title VII cases would be inconsistent with *Weber*'s focus on statistical imbalance, and could inappropriately create a significant disincentive for employers to adopt an affirmative action plan. . . .

As the Agency Plan recognized, women were most egregiously underrepresented in the Skilled Craft job category, since none of the 238 positions was occupied by a woman. . . .

[H]ad the Plan simply calculated imbalances in all categories according to the proportion of women in the area labor pool, and then directed that hiring be governed solely by those figures, its validity fairly could be called into question. This is because analysis of a more specialized labor pool normally is necessary in determining underrepresentation in some positions. If a plan failed to take distinctions in qualifications into account in providing guidance for actual employment decisions, it would dictate mere blind hiring by the numbers. . . .

The Agency's plan emphatically did not authorize such blind hiring. It expressly directed that numerous factors be taken into account. . . .

We next consider whether the Agency Plan unnecessarily trammeled the rights of male employees or created an absolute bar to their advancement. In contrast to the plan in *Weber*, which provided that 50% of the positions in the craft training program were exclusively for blacks, . . . the Plan sets aside no positions for women. The Plan expressly states that "[t]he 'goals' established for each Division should not be construed as 'quotas' that must be met." . . . Rather, the Plan merely authorizes that consideration be given to affirmative action concerns when evaluating qualified applicants. As the Agency Director testified, the sex of Joyce was but one of numerous factors he took into account in arriving at his decision. . . . The Plan thus resembles the "Harvard Plan" approvingly noted by Justice Powell in Regents of University of California v. Bakke, [1978,] which considers race along with other criteria in determining admission to the college. As Justice Powell observed [in *Bakke*]: "In such an admissions program, race or ethnic background may be deemed a 'plus' in a particular applicant's file, yet it does not insulate the individual from comparison with all other candidates for the available seats." Similarly, the Agency Plan requires women to compete with all other qualified applicants. No persons are automatically excluded from consideration; all are able to have their qualifications weighed against those of other applicants.

In addition, petitioner had no absolute entitlement to the road dispatcher position. Seven of the applicants were classified as qualified and eligible, and the Agency Director was authorized to promote any of the seven. Thus, denial of the promotion unsettled no legitimate, firmly rooted expectation on the part of petitioner. . . .

Finally, the Agency's Plan was intended to attain a balanced work force, not to maintain one. The Plan contains 10 references to the Agency's desire to "attain" such a balance, but no reference whatsoever to a goal of maintaining it. . . .

Express assurance that a program is only temporary may be necessary if the program actually sets aside positions according to specific numbers. . . . In this case, however, substantial evidence shows that the Agency has sought to take a moderate, gradual approach to eliminating the imbalance in its work force, one which establishes realistic guidance for employment decisions, and which visits minimal intrusion on the legitimate expectations of other employees. . . .

Justice STEVENS, concurring.

While I join the Court's opinion, I write separately to explain my view of this case's position in our evolving antidiscrimination law and to emphasize that the opinion does not establish the permissible outer limits of voluntary programs undertaken by employers to benefit disadvantaged groups.

I

Antidiscrimination measures may benefit protected groups in two distinct ways. As a sword, such measures may confer benefits by specifying that a person's membership in a disadvantaged group must be a neutral, irrelevant factor in governmental or private decisionmaking or, alternatively, by compelling decisionmakers to give favorable consideration to disadvantaged group status. As a shield, an antidiscrimination statute can also help a member of a protected class by assuring decisionmakers in some instances that, when they elect for good reasons of their own to grant a preference of some sort to a minority citizen, they will not violate the law. The Court properly holds that the statutory shield allowed respondent to take Diane Joyce's sex into account in promoting her to the road dispatcher position. . . .

II . . .

Given the interpretation of the statute the Court adopted in *Weber*, I see no reason why the employer has any duty, prior to granting a preference to a qualified minority employee, to determine whether his past conduct might constitute an arguable violation of Title VII. Indeed, in some instances the employer may find it more helpful to focus on the future. Instead of retroactively scrutinizing his own or society's possible exclusions of minorities in the past to determine the outer limits of a valid affirmative-action program — or indeed, any particular affirmative-action decision — in many cases the employer will find it more appropriate to consider other legitimate [diversity-related] reasons to give preferences to members of under-represented groups. Statutes enacted for the benefit of minority groups should not block these forward-looking considerations. . . . The Court today does not foreclose other voluntary decisions based in part on a qualified employee's membership in a disadvantaged group. Accordingly, I concur.

Justice O'CONNOR, concurring in the judgment. . . .

In my view, the proper initial inquiry in evaluating the legality of an affirmative action plan by a public employer under Title VII is no different from that required by the Equal Protection Clause. In either case, consistent with the congressional intent to provide some measure of protection to the interests of the employer's nonminority employees, the employer must have had a firm basis for believing that remedial action was required. An employer would have such a firm basis if it can point to a statistical disparity sufficient to support a prima facie claim under Title VII by the employee beneficiaries of the affirmative action plan of a pattern or practice claim of discrimination. . . .

As I read *Weber* . . . the Court . . . determined that Congress had balanced [its intent to root out invidious discrimination against any person on the basis of race or gender, and its goal of eliminating the lasting effects of discrimination against minorities] by permitting affirmative action only as a remedial device to eliminate actual or apparent discrimination or the lingering effects of this discrimination.

Contrary to the intimations in Justice Stevens' concurrence, this Court did not approve preferences for minorities "for any reason that might seem sensible from a business or a social point of view." . . . I concur in the judgment of the Court.

Justice SCALIA, with whom THE CHIEF JUSTICE joins, and with whom Justice WHITE joins in Parts I and II, dissenting. . . .

The Court today completes the process of converting [Title VII] from a guarantee that race or sex will *not* be the basis for employment determinations, to a guarantee that it often *will*. Ever so subtly, without even alluding to the last obstacles preserved by earlier opinions that we now push out of our path, we effectively replace the goal of a discrimination-free society with the quite incompatible goal of proportionate representation by race and by sex in the workplace. . . .

I . . .

Several salient features of the plan [at issue in this case] should be noted. Most importantly, the plan's purpose was assuredly not to remedy prior sex discrimination by the Agency. It could not have been, because there was no prior sex discrimination to remedy. The majority, in cataloging the Agency's alleged misdeeds . . . neglects to mention the District Court's finding that the Agency "has not discriminated in the past, and does not discriminate in the present against women in regard to employment opportunities in general and promotions in particular." . . . This finding was not disturbed by the Ninth Circuit.

Not only was the plan not directed at the results of past sex discrimination by the Agency, but its objective was not to achieve the state of affairs that this Court has dubiously assumed would result from an absence of discrimination—an overall work force "more or less representative of the racial and ethnic composition of the population in the community." . . . Teamsters v. United States, [1977]. Rather, the oft-stated goal was to mirror the racial and sexual composition of the entire county labor force, not merely in the Agency work force as a whole, but in each and every individual job category at the Agency. In a discrimination-free world, it would obviously be a statistical oddity for every job category to match the racial and sexual composition of even that portion of the county work force *qualified* for that job; it would be utterly miraculous for each of them to match, as the plan expected, the composition of the entire work force. Quite obviously, the plan did not seek to replicate what a lack of discrimination would produce, but rather imposed racial and sexual tailoring that would, in defiance of normal expectations and laws of probability, give each protected racial and sexual group a governmentally determined "proper" proportion of each job category. . . .

II

The most significant proposition of law established by today's decision is that racial or sexual discrimination is permitted under Title VII when it is intended to overcome the effect, not of the employer's own discrimination, but of societal attitudes that have limited the entry of certain races, or of a particular sex, into certain jobs. . . .

In fact, . . . today's decision goes well beyond merely allowing racial or sexual discrimination in order to eliminate the effects of prior societal discrimination. The majority opinion often uses the phrase "traditionally segregated job category" to describe the evil against which the plan is legitimately (according to the majority) directed. As originally used in *Weber*, that phrase described skilled jobs from which employers and unions had systematically and intentionally excluded black workers—traditionally segregated jobs, that is, in the sense of conscious, exclusionary discrimination. But that is assuredly not the sense in which the phrase is used here. It is absurd to think that the nationwide failure of road maintenance crews, for example, to achieve the Agency's ambition of 36.4% female representation is attributable primarily, if even substantially, to systematic exclusion of women eager to shoulder pick and shovel. It is a "traditionally segregated job category" not in the *Weber* sense, but in the sense that, because of longstanding social attitudes, it has not been regarded by women themselves as desirable work. . . . There are, of course, those who believe that the social attitudes which cause women themselves to avoid certain jobs and to favor others are as nefarious as conscious, exclusionary discrimination. Whether or not that is so (and there is assuredly no consensus on the point equivalent to our national consensus against intentional discrimination), the two phenomena are certainly distinct. And it is the alteration of social attitudes, rather than the elimination of discrimination, which today's decision approves as justification for state-enforced discrimination. This is an enormous expansion, undertaken without the slightest justification or analysis.

III . . .

It is impossible not to be aware that the practical effect of our holding is . . . effectively [to require] employers, public as well as private, to engage in intentional discrimination on the basis of race or sex. This Court's prior interpretations of Title VII, especially the decision in Griggs v. Duke Power Co., [1971,] subject employers to a potential Title VII suit whenever there is a noticeable imbalance in the representation of minorities or women in the employer's work force. Even the employer who is confident of ultimately prevailing in such a suit must contemplate the expense and adverse publicity of a trial. . . . If, however, employers are free to discriminate through affirmative action, without fear of "reverse discrimination" suits by their nonminority or male victims, they are offered a threshold defense against Title VII liability premised on numerical disparities. Thus, after today's decision the failure to engage in reverse discrimination is economic folly, and arguably a breach of duty to shareholders or taxpayers, wherever the cost of anticipated Title VII litigation exceeds the cost of hiring less capable (though still minimally capable) workers. (This situation is more likely to obtain, of course, with respect to the least skilled jobs—perversely creating an incentive to discriminate against precisely those members of the nonfavored groups least likely to have profited from societal discrimination in the past.) . . . A statute designed to establish a color-blind and gender-blind workplace has thus been converted into a powerful engine of racism and sexism, not merely permitting intentional race- and sex-based discrimination, but often making it, through operation of the legal system, practically compelled.

It is unlikely that today's result will be displeasing to politically elected officials, to whom it provides the means of quickly accommodating the demands of organized groups to achieve concrete, numerical improvement in the economic status of particular constituencies. Nor will it displease the world of corporate and governmental employers (many of whom have filed briefs as amici in the present case, all on the side of Santa Clara) for whom the cost of hiring less qualified workers is often substantially less—and infinitely more predictable—than the cost of litigating Title VII cases and of seeking to convince federal agencies by nonnumerical means that no discrimination exists. In fact, the only losers in the process are the Johnsons of the country, for whom Title VII has been not merely repealed but actually inverted. The irony is that these individuals—predominantly unknown, unaffluent, unorganized—suffer this injustice at the hands of a Court fond of thinking itself the champion of the politically impotent. I dissent.

NOTES

1. **Affirmative Action: Definitions and Background.**   Affirmative action plans vary across multiple dimensions: which employees are covered, whether the plans are voluntarily adopted or imposed under law or court order, and what measures they require. The most extreme type of affirmative action plan relies on "quotas,"

which measure success based on the hiring or promotion of a specific number or percentage of group members. But most affirmative action plans rely on less definitive measures such as forms of goals, timetables, and tie-breaking preferences that favor members of the underrepresented group without changing the applicable qualification standards.

Affirmative action became part of U.S. law in 1965, when President Lyndon Johnson approved Executive Order 11246, which was subsequently strengthened under President Nixon and further modified under President Clinton. The Order requires firms over a certain size doing a certain level of business with the federal government to employ qualified individuals from targeted groups in percentages roughly proportional to their representation in the available applicant pool. If those groups are underrepresented, the employer must develop a corrective plan and make good-faith efforts to implement it. Another form of affirmative action involves "set-asides"—preferences for targeted groups in the government contracting process. The concept originated in the 1950s as a way to help small businesses. Set-asides were expanded in the 1970s to encompass minority-owned businesses, and further extended in the 1980s to include women-owned businesses. However, the Supreme Court has cut back on race-based government set-aside plans that are not narrowly tailored to meet a compelling governmental interest—the same constitutional standard used to evaluate practices that discriminate *against* minorities.[8] For a race-based set-aside plan to pass strict scrutiny, it is not sufficient that a particular minority group is underrepresented in an industry; instead, there must have been a previous pattern of pervasive and systematic discrimination in which the government itself participated.[9] In contrast, the Supreme Court has upheld sex-based measures designed to remedy "mere" societal discrimination against women under a lower level of scrutiny, as in Kahn v. Shevin and Califano v. Webster.

The federal government has numerous other laws and regulations supporting some form of affirmative action. Most are aspirational: they express a desire for proactive strategies and goals but not methods of implementation or sanctions for noncompliance. One goal, which was reached in 2016, is that at least 5 percent of the federal government's contracting dollars go to businesses owned by women.[10] About one-fifth of American employees work for the U.S. government or for contractors and subcontractors who are subject to federal affirmative action requirements. Additional workers are covered by state or local mandates or voluntary private sector plans. Increasingly, however, voluntary affirmative action by employers has been supplanted by more amorphous "diversity" plans that do not require concrete actions to increase the hiring or promotion of women or minorities.[11]

---

8. See Adarand Constructors, Inc. v. Pena, 515 U.S. 200 (1995); City of Richmond v. J. A. Croson Co., 488 U.S. 469 (1989).

9. See, e.g., Associated Gen. Contractors of Ohio, Inc. v. Drabnik, 214 F.3d 730 (6th Cir. 2000).

10. See Stacy Cowley, Government Meets Goal Set in 1994 for Women's Business Contracts, N.Y. Times, Mar. 2, 2016, at B2.

11. See David B. Oppenheimer, The Disappearance of Voluntary Affirmative Action from the U.S. Workplace, 24 J. Poverty & Soc. Just. 37 (2016).

Since the Court decided *Johnson*, it has declared race-based affirmative action by a public employer to be constitutionally suspect and subject to strict scrutiny.[12] Although *Johnson* was decided under Title VII, Justice O'Connor would apply the same standard to affirmative action under Title VII as applies to a public employer under the Constitution. What would that mean for sex-based affirmative action? Given that the objective of affirmative action is to reverse the effects of past discrimination and/or to enhance diversity, is there any reason why gender-based affirmative action should be treated more leniently than race-based plans? Indeed, if race is the more suspect category, isn't it perverse to impose greater barriers to ending past race discrimination than to eliminating past sex discrimination?

Courts have not been entirely consistent in dealing with constitutional limits on affirmative action in the gender context, and there is conflicting authority on the question. The Sixth Circuit Court of Appeals has applied strict scrutiny to both race-based and sex-based affirmative action plans.[13] Several other circuits have applied intermediate scrutiny to sex-based affirmative action, with a lesser evidentiary burden.[14] Cases allowing gender-based affirmative action plans have generally required some showing of past discrimination, but not necessarily discrimination by the governmental entity whose affirmative action plan is in dispute.[15] Moreover, to an extent not apparent in judicial analysis of race-based affirmative action plans, courts emphasize that the purpose for reviewing gender-based discrimination is less to "smoke out" hidden, invidious discrimination than to make sure that sex-based rules are not based unintentionally on archaic stereotypes.[16] Does this difference justify a different legal standard?[17]

Notwithstanding the Court's tightening of the constitutional standard for race-based affirmative action in the interim, *Johnson* remains "good law" as a Title VII precedent. However, a subsequent Title VII case may cast doubt on *Johnson*'s longevity. In Ricci v. DeStefano,[18] the Court required the defendant, the City of New Haven, to show a strong basis in evidence for believing that it would have been liable for disparate impact if it had not thrown out the test results for promoting firefighters—results that would have largely excluded African Americans and Latinos from promotion. Failing that, the Court held the city liable for intentional race discrimination under Title VII. Although not an affirmative action case, *Ricci*'s tough approach to race-conscious measures designed to avoid shutting out

---

12. Public employers are bound by both the Constitution and Title VII; private employers, who are not state actors, need only comply with Title VII.

13. See Brunet v. City of Columbus, 1 F.3d 390, 403-04 (6th Cir. 1993).

14. See, e.g., Contractors Ass'n of E. Pa. v. City of Philadelphia, 6 F.3d 990 (3d Cir. 1993); Western States Paving Co. v. Wash. Dep't of Transp., 407 F.3d 983 (9th Cir. 2005).

15. See, e.g., Ensley Branch, N.A.A.C.P. v. Siebels, 31 F.3d 1548, 1580 (11th Cir. 1994).

16. See Contractors Ass'n of E. Pa. v. City of Philadelphia, 6 F.3d 990, 1010 (3d Cir. 1993).

17. See Rosalie Berger Levinson, Gender-Based Affirmative Action and Reverse Gender Bias: Beyond *Gratz, Parents Involved*, and *Ricci*, 34 Harv. J. Law & Gender 1, 36 (2011).

18. 557 U.S. 557 (2009).

a minority group from promotion opportunities is difficult to reconcile with the Court's more flexible approach in *Johnson*.[19]

The members of the *Johnson* Court held a wide range of views on employer promotion of diversity. For instance, in a conference argument over affirmative action in the 1980s, when Justice Scalia launched a tirade against any hiring preferences based on race or sex, Justice O'Connor, whom conservative President Ronald Reagan appointed as the first woman on the Court, reportedly interjected, "Why Nino, how do you think I got my job?"[20] Dissenting in *Johnson*, Justice Scalia, a virulent opponent of sex-conscious or race-conscious measures to promote equality, would permit voluntary affirmative action only by employers who previously engaged in discrimination against the group in question. In contrast, Justice O'Connor, concurring only in the judgment, would require that the disparity that the government is attempting to correct be substantial and provide a "firm basis for believing that remedial action is required." Justice Brennan, writing for a plurality of the Court, maintains that a voluntary affirmative action plan is justified to address a "manifest imbalance" (or substantial underrepresentation of women in "traditionally segregated job categories"). Justice Stevens, concurring in the plurality opinion, would give the employer even more leeway to achieve a "forward-looking" diversity. Who has the better approach?

Politically, affirmative action remains controversial. Sometimes supporters have emphasized gains to women and de-emphasized race in defending affirmative action. Most surveys reflect greater popular support for affirmative action programs on behalf of women than for programs on behalf of African Americans. Is this defensible as a pragmatic approach to preserving affirmative action in general? Or is any tactical advantage gained by prioritizing gender outweighed by reinforcing pernicious stereotypes about undeserving racial minorities? Does affirmative action itself, by identifying women and minorities as discrete classes of beneficiaries, reinforce dichotomous thinking about race and sex and erase women of color?[21]

Although the Court has, to date, left some room for affirmative action, the political process has sometimes gone farther to eliminate it. The first electoral test of affirmative action occurred in 1996 in California, when voters passed the California Civil Rights Initiative (Proposition 209), prohibiting "discrimination against, or . . . preferential treatment to, any individual on the basis of race, sex, color, ethnicity, or national origin in the operation of public employment, public education, or public contracting." Similarly, after the Supreme Court issued split decisions striking down the University of Michigan's undergraduate point-based affirmative action plan but upholding the law school's more nuanced, holistic plan, Michigan voters passed a referendum

---

19. See id. at 626 (Ginsburg, J., dissenting) (pointing out the irreconcilability of the *Ricci* and *Johnson* decisions); Sachin S. Pandya, Detecting the Stealth Erosion of Precedent: Affirmative Action After *Ricci*, 31 Berkeley J. Emp. & Lab. L. 285 (2010) (arguing that *Ricci* eroded *Johnson*'s precedential value).

20. Evan Thomas, First: Sandra Day O'Connor 259 (2019).

21. See, e.g., Rebecca Rifkin, Higher Support for Gender Affirmative Action Than Race, Gallup (Aug. 26, 2015) (67 percent of Americans support affirmative action for women, while 58 percent support affirmative action for minorities).

outlawing affirmative action in public education, employment, or contracting.[22] The Supreme Court upheld the constitutionality of the referendum in a case challenging it under the Equal Protection Clause.[23]

Analyzing several of the affirmative action initiatives, Sumi Cho observed that while white women in the State of Washington were targeted as potential supporters because they would have been the biggest beneficiaries, a majority of them voted to end affirmative action.[24] Why do you suppose they voted that way?

Race-based affirmative action in higher education remains under fire. In 2016, the Supreme Court rejected a challenge to the University of Texas's affirmative action plan, which considered race as one factor in each applicant's "Personal Achievement Index," a supplemental admissions program designed to augment the primary method of admitting applicants, the automatic admission of students who graduate in the top 10 percent of their class from a Texas high school.[25] More recently, the same organization that represented the plaintiff in *Fisher* is representing Asian-American students in a lawsuit against Harvard University, arguing that Harvard's use of affirmative action unfairly penalizes Asian-American students by preferentially admitting other racial minorities.[26] The suit alleges that Asian-American students have higher grades and test scores than other applicants who are admitted and are excluded due to adverse ratings on "personal" qualities, such as likability.[27] Not all Asian-American students have supported the lawsuit, pointing out that they are not a monolithic group and objecting to deploying the "model minority" myth as a wedge to divide persons of color over affirmative action.[28] Harvard's policy was upheld by both the district court and the First Circuit Court of Appeals, and the U.S. Supreme Court has agreed to review the case, along with a companion case challenging the University of North Carolina's admissions policy on the grounds that it discriminates against both whites and Asians.[29] Vinay Harpalani has studied the Harvard case and suggests that there may be some gender stereotyping in the "passive nerd" stereotype that seems to negatively influence

---

22. See Gratz v. Bollinger, 539 U.S. 244 (2003) (invalidating undergraduate affirmative action plan); Grutter v. Bollinger, 539 U.S. 306 (2003).

23. Schuette v. Coal. to Def. Affirmative Action, 572 U.S. 291 (2014).

24. Sumi Cho, Understanding White Women's Ambivalence Towards Affirmative Action: Theorizing Political Accountability in Coalitions, 71 UMKC L. Rev. 399, 401-02 (2002).

25. Fisher v. Univ. of Tex., 579 U.S. 365 (2016).

26. Anemona Hartocollis & Stephanie Saul, Asians Become Focus of Battle on Admissions, N.Y. Times, Aug. 3, 2017, at A1; Students for Fair Admissions, Inc. v. President and Fellows of Harv. Coll., 2019 U.S. Dist. LEXIS 170309 (D. Mass. Sept. 30, 2019).

27. Anemona Hartocollis, Harvard Rates Asian Americans as Less Likable, Plaintiffs Claim, N.Y. Times, June 15, 2018, at A1.

28. See Jo-Ann Yoo, Why Asian Americans Refuse to Be a Wedge in the War on Affirmative Action, Fortune (Aug. 6, 2017); Alia Wong, The Thorny Relationship Between Asians and Affirmative Action, Atlantic (Aug. 3, 2017).

29. Students for Fair Admission, Inc. v. President & Fellows of Harvard College, No. 20-1199 (filed Mar. 1, 2021); Students for Fair Admissions, Inc. v. Univ. of N.C., No. 21-707 (filed Nov. 15, 2021). See also Adam Liptak & Anemona Hartocollis, Supreme Court Will Hear Challenge to Affirmative Action Against Harvard and UNC, N.Y. Times, Jan. 22, 2022.

Asians' admittance to elite schools.[30] Do you agree? Can any consideration of diversity in school admissions be free of stereotypes?

Restrictions on affirmative action in higher education have had significantly greater impact on racial diversity than on gender diversity, and most of the continuing controversy concerns race-based plans.[31] One reason sex-based affirmative action in the educational setting is less of a hot-button issue than race-based affirmative action is that women earn about 58 percent of all bachelor's degrees[32] and represent 61 percent of enrollment in graduate programs.[33] Except in programs like science and engineering, where women are still underrepresented, some schools favor men in the application process in order to avoid having more than 60 percent women.[34] For consideration of whether this data warrants affirmative intervention on behalf of males, see Section C2 of this chapter.

2. **The Diversity Rationale.**   Although the Court recognized past discrimination as a compelling interest for affirmative action earlier, the diversity rationale is more persuasive to most people. In a 2019 poll, 75 percent of respondents said it was somewhat important or very important for companies and organizations to promote racial and ethnic diversity in the workplace,[35] and about six in ten U.S. adults in another study say that having an increasing number of people of different races, ethnic groups, and nationalities in the U.S. makes the country a better place to live.[36] Why do most people say they prefer a diverse work or school environment, even though they don't necessarily prefer to live in a racially integrated

---

30. Vinay Harpalani, Asian Americans, Racial Stereotypes, and Elite University Admissions, 102 B.U. L. Rev. 233, 258 (2022).

31. Susan W. Kaufmann, The History and Impact of State Initiatives to Eliminate Affirmative Action, 111 New Directions for Teaching and Learning 3, 5, 7 (Fall 2007).

32. See Nat'l Ctr. for Educ. Stats., Degrees Conferred by Race/Ethnicity and Sex (2022).

33. See Nat'l Ctr. for Educ. Stats., Postsecondary Education (May 2022). On the possible reasons for the new gender gap, see Claudia Goldin et al., The Homecoming of American College Women: The Reversal of the College Gender Gap, 20 J. Econ. Persps. 133 (2006) (finding that widening job prospects for women and girls led them to compete educationally and often win).

34. See Charlotte West, An Unnoticed Result of the Decline of Men in College: It's Harder for Women to Get In, Hechinger Rep. (Oct. 27, 2021); see also Hironao Okahana & Enyu Zhou, Council for Graduate Schs., Graduate Enrollment and Degrees: 2007 to 2017, at 12 (Oct. 2018) (women are 26.5 percent of graduate enrollment in engineering, 33.7 percent of graduate enrollment in math and computer science, and 40.8 percent of graduate enrollment in physical and earth sciences).

35. See Juliana Menasce Horowitz, Pew Rsch. Ctr., Americans See Advantages and Challenges in Country's Growing Racial and Ethnic Diversity (May 8, 2019).

36. See Hannah Fingerhut, Pew Rsch. Ctr., Most Americans Express Positive Views of Country's Growing Racial and Ethnic Diversity (June 14, 2018). In one poll of employed people, 68 percent said they had contact with people of other races and ethnicities on a daily basis, but only 50 percent had regular contact outside of work. See Taft Communications, New Poll: Attitudes on Diversity in U.S. Workplaces Show Significant Divisions by Race, Gender, Political Affiliation (Mar. 15, 2022).

one?[37] A partial explanation is that diversity feels good, at least if confined to public spaces. People may think that being in a diverse environment must mean that they are not racist, or sexist.

Another explanation is that people appreciate the extent to which diversity improves certain environments, especially work and school. It has become widely accepted that having individuals with diverse backgrounds and viewpoints make those environments more effective. Identity diversity (involving differences in race, gender, age, ethnicity, religion, and sexual orientation) is said to yield cognitive diversity because "identities influence what we know . . . and how we think, . . . and how others treat us."[38] Studies indicate that diverse viewpoints encourage critical thinking, creative problem solving, and the search for new information; they expand the range of alternatives considered and counteract "group think."[39] Diverse groups are more accepting of alternative viewpoints and foster more persistent and confident voicing of dissenting perspectives.[40] What kind of diversity, if any, do women bring to the table? Can you answer this question without engaging in the kind of gender stereotyping that undermines gender equality? The debate over women's differences is addressed in Chapter 4, Section A.

Notably, although most Americans want to work in an environment in which racial and ethnic diversity is supported (75 percent, in one poll), many fewer (24 percent in the same poll) think companies and organizations should take race or ethnicity into account in hiring and promotion decisions.[41] Can you explain this?

3. Women's "Choices": Explanation or Symptom of Gender Inequality?   In his dissent in *Johnson*, Justice Scalia attributes women's underrepresentation in traditionally male job categories to women's choices. In his view, it is "absurd" to think that women could be "eager to shoulder pick and shovel." Was he right at the time? What about today? If so, should a "lack of interest" by women generally in certain jobs be a defense to the absence, or severe underrepresentation, of women in those jobs?

This defense was the focus of an important lawsuit by the Equal Employment Opportunity Commission (EEOC) against Sears, Roebuck & Co. in the late 1980s. The suit alleged a nationwide pattern and practice of discriminating against women for commission sales positions. To support its claim, the EEOC offered extensive statistical evidence that women who applied for sales positions were less likely than men with similar qualifications to receive high-paying commission jobs involving

37. In 2018, 71 percent of whites lived in a white neighborhood, down from 79 percent in 2000. See Tracy Hadden Loh et al., Separate and Unequal: Persistent Residential Segregation Is Sustaining Racial and Economic Injustice in the U.S., Brookings (Dec. 16, 2020).

38. Scott E. Page, The Diversity Bonus: How Great Teams Pay Off in the Knowledge Economy 1133-34 (2017). See also Dominic Packer & Jay Van Bavel, The Power of Us: Harnessing Our Shared Identities to Improve Performance, Increase Cooperation, and Promote Social Harmony (2021).

39. Katherine W. Phillips, How Diversity Makes Us Smarter, Great Good Magazine, Sept. 18, 2017 (referring to specific studies).

40. Katherine W. Phillips, What Is the Real Value of Diversity in Organizations? Questioning Our Assumptions, in Page, The Diversity Bonus, supra note 38, at 233.

41. See Horowitz, supra note 35.

"big ticket" items, such as major appliances, furnaces, roofing, and tires. Rather, women disproportionately ended up in non-commission lower-paying jobs selling apparel, linen, toys, paint, and cosmetics. In defending its employment practices, Sears introduced testimony by a female historian, Rosalind Rosenberg, that such patterns were consistent with women's traditional preferences, including their reluctance to work irregular hours, their desire for "social contact and friendship," and their discomfort with the stress of competitive pay structures. The trial court found such evidence more credible than testimony by other historians called by the EEOC, who asserted that women are influenced by the opportunities presented to them and have been eager to take higher-paying nontraditional jobs when such options have been available.

Other evidence in the case showed that Sears relied on tests measuring applicants' "vigor" by reference to their views on boxing, wrestling, and swearing. One witness explained that female employees weren't in higher-paid retail sales positions because they "didn't like going outside when it's snowing, raining, or whatever." In addition, Sears had taken no steps that might have made the higher paid positions more attractive to women, such as flexible schedules or outreach and support programs.[42] Should this evidence have concerned the court? The judgment for Sears was affirmed on appeal, over the dissent of Judge Cudahy, who challenged the stereotypes implicit in the court's analysis and its failure to recognize the employer's role in shaping the interests of applicants.

Is the *Sears* case about the failure of courts to recognize stereotypes at work? Or does it simply recognize reality and decline to impose responsibility on employers to alter employee preferences? According to one commentator:

> The liberal prohibition against stereotyping assumes that the problem is that the employer has inaccurately identified the job interests of (at least some exceptional) women who have already formed preferences for nontraditional work. By stopping at this level of analysis, however, liberal courts fail to inquire into or discover the deeper process through which employers actively shape women's work aspirations along gendered lines. . . . [For example, through] their recruiting strategies, employers do more than simply publicize job vacancies to those who are already interested: They actually stimulate interest among those they hope to attract to the jobs.[43]

To what extent does the affirmative action plan at issue in *Johnson* address this concern?

Women do disproportionately "choose" lower-paying jobs, resulting in sex segregation in many occupation categories. For example, in 2019, women constituted 89.6 percent of paralegals and legal assistants, but only 36.4 percent of lawyers,

---

42. EEOC v. Sears, Roebuck & Co., 628 F. Supp. 1264, 1307 (N.D. Ill. 1986), aff'd, 839 F.2d 302 (7th Cir. 1988).

43. Vicki Schultz, Telling Stories About Women and Work: Judicial Interpretations of Sex Segregation in the Workplace in Title VII Cases Raising the Lack of Interest Argument, 103 Harv. L. Rev. 1749, 1808 (1990).

with the percentage of female lawyers having declined by 1 percent.[44] They also constitute 97.7 percent of preschool and kindergarten teachers and 92.2 percent of nurse practitioners, but less than 3 percent of electricians and carpenters.[45] Should these disparities be a concern? If so, what should be done about it? For further discussion of these differentials in pay, see Chapter 1, Section C.

4. **Affirmative Action and the "Merit" Principle.**   One of the differences between Kahn v. Shevin and Johnson v. Transportation Agency is that Florida's tax exemption, designed to address general societal discrimination against women, had no single, specific victim, while in *Johnson*, the district court found that the plaintiff would have gotten the job at issue were it not for Santa Clara's "affirmative action" plan. This finding allowed Justice Scalia in his dissent to conclude that affirmative action employers violate the merit principle.

> [Acceptance of the brief's contention] effectively constitutes appellate reversal of a finding of fact by the District Court in the present case ("[P]laintiff was more qualified for the position of Road Dispatcher than Diane Joyce. . . ."). More importantly, it has staggering implications for future Title VII litigation, since the most common reason advanced for failing to hire a member of a protected group is the superior qualification of the hired individual.[46]

Responding to this point, Justice Brennan, citing an amicus curiae brief from the American Society for Personnel Administration, disputes that underlying assumption:

> It is a standard tenet of personnel administration that there is rarely a single, "best qualified" person for a job. An effective personnel system will bring before the selecting official several fully-qualified candidates who each may possess different attributes which recommend them for selection. Especially where the job is an unexceptional, middle-level craft position, without the need for unique work experience or educational attainment and for which several well-qualified candidates are available, final determinations as to which candidate is "best qualified" are at best subjective.[47]

Who is right? Are you persuaded that Joyce was less "qualified" than Johnson? Note that her quantitative score included subjective interview evaluations. Is there an argument that a woman who compiled her record in a workplace with so much gender bias is at least as qualified as a man who ranked marginally higher? What do you make of Footnote 5 in the opinion?

How well is "merit" captured by standardized tests used to select applicants for higher education and employment? Research by Susan Sturm and Lani Guinier finds that standardized tests leave out criteria indicative of potential future success,

---

44. See U.S. Bureau of Labor Statistics, Women in the Labor Force: A Databook, Rep. 1077, tbl. 11, at 66 (Apr. 2021).

45. Id. at 66, 69, 76.

46. 480 U.S. 616, 675 n.5 (Scalia, J., dissenting).

47. Id. at 641 n.17.

such as discipline, emotional intelligence, commitment, drive to succeed, reliability, creativity, judgment, honesty, courage, ability to manage anger, and leadership, while overvaluing other criteria, such as the willingness to guess, conformity, and docility, in relation to their correlation with preparation for higher education or employment.[48] Professor Marjorie Shultz and others have questioned the overreliance of law school admissions on the LSAT, and argued for criteria that better measure potential as an effective lawyer.[49] What criteria do you think might be more relevant than test scores or GPAs?[50]

Recent highly publicized scandals involving large pay-outs and fraud by celebrity parents have sharpened skepticism about the role of "merit" in university admissions.[51] All agree that these abuses are outrageous, but they have prompted renewed public scrutiny of more ordinary preferences extended to children of alumni. Can affirmative action fairly be characterized as a departure from an otherwise meritorious admissions process? If "merit" admittedly does not explain admissions in many other circumstances—as, for example, in legacy admits—can it be a valid reason to reject admissions based on the diversity it would add to a school?

5. **State-Mandated Affirmative Action for Women.**   The European Union (as well as Canada) has explicit constitutional commitments to "positive action," or affirmative action programs for women. Tax breaks are available to firms that hire women in traditionally male-dominated fields, and advancement plans for women are sometimes mandatory. Still, these commitments are mixed with legal rules that reflect the same tensions apparent in U.S. debates on affirmative action, particularly when a man objects that he would have gotten a job but for gender preferences. In one case, the European Court of Justice struck down an affirmative action plan under facts strikingly similar to *Johnson*.[52] Yet European Union countries are considerably more generous in providing social and economic support for women when they are pregnant or raising small children (explored in Chapter 4, Section B). Are the two approaches to "special treatment" consistent? What do you make of the fact that sex segregation remains high even in Scandinavian countries with the most progressive work/family policies?

A number of European countries have passed legislation requiring companies to have a certain minimum percentage of women on their corporate boards. This

48. Susan Sturm & Lani Guinier, The Future of Affirmative Action: Reclaiming the Innovative Ideal, 84 Cal. L. Rev. 953, 957, 976-77 (1996); see also Lani Guinier & Susan Sturm, Trial by Firefighters, N.Y. Times, July 11, 2009, at A17 (*Ricci* case fails to question relevance of written tests for leadership skills).

49. See Jonathan D. Glater, Study Offers a New Test of Potential Lawyers, N.Y. Times, Mar. 10, 2009, at A22.

50. John Eligon & Audra D. S. Burch, To Those Facing Racial Inequity, Scandal Stings, N.Y. Times, Mar. 14, 2019, at A1.

51. Jennifer Medina et al., Actresses, Business Leaders and Other Wealthy Parents Charged in U.S. College Entry Fraud, N.Y. Times, Mar. 12, 2019, at A1.

52. Anderson v. Fogelqvist, Case C-407/98, 2000 E.C.R. I-5539. See also Thomas Trelogan et al., Can't We Enlarge the Blanket and the Bed? A Comparative Analysis of Positive/Affirmative Action in the European Court of Justice and the United States Supreme Court, 28 Hastings Int'l & Comp. L. Rev. 39, 40-41 (2004).

legislation is consistent with the European Union's explicit constitutional commitments to "positive action." With respect to corporate boards, Norway, Spain, France, and Iceland have quotas that set the minimum for women's representation at 40 percent. Italy has a quota of one-third, and Belgium and Germany require 30 percent. The Netherlands has a voluntary target of 30 percent, and Great Britain has launched a voluntary effort known as the 30% Club. The European Union considered measures to require up to 40 percent representation but these were not passed. Are these a good idea? From a formal equality perspective, what is the downside?[53] According to Viviane Reding, the EU's former Justice Commissioner, without intervention it would take more than 40 years for women to hold 40 percent of board positions in Europe's publicly traded companies.[54] Is that a sufficient reason?

As of 2020 in the United States, 28 percent of the boards of directors of publicly listed companies were female.[55] A third of companies, however, had two or fewer female directors, which is below the "critical mass" thought to prevent women from being mere "tokens," rather than a meaningful presence on the board.[56] Following the European model, in 2018, after voluntary efforts to increase female board representation failed, California passed the first law in the United States mandating quotas. Senate Bill 826 required that all publicly held companies that are headquartered or incorporated in California have at least one female director by the end of 2019; by the end of 2021, organizations with five board members were required to have at least two women, and organizations with six or more were required to have at least three.[57] Is this kind of legislation a good idea? Would it be constitutional?[58]

Are voluntary strategies that leverage public disclosure and institutional and client pressure a better approach? One such initiative was launched in the United States in 2017 as a way of obtaining a voluntary commitment by law firms to have 30 percent of their leadership and governance roles, equity partner promotions, formal client pitch opportunities, and senior lateral positions be filled by women, lawyers of color, LGBTQ+ lawyers, and lawyers with disabilities.[59] The "Mansfield

---

53. See Louisa Peacock, EU Quotas Would "Patronise Women," Telegraph, Mar. 5, 2012; James Kanter, Europe to Study Quotas for Women on Boards, N.Y. Times, Mar. 15, 2012, at B3.

54. Kanter, supra note 53.

55. Catalyst, Women on Corporate Boards (Nov. 5, 2021).

56. Id. For more on the effects of the failure to have a critical mass of women, see Oyvind Bohren & Siv Staubo, Does Mandatory Gender Balance Work? Change Organizational Form to Avoid Board Upheaval, 28 J. Corp. Fin. 152 (2013); Marleen A. O'Connor, Women Executives in Gladiator Corporate Cultures: The Behavioral Dynamics of Gender, Ego, and Power, 65 Md. L. Rev. 465, 468 (2006); Lisa Fairfax, Clogs in the Pipeline: The Mixed Data on Women Directors and Continued Barriers to Their Advancement, 65 Md. L. Rev. 579, 592-93 (2006).

57. Cal. Corp. Code § 301.3 (2022).

58. See Meland v. Weber, 2 F.4th 838 (9th Cir. 2021) (invalidating law under federal Equal Protection Clause).

59. For a statement of the rule by its instigator, Diversity Lab, in collaboration with Bloomberg Law and Stanford Law School, along with a running list of those companies who

Rule," as it is called, was named after Arabella Mansfield, the first female lawyer in the United States. It is a version of the NFL's "Rooney Rule," which requires every NFL team to interview at least one minority candidate for head coach vacancies.[60] Within three years of its launch, 118 firms had committed to the Mansfield Rule.[61]

Australia is a case study of the effectiveness of investor pressure coupled with voluntary quotas. In 2015, the Australian Institute of Company Directors set a goal of 30 percent female representation on boards for securities exchange-listed firms. A council that represents the country's largest investors asked members not to support companies that failed to meet the gender goals. By 2019, nearly one in three board members was female, which reflects a 10 percent increase in just three years. Is this a strategy that could work in the U.S.?

PUTTING THEORY INTO PRACTICE

2-3. Reconsider the issue of pay equity discussed in Chapter 1, Section C1. Is it a problem that teachers and secretaries, who are disproportionately women, are paid less than sanitation workers and mechanics, who are disproportionately men? If so, what additional tools does substantive equality add to address the problem?

2-4. A state university offers graduate degrees in a number of STEM fields, including engineering, math, and science. Although women are 59 percent of the university's undergraduate enrollment and 55 percent of its graduate enrollment overall, women are fewer than 10 percent of the students enrolled in the university's graduate programs in these fields. Seeking to redress this imbalance, the university is considering waiving the application fee ($100) for women applicants only. Would you recommend this as a way to increase the pool of women applicants for these programs? How would you compare the advantages and disadvantages of such an approach? Is it legal?

2-5. In 2014, only 2.7 percent of venture capital-funded companies had a female CEO. To address the absence of women in start-up companies, the law firm Perkins Coie offered to discount its services by 15 percent for all start-ups that are founded or led by a woman.[62] Is this a good idea? To what extent, if any, does it violate the principle of formal equality?

2-6. Unlike race, which gets strict scrutiny, or gender, which gets intermediate scrutiny but requires an "exceedingly persuasive" rationale, sex orientation and gender identity get rational basis scrutiny under the Equal Protection Clause. Suppose a state school created a strong preference for people with non-normative gender identities because of past societal discrimination and a desire for diverse classroom discussions. Would the plan survive scrutiny under the Equal Protection Clause? What would be the advantages and disadvantages of such plans as social policy?

---

have signed onto the policy and a set of measurable outcomes, see https://www.diversitylab.com/mansfield-rule-4-0.

60. Id.

61. See Diversity Lab, supra note 59.

62. Nell Gluckman, Perkins Coie Offers Discount to Female-Run Startups, Amer. Law. (Mar. 23, 2016).

2-7. Law reviews have long been criticized for using selection processes that have historically resulted in the underrepresentation of women and students of color compared to the student body. Some law reviews have recently changed their selection processes to consider additional criteria, beyond grades and writing competitions graded by current editors, such as the gender and racial diversity of candidates and/or personal statements in which students discuss their background and experiences. The Harvard Law Review amended its affirmative action policy in 2013 to include consideration of gender and, in 2016, for the first time in its history, selected a group of editors whose demographics (including race and gender) reflected that of the wider law school class. In 2018, a Texas group calling itself Faculty, Alumni and Students Opposed to Racial Preferences sued the Harvard Law Review, claiming that it discriminates against white men in the selection of editors, in violation of federal statutes (Title VI and Title IX) banning race and sex discrimination by educational institutions receiving federal funds. Is the Law Review's policy lawful affirmative action or unlawful discrimination?[63] The group also claims that the Law Review discriminates against articles authored by white men. If this can be proven, is it a problem?

B.   ELIMINATING THE DISADVANTAGES OF WOMEN'S DIFFERENCES

1.   Pregnancy

Different treatment of women might also be justified on the basis of genuine differences (i.e., not stereotypes) between men and women. The most obvious sex-based difference is reproductive capacity. Although this difference has a "real" biological basis, it has also given rise to gender stereotypes. Women's childbearing role was one of the nineteenth- and early twentieth-century justifications for excluding them from positions ranging from serving on juries to working as lawyers or bartenders. The question for contemporary sex discrimination law is whether different treatment based on pregnancy can reduce the disadvantages that childbearing produces, without also reinforcing other practices and attitudes that disadvantage women.

Geduldig v. Aiello

417 U.S. 484 (1974)

Mr. Justice STEWART delivered the opinion of the Court.

For almost 30 years California has administered a disability insurance system that pays benefits to persons in private employment who are temporarily unable to work because of disability not covered by workmen's compensation. The appellees

---

63. See Bob Van Voris, Harvard Law Review Suit Opens New Front in Admissions-Bias Fight, Bloomberg/Business (Oct. 8, 2018); Claire E. Parker, Law Review Inducts Most Diverse Class of Editors in History, Harv. Crimson, Sept. 6, 2016.

brought this action to challenge the constitutionality of a provision of the California program that, in defining "disability," excludes from coverage certain disabilities resulting from pregnancy. . . .

I.

California's disability insurance system is funded entirely from contributions deducted from the wages of participating employees. Participation in the program is mandatory unless the employees are protected by a voluntary private plan approved by the State. Each employee is required to contribute one percent of his salary, up to an annual maximum of $85. These contributions are placed in the Unemployment Compensation Disability Fund, which is established and administered as a special trust fund within the state treasury. It is from this Disability Fund that benefits under the program are paid.

An individual is eligible for disability benefits if, during a one-year base period prior to his disability, he has contributed one percent of a minimum income of $300 to the Disability Fund. In the event he suffers a compensable disability, the individual can receive a "weekly benefit amount" of between $25 and $105, depending on the amount he earned during the highest quarter of the base period. Benefits are not paid until the eighth day of disability, unless the employee is hospitalized, in which case benefits commence on the first day of hospitalization. In addition to the "weekly benefit amount," a hospitalized employee is entitled to receive "additional benefits" of $12 per day of hospitalization. "Weekly benefit amounts" for any one disability are payable for 26 weeks so long as the total amount paid does not exceed one-half of the wages received during the base period." "Additional benefits" for any one disability are paid for a maximum of 20 days.

In return for his one-percent contribution to the Disability Fund, the individual employee is insured against the risk of disability stemming from a substantial number of "mental or physical illness[es] and mental or physical injur[ies]." It is not every disabling condition, however, that triggers the obligation to pay benefits under the program. As already noted, for example, any disability of less than eight days' duration is not compensable, except when the employee is hospitalized. Conversely, no benefits are payable for any single disability beyond 26 weeks. Further, disability is not compensable if it results from the individual's court commitment as a dipsomaniac, drug addict, or sexual psychopath. Finally, § 2626 of the Unemployment Insurance Code excludes from coverage certain disabilities that are attributable to pregnancy. It is this provision that is at issue in the present case.

Appellant is the Director of the California Department of Human Resources Development. . . . Appellees are four women who have paid sufficient amounts into the Disability Fund to be eligible for benefits under the program. Each of the appellees became pregnant and suffered employment disability as a result of her pregnancy. With respect to three of the appellees. . ., the disabilities were attributable to abnormal complications encountered during their pregnancies.[13] The fourth, Jacqueline Jaramillo, experienced a normal pregnancy, which was the sole cause of her disability.

---

13. Aiello and Johnson suffered ectopic and tubal pregnancies, respectively, which required surgery to terminate the pregnancies. Armendariz suffered a miscarriage.

At all times relevant to this case, § 2626 of the Unemployment Insurance Code provided:

> " 'Disability' or 'disabled' includes both mental or physical illness and mental or physical injury. An individual shall be deemed disabled in any day in which, because of his physical or mental condition, he is unable to perform his regular or customary work. *In no case shall the term 'disability' or 'disabled' include any injury or illness caused by or arising in connection with pregnancy up to the termination of such pregnancy and for a period of 28 days thereafter.*" (Emphasis added.)

[Appellant ruled appellees ineligible under this provision], and they sued to enjoin its enforcement. The District Court, finding "that the exclusion of pregnancy-related disabilities is not based upon a classification having a rational and substantial relationship to a legitimate state purpose," held that the exclusion was unconstitutional under the Equal Protection Clause. [In the meantime,] the California Court of Appeal, in a suit brought by a woman who suffered an ectopic pregnancy, held that § 2626 does not bar the payment of benefits on account of disability that results from medical complications arising during pregnancy. Rentzer v. Unemployment Insurance Appeals Board, 108 Cal. Rptr. 336 (1973). The state court construed the statute to preclude only the payment of benefits for disability accompanying normal pregnancy.[15]. . .

Because of the *Rentzer* decision and the revised administrative guidelines that resulted from it, the appellees Aiello, Armendariz, and Johnson, whose disabilities were attributable to causes other than normal pregnancy and delivery, became entitled to benefits under the disability insurance program, and their claims have since been paid. . . . Thus, the issue before the Court on this appeal is whether the California disability insurance program invidiously discriminates against Jaramillo and others similarly situated by not paying insurance benefits for disability that accompanies normal pregnancy and childbirth.

II.

It is clear that California intended to establish this benefit system as an insurance program that was to function essentially in accordance with insurance concepts. Since the program was instituted in 1946, it has been totally self-supporting, never drawing on general state revenues to finance disability or hospital benefits. . . . [T]he one-percent contribution rate, in addition to being easily computable, bears a close and substantial relationship to the level of benefits payable and to the disability risks insured under the program. . . . Because any larger percentage or any flat dollar amount rate of contribution would impose an increasingly regressive levy bearing most heavily upon those with the lowest incomes, the State has resisted any attempt to change the required contribution from the one-percent level. . . .

———————

15. Section 2626 was later amended, and a new § 2626.2 was added, in order clearly to reflect this interpretation.

In ordering the State to pay benefits for disability accompanying normal pregnancy and delivery, the District Court acknowledged the State's contention "that coverage of these disabilities is so extraordinarily expensive that it would be impossible to maintain a program supported by employee contributions if these disabilities are included." There is considerable disagreement between the parties with respect to how great the increased costs would actually be, but . . . [f]or purposes of analysis, the District Court accepted the State's estimate, which was in excess of $100 million annually, and stated:

> "[I]t is clear that including these disabilities would not destroy the program. The increased costs could be accommodated quite easily by making reasonable changes in the contribution rate, the maximum benefits allowable, and the other variables affecting the solvency of the program."

Each of these "variables" — the benefit level deemed appropriate to compensate employee disability, the risks selected to be insured under the program, and the contribution rate chosen to maintain the solvency of the program and at the same time to permit low income employees to participate with minimal personal sacrifice — represents a policy determination by the State. The essential issue in this case is whether the Equal Protection Clause requires such policies to be sacrificed or compromised in order to finance the payment of benefits to those whose disability is attributable to normal pregnancy and delivery.

We cannot agree that the exclusion of this disability from coverage amounts to invidious discrimination under the Equal Protection Clause. California does not discriminate with respect to the persons or groups which are eligible for disability insurance protection under the program. The classification challenged in this case relates to the asserted underinclusiveness of the set of risks that the State has selected to insure. Although California has created a program to insure most risks of employment disability, it has not chosen to insure all such risks, and this decision is reflected in the level of annual contributions exacted from participating employees. . . . Particularly with respect to social welfare programs, so long as the line drawn by the State is rationally supportable, the courts will not interpose their judgment as to the appropriate stopping point. . . .

The District Court suggested that moderate alterations in what it regarded as "variables" of the disability insurance program could be made to accommodate the substantial expense required to include normal pregnancy within the program's protection. The same can be said, however, with respect to the other expensive class of disabilities that are excluded from coverage — short-term disabilities. If the Equal Protection Clause were thought to compel disability payments for normal pregnancy, it is hard to perceive why it would not also compel payments for short-term disabilities suffered by participating employees. . . .

The State has a legitimate interest in maintaining the self-supporting nature of its insurance program. Similarly, it has an interest in distributing the available resources in such a way as to keep benefit payments at an adequate level for disabilities that are covered, rather than to cover all disabilities inadequately. Finally, California has a legitimate concern in maintaining the contribution rate at a level that will not unduly burden participating employees, particularly low income employees who may be most in need of the disability insurance. . . .

There is no evidence in the record that the selection of the risks insured by the program worked to discriminate against any definable group or class in terms of the aggregate risk protection derived by that group or class from the program.[20] There is no risk from which men are protected and women are not. Likewise, there is no risk from which women are protected and men are not.[21]

Appellee simply contends that, although she has received insurance protection equivalent to that provided all other participating employees, she has suffered discrimination because she encountered a risk that was outside the program's protection. For the reasons we have stated, we hold that this contention is not a valid one under the Equal Protection Clause of the Fourteenth Amendment. . . . [T]he judgment of the District Court is reversed.

Mr. Justice BRENNAN, with whom Mr. Justice DOUGLAS and Mr. Justice MARSHALL join, dissenting.

[T]he Court today rejects appellees' equal protection claim and upholds the exclusion of normal pregnancy-related disabilities from coverage under California's disability insurance program on the ground that the legislative classification rationally promotes the State's legitimate cost-saving interests. . .

Because I believe that *Reed v. Reed* and *Frontiero v. Richardson* mandate a stricter standard of scrutiny which the State's classification fails to satisfy, I respectfully dissent. . . .

Despite the Code's broad goals and scope of coverage, compensation is denied for disabilities suffered in connection with a "normal" pregnancy—disabilities suffered only by women. Disabilities caused by pregnancy, however, like other physically disabling conditions covered by the Code, require medical

---

20. The dissenting opinion to the contrary, this case is thus a far cry from cases like *Reed v. Reed* and *Frontiero v. Richardson*, involving discrimination based upon gender as such. The California insurance program does not exclude anyone from benefit eligibility because of gender, but merely removes one physical condition—pregnancy—from the list of compensable disabilities. While it is true that only women can become pregnant, it does not follow that every legislative classification concerning pregnancy is a sex-based classification. . . . Normal pregnancy is an objectively identifiable physical condition with unique characteristics. Absent a showing that distinctions involving pregnancy are mere pretexts designed to effect an invidious discrimination against the members of one sex or the other, lawmakers are constitutionally free to include or exclude pregnancy from the coverage of legislation such as this on any reasonable basis, just as with respect to any other physical condition.

The lack of identity between the excluded disability and gender as such under this insurance program becomes clear upon the most cursory analysis. The program divides potential recipients into two groups—pregnant women and nonpregnant persons. While the first group is exclusively female, the second includes members of both sexes. The fiscal and actuarial benefits of the program thus accrue to members of both sexes.

21. Indeed, the appellant submitted to the District Court data that indicated that both the annual claim rate and the annual claim cost are greater for women than for men. As the District Court acknowledged, "women contribute about 28 percent of the total disability insurance fund and receive back about 38 percent of the fund in benefits." Several *amici curiae* have represented to the Court that they have had a similar experience under private disability insurance programs.

care, often include hospitalization, anesthesia and surgical procedures, and may involve genuine risk to life.[4] Moreover, the economic effects caused by pregnancy-related disabilities are functionally indistinguishable from the effects caused by any other disability: wages are lost due to a physical inability to work, and medical expenses are incurred for the delivery of the child and for postpartum care. In my view, by singling out for less favorable treatment a gender-linked disability peculiar to women, the State has created a double standard for disability compensation: a limitation is imposed upon the disabilities for which women workers may recover, while men receive full compensation for all disabilities suffered, including those that affect only or primarily their sex, such as prostatectomies, circumcision, hemophilia, and gout. In effect, one set of rules is applied to females and another to males. Such dissimilar treatment of men and women, on the basis of physical characteristics inextricably linked to one sex, inevitably constitutes sex discrimination.

The same conclusion has been reached by the Equal Employment Opportunity Commission, the federal agency charged with enforcement of Title VII of the Civil Rights Act of 1964. . . .

The Court's decision threatens to return men and women to a time when "traditional" equal protection analysis sustained legislative classifications that treated differently members of a particular sex solely because of their sex. *See, e.g., Muller v. Oregon; Goesaert v. Cleary; Hoyt v. Florida.*

I cannot join the Court's apparent retreat. I continue to adhere to my view [in Frontiero v. Richardson] that "classifications based upon sex, like classifications based upon race, alienage, or national origin, are inherently suspect, and must therefore be subjected to strict judicial scrutiny.". . .

The State has clearly failed to meet that burden in the present case. The essence of the State's justification for excluding disabilities caused by a normal pregnancy from its disability compensation scheme is that covering such disabilities would be too costly. To be sure, as presently funded, inclusion of normal pregnancies "would be substantially more costly than the present program." The present level of benefits for insured disabilities could not be maintained without increasing the employee contribution rate, raising or lifting the yearly contribution ceiling, or securing state subsidies. But whatever role such monetary considerations may play

---

4. On March 2, 1974, the American College of Obstetricians and Gynecologists adopted the following Policy Statement on Pregnancy-related Disabilities:

> Pregnancy is a physiological process. All pregnant patients, however, have a variable degree of disability on an individual basis, as indicated below, during which time they are unable to perform their usual activities. (1) In an uncomplicated pregnancy, disability occurs near the termination of pregnancy, during labor, delivery, and the puerperium. The process of labor and puerperium is disabling in itself. The usual duration of such disability is approximately six to eight weeks. (2) Complications of a pregnancy may occur which give rise to other disability. Examples of such complications include toxemia, infection, hemorrhage, ectopic pregnancy, and abortion. (3) A woman with preexisting disease which, in itself, is not disabling, may become disabled with the addition of pregnancy. Certain patients with heart disease, diabetes, hypertensive cardiovascular disease, renal disease, and other systemic conditions may become disabled during their pregnancy because of the adverse effect pregnancy has upon these conditions.

in traditional equal protection analysis, the State's interest in preserving the fiscal integrity of its disability insurance program simply cannot render the State's use of a suspect classification constitutional. . . .

Moreover, California's legitimate interest in fiscal integrity could easily have been achieved through a variety of less drastic, sexually neutral means. . . .

I would therefore affirm the judgment of the District Court.

***

Although the Court held in *Geduldig* that pregnancy-based classifications do not merit heightened scrutiny under the Equal Protection Clause, it considered another pregnancy discrimination case during the same term. In that case, Cleveland Board of Education v. LaFleur, the Court addressed the constitutionality under the Due Process Clause of a rule requiring public school classroom teachers to take unpaid maternity leave once they reached the fourth month of pregnancy and to stay out of the classroom until their child was at least three months old. The Court held that the policy was invalid as a matter of due process because, although the school district could prevent an individual woman from working if she was not fit for the job as a result of pregnancy, due process considerations prevented it from compromising her procreative rights by conclusively presuming an inability to work.[64] In effect, this gave people a right against pregnancy stereotyping but not against exclusion because of pregnancy.

Two years later, the Court in General Electric Co. v. Gilbert (1976) applied the reasoning in *Geduldig* in the Title VII context, holding that pregnancy discrimination is not a form of actionable sex discrimination.[65] That decision was overridden by Congress by an amendment to Title VII known as the Pregnancy Discrimination Act of 1978 (PDA). The PDA explicitly declares that discrimination based on pregnancy is discrimination based on sex, for purposes of Title VII:

> The terms "because of sex" or "on the basis of sex" include, but are not limited to, because of or on the basis of pregnancy, childbirth, or related medical conditions; and women affected by pregnancy, childbirth, or related medical conditions shall be treated the same for all employment-related purposes, including receipt of benefits under fringe benefit programs, as other persons not so affected but similar in their ability or inability to work, and nothing in section 703(h) of this title shall be interpreted to permit otherwise.[66]

The PDA amended Title VII, but only a constitutional amendment can override the Court's interpretation of the U.S. Constitution and *Geduldig* has never been overruled. Even though Justice Ginsburg repeatedly argued against *Geduldig*

---

64. 414 U.S. 632 (1974). For a comprehensive history of pregnancy discrimination law, see Deborah Dinner, The Costs of Reproduction: History and the Legal Construction of Sex Equality, 46 Harv. C.R.-C.L. L. Rev. 415 (2011).

65. 429 U.S. 125, 133-40 (1976).

66. 42 U.S.C. § 2000e(k) (2018).

and urged the Court to overrule it, the Court never did.[67] To the contrary, it relied on the holding in rejecting support for abortion rights rooted in equal protection principles in its 2022 opinion in Dobbs v. Jackson Women's Health Organization.[68] Accordingly, pregnancy discrimination can still be lawful where Title VII or other statutes are inapplicable. Where the PDA applies, employers cannot treat pregnant workers worse than other workers who are temporarily disabled. Can they treat them better? That question is taken up in the next case. The materials that follow explore two additional questions: (1) What constraints does the PDA place on an employer's ability to single out pregnant workers for adverse treatment; and (2) given the distinctiveness of pregnancy, how can courts tell when pregnant workers are unfairly disadvantaged, and compared to whom?

California Federal Savings & Loan Association v. Guerra

479 U.S. 272 (1987)

Justice MARSHALL delivered the opinion of the Court.

The question presented is whether Title VII of the Civil Rights Act of 1964, as amended by the Pregnancy Discrimination Act of 1978 (PDA), pre-empts a state statute that requires employers to provide leave and reinstatement to employees disabled by pregnancy.

I

California's Fair Employment and Housing Act (FEHA) . . . is a comprehensive statute that prohibits discrimination in employment and housing. In September 1978, California amended the FEHA to proscribe certain forms of employment discrimination on the basis of pregnancy. [At issue in this case is a provision that] requires these employers to provide female employees an unpaid pregnancy disability leave of up to four months. [It has been construed] to require California employers to reinstate an employee returning from such pregnancy leave to the job she previously held, unless it is no longer available due to business necessity. In the latter case, the employer must make a reasonable, good-faith effort to place the employee in a substantially similar job. The statute does not compel employers to provide paid leave to pregnant employees. Accordingly, the only benefit pregnant workers actually derive . . . is a qualified right to reinstatement. . . .

II

Petitioner California Federal Savings & Loan Association (Cal Fed) is a federally chartered savings and loan association based in Los Angeles; it is an employer covered by both Title VII and [the relevant state FEHA law]. Cal Fed has a facially

---

67. AT&T Corp. v. Hulteen, 556 U.S. 709, 717 (2009) (Ginsburg, J., dissenting); Coleman v. Ct. Appeals Md., 566 U.S. 30, 45 (2012) (Ginsburg, J., dissenting).

68. 142 S. Ct. 2228, 2245-46 (2022).

neutral leave policy that permits employees who have completed three months of service to take unpaid leaves of absence for a variety of reasons, including disability and pregnancy. Although it is Cal Fed's policy to try to provide an employee taking unpaid leave with a similar position upon returning, Cal Fed expressly reserves the right to terminate an employee who has taken a leave of absence if a similar position is not available.

Lillian Garland was employed by Cal Fed as a receptionist for several years. In January 1982, she took a pregnancy disability leave. When she was able to return to work in April of that year, Garland notified Cal Fed, but was informed that her job had been filled and that there were no receptionist or similar positions available. Garland filed a complaint with respondent Department of Fair Employment and Housing, which issued an administrative accusation against Cal Fed. . . . Prior to the scheduled hearing . . ., Fair Employment and Housing Commission, Cal Fed, joined by petitioners Merchants and Manufacturers Association and the California Chamber of Commerce, brought this action in the United States District Court for the Central District of California. They sought a declaration that [the California unpaid pregnancy disability leave requirement] is inconsistent with and preempted by Title VII and an injunction against enforcement of the section. The District Court granted petitioners' motion for summary judgment. . . .

The United States Court of Appeals for the Ninth Circuit reversed. . . .

We granted certiorari . . . and we now [uphold the statute.] . . .

III

Petitioners argue that the language of the federal statute itself unambiguously rejects California's "special treatment" approach to pregnancy discrimination. . . . They contend that the PDA forbids an employer to treat pregnant employees any differently from other disabled employees. . . .[6]

[S]ubject to certain limitations, we agree with the Court of Appeals' conclusion that Congress intended the PDA to be "a floor beneath which pregnancy disability benefits may not drop, not a ceiling above which they may not rise." . . .

The context in which Congress considered the issue of pregnancy discrimination supports this view of the PDA. Congress had before it extensive evidence of discrimination against pregnancy, particularly in disability and health insurance programs like those challenged in *Gilbert*. . . . Opposition to the PDA came from those concerned with the cost of including pregnancy in health and disability-benefit plans and the application of the bill to abortion, not from those who favored special accommodation of pregnancy. . . .

We . . . find it significant that Congress was aware of state laws similar to California's [including Connecticut and Montana requirements that employers

---

6. The PDA provides that] [t]he terms "because of sex" or "on the basis of sex" include, but are not limited to, because of or on the basis of pregnancy, childbirth, or related medical conditions; and women affected by pregnancy, childbirth, or related medical conditions shall be treated the same for all employment-related purposes, including receipt of benefits under fringe benefit programs, as other persons not so affected but similar in their ability or inability to work, and nothing in [this law] shall be interpreted to permit otherwise.

provide reasonable leave to pregnant workers], but apparently did not consider them inconsistent with the PDA. . . .

Title VII, as amended by the PDA, and California's pregnancy disability leave statute share a common goal. The purpose of Title VII is "to achieve equality of employment opportunities and remove barriers that have operated in the past to favor an identifiable group of . . . employees over other employees." . . . Rather than limiting existing Title VII principles and objectives, the PDA extends them to cover pregnancy. As Senator Williams, a sponsor of the Act, stated: "The entire thrust . . . behind this legislation is to guarantee women the basic right to participate fully and equally in the workforce, without denying them the fundamental right to full participation in family life." . . .

By requiring employers to reinstate women after a reasonable pregnancy disability leave, [the California law] ensures that they will not lose their jobs on account of pregnancy disability. California's approach is consistent with the dissenting opinion of Justice Brennan in General Electric Co. v. Gilbert . . .:

> [D]iscrimination is a social phenomenon encased in a social context and, therefore, unavoidably takes its meaning from the desired end products of the relevant legislative enactment, end products that may demand due consideration of the uniqueness of the "disadvantaged" individuals. A realistic understanding of conditions found in today's labor environment warrants taking pregnancy into account in fashioning disability policies. . . .

By "taking pregnancy into account," California's pregnancy disability-leave statute allows women, as well as men, to have families without losing their jobs.

We emphasize the limited nature of the benefits [this law] provides. The statute is narrowly drawn to cover only the period of *actual physical disability* on account of pregnancy, childbirth, or related medical conditions. Accordingly, unlike the protective labor legislation prevalent earlier in this century, [this law] does not reflect archaic or stereotypical notions about pregnancy and the abilities of pregnant workers. A statute based on such stereotypical assumptions would, of course, be inconsistent with Title VII's goal of equal employment opportunity. . . .

Moreover, even if we agreed with petitioners' construction of the PDA, we would nonetheless reject their argument that the California statute requires employers to violate Title VII. [The challenged statute] does not prevent employers from complying with both the federal law (as petitioners construe it) and the state law. This is not a case where "compliance with both federal and state regulations is a physical impossibility," . . . or where there is an "inevitable collision between the two schemes of regulation." . . . [The California law] does not compel California employers to treat pregnant workers better than other disabled employees; it merely establishes benefits that employers must, at a minimum, provide to pregnant workers. Employers are free to give comparable benefits to other disabled employees, thereby treating "women affected by pregnancy" no better than "other persons not so affected but similar in their ability or inability to work." Indeed, at oral argument, petitioners conceded that compliance with both statutes "is theoretically possible." . . .

Herma Hill Kay

Equality and Difference: The Case of Pregnancy

1 Berkeley Women's L.J. 1, 26-31 (1985)

Philosophers recognize that, just as the concept of equality requires that equals be treated equally, so it requires that unequals be treated differently. To treat persons who are different alike is to treat them unequally. The concept of formal equality, however, contains no independent justification for making unequals equal. A different concept, that of equality of opportunity, offers a theoretical basis for making unequals equal in the limited sense of removing barriers that prevent individuals from performing according to their abilities. The notion is that the perceived inequality does not stem from an innate difference in ability, but rather from a condition or circumstance that prevents certain uses or developments of that ability. As applied to reproductive behavior, the suggestion would be that women in general are not different from men in innate ability. During the temporary episode of a woman's pregnancy, however, she may become unable to utilize her abilities in the same way she had done prior to her reproductive conduct. Since a man's abilities are not similarly impaired as a result of his reproductive behavior, equality of opportunity implies that the woman should not be disadvantaged as a result of that sex-specific variation.

As applied to the employment context, the concept of equality of opportunity takes on the following form. Let us postulate two workers, one female, the other male, who respectively engage in reproductive conduct. Assume as well that prior to this activity, both were roughly equal in their ability to perform their similar jobs. The consequence of their having engaged in reproductive behavior will be vastly different. The man's ability to perform on the job will be largely unaffected. The woman's ability to work, measured against her prior performance, may vary with the physical and emotional changes she experiences during pregnancy. At times, her ability to work may be unaffected by the pregnancy; at other times, she may be temporarily incapacitated by it. Ultimately, she may require medical care to recover from miscarriage, or to complete her pregnancy by delivery, or to terminate it earlier by induced abortion. In order to maintain the woman's equality of opportunity during her pregnancy, we should modify as far as reasonably possible those aspects of her work where her job performance is adversely affected by the pregnancy. Unless we do so, she will experience employment disadvantages arising from her reproductive activity that are not encountered by her male co-worker . . . .

[P]regnancy differs from sex . . . in that pregnancy is an episodic occurrence, rather than an immutable trait. The category of pregnant persons is a sub-class within the larger category of women . . . .

This interpretation of Title VII based on an episodic analysis of biological reproductive differences will permit pregnancy to be recognized as the normal consequence of reproductive behavior that can and should be accommodated in the workplace. . . . If she is temporarily impaired from performing at work up to her normal level of ability, the concept of equal employment opportunity embodied in Title VII requires not only that she remain free of resulting job reprisals, but also that she secure compensatory benefits to offset any potential work-related disadvantage. Under this analysis, women will be equal to men in their ability to work and to make reproductive choices . . . .

Richard A. Posner

Conservative Feminism

1989 U. Chi. Legal F. 191, 195-198

Where the libertarian is apt to part company with the liberal or radical feminist in the field of employment is over the question whether employers should be forced to subsidize female employees, as by being compelled to offer maternity leave or pregnancy benefits, or to disregard women's greater longevity when fixing pension benefits. To the extent that women workers incur higher medical expenses than men (mainly but not entirely due to pregnancy), or live longer in retirement on a company pension, they cost the employer more than male workers do. So the employer should not be required to pay the same wage *and* provide the same package of fringe benefits. (Of course, to the extent that women impose lower costs—for example, women appear to be more careful about safety than men, and therefore less likely to be injured on the job—they are entitled to a correspondingly higher wage or more extensive fringe benefits.) This is not to suggest—which would be absurd—that women are blameworthy for getting pregnant or for living longer than men. It is to suggest merely that they may be more costly workers and that, if so, the disparity in cost should be reflected in their net compensation. If this disparity is not reflected, then male workers are being discriminated against in the same sense in which women would be discriminated against if they received a lower wage than equally productive (and no less costly) male workers. What is sauce for the goose should be sauce for the gander. More than symmetry is involved; we shall see in a moment that laws designed to improve the welfare of women may boomerang, partly though not wholly because of the economic interdependence of men and women.

I anticipate three objections to my analysis. The first is that in speaking of employers' subsidizing women I am taking as an arbitrary benchmark the costs and performance of male workers. I am not. Consider an employer who is female in a hypothetical female-dominated society and whose entire labor force is also female, so that for her the benchmark in setting terms of employment is female. A man applies for a job. He asks for a higher wage on the ground that experience shows that the average male employee's medical costs are lower than the average female employee's medical costs. If the employer refuses to pay him the higher wage, then, assuming that this worker is just as good as the employer's average female worker, the employer is discriminating against him. This should answer the second objection—that nature should not be allowed to determine social outcomes. I agree that natural law does not compel the conclusion that women should be penalized in the marketplace or anywhere else for living longer or for incurring greater medical costs on average than men. But neither is there any reason why men should be penalized for not living as long as women by being forced to pay for women's longer years of retirement. The matter should be left to the market.

The third objection to my analysis is that, in suggesting that the employer be allowed to make cost-justified differentiations based on sex, I am necessarily implying that he should be permitted to treat employees as members of groups whose average characteristics the particular employee may not share, rather than as individuals. That is true. Some women die before some men, just as some women are taller than some men. The difference is that while it is obvious on inspection whether a given woman is taller than a given man—and therefore it would be absurd for an employer to implement a (let us assume valid) minimum-height requirement of 5 feet 8 inches by refusing to accept job applications from women, it is not obvious which women employees will not live as long as which men employees or will not take as much leave or incur as high medical expenses. Any cost-based differentiation in these areas must be based on probabilistic considerations, of which sex may be the most powerful in the sense of having the greatest predictive power. The average differences between men and women are not invidious, and many cut in favor of women—they are safer drivers, and they live longer, and in a free insurance market would therefore be able to buy liability insurance and life insurance at lower rates than men. Women would not be stigmatized if the market were allowed to register these differences.

It is not even clear, moreover, that women benefit, on balance, from laws that forbid employers to take into account the extra costs that female employees can impose. Such laws discourage employers from hiring, promoting, and retaining women, and there are many ways in which they can discriminate in these respects without committing detectable violations of the employment-discrimination laws. Sometimes there is no question of violation, as when an employer accelerates the substitution of computers for secretaries in response to an increase in the costs of his female employees.

There is an additional point. Most women are married—and many who are not currently married are divorced or widowed and continue to derive a benefit from their husband's earnings. The consumption of a married woman is, as I have noted, a function of her husband's income as well as of her own (in the divorce and widowhood cases as well, for the reason just noted). Therefore a reduction in men's incomes as a result of laws that interfere with profit-maximizing and cost-minimizing decisions by employers will reduce women's welfare as well as men's. Moreover, women who are not married are less likely to have children than women who are married; and where employer benefits are child-related—such as pregnancy benefits and maternity leave—their effect is not merely to transfer wealth from men to women but from women to women. The effect could be dramatic. Compare the situation of a married woman with many children and an unmarried woman with no children. Generous pregnancy benefits and a generous policy on maternity leave will raise the economic welfare of the married woman. Her and her husband's wages will be lower, because all wages will fall in order to finance the benefit, but the reduction will probably be smaller than the benefits to her—in part because the unmarried female worker will experience the same reduction in wages but with no offsetting benefit. Feminists who support rules requiring employers to grant pregnancy benefits and maternity leave may therefore, and I assume unknowingly, be discouraging women from remaining single or childless. Feminists of all persuasions would think it outrageous if the government required fertile women to have children, yet many feminists support an oblique form of such a policy—a subsidy to motherhood. They do this, I suspect, because they have not considered the economic consequences of proposals that *appear* to help women.

UAW v. Johnson Controls, Inc.

499 U.S. 187 (1991)

Mr. Justice BLACKMUN delivered the opinion of the Court.

In this case we are concerned with an employer's gender-based fetal-protection policy. May an employer exclude a fertile female employee from certain jobs because of its concern for the health of the fetus the woman might conceive?

I

Respondent Johnson Controls, Inc., manufactures batteries. In the manufacturing process, the element lead is a primary ingredient. Occupational exposure to lead entails health risks, including the risk of harm to any fetus carried by a female employee.

Before [Title VII] became law, Johnson Controls did not employ any woman in a battery-manufacturing job. In June 1977, however, it announced its first official policy concerning its employment of women in lead-exposure work:

> [P]rotection of the health of the unborn child is the immediate and direct responsibility of the prospective parents. While the medical profession and the company can support them in the exercise of this responsibility, it cannot assume it for them without simultaneously infringing their rights as persons. . . .
>
> Since not all women who can become mothers wish to become mothers (or will become mothers), it would appear to be illegal discrimination to treat all who are capable of pregnancy as though they will become pregnant. . . .

Consistent with that view, Johnson Controls "stopped short of excluding women capable of bearing children from lead exposure," . . . but emphasized that a woman who expected to have a child should not choose a job in which she would have such exposure. The company also required a woman who wished to be considered for employment to sign a statement that she had been advised of the risk of having a child while she was exposed to lead. The statement informed the woman that although there was evidence "that women exposed to lead have a higher rate of [miscarriage]," this evidence was "not as clear . . . as the relationship between cigarette smoking and cancer," but that it was, "medically speaking, just good sense not to run that risk if you want children and do not want to expose the unborn child to risk, however small. . . ."

Five years later, in 1982, Johnson Controls shifted from a policy of warning to a policy of exclusion. Between 1979 and 1983, eight employees became pregnant while maintaining blood lead levels in excess of 30 micrograms per deciliter. . . . This appeared to be the critical level noted by the Occupational Health and Safety Administration (OSHA) for a worker who was planning to have a family. . . . The company responded by announcing a broad exclusion of women from jobs that exposed them to lead:

> [I]t is [Johnson Controls'] policy that women who are pregnant or who are capable of bearing children will not be placed into jobs involving lead

exposure or which could expose them to lead through the exercise of job bidding, bumping, transfer or promotion rights. . . .

The policy defined "women . . . capable of bearing children" as "[a]ll women except those whose inability to bear children is medically documented." . . . It further stated that an unacceptable work station was one where, "over the past year," an employee had recorded a blood lead level of more than 30 micrograms per deciliter or the work site had yielded an air sample containing a lead level in excess of 30 micrograms per cubic meter. . . .

II

In April 1984, petitioners filed in the United States District Court for the Eastern District of Wisconsin a class action challenging Johnson Controls' fetal-protection policy as sex discrimination that violated Title VII. . . . Among the individual plaintiffs were petitioners Mary Craig, who had chosen to be sterilized in order to avoid losing her job, Elsie Nason, a 50-year-old divorcee, who had suffered a loss in compensation when she was transferred out of a job where she was exposed to lead, and Donald Penney, who had been denied a request for a leave of absence for the purpose of lowering his lead level because he intended to become a father. . . .

[The District Court granted summary judgment for defendant and the court of appeals affirmed.] . . .

III

The bias in Johnson Controls' policy is obvious. Fertile men, but not fertile women, are given a choice as to whether they wish to risk their reproductive health for a particular job. [Title VII] prohibits sex-based classifications in terms and conditions of employment, in hiring and discharging decisions, and in other employment decisions that adversely affect an employee's status. Respondent's fetal-protection policy explicitly discriminates against women on the basis of their sex. The policy excludes women with childbearing capacity from lead-exposed jobs and so creates a facial classification based on gender. . . .

[The assumption by the appellate courts that sex-specific fetal-protection policies do not involve facial discrimination was incorrect.]

First, Johnson Controls' policy classifies on the basis of gender and childbearing capacity, rather than fertility alone. Respondent does not seek to protect the unconceived children of all its employees. Despite evidence in the record about the debilitating effect of lead exposure on the male reproductive system, Johnson Controls is concerned only with the harms that may befall the unborn offspring of its female employees. . . . Johnson Controls' policy is facially discriminatory because it requires only a female employee to produce proof that she is not capable of reproducing.

Our conclusion is bolstered by the Pregnancy Discrimination Act of 1978 (PDA), in which Congress explicitly provided that, for purposes of Title VII, discrimination "on the basis of sex" includes discrimination "because of or on the basis of pregnancy, childbirth, or related medical conditions." . . . In its use of the words "capable of bearing children" in the 1982 policy statement as the criterion for exclusion, Johnson Controls explicitly classifies on the basis of potential for pregnancy. Under the PDA, such a classification must be regarded, for Title VII purposes, in the same light as explicit sex discrimination. Respondent has chosen to treat all its female employees as potentially pregnant; that choice evinces discrimination on the basis of sex.

[T]he absence of a malevolent motive does not convert a facially discriminatory policy into a neutral policy with a discriminatory effect. Whether an employment practice involves disparate treatment through explicit facial discrimination does not depend on why the employer discriminates but rather on the explicit terms of the discrimination. . . .

We hold that Johnson Controls' fetal-protection policy is sex discrimination forbidden under Title VII unless respondent can establish that sex is a "bona fide occupational qualification."

IV . . .

The wording of the BFOQ defense contains several terms of restriction that indicate that the exception reaches only special situations. The statute thus limits the situations in which discrimination is permissible to "certain instances" where sex discrimination is "reasonably necessary" to the "normal operation" of the "particular" business. . . .

Johnson Controls argues that its fetal-protection policy falls within the so-called safety exception to the BFOQ. Our cases have stressed that discrimination on the basis of sex because of safety concerns is allowed only in narrow circumstances. In Dothard v. Rawlinson, . . . this Court indicated that danger to a woman herself does not justify discrimination. We there allowed the employer to hire only male guards in contact areas of maximum-security male penitentiaries only because more was at stake than the "individual woman's decision to weigh and accept the risks of employment." . . . Similarly, some courts have approved airlines' layoffs of pregnant flight attendants at different points during the first five months of pregnancy on the ground that the employer's policy was necessary to ensure the safety of passengers. . . . In two of these cases, the courts pointedly indicated that fetal, as opposed to passenger, safety was best left to the mother. . . .

We considered safety to third parties in Western Airlines, Inc. v. Criswell . . . in the context of the [Age Discrimination in Employment Act]. We focused upon "the nature of the flight engineer's tasks," and the "actual capabilities of persons over age 60" in relation to those tasks. Our safety concerns were not independent of the individual's ability to perform the assigned tasks, but rather involved the possibility that, because of age-connected debility, a flight engineer might not properly assist the pilot, and might thereby cause a safety emergency. . . .

Third-party safety considerations properly entered into the BFOQ analysis in *Dothard* and *Criswell* because they went to the core of the employee's job performance. Moreover, that performance involved the central purpose of the enterprise. . . . The concurrence attempts to transform this case into one of customer safety. The unconceived fetuses of Johnson Controls' female employees, however, are neither customers nor third parties whose safety is essential to the business of battery manufacturing. No one can disregard the possibility of injury to future children; the BFOQ, however, is not so broad that it transforms this deep social concern into an essential aspect of batterymaking. . . .

The PDA's amendment to Title VII contains a BFOQ standard of its own: unless pregnant employees differ from others "in their ability or inability to work," they must be "treated the same" as other employees "for all employment-related purposes." This language clearly sets forth Congress' remedy for discrimination on the basis of pregnancy and potential pregnancy. Women who are either pregnant or potentially pregnant must be treated like others "similar in their ability . . . to work." [Id.] In other words, women as capable of doing their jobs as their male counterparts may not be forced to choose between having a child and having a job. . . .

We conclude that the language of both the BFOQ provision and the PDA which amended it, as well as the legislative history and the case law, prohibit an employer from discriminating against a woman because of her capacity to become pregnant unless her reproductive potential prevents her from performing the duties of her job. We reiterate our holdings in *Criswell* and *Dothard* that an employer must direct its concerns about a woman's ability to perform her job safely and efficiently to those aspects of the woman's job-related activities that fall within the "essence" of the particular business.[4]

V

We have no difficulty concluding that Johnson Controls cannot establish a BFOQ. Fertile women, as far as appears in the record, participate in the manufacture of batteries as efficiently as anyone else. . . .

VI

A word about tort liability and the increased cost of fertile women in the workplace is perhaps necessary.

[The Court concedes the possibility that it may cost the employer more to protect pregnant women, at the risk of tort liability if it does not.] . . .

[T]he extra cost of employing members of one sex . . . does not provide an affirmative Title VII defense for a discriminatory refusal to hire members of that gender. . . . Indeed, in passing the PDA, Congress considered at length the considerable cost of providing equal treatment of pregnancy and related conditions, but made the "decision to forbid special treatment of pregnancy despite the social costs associated therewith." . . .

---

4. The concurrence predicts that our reaffirmation of the narrowness of the BFOQ defense will preclude considerations of privacy as a basis for sex-based discrimination. . . . We have never addressed privacy-based sex discrimination and shall not do so here because the sex-based discrimination at issue today does not involve the privacy interests of Johnson Control's customers. Nothing in our discussion of the "essence of the business test," however, suggests that sex could not constitute a BFOQ when privacy interests are implicated. See, e.g., Backus v. Baptist Medical Center [(E.D. Ark. 1981)] (essence of obstetrics nurse's business is to provide sensitive care for patient's intimate and private concerns).

We, of course, are not presented with, nor do we decide, a case in which costs would be so prohibitive as to threaten the survival of the employer's business. We merely reiterate our prior holdings that the incremental cost of hiring women cannot justify discriminating against them.

VII

Our holding today that Title VII . . . forbids sex-specific fetal-protection policies is neither remarkable nor unprecedented. Concern for a woman's existing or potential offspring historically has been the excuse for denying women equal employment opportunities. See, e.g., Muller v. Oregon. . . . Congress in the PDA prohibited discrimination on the basis of a woman's ability to become pregnant. We do no more than hold that the Pregnancy Discrimination Act means what it says. . . .

The judgment of the Court of Appeals is reversed and the case is remanded for further proceedings consistent with this opinion.

Justice WHITE, with whom THE CHIEF JUSTICE and Justice KENNEDY join, concurring in part and concurring in the judgment. . . .

I . . .

Common sense tells us that it is part of the normal operation of business concerns to avoid causing injury to third parties, as well as to employees, if for no other reason than to avoid tort liability and its substantial costs. This possibility of tort liability is not hypothetical; every State currently allows children born alive to recover in tort for prenatal injuries caused by third parties . . . and an increasing number of courts have recognized a right to recover even for prenatal injuries caused by torts committed prior to conception. . . .

The Court's narrow interpretation of the BFOQ defense in this case . . . means that an employer cannot exclude even pregnant women from an environment highly toxic to their fetuses. It is foolish to think that Congress intended such a result, and neither the language of the BFOQ exception nor our cases require it.[8]

II

Despite my disagreement with the Court concerning the scope of the BFOQ defense, I concur in reversing the Court of Appeals because that court erred in

---

8. The Court's cramped reading of the BFOQ defense is also belied by the legislative history of Title VII, in which three examples of permissible sex discrimination were mentioned — a female nurse hired to care for an elderly woman, an all-male professional baseball team, and a masseur. . . . In none of those situations would gender "actually interfer[e] with the employee's ability to perform the job," as required today by the Court. . . . the Court's interpretation of the BFOQ standard also would seem to preclude considerations of privacy as a basis for sex-based discrimination, since those considerations do not relate directly to an employee's physical ability to perform the duties of the job. The lower federal courts, however, have consistently recognized that privacy interests may justify sex-based requirements for certain jobs. . . .

affirming the District Court's grant of summary judgment in favor of Johnson Controls. First, the Court of Appeals erred in failing to consider the level of risk-avoidance that was part of Johnson Controls' "normal operation." . . . If the fetal protection policy insists on a risk-avoidance level substantially higher than other risk levels tolerated by Johnson Controls such as risks to employees and consumers, the policy should not constitute a BFOQ.

Second, even without more information about the normal level of risk at Johnson Controls, the fetal protection policy at issue here reaches too far. This is evident both in its presumption that, absent medical documentation to the contrary, all women are fertile regardless of their age . . . and in its exclusion of presumptively fertile women from positions that might result in a promotion to a position involving high lead exposure. . . .

Third, it should be recalled that until 1982 Johnson Controls operated without an exclusionary policy, and it has not identified any grounds for believing that its current policy is reasonably necessary to its normal operations. . . .

Finally, the Court of Appeals failed to consider properly petitioners' evidence of harm to offspring caused by lead exposure in males. . . . It seems clear that if the Court of Appeals had properly analyzed that evidence, it would have concluded that summary judgment against petitioners was not appropriate because there was a dispute over a material issue of fact.

Mr. Justice SCALIA, concurring in the judgment.

I generally agree with the Court's analysis, but have some reservations, several of which bear mention. . . . [T]he Court goes far afield, it seems to me, in suggesting that increased cost alone—short of "costs . . . so prohibitive as to threaten survival of the employer's business" . . . —cannot support a BFOQ defense . . . I think, for example, that a shipping company may refuse to hire pregnant women as crew members on long voyages because the on-board facilities for foreseeable emergencies, though quite feasible, would be inordinately expensive. In the present case, however, Johnson has not asserted a cost-based BFOQ.

Troupe v. May Department Stores Co.

20 F.3d 734 (7th Cir. 1994)

POSNER, Chief Judge.

The plaintiff, Kimberly Hern Troupe, was employed by the Lord & Taylor department store in Chicago as a saleswoman in the women's accessories department. . . . Until the end of 1990 her work was entirely satisfactory. In December of that year, in the first trimester of a pregnancy, she began experiencing morning sickness of unusual severity. The following month she requested and was granted a return to part-time status, working from noon to 5:00 p.m. Partly it seems because she slept later under the new schedule, so that noon was "morning" for her, she continued to experience severe morning sickness at work, causing what her lawyer describes with understatement as "slight" or "occasional" tardiness. In the month that ended with a warning from her immediate supervisor, Jennifer Rauch, on February 18, she reported late to work, or left early, on nine out of the 21 working days.

The day after the warning she was late again and this time received a written warning. After she was tardy three days in a row late in March, the company on March 29 placed her on probation for 60 days. During the probationary period Troupe was late eleven more days; and she was fired on June 7, shortly after the end of the probationary period. She testified at her deposition that on the way to the meeting with the defendant's human resources manager at which she was fired, Rauch told her that "I [Troupe] was going to be terminated because she [Rauch] didn't think I was coming back to work after I had my baby." Troupe was due to begin her maternity leave the next day. . . . [A]t argument Lord & Taylor's counsel said that employees of Lord & Taylor are entitled to maternity leave with half pay. . . .

The great, the undeniable fact is the plaintiff's tardiness. Her lawyer argues with great vigor that she should not be blamed — that she was genuinely ill, had a doctor's excuse, etc. That would be pertinent if Troupe were arguing that the Pregnancy Discrimination Act requires an employer to treat an employee afflicted by morning sickness better than the employer would treat an employee who was equally tardy for some other health reason. This is rightly not argued. If an employee who (like Troupe) does not have an employment contract cannot work because of illness, nothing in Title VII requires the employer to keep the employee on the payroll. . . .

Against the inference that Troupe was fired because she was chronically late to arrive at work and chronically early to leave, she has only two facts to offer. The first is the timing of her discharge: she was fired the day before her maternity leave was to begin. . . . Thus, her employer fired her one day before the problem that the employer says caused her to be fired was certain to end. If the discharge of an unsatisfactory worker were a purely remedial measure rather than also, or instead, a deterrent one, the inference that Troupe wasn't really fired because of her tardiness would therefore be a powerful one. But that is a big "if." We must remember that after two warnings Troupe had been placed on probation for sixty days and that she had violated the implicit terms of probation by being as tardy during the probationary period as she had been before. If the company did not fire her, its warnings and threats would seem empty. Employees would be encouraged to flout work rules knowing that the only sanction would be a toothless warning or a meaningless period of probation.

[I]t might appear to be an issue for trial whether it is superior to Troupe's interpretation. But what is Troupe's interpretation? Not (as we understand it) that Lord & Taylor wanted to get back at her for becoming pregnant or having morning sickness. The only significance she asks us to attach to the timing of her discharge is as reinforcement for the inference that she asks us to draw from Rauch's statement about the reason for her termination: that she was terminated because her employer did not expect her to return to work after her maternity leave was up. We must decide whether a termination so motivated is discrimination within the meaning of the pregnancy amendment to Title VII.

Standing alone, it is not. (It could be a breach of contract, but that is not alleged.) . . . We must imagine a hypothetical Mr. Troupe, who is as tardy as Ms. Troupe was, also because of health problems, and who is about to take a protracted sick leave growing out of those problems at an expense to Lord & Taylor equal to that of Ms. Troupe's maternity leave. If Lord & Taylor would have fired our hypothetical Mr. Troupe, this implies that it fired Ms. Troupe not because she was pregnant but because she cost the company more than she was worth to it.

The Pregnancy Discrimination Act does not, despite the urgings of feminist scholars . . . require employers to offer maternity leave or take other steps to make it easier for pregnant women to work . . . to make it as easy, say as it is for their spouses to continue working during pregnancy. Employers can treat pregnant women as badly as they treat similarly affected but nonpregnant employees. . . .

The plaintiff has made no effort to show that if all the pertinent facts were as they are except for the fact of her pregnancy, she would not have been fired. So in the end she has no evidence from which a rational trier of fact could infer that she was a victim of pregnancy discrimination. . . . The Pregnancy Discrimination Act requires the employer to ignore an employee's pregnancy, but . . . not her absence from work, unless the employer overlooks the comparable absences of nonpregnant employees. . . . Of course there may be no comparable absences . . . ; but we do not understand Troupe to be arguing that the reason she did not present evidence that nonpregnant employees were treated more favorably than she is that . . . there is no comparison group of Lord & Taylor employees. . . . We doubt that finding a comparison group would be that difficult. Troupe would be halfway home if she could find one nonpregnant employee of Lord & Taylor who had not been fired when about to begin a leave similar in length to hers. She either did not look, or did not find. Given the absence of other evidence, her failure to present any comparison evidence doomed her case.

Young v. United Parcel Service, Inc.

135 S. Ct. 1338 (2015)

Justice BREYER delivered the opinion of the Court.

The Pregnancy Discrimination Act makes clear that Title VII's prohibition against sex discrimination applies to discrimination based on pregnancy. It also says that employers must treat "women affected by pregnancy . . . the same for all employment-related purposes . . . as other persons not so affected but similar in their ability or inability to work." 42 U.S.C. §2000e(k). We must decide how this latter provision applies in the context of an employer's policy that accommodates many, but not all, workers with nonpregnancy-related disabilities.

In our view, the Act requires courts to consider the extent to which an employer's policy treats pregnant workers less favorably than it treats nonpregnant workers similar in their ability or inability to work. And here—as in all cases in which an individual plaintiff seeks to show disparate treatment through indirect evidence—it requires courts to consider any legitimate, nondiscriminatory, nonpretextual justification for these differences in treatment. See McDonnell Douglas Corp. v. Green (1973). Ultimately the court must determine whether the nature of the employer's policy and the way in which it burdens pregnant women shows that the employer has engaged in intentional discrimination. The Court of Appeals here affirmed a grant of summary judgment in favor of the employer. Given our view of the law, we must vacate that court's judgment.

I

The petitioner, Peggy Young worked as a part-time driver for the respondent, United Parcel Service (UPS). Her responsibilities included pickup and delivery of packages that had arrived by air carrier the previous night. In 2006, after suffering several miscarriages, she became pregnant. Her doctor told her that she should not lift more than 20 pounds during the first 20 weeks of her pregnancy or more than 10 pounds thereafter. UPS required drivers like Young to be able to lift parcels weighing up to 70 pounds (and up to 150 pounds with assistance). UPS told Young she could not work while under a lifting restriction. Young consequently stayed home without pay during most of the time she was pregnant and eventually lost her employee medical coverage.

Young subsequently brought this federal lawsuit. We focus here on her claim that UPS acted unlawfully in refusing to accommodate her pregnancy-related lifting restriction. Young said that her co-workers were willing to help her with heavy packages. She also said that UPS accommodated other drivers who were "similar in their . . . inability to work." She accordingly concluded that UPS must accommodate her as well.

UPS responded that the "other persons" whom it had accommodated were (1) drivers who had become disabled on the job, (2) those who had lost their Department of Transportation (DOT) certifications, and (3) those who suffered from a disability covered by the Americans with Disabilities Act of 1990 (ADA). UPS said that, since Young did not fall within any of those categories, it had not discriminated against on the basis of pregnancy but had treated her just as it treated all "other" relevant "persons."

This case requires us to consider the application of the second clause [of the PDA] to a "disparate-treatment" claim — a claim that an employer intentionally treated a complainant less favorably than employees with the "complainant's qualifications" but outside the complainant's protected class. . . .

In *McDonnell Douglas*, we considered a claim of discriminatory hiring. We said that, to prove disparate treatment, an individual plaintiff must "carry the initial burden" of "establishing a prima facie case" of discrimination by showing

> "(i) that he belongs to a . . . minority; (ii) that he applied and was qualified for a job for which the employer was seeking applicants; (iii) that, despite his qualifications, he was rejected; and (iv) that, after his rejection, the position remained open and the employer continued to seek applicants from persons of complainant's qualifications."

If a plaintiff makes this showing, then the employer must have an opportunity "to articulate some legitimate, nondiscriminatory reason for" treating employees outside the protected class better than employees within the protected class. If the employer articulates such a reason, the plaintiff then has "an opportunity to prove by a preponderance of the evidence that the legitimate reasons offered by the defendant [i.e., the employer] were not its true reasons, but were a pretext for discrimination." Texas Dep't of Community Affairs v. Burdine, 450 U.S. 248, 253 (1981). . . .

Young introduced further evidence indicating that UPS had accommodated several individuals when they suffered disabilities that created work restrictions similar to hers. UPS contests the correctness of some of these facts and the relevance of others. . . . [The District Court granted summary judgment to UPS; the Fourth Circuit affirmed, writing that] "UPS has crafted a pregnancy-blind policy" that is "at least facially a 'neutral and legitimate business practice,' and not evidence of UPS's discriminatory animus toward pregnant workers."

II

The parties disagree about the interpretation of the Pregnancy Discrimination Act's second clause. . . . [T]he Act's first clause specifies that discrimination " 'because of sex' " includes discrimination "because of . . . pregnancy." But the meaning of the second clause is less clear; it adds: "[W]omen affected by pregnancy, childbirth, or related medical conditions shall be treated the same for all employment-related purposes . . . as *other persons* not so affected but *similar in their ability or inability to work.*" 42 U.S.C. §2000e(k) (emphasis added). Does this clause mean that courts must compare workers *only* in respect to the work limitations that they suffer? Does it mean that courts must ignore all other similarities or differences between pregnant and nonpregnant workers? Or does it mean that courts, when deciding who the relevant "other persons" are, may consider other similarities and differences as well? If so, which ones? . . .

The parties propose very different answers to this question. Young and the United States believe that the second clause of the Pregnancy Discrimination Act "requires an employer to provide the same accommodations to workplace disabilities caused by pregnancy that it provides to workplace disabilities that have other causes but have a similar effect on the ability to work." In other words, Young contends that the second clause means that whenever "an employer accommodates only a subset of workers with disabling conditions," a court should find a Title VII violation if "pregnant workers who are similar in the ability to work" do not "receive the same [accommodation] even if still other non-pregnant workers do not receive accommodations."

UPS takes an almost polar opposite view. It contends that the second clause does no more than define sex discrimination to include pregnancy discrimination. Under this view, courts would compare the accommodations an employer provides to pregnant women with the accommodations it provides to others *within* a facially neutral category (such as those with off-the-job injuries) to determine whether the employer has violated Title VII.

We cannot accept either of these interpretations. . . .

The problem with Young's approach is that it proves too much. It seems to say that the statute grants pregnant workers a "most-favored-nation" status. As long as an employer provides one or two workers with an accommodation — say, those with particularly hazardous jobs, or those whose workplace presence is particularly needed, or those who have worked at the company for many years, or those who are over the age of 55 — then it must provide similar accommodations to *all* pregnant workers (with comparable physical limitations), irrespective of the nature of their jobs, the employer's need to keep them working, their ages, or any other criteria. . . .

We agree with UPS to this extent: We doubt that Congress intended to grant pregnant workers an unconditional most-favored-nation status. The language of the statute does not require that unqualified reading. The second clause, when referring to nonpregnant persons with similar disabilities, uses the open-ended term "other persons." It does not say that the employer must treat pregnant employees the "same" as "*any* other persons" (who are similar in their ability or inability to work), nor does it otherwise specify *which* other persons Congress had in mind.

Moreover, disparate-treatment law normally permits an employer to implement policies that are not intended to harm members of a protected class, even if their implementation sometimes harms those members, as long as the employer has a legitimate, nondiscriminatory, nonpretextual reason for doing so. There is no reason to believe Congress intended its language in the Pregnancy Discrimination Act to embody a significant deviation from this approach. . . .

We find it similarly difficult to accept the opposite interpretation of the Act's second clause. UPS says that the second clause simply defines sex discrimination to include pregnancy discrimination. But that cannot be so.

The first clause accomplishes that objective. . . . We have long held that " 'a statute ought, upon the whole, to be so construed that, if it can be prevented, no clause' " is rendered " 'superfluous, void, or insignificant.' " But that is what UPS' interpretation of the second clause would do. . . .

Moreover, the interpretation espoused by UPS and the dissent would fail to carry out an important congressional objective. As we have noted, Congress' "unambiguou[s]" intent in passing the Act was to overturn "both the holding and the reasoning of the Court in the *Gilbert* decision." Newport News Shipbuilding & Dry Dock Co. v. EEOC (1983). In *Gilbert*, the Court considered a company plan that provided "nonoccupational sickness and accident benefits to all employees" without providing "disability-benefit payments for any absence due to pregnancy." The Court held that the plan did not violate Title VII; it did not discriminate on the basis of sex because there was "no risk from which men are protected and women are not." Although pregnancy is "confined to women," the majority believed it was not "comparable in all other respects to [the] diseases or disabilities" that the plan covered. Specifically, the majority explained that pregnancy "is not a 'disease' at all," nor is it necessarily a result of accident. Neither did the majority see the distinction the plan drew as "a subterfuge" or a "pretext" for engaging in gender-based discrimination. In short, the *Gilbert* majority reasoned in part just as the dissent reasons here. The employer did "not distinguish between pregnant women and others of similar ability or inability *because of pregnancy*." It distinguished between them on a neutral ground — *i.e.*, it accommodated only sicknesses and accidents, and pregnancy was neither of those.

Simply including pregnancy among Title VII's protected traits (*i.e.*, accepting UPS' interpretation) would not overturn *Gilbert* in full — in particular, it would not respond to *Gilbert*'s determination that an employer can treat pregnancy less favorably than diseases or disabilities resulting in a similar inability to work. As we explained in California Fed. Sav. & Loan Assn. v. Guerra (1987), "the first clause of the [Act] reflects Congress' disapproval of the reasoning in *Gilbert*" by "adding pregnancy to the definition of sex discrimination prohibited by Title VII." But the second clause was intended to do more than that — it "was intended to overrule the holding in *Gilbert* and to illustrate how discrimination against pregnancy is to be remedied." The dissent's view, like that of UPS', ignores this precedent.

III

The statute lends itself to an interpretation other than those that the parties advocate and that the dissent sets forth. Our interpretation minimizes the problems we have discussed, responds directly to *Gilbert*, and is consistent with long-standing interpretations of Title VII.

In our view, an individual pregnant worker who seeks to show disparate treatment through indirect evidence may do so through application of the *McDonnell Douglas* framework. That framework requires a plaintiff to make out a prima facie case of discrimination. But it is "not intended to be an inflexible rule." Rather, an individual plaintiff may establish a prima facie case by "showing actions taken by the employer from which one can infer, if such actions remain unexplained, that it is more likely than not that such actions were based on a discriminatory criterion illegal under" Title VII. The burden of making this showing is "not onerous." In particular, making this showing is not as burdensome as succeeding on "an ultimate finding of fact as to" a discriminatory employment action. Neither does it require the plaintiff to show that those whom the employer favored and those whom the employer disfavored were similar in all but the protected ways.

Thus, a plaintiff alleging that the denial of an accommodation constituted disparate treatment under the Pregnancy Discrimination Act's second clause may make out a prima facie case by showing, as in *McDonnell Douglas*, that she belongs to the protected class, that she sought accommodation, that the employer did not accommodate her, and that the employer did accommodate others "similar in their ability or inability to work."

The employer may then seek to justify its refusal to accommodate the plaintiff by relying on "legitimate, nondiscriminatory" reasons for denying her accommodation. But, consistent with the Act's basic objective, that reason normally cannot consist simply of a claim that it is more expensive or less convenient to add pregnant women to the category of those ("similar in their ability or inability to work") whom the employer accommodates. After all, the employer in *Gilbert* could in all likelihood have made just such a claim.

If the employer offers an apparently "legitimate, non-discriminatory" reason for its actions, the plaintiff may in turn show that the employer's proffered reasons are in fact pretextual. We believe that the plaintiff may reach a jury on this issue by providing sufficient evidence that the employer's policies impose a significant burden on pregnant workers, and that the employer's "legitimate, nondiscriminatory" reasons are not sufficiently strong to justify the burden, but rather — when considered along with the burden imposed — give rise to an inference of intentional discrimination.

The plaintiff can create a genuine issue of material fact as to whether a significant burden exists by providing evidence that the employer accommodates a large percentage of nonpregnant workers while failing to accommodate a large percentage of pregnant workers. Here, for example, if the facts are as Young says they are, she can show that UPS accommodates most nonpregnant employees with lifting limitations while categorically failing to accommodate pregnant employees with lifting limitations. Young might also add that the fact that UPS has multiple policies that accommodate nonpregnant employees with lifting restrictions suggests that its reasons for failing to accommodate pregnant employees with lifting restrictions are not sufficiently strong—to the point that a jury could find that its reasons for failing to accommodate pregnant employees give rise to an inference of intentional discrimination.

This approach, though limited to the Pregnancy Discrimination Act context, is consistent with our longstanding rule that a plaintiff can use circumstantial proof to rebut an employer's apparently legitimate, nondiscriminatory reasons for treating individuals within a protected class differently than those outside the protected class. . . .

Our interpretation of the Act is also, unlike the dissent's, consistent with Congress' intent to overrule *Gilbert*'s reasoning and result. The dissent says that "[i]f a pregnant woman is denied an accommodation under a policy that does not discriminate against pregnancy, she *has* been 'treated the same' as everyone else." This logic would have found no problem with the employer plan in *Gilbert*, which "denied an accommodation" to pregnant women on the same basis as it denied accommodations to other employees—*i.e.*, it accommodated only sicknesses and accidents, and pregnancy was neither of those. . . .

IV

Under this interpretation of the Act, the judgment of the Fourth Circuit must be vacated. . . . Viewing the record in the light most favorable to Young, there is a genuine dispute as to whether UPS provided more favorable treatment to at least some employees whose situation cannot reasonably be distinguished from Young's. . . . Young also introduced evidence that UPS had three separate accommodation policies (on-the-job, ADA, DOT). Taken together, Young argued, these policies significantly burdened pregnant women. The Fourth Circuit did not consider the combined effects of these policies, nor did it consider the strength of UPS' justifications for each when combined. That is, why, when the employer accommodated so many, could it not accommodate pregnant women as well?

We do not determine whether Young created a genuine issue of material fact as to whether UPS' reasons for having treated Young less favorably than it treated these other nonpregnant employees were pretextual. We leave a final determination of that question for the Fourth Circuit to make on remand. . . .

NOTES

1. **The Debate over "Equal" vs. "Special" Treatment.** A broad coalition of feminist groups advocated the passage of the PDA, but after its passage they split over its meaning. The dispute centered on the legality and desirability of rules that attempt to eliminate some of the special disadvantages associated with pregnancy and childbirth.

Supporters of "special" treatment, like Professor Kay, argued that neutral rules cannot ensure equality between men and women when their circumstances are different, as in the case of pregnancy. By contrast, opponents like Wendy Williams claimed:

> Pregnancy [is] the centerpiece, the linchpin, the essential feature of women's separate sphere. The stereotypes, the generalizations, the role expectations [are] at their zenith when a woman [becomes] pregnant. . . .

[F]eminists who seek special recognition for pregnancy are starting from the same basic assumption, namely, that women have a special place in the scheme of human existence when it comes to maternity. . . .

The special treatment model has great costs. . . . [T]he reality [is] that conceptualizing pregnancy as a special case permits unfavorable as well as favorable treatment of pregnancy. Our history provides too many illustrations of the former. . . .[69]

Who is right? Judge Posner's analysis offers a market-based rationale against "special treatment." Does his analysis have the same consequences as Williams' rationale? To what extent is Judge Posner correct that maternity leave policies "subsidize" women? Are there ordinary employment policies that subsidize men?

Is *Cal Fed* consistent with *Johnson Controls*? *Cal Fed* permits special legislation or employer policies that give pregnant employees unique protection while *Johnson Controls* prohibits special protection. Is the rule that accommodations for pregnant women are permissible, but that protections that compromise their work opportunities are not? Is this distinction satisfactory? What would it mean to shift the focus away from comparisons of male and female workers and toward a critique of "gendered workplace structures," as Stephanie Bornstein argues?[70]

2. **Beyond Pregnancy.** The scope of protection under the PDA turns in part on the definition of pregnancy discrimination. The PDA extends to "pregnancy, childbirth, and related medical conditions," a phrase chosen, according to the Senate Report, to reflect those "physiological occurrences peculiar to women." Only people with female reproductive organs menstruate, use prescription contraceptives, utilize surgical impregnation procedures like in vitro fertilization, or lactate. Each of these things has physical effects that can, depending on the particular woman and her particular job, pose conflicts with job performance. Courts have been asked to consider the entire reproductive process within the rubric of pregnancy discrimination law. As the examples below illustrate, the law is often read broadly when it comes to preventing status-based discrimination but narrowly when the effects of the reproductive process might necessitate some accommodation.

Contraceptive Equity: Courts in the early 2000s considered several cases about whether it violates Title VII for an employer to omit coverage for prescription contraceptives, which are used only by women or people with female reproductive organs, from an otherwise comprehensive insurance plan. At the time, relatively few employers voluntarily provided coverage, and the contraceptive mandate under the Affordable Care Act ("ACA," discussed in Chapter 5, Section B) had not yet been enacted. Many plans did (and still do) cover surgical sterilization for both men and women. The EEOC issued a ruling, in 2000, concluding that a contraceptive exclusion constitutes pregnancy discrimination. Plaintiffs seeking to require contraceptive coverage in employer-sponsored insurance plans urged that access to contraception is an issue of sex equality—and constitutes unlawful discrimination

69. Wendy W. Williams, The Equality Crisis: Some Reflections on Culture, Courts, and Feminism, 7 Women's Rts. L. Rep. 175, 191, 195-96 (1982).

70. Stephanie Bornstein, The Politics of Pregnancy Accommodation, 14 Harv. L. & Pol'y Rev. 293 (2020).

under Title VII, as amended by the PDA.[71] Federal district courts split on the question.[72] In Erickson v. Bartell Drug Co., the court sided with the plaintiffs: "Title VII does not require employers to offer any particular type or category of benefit. However, when an employer decides to offer a prescription plan covering everything except a few specifically excluded drugs and devices, it has a legal obligation to make sure that the resulting plan does not discriminate based on sex-based characteristics and that it provides equally comprehensive coverage for both sexes."[73] Is *Erickson* correctly decided? What exactly is the nature of the discrimination? Does it matter whether the insurance plan covers drugs used only by men, such as Viagra? Only one federal appellate court has considered this issue, and it disagreed with *Erickson.* The Eighth Circuit, in Standridge v. Union Pacific Railroad Company, held that it was neither pregnancy nor sex discrimination for the employer to exclude coverage for all forms of contraception, including sterilization. Rejecting the earlier EEOC ruling, the court concluded that contraception is not a "related medical condition" under the terms of the PDA, despite the fact that the Supreme Court held in *Johnson Controls* that "potential pregnancy" is covered by that same language.[74] It also concluded that the employer's plan was gender-neutral because it excluded coverage for male contraception (condoms) and sterilization. Are you persuaded that omission of coverage is gender-neutral?[75]

Treatment for Infertility: The CDC estimates that as many as 7 million women suffer some degree of infertility.[76] With advances in reproductive technology, women have many more options for treating infertility. Twelve percent of women of childbearing age have sought medical help for infertility or prevention of miscarriage.[77] Assisted reproductive technology can be an effective way to overcome infertility, but it is expensive and financially out of reach for many women, making insurance coverage a necessity. By and large, however, plaintiffs have not succeeded in litigation challenging insurance exclusions under Title VII and the PDA. In Krauel v. Iowa Methodist Medical Center, the Eighth Circuit Court of Appeals held that infertility is not a "related medical condition" under the PDA because both men and women can suffer from it. It is thus unlike the "potential pregnancy" recognized in *Johnson Controls,* which is unique to women.[78] The Second Circuit in Saks v. Franklin Covey

---

71. Cornelia T. L. Pillard articulates an equality-based theory for contraceptive access in Our Other Reproductive Choices: Equality in Sex Education, Contraceptive Access, and Work-Family Policy, 56 Emory L.J. 941, 963-77 (2007).

72. Compare Stocking v. AT&T Corp., 436 F. Supp. 2d 1014 (W.D. Mo. 2006) (PDA requires coverage), and EEOC v. UPS, 141 F. Supp. 2d 1216 (D. Minn. 2001) (exclusion constitutes sex discrimination under Title VII), with Cummins v. Illinois, 2010 WL 334514 (S.D. Ill. 2010) (PDA does not require coverage).

73. 141 F. Supp. 2d 1266 (W.D. Wash. 2001).

74. 479 F.3d 936, 942 (8th Cir. 2007).

75. For further reading on this topic, see Jennifer Hickey, Insuring Contraceptive Equity, 17 Nw. J. L. Soc. Pol'y 1761 (2022); Greer Donley, Contraceptive Equity: Curing the Sex Discrimination in the ACA's Mandate, 71 Ala. L. Rev. 499 (2019).

76. Anjani Chandra et al., Nat'l Health Statistics Rep., Infertility Service Use in the United States: Data from the National Survey of Family Growth, 1982-2010, at 1 (Jan. 2014).

77. Id.

78. 95 F.3d 674, 679-80 (8th Cir. 1996).

Co. rejected a similar claim, ruling that it was neither pregnancy nor sex discrimination for an employer to deny insurance coverage for surgical impregnation procedures (such as artificial insemination and in vitro fertilization) performed only on women.[79] The court noted that including "infertility within the PDA's protection as a 'related medical condition[]' would result in the anomaly of defining a class that simultaneously includes equal numbers of both sexes and yet is somehow vulnerable to sex discrimination."[80] To fall under the PDA, the court concluded, the condition "must be unique to women." The Seventh Circuit, however, held in Hall v. Nalco that an employer could not fire a woman because she requested time off to undergo in vitro fertilization without violating the PDA. If her allegations were true, the plaintiff "was terminated not for the gender-neutral condition of infertility, but rather for the gender-specific quality of childbearing capacity."[81] Employees "terminated for taking time off to undergo IVF—just like those terminated for taking time off to give birth or receive other pregnancy-related care—will always be women."[82] Can *Saks* and *Hall* be reconciled? Which one has the better reading of *Johnson Controls*? Which is the more promising framework for developing a right to access to assisted reproductive technology—equality or autonomy?

Lactation Discrimination: A third set of cases raise the question of whether the PDA protects against lactation discrimination—or requires employers to accommodate breastfeeding workers. In EEOC v. Houston Funding, Inc., a federal district court ruled that lactation discrimination is not actionable under Title VII or the PDA because it does not qualify as a "related medical condition" because lactation doesn't begin until the pregnancy is over.[83] The Fifth Circuit reversed in part, disagreeing with the district court that lactation is unrelated to pregnancy—quite the contrary, "[l]actation is the physiological process of secreting milk from mammary glands and is directly caused by hormonal changes associated with pregnancy and childbirth."[84] But the PDA protects only against status-based discrimination, according to the appellate court's opinion. The plaintiff could not be fired because she asked for special facilities or breaks in order to pump breastmilk, but the employer did not have to provide any accommodations. As with contraceptive care, the ACA ameliorates this problem to a degree, requiring that hourly workers be provided regular breaks and a space other than a restroom to express breastmilk. Should the PDA be construed to provide broader protection for lactation?[85] Or should the law be expanded to require employers to provide reasonable accommodations for breastfeeding mothers? Why or why not?

3. **Stereotypes vs. Facts.** *Troupe* represents the prevailing interpretation of the PDA's first clause as a mandate to treat pregnant women like other similarly situated non-pregnant employees—no worse, but not necessarily any better. But the *LaFleur* case, discussed above, and the first clause of the PDA make clear that

---

79. 316 F.3d 337, 346-49 (2d Cir. 2003).

80. Id. at 346.

81. 534 F.3d 644, 649 (7th Cir. 2008).

82. Id. at 648-49.

83. EEOC v. Houston Funding II, Ltd., No. H-11-2442, 2012 WL 739494, at *2 (S.D. Tex. Feb. 2, 2012).

84. EEOC v. Houston Funding II, Ltd., 717 F.3d 425, 428 (5th Cir. 2013).

85. See generally Meghan Boone, Lactation Law, 106 Cal. L. Rev. 1827 (2020).

employers must base decisions on a pregnant woman's actual work capacity, rather than on stereotypes about how pregnant women or mothers behave.[86] Proving the basis for an employer's decision can be a challenge. Is it realistic to expect Ms. Troupe to show that she was treated worse because of her pregnancy, even if she was? Consider the view of Ruth Colker: "[w]hat was she supposed to find—a non-pregnant employee with a sudden record of tardiness after a nearly spotless work record who also had scheduled a lengthy leave?"[87] Troupe argued unsuccessfully that the problem was not her lateness, but the fact that the employer had impermissibly assumed that she would not return to work after her pregnancy leave. If she had proved this fact, should she have won?

In a case also from the Seventh Circuit Court of Appeals, Maldonado v. U.S. Bank, a new part-time bank employee was terminated, after notifying her supervisor that she was pregnant and due in July, because the bank needed a teller who could fill in for full-time tellers during summer vacations.[88] The court held that the bank could not take advance adverse action against Maldonado, noting that Maldonado had not asked for leave and had even hinted to her supervisor that she might not carry the pregnancy to term. The court qualified its holding, however, by suggesting that

> under narrow circumstances that we are not convinced are present here, [an employer may] project the normal inconveniences of pregnancy and their secondary effects into the future and take actions in accordance with and in proportion to those predictions. . . . But an employer cannot take anticipatory action unless it has a good faith basis, supported by sufficiently strong evidence, that the normal inconveniences of an employee's pregnancy will require special treatment.[89]

A growing number of mothers also have had success in court where they were harmed by stereotypical assumptions about their work commitments. These cases are discussed in the next section on caregiver discrimination. Chapter 4, Section B considers further the issue of work–family balance.

4. **Pregnancy Bias?** With many types of discrimination, the nature of the bias workers experience is clearly rooted in animus toward employees with a particular characteristic or trait. Is that the likely nature of bias with pregnancy? Pregnancy is not something people generally react to with disdain. Yet a New York Times article that reviewed court records and interviewed women, lawyers, and public officials found that "[m]any of the country's largest and prestigious companies still systematically sideline pregnant women. They pass them over for promotions and raises. They fire them when they complain. In physically demanding jobs . . . the discrimination can be blatant. In corporate office towers, the discrimination tends to be more subtle. Pregnant women and mothers are often perceived as less committed, steered away from prestigious assignments, excluded from client meetings and

---

86. 414 U.S. 632 (1974).
87. Ruth Colker, Pregnancy, Parenting, and Capitalism, 58 Ohio St. L.J. 61, 80 (1997).
88. 186 F.3d 759 (7th Cir. 1999).
89. Id. at 767.

slighted at bonus season."[90] The EEOC receives thousands of pregnancy discrimination charges every year, and a recent study estimates that 250,000 pregnant women
annually are denied workplace accommodations.[91]

Early studies found pregnancy to be a source of bias in almost every aspect
of employment—from hiring to performance appraisals to pay.[92] Mothers suffer a well-documented wage penalty, while fathers benefit from an equally well-
documented wage boost. The stereotypes that animate those pay effects are also
operative when employees are pregnant. Jennifer Shinall used empirical evidence
to document a "pregnancy" penalty—a gap in employment outcomes that cannot
be explained by any other factor.[93]

What do you suppose accounts for this widespread discrimination? If pregnancy discrimination is so pervasive despite strong laws against it, what can be done?
One study noted the contrasting reaction of store workers to pregnant customers
(soft and nurturing responses combined with overly friendly touches and terms)
and to pregnant job applicants (hostility).[94] Another noted especially hostile reactions to pregnant women applying for traditionally male-dominated jobs.[95] These
studies may suggest that pregnancy bias is more about an aversion to women combining work and motherhood than it is animus against pregnant women per se. If
so, what should be done about it?

What role does race play in pregnancy bias? Philosopher Iris Marion Young
captures our cultural depiction of pregnancy as a "time of quiet waiting," in which
the woman is simply "expecting."[96] It is not surprising that we tend then to see work
as presumptively incompatible with this passive and objectified state. But "[w]omen
of color historically have been both less revered while pregnant and presumed to

---

90. Natalie Kitroeff & Jessica Silver-Greenberg, Pregnancy Discrimination Is Rampant
Inside America's Biggest Companies, N.Y. Times, June 17, 2018, at A1; Liz Elting, Why Pregnancy Discrimination Still Matters, Forbes, Oct. 30, 2018.

91. EEOC, Pregnancy Discrimination Charges FY 2010-FY 2021 (2022); Nat'l P'ship for
Women & Fams., Fact Sheet: The Pregnant Workers Fairness Act 2 (May 2019).

92. Jane A. Halpert et al., Pregnancy as a Source of Bias in Performance Appraisals,
14 J. Org. Behav. 649 (1993) (finding negative stereotyping against pregnant workers with
significantly more negative performance appraisals, especially when reviews were done by
men); Sara J. Corse, Pregnant Managers and Their Subordinates: The Effects of Gender
Expectations on Hierarchical Relationships, 26 J. Applied Behav. Sci. 25 (1990) (finding that
pregnant managers are penalized for acting firmly in the face of a conflict, rather than con-
forming to expectations that pregnant women should be soft and nurturing).

93. Jennifer Bennett Shinall, The Pregnancy Penalty, 103 Minn. L. Rev. 749 (2018).

94. See Michelle R. Hebl et al., Hostile and Benevolent Reactions Toward Pregnant
Women: Complementary Interpersonal Punishments and Rewards That Maintain Tra-
ditional Roles, 92 J. Applied Psych. 1499 (2007); Shelley J. Correll et al., Getting a Job: Is
There a Motherhood Penalty?, 112 Am. J. Socio. 1297, 1306 (2007); Amy J. C. Cuddy et al.,
When Professionals Become Mothers, Warmth Doesn't Cut the Ice, 60 J. Soc. Issues 701, 703
(2004).

95. Hebl et al., supra note 94, at 1508-09.

96. Iris Marion Young, On Female Body Experience: "Throwing Like a Girl" and Other
Essays 54 (2005).

be less in need of protection from the rigors of work."[97] They are "more likely to be viewed as irresponsible reproducers, and are expected to work, while at the same time are predicted to be less reliable workers."[98] Studies show Black mothers are rated as less reliable than their equally qualified white counterparts; they also show that white mothers are viewed positively for staying home, while Black mothers are viewed positively for working.[99] What underlies these racial disparities, and what can be done to alleviate them?

5. **Pregnancy as a Disability.** Note that California's pregnancy leave requirement that was challenged in the *Cal Fed* case was a "disability leave." Should pregnancy be considered a disability under the Americans with Disabilities Act of 1990 (ADA)?[100] The ADA provides employees with a covered disability the right to reasonable accommodations that do not impose undue hardship.[101] The ADA does not expressly mention pregnancy, but most courts have interpreted it to exclude coverage for women who suffer temporary disability from the complications of normal pregnancy.[102] In 2008, Congress passed the Americans with Disabilities Act Amendments Act (ADAAA), which restores protections for the disabled that had been gutted by federal court rulings over two decades. Among other changes, the ADAAA expands the definition of disabled to include conditions that interfere with mundane, work-related tasks like standing, lifting, or bending.[103] It also directs courts to construe the statute broadly in favor of the disabled. In response, the EEOC issued an interpretive guidance stating that temporary disabilities can be covered if "substantially limiting," which is "not meant to be a demanding standard," and should be understood to encompass an employee with a "20-pound lifting restriction that lasts or is expected to last for several months." Yet, the EEOC guidance expressly excludes pregnancy from coverage under the ADAAA based on the theory that because "pregnancy is not the result of a physiological disorder," it is "not an impairment."[104] Given that the amended statute is designed to cover potentially short-term disabilities, including those whose only manifestation is a lifting restriction, can the continuing exclusion of pregnancy from the ADA be justified? Is there any benefit to women in refusing to treat pregnancy as a disability? On the one hand, the purpose of the ADA is to eliminate stereotyped thinking about disability.

---

97. Deborah L. Brake & Joanna L. Grossman, Unprotected Sex: The Pregnancy Discrimination Act at 35, 21 Duke J. Gender, L. & Pol'y 67, 105 (2013); Joanna L. Grossman, Expanding the Core: Pregnancy Discrimination Law as It Approaches Full Term, 52 Idaho L. Rev. 825 (2016) (retrospective look at the PDA).

98. Brake & Grossman, Unprotected Sex, supra note 97, at 106.

99. Correll et al., supra note 94, at 1324; Stephanie Bornstein, Work, Family, and Discrimination at the Bottom of the Ladder, 19 Geo. J. Poverty L. & Pol'y 1, 39-40 (2012).

100. 42 U.S.C. §§ 12101-12213 (2018).

101. 42 U.S.C. § 12102(1)(A) (2018).

102. See, e.g., Gorman v. Wells Mfg. Corp., 209 F. Supp. 2d 970, 976 (S.D. Iowa 2002); Gudenkauf v. Stauffer Commc'ns, Inc., 922 F. Supp. 465, 474 (D. Kan. 1996).

103. 42 U.S.C. § 12102(2)(A) (2018).

104. See EEOC Compliance Manual § 902.2(c)(3) (2022); see also 29 C.F.R. § 1630.2(j)(1)(ii) (2022). For detailed discussion of the law before and after the ADAAA, see Jeannette Cox, Pregnancy as "Disability" and the Amended Americans with Disabilities Act, 53 B.C. L. Rev. 443, 460-66 (2012).

On the other hand, this exclusion avoids associating pregnancy with the dependence implied in the notion of disability, upon which traditional legal restrictions against women were often based. Given the stereotypes associated with pregnancy, why exclude it from the Act, which requires reasonable accommodation?

6. **Accommodation Under the Second Clause of the PDA.** Unlike the ADA, the PDA provides only a comparative right of accommodation—employers need only accommodate the pregnant workers' needs if they accommodate the needs of those similar in their ability or inability to work, but unaffected by pregnancy. As interpreted in *Young*, this does not necessarily mean a pregnant woman is entitled to accommodations provided to *any* other person—the accommodation must be available to enough people to raise an inference of discrimination against the pregnant worker who is denied the accommodation. But the accommodation must be available to at least one person in order for the comparative right of accommodation to be activated. In one incident, Wal-Mart fired a pregnant woman who worked the fitting room for carrying a water bottle throughout the day because her doctor had advised that she drink water regularly to prevent recurring bladder infections.[105] Could the plaintiff have sought relief under the PDA? If Wal-Mart allows other employees to eat or drink on the job (say a diabetic in need of frequent snacks), then it would have to make a similar accommodation for a pregnant employee with a comparable medical need. But if the company makes no exceptions to its policy, can it deny her this medically indicated and costless accommodation?

In a post-*Young* case, Sanchez-Estrada v. Mapfre Praico Insurance Co., the trial court found no violation of the second clause when an employer refused to provide a pregnant employee with a maternity fit uniform because it had exhausted its uniform budget and was suffering significant financial losses.[106] Although, under *Young*, cost cannot be used to justify the failure to extend otherwise available accommodations to pregnant workers, the plaintiff could not point to any other employee whose need for a new uniform was accommodated. This decision illustrates how uniqueness of pregnancy can still be a trap, even under *Young*.

What if the employer *does* provide accommodations to some temporarily disabled workers, but not to pregnant women? In *Young*, the employer provided light-duty assignments to three broad classes of workers temporarily unable to perform certain requirements of their jobs. In theory, pregnant women were not the only ones excluded by the formal policy; other workers falling outside the three classes of accommodated workers were also denied light-duty work. Several federal appellate courts had ruled that similar policies did not violate the PDA,[107] but the Supreme Court held that this one might. How might employers justify such policies without reference to cost savings, which *Young* prohibits? What benefits to the employer are likely to be deemed sufficiently important in this context to avoid a

---

105. Wiseman v. Wal-Mart Stores, Inc., No. 08-1244-EFM, 2009 U.S. Dist. LEXIS 62079 (D. Kan. July 21, 2009).

106. 126 F. Supp. 3d 220 (D. P.R. 2015).

107. See, e.g., Reeves v. Swift Transp. Co., Inc., 446 F.3d 637 (6th Cir. 2006).

finding of discrimination? What burdens are too great to justify the benefits? How might you expect employers to draft light-duty policies in the wake of this ruling?[108]

Early cases in the wake of *Young* suggest that courts are doing as the Supreme Court instructed—taking a more careful look at the facts surrounding the denial of accommodation. A federal court in Louisiana, in the wake of *Young*, held that summary judgment for an employer in an accommodation case was inappropriate because there were disputed facts about whether the employer's explanation for the denial of accommodation was pretextual and whether it had offered accommodations to comparably restricted workers.[109] The Supreme Court of Iowa, interpreting a state law co-extensive with the PDA, held that the treatment of pregnant workers could not be compared only to those also injured off the job, but had to be compared to all workers with temporary disabilities.[110] But the results overall have been mixed for pregnant plaintiffs. One study found that in the first three years after *Young* was decided, courts ruled in two-thirds of the cases that the employer was not required to provide the requested accommodation.[111]

A bill entitled The Pregnant Women's Fairness Act was introduced in Congress in 2012, and again in several subsequent years. The House of Representatives passed the current version in 2021, and it awaits consideration in the Senate.[112] It proposes a right of reasonable accommodation for pregnancy-related disability, modeled after the Americans with Disabilities Act.[113]

Twenty-five states and some cities have passed laws to require at least some employers to provide reasonable pregnancy accommodations. Is this a better approach? What objections might you expect from employers? Are there any downsides to pregnant workers having a right of reasonable accommodation? Jennifer Shinall conducted an empirical analysis of different pregnancy laws and concluded that "[p]regnancy accommodation laws and paid family leave laws yield multiple positive labor market effects for recently pregnant women."[114] They yield at least a "short-term boost to new mothers' labor market outcomes" that may have benefits that last into the future.

   7. Disparate Impact Theory.   Another theory potentially available under existing law is that the failure to accommodate pregnancy has a disparate impact

---

108. On the potential implications of this ruling, see Joanna L. Grossman & Deborah L. Brake, Forceps Delivery: The Supreme Court Narrowly Saves the Pregnancy Discrimination Act in *Young v. UPS*; see also Joanna L. Grossman & Gillian A. Thomas, Making Sure Pregnancy Works: Accommodation Claims After *Young v. United Parcel Service, Inc.*, 14 Harv. J. L. & Pol'y 319 (2020).

109. Martin v. Winn-Dixie La., Inc., 132 F. Supp. 3d 794 (M.D. La. 2015).

110. McQuistion v. City of Clinton, 872 N.W.2d 817, 830 (Iowa 2015).

111. A Better Balance, Long Overdue: It Is Time for the Federal Pregnant Workers Fairness Act (May 2019).

112. H.R. 1065 (introduced Feb. 15, 2021). On the development of pregnancy discrimination law, see Joanna L. Grossman, Nine to Five: How Gender, Sex, and Sexuality Continue to Define the American Workplace (2016).

113. Nat'l P'ship for Women & Fams., Fact Sheet: Pregnant Workers Fairness Act (Feb. 2021).

114. Jennifer Bennett Shinall, Protecting Pregnancy, 106 Cornell L. Rev. 987 (2021).

against women.[115] In *Cal Fed*, the Court specifically declined to address the issue, and few plaintiffs have succeeded under this theory.[116] Consider the following analysis of disparate impact claims under the PDA:

> In theory, disparate impact law should compensate for some of the shortcomings of the PDA's comparative right of accommodation by invalidating some of the harsh employment policies that make it difficult for women to work through pregnancy. . . . The reality is that plaintiffs almost never prevail on such claims in the pregnancy context.
>
> There are a number of reasons why disparate impact theory has not turned out to be more useful for pregnant workers. Although most courts acknowledge the theoretical existence of disparate impact theory under the PDA, some refuse to apply it in its true form. These courts treat the second clause of the PDA . . . as a ceiling on what accommodations employers can be forced to provide. Judge Posner, for example, in *Troupe*, described disparate impact as a "permissible theory" under the PDA but cautioned that "properly understood," it was not a "warrant for favoritism" and could not be used to prevent employers from treating pregnant workers "as badly as they treat similarly affected but nonpregnant employees." Other courts have taken a similar tack—claiming to recognize disparate impact law but refusing to allow it to provide anything more than a comparative right to accommodation or leave. The Fifth Circuit . . . refused to apply disparate impact to claims "in which the plaintiff's only challenge is that the amount of sick leave granted to employees is insufficient to accommodate the time off required in a typical pregnancy. To hold otherwise would be to transform the PDA into a guarantee of medical leave for pregnant employees, something we have specifically held that the PDA does not do." . . .
>
> Even when courts are not openly dismissive of disparate impact claims, plaintiffs have not met with much success. One potential obstacle is the inability to identify, as required under the statute, a particular "employment practice" that produces the disparate impact. Courts have held, for example, that any discretionary decision—such as the decision to deny a particular woman's request for pregnancy-related leave—cannot be challenged as a practice. . . .
>
> A second obstacle arises when courts prejudge the merits of the claim by refusing to apply disparate impact analysis to "legitimate" job requirements like attendance. . . .
>
> A final, but important, obstacle is that courts tend to require statistical proof of a disparate impact. Courts have been largely unwilling to accept non-statistical showings of impact, or to rely on broader societal

---

115. See Christine Jolls, Antidiscrimination and Accommodation, 115 Harv. L. Rev. 643 (2001).

116. Several of the relevant cases are collected in Joan C. Williams & Nancy Segal, Beyond the Maternal Wall: Relief for Family Caregivers Who Are Discriminated Against on the Job, 26 Harv. Women's L.J. 77, 134-36 (2003).

data to support a claim of disparate impact. And plaintiffs have been mostly unsuccessful in making the requisite statistical showing. . . .[117]

Reva Siegel praises *Young* for affirming the possibility of disparate impact liability under the PDA. The proof structure set forth in *Young* expressly invites litigation over "rigid job descriptions" and the denial of low-cost accommodations.[118] Should courts be more accepting of disparate impact claims in the pregnancy context?[119] Is it consistent with the aims of the PDA? With its structure?

8. *Johnson Controls* **as a Reprise of the Protective Legislation Debate.** In Muller v. Oregon, excerpted in Chapter 1, the issue was whether the danger to women of a long work day was sufficient to overcome the Fourteenth Amendment freedom of contract rights of the employer. In *Johnson Controls*, the question was whether the danger to women and their fetuses justified their exclusion from certain job categories as a BFOQ under Title VII. Freedom of contract no longer has the recognition it once had and women's equality is now a protected value, both constitutionally and statutorily. Nonetheless, Justice Blackmun, and many legal commentators, have drawn parallels between fetal protection policies and protective legislation of the nineteenth century, which was also backed by "scientific" data. For contemporary law outside the employment context that reflects the "protective" approach toward pregnant women, see Chapter 5, Section B4. What are the costs and benefits of contemporary protective legislation? What, if anything, should be inferred from the fact that these policies are more common in certain industries — typically those with higher pay and benefits that have been traditionally dominated by men?[120] Is it unfair to employers to prevent them from excluding women but holding them potentially liable for miscarriages or birth defects attributable to lead exposure? Or is this simply a cost to the employer of being engaged in a risky business, which is best dealt with by ordinary business means, such as insurance, or passing the risks of business along to the consumer?

9. **Women Workers and "Choice."** The issue of women's choice with respect to fetal protection policies can be posed in different ways. Fetal protection policies do give women one kind of choice — between sterilization and losing their jobs. One woman at Johnson Controls, Betty Riggs, submitted to sterilization although she wanted more children because her marriage was breaking up and she needed the money. Not long after Betty Riggs and four other women were sterilized, the company shut down its pigments department and their jobs were eliminated.[121] The Court in *Johnson Controls*, in invalidating fetal protection policies, concludes

---

117. Joanna L. Grossman, Pregnancy, Work, and the Promise of Full Citizenship, 98 Geo. L.J. 567, 615-17 (2010).

118. Reva B. Siegel, Pregnancy as a Normal Condition of Employment: Comparative and Role-Based Accounts of Discrimination, 59 Wm. & Mary L. Rev. 969, 1004 (2018).

119. For analysis of disparate impact and pregnancy accommodation claims, see L. Camille Hebert, Disparate Impact and Pregnancy: Title VII's Other Accommodation Requirement, 24 Am. U. J. Gender Soc. Pol'y & L. 107 (2015).

120. Mary E. Becker, From *Muller v. Oregon* to Fetal Vulnerability Policies, 53 U. Chi. L. Rev. 1219, 1238-39 (1986).

121. David Kirp, Fetal Hazards, Gender Justice and the Justices: The Limits of Equality, 34 Wm. & Mary L. Rev. 101, 104-06 (1992).

that women workers should make their own decisions about whether to assume the risks of the workplace for themselves and their potential offspring. In fact, this has been the general response to the Court's decision in *Johnson Controls*.

Is this the best approach for women? Or should Johnson Controls have been required to make the workplace safer for pregnant women? The law in the United Kingdom requires employers to assess risks to expectant mothers and their fetuses and then to control the risk if possible. If the risk cannot be controlled, then suitable alternative work or paid leave must be given until the woman is no longer pregnant.[122] Could this approach be justified under formal equality, or does the possibility of paid leave treat women better than men?

10. **Equality Analysis in *Johnson Controls*.** The *Johnson Controls* case reveals a number of different ways to identify the groups to compare for purposes of equality analysis. The Seventh Circuit Court of Appeals, in effect, compared employees who could bear children to employees who could not. On that basis, the appellate court concluded that the policy was facially sex-neutral and justifiable as a way to protect women's unconceived offspring. This approach is similar to the one used by the U.S. Supreme Court in Geduldig v. Aiello, above. In Dobbs v. Jackson Women's Health Organization (discussed at length in Chapter 5, Section B), which eliminated federal constitutional protection for abortion under the Due Process Clause, the Court also held that a state abortion ban does not violate the Equal Protection Clause. As the majority wrote, resurrecting *Geduldig*,:

> We briefly address one additional constitutional provision that some of respondents' amici have now offered as another potential home for the abortion right: the Fourteenth Amendment's Equal Protection Clause. Neither *Roe* nor *Casey* saw fit to invoke this theory, and it is squarely foreclosed by our precedents, which establish that a State's regulation of abortion is not a sex-based classification and is thus not subject to the "heightened scrutiny" that applies to such classifications. The regulation of a medical procedure that only one sex can undergo does not trigger heightened constitutional scrutiny unless the regulation is a "mere pretext designed to effect an invidious discrimination against members of one sex or the other" [citing *Geduldig*]. And as the Court has stated, the "goal of preventing abortion" does not constitute "invidiously discriminatory animus" against women. Accordingly, laws regulating or prohibiting abortion are not subject to heightened scrutiny.[123]

Is this an appropriate application of *Geduldig*?

In contrast to the uniqueness analysis in *Geduldig* and *Dobbs*, Justice Blackmun's analysis in *Johnson Controls* compared fertile women to fertile men, concluding that the fetal protection policy violates Title VII because it treats these two groups differently. Justice Blackmun referred in his opinion to evidence that lead exposure may damage sperm as well as ova to strengthen his analysis that men and women are similarly situated and thus the relevant groups for comparison. Justice Scalia

---

122. See Michael Thomson, Reproductivity, the Workplace and the Gendering of the Body (Politic), 14 Cardozo Stud. L. & Lit. 565, 571 (2004).
123. 142 S. Ct. 2228, 2245-46 (2022).

did not specify the groups to be compared. In his view, whether or not the Court thought the policy in question was a form of sex discrimination, Congress unequivocally had determined with the Pregnancy Discrimination Act that it was. For the same reason, Justice Scalia's analysis is not affected by whether or not there are any comparable fetal risks to be passed through male employees.

If the *Johnson Controls* case satisfies formal equality requirements, does it also satisfy substantive equality—i.e., does it ensure that women and men enjoy the same opportunities? Arguably not, if women face damage to their reproductive capacities that men do not face. Emily Gold Waldman points out that while comparisons are often a useful tool in equality analysis, the "processes connected with the female reproductive cycle—menstruation, menopause, pregnancy, and breastfeeding—do not have perfect comparators" and yet impose "real costs and needs—unequally borne across the sexes."[124] She argues that accommodation of these unique biological processes is necessary "to achieve true social equality." Do you agree? Can Kay's "episodic approach" for pregnancy be used in these contexts? What would it require in this instance?

PUTTING THEORY INTO PRACTICE

2-8. Barbara works the 8-to-5 shift as a department store cashier. She is entitled to an hour break for lunch and two ten-minute breaks during the day. Ordinarily, the supervisor manages lunch hours and breaks for all employees by staggering the lunch hours on a rotating basis and trying to fit in the shorter breaks around lulls in store business. An employee may have her lunch hour at 11 a.m. one day, and 3 p.m. the next.

Barbara is returning to work after a maternity leave. She wants to have her breaks timed so that she can use her lunch break to breastfeed her baby (at an adjacent day-care center) and her short breaks to pump her breast milk. For this to work well, she needs a regular daily lunch hour and evenly spaced breaks. Should she be entitled to these accommodations? What if another mother returning to work wants a similar arrangement? Alternatively, what if such accommodations would prevent the supervisor from attending a management-training seminar given over the lunch break? How should fairness to other workers be juggled?

2-9. A local police department has a limited number of temporary desk-duty positions for its officers. Those officers injured on the job or in the course of military service are given priority; officers temporarily disabled for any other reason can hold a light-duty position only if no higher priority officer needs it. When Cynthia applied for a light-duty position during the last trimester of her pregnancy, when her doctor had told her to avoid long prolonged standing or physical exertion, she was told that none was available. Two of the three positions were held by men injured during a weekend training session with the military reserves, and the third was held by a man who broke his ankle at work. Without a temporary desk assignment, Cynthia was forced to go on unpaid leave until after she delivered her baby. Has she suffered actionable pregnancy discrimination under *Young*?

---

124. Emily Gold Waldman, Compared to What? Menstruation, Pregnancy, and the Complexities of Comparison, 41 Colum. J. Gender & L. 218 (2021).

2-10. A neighborhood community center runs after-school programs for teenage girls, many of whom lack positive adult role models. The center has a policy against hiring unmarried pregnant woman, on the theory that these individuals present negative role models. The center's employees and clients are almost all racial minorities, and the nonmarital birth rate for Black women is 70 percent. Does the policy wrongfully discriminate on the basis of sex?[125] Is intersectionality analysis relevant?

2-11. Plaintiff, who was the only female among her employer's four top-level executives, brought a lawsuit for sex discrimination after she was terminated. The employer claims that the dismissal was because of unsatisfactory performance. The plaintiff presents evidence of remarks by one vice president who questioned the ability of women to have children and still remain committed to work. She also presents evidence of a company hiring goal (or "profile") in favor of unmarried, childless women, which another vice president said was justified by the fact that such women are more committed to their work and available for long hours and travel. Should this evidence be sufficient to prove pretext in plaintiff's termination?[126]

2-12. A transgender man became pregnant while working at an Amazon warehouse.[127] He informed his supervisor that he was pregnant, after which his co-workers began to harass him. He then received unfavorable performance reviews and was put on leave. He complained to human resources but when he was reinstated, his supervisor forced him to carry heavy items despite a doctor's note stating that he could not lift anything over twenty-five pounds because of pregnancy. Is this actionable under Title VII?

2-13. A waitress at Hooters claims she was fired after disclosing her pregnancy. There were other pregnant waitresses at the time, but her boss complained that too many would make the restaurant "look like a circus." Will she prevail if she challenges her firing? Why or why not?

2-14. A friend asks you for advice about navigating her job as a lab technician during her first pregnancy. What advice would you give? Could you predict the challenges or conflicts she is likely to encounter? Could you explain her rights or how to enforce them? What additional information would you need?[128]

2-15. Black women face higher risks of many pregnancy-related complications, including high blood pressure and preeclampsia, and a higher maternal and infant mortality rate, and thus are disproportionally disadvantaged in jobs with inflexible structures and high physical demands.[129] Can pregnancy discrimination law address these disparities? How?

2-16. Is the U.S. military entitled to remove a pregnant soldier from combat duty?

---

125. See Chambers v. Omaha Girls Club, Inc., 834 F.2d 697 (8th Cir. 1987), reh'g en banc denied, 840 F.2d 583 (1988).

126. Santiago-Ramos v. Centennial P.R. Wireless Corp., 217 F.3d 46 (1st Cir. 2000).

127. See Dan Avery, Transgender Man Files Pregnancy Discrimination Suit Against Amazon, NBC News (Oct. 6, 2020).

128. See AAUW, Know Your Rights: The Pregnancy Discrimination Act (PDA).

129. Nat'l Latina Inst. for Reprod. Health & Nat'l Women's L. Ctr., Accommodating Pregnancy on the Job: The Stakes for Women of Color and Immigrant Women (May 2014); Creanga et al., Racial and Ethnic Disparities in Severe Maternal Morbidity: A Multistate Analysis 2008-10, 210 Am. J. Obstetrics & Gynecology 435 (2014).

2. *Caregiver Discrimination*

Discrimination against women because of their unique role in the reproductive process does not end with childbirth. Discrimination against mothers, especially those with young children, is well documented and can take a wide variety of forms. One problem for all new parents is the lack of adequate caretaking leave. This problem is even more acute for women of color, who are more likely to be in the work force than white women and more likely to be in households where they are the sole or primary wage earner. In 1993, Congress passed the federal Family and Medical Leave Act (FMLA).[130] The FMLA requires that employers with at least fifty workers allow up to twelve weeks of unpaid leave for the care of a new infant or ill family member, with the right to return to the same or an equivalent position without loss of pre-leave benefits. The Act covers employees who have worked for the employer for at least twelve months and for 1,250 hours during the year preceding the start of the leave. The law requires the employer to reinstate an employee at the end of an approved FMLA leave to the same position and prohibits the employer from retaliating against a leave-taker.

While the FMLA has helped many people resolve short-term conflicts between caregiving and work, it also has significant limitations. Only half of the work force is covered by the Act and the U.S. Department of Labor found that 88 percent of eligible employees who need time off do not take it, largely because they cannot afford to go without a paycheck. Even many who can afford to take leave sometimes do not do so because of resistance by supervisors and colleagues. One study of highly educated individuals found that about one-third of women and almost half of men reported that their workplace culture penalized employees for taking advantage of family-friendly policies.[131] Other research has indicated that many employees did not assert their rights because of well-founded concerns of informal retaliation and blacklisting; they feared being branded as a "troublemaker" or "slacker" and not getting favorable assignments, shifts, or recommendations if they changed jobs.[132] Fewer men take family leave than women, and fewer employers offer paid leave to men.[133] What accounts for this difference? Is it a problem that employers or public policy should address?[134] (The argument that the government should do more to subsidize caretaking through paid leave and other measures is addressed in Chapter 4, Section B.)

---

130. Pub. L. No. 103-03, 107 Stat. 6 (1993).

131. Sylvia Ann Hewlett & Carolyn Buck Luce, Off-Ramps and On-Ramps: Keeping Talented Women on the Road to Success, Harv. Bus. Rev. 43 (Mar. 2005).

132. Catherine R. Albiston, Bargaining in the Shadow of Social Institutions: Competing Discourses and Social Change in the Workplace Mobilization of Civil Rights, 39 Law & Soc'y Rev. 11, 23-27, 31-38 (2005); see also Catherine Albiston & Lindsey Trimble O'Connor, Just Leave, 39 Harv. J.L. & Gender 1 (2016).

133. See, e.g., Jane Herr et al., Dep't of Labor, Gender Differences in Needing and Taking Leave (Nov. 2020).

134. See Joanna L. Grossman, Job Security Without Equality: The Family and Medical Leave Act of 1993, 15 Wash. U. J.L. & Pol'y 17 (2004) (noting negligible impact of FMLA on caretaking leaves by men).

An important legal precedent is the U.S. Supreme Court's decision in Nevada Department of Human Resources v. Hibbs, upholding the constitutionality of the FMLA as applied to state employees.[135] The primary legal issue in the case concerned sovereign immunity and Congress's power to override it in order to enforce equal protection rights. The Eleventh Amendment to the U.S. Constitution prohibits money damages against a state except to the extent Congress has limited that immunity through specific legislation pursuant to a valid congressional power. *Hibbs* raised the question whether the FMLA constituted such a limitation and whether it was valid under Section Five of the Fourteenth Amendment as a congruent and proportional response to a state-sponsored history of discrimination. The plaintiff was a man and the expansive language of then-Chief Justice Rehnquist is noteworthy in its recognition of the power of gender stereotyping with respect to family care issues and the intent of the gender-neutral provisions of the FMLA to address the resulting disadvantages.

> The FMLA aims to protect the right to be free from gender-based discrimination in the workplace. . . . The history of the many state laws limit[ing] women's employment opportunities is chronicled in — and, until relatively recently, was sanctioned by — this Court's own opinions. . . . Congress responded to this history of discrimination by abrogating States' sovereign immunity in Title VII of the Civil Rights Act of 1964. . . . According to the evidence that was before Congress when it enacted the FMLA, states continue to rely on invalid gender stereotypes in the employment context, specifically in the administration of leave benefits. . . . Congress . . . heard testimony that . . . "Even . . . [w]here child-care leave policies do exist, men, *both in the public and private sectors*, receive notoriously discriminatory treatment in their requests for such leave." . . . Many States offered women extended 'maternity' leave that far exceeded the typical 4- to 8-week period of physical disability due to pregnancy and childbirth, but very few States granted men a parallel benefit: Fifteen States provided women up to one year of extended maternity leave, while only four provided men with the same. . . . This and other differential leave policies were not attributable to any differential physical needs of men and women, but rather to the pervasive sex-role stereotype that caring for family members is women's work.[136]

Note that the Act was inspired by a problem that disproportionately affects women, but by insisting that men receive the same parental leave benefits as similarly situated women, the FMLA reflects formal equality principles. If women disproportionately use parenting leave, is this benefit a "subsidy" for women?

In an interesting twist, nine years after *Hibbs*, the Supreme Court distinguished the FMLA's family leave provisions from the FMLA's provision entitling a covered employee to leave when that employee's own "serious health condition . . . interferes with the employee's ability to perform at work." According to the Court in Coleman v. Maryland Court of Appeals,[137] the FMLA's "self-care" provision was

---

135. 538 U.S. 721 (2003).
136. Id. at 728-31.
137. 566 U.S. 30 (2012).

not a response to any identified pattern of gender-based discrimination and thus does not constitute a valid Congressional abrogation of state sovereign immunity. Thus, while individuals under *Hibbs* can obtain money damages against a state for violations of the FMLA family-care provisions, sovereign immunity protects states against such suits under the FMLA's self-care provision. Is the Court's distinction between the FMLA's family-care and self-care persuasive? In a dissenting opinion, Justice Ginsburg emphasized the importance of job security for pregnant women with maternity-related disabilities before and after childbirth to the achievement of gender equality—an importance underlined in the legislative history of the Act. To Justice Ginsburg, an essential aspect of the FMLA is the way the family-care and the self-care provisions work together to protect women from discrimination on account of their pregnancies. "It would make scant sense to provide job-protected leave for a woman to care for a newborn, but not for her recovery from delivery, a miscarriage, or the birth of a stillborn baby."[138]

Does it matter that the plaintiff in *Coleman* was a man? According to Justice Ginsburg, the availability of FMLA rights to men was intended, among other things, to blunt the force of stereotypes of women as primary caregivers—in other words, to recognize the historic pattern of discrimination against pregnant women and female caregivers in a gender-neutral way. Does this intention supply the necessary connection between the self-care provision and an identified pattern of gender discrimination?

Even at its best, the FMLA only protects parents who need (and can afford) unpaid leave in the first months of caregiving; this limitation affects many wage earners, but people of color more so given racial disparities in household income. Moreover, both mothers and fathers often continue to face conflicts between work and the obligations of parenting for many more years. In the cases that follow, consider whether the mother in *Back* and the father in *Ayanna* faced the same type of discrimination. How well does the law protect them from caregiving discrimination? (The problem of work–family balance is revisited in Chapter 4 through the perspective of difference.)

Back v. Hastings on Hudson Union Free School District

365 F.3d 107 (2d Cir. 2004)

CALABRESI, Circuit Judge.

In 1998, Plaintiff-Appellant Elana Back was hired as a school psychologist at the Hillside Elementary School on a three-year tenure track. At the end of that period, when Back came up for review, she was denied tenure and her probationary period was terminated. . . . Defendants-Appellees contend that Back was fired because she lacked organizational and interpersonal skills. Back asserts that the real reason she was let go was that the defendants presumed that she, as a young mother, would not continue to demonstrate the necessary devotion to her job, and

---

138. Id. at 57 (Ginsburg, J., dissenting).

indeed that she could not maintain such devotion while at the same time being a good mother.

This appeal thus poses an important question, one that strikes at the persistent "fault line between work and family—precisely where sex-based overgeneralization has been and remains strongest." Nev. Dep't of Human Res. v. Hibbs, 538 U.S. 721 (2003). It asks whether stereotyping about the qualities of mothers is a form of gender discrimination, and whether this can be determined in the absence of evidence about how the employer in question treated fathers. We answer both questions in the affirmative. . . .

A. BACKGROUND

i. Back's Qualifications

[Plaintiff Elana Back was the school psychologist at Hillside Elementary School . . . Defendant-Appellee Marilyn Wishnie, the Principal of Hillside, and defendant-appellee Ann Brennan, the Director of Pupil Personnel Services for the District, were Back's supervisors. . . .

In the plaintiff's first two years at Hillside, Brennan and Wishnie consistently gave her excellent evaluations. . . . In her first annual evaluation, on a scale where the highest score was "outstanding," and the second highest score was "superior," Back was deemed "outstanding" and "superior" in almost all categories, and "average" in only one.

In her second year at Hillside, Back took approximately three months of maternity leave. After she returned, she garnered another "outstanding" evaluation from Brennan, who noted that she was "very pleased with Mrs. Back's performance during her second year at Hillside." Other contemporaneous observations also resulted in strongly positive feedback, for example, that Back "demonstrate[d] her strong social/emotional skills in her work with parents and teachers, and most especially with students," and that she was "a positive influence in many areas, and continues to extend a great deal of effort and commitment to our work." In her annual evaluation, Back received higher marks than the previous year, with more "outstandings" and no "averages." The narrative comments noted that she "continues to serve in an outstanding manner and provides excellent support for our students," and that her "commitment to her work and to her own learning is outstanding." At the beginning of Back's third year at Hillside, she again received "outstanding" and "superior" evaluations from both Brennan and Wishnie.

Defendant-Appellant John Russell, the Superintendent of the School District, also conducted ongoing evaluations of Back's performance. In January 1999, he . . . rated her performance "superior." In February 2000, he again . . . indicated that Back's performance was "superior." He also noted that she was effective without being overly directive, and worked well with the other members of the team. In addition, according to Back, all three individual defendants repeatedly assured her throughout this time that she would receive tenure.

ii. Alleged Stereotyping

Back asserts that things changed dramatically as her tenure review approached. The first allegedly discriminatory comments came in spring 2000, when Back's written evaluations still indicated that she was a very strong candidate for tenure. At that time, shortly after Back had returned from maternity leave, the plaintiff claims that Brennan, (a) inquired about how she was "planning on spacing [her] offspring," (b) said " '[p]lease do not get pregnant until I retire,' " and (c) suggested that Back "wait until [her son] was in kindergarten to have another child."

Then, a few months into Back's third year at Hillside, on December 14, 2000, Brennan allegedly told Back that she was expected to work until 4:30 p.m. every day, and asked " 'What's the big deal. You have a nanny. This is what you [have] to do to get tenure.' "Back replied that she did work these hours. And Brennan, after reportedly reassuring Back that there was no concern about her job performance, told her that Wishnie expected her to work such hours. But, always according to Back, Brennan also indicated that Back should "maybe . . . reconsider whether [Back] could be a mother and do this job which [Brennan] characterized as administrative in nature," and that Brennan and Wishnie were "concerned that, if [Back] received tenure, [she] would work only until 3:15 p.m. and did not know how [she] could possibly do this job with children."

A few days later, on January 8, 2001, Brennan allegedly told Back for the first time that she might not support Back's tenure because of what Back characterizes as minor errors that she made in a report. According to Back, shortly thereafter Principal Wishnie accused her of working only from 8:15 a.m. to 3:15 p.m. and never working during lunch. When Back disputed this, Wishnie supposedly replied that "this was not [Wishnie's] impression and . . . that she did not know how she could perform my job with little ones. She told me that she worked from 7 a.m. to 7 p.m. and that she expected the same from me. If my family was my priority, she stated, maybe this was not the job for me." A week later, both Brennan and Wishnie reportedly told Back that this was perhaps not the job or the school district for her if she had "little ones," and that it was "not possible for [her] to be a good mother and have this job." The two also allegedly remarked that it would be harder to fire Back if she had tenure, and wondered "whether my apparent commitment to my job was an act. They stated that once I obtained tenure, I would not show the same level of commitment I had shown because I had little ones at home. They expressed concerns about my child care arrangements, though these had never caused me conflict with school assignments." They did not—as Back told the story—discuss with her any concerns with her performance at that time. . . .

On April 30, 2001, Brennan and Wishnie purportedly repeated the same concerns about her ability to balance work and family, and told Back that they would recommend that she not be granted tenure and that Superintendent Russell would follow their recommendation. They reportedly also "stated they wanted another year to assess the child care situation."

iii. Denial of Tenure

Back retained counsel in response to Brennan and Wishnie's alleged statements, and in a letter dated May 14, 2001, informed [Superintendent] Russell of these comments, and of her fear that they reflected attitudes that would improperly affect her tenure review. On May 29, 2001, Brennan and Wishnie sent a formal memo to Russell informing him that they could not recommend Back for tenure. . . .

On or around June 13, 2001, Wishnie and Brennan filed the first negative evaluation of Back, which gave her several "below average" marks and charged her with being inconsistent, defensive, difficult to supervise, the source of parental complaints, and inaccurate in her reports. Their evaluation, which was submitted to Russell, concluded that Back should not be granted tenure. Around the same time, several parents who had apparently complained about Back were encouraged by Russell to put their concerns in writing. Several parents submitted letters, reporting a range of complaints about Back's work, including that she was defensive, immature, unprofessional, and had misdiagnosed children.

In September 2001, the Board notified Back that her probationary appointment would be terminated. . . .

Plaintiff presses three arguments on appeal. First, she contends that an adverse employment consequence imposed because of stereotypes about motherhood is a form of gender discrimination which contravenes the Equal Protection Clause. . . .

A. THEORY OF DISCRIMINATION . . .

[T]he plaintiff must prove that she suffered purposeful or intentional discrimination on the basis of gender. Discrimination based on gender, once proven, can only be tolerated if the state provides an "exceedingly persuasive justification" for the rule or practice. The defendants in this case have made no claim of justification. . . .

To show sex discrimination, Back relies upon a *Price Waterhouse* "stereotyping" theory. Accordingly, she argues that comments made about a woman's inability to combine work and motherhood are direct evidence of such discrimination. . . .

It is the law . . . that "stereotyped remarks can certainly be evidence that gender played a part" in an adverse employment decision. The principle of *Price Waterhouse*, furthermore, applies as much to the supposition that a woman *will* conform to a gender stereotype (and therefore will not, for example, be dedicated to her job), as to the supposition that a woman is unqualified for a position because she does *not* conform to a gender stereotype.

The instant case, however, foregrounds a crucial question: What constitutes a "gender-based stereotype"? *Price Waterhouse* suggested that this question must be answered in the particular context in which it arises, and without undue formalization. We have adopted the same approach, as have other circuits. Just as "[i]t takes no special training to discern sex stereotyping in a description of an aggressive female employee as requiring 'a course at charm school,'" *Price Waterhouse*, so it takes no special training to discern stereotyping in the view that a woman cannot "be a good mother" and have a job that requires long hours, or in the statement that a mother who received tenure "would not show the same level of commitment [she] had shown because [she] had little ones at home." These are not the kind of "innocuous words" that we have previously held to be insufficient, as a matter of law, to provide evidence of discriminatory intent.

Not surprisingly, other circuit courts have agreed. . . .

The defendants argue that stereotypes about pregnant women or mothers are not based upon gender, but rather, "gender plus parenthood," thereby implying that such stereotypes cannot, without comparative evidence of what was said about fathers, be presumed to be "on the basis of sex." *Hibbs* makes pellucidly clear, however, that, at least where stereotypes are considered, the notions that mothers are insufficiently devoted to work, and that work and motherhood are incompatible, are properly considered to be, themselves, gender-based. *Hibbs* explicitly called the stereotype that "women's family duties trump those of the workplace" a "*gender* stereotype," and cited a number of state pregnancy and family leave acts—including laws that provided *only* pregnancy leave—as evidence of "pervasive sex-role stereotype that caring for family members is women's work."

Defendants are thus wrong in their contention that Back cannot make out a claim that survives summary judgment unless she demonstrates that the defendants treated similarly situated men differently. . . . Although her case would be stronger had she provided or alleged the existence of such evidence, there is no requirement that such evidence be adduced. Indeed we have held that,

> In determining whether an employee has been discriminated against "because of *such individual's* . . . sex," the courts have consistently emphasized that the ultimate issue is the reasons for *the individual plaintiff's* treatment, not the relative treatment of different *groups* within the workplace. As a result, discrimination against one employee cannot be cured, or disproven, solely by favorable, or equitable, treatment of other employees of the same race or sex.

Brown v. Henderson, 257 F.3d 246, 252 (2d Cir. 2001) (citations omitted). . . .

Because we hold that stereotypical remarks about the incompatibility of motherhood and employment "can certainly be *evidence* that gender played a part" in an employment decision, we find that *Brown* applies to this case. As a result, stereotyping of women as caregivers can by itself and without more be evidence of an impermissible, sex-based motive.

* * *

We hold that Back has clearly produced sufficient evidence to defeat summary judgment as to Brennan and Wishnie. . . . We conclude that a jury could find, on the evidence proffered, that Brennan and Wishnie's cited justifications for their adverse recommendation and evaluation were pretextual, and that discrimination was one of the "motivating" reasons for the recommendations against Back's tenure.

Ayanna v. Dechert, LLP

914 F. Supp. 2d 51 (D. Mass. 2012)

GORTON, District Judge.

Plaintiff Ariel Ayanna sues defendant law firm Dechert, LLP for retaliation under the Family Medical Leave Act and sex discrimination in violation of M.G.L. c. 151B, §4(1). Currently before the Court is defendant's motion for summary judgment and plaintiff's opposition thereto.

Ayanna, a male attorney, was an associate at Dechert from September, 2006 until his termination in December, 2008. He is married and has two children. His wife suffers from chronic mental illness. During Ayanna's first year of employment at Dechert he met his assigned objective for billable hours, received positive performance reviews and was awarded a bonus.

During his second year, Ayanna requested to work from the Munich office of Dechert for nine months while his wife completed a Fulbright scholarship in Germany. Dechert did not transfer Ayanna to the Munich office, but, instead, agreed that he could work from Munich while remaining assigned to the Boston office. Ayanna contends that because attorneys in Munich worked fewer hours, he was told by his supervisors in Boston that he did not need to meet the billable hours requirement for United States based attorneys while working from Germany. Despite that reassurance, once in Germany, Ayanna expressed concern to the Boston office about his reduced hours. He requested additional work but was not assigned any. Although Ayanna's billable hours were lower than stateside attorneys, he billed more hours than the other associate in the Munich office.

During their time in Munich, Ayanna's wife became pregnant with their second child and experienced a deterioration of her mental health. After she attempted to commit suicide, Ayanna took emergency FMLA leave to care for his wife. Following the birth of their second child, he took four weeks of paid paternity leave. His wife's condition improved and he was able to return to the Boston office of Dechert in August 2008, despite being scheduled to remain on FMLA leave until September. As a result of his early return, Ayanna remained eligible for an additional four weeks of FMLA leave that year. He continued to care for his wife and children after returning to work.

When he returned to the Boston office Ayanna was assigned to be the "right hand man" to Partner Christopher Christian. Ayanna contends that Christian was immediately hostile to him due to his recent leave and monitored his work and presence in the office more closely than other associates. After Ayanna's wife was briefly hospitalized at the end of September 2008, the assignment of work from Christian to Ayanna dropped off and Christian began assigning work to other associates.

In his annual performance evaluation Ayanna was given an overall "fair" rating. Dechert claims that rating took into account both billable hours and supervisor evaluations but placed a far greater emphasis on the former. . . . Ayanna's "annualized" billable hours were adjusted to 1,460 to account for his FMLA and paternity leave. His total billable hours fell far short of the 1,950 target for associates in the Boston office and Ayanna ranked 62nd out of 65 associates in his practice group.

On December 17, 2008 Ayanna was terminated. . . .

1. Retaliation for Exercising Rights Afforded Under the Family Medical Leave Act (Count I)

Ayanna claims that Dechert retaliated against him for taking FMLA leave by withholding work assignments, thus decreasing his billable hours for the year and, ultimately, terminating him on the ground that his billable hours were too low.

To make out a prima facie case of retaliation under the FMLA [and applying the *McDonnell Douglas* three-step burden-shifting framework], an employee must prove that 1) he engaged in the protected conduct of taking FMLA leave, 2) he was fired, and 3) the protected conduct and the termination were causally connected. Only the third prong is in dispute in this case.

Although courts are hesitant to find a causal connection between an employee's FMLA leave and firing if the intervening time was several months, . . . when viewed in the light most favorable to Ayanna, there is sufficient evidence to support a finding that his FMLA leave and his termination were related, whether or not there was "temporal proximity."

[The court finds] that Ayanna has presented sufficient evidence to raise a genuine issue of material fact as to whether that proffered reason was actually a pretext for retaliation.

First, at the time he was fired, Ayanna was told by Dechert Partner Joseph Fleming that he was terminated due to his "fair" rating and his "personal issues." A reasonable jury could find that the comment was directed at Ayanna's recent need to take FMLA leave.

Furthermore, there remains a factual dispute as to whether Ayanna's billable hours were low because the firm purposefully withheld work from him in retaliation for taking FMLA leave. Viewing the facts in the light most favorable to Ayanna, Christian monitored Ayanna very closely following his return from FMLA leave. When Christian became aware that the condition of Ayanna's wife had worsened to the point that she needed further hospitalization, Christian shared his concern with other Dechert employees regarding Ayanna's ability to handle his workload. At the same time, Ayanna's work for Christian was curtailed. Christian informed Ayanna he no longer considered him "reliable" and was spreading work that previously would have gone to Ayanna to other associates thus decreasing his billable hours.

As proof that Ayanna was not denied work assignments in retaliation for taking FMLA leave, Dechert asserts that he billed more hours in September and October after returning from leave than he did prior to taking FMLA leave. However, Ayanna was working from Germany immediately prior to taking FMLA leave. Because it remains disputed whether the firm approved of his reduced billing while in Germany, his number of billable hours is not dispositive of his claim that he was denied work assignments.

When considering his annual billable hours, Dechert did not take into account Ayanna's time in Germany but, nevertheless, directly compared those billable hours to other Boston based associates when deciding whether to terminate him. The Court acknowledges that not adjusting the hours of associates temporarily working in foreign offices may have been standard practice at Dechert. Without evidence in the record of such a policy, however, and without knowing how many other retained associates failed to reach Dechert's billable hours target that year, a direct comparison of Ayanna's pre- and post-FMLA leave hours is not enough to disprove the inference that he was denied work in retaliation for taking leave. A reasonable jury could find that had Ayanna not taken FMLA leave, Dechert would have treated his reduced billable hours simply as an expected byproduct of his temporary assignment to Germany.

Finally, unlike most of the attorneys who were terminated contemporaneously, Ayanna met his billable hours requirement the previous year. While several other associates who were terminated were warned during 2008 that their billable hours were disappointingly low, Ayanna apparently was not given any such warning prior to his termination. That calls into question Dechert's claim that Ayanna was terminated solely because of his low billable hours.

Drawing all inferences in Ayanna's favor, there remains a genuine issue of material fact as to whether Dechert's termination of Ayanna on the ground of his low billable hours was actually a pretext for retaliation. . . . Dechert is not entitled to summary judgment.

2. Violation of M.G.L c. 151B §4(1) (Count II)

Ayanna alleges disparate treatment sex discrimination in violation of Chapter 151B on the grounds that he was fired because he was a male caregiver. Ayanna contends that his decision to take FMLA and paternity leave and to prioritize family obligations did not comport with Dechert's firm culture, which he asserts is dominated by a traditional male "macho" stereotype that promotes relegating family responsibilities to women.

Disparate treatment sex discrimination claims under Chapter 151B are also subject to the three step *McDonnell Douglas* burden-shifting test. . . . While Dechert asserts that Ayanna was fired for failing to meet performance expectations, as discussed above, there remains a dispute as to whether his low billable hours were actually caused by Dechert's alleged discriminatory treatment.

Even presuming that Ayanna can make out a prima facie case of disparate treatment sex discrimination, however, he has offered no evidence that his termination for low billable hours was actually a pretext for terminating him because he was a male who was also a caregiver. His broad claims about the "macho" culture at Dechert, without any facts specifically showing instances of discrimination against him, are inadequate to support a finding that he was fired due to his gender.

In fact, the record reflects that female attorneys who took on caregiving roles also experienced negative outcomes at Dechert. For example, a female attorney who was fired at the same time as Ayanna indicated that she was unable to obtain adequate work assignments when she returned from maternity leave. Further, the evidence does not support a finding that Christian was antagonistic to Ayanna because he is a male caregiver. At most the record suggests that Christian may have disfavored him because Ayanna prioritized his family over his employment responsibilities. While those facts suggest Ayanna may have been terminated because of the time he allotted to his caregiving duties, Chapter 151B does not provide protection for employees based on their caregiver status alone. Because Ayanna has proffered no evidence that his termination was based on his gender, Dechert is entitled to summary judgment on this count.

NOTES

1. **Caregiver Discrimination Lawsuits.**   Lawsuits alleging discrimination against caregivers are on the rise. One study noted a 590 percent increase between 1998 and 2012 (a time when employment discrimination lawsuits decreased overall), and a plaintiff success rate of 52 percent—far better than plaintiffs bringing other employment discrimination claims.[139] A small number of states, as well as

---

139. Cynthia Thomas Calvert, Ctr. WorkLife L., Caregivers in the Workplace Family Responsibilities Discrimination Litigation Update (2016). Plaintiffs in non-employment civil suits generally win their cases about 51 percent of the time. In contrast, plaintiffs in employment cases win only about 15 percent of their cases. Tom Spiggle, Winning an Employment

some municipalities, prohibit discrimination on the basis of familial status, which may provide some additional protection to caregivers.[140] *Ayanna* is one of the few alleging discrimination against a male caregiver.[141] Were you convinced that the plaintiff's family responsibilities in *Ayanna* were the reason for his adverse treatment at work? What is the difference in the stereotypes that were applied to the male plaintiff in *Ayanna* and the female plaintiff in *Back*? Does it matter whether their supervisors ever treated them favorably? One author has argued that although social psychology research has "thoroughly refuted the validity of the same-actor inference"—a "presumption of non-discrimination that arises when the same actor who engaged in an adverse action against the employee previously engaged in a positive action toward that employee"—courts continue to rely on it in caregiver discrimination cases.[142] Not surprisingly, stereotypes about caregivers can be racial as well as gendered. For example, studies show that the stereotypes about Black mothers are unique, e.g., that a pregnant Black woman is less likely to have a father available to share parenting responsibilities.[143]

In addition to problems of proof, caregiver discrimination suits are difficult because caregiving is not one of the protected characteristics under Title VII or any other federal anti-discrimination law. In 2007, however, the EEOC issued an enforcement guidance to explain the circumstances under which caregiver discrimination might nonetheless be actionable.[144] For example, it is unlawful, as a form of illegal sex stereotyping, for an employer to assume that female employees will have caregiving responsibilities that interfere with job performance or labor force commitment. Employers cannot assume that women with young children will not work long hours or be available for travel or that they will be more likely to leave the work force. In 2022, the EEOC supplemented its guidance on caregiver discrimination with a document designed to address the impact of Covid-19 on employees with caregiving responsibilities and the intersection

---

Lawsuit is Hard. What To Know About Evidence, Forbes (July 7, 2022); Jack Flynn, 31 Alarming Employment Discrimination Statistics [2022]: The State of Employment Discrimination in U.S., Zippia (April 5, 2022); (17.4 percent); Nathan Koppel, Job-Discrimination Cases Tend to Fare Poorly in Federal Court, W.J. Journal (Feb. 19, 2009) (plaintiffs won 15 percent of cases between 1979 and 2006).

140. Ctr. WorkLife L., State and Local FRD Laws Prohibiting Employment Discrimination Against Parents and Other Caregivers (2022).

141. See Keith Cunningham-Parmeter, Men at Work, Fathers at Home: Uncovering the Masculine Face of Caregiver Discrimination, 24 Colum. J. Gender & L. 253 (2013).

142. Andrea L. Miller, The Use (and Misuse) of the Same-Actor Inference in Family Responsibilities Discrimination Litigation: Lessons From Social Psychology on Flexibility Stigma, 41 Wm. Mitchell L. Rev. 1032, 1035 (2015); see also Victor D. Quintanilla & Cheryl R. Kaiser, The Same-Actor Inference of Nondiscrimination: Moral Credentialing and the Psychological and Legal Licensing of Bias, 104 Cal. L. Rev. 1 (2016).

143. See Lisa Rosenthal & Marci Lobel, Stereotypes of Black American Women Related to Pregnancy and Sexuality, 40 Psych. Women Q. 414 (2016).

144. EEOC, Enforcement Guidance: Unlawful Disparate Treatment of Workers with Caregiving Responsibilities, 915.002 (May 23, 2007), http://www.eeoc.gov/policy/docs/caregiving.html.

with discrimination law.[145] (The impact of Covid-19 on work/family balance is addressed in Chapter 4, Section B.)

In another case, Lust v. Sealy, the plaintiff was a sales representative who lost a promotion to a man. Evidence of discrimination included her supervisor's admission that he didn't consider recommending her for promotion because she had children. He didn't think she would want to relocate her family, even though she had not told him that and, in fact, had indicated frequently how much she wanted the promotion. When the plaintiff asked about that promotion, the supervisor also asked why her husband wasn't going to take care of her.[146] The plaintiff won at trial and the verdict was upheld on appeal in a decision written by Richard Posner, the same judge who wrote the opinion in *Troupe*. The court reduced the damages award to $150,000 — half the maximum statutorily allowed — because the employer had taken steps to remedy the discrimination.

A wide body of research and reported cases document adverse stereotypes that working mothers face, such as a presumed lack of dependability, productivity, and commitment.[147] Should such research be admissible in sex discrimination cases where women claim that they were subject to the "motherhood penalty" but lack explicit statements like those present in *Back* and *Sealy*? How else might this body of work be helpful in preventing workplace bias?

The EEOC guidance also makes clear that it is unlawful to treat male employees with caregiving responsibilities less favorably than female employees in the same situation (or vice versa), especially if motivated by the belief that men do not, or should not have to, assume such responsibilities. For example, an employer who told a male employee that he was not eligible for leave to take care of a newborn unless his wife was "in a coma or dead" committed actionable discrimination of this nature.[148] Two years later, in 2009, the EEOC issued a "best practices" document that encourages employers to provide accommodations for caregiving beyond those required by law in order to promote a better work/life balance for all employees.[149] The EEOC recommends that employers adopt a "caregiver" policy that describes common stereotypes or biases about caregivers and provides examples of prohibited discriminatory conduct. It also encourages employers to take proactive efforts to purge the hiring process of unfair stereotypes about caregivers and to ensure that applicants are not evaluated or steered into particular jobs on the basis of caregiving responsibilities. Finally, the EEOC recommends a number of policies to alleviate common conflicts faced by caregiving employees. Flexible work arrangements are at the top of the list, along with voluntary overtime, reasonable

145. See, e.g., EEOC, The Covid-19 Pandemic and Caregiver Discrimination Under Federal Employment Discrimination Laws (No. 2022-1) (Mar. 14, 2022); see also Ctr. Worklife L., Protecting Parents During Covid-19: State and Local FRD Laws Prohibit Discrimination at Work (2020).

146. Lust v. Sealy, 383 F.3d 580, 583 (7th Cir. 2004).

147. Stephen Benard et al., Cognitive Bias and the Motherhood Penalty, 59 Hastings L.J. 1359 (2008).

148. Knussman v. Maryland, 272 F.3d 625, 629-30 (4th Cir. 2001).

149. EEOC, Employer Best Practices for Workers with Caregiving Responsibilities (2009), http://www.eeoc.gov/policy/docs/caregiver-best-practices.html.

leave time for caregiving obligations, and other "family-friendly" modifications of conventional workplace rules. Should such policies be mandated? What objections do you see to them?

2. **Accommodation vs. Discrimination.** Should policies concerning childrearing, like childbearing, be seen as *accommodations* to employees with special needs, or as necessary components of a *nondiscriminatory* workplace? The former draws on a model of accommodation established with respect to religious beliefs or disabilities, requiring employers to undertake some expense and inconvenience if necessary to enable caretakers to participate fully in the work force. Viewed this way, measures to overcome disadvantages women experience from caretaking reflect values of substantive, rather than formal, equality.

Alternatively, it could be argued that the workplace is not a neutral structure that needs restructuring to accommodate women, but rather a set of arrangements already favoring an ideal worker, typically male, who lacks substantial caretaking responsibilities. On this view, reforming the workplace to acknowledge employees' caretaking responsibilities is not "special treatment" for women, but rather a recognition of the fundamental reality of women's lives and the importance of caretaking to society. Accordingly, Joan Williams calls for a "reconstructive feminism" that shifts attention from special treatment for women to more structural questions, like how household work is allocated, how the costs of childrearing should be shared between private households and the public, and how the workplace is structured.[150] Does this formulation escape the choice between nondiscrimination and accommodation?

How might this agenda be achieved? An important rationale for work/family reforms is that they can be effective for employers as well as society.

[E]mployers who provide family-friendly workplaces often save money because of decreased attrition and absenteeism, as well as enhancing recruitment and productivity. Practices that employees deem to reflect business necessity may in fact reflect business-irrational practices driven by gender stereotypes.[151]

Are employers who do not provide family-friendly workplaces overemphasizing short-term costs at the expense of long-term savings? If so, will the market eventually provide correctives or do we need policy interventions?

PUTTING THEORY INTO PRACTICE

2-17. In 2015, the Pentagon standardized maternity leaves for all branches of the service, offering women who give birth twelve weeks of paid leave. For the

---

150. Id.; Joan C. Williams, Reshaping the Work-Family Debate: Why Men and Class Matter (2010); Joan C. Williams, Do Women Need Special Treatment? Do Feminists Need Equality?, 9 J. Contemp. Legal Issues 279, 285-96 (1998).

151. Williams & Segal, supra note 116, at 79; see also Women and Leadership: The State of Play and Strategies for Change 16 (Barbara Kellerman & Deborah L. Rhode, eds., 2007); James T. Bond et al., Fams. and Work Inst., The 2002 National Study of the Changing Workforce 34-35 (2002).

Army, this represents a doubling of the available leave, but for the Navy and Marine Corps, this is a reduction from eighteen weeks. Then-Secretary of Defense Ash Carter noted that women at "peak ages" for childbearing leave the military at higher rates than other servicemembers and predicted that the new policy will "strengthen [the Pentagon's] position in the battle for top-tier talent."[152] The same policy, however, only grants men four days of paid leave. Is it possible that the reduction of leave for some servicewomen could actually promote equality? How? Does the new policy overall enhance equality?

2-18. If one problem with parental leaves is that men don't choose to take them, would it be a good idea to make paternity leave mandatory?[153] If not, why not?

2-19. You are the head of the litigation department at a mid-sized firm. A senior associate who has just had a second child asks not to be assigned to any cases requiring overnight travel. She also tends to avoid late or weekend hours at the firm, although she is accessible at home for conference calls and last-minute assignments. She is a hard-working and competent litigator but not a superstar. Other attorneys with families are annoyed that they are bearing a disproportionate share of document review work in other cities and tasks that require office face time. You believe that the woman's choices may signal a lack of commitment that will hurt her at partnership. When you raise this concern, she claims that it reflects gender bias. How do you respond? How should the firm?

2-20. Sharon worked as a billing specialist for a small medical practice. At the beginning of the Covid-19 pandemic, she was permitted to work remotely. After the first year, however, her employer told her that she would have to work in the office full time. Her 10-year-old daughter attended a school that continued to operate on a hybrid schedule, with half the students attending via Zoom each day. Sharon requested the same hybrid schedule so that her daughter would not be home alone during the school day, although her daughter would not require active supervision. Her employer denied the request and she was eventually fired.[154] Has she suffered actionable discrimination?

2-21. A major law firm's parental leave policy is to give eighteen weeks of paid leave to mothers who gave birth and are serving as the primary caretaker and ten weeks leave to fathers who are doing so.[155] Is the policy legal? Is it relevant that women continue to bear the brunt of caretaking responsibilities? How so?[156]

---

152. Max J. Rosenthal, Most Military Moms Just Got Expanded Benefits, But Here's How Dads Got Screwed, Mother Jones (Jan. 28, 2016).

153. See Michael Selmi, Family Leave and the Gender Wage Gap, 78 N.C. L. Rev. 707, 774-75 (2000).

154. Complaint, Wilder v. Advocare Ear, Nose, & Throat Specialists of Morristown, No. 2:21-CV-00848 (D.N.J. Jan. 18, 2021).

155. Dan Packel, Jones Day Parental Leave Bias Suit Likely to Reverberate, Am. Law, Aug. 16, 2019.

156. On disproportionate burdens, see data in Chapter 4, Section B, note 2.

C. *RECOGNIZING SEX-LINKED AVERAGE DIFFERENCES*

Some sex-based differences affect matters where group-based judgments remain highly relevant. For example, on average, women live longer than men, have fewer driving-related accidents, have higher health care costs, and stay out of the work force for longer periods. Does our commitment to sex equality require that we ignore such average differences—for example, in the setting of insurance rates? Similarly, researchers document some differences in the way girls and boys learn (again, on average). Does that justify "separate but equal" classroom treatment? Can athletic programs take account of average sex-based differences in strength, size, and speed?

1. *Fringe Benefit Plans, Insurance, and Other Actuarially Based Systems*

City of Los Angeles, Department of Water & Power v. Manhart

435 U.S. 702 (1978)

Mr. Justice STEVENS delivered the opinion of the Court.

As a class, women live longer than men. For this reason, the Los Angeles Department of Water and Power required its female employees to make larger contributions to its pension fund than its male employees. We granted certiorari to decide whether this practice discriminated against individual female employees because of their sex in violation of [Title VII].

For many years the Department has administered retirement, disability, and death-benefit programs for its employees. Upon retirement each employee is eligible for a monthly retirement benefit computed as a fraction of his or her salary multiplied by years of service. The monthly benefits for men and women of the same age, seniority, and salary are equal. Benefits are funded entirely by contributions from the employees and the Department, augmented by the income earned on those contributions. No private insurance company is involved in the administration or payment of benefits.

Based on a study of mortality tables and its own experience, the Department determined that its 2,000 female employees, on the average, will live a few years longer than its 10,000 male employees. The cost of a pension for the average retired female is greater than for the average male retiree because more monthly payments must be made to the average woman. The Department therefore required female employees to make monthly contributions to the fund which were 14.84% higher than the contributions required of comparable male employees. Because employee contributions were withheld from paychecks a female employee took home less pay than a male employee earning the same salary.[5] . . .

_____

5. The significance of the disparity is illustrated by the record of one woman whose contributions to the fund (including interest on the amount withheld each month) amounted to $18,171.40; a similarly situated male would have contributed only $12,843.53.

[The plan was subsequently amended based on state law. This action concerns the old plan, which the District Court found to violate Title VII. The United States Court of Appeals for the Ninth Circuit affirmed.] . . .

I

There are both real and fictional differences between women and men. It is true that the average man is taller than the average woman; it is not true that the average woman driver is more accident prone than the average man. Before [Title VII] was enacted, an employer could fashion his personnel policies on the basis of assumptions about the differences between men and women, whether or not the assumptions were valid.

It is now well recognized that employment decisions cannot be predicated on mere "stereotyped" impressions about the characteristics of males or females. Myths and purely habitual assumptions about a woman's inability to perform certain kinds of work are no longer acceptable reasons for refusing to employ qualified individuals, or for paying them less. This case does not, however, involve a fictional difference between men and women. It involves a generalization that the parties accept as unquestionably true: Women, as a class, do live longer than men. The Department treated its women employees differently from its men employees because the two classes are in fact different. It is equally true, however, that all individuals in the respective classes do not share the characteristic that differentiates the average class representatives. Many women do not live as long as the average man and many men outlive the average woman. The question, therefore, is whether the existence or nonexistence of "discrimination" is to be determined by comparison of class characteristics or individual characteristics. A "stereotyped" answer to that question may not be the same as the answer that the language and purpose of the statute command.

[Title VII] makes it unlawful "to discriminate against any individual with respect to his compensation, terms, conditions, or privileges of employment, because of such individual's race, color, religion, sex, or national origin." . . . The statute's focus on the individual is unambiguous. It precludes treatment of individuals as simply components of a racial, religious, sexual, or national class. If height is required for a job, a tall woman may not be refused employment merely because, on the average, women are too short. Even a true generalization about the class is an insufficient reason for disqualifying an individual to whom the generalization does not apply.

That proposition is of critical importance in this case because there is no assurance that any individual woman working for the Department will actually fit the generalization on which the Department's policy is based. Many of those individuals will not live as long as the average man. While they were working, those individuals received smaller paychecks because of their sex, but they will receive no compensating advantage when they retire.

It is true, of course, that while contributions are being collected from the employees, the Department cannot know which individuals will predecease the average woman. Therefore, unless women as a class are assessed an extra charge, they will be subsidized, to some extent, by the class of male employees. It follows, according to the Department, that fairness to its class of male employees justifies the extra assessment against all of its female employees.

But the question of fairness to various classes affected by the statute is essentially a matter of policy for the legislature to address. Congress has decided that classifications based on sex, like those based on national origin or race, are unlawful. Actuarial studies could unquestionably identify differences in life expectancy based on race or national origin, as well as sex. But a statute that was designed to make race irrelevant in the employment market . . . could not reasonably be construed to permit a take-home-pay differential based on a racial classification.

Even if the statutory language were less clear, the basic policy of the statute requires that we focus on fairness to individuals rather than fairness to classes. Practices that classify employees in terms of religion, race, or sex tend to preserve traditional assumptions about groups rather than thoughtful scrutiny of individuals. The generalization involved in this case illustrates the point. Separate mortality tables are easily interpreted as reflecting innate differences between the sexes; but a significant part of the longevity differential may be explained by the social fact that men are heavier smokers than women.

Finally, there is no reason to believe that Congress intended a special definition of discrimination in the context of employee group insurance coverage. It is true that insurance is concerned with events that are individually unpredictable, but that is characteristic of many employment decisions. Individual risks, like individual performance, may not be predicted by resort to classifications proscribed by Title VII. Indeed, the fact that this case involves a group insurance program highlights a basic flaw in the Department's fairness argument. For when insurance risks are grouped, the better risks always subsidize the poorer risks. Healthy persons subsidize medical benefits for the less healthy; unmarried workers subsidize the pensions of married workers; persons who eat, drink, or smoke to excess may subsidize pension benefits for persons whose habits are more temperate. Treating different classes of risks as though they were the same for purposes of group insurance is a common practice that has never been considered inherently unfair. . . .

An employment practice that requires 2,000 individuals to contribute more money into a fund than 10,000 other employees simply because each of them is a woman, rather than a man, is in direct conflict with both the language and the policy of the Act. Such a practice does not pass the simple test of whether the evidence shows "treatment of a person in a manner which but for that person's sex would be different." It constitutes discrimination and is unlawful unless exempted by the Equal Pay Act of 1963 or some other affirmative justification. . . .

III

[T]he Department argues that the absence of a discriminatory effect on women as a class justifies an employment practice which, on its face, discriminated against individual employees because of their sex. But even if the Department's actuarial evidence is sufficient to prevent plaintiffs from establishing a prima facie case on the theory that the effect of the practice on women as a class was discriminatory, that evidence does not defeat the claim that the practice, on its face, discriminated against every individual woman employed by the Department.

In essence, the Department is arguing that the prima facie showing of discrimination based on evidence of different contributions for the respective sexes is rebutted by its demonstration that there is a like difference in the cost of providing benefits for the respective classes. That argument might prevail if Title VII contained a cost justification defense comparable to the affirmative defense. . . . But neither Congress nor the courts have recognized such a defense under Title VII.

Although we conclude that the Department's practice violated Title VII, we do not suggest that the statute was intended to revolutionize the insurance and pension industries. All that is at issue today is a requirement that men and women make unequal contributions to an employer-operated pension fund. Nothing in our holding implies that it would be unlawful for an employer to set aside equal retirement contributions for each employee and let each retiree purchase the largest benefit which his or her accumulated contributions could command in the open market. Nor does it call into question the insurance industry practice of considering the composition of an employer's work force in determining the probable cost of a retirement or death benefit plan. . . .

Mr. Justice BRENNAN took no part in the consideration or decision of this case.

[The opinion of Mr. Justice BLACKMUN, concurring in part and concurring in the judgment, is omitted.]

Mr. CHIEF JUSTICE BURGER, with whom Mr. Justice REHNQUIST joins, concurring in part and dissenting in part. . . .

Gender-based actuarial tables have been in use since at least 1843, and their statistical validity has been repeatedly verified. The vast life insurance, annuity, and pension plan industry is based on these tables. As the Court recognizes . . . it is a fact that "women, as a class, do live longer than men." It is equally true that employers cannot know in advance when individual members of the classes will die. . . . Yet, if they are to operate economically workable group pension programs, it is only rational to permit them to rely on statistically sound and proved disparities in longevity between men and women. Indeed, it seems to me irrational to assume Congress intended to outlaw use of the fact that, for whatever reasons or combination of reasons, women as a class outlive men. . . .

Here, of course, petitioners are discriminating in take-home pay between men and women. . . . The practice of petitioners, however, falls squarely under the exemption provided by the Equal Pay Act of 1963 . . . [for] a differential based on any "other factor other than sex. . . ." The "other factor other than sex" is longevity; sex is the umbrella-constant under which all of the elements leading to differences in longevity are grouped and assimilated, and the only objective feature upon which an employer—or anyone else, including insurance companies—may reliably base a cost differential for the "risk" being insured.

This is in no sense a failure to treat women as "individuals" in violation of the statute, as the Court holds. It is to treat them as individually as it is possible to do in the face of the unknowable length of each individual life. Individually, every woman has the same statistical possibility of outliving men. This is the essence of basing decisions on reliable statistics when individual determinations are infeasible or, as here, impossible.

Of course, women cannot be disqualified from, for example, heavy labor just because the generality of women are thought not as strong as men — a proposition which perhaps may sometime be statistically demonstrable, but will remain individually refutable. When, however, it is impossible to tailor a program such as a pension plan to the individual, nothing should prevent application of reliable statistical facts to the individual, for whom the facts cannot be disproved until long after planning, funding, and operating the program have been undertaken. . . .

Mr. Justice MARSHALL's opinion, concurring in part and dissenting [to the Court's holding that the opinion should not be retroactive, is omitted].

NOTES

1. **Group-Based vs. Individual-Based Equality.**   In an important sense, *Manhart* chooses formal equality over a form of "reverse" substantive equality: women and men must be treated alike at the pay-in side, even though as a (substantive) result women, on average, will live longer and obtain greater pay-out benefits than men. Put another way, the employer may not take account of men's and women's differences and make adjustments so that the outcomes (again, on average) are the same. Formal equality in these circumstances means that each employee will be treated as an individual rather than as a member of a group, but it also means that women, because they live longer, will tend to obtain more benefits over their lifetimes than men, unless the employer shifts to a different system. Is that fair?

Despite the concern expressed by the defendant in *Manhart* that sex-neutral premiums would give women disproportionately higher pension benefits compared to men, women as a group historically were much less likely to be covered by a pension plan and received much lower pay-outs when they were.[157] Are these facts relevant to the legal issues in *Manhart?* Women have now caught up with men in their participation in retirement plans, but still receive about one-third less than men in pay-outs from both pensions and defined contribution (e.g., 401(k)) plans; moreover, they are 80 percent more likely than men to be impoverished at ages 65 and older.[158] Should these considerations affect whether formal equality or substantive equality is the governing legal model?

Justice Stevens concedes that an employer could simply give a fixed benefit to employees from which they could purchase their own retirement plan on the open insurance market. A functionally equivalent alternative to the plan in *Manhart* would be for employers to make fixed contributions to a private insurance carrier, which would then pay out different monthly amounts on retirement according to the employee's sex in recognition of the longer life expectancy of women. This alternative, too, has been found to violate Title VII when the employer requires

---

157. See Gillian Thomas, Because of Sex: One Law, Ten Cases, and Fifty Years That Changed American Women's Lives at Work 60 (2016).

158. Jennifer E. Brown et al., Shortchanged in Retirement: Continuing Challenges to Women's Financial Future, 2 J. Ins. & Fin. Mgmt. 78 (2016).

participating employees to use private insurance carriers that discriminate based on sex.[159]

The changing structure of employer retirement plans has all but obviated the practical effect of the restrictions imposed by *Manhart.* Employers now typically offer defined contribution plans that allow employee choice in investing their 401(k) funds in the private market upon retirement. Where that is the case, Title VII does not attribute sex discrimination in annuities in the private market to the employer. Did the plaintiffs in *Manhart* win the battle but lose the war?

2. **Efficiency vs. Nondiscrimination.**   Title VII covers employer-linked benefit plans, but no federal law bans sex discrimination in the private insurance market, with the recent exception of health insurance under the Affordable Care Act (discussed in note 4, below). Is sex discrimination in insurance more defensible than sex discrimination in employment, education, credit practices, and housing, all of which are covered by federal anti-discrimination laws? If so, is this because it is based on actuarial sex-based differences, such as longevity?

Critics of ignoring sex differences in actuarial-based systems have argued that sex is the most efficient proxy for the factors that affect cost in insurance markets and that monitoring these risks directly would be too expensive and inefficient.[160] Well-functioning insurance markets require reliance on actuarially sound risk classifications in order to accurately distribute the costs of insurance to those who are at higher risk and avoid a "death spiral" in insurance markets.[161]

Those who favor sex-neutrality, as in the result in *Manhart,* counter that arguments for reliance on sex-based actuarial differences confuse correlation with causation: the correlation between sex and longevity is largely explained by the fact that men engage in more self-destructive behaviors than women.[162] Consider the following:

> It is hard to understand why the use of merged-gender mortality tables is unfair to men. It has a disparate impact on men as a group because it disadvantages self-destructors, and more men than women are self-destructors. The total annuity payout to [men] is less than the total amount paid to [women] because the total number of years the men [live] would be less. But are men, especially non-self-destructors, entitled to cash in on the fact that many of their sex self-destruct, and is this "entitlement" one that rises to the level of a right protected by Title VII?[163]

---

159. See Ariz. Governing Comm. for Tax Deferred Annuity and Deferred Comp. Plans v. Norris, 463 U.S. 1073 (1983).

160. See, e.g., George J. Benston, The Economics of Gender Discrimination in Employee Fringe Benefits: *Manhart* Revisited, 49 U. Chi. L. Rev. 489, 517-19, 530-31 (1982).

161. Ronen Avraham et al., Understanding Insurance Antidiscrimination Rules, 87 So. Cal. L. Rev. 195, 204-14 (2014).

162. See, e.g., Lea Brilmayer et al., The Efficient Use of Group Averages as Nondiscrimination: A Rejoinder to Professor Benston, 50 U. Chi. L. Rev. 222, 223-25 (1983).

163. Id. at 226-27. For Benston's response to these arguments, see George J. Benston, Discrimination and Economic Efficiency in Employee Fringe Benefits: A Clarification of Issues and a Response to Professors Brilmayer, Laycock, and Sullivan, 50 U. Chi. L. Rev. 250 (1983).

The fairness argument for taking sex into account also assumes that insurers rely only on objective mathematical criteria to underwrite risks. Some scholars question this assumption, pointing out that actuarial classifications often reflect social judgments based on stereotypes and stigma.[164] Even if actuarially sound, setting rates based on membership in historically discriminated-against groups "trades on preexisting social inequities and stereotypes."[165]

One potential discrimination issue in the insurance industry concerns domestic violence victims. Until the mid-1990s, nearly half of insurers refused to insure domestic abuse victims because actuarial statistics showed that they are more likely to be victimized and thus draw disproportionately on health, life, and disability insurance plans. State laws vary widely in their approach to such discrimination. Some states have no legislation on the subject, or have only weak protections, such as a prohibition only against "irrational" discrimination against victims of domestic violence, or against denial or limitation of coverage "solely" because a person is a victim of domestic violence while still allowing insurers to limit coverage because abuse victims are at a higher risk of injury or death.[166] Should insurers be able to charge women higher rates because of what some men do to them? Is charging victims of domestic violence (a predominantly female group) more for insurance any different than charging victims of high blood pressure more?

3. **Life Insurance.**   More men than women get life insurance.[167] Is that a problem? If so, what should be done about it? On average, an individual's age is considered the most reliable predictor of how long they will live. Gender comes in second.[168] If women, on average, live longer than men, should they pay less for life insurance? At one time, life insurance rates were the same for men and women, although the amount of life insurance coverage available to a married woman sometimes depended upon the amount sold to her husband. Gender-distinct mortality tables emerged after the Civil War, especially for annuities, as these financial instruments substituted for the dower rights and other benefits of coverture that were in decline during this period.[169] One scholar has argued that gender-distinct life insurance rates reflected, in part, the growing emphasis on men's and women's

---

164. See Valerie V. Blake, Ensuring an Underclass: Stigma in Insurance, 41 Cardozo L. Rev. 1441 (2020).

165. Avraham et al., supra note 161, at 195, 214-20.

166. Emily C. Wilson, Stop Re-Victimizing the Victims: A Call for Stronger State Laws Prohibiting Insurance Discrimination Against Victims of Domestic Violence, 23 Am. U. J. Gender, Soc. Pol'y & Law 413, 424-25 (2015); see also Deborah S. Hellman, Is Actuarially Fair Insurance Pricing Actually Fair?: A Case Study in Insuring Battered Women, 32 Harv. C.R.-C.L. L. Rev. 355 (1997); Terry L. Fromson & Nancy Durborow, Insurance Discrimination Against Victims of Domestic Violence (Apr. 2016); see also Chapter 3, Section C, for discussion of violence against women in general.

167. See Yaron Ben-Zvi, Yes, There Is a Life Insurance Gender Gap, Forbes (Oct. 25, 2019).

168. Amy Fontinelle, Gender and Insurance Costs, Investopedia (Mar. 2, 2022).

169. See Mary L. Heen, From Coverture to Contract: Engendering Insurance on Lives, 23 Yale J. Law & Feminism 335, 373-83 (2011); Mary L. Heen, Nondiscrimination in Insurance: The Next Chapter, 49 Ga. L. Rev. 1, 12-13 (2014).

separate spheres after coverture rules were dismantled and the tendency thereafter to emphasize gender differences in order to support this ideology.[170]

Today, all states allow insurers to take sex into account in setting life insurance rates.[171] This includes Montana, which, in 2021, reversed its law banning the use of sex for any type of insurance.[172]

4. **Health Insurance.**   The only federal law specifically prohibiting sex discrimination in insurance is a provision of the federal Patient Protection and Affordable Care Act (ACA), which applies to health insurance only.[173] Based on this law, a number of complaints were filed in 2014 claiming that the nation's largest insurance companies continued to charge women more than men for the same coverage.[174]

Under the Obama administration, the Department of Health and Human Services (HHS) interpreted this provision to encompass protection from discrimination based on gender identity. Under the interpretation, the exclusion of medically appropriate care for transgender persons, puberty blockers (which temporarily block the onset of puberty), hormone therapy, and surgery discriminates on the basis of sex in violation of the ACA. Courts divided over the legality of this rule. In December 2016, a federal district court in Texas issued a nationwide injunction barring its enforcement based on the theory that it exceeded the agency's statutory authority, and that the absence of any religious exemption rendered it arbitrary and capricious, in violation of the Administrative Procedure Act.[175] The court held that the rule exceeded the agency's statutory authority and that the absence of any religious exemption rendered it arbitrary and capricious, in violation of the Administrative Procedure Act. A 2017 ruling from a federal district court in California, however, found that transgender individuals can still sue directly under the ACA and allege that the denial of coverage for gender-affirming care discriminates on the basis of sex.[176] Most recently, the Fourth Circuit Court of Appeals held that the state of North Carolina, in receiving federal assistance, was not immune from suit under the ACA for failure to provide gender-affirming health care for transgender individuals under the North Carolina State Health Plan.[177]

Is discrimination against transgender individuals in health insurance also covered by Title VII? Under Bostock v. Clayton County,[178] set forth in Chapter 1,

---

170. Heen, From Coverture to Contract, supra note 169, at 373-83.

171. Avraham et al., supra note 161, at 250.

172. Zoe Sagalow, Montana Drops "Unisex" Requirements for Setting Insurance Rates, Westlaw Today (Apr. 23, 2021).

173. See 42 U.S.C. § 18116 (2018); Nat'l Fed'n of Indep. Bus. v. Sebelius, 132 S. Ct. 2566 (2018).

174. Jessica Mason Pieklo, Four Insurance Companies Accused of Widespread Sex Discrimination, Rewire News (Jan. 17, 2014).

175. Franciscan Alliance, Inc. v. Burwell, No. 7:16-cv-00108-O, 2016 WL 7638311 (N.D. Tex. 2016).

176. See Prescott v. Rady Children's Hospital-San Diego, 265 F. Supp.3d 1090 (S.D. Ca. '2017).

177. Kadel v. Folwell, 12 F.4th 1222 (4th Cir. 2021).

178. 140 S. Ct. 1731 (2020).

discrimination against transgender individuals in the employment context is a violation of Title VII. Does that mean that gender-affirming medical treatment would be required under employer-sponsored health plans? Some employers thought so.[179] However, it is not obvious that denying insurance coverage for medical treatment to support gender transitioning discriminates on the basis of sex under the logic of *Bostock*. Does formal equality or substantive equality best support such a claim?

5. **Auto Insurance.** Nationwide, it costs about $7,400 to insure a male teenage driver, compared with $6,900 for a female teen.[180] Is this fair? The differential is based on the fact that male drivers under the age of 21, historically, are twice as likely to have accidents as female drivers under the age of 21.[181] If sex is a permitted consideration, should insurers have to show that actual differences justify the existence and size of the rate differentials? Studies in recent years suggest that female drivers text and talk on cell phones more while driving than male drivers, behaviors that significantly increase the risk of a collision.[182] Must insurers continuously update their behavioral assessments if they rely on sex as a proxy for risky driving?

In 2019, California became the seventh state to ban the use of gender in auto insurance. Is this fair? If men are riskier drivers, should women have to subsidize them? If sex is a prohibited factor, does it follow that such factors as education, occupation, and credit score should also be banned from insurance rate structures?[183] Or is sex particularly problematic as a basis for rate-setting?

One catalyst for the California law was that California no longer requires individuals to identify their sex as male or female on government records, and recognizes the category of non-binary gender identification. In the 40 states that permit the use of sex to set auto insurance rates, how should non-binary individuals be treated? Are the fairness considerations in the use of sex for auto insurance the same or different from the treatment of sex in pension plans, annuities, health insurance, and life insurance?

6. **Europe.** In March 2011, the European Court of Justice held in a case referred by the Constitutional Court of Belgium that insurance companies could not use sex as a risk factor in determining insurance rates.[184] Since 2012, new commercial insurance policies sold in Europe require unisex rates and benefits.[185] Some qualifications temper this approach; for example, safe-driver premiums may be charged, as long as sex itself is not used as a risk factor,[186] and family history

179. For an account of one Massachusetts case, see The Supreme Court and Healthcare for Transgender People, GLAD Blog (Oct. 7, 2021).

180. Fredrick Kunkle, Gender Can No Longer Be Used to Calculate Auto Insurance Rates in California and Other States, Wash. Post, Feb. 11, 2019.

181. See Jill Insley & Rupert Jones, ECJ Gender Ruling Hits Insurance Costs, Guardian, Mar. 1, 2011.

182. Katie Rosario, Females More Likely to Engage in Distracted Driving Than Male Drivers, Ins. J. (July 10, 2018).

183. See Kunkle, supra note 180 (some states have banned use of these factors as well in setting insurance rates).

184. Case C-236/09, Test-Achats v. Conseil des Ministres (Mar. 1, 2011), http://curia .europa.eu.

185. Heen, Nondiscrimination in Insurance, supra note 169, at 6.

186. See Press Release, European Commission (Dec. 22, 2011).

and health status may be used as factors.[187] Is Europe's sex-neutrality route the best approach?

After the European Court of Justice (ECJ) decision forbidding use of sex as a risk factor in determining insurance premiums, the Association of British Insurers estimated that women under age 25 could as a result pay 25 percent more for car insurance, while men's rates would likely fall by an average of 10 percent.[188] However, the experience to date shows that women have actually fared better under the ruling. Since the ECJ ruling, the overall gender gap in auto insurance (the amount by which male drivers pay more than female drivers) increased fourfold, contrary to predictions. Unable to consider gender, insurers apparently are taking greater account of more precise risk factors, such as occupation, miles driven, and type of vehicle, all of which tend to raise costs for male drivers more than female drivers.[189] The European example shows that a measure's effect on women can be difficult to predict. How should a substantive equality analysis, which focuses on the effects of a rule on men and women, deal with the risk of error in predicting a measure's impact on women? If banning consideration of sex in insurance pricing increases the costs for women in the short term, but lowers women's costs in the long term (as insurers recalibrate actuarial risk), how should a substantive equality model evaluate whether the measure is good or bad for women?

PUTTING THEORY INTO PRACTICE

2-22. Insofar as it is legal in every state for insurers to discriminate based on sex in setting life insurance rates, how does an individual with a non-binary gender identity apply? Should the individual be required to state a gender?[190] Oregon law since 2018 requires auto insurers using sex or gender as a factor in setting rates to accommodate consumers who designate their sex as neither male nor female on their driver's licenses, which they have been allowed to do in Oregon since 2017.[191] Should all states require this? What would constitute an "accommodation"?

2-23. As of March 2022, fifteen states have restricted access to gender-affirming medical care or are considering laws that would do so. In each of these states, the bills would either criminalize health care providers who provide gender-affirming care to minors, or subject them to discipline from state licensing boards. Bills in six states would provide penalties for parents who facilitate minors' access

---

187. Heen, Nondiscrimination in Insurance, supra note 169, at 75.

188. Insley & Jones, supra note 181.

189. Patrick Collinson, How an EU Gender Equality Ruling Widened Inequality, Guardian, Jan. 14, 2017.

190. For advice, see Amy Fontinelle, How Being Nonbinary Affects Getting Life Insurance, Investopedia (Mar. 15, 2022).

191. See Oregon Says Auto Insurers Must Accommodate Gender "X", JDSUPRA (May 8, 2018). A handful of other jurisdictions also allow individuals to designate a non-binary gender status on their drivers' licenses. See id.

to gender-affirming medical care. In Missouri and Texas, such treatment would be considered a form of child abuse.[192] What would be the impact of this legislation on the equality protections of the ACA and Title VII, discussed above?[193]

2-24.   The ACA does not classify infertility treatment, such as assisted reproductive technologies (ART), as an essential health benefit, leaving it up to the states and private market instead. Fifteen states prohibit exclusion of infertility treatment, but with varying levels of coverage. Only a handful of states require coverage of fertility services for some comprehensive private plans that are regulated by the state, and these requirements do not apply to health plans that are administered and funded directly by employers.[194] As a result, many women experience infertility and are unable to access infertility treatments due to lack of health insurance coverage, with sharp inequalities among women in the ability to access ART. Income, education, and marital status all strongly correlate with access to ART, as does race. African-American and Hispanic women are at higher risk of infertility than white women, and have less access to infertility treatment. Sexual orientation is also a factor in access to ART; some state definitions of infertility require proof of unprotected sexual intercourse for at least one year to prove infertility, leaving lesbian couples unable to prove eligibility for insurance coverage. Some definitions of infertility include age limits, restricting coverage to women above a certain age.

Given that pregnancy is a sex-linked condition, does the denial of health insurance coverage for infertility treatment violate the ACA's ban on sex discrimination in insurance coverage? How should this and other differences among women in access to covered services affect the sex equality argument?[195]

2.   *Sex-Segregated Education*

During much of early American history, it was often assumed that women needed no formal education; informal training in the household arts was thought sufficient. In the nineteenth century, as elementary and secondary education opportunities increased, prominent medical experts warned that women faced a deadly "brain-womb conflict." Rigorous study, it was asserted, would divert needed physical resources from reproductive to cognitive capacities. Even those who

---

192. See UCLA School of Law Williams Institute, Brief, Prohibiting Gender-Affirming Medical Care for Youth (Mar. 2022). For a description of the impact of these laws from a provider perspective, see Landon D. Hughes et al., "These Laws Will Be Devastating": Provider Perspectives on Legislation Banning Gender-Affirming Care for Transgender Adolescents, 69 J. Adolescent Health 976 (2021).

193. Adapted from William V. Padula & Kellan Baker, Coverage for Gender-Affirming Care: Making Health Insurance Work for Transgender Americans, 4 LGBT Health (Aug. 2017).

194. See Gabriela Weigel et al., Coverage and Use of Fertility Services in the U.S., Women's Health Pol'y (Sept. 15, 2020).

195. Madeline Curtis, Inconceivable: How Barriers to Infertility Treatment for Low-Income Women Amount to Reproductive Oppression, 25 Geo. J. Poverty L. & Pol'y 323 (2018).

favored expanded female education, such as Catherine Beecher, generally believed that its primary objective should be "the preparation of woman for her distinctive profession as housekeeper, mother, nurse, and chief educator of infancy and childhood." Defenders of academic rigor emphasized that the point of women's instruction in traditional disciplines was not only to "enlarge their sphere of thought" but also to render them "more interesting companions to men." Chemistry might be significant in its own right but its principles were also applicable in the kitchen. Smith College's first president and early administrators denied that the college would produce competitors with men or diminish the "innate capacities which have been the glory and charm of true womanhood."[196] Although the gender ideologies behind these views present as race-neutral, they implicitly reflect an ideal of white womanhood. Black women were never placed in a separate sphere from Black men to protect their "true womanhood." African Americans were denied education for different reasons: an ideology of racial inferiority that outlawed education for enslaved men and women alike and obstructed access to equal education for Black women and men long after slavery ended.[197]

Much has changed since women were formally denied access to education, but disputes still arise about whether girls and boys have different abilities, learning styles, or interests that should shape their educations. One issue concerns single-sex schools. In 1982, the U.S. Supreme Court held in Mississippi University for Women (MUW) v. Hogan that a traditionally all-female state nursing school could not exclude men. Underlying the Court's decision was evidence that the school's sex segregation reflected not legitimate educational or compensatory justifications, but rather stereotypical views of nursing as an exclusively female occupation.[198] This was not a constitutionally sufficient governmental interest in the wake of the Court's equal protection decisions of the 1970s. The Court in *Hogan* did not, however, declare all single-sex schools unconstitutional. Justice O'Connor reserved the possibility that under "limited circumstances," a gender-based classification favoring one sex might be justified "if it intentionally and directly assists members of the sex that is disproportionately burdened." Justice Powell, joined by Justice Rehnquist, wrote a strong dissent emphasizing the "honored" tradition of single-sex education, its benefits especially to women, and its contributions to educational diversity. Quoting from the Brief for the MUW Alumnae Association, Justice Powell noted the value of sex-segregated schools in freeing women from the distraction of romantic relationships:

> [I]n the aspect of life known as courtship or mate-pairing, the American female remains in the role of the pursued sex, expected to adorn and groom herself to attract the male. . . .

---

196. Sheila M. Rothman, Woman's Proper Place 40 (1978); see also Deborah L. Rhode, Association and Assimilation, 81 Nw. U. L. Rev. 106, 131-32 (1986); Deborah L. Rhode, Justice and Gender 291-292 (1989).

197. See Linda M. Perkins, The Role of Education in the Development of Black Feminist Thought, 1860-1920, 22 Hist. Educ. 265 (1993).

198. 458 U.S. 718 (1982).

An institution of collegiate higher learning maintained exclusively for women is uniquely able to provide the education atmosphere in which some, but not all, women can best attain maximum learning potential. It can serve to overcome the historic repression of the past and can orient a woman to function and achieve in the still male-dominated economy. It can free its students of the burden of playing the mating game while attending classes, thus giving academic rather than sexual emphasis.[199]

Fourteen years after *Hogan,* the Supreme Court was faced with another challenge — this time, to an all-male state military college, the Virginia Military Institute (VMI).

United States v. Virginia

518 U.S. 515 (1996)

GINSBURG, J., delivered the opinion of the Court, in which STEVENS, O'CONNOR, KENNEDY, SOUTER, and BREYER, JJ., joined.

Virginia's public institutions of higher learning include an incomparable military college, Virginia Military Institute (VMI). The United States maintains that the Constitution's equal protection guarantee precludes Virginia from reserving exclusively to men the unique educational opportunities VMI affords. We agree. . . .

II

From its establishment in 1839 as one of the Nation's first state military colleges, VMI has remained financially supported by Virginia and "subject to the control of the [Virginia] General Assembly." . . .

VMI today enrolls about 1,300 men as cadets. Its academic offerings in the liberal arts, sciences, and engineering are also available at other public colleges and universities in Virginia. But VMI's mission is special. It is the mission of the school to produce educated and honorable men, prepared for the varied work of civil life, imbued with love of learning, confident in the functions and attitudes of leadership, possessing a high sense of public service, advocates of the American democracy and free enterprise system, and ready as citizen-soldiers to defend their country in time of national peril. . . .

In contrast to the federal service academies, institutions maintained "to prepare cadets for career service in the armed forces," VMI's program "is directed at preparation for both military and civilian life;" "[o]nly about 15% of VMI cadets enter career military service."

VMI produces its "citizen-soldiers" through "an adversative, or doubting, model of education" which features "[p]hysical rigor, mental stress, absolute equality of treatment, absence of privacy, minute regulation of behavior, and indoctrination in desirable values." . . .

---

199. Id. at 739 n.5 (Powell, J., dissenting).

VMI cadets live in spartan barracks where surveillance is constant and privacy nonexistent; they wear uniforms, eat together in the mess hall, and regularly participate in drills. Entering students are incessantly exposed to the rat line, "an extreme form of the adversarial model," comparable in intensity to Marine Corps boot camp. Tormenting and punishing, the rat line bonds new cadets to their fellow sufferers and, when they have completed the 7-month experience, to their former tormentors.

VMI's "adversarial model" is further characterized by a hierarchical "class system" of privileges and responsibilities, a "dyke system" for assigning a senior class mentor to each entering class "rat," and a stringently enforced "honor code," which prescribes that a cadet " 'does not lie, cheat, steal nor tolerate those who do.' "

VMI attracts some applicants because of its reputation as an extraordinarily challenging military school, and "because its alumni are exceptionally close to the school." "[W]omen have no opportunity anywhere to gain the benefits of [the system of education at VMI]." . . .

In 1990, prompted by a complaint filed with the Attorney General by a female high-school student seeking admission to VMI, the United States sued the Commonwealth of Virginia and VMI, alleging that VMI's exclusively male admission policy violated the Equal Protection Clause of the Fourteenth Amendment. . . .

In the two years preceding the lawsuit, the District Court noted, VMI had received inquiries from 347 women, but had responded to none of them. "[S]ome women, at least," the court said, "would want to attend the school if they had the opportunity." The court further recognized that, with recruitment, VMI could "achieve at least 10% female enrollment"—"a sufficient 'critical mass' to provide the female cadets with a positive educational experience." And it was also established that "some women are capable of all of the individual activities required of VMI cadets." In addition, experts agreed that if VMI admitted women, "the VMI ROTC experience would become a better training program from the perspective of the armed forces, because it would provide training in dealing with a mixed-gender army."

[The District Court ruled in favor of VMI because admission of women would require alterations of some of the distinctive and beneficial aspects of VMI; the Fourth Circuit Court of Appeals reversed and remanded, holding that the state could not achieve its purposes by favoring one gender and that VMI had to either admit women, establish a parallel institution or program, or abandon state support. In response to the Fourth Circuit's ruling, Virginia proposed a parallel program at Mary Baldwin College, a private liberal arts school for women: Virginia Women's Institute for Leadership (VWIL). The program was to be open, initially, to 25 to 30 students. The District Court decided that the program plan met the requirements of the Equal Protection Clause, and a divided Court of Appeals affirmed.]

III

The cross-petitions in this case present two ultimate issues. First, does Virginia's exclusion of women from the educational opportunities provided by VMI—extraordinary opportunities for military training and civilian leadership development—deny to women "capable of all of the individual activities required of VMI cadets," the equal protection of the laws guaranteed by the Fourteenth

Amendment? Second, if VMI's "unique" situation, — as Virginia's sole single-sex public institution of higher education — offends the Constitution's equal protection principle, what is the remedial requirement?

IV ...

To summarize the Court's current directions for cases of official classification based on gender: Focusing on the differential treatment or denial of opportunity for which relief is sought, the reviewing court must determine whether the proffered justification is "exceedingly persuasive." The burden of justification is demanding and it rests entirely on the State. [See Mississippi Univ. for Women v. Hogan (1982).] The State must show "at least that the [challenged] classification serves 'important governmental objectives and that the discriminatory means employed' are 'substantially related to the achievement of those objectives.'" The justification must be genuine, not hypothesized or invented post hoc in response to litigation. And it must not rely on overbroad generalizations about the different talents, capacities, or preferences of males and females. . . .

The heightened review standard our precedent establishes does not make sex a proscribed classification. Supposed "inherent differences" are no longer accepted as a ground for race or national origin classifications. Physical differences between men and women, however, are enduring: "[T]he two sexes are not fungible; a community made up exclusively of one [sex] is different from a community composed of both." . . .

"Inherent differences" between men and women, we have come to appreciate, remain cause for celebration, but not for denigration of the members of either sex or for artificial constraints on an individual's opportunity. Sex classifications may be used to compensate women "for particular economic disabilities [they have] suffered," . . . to "promot[e] equal employment opportunity," . . . to advance full development of the talent and capacities of our Nation's people. But such classifications may not be used, as they once were, . . . to create or perpetuate the legal, social, and economic inferiority of women.

Measuring the record in this case against the review standard just described, we conclude that Virginia has shown no "exceedingly persuasive justification" for excluding all women from the citizen-soldier training afforded by VMI. We therefore affirm the Fourth Circuit's initial judgment, which held that Virginia had violated the Fourteenth Amendment's Equal Protection Clause. Because the remedy proffered by Virginia — the Mary Baldwin VWIL program — does not cure the constitutional violation, i.e., it does not provide equal opportunity, we reverse the Fourth Circuit's final judgment in this case.

V ...

Single-sex education affords pedagogical benefits to at least some students, Virginia emphasizes, and that reality is uncontested in this litigation.[8] Similarly, it

---

8. On this point, the dissent sees fire where there is no flame. "Both men and women can benefit from a single-sex education," the District Court recognized, although "the

is not disputed that diversity among public educational institutions can serve the public good. But Virginia has not shown that VMI was established, or has been maintained, with a view to diversifying, by its categorical exclusion of women, educational opportunities within the State. In cases of this genre, our precedent instructs that "benign" justifications proffered in defense of categorical exclusions will not be accepted automatically; a tenable justification must describe actual state purposes, not rationalizations for actions in fact differently grounded. . . .

Neither recent nor distant history bears out Virginia's alleged pursuit of diversity through single-sex educational options. In 1839, when the State established VMI, a range of educational opportunities for men and women was scarcely contemplated. Higher education at the time was considered dangerous for women; reflecting widely held views about women's proper place, the Nation's first universities and colleges—for example, Harvard in Massachusetts, William and Mary in Virginia—admitted only men. . . . VMI was not at all novel in this respect: In admitting no women, VMI followed the lead of the State's flagship school, the University of Virginia, founded in 1819. . . .

Debate concerning women's admission as undergraduates at the main university continued well past the century's midpoint. . . . If women were admitted, it was feared, they "would encroach on the rights of men; there would be new problems of government, perhaps scandals; the old honor system would have to be changed; standards would be lowered to those of other coeducational schools; and the glorious reputation of the university, as a school for men, would be trailed in the dust." . . .

Ultimately, in 1970, "the most prestigious institution of higher education in Virginia," the University of Virginia, introduced coeducation and, in 1972 [by court order], began to admit women on an equal basis with men. . . .

Virginia describes the current absence of public single-sex higher education for women as "an historical anomaly." But the historical record indicates action more deliberate than anomalous: First, protection of women against higher education; next, schools for women far from equal in resources and stature to schools for men; finally, conversion of the separate schools to coeducation. . . .

[I]t is uncontested that women's admission would require accommodations, primarily in arranging housing assignments and physical training programs for female cadets. It is also undisputed, however, that "the VMI methodology could be used to educate women." The District Court even allowed that some women may prefer it to the methodology a women's college might pursue. "[S]ome women, at least, would want to attend [VMI] if they had the opportunity," the District Court recognized, and "some women," the expert testimony established, "are capable of

---

beneficial effects" of such education, the court added, apparently "are stronger among women than among men." The United States does not challenge that recognition. Cf. C. Jencks & D. Riesman, The Academic Revolution 297-98 (1968): "The pluralistic argument for preserving all-male colleges is uncomfortably similar to the pluralistic argument for preserving all-white colleges. . . . The all-male college would be relatively easy to defend if it emerged from a world in which women were established as fully equal to men. But it does not. It is therefore likely to be a witting or unwitting device for preserving tacit assumptions of male superiority—assumptions for which women must eventually pay."

all of the individual activities required of VMI cadets." The parties, furthermore, agree that "some women can meet the physical standards [VMI] now impose[s] on men." In sum, as the Court of Appeals stated, "neither the goal of producing citizen soldiers," VMI's *raison d'etre*, "nor VMI's implementing methodology is inherently unsuitable to women."

In support of its initial judgment for Virginia, a judgment rejecting all equal protection objections presented by the United States, the District Court made "findings" on "gender-based developmental differences." These "findings" restate the opinions of Virginia's expert witnesses, opinions about typically male or typically female tendencies." For example, "[m]ales tend to need an atmosphere of adversativeness," while "[f]emales tend to thrive in a cooperative atmosphere." "I'm not saying that some women don't do well under [the] adversative model," VMI's expert on educational institutions testified, "undoubtedly there are some [women] who do"; but educational experiences must be designed "around the rule," this expert maintained, and not "around the exception."

The United States does not challenge any expert witness estimation on average capacities or preferences of men and women. Instead, the United States emphasizes that time and again since this Court's turning point decision in Reed v. Reed, [1971], we have cautioned reviewing courts to take a "hard look" at generalizations or "tendencies" of the kind pressed by Virginia, and relied upon by the District Court. . . .

It may be assumed, for purposes of this decision, that most women would not choose VMI's adversative method. As Fourth Circuit Judge Motz observed, however, in her dissent from the Court of Appeals' denial of rehearing en banc, it is also probable that "many men would not want to be educated in such an environment." . . . (On that point, even our dissenting colleague might agree.) Education, to be sure, is not a "one size fits all" business. The issue, however, is not whether "women — or men — should be forced to attend VMI"; rather, the question is whether the State can constitutionally deny to women who have the will and capacity, the training and attendant opportunities that VMI uniquely affords.

The notion that admission of women would downgrade VMI's stature, destroy the adversative system and, with it, even the school, is a judgment hardly proved, a prediction hardly different from other "self-fulfilling prophec[ies]," . . . once routinely used to deny rights or opportunities. When women first sought admission to the bar and access to legal education, concerns of the same order were expressed. . . .

[Such] fear, according to a 1925 report, accounted for Columbia Law School's resistance to women's admission, although

> [t]he faculty . . . never maintained that women could not master legal learning. . . . No, its argument has been . . . more practical. If women were admitted to the Columbia Law School, [the faculty] said, then the choicer, more manly and red-blooded graduates of our great universities would go to the Harvard Law School! . . .

More recently, women seeking careers in policing encountered resistance based on fears that their presence would "undermine male solidarity," . . . deprive male partners of adequate assistance, and lead to sexual misconduct. . . .

Women's successful entry into the federal military academies, and their participation in the Nation's military forces, indicate that Virginia's fears for the future of VMI may not be solidly grounded. . . .

The State's misunderstanding and, in turn, the District Court's, is apparent from VMI's mission: to produce "citizen-soldiers," individuals "imbued with love of learning, confident in the functions and attitudes of leadership, possessing a high sense of public service, advocates of the American democracy and free enterprise system, and ready . . . to defend their country in time of national peril." . . .

Surely that goal is great enough to accommodate women, who today count as citizens in our American democracy equal in stature to men. Just as surely, the State's great goal is not substantially advanced by women's categorical exclusion, in total disregard of their individual merit, from the State's premier "citizen-soldier" corps. Virginia, in sum, "has fallen far short of establishing the 'exceedingly persuasive justification' " . . . that must be the solid base for any gender-defined classification.

VI

In the second phase of the litigation, Virginia presented its remedial plan — maintain VMI as a male-only college and create VWIL as a separate program for women. . . .

The constitutional violation in this case is the categorical exclusion of women from an extraordinary educational opportunity afforded men. A proper remedy for an unconstitutional exclusion, we have explained, aims to "eliminate [so far as possible] the discriminatory effects of the past" and to "bar like discrimination in the future." . . .

Virginia chose not to eliminate, but to leave untouched, VMI's exclusionary policy. For women only, however, Virginia proposed a separate program, different in kind from VMI and unequal in tangible and intangible facilities. . . .

VWIL affords women no opportunity to experience the rigorous military training for which VMI is famed. . . . Instead, the VWIL program "deemphasize[s]" military education, and uses a "cooperative method" of education "which reinforces self-esteem."

VWIL students participate in ROTC and a "largely ceremonial" Virginia Corps of Cadets, but Virginia deliberately did not make VWIL a military institute. The VWIL House is not a military-style residence and VWIL students need not live together throughout the four year program, eat meals together, or wear uniforms during the school day. VWIL students thus do not experience the "barracks" life "crucial to the VMI experience," the spartan living arrangements designed to foster an "egalitarian ethic." "[T]he most important aspects of the VMI educational experience occur in the barracks," the District Court found, yet Virginia deemed that core experience nonessential, indeed inappropriate, for training its female citizen-soldiers.

VWIL students receive their "leadership training" in seminars, externships, and speaker series, episodes and encounters lacking the "[p]hysical rigor, mental stress, . . . minute regulation of behavior, and indoctrination in desirable values" made hallmarks of VMI's citizen-soldier training. Kept away from the pressures, hazards, and psychological bonding characteristic of VMI's adversative training,

VWIL students will not know the "feeling of tremendous accomplishment" commonly experienced by VMI's successful cadets.

Virginia maintains that these methodological differences are "justified pedagogically," based on "important differences between men and women in learning and developmental needs," "psychological and sociological differences" Virginia describes as "real" and "not stereotypes." The Task Force charged with developing the leadership program for women, drawn from the staff and faculty at Mary Baldwin College, "determined that a military model and, especially VMI's adversative method, would be wholly inappropriate for educating and training *most women*" . . . [and noted that while "some women would be suited to and interested" in a VMI-style experience, VMI's adversative method "would not be effective for *women as a group*."] . . .

As earlier stated, generalizations about "the way women are," estimates of what is appropriate for *most women*, no longer justify denying opportunity to women whose talent and capacity place them outside the average description. Notably, Virginia never asserted that VMI's method of education suits *most men*. It is also revealing that Virginia accounted for its failure to make the VWIL experience "the entirely militaristic experience of VMI" on the ground that VWIL "is planned for women who do not necessarily expect to pursue military careers." By that reasoning, VMI's "entirely militaristic" program would be inappropriate for men in general or *as a group*, for "[o]nly about 15% of VMI cadets enter career military service."

In contrast to the generalizations about women on which Virginia rests, we note again these dispositive realities: VMI's "implementing methodology" is not "inherently unsuitable to women," "some women . . . do well under [the] adversative model," "some women, at least, would want to attend [VMI] if they had the opportunity," "some women are capable of all of the individual activities required of VMI cadets," and "can meet the physical standards [VMI] now impose[s] on men." . . .

In myriad respects other than military training, VWIL does not qualify as VMI's equal. VWIL's student body, faculty, course offerings, and facilities hardly match VMI's. Nor can the VWIL graduate anticipate the benefits associated with VMI's 157-year history, the school's prestige, and its influential alumni network.

Mary Baldwin College, whose degree VWIL students will gain, enrolls first-year women with an average combined SAT score about 100 points lower than the average score for VMI freshmen. The Mary Baldwin faculty holds "significantly fewer Ph.D.'s," and receives substantially lower salaries than the faculty at VMI.

Mary Baldwin does not offer a VWIL student the range of curricular choices available to a VMI cadet. VMI awards baccalaureate degrees in liberal arts, biology, chemistry, civil engineering, electrical and computer engineering, and mechanical engineering. . . . VWIL students attend a school that "does not have a math and science focus," they cannot take at Mary Baldwin any courses in engineering or the advanced math and physics courses VMI offers. . . .

For physical training, Mary Baldwin has "two multi-purpose fields" and "[o]ne gymnasium." VMI has "an NCAA competition level indoor track and field facility; a number of multi-purpose fields; baseball, soccer and lacrosse fields; an obstacle course; large boxing, wrestling and martial arts facilities; an 11-laps-to-the-mile indoor running course; an indoor pool; indoor and outdoor rifle ranges; and a football stadium that also contains a practice field and outdoor track."

Although Virginia has represented that it will provide equal financial support for in-state VWIL students and VMI cadets, and the VMI Foundation has agreed to endow VWIL with $5.4625 million, the difference between the two schools' financial reserves is pronounced. Mary Baldwin's endowment, currently about $19 million, will gain an additional $35 million based on future commitments; VMI's current endowment, $131 million — the largest per-student endowment in the Nation — will gain $220 million.

The VWIL student does not graduate with the advantage of a VMI degree. Her diploma does not unite her with the legions of VMI "graduates [who] have distinguished themselves" in military and civilian life. . . . A VWIL graduate cannot assume that the "network of business owners, corporations, VMI graduates and non-graduate employers . . . interested in hiring VMI graduates," will be equally responsive to her search for employment. . . .

Virginia, in sum, while maintaining VMI for men only, has failed to provide any "comparable single-gender women's institution." Instead, the Commonwealth has created a VWIL program fairly appraised as a "pale shadow" of VMI in terms of the range of curricular choices and faculty stature, funding, prestige, alumni support, and influence.

Virginia's VWIL solution is reminiscent of the remedy Texas proposed 50 years ago, in response to a state trial court's 1946 ruling that, given the equal protection guarantee, African Americans could not be denied a legal education at a state facility. . . . Reluctant to admit African Americans to its flagship University of Texas Law School, the State set up a separate school for Herman Sweatt and other black law students. [In holding that the all-black school was not equivalent to the University of Texas facility, the Court emphasized not only the size of the full-time faculty, library, and extracurricular offerings, but also the alumni network.]

More important than the tangible features, the Court [in *Sweatt*] emphasized, are "those qualities which are incapable of objective measurement but which make for greatness" in a school, including "reputation of the faculty, experience of the administration, position and influence of the alumni, standing in the community, traditions and prestige." Facing the marked differences reported in the *Sweatt* opinion, the Court unanimously ruled that Texas had not shown "substantial equality in the [separate] educational opportunities" the State offered. Accordingly, the Court held, the Equal Protection Clause required Texas to admit African Americans to the University of Texas Law School. In line with *Sweatt*, we rule here that Virginia has not shown substantial equality in the separate educational opportunities the State supports at VWIL and VMI.

[Reversed and remanded.]

Justice SCALIA, dissenting.

Today the Court shuts down an institution that has served the people of the Commonwealth of Virginia with pride and distinction for over a century and a half. To achieve that desired result, it rejects (contrary to our established practice) the factual findings of two courts below, sweeps aside the precedents of this Court, and ignores the history of our people. As to facts: it explicitly rejects the finding that there exist "gender-based developmental differences" supporting Virginia's restriction of the "adversative" method to only a men's institution, and the finding that the all-male composition of the Virginia Military Institute (VMI) is essential to that institution's character. As to precedent: it drastically revises our established standards for reviewing sex-based classifications. And as to history: it counts for nothing the long tradition, enduring down to the present, of men's military colleges supported by both States and the Federal Government.

Much of the Court's opinion is devoted to deprecating the closed-mindedness of our forebears with regard to women's education, and even with regard to the treatment of women in areas that have nothing to do with education. Closedminded they were—as every age is, including our own, with regard to matters it cannot guess, because it simply does not consider them debatable. The virtue of a democratic system with a First Amendment is that it readily enables the people, over time, to be persuaded that what they took for granted is not so, and to change their laws accordingly. That system is destroyed if the smug assurances of each age are removed from the democratic process and written into the Constitution. So to counterbalance the Court's criticism of our ancestors, let me say a word in their praise: they left us free to change. The same cannot be said of this most illiberal Court, which has embarked on a course of inscribing one after another of the current preferences of the society (and in some cases only the counter-majoritarian preferences of the society's law-trained elite) into our Basic Law. Today it enshrines the notion that no substantial educational value is to be served by an all-men's military academy—so that the decision by the people of Virginia to maintain such an institution denies equal protection to women who cannot attend that institution but can attend others. Since it is entirely clear that the Constitution of the United States—the old one—takes no sides in this educational debate, I dissent.

I...

[I]n my view the function of this Court is to *preserve* our society's values regarding (among other things) equal protection, not to *revise* them; to prevent backsliding from the degree of restriction the Constitution imposed upon democratic government, not to prescribe, on our own authority, progressively higher degrees. For that reason it is my view that, whatever abstract tests we may choose to devise, they cannot supersede—and indeed ought to be crafted *so as to reflect*—those constant and unbroken national traditions that embody the people's understanding of ambiguous constitutional texts. More specifically, it is my view that "when a practice not expressly prohibited by the text of the Bill of Rights bears the endorsement of a long tradition of open, widespread, and unchallenged use that dates back to the beginning of the Republic, we have no proper basis for striking it down." ...

The all-male constitution of VMI comes squarely within such a governing tradition. Founded by the Commonwealth of Virginia in 1839 and continuously maintained by it since, VMI has always admitted only men. And in that regard it has not been unusual. For almost all of VMI's more than a century and a half of existence, its single-sex status reflected the uniform practice for government-supported military colleges. Another famous Southern institution, The Citadel, has existed as a state-funded school of South Carolina since 1842. And all the federal military colleges—West Point, the Naval Academy at Annapolis, and even the Air Force Academy, which was not established until 1954—admitted only males for most of their history. Their admission of women in 1976 (upon which the Court today relies), came not by court decree, but because the people, through their elected representatives, decreed a change. . . . In other words, the tradition of having government-funded military schools for men is as well rooted in the traditions of this country as the tradition of sending only men into military combat. The people may decide to change the one tradition, like the other, through democratic processes; but the assertion that either tradition has been unconstitutional through the centuries is not law, but politics-smuggled-into-law.

And the same applies, more broadly, to single-sex education in general, which, as I shall discuss, is threatened by today's decision with the cut-off of all state and federal support. Government-run *non*military educational institutions for the two sexes have until very recently also been part of our national tradition. "[It is] [c]o-education, historically, [that] is a novel educational theory. From grade school through high school, college, and graduate and professional training, much of the Nation's population during much of our history has been educated in sexually segregated classrooms." Mississippi Univ. for Women v. Hogan, [1982] (Powell, J., dissenting). These traditions may of course be changed by the democratic decisions of the people, as they largely have been.

Today, however, change is forced upon Virginia, and reversion to single-sex education is prohibited nationwide, not by democratic processes but by order of this Court. Even while bemoaning the sorry, bygone days of "fixed notions" concerning women's education, the Court favors current notions so fixedly that it is willing to write them into the Constitution of the United States by application of custom-built "tests." This is not the interpretation of a Constitution, but the creation of one.

II.

To reject the Court's disposition today, however, it is not necessary to accept my view that the Court's made-up tests cannot displace longstanding national traditions as the primary determinant of what the Constitution means. It is only necessary to apply honestly the test the Court has been applying to sex-based classifications for the past two decades. . . . We have denominated this standard "intermediate scrutiny" and under it have inquired whether the statutory classification is "substantially related to an important governmental objective." . . .

Only the amorphous "exceedingly persuasive justification" phrase, and not the standard elaboration of intermediate scrutiny, can be made to yield this conclusion that VMI's single-sex composition is unconstitutional because there exist several women (or, one would have to conclude under the Court's reasoning, a single woman) willing and able to undertake VMI's program. Intermediate scrutiny has never required a least-restrictive-means analysis, but only a "substantial relation" between the classification and the state interests that it serves. . . .

Not content to execute a *de facto* abandonment of the intermediate scrutiny that has been our standard for sex-based classifications for some two decades, the Court purports to reserve the question whether, even in principle, a higher standard (i.e., strict scrutiny) should apply. . . . [The Court's] statements are misleading, insofar as they suggest that we have not already categorically *held* strict scrutiny to be inapplicable to sex-based classifications. . . . And the statements are irresponsible, insofar as they are calculated to destabilize current law. Our task is to clarify the law — not to muddy the waters, and not to exact over-compliance by intimidation. The States and the Federal Government are entitled to know *before they act* the standard to which they will be held, rather than be compelled to guess about the outcome of Supreme Court peek-a-boo.

The Court's intimations are particularly out of place because it is perfectly clear that, if the question of the applicable standard of review for sex-based classifications were to be regarded as an appropriate subject for reconsideration, the stronger argument would be not for elevating the standard to strict scrutiny, but for reducing it to rational-basis review. The latter certainly has a firmer foundation in our past jurisprudence: Whereas no majority of the Court has ever applied strict scrutiny in a case involving sex-based classifications, we routinely applied rational-basis review until the 1970's. . . .

It is hard to consider women a "discrete and insular minorit[y]" unable to employ the "political processes ordinarily to be relied upon," when they constitute a majority of the electorate. And the suggestion that they are incapable of exerting that political power smacks of the same paternalism that the Court so roundly condemns. Moreover, a long list of legislation proves the proposition false. . . .

III . . .

There can be no serious dispute that, as the District Court found, single-sex education and a distinctive educational method "represent legitimate contributions to diversity in the Virginia higher education system." As a theoretical matter, Virginia's educational interest would have been best served (insofar as the two factors we have mentioned are concerned) by six different types of public colleges—an all-men's, an all-women's, and a coeducational college run in the "adversative method," and an all-men's, an all-women's, and a coeducational college run in the "traditional method." But as a practical matter, of course, Virginia's financial resources, like any State's, are not limitless, and the Commonwealth must select among the available options. Virginia thus has decided to fund, in addition to some 14 coeducational 4-year colleges, one college that is run as an all-male school on the adversative model: the Virginia Military Institute.

Virginia did not make this determination regarding the make-up of its public college system on the unrealistic assumption that no other colleges exist. Substantial evidence in the District Court demonstrated that the Commonwealth has long proceeded on the principle that " '[h]igher education resources should be viewed as a whole—public and private' "—because such an approach enhances diversity and because " 'it is academic and economic waste to permit unwarranted duplication.' " It is thus significant that, whereas there are "four all-female private [colleges] in Virginia," there is only "one private all-male college," which "indicates that the private sector is providing for th[e] [former] form of education to a much greater extent that it provides for all-male education." In these circumstances, Virginia's election to fund one public all-male institution and one on the adversative model—and to concentrate its resources in a single entity that serves both these interests in diversity—is substantially related to the State's important educational interests. . . .

IV . . .

In an odd sort of way, it is precisely VMI's attachment to such old-fashioned concepts as manly "honor" that has made it, and the system it represents, the target of those who today succeed in abolishing public single-sex education. The record contains a booklet that all first-year VMI students (the so-called "rats") were required to keep in their possession at all times. Near the end there appears the following period-piece, entitled "The Code of a Gentleman":

> Without a strict observance of the fundamental Code of Honor, no man, no matter how "polished," can be considered a gentleman. The honor of a gentleman demands the inviolability of his word, and the incorruptibility of his principles. He is the descendant of the knight, the crusader; he is the defender of the defenseless and the champion of justice . . . or he is not a Gentleman.
>
> A Gentleman . . .
>
> Does not discuss his family affairs in public or with acquaintances.
>
> Does not speak more than casually about his girlfriend.
>
> Does not go to a lady's house if he is affected by alcohol. He is temperate in the use of alcohol.
>
> Does not lose his temper; nor exhibit anger, fear, hate, embarrassment, ardor or hilarity in public.
>
> Does not hail a lady from a club window.
>
> A gentleman never discusses the merits or demerits of a lady. Does not mention names exactly as he avoids the mention of what things cost.
>
> Does not borrow money from a friend, except in dire need. Money borrowed is a debt of honor, and must be repaid as promptly as possible. Debts incurred by a deceased parent, brother, sister or grown child are assumed by honorable men as a debt of honor.
>
> Does not display his wealth, money or possessions.
>
> Does not put his manners on and off, whether in the club or in a ballroom. He treats people with courtesy, no matter what their social position may be.
>
> Does not slap strangers on the back nor so much as lay a finger on a lady.
>
> Does not "lick the boots of those above" nor "kick the face of those below him on the social ladder."
>
> Does not take advantage of another's helplessness or ignorance and assumes that no gentleman will take advantage of him.
>
> A Gentleman respects the reserves of others, but demands that others respect those which are his.
>
> A Gentleman can become what he wills to be. . . .

I do not know whether the men of VMI lived by this Code; perhaps not. But it is powerfully impressive that a public institution of higher education still in existence sought to have them do so. I do not think any of us, women included, will be better off for its destruction.

NOTES

1. **What's at Stake Here?**   The *VMI* case started with an anonymous complaint by a northern Virginia female high school student to the U.S. Department

of Justice that the school did not accept applications from women. One of the issues in the case was whether women would really attend VMI, although the record revealed that 347 women had made inquiries about VMI in the two years preceding the lawsuit.[200] Since VMI began admitting women in 1997, female students have typically accounted for between 12 and 15 percent of the entering class of cadets, peaking at 18 percent in 2018.[201] Another contested issue in the case was whether the presence of women would significantly change the school and eliminate its educational benefits for men. The government argued that women could thrive at VMI without changing it. Was this a realistic claim? VMI contended, and the District Court agreed, that women would change the fundamental dynamic of the school and ruin what was unique and valuable about it. Was this plausible? Or was it beside the point? Should women be excluded from a public institution simply because their presence might change that institution?

Despite claiming that VMI would not have to change, the Department of Justice pressured VMI to make changes to accommodate women after the Supreme Court decided the case, urging modifications such as more privacy in bedrooms and bathrooms and less severe haircuts. Does equal protection require such measures?[202] Which theory of equality best supports them?

Given VMI's highly gendered approach to education, was VMI's exclusion of women the only constitutional defect? Or should it also be unconstitutional for a state-supported institution to implement such a male-oriented pedagogy, no matter who has access to that institution?

While the exclusion of women from VMI was the central legal issue, another concern, not directly addressed in the parties' briefs or in the Supreme Court decision, was the propriety of the adversative method itself. Katharine Bartlett explains:

> The adversative system, which defined the essence of the institution, was deliberately and pervasively gendered. Its design was to create leaders by giving them near-impossible challenges, and then equating success in meeting those challenges to masculinity. Rat culture eschewed all things female except as objects of derision and humiliation. . . . The problem with admitting women to this environment was as much that they might succeed at these manly challenges as that they would fail. As one researcher put it, "if women could perform well on [the rat line], how could it continue to function as evidence of manhood?"[203]

---

200. See United States v. Virginia, 518 U.S. 515, 523 (1996).

201. Virginia Military Institute, Diversity, Equity, and Inclusion Review: 30 Day Report 15 (July 1, 2021).

202. A parallel case was filed against South Carolina's The Citadel, the only other state-supported, all-male military college. While the case was still on appeal, the Fourth Circuit ordered immediate admission of the named plaintiff, Shannon Faulkner, who dropped out less than a week later, "overcome by stress and terror as the only woman alone in the barracks with 1800 male cadets, most of whom hated her guts." Faulkner v. Jones, 10 F.3d 226 (4th Cir. 1993); Citadel's First Female Case Tells of the Stress of Her Court Fight, N.Y. Times, Sept. 10, 1995, at A36. After the ruling in *VMI*, The Citadel decided to admit women.

203. See Katharine T. Bartlett, Unconstitutionally Male?: The Story of United States v. Virginia, in Women and the Law Stories 133, 140-41 (Elizabeth Schneider & Stephanie

Language played an important part of the gendering of the adversative system, and sexual references saturated even the "official" VMI terminology. As Bartlett explains, to "reinforce the machismo ethos, gendered obscenities and hostility toward women served as quasi-official motivational techniques in the rat line."[204] In addition to the use of approved gendered terminology like "dyke," "bone," and "running a period," the administration tolerated "other familiar phrases [including] 'raping your virgin ducks' (peeling apart the stiffly starched legs of a new pair of white trousers), [and] 'rolling your hay tight as a tampon' (rolling up your thin mattress in the morning).[205]

The VWIL program at Mary Baldwin College remains the nation's only all-female undergraduate military training program and continues to attract women interested in military careers, many of whom receive military commissions and serve with distinction. Mary Anne Case visited both VMI and VWIL after the *VMI* decision. She found the "rats" at VMI "a sorry lot—terrified, sweating, shaking, and exhausted . . . they were unable to tell their left feet from their right."[206] By contrast, VWIL's equivalent to rats (nULLS) were working together, learning the same values of accountability and discipline in a more supporting, encouraging, and non-intimidating environment.[207] She noted, however, that VMI was still the more prestigious, sought-after alternative, even by many women.

> The paradoxes here are many: First, the dominant class, men, have selected what appears to be the less attractive standard for themselves. Second, in part because they have selected it, this standard is assumed unquestionably to be desirable; inquiry into it is generally limited only to how far it will be extended to women. Much less attention is paid to whether the separate standard sought to be applied to women might in fact make some sense for women and men alike.[208]

Does this analysis suggest that VWIL is actually the superior program for women?

What does VMI look like now, twenty-five years after first admitting female students? In 2020, in response to media reports of a campus environment rife with hostility on the basis of race and gender, the state ordered an investigation and equity audit of VMI. The report, prepared by an outside law firm, is scathing. After summarizing the investigation's findings of extensive racial hostility on campus

---

Wildman, eds., 2011) (quoting Philippa Strum, Women in the Barracks: The VMI Case and Equal Rights 109 (2002)); see also Valorie K. Vojdik, Gender Outlaws: Challenging Masculinity in Traditionally Male Institutions, 17 Berkeley Women's L.J. 68, 98-99 (2002) (describing the culture of hyper-masculinity at The Citadel).

204. Bartlett, supra note 203, at 140.

205. Id. at 174.

206. Mary Anne Case, Two Cheers for Cheerleading: The Noisy Integration of VMI and the Quiet Success of Virginia Women in Leadership, 1999 U. Chi. Legal F. 347, 378.

207. Id.

208. Id. at 349. See also Doe v. Bd. of Visitors of VMI, 494 F. Supp.3d 363 (W.D. Va. 2020) (dismissing male cadet's claim alleging hazing and physical assault by other male cadets for failure to state a claim under Title IX or the Equal Protection Clause).

including racial slurs, reverence for the Civil War and the Confederacy, and racial inequities, the report continues:

> On gender, many respondents — including men — stated that VMI's gender-equity issues are worse than its racial-equity issues. Respondents reported incidents of gender inequity; a culture of not taking women seriously; double-standards for women on matters of dress, social behavior, and sexual behavior; and disturbing sexist and misogynistic comments on social media apps such as Jodel. Some men reported resentment toward women for perceived preferential treatment in physical training standards, Rat line experience, discipline, and leadership opportunities. Female respondents had varying views about whether women are discriminated against at VMI. Many women expressed pride in VMI and the treatment of women by male cadets and a desire not to be given any preferential treatment simply because they are women.
>
> Sexual assault is prevalent at VMI yet it is inadequately addressed by the Institute. In the survey, 14 percent of female cadets reported being sexually assaulted at VMI, while 63 percent said that a fellow cadet had told them that he or she was a victim of sexual assault while a VMI cadet. Many female cadets reported a consistent fear of assault or harassment by their fellow male cadets. These fears are exacerbated by some procedures at VMI, including the inability to lock their doors. Many female cadets also feel that assault complaints are not or will not be taken seriously by the VMI administration or that a cadet will suffer retaliatory consequences for reporting them. . . . Although VMI conducts extensive sexual assault training on post, female cadets report that male cadets treat it as a joke and an opportunity for misogynistic humor, without consequences. Cadets perceive that the VMI-provided training is often not respected or taken seriously.[209]

The report also found problems with homophobia and bias toward the LGBTQ community on campus.[210] Why do you think the culture of VMI has been so resistant to change?

2. **Single-Sex Education at the Elementary and Secondary Level.** While the number of women's colleges has declined from just under 300 in 1960 to fewer than 40 today, single-sex education at the secondary level has increased significantly since the Supreme Court decided United States v. Virginia. In 1995, the nation had only two single-sex public high schools; by 2014-2015, there were more than 280 single-gender public schools.[211] The number of single-sex classrooms has also

---

209. Marching Toward Inclusive Excellence: An Equity Audit and Investigation of the Virginia Military Institute, Final Report of the Barnes & Thornburg LLP Special Investigation Team 5-6 (June 1, 2021). One of the articles that prompted the audit was Ian Shapira, At VMI, Black Cadets Endure Lynching Threats, Klan Memories and Confederacy Veneration, Wash. Post, Oct. 17, 2020.

210. Marching Toward Inclusive Excellence, supra note 209, at 132-33.

211. Snapshot: Single-Gender Education, Education Week, Nov. 15, 2017.

grown from about a dozen in 2002 to more than 500 in forty states in 2011.[212] Newer data are not readily available because the single-sex-education advocacy group that had been tallying it—to show that the idea was gaining interest—removed their list from the website to avoid triggering the interest of women's rights groups, which, as discussed below, have been challenging such programs as unlawfully discriminatory.[213]

Federal statutory law has long been a site of struggle over the extent to which single-sex education should be allowed. Title IX generally prohibits the exclusion of any person from federally funded education programs on the basis of sex, but contains several statutory exemptions that permit certain types of single-sex programs. For example, the statute exempts the admissions policies of private undergraduate institutions, public elementary and secondary schools, and the U.S. military academies.[214] In addition, the statute exempts public undergraduate institutions that have traditionally and continually admitted students of only one sex.[215] (This exemption protected VMI from a Title IX challenge, necessitating use of the Equal Protection Clause to challenge the exclusion of women.) Other exemptions exist for fraternities and sororities, Boys' and Girls' State programs, Boy Scouts and Girl Scouts, father-son and mother-daughter activities, and beauty pageants. What policies underlie these compromises? Can they be squared with a coherent theory of sex equality?

The Title IX regulations that took effect in 1975 set strict limits on single-sex classes within co-ed institutions, with narrow exceptions for physical education, sex education, and choral groupings based on vocal range, in addition to a more general provision allowing affirmative action to address the effects of limited opportunities for one sex.[216] By the late 1990s, however, interest in expanding access to single-sex education sparked a movement to change the regulations.

In 2001, Congress passed the No Child Left Behind Act, which included a clause stating that "funds made available to local educational agencies . . . shall be used for innovative assistance programs, which may include . . . programs to provide same-gender schools and classrooms (consistent with applicable law)."[217] In 2006, the U.S. Department of Education amended its regulations under Title IX to allow elementary and secondary non-vocational schools that receive federal funding to be single-sex as long as there is a "substantially equal" single-sex or coeducational school for students of the excluded sex. The revised regulations also permit single-sex classes or extracurricular activities when they are completely voluntary and substantially related to improving students' educational achievement, as long as a "substantially equal"

---

212. Elizabeth Weil, Teaching to the Testosterone, N.Y. Times Mag., Mar. 3, 2008, at 39, 40; Jennifer Medina, Schools Try Separating Boys from Girls, N.Y. Times, Mar. 10, 2009, at A24; Tamar Lewin, Single-Sex Education Is Assailed in Report, N.Y. Times, Sept. 22, 2011, at A19.

213. Sue Klein et al., Feminist Majority Found., Tracking Deliberate Sex Segregation in U.S. K-12 Public Schools (2018).

214. 20 U.S.C. § 1681(a)(1) (2018).

215. 20 U.S.C. § 1681(a)(5) (2018).

216. 34 C.F.R. § 106.34(a) (2022).

217. Pub. L. No. 107-110, 115 Stat. 1425 (2002).

opportunity is available to the excluded sex. Funding recipients must conduct at least biennial evaluations to ensure that single-sex opportunities are "based on genuine justifications and do not rely on overly broad generalizations about the different talents, capacities, or preferences of either sex to ensure they remain constitutional."[218]

What does it mean for single-sex classes to be "completely voluntary"?[219] How different can single-sex and co-ed classes be and still remain "substantially equal"? How will school districts determine whether their reasons for separating girls and boys are based on "genuine justifications" or "overly broad generalizations"?

Some of the impetus for the revival of girls-only educational opportunities in the 1990s came from research by the American Association of University Women (AAUW) identifying significant differences between boys and girls as they progress through educational institutions, with girls experiencing a much steeper decline than boys in self-image and in career aspirations, especially those related to math and science:

> Girls, aged eight and nine, are confident, assertive, and feel authoritative about themselves. They emerge from adolescence with a poor self-image, constrained views of their future and their place in society, and much less confidence about themselves and their abilities. Sixty percent of elementary school girls say they are "happy the way I am," a core measure of personal self-esteem. More boys, 67 percent of those surveyed, also strongly agreed with the statement. Over the next eight years, girls' self-esteem falls 31 percentage points, with only 29 percent of high school girls saying they are happy with themselves. Almost half of the high school boys (46 percent) retain their high self-esteem. By high school, this gender gap increases from 7 points to 17 points.[220]

The AAUW findings have been challenged by other experts who claim that the conclusion that schools shortchange girls is based on "soft and slippery issues, like the 'silencing' of girls in the classroom," rather than on educational achievement tests, college entrance and graduation rates, and earnings. Self-esteem measures may in part reflect boys' self-deception, bravado, and immaturity.[221] Moreover, on many measures, female students do better. They receive higher grades and more honors in every field but science and sports. On standardized tests, although boys do better on average in mathematics, science, and geopolitics, the margins are

---

218. 34 C.F.R. § 106.34(b)(4) (2022); see also U.S. Dep't of Educ. Office for Civil Rights, Questions and Answers Regarding OCR's Interpretation of Title IX and Single Sex Scholarships, Clubs, and Other Programs, Jan. 17, 2021, at 7.

219. See Doe v. Wood Cnty Bd. of Educ., 888 F. Supp. 2d 771 (S.D. W.Va. 2012) (holding that, to be "completely voluntary," single-sex offerings must require students to affirmatively choose them, and not merely provide an opt-out option).

220. Am. Ass'n of Univ. Women, Survey, Shortchanging Girls, Shortchanging America 4 (1991).

221. Judith Kleinfeld, The Myth That Schools Shortchange Girls: Social Science in the Service of Deception (Women's Freedom Network 1998); Kingsley R. Browne, Sex and Temperament in Modern Society: A Darwinian View of the Glass Ceiling and the Gender Gap, 37 Ariz. L. Rev. 971, 1032 (1995).

small; girls do better in reading comprehension and surpass boys in writing skills by a significant amount. Boys are also more likely to be at the bottom of their class, to be assigned to special education programs, to repeat a grade, to be diagnosed with a learning disability, and to create a discipline problem. They also participate less in extracurricular activities (other than athletics) and attend college at lower rates than their female counterparts, suggesting a "new gender gap."[222]

Indeed, concern about the negative effects of such educational disparities on boys has driven much of the recent advocacy in favor of single-sex education. One of the most prominent proponents of single-sex education at the elementary and secondary level, Leonard Sax, promotes a biological explanation for what he argues are gender differences in boys' and girls' learning styles.[223] Sax argues that boys and girls should be educated separately, without distraction from the other sex, by teachers trained to use different instructional methods for girls and boys, such as using a louder voice when teaching boys.[224] Sax's research is controversial, and other neuroscientists have taken issue with his findings and conclusions.[225]

Also open to dispute is whether single-sex education is likely to address the disadvantages confronting either girls or boys. Evidence on this point is mixed. A meta-analysis of controlled studies found no educational benefits of single-sex schooling compared to co-ed schooling.[226] Authors of another meta-analysis criticized the "pseudoscience" of single-sex education, arguing that it "is deeply misguided, and often justified by weak, cherry-picked, or misconstrued scientific claims rather than by valid scientific evidence." According to their analysis of existing studies, "[t]here is no well-designed research showing that single-sex education improves students' academic performance, but there is evidence that sex segregation increases stereotyping and legitimizes institutional sexism."[227] However, other evidence, including studies of Catholic schools, indicates that single-sex settings may benefit some students, particularly those from poor and minority communities.[228] A literature review by the Department of Education and American Institute

---

222. See, e.g., Kim Parker, Pew Rsch. Ctr., What's Behind the Growing Gap Between Men and Women in College Completion? (Nov. 8, 2021); Douglas Belkin, A Generation of American Men Give Up on College: 'I Just Feel Lost,' Wall St. J., Sept. 5, 2021.

223. Leonard Sax, Why Gender Matters: What Parents and Teachers Need to Know About the Emerging Science of Sex Differences (2006). For reviews of the evidence, see Rebecca A. Kiselewich, In Defense of the 2006 Title IX Regulations for Single-Sex Public Education: How Separate Can Be Equal, 49 B.C. L. Rev. 217, 229-30 (2008); Sara Mead, The Evidence Suggests Otherwise: The Truth About Boys and Girls (2006).

224. Leonard Sax, Six Degrees of Separation: What Teachers Need to Know About the Emerging Science of Sex Differences, 84 Educ. Horizons 190 (2006).

225. See, e.g., Lise Eliot, Single-Sex Education and the Brain, 69 Sex Roles 363 (2013).

226. Erin Pahlke et al., The Effects of Single-Sex Compared with Coeducational Schooling on Students' Performance and Attitudes: A Meta-Analysis, 140 Psych. Bulletin 1042 (2014).

227. Diane F. Halpern et al., The Pseudoscience of Single-Sex Schooling, 333 Science 1706 (2011); see also Rosalind C. Barnett & Caryl Rivers, The Truth About Girls and Boys (2011).

228. See Teresa A. Hughes, The Advantages of Single-Sex Education, 23 Nat'l F. Educ. Admin. & Supervision J. 5 (2006-2007); C. Kirabo Jackson, The Effect of Single-Sex Education

for Research found that 41 percent of existing studies documented advantages, 45 percent found no influence, 8 percent favored co-ed schools, and 6 percent found mixed effects (positive results for one sex but not the other).[229] When single-sex education does produce positive outcomes, it is unclear whether the gains are due to gender segregation or other factors, such as student background, small class size, favorable faculty-student ratio, or special mentoring programs—features that could be replicated in co-ed schools.[230] Legal scholars have varying views on whether the ramping up of single-sex education has been helpful or harmful to gender equality and student learning. David Cohen and Nancy Levit have argued that "seven years into an unconstitutional experiment that is promising a false bill of goods to parents and children and delivering significant damage in the form of stereotypes and sexism," the "arguments against sex segregation in public schools are even stronger than they were before," while Rosemary Salamone argues there is good evidence that single-sex education can be beneficial in some circumstances.[231]

Women's rights groups, including the Women's Rights Project of the American Civil Liberties Union and the National Organization for Women, have opposed the turn toward single-sex education and filed complaints against public school districts that have introduced single-sex classes. An ACLU report documents widespread instances of reliance on stereotyped attitudes and discredited science, including the idea that "boys are better than girls in math because boys' brains receive several daily 'surges' of testosterone, whereas girls can perform well on tests only a few days per month when they experience 'increased estrogen during the menstrual cycle.'"[232] Similarly, the AAUW cautions that "single-sex education without proper attention to civil rights protections can reinforce problematic gender stereotypes, increase discrimination, and restrict the educational opportunities open to both girls and boys. Where separate programs are established for boys and girls, such programs have tended to be distinctly unequal, with fewer resources allocated for girls' programs."[233]

---

on Academic Outcomes and Crime: Fresh Evidence from Low-Performing Schools in Trinidad and Tobago, Nw. Inst. Pol'y & Rsch. (May 2016).

229. Elizabeth Weil, Teaching Boys and Girls Separately, N.Y. Times Mag., Mar. 2, 2008, at 8; see also U.S. Dep't of Educ., Early Implementation of Public Single-Sex Schools: Perceptions and Characteristics (2008).

230. See Rebecca S. Bigler et al., Analysis and Evaluation of the Rationales for Single-Sex Schooling, in 47 Advances in Child Dev. & Behav. 225, 252-53 (Lynn S. Liben & Rebecca S. Bigler eds., 2014) (reviewing research showing benefits of single-sex education and concluding that the studies fail to control for selection effects and other variables unrelated to sex separation).

231. See David S. Cohen & Nancy Levit, 44 Seton Hall L. Rev. 339, 392 (2014); Rosemary Salamone, Rights and Wrongs in the Debate Over Single-Sex Schools, 93 B.U. L. Rev. 971 (2013).

232. ACLU, Preliminary Findings of ACLU "Teach Kids, Not Stereotypes" Campaign 3 (Aug. 20, 2012) (quoting Michael Gurian & Arlette Ballew, The Boys and Girls Learn Differently Action Guide for Teachers 100 (2003)); see also Feminist Majority Foundation, The State of Public School Sex Segregation in the United States (June 26, 2012).

233. AAUW, Position on Single-Sex Education.

In 2014, OCR issued a guidance cautioning school districts against reliance on generalized claims about teaching methods that work for "all boys" or "all girls" to support separate girls' and boys' classes.[234] Since issuing the Guidance, OCR has carefully scrutinized schools' justifications for single-sex classes. In 2016, OCR found that a public elementary school in Idaho violated Title IX by offering single-sex classes without a sufficient basis.[235] The district purportedly was responding to boys' deficits in reading and girls' lower achievement in math by using methods of instruction tailored to each sex. OCR concluded that the district failed to show that separate-sex classes were needed to address the specific needs of its students and failed to justify its decision to separate students by sex in other subjects. In addition, OCR faulted the district for having a better student-teacher ratio in the boys' classes than in either the girls' classes or the co-ed classes.

Case law has not resolved the legality of single-sex education, although some courts have considered arguments that these programs harm students in the context of standing. One federal court dismissed a lawsuit challenging separate-sex classes in a Kentucky school district.[236] Because the school offered voluntary single-sex classes and substantially equal co-ed classes, with no meaningful differences in content or instructional methods, the court ruled that plaintiffs — students who either chose co-ed classes or chose not to opt out of single-sex classes — lacked standing to sue. The court effectively rejected the plaintiffs' argument that single-sex classrooms are inherently unequal and harmful to the educational environment. The Fifth Circuit reached a different result on standing, based on allegations that the co-ed classes used different tests and taught to a lower level of ability than the single-sex classes.[237] If students have a choice between single-sex and co-ed classes, what type of harms should they have to prove in order to have standing to sue?

What role, if any, do you believe sex segregation should play in public education? Is it possible to devise a substantive equality approach to improve educational outcomes for girls and women, or for boys and men, that does not classify by sex?

3. **Race and Single-Sex Schooling.**   The most significant disparities in educational achievement are not based on gender, but on race, ethnicity, and income levels.[238] In the 1980s and 1990s, the rise in single-sex secondary schools was concentrated in areas with high populations of African-American students. During this period, schools for boys in inner-city neighborhoods were founded, and a Young Women's Leadership School in East Harlem was launched. Other urban centers later followed suit, including the District of Columbia, which established the Ron Brown College Preparatory High School for boys in 2016, a single-sex public high

---

234. U.S. Dep't of Educ., OCR, Questions and Answers on Title IX and Single-Sex Elementary and Secondary Classes and Extracurricular Activities (Dec. 1, 2014), http://www2.ed.gov/about/offices/list/ocr/docs/faqs-title-ix-single-sex-201412.pdf.

235. U.S. Dep't of Educ., OCR, Letter re Middleton School District 134 (Nov. 14, 2016), https://www2.ed.gov/about/offices/list/ocr/docs/investigations/more/10131040-a.pdf.

236. A.N.A. v. Breckinridge Cnty. Bd. of Educ., 833 F. Supp. 2d 673 (W. D. Ky. 2011).

237. Doe v. Vermilion Parish Sch. Bd., 421 Fed. Appx. 366 (5th Cir. 2011).

238. Tamar Lewin, Girls' Gains Have Not Cost Boys, Report Says, N.Y. Times, May 20, 2008, at A17.

school serving almost exclusively African-American boys (who are called "young Kings").[239] Public, single-gender high schools serve disproportionately Black and Latinx students; only 10 percent of students attending public single-sex high schools nationwide are white, compared to 50 percent in public schools overall.[240] Single-sex schools also serve large numbers of students in poverty; students attending public single-sex high schools are 1.5 times more likely to qualify for subsidized meals.[241] Supporters of single-sex schools claim that they increase positive role models, raise self-esteem, and nurture academic values. Some commentators hail all-female academies in particular for achieving high levels of college enrollments and low dropout rates.[242] But the main focus has been on all-male academies to address the challenges and inequities facing boys of color, especially African-American boys.

Opinion within the African-American community is mixed, with groups such as the NAACP opposing sex-segregated schools, and others welcoming the extra help they might bring to at-risk children who suffer from disproportionate homicide and school dropout rates, as well as poor grades and test performance. Verna Williams is critical of this perspective, arguing that such schools construct Black boys as unruly and hypersexualized, and that the case for sex separation in predominantly minority communities gained traction because of cultural fears of Black males.[243] In her view, the "crisis" discourse behind all-male urban academies assumes that Black males have too much feminization in their lives, having been raised by Black women, and need instruction, preferably by men, in socially acceptable forms of masculinity. In contrast, the discourse for all-female education in these communities focuses on Black female sexuality and the threat of teen pregnancy. More promising, but resource-intensive, educational reforms are shoved aside, as single-sex education is touted as a panacea for neutralizing disruptive racialized sexualities.[244] How persuasive are these criticisms, and should they affect the legality of single-sex education?

In an early challenge to an all-male urban academy, Garrett v. Board of Education of School District of Detroit, plaintiffs (represented by the ACLU and the NOW Legal Defense and Education Fund) succeeded in challenging the exclusion of girls from a newly established academy for Black male students in Detroit.[245] A federal district court held that excluding girls served no substantial interest and

---

239. Greg Toppo, All-Boys' High School Completes First Year; Boasts Wait List for Fall, USA Today, July 5, 2017.

240. Snapshot, supra note 211.

241. Id.

242. Nat'l Ass'n for Single Sex Pub. Educ., Advantages for Girls and Advantages for Boys (2006); Rosemary Salomone, Same, Different, Equal: Rethinking Single Sex Education (2003).

243. Verna L. Williams, Reform or Retrenchment? Single-Sex Education and the Construction of Race and Gender, 2004 Wisc. L. Rev. 15.

244. Id.; see also Freeden Blume Oeur, Black Boys Apart: Racial Uplift and Respectability in All-Male Public Schools (2019); Keisha Lindsay, In a Classroom of Their Own: The Intersection of Race and Feminist Politics in All-Black Male Schools (2018).

245. 775 F. Supp. 1004 (E.D. Mich. 1991).

violated both the federal and the state constitutions, as well as Title IX.[246] Critics of such academies argue that

> [t]he all-male black school is paternalistic. It stigmatizes boys, ignores girls, and brazenly discounts women as capable teachers of boys. In the minds of all-male black school advocates, only males can teach boys to become men.[247]

Does this analysis adequately contend with the inequities experienced by the boys who might have benefited from an all-male academy? Data at the time showed that the homicide rate for Black males between the ages of 18 and 24 in Wayne County, Michigan, was fourteen times the national rate, the dropout rate for males was twice that of females, boys were suspended three times as often as girls, and boys' scores on standardized tests were consistently lower.[248] Might such academies also be defended as a space for Black boys to escape racially oppressive practices and environments in mostly white schools—such as dress codes that penalize certain hairstyles like dreadlocks?[249] Critics of all-male academies point to the lack of evidence that boys' academic performance improves when separated from girls and to data showing that the achievement gap between Black girls and white girls often exceeds that between Black boys and white boys.[250] Recent scholarship on the phenomenon of "pushout" calls for greater attention to the distinctive blend of sexism and racism that derails the educational paths of African-American girls.[251] How should the law resolve these competing considerations? Is there any way to resolve these issues without getting mired in a debate over who is more oppressed by racism and sexism?

Explicitly all-Black academies would be difficult to sustain under existing equal protection doctrine, which requires showing that these schools are a narrowly tailored means to address specific prior intentional discrimination or to achieve a compelling state purpose.[252] General societal discrimination will not suffice. As a practical matter, however, given the small number of white residents in many inner-city school districts, de facto racial segregation is common.

---

246. Although Title IX exempts the admissions policies of elementary and secondary schools, the court interpreted this exemption as intended to apply to schools already in existence, and not to authorize newly created schools, especially where no equal alternative was provided to members of the excluded sex. Id. at 1009.

247. Michael Meyers, The Non-Viability of Single-Race, Single-Sex Schools, 21 N.Y.U. Rev. L. & Soc. Change 663, 665-66 (1994-1995).

248. Note, Inner-City Single-Sex Schools: Educational Reform or Invidious Discrimination?, 105 Harv. L. Rev. 1741, 1743-44 (1992).

249. Cf. Arnold v. Barbers Hill Indep. Sch. Dist., 479 F. Supp.3d 511 (S.D. Tex. 2020).

250. Lindsay, supra note 244, at 6, 13; see also Laura Lane-Steele, My Brother's Keeper. My Sister's Neglector: A Critique and Explanation of Single-Sex Initiatives for Black Boys, 39 Colum. J. Gender & L. 60 (2020).

251. See Monique W. Morris, Push-Out: The Criminalization of Black Girls in Schools (2018).

252. City of Richmond v. J.A. Croson Co., 488 U.S. 469 (1989).

4. **LGBTQ+ Students.**   Single-sex education classifies students based on a binary system of sex. But what if a student's assigned sex does not match the student's gender identity? A number of women's colleges have considered this question in recent years and have decided to permit transwomen to enroll, but not without controversy. Some critics of such a policy have argued that admitting persons who were assigned a male sex at birth and lived part of their lives as male changes the culture of an all-women's college.[253] All-male colleges, perhaps in part due to their very small numbers, have not grappled with this issue so publicly. The issue of how to classify transgender students also arises in assigning students to single-sex classes. Should transgender students be assigned to single-sex education programs based on their assigned sex at birth or according to gender identity? What about students who identify as neither male nor female? Some students identify as non-binary, rejecting any gender designation. Others may exhibit gender more fluidly or fluctuate between male and female identification. Where do non-binary and gender-fluid students fit into sex-segregated education? Should they be incorporated into a system of single-sex education or prompt its rejection?

Critics of single-sex education are also concerned about the environment for gay, lesbian, and bisexual students. To the extent that the rationale for separation by sex is based on a concern about sexuality and distraction caused by students of the "opposite" sex, as Justice Powell's opinion in *MUW* suggests, does single-sex education erase non-heterosexual identities? What implications does that have for the climate for lesbian, gay, and bisexual students? Critics of single-sex education warn that boys' schools and all-male classes, in particular, foster "hyper masculine environments" that are unsafe for gay students.[254]

Should any of these considerations affect the legality of single-sex education, and if so, how? How should a substantive equality model, focused on remedying women's historic and continuing disadvantages in educational opportunity, respond to these concerns?

PUTTING THEORY INTO PRACTICE

2-25.   How would you advise a private women's college that has historically admitted only cisgender women on whether to update its admissions policies? Should the college admit transgender women? What about non-binary students? Should the college open its doors to cisgender men who want to attend a "historically women's college," similar to the way historically Black colleges and universities have opened their doors to students of all races? Is it possible for a women's college to shift to gender-inclusive admissions and still serve the mission of a women's college to counter the marginalization of women in society?

---

253. See Anna North, Can Transgender Students Go to Women's Colleges? Across the Country, the Answer Is Evolving, Vox (Sept. 22, 2017) (citing views of some alumnae of women's colleges).

254. Kathy Sher & Galen Sherwin, MS 10 (Summer 2017) (quoting Pedro Noguera, a professor of education at UCLA).

2-26. A female women's studies professor at a co-educational public college does not permit men to enroll in her feminist ethics course, arguing that, in her experience, male students inhibit the participation of women. As an alternative for male students, she offers one-on-one tutorials, which about two dozen men have taken since she began teaching in 1966. She is sued by a male student under Title IX, and under the Fourteenth Amendment's Equal Protection Clause. Who should win?

2-27. Even when formally open to all students, women's studies departments have come under fire from men's groups claiming that such programs, and other women-centered initiatives such as women's centers and women's empowerment programs, discriminate against men in violation of Title IX. Under the Trump administration, the Office for Civil Rights opened investigations of several universities based on complaints that such programs incorporate preferences toward women and prioritize women's interests.[255] What room does the Court's decision in U.S. v. Virginia leave for university programs specifically designed to advance women's interests?

2-28. A 2013 study showed that the overall climate for LGBTQ students across the country had improved, but that 55 percent of LGBTQ students still reported feeling unsafe because of their sexual orientation.[256] In 2016, Atlanta established Pride School Atlanta, a private K-12 school designed specifically for LGBTQ students, although it was open to any student who felt unsafe or unsatisfied with their prior school. The school shut its doors in 2018 after only two years due to dwindling enrollment. In light of recent ramped-up attacks on transgender youth and the LGBTQ+ community, should this model be revisited?

2-29. Title IX's regulations prohibit the exclusion of any student from an education program based on pregnancy but permit separate schools for pregnant students if they are completely voluntary and the instructional component is comparable to the regular school. Pregnant students often face distinctive educational challenges and are at a high risk of dropping out of school. However, separate schools can stigmatize pregnant students, emphasize parenting at the expense of academics, and have often lacked the rigor of alternative programs. New York City ended its separate P-Schools for pregnant students in 2007, in response to complaints about the quality of the academic program. But pregnant and parenting students still face obstacles and bias in regular schools.[257] Are separate schools for pregnant students justified as a matter of substantive equality? Would another approach serve their interests better?

2-30. In the early 1970s, college enrollments in the United States were roughly 43 percent female and 57 percent male. Today, these figures are reversed—58 percent of undergraduates are female. The widening gender gap is especially acute in

---

255. See Maria Danilova, Education Department Probes Women's Studies Programs, Detroit News, Nov. 18, 2018.

256. Gay, Lesbian & Straight Education Network, 2013 National School Climate Survey, http://www.glsen.org/article/2013-national-school-climate-survey.

257. See Kendra Fershee, Hollow Promises for Pregnant Students: How the Regulations Governing Title IX Fail to Prevent Pregnancy Discrimination in School, 43 Ind. L. J. 79 (2009).

lower income categories.[258] One admissions officer explained the pressures: "gender balance matters in ways both large and small on a residential college campus. Once you become decidedly female in enrollment, fewer males, and, as it turns out, fewer females find your campus attractive."[259] Should it be permissible, under equal protection and Title IX, for a public university whose gender composition matches the national average to enact an affirmative plan that gives a plus factor to male applicants in order to boost male undergraduate enrollment?

2-31. A public law school has never matriculated a 1L class with more than 41 percent women, even though the school receives roughly equal numbers of male and female applicants and makes admissions offers to an equal percentage of men and women. In response, the school decides to increase its financial and merit aid awards to female students in a targeted effort to recruit a class that is roughly 50 percent female. Is this constitutional after U.S. v. Virginia? Does it violate Title IX?[260] Is it justified as a matter of substantive equality?

3. Sex Differentiation Within Mixed-Gender Educational Settings

Issues of sex separation and differentiation also arise in mixed-gender educational settings, especially with respect to restrooms and locker rooms. Transgender students have challenged school policies forbidding them from using sex-segregated restrooms and locker rooms that correspond to their gender identity. These cases have arisen when schools have required transgender students to use either the facilities corresponding to their sex assigned at birth or specially designated gender-neutral facilities. Transgender students claim that such policies stigmatize them; "out" them; and cause inconvenience, lost class time (when gender-inclusive facilities are less available), and even health risks (from curtailing restroom usage). Relying on Title IX and the Equal Protection Clause, transgender students have argued that the denial of access to the restroom aligned with their gender identity constitutes discrimination based on sex. Despite some early losses,[261] more recent cases have concluded that requiring transgender students to use the facilities based on their sex assigned at birth constitutes sex discrimination under both Title IX and equal protection.[262] Schools with inclusive restroom policies, permitting transgender students to use the restroom that aligns with their gender identity, have also been sued under Title IX and the Constitution. Parents of cisgender girls have argued that the presence of transgender girls (disparagingly

---

258. Nat'l Ctr. for Educ. Stat., Undergraduate Enrollment (May 2022). For further statistics, see note 1 in Section A.

259. Jennifer Delahunty Britz, To All the Girls I've Rejected, N.Y. Times, Mar. 23, 2006, at A25.

260. See Dep't of Educ., Questions and Answers Regarding OCR's Interpretation of Title IX and Single Sex Scholarships, Clubs, and Other Programs 3-4 (Jan. 14, 2021) (Question 4).

261. See Johnston v. Univ. of Pittsburgh, 97 F. Supp. 3d 657 (W.D. Pa. 2015).

262. See, e.g., Grimm v. Gloucester Cty. Sch. Bd., 972 F.3d 586 (4th Cir. 2020) (joining "a growing consensus of courts in holding" that excluding transgender students from school

referred to by the plaintiffs as "biological males") in the girls' restroom, locker room, and showers subjects their daughters to sexual harassment, creates a hostile environment, and invades their privacy. To date, courts have rejected these arguments, finding that gender-inclusive restroom policies do not discriminate aganst or otherwise invade the rights of cisgender girls.[263]

The Department of Education's position on how Title IX applies to single-sex bathrooms has whip-sawed in recent years. In 2016, the Obama administration issued a guidance explaining that Title IX's ban on sex discrimination encompasses discrimination against transgender students, and that Title IX requires schools with sex-segregated restrooms and locker rooms to allow transgender students to use facilities consistent with their gender identity.[264] The Trump administration rescinded the Obama guidance.[265] Soon after taking office, President Biden issued an Executive Order announcing a federal policy of prohibiting gender identity discrimination and directing federal agencies to review and rescind any policies inconsistent with this commitment.[266] In June 2021, the Department of Education issued a Notice of Interpretation officially reversing the Trump administration policy on transgender students, explaining that Title IX's ban on sex discrimination encompasses discrimination based on transgender status and sexual orientation for the same reasons articulated by the Supreme Court in Bostock v. Clayton County. The Department further explained that it need not take a position on the meaning of "sex" under Title IX, since even a traditional understanding of sex, based on "reproductive biology," would lead to the same result.[267] Denying a transgender student the ability to use the facility that corresponds to their gender identity treats that student differently than other students with the same gender identity who were assigned a different sex at birth. In June 2022, the Department announced a Notice of Proposed Rulemaking to codify this understanding in the Title IX regulations.[268] Is the Department's current understanding compatible with the continued existence of sex-separate facilities in schools? Would a shift to gender neutrality in school facilities be preferable to even an expansive approach to sex separation in such spaces?

---

restrooms that align with their gender identity violates Title IX and equal protection); Whitaker v. Kenosha Unified Sch. Dist. No. 1 Bd. of Educ., 858 F.3d 1034 (7th Cir. 2017); A.C. v. Metro. Sch. Dist. of Martinsville, 2022 U.S. Dist. LEXIS 78068 (S.D. Ind. 2022).

263. See Parents for Privacy v. Barr, 949 F.3d 1210 (9th Cir. 2021); Doe v. Boyertown Area Sch. Dist., 897 F.3d 518 (3d Cir. 2018).

264. U.S. Dep't of Justice, Civ. Rts. Div., and U.S. Dep't of Educ., Office for Civil Rights, Dear Colleague Letter (May 13, 2016), https://www2.ed.gov/about/offices/list/ocr/letters/colleague-201605-title-ix-transgender.pdf.

265. U.S. Dep't of Justice, Civ. Rts. Div., and U.S. Dep't of Educ., Office for Civil Rights, Dear Colleague Letter (Feb. 22, 2017), https://www.justice.gov/opa/press-release/file/941551/download.

266. Exec. Order 13988, 86 Fed.Reg. 7023 (Jan. 20, 2021).

267. Id. at 4.

268. Dep't of Educ., Federal Register Notice of Proposed Rulemaking: Title IX of the Education Amendments of 1972 (June 23, 2022).

Sex-separate restroom and locker room policies are not the only way sex differentiation is enforced in school settings. Consider the following materials.

Joanna L. Grossman & Grant Hayden

The Thin Pink Line: Policing Gender at Every Corner

Justia's Verdict (May 24, 2016)

A recent editorial in the *Tallahassee Democrat* reported on, and praised, the students at Leon High School, who elected two women to serve as prom king and queen. The two women had dated for three years and were viewed by their peers perhaps as the most popular couple. The surprising part of this story was that after the story reached over 200,000 people on Facebook, many of the comments were supportive and celebratory, or expressed the simple idea that this was no big deal.

But this story is the exception, as we see uproars across the country to people, rules, and events that challenge conventional gender norms. When students at a California high school tried to elect a lesbian couple as prom king and queen, school officials issued a royal edict that for all-important prom purposes, qualification for "king" or "queen" is defined by sex at birth. Meanwhile, across the country in Harrisburg, Pennsylvania, a girl who showed up in a tuxedo was turned away at the prom door for violating the established dress code that says "girls must wear formal dresses." And in nearby East Haddam, Connecticut, boys and girls walk in different lines at commencement, with boys dressed in blue, and girls in virginal white carrying flowers.

And if all this seems trivial—rules that affect people on only one night in high school—recall the sweeping (and unconstitutional) law passed by North Carolina recently, requiring that transgender individuals only use public bathrooms that align with their birth sex and wiping out the state's protections against employment discrimination simply to ensure that no LBGT person ever benefited from them. Or remember that the state refused to comply with a federal order stating that the bathroom portion of the bill violates Title IX and must be repealed. Or take notice of the efforts of Oklahoma legislators—at the same time they were passing an unconstitutional bill to ban *all* abortions (vetoed by their governor)—to pass a law that would grant students a right to avoid sharing a bathroom with a transgender student in the name of religious freedom.

Why all the hubbub? People simply cannot care this much about what people wear to a high school dance, whether the prom king is a boy (particularly when the students themselves don't care), or whether girls are both differentiated and robed in pristine white at a high school graduation.

Now people might care about sharing bathrooms with transgender people, but only because they are misinformed, acting out of a misplaced fear of predation, or bigoted. The transgender bathroom problem has been framed in some circles as one as one of safety—protecting girls and women from bathroom predators. But there is no empirical support for this fear. The number of transgender people is very low—the best estimate, by the Williams Institute, is that a mere 0.3 percent of the population is transgender. But, more importantly, as Mark Joseph Stern recently pointed out on Slate, there is "overwhelming evidence and professional consensus" that this fear is entirely baseless. (Not to mention that, with or without laws protecting transgender access to bathrooms, predatory men could dress up as women and enter women's rooms. Or, of course, they could just prey on little boys like Jerry Sandusky and Dennis Hastert, both of whom used all-male locker-rooms as their hunting grounds. But nobody is banning men from using communal restrooms).

There must, then, be some reason underlying all these scandals and stories. The real reason, we suggest, is that transgender people present a direct challenge to the existence of a simple division between the sexes. People who were born with one set of sexual organs but identify and present as members of the opposite sex blur the lines between sexes, and make clear there that the relationship between sex and gender is complicated. It's hard to maintain sexual inequality when you can't tell, exactly, what makes someone a boy or a girl, a man or a woman.

And when people are not transgender, but simply refuse to be segregated by sex or to conform to conventional sex norms, society has the same reaction: "make sure we can tell the difference between girls and boys." When the girls in East Haddam wrote an opinion piece in the local paper, it met with scores of angry comments (now deleted) about how their efforts to change the school's discrimination graduation robe policy were frivolous or stupid. But that argument cuts both ways. If it doesn't mean anything, then why don't the boys and girls wear the same graduation robes? Why wouldn't the default be that everyone earning the same degree wears the same genderless attire in the ceremony to honor their achievements?

What [bans on same-sex marriage, dress codes in the workplace, and gender restrictions in schools] have in common is that they are attempts to police the gender line. Maintaining the distinction between men and women wouldn't be important if, for most everything, they weren't treated differently. That is, when equality is the rule, then drawing a distinction really doesn't matter — whether you're on one side of the gender line or the other (or somewhere in between), you're treated the same. At home. At school. At work. At church. At the country club. The distinction matters precisely because equality isn't the rule in many of those places — the gender division reflects a longstanding hierarchy, with men on top. And if we can't tell who's who because people challenge gender conventions — by wearing the wrong color, or marrying someone of the wrong gender, or, even worse, trying to become someone of the other gender, chaos ensues.

This kind of behavior is not unique to sex discrimination. Systemic racial oppression depends, too, on a policing of boundaries. The "one drop" rule is the most notorious example. But a key facet of any system of oppression is the ability to clearly distinguish between classes of people. Any impediments to those distinctions, or suggestions that, even if they do exist, they don't really support the kind of radical distinctions that get drawn in the law or, more generally, society, are dismissed.

This isn't to say that people who are gay, transgender, or graduating from high school aren't being independently targeted for discrimination. They are, and their suffering is real. But they are also pawns in a larger game of gender oppression, one that depends on having clearly drawn battle lines.

Peltier v. Charter Day School, Inc.

37 F. 4th 104 (2022) (en banc)

KEENAN, Senior Circuit Judge:

Charter Day School (CDS), a public charter school in North Carolina, requires female students to wear skirts to school based on the view that girls are "fragile vessels" deserving of "gentle" treatment by boys (the skirts requirement). The plaintiffs argue that this sex-based classification grounded on gender stereotypes violates the Equal Protection Clause of the Fourteenth Amendment, and subjects them to discrimination and denial of the full benefits of their education in violation of Title IX of the Education Amendments of 1972. . . .

I.

CDS, a public charter school in Brunswick County, North Carolina, educates male and female[2] students in kindergarten through the eighth grade. The founder of the school, Baker A. Mitchell, Jr., incorporated defendant Charter Day School, Inc. in 1999. . . . CDS' policies are established by the volunteer members of its Board of Trustees (the Board). Mitchell initially served as the Board's chairman and now serves as its non-voting secretary.

Enrollment at CDS is open to all students who are eligible to attend North Carolina public schools. CDS receives 95% of its funding from federal, state, and local governmental authorities. . . .

Since its inception, CDS, at the direction of Mitchell and the Board, has "emphasize[d] traditional values," including a "traditional curriculum, traditional manners and traditional respect." These stated priorities pervade many areas of the school's practices. For example, CDS teaches a "classical curriculum," utilizing a "direct instruction" method. Overall, as one Board member explained, CDS operates "more like schools were 50 years ago compared to now."

As part of this educational philosophy, CDS has implemented a dress code to "instill discipline and keep order" among students. Among other requirements, all students must wear a unisex polo shirt and closed-toe shoes; "[e]xcessive or radical haircuts and colors" are prohibited; and boys are forbidden from wearing jewelry. Female students are required to wear a "skirt," "jumper," or "skort." In contrast, boys must wear shorts or pants. All students are required to comply with the dress code unless they have physical education class, when they wear unisex physical education uniforms, or an exception is made for a field trip or other special event. A student's failure to comply with the dress code requirements may result in disciplinary action, including notification of the student's parent, removal from class to comply with the dress code, or expulsion, though no student has been expelled for violating the dress code.

In 2015, plaintiff Bonnie Peltier, the mother of a female kindergarten student at CDS, informed Mitchell that she objected to the skirts requirement. Mitchell responded to Peltier in support of the policy, stating:

---

2. Because the plaintiffs challenge the skirts requirement only as discriminatory toward cisgender girls, we do not address the effects of the policy on any other students.

> The Trustees, parents, and other community supporters were determined to preserve chivalry and respect among young women and men in this school of choice. For example, young men were to hold the door open for the young ladies and to carry an umbrella, should it be needed. Ma'am and sir were to be the preferred forms of address. There was felt to be a need to restore, and then preserve, traditional regard for peers.

Mitchell later elaborated that chivalry is "a code of conduct where women are treated, they're regarded as a fragile vessel that men are supposed to take care of and honor." Mitchell further explained that, in implementing the skirts requirement, CDS sought to "treat[] [girls] courteously and more gently than boys.". . .

In support of their summary judgment motion, the plaintiffs submitted evidence of the tangible and intangible harms they suffer based on the skirts requirement. One plaintiff testified that the skirts requirement conveys the school's view that girls "simply weren't worth as much as boys," and that "girls are not in fact equal to boys." Another plaintiff stated that the skirts requirement "sends the message that girls should be less active than boys and that they are more delicate than boys," with the result that boys "feel empowered" and "in a position of power over girls."

The plaintiffs also described the impact of the skirts requirement on their ability to participate in school activities. On one occasion, when a first-grade female student wore shorts to school due to a misunderstanding of the dress code, she was removed from class and was required to spend the day in the school's office. The plaintiffs also explained that they avoid numerous physical activities, including climbing, using the swings, and playing soccer, except for days on which they are permitted to wear their unisex physical education uniforms. The plaintiffs further testified that they cannot participate comfortably in school emergency drills that require students to crawl and kneel on the floor, fearing that boys will tease them or look up their skirts. Both parties presented evidence from expert witnesses regarding the effects that the skirts requirement and gender stereotypes have on female students.

The district court concluded that CDS, in imposing and implementing the skirts requirement, was a state actor for purposes of the Equal Protection claim brought under 42 U.S.C. § 1983. . . . On the merits of the Equal Protection claim, the court held that the skirts requirement violates the Equal Protection Clause. The court therefore granted summary judgment to the plaintiffs on this claim against CDS.

The district court reached a different conclusion regarding the Title IX claim, holding that dress codes categorically are exempt from Title IX's prohibition against gender discrimination. The court reasoned that when the United States Department of Education rescinded a prior regulation governing dress codes, the Department reasonably had concluded that Congress did not intend for such policies to be subject to Title IX. The court thus granted summary judgment to the defendants on the Title IX claim. The district court denied summary judgment without prejudice on the plaintiffs' state law claims and entered partial final judgment on the remainder of the case.

On appeal, a panel of this Court reversed the district court's judgment on both the Equal Protection and the Title IX claims. That decision was vacated by a vote of the full Court, and we now consider this appeal en banc.

II. . . .

A.

Equal Protection Claim

[The Court concludes that the state action requirement is met against CDS because North Carolina has delegated to charter school operators like CDS part of the state's constitutional duty to provide free, universal elementary and secondary education, and designates its charter schools to be public institutions; CDS receives 95 percent of its funding from state; and CDS is subject to extensive state regulation. . . .]

[W]e turn to consider the merits of the plaintiffs' Equal Protection claim involving CDS. . . . We approach sex-based classifications with skepticism because of the dangers enmeshed in such arbitrary sorting of people. As we have explained: "[J]ustifications for gender-based distinctions that are rooted in overbroad generalizations about the different talents, capacities, or preferences of males and females will not suffice. . . . [W]e will reject sex-based classifications that "appear to rest on nothing more than conventional notions about the proper station in society for males and females." In view of this precedent, we reject CDS' argument that the skirts requirement satisfies intermediate scrutiny because the dress code as a whole is intended to "help to instill discipline and keep order." Instead, we must evaluate whether there is an exceedingly persuasive justification for the *sex-based classification being challenged*, namely, the skirts requirement. CDS cannot justify the skirts requirement based on the allegedly "comparable burdens" imposed by other portions of the dress code that are applicable only to male students. A state actor's imposition of gender-based restrictions on one sex is not a defense to that actor's gender-based discrimination against another sex.[13]

We also observe . . . that the agreement of some parents to the sex-based classification of the skirts requirement is irrelevant to our Equal Protection analysis. No parent can nullify the constitutional rights of other parents' children.

Applying the demanding lens of intermediate scrutiny, we conclude that the skirts requirement is not supported by any important governmental objective and, thus, falls woefully short of satisfying this constitutional test. CDS does not attempt to disguise the true, and improper, rationale behind its differential treatment of girls, which plainly does not serve an important governmental interest. In his initial response to a parent's objection to the requirement, Baker Mitchell, the founder

---

13. To the extent that other courts have endorsed a "comparable burdens" test for sex-specific dress codes, we respectfully disagree with that view. See Hayden v. Greensburg Comm. Sch. Corp., 743 F.3d 569, 577-82 (7th Cir. 2014) (in dicta, collecting cases and discussing principles of the comparable burdens test); cf. Jespersen v. Harrah's Operating Co., 444 F.3d 1104, 1109-10 (9th Cir. 2006) (en banc) (employing such a test in the Title VII context without considering the Equal Protection Clause). These cases rely heavily on precedent from the 1970s affirming the validity of dress codes based on "traditional" notions of appropriate gender norms. As explained above, any sex-specific dress or grooming policy, like any other sex-based classification, must be substantially related to an important governmental objective. *Virginia*, 518 U.S. at 533, 116 S.Ct. 2264. Thus, applying the holding in *Virginia*, we do not compare the relative "burdens" that CDS' dress code places on its female and male students.

of CDS, explained that the skirts requirement embodies "traditional values." According to Mitchell, the requirement for girls to wear skirts was part of CDS' effort "to preserve chivalry and respect among young women and men," which also included requiring boys "to hold the door open for the young ladies and to carry an umbrella" to keep rain from falling on the girls. Mitchell later elaborated that chivalry is "a code of conduct where women are . . . regarded as a fragile vessel that men are supposed to take care of and honor." Mitchell explained that in implementing the skirts requirement, CDS sought to "treat [girls] courteously and more gently than boys." CDS' Board members agreed with these stated objectives, including CDS' goal of fostering "traditional roles" for boys and girls.

It is difficult to imagine a clearer example of a rationale based on impermissible gender stereotypes. On their face, the justifications proffered by CDS "rest on nothing more than conventional notions about the proper station in society for males and females." . . . Thus, in the absence of any important governmental objective supporting CDS' skirts requirement, we hold that the skirts requirement fails intermediate scrutiny and facially violates the Equal Protection Clause.

In reaching this conclusion, we observe that nothing in the Equal Protection Clause prevents public schools from teaching universal values of respect and kindness. But those values are never advanced by the discriminatory treatment of girls in a public school. Here, the skirts requirement blatantly perpetuates harmful gender stereotypes as part of the public education provided to North Carolina's young residents. CDS has imposed the skirts requirement with the express purpose of telegraphing to children that girls are "fragile," require protection by boys, and warrant different treatment than male students, stereotypes with potentially devastating consequences for young girls. If CDS wishes to continue engaging in this discriminatory practice, CDS must do so as a private school without the sanction of the state or this Court.

B.

Title IX Claim

We next consider the plaintiffs' cross-appeal of the district court's summary judgment award on the Title IX claim in favor of the defendants. . . . Title IX provides that "[n]o person in the United States shall, on the basis of sex, be excluded from participation in, be denied the benefits of, or be subjected to discrimination under any education program or activity receiving Federal financial assistance." The statute enumerates several types of entities and activities that are excepted from this broad prohibition. Among other examples, certain religious organizations are exempted from Title IX's mandate, as are sororities, fraternities, and scouting organizations. Exempted activities also include "separate living facilities for the different sexes," as well as single-sex "beauty pageants" and "father-son" and "mother-daughter" activities when offered to members of both sexes. Notably, dress, appearance, and grooming policies are not included among the listed exceptions to Title IX.

Based on the plain language and structure of the statute, we conclude that Title IX unambiguously encompasses sex-based dress codes promulgated by covered entities. "Title IX is a broadly written general prohibition on discrimination, followed by specific, narrow exceptions to that broad prohibition." Jackson v. Birmingham Bd. of Educ. (2005). In selecting this format, "Congress did not list *any* specific discriminatory practices" and, thus, Congress' failure to prohibit explicitly sex-based dress codes does not suggest that such policies are beyond the reach of the statute.

Instead, we view Congress' decision to include specific exceptions in Title IX as a deliberate choice to "limit[] the statute to the [exceptions] set forth." In doing so, Congress clearly articulated its intent regarding what conduct falls outside the statute's scope. If Congress had intended to exclude sex-based dress codes from the broad reach of Title IX, Congress would have designated such policies along with the other enumerated exceptions. . . .

Because we conclude that the statute unambiguously covers such sex-based dress codes, we do not defer to the Department's rescission of its regulation applicable to such policies. . . . [F]or the plaintiffs to prevail under Title IX, they must show that: (1) they were excluded from participation in an education program or activity, denied the benefits of this education, or otherwise subjected to discrimination because of their sex; and (2) the challenged action caused them harm, which may include "emotional and dignitary harm." In this context, the term "discrimination" "means treating [an] individual worse than others who are similarly situated."

As with their Equal Protection claim, the defendants urge that a "comparable burdens" test should be applied to the Title IX claim, by comparing the burdens inflicted by the dress code on female students as a group compared with male students. We disagree. Title IX protects the rights of "individuals, not groups," and does not ask whether the challenged policy "treat[s] women generally less favorably than . . . men." Bostock v. Clayton Cnty., Ga. (2020). The Supreme Court has emphasized this distinction in the employment context:

> Suppose an employer fires a woman for refusing his sexual advances. It's no defense for the employer to note that, while he treated that individual woman worse than he would have treated a man, he gives preferential treatment to female employees overall. The employer is liable for treating *this* woman worse in part because of her sex. Nor is it a defense for an employer to say it discriminates against both men and women because of sex. [Title VII] works to protect individuals of both sexes from discrimination, and does so equally.

Discriminating against members of both sexes does not eliminate liability, but "doubles it."

The same reasoning applies here. Certain sex-based provisions of CDS' dress code may well violate the rights of both male and female students. However, the question that the district court must answer is not whether girls are treated less favorably than boys under the terms of the dress code. Instead, the court must determine whether the skirts requirement, the only challenged provision in this case, operates to exclude the plaintiffs from participation in their education, to deny them its benefits, or otherwise to discriminate against them based on their sex. For purposes of a claim of discrimination under Title IX, the plaintiffs are treated "worse" than similarly situated male students if the plaintiffs are harmed by the requirement that only girls must wear skirts, when boys may wear shorts or pants. Because the district court has not considered this question, we remand the Title IX claim for the district court to evaluate the merits of that claim in the first instance. . . .

WYNN, Circuit Judge, with whom Judge MOTZ, Judge THACKER, Judge HARRIS, and Senior Judge KEENAN join, concurring. . . .

I fully concur in the well-reasoned majority opinion.

Yet, our good colleague Judge Wilkinson disagrees and pens a separate opinion (the second dissent). But instead of offering concrete legal or factual arguments, the second dissent time travels back to the Middle Ages, dons knightly armor, and throws down the challenge gauntlet, presenting two broad policy arguments for why finding state action here is a bad idea.

First, the second dissent predicts a parade of horribles will follow in the wake of the majority's decision, including "collateral damage" to institutions like historically Black colleges and universities. Second, the second dissent claims that the majority opinion's holding will curtail "student and parental choice" by subjecting charter schools "to the slow strangulation of litigation." Both arguments are profoundly flawed.

The . . . second dissent posits that the majority opinion—an opinion on gender discrimination in charter schools—will effectively "extinguish the place of historically [B]lack colleges and universities (HBCUs) in the educational system." The apparent premise of the second dissent's argument is that HBCUs—and HBCUs alone—are engaging in unconstitutional racial discrimination, making them vulnerable to what the second dissent characterizes as the majority's "throw the baby out with the bath water" approach to righting constitutional wrongs.

But HBCUs are not segregated schools — like other modern higher-educational institutions, they are open to students of all races. Their notable attribute, of course, is that they are *historically* Black; just as other higher-educational institutions are *historically* white (HWCUs). . . .

Stripped of its euphemisms, the second dissent's argument seems to be that subjecting schools like Charter Day to the demands of the Constitution will frustrate parents' imaginary prerogative to send their children to free, state-funded public schools practicing unconstitutional discrimination, thereby "stifling" educational progress. The premise underlying this argument is that state schools must be allowed *to experiment with unconstitutional discrimination* to honor "consumer[]" demand and achieve said "educational progress."

That premise is so plainly wrong it borders on the offensive. Must state-designated public schools like Charter Day be allowed to experiment with blatantly unconstitutional gender discrimination to satisfy "consumer[]" demand? Must public schools be allowed to develop racially segregated institutions in the name of "educational progress"?[7] Must state schools be allowed to develop pilot programs promoting certain handpicked religions if enough parents ask for them?. . .

Under the second dissent's view, parents should have no constitutional remedy to address discrimination at their children's schools if those parents have *the option* of choosing between constitutional and unconstitutional alternatives. ("So what if certain charter schools . . . reside at the more [unconstitutional] side of the spectrum? I'm okay; you're okay."). But if that were true, a protestor unconstitutionally denied the right to assemble in one location has no claim if he could protest somewhere else; a Christian church denied the right to fly its flag in front of city hall has no constitutional redress if it could fly its flag at the courthouse next door; and a firearms enthusiast denied her constitutional right to carry a weapon in one city has no argument if she could exercise her right by moving up the interstate.

But no court has ever held that constitutional "dead zones" like these are permissible so long as enough people like them that way. . . .

Barbara Milano KEENAN, Senior Circuit Judge, with whom Judge THACKER joins, concurring:

The defendants would have us believe that the skirts requirement is merely another school regulation largely endorsed by CDS parents. According to the defendants, because girls at CDS "succeed" in academic and extracurricular activities, the skirts requirement is harmless in its effect on CDS' students.

I write separately to emphasize my strong disagreement with this view, which not only is antediluvian but also answers the wrong question. Left unanswered is the full spectrum of success that female students *might have achieved* if they had not been subjected to the pernicious stereotypes underlying the skirts requirement. It is irrelevant how well these students performed *despite* carrying the burden of unequal treatment. We cannot excuse discrimination because its victims are resilient enough to persist in the face of such unequal treatment. . . .

The record shows that these stereotypes can have dire psychological consequences for girls, including increased incidences of eating disorders, depression, anxiety, low self-esteem, and engagement in risky sexual behaviors.

This expert evidence confirms what we already know through common sense and lived experience, namely, that gender stereotypes are harmful to girls. As female students at CDS themselves explained, through the skirts requirement, CDS conveys its view that girls are not "worth as much as boys," are "not in fact equal to boys," and are "more delicate" than boys, which view results in boys being elevated to a "position of power over girls." What other conclusion can girls draw when they are told as kindergarteners to "sit like princesses" to avoid exposing their underwear, while boys may sit cross-legged? Or that girls cannot play as freely as boys during recess? Or that girls cannot participate comfortably in emergency drills for fear that boys will look up their skirts? When faced with this relentless messaging of inferiority, female students at CDS could only conclude that they must maintain constant vigilance about their physical appearance, and that the comfort of boys is more valued than their own. The negative impact of such gender stereotypes is not limited to girls. Evidence in the record shows that children who believe in such views are more likely to engage in gender-segregated play, which later can affect their communication skills and personal relationships. Most disturbingly, that evidence also shows that boys who hold stereotype-infused beliefs about gender are more likely to be the perpetrators of sexual harassment. Plainly, these outcomes are a far cry from "respect," traditional or otherwise, among and for all students.

Of course, the skirts requirement is merely one component of CDS' imposition of "traditional gender roles" on its young students. According to CDS, its female students are "fragile" and must acquiesce to having boys hold umbrellas over them when it rains. Considering this jaw-dropping assessment of girls' capabilities, we may never know the full scope or all the consequences of CDS' blatant, unapologetic discrimination against its female students. But the skirts requirement, harmless as it may seem to the defendants, requires only a pull of the thread to unravel the lifelong social consequences of gender discrimination. In 2022, there is no conceivable basis for allowing such obstacles to girls' progress in our public schools.

WILKINSON, Circuit Judge, with whom Judges NIEMEYER and AGEE join, dissenting. . . .

The majority misses the whole purpose of the development of charter schools. It has little clue about the problems that led to the formation of the charter school experiment or the function that it serves. Its opinion is all about conformity. It is essentially dismissive of what charter schools might have to contribute, prejudging them as miscreants that must be brought to heel. . . .

Student dress codes in particular are unsettling to those who believe, as plaintiffs do here, that they connote feminine inferiority. The codes are founded upon ideals of "chivalry," a word which to the majority suggests male condescension toward women and the need of women for male protection, which in turn robs women of their dignity and independence. As Justice Brennan said some years ago, such "romantic paternalism" can "put women, not on a pedestal, but in a cage." Frontiero v. Richardson (1973) (plurality). No doubt my concurring friend espouses that perspective and frowns upon this dress code. Fair enough. I understand and respect this view.

But the view is not universal. And the "cage" is one of imprisonment in our own perspective, a reluctance to recognize that across the great span of America, there are views that differ from the judge's own. To a great many people, dress codes represent an ideal of chivalry that is not patronizing to women, but appreciative and respectful of them. Far from being a pejorative term, chivalry is symbolic of the tone that CDS wishes to set. "Chivalry" harkens to the age of knighthood, defined as "[t]he brave, honourable, and courteous character attributed to the ideal knight." *Chivalry*, Oxford English Dictionary (2d ed. 1989). What the knights bestowed upon their ladies fair at the end of a tournament has become the bouquet of roses extended on stage at the close of an opera.

The majority seeks to portray the age of chivalry as a brutal time. But that is hardly the point. CDS uses chivalry in an aspirational sense, not to recreate an earlier time in all of its particulars, but to capture the contemporary connotations of a chivalric order as one in which women are due from the very inception of schooling the greatest measure of respect.

Whether a more chivalric order would in some way enhance mutual respect between the sexes, I hardly know. But one need only look to sexual assaults of women on campus, sexual harassment and belittlement of women in the workplace, sexual degradation of women on the internet, sexual trafficking of young women here and abroad, and spousal abuse of women in the home to know that all is not well. Views legitimately differ on the remedies for this condition. But CDS's chivalric approach should neither be legally banished from the educational system, nor should it be legally imposed.

For CDS, the dress code is an adjunct to an altogether lawful and legitimate view of education that relies upon a "classical curriculum espousing traditional western civilization values." But CDS's traditional perspective has not been respected by those who disagree with it. Instead, those who promulgated a dress code aimed at cultivating "mutual respect" among men and women have been greeted with a boundless determination to litigate their views out of the charter school setting.

That is a shame. It is altogether good that opportunities now exist for women that did not exist in earlier generations. Women today serve as lawyers, doctors, executives, professors and professional athletes, among countless other worthy and admirable professions. . . .

But the new need not banish the old. The present need not invariably rush to discredit the past, lest the future hold our own intolerance to poor account. The advent of new possibilities need not extinguish more traditional gender roles which lend stability to home and family and ultimately to society itself. Indeed, many women embrace and balance both modern and traditional elements in their lives, to the benefit of the worlds of both work and family life. So what if certain charter schools or private schools reside at the more traditional side of the spectrum? I'm okay; you're okay. There is room for all in an educational system worth its salt.

The crucial question is one of student and parental choice. North Carolina has designed a system that allows parents and students to choose among varied options, and charter schools seek to preserve precisely that choice. . . . .

While the parental right of choice is not unlimited, neither is this court's ability to restrict the options otherwise available to parents, either directly or by an expansive definition of state action. . . . Courts cannot allow the Fourteenth Amendment to become a self-contradiction by reading it to "constrain a State's neutral efforts to provide greater educational opportunity" and school choices. . . .

It is said that dress codes are themselves coercive and antithetical to student choice. That misses the point. Preserving variety is the very reason to have a menu. You need not eat, or even like, everything on offer, and others' tastes may well differ from your own. Castigating the chef for including salmon as an option (or a fellow customer for ordering it) makes little sense when you can order steak for yourself. So too here. No one is forced to go to a charter school, and certainly not to CDS. North Carolina offers a wide-ranging menu of educational options. While CDS may not suit the tastes of some, there should be no problem with letting others make that choice. . . .

And what is next? Will litigants seek to eradicate North Carolina's single-sex charter schools? Will some charter schools' recruiting and admissions decisions, undertaken in pursuit of serving underserved and dispossessed populations, be challenged on Equal Protection grounds? What about charter schools offering a progressive culture and curriculum? A state action finding here leaves charter schools of all stripes more vulnerable to attack. Regardless of the constitutional merits of such challenges, the costs of litigation may well accomplish opponents' lamentable goal of rendering such innovative and diverse programs an experiment that died aborning. Parents and students will feel a loss of participation in those very aspects of their lives that mean the most.

[As for the Title IX claim, it] simply "strains credulity" to believe that funding recipients such as CDS "should have known" that Title IX prohibits sex-specific dress codes when the Department of Education — the very agency charged by Congress with implementing and enforcing Title IX regulations in this sphere — did not have that understanding. The Department's published position, both in 1999 when CDS was incorporated and in 2015 when CDS signed its current charter, was that dress codes were not implicated by Title IX. And "liability is determined by[] the legal requirements in place when the grants were made" and "should be informed by the statutory provisions, regulations, and other guidelines provided by the [agency] at that time.". . .

Nobody has been clearly "excluded" from or "denied" anything; CDS offers the same educational programs to both sexes. And not all distinctions are discriminatory. "[T]he term 'discriminate against' refers to distinctions or differences in treatment that injure protected individuals," and "treat[] that individual worse than others who are similarly situated," Bostock v. Clayton Cnty. (2020). Though all agree that this dress code treats girls differently, eminently reasonable minds can and do disagree as to whether it treats them worse. For every parent that seeks to disparage a dress code like this one as harmful or discriminatory, there is another who would seek it out as beneficial. It is not our place to resolve this dispute right now, for whether or not a dress code that draws some sex-based distinctions *is* discriminatory, exclusionary, or benefit-denying, this very difference of opinion shows that it is certainly not *unambiguously* so. . . .

North Carolina has exercised its sovereignty by choosing to make a diverse assortment of school options available to its students, including independent charter schools. . . . To say that the federal government may prescribe student dress codes for the untold thousands of schools in the fifty states is to say that little lies beyond its competence, even where its directives themselves come clothed in ambiguity. . . .

NOTE

The charter school in *Peltier* sought to create a culture of "chivalry" toward girls and women, which reinforced stereotypes of female fragility and delicacy. The majority and concurring judges had little trouble finding the policy, and the skirt requirement in particular, to be discriminatory. Judge Wilkerson, in contrast, defends the school's dress code as an ameliorative measure to address widespread disrespect and degradation of women in society. Is his position an example of a substantive equality approach? Why or why not? Are there other measures likely to prevent or rectify the kind of inequalities and abuses he flags? Should the school instead adopt a code of conduct that requires the respectful treatment of girls? A curriculum that foregrounds women's history and seeks to instill values of respect and equality for girls and women? How far does *Peltier* go in requiring gender neutrality in school rules and policies? Judge Wilkerson argues that the majority's rationale sounds the death knell for single-sex education. Is he right?

Even school dress codes that are not as extreme as that in *Peltier* have been fraught with controversy. Some schools have adopted dress codes that are gender neutral in form but which critics contend incorporate cultural norms that are deeply gendered and biased against girls.[269] For example, policies forbidding students from wearing spaghetti straps, midriff-baring shirts, leggings, spandex, or short skirts necessarily target girls due to cultural norms of dress, and perhaps especially Black girls, whose bodies are more likely to draw administrators' scrutiny and register as sexualized and inappropriate.[270] Many Black girls have stories of being "dress coded" for wearing the exact same clothing that a white girl wore in school without incident.[271] Does the enforcement of such policies reflect and reinforce gender and racial stereotypes?[272] If such a policy was challenged, would *Peltier* support striking it down? Dress codes and appearance standards in employment are discussed in Chapter 1.

PUTTING THEORY INTO PRACTICE

2-32. A high school student who identifies as non-binary and uses they/them/theirs pronouns attends a public school that has only restrooms designated as either for male or female students. The student claims that this denies their gender identity and constitutes discrimination because of sex in violation of Title IX. How should a court decide this claim? Does the student have a right to use a gender-nonspecific restroom? If so, must it be as convenient, available, and non-stigmatizing as restroom access for cisgender students? As a matter of policy, how should the school structure its restrooms to protect this student and the interests of other students?

2-33. As mentioned in Problem 1-56, Harvard University recently rescinded its policy denying leadership opportunities and other forms of recognition to students who joined single-sex clubs or social organizations, such as fraternities and sororities. Sorority women condemned the policy, claiming that Harvard was mostly concerned with the problems attributable to fraternities, such as sexual assault, and had failed to account for the positive impact sororities have on women's college experiences and leadership opportunities. A legal challenge to the policy claimed that it violated Title IX because it could not be enforced without reference to a student's sex (e.g., punishing a man but not a woman seeking to join a men's club) and also because it was associational discrimination based on sex. Harvard

269. See, e.g., Deborah M. Ahrens & Andrew M. Siegel, Of Dress and Redress: Student Dress Restrictions in Constitutional Law and Culture, 54 Harv. C.R.-C.L. L. Rev. 48, 76 (2019); Stephan Wah, "Boys Will Be Boys, and Girls Will Get Raped": How Public School Dress Codes Foster Modern Day Rape Culture, 23 Cardozo J.L. & Gender 245, 261-62 (2016).

270. Sara Goodkind, Inequities Affecting Black Girls in Pittsburgh and Allegheny County 3 (2016).

271. Alyssa Pavlakis & Rachel Roegman, How Dress Codes Criminalize Males and Sexualize Females of Color, fig.1, Phi Delta Kappan (Sept. 24, 2015).

272. Rouhollah Aghasaleh, Oppressive Curriculum: Sexist, Racist, Classist, and Homophobic Practice of Dress Codes in Schooling, 22 J. Afr. Am. Stud. 94 (2018).

rescinded the policy, but do you think the policy could have been defended under Title IX? As a matter of policy?[273]

2-34. A public school adopts a unisex dress code with the goal of setting professional norms of dress for all students and inhibiting clothing that distracts or signals divisive affiliations, such as gangs. The new policy requires all students to wear "business casual" style clothing, consisting of tan khaki pants and a polo shirt of any color. Some girls object, claiming that the approved clothes conform to a typically masculine style and are more constraining of girls' clothing choices. Some Black girls have pointed out that the required clothing reflects an implicitly white standard of dress that is both uncomfortable and unflattering for bodies with curves. Is the policy vulnerable to challenge under Title IX and the Equal Protection Clause?

2-35. A transgender girl who attends the school discussed in Problem 2-36 objects that the "business casual" dress code causes her mental anguish and interferes with her learning. A statement from her medical provider explains that an important part of her gender transition is dressing and crafting her identity as a girl, and that it is important to her psychological and mental state to appear feminine and be recognizable as a girl. Does Title IX or the Equal Protection Clause require the school to make an exception for her? How should the school handle the student's request for an exception as a matter of policy?

2-36. After being forced to admit women, VMI initially applied its longstanding crew cut requirement without any exception for female cadets. Critics argued that mandating crew cuts had different cultural connotations for men and women and served to deter women from matriculating. VMI later changed its grooming standards for female cadets, requiring women to wear short hair (but not a crew cut) in the first year and allowing longer hair (appropriately fastened) in subsequent years. Are the different hair length requirements for male and female cadets justified by substantive equality? Do they violate equal protection principles?

2-37. May a school require boys to have short hair as a condition of playing a sport if female athletes have no hair length requirements?[274] Why or why not?

2-38. Gender pronouns are ubiquitous in and out of school settings. How should educators respond to the risks of misgendering and gender coercion when referring to students by pronouns? The issue may be more complex for very young children. Jessica A. Clarke notes that some preschools in Sweden avoid any reference to a child's gender until children are old enough to decide gender for themselves, calling students "friends" instead of boys and girls, and using the gender-neutral pronoun "hen."[275] Is this a solution that American educators should adopt?

2-39. A public high school requires male students to wear tuxedos and female students to wear drapes (a black velvet V-neck covering commonly worn by girls in formal pictures) when sitting for senior yearbook photographs. A cisgender girl

---

273. See Christine Scherer, Rushing to Get Rid of Greek Life and Social Clubs: The Impact of *Bostock* on Single-Sex College Organizations, 71 Case W. Res. L. Rev. 1165 (2021).

274. See Hayden v. Greensburg Cmty. Sch. Corp., 743 F.3d 569 (7th Cir. 2014).

275. Jessica A. Clarke, They, Them, and Theirs, 132 Harv. L. Rev. 894, 965 (2019).

who prefers more masculine clothing showed up for yearbook photos wearing a tuxedo, in violation of the rule. The photographer took her picture but the school excluded her portrait from the yearbook. Did the school engage in unlawful sex discrimination?[276]

2-40. Reconsider the practice of a school district requiring boys and girls to wear different color gowns at graduation.[277] Are complaints about such a practice too trivial to take seriously, or are they, as Grossman and Hayden contend, part of a "larger game of gender oppression" that are important to stop? Do you feel the same way about a school district rule requiring that a prom king and queen need to be, respectively, a boy and a girl?

4. Athletics

a. School Sports

Some of the issues raised by sex-differentiation and separation present particular difficulties in the context of school athletics. Differences in boys' and girls' experiences with sports begin early and have lasting consequences. Is this a product of biological sex differences? Socially constructed sex differences? Or is the perception of difference here itself a product of, or exaggerated by, sex stereotyping? What does substantive equality require in this setting?

A threshold issue concerns whether school sports teams should be segregated by sex. Separate teams explicitly discriminate on the basis of sex, but many proponents of women's sports believe sex separation is justified because if female athletes had to compete with male athletes for a place on the team, their opportunities would be more limited and less empowering. If there are relevant physical differences between the sexes, it seems fair to let girls compete against girls and boys against boys, as long as they have equal opportunities to participate in sports. Separate girls' and boys' basketball teams, for example, would seem to disadvantage neither sex. For these reasons, the regulations implementing Title IX, which went into effect in 1975, allow schools to offer separate teams for male and female students if team selection is based on competitive skill or if the team is a contact sport.[278] Is the reasoning behind sex-separate teams consistent with the *VMI* case?

Even if separate teams are generally permitted, what happens if, because of student demand, a school offers a particular sport to only one sex? Should a boy be able to join the girls' field hockey team, or a girl join the boys' football team? The Title IX regulations recognize a right for members of the excluded sex to try out for a team offered exclusively to members of the other sex, but only if opportunities for the excluded sex have been limited, and only if the sport is not a contact sport. Contact sports are defined to include "boxing, wrestling, rugby, ice hockey, football, basketball, and other sports the purpose or major activity of

---

276. See Sturgis v. Copiah Cnty. Sch. Dist., 2011 WL 4351355 (S.D. Miss. Sept. 15, 2011).
277. See Problem 1-4 in Chapter 1.
278. 34 C.F.R. § 106.41(b) (2022).

which involves bodily contact."[279] A girl who wants to wrestle or play football does not have a Title IX right to try out for the boys' teams in those sports. The contact sports exception has been severely criticized for reinforcing harmful stereotypes about female fragility.[280] Is the contact sports exemption consistent with the theory of equal protection in the *VMI* case? If not, why does it persist?

In contrast to Title IX, the Equal Protection Clause has forced schools to allow girls to try out for boys' teams in sports that are not offered to girls, even in contact sports.[281] That is because there is no contact sports exception to the Equal Protection Clause. The main practical significance of Title IX's contact sports exception, then, is that private schools — which are not state actors and are not governed by the Equal Protection Clause — may exclude female athletes from all-male contact sports.[282] In public schools, thanks to equal protection rights, female athletes have made significant inroads in traditionally male-only contact sports like wrestling. More than 28,000 young women now compete in high school wrestling, up from fewer than 5,000 in 2005; many still compete against male wrestlers and are on predominately male teams, although state athletic associations have increasingly added separate wrestling teams for girls.[283]

The experiences of female athletes in mixed-gender competition have been uneven. Girls are not always welcome on boys' wrestling teams, for example, and some boys have forfeited matches rather than compete against girls.[284] What accounts for this resistance and how should the law respond? Is it sex discrimination, under either Title IX or the Equal Protection Clause, for a school to permit male athletes in a sport to forfeit matches against girls if it results in diminished competitive opportunities for female athletes? Or is it a sex-neutral accommodation of individual choice to allow athletes of any gender to forfeit matches for any reason?

Male athletes have had very little success when asserting the right to try out for sports not offered to them.[285] Under Title IX, only persons whose athletic

---

279. Id.

280. See Michelle Margaret Smith, You Play Ball Like a Girl: Cultural Implications of the Contact Sports Exemption and Why It Needs to Be Changed, 66 Clev. St. L. Rev. 677 (2017); Suzanne Sangree, Title IX and the Contact Sports Exemption: Gender Stereotypes in a Civil Rights Statute, 32 Conn. L. Rev. 381 (2000).

281. See, e.g., Beattie v. Line Mountain Sch. Dist., 992 F. Supp. 2d 384 (M.D. Pa. 2014); Adams v. Baker, 919 F. Supp. 1496 (D. Kan. 1996); see also cases reviewed in Eileen McDonagh & Laura Pappano, Playing with the Boys: Why Separate Is Not Equal in Sports 137-44 (2008).

282. If an institution does allow a female athlete to join a previously all-male team in a contact sport, Title IX forbids the institution from discriminating against her on the basis of sex. See Mercer v. Duke Univ., 190 F.3d 643 (4th Cir. 1999). However, this caveat may only deepen an institution's commitment to keeping female athletes from trying out for all-male contact sports in the first place.

283. See Cody Porter, Nat'l Fed'n of State High Sch. Ass'ns Participation in Girls' Wrestling Explodes Across Country, (Dec. 20, 2021).

284. Id.; see also Deborah L. Brake, Wrestling with Gender, 13 Nev. L.J. 486 (2013).

285. See Petrie v. Illinois High Sch. Ass'n, 394 N.E.2d 855 (Ill. App. Ct. 1979); Williams v. Sch. Dist. of Bethlehem., 998 F.2d 168 (3d Cir. 1993).

opportunities have been historically limited by sex have the right to try out for a team offered exclusively to members of the other sex. This restriction means that male athletes rarely succeed in using Title IX to gain access to sports typically offered only to women, such as field hockey and volleyball. Male athletes have fared no better with constitutional equal protection rights (federal or state), on the grounds that their exclusion is substantially related to the important purpose of remedying athletic discrimination against girls and protecting girls' still-limited opportunities. Is this asymmetry defensible as a matter of sex equality? Is it wise as a matter of policy?

In an early, outlier case, the Massachusetts Supreme Judicial Court applied the state's equal rights amendment to permit boys to try out for female-only teams in sports not otherwise available to them, such as field hockey.[286] Critics of allowing boys to play on girls' teams have questioned whether such integration rights are fair to girls. For example, average height differences between boys and girls might create an advantage to boys in volleyball, where there is a nearly seven-inch difference in the height of the net used in girls' and boys' games. Skeptics also question whether letting boys onto a girls' team will change the experience of the game, making it less fun and empowering for girls. On the other hand, holding the line on all-female sports restricts the opportunities available to male athletes whose skills and interests do not match the sports typically offered to boys, and solidifies the gendering of particular sports as less suited for one sex than another.[287] How should the law address these concerns?

Even for girls, the right to try out for an all-male team is limited to sports that the school does not offer to girls. Neither Title IX nor the Equal Protection Clause guarantees an exceptional female athlete the right to play on the boys' team instead of the girls' team, even if doing so would better develop her skills; courts have uniformly rejected such claims.[288] Are these cases correctly decided? Why might a girl prefer to play on a boys' team? Is the existence of teams for both sexes a sufficient guarantee of equality for all players?

This question brings us back full circle to the justification for offering sex-separate athletic teams in the first place. Regardless of how integration rights are negotiated, the law's baseline determination to permit separate-sex teams remains controversial. Some scholars have disputed the biological basis for separating male and female athletes.[289] Nancy Leong argues that the biological justification for sex separation in sports is based on bad biology, both oversimplifying and overstating male athletic superiority.[290] Indeed, history has numerous, if forgotten, examples of

---

286. Atty. Gen. v. Mass. Interscholastic Athletic Ass'n, Inc., 393 N.E.2d 284 (Mass. 1979).

287. See Erin E. Buzuvis, Attorney General v. MIAA at Forty Years: A Critical Examination of Gender Segregation in High School Athletics in Massachusetts, 25 Tex. J. C.L. & C.R. 1 (2019).

288. See, e.g., O'Connor v. Bd. of Educ., 545 F. Supp. 376 (N.D. Ill. 1982); cf. Thomka v. Mass. Interscholastic Ath. Ass'n, 22 Mass. L. Rptr. 263 (2007).

289. See evidence reviewed in McDonagh & Pappano, supra note 281, at 53-68.

290. Nancy Leong, Against Women's Sports, 95 Wash. L. Rev. 1249 (2018).

women outshining men in high-profile athletic performances.[291] Leong questions why sex, but not other genetic variations linked to athletic advantage, serves as the basis for classifying athletes.[292] She points out that women have biological parity and even some biological advantages that go unnoticed in many athletic endeavors, such as distance swimming, rock climbing, distance running, skeet shooting, dog sledding, and fencing.[293] In 2019, for example, a woman was the overall winner in a 50K ultramarathon, which created a problem because the race organizers had ordered trophies for the overall (presumptively male) winner, plus the next two men and the top three women.[294] Leong criticizes as "sports essentialism" the view that those activities that are designed to showcase strength and speed count more for naturalizing male athletic superiority.[295] Moreover, even if men retain some biological advantage in certain sports, as women catch up in training, coaching, nutrition, and lifetime support for athletic competition, these performance gaps may narrow, particularly if more women regularly competed with men.

Critics of sex separation also contend that separate teams reinforce gender stereotypes that both construct and reinforce women's second-class status in sports.[296] Eileen McDonagh and Laura Pappano argue that the norm of separation codifies "historic myths about female physical inferiority and fosters a system which, while offering women more opportunities than ever before, still keeps them from being perceived as equal athletes to men."[297] Sex separation has also enabled the development of different rules of competition and standards of athlete dress and presentation that exacerbate this hierarchy.[298] There are also concerns about the effects of separate men's and women's teams on homophobia in sports. If sex separation reflects anxiety about sexually charged contact between male and female athletes, then separation itself may reinforce heterosexist assumptions that deny the possibility of same-sex attraction.[299]

But not everyone is ready to give up on sex separation in sports. Even if the biological case for separation eventually proves to be unfounded, separate sports for women might be defended based on the historic and continuing social and cultural influences that have inhibited the development of athleticism in girls and

---

291. Maria Cramer, How Women's Sports Teams Got Their Start, N.Y. Times, Apr. 28, 2022 (noting several examples of women outperforming men in elite sports, including in 1931 when 17-year-old Jackie Mitchell, a woman, struck out Babe Ruth and Lou Gehrig in an exhibition game).

292. Leong, supra note 290, at 1263-64.

293. Id. at 1265-69.

294. Hailey Middlebrook, Woman Wins 50K Ultra Outright, Trophy Snafu for Male Winner Follows, Runner's World (Aug. 15, 2019).

295. Leong, supra note 290, at 1278-80.

296. Elizabeth Sharrow, Sex Segregation as Policy Problem: A Gendered Policy Paradox, 9 Pol. Grps. & Identities 258 (2021).

297. McDonagh & Pappano, supra note 281, at 7.

298. For example, checking is an important part of the game in men's hockey, but forbidden in the women's game, and the clothing and appearance standards for gymnasts vary greatly for male and female participants.

299. See Sharrow, supra note 296, at 258.

women.[300] Whether due to biological or social and cultural forces, there is a real concern that shifting to a gender-neutral model of sport would eviscerate women's opportunities, at least in sports where height, upper body strength, and speed are advantageous.[301] Mixed-gender sport might also be a less empowering experience for girls and women due to the different treatment of girls in mixed-gender competition by coaches as well as male teammates and opponents.[302] Some research shows that separate sports environments enhance women's confidence, self-esteem, and skills development.[303]

The debate over sex segregation in sports is ultimately a debate over the merits of a substantive equality approach. Deborah Brake argues that neither sex separation nor integrated teams can fully solve the dilemma of difference as it plays out in this setting:

> Neither model is costless. Shifting to a framework that offers coed opportunities for all athletes with no attention to gender could potentially wipe out the biggest gains Title IX has produced: the burgeoning numbers of girls and women who participate in competitive school sports. With gender-blind team selection and competition, the majority of female athletes could well be relegated to second-tier teams or club and intramural games with only token representation at the varsity level. . . . Although some individual female athletes might be better off with coed teams because of their ability to excel in competition with male athletes, women as a group would likely face diminished opportunities to play sports at the most elite levels.
>
> On the other hand, accommodating gender difference has its costs, too. It reinforces an ideology that has historically been used to justify the outright denial of sports opportunities to women and, more recently, to place a lower value on women's sports. Having separate men's and women's teams risks sending the message that women are inherently lesser athletes. . . . As the feminist sport historian Jennifer Hargreaves explains the dilemma, separation can increase women's control over sport, mobilize women to fight for equal resources, and enable them to participate in sports free from male domination, but it also re-creates social gender

---

300. See Cheryl Cooky, "Girls Just Aren't Interested": The Social Construction of Interest in Girls' Sport, 52 Socio. Persps. 259 (2009).

301. See Susan K. Cahn, Coming on Strong: Gender and Sexuality in Women's Sport (U. Ill. Press, 2d ed. 2015) (contending that sports that emphasize speed or strength, such as basketball and track, would have few successful women athletes on mixed-gender teams at the elite level).

302. See Daniel Smith & Sarah Martiny, Stereotype Threat in Sport: Recommendations for Applied Practice and Research, 32 Sport Psych. 10 (2018); Nicole Zaerrett et al., Coaching Through a Gender Lens: Maximizing Girls' Play and Potential, Women's Sports Found. (2019) (noting that one-third of girls surveyed reported being made fun of by boys or harassed while playing their sport).

303. See Ellen Staurowsky et al., Women's Sports Found., Chasing Equity: The Triumphs, Challenges, and Opportunities in Sports for Girls and Women 16 (Jan. 2020).

divisions and can exaggerate sexism, with the message that biological sex, rather than culture, defines athleticism.[1]

This is the classic dilemma of difference, leaving advocates for gender equality damned if they ignore gender and damned if they don't. Title IX negotiates this terrain with a flexible and pragmatic approach. . . .[304]

How would you resolve this dilemma? Does segregation or integration best serve gender equality here?

The controversy over sex separation in sports has escalated in recent years as greater attention has been focused on transgender and non-binary students and where they fit into sex-segregated sports. Consider the following viewpoints.

Doriane Lambelet Coleman

Sex in Sport

80 Law & Contemp. Probs. 63, 85-86, 102-109, 113 (2017)

Competitive sport's institutional goals are to showcase the best athletes, to produce related benefits for stakeholders, and to use sport as a means to spread certain values throughout society. In all three respects, sport seeks specifically to reverse society's traditional subordination of women by providing females with opportunities for equal treatment and empowerment. It has chosen to fulfill this mission by classifying athletes according to their sex and setting aside the women's category for females only. . . .

Because male athletes in almost all modern sports and events go significantly faster and higher and are significantly stronger than female athletes, the only way to accomplish these ends is to segregate athletes on the basis of biological sex. Any other option that has males and females competing together works mainly to highlight, isolate, and display male bodies and hierarchies. . . .

The simple but powerful point is that sex-based classifications by definition exclude all trans and some intersex people because their biology does not match their identity. . . .

[T]he argument that switching out sex for identity does no cognizable harm erases exactly the harm that matters for many, if not most, females. That is, it threatens the movement to ensure equality for women who have been subjugated across millennia and cultures precisely because they are physically different from men. The goals of this movement are not primarily about identity; rather, they are about equal opportunity despite these physical differences which are, in the realm and dialect of sport, relative handicaps. . . .

Protecting these interests outweighs the interests of individual intersex and trans women to participate in and win sports events as women. It is doubtful that their being able to do so is more broadly beneficial given the inevitable backlash

---

1. Jennifer Hargreaves, Sporting Females: Critical Issues in the History and Sociology of Women's Sports 25-34, 207, 208 (1994).

304. Deborah L. Brake, Getting in the Game: Title IX and the Women's Sports Revolution 16-17 (2010).

that accompanies their entry into events, a backlash that muddies the optics for their purposes. But even if it is, because the stereotypes they need to counter are not based in any sense that they are physically fragile, there are other ways for them to accomplish these ends. On the other hand, participation and success in elite sport is truly a unique opportunity for females to combat the pervasiveness of damaging stereotypes.

Doriane Lambelet Coleman, Michael J. Joyner & Donna Lopiano

Re-Affirming the Value of the Sports Exception to Title IX's General Non-Discrimination Rule

27 Duke J. Gender L. & Public Pol'y 69, 108 (2020)

The case for re-affirming the sports exception is based in the goods produced by girls' and women's sport and in the causal link between sex segregation and those goods. The more specific case for not including—or conditioning the inclusion of—transgender women and girls in girls' and women's sport is related: If they haven't been on femininizing hormones for a relevant period of time, trans women and girls remain fully male-bodied in the respects that matter for sport; because of this, their inclusion effectively de-segregates the teams and events they join. Beyond this basic structural point is the fact that if they are just decent athletes, they will displace females who are the classification's *raison d'etre*, including in championship positions. This matters more for the individual females who are displaced, for those who would aspire to be champions, and for the broader expressive effects we expect from the classification. Even an exception risks swallowing the rule and defeating the category.

Finally, the position that there is no legally cognizable difference between females and trans women and girls destroys the legal basis for separate sex sport. This position—encapsulated in the movement mantra, "Girls who are transgender are girls. Period."—is presumably designed to erase sex-linked traits from consideration in the analysis of whether the two groups are similarly situated for purposes of equal protection doctrine. If we are not permitted legally to notice that girls who are female and girls who are transgender are dissimilarly situated with respect to their anatomy and physiology, and if we are not permitted to distinguish among them in circumstances where sex actually matters, we will have dismantled the scaffolding that supports separate sex sport.

Erin Buzuvis, Sarah Litwin & Warren K. Zola

Sport Is for Everyone: A Legal Roadmap for Transgender Participation in Sport

31 J. Legal Aspects of Sport 212, 232-36 (2021)

Efforts to restrict the participation of transgender athletes are rooted in protectionism of girls' and women's sports. Underscoring this argument is the belief that cisgender girls are incapable of competing alongside and against transgender girls, who may enjoy physical advantages as a result of their male, birth-assigned sex. We do not deny that post-puberty, generalized sex-based differences exist. But this does not mean that cisgender girls are categorically disadvantaged when it comes to sport. After all, cisgender girls compete with and against cisgender boys all the time. Ironically, one of the Connecticut high school athletes suing over the inter-scholastic athletic association's inclusive policy beat one of the transgender girls whose participation threatens her rightful victory. Even adult women routinely beat adult men in non-elite athletic contests, and elite competitions even have female winners at times. Additionally, the fact that many transgender girls delay puberty by treatment with testosterone blockers further dilutes the claim that transgender girls pose a categorical threat.

But more importantly, policies governing scholastic sports should not pursue the elimination of competitive advantage at the expense of promoting inclusion. Contest outcomes are far from the point of scholastic sport. . . . [T]he reason the government promotes, and why taxpayers support, school-sponsored athletic programs is not to benefit the elite few who may claim a state title on their way to an Olympic or professional career, it is because youth generally benefit from athletic participation.

Concerns that transgender inclusion will lead to the end of separate sports for boys and girls are unfounded. Scholastic sports are separated into sex-based categories in order to ensure generally that girls' opportunities are protected. Historically, girls have been excluded and marginalized from sport, so this protectionism is warranted. However, this protection is not undermined by the inclusion of transgender girls. First and foremost, this is because transgender girls are girls themselves, and anti-female bias in sport affects them as well. In addition, the small size of the transgender population and the imperfect proxy between birth-assigned sex and athletic performance support this conclusion as well.

But not only does transgender inclusion not undermine the protection of girls' athletic opportunities, the emphatic, high-profile exclusion of transgender girls could actually harm their athletic development. Stereotype threat is a well-documented phenomenon that calling an individual's attention to a generalized weakness of a group to which that individual belongs ensures that the individual's performance will reflect that weakness. Just as a well-timed message that "girls aren't good at math" will measurably diminish their performance on a math test, female athletes may internalize the message, inherent in transgender exclusion policies, that female athletes are so athletically inferior that they cannot safely or effectively compete against even a single transgender girl competitor. Moreover, when transgender athletes do raise the level of athleticism in girls' sport, their teammates and competitors benefit. A strong athlete raises the level of play of those around them both physically and motivationally. If the point of scholastic sport is to help develop athletic talent, athletes with diverse competitive abilities should be welcomed, not singled out for exclusion. . . .

Policies that require transgender youth to undergo hormone treatment as a condition for participation also impose problematic medical requirements. While many transgender youth elect hormone-based treatments such as puberty-blockers and cross-sex hormones, such medical interventions should never be a condition to athletic participation imposed on youth. Health risks associated with such treatments are, fortunately, low, but risks, particularly to one's fertility, nevertheless exist. To promote careful decisions and to respect the autonomy of transgender youth, their families, and their medical providers, school-sponsored sport should not influence the personal decision of when and if to begin a medical transition.

[T]ransgender athletes should be allowed to compete according to their gender identity in scholastic sports programs. . . .

Some have gone so far as to claim that transgender women's participation will lead to "the death of women's sport." Yet . . . the real threat to women's sport is legal and institutional failures to ensure equal access to opportunity.

NOTES

1. **Trans Panic or Protection of Women's Sports?** A wave of bills seeking to prohibit transgender girls—anyone not "biologically female" in the language of these bills—from participating in school sports on teams designated for girls has recently swept through state legislatures.[305] Backed by a group called the Alliance Defending Freedom, the bills are largely copycats of a sweeping ban pitched as a measure to protect girls' and women's sports from what the bills call "biological males."[306] All of the bills apply to high school sports, about half also extend to college sports, and just under a quarter include elementary students from kindergarten up.[307] Where applicable, these bans apply to all levels of sport competition, including varsity, club, and intramural, whenever a sport is designated a girls' or women's sport. The bills regulate athletic eligibility only in girls' sports; they do not set any limits on boys' sports, nor do they block transgender boys—even those taking testosterone—from playing on girls' teams. To date, eighteen states have adopted such statewide bans.[308] Many of these laws allow anyone with suspicions about a female athlete's "biological sex" to object to her eligibility, putting the burden on the athlete to prove, based on the criteria and process set out in the statute, that she is female. Idaho was the first state to pass such a law in 2020.[309] A Republican sponsor of the Idaho law described the threat facing girls' sports in dire terms: "The progress that we, as women, have made over the last 50 years will

305. See Legislative Tracker: Youth Sports Bans on the Freedom for All Americans website: https://freedomforallamericans.org/legislative-tracker/student-athletics. The website www.transathlete.com also compiles up-to-date information on state legislative action excluding transgender athletes from participating in sports.

306. See Elizabeth A. Sharrow, Sports, Transgender Rights and the Bodily Politics of Cisgender Supremacy, 10 Laws 1 (2021). The Alliance Defending Freedom positions itself as a defender of religious freedom, traditional marriage, and "the sanctity of life" among other issues; it is designated as a hate group by the Southern Poverty Law Center. Id.

307. Id.

308. David W. Chen, Transgender Athletes Face Bans from Girls' Sports in 10 U.S. States, N.Y. Times, Oct. 28, 2021.

309. See Talya Minsberg, "Boys Are Boys and Girls Are Girls": Idaho Is First State to Bar Some Transgender Athletes, N.Y. Times, Apr. 1, 2020.

be for naught and we will be forced to be spectators in our own sports."[310] Legal challenges to these laws have been brought under Title IX and the Constitution. Several courts have issued preliminary injunctions enjoining their application, finding the plaintiffs likely to prevail on the merits.[311]

Despite the frantic legislative pace, there is little evidence of a transgender takeover of girls' sports. Only 2 percent of high school students identify as transgender; not all of them are trans girls, nor do they all participate in sports.[312] In fact, sports participation by transgender girls is significantly lower than for cisgender girls. According to the Human Rights Campaign Fund, only 12 percent of transgender girls participate in school sports, compared to over two-thirds of high school students overall.[313] At the intercollegiate level, approximately 200,000 women competed in NCAA sports in 2021; only an estimated 50 of them were transgender.[314] Deborah Brake calls the anti-trans legislative fervor a quintessential moral panic, with several key features of a moral panic: the disproportionality of the sought-after response dwarfs the empirical evidence of a problem; the discourse has a high emotional pitch that defies nuanced policy analysis; the target of the panic, already marginalized, is portrayed unempathetically as a threat to the social order; and the specific issue (here, sports) is used strategically as a catalysis for altering the terms of engagement more broadly (e.g., reinstating traditional understandings of sex and gender roles).[315]

Some supporters of women's athletic equality contend that greater restrictions on participation by transgender women, at least those who went through male puberty without medical intervention, might be warranted, even if total bans are inappropriate, in order to protect women's competitive opportunities. This concern was heightened by the publicity trained on Lia Thomas, a transgender woman competing on the University of Pennsylvania's women's swim team, when she won the NCAA championship in one event.[316] Thomas had been a good but not stellar swimmer in men's events but earned top honors competing in women's events. The NCAA requires transgender women to receive hormone therapy reducing

---

310. Gillian R. Brassil & Jere Longman, Who Should Compete in Women's Sports? There Are "Two Almost Irreconcilable Positions," N.Y. Times, Aug. 18, 2020.

311. See A.M. v. Indianapolis Pub. Schs., No 1:22-cv-01075-JMS-DLP (S.D. Ind. July 26, 2022); Hecox v. Little, 479 F. Supp. 3d 930 (D. Idaho 2020); B.P.J. v. W. Va. State Bd. of Educ., 2021 WL 3081883 (S.D.W. Va. July 21, 2021).

312. Valerie Strauss, CDC: Nearly 2 Percent of High School Students Identify as Transgender—and More than One-Third of Them Attempt Suicide, Wash. Post, Jan. 24, 2019. The Trevor Project puts the figure at 1.8 percent of high school students who identify as transgender. National Survey on LGBTQ Youth Mental Health 2019, The Trevor Project (2019).

313. Human Rights Campaign Foundation, Play to Win: Improving the Lives of LGBTQ Youth in Sports; Women's Sports Foundation, Chasing Equity Report: Executive Summary 16 (2020).

314. Brassil & Longman, supra note 310.

315. See Deborah Brake, Title IX's Trans Panic, Wm. & Mary J. Race Gender & Soc. Justice, forthcoming 2022.

316. Michael Powell, Much Debate but Little Dialogue on Transgender Female Athletes, N.Y. Times, May 29, 2022, at A1, 14-15.

testosterone to typical female levels for at least a year in order to be able to compete in women's sports, and Thomas complied with that rule.[317] Critics of the rule contend that post-puberty hormone therapy does not fully neutralize transgender women's biological advantages. They argue that, at least for athletic events that prioritize speed, strength, and muscle development, going through male puberty gives transgender women an unfair advantage that undermines the purpose of reserving separate athletic events for women.[318]

Not everyone agrees. The effect of testosterone on athletic performance is hotly contested and some researchers point out that there is little evidence that transgender women—particularly those on hormone therapy—have any appreciable advantage over cisgender women in athletic competition.[319] Nor is male biological advantage the only plausible rationale for sex separation in sport; separate sports for women have been defended based on the social and institutional forces that have suppressed women's athleticism and the cultural influences that make separate sports empowering for women. Critics of transgender bans point out that human physiology varies in many ways that can affect athleticism, yet biological advantages besides sex (height, bone structure, and myriad genetic conditions that affect athletic performance) are not deemed unfair in competition.[320] And physiological advantage is just the beginning; rules of competition do nothing to even out the disparities of resources (year-round coaching, club sport experience, support for time- and travel-intensive sport) that give some athletes intractable competitive advantages over others.[321] Does singling out transgender athletes as a source of unfair competition reflect anti-trans bias and assume that cisgender girls are the only girls who matter for Title IX purposes?

The controversy can seem intractable, and it has divided women's sports equity advocates who have previously been united in seeking to advance women's

---

317. Id. at 14. In January 2022, the NCAA modified its policy on transgender eligibility to phase in a sport-by-sport approach that will align NCAA sports with the evolving requirements for Olympic sports in each sport. See NCAA, Transgender Student-Athlete Eligibility Review Procedures, Jan. 27, 2022, https://www.ncaa.org/sports/2022/1/27/transgender-participation-policy.aspx.

318. Powell, supra note 316, at 14-15.

319. Cordelia Fine, Testosterone Rex: Myths of Sex, Science, and Society (2017); Rebecca Jordan-Young & Katrina Karkazis, Testosterone: An Unauthorized Biography (2019); Jordan Buckwald, Outrunning Bias: Unmasking the Justifications for Excluding Non-Binary Athletes in Elite Sport, 44 Harv. J. L. & Gender 1, 25-32 (2021) (reviewing the evidence linking testosterone to enhanced athletic performance, and on transgender women and athletic advantage, and finding it lacking); Bethany Alice Jones et al., Sport and Transgender People: A Systematic Review of the Literature Relating to Sport Participation and Competitive Sport Policies, 47 Sports Med. 701 (2017) (similar findings).

320. Cheryl Cooky & Shari L. Dworkin, Policing the Boundaries of Sex: A Critical Examination of Gender Verification and the Caster Semenya Controversy, 50 J. Sex Rsch. 103, 106-107 (2013).

321. Michele Krech, To Be a Woman in the World of Sport: Global Regulation of the Gender Binary in Elite Athletics, 35 Berkeley J. Int'l L. 262, 265 (2017).

equality in sport.[322] Why do you think sport has been the site of such heated debate over where transgender girls and women belong? Do you think sex discrimination law should protect the rights of transgender girls and women to participate in girls' and women's sports? Or should it protect cisgender girls and women from competing against transgender girls and women in girls' and women's sports? Is there a middle path?

2. **Sport as Education.**   How should it affect the analysis of transgender inclusion that interscholastic and intercollegiate athletics are educational programs? The educational benefits of athletics are said to include teamwork, discipline, social relationships, leadership skills, self-esteem, and improved mental and physical health. The claim that women's sports must be protected from transgender women comes down to protecting the chances of cisgender women to win, not their chance to participate. The numbers of transgender women trying out for women's teams are unlikely to be large enough to displace cisgender women from participating. The "threat" raised by supporters of transgender restrictions, then, is the threat of cisgender girls being beaten by a transgender girl. How much of the educational value of athletics is attributable to winning as opposed to participating?

How should transgender women's opportunity to participate be weighed against cisgender women's chances to win? Supporters of transgender inclusion argue that the benefits of athletic participation are especially valuable for transgender girls and women, who are at heightened risk of negative mental, social, and educational outcomes. Is there any way to resolve this issue that avoids a zero-sum framing that pits the interests of transgender girls and cisgender girls against each other?

In early Title IX case law, when female superstar athletes sued their schools seeking a right to play on the boys' team, courts rejected their claims, citing the harms to women's sports from the talent drain if the very best women athletes were peeled off to join the men's team.[323] The rationale was that the other girls would benefit from playing with and against athletic superstars on the women's team and that playing with exceptional athletes raises the level of play for everyone. Should Title IX's response be different when the stellar athlete on the women's team is transgender?

3. **Rethink Sex Separation?**   How much of a challenge are transgender and non-binary students to the model of sex separation in sports? One view is that it is

---

322. An organization formed by former sport equity leaders and Olympic athletes, calling itself the Women's Sports Policy Working Group, advocates greater restrictions on transgender athletes competing in women's sports, while organizations such as the National Women's Law Center and Women's Sports Foundation side with full inclusion of transgender girls and women in women's sports. Compare The Resolution, Women's Sports Policy Working Group, https://womenssportspolicy.org/the-resolution/ with The Foundation Position, Participation of Transgender Athletes in Women's Sports, https://www.womenss portsfoundation.org/wp-content/uploads/2016/08/participation-of-transgender-athletes -in-womens-sports-the-foundation-position.pdf and National Women's Law Center, Fulfilling Title IX's Promise: Let Transgender and Intersex Students Play, https://nwlc.org/resource/ trans-and-intersex-inclusion-in-athletics.

323. Brake, Getting in the Game, supra note 304, at 23-26 (2010).

possible to accommodate transgender girls and non-binary students (who together are a small number of athletes) with a broader and more inclusive understanding of who counts as a girl or woman, and that sex separation is worth preserving to best support girls' and women's participation and experiences in sport. Alternatively, one might contend that it is time to reevaluate the structure of separation, and that the cracks exposed by greater attention to transgender and non-binary participants are more than minor glitches. On this view, separate but equal in sport was always based on a biological essentialism that is not worth salvaging. Which position do you find more persuasive?

Even if we accept sex segregation as an appropriate baseline in sports, complicated questions remain about what equality requires in this setting. What measure of nondiscrimination should the law adopt to ensure that women have equal, albeit separate, opportunities to participate in athletics?

Cohen v. Brown University

101 F.3d 155 (1st Cir. 1996)

BOWNES, Senior Circuit Judge.

This is a class action lawsuit charging Brown University, its president, and its athletics director (collectively "Brown") with discrimination against women in the operation of its intercollegiate athletics program, in violation of Title IX of the Education Amendments of 1972, and its implementing regulations. . . . The plaintiff class comprises all present, future, and potential Brown University women students who participate, seek to participate, and/or are deterred from participating in intercollegiate athletics funded by Brown.

This suit was initiated in response to the demotion in May 1991 of Brown's women's gymnastics and volleyball teams from university-funded varsity status to donor-funded varsity status. Contemporaneously, Brown demoted two men's teams, water polo and golf, from university-funded to donor-funded varsity status. As a consequence of these demotions, all four teams lost, not only their university funding, but most of the support and privileges that accompany university-funded varsity status at Brown.

[Following a bench trial, the district court found Brown to be in violation of Title IX, and ordered a comprehensive plan for compliance be submitted. The court found the plan submitted was not comprehensive and did not comply with the opinion. The court rejected the plan and ordered Brown to elevate and maintain the women's teams at university-funded varsity status.]

. . . Brown challenges on constitutional and statutory grounds the test employed by the district court in determining whether Brown's intercollegiate athletics program complies with Title IX. . . .

I . . .

As a Division I institution within the National Collegiate Athletic Association ("NCAA") with respect to all sports but football, Brown participates at the highest level of NCAA competition. Brown operates a two-tiered intercollegiate athletics program with respect to funding: although Brown provides the financial resources required to maintain its university-funded varsity teams, donor-funded varsity athletes must themselves raise the funds necessary to support their teams through private donations. The district court found . . . that it is difficult for donor-funded varsity athletes to maintain a level of competitiveness commensurate with their abilities and that these athletes operate at a competitive disadvantage in comparison to university-funded varsity athletes. . . .

Brown's decision to demote the women's volleyball and gymnastics teams and the men's water polo and golf teams from university-funded varsity status was apparently made in response to a university-wide cost-cutting directive. The district court found that Brown saved $62,028 by demoting the women's teams and $15,795 by demoting the men's teams, but that the demotions "did not appreciably affect the athletic participation gender ratio." . . .

Plaintiffs alleged that, at the time of the demotions, the men students at Brown already enjoyed the benefits of a disproportionately large share of both the university resources allocated to athletics and the intercollegiate participation opportunities afforded to student athletes. Thus, plaintiffs contended, what appeared to be the even-handed demotions of two men's and two women's teams, in fact, perpetuated Brown's discriminatory treatment of women in the administration of its intercollegiate athletics program.

The district court . . . summarized the history of athletics at Brown. . . . It found that, in 1993-94, there were 897 students participating in intercollegiate varsity athletics, of which 61.87% (555) were men and 38.13% (342) were women. During the same period, Brown's undergraduate enrollment comprised 5,722 students, of which 48.86% (2,796) were men and 51.14% (2,926) were women. . . . [I]n 1993-94, Brown's intercollegiate athletics program consisted of 32 teams, 16 men's teams and 16 women's teams. Of the university-funded teams, 12 were men's teams and 13 were women's teams; of the donor-funded teams, three were women's teams and four were men's teams. At the time of trial, Brown offered 479 university-funded varsity positions for men, as compared to 312 for women; and 76 donor-funded varsity positions for men, as compared to 30 for women. In 1993-94, then, Brown's varsity program — including both university- and donor-funded sports — afforded over 200 more positions for men than for women. Accordingly, the district court found that Brown maintained a 13.01% disparity between female participation in intercollegiate athletics and female student enrollment, and that "[a]lthough the number of varsity sports offered to men and women are equal, the selection of sports offered to each gender generates far more individual positions for male athletes than for female athletes." . . .

The district court found from extensive testimony that the donor-funded women's gymnastics, women's fencing and women's ski teams, as well as at least one women's club team, the water polo team, had demonstrated the interest and ability to compete at the top varsity level and would benefit from university funding. . . .

The district court did not find that full and effective accommodation of the athletics interests and abilities of Brown's female students would disadvantage Brown's male students.

II

Title IX provides that "[n]o person in the United States shall, on the basis of sex, be excluded from participation in, be denied the benefits of, or be subjected to discrimination under any education program or activity receiving Federal financial assistance." . . . As a private institution that receives federal financial assistance, Brown is required to comply with Title IX.

The agency responsible for administering Title IX is the United States Department of Education, through its Office for Civil Rights. Congress expressly delegated to Department of Education the authority to promulgate regulations for determining whether an athletics program complies with Title IX. The regulation at issue in this case . . . provides:

> (a) *General.* No person shall, on the basis of sex, be excluded from participation in, be denied the benefits of, be treated differently from another person or otherwise be discriminated against in any interscholastic, intercollegiate, club or intramural athletics offered by a recipient, and no recipient shall provide any such athletics separately on such basis.
>
> (b) *Separate teams.* Notwithstanding the requirements of paragraph (a) of this section, a recipient may operate or sponsor separate teams for members of each sex where selection of such teams is based upon competitive skill or the activity involved is a contact sport. However, where a recipient operates or sponsors a team in a particular sport for members of one sex but operates or sponsors no such team for members of the other sex, and athletic opportunities for members of that sex have previously been limited, members of the excluded sex must be allowed to try-out for the team offered unless the sport involved is a contact sport. For the purposes of this part, contact sports include boxing, wrestling, rugby, ice hockey, football, basketball and other sports the purpose or major activity of which involves bodily contact.
>
> (c) *Equal Opportunity.* A recipient which operates or sponsors interscholastic, intercollegiate, club or intramural athletics shall provide equal athletic opportunity for members of both sexes. In determining whether equal opportunities are available the Director will consider, among other factors:

> (1) Whether the selection of sports and levels of competition effectively accommodate the interests and abilities of members of both sexes;
> (2) The provision of equipment and supplies;
> (3) Scheduling of games and practice time;
> (4) Travel and per diem allowance;
> (5) Opportunity to receive coaching and academic tutoring;
> (6) Assignment and compensation for coaches and tutors;
> (7) Provision of locker rooms, practice and competitive facilities;
> (8) Provision of medical and training facilities and services;
> (9) Provision of housing and dining facilities and services;
> (10) Publicity. . . .

In 1978, several years after the promulgation of the regulations, the Office of Civil Rights published a proposed "Policy Interpretation," the purpose of which was to clarify the obligations of federal aid recipients under Title IX to provide equal opportunities in athletics programs. . . .

At issue in this appeal is the proper interpretation of the . . . so-called three-part test [developed to implement these regulations], which inquires as follows:

> (1) Whether intercollegiate level participation opportunities for male and female students are provided in numbers substantially proportionate to their respective enrollments; or
>
> (2) Where the members of one sex have been and are underrepresented among intercollegiate athletes, whether the institution can show a history and continuing practice of program expansion which is demonstrably responsive to the developing interest and abilities of the members of that sex; or
>
> (3) Where the members of one sex are underrepresented among intercollegiate athletes, and the institution cannot show a continuing practice of program expansion such as that cited above, whether it can be demonstrated that the interests and abilities of the members of that sex have been fully and effectively accommodated by the present program. . . .

The district court held that, "because Brown maintains a 13.01% disparity between female participation in intercollegiate athletics and female student enrollment, it cannot gain the protection of prong one." Nor did Brown satisfy prong two. While acknowledging that Brown "has an impressive history of program expansion," the district court found that Brown failed to demonstrate that it has "maintained a *continuing practice* of intercollegiate program expansion for women, the underrepresented sex." The court noted further that, because merely reducing program offerings to the overrepresented gender does not constitute program expansion for the underrepresented gender, the fact that Brown has eliminated or demoted several men's teams does not amount to a continuing practice of program expansion for women. As to prong three, the district court found that Brown had not "fully and effectively accommodated the interest and ability of the underrepresented sex 'to the extent necessary to provide equal opportunity in the selection of sports and levels of competition available to members of both sexes.'" . . .

The district court found that Brown predetermines the approximate number of varsity positions available to men and women, and, thus, that "the concept of any measure of unfilled but available athletic slots does not comport with reality." The district court concluded that intercollegiate athletics opportunities "means real opportunities, not illusory ones, and therefore should be measured by counting *actual participants.*" . . .

IV

Brown contends that . . . the district court's interpretation and application of the test is irreconcilable with the statute, the regulation, and the agency's interpretation of the law, and effectively renders Title IX an "affirmative action statute" that mandates preferential treatment for women by imposing quotas in excess of women's relative interests and abilities in athletics. Brown asserts, in the alternative, that if the district court properly construed the test, then the test itself violates Title IX and the United States Constitution. . . .

Brown's talismanic incantation of "affirmative action" has no legal application to this case and is not helpful to Brown's cause. While "affirmative action" may have different connotations as a matter of politics, as a matter of law, its meaning is more circumscribed. True affirmative action cases have historically involved a voluntary undertaking to remedy discrimination (as in a program implemented by a governmental body, or by a private employer or institution), by means of specific group-based preferences or numerical goals, and a specific timetable for achieving those goals [citing, among other cases, Johnson v. Transportation Agency . . .].

Title IX is not an affirmative action statute; it is an anti-discrimination statute. . . . No aspect of the Title IX regime at issue in this case — inclusive of the statute, the relevant regulation, and the pertinent agency documents — mandates gender-based preferences or quotas, or specific timetables for implementing numerical goals.

Like other anti-discrimination statutory schemes, the Title IX regime *permits* affirmative action. In addition, Title IX, like other anti-discrimination schemes, permits an inference that a significant gender-based statistical disparity may indicate the existence of discrimination. . . .

From the mere fact that a remedy flowing from a judicial determination of discrimination is gender-conscious, it does not follow that the remedy constitutes "affirmative action." Nor does a "reverse discrimination" claim arise every time an anti-discrimination statute is enforced. . . .

Brown maintains that the district court's decision imposes upon universities the obligation to engage in preferential treatment for women by requiring quotas in excess of women's relative interests and abilities. With respect to prong three, Brown asserts that the district court's interpretation of the word "fully" "requires universities to favor women's teams and treat them better than men's [teams] . . . forces them to eliminate or cap men's teams . . . [and] forces universities to impose athletic quotas in excess of relative interests and abilities." . . .

Brown simply ignores the fact that it is required to accommodate fully the interests and abilities of the underrepresented gender, not because the three-part test mandates preferential treatment for women *ab initio*, but because Brown has been found (under prong one) to have allocated its athletics participation opportunities so as to create a significant gender-based disparity with respect to these opportunities, and has failed (under prong two) to show a history and continuing practice of expansion of opportunities for the underrepresented gender. . . .

To adopt [Brown's] relative interests approach would be . . . to . . . entrench and fix by law the significant gender-based disparity in athletics opportunities found by the district court to exist at Brown. . . . According to Brown's relative interests interpretation of the equal accommodation principle, the gender-based disparity in athletics participation opportunities at Brown is due to a lack of interest on the part of its female students, rather than to discrimination, and any attempt to remedy the disparity is, by definition, an unlawful quota. This approach is entirely contrary to "Congress's unmistakably clear mandate that educational institutions not use federal monies to perpetuate gender-based discrimination" . . . and makes it virtually impossible to effectuate Congress's intent to eliminate sex discrimination in intercollegiate athletics. . . .

Interest and ability rarely develop in a vacuum; they evolve as a function of opportunity and experience. The Policy Interpretation recognizes that women's lower rate of participation in athletics reflects women's historical lack of opportunities to participate in sports. . . .

[T]here exists the danger that, rather than providing a true measure of women's interest in sports, statistical evidence purporting to reflect women's interest instead provides only a measure of the very discrimination that is and has been the basis for women's lack of opportunity to participate in sports. Prong three requires some kind of evidence of interest in athletics, and the Title IX framework permits the use of statistical evidence in assessing the level of interest in sports. Nevertheless, to allow a numbers-based lack-of-interest defense to become the instrument of further discrimination against the underrepresented gender would pervert the remedial purpose of Title IX. We conclude that, even if it can be empirically demonstrated that, at a particular time, women have less interest in sports than do men, such evidence, standing alone, cannot justify providing fewer athletics opportunities for women than for men. Furthermore, such evidence is completely irrelevant where, as here, viable and successful women's varsity teams have been demoted or eliminated. . . .

Finally, the tremendous growth in women's participation in sports since Title IX was enacted disproves Brown's argument that women are less interested in sports for reasons unrelated to lack of opportunity. . . .

V . . .

Of course, a remedy that requires an institution to cut, add, or elevate the status of athletes or entire teams may impact the genders differently, but this will be so only if there is a gender-based disparity with respect to athletics opportunities to begin with, which is the only circumstance in which prong three comes into play. Here, however, it has not been shown that Brown's men students will be disadvantaged by the full and effective accommodation of the athletics interests and abilities of its women students. . . .

There can be no doubt that Title IX has changed the face of women's sports as well as our society's interest in and attitude toward women athletes and women's sports. . . . In addition, there is ample evidence that increased athletics participation opportunities for women and young girls, available as a result of Title IX enforcement, have had salutary effects in other areas of societal concern. . . .

One need look no further than the impressive performances of our country's women athletes in the 1996 Olympic Summer Games to see that Title IX has had a dramatic and positive impact on the capabilities of our women athletes, particularly in team sports. These Olympians represent the first full generation of women to grow up under the aegis of Title IX. . . . What stimulated this remarkable change in the quality of women's athletic competition was not a sudden, anomalous upsurge in women's interest in sports, but the enforcement of Title IX's mandate of gender equity in sports. . . .

Affirmed in part, reversed in part, and remanded for further proceedings. . . .

NOTES

1. **Title IX and Women's Participation in Sports.** At one time, strenuous physical activity was thought to be harmful to women's reproductive capacities and competition antithetical to their femininity. "Unsexed Amazons" on the playing fields were widely viewed as unattractive and some physicians worried that they would damage women's delicate nerves and physiques, or drain the "vital forces" necessary for reproduction.[324] Of course this ideology of female fragility was implicitly racialized; only the delicacy of the reproductive systems of white, middle- and upper-class women was of concern.[325] Women of color were thought undeserving of sports, or leisure time altogether. The passage of Title IX reflected the more modern understanding that girls and women are equally deserving of athletic opportunities, and stand to gain important academic, psychological, health, and social benefits from participating in sports.[326]

Although Title IX enforcement got off to a slow start, it is now widely regarded as having led to substantially increased opportunities for female athletes.[327] In the post-Title IX era, girls' participation in high school sports has soared from approximately 294,000 in 1971 to over 3.4 million in the 2018-2019 school year.[328] Girls have gone from 7 percent of varsity high school athletes in 1972 to 43 percent today.[329] Women's participation in intercollegiate sports has also risen exponentially, from below 32,000 before Title IX was enacted[330] to more than 219,000 in 2021.[331] In 1972, women were 15 percent of all intercollegiate athletes, compared to 44 percent in 2021.[332] To what extent do you think Title IX's model of substantive equality is responsible for this growth? Would it have been possible under a gender-neutral model of sport?

Sport has often been lauded as a path to empowerment for girls and women, but is this a path that is open to all? The intersection of sport and disability has

---

324. Kathleen McCrone, Sport and the Physical Emancipation of English Women 1870-1914, at 6-7 (1988); Helen Lenskyi, Out of Bounds, Women, Sport, and Sexuality 38 (1986).

325. Dayna B. Daniels, Polygendered and Ponytailed 39 (2009).

326. Women's Sports Foundation, Teen Sport in America, Part II: Her Participation Matters 24-26 (2021).

327. See Betsey Stevenson, Title IX and the Evolution of High School Sports, 25 Contemp. Econ. Pol'y 486 (2007).

328. Nat'l Fed. of State High School Ass'ns, 2018-19 High School Athletics Participation Survey 54, www.nfhs.org. Due to a two-year hiatus in data collection during the Covid-19 pandemic, this is the most recent data currently available.

329. Women's Sports Foundation, 50 Years of Title IX: We're Not Done Yet 8 (May 2022). However, some research suggests the data are misreported and understates the actual gap in girls' athletic participation opportunities. Id. at 9.

330. See Dep't of Health, Educ., and Welfare Policy Interpretation, 44 Fed. Reg. 71419 (1979).

331. See NCAA Sports Sponsorship and Participation Rates Report 86 (Jan. 6, 2022), https://ncaaorg.s3.amazonaws.com/research/sportpart/2021RES_SportsSponsorshipParticipationRatesReport.pdf.

332. Women's Sports Foundation, 50 Years of Title IX, supra note 329, at 8.

often been overlooked in Title IX discussions, but only about 10 percent of girls with disabilities participate in sports,[333] compared to 60 percent of girls overall participating in high school sports.[334] Research on gender, sport, and disability is limited, but existing data suggest that male students with disabilities are significantly more likely than girls with disabilities to participate in sports.[335] Why do you think such a gender gap exists, and how should Title IX advocacy respond?

In the wake of the Covid-19 pandemic, which has had severe effects on college enrollment and university finances, some colleges and universities have contracted their sports programs, raising concerns about backsliding in women's intercollegiate athletic participation. As latecomers to the world of sport and without the deep pockets of alumni or the same investments and revenue as men's sports, women's intercollegiate sports have been particularly vulnerable to "Covid cuts." Title IX's three-part test discussed in *Brown* has been helpful in stemming these losses. Unless the university can demonstrate that it offers women athletic opportunities that are substantially proportionate to women's share of enrollment, the three-part test limits the ability of schools to cut women's sports, even in an austere budget environment.[336]

2. **Title IX and Race.** The growth in girls' and women's sports participation masks persistent racial disparities among the beneficiaries of Title IX. Girls and women of color have benefited from Title IX, but their sports participation has lagged behind that of white girls and women.[337] A 2015 report by the Women's Sports Foundation revealed that while the participation opportunities for women of color have increased dramatically since the passage of Title IX, they are still underrepresented when compared to enrollment; the report found women of color were 26 percent of college students, but fewer than 18 percent of intercollegiate athletes.[338] In recent years, college sports participation by women of color has risen to 32 percent of female undergraduate athletic participation, an increase of 9 percent since 2001; but with well over half of these athletes competing in just two sports — basketball and track — this growth has been uneven.[339] A deeper dive shows further disparities: Black women are only 11 percent of all female intercollegiate athletes, a figure that has held constant for ten years; Hispanic women make up 6 percent of female college athletes, and Asian women only 2 percent.[340] High

---

333. Id. at 57.

334. Women's Sports Foundation, Title IX Fast Facts, https://www.womenssportsfoundation.org/wp-content/uploads/2022/04/FINAL6_WSF-Title-IX-Infographic-2022.pdf.

335. Women's Sports Foundation, 50 Years of Title IX, supra note 329, at 13.

336. See, e.g., Ohlensehlen v. Univ. of Iowa, 2020 WL 7651974 (D. Iowa Dec. 24, 2020); Balow v. Mich. State Univ., 2021 WL 650712 (W.D. Mich. 2021), vacated and remanded, 24 F.4th 1051 (6th Cir. 2022).

337. See Deborah L. Brake & Verna L. Williams, The Heart of the Game: Putting Race and Educational Equity at the Center of Title IX, 7 Va. Sports & Ent. L.J. 199 (2008).

338. Women's Sports Foundation, Race and Sport (2015), https://www.womenssportsfoundation.org/en/home/advocate/title-ix-and-issues/title-ix-positions/race_and_sport.

339. NCAA, Title IX 50th Anniversary Report: The State of Women in College Sports 11 (June 2022).

340. Id. at 11, 52-54 (other categories include multiracial at 5 percent, international at 5 percent, and less than 1 percent for American Indian/Alaska Native and Native Hawaiian/Pacific Islander).

school data are harder to come by, but the disparities for girls of color appear to be even more pronounced at this level.[341] Education in the U.S. generally is stratified by race, and the gender disparity in athletic opportunity is greater at high schools attended predominantly by students of color, where girls have only 67 percent of the opportunities provided to boys, than at predominantly white schools, where girls have 82 percent of boys' opportunities.[342]

One reason Title IX has meant slower gains for women of color is that the sports added by schools to come into compliance with Title IX tend to be "country club" sports or sports that are popular in suburban areas, such as soccer, lacrosse, golf, and tennis, that are not widely accessible or affordable for many girls of color.[343] The list of "emerging sports" embraced by the NCAA to press colleges and universities to add additional women's sports — tumbling, equestrian, rugby, triathalon, and women's wrestling — has not helped matters, as these sports add little racial diversity to most programs.[344] Another problem is that girls of color are concentrated in majority-Black elementary and secondary schools; with little offered to boys in those typically underresourced schools, gender equality does not bring many new additions. In contrast, richer suburban schools with well-funded athletic programs have had to add substantially to the girls' athletic programs to keep up with what is available to boys.[345] The growing importance of youth sports and private club sports to varsity sport participation in high school and then college further deepens these disparities. Due to cost and access barriers, there are disparate class- and race-based impacts to participation in youth sport programs, which function as gatekeepers to varsity-level interscholastic sports.[346]

When girls and women of color do excel in sports, they are often depicted harshly, through a racialized lens, triggering unflattering scrutiny that complicates messages about sport as a path to female empowerment.[347] As a single-axis anti-discrimination law, Title IX addresses only sex inequality; it does not address racial inequality among women. While another anti-discrimination law, Title VI of the Civil Rights Act of 1964, prohibits race discrimination in federally funded schools, it does not address sex-based inequalities within racial groups. What legal or policy

---

341. Elizabeth Tang et al., Title IX at 50: A Report by the National Coalition for Women and Girls in Education 33 (June 2022).

342. Id.

343. Brake, Getting in the Game, supra note 304, at 112-18.

344. Women's Sports Foundation, 50 Years of Title IX, supra note 329, at 54.

345. See Regina Austin, Super Size Me and the Conundrum of Race/Ethnicity, Gender, and Class for the Contemporary Law-Genre Documentary Filmmaker, 40 Loy. L.A. L. Rev. 710 (2007); Katie Thomas, A City Team's Struggle Shows Disparity in Girls' Sports, N.Y. Times, June 14, 2009, at A1; Jeremy C. Fox, Minority Girls Given Fewer Chances in School Sports, Report Says, Bos. Globe, Apr. 26, 2015; William C. Rhoden, Black and White Women Far from Equal Under Title IX, N.Y. Times, June 11, 2012, at D5.

346. Women's Sports Foundation, 50 Years of Title IX, supra note 329, at 58-59.

347. See Cheryl Cooky & Lauren Rauscher, Girls and the Racialization of Female Bodies in Sport Contexts in Child's Play: Sport in Kids' Worlds 61 (2016); Jagger Blaec, Serena Williams Can't Force the Racism out of Tennis, Vice (Sept. 10, 2018) (discussing the role of race and gender in reactions to Serena Williams' response to being penalized in the U.S. Open women's final match against Naomi Osaka).

solutions would you propose to address the barriers to equal athletic opportunity facing girls and women of color?

3. **Title IX and Women's Interest in Sports.**   Since the ruling in *Cohen*, courts have uniformly upheld the three-part test against arguments from defendants that it amounts to reverse discrimination against men who, they argue, are more interested than women in playing sports.[348] Courts have ruled that men, as the overrepresented sex, are not protected by the three-part test, and that the test's focus on expanding opportunities for the underrepresented sex is constitutional. Courts have also applied the three-part test to high school sports,[349] as has OCR in its enforcement actions.[350]

The three-part test has been controversial and the subject of some political ping-pong as presidential administrations change. During the George W. Bush administration, OCR issued a policy clarification allowing schools to use email surveys to demonstrate a lack of student interest in additional women's sports offerings, and to infer a lack of interest from an absence of responses.[351] Critics condemned the policy for flaws in survey methodology and, most fundamentally, ignoring the key lesson of Title IX that, as Billie Jean King succinctly put it, "interest reflects opportunities."[352] The Obama administration rescinded the policy.[353] How else, apart from surveys, can institutions show that the interests and abilities of the underrepresented sex have been fully accommodated under the three-part test?[354]

Some commentators have criticized the three-part test for failing to account for asserted differences in men's and women's athletic interests. One strand of criticism takes a cultural feminist (or "difference") perspective, arguing that the three-part test locks women into a model of sport that is designed for men, and that women's athletic interests are more recreational, valuing participation over elite

---

348. See, e.g., Gonyo v. Drake Univ., 879 F. Supp. 1000 (S.D. Iowa 1995); Kelley v. Bd. of Trustees, 35 F.3d 265 (7th Cir. 1994); Miami Univ. Wrestling Club v. Miami Univ., 302 F.3d 608 (6th Cir. 2002); Equity in Athletics, Inc. v. Dep't of Educ., 639 F.3d 91 (4th Cir. 2011).

349. See, e.g., Ollier v. Sweetwater Union High Sch. Dist., 768 F.3d 843 (9th Cir. 2014); Horner v. Kentucky High School Athletic Ass'n, 43 F.3d 265 (6th Cir. 1994).

350. Bryan Toporek, Chicago Public Schools Reach Title IX Settlement with U.S. Dept. of Ed., Educ. Week, July 10, 2015; Bryan Toporek, N.Y.C. Public Schools in Violation of Title IX, Feds Find, Educ. Week, Feb. 24, 2015.

351. Office for Civil Rights, Additional Clarification of Intercollegiate Athletics Policy: Three Part Test—Part Three (2005). See also Erin E. Buzuvis, Survey Says . . . A Critical Analysis of the New Title IX Policy and a Proposal for Reform, 91 Iowa L. Rev. 821 (2006).

352. Don Sabo & Christine H. B. Grant, Ctr. for Research on Physical Activity, Sport and Health, D'Youville College, Limitations of the Department of Education's Online Survey Method for Measuring Athletic Interest and Ability on U.S.A. Campuses (2005).

353. Office for Civil Rights, Intercollegiate Athletics Policy Clarification, The Three-Part Test, Part Three (2010). For a discussion of the relevant history, see Brake, Getting in the Game, supra note 304, at 219-21.

354. See Robb v. Lock Haven Univ. of Pa., 2019 U.S. Dist. LEXIS 76762 (M.D. Pa. May 7, 2019).

competition.[355] This critique harkens back to early supporters of women's sports, who worried that Title IX would reproduce in female sports the same pressure to produce high-visibility and powerhouse teams endemic to male sports, rather than increasing female participation in intramural and club programs that promote the health and well-being of broad numbers of students. Before Title IX, the Association for Intercollegiate Athletics for Women (AIAW) pursued a less competitive model of sport than the NCAA. After the passage of Title IX, which the NCAA had initially opposed, the NCAA successfully managed to swallow up the AIAW and seize control over women's sports. This takeover, some critics have contended, imposed an overly commercial system on a program that initially had superior athlete-centered, educationally oriented values.[356] Do you agree? Would most female athletes? Could improving opportunities for women mean producing a more cooperative model of sport that better promotes physical and psychological health, teamwork, friendship, and recreation, rather than replicating a male model of sport?

4. **Affirmative Action or Nondiscrimination?**   Is the three-part test adopted in *Cohen* an example of affirmative action or is it a measure of nondiscrimination? This depends, of course, on what one understands as a neutral baseline, in relation to which some change might be understood as "affirmative" intervention.

Cohen rejects Brown's claim about the lack of greater women's interest in athletics based on factors partially controlled by institutions, such as Brown, that historically seemed to have contributed to the problem. Scholars have identified numerous ways in which educational institutions have suppressed women's athletic interest. These include (1) the dominance of men in leadership positions in college athletics; (2) disparities in hiring, promotion, and pay between male and female coaches and resource inequalities in other expenditures for women's sports; (3) the linkage of sports with masculinity, which is evidenced in training methods built on norms of masculinity ("you throw like a girl"); (4) hostile or demeaning characterizations of female athletes; (5) lesbian-baiting; and (6) the objectification of women in sports (starting with the "quintessentially 'feminine' role" of cheerleaders who "[stand] at the periphery, offering unconditional support for the athletes who play the traditionally masculine role of competing in the primary athletic event").[357] Cultural depictions of women in sports may also play a role in shaping girls' and women's interest in participating. Women continue to be starkly underrepresented in media coverage of sports.[358] Even when female athletes receive media attention,

---

355. See, e.g., B. Glenn George, Forfeit: Opportunity, Choice, and Discrimination Theory Under Title IX, 22 Yale J.L. & Feminism 1 (2010); Dionne L. Koller, Not Just One of the Boys: A Post-Feminist Critique of Title IX's Vision for Gender Equity in Sports, 43 Conn. L. Rev. 401 (2010).

356. See, e.g., Mary A. Boutilier & Lucinda SanGiovanni, The Sporting Woman 173-76 (1983); Murray Sperber, College Sports Inc.: The Athletic Department vs. The University 322-32 (1990).

357. Deborah Brake, The Struggle for Sex Equality in Sport and the Theory Behind Title IX, 34 U. Mich. J.L. Reform 13, 74-122 (2001).

358. See Cheryl Cooky et al., One and Done: The Long Eclipse of Women's Televised Sports, 1989-2019, 9 Communication & Sport 347 (2021) (finding little change in the disproportionate media coverage of men's and women's sports in the past thirty years).

they are often judged harshly and under a double standard for their appearance, condemned if they look too masculine or too feminine.[359]

To what extent should educational institutions such as Brown University be held accountable for the factors that suppress women's interest in sports? Should they be required to affirmatively reverse the effects of their own past practices? Would it help if more sports were open to men and women?[360] Or would shifting to a gender-inclusive model of sports only further marginalize female athletes?

One benefit to how Title IX has developed, imposing the three-part test for equal athletic opportunity onto a sex-separate structure of sports, is that any contraction of women's athletic opportunities, such as cutting a woman's team, registers doctrinally as disparate treatment rather than disparate impact.[361] Since the Supreme Court has cast doubt on the availability of a private right of action under Title IX for disparate impact, shifting to a gender-neutral model of sports would make it more difficult to prove a Title IX violation if a university took facially neutral action (such as cuts to gender-inclusive teams), with the effect of reducing women's participation opportunities.[362]

5. **Gaming Compliance.**   Under the first prong of the three-part test, compliance with substantial proportionality is determined by counting athletes on team rosters. Some colleges have found crafty ways to strategically manage rosters to demonstrate compliance on paper while inflating women's participation or understating men's actual participation levels. In 2009, female athletes sued Quinnipiac University over its roster manipulation inflating women's participation numbers.[363] The university cut its women's volleyball team but claimed that it remained in compliance with Title IX under prong one. The court disagreed, finding that the school artificially inflated its women's rosters by automatically counting its women's cross-country athletes as participants in indoor and outdoor track. Although Title IX generally permits counting each athlete for each sport in which she participates, Quinnipiac required its women's cross-country runners to join indoor and outdoor track — including runners who were injured or "red-shirted" and unable to participate — even though no other athletes were required to join multiple sports teams. In fact, Quinnipiac prohibited its male cross-country runners from competing individually in men's indoor and outdoor track. The lack of genuine athletic opportunity for the women cross-country runners in indoor and outdoor track prompted the court to reduce the women's participation numbers from what was reflected on the rosters, leaving Quinnipiac out of compliance with prong one, and require the school to reinstate volleyball.[364] Another common form of roster manipulation is to count male participants on women's practice squads toward female participation numbers, thereby artificially inflating women's participation.[365] On

---

359. Allison McCann, World Cup Players Say Muscles and Makeup Mix Just Fine, Thanks, N.Y. Times, June 20, 2019.

360. McDonagh & Pappano, supra note 281, at 252-55.

361. See Balow v. Mich. State Univ., 2021 WL 650712 (W.D. Mich. Feb. 19, 2021).

362. See Sandoval v. Alexander, 532 U.S. 275 (2001).

363. Biediger v. Quinnipiac Univ., 691 F.3d 85 (2d Cir. 2012).

364. Id. See also Lazor v. Univ. of Conn., 560 F. Supp.3d 674, 682 (D. Conn. 2021).

365. See Title IX: Falling Short at 50, USA Today, June 16, 2022.

the flip side, some colleges have undercounted men's numbers by deleting athletes from the roster prior to the first day of competition (the federal benchmark for reporting under the Equity in Athletics Disclosure Act), and then adding those athletes back on the roster once the first day of competition has passed.[366] How should the law respond to such compliance strategies?

Even when a school is found to be out of compliance, nothing in Title IX requires it to add or keep the sports that the plaintiffs wanted, instead of selecting sports for the institution's own fiscal or institutional reasons (for example, adding a sport that can use an existing field may be cheaper than keeping water sports, due to the cost of facilities and upkeep, and yet that choice may not best reflect women's athletic interests at the school).[367] Are there other measures of nondiscrimination, besides the three-part test, that might have avoided these complications? A simpler alternative, which was never seriously considered, would be to allocate equal financial resources for men's and women's athletic programs and allow each program to design and support the sports that best meet the interests of their students. Why do you think this approach was not adopted?

6. **Allocating Resources Under Title IX.** In addition to requiring equal participation opportunities — the issue litigated in *Cohen* — Title IX also requires equal treatment of men's and women's teams. Some of the litigated cases address matters of unequal scheduling, access to fields, and equipment. For example, one case involved schools that scheduled girls' soccer in the spring, and boys' soccer in the fall, in order to stagger use of field space. As a result, the girls' team was unable to compete in the New York Regional and State Championships, while the boys' team could compete. The appellate court found that this practice denied equality of athletic opportunity to the female team members, in violation of Title IX.[368]

An issue that frequently arises in equal treatment claims is the allocation of resources. The Title IX regulations reviewed in *Cohen* make it clear that Title IX does not require that women's sports receive equal expenditures. The regulation's only specific funding requirement is that the allocation of scholarships must match women's participation rates.[369] However, because men's athletic participation rates are higher, male intercollegiate athletes receive over $250 million more than women in athletic scholarship money.[370] With respect to athletic programs more generally, equal opportunity is measured by an overall comparison of the men's and women's programs, taking into account a variety of open-ended factors relating to the availability of teams and levels of competition, equipment, supplies, scheduling, travel, tutoring, locker rooms, practice facilities, housing, coaching, publicity, and the like. Women account for 54 percent of undergraduate enrollment at NCAA Division I institutions, but only 47 percent of intercollegiate athletes, and

---

366. See Biediger v. Quinnipiac Univ., 616 F. Supp.2d 277, 284-85 (D. Conn. 2009).

367. See, e.g., Mayerova v. E. Mich. Univ., 2019 U.S. App. LEXIS 9373 (6th Cir. Mar. 28, 2019); Berndsen v. N. Dakota Univ. Sys., 7 F.4th 782 (8th Cir. 2021).

368. See McCormick v. Sch. Dist. of Mamaroneck, 370 F.3d 275 (2d Cir. 2004).

369. See Barbara J. Osborne, Failing to Fund Fairly: Title IX Athletics Scholarship Compliance, 6 Tenn. J. Race, Gender, & Soc. Just. 83 (2017).

370. Women's Sports Foundation, 50 Years of Title IX, supra note 329, at 11.

the spending disparities are even more pronounced. Division I schools spend twice as much on men's sports than women's sports; the largest gaps are at schools with big football programs, where the disparity rises to two and a half times as much.[371] Even in Divisions II and III, where football is less of a resources hog, significant spending disparities remain.[372] When funds for recruiting and coaching salaries are taken into account, the gender spending gap approaches a three-to-one ratio.[373] High school funding data are harder to come by, since there is no equivalent to the federal Equity in Athletics Disclosure Act (which applies to intercollegiate athletics) at the high school level, so collecting information typically requires public records requests. Evidence from OCR complaints, litigation, and media reports suggests that the equal treatment problems at the high school level are endemic.[374]

Examples of unequal treatment in men's and women's sports are ubiquitous. One particularly egregious example made news in March 2021, when stark disparities came to light in the women's and men's NCAA basketball tournaments—including a state-of-the-art weight room for the men and a single dumbbell tree and yoga mats for the women. An outside report commissioned to review the incident found that the NCAA prioritizes men's basketball above all else, massively undervalues the market worth of women's basketball, and lacks any structure or system to identify, prevent, or address inequities between the men's and women's NCAA championship programs.[375]

A major problem, say many Title IX advocates, is enforcement. OCR does not routinely conduct Title IX compliance reviews on its own initiative. The insufficiency of penalties is another concern. Funding cutoffs are available in principle but not in practice. Universities' internal compliance procedures are also spotty. Although the Title IX regulations have long required educational institutions to appoint a Title IX coordinator to internally monitor compliance, institutional failures to appoint, publicize, and train such officials are still widespread.[376] The available data point to persistent violations of Title IX and a weak federal enforcement agency that is ill-equipped to ensure compliance.[377] Given the high levels of professed public support for Title IX,[378] why do you think the law has been so difficult to enforce?

371. NCAA, Title IX 50th Anniversary Report: The State of Women in College Sports 27, 28 (June 2022).

372. Id. at 30.

373. ESPN News Service, NCAA's Title IX Report Shows Stark Gap in Funding for Women, June 23, 2022.

374. See Women's Sports Foundation, 50 Years of Title IX, supra note 329, at 39 (discussing one case against a school district after which the plaintiffs' lawyers concluded, "almost all high schools are out of compliance with Title IX").

375. Alan Blinder, Report: N.C.A.A. Prioritized Men's Basketball "Over Everything Else," N.Y. Times, Aug. 3, 2021.

376. Women's Sports Foundation, 50 Years of Title IX, supra note 329, at 25-27.

377. See Alixandra B. Yanus & Karen O'Connor, To Comply or Not to Comply: Evaluating Compliance with Title IX of the Educational Amendments of 1972, 37 J. Women Pol. & Pub. Pol'y 341 (2016).

378. See Liz Clarke, Scott Clement & Emily Guskin, Most Americans Support Gender Equity in Sports Scholarships, Wash. Post, June 22, 2022.

7. **Pregnant Student Athletes**. Where do pregnant athletes fit into the existing model of sport, which was designed for men? This issue was thrust into the public eye in 2007 when ESPN's *Outside the Lines* ran a segment showcasing athletes who lost their athletic scholarships and dropped out of school when they became pregnant.[379] In response to the criticism and controversy that followed, OCR issued a "Dear Colleague" letter explaining the obligations under Title IX with respect to pregnant athletes.[380] The NCAA, which was taken to task in the ESPN program for not addressing pregnancy in its scholarship or eligibility rules, also took action. In 2008, it amended its scholarship rules to require members to treat pregnancy no worse than other injuries or illnesses, which means that a school cannot withdraw a scholarship based on pregnancy alone, and issued a model policy that includes other protections, including a right to reinstatement at the same level of competition after recovery from pregnancy or childbirth.[381] Still, most women participating in intercollegiate sports are unaware that they would have any rights under Title IX in the event of a pregnancy.[382] Why has intercollegiate athletics been so slow to respond to the reality of pregnancy among female athletes? What model of equality can best ensure that female athletic careers are not derailed by pregnancy, given the overlap between peak athletic and childrearing years?

8. **Redefining Sport**. What would a feminist reimagining of sport look like? In determining whether an activity is a sport for purposes of Title IX, OCR considers whether the primary purpose of the activity is to promote athletic competition.[383] Courts, too, have emphasized competition as a hallmark of intercollegiate sport, and some have rebuffed university attempts to count competitive cheerleading as an intercollegiate sport for purposes of measuring Title IX compliance, at least where competitive opportunities in the event are unequal to those provided varsity sports.[384] Competitive spirit team is a growing sport at the high school level, however.[385] Is it an implicitly male standard to emphasize competition over other values of sport, such as teamwork, dedication, cooperation, and physical fitness? For that matter, is physicality—as distinct from strategy and the nonphysical dimensions of

---

379. See Deborah L. Brake, The Invisible Pregnant Athlete and the Promise of Title IX, 31 Harv. J. Gender L. 323 (2008).

380. Office for Civil Rights, Dear Colleague Letter (June 25, 2007), http:// www.ed .gov/about/offices/list/ocr/letters/colleague-20070625.html.

381. NCAA Division I and II Bylaw 15, § 3.4.3; see also Bylaw 15, § 3.2.2; NCAA, Pregnant and Parenting Student-Athletes: Resources and Model Policies (2008).

382. Women's Sports Foundation, 50 Years of Title IX, supra note 329, at 60 (reporting study finding 69 percent of participants were unaware of their pregnancy-related rights prior to the survey).

383. U.S. Dep't of Educ., OCR, Dear Colleague Letter: Athletic Activities Counted for Title IX Compliance (Sept. 17, 2008), https://www2.ed.gov/about/offices/list/ocr/letters/ colleague-20080917.html.

384. See *Biediger*, 691 F.3d at 103-05 (competitive cheer at Quinnipiac was not a sport for purposes of Title IX, given insufficient competitive opportunities, inconsistency in scoring, and low quality of competition and postseason play compared to other varsity sports).

385. Women's Sports Foundation, 50 Years of Title IX, supra note 329, at 30 (competitive spirit now ranks ninth in the top ten most popular high school girls' sports).

sport—inherently a central aspect of what makes an activity a sport? The growing popularity of e-sports might suggest otherwise.[386] And yet, e-sports are no panacea for women's equality.[387] Does this cast doubt on biology-based explanations for sex inequality in sport? Is it possible to redesign sport to be less male-centric?

9. **Commercialization and Pay for Play**.   In recent years, controversy has peaked over what many view as the exploitation of college athletes, who earn vast sums of money for their institutions but are prohibited by NCAA amateurism rules from receiving monetary benefits themselves. Some critics analogize the structure of college sports to a plantation economy, in which predominantly white elites control and profit from the labor of a group that includes many athletes of color. In recent years, some steps have been taken to allow athletes to profit from playing college sports. In 2019, California was the first state to pass a Fair Pay to Play Act, allowing college athletes to secure endorsements and sponsorships without risking their athletic scholarships. Other states soon followed suit. In January 2021, the Supreme Court upheld a district court ruling holding that the NCAA's tight restrictions on education-related benefits to athletes violated federal antitrust law.[388] Soon after the decision, the NCAA voted to allow athletes to receive remuneration for their name, image, and likeness (NIL), but continued to set limits on the amount of education-related compensation schools can directly provide to athletes.[389] Further changes are likely.

What does this new landscape mean for women? On one hand, funneling more money to athletes, whether from schools or corporate sponsors, may disproportionately benefit male athletes, whose programs receive the biggest investments and market share. On the other hand, women athletes may have more to gain by the greater exposure made possible by the new rules on NIL.[390] So far, however, between 60 and 64 percent of endorsement deals awarded to intercollegiate athletes have gone to men.[391] Does Title IX put any obligation on schools to ensure that the money athletes receive for playing college sports, from whatever source, is distributed evenly to women and men?[392] If male intercollegiate athletes end up earning more than women from participating in their sports, should universities have to take action to equalize these outcomes? Does it matter if men's teams generate more revenue for their university, or should the main consideration be whether male and female athletes put equal amounts of time and effort into their sports?[393]

---

386. See Niraj Chokshi, What You Might Not Know About E-Sports, Soon to Be a $1 Billion Industry, N.Y. Times, Aug. 27, 2018, at B5.

387. See Yolanda L. Jackson, Sexism in eSports, Huff. Post (Nov. 14, 2017).

388. NCAA v. Alston, 141 S. Ct. 2141 (2021).

389. Leading Cases: NCAA v. Alston, 135 Harv. L. Rev. 471 (2021).

390. See Sarah Traynor, California Says Checkmate: Exploring the Nation's First Pay to Play Act and What It Means for the Future of the NCAA and Female Student-Athletes, 20 Wake Forest J. Bus. & Intell. Prop. L. 203 (2020) (arguing that female athletes and women's sports stand to gain, especially since women's professional opportunities are so limited).

391. Women's Sports Foundation, 50 Years of Title IX, supra note 329, at 13.

392. See Tan Boston, As California Goes, So Goes the Nation: A Title IX Analysis of the Fair Pay to Play Act, 17 Stan. J. C.R.& C.L. 1 (2021) (arguing that Title IX applies to NIL compensation, regardless of the source).

393. NCAA Research, GOALS Study: Understanding the Student Athlete Experience (2019).

PUTTING THEORY INTO PRACTICE

2-41. Connecticut's interscholastic athletic association permits transgender girls to compete in girls' sports. After two transgender girls won top medals in their track events, the parents of cisgender girls brought a Title IX lawsuit claiming that their equal opportunity to compete was denied by having to run against athletes with a biologically "male" advantage.[394] How should a court decide the case? Would it affect your analysis to know that the transgender girls involved were Black?[395] Should it matter that soon after filing suit, one of the plaintiffs finished first in her event, ahead of both transgender girls?[396]

2-42. Under Texas law, athletes must compete on the interscholastic team that aligns with their assigned sex, regardless of how they identify. A transgender boy taking testosterone, under medical supervision for his gender transition, won the state girls' wrestling championship. Parents of girls in the competition complained that this was unfair, since the transgender boy was on hormone therapy supplementing his testosterone levels. The transgender boy explained that he would have preferred to compete on the boys' team but was barred from doing so by the state. He added that it would have been unfair to him and medically inappropriate to stop hormone therapy as a condition for competing in sports.[397] Do the cisgender girls have an argument that the state policy violated their Title IX right to equal athletic opportunity? Does the transgender boy have a Title IX argument that the Texas rule discriminated against him by prohibiting him from competing as a boy? As a matter of policy, how should sport eligibility rules apply to transgender boys?

2-43. In June 2022, the Biden administration announced the intent to propose regulations addressing schools' obligations toward transgender students seeking to participate in sex-separate sports.[398] If you were advising the Department, how would you advocate regulating in this area? Try your hand at drafting a set of Title IX rules governing transgender athlete eligibility. Can you defend the lines you've drawn?

2-44. It is typical for mixed-gender intramural teams at colleges and universities to have requirements for participation by women in every game (for example, that at least two women be on the field, or in the batting lineup, at all times). How would you evaluate this approach from a gender equality perspective? Do you think rules requiring a certain gender balance on the field are likely to advance gender

---

394. See Soule v. Conn. Ass'n of Schools, Case No. 3:20-cv-00201 (RNC), 2021 WL 1617206 (D. Conn. Apr. 25, 2021).

395. See Elizabeth A. Sharrow, Sports, Transgender Rights and the Bodily Politics of Cisgender Supremacy, 10 Laws 1, 3 (2021).

396. See Teen Beats Transgender Competitor Amid Sports Participation Lawsuit, NBC Connecticut (Feb. 14, 2020).

397. See Catherine Jean Archibald, Transgender and Intersex Sports Rights, 26 Va. J. Soc. Pol'y & L. 246, 256 (2019).

398. U.S. Dep't of Educ., Federal Register Notice of Proposed RuleMaking: Title IX of the Education Amendments of 1972, at 541-42, https://www2.ed.gov/about/offices/list/ocr/docs/t9nprm.pdf.

equality in practice, or is it more likely women will be resented and marginalized on the field? Whatever the merits of this approach for recreational sports, is it a model that could be implemented at the varsity level?[399]

2-45. A male student on a high school swim team was hazed by his teammates. The hazing including dragging him into a bathroom and shaving his head against his will; applying Icy Hot to him without consent to create a burning sensation; stealing his swim equipment; and hitting him hard enough on the back to create a "five-star" handprint on his skin. He was not the only victim but was the only one to seek help from the school. The coach told his mother that "it's best if we don't do anything about it at this point." The athletic director said "the boys don't look at [these actions] as hazing," but rather as "initiation." The superintendent said: "[h]ey lady, your kid's hair got cut." The hazing continued unabated. In a lawsuit, the boy alleged that the school officials "were willfully turning a blind eye to all of the awful things going on in the male swimming program because 'boys will be boys,'" and that they did not permit similar types of hazing among female athletes.[400] Are the statements by the school officials sufficient to show the school's non-intervention was because of sex? If not, what other evidence would support or undermine his claim of sex discrimination?

2-46. In the United States, field hockey is typically a girls' sport. But when Keeling Pilaro moved to Long Island from Ireland, where he had been taught to play, he asked to play on the girls' team. As a sixth grader, he was invited to play for the local high school varsity field hockey team. He was a high scorer and earned "all-conference" honors. After two years, he was told that he was now "too skilled" to play for the girls' team. At 4 foot, 8 inches tall and 82 pounds, he is no larger than the average female player on his team. The school administrators said they looked only at his skill level, which gives him an "unfair advantage," and decided that his presence was interfering with meaningful athletic opportunities for girls. Should he be allowed to play? Does it matter that he has been playing for two years already?[401]

2-47. In the summer of 2017, reports surfaced about girls in youth soccer clubs (from different parts of the Midwest) who were barred from competition or harassed for sporting short haircuts that purportedly made them look like boys.[402] What does this incident say about the gendered structure of sport? Is it a product of the approach to equality that the law has taken in this area? Or is it the result of cultural and societal forces that are beyond the power of any model of equality adopted in the law to eradicate?

2-48. Under state high school league rules, only girls are permitted to compete in dance team competitions sanctioned by the state. A boy who joined his high

---

399. See B. Glenn George, Fifty/Fifty: Ending Sex Segregation in School Sports, 63 Ohio St. L. J. 1107 (2002).

400. These facts are taken from J.H. v. Sch. Town of Munster, 160 F. Supp. 3d 1079 (N.D. Ind. 2016).

401. Boy Wants to Play Girls' Field Hockey, timesunion.com (May 7, 2012).

402. Christopher Mele, Hairstyle Keeps Team from Tournament, N.Y. Times, June 7, 2017, at B9; Maddie Koss, No, They're Not Boys. But Madison Soccer Team Endures Criticism Because Players Have Short Hair, Milwaukee J. Sentinel, Aug. 5, 2017.

school dance team was forbidden from competing on the team. Is dance team a "sport" for purposes of Title IX? What considerations should determine whether an activity is a sport? Is the definition of sport gendered? If dance team is a sport, how should the Title IX rules governing athletics apply to the boy's challenge to his exclusion from competition?[403]

2-49. Highland Park High School in Dallas, Texas, maintains a strong sports program for both male and female athletes, with teams of each gender frequently bringing home state championship titles. All boys' teams are referred to as "The Scots," while all girls' teams are referred to as "The Lady Scots." Should female athletes object to this labeling? Why or why not? What arguments might persuade the administration to change this naming system?

b. Sports Outside of School Settings

Sex-separate competition is also characteristic of sports outside of schools, including both professional and amateur sports. Because these programs are not connected to educational institutions, Title IX does not apply; and because they are private, they are not bound by the Constitution's Equal Protection Clause. Title VII may come into play for athletes in professional sports if they are legally considered to be employees, as opposed to independent contractors; but so far at least, Title VII has not played a significant role in addressing sex equality in professional sports.[404] As a result, amateur and professional sports are far less regulated, from a sex equality perspective, than school-based athletics. The Amateur Sports Act, which establishes a governing structure for Olympic sports and their feeder programs, leaves the regulation of athletic eligibility and other matters of governance largely up to the athletic association for each particular sport.

Sex-separate teams are the norm for the vast majority of amateur and professional sports.[405] As in educational settings, there is much debate over the reasons and justifications for sex separation in Olympic sports.[406] Controversy has also arisen when individual athletes are not easily classifiable along a gender binary. The issue of how to determine an athlete's sex has arisen most prominently in Olympic sports, where the stakes are high and can include lucrative corporate sponsorships. As a result, in Olympic sports and their feeder amateur sports programs, an elaborate and shifting set of rules and procedures has developed to handle contested cases of athletes' sex. This process has not been without missteps. Sex verification in Olympic competition was originally enforced through "naked parades" in which

---

403. Lisa L. Kaczke, Title IX Complaint Filed over Minnesota Dance Team Policy, Duluth News Trib., Nov. 14, 2017. See also D. M. v. Minn. State High Sch. League, 917 F.3d 994 (8th Cir. 2019).

404. The Equal Pay Act was invoked by the U.S. women's soccer team to challenge their lower pay compared to male soccer players; that litigation is covered in Chapter 1, Section C.

405. The few exceptions in amateur sports include riflery and equestrian events.

406. For a critical take on the origins of separate women's Olympic sports, see Michele Krech, The Misplaced Burdens of "Gender Equality" in Caster Semenya v. IAAF: The Court of Arbitration for Sport Attempts Human Rights Adjudication, 19 Int'l Sports L. Rev. 66, 69 (2019).

a team of observers would identify athletes' sex based on the reviewers' perceptions of external genitalia.[407] Of course, only women were in the athlete parades. This degrading method was replaced by an evolving set of rules seeking to resolve disputed questions of sex.

A major difficulty in designing rules for athlete sex verification is the gap between a binary system of sex classification and the diversity of human physiology. Many persons — sometimes referred to as intersex — have chromosomes, external sex characteristics, or hormonal balances that defy a binary classification as either male or female.

With inherent ambiguity in drawing clear lines, cultural expectations about sex, gender, and feminine comportment necessarily come into play in determining whose sex is contested.[408] Critics of Olympic sport sex verification policies point out that the burden has fallen disproportionately on women of color.[409] Even before the highly publicized controversy over Black South African sprinter Caster Semenya, Indian sprinter Dutee Chand was singled out for medical scrutiny based on concerns expressed by other female athletes and coaches that she had a "masculine physique" and questionable "stride and musculature."[410] After initially being excluded from international women's track competition, Chand successfully appealed the ruling.[411]

Semenya's challenge to the sex verification rules that have disqualified her from international competition was less successful. After Semenya's exceptional speed triggered scrutiny of her eligibility to compete as a woman, she was subjected to mandatory sex testing. The results revealed that Semenya, who was classified as female at birth, raised as a girl, and identified throughout her life as a woman, had naturally elevated levels of testosterone, above the average levels typical for most women. The International Association of Athletics Foundation (IAAF) bars women from competition if they have "differences of sexual development," an umbrella term that includes hypoandrogenism, the condition used to disqualify Semenya, in which high levels of testosterone combine with androgen sensitivity.[412] In May 2019, the Court of Arbitration for Sport, based in Switzerland, ruled against Semenya's challenge to her exclusion under the rules and upheld the testosterone limits

---

407. Id.

408. Krech, To Be a Woman, supra note 321, at 286-87 (arguing that the "reasonable suspicion" standard for sex testing athletic eligibility in international women's competition incorporates "intersecting sexist and racist stereotypes" "that are culturally and historically specific, and often privilege white, middle-class, and Western standards of female beauty").

409. Krech, The Misplaced Burdens, supra note 406, at 70 (stating that "the IAAF's female eligibility regulations have almost exclusively affected women of colour from the Global South").

410. Krech, To Be a Woman, supra note 321, at 272.

411. The Court of Sport Appeals agreed with Chand that the IAAF regulations lacked sufficient scientific basis, but gave the IAAF two years to provide additional scientific evidence justifying the regulatory exclusion with regard to hyperandrogenism. Id. at 275-76.

412. Krech, The Misplaced Burdens, supra note 406, at 66 (criticizing the CAS decision).

as necessary to preserve the integrity of women's track competition.[413] The Swiss Supreme Court—the final court of appeal for Semenya—upheld the ruling, leaving Semenya disqualified from competition unless she underwent hormone therapy to comply with the IAAF regulation.[414] Semenya has refused to do so, a decision backed by the World Medical Association, which has opposed the IAAF regulation on ethical and medical grounds for conditioning athletic eligibility on hormone therapy that is not medically indicated for an athlete's health.[415]

Critics of such sex verification policies claim that these rules not only squeeze out athletes like Semenya, who identify as women but do not conform to a binary definition of sex; they also reinforce the stereotype of women's athletic inferiority.[416] Women who are "too good" for their sport may be called upon to prove their femaleness. Racialized conceptions of femininity inevitably play a role in determining which women are subjected to this scrutiny.[417] No such sex surveillance regime polices the athletes who compete in men's Olympic sports. On the other hand, if separate Olympic sports are worth preserving for women, how should the boundary between male and female be enforced? Would women Olympians be better off in a gender-blind sport structure in which men and women competed together? Does your analysis of the dilemma of separation here involve any different considerations than when considering sex separation in school sports?

Olympic sports have also wrestled with the issue of how to treat transgender athletes in a system of sex-separate opportunities, albeit more quietly. Only recently did an openly transgender woman compete in an Olympic women's sport. In 2021, Laurel Hubbard competed in the women's division of Olympic weightlifting. Her participation generated publicity and controversy, but it was somewhat more muted than the controversy over intercollegiate swimmer Lia Thomas, discussed above—perhaps because Hubbard did not complete her lifts or win a medal.[418] In November 2021, the International Olympic Committee announced a new policy, leaving it to each international sport body to set its own rules for transgender athlete eligibility.[419] In June 2022, the governing body for swimming made news when it issued rules barring an athlete who has gone through male puberty from the women's competition, and encouraged a new "open" category in some events

---

413. Jere Longman & Juliet Macur, Sports Court Backs Distinct Gender Lines, in Defeat for Olympian, N.Y. Times, May 2, 2019, at A1.

414. Jere Longman, Track's Caster Semenya Loses Appeal to Defend 800-Meter Title, N.Y. Times, Sept. 8, 2020.

415. Id.

416. See Erin Buzuvis, Hormone Check: Critique of Olympic Rules on Sex and Gender, 31 Wis. J. L. Gender & Soc'y 29 (2016).

417. See Katrina Karkazis & Rebecca M. Jordan-Young, The Powers of Testosterone: Obscuring Race and Regional Bias in the Regulation of Women Athletes, 30 Feminist Formations 1 (2018).

418. See Ken Belson & Tariq Panja, In Weight Lifting, a Historic Moment for Transgender Women, N.Y. Times, Aug. 2, 2020.

419. International Olympic Committee, IOC Framework on Fairness, Inclusion and Non-Discrimination on the Basis of Gender Identity and Sex Variations.

in which transgender athletes can compete.[420] Supporters claim the rule is necessary to protect the integrity of women's swimming competition, but critics question whether effectively banning transgender women from the sport is compatible with the Olympic Charter's principles of human rights, gender equality and inclusion, and athlete welfare.[421] Eligibility rules in other Olympic sports are in flux, as sport governing bodies grapple with the issue of transgender athlete eligibility in women's competition.[422]

What difference, if any, does it make that the issue of transgender inclusion in women's Olympic sports is not tied to an educational setting? Title IX's sex-conscious approach has been defended as a "tool-giving" measure to ensure that the educational benefits of sports are equally distributed to women and men.[423] If the purpose of Olympic sports is not to educate athletes but to showcase their talents, might that affect the analysis of why and how to separate sports by sex? Is there a stronger case for prioritizing individual athletes' competitive interests in Olympic sports than in intercollegiate and interscholastic sports? But whose competitive interests should prevail—those of cisgender women seeking to win medals, or of transgender women seeking a chance to compete and win?

Professional sports, too, are largely based on a structure of sex separation. As in the educational setting, separate does not mean equal. Where women have professional opportunities in sports—the WNBA, the Premier Hockey Federation (formerly National Women's Hockey League), and the Ladies Professional Golf Association, for example—they lag far behind in market share, salaries, and prestige of their male counterparts. To what extent do you think the sex-separate structure of sport is responsible for women's second-class status in professional sports? Would women be better off without separate women's teams, in a gender-blind system of tryouts for, say, a professional basketball team? Very few women have crossed the gender line to play a professional sport with men, at least in major sports markets. In 1977, a woman, Lusia Harris, was drafted by the New Orleans Jazz, the first and only woman to be drafted by any NBA team, but Harris was pregnant at the time and declined the opportunity.[424] Does this example speak to the need for separate professional sports for women, which would likely be better at accommodating women's distinctive needs and abilities? Yet even with separate leagues, the world of professional sports has struggled to accommodate players' pregnancies.[425] Consider whether the dilemma of difference plays out differently in the professional sport

---

420. Restrictions on Transgender Athletes Violate Olympic Charter- FIMS Chief, Reuters, July 1, 2022.

421. Id.

422. Policies on transgender athletes competing in Olympic and amateur sports are regularly updated at the Policies link on www.transathlete.com.

423. Kimberly A. Yuracko, One for You and One for Me: Is Title IX's Sex-Based Proportionality Requirement for College Varsity Athletic Positions Defensible?, 97 NW. Univ. L. Rev. 731 (2003).

424. Doug Harris, Lusia Harris, Only Woman Drafted by NBA Team, Dies, Assoc. Press, Jan. 18, 2022.

425. See Kevin Draper, Nike Plans to Stop Penalizing Pregnancy, N.Y. Times, Mar. 25, 2019, at B11.

setting, taking into account the distinctive interests and purposes of professional sports.

Policing the gender line in women's professional sports has also proven difficult. One of the most prominent controversies in this setting arose when tennis pro Richard Raskind publicly came out as a woman, Renee Richards, and competed on the women's circuit in the 1970s.[426] No overall governance structure applies to professional sports, leaving each professional sport body to create its own rules for eligibility in a woman's league, with varied results.[427] Unlike sports in schools, professional sports do not purport to be about providing educational opportunities for players. Does the distinctive nature and purpose of professional sports affect your analysis of how to draw the line on transgender inclusion in women's professional sports?

PUTTING THEORY INTO PRACTICE

2-50. The Ladies Professional Golf Association (LPGA) voted in 2010 to drop its requirement that players in the league be "female at birth." However, in order to compete, the LPGA requires a transgender woman to have completed gender reassignment surgery prior to competition in addition to at least one year of hormone therapy.[428] If a transgender woman met the hormone therapy requirement, but did not want to take the risk of undergoing sex reassignment surgery, should she be allowed to compete in the LPGA as a woman? If you were consulted by the LPGA on whether to revise its eligibility policy, how would you advise the association?

2-51. At a Hollywood award ceremony, acclaimed director Jane Campion, who is white, gratuitously quipped in her acceptance speech that, unlike herself, tennis greats Venus and Serena Williams never had to "play against the guys." Campion quickly apologized for her "thoughtless comment" and praised the legendary greatness of the Williams sisters, who in fact, Campion acknowledged, had "squared off against men on the court [in mixed doubles matches] (and off)."[429] By all indications, Campion's remark was not a deliberate attempt to slight Venus and Serena Williams, but it left many puzzling over why it seemed to bubble up from Campion's subconscious. To what extent do you think the separation of women's and men's professional sports contributes to a culture in which women are not seen as equals in sport unless they play and win against men? Does Campion's remark reflect the limits of sex segregation as a substantive equality strategy—indicating that separate sports for women reinforce a message of female athletic inferiority? What does the remark reveal about the challenges Black women face in achieving the recognition they deserve in sport?

---

426. For an overview and analysis of the Richards controversy, see Edward Schiappa, The Transgender Exigency: Defining Sex and Gender in the 21st Century 115-17 (2022).

427. The website www.transathlete.com also maintains a current list of the policies of professional sports leagues on transgender inclusion.

428. Beth Ann Nichols, Transgender Woman Wins Florida Mini-Tour Event, Sets Sights Squarely on LPGA, USA Today, May 14, 2021.

429. Jon Blistein, Jane Campion Apologizes to Venus and Serena Williams: "I Made a Thoughtless Comment," Rolling Stone (Mar. 14, 2022).

D. SUBSTANTIVE EQUALITY IN THE FAMILY

1. The Right to Marry for Same-Sex Couples

The last two decades were witness to a flurry of legislation and litigation over whether gay and lesbian couples could marry. The earliest lawsuits claiming a right of same-sex couples to marry were filed in the 1970s. Same-sex couples in several states applied for marriage licenses and then sued after the clerks refused to issue them. Although the marriage codes at the time generally did not specify that only heterosexual couples could marry, courts turned to dictionary definitions of marriage as the union between one man and one woman and held that same-sex couples are incapable of entering into it because what they proposed was not marriage.[430] The constitutional claims raised by the litigants in these early cases were dismissed out of hand. The U.S. Supreme Court granted certiorari in one of the cases, Baker v. Nelson, but ultimately dismissed the writ "for want of a substantial federal question."[431]

In the 1990s, a new round of lawsuits were filed alleging that state statutes that were silent on gender should be construed to permit same-sex couples to marry and that statutes that could not be so construed were unconstitutional under the Equal Protection and Due Process Clauses of the respective state constitutions.[432] In Baehr v. Lewin, the Hawaii Supreme Court issued the first decision finding that a denial of the right to marriage to same-sex couples constituted sex discrimination.[433] Under its reasoning, the state constitution's Equal Protection Clause required the government to show a compelling interest in denying marriage licenses to gay and lesbian couples. Before a ruling on remand, Hawaii voters approved an amendment to the state constitution giving the legislature the power "to reserve marriage to opposite-sex couples," which it did.[434]

The threat of same-sex marriage in Hawaii fueled efforts at the state and federal level to ban the celebration and recognition of such marriages. Congress jump-started this movement with passage of the Defense of Marriage Act (DOMA) in 1996, which purported to give states the right to refuse recognition to same-sex marriages from other states and, more importantly, defined marriage as a union between a man and a woman for all federal-law purposes.[435] States followed suit with their own so-called mini-DOMAs; at the high point of anti-marriage-equality efforts, more than forty states had enacted statutes or constitutional amendments to ban the celebration and recognition of marriages for same-sex couples. These

---

430. Jones v. Hallahan, 501 S.W.2d 588, 589-90 (Ky. Ct. App. 1973).

431. 191 N.W.2d 185 (Minn. 1971), appeal dismissed by Baker v. Nelson, 409 U.S. 810 (1972).

432. See Joanna L. Grossman & Lawrence M. Friedman, Inside the Castle: Law and the Family in 20th Century America (2011).

433. 852 P.2d 44, 59-68 (Haw. 1993).

434. See Haw. Rev. Stat. § 572-1 (2019) (amended to exclude same-sex marriage in 1997 and to include it in 2013).

435. 28 U.S.C. § 1738C (2018).

enactments prevented courts from applying the traditional rules of interstate marriage recognition, which generally followed the "place of celebration" rule that meant marriages that were valid where celebrated were valid everywhere. The tides began to turn in 1999, when the Vermont Supreme Court held that same-sex couples either had to be permitted to marry or had to be extended the same benefits under the state constitution.[436] This led to the creation of the civil union as a formal alternative to marriage. Then, in 2004, Massachusetts became the first state to legalize same-sex marriage. In Goodridge v. Department of Public Health (2008), the Supreme Judicial Court ruled that the state constitutional guarantees of equal protection and due process were violated by prohibiting gays and lesbians equal access to marriage.[437] In the years that followed, there were a multitude of court decisions with mixed results.[438] Meanwhile, on the international front, many countries legalized same-sex marriage, including some, like Spain and Argentina, with strong Catholic populations.

The U.S. Supreme Court eventually intervened to resolve questions about the legality of bans on same-sex marriage recognition and celebration. In United States v. Windsor, the Supreme Court held that Section 3 of DOMA, which provided that marriage is defined as a union between a man and a woman for all federal law purposes, was unconstitutional.[439] The case involved a lesbian couple who had married in Canada and then returned home to New York. Although New York did not allow same-sex couples to marry at that time, it later passed a law authorizing such marriages and recognized this couple's marriage as valid. However, when the first spouse died, the surviving spouse was assessed a large estate tax because she did not qualify for the marital exemption because of DOMA. Justice Kennedy, writing for the majority, reasoned as follows:

> When at first Windsor and Spyer longed to marry, neither New York nor any other State granted them that right. After waiting some years, in 2007 they traveled to Ontario to be married there. . . .
>
> By history and tradition the definition and regulation of marriage, . . . has been treated as being within the authority and realm of the separate States. Yet it is further established that Congress, in enacting discrete statutes, can make determinations that bear on marital rights and privileges. Just this Term the Court upheld the authority of the Congress to pre-empt state laws, allowing a former spouse to retain life insurance proceeds under a federal program that gave her priority, because of formal beneficiary designation rules, over the wife by a second marriage who survived the husband. . . .

---

436. Baker v. State, 744 A.2d 864 (Vt. 1999).

437. 798 N.E.2d 941 (Mass. 2003); Opinion of the Justices to the Senate, 802 N.E.2d 565 (2004) (holding that creation of a civil union status was insufficient to cure the constitutional violation).

438. Compare In re Marriage Cases, 43 Cal. 4th 757 (Cal. 2008) with Hernandez v. Robles, 855 N.E.2d 1 (N.Y. 2006).

439. 133 U.S. 2675 (2013).

Though these discrete examples establish the constitutionality of limited federal laws that regulate the meaning of marriage in order to further federal policy, DOMA has a far greater reach; for it enacts a directive applicable to over 1,000 federal statutes and the whole realm of federal regulations. And its operation is directed to a class of persons that the laws of New York, and of 11 other States, have sought to protect.

In order to assess the validity of that intervention it is necessary to discuss the extent of the state power and authority over marriage as a matter of history and tradition. State laws defining and regulating marriage, of course, must respect the constitutional rights of persons, see, *e.g.*, Loving v. Virginia, 388 U.S. 1 (1967); but, subject to those guarantees, "regulation of domestic relations" is "an area that has long been regarded as a virtually exclusive province of the States." . . .

The recognition of civil marriages is central to state domestic relations law applicable to its residents and citizens. . . . Consistent with this allocation of authority, the Federal Government, through our history, has deferred to state-law policy decisions with respect to domestic relations. . . . In order to respect this principle, the federal courts, as a general rule, do not adjudicate issues of marital status even when there might otherwise be a basis for federal jurisdiction. . . .

Against this background DOMA rejects the long-established precept that the incidents, benefits, and obligations of marriage are uniform for all married couples within each State, though they may vary, subject to constitutional guarantees, from one State to the next. . . . DOMA, because of its reach and extent, departs from this history and tradition of reliance on state law to define marriage. . . .

DOMA seeks to injure the very class New York seeks to protect. By doing so it violates basic due process and equal protection principles applicable to the Federal Government. . . . The Constitution's guarantee of equality "must at the very least mean that a bare congressional desire to harm a politically unpopular group cannot" justify disparate treatment of that group. In determining whether a law is motived by an improper animus or purpose, " '[d]iscriminations of an unusual character' " especially require careful consideration. [Romer v. Evans, 517 U.S. 620, 633.] DOMA cannot survive under these principles. The responsibility of the States for the regulation of domestic relations is an important indicator of the substantial societal impact the State's classifications have in the daily lives and customs of its people. DOMA's unusual deviation from the usual tradition of recognizing and accepting state definitions of marriage here operates to deprive same-sex couples of the benefits and responsibilities that come with the federal recognition of their marriages. This is strong evidence of a law having the purpose and effect of disapproval of that class. The avowed purpose and practical effect of the law here in question are to impose a disadvantage, a separate status, and so a stigma upon all who enter into same-sex marriages made lawful by the unquestioned authority of the States.

The history of DOMA's enactment and its own text demonstrate that interference with the equal dignity of same-sex marriages, a dignity conferred by the States in the exercise of their sovereign power, was more than an incidental effect of the federal statute. It was its essence. . . .

DOMA's principal effect is to identify a subset of state-sanctioned marriages and make them unequal. The principal purpose is to impose inequality, not for other reasons like governmental efficiency. Responsibilities, as well as rights, enhance the dignity and integrity of the person. And DOMA contrives to deprive some couples married under the laws of their State, but not other couples, of both rights and responsibilities. By creating two contradictory marriage regimes within the same State, DOMA forces same-sex couples to live as married for the purpose of state law but unmarried for the purpose of federal law, thus diminishing the stability and predictability of basic personal relations the State has found it proper to acknowledge and protect. By this dynamic DOMA undermines both the public and private significance of state-sanctioned same-sex marriages; for it tells those couples, and all the world, that their otherwise valid marriages are unworthy of federal recognition. This places same-sex couples in an unstable position of being in a second-tier marriage. The differentiation demeans the couple, whose moral and sexual choices the Constitution protects, see *Lawrence*, 539 U.S. 558, and whose relationship the State has sought to dignify. And it humiliates tens of thousands of children now being raised by same-sex couples. The law in question makes it even more difficult for the children to understand the integrity and closeness of their own family and its concord with other families in their community and in their daily lives. . . .

The federal statute is invalid, for no legitimate purpose overcomes the purpose and effect to disparage and to injure those whom the State, by its marriage laws, sought to protect in personhood and dignity. By seeking to displace this protection and treating those persons as living in marriages less respected than others, the federal statute is in violation of the Fifth Amendment.

Although the Supreme Court said in *Windsor* that its ruling applied only to the federal government's recognition of marriages validly celebrated, it held two years later that all states must permit same-sex couples to marry.

Obergefell v. Hodges

135 S. Ct. 2584 (2015)

Justice KENNEDY delivered the opinion of the Court. . . .

[F]our principles and traditions to be discussed demonstrate that the reasons marriage is fundamental under the Constitution apply with equal force to same-sex couples.

A first premise of the Court's relevant precedents is that the right to personal choice regarding marriage is inherent in the concept of individual autonomy. This abiding connection between marriage and liberty is why *Loving* invalidated interracial marriage bans under the Due Process Clause. Like choices concerning contraception, family relationships, procreation, and childrearing, all of which are protected by the Constitution, decisions concerning marriage are among the most intimate that an individual can make. Indeed, the Court has noted it would be contradictory "to recognize a right of privacy with respect to other matters of family life and not with respect to the decision to enter the relationship that is the foundation of the family in our society.". . .

A second principle in this Court's jurisprudence is that the right to marry is fundamental because it supports a two-person union unlike any other in its importance to the committed individuals. This point was central to Griswold v. Connecticut, which held the Constitution protects the right of married couples to use contraception. Suggesting that marriage is a right "older than the Bill of Rights," *Griswold* described marriage this way:

> "Marriage is a coming together for better or for worse, hopefully enduring, and intimate to the degree of being sacred. It is an association that promotes a way of life, not causes; a harmony in living, not political faiths; a bilateral loyalty, not commercial or social projects. Yet it is an association for as noble a purpose as any involved in our prior decisions."

And in Turner v. Safley (1987), the Court again acknowledged the intimate association protected by this right, holding prisoners could not be denied the right to marry because their committed relationships satisfied the basic reasons why marriage is a fundamental right. . . . Marriage responds to the universal fear that a lonely person might call out only to find no one there. It offers the hope of companionship and understanding and assurance that while both still live there will be someone to care for the other. . . .

A third basis for protecting the right to marry is that it safeguards children and families and thus draws meaning from related rights of childrearing, procreation, and education. The Court has recognized these connections by describing the varied rights as a unified whole: "[T]he right to 'marry, establish a home and bring up children' is a central part of the liberty protected by the Due Process Clause." *Zablocki.* Under the laws of the several States, some of marriage's protections for children and families are material. But marriage also confers more profound benefits. By giving recognition and legal structure to their parents' relationship, marriage allows children "to understand the integrity and closeness of their own family and its concord with other families in their community and in their daily lives." *Windsor.* Marriage also affords the permanency and stability important to children's best interests.

As all parties agree, many same-sex couples provide loving and nurturing homes to their children, whether biological or adopted. And hundreds of thousands of children are presently being raised by such couples. Most States have allowed gays and lesbians to adopt, either as individuals or as couples, and many adopted and foster children have same-sex parents. This provides powerful confirmation from the law itself that gays and lesbians can create loving, supportive families. . . .

Fourth and finally, this Court's cases and the Nation's traditions make clear that marriage is a keystone of our social order. Alexis de Tocqueville recognized this truth on his travels through the United States almost two centuries ago:

> "There is certainly no country in the world where the tie of marriage is so much respected as in America. . . . [W]hen the American retires from the

turmoil of public life to the bosom of his family, he finds in it the image of order and of peace . . . . [H]e afterwards carries [that image] with him into public affairs." 1 Democracy in America 309 (H. Reeve transl., rev. ed. 1990).

In Maynard v. Hill (1888), the Court echoed de Tocqueville, explaining that marriage is "the foundation of the family and of society, without which there would be neither civilization nor progress." Marriage, the *Maynard* Court said, has long been "'a great public institution, giving character to our whole civil polity.'" This idea has been reiterated even as the institution has evolved in substantial ways over time, superseding rules related to parental consent, gender, and race once thought by many to be essential. Marriage remains a building block of our national community.

For that reason, just as a couple vows to support each other, so does society pledge to support the couple, offering symbolic recognition and material benefits to protect and nourish the union. Indeed, while the States are in general free to vary the benefits they confer on all married couples, they have throughout our history made marriage the basis for an expanding list of governmental rights, benefits, and responsibilities. These aspects of marital status include: taxation; inheritance and property rights; rules of intestate succession; spousal privilege in the law of evidence; hospital access; medical decisionmaking authority; adoption rights; the rights and benefits of survivors; birth and death certificates; professional ethics rules; campaign finance restrictions; workers' compensation benefits; health insurance; and child custody, support, and visitation rules. Valid marriage under state law is also a significant status for over a thousand provisions of federal law. See *Windsor.* The States have contributed to the fundamental character of the marriage right by placing that institution at the center of so many facets of the legal and social order.

There is no difference between same- and opposite-sex couples with respect to this principle. Yet by virtue of their exclusion from that institution, same-sex couples are denied the constellation of benefits that the States have linked to marriage. This harm results in more than just material burdens. Same-sex couples are consigned to an instability many opposite-sex couples would deem intolerable in their own lives. As the State itself makes marriage all the more precious by the significance it attaches to it, exclusion from that status has the effect of teaching that gays and lesbians are unequal in important respects. It demeans gays and lesbians for the State to lock them out of a central institution of the Nation's society. Same-sex couples, too, may aspire to the transcendent purposes of marriage and seek fulfillment in its highest meaning.

The limitation of marriage to opposite-sex couples may long have seemed natural and just, but its inconsistency with the central meaning of the fundamental right to marry is now manifest. With that knowledge must come the recognition that laws excluding same-sex couples from the marriage right impose stigma and injury of the kind prohibited by our basic charter. . . .

The Due Process Clause and the Equal Protection Clause are connected in a profound way, though they set forth independent principles. Rights implicit in liberty and rights secured by equal protection may rest on different precepts and are not always co-extensive, yet in some instances each may be instructive as to the meaning and reach of the other. In any particular case one Clause may be thought to capture the essence of the right in a more accurate and comprehensive way, even as the two Clauses may converge in the identification and definition of the right. This interrelation of the two principles furthers our understanding of what freedom is and must become.

The Court's cases touching upon the right to marry reflect this dynamic. In *Loving* the Court invalidated a prohibition on interracial marriage under both the Equal Protection Clause and the Due Process Clause. . . . The reasons why marriage is a fundamental right became more clear and compelling from a full awareness and understanding of the hurt that resulted from laws barring interracial unions. . . .

Here the marriage laws enforced by the respondents are in essence unequal: same-sex couples are denied all the benefits afforded to opposite-sex couples and are barred from exercising a fundamental right. Especially against a long history of disapproval of their relationships, this denial to same-sex couples of the right to marry works a grave and continuing harm. The imposition of this disability on gays and lesbians serves to disrespect and subordinate them.

These considerations lead to the conclusion that the right to marry is a fundamental right inherent in the liberty of the person, and under the Due Process and Equal Protection Clauses of the Fourteenth Amendment couples of the same-sex may not be deprived of that right and that liberty. The Court now holds that same-sex couples may exercise the fundamental right to marry. . . .

These cases also present the question whether the Constitution requires States to recognize same-sex marriages validly performed out of State. As made clear by the case of Obergefell and Arthur . . . the recognition bans inflict substantial and continuing harm on same-sex couples. . . .

The Court, in this decision, holds same-sex couples may exercise the fundamental right to marry in all States. It follows that the Court also must hold—and it now does hold—that there is no lawful basis for a State to refuse to recognize a lawful same-sex marriage performed in another State on the ground of its same-sex character. . . .

No union is more profound than marriage, for it embodies the highest ideals of love, fidelity, devotion, sacrifice, and family. In forming a marital union, two people become something greater than once they were. As some of the petitioners in these cases demonstrate, marriage embodies a love that may endure even past death. It would misunderstand these men and women to say they disrespect the idea of marriage. Their plea is that they do respect it, respect it so deeply that they seek to find its fulfillment for themselves. Their hope is not to be condemned to live in loneliness, excluded from one of civilization's oldest institutions. They ask for equal dignity in the eyes of the law. The Constitution grants them that right.

Justice SCALIA, with whom Justice THOMAS joins, dissenting. . . .

The substance of today's decree is not of immense personal importance to me. The law can recognize as marriage whatever sexual attachments and living arrangements it wishes, and can accord them favorable civil consequences, from tax treatment to rights of inheritance. Those civil consequences—and the public approval that conferring the name of marriage evidences—can perhaps have adverse social effects, but no more adverse than the effects of many other controversial laws. So it is not of special importance to me what the law says about marriage. It is of overwhelming importance, however, who it is that rules me. Today's decree says that my Ruler, and the Ruler of 320 million Americans coast-to-coast, is a majority of the nine lawyers on the Supreme Court. The opinion in these cases is the furthest extension in fact—and the furthest extension one can even imagine—of the Court's claimed power to create "liberties" that the Constitution and its Amendments neglect to mention. This practice of constitutional revision by an unelected committee of nine, always accompanied (as it is today) by extravagant praise of liberty, robs the People of the most important liberty they asserted in the Declaration of Independence and won in the Revolution of 1776: the freedom to govern themselves.

Until the courts put a stop to it, public debate over same-sex marriage displayed American democracy at its best. Individuals on both sides of the issue passionately, but respectfully, attempted to persuade their fellow citizens to accept their views. Americans considered the arguments and put the question to a vote. The electorates of 11 States, either directly or through their representatives, chose to expand the traditional definition of marriage. Many more decided not to. Win or lose, advocates for both sides continued pressing their cases, secure in the knowledge that an electoral loss can be negated by a later electoral win. That is exactly how our system of government is supposed to work. . . .

But the Court ends this debate, in an opinion lacking even a thin veneer of law. Buried beneath the mummeries and straining-to-be-memorable passages of the opinion is a candid and startling assertion: No matter *what* it was the People ratified, the Fourteenth Amendment protects those rights that the Judiciary, in its "reasoned judgment," thinks the Fourteenth Amendment ought to protect. . . .

This is a naked judicial claim to legislative—indeed, *super*-legislative—power; a claim fundamentally at odds with our system of government. Except as limited by a constitutional prohibition agreed to by the People, the States are free to adopt whatever laws they like, even those that offend the esteemed Justices' "reasoned judgment." A system of government that makes the People subordinate to a committee of nine unelected lawyers does not deserve to be called a democracy.

Judges are selected precisely for their skill as lawyers; whether they reflect the policy views of a particular constituency is not (or should not be) relevant. Not surprisingly then, the Federal Judiciary is hardly a cross-section of America. Take, for example, this Court, which consists of only nine men and women, all of them successful lawyers who studied at Harvard or Yale Law School. Four of the nine are natives of New York City. Eight of them grew up in east- and west-coast States. Only one hails from the vast expanse in-between. Not a single Southwesterner or even, to tell the truth, a genuine Westerner (California does not count). Not a single evangelical Christian (a group that comprises about one quarter of Americans), or even a Protestant of any denomination. The strikingly unrepresentative character of the body voting on today's social upheaval would be irrelevant if they were functioning as *judges*, answering the legal question whether the American people had ever ratified a constitutional provision that was understood to proscribe the traditional definition of marriage. But of course the Justices in today's majority are not voting on that basis; *they say they are not.* And to allow the policy question of same-sex marriage to be considered and resolved by a select, patrician, highly unrepresentative panel of nine is to violate a principle even more fundamental than no taxation without representation: no social transformation without representation. . . .

NOTES

1. **Theories of Equality.**   Which theory best describes the Court's ruling in *Obergefell*? Why? Is Justice Kennedy focused on discriminatory animus, as in *Windsor*, or discriminatory effect?

2. **The Internal Debate on Same-Sex Marriage.**   The gay and lesbian community did not universally support the campaign for same-sex marriage. Early advocates argued that recognition of such marriages would ensure full legal benefits that were not otherwise available. In addition, it was thought, recognition of same-sex marriage would help to "normalize" the status of gays and lesbians, which could both stabilize those relationships and reduce the prejudice based on sexual orientation in society at large. But some worried that replicating the model of heterosexual unions would weaken the broader, extended relationships within lesbian communities; encourage possessive, patriarchal-style patterns of submission and dominance; and cultivate unacceptable distinctions between married and unmarried lesbians. This split was captured in a famous 1989 debate between Paula Ettelbrick, who was then the legal director of Lambda Legal Defense and Education Fund, and Tom Stoddard, her boss. Stoddard acknowledged that "marriage has been oppressive, especially (although not entirely) to women," but believed "strongly that every lesbian and gay man should have the right to marry the same-sex partner of his or her choice."[440] Ettelbrick, in contrast, argued as follows:

> [M]arriage will not liberate us as lesbians and gay men. In fact, it will constrain us, make us more invisible, force our assimilation into the mainstream, and undermine the goals of gay liberation. [A]ttaining the right to marry will not transform our society from one that makes narrow, but dramatic, distinctions between those who are married and those who are not married to one that respects and encourages choice of relationships and family diversity. Marriage runs contrary to two of the primary goals of the lesbian and gay movement: the affirmation of gay identity and culture; and the validation of many forms of relationships. . . .
>
> The moment we argue, as some among us insist on doing, that we should be treated as equals because we are really just like married couples and hold the same values to be true, we undermine the very purpose of our movement and begin the dangerous process of silencing our different voices. As a lesbian, I am fundamentally different from non-lesbian women. That's the point. . . .[441]

---

440. Thomas Stoddard, Why Gay People Should Seek the Right to Marry, Out/Look 8-12 (Autumn 1989).

441. Paula L. Ettelbrick, Since When Is Marriage a Path to Liberation?, 2 Out/Look, Nat'l Gay & Lesbian Q. 9, 14 (Fall 1989). For a related view, see Katha Pollitt, Gay Marriage? Don't Say I Didn't Warn You, in Subject to Debate: Sense and Dissents on Women, Politics, and Culture 109 (Katha Pollitt ed., 2001).

Despite Ettelbrick's argument, the fight for marriage equality became the centerpiece of the gay rights movement—culminating, successfully, in the *Obergefell* decision. But some gay rights advocates continue to oppose marriage, or at least its centrality to the movement's agenda. Nancy Polikoff and others have argued that expanding the right to marry to same-sex couples simply ensures that marriage will continue to be the "only worthy form of family relationship," one that is "economically privileged above all others."[442] Newly endowed with the right to marry, same-sex couples will be forced to choose marriage, just as heterosexual couples have done, in order to obtain the benefits of state and societal support. Katherine Franke, also a longstanding skeptic of the push for marriage equality, draws on the history and experience of freed African-American slaves who gained the right to marry to write a cautionary tale. "What have we gotten ourselves into?" is the question she poses to the LGBT community in the wake of *Obergefell*. She fears the loss of alternative types of relationship recognition, which might allow all couples to customize their level and type of commitment, as well as the assimilation of gay and lesbian couples into an institution that is perhaps inherently oppressive.[443] So too, Melissa Murray notes that in the aftermath of *Obergefell*, states began withdrawing recognition of alternative status protections for non-married families and eroded the "promise of a more pluralistic relationship-recognition regime."[444] Do you agree that this is a significant problem? If so, who is likely to suffer and what can be done to mitigate the harm?

3. **Backlash to Same-Sex Marriage.** Backlash against *Obergefell* has been extensive. A county clerk in Kentucky, for example, refused to issue marriage licenses to same-sex couples on grounds that doing so would violate her personal religious beliefs. She was sued by couples who were denied licenses, and ultimately lost the case. Unlike the refusals by private business discussed in Chapter 1, Section D, the refusal by a government official acting in her official capacity infringed the plaintiffs' constitutional right to marry. Her personal beliefs were irrelevant; as the district court noted, "this Court can find no example, nor has Davis provided one, where a defendant's constitutional rights were found to be a valid defense for violating the constitutional rights of others. Ultimately, this Court's determination is simple—Davis cannot use her own constitutional rights as a shield to violate the constitutional rights of others while performing her duties as an elected official."[445] Simple or not, it is not clear that this argument will carry the day. In a concurring opinion in Dobbs v. Jackson Women's Health Organization, in which the Supreme Court eliminated the constitutional right to obtain an abortion, Justice Clarence Thomas wrote that the entire substantive due process doctrine should be overruled, including the right of same-sex couples to marry.[446] How would such a decision affect our understanding of equality in constitutional law?

442. Beyond Same-Sex Marriage: A New Strategic Vision for All Our Families and Relationships (July 26, 2006); Nancy Polikoff, Beyond (Straight and Gay) Marriage: Valuing All Families Under the Law (2008).

443. See Katherine Franke, Wedlocked: The Perils of Marriage Equality (2015).

444. Melissa Murray, Obergefell v. Hodges and Nonmarriage Inequality, 104 Cal. L. Rev. 1207, 1244 (2016).

445. Ermold v. Davis, No. 15-46-DLB-EBA, 2022 WL 830606 (Mar. 18, 2022).

446. 142 S. Ct. 2228, 2301 (2022) (Thomas, J., concurring).

4. **Gender Identity, Marriage, and Documentation.**   Access to marriage has also been an issue for transgender individuals, who have struggled to be treated under the law according to their chosen sex, rather than their birth sex. In Littleton v. Prange, for example, the Court of Appeals of Texas held that Christie Littleton, a transgender woman, could not sue for wrongful death as the surviving spouse of a man because their marriage was legally invalid.[447] This case, the court began, "involves the most basic of questions. When is a man a man, and when is a woman a woman?" The court maintained that "[e]very schoolchild, even of tender years, is confident he or she can tell the difference," but considered whether a physician can "change the gender of a person with a scalpel, drugs and counseling." The court considered possible ways to define sex — chromosomal factors, gonadal factors, genital factors, and psychological factors — but concluded that sex at birth cannot be legally be changed.

> Christie Littleton is a transsexual. Through surgery and hormones, a transsexual male can be made to look like a woman, including female genitalia and breasts. Transsexual medical treatment, however, does not create the internal sex organs of a woman (except for the vaginal canal). There is no womb, cervix or ovaries in the post-operative transsexual female. The male chromosomes do not change with either hormonal treatment or sex reassignment surgery. Biologically a post-operative female transsexual is still a male. The evidence fully supports that Christie Littleton, born male, wants and believes herself to be a woman. She has made every conceivable effort to make herself a female, including a surgery that would make most males pale and perspire to contemplate. . . . Her female anatomy, however, is all man-made. The body that Christie inhabits is a male body in all aspects other than what the physicians have supplied. . . . There are some things we cannot will into being. They just are. . . . As a male, Christie cannot be married to another male.[448]

The legalization of marriage for same-sex couples has mooted the question of transgender marriage nationwide because a person's sex does not affect the validity of marriage. But whether one's legal sex can be changed and how it is determined continue to be relevant questions because of the many contexts in which people are categorized by gender.

The treatment of legal sex has evolved dramatically in a relatively short period of time.[449] Virtually every state permits gender markers on birth certificates to be changed, although there is variation on eligibility requirements and the process for making the change. Many states impose specific medical requirements before a change can be made. Tennessee is the only state that has a law prohibiting such a change.[450] Recall the readings on sex, gender, and gender identity from the

---

447. 9 S.W.3d 223 (Tex. App. San Antonio 1999).

448. Id. at 230-31.

449. For current statutes, see Transgender Law Center, State-by-State Overview: Changing Gender Markers on Birth Certificates, https://transgenderlawcenter.org/resources/id/state-by-state-overview-changing-gender-markers-on-birth-certificates.

450. See Tenn. Code Ann. § 68-3-203(d) (2022).

Introduction. Should the government continue to classify people on the basis of gender? What are the advantages and disadvantages of doing so?

PUTTING THEORY INTO PRACTICE

2-52. Justice Alito asked, during oral argument in *Obergefell*, whether a ruling in favor of the petitioners would necessarily require states to issue licenses to groups of more than two consenting adults who wish to marry. Does it? Does polygamy threaten women's rights in the family?[451]

2-53. Outside of the United States, there has been a successful movement to allow "gender self-identification," which means that people can determine their own legal sex without any medical requirements. Seventeen countries, including Brazil, India, France, and Ireland, have passed laws to allow people to change their sex through a simple declaration.[452] What do you think of this approach? Some women's rights advocates have opposed it because of concerns about effects on single-sex sports and sex-segregated housing in prisons and shelters. (Recall the debates about sex-segregation in sports in Section C.) Are those valid concerns?

2. *Marital Dissolution and Its Economic Consequences*

a. The Traditional View

To the extent that women's role in the home has limited their opportunities in the world outside it, the traditional, heterosexual family has been a principal site of women's social and economic vulnerability. Under early Anglo-American common law, when a woman married, her identity merged with that of her husband. He assumed an obligation to support his wife and, in return, obtained total control of her property. Because wives lost their separate identity on marriage, they could not form contracts, keep their own earnings, acquire property, or bring their own legal actions.[453]

Gradually throughout the nineteenth century, legislation known generally as "married women's property acts" loosened these restrictions. However, well into the second half of the twentieth century, family law still disfavored women. Only eight states provided for joint ownership of "community property" acquired during the marriage. In the others, property acquired by husbands and wives typically was the property of the spouse who earned it—the husband in traditional households. As a result, women at divorce were often left with little or no property, even what they helped their husbands acquire. At the same time, husbands typically owed their former wives continuing spousal support (often termed "maintenance" or "alimony"), unless the wife was determined to be at "fault" for the divorce.

---

451. See Deborah Rhode, Adultery: Infidelity and the Law (2016).
452. See Continental Europe Enters the Gender Wars, Economist (June 12, 2021).
453. See William Blackstone, 1 Commentaries on the Laws of England 430-32 (1765).

Beginning in the late 1960s and 1970s, states began to pass no-fault divorce statutes and "equitable distribution" laws, designed to allow courts to divide property by taking into account a range of factors having to do with the child care as well as economic contributions of both spouses. As Chapter 1 indicated, the *Orr* case decided in 1979 that alimony had to be available on a gender-neutral basis to men as well as women. About the same time, often in the name of "equality," states moved to limit spousal support obligations to shorter periods in an effort to encourage women's economic independence and avoid reinforcing traditional stereotypes about women's role. Many states also moved to reduce the significance of fault in defining post-divorce obligations between the spouses.

With respect to parental rights, traditionally fathers had complete authority over their children, including the right to custody in the event of the parents' divorce. In the nineteenth century during what is sometimes referred to as the "cult of domesticity," states reversed that practice, creating legal presumptions giving mothers custody unless they were shown to be unfit (due to adultery, drunkenness, neglect, and so forth). In the 1970s, explicit maternal presumptions were largely (although not entirely) eliminated in favor of the gender-neutral "best interests of the child" test.

Modern marriage and custody law reforms have been more controversial than one might expect because they have limited traditional protections for women without eliminating the economic vulnerability that women experience disproportionately at divorce. Most of the materials in this section explore the tension between formal and substantive equality principles: the desire to promote equal treatment and at the same time to ensure fairness for weaker parties, typically women, at divorce.

It bears emphasis that regulation of the family is primarily a matter of state, not federal, law. State statutes and court decisions vary widely on many questions, making it sometimes difficult to generalize about national trends. The cases and statutes discussed in this section should be viewed as representative of their own time and jurisdiction, but not necessarily of the nation as a whole.

b.   Modern Divorce

The divorce reforms that began in the 1970s had several objectives. One was the elimination of explicit gender distinctions, such as the rule invalidated in *Orr* that only wives could receive alimony and the presumptions favoring mothers in child custody cases. One of the questions explored in the next two sections is the extent to which this move to formal equality has promoted or undercut substantive equality between the sexes.

Not all aspects of the divorce reform movement explicitly concerned gender bias. One effort was to remove fault as a significant role in determining entitlement to divorce, custody, division of property, and spousal support. The requirement of fault often resulted in acrimony and false testimony, and was inconsistent with the modern notion of marriage as a complicated private relationship in which legal assignments of blame and innocence were often neither accurate nor constructive. It is not entirely clear whether the elimination of fault as a factor in divorce systematically favored, or disfavored, women. Although divorce is available now in every state on at least one ground that is not fault-based, fault continues to play a role in many divorces. Even in states that have only no-fault grounds for divorce, it is often hard to avoid fault considerations when judicial discretion is permitted in the distribution of property or the determination of spousal support.

Roughly 40 percent of first marriages today end in divorce.[454] Studies have consistently shown that women and children are, on average, worse off economically after divorce than men. The extent of the disparity has declined over time and varies by study, but remains especially acute for older women who divorce. One study showed that the standard of living of women who divorce drops on average by 45 percent, in comparison to 21 percent for men.[455]

Three factors affect economic well-being at divorce: property distribution, spousal support (or alimony or maintenance), and child support. Property distribution is a one-time distribution of the assets of the parties at divorce. Spousal support is an ongoing obligation of one spouse to the other after divorce. Child support is also a continuing obligation of one parent to the other, at least until the child reaches the age of majority.

It is relatively easy to make divorce laws in each of these areas formally equal; they simply have to apply the same rules to both sexes. Does equality require more than this? Should a substantive goal of divorce law be to ensure that women do not systematically leave marriage worse off than men? More broadly, what should be the priority of divorce law? Protecting the mutual expectations of the married couple when they got married? A clean break that encourages parties to get on with their lives? Equality? Justice? Women's autonomy? Self-sufficiency? Holding a guilty party accountable? What consequences follow from each of these possible goals?

Joan Williams

Do Wives Own Half? Winning for Wives After *Wendt*

32 Conn. L. Rev. 249, 253, 265-68 (1999)

[D]omesticity's peculiar organization of market work and family work first marginalizes mothers from market work, then limits their access to entitlements based on family work. The result is a system that is inconsistent with our commitment to gender equality, and leads to the widespread impoverishment of mothers and the children who depend on them. . . . [W]e need to deconstruct domesticity and develop in its place a new vision of morality in family life. . . .

The joint property theory begins from the principle that ideal workers who are parents are supported by a flow of family work from the primary caregiver of their children. If the ideal worker's performance depends on a flow of family work from his wife, then "his" wage is the product of two adults: his market work, and her family work. If an asset is produced by two family members, it makes no sense

---

454. Millennials may bring down the divorce rate; they are less likely to marry, but also less likely to divorce. See Marisa Lascala, The U.S. Divorce Rate Is Going Down, and We Have Millennials to Thank, Good Housekeeping (Feb. 27, 2019).

455. I-Fen Lin & Susan L. Brown, The Economic Consequences of Gray Divorce for Women and Men, 76 J. Gerontol: Series B. 2073 (2021).

to award ownership to only one of them. We should abandon the "he who earns it, owns it" rule as an outdated expression of coverture, and give the wife half the accumulated family wealth based on her family work, without which that wealth would not have been created.

This is true whether or not the children are in child care. In the vast majority of families, the primary caregiver provides much of the child care even when the children are cared for by relatives, a nanny, or a day care center. Recent studies show that mothers spend three times as much time as fathers interacting with children. . . . Even when mothers' caregiving consists in part of finding child care and training and supervising child care workers, this, too, is work: managerial work. Studies show that women still do roughly 80% of the management work, even in families where men contribute substantially to the actual caretaking. We do not refuse to pay managers because their employees "really do all the work"; the same principle should apply to mothers.

The joint property theory has implications both for property division and for alimony. In the context of property division, it explains why wives should jointly own the family wealth, eliminating the unexplained jump in human capital theory between joint ownership and an enumeration of the specific contributions of the wife. It also provides the basis for arguing that the household of the custodial parent, often composed of three people, should have a greater share of family wealth than the household of the noncustodial parent, composed of only one. Certainly, in this context, a 50/50 split should be the floor, not the ceiling. In assessing how to split the family assets of a middle class family, the court should take into consideration how such families use their assets: to buy housing that offers a secure home environment and access to good schools, and to send children to college. Children should not lose these entitlements simply because their parents divorce and fathers prefer to found a new family rather than support the old one. In dividing family property, courts should begin from the principle that parents have the duty to share their wealth with their children. They should award more than 50% of family assets if that is necessary to ensure that the life chances of the family's children, to the extent possible, are unaffected by divorce.

In the context of very large estates consisting of more assets than are required to preserve the expectations of the family's children to decent housing and a good education, the joint property theory mandates a 50/50 split.

In most divorces, the key issue is not property division but human capital. This is true because no rule concerning property division makes much difference in most divorces: in our cash flow society, most families have accumulated few assets. Therefore, the key issue is income sharing: who owns the family wage after divorce. The joint property theory offers a new rationale for income sharing that begins from the observation that—after as well as before the divorce—the father can perform as an ideal worker only because the mother's family work allows him to do so. In an economy where ideal workers need to be supported by a flow of family work, a divorced father can continue to perform as an ideal worker only because his ex-wife continues to support his ability to be one by continuing as the primary caregiver of his children. Evidence of this is that divorced fathers with custody often cannot perform as ideal workers because they lack the flow of family work that supports fathers without custody. The joint property theory mandates not a 50/50 split but an equalization of the standard of living in the post-divorce two households.

Because the joint property theory mandates post-divorce sharing on the basis of its analysis of dependence in the modern family, it avoids the language of partnership and other commercial metaphors. . . .

The joint property theory also is quite different from the established theory that wives deserve half because of their contributions, particularly when lawyers focus on wives' direct contributions to husbands' businesses (as when a wife helps decorate the company offices). The joint property theory shifts the focus away from market work onto family work. The point is not that the wife helped the husband in business development, but that the husband could not have performed as an ideal worker without the marginalization of his wife.

If the joint property regime were put into effect, the next question is when it should end. I have proposed that joint property in wages should equalize the standard of living of the two post-divorce households for the period of the children's dependence, followed by a period of years designed to allow the wife to regain her ability to recover her earning potential (if she is young enough) or save for her future (if she is not). This additional period should be set at one additional year of income sharing for each two years of the marriage. . . . [T]his formula is designed to give the father an incentive to support his former wife's return to nonmarginalized market work: the more she earns, the less income he needs to provide her. The formula also gives the mother herself the incentive to develop a career. Because income sharing does not last for life, mothers who are young enough to do so will have to prepare themselves for a time when income sharing has ended.

NOTES

1. **Property Distribution.** As noted earlier, the traditional rule in most states (which have "common law property regimes") was that ownership of property at divorce followed title of that property, which in turn usually reflected who earned the money with which the property was purchased. The title rule caused substantial inequalities in cases where spouses acted as partners during the marriage, both contributing to the value of assets that were assigned at divorce to only one of them, usually the husband.[456] A minority of states have community property regimes, which have long considered the earnings of each spouse to be the property of both marriage partners. With respect to property division, most women traditionally were better off at divorce in community property states than they were in common law property states.

Equitable distribution reform swept the nation in the 1970s and 1980s in an effort to promote greater fairness in the division of property. Implicit in most equitable distribution statutes is the principle of a marital partnership, similar to the premise of community property law. This principle assumes an equitable division of responsibility during the marriage, and thus the need for an equitable division of the property at divorce. In some states, particularly community property states, this means the assets are divided evenly, but the law in many jurisdictions recites a range

---

456. See, e.g., Saff v. Saff, 402 N.Y.S.2d 690 (App. Div. 1978), appeal dismissed, 415 N.Y.S.2d 829 (1979). On the changes to the American family and family law over the course of the twentieth century, see Grossman & Friedman, supra note 432.

of factors to consider, including how the assets were acquired (which tends to favor the spouse whose earnings or efforts produced the property), the contributions of the "homemaker" spouse, and need. Which approach is more consistent with principles of gender equality? Which is the fairest? Should the answer be affected by the length of the marriage or the presence of children living at home?

In Arneault v. Arneault, the West Virginia Supreme Court overturned the trial court's 65/35 division of a couple's assets. The statute provided for a 50/50 distribution in the absence of a compelling reason to deviate.[457] The husband, who had made a substantial amount of money in business operating video lottery terminals, had argued that he deserved more than half because his success was due to his intelligence and ability rather than simply his effort. The trial court agreed, explaining that he "must be given some additional weight and credit in equitable distribution for existence of those attributes, intelligences, and abilities, which helped him achieve the marital estate currently in question." The state Supreme Court, however, held that the trial court unfairly devalued the wife's non-economic contributions to the marriage, including homemaking and childrearing. Those contributions, the court explained, very likely were the reason the husband was able to pursue advanced decrees and obtain business experience that led to his accumulation of wealth. Should courts presume that spouses make equal contributions to the marital estate or require proof of who contributed in what ways? If the husband in *Arneault* was able to prove that his success was purely the product of his "innate abilities," should his wife share in the wealth accumulated during marriage?

2. **Spousal Support.** Traditional theories of spousal support called for compensation to a dependent wife for her divorcing husband's breach of marital vows and responsibilities. With the rise of no-fault divorce, a needs-based rationale supplanted the fault-based rationale. However, commentators have had difficulty constructing a viable theory for why one spouse should be the permanent insurer of the financial security of other, when modern marriage law generally allows either spouse to terminate the marriage.

The trend in the law has been (1) to disfavor spousal support, preferring to accomplish a "clean break" for the parties through property distribution alone, if possible; and (2) if spousal support is ordered, to favor short-term or "rehabilitative" awards designed to get a dependent spouse back on her (or his) feet so that a "clean break" can eventually be accomplished. Some states have adopted guidelines to constrain judicial discretion, which have tended to reduce the size and number of spousal support awards. When need comes into play, courts have applied relatively open-ended standards that produce widely varying results. About half of jurisdictions also consider fault in determining entitlement to support.

The American Law Institute has proposed to treat spousal support as a return of non-economic investments in the marital partnership on behalf of the family, investments, that would otherwise be irrational or inefficient. The theory of this approach is that spousal support encourages (socially useful) investments in the marriage. The proposal provides for "compensatory spousal payments" to close the post-marriage gap between the parties' earning capacities attributable to lost opportunities by one

457. 639 S.E.2d 720 (W. Va. 2006).

spouse as a result of investments in the marriage. It uses length of marriage as a multiplier in the income-gap closing formula, thereby serving as a proxy for "lost opportunity." It further increases the amount when the dependent spouse assumed primary caretaking responsibilities for the couple's children during the marriage.[458] Does this approach reinforce marital role specialization? If so, is it good or bad for women?

3. **Educational Degree: Property, Support, or Neither?** One problem that falls between the cracks of marital property distribution and spousal support is how to treat an educational degree or professional license earned during the marriage with the economic support of the other spouse. When the parties divorce shortly after the degree has been obtained, there is often no property to distribute, and the supporting spouse may not be "dependent" in the usual sense (after all, she has been supporting the party who has earned the degree or license). Yet without recognition of the degree or license, one party to the marriage will benefit unfairly from "owning" an asset to which the other spouse made important contributions.

Courts reject the theory that a degree is property subject to division, on the theory that it has none of the transferability attributes of property and its value depends entirely on the future efforts of the degree-holder.[459] However, a growing number of jurisdictions have applied theories of contract and equity, or other strained theories of spousal support, to arrive at awards that often combine features of maintenance and lump-sum property division.[460]

If an award is made for a spouse's contribution to the other spouse's degree, what about other human capital achieved through a partner's support? A working spouse typically enhances his or her income capacity through work experience. Should the spouse who has gained disproportionate earning capacity during the marriage be able to walk away with the benefits of that investment if the other spouse has sacrificed career opportunities in order to invest in the home and family?[461]

4. **Child Support.** Child support has also been a target of extensive reform. Close to one-third of American adults are either obligors or beneficiaries of such

---

458. American Law Institute, Principles of the Law of Family Dissolution, Chapter 4 (2002).

459. See In re Marriage of Graham, 574 P.2d 75, 77 (Colo. 1978). New York for some time treated educational degrees and other enhancements to one party's earning capacity acquired during the marriage as marital property subject to equitable division, O'Brien v. O'Brien, 489 N.E.2d 712 (N.Y. 1985), but a 2015 law has changed this approach. See N.Y. Dom. Rel. § 236 (2019) ("The court shall not consider as marital property subject to distribution the value of a spouse's enhanced earning capacity arising from a license, degree, celebrity goodwill, or career enhancement"); Lee Rosenberg, What a Difference a Year Makes: Changes to the Spousal Support Law and the End of *O'Brien*, 47 NYSBA Fam. L. Rev. 1 (Fall/Winter 2015).

460. See, e.g., Mace v. Mace, 818 So. 2d 1130 (Miss. 2002); Meyer v. Meyer, 620 N.W.2d 382 (Wis. 2000).

461. For New York's effort to develop administrable standards to carry out its degree-as-property approach, see Sebastian Weiss, Note, Preventing Inequities in Divorce and Education: The Equitable Distribution of a Career Absent an Advanced Degree or License, 9 Cardozo Women's L.J. 133 (2002).

awards. Traditionally, courts used their discretion in setting amounts, which led to inconsistent and often inadequate payments and increased the number of families needing welfare. In an effort to address these problems, federal law conditions receipt of certain federal funds on the adoption by states of measures to improve the quantity, quality, and enforceability of child support. Among other things, states must have formula guidelines, which act as rebuttable presumptions of amounts owed, and they must implement automatic wage withholding of support payments in most cases.

In choosing a formula for determining child support, most state guidelines either take a percentage of the obligor's income (percentage formula) or proportion liability based on the parents' relative incomes (income shares). Under both approaches, the level of support sought to be captured in a child support order is the marginal amount that a parent would be expected to spend on the child if the child still lived with the parent. Policymakers aim for this amount so that, theoretically at least, the obligor is paying only the child's expenses and not those of others in the household where the child primarily lives.[462]

The perceived fairness of child support awards under existing child support formulas depends on the goals one thinks should be achieved and, among other things, the relative earning powers of the two parents. When the parties' incomes are substantially different and the party with whom the child primarily lives is the lower-earning parent (as is typical), the standard of living enjoyed by the child in his or her primary residence is generally lower, sometimes far lower, than the standard of living enjoyed by the nonresidential parent. When the primary residential parent earns more, the child support order may require substantial sacrifice from the obligor parent in order to subsidize a household that is living quite comfortably. It is difficult for formulas to ensure results that are both consistent across cases and sensitive to such variations.[463]

Subsequent families pose especially difficult challenges. On the one hand, it seems fair to treat children of first families and second families alike, and thus make an adjustment in existing awards to reflect new family obligations. On the other hand, one might think that when parents undertake new family responsibilities, they do so as individuals with existing obligations to children whose needs remain the same. Sometimes the stepparent brings additional income, and the question arises whether that income should figure in the child support calculation as an asset of the obligor parent. None of these questions are answered consistently across states.[464]

Another issue is the effect of shared custody, when the obligor parent spends more parenting time with the child than the usual 20 percent arrangement.

---

462. For a comparison of child support systems, see Douglas W. Allen & Margaret F. Brinig, Child Support Guidelines: The Good, the Bad, and the Ugly, 45 Fam. L.Q. 135 (2011).

463. For an overview, see Ira Mark Ellman & Tara O'Toole Ellman, The Theory of Child Support, 45 Harv. J. Legis. 107 (2008).

464. For some of the recent cases and a proposal for more determinate rules, see Yitshak Cohen, Issues Subject to Modification in Family Law: A New Model, 62 Drake L. Rev. 313 (2014).

Typically states allow for a "shared custody child support adjustment" when the obligor's share of custody reaches a certain amount—say, 35 percent.[465] The adjustment reflects the extra costs that may be associated with custodial time, but not the fact that the primary custodian's fixed costs of raising the child are affected little, if at all. What do you think is the best way to handle this?

If a parent who is under a child support order loses a job and is unable to find another at the same wage, their ability to pay is affected, which may justify a modification of the child support award if the parent applies for it, although modification is not automatic and back awards, by federal law, are not retroactively modifiable.[466] But if the only job they can get pays much less than before, do they have to take it?

Every child support statute provides that the court can impute income to a parent who is not working or is determined to be underearning. In Chen v. Warner, the Wisconsin Supreme Court considered whether the father should pay additional child support because the mother decided to stop working. Both parents were physicians, with very high-paying jobs.[467] When the mother voluntarily left her job, she was earning $415,000 per year. The question was whether her decision to forego employment constituted "shirking" such that the court should treat her as if she were making that income for child support purposes. The court declined to do so. As it explained:

> Not working outside the home full time has enabled the mother to spend significantly more time with the children. This increased time with the children also includes periods during the weeks when the father has placement of the children. She shepherds the children to medical appointments, attends their school activities, does volunteer work at the school, communicates more with their teachers, transports the children to their various extracurricular activities (tae kwon do, ballet, knitting, dancing, piano lessons), and monitors their participation in all their endeavors.
>
> The record is also replete with evidence of the father's involvement in the children's lives.
>
> By all accounts, the children were doing well and their needs were met before the mother left employment at the Marshfield Clinic, and they have continued to do well thereafter. . . .
>
> This is a child support modification case. The father asserts that in determining child support the circuit court should have used the mother's earning capacity, not her actual earnings. Obviously, in the present case there is a significant difference between the two numbers. A circuit court would consider a parent's earning capacity rather than the parent's actual earnings only if it has concluded that the parent has been "shirking," to use the awkward terminology of past cases. To conclude that a parent

---

465. See Karen Syma Czapanskiy, The Shared Custody Child Support Adjustment: Not Worth the Candle, 49 Fam. L.Q. 409 (2015); Sanford L. Braver et al., Public Sentiments About the Parenting Time Adjustment in Child Support Awards, 49 Fam. L.Q. 433 (2015).

466. For the problem, see Julie Bosman, Fighting over Child Support After the Pink Slip Arrives, N.Y. Times, Mar. 29, 2009, at A1.

467. 695 N.W.2d 758 (Wis. 2005).

is shirking, a circuit court is not required to find that a former spouse deliberately reduced earnings to avoid support obligations or to gain some advantage over the other party. A circuit court need find only that a party's employment decision to reduce or forgo income is voluntary and unreasonable under the circumstances. . . .

The test of reasonableness under the circumstances is derived from the case law. . . . [T]he paying spouse should be afforded "a fair choice" of a means of livelihood as well as the ability to pursue what the spouse honestly feels are the best opportunities, even though the present financial return may be reduced from prior employment. The court further said that "[t]his rule is, of course, subject to reasonableness commensurate with [the spouse's] obligations to [the] children and [the former spouse]." The phrase "subject to reasonableness commensurate with a spouse's obligations to the children" has been repeated in numerous shirking cases, including unintentional shirking cases. The phrase "commensurate with a spouse's obligations to the children" does not explicitly refer to obligations of financial support; it includes other obligations, such as child care. . . .

The case law recognizes that the words "subject to reasonableness commensurate with a spouse's obligations to the children" mean that a court balances the needs of the parents and the needs of the child (both financial and otherwise, like child care) and the ability of both parents to pay child support.

Furthermore, Wis. Stat. § 767.25(1m)(d) and (e) provide that a court may modify the amount of child support payments under the percentage standard if, after considering the listed economic factors, "[t]he desirability that the custodian remain in the home as a full-time parent," and "the value of custodial services performed by the custodian if the custodian remains at home," the court concludes that the percentage standard is unfair to the child or to any of the parties. Thus the legislature has explicitly recognized that in establishing financial child support obligations a circuit court considers the desirability and value of child care services performed by a custodian. . . .

With appropriate deference to the circuit court's ruling, we now determine the reasonableness of the mother's decision to forgo employment outside the home to become an at-home full-time child care provider.

While a family is intact, the parents' choice of employment, child care, and standard of living are left to the parties, as long as the children's basic needs are met. Upon divorce, however, courts are plunged into the divorced parents' personal lives to ensure that the interests of minor children are protected.

A divorced parent who voluntarily leaves gainful employment outside the home, for however good a reason, may be subject to judicial inquiry into that parent's responsibility to furnish child support. A divorced parent may voluntarily terminate employment but may not do so if the conduct inures to the detriment of child support. There is a limit to the unemployment or underemployment of a parent when the other parent "is presented the bill for the financial consequences."

When a divorced parent decides to forgo employment outside the home to render at-home full-time child care (but not for the purpose of avoiding a support obligation) . . . [a] court must weigh the right of a parent to make such a choice, while keeping in mind the public's interests that children be adequately cared for, that the financial needs of the children be met, and that the financial burdens of child care be apportioned fairly between the parents.

If it determines that a parent's decision to forgo employment outside the home to provide at-home full-time child care is unreasonable, a court can impose an obligation on that parent to support a child by imputing income to the parent based on that parent's earning capacity. . . .

We do not adopt a position favoring or disfavoring a parent's decision to forgo employment outside the home to become an at-home full-time or part-time child care provider. . . .

The factors to be considered in determining the reasonableness of a parent's decision to forgo employment outside the home, become an at-home full-time child care provider, and increase the support obligation of the other parent include, but are not limited to, the following: the number of children at home and their ages, maturity, health, and special needs; the availability of child care providers; the financial needs of the children; any detrimental effect on the child's support level if a parent is a full- or part-time at-home child care provider; the age and mental and physical condition of the parents; the educational background, training, skills, prior employment, and wage earning history of each parent; the earning potential of the parent who forgoes employment outside the home and that parent's efforts to find and retain employment; the status of the job market; the assets and income of each parent and the available resources if a parent is an at-home full- or part-time child care provider; the hardship and burden on the parent employed outside the home caused by the other parent's decision to forgo employment; and any other factors bearing on the needs of the children and each parent's ability to fund child support.

The gender of the parent forgoing employment outside the home to provide at-home full- or part-time child care is not a relevant factor.

[W]e conclude that the circuit court correctly concluded that the mother's decision to remain unemployed to be an at-home full-time child care provider was reasonable under the circumstances. . . .

We do not set forth a general rule that it is always reasonable for a parent to terminate employment to become an at-home full-time child care provider when the other parent has the ability to support the children. . . .

Do you think *Chen* would have come out the same way if the father, rather than the mother, chose to forego highly paid employment in favor of staying home with the couple's school-aged children? Does *Chen* implicitly privilege a particular type of masculinity (e.g., that a man's value depends on his breadwinning capacity) over other, alternative masculinities in any of the court's assumptions about the parties regarding the allocation of labor and time?

Federal law also provides a complex set of rules and forms of assistance to help states enforce child support orders. Among other tools, federal law provides for the interception of tax refunds, garnishment of federal wages, and locator services for delinquent parents. The Federal Child Support Recovery Act of 1992 makes it a federal crime to cross state lines to avoid payment of child support. Aggressive state laws have been added to help improve child support collections. At least fifteen states provide for the suspension, revocation, or denial of occupational or business licenses of individuals delinquent in their child support obligations. Fifteen states provide for the suspension or revocation of delinquents' drivers' licenses. Other statutes provide for the suspension of permanent license plates or motor vehicle registrations, hunting or fishing licenses, and even passports and marriage licenses.[468]

In the last decade, policymakers and commentators have begun to focus greater attention on noncustodial parents who are overburdened by child support awards or arrearages and sought ways to alleviate some of the burden.[469] Ann Cammett argues that the child support system is detrimental to low-income families in a variety of ways and often drives fathers underground and away from their families rather than cementing ties.[470] On the other hand, some argue that efforts to relieve the burdens on noncustodial parents has been done at the expense of custodial parents (mostly women) and children who will see less money awarded or paid. If you were an advocate for single mothers, would you support or oppose this policy shift? Are there ways in which mothers and children might benefit from a less strict approach to enforcement of child support orders against poor fathers? Consider the observations of sociologists Kathryn Edin and Timothy Nelson, who conducted a field study of fatherhood among the urban poor:

> Most noncustodial fathers end up contributing very little to the support of their children over the eighteen-year span for which society holds them responsible. This leads to the question of how these men — who really want the kids — view the obligations that the fatherhood role typically carries. Almost no one among the fathers we spoke with believe that good fathers should "leave everything to the mother." Good fathers, they say, should provide. But the definition of good provider is unexpectedly broad. First, in the terms used by one father, he must be "all man" and provide for himself, not relying too much on his mother or his girlfriend. Though this point may seem obvious, it was often made explicit in our men's accounts, presumably because for many it is no easy feat. Second,

---

468. See Carmen Solomon-Fears, Child Support Enforcement and Driver's License Suspension Policies, Cong. Rsch. Serv. (Apr. 11, 2011), https://crsreports.congress.gov/product/pdf/R/R41762/5.

469. See, e.g., White House, Promoting Responsible Fatherhood (June 2012).

470. Ann Cammett, Deadbeats, Deadbrokes, and Prisoners, 18 Geo. J. Poverty L. & Pol'y 127, 129 (2011).

he must mollify those in his current household by paying some of the bills plus a little something for her kids now and then. After settling these accounts, he can offer his nonresident children some portion of what remains. This sharply abridged sense of financial responsibility—"doing the best I can . . . with what is left over"—is what drives both men's sense of obligation and their financial behavior.

American society tends to assess the unwed father's moral worth with a single question: how much money does he provide? But the men that we interviewed in Philadelphia and Camden vehemently reject the notion that they should be treated as mere paychecks. Instead, they desire, and even demand, at least a slice of the "whole fatherhood experience" in exchange for a portion of their hard-earned cash. When mom acts as gatekeeper or when a child refuses contact, even this relatively weak breadwinner norm can be eroded or nullified.[471]

Can the law account for the complex role gender plays in parenting and child support?

At the other end of the spectrum are issues concerning high-income families, where a percentage formula may overstate the child's "needs." Consider an earner, for example, who earns $2 million annually, and who would ordinarily be expected to pay one-third of that in child support. Some states set caps on child support amounts; others leave it to the court's discretion.[472] Should there be a limit? If so, what factors should be considered in setting it?

PUTTING THEORY INTO PRACTICE

2-54. Consider the following:
   (a) George has been a highly paid executive for a Fortune 500 company. As a result of his earnings, at the time of his divorce from Kate, the couple has $50 million of assets. Kate never worked during the marriage but she managed the household and did the majority of childrearing for their one child, who is now 30 years old. Under what sex-neutral principle should the parties' assets be divided?
   (b) In a case similar to (a), above, the husband complained of a judgment dividing the marital assets 50-50: "The biggest stress of the day for my wife was deciding what to tell the cook to make for dinner. There is a certain class of wealthy women who contribute nothing to the family wealth and then expect 50 percent on divorce. The court says she is entitled to continue the lifestyle you have provided. It's lunacy, absolute lunacy."[473] How would you respond to him?
   (c) In a case similar to (a), above, the wife rejected a settlement offer of $10 million from her corporate-executive husband whose net worth was close to $100 million. She explained: "Marriage is a partnership,

471. Kathryn Edin & Timothy J. Nelson, Doing the Best I Can 206-07 (2013).
472. See Lori W. Nelson, High-Income Child Support, 45 Fam. L.Q. 191 (2011).
473. Landon Thomas, Jr., Lawyer to Stars' Ex-Wives Has Never Been Busier, N.Y. Times, May 26, 2009, at B1 (quoting Brian Meyerson).

and I should be entitled to 50%. I gave thirty-one years of my life. I loved the defendant. I worked hard and I was very loyal." Although she admitted she could survive on $10 million, she asked "Why should he get $90 million? I entered this marriage as a partner. I don't know when he decided that it was not a partnership. [He] wanted to buy out my partnership, and I didn't want to be bought out. It's like a hostile takeover—he offered me a very small percentage, and I said that's not the price of a buyout."[474] Is her analogy persuasive?

2-55. Mary and Lewis both want to become lawyers and to open up a law practice together in their hometown. They do not have enough funds to support themselves while both of them go to law school, so they decide that Mary will support the couple as a data systems analyst while Lewis earns his law degree. Afterwards, Lewis will support them while Mary goes to law school.

They follow the plan, except that on the day he gets his law degree, Lewis announces to Mary that he has fallen in love with someone else and he now wants a divorce. They have no assets. Lewis has taken a Wall Street position making $220,000 a year.

What financial rights should Mary have? What theory of equality supports that result? What if she no longer wants to go to law school, and instead hopes to be a full-time painter?

2-56. Years before *Obergefell*, Mary Anne Case argued that feminists should support equal access to marriage by same-sex couples because it might disrupt some of the gender norms of traditional marriage that have been surprisingly persistent and, on the whole, oppressive for women. "It would complete," she argued, "the evolution away from sex-role differentiated, inegalitarian marriage law that began with nineteenth-century efforts to ameliorate the effects of coverture and continued in legislative reform and constitutional adjudication through the last third of the twentieth century."[475] In an article entitled Divorce Equality, Allison Tait makes the following observation about marriages by same-sex couples:

> [A] number of studies have shown that, in terms of labor specialization, same-sex couples adopt a more egalitarian approach: "Much research on same-sex domesticity points to a strong egalitarian ideal for division of labour, a reluctance for one spouse to be dependent on the other, and an emphasis on negotiation." Instead of allocating household labor by gender (wife cooks dinner, husband takes out the trash), "most couples in same-sex relationships do not assign gender roles. The tasks are flexible, often interchangeable between the partners and are often divided by time, ability, and consideration." This egalitarian concept of domestic labor and marital bargaining correlates with the fact that "most gay men

---

474. Judith H. Dobrzynski, A Corporate Wife Holds Out for a 50-50 Split of Assets, N.Y. Times, Jan. 24, 1997, at D1 (discussing divorce between Gary and Lorna Wendt); Wendt v. Wendt, 1998 Conn. Super. LEXIS 1023, at *55-56 (awarding wife $20 million in equitable distribution).

475. Mary Anne Case, What Feminists Have to Lose in Same-Sex Marriage Litigation, 57 UCLA L. Rev. 1199, 1202-03 (2010).

and lesbians are in dual-earner relationships, so neither partner is the exclusive breadwinner and each partner has some measure of economic independence."[476]

Is this egalitarian model likely to spill over into heterosexual marriages, as Case predicted? Should divorce law treat couples differently depending on whether they follow traditional gender roles or not?

2-57. An article in Forbes shares the stories of three women who were entitled to alimony upon divorce but declined it. One woman, who had married at 18 and stayed home to raise the daughter born soon thereafter before divorcing at 24, explained her decision to the reporter like this: "My marriage allowed me to stay home full-time with my daughter. . . . That was a luxury—not a job. I was compensated. I had a nice home, drove a nice car, had access to a bank account. Asking for alimony would be like asking for a pension for a job I no longer did. Why should he have to pay because he loved me enough to marry me? It just didn't seem fair."[477] If you were her lawyer, would you try to convince her to ask for alimony? If so, what arguments would you make?

2-58. In many states, spousal support payments terminate upon the remarriage of the payee spouse. Advocates, largely ex-husbands, have pushed to make cohabitation a trigger for termination as well, and a 2014 law in New Jersey provides that "cohabitation" can potentially be established even if the payee and significant other maintain separate residences.[478] What is the rationale for such a rule? Is it fair to women? Should any termination of the support award be permanent, or should it be reinstated if the cohabitation ends?

2-59. The Supreme Court in Japan upheld a law requiring married couples to have the same surname.[479] The law is gender neutral, in that a couple could choose either the husband's or the wife's surname, but more than 95 percent of couples pick the husband's surname. What arguments might you make about the relationship between this law and women's equality?

3. Child Custody

Although today's child custody standards focus on the best interests of the child, mothers continue to have custody of their children in the large majority of cases. About 80 percent of current custodial parents are mothers, a percentage

---

476. Allison Anna Tait, Divorce Equality, 90 Wash. L. Rev. 1246, 1268 (2015); see also Suzanne A. Kim & Edward Stein, Gender in the Context of Same-Sex Divorce and Relationship Dissolution, 56 Fam. Ct. Rev. 384 (2018).

477. Emma Johnson, "I Turned Down Alimony," 3 Women's Stories, Forbes, Nov. 13, 2014.

478. See N.J. Stat. Ann. § 2A:34-23(n) (West 2022).

479. See Jun Hongo, Japan's Top Court Rules Married Couples Must Have Same Surname, Wall St. J., Dec. 16, 2015.

largely unchanged over three decades.[480] The prevailing best interests test encompasses a wide range of factors, including the "quality of the emotional bonds between parent and child," "the ethical, emotional, and intellectual guidance the parent gives to the child throughout his formative years," the "moral fitness" and "ability" of the parents, and continuity of care. Such criteria have been criticized as overly subjective; they allow judges to act on their own instincts and biases (or those of the experts upon whom they rely), which results in uncertainty, inconsistency, recriminations among parents, and undesirable strategic behavior.[481]

Gender bias has been a particular problem. It can work both ways. Mothers sometimes benefit from traditional stereotypes and gender role expectations, but they also suffer if they fail to conform to idealized views of motherhood, or if fathers exceed the minimal expectations associated with fatherhood. In one case, for example, a father was awarded custody based on his "slightly more active engagement in their children's lives" even though the undisputed evidence showed that the father spent only nine waking hours per week with the children, as compared with twenty hours by the working mother.[482] Bias against lesbians, mothers with demanding jobs, and wives who have had extramarital affairs has also been apparent. Parenting expectations are racialized, as well. Black mothers do not benefit from the "good mother" stereotype and, when economically vulnerable, are disparaged as "welfare queens" instead.[483]

The difficulties of a standard focused on the best interests of the child have led many commentators to support a primary caretaker presumption. The main argument in favor of such a presumption is that it is a more determinate standard than the best interests test, and reduces the possibility of bias, stereotyping, uncertainty, and acrimonious litigation. It also is thought to encourage involvement in childrearing by rewarding parents who have assumed that responsibility. What should be the goal of custody law? To what extent should it reflect fairness to parents as well as the interests of their children? How important should gender neutrality be?

Patricia Ann S. v. James Daniel S.

435 S.E.2d 6 (W. Va. 1993)

Three children were born of the [parties'] marriage, [who are now ages 14, 11, and 7]. The [mother] was a kindergarten school teacher but left her employment upon the birth of their first child. The [father] is an architect. . . .

---

480. See U.S. Census Bureau, Current Population Reports, Custodial Mothers and Fathers and Their Child Support: 2017, at 3 (May 2020).

481. See Katharine T. Bartlett, Preference, Presumption, Predisposition, and Common Sense: From Traditional Custody Doctrines to the American Law Institute's Family Dissolution Project, 36 Fam. L.Q. 11 (2002).

482. See Hoover v. Hoover, 764 A.2d 1192, 1194 (Vt. 2000). According to the dissenting judge, time was credited to the father for activities such as helping with schoolwork in which the mother also engaged but for which she was not given credit.

483. See, e.g., Angela Onwuachi-Willig, The Return of the Ring: Welfare Reform's Marriage Cure as the Revival of Post-Bellum Control, 93 Cal. L. Rev. 1647 (2005).

The primary issue in this case is the [mother]'s contention that she should be awarded custody of the parties' children. . . .

The parties agree that the guidelines for establishing custody are clearly set forth in Garska v. McCoy, [1981]. We defined primary caretaker . . . in *Garska*, as "that natural or adoptive parent who, until the initiation of divorce proceedings, has been primarily responsible for the caring and nurturing of the child." The law presumes that it is in the best interests of young children to be placed in the custody of the primary caretaker. . . .

It is the circuit court's responsibility to determine which parent is the primary caretaker. . . . In *Garska*, we listed the factors to be considered by the circuit court in making this determination. However, . . . we pointed out, "[i]f the trial court is unable to establish that one parent has clearly taken primary responsibility for the caring and nurturing duties of a child neither party shall have the benefit of the primary caretaker presumption."

It is clear from the evidence that the parties shared the primary caretaker duties as discussed in *Garska*. While the evidence presented established the fact that the [mother] was the homemaker and the [father] was the wage earner, this Court has recognized that the length of time a parent has alone with a child is not determinative of whether the primary caretaker presumption should attach. . . . The [mother] was at home for the children when they would return from school while the [father] would work throughout the day. However, the [father] was also a substantial participant in the child care duties once he came home from work.

With respect to the child care duties, the [mother] testified that she was a night person, meaning she would stay up late at night and sleep later in the morning. As a result, both parties testified that the [father] would be responsible for getting the boys ready for school and fixing their breakfast. Both parties further testified that the [mother] would primarily plan and prepare the evening meals on the weekdays, but on the weekends the [father] would often prepare the evening meals. The parties also testified that they shared the responsibility for getting the children ready for bed each night.

In terms of school and social activities for the children, the evidence is indicative of the fact that both parties were active in their children's social lives. . . . [The mother] participated in PTO (Parent Teacher Organization) meetings and school activities. [A teacher] also testified that the [father] was involved with the children's school activities; and, the [father] testified that he was instrumental in helping the children with their homework in the evenings.

Furthermore, each parent organized and participated in social activities with the children. [The mother] would organize birthday parties for the children, and she would often host pool parties for the children and their friends at the parties' home. On the other hand, the [father] would arrange and participate in camping, hiking, and biking trips as well as other sporting events with the children. . . .

Finally, the evidence suggests that the parties shared in the responsibility of disciplining the children. The [father] admitted that he used a belt to whip the boys, but he stated that he used his hand to whip Jennifer. The [mother], however, stated that she no longer uses the belt to whip the children. Rather, the [mother] testified that she had attended parenting classes, and as a result, she employed a new method of discipline such as taking away the children's privileges and grounding them for their wrongdoings. . . .

[W]e agree . . . that neither party is entitled to the status of primary caretaker because the child care duties were shared equally by the parties. Therefore, the issue of custody properly rests on the best interests of the child. . . .

With this in mind, we turn to the [mother's contention] that the circuit court erred in utilizing psychological expert witnesses prior to the circuit court's determination as to who was entitled to the status of primary caretaker. . . .

[The father] called psychologist, Mari Sullivan Walker, to testify before the family law master. Ms. Walker met with the [father] and the three children for approximately ninety minutes on September 22, 1990. Ms. Walker was of the opinion that the children perceive their father as the more nurturing person rather than their mother. Ms. Walker testified that all three children told her that the [mother] "beat" them. . . . Based upon the children's responses [to her question how they thought life would be with their father versus life with their mother,] Ms. Walker opined that the children have more faith in their father as opposed to their mother whom they were afraid of and with whom they were angry. . . .

Dr. Charles Yeargan, a child psychologist, . . . was initially hired by the [mother], but later the parties agreed to use him as a neutral expert to give his opinion regarding the welfare of the children. In October of 1990, Dr. Yeargan interviewed the entire S. family.

In response to questions asked by [father]'s counsel, Dr. Yeargan stated that he didn't ask the children where and with whom they wanted to live; however, based upon the children's comments, it was Dr. Yeargan's opinion that the children feel emotionally safer with the [father and that they would prefer to live with him].

Dr. Yeargan stated that the children perceive the [father] as emotional and supportive, and the [mother] is perceived as angry. Further, Dr. Yeargan testified that Jennifer told him that if her brothers live with the [father], then that is where she wants to live. Dr. Yeargan also opined that both parents have behavioral traits that they need to work out in order for them to be able to better cope with and relate to their children.

Ultimately, it was Dr. Yeargan's opinion that it was in the best interests of the two boys, Jason and Justin, that they live with the [father]. With respect to Jennifer, Dr. Yeargan admitted he did not have a lot to go on, but he recommended that Jennifer live with her mother because of "the interests of the two different parties," "the activity levels," "the socialization issues" and "the involvements."

Dr. Carl McGraw . . . interviewed all three children, the [father], and the [father]'s mother, because she had been helping care for the children. Dr. McGraw stressed the importance of keeping the children together in order to keep the family unit intact. Dr. McGraw noted that he had difficulty understanding Dr. Yeargan's reasoning for splitting the children between each parent. Dr. McGraw testified that the children told him they felt their mother was mean. Dr. McGraw stated he didn't ask the children who they wanted to live with, but he testified that they were adamant about wanting to live with their father. It was Dr. McGraw's opinion that the children would "have a better chance" if all three of them were to live with the [father], considering the rapport [he] has with [them]. . . .

The circuit court determined that the best interests of the children would be served by awarding custody to the [father]. There was an abundance of evidence presented in this case, which included the testimony of the parties, neighbors, teachers, family members, friends, and psychologists.

[In addition to the psychological testimony,] Jessica Halstead Sharp, a neighbor and friend of the parties, testified that she found the [father] to be loving and nurturing towards the children unlike the [mother] who, in Mrs. Sharp's opinion, had a problem dealing with the children. Mrs. Sharp also stated that, on more than one occasion, she overheard the [mother] calling the children vulgar names.

In addition, Nancy Jo S. and Reese and Ron Webb, Jr. testified that the children interact well with the [father]. However, they all felt the [mother] acted hostile with the children, and thus, the children did not respond well to her. All three witnesses further confirmed Mrs. Sharp's testimony that the [mother] called the children vulgar names, and they added, she used bad language around the children as well. . . .

Jason, the eldest son at fourteen years of age, is old enough to make a decision as to which parent he wants to live with, and the record clearly supports the circuit court's finding that Jason should live with his father. . . . Justin, on the other hand, is eleven years of age and not quite capable of making such a decision, but the evidence supports the circuit court's finding that he should live with his father. In addition, the [mother] admits that there is a lot of hostility between the boys and her, and because of this anger she might not be able to manage them. . . .

However, with respect to Jennifer, we do not believe that the record has been adequately developed. . . .

[W]e hold that the circuit court judge did not abuse his discretion by concluding that the best interests of the two boys would be served by awarding custody to the [father]. With respect to Jennifer, we remand the case to the circuit court for further development of the record in order to determine what is in her best interests. . . .

WORKMAN, CHIEF JUSTICE, dissenting.

The majority opinion marks a sharp departure from the primary caretaker rule which has been a viable and working concept in West Virginia for more than a decade. More disturbing, however, is the determination that it is in the best interests of children to place them in the custody of a parent who has abused both the wife and the children. In doing so, the majority implicitly places its stamp of approval on physical and emotional spousal abuse.

Deaths by domestic violence are increasing dramatically every year in West Virginia, and there is much discussion about the inefficacy of the judicial system in dealing with family violence. But until judicial officers on every level come to a better understanding of the phenomenon of family violence in its finer gradations, the response of the court system will continue to fall short. The majority demonstrates a tragic lack of understanding of the true nature of the dynamics that underlie family violence.

EROSION OF PRIMARY CARETAKER PRESUMPTION

The primary caretaker rule as set forth in Garska v. McCoy . . . has been an important part of domestic relations law . . . for more than twelve years. . . .

After stating the rationale for implementing the primary caretaker rule, this Court [in *Garska*] ruled that "in any custody dispute involving children of tender years it is incumbent upon the circuit court to determine as a threshold question which parent was the primary caretaker parent before the domestic strife giving rise to the proceeding began." . . .

In the instant case, it was clearly an abuse of discretion for the family law master and the circuit court to deny primary caretaker status to the mother. It is unfathomable that a woman who gives up her career (in this case, that of being a kindergarten teacher) to stay home to raise three children does not qualify as the primary caretaker, when as a full-time stay-at-home mother she breast-fed all three children; was so concerned about unnecessary additives and excess sugar that she processed her own baby food; was responsible for the majority of meal planning and preparation; was primarily responsible for laundering the family's clothing and housecleaning; was a Girl Scout troop leader; was a regular volunteer at her children's school and an active member of the parent-teacher organization; was responsible for scheduling and taking the children to their medical appointments; and was primarily responsible for managing the children's social activities. For some unarticulated reason, both the family law master and the circuit court appear to have been bowled over by the fact that the father helped in the evenings and weekends. Not unlike many modern fathers, the [father] did participate in some of the household and childrearing responsibilities. The mother and father jointly oversaw the bedtime routine of the children. Upon the birth of the third child, the father, by agreement of the parties, awoke the two oldest children and prepared their breakfasts, because the baby (Jennifer) was up a lot at night. As Jennifer grew older and began sleeping all night, the parties continued this routine. Although the mother stayed up late, during those evening hours she cleaned up from dinner, prepared lunches for the children to take to school the next day, and did other household duties. The [father] planned recreational activities such as camping and hiking trips, primarily for the boys. Given the father's admitted ten to twelve-hour work days combined with frequent business trips which took him away from home, it is difficult to conceive how he could ever qualify as having equal caretaking responsibility. . . . The majority in essence places a higher value on a father's time and contribution.

By upholding the circuit court's ruling, the majority begins an erosion of the primary caretaker rule, or at least sends a signal to domestic relations practitioners that it will be situationally ignored when expedient. . . . Sadly, . . . this case boils down to . . . one expert versus another [which the primary caretaker presumption was intended to avoid]. . . .

MAJORITY OKAYS SPOUSAL ABUSE

This father not only takes a belt to the three children regularly, but he also has taken a belt to his wife. Phenomenally, the family law master did not permit the wife to testify in detail to the physical abuse she endured throughout the marriage, as he apparently concluded it had nothing to do with the children. In fact, spousal abuse has a tremendous impact on children.

> Children learn several lessons in witnessing the abuse of one of their parents. First, they learn that such behavior appears to be approved by their most important role models and that the violence toward a loved one is acceptable. Children also fail to grasp the full range of negative

consequences for the violent behavior and observe, instead, the short term reinforcements, namely compliance by the victim. Thus, they learn the use of coercive power and violence as a way to influence loved ones without being exposed to other more constructive alternatives.

In addition to the effect of the destructive modeling, children who grow up in violent homes experience damaging psychological effects. There is substantial documentation that the spouse abuser's violence causes a variety of psychological problems for children. Children raised in a home in which spouse abuse occurs experience the same fear as do battered children. . . .

Spouse abuse results not only in direct physical and psychological injuries to the children, but, of greatest long-term importance, it breeds a culture of violence in future generations. Up to 80 percent of men who abuse their wives witnessed or experienced abuse in their family of origin. Abused children are at great risk of becoming abusive parents. Thus, the ultimate question in assessing the relative fitness for custody of the abuser and victim is which parent is most likely to provide the children with a healthy, caring and *nonviolent* home. . . .

There is yet another aspect of spousal abuse that judges and many others find difficult to understand. These relationships are characterized not only by physical abuse, but also by repeated humiliation and other psychological abuse that " 'reaches the level of a campaign to reduce the partner's sense of self-worth and to maintain control' "[;] and "a pattern on the part of the abusive partner to control the victim's daily actions. . . . " . . .

It is clear from Mr. S.'s testimony that he ran this family with an iron hand, a significant trait in abusive relationships being the total power and control of one party. The evidence reflects that for some period of time Mrs. S. was not allowed to have a cent, not even grocery money. She was permitted to write a grocery list, and if her husband was ever-so-gracious, he would include her requests. . . . Once she attempted to take $20 from his wallet and wound up in the emergency room after he wrestled with her over it. Mr. S. testified that he actually found the whole episode rather humorous, likening his wife clinging desperately to the $20 bill by hiding it in her mouth as resembling a lizard with lettuce sticking out of its mouth.

One of the complaints made about this mother is that she lacked the ability to manage the boys, ages twelve and ten at the time of the hearings, and surely the record is clear that it was difficult for her to manage these boys, especially Jason, the older of the two. In her petition for review, she pointed out that for several years, her husband had been "mentally, emotionally, and physically cruel" to her. Studies demonstrate that after ages five or six, children show strong indications of identifying with the aggressor and losing respect for the mother. . . .

In her personal petition for review to the circuit court, she [the mother] stated:

My two boys in particular identify with their father. Unfortunately, their father has downgraded me for years in front of them and continues to do so. I would become angry in response. The children have seen their father hit me with a belt. My oldest son Jason has bit me and kicked me so hard to have left bruises on me. Jason repeats to me in arguments what his father tells him happens in court. . . . My second son Justin is ten years old and is having difficulty adjusting. Since he has been with his father, his grades have gone from "A's" and "B's" to some "C's," "D's," and one "F." My six year old daughter, Jennifer is a 4.0 student in first grade. She is also in the gifted program. She has done fine under my care alone this past year.

The evidence reflects that Mr. S. modeled for these children the behavior of demeaning, discrediting, and otherwise disempowering the mother. For example, the father devised a point system to reward good behavior and punish bad behavior. When the mother attempted to participate in the system as a method of encouraging good behavior and managing the children, the children were told that "mommy's points don't count" and "mommy is crazy." The mother testified that the children's response was that "you're not the boss, daddy's the boss. . . ." Furthermore, the father would tally the points and take the children to the toy store for the payoff, which the mother had no financial resources to do. . . .

From Dr. Yeargan's report:

Mr. S. reported that he can't see himself trying to tell the boys to be kinder and gentler to their mother for fear that he'll lose credibility with them. He said, "I'm not too interested in finding a way to help the enemy camp look good or better . . . until all three kids are together and this is resolved. My primary objective is to have the three kids."

Mrs. S. testified that she attended counselling, both in an effort to save the marriage and in an effort to get help in working with the children, and that she read a number of books on parenting and divorce. She admitted that she used bad language (as did the whole family) and that the husband's constant demeaning of her in front of the children made her angry. She acknowledged she had made mistakes and was working to correct them.

Mr. S., however, presents himself as the perfect father as demonstrated by his testimony that his rapport with the children was "exemplary," and "that it would be very difficult to improve upon." He described himself as "nurturing," "kind," "loving," "caring," "understanding," and "patient."

But a look at Dr. Yeargan's report presents a very different picture of this man:

Some of the same parental behaviors that previously contributed to the children feeling torn between parents is continuing; those behaviors are (a) increasing the alienation between the children and their mother and (b) exacerbating the loneliness which the boys feel for their sister and vice versa. In this examiner's opinion the behaviors of Mr. [S.] . . . are of primary importance in the creation of more alienation and loneliness in the children. . . .

Mr. S. acknowledges that (although less frequently on five-year-old Jennifer), yes, he does use a belt on all three children, and according to unrefuted testimony he also has grabbed Jason by the shoulders and banged Jason's head against a tree. His own description of how he handles physical discipline shows best the kind of fear he uses to exert control over this family:

Normally, the punishment is a smack on the behind with a belt. And I tell them what will happen if they transgress or exceed certain limitations;

and, when they, on occasion—not recently, but on occasion—test an adult's authority, which all children are want (sic) to do, I have no choice but to follow through consistently with what I told them would happen. . . .

On the occasions when I do smack their behinds with a belt, I will always make sure, after I have done it in a controlled and unemotional way—never in anger—that they understand what the punishment was for and why I had to do it, and I will always check their little bottoms to make sure that there is not sufficient force to seriously damage them, say bruising or whatever.

With all of these circumstances, one may wonder why the children were taken from the mother. A close reading of the record reveals that the most damaging things that can be said about Mrs. S. are that 1) she uses bad language; 2) she is very angry; 3) the children told the psychologists that they wanted to live with their father; and 4) one of the psychologists concluded that they "feel safer with their father."

ANGER

What judges and indeed many therapists usually fail to understand is the behavior manifestations battered women frequently demonstrate. . . . Psychologists unfamiliar with all the circumstances and with the unique dynamics of family abuse may make these mistakes:

1. They fail to see that the victim's anger is appropriate and normal. . . .
2. They look to the victim's behavior and personality problems to explain the abuse. . . . Such blaming of the victim tends to reinforce the abuser's position that . . . the victim is crazy. 3. They seem to identify with the seemingly sociable, "appropriate" male as a man who has been pushed beyond his limits by an "angry woman." 4. They fail to see beneath the sincere, positive image of the abuser, but look instead for the "typical" abuser personality. . . . 7. Finally, they criticize [the woman] for focusing her anger on her husband. . . .

It does not appear that any of the psychologists had any information on the domestic abuse and none dealt with the physical abuse; only Dr. Yeargan seems to have had any information on the psychological abuse and domination. If family law masters and judges are to make decisions on the lives of troubled families, they must become sufficiently knowledgeable about physical and emotional domination to enable them to recognize that these factors are just as invidious, and probably more pervasive, than physical abuse alone. And we must begin to see anger on the part of the victim as healthy.

CHILDREN'S PREFERENCE

These children learned from their father that their mother did not have even sufficient authority to purchase a package of Oreo cookies for them, that it was okay to demean, disobey, and verbally abuse her, and that physical violence awaited those who did not do as he said. The mother reacted with anger, and the father by word, deed, and dollar delivered the message that mommy's crazy and mommy's contemptible.

Jason was twelve years old at the time of the hearings before the family law master and thirteen by the time of the divorce. . . . Consequently, even though the mother was the primary caretaker, the circuit court cannot be said to have abused its discretion in giving weight to Jason's preference and placing him in the custody of his father. In all likelihood, and by all the evidence, this young man has already demonstrated a propensity to act out anger with violence, and we can only hope we do not see him in court in another generation.

Justin was ten years old and Jennifer six years old at the time their preferences were expressed. Although it could be argued that a ten-year-old's preference could be given some weight, Jennifer at six was too young to express a meaningful preference. Furthermore, a reading of the record makes it quite clear that Jennifer was spirited off to see psychologists by her father and instructed rather specifically on the way by her father and older brother regarding what to say. She related to her mother after-the-fact that she told lies and even Dr. Yeargan discerned that she had been coached.

Justin and Jennifer should have been placed in the custody of their mother. The majority wreaks further havoc on this family (especially Jennifer) by a remand for further evidence. It appears that anxiety and manipulation will again be the order of the day for this little girl, and life's most basic uncertainties will resume as the family is figuratively killed with due process. . . .

NOTES

1. **Primary Caretaker Presumption.**   Although the primary caretaker presumption has been favored by many academics, only three states have ever enacted it.[484] Did the West Virginia Supreme Court apply the presumption accurately in the *Patricia Ann S.* case?

Some commentators have argued that the primary caretaker test is too heavily weighted in favor of the functions usually performed by women.[485] Is that a sufficient reason to abandon the test? What tasks are missing that ought to be on the list? Should wage-earning be a function that counts as "caretaking"? Even if a primary caretaker presumption does not reflect gender preferences, is it a problem that the rule perpetuates them? Even without the presumption, primary caretaking figures strongly in custody decisions.[486] Is that a problem?

West Virginia replaced its primary caretaker presumption in 2000 in favor of a past caretaking standard. See note 3 below. Minnesota and Montana also tried the primary caretaker presumption, but neither retained it for long. Does

---

484. See, e.g., Martha Albertson Fineman, The Illusion of Equality: The Rhetoric and Reality of Divorce Reform 180-85 (1991) (for all children); David L. Chambers, Rethinking the Substantive Rules for Custody Disputes in Divorce, 83 Mich. L. Rev. 477 (1985) (for children between six months and five years).

485. Ronald K. Henry, Primary Caretaker: Is It a Ruse?, 17 Fam. Advoc. 53 (Summer 1994).

486. See, e.g., In re Custody of Kali, 792 N.E.2d 635 (Mass. 2003); In re McBrayer, 83 P.2d 936 (Or. Ct. App. 2004).

the *Patricia Ann S.* case suggest any reasons why the presumption has not gained greater traction?

2. **Joint Custody.** All states allow some form of joint custody, and some provide a presumption or preference in its favor. Most commonly, however, despite statutory language encouraging participation in the child's life by both parents,[487] joint custody is but one among a number of custody alternatives and not necessarily the favored one.[488] In states with a preference for joint custody, some narrow it to circumstances in which the parents jointly agree,[489] or allow the presumption to be overcome by a showing that joint custody would not be in the child's best interests, or would be detrimental to the child.[490] Iowa requires the court to order joint custody on the request of either parent, unless clear and convincing evidence indicates that such an arrangement is unreasonable and not in the child's best interests, but joint custody in Iowa does not necessarily mean joint physical care.[491] A few states disfavor joint custody awards.[492]

Critics of joint custody argue that to the extent it reduces gender stereotypes, it does so by sacrificing the custodial rights of mothers who have acted as primary parents in favor of fathers who have not earned those rights. Another concern is "custody blackmail"—that laws favoring joint custody provide additional bargaining leverage to men at divorce, who use it to exact financial concessions from mothers who fear litigation over parental rights. A third criticism is that it gives spouses opportunities to harass their former partner and to prevent them from relocating. Similar critiques are leveled against "friendly parent" custody standards, which take into account the willingness and ability of a parent to cooperate in contact between the child and the other parent.[493] For example, Florida requires courts to examine "the demonstrated capacity and disposition of each parent to facilitate and encourage a close and continuing parent-child relationship, to honor the time-sharing schedule, and to be reasonable when changes are required."[494] Critics of such provisions argue that they enable vindictive individuals to harass and manipulate their former spouses and discourage well-intentioned parents—usually mothers—from opposing joint custody for fear that this opposition might be used to label them as a "non-friendly" parent and therefore an inappropriate candidate for primary

---

487. See, e.g., Colo. Rev. Stat. § 14-10-124(1) (West 2022).

488. See Michael Alison Chandler, More Than 20 States in 2017 Considered Laws to Promote Shared Custody of Children After Divorce, Wash. Post, Dec. 11, 2017; Ryland Barton, Joint Custody Will Be the Default Under New Kentucky Law, WFPL News (Apr. 29, 2018). For current state statutes, see FindLaw, Child Custody: Summaries of State Laws, https://family.findlaw.com/child-custody/child-custody-summaries-of-state-laws.html.

489. See, e.g., Cal. Fam. Code § 3080 (West 2022).

490. See, e.g., D.C. Code Ann. § 16-914(a)(2) (West 2022); Fla. Stat. Ann. § 61.13(2)(c)(2) (West 2022).

491. Iowa Code Ann. § 598.41(2) & (5) (West Supp. 2022).

492. Oregon, for example, prohibits an order unless both parents agree. Or. Rev. Stat. § 107.169(3) (2022); see also Vt. Stat. Ann. tit. 15, § 665(a) (2022) (when parents cannot agree, court must order primary or sole custody to one parent).

493. See Margaret K. Dore, The "Friendly Parent" Concept: A Flawed Factor for Child Custody, 6 Loy. J. Pub. Int. L. 41 (2004).

494. Fla. Stat. Ann. § 61.13(3)(a) (West 2022).

custodian. These concerns are heightened where there is a history of family violence. Fathers' rights advocates, by contrast, argue that mothers sometimes falsely claim abuse in order to obtain custody and that such allegations can be difficult to refute.

The effects of joint custody on child support are open to dispute. Supporters of joint custody note that it results in greater child support compliance than other arrangements. However, researchers note that it is unclear whether joint custody encourages compliance or whether the kind of parents who seek joint custody are also the kind of parents who tend to take their child support obligations most seriously. Moreover, as discussed in note 4 to Section 2, above, shared custody may reduce the amount of a child support order in a way that puts a greater strain on the lower earning parent, even when the expenses of that parent on behalf of the child are not affected by the enhanced involvement of the other parent.

More generally, whether joint custody benefits children appears to depend upon the family circumstances. Children generally do well under shared arrangements when parents are able to value each other's contribution and have good psychological functioning, high self-esteem, and a low level of anger. By contrast, when parents have intense hostility, low self-esteem, and a tendency to blame or punish their former spouse, the children are likely to suffer.[495]

3. **The "Approximation" or "Past Caretaking" Standard.**   The primary caretaking test was intended to give greater determinacy to the best interests test, which gave judges free rein to decide custody matters according to their own, subjective ideas about what is best for children. But the *Patricia Ann S.* case demonstrates that gender stereotypes can control a case, even in the face of a primary caretaker presumption.

If the best interests test is too subjective, the primary caretaker presumption too unfair to primary breadwinners, and the joint custody alternative too unrealistic for many couples, is there a preferable alternative?[496] Given the variety in circumstances in today's families and the importance of the actual custodial arrangements that parents make on their own, Elizabeth Scott suggests an alternative presumption, which she calls the "approximation standard." That standard calls for the custody arrangement that best approximates parenting patterns while the family was intact. Such an approach, Scott argues, promotes continuity and stability for children, encourages cooperative rather than adversarial behavior by parents, and provides incentives for both parents to invest in parenting before as well as after

---

495. On the relationship between high conflict and joint custody, see Janet Johnston, Building Multidisciplinary Professional Partnerships with the Court on Behalf of High-Conflict Divorcing Families and Their Children: Who Needs What Kind of Help?, 22 U. Ark. Little Rock L. Rev. 4543 (2000); Muriel Brotsky et al., Joint Custody Through Mediation: A Longitudinal Assessment of the Children, in Joint Custody and Shared Parenting 167 (1991).

496. The Supreme Court of Wyoming reversed a trial court's finding that a husband's breadwinning was sufficient to allow him to share "primary caretaker" status with the child's mother. See Williams v. Williams, No. S-15-0148, 2016 WL 662020, at *6 (Wyo. Feb. 18, 2016); see also Laurie S. Kohn, Money Can't Buy You Love: Valuing Contributions by Nonresidential Fathers, 81 Brook. L. Rev. '53 (2015).

divorce.[497] This is also the approach taken by the American Law Institute, which calls it the "past caretaking standard."[498] Does this approach make gender bias less likely? Does it unfairly penalize fathers who are primary breadwinners? Douglas NeJaime argues that the marriage equality movement, because of its recognition of the needs of children being raised by same-sex couples, will help to promote a more intentional and functional view of parenthood.[499] Is that a good thing?

Another possibility is to give a custodial preference to the parent who is the same sex as the child. A few states have such a preference for children who are at or near adolescence; a few states expressly prohibit it.[500] Social science evidence on the benefits of such placements is mixed and may reflect gendered assumptions about what is healthy "sex role identification." Would you expect that successful role modeling depends upon sharing a primary residence with the same-sex parent?

4. **LGBTQ+ Parents.** Gay, lesbian, bisexual, or transgender parents may have custody issues even if they are the child's biological parent. Under the traditional view, homosexuality was sufficient to render a parent unfit to have custody of a child. While no court currently embraces such a categorical approach, a number of states permit the fact-finder to draw an inference that a parent's homosexual conduct is harmful to a child. In some cases, gay or lesbian parents have lost custody based upon kissing a same-sex partner in front of the children, admitting their homosexuality, or enrolling a child in a conservative school where it would cause embarrassment to the child to have a gay or lesbian parent.[501] In contrast, the rule today in most jurisdictions is that the sexual orientation of a parent may not be taken into account in a custody determination unless there is a nexus with the child's well-being.[502] Only the District of Columbia, however, specifically limits courts' ability to consider a parent's LGBT status in a custody proceeding.[503]

---

497. Elizabeth S. Scott, Pluralism, Parental Preference, and Child Custody, 80 Cal. L. Rev. 615 (1992).

498. Amer. L. Inst., Principles of the Law of Family Dissolution § 2.08 (2002).

499. Douglas NeJaime, Marriage Equality and the New Parenthood, 129 Harv. L. Rev. 1185 (2016); see also Joanna L. Grossman, Parentage Without Gender, 17 Cardozo J. Conflict Resol. 717 (2016).

500. Alabama appears to allow a same-sex parent preference, by statute. Other states, such as Arizona and Maine, explicitly prohibit it. See Ariz. Rev. Stat. Ann. § 25-403.01(A) (West 2022); Me. Rev. Stat. Ann. tit. 19-A, § 1653(4) (West 2022). In a few jurisdictions, including Illinois and North Dakota, courts have allowed a preference for a parent of the same sex during or right before adolescence on various role-modeling hypotheses. The majority rule, however, is that courts may not prefer a parent because he or she is the same sex as the child.

501. See Suzanne A. Kim, The Neutered Parent, Yale J.L. & Feminism 1 (2012) (observing the tendency in custody law to prefer "sexually neutral" parenting, where parental sexuality is kept at a safe distance from children).

502. This is also the recommendation of the American Law Institute. See Amer. L. Inst., Principles of the Law of Family Dissolution, § 2.12(1)(d), (e) (2002); Sonia K. Katyal & Ilona M. Turner, Transparenthood, 117 Mich. L. Rev. 1593 (2019). For a breakdown of the law among the states and a discussion of some of the early cases, see Jovana Vujovic, Child Custody and Visitation, 5 Geo J. Gender & L. 477, 493 (2004). See In re Marriage of Black, 393 P.3d 1041 (Wash. 2017) (finding an abuse of discretion where trial court used mother's sexual orientation as factor to deny custody, reflecting judicial bias).

503. D.C. Code § 16-914(a)(1)(A) (2022).

Generally, under the harm standard, real or imagined stigma from having a gay or lesbian parent is insufficient. The following analysis is increasingly typical:

> [O]ne of life's realities is that one of his parents is homosexual. In the absence of evidence that the homosexuality in some way harms the boy, limiting [his] relationship with that parent fails to permit him to confront his life situation, however unconventional it may be. . . . [The child's] best interest is served by exposing him to reality and not fostering in him shame or abhorrence for his mother's non-traditional commitment.[504]

Shannon Minter observes that while courts have grown to understand that sexual orientation is irrelevant to parental ability, transgender parents still face considerable discrimination.[505] Why do you think the issues are treated differently?

In those states that subscribe to a same-sex custodial preference, how should such a rule apply when a child and/or a parent is transgender or non-binary? Should sexual orientation of either the child or the parent be considered — for example, should a child who identifies as gay be presumptively placed in the custody of a gay parent, where one parent is gay and the other is not? Does the logic of pairing children with a same-gender parent for role modeling purposes apply here?

Another set of issues arises with respect to a nonbiological, lesbian co-parent who has acted as a parent with the consent of her partner, who is the biological mother, and who seeks some custodial rights when the couple's relationship ends.[506] Traditionally, courts denied visitation and custody rights to lesbians who were de facto nonbiological parents, either because they lacked standing or because they failed to meet the substantive criteria for parenthood under the state's custody statute.[507] Starting in 1995, some states began developing a doctrine variously labeled de facto parentage, equitable parenthood, parenthood by estoppel, or in loco parentis (taking on all or some responsibilities of a parent), which allowed courts to award visitation rights to a lesbian co-parent who had raised the child on an equal basis with the biological parent, with that parent's approval.[508] New York's highest court recently recognized de facto parentage in some circumstances, after rejecting it twice, seventeen years apart.[509] Some states have codified this doctrine.[510] Same-sex co-parents may also obtain recognition in some states under parentage laws

---

504. Blew v. Verta, 617 A.2d 31, 36 (Pa. Super. Ct. 1992); see also Jacoby v. Jacoby, 763 So. 2d 410, 413 (Fla. Dist. Ct. App. 2000) (law cannot give effect to private biases, which in any event "flow not from the fact that the children were living with a homosexual mother, but from the fact that she is a homosexual").

505. Shannon Price Minter, Transgender Family Law, 56 Fam. Ct. Rev. 410 (2018).

506. See generally Emily Kazyak et al., Law and Family Formation Among LGBQ-Parent Families, 56 Fam. Ct. Rev. 364 (2018).

507. See, e.g., Debra H. v. Janice R., 930 N.E.2d 184 (N.Y. 2010); Hawkins v. Grese, 809 S.E.2d 441 (Va. Ct. App. 2018) (holding lesbian partner to be nonparent).

508. In re Custody of H.S.H.-K., 533 N.W.2d 419 (Wis. 1995); Rubano v. DiCenzo, 759 A.2d 959 (R.I. 2000); Nguyen v. Boynes, 396 P.3d 774 (Nev. 2017).

509. See Brooke S.B. v. Elizabeth A. C.C., 61 N.E.3d 488 (N.Y. 2016).

510. See, e.g., Conn. Gen. Stat. §§ 46b-56, 46b-59 (2022).

based on intent to parent with the consent of the biological mother.[511] Under these theories, courts have also imposed support obligations on members of same-sex couples.[512] Courts in several states, however, have continued to reject de facto parentage, citing concerns about intruding on the biological mother's constitutionally protected parental rights and the lack of certainty about parental status that arises from a functional approach.[513]

Before the legalization of same-sex marriage nationwide, same-sex co-parents in some states were able to adopt the child they were co-parenting, notwithstanding the traditional prohibition against a child having more than one mother (or more than one father). Over a dozen states allowed "second-parent adoptions," a term developed as an equitable work-around for committed same-sex couples that could not avail themselves of stepparent adoptions because they were not permitted to marry.[514] When the California Supreme Court ruled in favor of same-sex, second-parent adoptions in 2003, more than 20,000 had already been granted by family court judges.[515] The American Academy of Pediatrics has long supported same-sex co-parent adoption as beneficial to children.[516]

Because state laws vary, questions arose about whether same-sex adoptions obtained in one state need to be recognized in another. The U.S. Supreme Court resolved this issue in V.L. v. E.L., in which it held, even without the benefit of briefing on the merits, that a final judgment of adoption in one state is entitled to full faith and credit in another.[517]

Obergefell has eliminated the need for second-parent adoptions for couples who choose to marry because they can use the stepparent adoption process that is available in every state. Mississippi had a separate law barring two people of the same sex from jointly adopting a child, but it was challenged in the wake of *Obergefell* and struck down by a federal court.[518] The Supreme Court, however, held in Fulton v. City of Philadelphia that a taxpayer-funded social service organization could

---

511. See, e.g., Chatterjee v. King, 280 P.3d 283 (N.M. 2012); Frazier v. Goudschaal, 295 P.3d 542 (Kan. 2013). For the argument, see Nancy D. Polikoff, From Third Parties to Parents: The Case of Lesbian Couples and Their Children, 77 L. & Contemp. Probs. 195, 209-19 (2014).

512. See, e.g., Elisa B. v. Superior Court, 117 P.3d 660, 663 (Cal. 2005).

513. See, e.g., Sheardown v. Guastella, 324 Mich. App. 251 (2018); Smith v. Gordon, 968 A.2d 1 (Del. 2009); White v. White, 293 S.W.3d 1 (Mo. Ct. App. 2009). A similar case in Maryland, Janice M. v. Margaret K., 948 A.2d 73 (Md. 2008), was overruled in Conover v. Conover, 146 A.3d 433 (Md. 2016).

514. Courtney G. Joslin, The Legal Parentage of Children Born to Same-Sex Couples, 39 Fam. L.Q. 683, 691 (2005).

515. Sharon S. v. Superior Court, 73 P.3d 554, 568 (Cal. 2003).

516. Amer. Acad. of Pediatrics, Co-Parent or Second Parent Adoption by Same-Sex Parents, 109 Pediatrics 339 (2002).

517. 577 U.S. 404 (2016).

518. See Campaign for Southern Equality et al. v. Mississippi Dep't Human Servs., 175 F. Supp. 3d 691 (S.D. Miss. 2016) (invalidating Miss. Code Ann. § 93-17-3(5) (2010)). The Movement Advancement Project provides helpful tracking on these issues. Foster and Adoption Laws, MAP: Movement Advancement Project (2019), http://www.lgbtmap.org/equality-maps/foster_and_adoption_laws.

refuse to certify married same-sex couples as licensed foster families because of its religious belief that marriage is limited to a union between a man and a woman.[519]

Now that same-sex couples have equal access to marriage, will courts be even less willing to recognize de facto parentage or second-parent adoption for unmarried same-sex couples, remedies that were designed to fill the gap left by discriminatory marriage laws? A Missouri appellate court recently observed that "the justification for rejecting an equitable parentage argument is stronger today" than in 2009 when it first rejected the doctrine.[520] Indeed, the court noted, "[w]e anticipate that in the wake of *Obergefell*, situations like this one, in which important issues involving children must be decided outside the established legal framework applicable to married couples, will occur less frequently."[521] The Supreme Court issued a second per curiam parentage decision after *Obergefell*, in which it summarily reversed a ruling of the Arkansas Supreme Court that would have prevented a biological mother's wife's name from being listed on her child's birth certificate. The Court held that parentage-by-marriage is one of the "constellation of benefits" of marriage to which same-sex couples are equally entitled.[522]

5. **Relocation.** Many families relocate after divorce. In 2020, approximately 8.5 percent of divorced or separated U.S. families reported having changed living quarters within the previous year. Of these, 58.7 percent relocated within the same county, 23.8 percent to a different county within the same state, and 17.5 percent to a different state or abroad.[523] One study of college students from divorced families found that in only 39 percent of cases did neither parent relocate after the divorce. It was equally likely that the child remained with the mother while the father relocated or that the child relocated with the mother.[524]

The law in this area has been unstable, at best, but the clear trend has been toward increasing deference to the parent with whom the child has been primarily living.[525] Typically, the kinds of reasons for relocation that courts view as acceptable are to take a significantly better job (or to allow a new spouse to take a significantly better job), to address significant health issues, to pursue educational opportunities not available in the original jurisdiction, to be close to other relatives, or to bring significant improvement in the family's quality of life.

---

519. 141 S. Ct. 1848 (2021).

520. McGaw v. McGaw, 468 S.W.3d 435, 442 (Mo. Ct. App. 2015).

521. Id. at 438.

522. Pavan v. Smith, 137 S. Ct. 2075 (2017).

523. See U.S. Census Bureau, Population Division, Current Population Survey, Geographic Mobility: 2020-21 (Nov. 2021).

524. Sanford L. Braver et al., Relocation of Children After Divorce and Children's Best Interests: New Evidence and Legal Considerations, 17 J. Family Psych. 206, 212 (2003); Matthew M. Stevenson et al., Associations Between Parental Relocation Following Separation in Childhood and Maladjustment in Adolescence and Young Adulthood, 24 Psych. Pub. Pol'y & L. 365 (2018).

525. See, e.g., Miller v. Miller, 88 N.E.3d 843, 848 (Mass. 2018); Burnett v. Parra, No. A17-1107, 2018 WL 817783 (Minn. Ct. App. Feb. 12, 2018). But see Ainsworth v. Ainsworth, 186 A.3d 1074, 1084 (R.I. 2018). See generally Robert G. Spector & Melissa A. Kucinski, International Family Law, 49 Int'l L. 147 (2015).

Which of these reasons seem significant enough to deprive the non-custodial parent and the child of frequent contact with each other? On the one hand, depriving a custodial parent of the right to move with his or her children is a high price to pay for custody. It often seems unfair to make the parent who has borne the primary responsibility for the children during the marriage incur relocation limitations that the other parent does not incur at divorce. On the other hand, the non-custodial parent will often face significant constraints in maintaining a close relationship to a child who resides a long distance away. These challenges can be insurmountable, especially for low-income parents. Yet preventing both parents from relocating may impose significant economic as well as personal disadvantages.

Because most children of divorced families are in the physical custody of their mothers, the relocation standard a court applies will have a gender impact. Should that impact be taken into account? If one objective of custody law is to encourage parenting by fathers, should the standard prefer protecting the custodial and visitation rights of fathers or the caretaking roles already assumed during the marriage?

6. **Fairness and Custody.** To what extent should fairness be a factor in custody rules? What if *Patricia Ann S.* is read, for example, to mean that (1) the children are more comfortable with their father and want to live with him; (2) the reason for this is that the father has physically and emotionally abused the mother, eliminating her self-esteem and impairing her parental abilities; and (3) it is a reasonable prediction that the mother will not be able to regain the confidence and trust of her children? In these circumstances (which represent one reading of the case), should fairness to the mother be a factor in her favor?

PUTTING THEORY INTO PRACTICE

2-60. Since the birth of her son, David, two years ago, Rhonda quit her job as an assistant office manager to care for her son at home, relying on support by her husband Hugh, who is a high school teacher. They are divorcing. Since Hugh does not make enough money to support two households, Rhonda has agreed that she must return to full-time employment and that David will have to be placed in day care. Rhonda seeks primary custody of David based on her primary caretaking role during the marriage. Hugh argues that he should have primary custody because his mother has agreed to take care of David while he works, which he believes would be preferable to care by strangers. What rules should govern such a case? What further information should the court have to make its decision?

What if Hugh is about to remarry and his new wife is prepared to provide full-time, in-home care for David along with her own young child? Is this a stronger or weaker case for Rhonda?

2-61. When Janet and Mark divorced after an eight-year marriage, Janet had no job skills or training. During the marriage, she stayed at home to care for her three children, the first of whom was born almost immediately upon her graduation from high school. At the divorce, Janet decided to give up primary custody of the children, then ages 3, 5, and 8, to Mark, who was planning to remarry, so that Janet would have two years to attend community college full-time. Still, Janet had custody of the children every weekend and during school vacations, talked to them every night on the telephone, and continued to take primary responsibility for such things as doctor appointments, clothing, haircuts, birthday presents, and the like. Janet missed seeing the children every day, but felt the arrangement was the only way she would be able to make herself economically independent. The children were cared for during the day, when they weren't in school, by their stepmother, who did not work outside the home.

The arrangement seemed to be working well, until one year into the arrangement, Mark announced that he had received a very large promotion and was moving to another state, 1,500 miles away. He intends to take the children with him. Should Janet be able to stop him from moving with the children? Under what general rule?

2-62. At a custody trial between biological parents, the father offers evidence to show that a mother snuggles with her children and her female companion in bed, has the children march with her in a gay and lesbian rights parade, and has her children participate in their wedding. Her children also have an "astonishing grasp of anatomical terminology." Is this evidence proof of harm to the children? What are the arguments on each side?[526]

2-63. The parents of a 7-year-old are fighting over the child's custody. The mother believes the child, who was born a boy but now identifies as female, is a transgender girl; she does not seek any surgical or chemical interventions but she thinks the child should be affirmed as a girl both inside and outside the home. The father believes the child is a boy and refuses to cooperate with the mother's wishes to treat the child as a girl. The judge in the case, finding that the child "appears comfortable as a girl, boy or gender nonspecific," orders joint custody. Does this make sense? If you were the judge, how would you approach the case?

2-64. Two researchers have concluded, from a comparative longitudinal study, that while there is no significant difference in sexual attraction to someone of the same gender between those raised by lesbian single mothers and those raised by heterosexual single mothers, children raised in lesbian families are somewhat more likely to consider, and to have, homosexual involvement than are their peers raised by heterosexual mothers.[527] Should these findings play any role in custody decisions?

2-65. John seeks to have his 11-year-old son undergo "gay conversion" therapy so that he will live a happier life and because John's religion, in which the child was raised, believes that gays and lesbians will spend eternity in hell. His ex-wife, Louise, who is the child's mother, objects. Many states, although not their home state, have banned this type of therapy by law. How should this dispute be resolved? Should the dispute affect who gets custody of the child?[528]

---

526. See Hertzler v. Hertzler, 908 P.2d 946 (Wyo. 1995).

527. See Judith Stacey and Timothy J. Biblarz, (How) Does the Sexual Orientation of Parents Matter?, 66 Am. Socio. Rev. 159 (2001); Susan Golombok & Fiona Tasker, Do Parents Influence the Sexual Orientation of Their Children? Findings from a Longitudinal Study of Lesbian Families, 32 Developmental Psych. 3, 7 (1996); Fiona Tasker & Susan Golombok, Growing Up in a Lesbian Family: Effects on Child Development 102-14 (1997).

528. Eighteen states and the District of Columbia prohibit the practice — a fourfold increase in just three years. See Movement Advancement Project, Conversion Therapy Laws (2019), https://www.lgbtmap.org/equality-maps/conversion_therapy. The laws are predicated on varying legislative findings, most notably harm to children and consumer fraud (on

2-66. As many as 40 percent of children who reside with their mothers haven't seen their fathers in the last year.[529] If making divorced men more involved in parenting is an important goal, how can it be achieved? What would you think of a requirement that each parent exercise approximately 50 percent of physical custody of his or her children? What are the advantages and disadvantages of such an approach?[530]

4. Unmarried Parents

One area in which many sex-based distinctions persist involves the rights of unmarried parents. The issue is increasingly important given the meteoric rise in nonmarital births. In 2020, just over 40 percent of all births in the United States were to unmarried women, as many as 70 percent in some racial groups.[531] At common law, the child of unmarried parents was *filius nullius*—the child of no one. In the nineteenth century, states began to recognize legal ties between unwed mothers and their children, but unwed fathers were generally denied parental rights (though not always parental obligations) well into the twentieth century.[532] That system crumbled beginning in the 1970s when the Supreme Court held, in a series of cases, that unwed fathers could not be categorically stripped of legal parentage without violating Fourteenth Amendment protections. These cases followed a series of cases recognizing the equal protection rights of illegitimate children not to be unfairly penalized by their parents' actions.[533]

In Stanley v. Illinois, the U.S. Supreme Court held that the state could not make children of an unmarried father wards of the state when their mother died based on a conclusive presumption that he was unfit.[534] Peter Stanley had lived with his children and their mother for most of the eighteen years before her death. But because he was not married to the mother, he was not considered a legal parent under the applicable statute. The Court invalidated the statute on substantive and procedural due process grounds, holding that the children could not be removed from their father unless he was first shown to be unfit. It found the state's proffered justifications — to protect "the moral, emotional, mental, and physical welfare of

---

the theory that sexual orientation is innate and not subject to "conversion"). The American Psychological Association and American Academy of Pediatrics both condemn the practice.

529. Jane Anderson, The Impact of Family Structure on the Health of Children: Effects of Divorce, 81 Sage J. 378 (Nov. 1, 2014).

530. See Ariel Ayanna, From Children's Interests to Parent Responsibility: Degendering Parenthood Through Custodial Obligation, 19 UCLA Women's L.J. 1 (2012).

531. Michelle J. K. Osterman et al., Births: Final Data for 2020, 70 Nat'l Vital Stat. Reps. 5 & tbl. 9 (Feb. 7, 2022).

532. See Mary Ann Mason, From Father's Property to Children's Rights: The History of Child Custody in the United States 24 (1994).

533. See, e.g., Levy v. Louisiana, 391 U.S. 68 (1968). On the development of rights for unwed fathers, see Joanna L. Grossman, The New Illegitimacy: Tying Parentage to Marital Status for Lesbian Co-Parents, 20 J. Gender, Soc. Pol'y & L. 101, 122-32 (2012).

534. 405 U.S. 645 (1972).

the minor and the best interests of the community" and to "strengthen the minor's family ties whenever possible"—to be undermined by cutting off custodial, biological fathers solely based on marital status.[535]

Although *Stanley* put an end to the categorical denial of unwed fatherhood, the Court considered in other cases the degree to which states could still differentiate between unmarried fathers and unmarried mothers. In Caban v. Mohammed (1979), the Supreme Court decided that a stepparent could not adopt a child without the biological father's consent if the father had developed an ongoing, meaningful relationship with the child.[536] If state law would not allow the termination of a mother's rights in similar circumstances, the Court reasoned, it could not allow the termination of the rights of a father who had accepted his responsibilities as a parent. The Court rejected the state's justification that "a natural mother" usually has a "closer relationship with her child . . . than a father does."[537] Finally, in Lehr v. Robertson (1983), the Court considered an unwed father's rights to an infant before a substantial relationship has had time to develop.[538] The mother in that case married a man other than the biological father of her eight-month-old infant and petitioned for the stepfather to adopt the child when she was two. A court approved the adoption without notifying the biological father of the proceeding. New York maintained a "putative father registry" that allows men to notify the state of their intent to assert paternity over an actual or potential child. But the father had not registered nor satisfied any other criteria such as being listed on the birth certificate or living with the child that would entitle him to notice. The Court upheld the New York law, concluding that the father's biological tie to the child was not enough to justify full constitutional protection of his parental rights. While a "developed parent-child relationship" deserves robust protection, an undeveloped one is only protected if the father has grasped every opportunity to develop one.[539]

Together, these rulings allow states to grant legal parentage automatically to unwed mothers, but to impose preconditions on legal parentage for unwed fathers. Most states have adopted a system similar to the one endorsed by the Uniform Parentage Act, in which a man is the legal father of a child if one of several criteria is met, including marriage to the mother, adjudication or acknowledgment of paternity, open and notorious acknowledgment of fatherhood, cohabitation with the mother and child in the first two years of life, or clear and convincing evidence of biological paternity.[540] The 2017 version of the Uniform Parentage Act makes all rules of parentage gender neutral, including the rules regarding paternity. With respect to legally married couples, this is arguably required pursuant to the Supreme Court's per curiam ruling in *Pavan*, discussed above.[541] Is it more

---

535. Id. at 652.
536. 441 U.S. 380 (1979).
537. Id. at 388.
538. 463 U.S. 248 (1983).
539. Id. at 250-62.
540. Unif. Parentage Act, Articles 2, 3, & 6 (2017).
541. See generally NeJaime, supra note 499; Douglas NeJaime, The Nature of Parenthood, 126 Yale L.J. 2260 (2017).

acceptable to differentiate between mothers and fathers who are not married? Why or why not?

The federal government makes sex-based distinctions between unmarried mothers and unmarried fathers in circumstances that can produce harsh consequences. The Supreme Court has three times upheld various provisions of immigration law that disallow citizen-fathers from passing citizenship to their offspring born abroad in situations when a citizen-mother could have transmitted citizenship.[542] The Supreme Court in Nguyen v. Immigration and Naturalization Service (2001), for example, upheld a federal statute that sets forth different requirements for citizenship claimed through an American-born father than through the American-born mother.[543] Even though the child was abandoned by his Vietnamese mother and raised exclusively by his American father in Texas, he was not eligible for citizenship because his father had not taken the right administrative steps within the allotted time to establish a legal parent-child relationship. Had his mother been the citizen, he would have inherited it automatically regardless of whether she actively participated in childrearing or took any affirmative steps to establish their relationship. But because his citizen-parent was his father, he was no longer eligible to apply for citizenship and was deported to Vietnam after conviction for a crime of moral turpitude. The Court upheld this gender differentiation against an equal protection challenge as justified by "a biological difference between the parents" because "the mother is always present at birth," but "the father need not be."[544]

The Court has not revisited *Nguyen*, but it did subsequently invalidate a different provision of immigration law that imposed different residency requirements on mothers and (legally recognized) fathers necessary to transmit citizenship. Mothers had to live in the United States for only one year before the child's birth, at any time, while fathers had to live there for ten years, five of which had to be before the age of 14. In Sessions v. Morales-Santana, the Court held this distinction violated the Equal Protection Clause because it drew on the "obsolescing view that 'unwed fathers [are] invariably less qualified and entitled than mothers' to take responsibility for non-marital children."[545] The majority noted that laws based on "overbroad generalizations" might create a "self-fulfilling cycle of discrimination that force[s] women to continue to assume the role of primary family caregiver."[546] Despite this ruling, *Nguyen* still permits Congress to draw sex-based distinctions based on relevant biological differences.

---

542. See Miller v. Albright, 523 U.S. 420 (1998); Nguyen v. INS, 533 U.S. 53 (2001); United States v. Flores-Villar, 564 U.S. 210 (2010) (affirming without opinion, by a vote of 4-4, the appellate ruling, 536 F.3d 990 (9th Cir. 2008)).

543. 533 U.S. at 53. On how the citizenship-by-descent rules were used historically to deny citizenship to non-white children, see Kristin A. Collins, Illegitimate Borders: Jus Sanguinis Citizenship and the Legal Construction of Family, Race, and Nation, 123 Yale L.J. 2134 (2014).

544. *Nguyen*, 533 U.S. at 64.

545. 137 S. Ct. 1678, 1692 (2017) (citing Caban v. Mohammed, 441 U.S. 380, 382 (1979)).

546. Id. at 1693 (quoting Nevada Dept. of Human Resources v. Hibbs, 538 U.S. 721, 736).

Both lines of cases — considering the legality of state and federal distinctions between unwed mothers and fathers — are controversial. Some commentators argue that the rights of unmarried fathers and mothers should be identical; others claim that fathers and mothers are not similarly situated, and that the same rules should not apply. Justice Stevens has consistently followed the latter reasoning. Consider the following, from his dissent in Caban v. Mohammed:

> Men and women are different, and the difference is relevant to the question whether the mother may be given the exclusive right to consent to the adoption of a child born out of wedlock. Because most adoptions involve newborn infants or very young children, it is appropriate at the outset to focus on the significance of the difference in such cases.

> Both parents are equally responsible for the conception of the child out of wedlock. But from that point on through pregnancy and infancy, the differences between the male and the female have an important impact on the child's destiny. Only the mother carries the child; it is she who has the constitutional right to decide whether to bear it or not. In many cases, only the mother knows who sired the child, and it will often be within her power to withhold that fact, and even the fact of her pregnancy, from that person. If during pregnancy the mother should marry a different partner, the child will be legitimate when born, and the natural father may never even know that his "rights" have been affected. On the other hand, only if the natural mother agrees to marry the natural father during that period can the latter's actions have a positive impact on the status of the child; if he instead should marry a different partner during that time, the only effect on the child is negative, for the likelihood of legitimacy will be lessened.

> These differences continue at birth and immediately thereafter. During that period, the mother and child are together; the mother's identity is known with certainty. The father, on the other hand, may or may not be present; his identity may be unknown to the world and may even be uncertain to the mother. These natural differences between unmarried fathers and mothers make it probable that the mother, and not the father or both parents, will have custody of the newborn infant.

> In short, it is virtually inevitable that from conception through infancy the mother will constantly be faced with decisions about how best to care for the child, whereas it is much less certain that the father will be confronted with comparable problems. There no doubt are cases in which the relationship of the parties at birth makes it appropriate for the State to give the father a voice of some sort in the adoption decision. But as a matter of equal protection analysis, it is perfectly obvious that at the time and immediately after a child is born out of wedlock, differences between men and women justify some differential treatment of the mother and father in the adoption process.

> Most particularly, these differences justify a rule that gives the mother of the newborn infant the exclusive right to consent to its adoption. Such

a rule gives the mother, in whose sole charge the infant is often placed anyway, the maximum flexibility in deciding how best to care for the child. It also gives the loving father an incentive to marry the mother, and has no adverse impact on the disinterested father. Finally, it facilitates the interests of the adoptive parents, the child, and the public at large by streamlining the often traumatic adoption process and allowing the prompt, complete, and reliable integration of the child into a satisfactory new home at as young an age as is feasible. Put most simply, it permits the maximum participation of interested natural parents without so burdening the adoption process that its attractiveness to potential adoptive parents is destroyed.[547]

Consider also Justice Kennedy's plurality opinion in *Nguyen*:

To fail to acknowledge even our most basic biological differences—such as the fact that a mother must be present at birth but the father need not be—risks making the guarantee of equal protection superficial, and so disserving it. Mechanistic classification of all our differences as stereotypes would operate to obscure those misconceptions and prejudices that are real.[548]

Are Justices Stevens and Kennedy right? Granting the differences between mothers and fathers with respect to the birth process, should these differences have legal consequences? Does distinguishing between unmarried mothers and fathers promote, or undermine, gender equity?[549]

Feminists were split over the rights of unmarried fathers. On the one hand, greater recognition of unwed fathers' rights might help disrupt the deeply entrenched gender stereotypes about parenting. On the other, some worried that greater recognition might invite greater second-guessing of parenting decisions without much meaningful help with caretaking. Consider Professor Serena Mayeri's discussion of the conflicting feminist views of the law regarding unwed fathers, on display in Kirkpatrick v. Christian Homes of Abilene,[550] which raised equality questions before the Supreme Court but was remanded for a decision on state-law grounds.

---

547. Caban v. Mohammed, 441 U.S. 380, 404-08 (1979) (Stevens, J., dissenting).

548. 533 U.S. at 73.

549. For feminist support of the *Lehr* line of cases, see Jennifer S. Hendricks, Essentially a Mother, 13 Wm. & Mary J. Women & L. 429 (2007); E. Gary Spitko, The Constitutional Function of Biological Paternity: Evidence of the Biological Mother's Consent to the Biological Father's Co-parenting of Her Child, 48 Ariz. L. Rev. 97 (2006). For feminist commentary that is critical of the same line of cases, see Dara Purvis, The Origin of Parental Rights: Labor, Intent, and Fathers, 41 Fla. St. L. Rev. 645 (2014); Albertina Antognini, From Citizenship to Custody: Unwed Fathers Abroad and at Home, 36 Harv. J.L. & Gender 405 (2013).

550. 460 U.S. 1074 (1983).

Serena Mayeri

Foundling Fathers: (Non-)Marriage and Parental Rights in the Age of Equality

125 Yale L.J. 2292, 2354-57 (2016)

Kirkpatrick was the first case to present the Court with a feminist argument against sex neutrality in non-marital parental rights. In a small Nebraska town, Donald Kirkpatrick and Laura S. began an intimate relationship when he was 22 and she was 14. At 15, Laura became pregnant, and decided, in consultation with her parents, to place the child for adoption. An adoptee herself, Laura "had great concern for the stigma attached to a child born out of wedlock in a small town." . . .

When Laura informed [Kirkpatrick] of the pregnancy, Kirkpatrick proposed marriage, but Laura declined. In Texas, biological fathers were entitled to receive notice of adoption proceedings, but could not veto an adoption and take custody of an unlegitimated child unless a court agreed that legitimation was in the child's best interests. The trial court denied Kirkpatrick's legitimation petition and placed the infant in foster care pending appeal. The state appellate court affirmed. . . .

Supporters said Kirkpatrick was a responsible, upstanding young man devoted to his daughter and eager to marry her mother; detractors claimed he was an irreligious statutory rapist with inconstant paternal instincts who planned to turn the child over to the care of his female relatives. Both characterizations enjoyed some support in the record. . . .

[T]he national ACLU agreed to represent Kirkpatrick before the U.S. Supreme Court. The ACLU argued that substantive due process and equal protection required that unmarried fathers be permitted to legitimate their children over the mother's objection, veto an adoption, and obtain custody unless they were proven unfit. The Court should, the ACLU argued, declare the best-interests standard unconstitutionally vague, at least with respect to terminations of parental rights. And the Texas statute was "freighted with the 'baggage of sexual stereotypes'" so often condemned by this Court." The injury to "caring fathers" was "patent." "Less obvious but equally invidious" was "the harm done to women," who were "inevitably locked into the childcare role, unable to share childrearing responsibilities equally with men."

. . . Feminist attorney Nancy Erickson authored an amicus brief on behalf of "unwed mothers" who opposed unmarried fathers' asserted right to veto an adoption and obtain custody for themselves. She quoted unmarried mothers who said they would not have pursued adoption if it meant that the father might gain custody. Instead, these mothers might have felt pressured to have an abortion or to raise an unwanted child, Erickson asserted, violating their right to privacy and decisional autonomy and flouting the child's best interests. Mothers should also have the right to give up their children for adoption anonymously, Erickson argued, and men should not be allowed to use their sexual partners as involuntary surrogate mothers.

Erickson denied that the Texas statutory scheme reflected "an impermissible gender bias" or promoted "sexual stereotypes that portray men as incapable of good parenting." Kirkpatrick himself seemed to assume that various female relatives—his mother, sister, or grandmother—would care for the baby if he were to obtain parental rights and custody. Most recently, Kirkpatrick had married a "full-time homemaker" who allegedly was eager to raise the child, leading Erickson to observe that awarding custody to a man who did not intend to assume a caregiving role hardly served feminist objectives. Feminists like Erickson embraced the goal of greater paternal involvement in the care of children, but they worried about the effects of formal equality on unequal social circumstances. . . .

PUTTING THEORY INTO PRACTICE

2-67. Delaware law allows for the changing of a child's name, upon petition of a parent, if the change is in the child's best interests. A mother petitioned the court seeking to change the surname of her 5-year-old daughter from her father's surname alone to a name that combined it with her mother's surname, without a hyphen. Denying the petition, the judge said the only benefit of the name change would be to "superficially execute [the mother's] desire to draw the child closer to her heritage," which was insufficient to make the change in the child's best interests.[551]

What arguments would you make on appeal for the mother?

2-68. Aala, a Muslim born of Syrian parents, had sex for the first time with John, after he had convinced her to try alcohol for the first time. She became pregnant, but did not tell John because she did not want him to interfere with her decision about the pregnancy. Aala placed the child for adoption without his knowledge for four reasons: (1) her parents are fundamentalist Muslims with strict views against pre-marital sex; (2) she is a college student and could not support a child; (3) she does not want her child raised by John because of his liberal cultural and political views; and (4) she believes that her child will be better off if raised in a two-parent family. During a statutory waiting period, John found out about the baby and petitioned to block the adoption. State law allows an unmarried mother to place a baby for adoption without the father's consent unless he has provided support during pregnancy or after birth.

Is this law constitutional? Is it wise? If the adoption is blocked, how should a court decide a custody dispute between Aala and John?

2-69. A newspaper article examining putative father registries, critical to the ruling in Lehr v. Robertson, described above, concluded that "it's all smoke and mirrors. How can registries work if no one's heard of them? And it's just not reasonable to expect that men will register every time they have sex." It also reported that, in Florida in 2004, 47 men signed up for the state's registry, while there were 89,436 out-of-wedlock births.[552] Do those numbers signal an equality problem? Should states have the obligation to educate men of the steps necessary to protect parental rights?

---

551. In re Sophie LaVoie Boone, C.A. No. CPU 4-15-003549 (Ct. Common Pleas New Castle Cty. Del., Dec. 21, 2015).

552. Tamar Lewin, Unwed Fathers Fight for Babies Placed for Adoption by Mothers, N.Y. Times, Mar. 19, 2006.

2-70. The parents of a 7-year-old are fighting over the child's custody. The mother believes the child, who was born a boy but now identifies as female, is a transgender girl; she does not seek any surgical or chemical interventions but she thinks the child should be affirmed as a girl both inside and outside the home. The father believes the child is a boy and refuses to cooperate with the mother's wishes to treat the child as a girl.

The judge in the case, finding that the child "appears comfortable as a girl, boy or gender nonspecific," orders joint custody. Does this make sense? If you were the judge, how would you approach the case?

CHAPTER 3

NONSUBORDINATION

A nonsubordination perspective shifts the focus of attention from whether women and men are the same or different to whether a rule or practice serves to subordinate women to men. From this perspective, concentrating on sex differences often distracts from the central issue of women's subordination, and even helps to legitimate the power imbalance between men and women. A focus on subordination brings this power imbalance front and center, unmasking the extent to which what leading feminist legal theorist Catharine MacKinnon calls "gender-neutral absolutes, such as difference and sexuality and speech and the state"[1] further that imbalance.

This chapter introduces nonsubordination theory by pairing John Stuart Mill's description of women's nineteenth-century "subjection" as a "solitary breach" in the fundamental laws of modern civilization with MacKinnon's characterization of women's legal subordination as the ability of those with power — men — to identify their own point of view, systematically, as universal "point-of-viewlessness." A third excerpt by Nancy Dowd speaks to the position of men in a system of gender subordination. The remainder of the chapter explores nonsubordination theory's claim that the law defines sex and sexual difference in ways that naturalize women's relative powerlessness in this society, primarily through legal materials relating to sexual harassment, pornography, domestic violence, and heterosexuality.

It is no accident that most of the topics of this chapter relate to sexual behavior. Traditional modes of analysis have been useful in achieving improvements for women in employment, education, and public benefits, but less helpful in addressing some of the problems that have most served to keep women "in their place"—sexual harassment, violence against women, poverty, and control of women's sexuality. Advocates contend that we must move beyond questions of sameness and difference to an understanding of the construction of women's sexuality and gender roles that underpin these realities. While MacKinnon developed the theoretical concepts upon which much of the nonsubordination theory set forth here is based, she considers her theory to be one of substantive equality. For MacKinnon, the "substantive equality alternative . . . aims to eliminate systemic patterns of group advantage and disadvantage—i.e., hierarchies of social dominance and subordination—on the concrete often intertwined bases like sex and race that have

---

1. See Catharine A. MacKinnon, Feminism Unmodified: Discourses on Life and Law 16 (1987).

historically been their grounds."[2] Nonsubordination theory's emphasis on sexuality has generated criticism both from within and outside feminism, including a "governance feminism" critique that examines the costs of feminist policies prioritizing sexual violence above other feminist agendas, and an anti-carceral perspective that highlights the negative consequences of collaborating with state power to punish sexual subordination. As you study the materials in this chapter, consider what nonsubordination theory contributes to the equality principles studied thus far. Is it a supplement, a full replacement, or something else?

A.   WOMEN'S RIGHTS AND POWER IN THE LIBERAL STATE

In the readings below, John Stuart Mill — the leading spokesman for nineteenth-century liberalism — finds the subordination of women an aberrational blind spot of liberalism. Catharine MacKinnon, on the other hand, finds the subordination of women a more or less inevitable consequence of liberalism's emphasis on the individual, its claim to objectivity, and its idealism. These two starting points frame much of the material in this chapter.

MacKinnon's theory is sex specific. The system of subordinations she describes is one of men subordinating women. A third excerpt in this section takes a different tack, offering insights from the field of masculinities studies about the position of men in a system of gender subordination. Are the views Dowd advances compatible with those raised by MacKinnon?

John Stuart Mill

The Subjection of Women
_____

> Three Essays by John Stuart Mill 427-28, 443-44, 449-50 (World's
> Classics ed. 1912) (1869)

[T]he principle which regulates the existing social relations between the two sexes — the legal subordination of one sex to the other — is wrong in itself, and now one of the chief hindrances to human improvement; . . . it ought to be replaced by a principle of perfect equality, admitting no power or privilege on the one side, nor disability on the other.

The . . . difficulty . . . is that which exists in all cases in which there is a mass of feeling to be contended against. So long as an opinion is strongly rooted in the feelings, it gains rather than loses in stability by having a preponderating weight of argument against it. For if it were accepted as a result of argument, the refutation of the argument might shake the solidity of the conviction; but when it rests solely on feeling, the worse it fares in argumentative contest, the more persuaded its adherents are that their feeling must have some deeper ground, which the arguments do not reach; and while the feeling remains, it is always throwing up fresh

_____

2. Catharine A. MacKinnon, Butterfly Politics 306 (2017).

entrenchments of argument to repair any breach made in the old. And there are so many causes tending to make the feelings connected with this subject the most intense and most deeply-rooted of all those which gather round and protect old institutions and customs, that we need not wonder to find them as yet less undermined and loosened than any of the rest by the progress of the great modern spiritual and social transition; nor suppose that the barbarisms to which men cling longest must be less barbarisms than those which they earlier shake off.

All causes, social and natural, combine to make it unlikely that women should be collectively rebellious to the power of men. They are so far in a position different from all other subject classes, that their masters require something more from them than actual service. Men do not want solely the obedience of women, they want their sentiments. All men, except the most brutish, desire to have, in the woman most nearly connected with them, not a forced slave but a willing one; not a slave merely, but a favorite. They have therefore put everything in practice to enslave their minds. The masters of all slaves rely, for maintaining obedience, on fear; either fear of themselves, or religious fears. The masters of women wanted more than simple obedience, and they turned the whole force of education to effect their purpose. All women are brought up from the very earliest years in the belief that their ideal of character is the very opposite to that of men; not self-will, and government by self-control, but submission, and yielding to the control of others. All the moralities tell them that it is their nature, to live for others; to make complete abnegation of themselves, and to have no life but in their affections. And by their affections are meant the only ones they are allowed to have — those to the men with whom they are connected, or to the children who constitute an additional and indefeasible tie between them and a man. When we put together three things — first, the natural attraction between opposite sexes; secondly, the wife's entire dependence on the husband, every privilege or pleasure she has being either his gift, or depending entirely on his will; and lastly, that the principal object of human pursuit, consideration, and all objects of social ambition, can in general be sought or obtained by her only through him — it would be a miracle if the object of being attractive to men had not become the polar star of feminine education and formation of character. And, this great means of influence over the minds of women having been acquired, an instinct of selfishness made men avail themselves of it to the utmost as a means of holding women in subjection, by representing to them meekness, submissiveness, and resignation of all individual will into the hands of a man, as an essential part of sexual attractiveness. . . .

The social subordination of women thus stands out an isolated fact in modern social institutions; a solitary breach of what has become their fundamental law; a single relic of an old world of thought and practice exploded in everything else, but retained in the one thing of most universal interest. . . .

Catharine A. MacKinnon

Feminism Unmodified: Discourses on Life and Law

34-38, 40-41 (1987)

Under the sameness standard, women are measured according to our correspondence with man, our equality judged by our proximity to his measure. Under the difference standard, we are measured according to our lack of correspondence with him, our womanhood judged by our distance from his measure. Gender neutrality is thus simply the male standard, and the special protection rule is simply the female standard, but do not be deceived: masculinity, or maleness, is the referent for both. . . .

Feminists have this nasty habit of counting bodies and refusing not to notice their gender. As applied, the sameness standard has mostly gotten men the benefit of those few things women historically had—for all the good they did us. Almost every sex discrimination case that has been won at the Supreme Court level has been brought by a man. . . .

In reality, which this approach is not long on because it is liberal idealism talking to itself, virtually every quality that distinguishes men from women is already affirmatively compensated in this society. Men's physiology defines most sports, their needs define auto and health insurance coverage, their socially designed biographies define workplace expectations and successful career patterns, their perspectives and concerns define quality in scholarship, their experiences and obsessions define merit, their objectification of life defines art, their military service defines citizenship, their presence defines family, their inability to get along with each other—their wars and rulerships—defines history, their image defines god, and their genitals define sex. For each of their differences from women, what amounts to an affirmative action plan is in effect, otherwise known as the structure and values of American society. But whenever women are, by this standard, "different" from men and insist on not having it held against us, whenever a difference is used to keep us second class and we refuse to smile about it, equality law has a paradigm trauma and it's crisis time for the doctrine. . . .

The women that gender neutrality benefits, and there are some, show the suppositions of [the difference] approach in highest relief. They are mostly women who have been able to construct a biography that somewhat approximates the male norm, at least on paper. They are the qualified, the least of sex discrimination's victims. When they are denied a man's chance, it looks the most like sex bias. The more unequal society gets, the fewer such women are permitted to exist. Therefore, the more unequal society gets, the less likely the difference doctrine is to be able to do anything about it, because unequal power creates both the appearance and the reality of sex differences along the same lines as it creates its sex inequalities. . . .

There is an alternative approach, one that threads its way through existing law and expresses, I think, the reason equality law exists in the first place. . . . In this approach, an equality question is a question of the distribution of power. Gender is also a question of power, specifically of male supremacy and female subordination. The question of equality, from the standpoint of what it is going to take to get it, is at root a question of hierarchy, which—as power succeeds in constructing social perception and social reality—derivatively becomes a categorical distinction, a difference. Here, on the first day that matters, dominance was achieved, probably by force. By the second day, division along the same lines had to be relatively firmly in place. On the third day, if not sooner, differences were demarcated, together with social systems to exaggerate them in perception and in fact, because the systematically differential delivery of benefits and deprivations required making no mistake about who was who. Comparatively speaking, man has been resting ever since. Gender might not even code as difference, might not mean distinction epistemologically, were it not for its consequences for social power.

I call this the dominance approach. . . . The goal of this dissident approach is not to make legal categories trace and trap the way things are. It is not to make rules that fit reality. It is critical of reality. . . .

The dominance approach centers on the most sex-differential abuses of women as a gender, abuses that sex equality law in its difference garb could not confront. It is based on a reality about which little of a systematic nature was known before 1970. . . . This new information includes not only the extent and intractability of sex segregation into poverty, which has been known before, but the range of issues termed violence against women, which has not been. It combines women's material desperation, through being relegated to categories of jobs that pay nil, with the massive amount of rape and attempted rape . . . which is apparently endemic to the patriarchal family; the battery of women that is systematic in one quarter to one third of our homes; prostitution, women's fundamental economic condition, what we do when all else fails, and for many women in this country, all else fails often; and pornography, an industry that traffics in female flesh, making sex inequality into sex to the tune of eight billion dollars a year in profits largely to organized crime.

These experiences have been silenced out of the difference definition of sex equality largely because they happen almost exclusively to women. Understand: for this reason, they are considered not to raise sex equality issues. Because this treatment is done almost uniquely to women, it is implicitly treated as a difference, the sex difference, when in fact it is the socially situated subjection of women. The whole point of women's social relegation to inferiority as a gender is that for the most part these things aren't done to men. . . .

Nancy E. Dowd

Asking the Man Question: Masculinities Analysis and Feminist Theory

33 Harv. J. Law & Gender 415, 416-19 (2010)

Masculinities [studies] can be used to understand more clearly how male privilege and dominance are constructed. . . . .

These are what I have identified as core propositions [of masculinities studies]:

1. Men are not universal or undifferentiated.
2. Men pay a price for privilege.
3. Intersections of manhood, particularly with race, class, and sexual orientation, are critical to the interplay of privilege and disadvantage, to hierarchies among men, and factors that may entirely trump male gender privilege.
4. Masculinity is a social construction and not a biological given.
5. Hegemonic masculinity recognizes that one masculinity norm dominates multiple masculinities.
6. The patriarchal dividend is the benefit that all men have from the dominance of men in the overall gender order.

7. The two most common pieces defining masculinity are, at all costs, to not be like a woman and not be gay.
8. Masculinity is as much about relation to other men as it is about relation to women.
9. Men, although powerful, feel powerless.
10. Masculinities study exposes how structures and cultures are gendered male.
11. The spaces and places that men and women daily inhabit and work within are remarkably different.
12. The role of men in achieving feminist goals is uncertain and unclear.
13. The asymmetry of masculinities scholarship and feminist theory reflects the differences in the general position of men and women.

The implications of these teachings . . . are that feminists should "ask the man question."

As you read the remainder of Chapter 3, consider how the materials raise issues of male subordination of women. Are they anomalies in an otherwise egalitarian order or fundamental to the position of women in society? Is nonsubordination a useful lens in understanding gender oppression more broadly, or does it assume a male/female binary? What does it mean to "ask the man question" when studying gender subordination, and how does that question shape your understanding of the problem or possible solutions?

B.   SEXUAL HARASSMENT

1.   Sexual Harassment in the Workplace

The term "sexual harassment" did not come into use until the mid-1970s and was not fully articulated as a form of discrimination based on sex until 1979, with the publication of Catharine MacKinnon's The Sexual Harassment of Working Women, excerpted below. This theory and the framework MacKinnon proposed was embraced by the EEOC in a set of guidelines issued in 1980, in which it interpreted Title VII to prohibit two types of harassment: (1) *quid pro quo* harassment, in which the harasser requires sexual contact or favors as a condition of employment or advancement, and (2) hostile environment harassment, based on unwelcome conduct of a sexual nature that "has the purpose or effect of unreasonably interfering with an individual's work performance or creating an intimidating, hostile, or offensive working environment."[3] Three major Supreme Court cases defining the contours of sexual harassment doctrine are excerpted below. The EEOC also proposed standards for determining when employers should be held liable for harassment by supervisors, co-workers, and third parties, a doctrinal question that spawned significant litigation and was eventually addressed by the Supreme Court.

Estimates of how many women have experienced sexual harassment range from 30 to 80 percent, depending upon who is asked and how sexual harassment is

---

3. 29 C.F.R. § 1604.11(a)(1)-(3) (1980); see also Joanna L. Grossman, Moving Forward, Looking Back: A Retrospective on Sexual Harassment Law, 95 B.U. L. Rev. 1029 (2015).

defined.[4] The prevalence of harassment did not change much from the earliest surveys, in the late 1970s, through 1994, when the federal government did the last in a series of comprehensive harassment surveys of its own workforce.[5] A 2016 report from the EEOC Select Task Force on the Study of Harassment in the Workplace noted that 43 percent of all discrimination complaints filed by federal employees in 2015 alleged harassment, almost a third of all charges of employment discrimination included a harassment allegation, and 60 percent of women surveyed reported having experienced sex-based harassment.[6] Sexual harassment charges filed with the EEOC generally decreased between 1997 and 2017 before increasing again, likely in response to the #MeToo movement.[7] Charges represent only the tip of the iceberg, as studies show that victims report only 5 to 15 percent of harassment incidents, and less than 3 percent end up in litigation. Major barriers to reporting include guilt, shame, fears of retaliation or blacklisting, an unwillingness to jeopardize working relationships or to be known as a humorless whiner, concerns about loss of privacy, and doubts that an effective response to a complaint would be forthcoming. Women of color experience disproportionate rates of abuse: they account for 16 percent of the female labor force but 33 percent of women's sexual harassment claims. Women of color are also ten times less likely to report harassing incidents internally than their white counterparts. Men file 16 to 17 percent of claims, up from approximately 9 percent of claims in 1992; about half of these are complaints about the behavior of other men.[8] Other than large surveys, how else might we gauge whether the prevalence of harassment has gone down in response to greater enforcement efforts?

In what sense is sexual harassment a form of sex discrimination?

Catharine A. MacKinnon

The Sexual Harassment of Working Women

1, 9-10 (1979)

Intimate violation of women by men is sufficiently pervasive in American society as to be nearly invisible. Contained by internalized and structural forms of power, it has been nearly inaudible. Conjoined with men's control over women's

---

4. See, e.g., Theresa M. Beiner, Gender Myths v. Working Realities: Using Social Science to Reformulate Sexual Harassment Law 1 (2004); Joanna L. Grossman, The First Bite Is Free: Employer Liability for Sexual Harassment, 61 U. Pitt. L. Rev. 671, 673-74 (2000).

5. Joanna Grossman, The Culture of Compliance: The Final Triumph of Form over Substance in Sexual Harassment Law, 26 Harv. Women's L.J. 3, 5-7 (2003).

6. Chai R. Feldblum & Victoria A. Lipnic, U.S. Equal Emp. Opportunity Comm'n, Select Task Force on the Study of Harassment in the Workplace 5, 8 (June 2016).

7. U.S. Equal Emp. Opportunity Comm'n, Sexual Harassment Charges Combined: FY 1997-FY 2011; see also U.S. Equal Emp. Opportunity Comm'n, Charges Alleging Sexual Harassment, FY 2010-FY 2021.

8. U.S. Equal Emp. Opportunity Comm'n, Sexual Harassment Charges: EEOC & FEPAs Combined: FY 1997-FY 2011; U.S. Equal Emp. Opportunity Comm'n, Sexual Harassment Charges FY 2010-FY 2021.

material survival, as in the home or on the job, or over women's learning and educational advancement in school, it has become institutionalized. . . .

Sexual harassment, most broadly defined, refers to the unwanted imposition
of sexual requirements in the context of a relationship of unequal power. Central
to the concept is the use of power derived from one social sphere to level benefits or impose deprivations in another. The major dynamic is best expressed as the
reciprocal enforcement of two inequalities.

When one is sexual, the other material, the cumulative sanction is particularly potent. American society legitimizes male sexual dominance of women and
employer's control of workers. . . .

[T]he sexual harassment of women can occur largely because women occupy
inferior job positions and job roles; at the same time, sexual harassment works to
keep women in such positions. Sexual harassment, then, uses and helps create
women's structurally inferior status.

Kathryn Abrams

Gender Discrimination and the Transformation of Workplace Norms

42 Vand. L. Rev. 1183, 1207-09 (1989)

[S]exually oriented behavior in the workplace produces at least two responses
among women that contribute to their subordination. . . . One response is a fear
of sexual coercion. Sexually oriented behavior brings into the workplace echoes of
a context in which men and women often are radically unequal. A woman struggling to establish credibility in a setting in which she may not be, or may not feel,
welcome, can be swept off balance by a reminder that she can be raped, fondled,
or subjected to repeated sexual demands. Her employment setting, already precarious, can be transformed instantly into an unwanted sexual encounter in which
she is likely to feel even less control, a transformation that can cast shadows even
when demands are not being made. The feelings of anxiety, fear, or vulnerability
produced by the spectre of sexual coercion prevent women from feeling, or being
viewed as, the equals of their male counterparts in the workplace.

But a woman need not be threatened with sexual coercion to feel, and to be
perceived as, unequal in the workplace. Sexual inquiries, jokes, remarks, or innu-
endoes sometimes can raise the spectre of coercion, but they more predictably
have the effect of reminding a woman that she is viewed as an object of sexual
derision rather than as a credible co-worker. A woman who is continuously que-
ried by male colleagues about her sexual preferences, referred to by co-workers
as "the fucking flag girl," or depicted on the walls of men's restrooms in sexual
poses is being told that she is not, first and foremost, a credible colleague and
an equal. This message would be disturbing to any worker, even one who felt
comfortable and secure in the workplace. For a woman worker, who may not have
been socialized to feel comfortable in that role, and who may have faced numerous men who have difficulty viewing women as workers rather than wives or dates,
this message can be devastating. Treatment that sexualizes women workers prevents them from feeling, and prevents others from perceiving them, as equal in
the workplace.

Vicki Schultz

Reconceptualizing Sexual Harassment

107 Yale L.J. 1683, 1755, 1761, 1801 (1998)

Contrary to the assumption of the cultural-radical feminist tradition that inspired the development of harassment law, men's desire to exploit or dominate women sexually may not be the exclusive, or even the primary, motivation for harassing women at work. Instead, a drive to maintain the most highly rewarded forms of work as domains of masculine competence underlies many, if not most, forms of sex-based harassment on the job. . . . [B]y portraying women as less than equal at work, men can secure superior jobs, resources, and influence—all of which afford men leverage over women at home and everyplace else. . . . [The focus of legal inquiry should be whether the conduct at issue has] the purpose or effect of undermining women's "right to participate in the workplace on [an] equal footing."

Katherine M. Franke

What's Wrong with Sexual Harassment

49 Stan. L. Rev. 691, 693, 696 (1997)

According to the theory I develop . . ., the sexual harassment of a woman by a man is an instance of sexism precisely because the act embodies fundamental gender stereotypes: men as sexual conquerors and women as sexually conquered, men as masculine sexual subjects and women as feminine sexual objects. . . . Sexual harassment is a technology of sexism. It is a disciplinary practice that inscribes, enforces, and polices the identities of both harasser and victim according to a system of gender norms that envisions women as feminine, (hetero)sexual objects, and men as masculine, (hetero)sexual subjects. . . .

Similarly, sexual harassment operates as a means of policing traditional gender norms particularly in the same-sex context when men who fail to live up to a societal norm of masculinity are punished by their male co-workers through sexual means.

Meritor Savings Bank v. Vinson

477 U.S. 57 (1986)

Justice REHNQUIST delivered the opinion of the court.

This case presents important questions concerning claims of workplace "sexual harassment" brought under Title VII of the Civil Rights Act of 1964. . . .

I

In 1974, respondent Mechelle Vinson met Sidney Taylor, a vice president of what is now petitioner Meritor Savings Bank (bank) and manager of one of its branch offices. . . . With Taylor as her supervisor, respondent started as a teller-trainee, and thereafter was promoted to teller, head teller, and assistant branch manager. She worked at the same branch for four years, and it is undisputed that her advancement there was based on merit alone. In September 1978, respondent notified Taylor that she was taking sick leave for an indefinite period. On November 1, 1978, the bank discharged her for excessive use of that leave.

Respondent brought this action against Taylor and the bank, claiming that during her four years at the bank she had "constantly been subjected to sexual harassment" by Taylor in violation of Title VII. She sought injunctive relief, compensatory and punitive damages against Taylor and the bank, and attorney's fees.

At the 11-day bench trial, the parties presented conflicting testimony about Taylor's behavior during respondent's employment. Respondent testified that during her probationary period as a teller-trainee, Taylor treated her in a fatherly way and made no sexual advances. Shortly thereafter, however, he invited her out to dinner and, during the course of the meal, suggested that they go to a motel to have sexual relations. At first she refused, but out of what she described as fear of losing her job she eventually agreed. According to respondent, Taylor thereafter made repeated demands upon her for sexual favors, usually at the branch, both during and after business hours; she estimated that over the next several years she had intercourse with him some 40 or 50 times. In addition, respondent testified that Taylor fondled her in front of other employees, followed her into the women's restroom when she went there alone, exposed himself to her, and even forcibly raped her on several occasions. These activities ceased after 1977, respondent stated, when she started going with a steady boyfriend. . . .

Taylor denied respondent's allegations of sexual activity, testifying that he never fondled her, never made suggestive remarks to her, never engaged in sexual intercourse with her, and never asked her to do so. He contended instead that respondent made her accusations in response to a business-related dispute. The bank also denied respondent's allegations and asserted that any sexual harassment by Taylor was unknown to the bank and engaged in without its consent or approval.

The District Court denied relief . . . [and the] Court of Appeals for the District of Columbia Circuit reversed. . . .

II . . .

Respondent argues . . . that unwelcome sexual advances that create an offensive or hostile working environment violate Title VII. Without question, when a supervisor sexually harasses a subordinate because of the subordinate's sex, that supervisor "discriminate[s]" on the basis of sex. Petitioner apparently does not challenge this proposition. It contends instead that in prohibiting discrimination with respect to "compensation, terms, conditions, or privileges" of employment, Congress was concerned with what petitioner describes as "tangible loss" of "an economic character," not "purely psychological aspects of the workplace environment." . . . In support of this claim petitioner observes that in both the legislative history of Title VII and this Court's Title VII decisions, the focus has been on tangible, economic barriers erected by discrimination.

We reject petitioner's view. First, the language of Title VII is not limited to "economic" or "tangible" discrimination. The phrase "terms, conditions, or privileges of employment" evinces a congressional intent " 'to strike at the entire spectrum of disparate treatment of men and women' " in employment. . . .

Second, in 1980 the EEOC issued Guidelines specifying that "sexual harassment," as there defined, is a form of sex discrimination prohibited by Title VII. . . . The EEOC Guidelines fully support the view that harassment leading to noneconomic injury can violate Title VII.

In defining "sexual harassment," the Guidelines first describe the kinds of workplace conduct that may be actionable under Title VII. These include "[u]nwelcome sexual advances, requests for sexual favors, and other verbal or physical conduct of a sexual nature." . . . Relevant to the charges at issue in this case, the Guidelines provide that such sexual misconduct constitutes prohibited "sexual harassment," whether or not it is directly linked to the grant or denial of an economic *quid pro quo*, where "such conduct has the purpose or effect of unreasonably interfering with an individual's work performance or creating an intimidating, hostile, or offensive working environment." . . .

In concluding that so-called "hostile environment" (i.e., non *quid pro quo*) harassment violates Title VII, the EEOC drew upon a substantial body of judicial decisions and EEOC precedent holding that Title VII affords employees the right to work in an environment free from discriminatory intimidation, ridicule, and insult. . . . Courts applied this principle to harassment based on race, religion, and national origin. Nothing in Title VII suggests that a hostile environment based on discriminatory sexual harassment should not be likewise prohibited. The Guidelines thus appropriately drew from, and were fully consistent with, the existing case law.

Since the Guidelines were issued, courts have uniformly held, and we agree, that a plaintiff may establish a violation of Title VII by proving that discrimination based on sex has created a hostile or abusive work environment. As the Court of Appeals for the Eleventh Circuit wrote in Henson v. Dundee, 682 F.2d 897, 902 (1982): "Sexual harassment which creates a hostile or offensive environment for members of one sex is every bit the arbitrary barrier to sexual equality at the workplace that racial harassment is to racial equality. Surely, a requirement that a man or woman run a gauntlet of sexual abuse in return for the privilege of being allowed to work and make a living can be as demeaning and disconcerting as the harshest of racial epithets." . . .

Of course, . . . not all workplace conduct that may be described as "harassment" affects a "term, condition, or privilege" of employment within the meaning of Title VII. . . . For sexual harassment to be actionable, it must be sufficiently severe or pervasive "to alter the conditions of [the victim's] employment and create an abusive working environment." Respondent's allegations in this case — which include not only pervasive harassment but also criminal conduct of the most serious nature — are plainly sufficient to state a claim for "hostile environment" sexual harassment. . . .

[T]he District court apparently believed that a claim for sexual harassment will not lie absent an economic effect on the complainant's employment. . . . Since it appears that the District Court made its findings without ever considering the "hostile environment" theory of sexual harassment, the Court of Appeals' decision to remand was correct.

[T]he District Court's conclusion that no actionable harassment occurred might have rested on its earlier "finding" that "[i]f [respondent] and Taylor did engage in an intimate or sexual relationship . . ., that relationship was a voluntary one." But the fact that sex-related conduct was "voluntary," in the sense that the complainant was not forced to participate against her will, is not a defense to a sexual harassment suit brought under Title VII. The gravamen of any sexual harassment claim is that the alleged sexual advances were "unwelcome." While the question whether particular conduct was indeed unwelcome presents difficult problems of proof and turns largely on credibility determinations committed to the trier of fact, the District Court in this case erroneously focused on the "voluntariness" of respondent's participation in the claimed sexual episodes. The correct inquiry is whether respondent by her conduct indicated that the alleged sexual advances were unwelcome, not whether her actual participation in sexual intercourse was voluntary.

Petitioner contends that even if this case must be remanded to the District Court, the Court of Appeals erred in one of the terms of its remand. Specifically, the Court of Appeals stated that testimony about respondent's "dress and personal fantasies", which the District Court apparently admitted into evidence, "had no place in this litigation." The apparent ground for this conclusion was that respondent's voluntariness vel non in submitting to Taylor's advances was immaterial to her sexual harassment claim. While "voluntariness" in the sense of consent is not a defense to such a claim, it does not follow that a complainant's sexually provocative speech or dress is irrelevant as a matter of law in determining whether he or she found particular sexual advances unwelcome. To the contrary, such evidence is obviously relevant. The EEOC Guidelines emphasize that the trier of fact must determine the existence of sexual harassment in light of "the record as a whole" and "the totality of circumstances, such as the nature of the sexual advances and the context in which the alleged incidents occurred." Respondent's claim that any marginal relevance of the evidence in question was outweighed by the potential for unfair prejudice is the sort of argument properly addressed to the District Court. In this case the District Court concluded that the evidence should be admitted, and the Court of Appeals' contrary conclusion was based upon the erroneous, categorical view that testimony about provocative dress and publicly expressed sexual fantasies "had no place in this litigation." While the District Court must carefully weigh the applicable considerations in deciding whether to admit evidence of this kind, there is no *per se* rule against its admissibility. . . .

IV. . . .

Accordingly, the judgment of the Court of Appeals reversing the judgment of the District Court is affirmed. . . .

Harris v. Forklift Systems, Inc.

510 U.S. 17 (1993)

Justice O'CONNOR delivered the opinion of the Court.

In this case we consider the definition of a discriminatorily "abusive work environment" (also known as a "hostile work environment") under Title VII. . . .

I

Teresa Harris worked as a manager at Forklift Systems, Inc., an equipment rental company, from April 1985 until October 1987. Charles Hardy was Forklift's president.

The Magistrate found that, throughout Harris' time at Forklift, Hardy often insulted her because of her gender and often made her the target of unwanted sexual innuendos. Hardy told Harris on several occasions, in the presence of other employees, "You're a woman, what do you know" and "We need a man as the rental manager"; at least once, he told her she was "a dumb ass woman." . . . Again in front of others, he suggested that the two of them "go to the Holiday Inn to negotiate [Harris'] raise." . . . Hardy occasionally asked Harris and other female employees to get coins from his front pants pocket. He threw objects on the ground in front of Harris and other women, and asked them to pick the objects up. . . . He made sexual innuendos about Harris' and other women's clothing.

In mid-August 1987, Harris complained to Hardy about his conduct. Hardy said he was surprised that Harris was offended, claimed he was only joking, and apologized. . . . He also promised he would stop, and based on this assurance Harris stayed on the job. But in early September, Hardy began anew: While Harris was arranging a deal with one of Forklift's customers, he asked her, again in front of other employees, "What did you do, promise the guy . . . some [sex] Saturday night?" . . . On October 1, Harris collected her paycheck and quit.

Harris then sued Forklift, claiming that Hardy's conduct had created an abusive work environment for her because of her gender. The United States District Court for the Middle District of Tennessee, adopting the report and recommendation of the Magistrate, found this to be "a close case," . . . but held that Hardy's conduct did not create an abusive environment. The court found that some of Hardy's comments "offended [Harris], and would offend the reasonable woman," . . . but that they were not "so severe as to be expected to seriously affect [Harris'] psychological well-being." A reasonable woman manager under like circumstances would have been offended by Hardy, but his conduct would not have risen to the level of interfering with that person's work performance. "Neither do I believe that [Harris] was subjectively so offended that she suffered injury. . . . Although Hardy may at times have genuinely offended [Harris], I do not believe that he created a working environment so poisoned as to be intimidating or abusive to [Harris]." . . . The United States Court of Appeals for the Sixth Circuit affirmed. . . .

II

Title VII . . . makes it "an unlawful employment practice for an employer . . . to discriminate against any individual with respect to his compensation, terms, conditions, or privileges of employment, because of such individual's race, color, religion, sex, or national origin." As we made clear in Meritor Savings Bank v. Vinson, this language "is not limited to 'economic' or 'tangible' discrimination. The phrase 'terms, conditions, or privileges of employment' evinces a congressional intent 'to strike at the entire spectrum of disparate treatment of men and women' in employment," which includes requiring people to work in a discriminatorily hostile or abusive environment. When the workplace is permeated with "discriminatory intimidation, ridicule, and insult," that is "sufficiently severe or pervasive to alter the condition of the victim's employment and create an abusive working environment," Title VII is violated.

This standard, which we reaffirm today, takes a middle path between making actionable any conduct that is merely offensive and requiring the conduct to cause a tangible psychological injury. As we pointed out in *Meritor*, "mere utterance of an . . . epithet which engenders offensive feelings in an employee," . . . does not sufficiently affect the conditions of employment to implicate Title VII. Conduct that is not severe or pervasive enough to create an objectively hostile or abusive work environment—an environment that a reasonable person would find hostile or abusive—is beyond Title VII's purview. Likewise, if the victim does not subjectively perceive the environment to be abusive, the conduct has not actually altered the conditions of the victim's employment, and there is no Title VII violation.

But Title VII comes into play before the harassing conduct leads to a nervous breakdown. A discriminatorily abusive work environment, even one that does not seriously affect employees' psychological well-being, can and often will detract from employees' job performance, discourage employees from remaining on the job, or keep them from advancing in their careers. Moreover, even without regard to these tangible effects, the very fact that the discriminatory conduct was so severe or pervasive that it created a work environment abusive to employees because of their race, gender, religion, or national origin offends Title VII's broad rule of workplace equality. The appalling conduct alleged in *Meritor*, and the reference in that case to environments "so heavily polluted with discrimination as to destroy completely the emotional and psychological stability of minority group workers," merely present some especially egregious examples of harassment. They do not mark the boundary of what is actionable.

We therefore believe the District Court erred in relying on whether the conduct "seriously affect[ed] plaintiff's psychological well-being" or led her to "suffe[r] injury." Such an inquiry may needlessly focus the factfinder's attention on concrete psychological harm, an element Title VII does not require. Certainly Title VII bars conduct that would seriously affect a reasonable person's psychological well-being, but the statute is not limited to such conduct. So long as the environment would reasonably be perceived, and is perceived, as hostile or abusive, *Meritor*, there is no need for it also to be psychologically injurious.

This is not, and by its nature cannot be, a mathematically precise test. We need not answer today all the potential questions it raises. . . . But we can say that whether an environment is "hostile" or "abusive" can be determined only by looking at all the circumstances. These may include the frequency of the discriminatory conduct; its severity; whether it is physically threatening or humiliating, or a mere offensive utterance; and whether it unreasonably interferes with an employee's work performance. The effect on the employee's psychological well-being is, of course, relevant to determining whether the plaintiff actually found the environment abusive. But while psychological harm, like any other relevant factor, may be taken into account, no single factor is required. . . .

We therefore reverse the judgment of the Court of Appeals, and remand the case for further proceedings consistent with this opinion.

Justice SCALIA, concurring. . . .

"Abusive" (or "hostile," which in this context I take to mean the same thing) does not seem to me a very clear standard — and I do not think clarity is at all increased by adding the adverb "objectively" or by appealing to a "reasonable person's" notion of what the vague word means. Today's opinion does list a number of factors that contribute to abusiveness, . . . but since it neither says how much of each is necessary (an impossible task) nor identifies any single factor as determinative, it thereby adds little certitude. As a practical matter, today's holding lets virtually unguided juries decide whether sex-related conduct engaged in (or permitted by) an employer is egregious enough to warrant an award of damages. One might say that what constitutes "negligence" (a traditional jury question) is not much more clear and certain than what constitutes "abusiveness." Perhaps so. But the class of plaintiffs seeking to recover for negligence is limited to those who have suffered harm, whereas under this statute "abusiveness" is to be the test of whether legal harm has been suffered, opening more expansive vistas of litigation.

Be that as it may, I know of no alternative to the course the Court today has taken. One of the factors mentioned in the Court's nonexhaustive list — whether the conduct unreasonably interferes with an employee's work performance — would, if it were made an absolute test, provide greater guidance to juries and employers. But I see no basis for such a limitation in the language of the statute. Accepting *Meritor*'s interpretation of the term "conditions of employment" as the law, the test is not whether work has been impaired, but whether working conditions have been discriminatorily altered. I know of no test more faithful to the inherently vague statutory language than the one the Court today adopts. For these reasons, I join the opinion of the Court.

Justice GINSBURG, concurring.

Today the Court reaffirms the holding of Meritor Savings Bank v. Vinson . . .: "[A] plaintiff may establish a violation of Title VII by proving that discrimination based on sex has created a hostile or abusive work environment." The critical issue, Title VII's text indicates, is whether members of one sex are exposed to disadvantageous terms or conditions of employment to which members of the other sex are not exposed. . . . As the Equal Employment Opportunity Commission emphasized . . . the adjudicator's inquiry should center, dominantly, on whether the discriminatory conduct has unreasonably interfered with the plaintiff's work performance. To show such interference, "the plaintiff need not prove that his or her tangible productivity has declined as a result of the harassment." . . . It suffices to prove that a reasonable person subjected to the discriminatory conduct would find, as the plaintiff did, that the harassment so altered working conditions as to "ma[k]e it more difficult to do the job." . . .

The Court's opinion, which I join, seems to me in harmony with the view expressed in this concurring statement.

Oncale v. Sundowner Offshore Servs., Inc.

523 U.S. 75 (1998)

Justice SCALIA delivered the opinion of the Court.

This case presents the question whether workplace harassment can violate Title VII's prohibition against "discrimination . . . because of . . . sex" when the harasser and the harassed employee are of the same sex.

I

The District Court having granted summary judgment for respondent, we must assume the facts to be as alleged by petitioner Joseph Oncale. The precise details are irrelevant to the legal point we must decide. . . . In late October 1991, Oncale was working for respondent Sundowner Offshore Services on a Chevron U.S.A., Inc., oil platform in the Gulf of Mexico. He was employed as a roust about on an eight-man crew which included respondents John Lyons, Danny Pippen, and Brandon Johnson. Lyons, the crane operator, and Pippen, the driller, had supervisory authority. On several occasions, Oncale was forcibly subjected to sex-related, humiliating actions against him by Lyons, Pippen and Johnson in the presence of the rest of the crew. Pippen and Lyons also physically assaulted Oncale in a sexual manner, and Lyons threatened him with rape.

Oncale's complaints to supervisory personnel produced no remedial action; in fact, the company's Safety Compliance Clerk, Valent Hohen, told Oncale that Lyons and Pippen "picked [on] him all the time too," and called him a name suggesting homosexuality. Oncale eventually quit — asking that his pink slip reflect that he "voluntarily left due to sexual harassment and verbal abuse." When asked at his deposition why he left Sundowner, Oncale stated, "I felt that if I didn't leave my job, that I would be raped or forced to have sex."

Oncale filed a complaint against Sundowner in the United States District Court for the Eastern District of Louisiana, alleging that he was discriminated against in his employment because of his sex. . . . [T]he district court held that "Mr. Oncale, a male, has no cause of action under Title VII for harassment by male co-workers." On appeal, a panel of the Fifth Circuit . . . affirmed. We granted certiorari.

II . . .

Title VII's prohibition of discrimination "because of . . . sex" protects men as well as women, and in the related context of racial discrimination in the workplace we have rejected any conclusive presumption that an employer will not discriminate against members of his own race. "Because of the many facets of human motivation, it would be unwise to presume as a matter of law that human beings of one definable group will not discriminate against other members of that group." Castaneda v. Partida, 430 U.S. 482 (1977). In Johnson v. Transportation Agency, Santa Clara Cty., 480 U.S. 616 (1987), a male employee claimed that his employer discriminated against him because of his sex when it preferred a female employee for promotion. Although we ultimately rejected the claim on other grounds, we did not consider it significant that the supervisor who made that decision was also a man. If our precedents leave any doubt on the question, we hold today that nothing in Title VII necessarily bars a claim of discrimination "because of . . . sex" merely because the plaintiff and the defendant (or the person charged with acting on behalf of the defendant) are of the same sex.

Courts have had little trouble with that principle in cases like *Johnson*, where an employee claims to have been passed over for a job or promotion. But when the issue arises in the context of a "hostile environment" sexual harassment claim, the state and federal courts have taken a bewildering variety of stances. Some, like the Fifth Circuit in this case, have held that same-sex sexual harassment claims are never cognizable under Title VII. Other decisions say that such claims are actionable only if the plaintiff can prove that the harasser is homosexual (and thus presumably motivated by sexual desire). Still others suggest that workplace harassment that is sexual in content is always actionable, regardless of the harasser's sex, sexual orientation, or motivations.

We see no justification in the statutory language or our precedents for a categorical rule excluding same-sex harassment claims from the coverage of Title VII. As some courts have observed, male-on-male sexual harassment in the workplace was assuredly not the principal evil Congress was concerned with when it enacted Title VII. But statutory prohibitions often go beyond the principal evil to cover reasonably comparable evils, and it is ultimately the provisions of our laws rather than the principal concerns of our legislators by which we are governed. Title VII prohibits "discrimination . . . because of . . . sex" in the "terms" or "conditions" of employment. Our holding that this includes sexual harassment must extend to sexual harassment of any kind that meets the statutory requirements.

Respondents and their *amici* contend that recognizing liability for same-sex harassment will transform Title VII into a general civility code for the American workplace. But that risk is no greater for same-sex than for opposite-sex harassment, and is adequately met by careful attention to the requirements of the statute. Title VII does not prohibit all verbal or physical harassment in the workplace; it is directed only at "*discrimination* . . . because of . . . sex." We have never held that workplace harassment, even harassment between men and women, is automatically discrimination because of sex merely because the words used have sexual content or connotations. "The critical issue, Title VII's text indicates, is whether members of one sex are exposed to disadvantageous terms or conditions of employment to which members of the other sex are not exposed." *Harris*, (Ginsburg, J., concurring).

Courts and juries have found the inference of discrimination easy to draw in most male-female sexual harassment situations, because the challenged conduct typically involves explicit or implicit proposals of sexual activity; it is reasonable to assume those proposals would not have been made to someone of the same sex. The same chain of inference would be available to a plaintiff alleging same-sex harassment, if there were credible evidence that the harasser was homosexual. But harassing conduct need not be motivated by sexual desire to support an inference of discrimination on the basis of sex. A trier of fact might reasonably find such discrimination, for example, if a female victim is harassed in such sex-specific and derogatory terms by another woman as to make it clear that the harasser is motivated by general hostility to the presence of women in the workplace. A same-sex harassment plaintiff may also, of course, offer direct comparative evidence about how the alleged harasser treated members of both sexes in a mixed-sex workplace.

Whatever evidentiary route the plaintiff chooses to follow, he or she must always prove that the conduct at issue was not merely tinged with offensive sexual connotations, but actually constituted "*discrimination . . .* because of . . . sex."

And there is another requirement that prevents Title VII from expanding into a general civility code: As we emphasized in *Meritor* and *Harris*, the statute does not reach genuine but innocuous differences in the ways men and women routinely interact with members of the same sex and of the opposite sex. The prohibition of harassment on the basis of sex requires neither asexuality nor androgyny in the workplace; it forbids only behavior so objectively offensive as to alter the "conditions" of the victim's employment. "Conduct that is not severe or pervasive enough to create an objectively hostile or abusive work environment—an environment that a reasonable person would find hostile or abusive—is beyond Title VII's purview." *Harris*, citing *Meritor*. We have always regarded that requirement as crucial, and as sufficient to ensure that courts and juries do not mistake ordinary socializing in the workplace—such as male-on-male horseplay or intersexual flirtation—for discriminatory "conditions of employment."

We have emphasized, moreover, that the objective severity of harassment should be judged from the perspective of a reasonable person in the plaintiff's position, considering "all the circumstances." *Harris*. In same-sex (as in all) harassment cases, that inquiry requires careful consideration of the social context in which particular behavior occurs and is experienced by its target. A professional football player's working environment is not severely or pervasively abusive, for example, if the coach smacks him on the buttocks as he heads onto the field—even if the same behavior would reasonably be experienced as abusive by the coach's secretary (male or female) back at the office. The real social impact of workplace behavior often depends on a constellation of surrounding circumstances, expectations, and relationships which are not fully captured by a simple recitation of the words used or the physical acts performed. Common sense, and an appropriate sensitivity to social context, will enable courts and juries to distinguish between simple teasing or roughhousing among members of the same sex, and conduct which a reasonable person in the plaintiff's position would find severely hostile or abusive.

III

Because we conclude that sex discrimination consisting of same-sex sexual harassment is actionable under Title VII, the judgment of the Court of Appeals for the Fifth Circuit is reversed. . . .

Justice THOMAS, concurring.

I concur because the Court stresses that in every sexual harassment case, the plaintiff must plead and ultimately prove Title VII's statutory requirement that there be discrimination "because of . . . sex."

NOTES

1. **Distinguishing "Ordinary" Social Exchange from Sexual Harassment.** Courts have struggled with finding the line between "ordinary" social behavior between men and women and actionable sexual harassment, requiring

that the conduct be sufficiently severe or pervasive, offensive (not only to the plaintiff, but to a reasonable person in the plaintiff's position), and unwelcome. Does the prohibition against sexual harassment leave room for ordinary sexual banter between men and women in the workplace? Under nonsubordination analysis, the ordinary is the problem—i.e., sex has been defined so that what has come to be accepted as everyday behavior, in fact, subordinates women. The ordinariness of sexual subordination makes it invisible and thus all the more effective.

Those who have resisted recognizing sexual harassment as a wrong, on the other hand, see the law as a clumsy tool for restraining what is a "natural" attraction between the sexes. In one early case, in which defendant president of a company kissed the plaintiff, touched her breasts and buttocks, and put his hands up her dress, the court observed that "one of the traditional places where man meets woman is at the workplace," and a "man should not have to gamble on civil liability on her 'yes' response."[9]

In another widely publicized case, the plaintiff introduced the following evidence of harassment: (1) her supervisor referred to her as a "pretty girl," as in "There's always a pretty girl giving me something to sign off on." (2) Once when she commented on how hot his office was, he raised his eyebrows and said, "Not until you stepped your foot in here." (3) Once when the announcement "May I have your attention, please" was broadcast over the public-address system, the supervisor stopped at her desk and said, "You know what that means, don't you? All pretty girls run around naked." (4) The supervisor once told her that his wife had told him "I had better clean up my act" and "better think of you as Ms. Anita Hill." (5) Once when she complained that his office was "smoky" from cigarette smoke, the supervisor replied, "Oh, really? Were we dancing, like in a nightclub?" (6) When she asked him whether he had gotten his wife a Valentine's Day card, he responded that he had not but he should because it was lonely in his hotel room, at which point he looked ostentatiously at his hand with a gesture suggesting masturbation. Judge Richard Posner analyzed this conduct as follows:

> He never touched the plaintiff. He did not invite her, explicitly or by implication, to have sex with him, or to go out on a date with him. He made no threats. He did not expose himself, or show her dirty pictures. He never said anything to her that could not be repeated on prime time television. The comment about Anita Hill was the opposite of solicitation, the implication being that he would get into trouble if he didn't keep his distance. . . . Some of his repartee . . . has the sexual charge of an Abbott and Costello movie. The reference to masturbation completes the impression of a man whose sense of humor took final shape in adolescence. It is no doubt distasteful to a sensitive woman to have such a silly man as one's boss, but only a woman of Victorian delicacy—a woman mysteriously aloof from contemporary American popular culture in all its sex-saturated vulgarity—would find [his] patter substantially more distressing than the heat and cigarette smoke of which the plaintiff does not complain.[10]

---

9. Jones v. Wesco Invs., Inc., 846 F.2d 1154, 1157 n.6 (8th Cir. 1988).
10. Baskerville v. Culligan Int'l Co., 50 F.3d 428, 431 (7th Cir. 1995).

How would you respond? Should such dated cases, decided decades before #MeToo (discussed in note 11 below), lack precedential value today?[11]

2. **Same-Sex Harassment and Sex-Stereotyping.**   Since the Supreme Court's ruling in Oncale v. Sundowner Offshore Services,[12] it has been clear that male-on-male harassment can violate Title VII as long as the plaintiff can prove the harassment occurred because of sex. The Court in that case reasoned that a sexual harassment claim is not precluded simply because the complainant and the harasser are of the same sex. In *Oncale,* the harassers appear to have thought that the complainant was gay, although he claimed he was straight. At the time, the Supreme Court had not yet decided that Title VII's ban on sex discrimination encompasses sexual orientation and gender identity discrimination. But some courts drew on *Oncale* and *Price Waterhouse* to recognize same-sex harassment as actionable when the conduct reflected sex stereotyping. For example, in Nichols v. Azteca Restaurant Enterprises, Inc., the Ninth Circuit applied *Oncale* and *Price Waterhouse* to hold that harassment of a gay man for his effeminacy was actionable.[13] The plaintiff was "subjected to a relentless campaign of insults, name-calling, and vulgarities. Male co-workers and a supervisor repeatedly referred to Sanchez in Spanish and English as 'she' and 'her.' Male co-workers mocked Sanchez for walking and carrying his serving tray 'like a woman,' and taunted him in Spanish and English as, among other things, a 'faggot' and a 'fucking female whore.' The remarks were not stray or isolated. Rather, the abuse occurred at least once a week and often several times a day." The court agreed with the plaintiff that the harassment occurred because of "the perception that he is effeminate" and "because he failed to conform to a male stereotype," and was actionable under Title VII. As the court explained,

> At its essence, the systematic abuse directed at Sanchez reflected a belief that Sanchez did not act as a man should act. Sanchez was attacked for walking and carrying his tray "like a woman" — i.e., for having feminine mannerisms. Sanchez was derided for not having sexual intercourse with a waitress who was his friend. Sanchez's male co-workers and one of his supervisors repeatedly reminded Sanchez that he did not conform to their gender-based stereotypes, referring to him as "she" and "her." And, the most vulgar name-calling directed at Sanchez was cast in female terms. We conclude that this verbal abuse was closely linked to gender. *Price Waterhouse* sets a rule that bars discrimination on the basis of sex stereotypes. That rule squarely applies to preclude the harassment here.[14]

The theory recognized in *Nichols* posits that men often harass other men to enforce "the traditional heterosexual male gender role" by encouraging "stereotypical forms of 'masculine' behavior" and punishing or devaluing "feminine" conduct. Mary Anne Case provides this analysis:

---

11. See Joan C. Williams et al., What's Reasonable Now? Sexual Harassment Law After the Norm Cascade, 2019 Mich. St. L. Rev. 139 (arguing that older cases ruling harassment insufficiently severe or pervasive should no longer be credited as precedent).

12. 523 U.S. 75 (1998).

13. 256 F.3d 864 (9th Cir. 2001).

14. Id. at 874-75.

By examining the similarity of the taunts typically hurled at both women and gay or effeminate men in hostile environments, taunts that stress feminine sexual passivity . . . [it is apparent] that the sexual harassment inflicted on all three groups may have in common the desire of certain "active" masculine males to drive out of the workplace those they see as contaminating it with the taint of feminine passivity. Such harassment is, therefore, a form of gender discrimination against the feminine, one with serious effects on the job performance and security of its victims, who should have a legal remedy against it regardless of their sex.[15]

As a practical matter, this theory is less important after the Supreme Court's ruling in *Bostock v. Clayton County* (excerpted in Chapter 1, Section C) because sexual orientation discrimination (including harassment) is now actionable under Title VII regardless of whether it explicitly draws on sex stereotypes.

Given the reasoning cited above from the *Oncale* decision, do you see a risk, as commentators like Janet Halley have warned, that recognition of harassment based on sexual orientation may expose gays and lesbians to unwarranted claims of harassment by individuals who are threatened by any display of homosexual conduct in the workplace?[16]

3. When Is Sexual Conduct "Unwelcome"? As discussed in *Meritor*, the plaintiff in a hostile environment sexual harassment case must prove that the conduct was "unwelcome." One function of this requirement is to prevent parties from using sexual harassment charges to punish each other when a consensual relationship fails. Critics have argued that, as in the case of proving rape, this requirement often seems to put on trial the plaintiff, whose sexually provocative speech or dress was thought by Justice Rehnquist in *Meritor* to be "obviously relevant." Evaluating it, according to Louise Fitzgerald and others, also reinforces double standards of morality that treat women's sexual expression more harshly than men's.[17] The Federal Rules of Evidence impose some limits on the admissibility of evidence of the plaintiff's dress or lifestyle: such evidence must be more probative than prejudicial.[18]

Evidence of the plaintiff's participation in workplace banter has been still more controversial. Court decisions concerning the relevance of such evidence are divided. In one case, the plaintiff admitted at trial that she cursed and used vulgar language while at work. Her co-workers also testified that she often made jokes

---

15. Mary Anne Case, Disaggregating Gender from Sex and Sexual Orientation: The Effeminate Man in the Law and Feminist Jurisprudence, 105 Yale L.J. 1, 7 (1995); see also Craig R. Waldo et al., Are Men Sexually Harassed? If So by Whom?, 22 Law & Hum. Behav. 59, 61 (1998).

16. Janet Halley, Split Decisions: How and Why to Take a Break from Feminism 293-96 (2006).

17. Louise Fitzgerald, Who Says? Legal Psychological Construction of Women's Resistance to Sexual Harassment, in Directions in Sexual Harassment Law 94, 102 (Catharine A. MacKinnon & Reva B. Siegel eds., 2004).

18. See Theresa M. Beiner, Sexy Dressing Revisited: Does Target Dress Play a Part in Sex Harassment Cases?, 14 Duke J. Gender L. & Pol'y 125, 149 (2007).

about sex, including jokes about "screwing her boss," and that she participated in frequent discussions and bantering about sex. In light of this testimony, the trial judge concluded that "[a]ny harassment plaintiff received . . . was prompted by her own actions, including her tasteless joking. Considering plaintiff's contribution to and apparent enjoyment of the situation, it cannot be said that the defendants created 'an intimidating, hostile, or offensive working environment.' "[19] The Eleventh Circuit held that a plaintiff did not prove unwelcomeness of a co-worker's repeated crotch-grabbing and requests for oral sex, once at knifepoint, because she sometimes told jokes with sexual innuendo.[20] Other courts, however, have found that a plaintiff who has participated in some of the exchanges involving foul language and sexual innuendo does not lose all protection to be free from sexual harassment.[21]

What, besides consent to sexual advances, might explain an employee's participation in such conduct? Research suggests that such behavior might sometimes serve as a survival technique — a way to achieve acceptance or to defuse a potentially unpleasant situation.[22] A similar motive might explain situations in which a plaintiff discounts the significance of harassing behavior as "[not] that big of a deal" or maintains friendly relations with the harasser. Yet courts have sometimes considered such responses as proof that the conduct was not sufficiently abusive to establish liability.[23] Do such outcomes "ignore[] the reality of what women must do to make life bearable in an all-male workplace"?[24]

The most obvious way for an employee to signal that particular behavior is offensive and unwelcome is to complain about it. Courts have increasingly required such complaints, but questions remain about when an employee must register objections: After the first instance? When it becomes intolerable? Somewhere in between? Note, again, the potential Catch-22 situation: if the woman complains too early, she is hypersensitive, humorless, and unreasonable; if she waits too long, she may have difficulty proving that the behavior was unwelcome.[25] What does it tell

---

19. Loftin-Boggs v. City of Meridian, 633 F. Supp. 1323, 1327 (S.D. Miss. 1986), aff'd, 824 F.2d 971 (5th Cir. 1987).

20. Weinsheimer v. Rockwell Int'l Corp., 754 F. Supp. 1559, 1564 (M.D. Fla. 1990), aff'd, 949 F.2d 1162 (11th Cir. 1991).

21. See, e.g., Carr v. Allison Gas Turbine Div., Gen. Motors Corp., 32 F.3d 1007, 1011 (7th Cir. 1994) (plaintiff's vulgar language and dirty jokes could not justify a barrage of derogatory language, pranks, and graffiti); Spencer v. Gen. Elec. Co., 697 F. Supp. 204 (E.D. Va. 1988), aff'd, 894 F.2d 651 (4th Cir. 1990), overruled on other grounds by Farrar v. Hobby, 506 U.S. 103 (1992) (joining in milder forms of sexual horseplay that occurred in the office did not waive plaintiff's protection against sexual harassment).

22. See Beth A. Quinn, The Paradox of Complaining: Law, Humor, and Harassment in the Everyday Work World, 25 L. & Soc. Inquiry 1151, 1179-81 (2000).

23. Highlander v. K.F.C. Nat'l Mgmt. Co., 805 F.2d 644 (6th Cir. 1986); Scott v. Sears, Roebuck & Co., 798 F.2d 210, 212-14 (7th Cir. 1986).

24. Wendy Pollack, Sexual Harassment: Women's Experience vs. Legal Definitions, 13 Harv. Women's L.J. 35, 72-73 (1990).

25. See Reed v. Shepard, 939 F.2d 484, 492 (7th Cir. 1991) (female police officer's receptiveness to co-workers' sexually suggestive jokes and activities because she wanted to be accepted by others on the police force was fatal to her sexual harassment claim).

you, if anything, that filing a formal complaint is the least likely response of a victim of workplace harassment?[26]

4. **Sexual Harassment as Discrimination "Because of Sex"?**   As discussed in *Oncale*, sexual harassment is a form of intentional discrimination under Title VII as long as it occurs *because of* sex. Given its foundation in equality analysis, under what circumstances should abusive or degrading behavior be considered actionable sexual harassment?

For example, what if a supervisor treats every worker in exactly the same way—abusively, and as a sexual object? Can this still be sex discrimination? Courts have not been consistent. Some have applied a comparative equality analysis and only recognized as discriminatory vulgar language, pictures, jokes, and other behaviors that affected plaintiffs in a particular way, or to a greater degree, because of their sex.[27] Other courts have concluded that a harasser cannot insulate him or herself from a sexual harassment charge simply because his or her conduct is sufficiently egregious as to offend everyone.[28] For still other courts, the "because of sex" dimension is satisfied by the sexual nature of the offending behavior—although *Oncale* admonishes that just because conduct takes a sexual form does not necessarily mean it was "because of sex" under the terms of the statute. For male-female proposals of sexual activity, however, the Court appears to endorse a presumption that the conduct was because of sex. Which approach would best address the harms of sexual harassment?

What if a supervisor's abusive conduct is not sexual or gendered in nature, but is targeted only at women? In EEOC v. National Education Association,[29] the Ninth Circuit allowed plaintiffs to proceed with a hostile environment harassment lawsuit on the basis of their supervisor's bullying. While his conduct did not include sexual advances or gendered slurs, he yelled at the plaintiffs with "little or no provocation," and his shouting rants were often accompanied by aggressive physical gestures like lunging, pumping fists, and grabbing plaintiffs while barking commands or complaints at them. The evidence showed that he behaved this way only toward women. The court held that this comparative evidence could satisfy the "because of sex" requirement, as elucidated in *Oncale*.

What if, in contrast, the conduct *is* very sexual in nature, but not targeted at anyone in particular or even women in general? In Lyle v. Warner Brothers Television Productions, a writer's assistant for the long-running sitcom *Friends* alleged she had been sexually harassed by being forced to be present and take notes during meetings where the comedy writers engaged in sexually explicit conversation, gestures (including pantomimed masturbation), and cartoon drawings.[30] The plaintiff complained especially about the writers' discussions of their own sexual preferences

---

26. See Dan Cassino & Yasemin Besen-Cassino, Race, Threat and Workplace Sexual Harassment: The Dynamics of Harassment in the United States, 1997-2016, 26 Gender, Work & Org. 1221, 1222 (2019) (citing research finding that 99.8 percent of women who experience sexual harassment in the workplace never file formal charges).

27. See, e.g., Carpenter v. City of Torrington, 100 Fed. Appx. 858 (2d Cir. 2004).

28. McDonnell v. Cisneros, 84 F.3d 256, 260 (7th Cir. 1996).

29. 422 F.3d 840 (9th Cir. 2005).

30. 132 P.3d 211 (Cal. 2006).

and experiences and their fantasies about the sex lives of the actresses on the show, as well as other topics like anal sex and naked cheerleaders. The defendant offered "creative necessity" as a defense, arguing that comedy writers needed to have "frank sexual discussions and tell colorful jokes and stories (and even make expressive gestures) as part of the creative process."[31] The California Supreme Court, interpreting a state law provision similar to Title VII, concluded that while there is no categorical defense to sexual harassment lawsuits for creative workplaces, the plaintiff could not prevail because she did not prove that the conduct was either targeted at her directly or created hostility for women in general. To be actionable, the court held, undirected conduct must be even more severe and pervasive than targeted conduct. It also held that workplace context is relevant to determining whether actionable harassment occurred.

What if the sexual conduct is consensual between a supervisor and employee, but unfair to other employees? So-called sexual favoritism complaints have not fared well under Title VII generally due to the "because of sex" requirement. If a male supervisor has an affair with a female subordinate, other employees, both male and female, may have a grievance if the supervisor treats his subordinate more favorably than he treats them; however, those effects are not obviously "because of sex" in the sense required by Title VII. But what if it was clear to women that employees who slept with the boss would be treated more favorably? Does that create an implied *quid pro quo* for other female employees and create a hostile environment? The EEOC issued a policy guidance in 1990 stating the agency's position that while isolated incidents of sexual favoritism do not violate Title VII, widespread favoritism can create a hostile environment, as well as support an implicit *quid pro quo* claim.[32] The California Supreme Court, interpreting state anti-discrimination law, followed this guidance in a 2005 case, Miller v. Department of Corrections, which presents a textbook case of sexual favoritism.[33] There, the warden at a women's prison had sexual relationships with at least three female subordinates, often involving public displays of affection and emotional fights among the women over competing affairs. He admittedly treated these women more favorably than other employees, defending the decision to give one of them a promotion over more qualified applicants because he had no choice lest she "take him down" by revealing "every scar on his body." Plaintiffs claimed that female employees repeatedly questioned whether this was the type of workplace where they would have to " 'F' my way to the top."[34] The court ruled that sexual favoritism is a valid claim when it is "sufficiently widespread" such that "the demeaning message is conveyed to female employees that they are viewed by management as 'sexual playthings' or that the way required for women to get ahead in the workplace is by engaging in sexual conduct with their supervisors or management." If you were an employer, what steps would you take to

31. Lyle v. Warner, 12 Cal. Rptr. 3d 511, 518 (Cal. Ct. App. 2004).

32. U.S. Equal Emp. Opportunity Comm'n, Policy Guidance on Employer Liability Under Title VII for Sexual Favoritism No. N-915-048 (Jan. 12, 1990). See also Nancy Leong, Them Too, 96 Wash. U. L. Rev. 941 (2019) (discussing third-party harms of consensual sexual conduct at work).

33. 115 P.3d 77 (Cal. 2005).

34. Id. at 82.

avoid liability for sexual favoritism? For further discussion of office romances, see Note 10.

How does MacKinnon's theory apply to sexual harassment of men by women? If sexual harassment is viewed primarily as a means of reinforcing gender subordination, what accounts for cases in which women harass male subordinates or co-workers? Although cases with male plaintiffs alleging sexual harassment by a woman have been relatively rare, they have resulted in some of the largest verdicts, including the first $1 million damage award in a sexual harassment case.[35] Most of these cases involve *quid pro quo* harassment. Do these claims support the suspicion that sexual harassment charges are sometimes simply an act of revenge following a romantic attraction that ends badly? Or do they indicate that women, too, are capable of abusing power in the workplace? Men have also received unusually high verdicts for the harm of being wrongly accused in sexual harassment cases.[36]

5. **The Standard for Determining Hostile Work Environment.** *Harris* imposes both a subjective and an objective standard for determining a hostile work environment. The plaintiff must have been actually offended, and the offense taken must have been reasonable. A longstanding issue is whether "reasonable" should be interpreted in light of the plaintiff's sex — i.e., can conduct that would not be offensive to a male employee, if the tables were turned, be sufficiently offensive to the female plaintiff to be actionable as sexual harassment? Only the Ninth Circuit Court of Appeals has specifically applied a "reasonable woman" standard.[37] *Harris* and subsequent U.S. Supreme Court cases have instructed courts to apply the objective standard "from the perspective of a reasonable person in the plaintiff's position, considering 'all the circumstances.' "[38] In *Oncale,* Justice Scalia reaffirmed that the "objective severity of harassment should be judged from the perspective of a reasonable person in the plaintiff's position, considering 'all the circumstances.' " Is this broad enough to encompass a "reasonable woman" standard if the plaintiff is female? Must a jury take that perspective? What if the plaintiff is a man? Which of a plaintiff's other socially salient identities should be taken into account? Race? Sexual orientation?[39]

Some research shows that women are more likely than men to perceive certain behaviors, such as unsolicited invitations for sex, as harassing.[40] If such findings are correct, does a gender-neutral reasonable person standard risk legitimating behaviors that many female workers find offensive?[41] Or would women be harmed

---

35. See Man Wins $1 Million Sex-Harassment Suit, N.Y. Times, May 21, 1993, at A12.

36. Mackenzie v. Miller Brewing Co., 623 N.W.2d 739 (Wis. 2001) ($26 million jury award, later overturned, for man who was fired for sexual harassment, including his description of a racy *Seinfeld* episode to a female co-worker).

37. See Steiner v. Showboat Operating Co., 25 F.3d 1459, 1464 (9th Cir. 1994).

38. See Oncale v. Sundowner Offshore Servs., Inc., 523 U.S. 75, 81 (1998).

39. See Angela Onwuachi-Willig, What About #UsToo?: The Invisibility of Race in the #MeToo Movement, 128 Yale L.J.F. 105, 119-20 (2018) (arguing that the reasonable woman standard "must also be rooted in an intersectional and multi-dimensional lens").

40. See Hank Rothgerber et al., Is a Reasonable Woman Different from a Reasonable Person? Gender Differences in Perceived Sexual Harassment, 84 Sex Roles 208 (2021).

41. Caroline A. Forrell & Donna M. Mathews, A Law of Her Own: The Reasonable Woman as a Measure of Man 35-58 (2000).

more than helped by a legal standard that incorporates an assumption that women are all alike and easily offended?[42]

How should courts determine what acts are sufficiently pervasive and abusive to justify liability? Sandra Sperino and Suja Thomas argue that the "severe or pervasive" test articulated in *Meritor* operates to limit liability even in cases where the harassment clearly interferes with a person's working environment; they identify cases where supervisors kissed or grabbed the breasts of subordinates but the claims were dismissed.[43] Consider the proposal of Gillian Hadfield, who would define sex-based harassment as "sex-based non-job-related workplace conduct that would lead a rational woman to alter her workplace behavior—such as by refusing overtime, projects, or travel that will put her in contact with a harasser, requesting a transfer, or quitting. . . ." In Hadfield's view, "the issue is whether a workplace practice has systematically negative consequences for women vis-à-vis men. Even if significant numbers of women enjoy an atmosphere in which sexual jokes abound, if systematically more women than men find this costly, then the practice is discriminatory. . . ." Such a standard would place "the onus on men, employers, and organizations to become educated about what behavior on their subordinates' part would prompt employment changes by a rational female employee. The test rejects the notion that men are entitled to the protection of their misimpressions about how such behavior is interpreted by women."[44] Is Hadfield's approach preferable to existing law?

6. **Race and Sexual Harassment.**   The Supreme Court's first sexual harassment case, Meritor Savings Bank v. Vinson, does not present as a case about race. Yet Tanya Kateri Hernandez argues that racial dynamics fundamentally influenced how the plaintiff, Mechelle Vinson, an African-American woman, experienced the harassment by Sidney Taylor, an African-American man, and how the courts responded to her claim.[45] Hernandez argues that the Supreme Court's failure to appreciate the salience of race in the case led it to a problematic conceptualization of welcomeness. By accepting that a complainant's "sexually provocative speech or dress" is "obviously relevant" to the legal standard, the Court

> embeds unconscious historical presumptions about the wantonness of Black women into the legal doctrine. The examination of the attire of Black women (such as Mechelle Vinson) dovetails with stereotypic notions of the sexuality availability of Black women. By ignoring the race of the plaintiff, the Supreme Court was able to overlook the significance

42. See Linda Kelly Hill, The Feminist Misspeak of Sexual Harassment, 57 Fla. L. Rev. 133, 172-80 (2005); Barbara A. Gutek et al., The Utility of the Reasonable Woman Standard in Hostile Environment Sexual Harassment Cases: A Multimethod Multistudy Examination, 5 Psych. Pub. Pol'y & L. Rev. 596, 623 (1999).

43. Sandra F. Sperino & Suja A. Thomas, Unequal: How America's Courts Undermine Discrimination Law (2017).

44. Gillian K. Hadfield, Rational Women: A Test for Sex-Based Harassment, 83 Calif. L. Rev. 1151, 1182, 1185-86 (1995).

45. Tanya Kateri Hernandez, "What Not to Wear"—Race and Unwelcomeness in Sexual Harassment Law: The Story of *Meritor Savings Bank v. Vinson*, in Women and the Law Stories 277 (Elizabeth M. Schneider & Stephanie M. Wildman eds., 2011).

of racial stereotypes that pervade the question of appropriate evidence of welcomeness.[46]

Indeed, some of Vinson's co-workers harshly criticized her for how she dressed, with testimony exclaiming that her "dress wear was very explosive," that "most of the days she would come in with, if not a third of her breasts showing, about half of her breasts showing; and some days, short dresses; or if she did wear a skirt, something that had a slit in it."[47] Another co-worker's testimony derided her for wearing "low-cut blouses" and "extremely tight pants."[48] According to Vinson's lawyer, the district court judge allowed into evidence testimony that obsessively focused on Vinson's sexual presentation at work, stereotyping her as "a temptress, a seductress, a lascivious woman."[49] Hernandez cites research showing that Black women are subjected to a double standard scrutinizing their attire and sexual appearance in the workplace, pointing to evidence that the same clothing worn by white women is more likely to be characterized as sexual and offensive when worn by Black women.[50] Does the standard the Court adopted invite racial stereotypes to come into play in evaluating whether the plaintiff, by her conduct, demonstrated that the sexual conduct was unwelcome? If so, what might be done to mitigate this?

Women of color account for a disproportionately high percentage of sexual harassment claimants.[51] Black women, in particular, have played a central role as plaintiffs in the leading foundational cases setting important precedents in sexual harassment law, including in *Vinson*.[52] Yet, they often have difficulty fitting their experiences of harassment into winnable legal claims and are still only rarely centered in the analysis of sexual harassment in legal scholarship.

Part of the problem is that the legal standards for sexual harassment may, for practical reasons, be particularly onerous for women of color to meet. In addition to the problem of scrutinizing plaintiffs' displays of sexiness, discussed above, the welcomeness standard requires a plaintiff to show "by her conduct" that she did not welcome the advances. Women of color, fearing disbelief and unable to risk job loss, may not be in a position to risk openly demonstrating their objection. Likewise, the standards for employer liability, discussed below, place an obligation on the plaintiff to act "reasonably" in reporting and preventing abuse. Speaking up and reporting a harasser is enormously difficult for women across the board, but women of color are even less likely than white women to report sexual

---

46. Id. at 280.

47. Id. at 286.

48. Id.

49. Id. at 301 (quoting Vinson's attorney, Patricia Barry).

50. Id. at 303-04.

51. See Trina Jones & Emma E. Wade, Me Too: Race, Gender, and Ending Workplace Sexual Harassment, 27 Duke J. Gender L. & Pol'y 203, 209 (2020).

52. Hernandez, supra note 45, at 278 (noting that an African American woman was the plaintiff in the first successful sexual harassment case decided by a federal district court, a federal circuit court, and the Supreme Court, as well as in the first cases involving sexual harassment by a co-worker and of sexual harassment of a student under Title IX).

harassment.[53] Reasons for the disparity include greater economic vulnerability, lack of mobility in the marketplace, fear of not being believed, fear of being shut out from other jobs, lack of support from co-workers or superiors, and distrust of authorities and internal complaint procedures. If the harasser is also a person of color, an added obstacle to calling out the harasser is fear of being labeled a "race traitor" and difficulty breaking from norms of intraracial solidarity in a racist society.[54]

The severity or pervasiveness element is also a hurdle for all plaintiffs, but racialized sexual stereotypes can make it all the more so for women of color. Black women, for example, have long been denied the capacity to claim sexual injury as a legacy from slavery, and continue to be vulnerable to stereotypes that depict them as hypersexual and impervious to offense. One witness for the bank in *Vinson*, an ex-boyfriend, belittled Vinson and the other women who accused Taylor of sexual misconduct by saying, "They're not little innocent girls. They are streetwise."[55] Sumi Cho has exposed the "converging racial and gender stereotypes" that depict Asian Pacific American women as one-dimensional and hypersexual, ranging from "tragically passive to demonically aggressive," and always "receptive to . . . aggressively heterosexual advances," leaving them vulnerable to racialized sexual harassment.[56] Maria Ontiveros observes that "Latinas are often perceived as readily available and accessible for sexual use, with few recriminations to be faced for abusing them."[57] The burden to prove that sexual harassment rises to the level of an abusive work environment is a high hurdle for all women, but the power of racialized sexual stereotypes may set the bar higher in claims brought by women of color.

On the other hand, some commentators have suggested that standards of what is offensive should be calibrated to account for distinctive cultural expectations, including those based on race. Consider the highly publicized Senate confirmation hearing in which Clarence Thomas, nominated to serve on the U.S. Supreme Court, faced accusations of sexual harassment. Anita Hill, a former staff attorney under Thomas' supervision at the EEOC, claimed that she had been subject to repeated and unwelcome sexual comments and advances. In assessing Hill's claims, Harvard sociologist Orlando Patterson argued that "what constitutes proper and effective male-female relations varies across gender, class, ethnicity, and religion." To "most American feminists . . . an obscenity is always an obscenity . . .; to everyone else . . . an obscene expression . . . has to be understood in context." With his "mainstream cultural guard down," Thomas may have engaged in conduct that might be offensive to some but not to others like Hill. To those of African-American Southern working-class backgrounds, such conversation might have seemed reflective of a "down home style of courting." Patterson also claimed that "[i]f women are

---

53. Hernandez, supra note 45, at 295.

54. See Jones & Wade, supra note 51, at 212-13.

55. Hernandez, supra note 45, at 292.

56. Sumi K. Cho, Converging Stereotypes in Racialized Sexual Harassment: Where the Model Minority Meets Suzie Wong, 1 J. Gender Race & Just. 177, 181, 185, 190-94 (1997).

57. Maria L. Ontiveros, Three Perspectives on Workplace Harassment of Women of Color, 23 Golden Gate U. L. Rev. 817, 820 (1993).

to break through the glass ceiling, they must escape the trap of neo-Puritan feminism with its reactionary sacralization of women's bodies."[58]

Kimberlé Crenshaw criticizes this "cultural defense" on the grounds that it "effectively deflects criticism of sexist attitudes and practices that subordinate Black women and other women of color in our communities."[59] Does it also draw on and reinforce race and sex stereotypes about Black masculinity that are harmful to African-American men?

7. **Sexual Harassment in the Legal Profession.** The legal profession has a significant problem with sexual harassment. In a study by the ABA Commission on Women, Minority Corporate Counsel Association, and the Center for Work-Life Law, about 25 percent of women, 7 percent of white men, and 11 percent of men of color reported that they had encountered unwelcome sexual harassment at work, including unwanted sexual comments, physical contact, and/or romantic advances. More than 70 percent of all groups reported encountering sexist comments, stories, and jokes. About one in eight white women and one in ten women of color reported having lost career opportunities because they received sexual advances at work.[60] In other studies, as many as half of female lawyers have reported experiencing sex harassment in their current or previous jobs.[61] These numbers may understate the problem because more marginalized lawyers may be less willing to report sexual harassment for fear of heightened retaliation based on their race, gender, sexuality, or gender identity. As in other workplaces, targets of harassment in the legal profession understand the costs of coming forward to complain. Many are shunned or stigmatized as "oversensitive, whiny, and vindictive."[62] Others fear coming forward and suffering similar retaliation, particularly if their harassers are powerful partners.[63] As one woman noted, those who complained "were no longer employed there and these men were. Is there anything more to be said?"[64]

Even when law firms do sanction abusers, the lack of adequate vetting makes it possible for serial offenders to find new employment without accurately disclosing their work history. Many firms do not ask for references or confirming details due to fear of alerting competitors or lack of confidence that they will get candid

---

58. Orlando Patterson, Race, Gender and Liberal Fallacies, N.Y. Times, Oct. 10, 1991, at A15; see also Waleska Suero, We Don't Think of It as "Sexual Harassment": The Intersection of Gender and Ethnicity on Latinas' Workplace Sexual Harassment Claims, 33 Chicano/a-Latino/a L. Rev. 129 (2015).

59. Kimberlé Crenshaw, Race, Gender, and Sexual Harassment, 65 S. Cal. L. Rev. 1467, 1472 (1992).

60. Joan C. Williams et al., ABA Commission on Women in the Pro., Minority Corporate Counsel Association, and the Center for WorkLife Law, You Can't Change What You Can't See: Interrupting Racial & Gender Bias in the Legal Profession: Executive Summary 9 (2018); see also Int'l Bar Ass'n, Us Too: Bullying and Sexual Harassment in the Legal Profession (2019).

61. ABA Comm'n on Women in the Pro., Zero Tolerance: Best Practices for Combating Sex-Based Harassment in the Legal Profession 3 (2018).

62. Id. at 55.

63. Id. at 4.

64. Lauren Still Rikleen, Survey of Workplace Conduct and Behaviors in Law Firms 10 (2018).

reports.[65] In one notorious case, a partner who left two major firms following sexual harassment allegations was just settling happily into a third firm when some of his former colleagues sent that firm a bouquet of flowers with a note reading, "Thanks for taking him," signed "the women."[66] That led to an investigation and his resignation soon after. Strategies to address sexual harassment in the legal profession include training, multiple reporting channels, use of ombuds, prompt and unbiased investigation, bans on retaliation, significant sanctions, and monitoring of these structures through exit interviews and anonymous surveys.[67] Are there other measures that you would recommend? What can be done to address men who report reluctance to mentor women for fear of being targeted by harassment claims?[68]

8. **Sexual Harassment as an Offense Against Dignity.** A European Union Recommendation on the Protection of Dignity of Women and Men at Work defines the issue in terms of workplace dignity, rather than sex discrimination. Western European countries generally recognize harassment as an offense whether or not it is based on sex. "Bullying" is an actionable tort that includes everything from verbal harangues to social ostracism.[69] More than thirty states have considered legislation known as the Healthy Workplace Bill that would make unlawful behaviors that are threatening, intimidating, or humiliating but none has passed it.[70] Some commentators have recommended remedies for harassment by extending current tort law concepts of intentional infliction of emotional distress. Such a remedy would allow victims to sue the persons responsible, rather than just the employer, and would encompass conduct that is not sexual or aimed at only certain groups.[71]

A 2014 national survey found that 38 percent of surveyed American workers either experienced or witnessed bullying behavior, defined as verbal or psychological forms of aggressive (hostile) conduct that persists for at least six months. About 70 percent of the bullies were male, and 60 percent of targets were female.[72] What are the likely gendered dimensions of bullying?

Is the dignity approach preferable to the discrimination approach as a response to workplace harassment? Some critics worry that such legislation would

---

65. Sara Randazzo & Nicole Hong, At Law Firms, Rainmakers Accused of Harassment Can Switch Jobs with Ease, Wall St. J., July 30, 2018.

66. Id.

67. ABA Comm'n on Women in the Pro., supra note 61, at 42-50.

68. Katrin Bennhold, Another Side of #MeToo: Male Managers Fearful of Mentoring Women, N.Y. Times, Jan. 27, 2019, at A6.

69. See generally Susanne Baer, Dignity or Equality?: Responses to Workplace Harassment in European, German, and U.S. Law, in Directions in Sexual Harassment Law, supra note 17, at 582.

70. See WBI Healthy Workplace Bill to Prevent and Correct Abuse at Work, Healthy Workplace Bill.

71. Wendy N. Davis, No Putting Up with Put Downs, ABA J. 16 (Feb. 2008); Martha Chamallas, Discrimination and Outrage: The Migration from Civil Rights to Tort Law, 48 Wm. & Mary L. Rev. 2115 (2007); L. Camille Hébert, Conceptualizing Sexual Harassment in the Workplace as a Dignitary Tort, 75 Ohio St. L.J. 1345 (2014).

72. Gary Namie, Workplace Bullying Inst., U.S. Workplace Bullying Survey (2017).

encompass too much trivial behavior and impose undue legal costs. Others believe that it would prove largely meaningless since few victims could afford the costs of proceeding except in egregious cases. What is your view?

9. **Employer Liability.** An employee may experience sexual harassment in the workplace but still not be able to recover against the employer. Sexual harassment law involves two separate questions: (1) did actionable harassment occur; and (2) can the employer be held liable for it? Individual harassers cannot be held liable under Title VII, thus employer liability is a crucial part of the case.[73]

In *Meritor*, the Supreme Court declined to issue "a definitive rule" on employer liability, but the Court revisited the issue in 1998, when it established the governing standard for employer liability for harassment by supervisors. In Faragher v. City of Boca Raton, a college student who worked as a city lifeguard alleged that her supervisors had created a "sexually hostile atmosphere" by repeatedly subjecting female lifeguards to "'uninvited and offensive touching,' by making lewd remarks, and by speaking of women in offensive terms."[74] One lifeguard allegedly told her, "Date me or clean the toilets for a year." Although the city had a sexual harassment policy, it was not distributed to her supervisors, and they were unaware of its requirements.

The Supreme Court, speaking through Justice Souter, held:

> [W]e . . . agree with Faragher that in implementing Title VII it makes sense to hold an employer vicariously liable for some tortious conduct of a supervisor made possible by abuse of his supervisory authority. . . .
>
> In order to accommodate the principle of vicarious liability for harm caused by misuse of supervisory authority, as well as Title VII's equally basic policies of encouraging forethought by employers and saving action by objecting employees, we adopt the following holding. . . . An employer is subject to vicarious liability to a victimized employee for an actionable hostile environment created by a supervisor with immediate (or successively higher) authority over the employee. When no tangible employment action is taken, a defending employer may raise an affirmative defense to liability or damages, subject to proof by a preponderance of the evidence. The defense comprises two necessary elements: (a) that the employer exercised reasonable care to prevent and correct promptly any sexually harassing behavior, and (b) that the plaintiff employee unreasonably failed to take advantage of any preventive or corrective opportunities provided by the employer or to avoid harm otherwise. While proof that an employer had promulgated an antiharassment policy with complaint procedure is not necessary in every instance as a matter of law, the need for a stated policy suitable to the employment circumstances may appropriately be addressed in any case when litigating the first element of the defense. And while proof that an employee failed to fulfill the corresponding obligation of reasonable care to avoid harm is not limited to showing an unreasonable failure to use any complaint procedure provided by the

---

73. See, e.g., Williams v. Banning, 72 F.3d 552, 555 (7th Cir. 1995); Grossman, supra note 5, at 9 n.25.

74. 524 U.S. 775 (1998).

employer, a demonstration of such failure will normally suffice to satisfy the employer's burden under the second element of the defense. No affirmative defense is available, however, when the supervisor's harassment culminates in a tangible employment action, such as discharge, demotion, or undesirable reassignment. . . .

The City points to nothing that might justify a conclusion by the District Court on remand that the City had exercised reasonable care. Nor is there any reason to remand for consideration of Faragher's efforts to mitigate her own damages, since the award to her was solely nominal. . . .

[Reversed and remanded for entry of judgment for Faragher.][75]

In Burlington Industries v. Ellerth, a companion case decided on the same day as *Faragher*, the plaintiff was a salesperson who alleged that she was subjected to constant sexual harassment by her supervisor, a mid-level manager. The misconduct consisted of "repeated boorish and offensive remarks and gestures," including repeated warnings to "loosen up" in response to sexual comments and pressure to meet him at a hotel lounge under the threat that "you know, Kim, I could make your life very hard or very easy at Burlington."[76] The plaintiff never reported her supervisor's conduct to her employer, despite being aware that it had a policy against sexual harassment. The Court adopted the same legal standard for employer liability, but remanded Ellerth's case for application of it. The employer was likely to prevail given that she failed to take advantage of an available internal grievance procedure.

Three subsequent cases further refined employer liability standards. In one, the Court established that where an employee resigns as a result of conditions that have become intolerable (constructive discharge), the employer may avoid liability by showing that there was an effective remedial process that the employee unreasonably failed to use.[77] In another, the Court limited punitive damages to cases in which the employer has not made good-faith efforts to comply with Title VII.[78] In a third, the Court clarified the definition of "supervisor" for purposes of applying the *Fargaher/Ellerth* liability framework. A threshold issue in this framework is whether the harasser was a supervisor or co-worker; the Supreme Court adopted a narrow definition of "supervisor" in Vance v. Ball State University, making it even harder to holder employers accountable.[79]

Under the affirmative defense, employers who wish to avoid liability must make prompt and thorough investigations and take remedial actions reasonably calculated to prevent further harassment and to protect the complainant. Thus, *Faragher* and *Ellerth* spurred many employers to adopt formal, written anti-harassment policies and procedures; some also adopted anti-harassment training programs. But there has been considerable litigation over what types of responses are required of employers and complainants under the affirmative defense. For example, what constitutes a reasonable remedial action? Case law suggests that employers may

---

75. Id. at 792, 802, 807-09.
76. 524 U.S. 742, 748-49 (1998).
77. Pennsylvania State Police v. Suders, 542 U.S. 129 (2004).
78. See Kolstad v. American Dental Ass'n, 527 U.S. 526, 545 (1999).
79. 570 U.S. 421 (2013).

avoid liability if they transfer complainants out of range of the harasser unless that involves a less desirable assignment.[80] As long as employers take some responsive measures, failure to stop the harassment is not necessarily fatal to the affirmative defense.[81] As interpreted by lower courts, the law does not require employers to be very proactive. A survey of some 200 post-*Faragher* and post-*Ellerth* cases found that as long as the employer had a viable anti-harassment policy and a grievance procedure that allows an employee to bypass a harassing supervisor, *Ellerth* and *Faragher* "did little to change employer incentives to reduce the incidence of sexual harassment by supervisors in the workplace."[82]

Another set of questions focuses on victim behavior. When is a victim's failure to complain unreasonable? As noted above, the obstacles to reporting are likely to be greater for women of color, but many women fail to report harassment out of concerns for retaliation, blacklisting, loss of privacy, and doubts that effective responses will be forthcoming.[83] Although employers must demonstrate that a victim's failure to complain was unreasonable, judges have been skeptical of plaintiffs' reasons for delaying or failing to complain. A "generalized fear of retaliation" is insufficient. As one circuit court put it, "the bringing of a retaliation claim, rather than failing to report harassment, is the proper method for dealing with retaliation."[84] Courts have imposed strict standards on plaintiffs, ruling in one case that an employee who complained on her eighth day at a new job that she had been harassed daily since the first day had waited too long.[85] Yet the majority of surveyed victims say that complaints make the situation worse.[86] Studies support this perception, with one study finding that as many as 60 percent of employees who complain about harassment are subjected to retaliation.[87] How can the law take

---

80. Compare Robinson v. Sappington, 351 F.3d 317 (2003), with Sparks v. Reg'l Med. Ctr. Bd., 792 F. Supp. 735 (N.D. Ala. 1992). See also Smith v. Rock-Tenn Serv., No. 1505534, 2016 WL 520073 (6th Cir. 2016).

81. See cases cited in Grossman, supra note 4, at 699.

82. Anne Lawton, Operating in an Empirical Vacuum: The *Ellerth* and *Faragher* Affirmative Defense, 13 Colum. J. Gender & L. 197, 210 (2004); see also David Sherwyn et al., Don't Train Your Employees and Cancel Your "1-800" Harassment Hotline: An Empirical Examination and Correction of the Flaws in the Affirmative Defense to Sexual Harassment Charges, 69 Fordham L. Rev. 1265, 1304 (2001).

83. Vicki Schultz, The Sanitized Workplace, 112 Yale L.J. 2061, 2140 (2003); Tanya Kateri Hernandez, A Critical Race Feminism Empirical Research Project: Sexual Harassment and the Internal Complaints Black Box, 39 U.C. Davis L. Rev. 1235, 1262-68 (2006); Angela Onwuachi-Willig, What About #UsToo?: The Invisibility of Race in the #MeToo Movement, 128 Yale L.J. F. 105 (2018); Julie Konik & Lilia M. Cortina, Policing Gender at Work: Intersections of Harassment Based on Sex and Sexuality, 21 Soc. Justice Rsch. 313 (2008).

84. Matvia v. Bald Head Island Mgmt., Inc., 259 F.3d 261, 270 (4th Cir. 2001).

85. Marsicano v. American Soc'y of Safety Eng'rs, No. 97-C7819, 1998 WL 603128 (N.D. Ill. Sept. 4, 1998).

86. Louise Fitzgerald et al., Why Didn't She Just Report Him? The Psychological and Legal Implications of Women's Responses to Sexual Harassment, 13 Harv. Women's L.J. 35, 100 (1995).

87. See id. at 122-23; see also Deborah L. Brake & Joanna L. Grossman, The Failure of Title VII as a Rights-Claiming System, 86 N.C. L. Rev. 859, 902-05 (2008).

account of this reality while providing adequate incentives for employees to report harassment?[88]

Some critics of the current law have charged that having an anti-harassment policy and a grievance process is not enough to change behaviors in the workplace. The law generally fails to require more proactive measures, such as training, and some management experts advise against strategies that would encourage reporting.[89] About 40 percent of surveyed businesses offer no training, and many programs that are in place have demonstrated no long-term positive effect on attitudes or behaviors.[90] There are also questions about the quality of employer trainings, with some critics contending that employers overemphasize relatively minor sexual behaviors, contributing to employee resentment and trivializing the problem of harassment.[91] Internal complaint mechanisms are often structured in ways that inadvertently discourage their use and diminish their ability to address underlying discrimination issues. For example, because employers cannot promise confidentiality during investigation of a complaint, many victims are unwilling to come forward.[92] Moreover, because internal grievance procedures tend to recast harassment as a problem of interpersonal conflict that must be addressed to preserve harmonious working relationships, experts have noted that they fail to address the broader systemic conditions that perpetuate discrimination, such as gender segregation and stratification in the work force.[93]

10. **Harassment Prevention Policies: Do They Go Too Far?**   While some believe that harassment policies do not effectively address discriminatory behaviors in the workplace, others argue that the current liability structure gives employers too great an incentive to regulate harmless behaviors, including "trivial" sexual conduct. According to Vicki Schultz:

> [T]he federal agency and the lower courts charged with interpreting Title VII define[d] harassment primarily in terms of sexual advances and other sexual conduct—an approach I call the sexual model. . . . [T]his sexual model is too narrow, because the focus on sexual conduct has obscured more fundamental problems of gender-based harassment and discrimination that are not primarily "sexual" in content or design. . . . [T]he sexual model is also too broad, because . . . [it is] leading *companies* to prohibit a broad range of relatively harmless sexual conduct, even when that conduct does not threaten gender equality on the job. . . . Many firms are banning or discouraging intimate relationships between their employees. Worst of all, companies are disciplining (and even firing) employees

---

88. See Brake & Grossman, supra note 87, at 879-84.

89. Sherwyn et al., supra note 82, at 1304; Lua Kamal Yuille, Liberating Sexual Harassment Law, 22 Mich. J. Gender & L. 345 (2015).

90. Train Right Solutions, EE Compliance Practices Benchmarking (2006); Deborah L. Rhode, Social Research and Social Change: Meeting the Challenge of Gender Inequality and Sexual Abuse, 30 Harv. J.L. & Gender 11, 14 (2007).

91. See Elizabeth Tippett, Harassment Trainings: A Content Analysis, 39 Berkeley J. Emp. & Lab. L. 481 (2018).

92. See Grossman, supra note 5, at 61-63; Schultz, supra note 83, at 2140.

93. See Grossman, supra note 5, at 42-47.

for these perceived sexual transgressions without bothering to examine whether they are linked to sex discrimination in purpose or effect.[94]

Schultz worries, in addition, that both employers and employees use trivial examples of sexual conduct as a pretext for other concerns.[95] Schultz maintains that efforts to "sanitize the workplace" will "induce[] social stigma and enforce[] sexual conformity in a way that impoverishes life for everyone."

Is there also a First Amendment issue with the "sanitizing" approach? One court ordered an employer who was found to have established a "hostile environment" pervaded by pornographic pictures and repeated sexual and demeaning remarks and jokes to prohibit the display, reading, or viewing of "sexually suggestive, sexually demeaning, or pornographic" materials. The court concluded there was no First Amendment issue because (1) the employer had "no intention to express itself through the sexually-oriented pictures" and had banned other speech as well (such as political campaign literature and buttons); (2) pictures and verbal harassment were "not protected speech [when] they act as discriminatory conduct in the form of a hostile work environment"; (3) "regulation of discriminatory speech in the workplace constitutes nothing more than time, place, and manner regulation of speech"; (4) "female workers were a captive audience in relation to the speech that comprised the hostile work environment"; (5) even if the speech is "treated as fully protected by the First Amendment," the governmental interest in "cleansing the workplace of impediments to the equality of women is . . . a compelling interest that permits [a regulation] . . . narrowly drawn to serve this interest"; and (6) even a governmental employer has the power to enforce workplace rules impinging on free speech rights, in order to maintain discipline and order in the workplace.[96] Do you agree?

Eugene Volokh and Kingsley Browne, both strong critics of restrictions on workplace expression, argue that harassment laws should target only offensive conduct directed at a particular employee; they worry that broader, vaguer prohibitions will encourage employers to avoid liability by unduly limiting workplace speech.[97] What is your view? Is the standard adopted by the court in Lyle v. Warner Bros. (*Friends*), discussed in Note 4, above, a fair compromise?

Schultz, along with other commentators, is critical of the growing tendency of employers to become "cupid cops." The limited research available suggests that somewhere between 20 and 40 percent of companies have policies or clear norms on workplace romances and that the vast majority prohibits or discourages such relationships.[98] Critics of prohibitions on workplace romances worry that attempts

---

94. Schultz, supra note 83, at 2065.

95. Id. at 2113-16, 2156.

96. Robinson v. Jacksonville Shipyards, 760 F. Supp. 1486, 1534-36, 1542 (Appendix) (M.D. Fla. 1001).

97. See Eugene Volokh, What Speech Does "Hostile Work Environment" Restrict?, In Sexual Harassment: Cases, Case Studies, and Commentary 180, 202 (Paul I. Weizer ed., 2002); Kingsley Browne, The Silenced Workplace: Employer Censorship Under Title VII, in Directions in Sexual Harassment Law, supra note 17, at 399.

98. Schultz, supra note 83, at 2129.

to enforce them are often ineffective and intrusive, and likely to drive relationships underground. Enforcement is also likely to have gender-biased results; those in subordinate positions, typically women, are the ones most likely to be subject to transfer or termination. Do categorical bans on workplace relationships ignore courtship realities? For a growing number of employees, the increasing length of workweeks means that they have less time to find potential partners outside of the workplace. In representative surveys, 40 to 50 percent of employees had dated someone at work, one-fifth had dated a subordinate, over one-quarter ended up marrying a colleague, and three-quarters felt that they should be able to date anyone they wished.[99] Would it be reasonable for an employer to ask romantically involved employees to sign a "love contract" acknowledging the relationship and promising it will not interfere with work? Do some workplace relationships—those marked by disparities of position—warrant more surveillance than others?[100]

11. **Sexual Harassment and the #MeToo Movement.** In October 2017, the New York Times published an investigative journalism piece detailing three decades of sexual misconduct by Hollywood mega-producer Harvey Weinstein.[101] Subsequent coverage revealed even more egregious behavior, including retaliation and intimidation.[102] The revelations led to Harvey Weinstein's removal from his own company, a Pulitzer Prize for Public Service for the New York Times authors, and a collective wake-up call about the problem of sexual harassment.[103] Ten days later, actress Alyssa Milano tweeted the following invitation: "If you've been sexually harassed or assaulted, write 'me too' as a reply to this tweet." Within just a few days of Milano's tweet, the hashtag #MeToo was used millions of times in eighty-five different countries. Since then, #MeToo has become the one-word descriptor of a movement, as well as a shorthand for single incidents or a workplace culture—"We've got a #MeToo problem." Although Milano was not the first to use the "me too" framing—civil rights activist Tarana Burke founded the Me Too campaign over a decade earlier, through a nonprofit organization designed to help victims of sexual harassment and assault, especially Black girls and women[104]—the 2017 hashtag sparked a movement.

99. Rosemary Haefner, Office Romances Rarely Kept Secret, CNN.com (Feb. 13, 2008).

100. See Michael Z. Green, A New #MeToo Result: Rejecting Notions of Romantic Consent with Executives, 23 Emp. Rts. & Emp. Pol'y J. 115 (2019).

101. Jodi Kantor & Megan Twohey, Harvey Weinstein Paid Off Sexual Harassment Accusers for Decades, N.Y. Times, Oct. 5, 2017, at A1. The reporters subsequently published a fuller account of Weinstein's misconduct and the efforts required to expose it. See Jodi Kantor & Megan Twohey, She Said: Breaking the Sexual Harassment Story That Helped Ignite a Movement (2019).

102. See Ronan Farrow, From Aggressive Overtures to Sexual Assault: Harvey Weinstein's Accusers Tell Their Stories, New Yorker (Oct. 23, 2017).

103. See Megan Twohey & Niraj Chokshi, Company Scrambles as Weinstein Takes Leave and a Third of the Board Resigns, N.Y. Times, Oct. 6, 2017, at A1. Weinstein was ultimately convicted of felony sex crime and rape in New York and is serving a lengthy prison sentence. See Jonah E. Bromwich & Jodi Kantor, Weinstein's Sex Crime Conviction, a Milestone for #MeToo, is Upheld, N.Y. Times, June 3, 2022.

104. See Sandra E. Garcia, The Woman Who Created #MeToo Long Before Hashtags, N.Y. Times, Oct. 20, 2017.

In the days and months that followed the Weinstein article, numerous women came forward with allegations of sexual misconduct by powerful men, including Garrison Keilor (public radio figure), Alex Kozinski (federal judge), Al Franken (U.S. Senator), and Matt Lauer (television news host). Between October 2017 and April 2019, more than 1,200 high-profile figures were publicly accused of sexual harassment, assault, and other related workplace misconduct, and half are known to have lost their jobs.[105] Although men accounted for a significant percentage of complainants, only 3 percent of the alleged perpetrators were female.[106] After the initial focus on individual men in positions of power, journalists turned to focus on particular companies and industries in which sexual harassment was a significant problem.[107]

Has anything changed as a result of #MeToo? Arguably, yes. First, women are showing greater willingness to come forward and report harassment. Studies have repeatedly shown that harassment victims rarely file formal complaints. Victims tend to complain only about severe harassment, and only when they've exhausted all other avenues. Yet, the #MeToo movement consists of countless women naming what has happened to them and blaming the harasser (or the harasser's employer) for the harm. Once the dam broke, we witnessed, in Catharine MacKinnon's words, "mass mobilization against sexual abuse . . . through an unprecedented wave of speaking out in conventional and social media."[108] One study found that although accusations were at their highest in November 2017, and the initial spike has subsided, the rates per month still far exceed the pre-Weinstein levels.

Second, the voices of accusation have been greatly amplified by technology and social media. A viral Facebook post or tweet will reach more people, more quickly, and the Internet makes it easy to find other people dealing with similar issues. The age of social media has also transformed notions of privacy in favor of more openness about almost every aspect of life. The sharing raised the stakes, as women realized they, collectively, "live under threat. Not sometimes, but all the time."[109] The swell of stories and support moved Monica Lewinsky, the intern involved in the sex scandal that led to the impeachment of President Bill Clinton,

---

105. E-mail from Davia B. Temin to Deborah L. Rhode (Apr. 29, 2019), discussed in Deborah L. Rhode, #MeToo: Why Now? What Next?, 69 Duke L. J. 377 (2019).

106. Id.

107. See, e.g., Bethany McLean, "We All Wear All Black Every Day": Inside Wall Street's Complex, Shameful, and Often Confidential Battle With #MeToo, Vanity Fair (Mar. 2018); Working Mother Research Inst., #MeToo Workplace Study (2018); Elyse Shaw et al., Inst. Women's Pol'y Rsch., Sexual Harassment and Assault at Work: Understanding the Costs (Oct. 2018); Jocelyn Frye, Ctr. Am. Progress, Not Just the Rich and Famous: The Pervasiveness of Sexual Harassment Across Industries Affects All Workers, americanprogress.org (Nov. 11, 2017); Amanda Rossie et al., Nat'l Women's L. Ctr., Out of the Shadows: An Analysis of Sexual Harassment Charges Filed by Working Women (2018).

108. Catharine A. MacKinnon, #MeToo Has Done What the Law Could Not, N.Y. Times, Feb. 4, 2018, at A29; see also Johana Bhuiyan, With Just Her Words, Susan Fowler Brought Uber to Its Knees, Vox (Dec. 6, 2017).

109. Barbara Kingsolver, #MeToo Isn't Enough, Now Women Need to Get Ugly, Guardian, Jan. 16, 2018.

to reflect on how different her experience might have been two decades later: "If the Internet was a bête noire to me in 1998, its stepchild — social media — has been a savior for millions of women today. . . . Virtually anyone can share her or his #MeToo story and be instantly welcomed into a tribe."[110] The chorus of voices became a "hashtag, a movement, a reckoning," and the "silence breakers" were chosen by *Time* magazine as Person of the Year for 2017.[111] Hollywood A-listers and women's rights activists teamed up to form Time's Up, a campaign based on the idea that the "clock has run out on sexual assault, harassment and inequality in the workplace. It's time to do something about it."[112]

Third, men facing credible accusations of harassment are suffering consequences. Much of the history of sexual harassment law has been characterized by employers taking insufficient action — often no action — despite credible evidence of harassment. Internal investigations are often biased and employers tend to recast harassment as a problem of interpersonal conflict that does not warrant discipline and to overlook misconduct when the harasser is too valuable to lose.[113] "Now, all at once," Barbara Kingsolver wrote, "women are refusing to accept sexual aggression as any kind of award, and men are getting fired from their jobs. It feels like an earthquake."[114] Catherine MacKinnon commented that today's survivors, "no longer liars, no longer worthless,. . . are initiating consequences none of them could have gotten through any lawsuit — in part because the laws do not permit relief against individual perpetrators, but more because they are being believed and valued as the law seldom has."[115] Of the 417 men profiled in one study, 60 percent were fired; some additional number were subject to some formal repercussion for their behavior.[116] As author Lindy West wrote, "[a]fter decades of debates and doubts and dissertations and settlements and nondisclosure agreements and whisper networks and stasis and silence, all of a sudden, in one great gust, powerful men are toppling. . . . This is new."[117]

Fourth, the movement has shed light on the role of nondisclosure agreements (NDAs) in allowing harassers to stay in power and concealing problems of harassment. NDAs are not new, but many of the high-profile men at the center of the #MeToo movement had a history of similar misconduct that had been kept quiet in part through such agreements.[118]

---

110. Monica Lewinsky, Monica Lewinsky: Emerging from "The House of Gaslight" in the Age of #MeToo, Vanity Fair (Feb. 25, 2018).

111. See Edward Felsenthal, The Choice, Time (Dec. 18, 2017).

112. See http://timesupnow.com.

113. See, e.g., Lauren B. Edelman et al., Internal Dispute Resolution: The Transformation of Civil Rights in the Workplace, 27 Law & Soc'y Rev. 497, 506 (1993).

114. Kingsolver, supra note 109.

115. See Catharine A. MacKinnon, Where #MeToo Came From, and Where It's Going, Atlantic (Mar. 24, 2019).

116. Jeff Green, #MeToo Snares More Than 400 High-Profile People, Bloomberg (June 25, 2018).

117. Lindy West, We Got Rid of Some Bad Men. Now Let's Get Rid of Bad Movies., N.Y. Times, Mar. 3, 2018, at SR1.

118. See, e.g., Jim Rutenberg, A Long-Delayed Reckoning of the Cost of Silence on Abuse, N.Y. Times, Oct. 22, 2017, at A1; On the role of NDAs in harassment cases, see Ian

Legal reform has been limited so far.[119] A handful of states passed laws to limit or ban the use of NDAs in sexual harassment or assault cases.[120] Such prohibitions reduce the likelihood of serial harassment, but at the expense of individual victims, who will find it harder to obtain settlements or ensure the privacy that often they, as well as employers, would like. Is the trade-off worth it? If so, why do you think legislatures have been so slow to adopt such prohibitions? Congress passed a law requiring mandatory arbitration for employment claims involving sexual misconduct, which has some of the benefits of limiting NDAs without the same costs.[121]

Within the legal profession, there have been some changes in response to the movement. For example, the ABA House of Delegates passed one resolution urging legal employers not to require mandatory arbitration for sexual harassment claims and another to urge them to "prohibit, prevent, and promptly redress" harassment and retaliation, with intersectionality in mind.[122] Several other professions and academic associations have redefined professional misconduct to include sexual harassment.[123] Is that a reasonable strategy? What changes do you think are appropriate?

In January 2018, a Federal Judiciary Workplace Conduct Working Group was launched to consider whether adequate safeguards were in place within the federal judiciary to protect court employees from inappropriate workplace conduct. In its initial report, the working group recommended a variety of changes endorsed by Chief Justice John Roberts, including:

- Changing codes of conduct for both judges and employees to make clear that both harassment and retaliation against those who report misconduct are prohibited.

Ayres, Targeting Repeat Offender NDAs, 71 Stan. L. Rev. Online 76 (June 2018); Vasundhara Prasad, If Anyone Is Listening, #MeToo: Breaking the Culture of Silence Around Sexual Abuse Through Regulating Non-Disclosure Agreements and Secret Settlements, 59 B.C. L. Rev. 2507 (2018); Kathleen McCullough, Mandatory Arbitration and Sexual Harassment Claims: #MeToo- and Time's Up-Inspired Action Against the Federal Arbitration Act, 87 Fordham L. Rev. 2653 (2019).

119. See generally L. Camille Hébert, Is "MeToo" Only a Social Movement or a Legal Movement Too?, 22 Emp. Rts. & Emp. Pol'y J. 321 (2018); Elizabeth C. Tippett, The Legal Implications of the MeToo Movement, 103 Minn. L. Rev. 229 (2018).

120. See, e.g., Cal. Civ. Pro. § 1001 (2022) (providing that a settlement agreement that "prevents the disclosure of factual information" related to claims of sexual harassment or assault is "void as a matter of law and against public policy"). Vermont passed a law mandating that agreements to settle sexual harassment cases be accompanied by an express disclosure that the victim is still able to disclose the harassment to any government agency or to comply with a valid request for discovery in civil litigation. See Vt. Stat. Ann. Tit. 2, § 495h (2022). See, e.g., Cal. Civ. Pro. § 1001 (2022).

121. See Ending Forced Arbitration of Sexual Assault and Sexual Harassment Act of 2021, Pub. L. No. 117-90, 136 Stat. 26 (2022).

122. See ABA Comm'n on Women in the Pro., Resolutions, https://www.americanbar.org/groups/diversity/women/resolutions.

123. Nat'l Acad. of Scis., Sexual Harassment of Women: Climate, Culture, and Consequences in Academic Sciences, Engineering, and Medicine (2018).

- Strengthening internal procedures for identifying and correcting misconduct.
- Expanding training programs to prevent inappropriate and uncivil conduct.[124]

A report of the Working Group in 2022 recommended additional changes, including a comprehensive climate survey of the federal judiciary and the adoption of a policy on romantic relationships within supervisory working relationships.[125] Why might sexual harassment be a difficult problem to tackle within the judiciary?

Will #MeToo bring about lasting change? Certainly some of the intensity of the focus on sexual harassment has waned since 2017. Do you think the movement has changed the way people think or talk about sexual harassment, or caused them to react differently when it happens to them?

Is the #MeToo movement empowering for all women? Angela Onwuachi-Willig argues that it has ignored and marginalized women of color.[126] From appropriating a phrase first used by an African-American activist to empower sexually abused girls and women of color, to the focus on the stories of powerful white women, Onwuachi-Willig calls the movement to task for ingrained racial bias. She blames not just the racial disparity in whose stories are elevated, but more important, the movement's failure to contend with the heightened vulnerability of women of color. Jamillah Bowman Williams argues that the movement should focus more on the intersectional harms experienced by Black women.[127] As she explains:

> The #MeToo movement prompted millions globally to speak out against sexual harassment, sexual assault, and violence against women, and is now known as the most significant mobilization in the women's movement in decades. Although many theorize that social media activism, like #MeToo, broadens access to movements and builds bridges across demographic groups, women of color are largely left out of the conversation. Offline organizing efforts that pre-dated #MeToo also gained legitimacy and momentum from the hashtag, but women of color again were in the shadows. This is particularly problematic given the unique ways that women of color experience harassment combined with the law's failure to remedy these offenses. . . .
>
> Although some are hopeful that the #MeToo movement has helped fill these gaps through seemingly positive legal strides, such as

---

124. 2018 Year End Report on the Federal Judiciary 5-6, supremecourt.gov (Dec. 31, 2018); Report of the Federal Judiciary Workplace Conduct Working Group to the Judicial Conference of the United States, uscourts.gov (June 1, 2018).

125. Report of the Federal Judiciary Workplace Conduct Working Group to the Judicial Conference of the United States, uscourts.gov (Mar. 16, 2022).

126. Angela Onwuachi-Willig, What About #UsToo?: The Invisibility of Race in the #MeToo Movement, 128 Yale L. J. F. 105 (2018). See also Symposium, Race-ing Justice Engendering Power: Black Lives Matter, #MeToo, and the Role of Intersectional Legal Analysis in the Twenty-First Century, Wis. Women's L.J. (Apr. 12, 2019).

127. Jamillah Bowman Williams, Maximixing #MeToo: Intersectionality & The Movement, 62 B.C. L. Rev. 1797 (2021).

stronger enforcement by the Equal Employment Opportunity Commission (EEOC), increased lawsuits, and new legislation, I argue that the law is less than promising for women of color seeking justice. Numerous legal, organizational, and cultural barriers make it nearly impossible for women of color to exercise their civil rights.

It is no surprise. . . that intersectionality figures prominently in women of colors' experiences of sexual harassment. Harassment and assault are often layered with complexities of segregation, stereotypes, racial subordination, and low-wage work, related to both their race *and* sex. For example, women of color are often targets of sexual harassment because of racialized stereotypes about their sexuality. . . . In addition to the specific racial tropes that factor into their harassment experiences, women of color are often not viewed with compassion. Racialized stereotypes not only lead to victim-blaming, but also cause the experiences of Black women and other women of color to be downplayed and not perceived as requiring a protective response. Stereotypical perceptions of their gendered racial identity means that employers see women of color not only as more dispensable, but they also see them as less sympathetic or trustworthy when they do report harassment. . . .

Although the #MeToo movement has presented an opportunity for united activism that could have led to advances for all women, . . . it has largely left women of color at the margins, whose plight can be better understood by applying Crenshaw's framework of intersectionality. . . .

How would intersectional analysis change the approach to sexual harassment at the individual, institutional, or legal level? What do you expect will come of the #MeToo movement in the long term? How should we measure its success or failure?[128]

PUTTING THEORY INTO PRACTICE

3-1. Analyze each of the following situations to determine whether it establishes a case of "discrimination based on sex." What theories of sex discrimination help you make the determination?

(a) At an all-female mortgage company office, female employees make lewd jokes, ask each other about their sexual experiences, discuss whose breasts are bigger, and change clothes in front of one another. One administrative assistant is offended and claims that it interferes with her work.

(b) In a correctional facility, a female officer discovers that night-shift workers have been using her desk at night for sexual liaisons.[129]

---

128. For a range of scholarly takes on the #MeToo movement, see, e.g., Margaret Ryznar, #MeToo & Tax, 75 Wash. & Lee L. Rev. Online 53 (2018); Lesley Wexler et al., #MeToo, Time's Up, and Theories of Justice, 2019 U. Ill. L. Rev. 45 (2019); Jamie R. Abrams, The #MeToo Movement: An Invitation for Feminist Critique of Rape Crisis Framing, 52 U. Rich. L. Rev. 749 (2018).

129. Orton-Bell v. Indiana, 759 F.3d 768 (7th Cir. 2014).

(c) A secretary who works in a physician's office announces that she is pregnant. The doctor's wife believes her husband was having an affair with the secretary and that the child might be his. After other measures to alleviate his wife's fears, the doctor fires his secretary to save his marriage. Does it matter whether they were actually having an affair?[130]

(d) A U.S. Congressman asks a young female staffer in his office whether she would be willing to serve as a surrogate for him and his wife. He offers her $5 million and suggests "insemination" through sex.[131]

3-2. Of the things that a male boss might ask of a female employee, which is the most objectionable: (1) to kiss him, (2) to babysit his kids, or (3) to be responsible for serving coffee at staff meetings?[132] Does the law reflect your opinion?

3-3. Julie is a dedicated young scientist who received the following e-mail from a senior scientist in the research institute for which they both work: "Forgive the truth bomb, but from the first day I talked to you, there hasn't been a single day or hour when you weren't on my mind. I find you incredibly attractive, adorably dorky, and worth promoting in all the ways I have done—some known to you, and some unknown. Being near you is wildly exhilarating and at the same time frustrating, as I am utterly unable to get a grip on myself. That's just the way things are and you're gonna have to deal with me until one of us leaves."[133] Is this sexual harassment? What should Julie do?

3-4. Vice President Pence made news when he stated that he would never meet alone with a woman who is not his wife. "Gender sidelining" is a well-documented phenomenon that involves the practice some men follow of minimizing the risk of a sexual harassment accusation (true or false) by limiting contact at work with women. In the wake of #MeToo, the Harvard Business Review found that 64 percent of male executives were reluctant to meet one-on-one with junior female colleagues, and a New York Times survey found that 45 percent of men felt it was inappropriate to have dinner alone with a female co-worker, and 22 percent felt it was inappropriate to have a one-on-one meeting.[134] Men give various reasons for avoiding contact with female co-workers in certain situations, including the desire to avoid the appearance of impropriety, to avoid false accusations of sexual misconduct, and to prevent their wives from getting jealous. Do any of these reasons justify the avoidance behavior? If a female friend felt like she was being avoided by a male executive or partner, what would you advise her to do? If she sued in court, would she be likely to prevail? On what theory?

---

130. Mittl v. N.Y. State Div. of Hum. Rts., 794 N.E.2d 660 (N.Y. 2003); see also Kahn v. Objective Sols., Int'l, 86 F. Supp. 2d 377 (S.D.N.Y 2000).

131. Katie Rogers, Trent Franks, Accused of Offering $5 Million to Aide for Surrogacy, Resigns, N.Y. Times, Dec. 8, 2017, at A1.

132. These examples are taken from Laura Rosenbury, Work Wives, 36 Harv. J. Gender & L. 345 (2013).

133. A. Hope Jahren, She Wanted to Do Her Research. He Wanted to Talk "Feelings," N.Y. Times, Mar. 4, 2016, at SR4.

134. Sylvia Ann Hewlett, As a Leader, Create a Culture of Sponsorship, Harv. Bus. Rev. (Oct. 8, 2013).

3-5. How should the law handle "street hassling" — crude behaviors such as wolf whistles, leers, catcalls, grabs, pinches, and sexual invitations? Some feminists have proposed liability for such conduct under tort doctrine or misdemeanor statutes.[135] What problems and benefits do you see from such efforts? An anti-harassment campaign was launched on Philadelphia transit, featuring ads such as "Nice a** is not a compliment," and "In a perfect world, what would your sister/daughter/girlfriend hear as she walks to the subway? Hey sexy? Can I have a smile? What, you gay? Good Morning!"[136] Are public awareness campaigns such as this one likely to change attitudes or behavior (or both)?

3-6. Catharine MacKinnon has written that while the law of sexual harassment was a precondition for the #MeToo movement, that movement "is surpassing the law in changing norms and providing relief that the law did not."[137] What does she mean? In what sense does the #MeToo movement exemplify nonsubordination theory?

3-7. What should redemption look like for sexual harassers terminated or otherwise punished for sexual harassment? Many of the men caught up in the early firings in the 2017 #MeToo movement issued statements in which they apologized for anything they had said or done that might have been misunderstood and said they were going to take time to focus on themselves and become better men. Is that sufficient? What would a genuine apology look like? Is an apology enough to make amends? Michelle Goldberg suggests that most of these men were not "proposing paths to restitution. They're asking why women won't give them absolution" — and what they should do is propose "ideas to make things better . . . [now that] they've got time on their hands."[138] How long should an ousted harasser remain a "professional pariah"?[139] What would you advise a person in this situation to do?

3-8. One of the most controversial forms of #MeToo activism involved the online circulation of "shitty men" lists in various fields — entertainment, tech, academia.[140] There is a long history of such anonymous postings of sexual abusers,

---

135. Olatokunbo Olukemi Laniya, Street Smut: Gender, Media, and the Legal Power Dynamics of Street Harassment, or "Hey Sexy" and Other Verbal Ejaculations, 14 Colum. J. Gender & L. 91 (2005); Cynthia Grant Bowman, Street Harassment and the Informal Ghettoization of Women, 106 Harv. L. Rev. 517 (1993).

136. Details of the SEPTA campaign can be found at http://www.stopstreetharassment .org/2013/4/septaads.

137. MacKinnon, supra note 115.

138. Michelle Goldberg, The Shame of the MeToo Men, N.Y. Times, Sept. 14, 2018, at SR9; see also It'll Never Be the Right Time for Famous Sexual Predators to Make Their Comebacks, Time (May 10, 2018); see also Alexandra Brodsky, Meeting "The Other Side": Conversations with Men Accused of Sexual Assault, New Yorker (Aug. 20, 2021). Notably, five years after calling for Senator Franken's resignation after he was accused of groping several women, Goldberg said she regretted doing so before he had had a proper hearing. Michelle Goldberg, I Was Wrong About Al Franken, N.Y. Times, July 21, 2022.

139. Rhode, supra note 105; see also Editorial, Alex Kozinski's Retirement Doesn't End the Discussion About Sexual Harassment in the Judiciary, L.A. Times, Dec. 19, 2017.

140. Rhode, supra note 105.

including graffiti in college women's bathrooms identifying alleged rapists. How would you evaluate this form of activism in particular—the costs to men who are unfairly accused and have no ready way to remove themselves from the lists, versus the benefits to victims from deterring or alerting them to potential abuse?

3-9. In a highly publicized trial, actor Johnny Depp successfully sued his ex-wife, Amber Heard, for defamation because she alleged that he had abused her. He won, even though he had admitted to some physical abuse, and there was written evidence of his threats to kill her. Will cases like this cause survivors to keep quiet about sexual harassment or other forms of violence against women? Is the verdict a sign, as one journalist wrote, that the #MeToo Movement is dying?[141] Is Susan Faludi right that "[u]sing celebrity and hashtag feminism is a perilous way to pursue women's advance because it falls victim so easily to its own tools and methods?"[142]

2.   *Sexual Harassment in Educational Institutions*

a.   School Liability for Sexual Harassment

Title IX of the Education Amendments of 1972 broadly prohibits sex discrimination by educational institutions that receive any federal funding.[143] Although it is most closely associated with gender equity in athletics, discussed in Chapter 2, Title IX also has substantial application to sexual harassment in educational settings. The Supreme Court has interpreted Title IX to prohibit both *quid pro quo* harassment and hostile environment harassment as forms of intentional sex discrimination and to permit lawsuits for money damages.[144] The standards of liability, however, are more favorable to educational institutions than to employers under Title VII. A pair of Supreme Court cases decided in the late 1990s set the liability standard for both teacher-student and student-to-student (peer) sexual harassment under Title IX.

The first of these, Gebser v. Lago Vista Independent School District, was brought by parents of a female student who sued the school district after police found that a teacher was having sex with their eighth-grade daughter.[145] By a 5-4 vote, the Court held that schools are not liable for harassment of a student by an employee unless officials had actual notice of the specific misconduct and responded with "deliberate indifference." The school's failure in that case to have a nondiscrimination policy and internal grievance procedure, both of which are required by Title IX's implementing regulations, was not sufficient to render it liable for the harassment. This sort of

---

141. Spencer Bokat-Lindell, Is the #MeToo Movement Dying?, N.Y. Times, June 8, 2022. See also Michelle Goldberg, Amber Heard and the Death of #MeToo, N.Y. Times, May 18, 2022.

142. Susan Faludi, Feminism Made a Faustian Bargain with Celebrity Culture. Now It's Paying the Price, N.Y. Times, June 20, 2022.

143. 20 U.S.C. § 1681 (2018).

144. See Franklin v. Gwinnett Cnty. Pub. Schs., 503 U.S. 60 (1992).

145. 524 U.S. 274 (1998).

violation, however, can trigger enforcement and penalties by the Department of Education's Office for Civil Rights, the agency charged with implementing Title IX.

In explaining the result in *Gebser*, Justice O'Connor's majority opinion reasoned that any stricter standard would be at odds with the overall compliance scheme of Title IX, which requires federal enforcement agencies to provide notice of any violation of nondiscrimination requirements before initiating enforcement actions. The "central purpose" of this notice is to "avoid diverting education funding from beneficial uses where a recipient was unaware of discrimination in its programs and is willing to institute prompt corrective measures." Justice Stevens' dissenting opinion countered that the Court's opinion creates incentives to avoid the knowledge that should trigger corrective action. According to some commentators, the liability standard in *Gebser* may encourage the see-no-evil/hear-no-evil attitudes already in place in many school districts. "When ignorance is bliss, and a defense to legal judgments, why should schools establish effective complaint strategies?"[146] To some, this double standard for educational and employment settings seems perverse. "Students often have fewer options for avoiding an abusive situation than an adult employee, their capacities for resistance are less developed, and their values are more open to influence. Schools are powerful socializing institutions and their failure to address harassment perpetuates the attitudes that perpetuate problems."[147] What is your view?

The following year, the Court addressed Title IX's applicability to sexual harassment by a fellow student. In Davis v. Monroe County Board of Education, a divided Supreme Court recognized for the first time that peer sexual harassment may support a Title IX case against the school, but set a high standard for liability.[148] There, a fifth-grade African-American female student alleged repeated acts of harassment by one of her male classmates, including verbal and physical assaults such as attempts to touch her genital area. Despite several complaints by the girl's mother to the teacher, principal, and, eventually, the school board, the school failed to take adequate remedial action. At one point, the principal responded dismissively to the girl's complaints, asking why she was the only one complaining. Even though the boy pled guilty to criminal sexual battery, the school took three months even to agree to change the girl's seat so she wouldn't have to sit next to him in every class. The majority in *Davis* held that a school district's "deliberate indifference to known acts of harassment" by students could give rise to liability, but only when the district "exercises substantial control over the harasser and the context in which the known harassment occurs" and the conduct is so "severe, pervasive, and objectively offensive that it can be said to deprive the victims of access to the educational opportunities or benefits provided by the school."[149] In assessing the adequacy of remedial responses, the majority continued, courts should not expect that administrators can entirely "purg[e] their schools of actionable peer harassment" and "should refrain from second-guessing [administrators'] disciplinary

---

146. Deborah L. Rhode, Sex in Schools: Who's Minding the Adults, in Directions in Sexual Harassment Law, supra note 17, at 290, 297.

147. Id.

148. 526 U.S. 629 (1999).

149. Id. at 633.

decisions."[150] The Court remanded the case, which ultimately settled for an undisclosed amount of damages.

Critics found *Davis* problematic on the same grounds as *Gebser*, in that it creates an incentive for educators to avoid knowledge that might subject them to legal accountability. Given the reluctance of students to complain to anyone, reporting requirements are said to create an unrealistic limitation on accountability where some school personnel have knowledge of a likely problem and fail to investigate or take reasonable remedial action. Indeed, expecting students to report harassment to the proper authorities may well exceed the capabilities of many young students and those experiencing the effects of trauma.[151] School officials have generally opposed stricter liability standards on the ground that they have limited control over abusive conduct, especially by students. While other employers can more easily dismiss workers who persist in harassment, administrators believe that they have fewer options in the face of recalcitrant students and teachers who have due process and contractual rights. Especially where facts are contested or ambiguous, officials feel "caught in the middle. . . . We weren't doing the harassing. We're the entity with the deep pockets."[152] How would you respond?

School officials may be liable under another civil rights law, Section 1983, which creates liability for deprivations of constitutional rights. In Fitzgerald v. Barnstable School Committee, the Supreme Court held that parents could sue school officials for sex discrimination that denies their equal protection rights under that statute when the school allegedly failed to respond to serious harassment of their daughter by another classmate.[153] However, it is not clear that this avenue provides an easier path for plaintiffs than proceeding under Title IX.

Has the Supreme Court struck the right balance between avoiding undue liability and providing incentives for schools to prevent or remedy harassment? How proactive should schools be? Is there a danger of overreaction? How should schools deal with online harassment?

Feminist Majority Foundation v. Hurley

911 F. 3d 674 (4th Cir. 2018)

KING, Circuit Judge.

Plaintiffs Feminist Majority Foundation, Feminists United on Campus, and several Feminists United members appeal from the district court's dismissal of their civil action, filed pursuant to Title IX of the Education Amendments of 1972, as well as 42 U.S.C. §1983. . . . The plaintiffs seek the reinstatement of three claims: a Title IX sex discrimination claim against the University of Mary Washington ("UMW,"

---

150. Id. at 648.

151. See Emily Suski, The Title IX Paradox, 108 Cal. L. Rev. 1147 (2020).

152. Guy W. Horsley, quoted in Robin Wilson, William and Mary Seeks to Shift Liability for Damages to Professor in Federal Sexual Harassment Case, Chron. of Higher Educ., June 9, 1995, at A20.

153. 555 U.S. 246 (2009).

or "the University"); a Title IX retaliation claim against UMW; and a §1983 claim against UMW's former president, Dr. Richard Hurley, for violating the Equal Protection Clause of the Fourteenth Amendment. . . . [W]e affirm the dismissal of the §1983 claim and part of the Title IX retaliation claim. We vacate, however, the dismissal of the Title IX sex discrimination claim and the balance of the retaliation claim. We . . . remand.

I

Plaintiff Feminists United is a student organization at UMW and a local affiliate of plaintiff Feminist Majority Foundation, a national organization. During the 2014-2015 academic year, plaintiffs Paige McKinsey, Julia Michels, Kelli Musick, Jordan Williams, and Alexis Lehman were UMW students who served on Feminists United's executive board.

In November 2014, UMW's student senate voted to authorize male-only fraternities at the University. During a campus town hall meeting following the senate's authorization, Feminists United members questioned the wisdom of having such fraternities at UMW, in light of "research that showed that Greek life on campus increased the number of [on-campus] sexual assaults." Plaintiff McKinsey was particularly troubled by the vote of approval, and she believed that UMW had failed to support victims of sexual assault in the past. Soon after the town hall meeting, UMW students debated the Greek life vote on Yik Yak, a now-defunct social media application. Yik Yak allowed its users within a limited geographic range to create and view anonymous messages known as "Yak." Within the Yik Yak conversational thread available at UMW, several students expressed—in offensive terms—strong criticism of Feminists United and its members for their opposition to on-campus fraternities.

On November 21, 2014, several Feminists United members met with UMW's Title IX coordinator, Dr. Leah Cox, to explain their concerns about the University's past failures in responding to student sexual assault complaints. As the Feminists United members walked home from the meeting, other UMW students drove by and screamed "Fuck the feminists!"

Two days later, on November 23, a UMW student videotaped members of the UMW men's rugby team performing a chant that glorified violence against women, including rape and necrophilia.[2] Later that month, the student who recorded the rugby team video provided it to the UMW administration and informed plaintiff McKinsey about the video. Members of Feminists United subsequently met with then-President Hurley to discuss the rugby team's offensive chant. They were assured by Hurley that some unspecified "action" was being taken in response thereto. . . .

On January 29, 2015, McKinsey published an opinion piece in UMW's student newspaper explaining "[w]hy UMW is not a feminist-friendly campus." . . . That

---

2. Necrophilia generally refers to sexual intercourse with, or attraction towards, dead bodies. The repulsive rugby team chant included the following: "Finally found a whore/she was right and dead/well God damn son of a bitch we're gonna get it in . . . Finally got it out/ it was red and sore/moral of the story is never fuck a whore."

article . . . was not well-received by some members of the UMW community and "led to an escalation of verbal assaults and cyber-attacks on members of Feminists United." For example, various comments of a "derogatory, sexist, and threatening" nature were posted to the school newspaper's website.

On February 20, 2015, members of the UMW men's rugby team approached plaintiff McKinsey in the University's dining hall and confronted her about the newspaper article. That same day, McKinsey informed Dr. Cox—UMW's Title IX coordinator—that McKinsey felt unsafe on the UMW campus after her encounter with the rugby team members, particularly in light of the threats lodged against her and other Feminists United members on Yik Yak and the school newspaper's website. McKinsey requested that the UMW administration take "some sort of action." . . .

[O]n February 24 . . . Cox offered . . . to schedule a mediated discussion between the men's rugby team and Feminists United. About that time, a UMW professor—concerned with the threatening nature of recent Yik Yak posts— emailed various Feminists United members to request their participation in what the professor called "listening circles." As proposed, UMW students, including Feminists United members, would meet with UMW faculty and administrators in small groups and explain how the offending Yaks were affecting them.

On March 11, 2015, UMW held an open forum about sexual assault on campus, at which President Hurley downplayed the seriousness of the rugby team's chant. Several days later, plaintiff Michels emailed Hurley and notified him that she planned to release a transcript of the rugby team's chant to UMW's student newspaper because the administration had not yet punished those responsible for it. Michels reiterated that Feminists United members felt unsafe on campus. In response, Hurley disclosed that some students had been sanctioned for their participation in the repulsive chanting and that those sanctions had been appealed. Hurley added that he took student safety concerns "quite seriously."

About a week after the open forum, President Hurley emailed the UMW student body, "generally discussing UMW's efforts to end sexual assault, violence against women, and other forms of discrimination and harassment." Without referencing the rugby team's chant or any other specific acts, Hurley described certain students' recent behavior as "repugnant and highly offensive." That same day, Hurley met with several Feminists United members, who questioned why Hurley's email . . . had not mentioned the rugby team's repulsive chant or the sanctions imposed on the students who had participated therein. Hurley responded that he was following his lawyer's advice and that "he would rather rely on the student grapevine to spread the word about what happened with the rugby team and why."

On March 19, 2015, after several UMW students expressed outrage on Facebook over the rugby team's chant, President Hurley announced that all rugby activities had been suspended indefinitely and that the rugby players would be required to participate in anti-sexual assault and violence training. Immediately after Hurley's announcement, a flurry of harassing and threatening Yaks were directed at members of Feminists United, blaming them for the rugby team's suspension. The Yaks named plaintiffs McKinsey and Musick, along with Feminists United member Grace Mann, and contained threats of physical and sexual violence. By way of example, the Yaks threatened:

- "Gonna tie these feminists to the radiator and [g]rape them in the mouth";
- "Dandy's about to kill a bitch . . . or two"; and
- "Can we euthanize whoever caused this bullshit?"

Several of the offending Yaks . . . also referred to Feminists United members by such terms as "femicunts, feminazis, cunts, bitches, hoes, and dikes."

In addition to naming plaintiff McKinsey, some of the offending Yaks shared her whereabouts so that she could personally be confronted. After McKinsey agreed to speak at the March 24, 2015 meeting of UMW's Young Democrats Club, an anonymous poster shared McKinsey's schedule and outlined a plan to accost her at that meeting. [McKinsey again sought assistance from UMW administrators.] The campus police believed the threat serious enough to assign an officer to the Feminists United and Young Democrats meetings that evening.

On March 25, plaintiff Michels sent an email to President Hurley, Dr. Cox, and UMW's vice president, Douglas Searcy. The email explained that Feminists United members had documented "nearly 200 examples of students using Yik Yak to post either violent, vitriolic hate or threats against [them]," and that they feared for their safety on the UMW campus. [At a subsequent meeting], members . . . requested that the UMW administration take a number of steps. Those requests included: (1) contacting Yik Yak to have the Yik Yak application disabled on UMW's campus; (2) barring access to Yik Yak on UMW's wireless network; (3) communicating "more transparent[ly]" with students; (4) announcing to UMW's student body that Feminists United "had no role in . . . UMW's decision [to suspend rugby activities]"; and (5) hosting an "assembly to explain rape culture and discuss harassment, cyber bullying[,] and social media issues."

Rather than grant the requests . . . Dr. Cox sent a schoolwide email on March 27, . . . [that] asserted that the University had "no recourse for . . . cyberbullying." Instead, she encouraged UMW students to report any threatening online comments to Yik Yak and other platforms where such comments were made.

[Plaintiffs expressed disappointment with the response and, on March 30,] emailed President Hurley that UMW's hands-off response to the offending Yaks had contravened . . . Title IX. By that time, more than 700 harassing and threatening Yaks had been directed at Feminists United and its members. . . . [One emailer informed Hurley that she felt] "so unsafe . . . that she could not concentrate on her classwork." . . .

[In further exchange after a Feminists United march on the UMW campus and discussions between its members and President Hurley,] Hurley responded that he had discussed the option of banning Yik Yak with "several experts" and was concerned about violating the First Amendment.

Two listening circles were held at which plaintiffs stressed the danger they felt on campus but UMW administrators took no further action. A UMW professor recommended that the University provide "better training" and engage in "more transparency and communication at all levels." Dr. Cox responded, however, that "such solutions would violate privacy rights," and she otherwise failed to offer any plan to address the harassment and threats. . . .

On April 17, 2015 — in an event later determined to be unrelated to the offending Yaks — UMW student and Feminists United member Grace Mann was killed by another student who was her roommate. During the immediate aftermath of that terrible event, Feminists United members were unaware that it had no apparent connection to the harassing and threatening Yaks. Mann's demise prompted one Feminists United member to send an email to UMW administrators chastising the University for its failure to respond to the Yik Yak bullying and threats. UMW administrators did not respond to that email.

On May 7, 2015, the plaintiffs filed a complaint with the Department of Education's Office of Civil Rights (the "OCR complaint"), alleging that UMW had contravened Title IX by failing to address the hostile environment at the University resulting from the sexually harassing and threatening posts. That same day, UMW issued a statement denying the allegations . . . After the University's denials, several messages were posted on Yik Yak that again harassed Feminists United members, and also criticized the filing of the OCR complaint.

A month later, on June 8, President Hurley wrote to the president of the Feminist Majority Foundation . . . . Hurley's letter falsely asserted that the OCR complaint drew a connection between Grace Mann's death and the threatening media posts. Hurley also inaccurately claimed that neither UMW nor its campus police had received any reports of Yik Yak threats directed at Feminists United members. Additionally, Hurley suggested that the safety concerns of Feminists United members were exaggerated because some of the online threats simply derived from "pop culture."

In the wake of President Hurley's June 2015 letter, additional harassing and threatening messages were directed at Feminists United members on Yik Yak. [Such Yaks continued . . . throughout the summer of 2015.] According to the Complaint, "[t]he new posts expressed a sense of validation regarding the earlier posts along with a newfound sense of outrage toward Feminists United for filing their OCR [c]omplaint. The plaintiffs thereafter amended the OCR complaint to allege retaliatory conduct by UMW.

In May 2017, the plaintiffs withdrew the OCR complaint and initiated this lawsuit . . . .

[UMW does not dispute that] (1) UMW receives federal funds; (2) many of the harassing and threatening Yaks targeted the plaintiffs . . . on the basis of sex; and (3) those Yaks, along with only online posts and in-person interactions, created a hostile and abusive environment. But UMW maintained . . . — and the district court agreed — that [the claim] lacks a basis for imputing liability to UMW.

The district court explained that the sexual harassment endured by [plaintiffs] "took place in a context over which UMW had limited, if any, control.". . .

III . . .

[W]e remain mindful that the Supreme Court's Davis [v. Monroe County Board of Education] decision limits an education institution's Title IX liability for student-on-student sexual harassment to those situations where the defendant institution "exercises substantial control over both the harasser and the context in which the known harassment occurs." . . .

Although [the harassment] occurred through Yik Yak, the Complaint shows that UMW had substantial control over the context of the harassment because it actually transpired on campus. Specifically, due to Yik Yak's location-based feature, the harassing and threatening messages originated on or within the immediate vicinity of the UMW campus. In addition, some of the offending Yaks were posted using the University's wireless network, and the harassers necessarily created those Yaks on campus. Moreover, the harassment concerned events occurring on campus and specifically targeted UMW students. *See Davis*, 526 U.S. at 646 ("Where . . . the misconduct occurs during school hours and on school grounds[,] . . . the [educational institution] retains substantial control over the context in which the harassment occurs."

Furthermore, to the extent the sexual harassment was communicated through UMW's wireless network, the Complaint alleges that the University could have disabled access to Yik Yak campuswide. The Complaint also alleges that the University could have sought to identify those students using UMW's network to harass and threaten Feminists United members. If the University had pinpointed the harassers, it could then have circumscribed their use of UMW's network. Indeed, it is widely known that a university can control activities that occur on its own network. . . .

[In addition,] UMW administrators could have more clearly communicated to the student body that the University would not tolerate sexually harassing behavior either in person or online. The University also could have conducted mandatory assemblies to explain and discourage cyber bullying and sex discrimination, and it could have provided anti-sexual harassment training to the entire student body and faculty. . . .

The substantial control analysis [under *Davis*, 526 U.S. at 647] also requires us to consider the educational institution's control over the harasser, especially its "disciplinary authority." Under the Complaint, UMW had the ability to punish those students who posted sexually harassing and threatening messages online. Indeed, the Complaint recounts that UMW had previously disciplined students—members of the men's rugby team—for derogatory off-campus speech. . . .

The University cannot escape liability based on facially anonymous posts when . . . UMW never sought to discern whether it could identify the harassers. . . .

At bottom, in assessing whether UMW . . . had sufficient control over the harassers and the context of the harassment, we cannot conclude that UMW could turn a blind eye to the sexual harassment that pervaded and disrupted its campus solely because the offending conduct took place through cyberspace. . . .

[T]he Complaint [also] demonstrates that—although UMW was not entirely unresponsive to allegations of harassment—the University did not engage in efforts that were "reasonably calculated to end [the] harassment." . . .

On the allegations of the complaint, we are satisfied that the plaintiffs sufficiently allege that UMW exhibited deliberate indifference to known instances of sexual harassment. . . . UMW's decision to have a campus police officer at two student meetings was a short-term countermeasure—a one-off—that failed to address the more than six-month harassment campaign directed at Feminists United and its members . . . [v]iewed in the proper light, UMW's position is undermined by the fact that its campus environment was such that a police officer's presence was necessary at two student meetings.

As for the listening circles, we agree that university administrators listening to students' reports of harassment and threats is an important step in seeking to rectify a sexually hostile environment. But the mere act of listening to students is not a remedy in and of itself. Significantly, after the Feminists United members placed the UMW administration on notice of the hostile environment permeating the campus, the university made no real effort to investigate or end the harassment and threats contained in the Yaks. . . .

First Amendment concerns do not render the University's response to the sexual harassment and threats legally sufficient for two sound reasons: (1) true threats are not protected speech, and (2) the University had several responsive options that did not present First Amendment concerns. . . .

The Supreme Court and our Court have consistently recognized the principle that threatening speech is not protected by the Constitution . . .

Moreover, although the student culprits in these proceedings made their threats through an anonymous messaging application, the anonymity of the threats does not excuse UMW's deficient response. We are satisfied that the University was obliged to investigate and seek to identify those students who posted the threats and to report the threats to appropriate law enforcement agencies. . . .

Furthermore, . . . the University could have more vigorously denounced the harassing and threatening conduct, clarified that Feminists United members were not responsible for the rugby team's suspension, conducted a mandatory assembly of the student body to discuss and discourage such harassment through social media, or hired an outside expert to assist in developing policies for addressing and preventing harassment. Additionally, UMW could have offered counseling services for those impacted by the targeted harassment. To be sure, Title IX required none of those specific actions. Consideration of an educational institution's remedial options, however, inheres in the deliberate indifference analysis. In other words, when an education institution claims that it has done all it can to address instances of sexual harassment and threats, a reviewing court should consider whether the institution failed to take other obvious and reasonable steps.

At bottom, we are satisfied that the plaintiffs have sufficiently alleged a sex discrimination claim under Title IX, predicated on UMW's deliberate indifference to the specified student-on-student harassment. We will therefore vacate the dismissal of that claim. . . .

[On the retaliation claim, the Court holds that "if an education institution can be liable for student-on-student sexual harassment, it can also be liable for student-on-student retaliatory harassment." It concludes "that the district court erred in dismissing the retaliation claim insofar as it is predicated on UMW's deliberate indifference to student-on-student retaliatory harassment," but it upholds the dismissal of that part of the retaliation claim that is predicated on President Hurley's June 2015 letter, insofar as "an educational institution and its administrators are entitled to defend against accusations of discrimination."]

[The Court upholds the dismissal of the Equal Protection claim on the grounds that President Hurley is entitled to qualified immunity for his acts because the equal protection right to be free from a university administrator's deliberate indifference to student-on-student sexual harassment was not clearly enough established by either controlling authority or by a robust consensus of persuasive authority.]

NOTES

1. **The Problem.**   Decades after the Court recognized sexual harassment as a form of sex discrimination under Title IX, it remains prevalent. A 2011 survey

of students in grades 7-12 found that harassment is "part of everyday life."[154] The survey found that 56 percent of girls and 40 percent of boys in these grades are sexually harassed during a given school year, with girls more likely to be harassed more than once. Boys describe being called gay as the worst type of harassment, while girls respond that unwelcome sexual comments, jokes, or gestures are the most troubling and online sexual rumors the second most troubling. Physical harassment is also widespread. More than one in five girls ages 14 to 18 has been kissed or touched without her consent (21 percent), a figure that is higher for Latina girls (24 percent), Native American girls (23 percent), and Black girls (22 percent), and highest for girls who identify as LGBTQ (38 percent).[155] While harassment occurs most often by other students, it is all too common by teachers and other adults in schools. An estimated 10 percent of K-12 students are subjected to sexual misconduct by a school employee.[156]

Sexual harassment is also prevalent at the college level. A 2019 survey found that 42 percent of college students reported having experienced sexual harassment on campus.[157] Such conduct can include sexual comments, rumors, grabbing, propositions, and in the extreme, sexual assault and rape. (Campus sexual assault and Title IX is covered in more detail in Chapter 5, Section A) At all levels of schooling, sexual harassment rates tend to be higher for students of color, LGBTQ+ students, disabled students, and pregnant or parenting students.[158]

The impact of harassment on students includes a variety of physical, emotional, and educational consequences, including, most frequently, a desire not to go to school. Women are more likely than men to be adversely affected by sexual harassment—a finding that may reflect differences in the types of harassment men and women are likely to experience.[159] The adverse effects can lead to emotional and social difficulties at school that register as disciplinary problems, leading to punitive responses by school officials that compound the harm.

Despite the negative effects of harassment, the most common response by students is to do nothing and try to ignore it. Only 2 percent of girls who are harassed or assaulted in school told a school principal or administrator.[160] It can be particularly difficult for girls with intersecting identities to decide whether to complain and to whom because they are more vulnerable to doubt and systemic bias. For example, Black girls

154. See Am. Ass'n of Univ. Women, Crossing the Line: Sexual Harassment at School (2011).

155. Nat'l Women's L. Ctr., Let Her Learn: Stopping School Pushout for Girls Who Have Suffered Harassment and Sexual Violence 3 (2017).

156. Billie-Jo Grant et al., Nat'l Crim. Just. Reference Serv., A Case Study of K-12 School Employee Sexual Misconduct: Lessons Learned from Title IX Policy Implementation (Dec. 2017).

157. David Cantor et al., Report on the AAU Campus Climate Survey on Sexual Assault and Sexual Misconduct 79 (Jan. 17, 2020).

158. Nat'l Coal. for Women and Girls in Educ., Title IX at 50, at 10 (June 2022).

159. Am. Ass'n of Univ. Women, Drawing the Line: Sexual Harassment on Campus (2005) (men are more likely to be verbally harassed with homophobic name-calling, for example).

160. Id. at 2.

may feel pressure not to report Black boys, who are at higher risk than white boys of ending up in the school-to-prison pipeline, and may fear rejection by their communities if they choose to report.[161] The risk of not being believed or being blamed for what happened after reporting sexual harassment is also of particular concern for girls of color.[162]

2. **Legal Issues Under *Gebser* and *Davis*.**   Four key issues arise in Title IX lawsuits alleging sexual harassment of students by teachers or other students. First, who in the school's chain of command must receive "actual notice" of the harassment? It depends on who has authority to respond to the problem. For harassment by students, some courts have said notice to a teacher is sufficient given that teachers have the authority to discipline students.[163] Notice to a principal or other administrator almost certainly suffices.[164] For harassment by teachers, the notice must reach higher in the chain. Knowledge by other teachers has been held insufficient, and even notice to department chairs and other mid-level administrators may be insufficient.[165] Second, what kind of notice must be provided? Some courts require that the official have actual knowledge of the harassment of the complaining victim, while others say that knowledge of previous victims or other incidents can be enough.[166] Third, did the school respond to actual knowledge of the harassment with deliberate indifference? This standard is very hard for plaintiffs to meet unless school officials did absolutely nothing.[167] Not all courts are so draconian, though; some, like the court in *Hurley*, have found the standard met when some responsive action—albeit inadequate—was taken.[168] Fourth, was the harassment so severe and pervasive that it effectively deprived the students of access to education? This, too, can set a high bar, demanding tangible proof of harm such as lower grades, greater absenteeism, physical injury that prevents schooling, or other educational difficulties.[169] Courts' interpretation of this prong is a rejection of the rule in employment cases under Harris v. Forklift Systems that harassment can be

---

161. Id. at 4.

162. See Sonja C. Tonnensen, "Hit It and Quit It": Responses to Black Girls' Victimization in School, 28 Berkeley J. Gender L. & Just. 1 (2013).

163. See, e.g., Murrell v. School Dist. No. 1, 186 F.3d 1238 (10th Cir. 1999).

164. See, e.g., S.K. v. North Allegheny School Dist., No. 2:14cv1156, 2016 WL 806483 (W.D. Pa. Mar. 2, 2016).

165. See, e.g., Miller v. Kentosh, No. 97-6541, 1998 U.S. Dist. LEXIS 9497 (E.D. Pa. June 29, 1998).

166. See, e.g., Doe v. Blackburn Coll., No. 06-3205, 2012 U.S. Dist. LEXIS 24797, at *23-25 (C.D. Ill. Feb. 27, 2012) (no liability where college had no notice of prior harassment of plaintiff).

167. See Emily Suski, Subverting Title IX, 105 Minn. L. Rev. 2259, 2268-78 (2021) (collecting cases and arguing that courts set a particularly high bar for deliberate indifference in the K-12 cases).

168. See, e.g., Doe v. Brown Univ., 304 F. Supp.3d 252 (D. R.I. 2018) (although Brown's response was "far from perfunctory," summary judgment denied where its investigation was "bungled" and "carried out so inartfully as to render it clearly unreasonable"); S.K. v. North Allegheny Sch. Dist., 168 F. Supp.3d 786 (W.D. Pa. 2016).

169. See, e.g., Gabrielle M. v. Park Forest-Chicago Heights, 315 F.3d 817, 822-23 (7th Cir. 2003); Burwell v. Pekin Cmty. High Sch., 213 F. Supp. 2d 917 (C.D. Ill. 2002).

actionable regardless of whether it caused severe psychological injury or other tangible harm.[170] In addition, plaintiffs must overcome the usual hurdles in harassment litigation such as proving that the conduct was unwelcome, because of sex, and sufficiently severe or pervasive.[171]

Recently, some courts have gone further and required proof that the school's deliberately indifferent response to the harassment subjected the plaintiff to additional harassment.[172] Their rationale is that Title IX holds institutions liable for "subjecting" students to peer sexual harassment, which occurs only when the school's response to prior harassment "caused" more harassment to occur. Other courts have rejected such a requirement, on the theory that a deliberately indifferent response to prior known harassment subjects the plaintiff to a hostile environment and makes future harassment more likely (whether or not it actually occurred).[173] The split stems from the Court's language in *Davis* stating, "deliberate indifference must, at a minimum, cause students to undergo harassment or make them liable or vulnerable to it."[174] Does this mean schools are immune from liability for deliberate indifference to known harassment as long as the plaintiff is not sexually harassed again by the same harasser? Is there another way to understand the Court's language? Short of repeated harassment, how might a school's response make a harassment victim "vulnerable" to harassment? Might the school's indifference to sexual harassment itself be a form of sex discrimination?[175] How so, absent proof that the school would respond any better to a sexually harassed student of the other sex? Does nonsubordination theory help in developing a response to this question?

One issue that has received relatively little attention in the case law is whether educational institutions can be held liable under Title IX for an inadequate response to peer retaliation against a student who alleges sexual assault by another student. The court in *Hurley* answered this question in the affirmative.[176] What obligations should Title IX place on schools to respond to known peer retaliation by students, and how can schools fulfill such obligations without suppressing student speech?

3. **Administrative Versus Judicial Enforcement.**   *Gebser* and *Davis* set forth the standards for institutional liability for sexual harassment in schools when victims seek money damages in court. As noted at the beginning of this section, however, educational institutions covered by Title IX are independently subject to enforcement by the Department of Education's Office for Civil Rights (OCR). OCR has

---

170. See Harris v. Forklift Sys., Inc., 510 U.S. 17 (1993).

171. See, e.g., Morgan v. Town of Lexington, No. 14-13781-DJC, 2015 WL 5634463 (D. Mass. Sept. 30, 2015); Hankey v. Town of Concord-Carlisle, 136 F. Supp. 3d 52 (D. Mass. 2015).

172. See, e.g., Kollaritsch v. Mich. State Univ. Bd. of Trs., 944 F.3d 613 (6th Cir. 2019).

173. See Farmer v. Kan. State Univ. 918 F.3d 1094 (10th Cir. 2019).

174. 526 U.S. 629, 645 (1999).

175. See Emily Suski, Institutional Betrayals as Sex Discrimination, 107 Iowa L. Rev. 1685 (2022).

176. See also Niesen v. Iowa State Univ., No. 4:17-cv-201-RAW, 2017 U.S. Dist. LEXIS 221061 (S.D. Iowa Nov. 3, 2017).

broad authority to punish schools for noncompliance, up to and including the termination of federal funding. Soon after *Gebser* and *Davis* were decided, OCR clarified, through a series of policy guidances known as "dear colleague" letters, that it applies a stricter standard than courts to determine schools' compliance with Title IX.[177] In its 2001 Revised Sexual Harassment Guidance, OCR explained that it holds recipients to a standard of actual or constructive notice and requires a more robust response to harassment than merely avoiding deliberate indifference. If a school knows or should have known about a hostile environment and "fails to take prompt and effective corrective action," it has "violated Title IX even if the student failed to use the school's existing grievance procedures or otherwise inform the school of the harassment."[178] During the Trump administration, however, the Department of Education issued new Title IX regulations on sexual harassment that jettisoned this and many other longstanding OCR interpretations.[179] The new regulations require OCR to use the same standard in its administrative enforcement actions as used by courts in damages actions: actual notice and deliberate indifference. The regulations also impose the high threshold courts use for finding harassment in violation of Title IX — that it is severe, pervasive, objectively offensive, and effectively deprives the student of equal access to education — and lift the obligation on schools to respond to off-campus harassment, unless connected to an educational program or activity. Would it change the result in *Hurley* if the court had applied this rule?

Because the regulations are a product of the formal rulemaking process, they are more difficult to change than an agency interpretation such as a "dear colleague" letter. The Biden administration has issued a Notice of Proposed Rulemaking that would rescind these new requirements and replace them with regulations restoring OCR's prior standards.[180] As this book goes to press, the administrative process is still ongoing. (Additional discussion of these regulatory changes and their application to campus sexual assault is taken up in Chapter 5, Section A.)

b. Speech and Conduct Codes to Prevent Harassment

One approach to addressing sexual and racial harassment in educational institutions, especially at the college and university level, has been speech codes that prohibit "verbal conduct" or "expression" that interferes with a student's educational environment. Some proposals relate specifically to online harassment and social media. These codes have drawn fierce criticism from conservative free speech advocates who consider them censorship and urge that the remedy for hurtful

---

177. See Off. for Civ. Rts, Dep't of Educ., Revised Sexual Harassment Guidance: Harassment of Students by School Employees, Other Students, or Third Parties 19, at iv (Jan. 2001).
178. Id. at 13-14.
179. Dept. of Educ., 34 C.F.R. § 106, Nondiscrimination on the Basis of Sex in Education Programs or Activities Receiving Federal Financial Assistance; Final Rule, 85 Fed. Reg. 30026 (May 19, 2020).
180. Dept. of Educ., 34 C.F.R. § 106, Nondiscrimination on the Basis of Sex in Education Programs or Activities Receiving Federal Financial Assistance; Notice of Proposed Rulemaking, 87 Fed. Reg. 41390 (July 12, 2022).

speech is more speech. By contrast, advocates of such restrictions argue that in a sexist, racist society, "free speech" is available only to those with the power to use it. They contend that racist and sexist speech prevents some students from learning and participating fully in university life.[181]

The tension between schools' interests in preventing harassment and protecting expression has provoked increasing disputes, but no Supreme Court decision. Conservative groups such as Speech First and FIRE (Foundation for Individual Rights in Education) have launched targeted campaigns against what they call "woke" culture and political correctness on campus. Speech codes generally have not fared well in First Amendment challenges.[182] For example, a federal district court in Texas recently granted a preliminary injunction enjoining a university's anti-discrimination policy disciplining students who "subject an individual on the basis of their membership in a protected class to unlawful severe, pervasive, or persistent treatment," defined to include behavior that "is humiliating, abusive, or threatening and denigrates or shows hostility or aversion towards an individual or group."[183] The court cited the "chilling effect" of self-censorship and noted that the policy did not comport with the standard for harassment adopted in *Davis*. When anti-harassment policies have been enforced against professors for conduct in the classroom, courts have been particularly protective of First Amendment concerns.[184] The First Amendment does not prevent schools from maintaining anti-harassment policies altogether, but they must be narrowly drawn.[185] Explicitly sexual or lewd statements, for example, are not protected speech within an educational environment, at least in the K-12 setting.[186] Schools may also defend such policies and their enforcement under the standard in Tinker v. Des Moines Independent School District if the speech might "substantially interfere with the work of the school or impinge upon the rights of other students."[187] Even universities may

---

181. For classic works debating the merits of such policies, compare Nadine Strossen, Defending Pornography: Free Speech, Sex, and the Fight for Women's Rights (1995) with Mari J. Matsuda et al., Words That Wound: Critical Race Theory, Assaultive Speech, and the First Amendment (1993). For more recent consideration of these arguments, see Jamal Greene, Constitutional Moral Hazard and Campus Speech, 61 Wm. & Mary L. Rev. 223 (2019).

182. See, e.g., Saxe v. State Coll. Area School Dist., 240 F.3d 200 (3d Cir. 2001).

183. Speech First, Inc. v. Renu Khator, No. H-22-582, 2022 WL 1638773 (S.D. Tex. May 19, 2022).

184. See, e.g., Cohen v. San Bernardino Valley College, 92 F.3d 968 (9th Cir. 1996); Silva v. Univ. of New Hampshire, 888 F. Supp. 293 (D.N.H. 1994).

185. For cases striking down university anti-harassment policies under the First Amendment, see McCauley v. Univ. of the Virgin Islands, 618 F.3d 232 (3d Cir. 2010); DeJohn v. Temple Univ., 537 F.3d 301 (3d Cir. 2008); College Republicans at San Francisco State Univ. v. Reed, 523 F. Supp. 2d 1005 (N.D. Cal. 2007); Bair v. Shippensburg Univ., 280 F. Supp.2d 357 (M.D. Pa. 2003); Booher v. Bd. of Regents, No. 2:96-CV-135, 1998 U.S. Dist. LEXIS 11404 (E.D. Ky. Jul. 21, 1998).

186. See Bethel Sch. Dist. v. Fraser, 478 U.S. 675 (1986) (upholding school's right to discipline student for making sexually explicit speech at school function).

187. 393 U.S. 503, 509 (1969); see also West v. Derby Unified Sch. Dist., 206 F.3d 1358 (10th Cir. 2000); Zamecnik v. Indian Prairie Sch. Dist., 636 F.3d 874 (7th Cir. 2011).

be able to justify speech-restrictive anti-harassment policies under strict scrutiny because of the compelling interest in preventing discrimination. Still, the trend has been unfavorable for campus policies that extend beyond the limits of what sexual harassment law proscribes.

The law has developed in Canada in a direction more supportive of speech codes. There, the Supreme Court of Canada upheld a statute penalizing the communication of statements that willfully promote hatred against any identifiable racial, religious, or ethnic group, as applied to a high school teacher who expressed anti-Semitic views, including the belief that the Holocaust was a myth.[188]

How should academic institutions deal with offensive and harassing speech? How should hateful or threatening posts on social media be handled? Does *Hurley* subject universities to liability for not monitoring and reacting to harassing speech? Are strategies other than prohibitions preferable, such as student protests, negative course evaluations, and open forums?

c.   Faculty-Student Relationships

Faculty-student dating has been another subject of campus concern. The limited available data suggest such relationships are not uncommon. The conventional assumption has been that broad prohibitions are unnecessary, unenforceable, or unduly paternalistic. As one commentator put it:

> Being sexually propositioned . . . is a normal and healthy part of life. (The real psychological and emotional tragedy probably befalls those who are not.) . . . It is hardly self evident that the "power imbalance" in such [relationships] favors the teacher. . . . If matters turn out badly, his career is finished.[189]

Feminist literary critic Jane Gallop acknowledges that women are at a "disadvantage" in a faculty-student relationship but argues that "denying women the right to consent further infantilizes us."[190]

Compare Robin West's analysis:

> Smart male students view themselves as all sorts of things, including young intellectuals. A good male student will often attach himself to a brilliant professor, and will aspire to *be like* him. . . . Unlike the male student, [the good female student] is more likely to be attracted to the brilliant professor, and aspire not to be like him, but to give herself *to* him. . . .
>
> "Falling-in-love" with high school teachers, college professors, or research assistants really does destroy the productivity, the careers, the earning potential, and eventually the self-respect of many gifted women.

---

188. See Regina v. Keegstra, 3 S.C.R. 697 (S.C.C. 1990).

189. Edward Greer, What's Wrong with Faculty-Student Sex? Response I, 47 J. Legal Educ. 437, 438 (1997).

190. Jane Gallop, Sex and Sexism: Feminism and Harassment Policy, 80 Academe 16, 22 (Sept.-Oct. 1994); see also Sherry Young, Getting to Yes: The Case Against Banning Consensual Relationships in Higher Education, 4 Am. U. J. Gender & L. 269, 298, 302 (1996).

> Smart women drop out of high school, college and graduate school (and pretty women are at the highest risk) to date, to marry, to help, and to serve those they perceive as intellectual giants. Eventually they learn boredom, the weariness of inactivity, and the self-contempt of nonproductivity.[191]

Students' own accounts of sexual overtures by faculty echo these concerns. In one study, almost three-quarters of those surveyed who rejected a professor's advances considered them coercive and about half of those who had sexual relationships believed that some degree of coercion was involved.[192] Except in egregious cases, however, few students file complaints, and few institutions impose serious sanctions. One analysis of all publicly reported faculty-student harassment cases found that over half involve professors who allegedly engaged in serial harassment.[193] The same study found graduate students particularly vulnerable to sexual overtures by faculty—three times as much as undergraduates—with a high cost to their studies and careers.[194] Even if some relationships between students and faculty are fully consensual, does the lack of a prohibitive policy give too much space for faculty overtures to gauge a student's interest?

Another consideration is the effect of such relationships on other students. In a recent opinion piece, Amia Srinivasan, a professor of social and political theory, argues that too much emphasis has been placed on the power dynamics between professors and students in these debates, and not enough on the effect on the educational environment for other students.[195] She argues that teaching and learning are compromised when professors have sex with students, even if the relationship is consensual and not oppressive. What is your view?

A growing number of institutions have adopted policies banning or discouraging faculty-student relationships and the vast majority now have some restrictive policy.[196] The trend is toward tightening up university policies on faculty-student consensual relationships to make them more restrictive.[197] In the past decade, many schools have moved to a flat-out ban on sexual relationships between professors and students, replacing previous policies that had set limits based on whether the professor had supervisory responsibility over the student.[198] What kind of policy would you recommend for your own school?

---

191. Robin L. West, The Difference in Women's Hedonic Lives: A Phenomenological Critique of Feminist Legal Theory, 3 Wis. Women's L.J. 81, 109-11 (1987).

192. See surveys discussed in Caroline Forrell, What's Wrong with Faculty-Student Sex? The Law School Context, 47 J. Legal Educ. 47 (1997).

193. Nancy Chi Cantalupo & William C. Kidder, A Systemic Look at a Serial Problem: Sexual Harassment of Students by University Faculty, 2018 Utah L. Rev. 671 (2018).

194. Id. at 674-75.

195. Amia Srinivasan, The Right to Sex: Feminism in the Twenty-First Century (2021).

196. Srinivasan, supra note 195 (citing 2014 study finding that 84 percent of universities surveyed had some policy restricting or banning such relationships).

197. See Tara N. Richards & Alyssa Nystrom, Examining Faculty-to-Student Consensual Sexual Relationship Policies on Campus: Have There Been Changes in the Era of #MeToo?, 37 J. Interpersonal Violence 1835 (2022).

198. Srinivasan, supra note 195.

PUTTING THEORY INTO PRACTICE

3-10. Administrators at a middle school sent a notice to parents announcing that female students would no longer be allowed to wear shorts, leggings, or yoga pants because those types of clothing might be "too distracting" for their male peers. Many students and parents complained in a letter sent to the school saying, "this kind of message lands itself squarely on a continuum that blames girls and women for assault by men. It also sends the message to boys that their behaviors are excusable, understandable given what the girls are wearing. We really hope that you will consider the impact of these policies and how they contribute to rape culture."[199] If the school refuses to change the policy and later receives an uptick of complaints about boys sexually harassing girls at the school, is the dress code policy relevant to a Title IX lawsuit for sexual harassment? Should it be?

3-11. A faculty member was disciplined under his college's harassment policy for refusing to refer to a transgender student in his class by the student's preferred pronouns. The student filed a complaint, claiming that the professor's misgendering created a hostile environment based on gender identity, a form of sex-based harassment. The college found that the professor's classroom conduct violated its policy prohibiting "knowingly disparaging members of the university community based on the individual's sex, race, ethnicity, sexual orientation or gender identity." If the professor challenges the discipline as a violation of his First Amendment rights and academic freedom, who should win? What if the professor had sought, but was denied, a religious exemption from the policy on the grounds that it violated his religious beliefs?[200]

3-12. A male university professor is fired for having what both parties agree was a consensual relationship with a female undergraduate, in violation of the university's policy on faculty-student relationships. The professor sues the university, alleging sex discrimination against him under Title IX. Because his relationship with the student was consensual, he claims, "the university exhibited gender bias because the infantilization of women plays into archaic gender stereotypes about women as chaste, sexually innocent, naïve, lacking sexual autonomy, and needing protection from men, who are considered the sexual aggressors." The university's policy is gender-neutral, not dependent on the sex of the either the student or the faculty member. However, the discussions and debates when it was adopted all focused on the problematic power imbalance of male faculty members having sex with female students. How should the court decide the case? Are his concerns valid even if not actionable?[201]

---

199. Tara Culp-Ressler, Middle School Girls Protest Sexist Dress Code: "Are My Pants Lowering Your Test Scores?", Think Progress (Mar. 25, 2014).

200. Adapted from Meriwether v. Hartop, 992 F.3d 492 (6th Cir. 2021); for analysis of related cases, see Chan Tov McNamarah, Some Notes on Courts and Courtesy, 107 Va. L. Rev. Online 317 (Dec. 2021).

201. See Verdu v. Trustees of Princeton Univ., No. 19-12484, 2020 WL 1502849 (D. N.J. Mar. 30, 2020).

C. DOMESTIC VIOLENCE

1. Domestic and Intimate Partner Violence: The Problem and Legal Responses

According to William Blackstone, the husband at English common law was legally entitled to use some physical force to provide his wife with "moderate correction."[202] So, too, under early American common law, a husband, as master of his household, could subject his wife to "chastisement" short of permanent physical injury.[203] By the end of the Civil War, partly through efforts by early feminists, the American legal system had repudiated the doctrine of chastisement. However, during the Reconstruction Era, a new body of common law emerged under which judges concluded that "the legal system should not interfere in cases of wife beating, in order to protect the privacy of the marriage relationship and to promote domestic harmony."[204]

By the end of the nineteenth century, wife beating was viewed as a crime, but increasingly characterized as solely the practice of drunkards, or "lawless or unruly men of the 'dangerous classes,'" particularly African-American men and men from low-status immigrant ethnic groups such as Germans and Irish Americans.[205] Domestic violence among the economically and racially privileged classes disappeared from public view.[206] By the 1920s, the victims of wife beating and child abuse had been transferred from "protection societies," which sought to provide women and children a safe haven from abusive men, to "child welfare agencies," which attempted to regulate domestic life more broadly. In the process, women were increasingly seen as part of the problem and "domestic trouble cases" often became an occasion to help wives "master the habits of cleanliness, nutrition, and child care."[207] The goal of the new family court system was to keep the family intact; accordingly, judges encouraged battered women to accept responsibility for their role in provoking the violence and discouraged them from filing criminal charges. Those views, and the perception of domestic violence as a private matter, lasted well into the 1970s.

---

202. William Blackstone, Commentaries on the Laws of England Book I: The Rights of Persons 432-33 (David Lemmings ed., 2016).

203. Reva B. Siegel, "The Rule of Love": Wife Beating as Prerogative and Privacy, 105 Yale L.J. 2117, 2118 (1996).

204. Id. at 2120.

205. Id. at 2137-39. For the temperance movement's link of wife abuse and alcohol abuse, see Carolyn B. Ramsey, The Stereotyped Offender: Domestic Violence and the Failure of Intervention, 120 Penn St. L. Rev. 337, 349-53 (2015).

206. Siegel, supra note 203, at 2137-39.

207. Evan Stark, Re-Presenting Woman Battering: From Battered Woman Syndrome to Coercive Control, 58 Alb. L. Rev. 973, 992-93 (1995). For further historical accounts of violence against women in Anglo-American social life and efforts to control it, see Linda Gordon, Heroes of Their Own Lives: The Politics and History of Family Violence: Boston 1880-1960 (1988); Elizabeth Pleck, Domestic Tyranny: The Making of Social Policy Against Family Violence from Colonial Times to the Present (1987).

Beginning in the 1960s, the women's movement sought to make "private" violence a public issue. Activists created shelters to protect the health and safety of battered women and children, and undertook public education campaigns to call attention to male violence and state inaction. During this same period, legal advocates initiated efforts to change how law enforcement officials responded to cases of intimate abuse.

As the legal landscape has changed, so has the language used to describe it. Women's rights advocates initially introduced the term "domestic violence" to replace more colloquial terms such as "wife beating." Domestic violence (DV) is a term used to describe violence between people who live in the same household. Intimate partner violence (IPV) is a more recent term, and the preferred term, to describe violence that occurs between romantic partners whether or not they live together. Descriptions of all forms of IVF also have evolved from a focus on "battering" or physical assault, to a broader range of abusive and manipulative behaviors—including threats, isolation, the withholding of resources, and stalking—through which perpetrators gain and maintain power and control over their victims. This expansion reflects, in part, the recognition that psychological abuse can be at least as harmful to victims as physical assaults.[208]

Annually, more than 10 million adults in the United States experience some form of domestic violence.[209] The lifetime risk of experiencing physical violence, sexual violence, or stalking by an intimate partner or acquaintance is estimated at one in four for women and one in nine for men.[210] Those numbers are higher if psychological or economic abuse is included.

About four out of five victims of IPV are female.[211] In fact, harm from IPV is one of the most significant lifetime risks for women. One of the Congressional findings that animated passage of the Violence Against Women Act was that "violence is the leading cause of injuries to women between the ages of 15 and 44—more than car accidents, muggings, and rapes combined."[212] Today, about one in three female murder victims are killed by intimate partners.[213] Pregnancy is a risk factor, with about 8 percent of maternal mortality deaths resulting from homicide, the largest proportion of which are killed by an intimate partner.[214] So is the effort to

---

208. Margaret E. Johnson, Balancing Liberty, Dignity, and Safety: The Impact of Domestic Violence Lethality Screening, 32 Cardozo L. Rev. 519, 526 (2010).

209. Nat'l Coal. Against Domestic Violence (NCADV), National Statistics (2022).

210. Id. See also Ctr. for Disease Control and Prevention (CDC), National Intimate Partner and Sexual Violence Survey: 2015 Data Brief Updated Release (2018) ("NISVS") (25 percent for women and 10 percent for men).

211. Bureau of Just. Stats., Intimate Partner Violence, 1993-2010 (rev. 2015). For further data, see Violence Policy Ctr., When Men Murder Women (2014).

212. S. Rep. No. 103-138, at 38 (1993).

213. CDC, Racial and Ethnic Differences in Homicides of Adult Women and the Role of Intimate Partner Violence—United States, 2003-2014 (2017) [hereinafter Ethnic Difference in Homicides of Women]; NCADV, Domestic Violence Fact Sheet (2018). This figure compares to one in twenty male victims who are killed by their intimate partners. Id.

214. See Jacquelyn Campbell et al., Pregnancy-Associated Deaths from Homicide, Suicide, and Drug Overdose: Review of Research and the Intersection with Intimate Partner Violence, 30 J. Women's Health 236 (2021).

leave one's partner. As the Mahoney reading excerpted below emphasizes, women are most likely to be injured in the course of trying to end an intimate relationship. According to one Department of Justice study, almost half of survivors of violence were abused while attempting to leave their partners.[215] The availability of guns also matters. An abuser's access to guns increases the risk of femicide by at least 400 percent.[216]

Although there was an effort within the domestic violence movement to organize around the idea of "universal risk" to women "by virtue of being women in a male-privileged society," the data show significant differences among women in the risk of experiencing violence, the risk of intimate partner homicide, and also the likely response both by the survivor and the institutions ostensibly designed to help.[217] Black women experience IPV at a disproportionately high rate (41 percent), while rates among Asian and Pacific Islander women (15 percent) are significantly lower than the average (25 percent). Native American women experience higher rates of IPV than any category of women of color.[218] The likelihood of a fatal outcome is also higher for women of color. African-American women and Native American women are at the highest risk of intimate partner homicide.[219] "An estimated 51.3% of black adult female homicides are related to IPV."[220] Black women ages 25 to 29 are eleven times more likely than white women at that age to be murdered while pregnant or in the first year after childbirth.[221]

Despite having a victimization rate higher than that of white women, Black women are less likely to use social services, medical services, and battered women's programs.[222] Studies show that Latinas also face barriers to reporting, stemming in part from family and cultural pressures. When they do report, women of color are often treated differently. A "cross-sectional study of 484 medical students found

---

215. Walter S. DeKeseredy, U.S. Dep't of Just., Sexual Assault During and After Separation/Divorce: An Exploratory Study, ix (2007); see also Molly Dragiewicz & Yvonne Lindgren, The Gendered Nature of Domestic Violence: Statistical Data for Lawyers Considering Equal Protection Analysis, 17 Am. U. J. Gender Soc. Pol'y & L. 229 (2009).

216. NCADV, Guns and Domestic Violence Fact Sheet (2018). There is also a link between domestic violence and mass killings. Over half of mass shooters have histories of domestic violence and targeted intimate partners or family members in mass killings. See Pamela Shifman & Salamishah Tillet, To Stop Violence, Start at Home, N.Y. Times, Feb. 3, 2015, at A23; Natalie Schreyer, A Lethal Combination, Ms. 30 (Spring 2018); Melissa Jeltsen, We're Missing the Big Picture on Mass Shootings, HuffPost (Jan. 11, 2017).

217. Deborah M. Weissman, The Community Politics of Domestic Violence, 82 Brook. L. Rev. 1479, 1497 (2017); see also Melissa Broaddus, The Intersectionality of Race, Gender, Poverty, and Intimate Partner Violence, 17 Ind. Health L. Rev. 207 (2020).

218. Id.

219. NCADV, Domestic Violence Against American Indian and Alaska Native Women Fact Sheet (2018).

220. Inst. Domestic Violence in the African American Cmty., Facts About Domestic Violence & African American Women (2015).

221. Id.

222. Id.

that they systematically discounted the pain, distress and discomfort of non-white survivors and adjusted their treatment recommendations accordingly."[223]

Race is just one of the intersectional identities that affects the likelihood and experience of IPV. One study found, for example, that 70 percent of respondents with disabilities had experienced some form of abuse, many at the hands of an intimate partner, family member, or caregiver.[224] By one estimate, "a staggering 92% of homeless women report having experienced severe physical or sexual violence at some point in their lives, and upwards of 50% of all homeless women report that domestic violence was the immediate cause of their homelessness."[225] Being a member of a highly observant religious community also makes individuals particularly vulnerable.[226] Unresponsive clergy, pressure to preserve the family unit, and an absence of targeted support services pose ongoing challenges.[227]

Rates of IPV in the LGBTQ+ community are also higher than average. According to a study co-sponsored by the National Institute of Justice and the Centers for Disease Control and Prevention, the lifetime prevalence of rape, physical violence, or stalking by an intimate partner was 61 percent for bisexual women, 44 percent for lesbian women, and 35 percent for heterosexual women. Among men, it was 37 percent for bisexuals, 29 percent for heterosexuals, and 26 percent for gay men.[228] Transgender persons, especially those of color, also face dramatically higher rates of IPV.[229] Like racial minority women, LGBTQ+ survivors are less likely to seek help and receive adequate help if they do seek it. A fear of encountering homophobia or "making the community look bad" keeps many survivors from seeking help.[230] Research by the National Coalition of Anti-Violence Programs found that only 17 percent of LGBT survivors reported abuse to the police, and only 4 percent reported seeking shelters.[231] Biases based on sexual orientation and gender identity remain all too common within the domestic violence community.[232]

---

223. Laura Brignone et al., Access to Domestic Violence Advocacy by Race, Ethnicity, and Gender, 17 PLoS ONE (Mar. 18, 2022); K. M. Hoffman, Racial Bias in Pain Assessment and Treatment Recommendations, and False Beliefs About Biological Differences Between Blacks and Whites, 113 Proc. Nat'l Acad. Sci. 4296 (2016).

224. Spectrum Inst. Nat'l Disability and Abuse Project, 2012 National Survey on Abuse Against People with Disabilities (2012).

225. Monica McLaughlin & Debbie Fox, Housing Needs of Victims of Domestic Violence, Sexual Assault, Dating Violence, and Stalking 6 (2019).

226. Michal Gilad, In God's Shadow: Unveiling the Hidden World of Victims of Domestic Violence in Observant Religious Communities, 11 Rutgers J.L. & Pub. Pol'y 471 (2014).

227. Id. at 538, 541-42.

228. CDC, An Overview of 2010 Findings on Victimization by Sexual Orientation (2013).

229. Sarah M. Peitzmeier, Intimate Partner Violence in Transgender Populations: Systematic Review and Meta-Analysis of Prevalence and Correlates, 110 Am. J. Public Health 1 (2020).

230. Maya Shwayder, Same Sex Domestic Violence Epidemic Is Silent, Atlantic, Nov. 5, 2013 (quoting Jesse Newman of Violence Recovery Program in Boston).

231. Id.

232. Deborah M. Weissman, Rethinking a New Domestic Violence Pedagogy, 5 U. Miami Race & Soc. Just. L. Rev. 635, 653 (2015).

Research on the incidence of domestic violence across class consistently finds a link between poverty and abuse. Low-income women have rates of IPV that are about four times greater than rates among high-income women.[233] Residents of rural communities also face disproportionate dangers both because of the inaccessibility of shelters and support services, and the persistence of "old boy networks" that trivialize abuse.[234] Poor women are particularly vulnerable to violence because their lack of financial resources and employment skills traps them in abusive relationships. By the same token, violence impairs individuals' ability to find and retain work, which perpetuates economic dependence. Research finds that between one-third and two-thirds of women who were welfare recipients have been victims of domestic violence.[235]

Teens and elderly Americans are also targets for abuse. The Centers for Disease Control and Prevention reports that about 10 percent of high school students reported physical victimization and 10 percent reported sexual victimization from a dating partner in the preceding year.[236] Women ages 18 to 24 face the highest risk of violence.[237] Accurate estimates of elder abuse are unavailable, but the most comprehensive recent research estimates that approximately 10 percent of senior adults are subject to some form of physical, psychological, or sexual abuse, financial exploitation, or neglect in the prior year.[238]

It should be noted that men are also victims of intimate partner abuse. The National Coalition Against Domestic Violence reports that one in seven men have been severely physically abused by an intimate partner; other men are responsible for most of the sexual abuse and stalking.[239] When women are the abusers of men, research suggests that they are as physically aggressive as men, but less likely to inflict serious injury.[240]

---

233. U.S. Dept. of Justice, Bureau of Just. Stats., Household Poverty and Nonfatal Violent Victimization, 2008-2012 (2014); see also Amy E. Bonomi et al., Intimate Partner Violence and Neighborhood Income: A Longitudinal Analysis, 20 Violence Against Women 42 (2014).

234. Sara R. Benson, Failure to Arrest: A Pilot Study of Police Response to Domestic Violence in Rural Illinois, 17 Am. J. Gender Soc. Pol'y & L. 685, 697-99 (2009).

235. Angelo M. Moe & Myrtle Bell, Abject Economics: The Effects of Battering and Violence on Women's Work and Employability, 10 Violence Against Women 29, 35-36 (2004); Rachel Gallagher, Welfare Reform's Inadequate Implementation of the Family Violence Option: Exploring the Dual Oppression of Poor Domestic Violence Victims, 19 Am. U. J. Gender, Soc. Pol'y & L. 987 (2011).

236. CDC, Prevent Teen Dating Violence (2022).

237. R. E. Morgan & B. A. Oudeker, Bureau of Just. Stats., Criminal Victimization, 2018 (2019).

238. Nat'l Ctr. on Elder Abuse, Research Statistics (2018); Mark S. Lachs & Karl A. Pillemer, Elder Abuse, 373 New England J. Medicine 1947 (2015).

239. NCADV, Male Victims of Intimate Partner Violence: Fact Sheet (2015).

240. For data on female violence and male victims, see Cathy Young, The Surprising Truth About Women and Violence, Time (June 25, 2014); see also Jamie R. Abrams, The Feminist Case for Acknowledging Women's Acts of Violence, 27 Yale J.L. & Feminism 287 (2016).

In addition to the human costs, the financial costs of IPV reverberate throughout the economy. Estimates suggest that domestic violence in the United States may cost nearly $3.5 trillion annually in medical and criminal legal expenses and lost productivity and earnings.[241] According to Legal Momentum, an advocacy group, between one-quarter and one-half of domestic violence victims report that they have lost a job due, at least in part, to domestic violence. This may be because they need time off from work to seek medical attention, a restraining order, or a safe place to stay. Or they may not be able to get to work when an abuser disables their car, sabotages childcare arrangements, or leaves them without cash for public transportation. The Centers for Disease Control and Prevention estimates that the annual cost of lost productivity due to domestic violence is $727.8 million.[242]

In a Washington Post/Kaiser Family Foundation survey, reducing domestic violence and sexual assault were the top priorities for improving women's lives. How should that ranking inform the policies described below?[243]

Consider the following perspectives on intimate partner violence.

Karla Fischer, Neil Vidmar & René Ellis

The Culture of Battering and the Role of Mediation in Domestic Violence Cases

46 SMU L. Rev. 2117, 2120-21, 2126-29, 2137-38 (1993)

The culture of battering refers to the relationship context of an abusive relationship. The first of the three elements of the culture of battering is the abuse, which includes at least one of the following types: physical, emotional, sexual, familial, and property. Professionals have increasingly recognized non-physical forms of abuse as harmful to domestic violence victims. The second element is the systematic pattern of domination and control that the batterer exerts over his victim. This pattern may be initiated by the batterer's gradual imposition of a series of rules that his victim must follow or be punished for violating. Over time, victims may censor their own behavior in anticipation of yet-unexpressed rules. The abuser's rein on the members of the household is enhanced by the use of emotional abuse and financial and social isolation, all of which help keep the victim in fear of impending abuse. Victims may engage in episodes of rebellion or resistance to the rules, which are nearly always met with more serious violence. Even separating from the abuser, an act of rebellion by itself, does not secure the end of the abuse; rather, it frequently escalates it. The third element, hiding, denying, and minimizing the abuse, refers to typical coping strategies that battered women use to reduce

---

241. Cora Peterson, Lifetime Economic Burden of Intimate Partner Violence Among U.S. Adults, 55 Am. J. Preventive Med. 433 (2018).

242. Legal Momentum, The Women's Legal Defense and Education Fund, Domestic and Sexual Violence in the Workplace (2014).

243. Liz Hamel et al., Washington Post/Kaiser Family Foundation Feminism Survey (Jan. 28, 2016).

the psychological impact of the abuse. Each of these elements to some degree must be present in order for a culture of battering to be established. . . .

Battered women have frequently reported that abusers are extremely controlling of the everyday activities of the family. This domination can be all encompassing: as one of the batterers from Angela Browne's study was fond of stating, "[y]ou're going to dance to my music . . . be the kind of wife I want you to be." Charlotte Fedders' account of the escalating rules imposed by her husband [who was a prominent lawyer and high-level government official] over the course of their seventeen year, extremely violent marriage is particularly illuminating about the range of control that abusers can exert. Her husband insisted that no one (including guests and their toddler children) wear shoes in the house, that the furniture be in the same indentations in the carpet, that the vacuum marks in the carpet be parallel, and that any sand spilled from the children's sandbox during their play be removed from the surrounding grass. Charlotte was not allowed to write checks from their joint checking account. Any real or perceived infraction of these rules could result in her husband beating her, or at the very least, the expression of his irritation that was frequently a harbinger to a beating.

Typically, battered women talk to the men about the abuse, partly as an attempt to concretize the rules that are connected to the absence of abuse. In turn, many abusers promise to stop the abuse. One abuser in Browne's study formalized such discussions into a written document, where he set forth a list of conditions that his victim was to agree to in exchange for cessation of his violence. These conditions were: (1) the children were to keep their rooms clean without being told; (2) the children could not argue with each other; (3) he was to have absolute freedom to come and go as he wished, and could have a girlfriend if he wanted one; (4) she would perform oral sex on him anytime he requested; and (5) she would have anal sex with him. He enforced this document shortly after she "agreed" to it and continued to sexually assault her until his death. This abuser simply made explicit the rules in the relationship and made it obvious that abuse was the punishment for violating the rules.

In many abusive relationships, however, the rules do not need to be verbally expressed to create a family atmosphere controlled by the batterer. Charlotte Fedders' story is a prototype of a battered woman who becomes very good at reading nonverbal messages from her abuser. She writes of how she restricted the play of her four young boys in order to avoid her husband's increasingly subtle signs of displeasure:

> "Eventually . . . we just stopped using the living room and the family room because little things out of place would make him angry. . . . If [the boys'] rooms were a mess, he'd complain to me, so I was reluctant to let them play there. So they pretty much played in the basement. . . ."

What fuels this . . . process is the responsibility the victim feels, both as a woman socialized into believing that making relationships work is her job, and the responsibility added by the abuser, who blames her for the "failure" of the relationship, as evidenced by the occurrence of abuse. . . .

Our argument that abuse occurs within a relationship context of control and domination is an explicit rejection of the popular belief that abuse is simply a logical extension of a heated argument or disagreement. . . . Battered women's narratives of the context of abuse suggest quite the opposite of conflict. Women are typically beaten in a variety of situations that could hardly be classified as conflict: while sleeping, while using the toilet, and while in another room that the batterer suddenly entered to begin his beating. The usual scenario women describe is that at one moment all is calm and in the next, there is a major, seemingly untriggered explosion:

> I remember walking in, got undressed, and put my robe on, and I was going to get a glass of milk. At one moment we were laying together and kissing and everything seemed fine. And, it was like a second later, he was saying that I stayed out too late, and asked who was there and stuff, and then just . . . everything blew up. I know he threw me off the bed. And he told me he was going to beat me to death. And, then he said, "I'm going to set the trailer on fire with you and your daughter in it." And then he goes, "well, first, bitch, you are going to get me a glass of ice water."

In addition to the information about context, batterers' behavior during abusive incidents does not support an image that these men are out of control with anger. Women have reported deliberate, calculating behavior, ranging from searching for and destroying a treasured object of hers to striking her in areas of her body that do not show bruises (e.g. her scalp) or in areas where she would be embarrassed to show others her bruises.

Anger and conflict may be frequently confused with violence because both can be a proxy for abuse. The abuser may in fact be angry when he beats his victim or a conflict over what she has served for dinner may have developed before the incident of violence. But this simple coexistence in time does not mean that the anger or conflict has caused the violence. Lurking underneath the surface anger or conflict is the batterer's need to express his power over his victim. Even if the anger is controlled and all sources of conflict are removed from the relationship, violence still occurs. After all, batterers are usually involved in other social relationships, at work or elsewhere, where they become angry or have conflicts with others that they do not abuse. Their ability to cope with anger in some situations but not at home suggests that conflict and anger are not at the root of domestic violence. Perhaps the best evidence, however, that abuse is not about anger or conflict is that violence continues to occur, frequently escalating, after women leave their abusers.

Deborah Epstein & Lisa A. Goodman

Discounting Women: Doubting Domestic Violence Survivors' Credibility and Dismissing Their Experiences

167 U. Pa. L. Rev. 399, 405-06 (2019)

Women survivors of abuse inflicted by their intimate partners encounter doubt, skepticism, or disbelief in their efforts to obtain justice and safety from judges and other system gatekeepers. First, their stories of abuse appear less plausible than other stories told in the justice system. We tend to believe stories that are internally consistent — they have a linear thread and are emotionally and logically coherent. But domestic violence often results in neurological and psychological trauma, both of which can affect a survivor's comprehension and memory. The result is a story that, to the untrained ear, sounds internally inconsistent and therefore implausible. In addition, we tend to believe stories that are externally consistent — that fit in with how we believe the world works. But many aspects of the domestic violence experience are foreign, and therefore incomprehensible, to most nonsurvivors. The result is a story that appears on its surface to lack external consistency, and therefore — again — to be less plausible. Second, our assessments of women's personal trustworthiness suffer from skepticism rooted in perceptions of survivors' apparent "inappropriate" demeanor, prejudicial stereotypes regarding women's false motives, and the longstanding cultural tendency to disbelieve women simply because they are women.

Stevenson v. Stevenson

714 A.2d 986 (N.J. Super. Ct. Ch. Div. 1998)

COOK, J.S.C. . . .

In what appears as a matter of first impression in New Jersey, this case presents the question whether a final restraining order issued under the Prevention of Domestic Violence Act . . . must be dissolved in all cases where the plaintiff so requests. For the reasons expressed below, this court determines that dissolution of a final restraining order at the request of plaintiff is not mandatory. Rather, dissolution in such cases is at the court's discretion, and should depend upon a showing of good cause, with an independent finding by the court based upon the facts presented in each case. . . .

On November 6, 1997, the parties appeared before this court for a hearing on plaintiff's complaint charging defendant with numerous violations of the Prevention of Domestic Violence Act (the Act). The testimony of plaintiff, the photographic exhibits offered by her counsel, and the graphic appearance at the hearing of the residual effects of the severe physical injuries she suffered, established by a clear preponderance of the evidence that defendant was guilty of attempted criminal homicide, aggravated assault, terroristic threats, criminal restraint and burglary, all in violation of the Act. These violations arose from a brutal, sadistic and prolonged attack by defendant on his wife during the late evening and early morning hours of October 29-30, 1997.

Plaintiff, who appeared at the hearing with two black and severely swollen eyes, testified that on the late evening of October 29, 1997, defendant came into the marital bedroom, went into a total rage, punched plaintiff with both fists, held her down with his knees, kicked her in the back and ribs, and continued beating her there for approximately 25 minutes. Defendant then dragged her by her hair down the stairs and out of the house, and shoved her into his van, saying that they were going to go to a friend's house. Plaintiff was bleeding from her ears, nose and mouth. She got out of the van, ran to a neighbor's house and banged on the door. Defendant chased her, screaming he would kill her, and that he should have killed her before. She was "petrified." He caught up to her outside the neighbor's house, and choked her with both hands around her throat. He then dragged her down the street and pushed her back into the van. She escaped again and ran to another neighbor's house. At that point, defendant's vicious attack on his wife had been going on for 45 minutes. She went inside the neighbor's house and asked her neighbor to call the police, while she went into a powder room, closed the door, and tried to hide from defendant. Defendant went into the neighbor's house and proceeded to rip the powder room door off its hinges. The door landed on plaintiff. He dragged her out of the house, and back towards their house. Plaintiff grabbed onto trees along the way, trying to resist. He was furious because she had asked her neighbor to call the police. Finally, he let go of her, got into the van and left. She was badly injured and very scared. A neighbor came with a blanket and rendered first aid. She was rushed by ambulance to the Emergency Room . . . [and] medevac'd by helicopter to the Cooper Hospital Trauma Center. She had a fractured skull, a concussion, four broken ribs, and a punctured lung (pneumothorax), in addition to the injuries noted above. She remained hospitalized at Cooper for several days, and was still under medical care at the time of the hearing on November 6, 1997.

At the hearing, the court had the opportunity not only to hear the testimony of plaintiff, but to observe her injuries and review the photographic exhibits submitted by her counsel as well. . . . The photographic exhibits submitted by plaintiff's counsel depicted her injuries, as well as the powder room door that defendant ripped off its hinges in the neighbor's home where plaintiff sought refuge. The photos, including those of plaintiff's facial and head injuries, and the hole in her chest where a tube was inserted to re-inflate her punctured lung, depicted a severally beaten and battered woman.

Plaintiff testified she was in fear of defendant. She related a prior history of domestic violence on his part, including previous assaults. She was afraid he would take their ten year-old son and leave the area, noting that he would do anything and everything to get physical custody and keep their son away from her. She added that their ten year-old son was in the house throughout the forty-five minute period that the beating of his mother took place.

Defendant, who was represented by counsel at the hearing, did not testify. No evidence was presented to controvert plaintiff's testimony, or the domestic violence charges she made against him. . . .

Because of (1) the barbaric conduct of the defendant during the nightmarish incident of October 29-30, 1997; (2) the evidence of his drunkenness that night and in the past; (3) his prior history of domestic violence; and (4) plaintiff's clearly expressed fear that defendant would take her son away if not restrained, a final restraining order was entered. The order prohibited any further acts of domestic violence, and barred him from having any contact or communication with the plaintiff and from harassing or stalking her. The order also required defendant to undergo substance abuse and psychological evaluations, and restricted him to supervised visitation only. He was also ordered to pay plaintiff's attorneys' fees of $2,400 by December 12, 1997; child and spousal support; all household expenses; and other expenses enumerated in the order.

At the hearing on plaintiff's request that the court dissolve the final restraining order, several violations of the order came to light. For example, it appeared that the defendant has engaged in *unsupervised visitation* with the child, including trips out-of-state. He has continually attempted to contact plaintiff. He has not abided by the psychotherapy recommendations of the Steininger Center, nor with the substance abuse recommendations of Segaloff. Both of those reports are discussed below. He has not paid any of the attorney's fees he was ordered to pay. In short, the defendant has flouted and violated the final restraining order. . . .

At the hearing on March 13, 1998, plaintiff asked the court to dissolve the final restraining order. She claimed she had reconsidered her relationship with the defendant and wanted him to be involved with their son's life. She requested that the restraints be dissolved, but only on the condition that he commit no future violence.

The final restraining order permitted *supervised visitation only*, pending a risk assessment and further order of the court. Risk assessment evaluations, substance abuse evaluations, and psychological evaluations of defendant were received by the court. At the request of and by agreement of both parties, through their counsel, copies of those evaluation reports were provided to the parties and their counsel. Plaintiff testified she had read the reports. . . .

Those reports include (1) a psychological evaluation of defendant by Dr. Stuart Kurlansik, Chief Psychologist, The Steininger Center; and (2) a drug and alcohol abuse evaluation of defendant by Patricia Thurman, a substance abuse counsellor. . . .

Dr. Karlansik reported inter alia that:

> When asked to describe the events which resulted in his referral to this office, Mr. Stevenson reported that "I assaulted my wife. I beat her up very badly." . . .
>
> He reported prior fights with his wife, but "nothing to this degree." He claimed that *every time they fought, he was drunk.* He stated that she never had to go to the hospital in previous fights. He stated that the previous fights involved punching, although not to the face. He stated that he bruised her in prior fights, but then claimed that she bruises easily. He reported that he had been in fights with other people during the period of his marriage as well. He stated that he boxes and plays hockey, and fought during the course of a game. He stated that he has had a few fights outside of the sport events, however. He then said there had been a handful, the most recent occurring [a year ago] at a roller rink [when] the other coach had been a poor sport, and "we ended up in a physical confrontation." . . . Another time, four years ago, he stated that he was a spectator at an ice hockey [game] in which his son was playing. He stated that a parent of one of his teams' children became involved in a fight with three of the opposing team's parents, and he "intervened." *He reported having a fight five years ago in a bar, and stated that he was intoxicated at the time.* He stated that he had played a game of pool for twenty dollars and the other person lost the game, and did not want to pay, "so I hit him." . . .
>
> He denied any arrests as a result of fighting as an adult. As a juvenile, he stated that he was incarcerated at Glen Mills for a total of three years, and stated that "we could go on for hours" regarding juvenile incidents. He stated that he was at Glen Mills twice — once at age thirteen for assault, and the second time at age fourteen for robbery.

His current marriage has been his only marriage. He married on December 28, 1986. The most recent separation occurred October 29, 1997. He reported one other separation, two years ago. He stated that "things just weren't working well." This separation lasted about three months.

He reported that he has a *short temper*, although "not now." He claimed that the experience which brought him here has changed his life and a short temper is "not gonna be a trait for me anymore." . . .

An objective measure of personality functioning, the Million Clinical Multiaxial Inventory–III, was administered. . . . [T]he interpretive report stated that "on the basis of the test data (assuming denial is not present), it may be reasonable to assume that the patient is exhibiting psychological dysfunction of mild to moderate severity." An Axis I (an "acute" disorder) diagnosis of Generalized Anxiety Disorder is suggested, while Axis II (enduring features of an individual's personality, and therefore more "chronic") diagnosis of: "*Antisocial Personality Traits*," "*Passive-Aggressive Personality Traits*," "*Avoidant Personality Traits*," and "*Sadistic Personality Features*" are suggested. The NCS report hypothesizes . . . that he may manifest (among other things) a lack of empathy, intolerance, and display "impulsive and quixotic emotionality." It goes on to state that *individuals with his profile can "be easily provoked into sudden and unpredictable reactions," which "may be punctuated periodically by angry outbursts."*

Recommendations:

It is strongly urged that Mr. Stevenson participate in psychotherapy, to help him learn to control his anger (and to find more appropriate ways of expressing it), as well as to reduce his anxiety. Psychotherapy might also address what appears to be an issue with *excessive use of alcohol at times.*

In her substance abuse evaluation of defendant, Ms. Thurman, a substance abuse counsellor . . . reported that: . . .

Robert, a 34 year-old white male, was interviewed on November 29, 1997, at 8:30 a.m. Eye contact was fair, affect closed, guarded and *very accusatory toward his estranged wife, Melody.*

When asked about his use of drugs and alcoholic beverages, Mr. Stevenson states he's never used drugs of any kind and attempts to portray himself as a modest drinker, however, says the day he was charged "*I had a little too much to drink*". . . . But, Robert was quick to defend his actions by blaming the problem on "I caught my wife trying to buy drugs on the phone" and sees no relationship between his drinking and his current family problems. . . .

Concluding, based upon the limited information available to us, we strongly suspect Mr. Stevenson is drinking more than he reports and we feel he would greatly benefit from outpatient counseling to enable him to cease drinking and evaluate his family problems in a drug free state. The fact the client admits he was under the influence at the time of the altercation with his wife prompts us to question the severity of his drinking and its relationship to his family problems. . . . If Mr. Stevenson is not already in treatment for substance abuse, *we would then recommend he be mandated to complete at least 3 months in substance abuse treatment. . . .*

At a risk assessment conference with a Family Court staff therapist, plaintiff expressed concern over defendant's "*need for control,*" and again said she feared he would flee with their son, perhaps to Arizona. . . . She also said that on more than one occasion, defendant has threatened that he "will do anything and everything he has to" in order to gain custody of his son. Plaintiff requested that supervised visitation continue.

There remain several criminal charges pending against defendant as a result of his sadistic attack on his wife, including criminal attempt–murder; aggravated assault; burglary; criminal mischief; threatened violence; and criminal restraint. He is reportedly free on $75,000 cash bail, and is awaiting further proceedings in the criminal case.

When considering a plaintiff's request to dissolve the Final Restraining Order, a court must not forget that it is the public policy of the State of New Jersey, expressed by the Legislature in the Act, *that victims of domestic violence must be assured the maximum protection from abuse the law can provide; that the official response to domestic violence, including that of the courts, shall communicate the attitude that domestic violent behavior will not be excused or tolerated; and that it is the responsibility of the courts to protect victims of domestic violence* by ordering those remedies and sanctions that are *available to assure the safety of the victims* and the public. . . .

In addition, the Legislature has mandated that a final restraining order cannot be dissolved [or modified], *unless good cause is shown.* . . . Even where good cause is shown, the language of the statute, [the Act] expressly makes dissolution *discretionary*, not mandatory (". . . final order *may* be dissolved").

Plaintiff's dissolution request, made despite the latest brutal beating she suffered at the hands of a drunken husband who has a past history of wife-beating and an alcohol abuse problem, is consistent with phase three of "the battered woman's syndrome." That phase of the battering cycle is characterized by a period of loving behavior by the batterer, during which pleas for forgiveness and protestations of devotion are often mixed with promises to seek counselling, stop drinking and refrain from further violence. A period of relative calm may last as long as several months, but in a battering relationship the affection and contrition of the batterer will eventually fade, and phases one and two, the "tension-building" phase and the "acute battering incident" phase, will start anew. . . . Plaintiff has gone through the battering cycle with defendant at least twice. Through this dissolution request she seeks to remain in the situation. She thus meets the definition of a "battered woman." . . . The New Jersey Legislature recognized the plight of battered women when it enacted the Act and provided battered women with the remedy of *permanent* restraining orders against wife-beaters and other batterers of women.

Obviously, if there were no basis at all for plaintiff to fear further violence — as most certainly there is, given the nature and extent of this attack and defendant's past history of violence, including domestic violence against plaintiff; then there would be no need to condition dissolution on the absence of further violence. But there is that inherent fear, a fear that this court and any reasonable person viewing this situation would certainly share.

[Because fear is vital to the continuance of power and control in a domestic violence relationship, and this fear can impact the victim's ability to act in the best interests of her child, it is important to consider the victim's fear of the defendant.] When considering the question of fear of defendant, . . . the test should not be the victim's subjective fear. Rather, the test is one of objective fear, i.e., that fear which a reasonable victim similarly situated would have under the circumstances. . . .

When considering a victim's application to dissolve, and whether there is good cause to do so, a court must determine whether objective fear can be said to continue to exist, and also whether there is a real danger of domestic violence recurring, in the event the restraining order is dissolved. . . . Whether or not this plaintiff would agree, it is clear that *from the standpoint of objective fear*, that a reasonable victim of such a brutal beating by a husband, who has assaulted her in the past and has a history of other violent behavior, and is the subject of experts' findings of uncontrolled anger and excessive use of alcohol, would have a reasonable fear that future violence by her husband would occur, were the restraining order dissolved.

Even in cases of reconciliation, the court must still make *an independent finding* that continued protection is unnecessary before vacating a restraining order. . . . In this case, given the uncontroverted evidence of defendant's brutality against his wife, his history of violence both within and without the domestic arena, his alcohol abuse and uncontrolled assaultive behavior when under the influence, and the reports before the court, including those of The Steininger Center and Segaloff, a reasonable, objective and independent determination of the facts leads to the inescapable conclusion that a real threat of recurrence of domestic violence by defendant upon his battered wife will exist, if the Final Restraining Order is dissolved. This court will not be an accomplice to further violence by this defendant, by wholly dissolving at this point the restraints that have been entered against him. Accordingly, and for lack of good cause shown, plaintiff's application to dissolve the Final Restraining Order is denied.

The court does find cause to modify the Final Restraining Order with respect to certain matters concerning the child of the parties, as follows. The final restraining order shall remain in full force and effect, except that contact or communication between plaintiff and defendant relating to supervised visitation, and to the safety, health, education, welfare, status or activities of the minor child of the parties, shall be permitted. There shall be no further modification of the final restraining order, without application to and with the express approval of the court.

Defendant shall promptly undergo psychotherapy as recommended in the report of Dr. Kurlansik of The Steininger Center. He shall also promptly undergo at least three months of substance abuse treatment. . . . Upon completion of psychotherapy and substance abuse treatment, the court will consider unsupervised visitation.

Aya Gruber

A "Neo-Feminist" Assessment of Rape and Domestic Violence Law Reform

15 J. Gender Race & Just. 583 (2012)

[T]he personal really became the political [for me] after I practiced as a public defender in a specialized domestic violence court. Prior to that, I believed that women are universally united and similarly situated in their subordinate status to men. I bought into the idea that all abused women are trapped in a cycle of violence perpetuated solely by a cunning, socially empowered abuser. I adhered to the concept that equal rights and the use of criminal strategies to combat gender crimes are the logical solutions to the problem of sexism. . . .

Later, as an eager-eyed new public defender, I absolutely dreaded the prospect of defending horrible macho male abusers in domestic violence court. Soon, however, I began to dread domestic violence court for a host of other reasons. Not only did I see the rampant destruction of domestic relations, entrenchment of economic disempowerment, and mass incarceration of minority men, but I also saw distinctly anti-female ideologies at work. I observed government actors systematically ignore women's desires to stay out of court, express disdain for ambivalent victims, and even infantilize victims to justify mandatory policies while simultaneously prosecuting the victims in other contexts. It seemed to me that feminist criminal law reform had become less about critiquing the state and society's treatment of women and more about allying with police power to find newer and better ways of putting men, who themselves often occupy subordinate statuses, in jail. . . .

As feminist scholars responded to the limits of liberal reform efforts, feminism, a quintessentially progressive movement, veered in a curious direction. In responding to the failure of equal opportunity to bring about substantive results, certain feminist legal theories moved toward authoritarian policies and obdurate views of right and wrong. So-called "dominance" feminism . . . views the inequality of men and women, not solely as a matter of unequal rights and formal institutional disparities, but as a matter of the ubiquitous power differential between men and women in all aspects of life. From the point of view of dominance feminists, establishing uniform rights would not adequately address the "patriarchy," a system of norms, practices, instincts, and signals that keeps men dominant and women subordinate. . . .

In defining the patriarchal structure as a sexual structure, dominance feminism centers on a fairly uncompromising and absolutist idea of bad and good—bad being things that sexualize women and good being the eradication of those things through prohibitory law. . . . Dominance feminism accordingly calls for the reversal of the gender power structure by utilizing penal law to stamp out instances of sexual domination. . . .

[M]any scholars note that mandatory policies inevitably force certain domestic violence victims to proceed with prosecutions that they would rather avoid for a variety of reasons. . . . The reductionist characterization of all abused women as simply too scared to prosecute hides the complex reality of many battered women's lives. Abused women decline to ally with police actors for a number of reasons—money, children, fear of the state, immigration concerns, race-related reasons, and even emotional attachment to the abuser. . . .

The autonomy-stripping aspects of domestic violence reform appear blatantly at odds with the philosophical commitments of feminism. . . . [My] neo-feminist approach accordingly supports a focus on legal approaches that are more responsive to social welfare concerns. [I]t advocates turning the bulk of efforts away from purely legal solutions toward policy efforts that transform economic distributions and cultural attitudes. . . . Rather than being a grand narrative of women's condition, the neo-feminist approach can be practical in its support of strategies whose benefits to women's conditions outweigh the drawbacks. As a result, a neo-feminist theory can account for the differing ways in which women from different subgroups experience male domination and other forms of subordination.

[T]his neo-feminist moment in criminal law scholarship can be seen as a return to the feminist first principles of non-subordination, distributive equality, and skepticism of the status quo.

NOTES

1. **The Violence Against Women Act and Other Federal Legislation.**   The Violence Against Women Act of 1994 (VAWA) responded to domestic violence on multiple fronts. For example, it tightened sanctions by requiring courts to sentence first-time offenders to prison or probation rather than to general deferred or diverted prosecution programs, and to condition probation on participation in an approved nonprofit rehabilitation program. Assault with intent to rape, sexual abuse, and an attempt or solicitation to commit these offenses qualify as "serious violence felonies" under the federal "three strikes and you're out" sentencing structure. The Safe Homes for Women Act, created under VAWA, provides law enforcement personnel with the authority to enforce civil protection orders from other states, and provides databases and technical assistance to courts handling domestic violence. VAWA also expanded the State Justice Institute's authority and mission to study and eliminate gender bias in all criminal justice and court systems. On issues related to women of color, VAWA provided for the improvement of delivery services to racial, cultural, ethnic, and language minorities. It also expanded the remedies available to battered immigrant women, which were further broadened in the 2005 VAWA reauthorization legislation. Finally, VAWA created new substantive law, making it a federal crime to cross state lines for the purpose of, or in the course of, "harassing, intimidating, or injuring a spouse or intimate partner."[244] The original VAWA also created a federal civil rights remedy for sex-based violence, but the U.S. Supreme Court declared that the regulation of domestic violence was a matter for states, not the federal government.[245]

In 2013, the reauthorization of VAWA concentrated on improving prevention and response services among communities that have traditionally been underserved: Native Americans, LGBT individuals, and immigrant women.[246] For example, VAWA 2013 included provisions that ensure access to services and programs to all victims of domestic violence, regardless of their sexual orientation or gender identity, and allowed states to use federal funding to improve responses to domestic violence among the LGBT community. As indicated in note 3, below, however, financial support for counseling and intervention programs remains inadequate. In 2022, Congress reauthorized VAWA through 2027.[247]

---

244. 18 U.S.C. § 2261 (2018).

245. United States v. Morrison, 529 U.S. 598, 617 (2000).

246. Violence Against Women Reauthorization Act of 2013, Pub L. No. 113-4, 127 Stat. 54 (2013).

247. The Violence Against Women Reauthorization Act was passed as part of a budget bill. See Consolidated Appropriations Act, Pub L. No. 117-103, 136 Stat. 49 (2022).

Another federal law prohibits individuals convicted of domestic violence misdemeanors involving force or attempted use of physical force from owning a firearm.[248] That statute was enacted to close a loophole that had allowed access to guns by abusers who had not been convicted of a felony. The new gun law passed in the wake of a mass school shooting in Texas closes the "boyfriend loophole," which had allowed non-spousal partners convicted of domestic abuse to remain eligible to own firearms.[249] In United States v. Castleman, the Supreme Court held that a crime satisfying the common law definition of battery satisfied the force requirement of the federal statute.[250] In Voisine v. United States, the Court concluded that a misdemeanor crime with the mens rea of recklessness qualified as a misdemeanor crime of domestic violence under the statute.[251] The Court did not review claims that the statute was unconstitutional. However, gaps in statutory coverage and enforcement enable many abusers to gain access to guns. Records are often incomplete, offenders can make purchases from private sellers or gun show distributors, restraining orders expire, and statutes do not cover former dating partners or other individuals subject to temporary restraining orders.[252]

2. **Reporting Laws.**   Medical screening for violence and mandatory reporting laws are another form of legal intervention. Almost every state requires reporting by health care providers if the patient has one of a number of injuries that appears to be non-accidental, such as injuries inflicted by a deadly weapon.[253] In some states, that reporting obligation extends to service providers at Family Justice Centers, which coordinate the provision of services to domestic violence victims by a number of different agencies and community services.[254] Advocates of these requirements see them as a way to ensure early law enforcement intervention when survivors' lives and health are at risk because they are more likely to visit doctors than call the police. In an effort to encourage screening that too often falls through the cracks, the Patient Protection and Affordable Care Act provides that covered insurance plans must include domestic violence screening and counseling free of copays by the insured individual.[255]

Critics of mandatory reporting requirements worry that women whose history of abuse makes them aware of requirements may be deterred from seeking treatment. Alternatively, their abusive partners may prevent victims from seeking medical assistance. Some research suggests that most women fear that mandatory

---

248. 18 U.S.C. § 922 (g)(9) (2018).

249. Bipartisan Safer Communities Act, Pub. L. 117-159, 136 Stat. 1313 (2022).

250. United States v. Castleman, 572 U.S. 157, 163 (2014).

251. 579 U.S. 686, 698-99 (2016).

252. NCADV, Guns and Domestic Violence, supra note 216.

253. For a listing of statutes as of 2014, see Victim Rights Law Center, Mandatory Reporting of Non-Accidental Injuries: A State-by-State Guide (updated May 2014).

254. See Jane K. Stoever, Mirandizing Family Justice, 39 Harv. J.L. & Gender 189 (2016).

255. Health Res. & Servs. Admin., Women's Preventive Service Guidelines (2018). For discussion of the inadequacy of screening and new Affordable Care Act provisions, see Karen Oehme et al., Unheard Voices of Domestic Violence Victims: A Call to Remedy Physician Neglect, 15 Geo. J. Gender & L. 613, 615-22 (2014).

reporting would increase their risk of abuse.[256] Out of concern for patients' safety, confidentiality, and autonomy, the American Medical Association opposes mandatory reporting. A few states require health care providers to obtain the consent of victims before reporting injuries caused by domestic violence or sexual assault.[257] Is this a sound approach?

3. **Victim Services.**   Domestic violence advocates argue that providing women with material resources such as housing, food, clothing, or money should take priority over policies that seek greater punishment of batterers.[258] As indicated in note 1, above, some of the emphasis in the Violence Against Women Act has been on such services. Spurred by federal assistance, states have also expanded services for victims of domestic violence, including shelters and counseling centers, Family Justice Centers that consolidate services under one roof, and short-term financial assistance that enables victims to put down security deposits on safe housing, pay off crippling debts created by abusive partners, or otherwise restart their lives. However, in most jurisdictions, the need substantially exceeds the resources of the programs available. Every year, the National Network to End Domestic Violence conducts a one-day count of individuals seeking services from U.S. domestic violence shelter programs. In the 2021 survey, of the more than 70,000 victims of domestic violence who were seeking help across the U.S., almost 10,000 requests remained unmet, mainly from women seeking housing and emergency shelter.[259]

A separate issue for victim services is which women should have access to shelters. Thirty years ago, Kimberlé Crenshaw raised this issue with respect to women who might need a bilingual male friend or relative to help them translate.[260] Today the issue might also arise with transgender women who have been unable or unwilling to have a complete reconstruction of their bodies. Consider the following excerpt:

> Domestic violence shelters are often marked "women-only" with the goal of creating spaces for female empowerment, wherein women learn feminist principles of liberation, engage with theories of male domination, and find a "sisterhood" of support by forging healthy female relationships. However, as a result, shelters frequently deny transgender women access because shelter staff perceive them to be a threat to survivor comfort and to be disruptive to shelters' female-empowerment model. Consequently, though transgender women face similar gender-based oppression and a

---

256. Thomas L. Hafemeister, If All You Have Is a Hammer: Society's Ineffective Response to Intimate Partner Violence, 60 Cath. U. L. Rev. 919, 962 (2011); Tribute to Lenora Lapidus, 43 Harbinger 1, 2 (2019).

257. Victim Rights Law Center, supra note 253.

258. Elizabeth M. Schneider, Domestic Violence Law Reform in the Twenty-First Century: Looking Back and Looking Forward, 42 Fam. L.Q. 353, 361 (2008); Donna Coker, Shifting Power for Battered Women: Law, Material Resources, and Poor Women of Color, 33 U.C. Davis L. Rev. 1009 (2000).

259. See Nat'l Network to End Domestic Violence, 16th Annual Domestic Violence Counts Report: National Summary 1 (2021).

260. Kimberlé Crenshaw, Mapping the Margins: Intersectionality, Identity Politics, and Violence Against Women of Color, 43 Stan. L. Rev. 1241, 1262-63 (1991).

relatively higher risk of violence as compared to cisgender women, shelters commonly deny transgender women equal protection.[261]

How should this issue be handled?

4. **Stalking and Domestic Violence in the Workplace.**   Government research estimates that about 16 percent of women and 5.8 percent of men have been victims of stalking, defined as a pattern of threatening or harassing behavior that is unwanted and causes reasonable persons to fear for their safety.[262] Employers sometimes respond by penalizing or terminating employees who are victims, which compounds their problems and reinforces economic dependence on abusers. Workplaces that do not provide adequate security force many women to leave their jobs out of safety concerns.

All states now have anti-stalking laws, and almost all have criminal statutes that make violating a protection order a criminal offense. A growing number of stalking victims who lose a job have recourse under federal or state law. The EEOC notes that although federal law does not explicitly protect domestic violence victims from employment discrimination, they may be entitled to protection under federal anti-discrimination law.[263] For example, an employer that terminates an employee subject to domestic violence out of fear of the potential "drama battered women bring to the workplace" may be liable for discrimination on the basis of sex.[264] An increasing number of states expressly prohibit employment discrimination against domestic violence survivors or have common law remedies for wrongful termination or for negligence in response to foreseeable violence.[265]

Strategies to increase workplace protections have included a variety of approaches. Some states have passed laws not only banning ban discrimination based on domestic violence but also providing unpaid leave for employees to deal with violence-related concerns. About half of the states have enacted laws explicitly granting unemployment benefits in some circumstances, such as where loss of employment reflects individuals' reasonable actions to protect themselves or their families from domestic violence.[266] Congress has also considered federal legislation such as the Security and Financial Empowerment Act, which would prohibit discrimination based on

261. Rishita Apsani, Are Women's Spaces Transgender Spaces? Single-Sex Domestic Violence Shelters, Transgender Inclusion, and the Equal Protection Clause, 106 Cal. L. Rev. 1689, 1692–93 (2018).

262. Cora Peterson, Lifetime Economic Burden of Intimate Partner Violence Among U.S. Adults, 55 Am. J. Preventive Med. 433 (2018). For other estimates, see McKinsey Global Institute, The Power of Parity: Advancing Women's Equality in the United States (Apr. 2016); NISVS, supra note 210, at 5.

263. EEOC, The Application of Title VII and the ADA to Applicants or Employees Who Experience Domestic or Dating Violence, Sexual Assault, or Stalking (2012).

264. Id.

265. Legal Momentum, State Law Guide: Employment Rights for Victims of Domestic or Sexual Violence (Aug. 27, 2019. For an example, see Danny v. Laidlaw Transit Servs., Inc. 193 P.3d 128 (Wash. 2008) (finding public policy of prohibiting an employer from discharging an employee because of domestic violence).

266. Legal Momentum, State Law Guide: Employment Rights, supra note 265.

domestic violence, guarantee eligible employees time off to address domestic violence issues, and ensure unemployment compensation for those who lose employment due to domestic violence.[267] Some commentators have urged that state and local governments require employers to offer reasonable accommodations to employees subject to domestic violence that would enable them to maintain their employment.[268] A few states and localities have enacted such requirements, which include measures such as modifying work schedules or transferring the employee to another location.[269]

What strategies do you believe are most essential to deal with the impact of IPV on the workplace? What stands in the way? Do employers have legitimate concerns? How would you respond to them? Would it be appropriate, for example, to require individuals who are under a restraining order to wear Global Positioning System (GPS) devices that track their location and alert police when they enter a prohibited zone?[270] A growing number of states have legislation authorizing courts to require electronic monitoring under certain conditions.[271] A number of studies suggest that such monitoring has reduced offenders' likelihood of reoffending.[272] Would such safety benefits outweigh concerns about intrusive government and due process rights for defendants?

5. **Domestic Violence and Housing Discrimination.**   A related issue involves housing discrimination based on domestic violence. The Violence Against Women Act and the federal Fair Housing Act both offer protection to victims of domestic violence living in federally subsidized housing and give them priorities in placement when justified by safety concerns.[273] The U.S. Department of Housing and Urban Development has pursued a growing number of enforcement actions involving such issues. In one typical case, the Department settled complaints against two New Hampshire landlords who refused to rent or renew a lease because of police visits responding to domestic violence incidents.[274] Women's rights advocates have also successfully challenged local nuisance laws that penalize victims for seeking police protection. In one case, the ACLU settled a case involving an ordinance under which three calls to the police

---

267. Security and Financial Empowerment Act of 2015, HR 3841 & S 2208, 114th Congress (2015).

268. See, e.g., Stephen R. Arnott & Margaret C. Hobday, It's a Human Right: Using International Human Rights Principles to Assist Employees Experiencing Domestic Violence, 18 Emp. Rts. & Emp. Pol'y J. 6, 15, 31-34 (2014); see also Joan Zorza, New Study on Domestic Violence in the Workplace, 3 Fam. & Intimate Partner Violence Q. 217 (2011).

269. Arnott & Hobday, supra note 268, at 15.

270. Chaz Arnett, From Decarceration to E-Carceration, 41 Cardozo L. Rev. 641, 672 (2019). See also Suraji R. Wagage, When the Consequences Are Life and Death: Pretrial Detention for Domestic Violence Offenders, 7 Drexel L. Rev. 195, 210 (2014).

271. Hannah Brenner, Transcending the Criminal Law's One Size Fits All Response to Domestic Violence, 19 Wm. & Mary Women & L. 341 (2012-2013).

272. Wagage, supra note 270, at 210.

273. U.S. Dep't of Housing and Urban Development, Assessing Claims of Housing Discrimination Against Victims of Domestic Violence Under the Fair Housing Act and the Violence Against Women Act (2011); see also McLaughlin & Fox, supra note 225 (policy guidance).

274. Mary C. Curtis, HUD Settles Case Alleging Housing Discrimination Against Domestic Violence Victim, Wash. Post, July 22, 2014.

in four months could result in revocation of a landlord's rental license and fines that could be avoided if the landlord evicted the tenant initiating the calls.[275]

6. **Domestic Violence and Child Custody.** Children can give abusers additional ways to exercise domination and control. Scholars contend that courts do not adequately consider IPV in custody cases, where male batterers are more likely than non-abusive men to seek custody of their children.[276] A mother may be more reluctant to leave her batterer if by doing so she jeopardizes the safety and economic support of her children. As has been noted, the period after separation — when a custody action is most likely to be filed — is one of the most dangerous times for abused women and their children.[277] Moreover, victims' psychological profiles or reluctance to cooperate with an abuser may work against their efforts to secure permanent custody of the children, and they may even be blamed for failing to protect children from abuse.[278] Visitation rights and joint custody arrangements may also provide opportunities for continued abuse.

In principle, family law recognizes such problems. At least twenty-two states have some form of a rebuttable presumption against awarding custody to a parent who has engaged in domestic violence, and many other states direct the court to take such violence into account in making custody and visitation decisions.[279] However, critics claim that judges and experts who make custody evaluations often fail to accord sufficient weight to evidence of domestic violence and discount incidents as "occasional," provoked, uncorroborated, or unlikely to recur.[280] The existence of "friendly parent" provisions, discussed in Chapter 2, Section D, can further complicate the matter by penalizing a battered mother who "alienates" the child from the abuser.

---

275. Sandra Park, Victory! Town Will No Longer Treat Domestic Violence Victims as Nuisances, ACLU Blog (Sept. 8, 2014).

276. Debra Pogrund Stark et al., Properly Accounting for Domestic Violence in Child Custody Cases: An Evidence-Based Analysis and Reform, 26 Mich. J. Gender & L. 1, 4 (2019); see Allen M. Bailey, Prioritizing Child Safety as the Prime Best-Interest Factor, 47 Fam. L.Q. 35, 38 (2013) (citing sources).

277. Bailey, supra note 276, at 37.

278. Lynn F. Beller, When in Doubt, Take Them Out: Removal of Children from Victims of Domestic Violence Ten Years After *Nicholson v. Williams*, 22 Duke J. Gender L. & Pol'y 205 (2015); see Nicholson v. Scoppetta, 820 N.E.2d 840 (N.Y. 2004) (holding that a policy of removing children from their mother's custody was not justified where the only allegation of neglect was that the child witnessed the mother's abuse; the reasonableness of the mother's action must be considered in light of all the circumstances).

279. For the latest reliable inventory, along with a review of legislative approaches to domestic violence and custody, see Nina Jaffe-Geffner, Gender Bias in Cross-Allegation Domestic Violence-Parental Alienation Custody Cases: Can States Legislate the Fix?, 42 Colum. J. Gender & L. 58, 84-95 (2022).

280. Id.; Schneider, supra note 258, at 360 (describing inadequate consideration of violence in custody cases); Leigh Goodmark, When Is a Battered Woman Not a Battered Woman? When She Fights Back, 20 Yale J.L. & Feminism 75, 116 (2008) (describing judicial belief that women fabricate claims to gain custody leverage); Deborah Epstein & Lisa A. Goodman, Discounting Women: Doubting Domestic Violence Survivors' Credibility and Dismissing Their Experiences, 167 U. Pa. L. Rev. 399, 431-32 (2019).

Another difficult issue in battering relationships is allocating culpability when the children themselves are abused. If children are present when police arrive at the home of a domestic violence incident, in some jurisdictions "the officers, as mandated reporters of child maltreatment, will routinely report not only the perpetrator, but also the abused adult victim to the child protection agency"; the government may then "charge a victim with 'failure to protect' her children by permitting domestic violence to occur while they are living in the home."[281] Such practices can deter women from reporting violence.

Finally, how should the law respond when a battered woman flees with the children — or when an abuser does? Various federal statutes seek to protect victims of abduction and promote coordination among states.[282] When abductors flee the United States altogether, the Hague Child Abduction Convention mandates the return of children to their place of "habitual residence" for a custody determination unless that would pose a "grave risk of harm."[283] Judicial remedies known as "undertakings" can return families to the country of origin to arrange custody. Whether courts have interpreted the Convention in ways responsive to domestic violence that prompts abduction remains open to dispute. Some commentators charge that courts do not consider violence directed only against mothers when assessing harm. If their children are subject to return, these mothers may accompany them and become vulnerable to further abuse.[284]

7. **Prevention and Rehabilitation Services.**   Many experts believe that more attention needs to center on prevention and rehabilitation. Since the late 1970s, at least 2,000 batterer treatment programs have been developed in prisons or as alternatives to incarceration.[285] Such programs aim to change attitudes, improve anger management skills, and thus reduce the likelihood of future violence. Despite the prevalence of such initiatives, there is surprisingly little data on their long-term effectiveness, and much of the research available is conflicting or hampered by small and nonrandom samples and large dropout rates.[286] However, what limited data are available "suggest that batterer programs have little or no effect" even on

---

281. Leslie Joan Harris, Failure to Protect from Exposure to Domestic Violence in Private Custody Contests, 44 Family L.Q. 169, 178-83 (2010); Emily J. Sack, Battered Women and the State: The Struggle for the Future of Domestic Violence Policy, 2004 Wis. L. Rev. 1684 (2004). For consideration of these issues, see Jeanne M. Kaiser & Caroline M. Foley, Family Law — The Revictimization of Survivors of Domestic Violence and Their Children: The Heartbreaking Unintended Consequence of Separating Children from Their Abused Parent, 43 W. New Eng. L. Rev. 167, 184 (2021).

282. The Uniform Child Custody Jurisdiction and Enforcement Act (UCCJEA) generally favors the "home state" of the child and custodial parent. Other relevant statutes are the Parental Kidnapping Prevention Act (PKPA) and the full faith and credit requirements of the Violence Against Women Act (VAWA).

283. Hague Convention of October 25, 1980 on the Civil Aspects of Child Abduction, Article 13(b), Oct. 25, 1980.

284. Merle H. Weiner, Using Article 20, 38 Fam. L.Q. 583 (2004).

285. D. Kelly Weisberg, Domestic Violence: Legal and Social Reality 803 (2012).

286. Deborah L. Rhode, Social Research and Social Change: Meeting the Challenge of Gender Inequality and Sexual Abuse, 30 Harv. J.L. & Gender 11, 21 (2007) (reviewing studies).

those who complete them.[287] In an article in The Atlantic magazine, reporter Matthew Wolfe describes the most commonly prescribed anti-battering program, the Domestic Abuse Intervention Project (DAIP), also known as the Duluth model.[288] It is based in the feminist insight that our society is structured around male power over women and individual men may thus feel entitled to exercise power over individual women. The Atlantic article questions the Duluth model's efficacy, saying "In the view of most psychologists, domestic violence can be caused by many things. While culture—particularly the degree to which domestic violence is tolerated or encouraged by a society—plays a role in producing batterers, scholars argue that it is impossible to isolate a single element, like male entitlement, from what is often a grisly gnarl of psychological and biological influences."

Wolfe does provide some hope by discussing the Achieving Change Through Values-Based Behavior (ACTV) program, which does not assume the motivation for battering. It allows batterers to think whatever they want—including that they are the victim—as long as they identify a value that motivates them to change their behaviors. This may be a fruitful approach: "In a pilot study, published in 2017, men who successfully completed an ACTV program were nearly 50 percent less likely to be rearrested for domestic violence as participants in Iowa's old program." Is rehabilitation worthwhile even if it is predicated upon a batterer's goal of staying out of jail rather than respecting their partner? Does such an individual focus miss or even exacerbate structural problems?

Researchers such as Carolyn Ramsey argue that a large part of the problem is that too few programs differentiate between different categories of offenders and abuses, and many fail to take into account relevant factors such as sex, race, ethnicity, socioeconomic status, sexual orientation, mental health, and substance abuse.[289] Interventions need to address the particular challenges facing individual offenders and to employ culturally sensitive strategies with adequate therapeutic, educational, and employment services.

It is especially important to address both structural and individual factors when dealing with youth victims of violence. A significant number of high school students report being physically hurt by a partner and these youths are more likely to do poorly in school and to suffer from mental health and substance abuse problems.[290] Perpetrators of teen violence may also carry those patterns into future relationships. Among adult victims of rape, stalking, or violence by an intimate partner, almost a quarter of women first experienced some form of partner violence when they were adolescents.[291] The Centers for Disease Control and Prevention has a project aimed at promoting healthy teen dating relationships.[292]

---

287. Edward Gondolf, The Future of Batterer Programs: Reassessing Evidence-Based Practice 71, 125 (2012); see also Carolyn B. Ramsey, The Stereotyped Offender: Domestic Violence and the Failure of Intervention, 120 Penn St. L. Rev. 337, 369 (2015).

288. See Matthew Wolfe, Can You Cure a Domestic Abuser?, Atlantic (Jan. 17, 2020).

289. Ramsey, supra note 287, at 373, 381.

290. Id.

291. CDC, Preventing Teen Dating Violence (2022).

292. CDC, Dating Matters, The Science (2020).

8. **Mandatory Arrest Policies.**   The primary approach to IPV has been through criminalization. Mandatory or pro-arrest policies require police officers to arrest a suspect if there is probable cause to believe that an assault or battery has occurred, or that a domestic restraining order has been violated, without regard to the victim's consent or objection. These policies began to appear in the wake of a landmark Minneapolis study showing that arrest lowered recidivism rates in domestic violence cases. This study, along with several high-profile lawsuits against unresponsive police departments, helped launch policies now in force in about half of the states.[293]

Evidence concerning the effectiveness of these policies is mixed.[294] Some studies indicate that some police officers remain unresponsive even under mandatory policies because they retain discretion to determine the existence of probable cause to believe that domestic violence has occurred.[295] Some criticize the laws because of the decreased likelihood that victims will contact police or service providers.[296] Some research finds that mandatory arrest policies increase the frequency of arrests, but not successful prosecutions or victim safety.[297] One study found an increased death rate among domestic violence survivors whose partners were jailed.[298] Research also indicates that arrest and prosecution work best with those who have the most to lose from criminal sanctions, and that the risks of violence escalate among those who have the least to lose: those who are unemployed, poorly educated, unmarried, and who already have a criminal record.[299]

Mandatory arrest laws also increase the likelihood of dual arrests, in which victims who fight back are also charged, although rates of dual arrest are still relatively low.[300] In some jurisdictions, victims have even been jailed for refusing to testify after filing an abuse complaint.

---

293. For a review of policies, see Xinge He et al., Domestic Violence, 21 Geo. J. Gender & L. 253, 279-82 (2020); Emerson Beishline, An Examination of the Effects of Institutional Racism and Systematic Prejudice on Intimate Partner Violence in Minority Communities, 4 Wm. Mitchell L. Raza J. 2, 23-24 (2013).

294. For an overview, see He et al., supra note 293; see also Leigh Goodmark, Decriminalizing Domestic Violence: A Balanced Policy Approach to Intimate Partner Violence 12-15 (2018).

295. Kimberly Bailey, Lost in Translation: Domestic Violence, "The Personal Is Political," and the Criminal Justice System, 100 J. Crim. L. & Criminology 1255, 1257 (2010).

296. For an overview, see Laurie S. Kohn, The Justice System and Domestic Violence: Engaging the Case but Divorcing the Victim, 32 N.Y.U. Rev. L. & Soc. Change, 237-38 (2008); Sally F. Goldfarb, Reconceiving Civil Protection Orders for Domestic Violence: Can Law Help End the Abuse Without Ending the Relationship?, 29 Cardozo L. Rev. 1511, 1537 (2008).

297. Leigh Goodmark, Autonomy Feminism: An Anti-Essentialist Critique of Mandatory Interventions in Domestic Violence Cases, 37 Fla. St. U. L. Rev. 1, 35 (2009).

298. Lawrence W. Sherman & Heather M. Harris, Increased Death Rates of Domestic Violence Victims from Arrests vs. Warning Suspects in the Milwaukee Domestic Violence Experiment, 11 J. Experimental Criminology 1 (2015).

299. See Keith Guzik, The Forces of Conviction: The Power and Practice of Mandatory Prosecution upon Misdemeanor Domestic Battery Suspects, 32 L. & Soc. Inquiry 44 (2007).

300. Alexandra Masri, Equal Rights, Unequal Protection: Institutional Failures in Protecting and Advocating for Victims of Same-Sex Domestic Violence in Post-Marriage Equality

9. **Mandatory No-Drop Policies.**   Another initiative has been mandatory or no-drop policies, which require prosecutors to pursue domestic violence cases regardless of victims' wishes. These policies take two forms. The "hard approach" requires the victim to cooperate or face penalties; the "soft" approach does not penalize the victim for refusing to participate.[301] The limited evidence available suggests that the vast majority of victims are reluctant to testify against an abuser due to fear of retaliation, financial dependence, emotional attachment, or family and community pressure.[302] Under these circumstances, prosecutors may use strategies similar to those used in murder cases where victims are unavailable: introducing spontaneous statements made by the victim at the time of arrest, police officers' testimony, and videos or photographs taken at the time of the injury. However, while statements given by the victim in an effort to obtain help are admissible, statements elicited by the police as part of their investigation (known as "testimonial evidence") are not admissible against a criminal defendant unless the witness who made the statements at issue is unavailable and the defendant had a prior opportunity for cross-examination. Except in cases involving serious documented injuries, juries tend to be reluctant to convict if victims are uncooperative.[303] But prosecutors in many of these cases are able to obtain plea agreements at least to misdemeanors by charging defendants with more serious offenses, or by threatening to prosecute violations of restraining orders. The *Stevenson* case illustrates the further instance of not allowing women themselves to end civil restraining orders.

Proponents of these mandatory policies argue that they are the best way to force law enforcement officials and various service providers to take domestic violence seriously. In advocates' view, a mandatory approach can deter future abuse and reduce the exposure of victims.

Critics charge that interventions over which victims have no control compound victims' trauma and erode their senses of efficacy, autonomy, and self-esteem — all aspects of their lives that are already weakened by the violence itself.[304] Some advocates propose that law enforcement agencies should make victims' long-term safety the preeminent concern. A "survivor-centered" strategy might suggest more flexible policies that, say, permit dropping charges where victims are at high risk for retaliation; where abusers are unlikely to get lengthy sentences; or where an alternative like completion of a substance abuse and counseling program might assist the parties more than prosecution. Such a strategy could also provide more outreach to victims to ensure that protective orders are effective. The limited available evidence suggests that focusing on women's

Era, 27 Tul. J.L. & Sexuality 75, 84 (2018) (26 percent and 27 percent of female and male same-sex couples are both arrested, only 1.3 percent in all IPV cases); see also David Hirschel et al., Domestic Violence and Mandatory Arrest Laws: To What Extent Do They Influence Police Arrest Decisions, 98 J. Crim. L. & Criminology 255 (2007).

301. Leigh Goodmark, A Troubled Marriage: Domestic Violence and the Legal System 112 (2012).

302. See id.

303. Guzik, supra note 299, at 49.

304. Goodmark, supra note 301, at 118-24.

needs increases their willingness to cooperate with prosecutors and reduces their exposure to repeated abuse.[305]

What is your view? Are mandatory policies a logical application of nonsubordination theory? Can women be counted on to make the right decisions to protect themselves when subject to the pressures that domestic violence exerts upon them?

Some judges have imposed fines or jail sentences for a battered woman's contempt of a civil protection order. For example, Kentucky Judge Megan Lake Thornton fined an impoverished woman $100 for reconciling with her husband a few days after she had obtained a protective order. Thornton explained, "I find that offensive. It drives me nuts when people just decide to do whatever they want." Like a vocal minority of family court judges, she has made it clear that no-contact orders apply equally to abusers and targets of abuse. "People are ordered to follow them and I don't care which side you are on."[306] Domestic violence advocates view this kind of formalistic egalitarian approach as unrealistic, unjust, and "a barrier that stops abused women from seeking protection of the court."[307] They believe that victims should be able to request orders that do not bar all contact. When parties have children, financial difficulties, or continuing love for their abusers, "[i]t's pretty hard to say, 'Never speak again.'"[308] Jeannie Suk argues that insofar as violations of protective orders are usually a crime, such orders can amount to a de facto divorce, especially in poorer families.[309] Should victims have the option of requesting protection orders that do not prohibit all contact with the requesting party?

Practices with respect to restraining orders vary. In some jurisdictions, courts defer to victims' preferences; in others they make independent inquiries concerning coercion and risks; and in some instances they deny requests as a matter of policy. However, pressure on the victim from the abuser is hard to assess, and when in doubt many judges err on the side of keeping protections in place; no one wants to be the one who dissolved an order for a woman "found face down in the morning."[310]

10. **Domestic Violence and the Overincarceration Problem.**   In considering the legal options available for domestic violence, should the effects of mass

305. See Deborah Epstein et al., Transforming Aggressive Prosecution Policies: Prioritizing Victims' Long-Term Safety in the Prosecution of Domestic Violence Cases, 11 Am. U. J. Gender Soc. Pol'y & L. 465, 486-98 (2003).

306. Francis X. Clines, Judge's Domestic Violence Ruling Creates an Outcry in Kentucky, N.Y. Times, Jan. 8, 2002, at A14 (quoting Thornton).

307. Id. (quoting Carol Jordan, director of the Kentucky Governor's Office of Child Abuse and Domestic Violence).

308. Id. at A14 (quoting Sherry Currens, Executive Director of the Kentucky Domestic Violence Ass'n). For arguments supporting orders that do not ban all contact, see generally Sally F. Goldfarb, Reconceiving Civil Protection Orders for Domestic Violence: Can Law Help End the Abuse Without Ending the Relationship?, 29 Cardozo L. Rev. 1487 (2008).

309. See Jeannie Suk, At Home in the Law: How the Domestic Violence Revolution is Transforming Privacy (2009).

310. Tamara L. Kuennen, Analyzing the Impact of Coercion on Domestic Violence Victims; How Much Is Too Much?, 22 Berkeley J. Gender, L. & Just. 2, 25 (2007).

incarceration, particularly on poor, minority populations, be relevant?[311] Tonya Jacobi and Ross Berlin note that "[u]ntil around 1975, the rate of imprisonment in the United States remained stable and in line with global averages, before increasing more than sevenfold in the following forty years." This coincides with most of the growth of the anti-domestic violence movement.[312] Some feminists, organized as anti-carceral/decarceration feminists, point out that criminal legal responses to gender violence often disserve victims, too, failing to result in healing and aggravating their distress. Women of color, lesbian and transgender women, poor women, and immigrant women often have heightened skepticism of "law and order" responses to domestic violence, based on their own or friends' and relatives' experiences of being doubted, disbelieved, abused, or unfairly treated by police and law enforcement authorities.[313] Deborah Weissman extends anti-carceral feminism into class analysis, arguing there is a "convergence of interests between anti-carceral groups, anti-domestic violence groups, and labor groups."[314]

Increasingly, scholars of domestic violence, including Aya Gruber, excerpted above, are urging solutions that avoid exacerbating these problems. In her critique of mandatory prosecution policies and the like, does Professor Gruber give a fair description of dominance (referred to in this chapter as nonsubordination) feminism? Which parts of it does she accept, and which parts does she reject? How important are intersectionality concerns to her analysis?

Greater community resources both for victims of domestic violence and its perpetrators, described in notes 3 and 7 above, are a relatively uncontroversial reaction to concerns about overincarceration. Leigh Goodmark goes further and offers a different justice model for addressing domestic violence — the restorative justice model.

> Restorative justice focuses on harm rather than crime, allowing victims to define the harm done to them, requiring offenders to acknowledge the harm, and bringing victims, offenders, and their supporters together to craft a plan that holds offenders accountable for and addresses the harm. Restorative processes allow victims the opportunity to confront their perpetrators directly and to speak to them openly about how they have been affected, a much more direct form of accountability than that which is available through the criminal legal system. Restorative justice engages community members in supporting people subjected to abuse and developing solutions that hold perpetrators accountable, making intimate partner violence more visible within the community. Restorative justice has

---

311. See Donna Coker & Ahjané D. Macquoid, Why Opposing Hyper-Incarceration Should Be Central to the Work of the Anti-Domestic Violence Movement, 5 U. Miami Race & Soc. Just. L. Rev. 585 (2015).

312. Tonja Jacobi & Ross Berlin, Supreme Irrelevance: The Court's Abdication in Criminal Procedure Jurisprudence, 51 U.C. Davis L. Rev. 2033, 2081 (2018).

313. See Chloe Taylor, Anti-Carceral Feminism and Sexual Assault — A Defense, 34 Soc. Phil. Today 29 (2018).

314. Deborah M. Weissman, Gender Violence, the Carceral State, and the Politics of Solidarity, 55 U.C. Davis L. Rev. 801, 871 (2021).

been widely used in criminal cases, most often with juvenile offenders, with very positive results. Both victims and offenders report high levels of satisfaction with both restorative processes and outcomes. Victims who opt for restorative justice have more information, are more likely to meet with and confront their perpetrator, are more likely to have some understanding of the reasons behind the offending, are more likely to receive some kind of repair for the harm done . . . are more likely to be satisfied with the agreements reached, are more likely to feel better about their experience and are less likely afterwards to feel angry or fearful than those victims whose perpetrators were dealt with by the courts. Perpetrators, in turn, are more likely to understand the impact of their actions, be held accountable in meaningful ways, and provide the kinds of redress requested by victims.[315]

Is Goodmark's suggestion realistic? Feminist scholars have long opposed mediation in domestic violence cases, on numerous grounds, including its risks to the victims.[316] Should the same concern extend to restorative justice? Is the restorative justice model consistent with Aya Gruber's neo-feminist approach?

11. **Civil Damage Claims.**   Apart from what is to be done with batterers is the question of how to heal their victims. Civil damages suits provide a legal resource for survivors of intimate violence. VAWA had created a federal civil rights remedy for "crimes of violence motivated by gender," but the Supreme Court in United States v. Morrison determined that it was up to the states to create such a cause of action and beyond Congress' constitutional authority.[317] However, a few states and localities have adopted gender-motivated violence civil rights laws that cover domestic assaults.[318] State tort law also generally provides remedies for assault, and 48 jurisdictions have abolished barriers to spouses suing each other.[319] Such claims are, however, infrequent, partly because defendants lack deep pockets and insurance policies do not cover intentional torts.[320]

Beginning in the 1980s, some leading decisions allowed actions under Section 1983 of the Federal Civil Rights Act against municipalities whose police were grossly negligent in responding to domestic violence complaints. However, in 2005, the Supreme Court limited such remedies. In Castle Rock v. Gonzales, the Court held that a jurisdiction's mandatory arrest policy does not create the necessary "special relationship" with the state or an entitlement under the Due Process Clause that

---

315. Leigh Goodmark, Should Domestic Violence Be Decriminalized?, 40 Harv. J. L. & Gender 53, 94-95 (2017).

316. See, e.g., Sara Cobb, The Domestication of Violence in Mediation, 31 Law & Soc'y Rev. 397, 398 (1997).

317. United States v. Morrison, 529 U.S. 598 (2000). The case arose from a sexual assault by two college football players. One of them announced in the dormitory's dining room that "I like to get girls drunk and fuck the shit out of them."

318. Camille Carey, Domestic Violence Torts: Righting a Civil Wrong, 62 Kan. L. Rev. 695, 712 (2014); Domestic Violence, 0030 SURVEYS 7 (2022).

319. Caitlin Valiulis, Domestic Violence, 15 Geo. J. Gender & L. 123, 145 (2014).

320. Carey, supra note 318, at 728-29.

would justify liability under Section 1983.[321] There, Jessica Gonzales repeatedly requested that local police arrest her ex-husband for violation of a civil restraining order after he abducted their three daughters who were playing in the family's front yard.[322] According to the facts in the complaint, which the Court accepted for purposes of the decision, the respondent contacted the police six times between 7:30 p.m. and 1:00 a.m. the next morning. She even went to the police station to file an incident report and begged the officers to look for her husband, who had a history of instability and violence. The officer who took the report made "no reasonable effort to enforce the [restraining order] or locate the three children. Instead he went to dinner." Shortly after 3:00 a.m., the husband arrived at the police station and opened fire. Officers shot back, killing him in the exchange, and then discovered the dead bodies of his daughters in his pickup truck.

Colorado has a mandatory arrest law for violations of restraining orders. It provides that:

> (a) Whenever a protection order is issued, the protected person shall be provided with a copy of such order. A peace officer shall use every reasonable means to enforce a protection order.
> (b) A peace officer shall arrest, or, if an arrest would be impractical under the circumstances, seek a warrant for the arrest of a restrained person when the peace officer has information amounting to probable cause that [the order has been violated].

Speaking for the majority, Justice Scalia reasoned that these statutory provisions have not "truly made enforcement of restraining orders mandatory. A well-established tradition of police discretion has coexisted with apparently mandatory arrest statutes." Moreover, even if Gonzales had been entitled to enforcement, the majority concluded that such an entitlement would not constitute a property interest protected by the Due Process Clause and enforceable under Section 1983.[323] Justice Souter, joined by Justice Breyer, concurred in the judgment but wrote separately to emphasize the concern that finding a property right to enforcement would in effect "federalize every mandatory state-law direction to executive officers whose performance on the job can be vitally significant to individuals affected."[324] Justice Stevens, joined by Justice Ginsburg, dissented. As Stevens read the statute, in light of its legislative history, "the police were required to provide enforcement. They lacked the discretion to do nothing."[325]

Following that decision, the mother brought a suit before the Inter-American Commission on Human Rights, affiliated with the Organization of American States. In essence, she claimed that the United States violated her rights under the American Declaration of the Rights and Duties of Man, denying her right to be free from gender-based violence and discrimination. State Department lawyers countered

---

321. 545 U.S. 748 (2005).
322. Id.
323. Id. at 760.
324. Id. at 772 (Souter, J., concurring in the judgment).
325. Id. at 784-85 (Stevens, J., dissenting).

that the Declaration imposes no duty to prevent crimes inflicted by private individuals and that the state acted reasonably on the information it had available. In rejecting that argument, the Commission found that the State failed to act with "due diligence" to protect the Gonzales children and their mother from domestic violence, which violated "the State's obligation not to discriminate and to provide for equal protection before the law under the American Declaration." The Commission also found that the state failed to undertake reasonable measures to protect the lives of the children, in violation of their right to life under the Declaration. Under the Commission's analysis, the "state apparatus was not duly organized, coordinated, and ready to protect these victims from domestic violence by adequately and effectively implementing the restraining order at issue . . . [which] constituted a form of discrimination in violation of Article II of the American Declaration."[326] Based on those conclusions, the Commission made recommendations to the United States including that:

- it undertake a "serious, impartial and exhaustive investigation" into the deaths of the Gonzales children and the failures to enforce Jessica Lenahan Gonzales's protection order, and hold those responsible accountable;
- it offer full reparations to Jessica Lenahan Gonzales;
- it adopt multifaceted legislation at the federal and state levels, or reform existing legislation to protect women and children from imminent violence and to ensure effective implementation mechanisms.[327]

How would you evaluate the Commission's ruling? If the United States were to follow its recommendations, what initiatives would be likely?

Lower federal courts have also sometimes been willing to hold states liable under civil rights law where law enforcement officials increase the danger to domestic violence victims. Circuits are split on the evidence required to make such a showing. Some have required more than inaction, such as failure to arrest.[328] The Second Circuit, however, in Okin v. Village of Cornwall-on-Hudson Police Department, has held that "repeated sustained inaction by government officials, in the face of potential acts of violence, might . . . [give rise] to the level of an affirmative condoning of private violence," and if the indifference is so egregious as to "shock the conscience" the victim can recover damages under Section 1983.[329] In *Okin*, police officers' failure to arrest a batterer, and discussion of football with him, could be taken as condoning future violence. However, because of the U.S. Supreme Court's Deshaney v. Winnebago County Department of Social Services case, which refuses liability for police failure to act,[330] most cases distinguish *Okin*.[331] What legal standards should courts apply to civil cases challenging police inaction?

---

326. Jessica Lenahan (Gonzales) et al. v. United States, Report No. 80/11, Case 12.626, paragraphs 5 & 60 (Merits, July 21, 2011).

327. Id. at para. 201.

328. See cases discussed in Julie Goldscheid, Rethinking Civil Rights and Gender Violence, 14 Geo. J. Gender & L. 43, 67-69 (2013).

329. 577 F. 3d 415, 428, 431 (2d Cir. 2009).

330. DeShaney v. Winnebago Cnty. Dep't of Soc. Servs., 489 U.S. 189 (1989).

331. See, e.g., Zubko-Valva v. Cnty. of Suffolk, No. 220CV2663ERKARL, 2022 WL 2161193, at *6 (E.D.N.Y. June 15, 2022) (quoting *DeShaney*, 489 U.S. at 201).

12. **Immigration and Asylum Law.** Experts estimate that between one-third and one-half of immigrant women in the United States experience domestic violence, and are at particular risk for lethal abuse.[332] Their special vulnerability reflects lack of English language ability, unfamiliarity with the U.S. legal system and local social services as well as dependence on partners for financial support and immigration status. Abused immigrants who meet rigorous conditions, including cooperation with law enforcement, are eligible for U visas, but these have been capped at levels wholly inadequate to the demand.[333] In the most recent years, three times as many crime victims applied for U visas as were available, and insufficient adjudicative resources have led to a huge backlog.[334] Moreover, many women fail to meet the conditions for the U visa due to lack of knowledge, distrust of government officials, and fear of deportation for themselves or for partners.[335]

Should the U visa system provide exceptions similar to those for trafficking victims who are too traumatized to cooperate or whose safety would be compromised by cooperation?[336] Should these survivors have a special right to legal assistance and adequate court services, including interpreters and appropriate social services, even if these are not available to other individuals who need them?

Whether domestic violence should be treated as a human rights violation has arisen in several contexts, including asylum. In the United States, the right to asylum is governed by the international definition of a "refugee." The United Nations Convention Relating to the Status of Refugees defines a refugee in part as any person who "owing to a well-founded fear of being persecuted for reasons of race, religion, national origin, membership in a particular social group or political opinion, is outside the country of his nationality and is unable or, owing to such fear, is unwilling to avail himself of the protection of that country." Victims of domestic violence have generally based their claims for asylum on the "membership in a particular social group."[337]

For two decades, courts and immigration authorities struggled with such claims. In 2014, in the Matter of A-R-C-G-, the Board of Immigration Appeals held in a published opinion that an applicant can qualify for asylum based on domestic violence.[338] The principal respondent in the case was a Guatemalan mother of three whose husband raped and beat her repeatedly. When calls to the police and attempts to escape proved unavailing, she entered the United States and filed for asylum soon after. On appeal, a unanimous Board held that the respondent

---

332. Natalie Nanasi, The U Visa's Failed Promise for Survivors of Domestic Violence, 29 Yale J. L. & Feminism 273, 277, 284-85 (2018).

333. Id. at 277.

334. U.S. Citizenship & Immig. Serv., Number of Form I-918, Petition for U Nonimmigrant Status by Fiscal Year, Quarter, and Case Status 2009-2022 (2022).

335. Nanasi, supra note 332, at 297-303.

336. Id. at 315-16.

337. See Theresa A. Vogel, Critiquing Matter of A-B-: An Uncertain Future in Asylum Proceedings for Women Fleeing Intimate Partner Violence, 19-07 Immigr. Briefings 1.

338. 26 I. & N. Dec. 388 (B.I.A. 2014). For discussion see, Recent Adjudication, Asylum Law, 128 Harv. L. Rev. 2090 (2015).

belonged to a social group — married women in Guatemala who are unable to leave their relationship — that could form the basis of an asylum claim.[339]

However, in 2018, Attorney General Jeff Sessions used another case, *Matter of A-B-*, to overrule *Matter of A-R-C-G-*. In nonbinding dicta, Sessions stated that "generally claims by aliens pertaining to domestic violence or gang violence perpetrated by nongovernmental actors will not qualify for asylum."[340] There is, he wrote, "significant room for doubt that Guatemalan society views these women, as horrible as their personal circumstances may be, as members of a distinct group in society, rather than each as a victim of a particular abuser in highly individualized circumstances. . . . Rather, he attacked her because of his preexisting personal relationship with the victim."[341] How would you critique the perspective on domestic violence reflected in this opinion?

This approach runs counter to that advocated by international law authorities, who treat domestic violence as a human rights issue. The Declaration on the Elimination of Violence Against Women and the UNHCR Guidelines on the Protection of Refugee Women recognize domestic violence as a form of gender discrimination, and thus a human rights violation. The UN Convention Against Torture is another possible mechanism for protection of women fleeing domestic violence. The United Nations Special Rapporteur on Violence Against Women has "recommended that bodies that report on human rights abuses and violence against women and treaty bodies consider treating domestic violence as an internationally proscribed form of torture."[342] Should all women fleeing domestic violence in their home countries be entitled to claim asylum in the United States? If not, what limiting principles should be applicable?[343]

President Biden reinstated the opinion in *Matter of A-R-C-G-* but the Fifth Circuit has put that order on hold.[344] If the Biden administration promulgates new regulations to address this issue, what should they say?

PUTTING THEORY INTO PRACTICE

3-13. When a terrified Oregon woman called a 911 operator to report that a violent former boyfriend was trying to break into her home, the dispatcher had no one to send. The local sheriff's department had insufficient funds to staff anyone on weekends to take such calls. The operator unsuccessfully tried to coach the woman into how to hide or negotiate with the intruder, who ended up breaking in

---

339. A-R-C-G-, 26 I & N. Dec. at 388-89. (2014).

340. 27 I & N Dec. 316 (A.G. 2018); Katie Benner & Caitlin Dickerson, Sessions Says Domestic and Gang Violence Are Not Grounds for Asylum, N.Y. Times, June 11, 2018, at A1.

341. A-R-C-G-, 26 I & N. Dec. at 336, 339.

342. Amanda Blanck, Domestic Violence as a Basis for Asylum Status: A Human Rights Based Approach, 22 Women's Rts. L. Rep. 47, 72 (2001).

343. See Spencer Kyle, Safety Over Semantics: The Case for Statutory Protection for Domestic Violence Asylum Applicants, 16 The Scholar: St. Mary's L. Rev. & Soc. Just. 505, 535 (2014).

344. Jaco v. Garland, 24 F.4th 395 (5th Cir. 2021).

and raping her. The following week, the county sheriff issued a press release, warning victims of domestic violence with restraining orders to "consider relocating to an area with adequate law enforcement services."[345] If the Oregon woman brought suit against the county, would she win? Should she? Would authorizing damage awards exacerbate the financial difficulties that exposed her to risk? Or would such judgments force state and local authorities to readjust their funding priorities in ways that took account of safety risks to women?

3-14. Rendez-Vous is a small, upscale restaurant that caters to the Manhattan theater crowd. One of its best waitresses is being stalked by an ex-boyfriend who has come to the restaurant several times to harass her and has occasionally prevented her from arriving on time. After one loud, abusive incident in which the owner had to call the police, he fires the waitress. "I don't need this," he tells her. "Business is bad enough as it is." Would it be fair to the employer to hold him liable for firing her? The boyfriend also has stalked her apartment complex, and his violent actions have alarmed other tenants. Should the landlord be able to evict her? If not, what remedies should be available to the landlord?

3-15. Pamela Hird obtained a protective order against the defendant based on domestic violence. She subsequently allowed him to live in her basement and have occasional meals with her because she felt sorry for him when he was intoxicated and had no place to go, and because she worried that she might be in trouble for not calling the police immediately when he showed up. Should her consent be relevant in a prosecution of the defendant for violating the protective order?[346]

3-16. Fawn Balliro, an Assistant District Attorney in Massachusetts, was assaulted by her partner in Tennessee after he became jealous when she talked to another man in a bar. Her screams when he punched her in the face alerted the neighbor, who called 911. The police charged the man with misdemeanor assault. He told Balliro that he was on probation for drug offenses and if he was convicted he would be incarcerated and no one would be available to support his two minor daughters. Balliro then told the prosecutor that she had been injured while falling. Other evidence suggested her story about falling was not credible, and the prosecutor tried the case and called her as a witness. She told the same story exculpating the defendant at trial, and the case was dismissed. The Tennessee prosecutor then informed the District Attorney's office in Massachusetts, which put her on leave until she agreed to undergo counseling. It also reported her conduct to disciplinary authorities, who recommended a public reprimand, partly on the basis of psychiatric testimony indicating that she was highly unlikely to commit such an act again. The Massachusetts Supreme Court, however, held that false testimony under oath could not be condoned, irrespective of the circumstances, and suspended her from practice for six months. The Court noted the perceived inequity of giving her a greater penalty than the two-month suspension for a lawyer guilty of misdemeanor assault against his wife from whom he was separated. However, lying under oath was in the court's view a more serious offense.[347] Do you agree?

---

345. Michelle Anderson, We Are Not Dead: Local Government in the Post-Industrial Era (unpublished manuscript) (on file with author).

346. State v. Branson, 167 P.3d 370 (Kan. Ct. App. 2007).

347. In re Balliro, 899 N.E. 2d 794 (Mass. 2009).

3-17. Numerous professional sports figures have been involved in highly publicized instances of domestic violence, including battery and sexual assault. In response, the National Football League, Major League Baseball, the National Hockey League, and the National Basketball Association have all instituted policies related to domestic violence. For example, the NFL prohibits a broad range of violent and abusive behaviors by its players, requiring that while a charge is being investigated a player be placed on paid leave, and that the minimum suspension for a player found to have engaged in assault (including sexual assault) or domestic violence is six games, without pay. "A player who violates the policy again will be banned from the league."[348] Why do you suppose domestic violence is such a problem among professional sports players? How should the leagues handle it? What is the appropriate punishment for a professional football player who beat his fiancée to a state of unconsciousness?[349]

2. Domestic Violence and Substantive Criminal Law

Under longstanding Anglo-American law, killing in the "sudden heat of passion" is not murder, but rather the lesser crime of voluntary manslaughter; the theory is that "adequate provocation" by the victim may cause reasonable people to lose their reason.[350] Catching one's spouse in the act of adultery traditionally has been described as the quintessential example of adequate provocation. Sexual taunting, as in People v. Berry, excerpted below, provides a classic illustration. Until the 1960s, juries in some states also recognized an "unwritten law" of "honor defense" that allowed for acquittal of a defendant who killed his wife or his wife's lover out of sexual jealousy.

Under the Model Penal Code (MPC), a homicide that would otherwise be murder may be reduced to manslaughter if defendants can show that they acted under the influence of "extreme mental or emotional disturbance for which there is reasonable explanation or excuse." Whether there is such an explanation or excuse is to be judged from the point of view of "a person in the actor's situation under the circumstances as he believes them to be." The intention of the MPC drafters was to focus on the defendant's disturbed state of mind, rather than on the existence of justifying circumstances. *Berry* reflects this approach.

Another criminal law doctrine that applies in some domestic violence cases is the law of self-defense. This doctrine exonerates a killing when reasonably necessary to save oneself from imminent death or great bodily harm. This is the law at issue in State v. Norman, excerpted below. Both *Berry* and *Norman* involve a lapse

---

348. Charlotte Edmonds, Notable Cases of Domestic Violence and Assault in Sports, NBC Sports, May 23, 2022.

349. Baltimore Ravens running back Ray Rice was suspended for two games after a third-degree aggravated assault charge was dropped in favor of court-ordered counseling. When a more conclusive video was released, Rice was suspended indefinitely. This suspension was overturned, but the Ravens dropped Rice and no team thereafter would sign him. Id.

350. See Cynthia Lee, The Trans Panic Defense Revisited, 57 Am. Crim. L. Rev. 1411, 1425 (2020).

of time between the victim's provocation of the defendant and defendant's violent acts. How does that lapse of time factor in? How should it? When a claim of self-defense is raised, evidence of Battered Person Syndrome (the newer term for Battered Woman Syndrome) may be used in domestic violence cases to help the jury understand the reasonableness of a defendant's actions, as in the *Norman* case. Has the law been able to maintain gender neutrality in this area? Does it ameliorate or reinforce gender subordination?

People v. Berry

556 P.2d 777 (Cal. 1976)

Sullivan, Justice.

Defendant Albert Joseph Berry was charged by indictment with one count of murder and one count of assault by means of force likely to produce great bodily injury. . . . The assault was allegedly committed on July 23, 1974, and the murder on July 26, 1974. In each count, the alleged victim was defendant's wife, Rachel Pessah Berry. A jury found defendant guilty as charged and determined that the murder was of the first degree. Defendant was sentenced to state prison for the term prescribed by law. He appeals from the judgment of conviction.

Defendant contends that there is sufficient evidence in the record to show that he committed the homicide while in a state of uncontrollable rage caused by provocation and flowing from a condition of diminished capacity and therefore that it was error for the trial court to fail to instruct the injury on voluntary manslaughter as indeed he had requested. . . .

Defendant, a cook, 46 years old, and Rachel Pessah, a 20-year-old girl from Israel, were married on May 27, 1974. . . .

After their marriage, Rachel lived with defendant for only three days and then left for Israel. Immediately upon her return to San Francisco she told defendant about her relationship with and love for Yako. This brought about further argument and a brawl that evening in which defendant choked Rachel and she responded by scratching him deeply many times. Nonetheless they continued to live together. Rachel kept taunting defendant with Yako and demanding a divorce. She claimed she thought she might be pregnant by Yako. She showed defendant pictures of herself with Yako. Nevertheless, during a return trip from Santa Rosa, Rachel demanded immediate sexual intercourse with defendant in the car, which was achieved; however upon reaching their apartment, she again stated that she loved Yako and that she would not have intercourse with defendant in the future.

On the evening of July 22d defendant and Rachel went to a movie where they engaged in heavy petting. When they returned home and got into bed, Rachel announced that she had intended to make love with defendant, "But I am saving myself for this man Yako, so I don't think I will." Defendant got out of bed and prepared to leave the apartment, whereupon Rachel screamed and yelled at him. Defendant choked her into unconsciousness.

Two hours later defendant called a taxi for his wife to take her to the hospital. He put his clothes in the Greyhound bus station and went to the home of his friend Mrs. Berk for the night. The next day he went to Reno and returned the day after.

Rachel informed him by telephone that there was a warrant for his arrest as a result of her report to the police about the choking incident. On July 25th defendant returned to the apartment to talk to Rachel, but she was out. He slept there overnight. Rachel returned around 11 a.m. the next day. Upon seeing defendant there, she said, "I suppose you have come here to kill me." Defendant responded, "yes," changed his response to "no," and then again to "yes," and finally stated "I have really come to talk to you." Rachel began screaming. Defendant grabbed her by the shoulder and tried to stop her screaming. She continued. They struggled and finally defendant strangled her with a telephone cord.

Dr. Martin Blinder, a physician and psychiatrist, called by the defense, testified that Rachel was a depressed, suicidally inclined girl and that this suicidal impulse led her to involve herself ever more deeply in a dangerous situation with defendant. She did this by sexually arousing him and taunting him into jealous rages in an unconscious desire to provoke him into killing her and thus consummating her desire for suicide. Throughout the period commencing with her return from Israel until her death, that is from July 13 to July 26, Rachel continually provoked defendant with sexual taunts and incitements, alternating acceptance and rejection of him. This conduct was accompanied by repeated references to her involvement with another man; it led defendant to choke her on two occasions, until finally she achieved her unconscious desire and was strangled. Dr. Blinder testified that as a result of this cumulative series of provocations, defendant at the time he fatally strangled Rachel, was in a state of uncontrollable rage, completely under the sway of passion.

We first take up defendant's claim that on the basis of the foregoing evidence he was entitled to an instruction on voluntary manslaughter as defined by statute which is "the unlawful killing of a human being, without malice . . . upon a sudden quarrel or heat of passion." [In an earlier case the court approved the following quotation of the law:] "[T]he fundamental of the inquiry is whether or not the defendant's reason was, at the time of his act, so disturbed or obscured by some passion — not necessarily fear and never, of course, the passion for revenge — to such an extent as would render ordinary men of average disposition liable to act rashly or without due deliberation and reflection, and from this passion rather than judgment."

We further held . . . that there is no specific type of provocation required . . . and that verbal provocation may be sufficient. [In a previous case] in the course of explaining the phrase "heat of passion" used in the statute defining manslaughter we pointed out that "passion" need not mean "rage" or "anger" but may be any "[v]iolent, intense, high-wrought or enthusiastic emotion" and concluded there "that defendant was aroused to a heat of 'passion' by a series of events over a considerable period of time. . . ." Accordingly we there declared that evidence of admissions of infidelity by the defendant's paramour, taunts directed to him and other conduct, "supports a finding that defendant killed in wild desperation induced by [the woman's] long continued provocatory conduct." We find this reasoning persuasive in the case now before us. Defendant's testimony chronicles a two-week period of provocatory conduct by his wife Rachel that could arouse a passion of jealousy, pain and sexual rage in an ordinary man of average disposition such as to cause him to act rashly from this passion. It is significant that both defendant and Dr. Blinder testified that the former was in the heat of passion under an uncontrollable rage when he killed Rachel.

The Attorney General contends that the killing could not have been done in the heat of passion because there was a cooling period, defendant having waited in the apartment for 20 hours. However, the long course of provocatory conduct, which had resulted in intermittent outbreaks of rage under specific provocation in the past, reached its final culmination in the apartment when Rachel began screaming. . . .

. . . There was no clear direction to the jury to consider the evidence of Rachel's course of provocatory conduct so as to determine whether defendant, as an ordinary man of average disposition, having been exposed to such conduct, was provoked into committing the homicide under a heat of passion. [The failure to give the jury proper instructions on this question was prejudicial error and requires us to reverse the conviction of murder of the first degree.]

Donna K. Coker

Heat of Passion and Wife Killing: Men Who Batter/Men Who Kill

2 S. Cal. Rev. L. & Women's Stud. 71, 93-94, 118-20, 128 (1992)

[H]omicide law divides sane individuals who intentionally kill into two major categories: those who premeditate murder and those who act in the heat of passion. Social stereotypes of wife-killing that characterize the killer as a previously non-violent man who "snapped" under pressure, roughly parallel the understandings which underlie heat-of-passion doctrine. However, this social stereotype is grossly inaccurate when applied to men who are identified as "batterers" and when applied to the general category of husband-wife killings. Violence perpetrated by abusive men is purposeful, not spontaneous; the majority of men who kill their wives have a documented history of violent assaults. Furthermore, one would expect to find empirical evidence of wife-killers who fit the stereotype of the heat-of-passion killer in those reports of forensic psychiatrists whose job it is to aid defense counsel, yet these reports seem to confirm that men who kill and men who batter have remarkably similar personality traits and similar motivations. . . .

In essence, Berry's defense was that he was the sort of man who abused women — but the twist was [Dr.] Blinder's psychiatric explanation that Berry's violence was a result of his choosing women who enraged him and provoked him to violence. The fact that Berry had a prior conviction for assaulting his ex-wife with a butcher knife, that in past relationships with other women he had destroyed their property, forcing former girlfriends to "put him out of the house, locking the door," indicated to Blinder the personality of the women with whom Berry involved himself, more than it demonstrated Berry's dangerous and abusive nature. Blinder testified that these women "offer[ed] him the promise of comfort but ultimately deliver[ed] emotional pain." Yet Blinder's testimony provides a classic portrait of an abuser. Berry was most dangerous when women threatened to leave him. Berry was "emotionally dependent" on wives and girlfriends; he threatened physical violence in order to control women; he destroyed women's property; and he had a history of violent relationships with wives and lovers. The Supreme Court's opinion read Dr. Blinder's testimony to focus narrowly on the effect of Rachel's "provocative" behavior on Berry's mental state. Dr. Blinder's testimony, however, refers to a cumulative rage resulting from the provocation of all the women in Berry's entire life:

> **Q.**   . . . How would you characterize [Berry's] state of mind . . . [at the time of the homicide]?
>
> **A:**   . . . I would say that he was in a state of uncontrollable rage which was a product of having to contend with what seems to me an incredibly provacative [sic] situation, an incredibly provacative [sic] young woman, and that this immediate situation was superimposed upon Mr. Berry having encountered the situation time and time again. So that we have a cumulative effect dating back to the way his mother dealt with him. . . .
>
> **Q:**   . . . [Y]ou say that the situation involving Rachel Berry and Albert Berry . . . was the product of . . . cumulative . . . provocations. Now, specifically, what would you base your opinion as to provocations on? . . .
>
> **A:**   . . . We have two factors here. . . . The past history, that is, the history of this man well in advance of his meeting the deceased. And then the history of his relationship with her. And I think the two go together. . . . After 15 years [of marriage to his second wife] and five children, his wife leaves him for . . . another man. . . . They continued to live together, during which time his wife taunted him about her boyfriend. . . .
>
> One night while they were having sex, his wife [called him by the name of her boyfriend]. Despondent and enraged at the same time, he went into the kitchen, obtained a knife, and stabbed his wife in the abdomen. And she was not serious [sic]. He only got to spend a year in jail for that. . . .
>
> So we have this pattern of enormous dependency on these women and then rupture of the relationship with tremendous rage, almost uncontrollable. I think in one instance he put his foot through the stereo . . . he had purchased for one of these girls [sic]. . . .
>
> So we see a succession of women, beginning with his mother, who offer the promise of comfort but ultimately deliver indifference and emotional pain. . . .

The irony of this defense . . . [is that] Berry's past abuse of other women was used to strengthen his claim of Rachel's provocative nature: Berry had a pattern of involvement with emotionally abusive women; his violence was in response to their "abuse" — never the other way around. . . .

The California Supreme Court opinion repeatedly echoes the tenor of Blinder's words — using terms such as "the result" or "culmination" — terms that diffuse responsibility and make Berry's violence seem inevitable and uncontrollable. . . .

Though Blinder's testimony focused on Rachel's "provocative" sexual behavior, the truth is that Berry didn't kill Rachel until it appeared that she might make good on her threat to leave him. . . . [*Berry's*] perspective . . . suggests that a woman's "abandonment" of a husband is provocative — and that a woman's preference of another lover is provocation of the worst sort.

State v. Norman

378 S.E.2d 8 (N.C. 1989)

MITCHELL, Justice. . . .

At trial, the State presented the testimony of Deputy Sheriff R.H. Epley of the Rutherford County Sheriff's Department, who was called to the Norman residence on the night of 12 June 1985. Inside the home, Epley found the defendant's husband, John Thomas Norman, lying on a bed in a rear bedroom with his face toward the wall and his back toward the middle of the room. He was dead. . . . A later autopsy revealed three gunshot wounds to the head, two of which caused fatal brain injury. The autopsy also revealed a .12 percent blood alcohol level in the victim's body.

Later that night, the defendant related an account of the events leading to the killing. . . . The defendant told Epley that her husband had been beating her all day and had made her lie down on the floor while he slept on the bed. After her husband fell asleep, the defendant carried her grandchild to the defendant's mother's house. The defendant took a pistol from her mother's purse and walked the short distance back to her home. She pointed the pistol at the back of her sleeping husband's head, but it jammed the first time she tried to shoot him. She fixed the gun and then shot her husband in the back of the head as he lay sleeping. After one shot, she felt her husband's chest and determined that he was still breathing and making sounds. She then shot him twice more in the back of the head. The defendant told Epley that she killed her husband because "she took all she was going to take from him so she shot him."

The defendant presented evidence tending to show a long history of physical and mental abuse by her husband due to his alcoholism. At the time of the killing, the thirty-nine-year-old defendant and her husband had been married almost twenty-five years and had several children. The defendant testified that her husband had started drinking and abusing her about five years after they were married. His physical abuse of her consisted of frequent assaults that included slapping, punching and kicking her, striking her with various objects, and throwing glasses, beer bottles and other objects at her. The defendant described other specific incidents of abuse, such as her husband putting her cigarettes out on her, throwing hot coffee on her, breaking glass against her face and crushing food on her face. Although the defendant did not present evidence of ever having received medical treatment for any physical injuries inflicted by her husband, she displayed several scars about her face which she attributed to her husband's assaults.

The defendant's evidence also tended to show other indignities inflicted upon her by her husband. Her evidence tended to show that her husband did not work and forced her to make money by prostitution, and that he made humor of that fact to family and friends. He would beat her if she resisted going out to prostitute herself or if he was unsatisfied with the amounts of money she made. He routinely called the defendant "dog," "bitch" and "whore," and on a few occasions made her eat pet food out of the pets' bowls and bark like a dog. He often made her sleep on the floor. At times, he deprived her of food and refused to let her get food for the family. During those years of abuse, the defendant's husband threatened numerous times to kill her and to maim her in various ways.

The defendant said her husband's abuse occurred only when he was intoxicated, but that he would not give up drinking. She said she and her husband "got along very well when he was sober," and that he was "a good guy" when he was not drunk. She had accompanied her husband to the local mental health center for sporadic counseling sessions for his problem, but he continued to drink.

In the early morning hours on the day before his death, the defendant's husband, who was intoxicated, went to a rest area off I-85 near Kings Mountain where the defendant was engaging in prostitution and assaulted her. While driving home, he was stopped by a patrolman and jailed on a charge of driving while impaired. After the defendant's mother got him out of jail at the defendant's request later that morning, he resumed his drinking and abuse of the defendant.

The defendant's evidence also tended to show that her husband seemed angrier than ever after he was released from jail and that his abuse of the defendant was more frequent. That evening, sheriff's deputies were called to the Norman residence, and the defendant complained that her husband had been beating her all day and she could not take it anymore. The defendant was advised to file a complaint, but she said she was afraid her husband would kill her if she had him arrested. The deputies told her they needed a warrant before they could arrest her husband, and they left the scene.

The deputies were called back less than an hour later after the defendant had taken a bottle of pills. The defendant's husband cursed her and called her names as she was attended by paramedics, and he told them to let her die. A sheriff's deputy finally chased him back into his house as the defendant was put into an ambulance. The defendant's stomach was pumped at the local hospital, and she was sent home with her mother.

While in the hospital, the defendant was visited by a therapist with whom she discussed filing charges against her husband and having him committed for treatment. Before the therapist left, the defendant agreed to go to the mental health center the next day to discuss those possibilities. The therapist testified at trial that the defendant seemed depressed in the hospital, and that she expressed considerable anger toward her husband. He testified that the defendant threatened a number of times that night to kill her husband and that she said she should kill him "because of the things he had done to her."

The next day, the day she shot her husband, the defendant went to the mental health center to talk about charges and possible commitment, and she confronted her husband with that possibility. She testified that she told her husband later that day: "J.T., straighten up. Quit drinking. I'm going to have you committed to help you." She said her husband then told her he would "see them coming" and would cut her throat before they got to him.

The defendant also went to the social services office that day to seek welfare benefits, but her husband followed her there, interrupted her interview and made her go home with him. He continued his abuse of her, threatening to kill and to maim her, slapping her, kicking her, and throwing objects at her. At one point, he took her cigarette and put it out on her, causing a small burn on her upper torso. He would not let her eat or bring food into the house for their children.

That evening, the defendant and her husband went into their bedroom to lie down, and he called her a "dog" and made her lie on the floor when he lay down on the bed. Their daughter brought in her baby to leave with the defendant, and the defendant's husband agreed to let her baby-sit. After the defendant's husband fell asleep, the baby started crying and the defendant took it to her mother's house so it would not wake up her husband. She returned shortly with the pistol and killed her husband.

The defendant testified at trial that she was too afraid of her husband to press charges against him or to leave him. She said that she had temporarily left their home on several previous occasions, but he had always found her, brought her home and beaten her. Asked why she killed her husband, the defendant replied: "Because I was scared of him and I knowed when he woke up, it was going to be the same thing, and I was scared when he took me to the truck stop that night it was going to be worse then he had ever been. I just couldn't take it no more. There ain't no way, even if it means going to prison. It's better than living in that. That's worse hell than anything."

The defendant and other witnesses testified that for years her husband had frequently threatened to kill her and to maim her. When asked if she believed those threats, the defendant replied: "Yes. I believed him; he would, he would kill me if he got a chance. If he thought he wouldn't a had to went to jail, he would a done it." . . .

Two expert witnesses in forensic psychology and psychiatry who examined the defendant after the shooting, Dr. William Tyson and Dr. Robert Rollins, testified that the defendant fit the profile of battered wife syndrome. This condition, they testified, is characterized by such abuse and degradation that the battered wife comes to believe she is unable to help herself and cannot expect help from anyone else. She believes that she cannot escape the complete control of her husband and that he is invulnerable to law enforcement and other sources of help.

Dr. Tyson, a psychologist, was asked his opinion as to whether, on 12 June 1985, "it appeared reasonably necessary for Judy Norman to shoot J.T. Norman?" He replied: "I believe that . . . Mrs. Norman believed herself to be doomed . . . to a life of the worst kind of torture and abuse, degradation that she had experienced over the years in a progressive way; that it would only get worse, and that death was inevitable. . . ." Dr. Tyson later added: "I think Judy Norman felt that she had no choice, both in the protection of herself and her family, but to engage, exhibit deadly force against Mr. Norman, and that in so doing, she was sacrificing herself, both for herself and for her family."

Dr. Rollins, who was the defendant's attending physician at Dorothea Dix Hospital when she was sent there for evaluation, testified that in his opinion the defendant was a typical abused spouse and that "[s]he saw herself as powerless to deal with the situation, that there was no alternative, no way she could escape it." Dr. Rollins was asked his opinion as to whether "on June 12th, 1985, it appeared reasonably necessary that Judy Norman would take the life of J.T. Norman?" Dr. Rollins replied that in his opinion, "that course of action did appear necessary to Mrs. Norman."

Based on the evidence that the defendant exhibited battered wife syndrome, that she believed she could not escape her husband nor expect help from others, that her husband had threatened her, and that her husband's abuse of her had worsened in the two days preceding his death, the Court of Appeals concluded that a jury reasonably could have found that her killing of her husband was justified as an act of perfect self-defense. The Court of Appeals reasoned that the nature of battered wife syndrome is such that a jury could not be precluded from finding the defendant killed her husband lawfully in perfect self-defense, even though he was asleep when she killed him. We disagree.

The right to kill in self-defense is based on the necessity, real or reasonably apparent, of killing an unlawful aggressor to save oneself from *imminent* death or great bodily harm at his hands. . . . Our law has recognized that self-preservation under such circumstances springs from a primal impulse and is an inherent right of natural law. . . .

The killing of another human being is the most extreme recourse to our inherent right of self-preservation and can be justified in law only by the utmost real or apparent necessity brought about by the decedent. For that reason, our law of self-defense has required that a defendant claiming that a homicide was justified and, as a result, inherently lawful by reason of perfect self-defense must establish that she reasonably believed at the time of the killing she otherwise would have immediately suffered death or great bodily harm. Only if defendants are required to show that they killed due to a reasonable belief that death or great bodily harm was imminent can the justification for homicide remain clearly and firmly rooted in necessity. The imminence requirement ensures that deadly force will be used only where it is necessary as a last resort in the exercise of the inherent right of self-preservation. . . .

The term "imminent," as used to describe such perceived threats of death or great bodily harm as will justify a homicide by reason of perfect self-defense, has been defined as "immediate danger, such as must be instantly met, such as cannot be guarded against by calling for the assistance of others or the protection of the law." . . .

The evidence in this case did not tend to show that the defendant reasonably believed that she was confronted by a threat of imminent death or great bodily harm. The evidence tended to show that no harm was "imminent" or about to happen to the defendant when she shot her husband. The uncontroverted evidence was that her husband had been asleep for some time when she walked to her mother's house, returned with the pistol, fixed the pistol after it jammed and then shot her husband three times in the back of the head. The defendant was not faced with an instantaneous choice between killing her husband or being killed or seriously injured. Instead, *all* of the evidence tended to show that the defendant had ample time and opportunity to resort to other means of preventing further abuse by her husband. . . .

Dr. Tyson . . . testified that the defendant "believed herself to be doomed . . . to a life of the worst kind of torture and abuse, degradation that she had experienced over the years in a progressive way; that it would only get worse, and that death was inevitable." Such evidence of the defendant's speculative beliefs concerning her remote and indefinite future, while indicating she had felt generally threatened, did not tend to show that she killed in the belief — reasonable or otherwise — that her husband presented a threat of imminent death or great bodily harm. . . .

The reasoning of our Court of Appeals in this case . . . proposes justifying the taking of human life not upon the reasonable belief it is necessary to prevent death or great bodily harm—which the imminence requirement ensures—but upon purely subjective speculation that the decedent probably would present a threat to life at a future time and that the defendant would not be able to avoid the predicted threat. . . .

The relaxed requirements for perfect self-defense proposed by our Court of Appeals would tend to categorically legalize the opportune killing of abusive husbands by their wives solely on the basis of the wives' testimony concerning their subjective speculation as to the probability of future felonious assaults by their husbands. Homicidal self-help would then become a lawful solution, and perhaps the easiest and most effective solution, to this problem. . . . It has even been suggested that the relaxed requirements of self-defense found in what is often called the "battered woman's defense" could be extended in *principle to any type of case* in which a defendant testified that he or she subjectively believed that killing was necessary and proportionate to any perceived threat. . . .

In conclusion, we decline to expand our law of self-defense beyond the limits of immediacy and necessity which have heretofore provided an appropriately narrow but firm basis upon which homicide may be justified. . . .

Reversed.

MARTIN, Justice, dissenting.

At the outset it is to be noted that the peril of fabricated evidence is not unique to the trials of battered wives who kill. The possibility of invented evidence arises in all cases in which a party is seeking the benefit of self-defense. Moreover, in this case there were a number of witnesses other than defendant who testified as to the actual presence of circumstances supporting a claim of self-defense. This record contains no reasonable basis to attack the credibility of evidence for the defendant. . . .

Evidence presented by defendant described a twenty-year history of beatings and other dehumanizing and degrading treatment by her husband. In his expert testimony a clinical psychologist concluded that defendant fit "and exceed[ed]" the profile of an abused or battered spouse, analogizing this treatment to the dehumanization process suffered by prisoners of war under the Nazis during the Second World War and the brainwashing techniques of the Korean War. The psychologist described the defendant as a woman incarcerated by abuse, by fear, and by her conviction that her husband was invincible and inescapable:

> Mrs. Norman didn't leave because she believed, fully believed that escape was totally impossible. There was no place to go. He, she had left before; he had come and gotten her. She had gone to the Department of Social Services. He had come and gotten her. The law, she believed the law could not protect her; no one could protect her, and I must admit, looking over the records, that there was nothing done that would contradict that belief.

[F]or the battered wife, if there is no escape, if there is no window of relief or momentary sense of safety, then the next attack, which could be the fatal one, is imminent. In the context of the doctrine of self-defense, "imminent" is a term the meaning of which must be grasped from the defendant's point of view. Properly stated, the second prong of the question is not whether the threat was in fact *imminent*, but whether defendant's belief in the impending nature of the threat, given the circumstances as she saw them, was reasonable in the mind of a person of ordinary firmness.

Defendant's intense fear, based on her belief that her husband intended not only to maim or deface her, as he had in the past, but to kill her, was evident in the testimony of witnesses who recounted events of the last three days of the decedent's life. This testimony could have led a juror to conclude that defendant reasonably perceived a threat to her life as "imminent," even while her husband slept. . . .

From this evidence of the exacerbated nature of the last three days of twenty years of provocation, a juror could conclude that defendant believed that her husband's threats to her life were viable, that serious bodily harm was imminent, and that it was necessary to kill her husband to escape that harm. And from this evidence a juror could find defendant's belief in the necessity to kill her husband not merely reasonable but compelling. . . .

Martha R. Mahoney

Legal Images of Battered Women: Redefining the Issue of Separation

90 Mich. L. Rev. 1, 5-7 (1991)

The question "why didn't she leave?" shapes both social and legal inquiry on battering; much of the legal reliance on academic expertise on battered women has developed in order to address this question. At the moment of separation or attempted separation—for many women, the first encounter with the authority of law—the batterer's quest for control often becomes most acutely violent and potentially lethal. Ironically, although the proliferation of shelters and the elaboration of statutory structures facilitating the grant of protective orders vividly demonstrate both socially and legally the dangers attendant on separation, a woman's "failure" to permanently separate from a violent relationship is still widely held to be mysterious and in need of explanation, an indicator of her pathology rather than her batterer's. We have had neither cultural names nor legal doctrines specifically tailored to the particular assault on a woman's body and volition that seeks to block her from leaving, retaliate for her departure, or forcibly end the separation. I propose that we name this attack "separation assault."

Separation assault is the common though invisible thread that unites the equal protection suits on enforcement of temporary restraining orders, the cases with dead women that appear in many doctrinal categories, and the cases with dead men—the self-defense cases. As with other assaults on women that were not cognizable until the feminist movement named and explained them, separation assault must be identified before women can recognize our own experience and before we can develop legal rules to deal with this particular sort of violence. Naming one particular aspect of the violence then illuminates the rest: for example, the very concept of "acquaintance rape" moves consciousness away from the stereotype of rape (assault by a stranger) and toward a focus on the woman's volition (violation of her will, "consent"). Similarly, by emphasizing the urgent control moves that seek to prevent the woman from ending the relationship, the concept of separation assault raises questions that inevitably focus additional attention on the ongoing struggle for power and control in the relationship.

NOTES

1. **"Heat of Passion" Law and Sex Equality.** The traditional elements for mitigation from murder (which usually would have been first-degree murder) to voluntary manslaughter were that the defendant killed while in a heat of passion, upon sudden adequate provocation. One of the requirements was that a "reasonable person" would have been thrown into a heat of passion by the provoking incident. The standard itself can be gendered. Victoria Nourse's landmark study compiled heat of passion cases from across several jurisdictions. She found that a woman's attempt to leave the relationship, or the man's belief in her infidelity, were the most common "provocations" when men killed women and then sought reduction of their crime to manslaughter. Should it be considered "reasonable" for men to be provoked into murder in these circumstances? In Model Penal Code jurisdictions, Nourse found that there were three times as many infidelity cases involving separation as cases involving infidelity in a continuing relationship. Nourse asked: "If intimate homicide frequently involves separated couples why does our canonical legal image still revolve around sexual infidelity?"[351] In another study of separation assaults, male partners frequently warned women whom they later killed, "If I can't have you, nobody can."[352] Should a man with the attitude this statement suggests be able to obtain a lesser sentence if he kills his wife?

For three centuries, English courts reserved the heat of passion defense to men, and early American law followed suit. Before the 1960s, many states retained laws that allowed a husband to kill his wife's lover but made no concession for the wife who killed her husband or her husband's lover. Today, the doctrine is gender neutral in form but women rarely assert it, perhaps because they are socialized to respond less aggressively than men to most provocation, including infidelity.[353]

When heat of passion is asserted, are juries likely to react the same way to women and men who invoke the defense? No statistical evidence is available, but some experts cite representative examples to suggest gender bias. A case in point is that of Clara Harris, who killed her husband after he failed to keep his promise to end his extramarital affair with his office's receptionist. Harris confronted her husband and his mistress at a hotel, and the two women became involved in a violent fight. Hotel

---

351. Victoria Nourse, Passion's Progress: Modern Law Reform and the Provocation Defense, 106 Yale L.J. 1331, 1345 (1997). For an argument that infidelity killing should not be mitigated at all, see Roni Rosenberg, A New Rationale for the Doctrine of Provocation: Applications to Cases of Killing an Unfaithful Spouse, 37 Colum. J. Gender & L. 220, 222 (2019).

352. Ruth E. Fleury et al., When Ending the Relationship Does Not End the Violence, 6 Violence Against Women 1363, 1365 (2000).

353. See Christine R. Harris, A Review of Sex Differences in Sexual Jealousy, Including Self-Report Data, Psychosociological Responses, Interpersonal Violence, and Morbid Jealousy, 2 Personality & Soc. Psych. Rev. 102 (2003).

employees separated them, and Harris, still enraged, got in her car and ran over her husband twice in the parking lot. She was convicted of murder, despite her testimony that she was "in a fog" at the time, and that it was a "blackout" period, a "crazy time." Eyewitnesses reported that after she had hit her husband, she jumped from the car, asked him repeatedly whether he was "okay" and screamed, "I am sorry." The jury convicted her of murder, and of using a deadly weapon, which enhanced the offense. During the sentencing phase, the jury found that she had acted in the heat of passion but imposed the maximum sentence of twenty years.[354] During the trial, both sides capitalized on gender stereotypes. The prosecution painted Harris as a wife who ignored her husband's needs and who was a selfish spendthrift. The defense painted the mistress as an unscrupulous and promiscuous woman with a history of "abnormal relationships," including an alleged lesbian affair.[355]

Should "hot-blooded" separation murders and assaults, whether committed by men or women, be seen as deserving of less culpability? Or would you favor the approach of Minnesota, which authorizes a finding of first-degree murder if the perpetrator has engaged in a "past pattern of domestic abuse" and the murder reflects an "extreme indifference to human life"?[356]

If equality is a goal in these cases, is it best achieved by restricting the heat of passion doctrine or by enlarging it to mitigate women's killings, such as those described below? What other changes to the law might be beneficial?[357]

2. **Battered Person Syndrome.**   Every year, a small percentage of women kill their abusers and base their claim of self defense, which might otherwise lack necessary elements such as the immediacy or imminence of the threat, on the fact that they exhibit signs of battered women's syndrome (BWS) and thereby acted reasonably.[358] All states, either by statute or case law, admit this type of evidence, often with the use of an expert.[359] Now called battered person syndrome, this label describes a subcategory of post-traumatic stress disorder involving "thoughts, feelings, and actions that logically follow a frightening experience that one expects could be repeated." It is associated with three major symptom clusters, each of which can

---

354. Nick Madigan, Wife Testifies She Was "In a Fog" Just Before Her Car Struck Husband, N.Y. Times, Feb. 8, 2003, at A11; Antonia Elise Miller, Inherent Gender Unreasonableness of the Concept of Reasonableness in the Context of Manslaughter Committed in the Heat of Passion, 17 William & Mary J. Women & L. 249 (2010).

355. Lucas Wall, Clara Harris: Mother of Twins Kept to Herself, Hous. Chron., Aug. 4, 2002, at 37.

356. See Minn. Stat. § 609.185(6) (West 2022).

357. For further discussion of law reform in this area, see Caroline Davidson, Speaking Femicide, 71 Am. U. L. Rev. 377, 446 (2021); Carolyn B. Ramsey, Provoking Change: Comparative Insights on Feminist Homicide Law Reform, 100 J. Crim. L. & Criminology 33 (Winter 2010).

358. See generally Martha Mahoney, Misunderstanding Judy Norman: Theory as Cause and Consequence, 51 Conn. L. Rev. 671, 702-12 (2019) (exploring origin and application of theory); Jessica R. Holliday et al., The Use of Battered Woman Syndrome in U.S. Criminal Courts, 50 J. Am. Acad. Psychiatry Law 1 (2022).

359. For a discussion of the feminist movement for such laws, see Claire Houston, The Trouble with Feminist Advocacy Around Child Victims of Domestic Violence, 39 Women's Rts. L. Rep. 85, 94 (2018).

be accompanied by neurochemical and other physical changes. These clusters are (1) cognitive disturbances, including repetitive memories that cause battered women to re-experience previous abusive incidents and that increase their perception of danger; (2) high arousal symptoms that cause battered women to be nervous and hypervigilant to cues of potential danger; and (3) avoidance symptoms, including depression, denial, minimization, and repression, often leading to isolation as the batterer exerts his power and control.[360] Researchers initially offered two psychological theories to help juries understand the syndrome: learned helplessness and the cycle theory of violence. The theory of learned helplessness was first developed by experimental psychologist Marvin Seligman to explain the fact that dogs and other animals subjected to electric shocks that they are powerless to control will soon stop trying to escape or to avert the shocks. In the context of battered women, Lenore Walker pioneered the theory of learned helplessness to explain a cycle that traps women in abusive relationships. That cycle includes a tension-building phase, an acute battering incident, and a period of loving-contrition or absence of tension. The pattern leads the battered woman to believe that she is unable to help herself, that others cannot help her, and that the batterer might in fact reform.

In this state of learned helplessness, what would cause a victim of abuse to kill a batterer? Many abused individuals do not, but others at some point experience a "turning point." This point may come when there is a marked increase in the severity of the abuse, when the abuse becomes visible to others who question the victim's denial or rationalizations, or when the "loving-contrition" phase becomes increasingly short or disappears altogether. According to Walker, at that point, victims move from the state of learned helplessness to a state of the "victimized self," and conclude that they must either assert themselves or be killed. For some victims, this means finally being able to leave their batterers; others stay, and a few kill.

3. **The Reasonable Battered Woman?**   The most common criticism of the law of self-defense in the battered person context is that it reflects patterns of male aggression: a "fair fight" between physical equals meeting in a single, discrete confrontation. Critics say this approach fails to take into account the realities of battered persons. Its "objective" standard of reasonableness ignores the special circumstances facing individuals in abusive relationships and fails to consider the risk that verbal threats may convey in light of the history of battering. Requirements of "imminence" and proportionate force also discount women's lesser strength, which may make delay seem untenable and deadly force seem necessary. Do these criticisms seem justified in the context of *Norman*? If so, do they support some critics' call for a "reasonable woman" or a "reasonable battered woman" standard? Assuming that expert testimony on the battered person syndrome should have gone to the jury in *Norman*, should the defendant's circumstances constitute a justification, exonerating her from guilt, or merely an excuse (mitigating factor) affecting the degree of crime or the sentence?[361]

---

360. Lenore E. A. Walker, Battered Women Syndrome and Self-Defense, 6 Notre Dame J.L. Ethics & Pub. Pol'y 321, 327-28 (1992).

361. See Maryland v. Elzey, 244 A.3d 1068 (2021); U.S. v. Lopez, 913 F.3d 807 (9th Cir. 2019); see Mahoney, supra note 358.

4. Concerns About Battered Person Syndrome. Uneasiness about use of the battered person syndrome reflects various concerns. The *Norman* court's objection was that such evidence could be too easily manipulated and might encourage opportunistic premeditated killings. Other critics similarly warn that the defense could permit "vigilante justice" and give battered persons a "license to kill."[362] How would you respond?

In response to such concerns, one scholar collected data from numerous studies comparing battered women who killed their husbands to those who did not. He concluded that women who kill their husbands suffer from far more frequent, more severe, and more prolonged abuse than other battered women; they have less ability to support themselves and thus to escape from their situations; they are more likely to have children who are also being abused by the batterer; and they are more likely to live in an environment where a gun is present and where the batterer abuses alcohol or other drugs.[363] Other research indicates that some groups of women are more likely than others to respond with force. African-American women are disproportionately likely to resort to physical violence probably because they have less access to services than more affluent white women; they feel pressure not to shame or force imprisonment of a "black brother"; and they do not "really trust" law enforcement officials to help them.[364] Lesbians also have disproportionately high rates of violent responses presumably because they, too, lack confidence that police and courts would be responsive, and because they experience bias based on sexual orientation from police, judges, and service providers.[365] A reluctance to expose violence in the lesbian community, along with greater comfort and capacity in fighting back, also help to explain the use of force rather than other strategies of resistance.[366] What are the reform implications of these conclusions?

Some scholars, even if sympathetic to the plight of battered women, question the science bethind the theory. David L. Faigman and Amy J. Wright assert that "[t]he battered woman syndrome illustrates all that is wrong with the law's use of science."[367] They and other critics note that Lenore Walker's research, based on a small group of racially homogeneous women, failed to establish either the duration of the cycle of violence or that all subjects experienced all three stages. The relevance of research on dogs to battered women is also problematic, particularly

---

362. Donald A. Downs & James Fisher, Battered Woman's Syndrome: Tool of Justice or False Hope in Self-Defense Cases, in Current Controversies on Family Violence 241, 252 (Donileen R. Loseke et al., eds., 2005).

363. See Charles Patrick Ewing, Battered Women Who Kill: Psychological Self-Defense as Legal Justification 23-40 (1987). For recent affirmation of that research, see Avlana K. Eisenberg, Discontinuities in Criminal Law, 22 Theoretical Inquiries L. 137, 153 (2021).

364. Leigh Goodmark, When Is A Battered Woman Not A Battered Woman? When She Fights Back, 20 Yale J.L. & Feminism 75, 96-98 (2008).

365. Id. at 102.

366. Id.; Adele M. Morrison, Queering Domestic Violence to "Straighten Out" Criminal Law: What Might Happen When Queer Theory and Practice Meet Criminal Law's Conventional Responses to Domestic Violence, 13 S. Cal. L. & Women's Stud. 8, 147 (2003).

367. David L. Faigman & Amy J. Wright, The Battered Woman's Syndrome in the Age of Science, 39 Ariz. L. Rev. 67, 68 (1997).

given that the dogs exhibited total passivity, while battered women generally resist in some form, including instances in which they assault or kill their batterers.[368]

Moreover, when invoked in court, the battered person syndrome implies an excuse through mitigation based on the victim's passivity, while self-defense generally requires justification based on the reasonableness of the defendant's behavior. Women who do not match the battered person profile may be assumed (by themselves as well as others) to fail to meet standards for self-defense.[369] The risk appears particularly great for African-American and lesbian women; their resistance, viewed through the lens of racist and homophobic stereotypes, is inconsistent with the image of helpless victim.[370] What should be done about this? Should Black women be coached to act more like the jury's imagined victim?[371] A final concern is that the syndrome will reinforce the view of woman as passive, dysfunctional, powerless, and victimized, a view from which so many negative consequences flow, especially in child custody contexts.

How could these harms be mitigated? Sarah Buel proposes jettisoning BWS in favor of an approach that focuses on "battering and its effects." Instead of a psychological syndrome purporting to typecast victims, expert testimony would educate judges and juries about battering behaviors and how they affect victims' state of mind and range of possible actions.[372] To what extent would more accurate testimony about the effects of battering help in cases like *Norman*? Would it be enough to show that a "reasonable" person, in the face of past experiences of abuse and no certain options for escaping it, might respond with deadly force? Could a defendant reasonably claim that "a sleeping abuser is merely seconds away from being an awakened abuser" who poses an imminent threat?[373]

5. **Post-Conviction Remedies for Battered Persons Who Kill.** After Judy Norman had served four years of her six-year sentence, the state governor commuted her sentence to time served. He gave no reasons.[374] What would you have done as governor, or as a member of her jury?

---

368. For critiques, see Kit Kinports, The Myth of Battered Woman Syndrome, 24 Temple P. & Civ. Rts. L. Rev. 313 (2015).

369. See, e.g., New York v. Addimando, 120 N.Y.S. 3d 596, 618 (2020) (finding that the defendant's actions in response to the abuse and killing of her batterer did not fit the behavior of a real victim). See also Sarah M. Buel, Beyond Battered Women's Syndrome, in The Oxford Handbook of Feminism & Law in the United States (Deborah L. Brake, Martha Chamallas & Verna L. Williams, forthcoming 2022) (critiquing the case and using it to illustrate the pitfalls of BWS).

370. See Buel, supra note 369.

371. See Amber Simmons, Why Are We So Mad? The Truth Behind "Angry" Black Women and Their Legal Invisibility as Victims of Domestic Violence, 36 Harv. BlackLetter L.J. 47, 59 (2020). For more on this problem, see Alafair S. Burke, Rational Actors, Self-Defense, and Duress: Making Sense, Not Syndromes, Out of the Battered Woman, 81 N.C. L. Rev. 211, 230-47 (2002); Adele M. Morrison, Changing the Domestic Violence (Dis)course: Moving Away from White Victim to Multi-Cultural Survivor, 39 U.C. Davis L. Rev. 1061 (2006).

372. Buel, supra note 369.

373. Joan Krause, Distorted Reflections of Women Who Kill: A Response to Professor Dressler, 4 Ohio St. J. Crim. L. 555, 563 (2007); Burke, supra note 371, at 266.

374. Elizabeth Leland, Abused Wife's Sentence Commuted, Charlotte Observer, July 8, 1989, at B1.

Systematic efforts for clemency on behalf of convicted women have sometimes yielded similar results. However, despite gains in granting clemency petitions
during the 1980s and early 1990s, success slowed in the next decade, with some
states rejecting all such requests, even in cases where defendants were convicted
before expert testimony on battered women was available at trial.[375] More recently,
the #SurvivedandPunished movement has succeeded in raising the profile of
unjust convictions of women charged with crimes against their abusers, and online
and social media campaigns have resulted in the release of some women convicted
in such cases.[376] Do you think this is a more promising strategy than law reform in
this area?

Men's rights groups generally oppose efforts to mitigate penalties for battered
women. According to Warren Farrell, feminists argue "'there's never an excuse for
violence against women.' Now they [are] saying 'but there's always an excuse for
violence against men.'"[377] How would you respond? What criteria would you advise
governors to apply in considering clemency requests by battered persons convicted
of killing their abusers?

PUTTING THEORY INTO PRACTICE

3-18. In People v. Beltran, the defendant killed a woman with whom he had
previously cohabitated and who was involved with another man. He testified that he
acted in the heat of passion after the woman stated that she "could get better than
[him]" and that "I knew you were going to walk away someday. That's why I killed
your bastard. I got an abortion."[378] The test for reducing a murder charge to manslaughter under California law at the time was a generous version of the common
law test: whether the defendant's reason was "at the time of his act, so disturbed
or obscured by some passion to such an extent as would render ordinary men of
average disposition liable to act rashly or with due deliberation and reflection, and
from this passion rather than from judgment."[379] If the jury had believed the defendant in this case, would that be a sufficient basis for finding that the defendant was
guilty only of manslaughter?

3-19. Debra and Terrance are both addicted to cocaine and were arrested for
the commission of several armed robberies. Debra admits the crimes, but claims
a defense of duress, which is unlawful threat or coercion creating an immediate
threat of injury that causes someone to act as he or she would not otherwise act.
Debra argues that she participated in the robberies out of fear that Terrance would

---

375. See Burke, supra note 371.

376. See End the Criminalization of Survival, Survived and Punished, https://survived
andpunished.org; Leigh Goodmark, The Anti-Rape and Battered Women's Movements of
the 1970s and 80s, in The Oxford Handbook of Feminism & Law, supra note 369 (discussing
several successful recent campaigns to free individual survivors).

377. Deborah L. Rhode, Speaking of Sex: The Denial of Gender Equality 115 (1997)
(quoting Farrell).

378. People v. Beltran, 301 P.3d 1120, 1124 (Cal. 2013).

379. Id. at 1120. The Court rejected the prosecution's argument that the provocation
must be of a kind that would cause an ordinary person of average disposition to kill.

kill her if she did not. In support of her defense, Debra seeks to present expert testimony indicating that she suffers from battered person's syndrome; she has a history of physical and emotional abuse that escalated every time she tried to leave Terrance.

Evidence of battered person's syndrome has been admitted in the jurisdiction in cases in which victims of domestic violence have killed their batterers and claim self-defense. Duress in the criminal law ordinarily does not exonerate a defendant but it can reduce the severity of the crime or the sentence. Should the defense of duress be available in Debra's circumstances? In any felony case?[380]

3-20. Child welfare authorities removed Sharon's three children from her home based on findings that her husband had subjected them to repeated abuse, such as cursing at and beating them. A mental health evaluation of Sharon showed that she did not always put the needs of the children first, that her parenting skills were weak, and that she was a battered wife who had a history of relationships with batterers. Her social profile and personality type suggested that she was particularly vulnerable to abuse. The child welfare authorities now seek to terminate Sharon's parental rights to her children on the theory that even if she leaves her current husband, she is likely to enter into another relationship that will be dangerous to the children.

Under your state's abuse and neglect law, parental rights can be terminated on a showing that a parent has failed to prevent another person from abusing a child and that it is reasonably likely that the child will be abused if returned to the parent.

As Sharon's lawyer, what arguments would you make against termination of her parental rights? Should she win?

3-21. What would you have done if you had been Laura Beth Lamb, an attorney who fraudulently took the bar exam in her husband's place, after he physically abused her and threatened to kill both her and her unborn child if she did not take the exam? She pled guilty to felony impersonation and received probation on condition of paying a fine and completing 200 hours of community service. The California Bar then recommended disbarment. Is disbarment appropriate? If so, what should she have to prove when she later seeks reinstatement?[381]

3-22. In France, Jacqueline Sauvage married her husband when they were teenagers. She sustained 47 years of physical and psychological abuse. She had once tried to kill herself but the doctor who treated her never asked the reason. Her husband also physically and sexually abused their three daughters. One of her daughters complained to the police about the sexual abuse, but instead of taking the charges seriously, the police called the father, causing the daughter to recant. One night, the husband woke Ms. Sauvage from a nap with a blow to the face demanding that she make him dinner. Instead, she retrieved a hunting rifle from the closet, went to the terrace where he was sitting drinking whiskey, and shot him three times in the back. She was found guilty of murder and given a ten-year prison

---

380. Dixon v. United States, 548 U.S. 1 (2006). See also Burke, supra note 371, at 263.
381. See In re Lamb, 776 P.2d 765 (Cal. 1989).

sentence. President Francois Hollande commuted part of her sentence in 2016.[382] What punishment would you have imposed?

D.   PORNOGRAPHY

Sex sells. That has always been true, but increased technological innovations have created increased opportunities for profit from private consumption of sexually explicit materials. Accurate revenue data on the pornography industry are unavailable because of piracy and private company involvement, but in 2018 most estimates range from $6 billion to $15 billion annually from U.S. video sales and rentals, pay-per-view movies on cable and websites, phone sex, and Internet websites.[383] Reported revenues did not capture all porn usage, because popular places to see porn are "tube sites," where users upload clips, whether self-produced or pirated outside the scope of regulation.[384] Pornhub receives more than 78 billion page views a year, and 29 percent of viewers are women; some porn sites get more traffic than news sites such as CNN.[385] More and more pornography is self-produced and distributed, leading to the growth of niche markets and a greater diversity in "who gets to be sexy."[386]

There is no uncontested definition of pornography and how it differs from erotica. The etymology of both terms is Greek; the term *graphos* means description, *porne* refers to whores, and *eros* means passion or love. Some commentators argue that what distinguishes pornography is its intentional violation of widely accepted moral and social taboos in an effort to cause arousal.[387] Cultural critic Ruby Rich argues that distinctions among sexually explicit materials rely on subjective judgments: "if I like it, it's erotic; if you like it, it's pornographic."[388]

Pornography has long been a contested topic because it implicates issues of religion, morality, equality, free speech, and free will. Since the early 1980s, some feminists have joined with religious conservatives and other activists to combat pornography on several fronts. While the conservative case against pornography has focused on the corruption of morals, erosion of "family values," and risks to

---

382. Lilia Blaise, He Abused Her for Years. She Shot Him. France Asks: Is It Self-Defense?, N.Y. Times, Mar. 11, 2016, at A8.

383.   See Ross Benes, Porn Could Have a Bigger Economic Influence on the US than Netflix, Yahoo!Finance (June 20, 2018).

384. Malcolm Harris, Kids These Days: Human Capital and the Making of Millennials 197 (2017).

385. Katrina Forrester, Lights. Camera. Action, New Yorker 64 (Sept. 26, 2016); Pornhub, 2018 Year in Review (Dec. 11, 2018).

386. Amanda Hess, Who Gets to Be Sexy?, N.Y. Times, May 6, 2018, at ST4.

387. Lynn Hunt, The Invention of Pornography: Obscenity and the Origins of Modernity (1996).

388. B. Ruby Rich, Anti-Porn: Soft Issue, Hard World, 13 Feminist Rev. 60 (1983).

children, the feminist rationale emphasizes the role of pornography in subordinating women through objectifying and degrading images and eroticization of abuse.

The traditional legal approach to pornography is reflected in obscenity doctrine. The leading case, Miller v. California, permits the government to ban material if, under contemporary community standards, the work as a whole appeals to the "prurient interest," depicts sex in a "patently offensive" way, and lacks serious literary, artistic, political, or scientific value.[389] Feminists charge that this standard cannot be effective in challenging pornographic materials because it incorporates the very community standards that have made subordination sexually appealing. Moreover, it asks judges to admit to an uncomfortable psychological state of finding material both sexually arousing *and* patently offensive.[390]

What legal theories best apply to pornography? Is pornography a form of discrimination based on sex? Is it a form of subordination?

1. The Feminist Critique of Pornography

Catharine A. MacKinnon

Feminism Unmodified: Discourses on Life and Law

171-72 (1987)

Pornography sexualizes rape, battery, sexual harassment, prostitution, and child sexual abuse; it thereby celebrates, promotes, authorizes and legitimizes them. More generally, it eroticizes the dominance and submission that is the dynamic common to them all. It makes hierarchy sexy and calls that "the truth about sex" or just a mirror of reality. Through this process pornography constructs what a woman is as what men want from sex. . . .

The content of pornography is one thing. There, women substantively desire dispossession and cruelty. We desperately want to be bound, battered, tortured, humiliated, and killed. . . . What pornography does goes beyond its content: it eroticizes hierarchy, it sexualizes inequality. It makes dominance and submission into sex. Inequality is its central dynamic; the illusion of freedom coming together with the reality of force is central to its working. . . .

From this perspective, pornography is neither harmless fantasy nor a corrupt and confused misrepresentation of an otherwise natural and healthy sexual situation. It institutionalizes the sexuality of male supremacy, fusing the eroticization of dominance and submission with the social construction of male and female. To the extent that gender is sexual, pornography is part of constituting the meaning of that sexuality.

---

389. 413 U.S. 15 (1973).
390. Deborah L. Rhode, Speaking of Sex: The Denial of Gender Equality 130-36 (1997).

Catharine A. MacKinnon

Pornography as Defamation and Discrimination

71 B.U. L. Rev. 793, 796-97, 801-02 (1991)

Pornography has a central role in actualizing . . . [a] system of subordination in the contemporary West, beginning with the conditions of its production. Women in pornography are bound, battered, tortured, harassed, raped, and sometimes killed; or in the glossy men's entertainment magazines, "merely" humiliated, molested, objectified, and used. In all pornography, women are prostituted. . . . It is done because someone who has more power than they do, someone who matters, someone with rights, a full human being and a full citizen, gets pleasure from seeing it, or doing it, or seeing it as a form of doing it. In order to produce what the consumer wants to see, it must first be done to someone, usually a woman, a woman with few real choices. . . .

The evidence shows that the use of pornography makes it impossible for men to tell when sex is forced, that women are human, and that rape is rape. Pornography makes men hostile and aggressive toward women, and it makes women silent. While these effects are not invariant or always immediate, and do not affect all men to the same degree, there is no reason to think they are not acted upon and every reason and overwhelming evidence to think that they are — if not right then, then sometime, if not violently, then through some other kind of discrimination. . . . When men use pornography, they experience in their bodies, not just their minds, that one-sided sex — sex between a person (them) and a thing (it) — is sex, that sexual use is sex, sexual abuse is sex, sexual domination is sex. This is the sexuality that they then demand, practice, purchase, and live out in their everyday social relations with others. Pornography works by making sexism sexy.

2.   *The Judicial, First Amendment Response*

American Booksellers Association, Inc. v. Hudnut

771 F.2d 323 (7th Cir. 1985), aff'd mem., 475 U.S. 1001, reh'g denied, 475 U.S. 1132 (1986)

EASTERBROOK, Circuit Judge.

Indianapolis enacted an ordinance defining "pornography" as a practice that discriminates against women. "Pornography" is to be redressed through the administrative and judicial methods used for other discrimination. The City's definition of "pornography" is considerably different from "obscenity," which the Supreme Court has held is not protected by the First Amendment.

To be "obscene" under Miller v. California, . . . "a publication must, taken as a whole, appeal to the prurient interest, must contain patently offensive depictions or descriptions of specified sexual conduct, and on the whole have no serious literary, artistic, political, or scientific value." . . . Offensiveness must be assessed under the standards of the community. Both offensiveness and an appeal to something other than "normal, healthy sexual desires" are essential elements of "obscenity."

"Pornography" under the ordinance is "the graphic sexually explicit subordination of women, whether in pictures or in words, that also includes one or more of the following: (1) Women are presented as sexual objects who enjoy pain or humiliation; or (2) Women are presented as sexual objects who experience sexual pleasure in being raped; or (3) Women are presented as sexual objects tied up or cut up or mutilated or bruised or physically hurt, or as dismembered or truncated or fragmented or severed into body parts; or (4) Women are presented as being penetrated by objects or animals; or (5) Women are presented in scenarios of degradation, injury, abasement, torture, shown as filthy or inferior, bleeding, bruised, or hurt in a context that makes these conditions sexual; or (6) Women are presented as sexual objects for domination, conquest, violation, exploitation, possession, or use, or through postures or positions of servility or submission or display." . . . The statute provides that the "use of men, children, or transsexuals in the place of women in paragraphs (1) through (6) above shall also constitute pornography under this section." . . . The Indianapolis ordinance does not refer to the prurient interest, to offensiveness, or to the standards of the community. It demands attention to particular depictions, not to the work judged as a whole. It is irrelevant under the ordinance whether the work has literary, artistic, political, or scientific value. The City and many amici point to these omissions as virtues. They maintain that pornography influences attitudes, and the statute is a way to alter the socialization of men and women rather than to vindicate community standards of offensiveness. And as one of the principal drafters of the ordinance has asserted, "if a woman is subjected, why should it matter that the work has other value?" . . .

The plaintiffs are a congeries of distributors and readers of books, magazines, and films. . . . Civil rights groups and feminists have entered this case as amici on both sides. Those supporting the ordinance say that it will play an important role in reducing the tendency of men to view women as sexual objects, a tendency that leads to both unacceptable attitudes and discrimination in the workplace and violence away from it. Those opposing the ordinance point out that much radical feminist literature is explicit and depicts women in ways forbidden by the ordinance and that the ordinance would reopen old battles. It is unclear how Indianapolis would treat works from James Joyce's Ulysses to Homer's Iliad; both depict women as submissive objects for conquest and domination. . . .

"If there is any fixed star in our constitutional constellation, it is that no official, high or petty, can prescribe what shall be orthodox in politics, nationalism, religion, or other matters of opinion or force citizens to confess by word or act their faith therein." . . . Under the First Amendment the government must leave to the people the evaluation of ideas. Bald or subtle, an idea is as powerful as the audience allows it to be. A belief may be pernicious—the beliefs of Nazis led to the death of millions, those of the Klan to the repression of millions. A pernicious belief may prevail. Totalitarian governments today rule much of the planet, practicing suppression of billions and spreading dogma that may enslave others. One of the things that separates our society from theirs is our absolute right to propagate opinions that the government finds wrong or even hateful. . . .

Under the ordinance graphic sexually explicit speech is "pornography" or not depending on the perspective the author adopts. Speech that "subordinates" women and also, for example, presents women as enjoying pain, humiliation, or rape, or even simply presents women in "positions of servility or submission or display" is forbidden, no matter how great the literary or political value of the work taken as a whole. Speech that portrays women in positions of equality is lawful, no matter how graphic the sexual content. This is thought control. It establishes an "approved" view of women, of how they may react to sexual encounters, of how the sexes may relate to each other. Those who espouse the approved view may use sexual images; those who do not, may not.

Indianapolis justifies the ordinance on the ground that pornography affects thoughts. Men who see women depicted as subordinate are more likely to treat them so. Pornography is an aspect of dominance. It does not persuade people so much as change them. It works by socializing, by establishing the expected and the permissible. In this view pornography is not an idea; pornography is the injury.

There is much to this perspective. Beliefs are also facts. . . . Depictions of subordination tend to perpetuate subordination. The subordinate status of women in turn leads to affront and lower pay at work, insult and injury at home, battery and rape on the streets. In the language of the legislature, "[p]ornography is central in creating and maintaining sex as a basis of discrimination. Pornography is a systematic practice of exploitation and subordination based on sex which differentially harms women. The bigotry and contempt it produces, with the acts of aggression it fosters, harm women's opportunities for equality and rights [of all kinds]."

Yet this simply demonstrates the power of pornography as speech. All of these unhappy effects depend on mental intermediation. Pornography affects how people see the world, their fellows, and social relations. If pornography is what pornography does, so is other speech. Hitler's orations affected how some Germans saw Jews. . . . Racial bigotry, anti-[S]emitism, violence on television, reporters' biases — these and many more influence the culture and shape our socialization. None is directly answerable by more speech, unless that speech too finds its place in the popular culture. Yet all is protected as speech, however insidious. Any other answer leaves the government in control of all of the institutions of culture, the great censor and director of which thoughts are good for us. . . .

Much of Indianapolis's argument rests on the belief that when speech is "unanswerable," and the metaphor that there is a "marketplace of ideas" does not apply, the First Amendment does not apply either. The metaphor is honored; Milton's Areopagitica and John Stewart [sic] Mill's On Liberty defend freedom of speech on the ground that the truth will prevail, and many of the most important cases under the First Amendment recite this position. The Framers undoubtedly believed it. As a general matter it is true. But the Constitution does not make the dominance of truth a necessary condition of freedom of speech. To say that it does would be to confuse an outcome of free speech with a necessary condition for the application of the amendment.

A power to limit speech on the ground that truth has not yet prevailed and is not likely to prevail implies the power to declare truth. At some point the government must be able to say (as Indianapolis has said): "We know what the truth is, yet a free exchange of speech has not driven out falsity, so that we must now prohibit falsity." If the government may declare the truth, why wait for the failure of speech? Under the First Amendment, however, there is no such thing as a false idea, . . . so the government may not restrict speech on the ground that in a free exchange truth is not yet dominant. . . .

We come, finally, to the argument that pornography is "low value" speech, that it is enough like obscenity that Indianapolis may prohibit it. Some cases hold that speech far removed from politics and other subjects at the core of the Framers' concerns may be subjected to special regulation. . . . These cases do not sustain statutes that select among viewpoints, however. In [one case], the FCC sought to keep vile language off the air during certain times. The Court held that it may; but the Court would not have sustained a regulation prohibiting scatological descriptions of Republicans but not scatological descriptions of Democrats, or any other form of selection among viewpoints.

At all events, "pornography" is not low value speech within the meaning of these cases. Indianapolis seeks to prohibit certain speech because it believes this speech influences social relations and politics on a grand scale, that it controls attitudes at home and in the legislature. This precludes a characterization of the speech as low value. True, pornography and obscenity have sex in common. But Indianapolis left out of its definition any reference to literary, artistic, political, or scientific value. The ordinance applies to graphic sexually explicit subordination in works great and small. The Court sometimes balances the value of speech against the costs of its restriction, but it does this by category of speech and not by the content of particular works. . . . Indianapolis has created an approved point of view and so loses the support of these cases.

Any rationale we could imagine in support of this ordinance could not be limited to sex discrimination. Free speech has been on balance an ally of those seeking change. Governments that want stasis start by restricting speech. Culture is a powerful force of continuity; Indianapolis paints pornography as part of the culture of power. Change in any complex system ultimately depends on the ability of outsiders to challenge accepted views and the reigning institutions. Without a strong guarantee of freedom of speech, there is no effective right to challenge what is. . . .

The offense of coercion to engage in a pornographic performance . . . has elements that might be constitutional. Without question a state may prohibit fraud, trickery, or the use of force to induce people to perform—in pornographic films or in any other films. Such a statute may be written without regard to the viewpoint depicted in the work. New York v. Ferber . . . suggests that when a state has a strong interest in forbidding the conduct that makes up a film (in *Ferber* sexual acts involving minors), it may restrict or forbid dissemination of the film in order to reinforce the prohibition of the conduct. A state may apply such a rule to non-sexual coercion (although it need not). . . .

But the Indianapolis ordinance, unlike our hypothetical statute, is not neutral with respect to viewpoint. . . . The ban on distribution of works containing coerced performances is limited to pornography; coercion is irrelevant if the work is not "pornography," and we have held the definition of "pornography" to be defective root and branch. A legislature might replace "pornography" in [the ordinance] with "any film containing explicit sex" or some similar expression, but even the broadest severability clause does not permit a federal court to rewrite as opposed to excise. Rewriting is work for the legislature of Indianapolis. . . .

No amount of struggle with particular words and phrases in this ordinance can leave anything in effect. The district court came to the same conclusion. Its judgment is therefore Affirmed.

NOTES

1. **Pornography and the First Amendment.**   Some commentators have argued that regulation of pornography is consistent with the First Amendment, in that pornography is like other forms of speech that can be regulated because of their low value (such as advertising) or their social harm (such as libel, fraud, and sexual harassment). They also claim that pornography ordinances are no less vague than existing obscenity law. In MacKinnon's view,

> while the First Amendment supports pornography on the belief that consensus and progress are facilitated by allowing all views, however divergent and unorthodox, it fails to notice that pornography . . . is not at all divergent or unorthodox. It is the ruling ideology. Feminism, the dissenting view, is suppressed by pornography.[391]

How does *Hudnut* respond to these claims? How would you? The technologies of producing and disseminating pornography have changed radically since *Hudnut* was decided; should that affect the First Amendment analysis?[392]

Legislation somewhat similar to the Indianapolis ordinance has been upheld by the Canadian Supreme Court. In Regina v. Butler, the Court sustained a statute that criminalizes "any publication a dominant characteristic of which is the undue exploitation of sex, or of sex and any one or more of the following subjects, namely crime, horror, cruelty and violence." The Court interpreted the statute to prohibit any "materials that subordinate, degrade or dehumanize women."[393] In determining that the restriction of speech expression was justified, the Court concluded:

> [T]his kind of expression lies far from the core of the guarantee of freedom of expression. It appeals only to the most base aspect of individual fulfillment and it is primarily economically motivated. The objective of the legislation on the other hand is of fundamental importance in a free and democratic society. . . . It thus seeks to enhance respect for all members of society and non-violence and equality in their relations with each other.[394]

Is this a desirable approach? Is your view affected by the fact that the first targets of the legislation included a gay and lesbian bookstore, a lesbian magazine, and two books by anti-pornography activist Andrea Dworkin?[395] No other Western democracies have followed Canada's example. Why do you suppose they haven't?

Under the right circumstances, some of the types of cases advocates of the Minneapolis ordinance had in mind may be pursued under existing tort theories.

---

391. Catharine A. MacKinnon, Toward a Feminist Theory of the State 205 (1989).

392. See Mary Anne Franks & Ari Ezra Waldman, Sex, Lies, and Videotape: Deep Fakes and Free Speech Delusions, 78 Md. L. Rev. 892 (2019) (arguing that practices such as deep fake manipulation and digital alteration render such images deliberately deceptive and no part of the "marketplace of ideas").

393. 89 D.L.R.4th 449 (S.C.C. 1992).

394. Id. at 487-88.

395. Nadine Strossen, A Feminist Critique of "the" Feminist Critique of Pornography, 79 Va. L. Rev. 1099, 1145-46 (1993).

In one such case, fifty women brought an action for fraud and coercion again Mind-Geek, the parent company of Pornhub, based on Pornhub's partnership with Girls-DoPorn—a porn producer shut down by the U.S. Department of Justice in 2019 after its senior staff were arrested for sex trafficking and other offenses. The women claimed that they were recruited as models, but the jobs turned out to be making pornographic videos. They were told that their videos were for private collectors or far-flung markets and would not be posted on the web, but in fact they were distributed and posted publicly, including on Pornhub. The women eventually settled for an undisclosed amount of damages.[396] In the criminal action, defendants were ordered to pay $18 million in restitution to the victims of the GirlsDoPorn fraud.[397]

2. **Evaluating the Harm of Pornography.**   Evidence concerning the harms of pornography remains conflicting and contested. Part of the problem is that controlled studies are difficult to conduct in real-world settings, laboratory findings about attitudes may not generalize into behavioral differences, and correlations between pornography consumption and adverse outcomes may not reflect causation, nor distinguish between different kinds of materials.[398] Still, evidence of harm does exist. Experts cite data showing that frequent viewing of pornography leads to unrealistic expectations concerning female appearance and behavior, greater acceptance of sexual aggression and harassment, and difficulties in forming sexually satisfying relationships.[399] Part of the reason is that the bestselling pornography emphasizes physical aggression by men apparently enjoyed by women.[400] Other research suggests that exposure to degrading pornography (but not erotica) is linked to sexist beliefs and objectification of women.[401] One study of college men found that those who viewed violent, degrading pornography (but not those who viewed explicit but nondegrading sexual material) were less likely to intervene as a bystander to rape.[402] A review of research by the Children's Commissioner in Great

---

396. See Pornhub Owner Settles with Girls Do Porn Victims over Videos, BBC News, Oct. 19, 2021.

397. See Charlie Osborne, Victims Awarded $18 million in GirlsDoPorn Online Video case, Boss on the Run, ZDNet (Dec. 15, 2021).

398. David Segal, Does Porn Hurt Children?, N.Y. Times, Mar. 29, 2014, at SR1; Ronald Weitzer, Interpreting the Data: Assessing Competing Claims in Pornography Research, in New Views on Pornography: Sexuality, Politics, and the Law 249-54, 259 (Lynn Comella & Shira Tarrant eds., 2015).

399. Report of the American Psychological Association Task Force on the Sexualization of Girls 29, 31, 34 (2006); Belinda Luscombe, Porn and the Threat to Virility, Time, Apr. 11, 2016, 42-46; Alison Baxter, How Pornography Harms Children: The Advocates' Role, 33 Child. L. Prac. 113 (2014); Lihi Yona, Politicizing Health, Medicalizing Porn: Rethinking Modern Pornography, 16 Marq. Elder's Advisor 113, 149 (2014).

400. Ana Bridges et al., Aggression and Sexual Behavior in Best-Selling Pornography Videos: A Content Analysis Update, 16 Violence Against Women 1065 (2010).

401. Malvina N. Skorska et al., Experimental Effects of Degrading Versus Erotic Pornography Exposure in Men on Reactions Toward Women (Objectification, Sexism, Discrimination), 27 Canadian J. Hum. Sexuality 26, 271 (2018).

402. John D. Foubert & Ana J. Bridges, Predicting Bystander Efficacy and Willingness to Intervene in College Men and Women: The Role of Exposure to Varying Levels of Violence in Pornography, 21 Violence Against Women 692 (2016).

Britain found a link between exposure to pornography among children and adolescents with unrealistic attitudes about sex, a belief in less progressive gender roles, and greater likelihood of engagement in sexually risky behaviors.[403] Research on young American women finds that many feel that they are "in competition with porn, and if they don't put out, it's easy for the guy to go home, log in to Pornhub and get what he needs there. They're sublimating their own needs to try and please the guy. Then they realize their needs weren't being met at all."[404] A study of battered women also found that pornography use by the batterer was correlated with an increased likelihood of sexual as well as physical abuse.[405] Longitudinal data indicate that frequently viewing pornography results in a significantly lower quality of marital relations for men, but not women.[406]

In elaborating the harms to men, sociologist Michael Kimmel argues that "porn gives guys a world in which no one has to take no for an answer." It serves as a "refuge from the harsh reality of a more gender equitable world. . . . It's about anger at the loss of privilege." Escape into this world, Kimmel argues, fosters attitudes "that won't serve [men] in the long term. . . . They're missing out on developing the skills, sexual and otherwise, that might help them to sustain relationships with women in the real world," relationships that demand "at least a modicum of dignity, respect, and care."[407] Is he right? Is it worrisome that researchers find that porn is the primary source of information about sex for most teens, and that only one in six boys and one in four girls believed that women in online porn were not actually experiencing pleasure?[408]

Extensive use of pornography has also been correlated to high levels of depression, anxiety, and stress among its consumers. One survey of more than 1,000 college students showed a strong association between compulsive, Internet pornography use and an elevation in each of these three mental health indicators.[409]

Some experts maintain that the vast majority of pornography viewers are occasional, recreational users, not addicts, and that such use can be beneficial in sparking desire, enhancing satisfaction, and constructively channeling sexual fantasies. Some also believe that even if the causal relationship between the most common kinds of pornography and sexual violence was established, attempts to prohibit it are counterproductive.[410] Law professor David Cole argues:

---

403. Miranda A. H. Horvath et al., Basically . . . Porn Is Everywhere: A Rapid Evidence Assessment on the Effects That Access and Exposure to Pornography Has on Children and Young People (2013).

404. Maureen Dowd, What's Lust Got to Do With It?, N.Y. Times, Apr. 8, 2018, at SR9 (quoting Joann Coles); see Peggy Orenstein, Girls & Sex: Navigating the Complicated New Landscape (2017).

405. Janet Hinson Shope, When Words Are Not Enough: The Search for the Effect of Pornography on Abused Women, 10 Violence Against Women 56, 67-68 (2004).

406. Samuel L. Perry, Does Viewing Pornography Reduce Marital Quality Over Time? Evidence from Longitudinal Data, 46 Arch. Sex. Behavior (2017).

407. Michael Kimmel, Guyland 173, 177, 188 (2008).

408. Maggie Jones, When Porn Is Sex Ed, N.Y. Times Mag., Feb. 11, 2018, at 30.

409. See Christina Camilleri et al., Compulsive Internet Pornography Use and Mental Health: A Cross-Sectional Study in a Sample of University Students in the United States, Frontiers in Psych. (Jan. 12, 2021).

410. For discussion of studies, see Horvath et al., supra note 403; Segal, supra note 398.

Sexual expression . . . inevitably confounds society's attempts to regulate it. It subverts every taboo by making it a fetish. The forbidden is simultaneously eroticized. As a result, attempts to regulate sexual expression are doomed to failure; by creating taboos to transgress, regulation only adds to sexual expression's appeal.[411]

Feminists opposing the *Hudnut* decision argued that pornography regulation reinforces damaging stereotypes — stereotypes that men are "attack dogs" or "irresponsible beasts;" that only women are demeaned or degraded by pornography; that women are incapable of consent to sex; or that good women do not seek and enjoy sex.[412] Are they right? What is your view? Is the answer to regulate more, or less?

How does thinking about race and ethnicity complicate these questions? Some scholars have pointed out that pornography "sexualizes racialized oppression," and that it is not enough to just emphasize that women of color "have it worse."[413] These scholars argue that feminists have failed to generate a theory that "attends to pornography's complexity, multiplicity of meanings, or connections to the maintenance (and possible disruption) of both white supremacy and patriarchy."[414] One way to bring an intersectional approach to pornography issues would be to explore how racial and ethnic stereotypes work together with gender stereotypes in uniquely harmful ways for women of color. An example is how images of Asian-American sex workers have functioned to reinforce oppression in contexts involving sex tourism, sexual harassment, and regulation of prostitution.[415] Can you identify other examples?

3. **Sex-Positive Feminism and Feminist, Ethical, and Queer Pornography.** Sex-positive or pro-sex feminism is a movement that began in the early 1980s that emphasizes the importance of sexual freedom as part of women's overall autonomy. Some activists became involved in the movement in response to anti-pornography feminist efforts. Wendy McElroy, an early defender of the sex-positive position, opens her book, **XXX: A Woman's Right to Pornography**, with the claim, "Pornography benefits women, both personally and politically."[416] In her view, "every woman has the right to define what is degrading and liberating for herself." Pornography can be liberating by (1) giving a "panoramic view of the world's sexual possibilities"; (2) allowing women to avoid shame and "enjoy scenes and situations

411. David Cole, Playing by Pornography's Rules: The Regulation of Sexual Expression, 143 U. Pa. L. Rev. 111, 116 (1994).

412. See Nan D. Hunter & Sylvia A. Law, Brief Amici Curiae of Feminist Anti-Censorship Taskforce et al., in American Booksellers Association v. Hudnut, 21 U. Mich. J.L. Reform 69, 125-31 (Fall 1987-Winter 1988).

413. Jennifer C. Nash, Bearing Witness to Ghosts: Notes on Theorizing Pornography, Race, and Law, 21 Wis. L. Rev. 47, 64 (2006); see also Patricia Hill Collins, Pornography and Black Women's Bodies, Black Feminist Thought (Patricia Hill Collins, ed., 2d ed. 2000).

414. Nash, supra note 413, at 71.

415. See Suzie K. Cho, Converging Stereotypes in Racialized Sexual Harassment: Where the Model Minority Meets Suzie Wong, 1 J. Gender, Race, and Just. 177, 183-94 (1997).

416. Wendy McElroy, XXX: A Woman's Right to Pornography (1997). For a more recent account, see Wendy McElroy, A Feminist Overview of Pornography Ending in a Defense Thereof, http://www.wendymcelroy.com/freeinqu.htm.

that would be anathema in real life"; and (3) providing a sexual outlet for those who have no sexual partner.[417] Some sex-positive feminists are committed to "ethical porn," which seeks to provide equitable financial agreements, including flat rates for sexual acts so no performer feels pressure to engage in behaviors that they find uncomfortable.[418] This movement has been compared to the campaign for fair trade food, which leads some commentators to suggest that "it's a harder sell. Few people want ethics with their porn."[419] Other feminists create what they term "feminist porn," which stresses women's agency and pleasure even as it sometimes depicts sado-masochistic acts that anti-porn activists find subordinating.[420] Candida Royalle, a prominent creator of feminist porn, argues that it can "help people become comfortable with a particular fantasy they or their partner may have. Pornography can reboot a couple's sex life. It can give ideas or help you get in touch with what turns you on."[421] One former porn star similarly argues that she provides materials that are "helping peoples' lives," including men who for various reasons find it difficult to find sexual partners, or couples who are "unhappy sexually." Porn can "stimulate their relationship," or provide an outlet that is better than having an affair.[422]

Other identity groups have carved out their own niches for positive representation. Makers of queer porn and transgender porn stress authentic desire and inclusive forms of sexual representation, including diversity in performers and behaviors.[423] Studies of Black women performers have similarly found that some are "working hard to create their own images, express their own desires, and shape their own labor choices and conditions."[424] Older performers, people with disabilities, and fat activists have all widened the definition of what kinds of sex can be "sexy."[425]

Some feminists have objected to the label "sex positive," which implies that others are "sex negative." Meghan Murphy argues that those who are seen as sex negative are actually critical of pornography because they "want to work towards a real, liberated, *feminist* understanding of sex and sexuality, rather than one that sexualizes inequality, domination, and subordination."[426] Other feminists argue that "it's saddening to see us fighting each other; women who have been called prudes for asserting their sexual choices attacking women who have been called whores for

---

417. McElroy, A Feminist Overview, supra note 416.

418. Shirra Tarrant, The Pornography Industry: What Everyone Needs to Know 29 (2016).

419. Forrester, supra note 385, at 26.

420. Rebecca Santiago, Feminist Porn 101: Your Guide to Empowering Sexytimes, Bustle.com (Dec. 12, 2013).

421. Candida Royalle, Room for Debate: Pornography Can Be Good for Consumers, N.Y. Times, Nov. 11, 2012).

422. Brad Armstrong, Porn Star, in Gig: Americans Talk About Their Jobs at the Turn of the Millennium 359, 364 (John Bowe et al. eds., 2000).

423. Tarrant, supra note 418, at 171 (discussing examples such as the documentary Doing It for Ourselves: The Transwoman Porn Project).

424. Mireille Susan Miller-Young, A Taste for Brown Sugar x-xi (2014).

425. Hess, supra note 386.

426. Meghan Murphy, The Divide Isn't Between "Sex Negative" and "Sex Positive" Feminists—It's Between Liberal and Radical Feminism, Feminist (Apr. 11, 2014).

asserting their sexual choices . . . and vice versa."[427] These feminists note research finding that large numbers of women have fantasies that include sexual submission, and that higher rates of female than male users of sites such as Pornhub browse sections like "rough sex" and "gangbang."[428] Some have questioned whether it makes sense to even try to reach agreement on what constitutes "good porn." As one puts it, "What right do we have to dictate the way adult performers have sex with one another, or what is good and normal, aside from requiring that it be consensual."[429] Where do you situate yourself in this debate? Is it productive? Is it unavoidable?

Is there some "natural" set of sexual drives and desires that pornography, advertising, and other social forces distort? Or is sexuality always socially constructed? If the latter, how should society promote the healthiest understandings of sex and sexuality?

4. **Pornography, the Internet, and Children.** In New York v. Ferber,[430] the U.S. Supreme Court categorically excluded child pornography from First Amendment protections because of its intrinsic relationship to the inevitable physiological, emotional, and mental harm to children, not only from its production, but also from its distribution, which makes a permanent record of the exploitation. The opportunities for distribution of child pornography have since exploded due to the Internet. Data indicate that the number of global reports of child sexual abuse imagery by online platforms and other sources has increased from 3,000 in 1998 to 18.4 million in 2018, with more than 45 million images and videos flagged as including such imagery.[431] There is the further harm of adolescent exposure to online pornography, which has led to more unrealistic sexual beliefs, and, in the case of violent pornography, to increased sexually aggressive behavior. In the absence of education, exposure to high-risk practices is correlated with high-risk behavior.[432]

Online pornography poses special challenges for regulation. The first problem is detection. The sheer size of cyberspace and the growth of the encrypted "dark web" make it difficult to police. A second problem is accountability. Even if illegal content is discovered online, the responsible party may be impossible to track. Both of these difficulties are exacerbated by encryption technology, which allows parties to disguise their identities. A third problem is jurisdiction: How can courts exercise authority over out-of-state providers? Other difficulties arise in determining which "community standards" govern online materials that can be downloaded anywhere. The Internet's decentralized structure also resists regulation by permitting users to reroute access and evade recognition. In addition, users can post messages anonymously through the use of remailers, making it difficult to suspend privileges or identify senders. Finally, enforcement resources have been

---

427. Kitty Stryker, The 80s Called and They Want Their Sex Wars Back, The Frisky (Apr. 10, 2014).

428. Tarrant, supra note 418, at 95.

429. Stoya, Can There Be Good Porn?, N.Y. Times, Mar. 4, 2018, at A27.

430. 458 U.S. 747, 748 (1982).

431. Michael H. Keller & Gabriel J.X. Dance, Child Sex Abuse on the Internet: Stolen Innocence Gone Viral, N.Y. Times, Sept. 29, 2019.

432. Eric W. Owens et al., The Impact of Internet Pornography on Adolescents: A Review of the Research, 19 Sexual Addiction & Compulsivity 99, 116 (2012).

grossly inadequate to keep up with either the abuse of children in the production of pornography or adolescents' access to adult pornography.[433]

Notwithstanding the Court's initial determination in *Ferber* that child pornography constituted a categorical exemption from the First Amendment, the Supreme Court has since struck down some congressional efforts to police child pornography as overly broad restrictions on speech.[434] In Ashcroft v. Free Speech Coalition,[435] the Court struck down provisions of the Child Pornography Prevention Act (CPPA), which prohibited virtual child pornography, on the grounds that only obscene depictions of actual children were unprotected by the First Amendment. The Court rejected the government's argument that such works could be banned because pedophiles used them to stimulate their appetite for sexual contact or to lure children into criminal acts, calling it "contingent and indirect."[436]

Other important legislation includes the PROTECT Act, passed in 2003, which attempts to curb the spread of child pornography on the Internet by making it a crime to offer or solicit sexually explicit images of children. More recent federal legislation, FOSTA-SESTA, ends legal immunity for online platforms that facilitate sex trafficking, such as Backpage.com.[437]

How serious is the crime of possession of child pornography? In some instances, punishments for the possession of child pornography have exceeded those for actual child abuse.[438] In contrast, some courts have used their discretion to revise sentences downward on the ground that penalties are too high for a victimless offense and that offenders are themselves victims of mental health disorders.[439] The Violence Against Women Act authorizes restitution to victims who are harmed as a result of commission of a crime involving sexual exploitation of children.[440] Lower courts have divided over this remedy in pornography possession cases because the number of potential victims and offenders is "staggering," the amount of losses directly attributable to a single owner is difficult to calculate, and inconsistent verdicts are likely.[441]

---

433. Id.

434. Reno v. ACLU, 521 U.S. 844 (1997); Ashcroft v. ACLU, 542 U.S. 656 (2004); ACLU v. Gonzales, 478 F. Supp. 2d 775 (E.D. Pa. 2007).

435. 535 U.S. 234 (2002).

436. Id. at 250. The Court upheld the Children's Internet Protection Act, which gave public schools and libraries authority to block or filter access to Internet sites depicting child pornography. See U.S. v. Am. Library Ass'n, 539 U.S. 194 (2003).

437. See Aja Romano, A New Law Intended to Curb Sex Trafficking Threatens the Future of the Internet as We Know It, Vox (July 2, 2018).

438. Carissa Byrne Hessick, The Limits of Child Pornography, 89 Ind. L.J. 1437, 1439 (2014).

439. United States v. Irey, 612 F.3d 1160 (11th Cir. 2010) (en banc); Melissa Hamilton, Sentencing Adjudication: Lessons from Child Pornography Policy Nullification, 30 Ga. St. U. L. Rev. 375, 378 (2014).

440. 18 U.S.C. § 2259 (2018).

441. Dina McLeod, Section 2259 Restitution Claims and Child Pornography Possession, 109 Mich. L. Rev. 1327, 1342 (2011) (noting that each year there are about 200 victims of child pornography and 3,000 prosecutions for possession). The Supreme Court has held that where it is impossible to trace a particular amount of the plaintiff's losses to an

Is a life sentence appropriate for a 26-year-old man convicted of 454 counts of possessing child pornography?[442] In her nomination hearings for a seat on the U.S. Supreme Court, Judge Ketanji Brown Jackson was excoriated by some senators for sentencing an 18-year-old to only three months in prison for downloading four videos of children engaged in sex acts.[443] Is that too little? What would you need to know to answer that question? Should pretrial diversion for offenders be available?[444] If restitution is appropriate, how should damages be measured?

5. **Sexting.** An issue that is gaining increased attention is sexting — sending nude or seminude pictures over cell phones. Sexting has evolved against a growing cultural backdrop of sexualization of adolescents.[445] Girls often use sexting as a form of "relationship currency" to initiate or sustain intimacy, as well as to entertain friends and humiliate enemies.[446] A 2018 meta-analysis of studies found that the mean prevalence of receiving sexts by adolescents younger than 18 was 27 percent, of sending sexts was 15 percent, of forwarding sexts without consent was 12 percent, and of having a sext forwarded without consent was 8 percent. No significant gender differences emerged in the frequency of sending or receiving such messages.[447] However, differences are apparent in the motivations for such behavior. Girls in middle school and high school often feel pressure from boys to engage in sexting. This exchange tends to uplift boys' popularity while subjecting girls to social disapproval. Some boys collect photos of girls like playing cards, assigning values to each image. In effect, "girls are treated as sex objects and punished for doing what is expected of them."[448] Adolescents have faced exploitation, harassment, bullying,

---

individual defendant's possession, the court should order restitution in an amount "that comport[s] with the defendant's relative role in the causal process that underlay the victim's general losses," taking into account such things as the number of images the defendant possessed and whether the defendant reproduced or distributed them. Paroline v. U.S., 572 U.S. 434 (2014). For a discussion of reform proposals designed to address the difficulties of enforcing restitution remedies, see Alanna D. Francois, *Paroline v. United States*: Mandatory Restitution: An Empty Gesture, Leaving Victims of Child Pornography Holding the Bag, 42 S. U. L. Rev. 293, 324-25 (2015).

442. Jacob Carpenter, East Naples Man's Life Sentence for Child Porn Too Harsh, Attorney Says, Naplesnews.com (Nov. 3, 2011).

443. See Aaron C. Davis & Spencer S. Hsu, The Child Pornography Case at the Center of Ketanji Brown Jackson's Hearing, Wash. Post, Mar. 24, 2022.

444. Sarah J. Long, The Case for Extending Pretrial Diversion to Include Possession of Child Pornography, 9 U. Mass. L. Rev. 306 (2014).

445. M. Gigi Durham, The Lolita Effect: The Media Sexualization of Young Girls and What We Can Do About It (2008).

446. Andrea Lenhart, Teens and Sexting (2009); Alex Morris, They Know What Boys Want, N.Y. Mag., Jan. 30, 2011; Jim Hoffman, Girl's Nude Photo and Altered Life, N.Y. Times, Mar. 27, 2011, at A1.

447. Sheri Madigan et al., Prevalence of Multiple Forms of Sexting Behavior Among Youth: A Systematic Review and Meta-analysis, 172 JAMA Pediatrics 327, 331-33 (2018). Some confirming studies are summarized in Victor Strasburger et al., Teenagers, Sexting, and the Law, 143 Pediatrics 1 (May 2019).

448. Soraya Chemaly, Rage Becomes Her: The Power of Women's Anger 28 (2018); Leora Tanenbaum, I Am Not a Slut: Slut-Shaming in the Age of the Internet (2015).

blackmail, and psychological trauma as a result of nonconsensual distribution of such images, and a number have committed suicide.[449] Research also suggests that sexting is increasing despite prevention efforts.[450]

A number of states now have specific laws addressing sexting, with other states handling the issue under their existing obscenity or child pornography statutes.[451] Depending on the circumstances, sexting may also be covered under federal law by PROTECT, discussed in Note 4, above. Students have been expelled or suspended or denied the right to participate in school activities in response to such offenses.[452] Prosecutors in several states also have filed or threatened child pornography charges against students involved in sending or forwarding such photos.[453] Opponents of prosecution point out that even if students aren't convicted, searchable records exist of charges that may affect college admissions and job applications.[454] Prosecutors, by contrast, defend the charges as a way to "protect these kids from themselves" and from acting in ways that can "follow them for the rest of their lives."[455]

In a 2019 decision, Maryland's highest court sustained the conviction of a 16-year-old girl who had distributed a video of herself performing fellatio on another student.[456] She was convicted under the state's child pornography statute and sentenced to probation with conditions of electronic monitoring and drug testing. The majority determined that she fell under the plain meaning of the statute, and that Maryland was one of twenty-one states that had not amended its laws to create special treatment for sexting. Given the frequency of the practice, the majority advised the legislature to consider such legislation. Judge Michele Hotten, the lone dissenter, argued that the law was intended to "protect children from exploitation and abuse" by others, not to criminalize consensual sex between minors.[457] Other courts have attempted to mitigate the punishment of minors by imposing limits on the sanctions that can be imposed. In Miller v. Mitchell, the Third Circuit Court of Appeals granted a preliminary injunction against requiring a student to attend an

---

449. Jane Bailey & Mouna Hanna, The Gendered Dimensions of Sexting: Assessing the Applicability of Canada's Child Pornography Provision, 23 Canadian J. W. & L. 405, 407, 411-21 (2011); April Gile Thomas & Elizabeth Cauffman, Youth Sexting as Child Pornography? Developmental Science Supports Less Harsh Sanctions for Juvenile Sexters, 17 New Crim. L. Rev. 631, 639-40 (2014).

450. Madigan et al., supra note 447, at 333.

451. For a listing, see Is Sexting Illegal, Mobicip, Feb. 17, 2021; Haley Zapal, State-by State Differences in Sexting Laws, Bark (Apr. 9, 2019).

452. Bailey & Hanna, supra note 449, at 413-14.

453. Erik Eckholm, Prosecutors Weigh Teenage Sexting: Folly or Felony?, N.Y. Times, Nov. 14, 2015, at A13.

454. Id. at A17.

455. Comments of Michal McAlexander, Chief Deputy, Prosecutor's Office, Allen County, PA, in Racy Teen Messaging Could Be Illegal, Talk of the Nation, NPR (Feb. 18, 2009).

456. In re S.K., 2019 WL 4051636 (Md. 2019).

457. Id. at *19 (Hotten, J., dissenting).

educational class on sexting on the grounds that it infringed her parent's autonomy and her own right of free expression.[458]

How would you respond to "sexting," as a parent, principal, or prosecutor? Is it sexually subordinating to girls? Or are there legitimate issues of sexual self-expression and agency at issue? Should punishment extend to those who send sexts as part of a relationship, or only to those who forward them or pressure others to engage in the practice?[459] About twenty states have adopted laws to address juvenile sexting, with penalties such as misdemeanor charges that may be expunged, required community service, or counseling.[460] Are these good policies?

6. **Nonconsensual Pornography: Revenge Porn.** A practice that has attracted increasing concern is nonconsensual pornography — the distribution of sexually explicit images without the subject's consent. A subset involves "revenge porn," where the disclosure is done with the intent to harm, harass, intimidate, threaten, or coerce the victim, usually in the context of an intimate relationship. Often the images are posted alongside the victim's name and other identifying information, such as phone number, email address, or social media links. One study estimates that one in eight people 18 years or older have experienced sexually explicit image-based abuse.[461] Another puts the figure at one in twelve.[462] Over 90 percent of the victims are women.[463]

In 2015, many of the primary websites for hosting nonconsensual porn, like IsAnyoneUp or U Got Posted, were removed from the Internet, and a number of major players, such as Facebook, Reddit, Twitter, and Google, have incorporated ways for victims to remove nonconsensual porn.[464] Almost every state has criminalized this conduct.[465] Do you see any constitutional problems with criminalizing revenge porn?[466]

By now, a number of state statutes have faced constitutional scrutiny, and while some lower courts have found such statutes overbroad, vague, or unconstitutional under the First Amendment, they have generally been reversed on appeal.

---

458. 598 F.3d 139 (3d Cir. 2010).

459. See Lenhart, supra note 446, at 439-41 (arguing against compounding the adverse consequences for girls who naively trust an intimate partner not to share sexualized representations).

460. Eckholm, supra note 453, at A13.

461. See Jillian McKoy, The Social Consequences of Nonconsensual Pornography, J. Interpersonal Violence BU School of Pub. Health (2020).

462. See Y. Ruvalcaba & E. A. Eaton, Nonconsensual Pornography Among U.S. Adults: A Sexual Scripts Framework on Victimization, Perpetration, and Health Correlates for Women and Men, 10 Psych. Violence 68 (2020).

463. Carolyn A. Uhl et al., An Examination of Nonconsensual Pornography Websites, 28 Feminism & Psych. 50 (2018).

464. See Chance Carter, Nat'l Ass'n Att'y Gen., An Update on the Legal Landscape of Revenge Porn (Nov. 6, 2021).

465. For a continuously updated list of laws relating to nonconsensual pornography, see Cyber Civil Rights Initiative, Existing Nonconsensual Pornography, Sextortion, and Deep Fake Laws, https://cybercivilrights.org/existing-laws.

466. See Danielle Keats Citron & Mary Ann Franks, Criminalizing Revenge Porn, 48 Wake Forest L. Rev. 345 (2014).

In upholding the statutes, courts have been reluctant to carve out a new category of unprotected speech for substantial invasions of privacy or to conclude that the conduct at issue satisfies the definition of obscenity, but they have found, under either a strict scrutiny analysis or intermediate scrutiny, that the state's interest in protecting victims from the harms prohibited by the statutes are sufficiently strong justifications.[467]

The European Union passed the General Data Protection Regulation law in 2018, which allows Internet users to go directly to a platform and request the delisting of "inaccurate, inadequate, irrelevant, or excessive" personal information.[468] Cases of nonconsensual pornography have continued to rise dramatically, however, at least in part because the procedure can be lengthy, expensive, and depend on the website's willingness to collaborate.[469] Stronger regulations continue to be debated.[470]

Is revenge porn a gender equality issue? Does it affect your answer that some prosecutions have been against women?[471]

7. **Misogyny Online and In-Person Violence.**   Since its inception, the Internet has been a breeding ground for virulent forms of misogyny, and in recent years, participants steeped in this culture have been increasingly engaged in terrorist acts, including mass shootings.[472] This misogyny takes various forms in addition to violence and threats of violence: "ridiculing, humiliating, mocking, slurring, vilifying, demonizing, silencing shunning, shaming, blaming, patronizing, condescending disparaging."[473] Some victims are the targets of organized and sustained campaigns. These include Google bombing (the manipulation of search results associated with a victim's name to prioritize negative results),[474] digitally manipulating a victim's images onto pornography or violent imagery,[475] doxxing (the publishing and distributing of a victim's identifying information, such as home address, workplace, telephone number, email address, or Social Security number to enable others to harass them, both online and offline),[476] swatting (putting in hoax calls

---

467. See, e.g., State v. Casillas, 952 N.W.2d 629 (Minn. 2019) (applying strict scrutiny); Illinois v. Austin, 155 N.E. 3d 439 (Ill. 2019) (intermediate scrutiny); Vermont v. VanBuren, 214 A.3d 791 (Vt. 2018) (strict scrutiny).

468. Leonie Cater, How Europe's Privacy Laws Are Failing Victims of Sexual Abuse, Politico, Jan. 13, 2021.

469. Id.

470. See Lorna Woods et al., London Sch. Econ., Pornography Platforms, the EU Digital Services Act and Image-Based Sexual Abuse (Jan. 26, 2022).

471. See, e.g., People v. Austin, 155 N.E.3d 439 (Ill. 2019) (prosecuting a woman who sought to tell her side of the story after a broken engagement, by posting a letter accompanied by naked pictures of the victim).

472. Emma A. Jane, Misogyny Online: A Short and Brutish History 55 (2017); Kate Manne, Down Girl: The Logic of Misogyny (2018); Mediating Misogyny: Gender, Technology, and Harassment 111 (Jacqueline Ryan Vickery & Tracy Everbach eds., 2018); Tamara Shepherd et al., Histories of Hating, 2015 Soc. Media & Soc'y 1, 2 (2015).

473. Manne, supra note 472, at 68.

474. Danielle Keats Citron, Hate Crimes in Cyberspace 69-71 (2014).

475. Karla Mantilla, Gendertrolling: How Misogyny Went Viral 11-12 (2015).

476. Bailey Poland, Haters: Harassment, Abuse, and Violence Online 54 (2016).

to authorities such as the FBI to have them come to the victim's home expecting a crime to be taking place),[477] and threatening the victim's family.[478] Women are disproportionately subject to such abuse, with one study finding that women age 18 to 29 were twice as likely to suffer as male counterparts.[479] Online threats of violence are almost exclusively directed toward female candidates.[480] Women of color are at greatest risk and often face racist as well as sexist content.[481]

The harms of this abuse are obvious, often debilitating, and occasionally fatal. Victims have experienced serious mental health consequences, such as depression, anxiety, insomnia, and suicidal tendencies following online abuse.[482] They also suffer economic, reputational, and other professional consequences. Law enforcement officials were generally unresponsive or ineffectual.[483]

Most disturbingly, online threats have translated into offline violence against women, particularly by "doxxers" and "Men's Rights Activists."[484] Increasing numbers of mass killings have been committed by men who had previously engaged in misogynistic abuse online and described their motivations as exacting revenge on women.[485] One of the first of this trend was George Sodini, who opened fire on a women's fitness class in Pennsylvania in 2009 that killed three women and wounded nine others in order to "prevail over . . . female vipers."[486] More recently, the 18-year-old responsible for shooting nineteen children and two teachers in Uvalde, Texas, had an extensive presence on various social media websites, where he regularly made hate-filled threats of sexual assault, rape, and murder against young women.[487] Several women complained to Yubo, one of the gunman's favorite sites, but nothing was done about it. Many women indicated that such threats happen so often, they have become a normal, expected part of the digital landscape.[488] A particularly alarming subculture on the Internet are Incels (involuntary

---

477. Id. at 55.

478. Catherine Piner, Feminist Writer Jessica Valenti Takes a Break from Social Media After Threat Against Her Daughter, Slate (July 28, 2016).

479. Maeve Duggan, Men, Women Experience and View Online Harassment Differently, Pew Rsch. Ctr. (July 14, 2017); Amanda Lenhart et al., Online Harassment, Digital Abuse, and Cyberstalking in America, Data & Soc'y 3, 25-26 (Nov. 21, 2016).

480. Caitlin Moscatello, See Jane Win; The Inspiring Story of the Women Changing American Politics 139 (2019).

481. Citron, supra note 474, at 14; Poland, supra note 476, at 57-60; Lenhart et al., supra note 479, at 36-37, 39; Mantilla, supra note 475, at 34-36.

482. Citron, supra note 474, at 10-11; Hunt, supra note 387 (finding 22 percent of respondents who had experienced online harassment felt depressed and that 5 percent felt suicidal).

483. Briana Wu, Why Was There No Reckoning, N.Y. Times, Aug. 19, 2019.

484. Mantilla, supra note 475; Poland, supra note 476, at 139-40.

485. Jessica Valenti, When Misogynists Become Terrorists, N.Y Times, Apr. 26, 2018, at A27.

486. Michael Kimmel, The Aggrieved Entitlement of Elliot Rodger, Shriver Rep. (June 2, 2014). See also Post Staff Report, Full Text of Gym Killer's Blog, N.Y. Post, Aug. 5, 2009.

487. See Silvia Foster-Frau et al., Before Massacre, Uvalde Gunman Frequently Threatened Teen Girls Online, Wash. Post, May 28, 2022.

488. Id.

celibates), who are willing to punish all women for the refusal of chosen women to have sex with them on demand.[489] Elliot Rodger posted his misogynistic manifesto on YouTube before killing six people and wounding thirteen others in Isla Vista, California.[490] In that manifesto, "Tomorrow Is the Day of Retribution," Rodger explained how he had been "forced to endure an existence of loneliness, rejection and unfilled desires, all because girls have never been attracted to me." His retribution was to enter the "hottest sorority house of UCSB; and I will slaughter every single spoiled, stuck-up blonde slut I see inside there. . . . I'll take great pleasuring in slaughtering all of you."[491] Citing Rodger as one of his icons, Chris Harper-Mercer shot nine people on a college campus in Oregon in 2015 after complaining about his lack of a sex life.[492] Law enforcement officials note increasing concern about the dangers of violence and terrorism generated on the Internet.[493] Facing mounting pressures to do something about the problem, some platforms, including Facebook, Twitter, and YouTube, have made an effort to crack down on extremist content, although this may do little more than send the most objectionable elements to other platforms.[494]

Some commentators recommend expanding tort liability and making platforms accountable for negligent failure to respond to threats and other illegal online conduct. This would require amending Section 230 of the Communications Decency Act, which protects online intermediaries such as Facebook and YouTube from liability for what users post. Danielle Citron and Benjamin Wittes, for example, proposed extending immunity only to providers that "take[] reasonable steps to address known unlawful uses of its services that create serious harm to others."[495] Others, citing the importance of protections for providers on the Internet to innovation and free speech, resist calls for reform, calling Section 230 "the most important law protecting internet speech."[496]

If you were a legislator or a general counsel for a leading social media company, what regulatory responses would you support?

---

489. Melissa J. Gismondi, Why Are "Incels" So Angry? The History of The Little-Known Ideology Behind the Toronto Attack, Wash. Post, Apr. 27, 2018.

490. Ian Lovett & Adam Nagourney, Video Rant, then Deadly Rampage in California Town, N.Y. Times, May 24, 2014, at A1.

491. Rodger's video is quoted in Manne, supra note 472, at 34-35.

492. Rick Anderson, "Here I Am, 26, With No Friends, No Job, No Girlfriend": Shooter's Manifesto Offers Clues to 2015 Oregon College Rampage, L.A. Times, Sept. 23, 2017.

493. See Olafimihan Oshin, Secret Service Report Points to Rising "Incel" Threats, The Hill, Mar. 15, 2022.

494. See Adam Clark Estes, How Neo-Nazis Used the Internet to Instigate a Right-Wing Extremist Crisis, Vox (Feb. 2, 2021).

495. See, e.g., Danielle Keats Citron & Benjamin Wittes, The Internet Will Not Break: Denying Bad Samaritans § 230 Immunity, 86 Ford. L. Rev. 401 (2017); Danielle Citron and Benjamin Wittes, The Problem Isn't Just Backpage: Revising Section 230 Immunity, 2 Geo. L. Tech. Rev. 453 (2018).

496. See, e.g., Electronic Frontier Foundation, CDA 230: The Most Important Law Protecting Internet Speech, https://www.eff.org/issues/cda230.

PUTTING THEORY INTO PRACTICE

3-23. You are a university lawyer who is contacted by the campus women students' organization that is offended by the practices of several fraternities, which show porn films and invite strippers to perform on campus at all-male parties. The students believe that these practices encourage date rape. They also protest the fraternities' practice of circulating provocative photos that members receive from their girlfriends. The fraternity officers believe that their members are entitled to exercise their First Amendment rights. How would you respond? What strategies would you propose?

3-24. After a woman sent naked photos of herself to an ex-boyfriend, the boyfriend's then-girlfriend accessed his account, saw the photos, and posted them. After the victim left a voicemail for her ex-boyfriend asking him to take them down, the girlfriend called back from the boyfriend's phone, said she was going to "ruin" the victim, called her a "moraless [sic] pig" and said she would tell the victim's employer, a child-care facility, about "what kind of person work[ed] there." The girlfriend was prosecuted under a Vermont statute that prohibits "knowingly disclos[ing] a visual image of an identifiable person who is nude or who is engaged in sexual conduct, without his or her consent," "with the intent to harm, harass, intimate, threaten, or coerce the person depicted."[497] The state supreme court upheld the constitutionality of the statute, but determined that the victim had no reasonable expectation of privacy when she sent the photos to someone with whom she no longer had a relationship.[498] Do you agree?[499]

3-25. The Boston public health agency sponsors a peer leadership program on porn literacy for selected youth from primarily disadvantaged communities of color. The course, The Truth About Pornography: A Pornography Literacy Curriculum for High School Students Designed to Reduce Sexual and Dating Violence, has given students a more informed understanding of sexuality and a more critical perspective on porn.[500] Sex education guidelines by the World Health Organization's European office recommend that educators include discussions about pornography starting in late elementary school and continuing through high school.[501] Some schools, such as those in Denmark, have done so.[502] Proposals to encompass such discussions in U.S. public schools have been largely unsuccessful. Would you support such efforts? If schools resist, what other strategies would you recommend?

3-26. There is no law that prevents a consenting adult from engaging in sexual acts for money for purposes of making a pornographic movie or image. Why, then, is prostitution illegal in most jurisdictions? Are the autonomy interests different? Reconsider this problem when you read the materials on sex work in Chapter 5.

---

497. State v. VanBuren, 214 A.3d 791 (2018).

498. Id.

499. See State v. VanBuren: Vermont Supreme Court Holds That Privacy Expectations Depend on the Context of Relationships, 133 Harv. L. Rev. 2427 (2020).

500. Jones, supra note 408, at 32, 48.

501. Id. at 48.

502. Porn (1): A User's Manual, Economist (Sept. 24, 2015) (quoting Christian Graugaard).

3-27. If courts had upheld the Indianapolis ordinance, what other measures to reduce gender stereotyping might also be legal? For example, the United Kingdom's Advertising Standards Authority now bans ads that perpetuate harmful gender stereotypes, insofar as they limit "how people see themselves and how others see them and the life decisions the take."[503] Under the rules, a Philadelphia cream cheese ad depicting new fathers bungling the care of their babies and a Volkswagen ad showing a woman sitting next to a stroller have been banned.[504] What do you think of this approach to advancing gender equity?

---

503. See Mark Sweney, First Ads Banned for Contravening UK Gender Stereotyping Rules, Guardian, Aug. 13, 2019.

504. Id.

CHAPTER 4
DIFFERENCE

Formal equality assumes a basic sameness between men and women, and the obligation of law to respect that sameness. Substantive equality assumes some meaningful differences and seeks to eliminate the disadvantages of those differences through various legal strategies. Nonsubordination theory treats sameness and difference both as distractions from the fundamental question of how rules and social norms and practices keep women in their place.

Difference theory (also referred to as cultural feminism, relational feminism, or the ethic of care) offers still another perspective on gender and the law. Like substantive equality, difference theory underscores important differences between women and men. Unlike substantive equality, however, difference theory sees at least some of these differences not as problems to be overcome, but rather as potentially valuable resources that might improve the legal and social institutions that currently place too high a premium on "male" characteristics and values. Thus, rather than trying to eliminate or offset women's differences, difference theory seeks to include them, and possibly even redesign the law and societal institutions in order to reflect them. Among these values are said to be a greater emphasis on relationships, empathy, and protection of the vulnerable, as contrasted to the supposed male emphasis on autonomy and individualism. Difference theory also affirms the values of collaboration and cooperation, as correctives to a society that is overly competitive and individualistic. This chapter investigates the nature of these claimed differences and their implications for law.

A simple example may help distinguish difference theory from the theories examined thus far in this book. Until 1975, it was considered constitutional for the state to require only men, and not women, to report for jury service.[1] On what grounds should this distinction have been invalidated? The principle of equality would object to treating women different from men on the grounds that, for all purposes that matter, women are the same as men and thus should be subject to the same rules. Difference theory supports an alternative rationale — that women are different from men, with different experiences and perspectives. When they are not present on juries, the argument goes, those experiences and perspectives are not represented, and thus the jury could not fairly be said to be a jury of "peers." In a 1946 case about whether the exclusion of women from juries violated a federal defendant's statutory right to a jury drawn from a "cross-section of the community," the Supreme Court observed: "The truth is that the two sexes are not fungible; a

---

1. See Hoyt v. Florida, 368 U.S. 57 (1961), overturned by Taylor v. Louisiana, 419 U.S. 522 (1975).

community made up exclusively of one is different from a community composed of both; the subtle interplay of influence one on the other is among the imponderables."[2] To what extent are the sameness and difference rationales inconsistent? Do you prefer one to the other? Is it necessary to choose?

Many feminist theorists view difference theory with suspicion because of the risk that attributing certain traditional virtues to women will reinforce the stereotypes upon which ideologies of subordination rest. For example, in one high-profile employment discrimination case, the employer successfully defended its low numbers of women in higher paid commission sales jobs by relying on expert testimony from a cultural feminist perspective contending that women were simply less interested in the hypercompetitive and risky model of selling on commission.[3] At the same time, it is generally assumed that the increasing presence of women in law schools, legal practice, elected office, juries, and the judiciary will affect how law is created, taught, practiced, and applied. This chapter explores the tension between the embrace of gender differences as a means of improving legal and societal institutions and the rejection of gender stereotypes.

A.   THE ETHIC OF CARE AND ITS LEGAL IMPLICATIONS

This section sets forth the basic case for difference theory: that women have distinctive traits and values that should be affirmatively valued in the public realm as well as the realm of private relationships and family. In the business context, for example, women are found to outperform men when it comes to developing others, inspiring and motivating colleagues, relationship building, collaboration, and teamwork. Perhaps surprisingly, women also rank higher than men in taking initiative, showing resilience, practicing self-development, displaying integrity and honesty, and driving for results.[4] Whether these traits are biologically based or culturally cultivated, or a bit of both, is, as might be expected, a matter of some debate.[5]

Some feminist scholars who helped develop difference theory in law were influenced by Carol Gilligan's 1982 publication, In a Different Voice: Psychological Theory and Women's Development. This work challenged a widely accepted model of moral development articulated by psychologist Lawrence Kohlberg, a model that charted a progression in moral thinking through increasingly abstract levels of reasoning. Gilligan argued that this model missed the more contextualized, relationship-sensitive style of reasoning more typical of girls. In one of her

---

2. Ballard v. U.S., 329 U.S. 187, 193 (1946).

3. EEOC v. Sears, Roebuck & Co., 839 F.2d 302 (7th Cir. 1988) (relying on Sears' expert witness, Dr. Rosalind Rosenberg, a historian at Barnard College).

4. See Jack Zenger & Joseph Folkman, Research: Women Score Higher Than Men in Most Leadership Skills, Harv. Bus. Rev. (June 25, 2019); Bob Sherwin, Why Women Are More Effective Leaders Than Men, Bus. Insider (Jan. 25, 2014).

5. See Leonardo Christov-Moore et al., Gender Effects in Brain and Behavior, 46 Neuroscience & Behav. Rev. 604 (2014); Agneta H. Fisher et al., Gender Differences in Emotion Perception and Self-Reported Emotional Intelligence: A Test of the Emotional Sensitivity Hypothesis, 13 PLoS ONE (Jan. 2018).

most well-known studies, Gilligan compared how boys and girls responded to "Heinz's dilemma," in which Heinz's wife is dying of cancer and requires a drug that Heinz cannot afford to purchase from the local pharmacist. The children are asked whether Heinz should steal the drug. Summarizing Gilligan's findings, Carrie Menkel-Meadow explains:

> Jake, an eleven-year-old boy, sees the problem as one of "balancing rights," like a judge who must make a decision or a mathematician who must solve an algebraic equation. Life is worth more than property, therefore Heinz should steal the drug. For Amy, an eleven-year-old girl, the problem is different. Like a "bad" law student who "fights the hypo" she wants to know more facts. Have Heinz and the druggist explored other possibilities, like a loan or credit transaction? Why couldn't Heinz and the druggist simply sit down and talk it out so that the druggist would come to see the importance of Heinz's wife's life? In Gilligan's terms, Jake explores the Heinz dilemma with the "logic of justice" while Amy uses the "ethic of care." Amy scores lower on the Kohlberg scale because she sees the problem rooted in the persons involved rather than in the larger universal issues posed by the dilemma.[6]

It is important to note that Gilligan did not reject abstract reasoning; rather, she believed that the more contextualized form of reasoning (at which girls were more likely to excel) was no less valuable or advanced a way of thinking. In using Gilligan's research, however, some feminist legal scholars in the 1980s and 1990s were highly critical of "masculine" values and forms of reasoning and proposed legal reforms that they associated with "feminine" alternatives. The excerpts below illustrate classic applications of the ethic of care and arguments against it. They also explore the socio-biological account of women's differences, and the possible consequences of this account.

Robin West

Relational Feminism and Law

in Research Handbook on Feminist Jurisprudence
(Robin West & Cynthia Grant Bowman eds., 2019)

At the heart of the movement sometimes called relational feminism is the claim that we might best address all the problems, or limits, within liberal feminism . . . by reconceptualizing the human being and doing so in a way that centralizes precisely the experiences, emotions, ambitions, fears and dreams shared by many women that are marginalized by liberal conceptions of the human. Perhaps human beings are not, contrary to any number of political theorists writing within

---

6. Carrie Menkel-Meadow, Portia in a Different Voice: Speculations on a Women's Lawyering Process, 1 Berkeley Women's L.J. 39, 46 (1985). For an overview of the foundational "connection thesis" literature, see Patricia W. Hatamyar & Kevin M. Simmons, Are Women More Ethical Lawyers? An Empirical Study, 31 Fla. St. L. Rev. 785, 839-41 (2004).

the liberal tradition, essentially separated from or disconnected from other human and animal life and uniquely knowledgeable of that separation. . . . If we centralize women's experiences to the definitional and tentative accounts we give of humanity, a different and truer picture might emerge.

Perhaps human beings are essentially connected to rather than separated from human life. Women clearly are connected to human life when pregnant; all of humanity is connected to human life when in utero; and women and men both are all culturally connected to others through ties of kinship and friendship and membership in political and civil communities. . . . The significance of these connective experiences to our understanding of the human, though, is obscured by a liberal jurisprudence that prioritizes production over reproduction and isolation over connection. . . . It is no wonder then that a liberal legal order that does so also marginalizes both the harms and the moral aspirations to which those experiences give rise. . . .

If we centralized women's experiences of both the harms and the aspirations that are rooted in some way in this fundamental fact of human connectivity to the understanding of humanity that undergirds our liberal legal orders, we might thereby construct a more humane as well as more inclusive liberal legal order.

Leslie Bender

A Lawyer's Primer on Feminist Theory and Tort

38 J. Legal Educ. 3, 31-36 (1988)

Negligence law could begin with Gilligan's articulation of the feminine voice's ethic of care—a premise that no one should be hurt. We could convert the present standard of "care of a reasonable person under the same or similar circumstances" to a standard of "conscious care and concern of a responsible neighbor or social acquaintance for another under the same or similar circumstances." . . .

The recognition that we are all interdependent and connected and that we are by nature social beings who must interact with one another should lead us to judge conduct as tortious when it does not evidence responsible care or concern for another's safety, welfare, or health. Tort law should begin with a premise of responsibility rather than rights, of interconnectedness rather than separation, and a priority of safety rather than profit or efficiency. The masculine voice of rights, autonomy, and abstraction has led to a standard that protects efficiency and profit; the feminine voice can design a tort system that encourages behavior that is caring about others' safety and responsive to others' needs or hurts, and that attends to human contexts and consequences. . . .

One of the most difficult areas in which questions of duty and the standard of care arise is the "no duty to rescue" case. The problem is traditionally illustrated by the drowning-stranger hypothetical and the infamous case of Yania v. Bigan [in which one businessman jumped into a trench partially filled with water and drowned, although his business competitor was also in the trench and could have saved him if he had tried].

Each year that I teach torts I watch again as a majority of my students initially find this legal "no duty" rule reprehensible. After the rationale is explained and the students become immersed in the "reasoned" analysis, and after they take a distanced, objective posture informed by liberalism's concerns for autonomy and liberty, many come to accept the legal rule that intuitively had seemed so wrong to them. They are taught to reject their emotions, instincts, and ethics, and to view accidents and tragedies abstractly, removed from their social and particularized contexts, and to apply instead rationally-derived universal principles and a vision of human nature as atomistic, self-interested, and as free from constraint as possible. They are also taught that there are legally relevant distinctions between acts and omissions.

How would this drowning-stranger hypothetical look from a new legal perspective informed by a feminist ethic based upon notions of caring, responsibility, interconnectedness, and cooperation? If we put abstract reasoning and autonomy aside momentarily, we can see what else matters. In defining duty, what matters is that someone, a human being, a part of us, is drowning and will die without some affirmative action. That seems more urgent, more imperative, more important than any possible infringement of individual autonomy by the imposition of an affirmative duty. If we think about the stranger as a human being for a moment, we may realize that much more is involved than balancing one person's interest in having his life saved and another's interest in not having affirmative duties imposed upon him in the absence of a special relationship, although even then the balance seems to me to weigh in favor of imposing a duty or standard of care that requires action. The drowning stranger is not the only person affected by the lack of care. He is not detached from everyone else. He no doubt has people who care about him — parents, spouse, children, friends, colleagues; groups he participates in — religious, social, athletic, artistic, political, educational, work-related; he may even have people who depend upon him for emotional or financial support. He is interconnected with others. If the stranger drowns, many will be harmed. It is not an isolated event with one person's interests balanced against another's. When our legal system trains us to understand the drowning-stranger story as a limited event between two people, both of whom have interests at least equally worth protecting, and when the social ramifications we credit most are the impositions on personal liberty of action, we take a human situation and translate it into a cold, dehumanized algebraic equation. We forget that we are talking about human death or grave physical harms and their reverberating consequences when we equate the consequences with such things as one person's momentary freedom not to act. People are decontextualized for the analysis, yet no one really lives an acontextual life. . . .

If instead we impose a duty of acting responsibly with the same self-conscious care for the safety of others that we would give our neighbors or people we know, we require the actor to consider the human consequences of her failure to rescue. . . .

The duty to act with care for another's safety, which under appropriate circumstances would include an affirmative duty to act to protect or prevent harm to another, would be shaped by the particular context. One's ability to aid and one's proximity to the need would be relevant considerations. Whether one met that duty would not be determined by how a reasonable person would have acted under the circumstances but by whether one acted out of a conscious care and concern for the safety, health, and well-being of the victim in the way one would act out of care for a neighbor or friend. . . . This seemingly minor change would transform the core of negligence law to a human, responsive system.

Richard A. Posner

Conservative Feminism

1989 U. Chi. Legal F. 191, 214

[Most] people are what they are; most neighbors are not caring, and most accident victims are not neighbors. Human nature will not be altered by holding injurers liable for having failed to take the care that a caring neighbor would have taken. The only effect of adopting Bender's proposal would be to shift negligence liability in the direction of strict liability. Her "caring neighbor" is an unnecessary step in the analysis. Bender might as well argue directly for strict liability on the ground that it is the more altruistic regime than negligence.

Is it? Strict liability is sometimes defended on the ground that it provides more compensation to more accident victims. This is a partial analysis. Strict liability can also result in higher prices, and the burden may be borne by consumers. The net distributive impact is unclear. If these complications are ignored, maybe a feminine outlook on law could be expected to stress compensation — obviously Bender associates altruism with women. On the other hand, strict liability is more rule-like, less standard-like, less contextualist, less sensitive to the particulars of the individual accident, than negligence is; in that respect it is the more masculine standard.

NOTES

1. **Mainstreaming the Ethic of Care in the Law.** As both a critique of existing "male" law and a substantive reform agenda, difference theory or the "ethic of care" has been applied to virtually every area of law. For example, more than twenty-five years ago, Kathleen Lahey and Sarah Salter challenged the "patriarchal nature of the dominations upon which corporate culture depends" and urged legal reforms in corporate law that reflect "the ethics of care, responsibility, connection and sharing" and are organized around the "values of contextuality, continuity, and holistic participation."[7] Other commentators argue that because women and men use different factors and processes in deciding whom to trust, and women tend to be "more prudent" and "less ego driven" than men, greater gender diversity on corporate boards will enhance the independence and decisionmaking of corporate boards.[8] Marjorie Kornhauser has defended progressive income tax rules from a "female voice" perspective that emphasized interdependence and

---

7. Kathleen A. Lahey & Sarah W. Salter, Corporate Law in Legal Theory and Legal Scholarship: From Classicism to Feminism, 23 Osgoode Hall L.J. 543, 555-56, 570 (1985); see also Kellye Y. Testy, Capitalism and Freedom—For Whom?: Feminist Legal Theory and Progressive Corporate Law, 67 Law & Contemp. Probs. 87, 99 (2004); Theresa A. Gabaldon, Assumptions About Relationships Reflected in the Federal Securities Laws, 17 Wis. Women's L.J. 215 (2002); Barbara Ann White, Feminist Foundations for the Law of Business: One Law and Economics Scholar's Survey and (Re)View, 10 UCLA Women's L.J. 39 (1999).

8. See Joan MacLeod Heminway, Sex, Trust, and Corporate Boards, 18 Hastings Women's L.J. 173 (2007); Deborah L. Rhode, Women and Leadership 114 (2017). The issue of women on corporate boards is addressed further in Note 3, below.

altruism.[9] Aviva Orenstein has proposed a new "apology exception" to evidentiary rules relating to admissions by party opponents based on feminist relational values.[10] Judith Resnik has criticized the relegation of mundane, fact-specific cases, such as prisoner petitions and Social Security cases, to Article I judges or state courts, as well as the treatment of "the complex and messy activity of interacting with litigants, witnesses, and lawyers" as "mere housekeeping." She urges "[r]etrieving — without romanticizing — the importance of 'humble' activities" that may be "repetitive and non-engaging," but that are nonetheless necessary to maintain the daily maintenance of a judicial system.[11]

In recent years, many proposals by legal scholars that incorporate the values associated with women in this chapter have focused on work structures and family support policies that would better account for the needs of both children and their mothers, addressed in the next section of this chapter.

2. **Carol Gilligan 2.0.** In a 2015 speech, Carol Gilligan revisited her book on women's "different voice." That work, she wrote, had "challenged the separation of the self from relationships, . . . considered a milestone of development, by showing how this separation impairs our relational intelligence and moral capacity."[12] Child development studies have pinpointed times when the initiation of this separation, which is "driven by gender," "is culturally sanctioned and enforced through shaming."[13] She argues that the "disruption of human relational capacities" is "essential to the establishment of hierarchy" and "the building blocks of a patriarchal order, where being a man means not being a woman or like a woman, and also being on top." She continues, arguing that a "gender binary that bifurcates human qualities into 'masculine' or 'feminine' and a gender hierarchy force rifts in the psyche, impairing basic human capacities and dividing everyone from parts of their humanity. Reason and self (masculine) become separated from and privileged over emotions and relationships (feminine), compromising the ability to love and to participate as citizens in a democratic society."[14]

How significant are Gilligan's advancements to difference theory? Is it possible to embrace difference theory and also believe gender is more a spectrum than a set of binary categories?

---

9. Marjorie Kornhauser, The Rhetoric of the Anti-Progressive Income Tax Movement: A Typical Male Reaction, 86 Mich. L. Rev. 464 (1987); see also Nancy E. Shurtz, Long-Term Care and the Tax Code: A Feminist Perspective on Elder Care, 20 Geo. J. Gender & L. 107 (2018).

10. Aviva Orenstein, Apology Excepted: Incorporating a Feminist Analysis into Evidence Policy Where You Would Least Expect It, 28 Sw. U. L. Rev. 113 (1999); see also Kit Kinports, Evidence Engendered, 1991 U. Ill. L. Rev. 413; Rosemary C. Hunter, Gender in Evidence: Masculine Norms vs. Feminist Reforms, 19 Harv. Women's L.J. 127, 129 (1996) (criticizing rules of evidence for privileging "fact over value, reason over emotion, presence over absence, physical over psychological, perception over intuition").

11. See Judith Resnik, Housekeeping: The Nature and Allocation of Work in Federal Trial Courts, 24 Ga. L. Rev. 909, 945, 960-61 (1990).

12. Carol Gilligan, Revisiting "In a Different Voice," 39 Harbinger 19, 24 (2015).

13. Id. at 24-25.

14. Id.

3. **Women and Leadership**. There is some evidence that women tend to be less subject than men to the arrogance and overconfidence that contribute to leadership failures, and some evidence that they are also better decision-makers under stress. Such differences prompted the quip by the International Monetary Fund's managing director, Christine Lagarde, that the global financial crisis would have played out quite differently "if Lehman Brothers had been 'Lehman Sisters.'"[15]

The case for including more women on corporate boards is based, at least in part, on the additional viewpoints that women would add.[16] The evidence is mixed, however, on whether there is really a "business case" to be made for greater gender diversity, at least when the measure used is shareholder profit.[17] By what criteria do you think it should be determined whether the greater presence of women on corporate boards benefits a company? Stock price? Responses to quality control issues? The quality of board discussions? Promoting diversity within society more generally? Should advocates of greater representation by women on corporate boards have the burden of showing the benefits accruing to the company from greater diversity?

Would you expect gender to affect particular decisions leaders make? In the political arena, there is considerable research showing that in the United States, party affiliation is more important than gender in predicting legislators' votes on women's issues and that ideology is more important than gender in predicting sponsorship of legislation on these issues.[18] However, female legislators at both state and federal levels are disproportionately Democratic and progressive, and thus are more likely than their male colleagues to support women's issues, rank them as priorities, and spend political capital on their behalf.[19] Is this an example of the benefits of diversity, or of gender bias? Is it a problem that fewer female politicians are Republican?

---

15. See Deborah L. Rhode, Women and Leadership 7 (2017).

16. The issue of whether the case for greater diversity on corporate boards is one of fairness or diversity is discussed in Chapter 2, Section A2.

17. For a review of the research, see Corinne Post & Kris Byron, Women on Boards and Firm Financial Performance: A Meta-Analysis, 58 Acad. Mgmt. J. 1546 (2015).

18. Tracy L. Osborn, How Women Represent Women: Political Parties, Gender, and Representation in the State Legislatures 12 (2012); Michele Swers, The Difference Women Make: The Policy Impact of Women in Congress 124 (2002); Michele Swers & Amy Caiazza, Inst. for Women's Pol'y Rsch., Transforming the Political Agenda? Gender Differences in Bill Sponsorship on Women's Issues, Research-in-Brief (Oct. 2000).

19. Pamela Paxton & Melanie M. Hughes, Women, Politics and Power: A Global Perspective 2, 193 (2007). For Congress, see Jessica C. Gerrity et al., Women and Representation: A Different View of the District?, 3 Pol. & Gender 179 (2007); Michele Swers, Women in the Club: Gender and Policy Making in the Senate 38, 62, 93-94, 100 (2013); Christina Wolbrecht, The Politics of Women's Rights: Parties, Positions and Change (2000). For state legislatures, see Osborn, supra note 18, at 12, 118; Swers, The Difference Women Make, supra note 18, at 8, 72; Kathleen A. Bratton, Critical Mass Theory Revisited: The Behavior and Success of Token Women in State Legislatures, 1 Pol. & Gender 97 (2005). For consideration of this issue in the context of female judges, see Section C, infra.

Women of color are particularly likely to champion issues of special concern to women and communities of color.[20] It is also widely reported that female state legislators do more to help constituents and adopt more collaborative, consensual styles than men, and that women in Congress have an approach that is "more collaboration, less confrontation; more problem-solving, less ego; more consensus building, less partisanship."[21] Political party pressures have constrained these tendencies, but research finds that the value women place on collegiality "make[s] Congress a better to place to work even if it doesn't translate into voting across the aisle."[22]

4. **The Sociobiological Explanation.** One consequence of the proposition that women are naturally more nurturing and relationship-oriented than men is that it provides an alternative to the explanation that the gender disparities in employment are a result of discrimination. Kingsley Browne argues that pay disparities between women and men and the so-called "glass ceiling" that keeps women from advancing as far and as fast as men are less a result of discrimination than of the "basic biological sex differences in personality and temperament."[23] Browne's analysis draws on a branch of social science called sociobiology—one that explains personality traits and temperament by the same evolutionary forces as those that produced such things as bipedal locomotion and opposable thumbs in human beings.[24] "Evolutionary theory predicts that men will tend to exhibit greater status-seeking, competitiveness, and risk-taking than women, and that women will exhibit more nurturance and affiliative behavior."[25] Richard Epstein states the case in terms of nature's efficiency.

> So long as there is any division of labor between the two sexes, it must be decided who will stay with the newborn child and who will venture forth to explore, to fight, and to hunt. This is true because there are clear losses to the family unit if both parents have identical tasks. In economic terms, the potential gains from specialization and trade are too large to be ignored, especially under conditions of extreme scarcity. The mere fact that the mother carries with her a supply of milk makes it clear that she is the better candidate for staying with the child, consequently leaving the male of the species to engage in a broad class of explorative activities. The

---

20. Kira Sanbonmatsu, Why Women? The Impact of Women in Elective Office, Political Parity (2015); Rhode, Women and Leadership, supra note 15, at 47.

21. Rhode, supra note 15, at 51 (quoting Ziegler); Caitlin Moscatello, See Jane Win; The Inspiring Story of the Women Changing American Politics 139 (2019); Jill Lawrence, Do Women Make Better Senators Than Men?, Atlantic (July 11, 2013); see also Jay Newton-Small, Broad Influence: How Women Are Changing the Way America Works 56 (2016) (quoting Nancy Pelosi).

22. Sarah Kellogg, The Ripple Effect of the Women's Wave, Wash. Law. 17 (Mar. 2019); see also Jennifer L. Lawless et al., Nice Girls? Collegiality and Bipartisan Cooperation in the U.S. Congress, 80 J. Pol. 1268 (2018).

23. Kingsley R. Browne, Sex and Temperament in Modern Society: A Darwinian View of the Glass Ceiling and the Gender Gap, 37 Ariz. L. Rev. 971, 984 (1995).

24. Id. at 984.

25. Id. at 1016.

nurturing instincts usually attributable to women are a set of attitudinal adaptations that reduce the cost of doing activities that help promote the survival of both her and her offspring. Although modern women operate in settings far different from those of their ancient mothers, the initial tendency still remains: If nurturing brings greater pleasure or requires lower cost for women than for men, then we should expect to see women devote a greater percentage of their resources to it than men. This specialization will endure in the aggregate and should be accepted for what it is: a healthy adaptation that works for the benefit of all concerned, and not as a sign of inferiority or disrespect.[26]

What are the implications of Epstein's and Browne's analysis? According to Browne, to the extent compensation differences are due to women's priorities, which cause them to invest less in their human capital than men, work fewer hours, seek less job-related training, and select jobs that give them the flexibility they need for their children, "it is not clear why there should be societal intervention."[27] Does this follow? Elsewhere, Browne states that efforts to prohibit sexual harassment are doomed, insofar as they go "against the grain" of human psychology.[28] Is this a logical implication of the sociobiological account?

Feminist legal scholars have challenged the sociobiological account on both factual and normative grounds. For example, Kathryn Abrams challenges the factual premises of Richard Epstein's sociobiological analysis:

> Breast milk is not, nor has it in memory been, the only alternative for nourishing infants. . . . To enshrine this difference as central, at a time when we have the technological capacity to generate adequate substitutes is a bit like describing the structure of contemporary society as arising from the human inability to master air travel. . . . [Moreover,] it is not clear . . . why the initial division of labor arising from breastfeeding would necessarily reinforce [his explorative and spatial perception advantages]. Why should the male adventurer have more opportunity to develop these capacities than the female, who is constantly balancing and shifting her infants, or cannily judging the distance between her children and danger?[29]

Another line of factual attack on scholars such as Epstein and Browne is that even if sex-based differences exist, they do not account for the full range of occupational segregation and wage differentials that exist. Deborah Weiss argues, for example, that "heritable" (i.e., genetic) differences interact with various forms of discrimination, including unconscious discrimination, irrational discrimination, and structural discrimination, in ways that are impossible to untangle.[30]

---

26. Richard A. Epstein, Gender Is for Nouns, 41 DePaul L. Rev. 981, 989-90 (1992).

27. Browne, supra note 23, at 1081-82.

28. Kingsley R. Browne, An Evolutionary Perspective of Sexual Harassment: Seeking Roots in Biology Rather Than Ideology, 8 J. Contemp. Legal Issues 5 (1997).

29. Kathryn Abrams, Social Construction, Roving Biologism, and Reasonable Women: A Response to Professor Epstein, 41 DePaul L. Rev. 1021, 1024-25 (1992).

30. See Deborah Weiss, The Annoyingly Indeterminate Effects of Sex Differences, 19 Tex. J. Women & L. 99 (2010).

Other feminists have taken the position that even if there is a biological basis for some statistical differences between men and women, this does not mean that these differences should be accepted or embraced. After all, society does not excuse rape because sexual urges are natural or even inevitable.

Feminist scholars June Carbone and Naomi Cahn put the point this way:

> The most critical development in our evolutionary past may be not so much the development of any particular behavior or trait, but the ability to reshape our behavior with others. As our biological knowledge grows, we are almost certain to find that our genes create the capacity for various behaviors and virtues, with love, loyalty, and commitment among them, but that these values do not happen automatically. Instead, the right conditions in childhood, including parent-child attachment, family stability, appropriate role models, and education, prime the neural pathways that allow[] some behavior to develop and become deeply ingrained. Over longer periods of time, the prevalence of certain norms within a group can favor the passing on of the genes associated with that behavior, so that these genes, whether they are the genes that control the ability to learn, the discipline to conform behavior to norms, or the tendency to [do] so with a minimum of external coercion, become more common over time.[31]

Some feminist scholars affirm both a social and a biological dimension to women's distinctive experiences and perspectives. Consider the views of Robin West:

> It truly would be extremely odd, as [Gilligan] argued, if it turned out that the vastly greater amount of child raising and homekeeping, the world over and throughout history, in which women engage—a fact apparently conceded by all—has *no impact whatsoever* on the moral orientations of the two sexes. Similarly it really would be extremely odd if it turned out that our shared experience as infants and children under the protection and tutelage and love of *women*—our shared experiences derived from the fact that we are all *to woman* born—also has *no* differentiating effect or impact on the way the two sexes view relational ethics. It would be odd if it turned out that the experiences of pregnancy and childbirth, shared by the majority of all women everywhere, have no effect, and lend to women's perspectives no unifying and distinguishing threads. The null hypothesis, if we are questioning sameness or difference, might more defensibly be identified as the claim of difference, rather than the claim of sameness, in the face of these quite different early experiences of the world.[32]

Do you agree? Are West's views closer to Browne's, or to Carbone and Cahn's?

5. **Feminist Critiques of an Ethic of Care.** The primary normative criticism of difference theory is that the values that it seeks to redeem and celebrate are the same as those that have been used to justify women's subordination to men. Catharine MacKinnon argues, for example, that the theory "mak[es] it seem as though

---

31. See, e.g., June Carbone & Naomi Cahn, The Biological Basis of Commitment: Does One Size Fit All?, 25 Women's Rts. L. Rep. 223, 247-48 (2004).

32. Robin West, Caring for Justice 18-19 (1997).

[women's] attributes, with their consequences, really are somehow ours, rather than what male supremacy has attributed to us for its own use. For women to affirm difference, when difference means dominance, as it does with gender, means to affirm the qualities and characteristics of powerlessness."[33] Does she have a point?

Linda McClain, after reviewing the dangers of difference theory, concludes that the voice of care is important but is better attributed to liberal humanist values than specifically "female" values. Liberalism has plenty of room for these values, she argues. Rather than forcing a "stark pick between mothering and contract, or care and justice, or connection and separation," feminists should engage in dialogue about how their insights about interdependency, connection, and responsibility can be incorporated within the liberal legal system. "[P]rinciples of justice, equality, and autonomy can coexist with and inform care and responsibility, just as care and connection, for both liberals and feminists, aid in the pursuit of justice."[34] Joan Tronto echoes this theme, arguing that "we need to stop talking about 'women's morality' and start talking instead about a care ethic that includes the values traditionally associated with women."[35]

Is this gender-neutral approach appealing? Consider Leslie Bender's objection:

> [S]ome who have been attracted by the advantages of an ethic of care have argued that it has non-gender-based sources and could be adopted as a "humanist" approach to law, that is, one that promotes the value of caring apart from any language of gender relations. Frankly, while I am sympathetic to feminists who make this argument, I believe it is politically, theoretically, and factually unsound to move women from center stage in this proposed reconstruction of legal and ethical discourse based on an ethic of care. Interpersonal caregiving is something that women have specialized in for years. We have special knowledge and insights to offer. After many, many years of being submerged, we have finally come above the surface and caught our long-awaited breath. The air tastes good. A change to "humanism," I fear, will ultimately press us under water again. While we clearly must be very cautious about perpetuating disempowering or disadvantaging stereotypes, the move from "women" to "human" seems to dupe us into an even worse co-optation of being reabsorbed, resilenced, and resubmerged into a newly invisible system of male dominance. Consequently, I reject critiques of a gender-based ethic of care that locate the ethic of care in a humanist approach.[36]

33. Catharine A. MacKinnon, Feminism Unmodified: Discourses on Life and Law 38-39 (1987).

34. Linda C. McClain, "Atomistic Man" Revisited: Liberalism, Connection, and Feminist Jurisprudence, 65 S. Cal. L. Rev. 1171, 1196-1202, 1263 (1992).

35. Joan C. Tronto, Moral Boundaries: A Political Argument for an Ethic of Care 3 (1993).

36. Leslie Bender, From Gender Difference to Feminist Solidarity: Using Carol Gilligan and an Ethic of Care in Law, 15 Vt. L. Rev. 1, 40 (1990).

What is your view? What is gained, or lost, by a gender-neutral strategy? If the ethic of care is distinctively feminine, what does that say about what ethic is ascribed to men and masculinity?

Janet Halley notes the longstanding tension within feminism between those who want to compensate and reward women's crucial caretaking contributions and "centrist liberal feminists" who regard many claims about women's special altruism as a "return to outmoded conventions and false stereotypes, an entrenching social bride that will keep women bound to care, and a bid for redistribution from working women to homemakers." Leftist feminists, Halley argues, are also troubled about encouraging women to accept "social vulnerability that they could avoid."[37] Can this tension be resolved?

PUTTING THEORY INTO PRACTICE

4-1. A study looking at co-authored publications at fifty North American universities found that male professors were more likely than female professors to co-author a publication with someone below their own rank, but female professors were more likely to work with equally ranked colleagues.[38] Is there a difference between women and men that might help explain this disparity? To what extent is this disparity a problem for which a solution should be found?

4-2. A memorandum written by a Google engineer in 2017 went viral and created controversy, resulting in the company firing the author. The memo made a number of controversial claims about why women are not better represented in the technology sector, including:

> "Differences in distributions of traits between men and women may in part explain why we don't have 50% representation of women in tech and leadership."

> "[W]hen it comes to diversity and inclusion, Google's left bias has created a politically correct monoculture that maintains its hold by shaming dissenters into silence."

> "On average, men and women biologically differ in many ways . . . women relatively prefer jobs in social or artistic areas. More men may like coding because it requires systemizing. . . . We need to stop assuming that gender gaps imply sexism."

> "Women on average are more prone to anxiety."

Did Google do the right thing in firing the author? Is the memo indicative of a sexist culture at Google? If so, what additional measures should the company take to address its corporate culture?[39]

---

37. Janet Halley, Which Forms of Feminism Have Gained Inclusion?, in Governance Feminism: An Introduction (Janet Halley et al., eds., 2018).

38. See Eliana Dockterman, Leaning Out: Men Like to Be the Boss More Than Women Do, Study Says, Time (Mar. 4, 2014).

39. Daisuke Wakabayashi, Google Fired Worker Legally Over Memo, N.Y. Times, Feb. 17, 2018, at B2. For the full memo, see https://gizmodo.com/exclusive-heres-the-full-10-page-anti-diversity-screed-1797564320.

4-3. Michael Mattioli is a 66-year-old retired psychologist. For over thirty years, he lived in a Manhattan apartment complex owned by New York University. He then moved "temporarily" to Rochester to care for his aging parents so that they would be spared the "indignity of dying in a nursing home." His mother died four years later; his father was still alive at age 103. NYU sought to evict him based on a statute allowing eviction of tenants who do not use the premises as their primary residence. Mattioli believed he should be able to keep his apartment, because he intended to return there as soon as his father no longer needed him. "I'm sure that at N.Y.U.'s medical school and law school and nursing school, they're teaching about the problems of the elderly," he said. "I don't think they're teaching that people who are taking responsibility for their own parents should be driven out of their apartments."[40]

Should the circumstances of Mattioli's departure from his apartment and his intention to return some time in the indefinite future provide a defense to the eviction action? If the applicable rules reflected an "ethic of care," what would they be?

4-4. Reconsider the materials on women and sport in Chapter 2, including the dispute over whether cheerleading counts as a sport. Does Title IX disadvantage women by embracing a male model of sport that rewards characteristics such as competitiveness, aggressiveness, and physicality? Can you think of activities that reward interconnectedness, trust, or reliance on others that could be recognized as sports?[41] Should they be?

4-5. To what extent is empathy a good thing? Researchers generally agree that selfless action is good for the self. For example, people who contribute more in time and money to those less fortunate have greater senses of well-being.[42] Experts also agree that there are downsides to "preferential empathy"—people's tendency to care more about those who are like them or whose concerns seem concrete and immediate (unlike the concerns of future generations).[43] How might society encourage the kind of empathy that is healthy and discourage the kind that makes society more tribal?

4-6. How well do transgender individuals fit difference theory? In a society that was less gender-coded than our own, would it be as necessary to conform one's gender presentation to match one's gender identity? Does difference theory reinforce gender coding or lessen it? Does difference theory have anything to say to, or about, individuals who do not identify as either male or female?

4-7. If one believes that either biology or cultural division of roles has given women certain distinctive capabilities, does it follow that putting them in power will

---

40. David Margolick, At the Bar, N.Y. Times, July 10, 1992, at B8.

41. For a cultural feminist analysis of sports, see Dionne L. Koller, Not Just One of the Boys: A Post-Feminist Critique of Title IX's Vision for Gender Equity in Sports, 43 Conn. L. Rev. 401 (2010).

42. Jamil Zaki, The War for Kindness: Building Empathy in a Fractured World 166 (2019).

43. Id. at 56; Paul Bloom, Against Empathy: The Case for Rational Compassion 112 (2008) (discussing people's willingness to empathize with those harmed by efforts to reduce climate change and to discount concerns of unborn generations who seem like "statistical abstractions").

change the way power is exercised? Consider an op-ed in which Tina Brown notes the recent "second wave of masculine mayhem" in many countries with autocratic and narcissistic leaders and asks "Can Women Save the World?"[44] Brown argues that electing more female leaders is a partial answer but not because women "are naturally and invariably better at running governments than men" (citing Theresa May's handling of Brexit as an example). It is rather that

> During thousands of years of civilization, women have evolved to deal with the intractable perplexities of life and find means of peaceful coexistence where men have traditionally found roads to conflict. Women have accumulated rich ways of knowing that until recently were dismissed in male circles of power. . . . In drawing on women's wisdom [as caregivers] without apology and pushing that wisdom forward into positions of power, we can soothe our world and, maybe, even save it.[45]

Do you agree?

4-8. Choose an area of law — like environmental law or international law — and explain how incorporating an "ethic of care" into legal doctrine might make a difference. How would you evaluate that difference?

4-9. On many issues, public opinion polls show differences between women as a group and men as a group. For example, women are more likely to support strict gun control laws than men. To what extent do you think these findings are explained by difference theory, and to what extent by something else?

B. WORK AND FAMILY

Chapter 2 examined issues of work and family from the point of view of equality for women and considered whether employers should accommodate the extra burdens of pregnancy and parenthood in order to avoid disadvantaging women. This chapter examines goals other than equality, such as care for society's dependents, that might ground policies affecting work and family. As you read these materials, consider what difference theory has to offer in reconceptualizing caretaking, how it is valued, and what role the government should play in supporting families.

Anne-Marie Slaughter

The Failure of the Phrase "Work-Life" Balance

Atlantic, Dec. 16, 2015

If society valued care, it would be accounted for in measurements of the economy and assessments of the country's health and wealth. If society valued care,

44. Tina Brown, Can Women Save the World?, N.Y. Times, Mar. 31, 2019, at SR6.
45. Id.

workplaces would adopt an entire set of new practices, from a right to request flexible work to the routine creation of work coverage plans for every worker, on the expectation that all workers must make room for caring for someone in their lives at some point in their lives. And if society valued care, the roles of teacher, lead parent, coach, nurse, therapist, or any other caring profession would have a degree of prestige and compensation that reflect the enormous importance of the work these people do.

"Balance" is a luxury, something only the very luckiest can ever attain. Equality—of the activities that are equally necessary for our survival and flourishing—is a better framework, as it demonstrates why care is something everyone needs to do and everybody needs access to. That's not about balancing work and life. That's about valuing all the activities that society needs for humans to flourish.

Dorothy Roberts

Spiritual and Menial Housework

9 Yale J.L. & Feminism 51, 55-59 (1997)

The "cult of domesticity" legitimized the confinement of women to the private sphere by defining women as suited for motherhood (and unsuited for public life) because of their moral or spiritual nature. Thus, the very idealization of women's spirituality bolstered the opposition between maternal nurturing in the home and masculine work in the cutthroat marketplace.

Household labor, however, is not all spiritual. It involves nasty, tedious physical tasks—standing over a hot stove, cleaning toilets, scrubbing stains off of floors and out of shirts, changing diapers and bedpans. The notion of a purely spiritual domesticity could only be maintained by cleansing housework of its menial parts. The ideological separation of home from market, then, dictated the separation of spiritual and menial housework. Housework's undesirable tasks had to be separated physically and ideologically from the moral aspects of family life.

This dichotomy has two important consequences. First, women may delegate housework's menial tasks to others while retaining their more valuable spiritual duties. Second, this fragmentation fosters a hierarchy among women because the menial aspects of housework are typically delegated by more privileged women to less privileged ones. At the same time, the availability of a class of menial workers, sustained by race and class subordination, makes this division of women's housework possible. Although women's participation in the market is now widely accepted, the assignment of household work to women and the distinction between spiritual and menial housework both persist. In the hit movie *The First Wives' Club*, the character played by Diane Keaton complains to her friends about the work she did for her ex-husband: "I washed his shorts, I ironed them, and I starched them." "You did?" her friends respond in amazement. "Well, I supervised," Keaton clarifies. This scene conveys the spiritual housewife's relationship to menial housework: she supervises the labor of less privileged women.

An early example of the distinction between spiritual and menial housework is embodied in the relationship between Mammy and her mistress. The image of

Mammy was that of a rotund, handkerchiefed house servant who humbly nursed her master's children. Mammy was both the perfect mother and the perfect slave; whites saw her as a "passive nurturer, a mother figure who gave all without expectation of return, who not only acknowledged her inferiority to whites but who loved them." It is important to recognize, however, that Mammy did not reflect any virtue in Black motherhood. The ideology of Mammy placed no value in Black women as the mothers of their own children. Rather, whites claimed Mammy's total devotion to the master's children, without regard to the fate of Mammy's own offspring. Moreover, Mammy, while caring for the master's children, remained under the constant supervision of her white mistress. She had no real authority over either the white children she raised or the Black children she bore. Mammy's domestic labor is the perfect illustration of menial housework; her mistress, on the other hand, performed the spiritual work in the house.

Today, the spiritual/menial split enables many professional women to go to work without disturbing the sexual division of housework or relinquishing their role as spiritual housekeepers. . . .

The modern household worker's job is defined in a way that prevents its interference with the female employer's spiritual prerogatives. Even if a child spends the entire day with her nanny while her mother is at work, the hour of "quality time" mother and child share at bedtime is considered most important. Of course, the mother expects the nanny to develop a warm and caring relationship with the child. She wants the nanny to treat the child as a special person, and not as a chore. But the mother nevertheless desires her own relationship with her child to be superior to—closer, healthier, and more influential than—the relationship the child has with the nanny. . . .

These incompatible motives parallel another dilemma that mothers face in delegating childcare to a less privileged employee. In another study of private childcare arrangements, Julia Wrigley discovered that parents were torn between their desire to hire a high-status substitute mother and their preference for a manageable subordinate. "They would like caregivers who share their child-rearing values and who operate independently," Wrigley explains, "but they also want inexpensive, reliable, controllable employees." Parents often resolve this dilemma by relying on their spiritual supervision of the low-status employees' menial work. For example, one employer commented that "sometimes it was better to accept 'dumb' employees who are under the parents' control rather than deal with cocky ones." In both studies, employers resolved their contradictory desires by distinguishing between their own spiritual and the employees' menial housework.

Thus, the mother's spiritual moments with her child are far more valuable than the long hours the nanny spends caring for the child. Moreover, the working mother might not be able to devote quality time to her child at all if she came home to face the chores that the nanny took care of during the day. Some working mothers also hire another woman, who has even lower status, to clean the house and run errands. By delegating work to a nanny and/or maid, affluent women can fulfill their spiritual calling as mother despite their career in the market.

What is wrong with distinguishing between the roles played by the mother and by the woman she hires to care for her children? Would we not expect to find a difference between a child's relationship with her parents and with the paid household help? My point is not that we should eradicate all distinctions among people who perform housework, but to demonstrate how the distinction made between spiritual and menial housework fosters both a gendered and racialized devaluation of this type of labor. By separating spiritual from menial housework, both the mother and the nanny continue to be undercompensated for their work in the home despite working women's supposed liberation from domestic confinement.

Darren Rosenblum

Unsex Mothering: Toward a New Culture of Parenting

35 Harv. J. Law & Gender 57, 58 (2012)

I was, until recently, a pregnant man. . . . My husband and I began the process of having a child several years ago when we hired a surrogacy agency that works primarily with gay male couples. After a complex process, we are now raising our daughter.

As a parent, I confront a far more sexed area of life than I have ever encountered before. Everyone congratulates my partner and me on being "fathers," even though within our home we share responsibilities and flip roles, including a mothering role, with some fluidity. The outside world, it seems, needs to box us into the "daddy" category as much as it invests women with the power of motherhood.

Some time ago, I was in a taxi with my daughter. . . . She fussed a bit and the driver said, "Where's the mother? Only the mother knows how to do this." Avoiding a complex explanation that I view myself as both mother and father, I said she has two dads. He still seemed perplexed that a man could know how to care for a child. I left the taxi and wiped a saliva-soaked Cheerio from my daughter's chin, feeling less of a parent because I was perceived as only a father, and not the primary parent—a mother. It is a feeling constantly reinforced for gay male parents I know who report that when in public, at markets, stores, and restaurants—they get asked by women: "Is it mommy's day off?" It is challenging to come up with a responsible response.

Maxine Eichner

The Free-Market Family: How the Market Crushed the American Dream (and How It Can Be Restored)

51-52, 61 (2019)

We don't have to look far to come up with an explanation for Americans' long work hours. Other wealthy democracies have adopted a range of laws that help workers of both sexes balance work and family. In contrast, U.S. policymakers insist that unregulated markets alone will provide for American families.

Compare the regulation of work hours. Most European Union countries make it easy for adults to go home at the end of the workday by setting the number of hours in a standard workweek by law or by empowering collective-bargaining agreements.

Our Fair Labor Standards Act, in contrast, simply requires that employees be paid time-and-a-half wages when they work more than forty hours a week. Other countries have also passed other laws that help employees balance work with family life like requiring paid vacation days and national holidays. Finally, these countries have passed laws allowing parents taking time off to care for young children.

In the United States, by contrast, free-market proponents claim that employees can negotiate time off if they truly value it. But it isn't that simple in the real world. Many factors shape work hours beyond a worker's independent preferences. The most important of these are rising economic inequality and insecurity. These create in the words of the Harvard economist Richard Freeman, both a carrot and stick that push Americans to work long hours:

> The carrot is that Americans who work hard have a better chance of being promoted, moving up in the wide distribution of earnings, and experiencing substantial earnings increases. The stick is that Americans who lose their jobs suffer greatly because the United States has a minimal safety net for the unemployed.

[T]o add to their time crunch, parents have substantially *increased* their time with their kids in response to growing anxiety about their children's economic futures, a product of our increasingly unequal and insecure economy.

Martha Albertson Fineman

The Vulnerable Subject and the Responsive State

60 Emory L.J. 251, 263-65, 274 (2011)

Recognition of human dependency and vulnerability should present the traditional political and legal theorist with a dilemma. Unfortunately, dependency is not part of many approaches to theory in politics or law. Instead, a structure and set of social orderings have been constructed in which the family has been deemed the primary societal institution responsible for dependency. The family is the mechanism by which we privatize, and thus hide dependency and its implications. This allows simplistic assertions of the attainability, as well as the superiority, of individual independence and self-sufficiency, which are spun out in an ideology of autonomy and personal responsibility that bears little relationship to the human condition.

This obfuscatory approach to dependency and vulnerability has to be confronted and contested. . . . In one basic form, dependency should be thought of as unavoidable and inevitable; it is developmental and biological in nature. All of us are dependent on others for care and provision as infants, and many will become dependent as we age, are taken ill, or become disabled. This form of dependency is the type that generally is viewed sympathetically and sparks our charitable impulses, as well as government programs. In policy terms, inevitably dependent persons are the "deserving poor" in terms of social welfare programs.

There is a second form of dependency that needs to be discussed in relation to, but separate from, inevitable dependency, however. This form of dependency is much less obvious, but when it is noticed it is often stigmatized and condemned.

I label[] this form of dependency *derivative* to reflect the very simply but often over-looked fact that those who cared for inevitable dependents were themselves depen-dent on resources in order to accomplish that care. This form of dependency is *neither* inevitable, *nor* is it universally experienced. Rather, it is socially imposed through our construction of institutions such as the family, with roles and relation-ships traditionally defined and differentiated along gendered lines. . . .

I argue[] for a more collective and institutionally shared notion approach to dependency: a reallocation of primary responsibility for dependency that would place some obligation on other societal institutions to share in the burdens of dependency, particularly those associated with the market and the state. This real-location of responsibility seem[s] particularly appropriate, since both state and market institutions reap[] the benefits that care work produce[s] in the form of the reproduction and regeneration of society. . . .

Our present insistence that the state need be constrained underestimates or even ignores the many ways in which the state — through law — shapes institutions from their inception to their dissolution, and the ways in which those institutions produce and replicate inequalities. . . .

We all benefit from society and its institutions, but some are relatively advan-taged and privileged in their relationships, while others are disadvantaged. Under a vulnerability analysis, the inquiry would be into the organization, operation, and outcomes of the institutions and structures through which societal resources are channeled. . . . Under a vulnerability analysis, the state has an obligation not to tolerate a system that unduly privileges any group of citizens over others. It has a responsibility to structure conditions in which individuals can aspire to meaning-fully realize their individual capabilities as fully as possible. . . .

Th[e] theoretical task of reconceptualizing the role of the state requires that we imagine responsible structures whereby state involvement actually empowers a vulnerable subject by addressing existing inequalities of circumstances that result from undue privilege or institutional advantage.

Vicki Schultz

Life's Work

100 Colum. L. Rev. 1881, 1883, 1885, 1900-05 (2000)

Some feminist legal scholars now advocate paying women to care for their own families in their own households; many seem to have given up on achieving genuine gender integration of the work done in both households and workplaces. Some liberal thinkers urge that we provide everyone a guaranteed income or cap-ital allotment; they believe tying the distribution of social goods to work interferes with individual freedom and choice. The presence of these discourses has moved me to articulate a feminist vision of the significance of paid work to the good life, to equality, and to women. I agree that it is vitally important to create society-wide mechanisms for allocating the costs of household labor and for allowing people to realize their preferences. But, unless we pay attention to the institutional con-texts through which housework is valued and individual choice realized, stubborn patterns of gender inequality will continue to reassert themselves—including the gender-based distribution of work that is at the root of women's disadvantage. In the search for social justice, separatism simply won't suffice. . . .

In my view, a robust conception of equality can be best achieved through paid work, rather than despite it. Work is a site of deep self-formation that offers rich opportunities for human flourishing (or devastation). To a large extent, it is through our work—how it is defined, distributed, characterized, and controlled—that we develop into the "men" and "women" we see ourselves and others see us as being. . . .

Paid work has the potential to become the universal platform for equal citizenship it has been imagined to be, but only if we ensure meaningful participation in the workforce by attending to the specific needs of various social groups and individuals. . . . This means that, in the future, we will have to supplement employment discrimination law with measures like job-creation programs, wage subsidies, universal child care and health care programs, enhanced employee representation, and a reduced workweek for everyone. . . .

It is vitally important to acknowledge the hidden labor that is performed in households, and to create society-wide mechanisms for allocating its costs rather than continuing to impose them on individual family members (too often, women). One method of doing so is already being implemented on a massive scale: collectivizing housework by converting it into employment. . . . Converting household work into paid employment not only provides jobs for many people who need them, it also frees those who provide unpaid family labor to pursue more fully for pay the work that suits them best. . . . Some services could be subsidized for those who cannot afford them, or even made available for free to everyone (like public schooling, a now universal service that was once provided exclusively within the family setting).

Despite the fact that converting household labor into paid work collectivizes it and renders it more visible and publicly accountable, feminists in the movement to value housework tend to shun this approach. Instead, these feminists are proposing schemes to compensate women for performing household labor in private homes. . . . [Some] feminists promote state-based "welfare" strategies in which the government pays caregiver stipends that are not tied to paid employment, but are instead intended to permit women to choose full-time or near full-time homemaking and child care. . . .

Wittingly or unwittingly, advocates of these family-based approaches replicate some of the same conservative assumptions that have been used traditionally to justify women's disadvantage. Indeed, feminists in this movement tend to rely on the human capital literature to assert that it is women's disproportionate responsibility for housework and child care that accounts for our lower wages and our inferior position in the workforce. Unfortunately, many of these feminists seem unaware of (or uninformed about) the body of sociological work that casts doubt on the validity of human capital theory. Within the social sciences, the debate is between conventional economists—who pin women's plight on our family roles—and feminist sociologists (and sociologically-inclined economists)—who have produced evidence that discriminatory workplace dynamics are a more fundamental cause. The sociological literature points toward a more contextual approach that rejects static family-based conceptions of women's difference; it shows instead that socially-constructed features of the work world help create the very gender differences (manifested in work aspirations, employment patterns, and familial divisions of labor) that human capital theory attributes to women themselves. Such an approach creates greater possibilities for change. If the sources of women's disadvantage lie not in sociobiological forces that commit women more heavily to child care and housework but instead in the political economy of paid work, we can challenge the sex bias in allegedly gender-neutral forces in labor markets and work places. We can create more empowering gender arrangements by demanding work and working conditions that will give women more economic security, more political clout, more household bargaining power, and perhaps even more personal strength with which to pursue our dreams.

Naomi R. Cahn & Linda C. McClain

Gendered Complications of COVID-19: Towards a Feminist Recovery Plan

22 Geo. J. Gender & L. 1 (2020)

The COVID-19 pandemic made pre-existing gender disparities worse globally, and pre-existing problems within social, political, and economic systems amplified the pandemic's impact. In the United States, the pandemic has exposed the structural limitations on public and private support for gender equity, and the intersecting impact of gender, race, and class in that lack of support. . . .

The catalogue of COVID-19's impact covers all aspects of women's lives: work, family, education, health, reproduction, mental and physical well-being, leisure, and even retirement security. The unprecedented job losses during the pandemic hit women harder than men, and reports repeatedly emphasized how the loss of child care set women back in the workplace and had a negative effect on their children, particularly children in low-income families. Women are a larger percentage of workers in the service-related jobs in which businesses furloughed or laid off employees to ensure social distancing. At the same time, the nature of women's employment also resulted in greater vulnerability to exposure to COVID-19. Women are the overwhelming majority of health and home care workers and child care workers, and thus are on the frontlines of providing paid care to both children and the elderly. More than half of home health care workers are women of color; one in five workers is a single mother.

These gendered patterns intersect with a "racial justice paradox" that reveals what Catherine Powell calls the "color of COVID": "people of color [are] overrepresented among both the unemployed and among essential workers" being asked to take risks at work. Further, the "color of COVID" and the "the gender of COVID" mean that women of color, particularly those who are Black, Latina, and Native American, are at the intersection of the inequities exposed by the pandemic, a result that reflects longstanding intersectional inequities. They are a prominent part of the female workforce in low-paid and undervalued frontline jobs—including care work—vital to the economy but lacking the flexibility of being able to work from home and have been disproportionately affected by the so-called "shecession" of pandemic-related job loss. Women of color are also disproportionately represented among those women in poverty in the U.S., and the lack of adequate policy responses to the pandemic's impact on work and family is increasing that economic insecurity.

At the same time, the pandemic also reveals the protective effects of class for some women: women in professions where working from home is feasible, or who are not essential workers, or who depend upon or benefit from the domestic labor of other women. However, the pandemic has had gendered effects even among more privileged professional women—such as women in academia: their greater likelihood than male colleagues to be engaged in domestic chores and child care during the pandemic has negatively affected their productivity more than that of their male peers.

When it comes to family responsibilities, mothers have assumed the majority of child care and schoolwork responsibilities for children who can no longer attend day care or whose schools have closed. In September 2020, as the new school year began (often virtually), a staggering "865,000 women dropped out of the labor force"—four times the rate of drop out by men (216,000). Mothers of young children are disproportionately among this group who feels "driven out" by the impossibility of managing work and family demands.

Although the pace of job loss and the increased amount of child care affecting women are new, the weaknesses in support for gender equity are not. Prior to the pandemic, women faced barriers affecting work, family leave, and child care; they also experienced unequal parenting burdens. Those unequal burdens flowed both from women doing more work in dual-parent heterosexual households and from the fact that almost five times as many children live with a single mother than with a single father. As with child care, the COVID-19 pandemic has highlighted the care needs of older Americans and of the precarious condition of the undervalued—and predominantly female—workforce that provides elder care. . . .

While a recovery process might focus on a return to the status quo, the development of a recovery plan also opens up an opportunity to address the intersecting inequities of gender, race, and class made more visible by the pandemic—that is, to go beyond a return to the status quo and instead move forward. Consequently, rather than simply focus on economics, a feminist recovery plan could approach the goals of recovery and "resilience" in a way mindful of such inequities. Such a plan would insist that building resilience requires addressing such inequities and—as Professor Martha Fineman has argued—focusing upon how society and its institutional structures allocate benefits and burdens in ways that mitigate or worsen human vulnerability. . . .

A feminist economic recovery plan needs to address a cluster of workplace issues, including mandated paid leave, closing the gender pay gap, and supporting the care economy. Such a plan must also ensure access to social services that are integral to gendered aspects of family and work, such as reproductive health care and domestic violence resources. Moreover, concerns about workplace flexibility, both in terms of managing a work-from-home economy and acknowledging that such a form of work is less available for women in lower-paid jobs, must also inform any feminist economy recovery plan. Thus, for example, supporting child care supports working mothers, regardless of whether they must work at a workplace (such as a hospital or nursing home) or are able to work from home.

NOTES

1. **Substantive Equality vs. Difference Theory as a Basis for Legal Reform.**   Both substantive equality and difference theory support greater public responsibility for children and family leave policies, as well as more flexible work policies. However, while substantive equality models justify supportive measures as necessary to eliminate the disadvantages women experience, and thus to equalize the sexes' legal and economic status (see Chapter 2, Section B), difference theory justifies such measures as part of a better, more nurturing world for everyone. Which approach is reflected in each of the readings, above? Which approach seems more compelling? More politically viable? Are there any advantages, or disadvantages, to characterizing these measures as a positive, societal ideal, rather than as an accommodation to women's "difference"?

Why does Anne-Marie Slaughter resist "balance" as the ideal? Susan Dominus writes that the term "balance" suggests some zero-sum game in which one achieves a "state of grace" between "work" at one end of the fulcrum and "life" on the other. An alternative is the term "work-life fit," which "capture[s] the way workers try to piece the disparate parts of their lives together."[46] Is there enough commonality in women's experiences with respect to these issues that it makes sense to talk about it in gendered terms? Or is Dorothy Roberts right to suggest that these broad narratives obscure important class and race issues and deny the possibility that "equality" for privileged women might come at the expense of those women with less privilege?

Martha Fineman's emphasis on "derivative dependency" leads her to focus on restructuring society's institutions to better accommodate caretaking functions.[47] Maxine Eichner considers how the free market sets up many parents, especially mothers, for failure by neglecting to impose any meaningful controls on hours of work. Vicki Schultz's emphasis on the importance of women's work as a path to equal citizenship leads her toward reforming workplace institutions and improving the treatment of household workers. Joan Williams has focused on workplace changes, including flexible, reduced hours and leave policies, that do not penalize those who take advantage of them.[48] Are these all alternative ways of getting to the same policy recommendations, or are there important differences?

---

46. Susan Dominus, Rethinking the Work-Life Equation, N.Y. Times Mag., Feb. 25, 2016, at MM46.

47. See also Martha Albertson Fineman, Cracking the Foundational Myths: Independence, Autonomy, and Self-Sufficiency, 8 Am. U.J. Gender Soc. Pol'y & L. 13, 18 (2000) ("[C]aretaking work creates a collective or societal debt. . . . In order to move . . . to a more just resolution for the dilemma of caretaking and dependency, . . . [t]he active state must . . . structure accommodation of the needs of caretaking into society's institutions.").

48. See Joan Williams, Reshaping the Work-Family Debate (2010); see also Sylvia Ann Hewlett & Carolyn Buck Luce, Off-Ramps and On-Ramps: Keeping Talented Women on the Road to Success, Harv. Bus. Rev. (Mar. 2005).

Do workers have a legal right to work-life balance (or "fit")? One district court, in dismissing a class-action complaint brought by mothers against Bloomberg News alleging that the company had reduced the pay of pregnant women and mothers, reduced their responsibilities, excluded them from management meetings, and subjected them to stereotypes about female caregivers, stated that the law "does not mandate 'work-life balance.' . . . In a company . . . which explicitly makes all-out dedication its expectation, making a decision that preferences family over work comes with consequences."[49] The court concluded that the plaintiffs could not show a pattern and practice of treating pregnant women and mothers differently from other workers. Does this reasoning show the need for a theory that is not tied to the concept of equality?

Research shows that, in some industries at least, workplace reform can help workers achieve a better work-life fit without compromising work productivity. A pilot program at Best Buy found that workers randomly assigned to have their productivity measured by results rather than the number of hours worked met their goals just as reliably and were much happier.[50] A study by the Center for Work-life Law found that stable work schedules (a rarity in many female-dominated occupations like retail and food service) increase productivity and sales.[51] What do you take from these studies?

2. **Women's Disproportionate Caretaking Burdens.** Sociologist Arlie Hochschild coined the term "second shift" to describe the social norm by which women who work for wages are also expected to take care of the house and the children.[52] Despite more egalitarian attitudes toward housework and care of children, women continue to bear a disproportionate burden. According to one study, for example, women work an average of four hours a day on unpaid, household work, while men's average is 2.5 hours.[53] Tellingly, men's and women's perceptions do not always match reality. In one Pew Research study, 50 percent of women thought they did more household chores than their partners, while 46 percent of men thought the workload was distributed equally.[54] One might expect this to change with the next generation with its more progressive attitudes, but the data are not promising. According to one report, men between the ages of 18 and 34 in opposite-sex relationships are no more likely to divide household responsibilities equally than their older counterparts.[55]

Drawing on sociological theory, Naomi Cahn suggests that wives take responsibility for a disproportionate share of housework and child care as a way of

---

49. EEOC v. Bloomberg L.P., 778 F. Supp. 2d 458, 485-86 (S.D.N.Y. 2011).

50. Dominus, supra note 46.

51. See Joan Williams et al., Stable Scheduling Increases Productivity and Sales: The Stable Schedules Study (2018).

52. Arlie Russell Hochschild, The Second Shift: Working Parents and the Revolution at Home (1989).

53. See Francesca Donner, The Household Work Men and Women Do, and Why, N.Y. Times, Feb. 12, 2020.

54. See Amanda Borroso, Pew Rsch. Ctr., For American Couples, Gender Gaps in Sharing Household Responsibilities Persist Amid Pandemic (Jan. 25, 2021).

55. Donner, supra note 53.

"performing gender": Since women are expected to mother and to take care of the house, doing so gives wives both social approval and interpersonal power.[56] By contrast, men may suffer social stigma when they are full-time "househusbands." How do stereotypical attitudes about mothering versus fathering play out in the daily lives of parents? What assumptions underlie the reaction fathers get from onlookers while they carry out basic parenting tasks? Do you think Darren Rosenblum's experience is typical? How does intensive parenting affect a man's masculinity?[57] Are there culturally validated masculinities that are available to men who serve as the "default" parent?[58]

The "chore gap" is not confined to married American couples. Melinda Gates focused on the unpaid labor chore gap in her 2016 philanthropy letter, noting that "[u]nless things change, girls today will spend hundreds of thousands more hours than boys doing unpaid work simply because society assumes it's their responsibility. . . . It ends up robbing them of their potential."[59] She cited data from the Organisation for Economic Co-operation and Development showing that women do more unpaid labor than men in virtually every country, even Finland.[60]

Do same-sex couples fall into similar traps? One study found that same-sex couples were more likely to share chores like laundry and household repair that might be allocated more along gender lines in different-sex couples, as well as routine and sick child care.[61] It also found that, unlike with different-sex couples, relative income and work hours are not a reliable predictor of which partner will perform more child care. For both same-sex and different-sex couples, the study found that satisfaction was highest when the couple had a conversation about how to allocate responsibilities.

If we focus only on caretaking patterns, are we missing other tasks that also fall disproportionately on women's shoulders? Consider Elizabeth Emens's analysis of "life admin":

> Admin is the office-type work that it takes to run a life and a household. [T]his life admin involves both secretarial and managerial labor—filling out forms, scheduling doctors' appointments, sorting mail, making shopping lists, returning faulty products, paying bills and taxes, applying for government benefits or identification, making financial decisions, managing any outsourcing, and keeping track of everything that needs doing. This list covers only a fraction of the job description. . . .

---

56. Naomi Cahn, Gendered Identities: Women and Household Work, 44 Vill. L. Rev. 525, 532 (1999); Naomi Cahn, The Power of Caretaking, 12 Yale J.L. & Feminism 177 (2000).

57. Sarah C. Hunter et al., Constructions of Primary Caregiving Fathers in Popular Parenting Texts, Men and Masculinities (Sept. 23, 2017).

58. Beth A. Burkstrand-Reid, Dirty Harry Meets Dirty Diapers: Masculinities, At-Home Fathers, and Making the Law Work for Families, 22 Tex. J. Women & L. 1 (2012).

59. Olga Khazan, The Scourge of the Female Chore Burden, Atlantic (Feb. 23, 2016).

60. Id.

61. Kenneth Matos, Fams. and Work Inst., Modern Families: Same- and Different-Sex Couples Negotiating at Home (2015); Leanne Roncolato & Michael E. Martell, Modern Families: Bargaining and Time-Use in Same-Sex Households (Dec. 28, 2016).

The *second shift* has become the term for women's household labor after a day's market work. Admin—with its pervasive presence in the margins of everything else—should be understood as everyone's *parallel shift.* Admin is like a second (or third or fourth) job we are each asked to do in the margins of our other roles. . . .

Researchers have observed that . . . household management—the "essential planning, coordinating, and budgeting . . . above and beyond the physical demands of household work"—is "the last barrier to gender-egalitarian marriages." In other words, as feminists have observed for decades, "some tasks are easier to delegate than others," and management tasks are particularly hard to delegate (though not impossible). . . .

[T]he labor of "managing the children's schedule and activities"—a subset of what we might call . . . kidmin—is the one category that both mothers (64 percent) and fathers (53 percent) agreed that mothers do more of. . . .

Some forms of admin are especially likely to be characterized as women's work. Social admin is a prime example: party planning and inviting and RSVPing; remembering birthdays and anniversaries; keeping up extended family relationships through letters, calls, gifts. . . .

[H]andling finances might sound like a traditionally masculine domain. But the research suggests a more complicated picture. These days women more often pay the bills, as part of their role of feeding and clothing the family. . . .

Those who aspire to equity between the sexes may find it unfair if women are more burdened by life admin, which is often deemed trivial and taxing. The invisibility of admin also raises the concern that couples won't discuss it and so women (or other doers) may not be clearly consenting to their disproportionate burden. Note that admin is invisible not just because multi-tasking, especially on a device, is literally harder to see.[62]

Is it important to address gender inequality in life's "paperwork"? How might a couple avoid falling into typical gender patterns?

3. **Women's "Opting Out."**   One of the explanations for why, despite an upward trend in women's labor force participation, women continue to bear an unfair share of housework and child-care work is that women disproportionately drop out of the work force. Although women make up approximately half of the graduates of graduate programs in law, medicine, and business, their representation in these fields is much lower.[63] The opt-out explanation gained popularity with an influential 2003 New York Times article by Lisa Belkin, who told the stories of professional women who found that they could not both raise families and pursue demanding professions.[64] This narrative was fed by research purportedly

---

62. Elizabeth Emens, Life Admin: How I Learned to Do Less, Do Better, and Live More (2019).

63. See Lisa Belkin, The Opt-Out Revolution, N.Y. Times Mag., Oct. 26, 2003.

64. Id.

Chapter 4. Difference

documenting a high "opt-out" rate among women, especially professional women. For example, a study by the Center for Work-Life Policy of some 3,000 high-achieving American women and men (defined as those with graduate or professional degrees or high honors undergraduate degrees) showed that nearly four in ten women reported leaving the work force voluntarily at some point over their careers. The same proportion reported sometimes choosing a job with lesser compensation and fewer responsibilities than they were qualified to assume in order to accommodate family responsibilities. By contrast, only one in ten men left the work force primarily for family-related reasons.[65] Subsequent research has continued to highlight the difficulties women have in both raising a family and holding down a demanding job.[66]

The opt-out narrative suggests that the women in these stories are, at least for some period in their lives, choosing family over work. However, "choice"—a construct explored more deeply in Chapter 5—is complicated and always constrained. Joan Williams takes issue with the choice rhetoric in the opt-out explanation, arguing that many women do not leave work or scale back voluntarily, in any meaningful sense, but are pushed out by family-hostile workplace policies.[67] Has the popularity of the opt-out narrative, even though not necessarily supported by current data, hurt the case for structural change to make workplaces more supportive of employees in balancing family demands? Do you think the opt-out narrative functions like the idea of women's choosing lower paying jobs, as discussed in Chapter 1, Section C, by letting institutions off the hook and locating responsibility for unequal outcomes with women themselves?

Would Kingsley Browne, whose views are described in Note 4 of the previous section, find women's opting out problematic? How about Martha Fineman? Vicki Schultz? Dorothy Roberts? Linda Hirshman writes that when women opt out, they are "cutting their ambitions off at the knees." In her view, those who put family first have "fewer opportunities for full human flourishing" in public life. Assigning this role to women "is unjust. Women assigning it themselves is equally unjust."[68] Is that a bad example for their children? Leslie Bennetts argues that it has become "inescapably clear that choosing economic dependency as a lifestyle is the classic feminine mistake."[69] Do you agree?

4. **Parental Leave Laws.** As discussed in Chapter 2, Section B, the federal Family and Medical Leave Act requires employers with at least 50 employees to provide

65. See Hewlett & Luce, supra note 48, at 43-45. Beth Burkstrand-Reid, Trophy Husbands & Opt-Out Moms, 34 Seattle U. L. Rev. 663, 667-69 (2011), explains why it is difficult to come up with an accurate number of "opt-out" parents.

66. See, e.g., Anne-Marie Slaughter, Unfinished Business: Women Men Work Family (2015).

67. Joan C. Williams, Reshaping the Work-Family Debate: Why Men and Class Matter 1 (2010).

68. Linda Hirshman, Get to Work 23, 24-25 (2006). For the popularized version of this theme, see Sheryl Sandberg, Lean In: Women, Work, and the Will to Lead (2013).

69. Leslie Bennetts, The Feminine Mistake: Are We Giving Up Too Much? xxivii-xxiv (2007).

up to twelve weeks unpaid leave per year for employees with a newborn or newly adopted child.[70] But should the government require employers to offer *paid* family leave? If so, who should subsidize it? Should such legislation be a top priority? Paid leave has increasingly garnered support from both major political parties, yet a broad-based paid leave bill has not yet passed.[71] Congress did pass a law providing twelve weeks of paid parental leave for federal workers with a qualifying birth or placement of a child.[72] The Families First Coronavirus Response Act provided workers up to two weeks of paid leave if they needed time off because of quarantine or because a child's school or daycare had closed due to the pandemic, but it expired at the end of 2020.[73] President Biden's Build Back Better Act would provide four weeks of paid family and medical leave, funded through general revenues rather than by employers, but the bill has yet to make it through the Senate.[74] As a result, the United States is now the only high-income country without paid maternity leave and one of only two that do not require paid paternity leave.[75] Some states have stepped in to increase the availability of paid parental leave. In 2002, California became the first state to amend a state disability program to include up to six weeks of compensation for leave to care for an ill family member, or the birth, adoption, or foster care placement of a new child. Eleven states and the District of Columbia now offer some form of paid family leave.[76] Polls show that Americans overwhelmingly support paid family leave.[77] Why has it been so hard to change federal law to provide it?

Paid leave programs may do more to reveal than to reduce the gap between high- and low-wage workers. California's Paid Family Leave program (which provides 55 percent wage replacement with a capped ceiling on weekly benefits) was designed to close the socioeconomic gap in access to and use of paid family leave; yet California workers who are eligible for family leave but do not take one are disproportionately nonwhite, older, foreign-born, and less educated. Over 60 percent of respondents who could have taken a leave but didn't earn less than $35,000 annually. The main reason appears to be fear of retaliation at work for taking family leave.[78] Studies show that women of color are more likely to work

---

70. Pub. L. No. 103-03, 107 Stat. 6 (1993).

71. Tara Golshan, There's a Bipartisan Push Around Paid Family Leave Brewing in the Senate, Vox (Apr. 3, 2019).

72. Federal Employee Paid Leave Act, 5 U.S.C. § 6382(d)(2)(B) (Supp. 2022).

73. FFCRA, Pub. L. No. 116-127, 134 Stat. 178 (2020).

74. H.R. 5376, 117th Cong. (2021-2022); see also Tony Romm, How the House Spending Bill Offers the First Federal Paid Leave Program, Wash. Post, Nov. 19, 2021.

75. See Amy Raub et al., World Pol'y Analysis Ctr., Paid Parental Leave: A Detailed Look Across OECD Countries (2018); Joe Pinsker, Parental Leave Is American Exceptionalism at Its Bleakest, Atlantic (Nov. 9, 2021).

76. Bipartisan Pol'y Ctr., State Paid Family Leave Laws Across the U.S. (Jan. 13, 2022).

77. See, e.g., Audrey Goodson Kingo, A New Survey Shows Paid Family Leave Is Popular Across Party Lines . . . So Why Isn't It Happening?, Working Mother (Aug. 9, 2018).

78. See Catherine Albiston & Lindsey Trimble O'Connor, Just Leave, 39 Harv. J.L. & Gender 1, 25, 29, 32 (2016).

than white women, are paid substantially less, and suffer greater penalties for using benefits like family leave.[79] How could these disparities be addressed?

Should the government do more to disrupt the gendered patterns of care-taking and leave-taking? Or to better support all families, regardless of who performs caretaking? Income supplements for families with dependents, greater tax subsidies for child-care expenses, and mandatory paid leave tend to leave existing employment and family patterns relatively intact, with government assistance to lessen their burdens. Does an ethic of care demand more? What kinds of measures would satisfy Anne-Marie Slaughter's call for truly valuing care? The proposals that go beyond economic measures tend to emphasize a revamping of the workplace itself to make it more flexible and amenable to parents. Clare Huntington looks beyond these measures to changes in family law that might strengthen family relationships, and even to changes in zoning laws that would better facilitate family life.[80] To what extent do you think it is the responsibility of the government to support families?

5. **Parenting Leave: An International Perspective.** When women started entering the workforce in greater numbers in the 1960s and 1970s, many countries acted more aggressively than the United States, implementing policies to help women "reconcile careers and motherhood." These policies, including job-protected maternity leave, income support during leaves, and, eventually, paternity leave, "contributed to eroding the male breadwinner model in most high-income countries."[81] Three years after the passage of the FMLA in the United States, the European Council adopted the European Union Directive on Parental Leave, which provides minimum standards with which the member states must comply. These standards include a right to parental leave for at least three months (in addition to childbirth leave), protection against dismissal, and the right to return to the same or similar position. The length of parental leave was extended to four months in the EU's 2010 Parental Leave Directive. Among OECD countries today, the average maternity leave for childbirth is around eighteen weeks, which is consistent with the standards set by the International Labour Organization Convention and the current European Union Directive.[82] In many countries, mothers have access to even longer childbirth leaves as well as additional periods of parental leave. In France, for example, mothers are entitled to sixteen weeks paid maternity leave

---

79. See Asha DuMonthier et al., Inst. for Women's Policy Res., The Status of Black Women in the United States (2017); Elise Gould, Econ. Policy Inst., State of Working America Wages 2018 (2019) (reporting that Black/white wage gap is persistent in some situations and worsening in others); see also Kimberly Seals Allers, Rethinking Work-Life Balance for Women of Color (and How White Women Got It in the First Place), Slate (Mar. 5, 2018).

80. See Clare Huntington, Failure to Flourish: How Law Undermines Family Relationships (2014).

81. See Claudia Olivetti & Barbara Petrongolo, The Economic Consequences of Family Policies: Lessons from a Century of Legislation in High-Income Countries, 31 J. Econ. Persps. 205, 207-08 (2017).

82. OECD Family Database 1 (Oct. 2021), https://www.oecd.org/els/soc/PF2_1 _Parental_leave_systems.pdf.

and an additional twenty-six weeks of parental leave; payment during the first leave averages 95 percent of salary but drops dramatically for the weeks of parental leave (14 percent).[83] Romania mandates eighteen weeks of paid maternity leave followed by ninety weeks of paid parental leave.[84] One measure of leave policies is the number of full-rate equivalent weeks—how many weeks an employee can take without losing any salary. On this ranking, the countries that score near the top are Estonia (82 weeks), Czech Republic (55 weeks), and Turkey (52 weeks); the countries at the bottom are Switzerland (8 weeks), Australia (7 weeks), Ireland (7 weeks), and the United States (0 weeks).[85]

A study of maternity leave in low- and middle-income countries found that "[m]ore generous maternity leave increases gender equality in economic decision making in the household and improves gender norms related to work."[86] For example, a one-month increase in the paid maternity leave mandated by law "was associated with 41.5 percentage-point increase in the prevalence of individuals disagreeing with the statement that "when jobs are scarce, men should have more right to a job than women."[87]

The comparative generosity of other countries' family leave policies, however, obscures complex issues about implementation and equity. For one thing, there is some evidence from high-income countries that the long absences from work allowed by guaranteed leaves may encourage women to detach from the workforce and reinforce employer negative beliefs about women's work attachment.[88]

In addition, the policies have done little to change the fact that mothers provide a disproportionate amount of child care, which lessens their opportunities in the workplace. Should policy makers create incentives for men to get more involved in parenting? Some countries have achieved much higher rates of male involvement by a "use it or lose it approach." Sweden gives new parents 480 days paid parental leave to split, 90 of which cannot be transferred from one to the other and thus is lost unless both parents take a leave. Similar "use it or lose it" policies to encourage males to taking parental leave are in place in Portugal, Belgium, Iceland, and France.[89] Italy mandates a 10-day paid paternity leave for fathers, along with a five-month maternity leave at 80 percent pay for mothers. France provides for a 25-day paternity leave, one week of which is compulsory.[90]

---

83. Id. at 3.

84. Id. For highlights from other countries, see Ellen Francis et al., How Does the U.S. Compare to Other Countries on Paid Parental Leave?, Wash. Post, Nov. 11, 2021.

85. Id. See also Jan Tormod Dege & Erik Aas, Norway, in Employment Law in Europe 710, 714 (Susan Mayne & Susan Maylon, eds., 2001).

86. Yan Chai et al., Does Enhancing Paid Maternity Leave Policy Help Promote Gender Equality? Evidence from 31 Low- and Middle-Income Countries, 39 Gender Issues 335 (2022).

87. Id.

88. Olivetti & Petrongolo, supra note 81, at 221.

89. See How a Parental Leave Policy Changed the Way Sweden Sees Fatherhood, Apolitical (June 6, 2017).

90. See Ekaterina Mouromtseva, Doing It for the Dads: All About France's New Paternity Leave Law, Transcontinental Times, Sept. 6, 2022.

However, even the most generous policies abroad do not necessarily translate into gender equality. For example, Swedish women take most of the sixteen months in parental leave to which they are entitled; fathers use only about one-fourth of that amount.[91] Studies of Scandinavian approaches find that when fathers take more leave, it results in shorter leave by mothers and a smaller loss in their earning potential. One study found that a mother's income increased 7 percent for every month of paternity leave her husband takes.[92] However, Swedish fathers account for only about 12 percent of total benefit days claimed. One reason is employer resistance. Another is mothers' preferences: About half of those surveyed wanted all the days for themselves. Gender differences persist after the parental leave period—a higher percentage of employed fathers with young children work full time (95%) than employed mothers of young children (77%).[93]

Several American commentators argue that the FLMA should be amended to reward employers for encouraging men to take more parental leave.[94] Are these proposals worth considering?

6. **Child Care.**   Early in the "second wave" of feminism, a common assumption was that the state would step in to provide quality child care for families.

When Betty Friedan wrote [The Feminine Mystique (1963)], she assumed that very soon there would be a national system of subsidized child care centers that would be as free, accessible, and high in quality as public libraries. She actually believed this. Not only did she believe this, it was not an implausible vision. After all, that is what has happened in Belgium. That's what happened in France. . . . Ninety-five percent of nursery school age children in those countries are in government-subsidized child care.[95]

Friedan's vision came nowhere close to realization. Instead, as Joan Williams notes:

In 1971, when Congress passed a Comprehensive Child Development Act, President Nixon vetoed it under pressure from an intense lobbying campaign that decried the proposal as "a radical piece of social legislation" designed to deliver children to "communal approaches to child-rearing over and against the family-centered approach." A 1975 proposal was also defeated, decried as an effort to "[s]ovietize the family." As a result, the

---

91. Swedish Inst., Gender Equality: Equal Power and Influence for Women and Men – That's What Sweden is Aiming For, Sweden.se (July 15, 2022). See also Bryce Covert, Women Won't Have Equality Until Dads Stay Home, Nation (Apr. 20, 2016).

92. Elly-Ann Johansson, The Effect of Own and Spousal Parental Leave on Earnings 28 (2010).

93. Bureau of Lab. Stats., Employment Characteristics of Families—2021, https://www.bls.gov/news.release/pdf/famee.pdf.

94. See, e.g., Keith Cunningham-Parmeter, (Un)Equal Protection: Why Gender Equality Depends on Discrimination, 109 Nw. U. L. Rev. 1 (2014); Gillian Lester, A Defense of State Paid Family Leave, 28 Harv. J.L. & Gender 1, 80-81 (2005).

95. Symposium, Unbending Gender: Why Family and Work Conflict and What to Do About It, 49 Am. U. L. Rev. 901, 904 (2000) (remarks by Joan Williams).

U.S. offers less governmental support for child care than does any other industrialized nation.[96]

Current law provides federal funds for various child-care assistance programs for disadvantaged children. The federal Child and Dependent Care Tax Credit allows a credit for a percentage of money certain taxpayers spend on child care.[97] The Personal Responsibility and Work Opportunity Reconciliation Act of 1996 offsets some of the losses to poor families under "welfare reform" through a $4 billion increase in child-care funding. This Act is discussed more broadly in Chapter 5, Section C. As a general matter, however, funding for federal programs has failed to keep up with inflation. Moreover, states vary widely in their use of federal funds and their own resources to support child-care assistance programs. As a result, children in some states are better off than before, while others are worse off.[98] During the Covid-19 pandemic, Congress included relief payments for families with children to alleviate some of the burdens of caring for children with reduced access to day care and in-person schools and while suffering Covid-related job losses. Policy analysis shows that these payments had a significant effect on reducing child poverty.[99] Should they have been made permanent?

Employer-subsidized child care is another option for some families. Employers can establish a Dependent Care Assistance Plan through which their employees can put a certain percentage of their earnings up to $5,000 into tax-free savings accounts.[100] More than a third of workers in private industry have access to this benefit.[101] Employers may also choose to provide on-site or off-site day care, or subsidize their employees' day-care costs as a part of their compensation packages. Indeed, demand is sufficiently high that businesses have sprung up specifically to address the day-care needs of the employees of their corporate clients. Ten percent of workers in private industry have access to subsidized child care. Workers in white-collar occupations are much more likely to have employer subsidies for child care than blue-collar or service workers.[102]

---

96. Joan Williams, Toward a Reconstructive Feminism: Reconstructing the Relationship of Market Work and Family Work, 19 N. Ill. U. L. Rev. 89, 150-51 (1998). On the feminist campaign for universal child care, see Deborah Dinner, The Universal Childcare Debate: Rights Mobilization, Social Policy, and the Dynamics of Feminist Activism, 1966-74, 28 Law & Hist. Rev. 577 (2010).

97. 26 U.S.C. § 21 (2018).

98. See Karen Schulman & Helen Blank, Nat'l Women's L. Ctr., Pivot Point: State Child Care Assistance Policies (2013).

99. Kris Cox et al., Ctr. Budget & Pol'y, Priorities, Stimulus Payments, Child Tax Credit Expansion Were Critical Parts of Successful Covid-19 Policy Response (June 22, 2022).

100. 26 U.S.C. § 129 (2018). For a summary of the detailed rules, see https://www.law.cornell.edu/uscode/text/26/129.

101. Eli R. Stolzfus, Bureau of Lab. Stats., Access to Dependent Care Reimbursement Accounts and Workplace-Funded Childcare, 4 Beyond the Numbers: Pay and Benefits (Jan. 2015).

102. Bureau of Lab. Stats., National Compensation Survey: Employee Benefits in Private Industry in the United States 26, tbl. 22 (Mar. 2005).

Most Western countries have gone considerably further than the United States in assisting families with children. Sweden, for example, not only provides paid caretaking leave for more than one caregiver, but also a basic child allowance for all families, increased allowances for families with three or more children, and additional subsidies to replace support that a non-custodial parent is unable or unwilling to pay. There are additional income supports for post-childbirth leave and for care of children with disabilities, as well as an extensive publicly financed child-care system. Single parents receive preferential treatment for housing and child care. The tax system encourages the entry of women into the work force by taxing the second earner separately, rather than at the marginal rate of the primary wage earner. France, like Sweden, has a family allowance system that is particularly generous to large families. France also has a nearly universally available child-care and preschool education system, regardless of whether the parent or parents are in the paid work force. Are these countries to be emulated? Economists have found that spending on early childhood education and child care is "across the board associated with more gender equal outcomes."[103] What do you think of the argument that the U.S. approach is appropriate because our culture is based on a different set of principles and values?[104] Many sectors shifted to full or partial remote work during the Covid-19 pandemic, and, although employers largely want to return to in-person work requirements, employees have resisted.[105] Would the continuation of remote work be good for mothers and fathers?[106] Working women without children? For children, other dependents, and society? Would it ease the burdens associated with finding safe, affordable child care?

7. **Is Caretaking a Public Good?** From an equality perspective, the debate over caretaking is about the disadvantages women experience when the family is organized to give them primary responsibility for their "private" decision to have children while the "ideal worker" in the workplace is assumed to be available full time, unburdened by significant family responsibilities. But theorists such as Martha Fineman stress that caretaking is not just a private consumption decision; it is a public good, upon which society depends, and for which society bears some responsibility.[107]

---

103. Olivetti & Petrongolo, supra note 81, at 221.

104. Compare Thomas B. Edsall, Why Can't America Be Sweden?, N.Y. Times, May 29, 2013, with David Brooks, Livin' Bernie Sanders's Danish Dream, N.Y. Times, Feb. 12, 2016, at A27.

105. See, e.g., Tim Henderson, Pew Rsch. Ctr., As Women Return to Jobs, Remote Work Could Lock in Gains (May 3, 2022); Kim Parker et al., Pew Rsch. Ctr., Covid-19 Pandemic Continues to Reshape Work in America (Feb. 16, 2022).

106. See, e.g., Jeff Green et al., The Return to the Office Is Pushing Even More Women Out of Work, Bloomberg (June 16, 2021); Matthew A. Ng. et al., Has the Covid-19 Pandemic Accelerated the Future of Work or Changed Its Course? Implications for Research and Practice, 18 Int'l J. Env't Rsch. Pub. Health 10199 (2021).

107. For another robust political theory calling for a "supportive state," see Maxine Eichner, The Supportive State: Families, Government, and America's Political Ideals (2010); see also Huntington, supra note 80; Linda C. McClain, The Place of Families: Fostering Capacity, Equality, and Responsibility (2006).

A number of feminist theorists take issue with the premise that caretaking is a public good. Katherine Franke's primary concern is the further privileging of reproduction, along with its various cultural associations and a sexual division of labor that oppresses women.

> Reproduction has been so taken for granted that only women who are not parents are regarded as having made a choice—a choice that is constructed as nontraditional, nonconventional, and for some, non-natural.[108]

Franke also raises fairness issues about the public support for an activity over which the public retains so little control.

> The politics of public value, public subsidy, but private accountability with respect to raising children is revealed to be quite paradoxical under close examination. . . . [For example, a] large number of home schoolers are fundamentalist Christian families who . . . "are no longer fighting against the mainstream—they're 'dropping out' and creating their own private America." Many families . . . are heeding the call of Paul Weyrich, a founder of the Christian Right, to "drop out of this culture, and find places . . . where we can live godly, righteous, and sober lives." Not coincidentally, these families, and many others like them, are also making the loudest demands for public subsidies or vouchers that will finance homeschooling as well as private, parochial school tuition for families that seek to remove their children from the public school system. It must be worth at least thinking about the carte blanche we give the privatized family to refuse to teach "our" future citizens public norms of tolerance, equality, and humanity—or worse. . . .
>
> What also strikes me as worthy of examination is the degree to which parenting is described as productive society activity while, in many regards, parenting has become as much or more about consumption than production. Sylvia Anne Hewlett, the founder of the National Parenting Association, mused in a recent op-ed piece . . . about how the public fails to recognize the financial sacrifices that mothers make to raise children. What with "therapy, summer camp, computer equipment and so on," kids are just darn expensive, she argued. The "and so on" explicitly entails Pokemon accessories, My Little Pony dolls, Barbies, fancy sneakers, and other expensive articles of consumption that are aggressively marketed to children these days. While I don't think that children of any economic class should be deprived of the toys and other items that bring joy into their lives, I am concerned about the bourgeois framing of an issue that gives the larger public the tab for the marketing-induced "needs" of children. And all in the name of "society-preserving work." That children want things, or their parents wish to provide them to their children, is an insufficient justification for shifting the costs of those needs to the public.[109]

---

108. Katherine Franke, Theorizing Yes: An Essay on Feminism, Law, and Desire, 101 Colum. L. Rev. 181, 186-87 (2001).

109. Id. at 191-92.

Another critic, Mary Anne Case, focuses on the unfairness of shifting the burden of caretaking to those who choose not to have children.

> The difficulty I have experienced goes beyond privileging certain kinds of family over others, and more broadly extends to a privileging of family matters over an employee's other life concerns.
>
> [I]f the premise of some parents' advocates really is one of strong equality of result (i.e., that parents should, in effect, be held harmless in time and money from their decision to have children; that their decision to have children should be made as close as possible to costless), then we really are talking, if not quite about a zero-sum game, then at least about a massive redistribution from nonparents to parents, one which, on grounds, *inter alia*, of inequity to people like myself, I would strongly oppose.[110]

Are efforts to create family-friendly workplaces and provide subsidies for workers with children in fact a form of discrimination against people who do not have children? If so, is this discrimination illegal under the various doctrines in this book?[111] Is it sound public policy?

Even if caretaking is a public good, is there a reason why it should be singled out for priority over other public goods such as health care or the environment? Is there such a thing as too much caretaking?[112]

How far should caretaking obligations extend? In his influential 2009 book, The Life You Can Save, philosopher Peter Singer argues that if relatively well-off individuals can save the lives of starving children in other nations with little harm to themselves, they have a moral obligation to do so. Do you think that feminists like Fineman and Bender (excerpted in Section A) would agree? Is there a logical stopping point to an ethic of care?

8. **Dependent Care and the Market in Domestic Workers.** As Martha Fineman observes, the primary approach to child and elder care in the United States has been to treat it as a "private" issue to be negotiated by individual women. Government involvement has largely been limited to providing mothers with resources to track down "deadbeat dads." Women who must work but cannot afford high-quality in-home assistance or day care look to their own relatives, to babysitters, or to low-cost, frequently unlicensed family day-care centers that feature regular turnover and poorly trained workers. Those workers are 95 percent female

---

110. Mary Anne Case, How High the Apple Pie? A Few Troubling Questions About Where, Why, and How the Burden of Care for Children Should Be Shifted, 76 Chi.-Kent L. Rev. 1753, 1767, 1771 (2001). For a rich historical analysis of how feminism came to "abandon" the interests of single women, see Rachel F. Moran, How Second-Wave Feminism Forgot the Single Woman, 33 Hofstra L. Rev. 223 (2004).

111. For the argument that it should be, see Trina Jones, Single and Childfree! Reassessing Parental and Marital Status Discrimination, 46 Ariz. State L.J. 1253 (2014).

112. See Judith Warner, Perfect Madness: Motherhood in the Age of Anxiety 220 (2005) (on the "helicopter parent" phenomenon).

and poorly paid.[113] And, as Dorothy Roberts argues, the convergence of gender roles, racial norms, and market forces has meant that a disproportionate part of that undervalued labor force is nonwhite. A sizable proportion of domestic workers are immigrants who typically do not have the protections of traditional labor and employment laws. By one count, 46 percent of domestic workers were born abroad.[114]

Domestic workers also lack effective legal protections. They are explicitly excluded from coverage under the National Labor Relations Act (which guarantees the right to organize and engage in collective bargaining). Why do you think they were excluded? Domestic workers are also outside the protection of the Occupational Safety and Health Act, Title VII, and most state workers' compensation acts. They typically have only limited eligibility for unemployment benefits. Further, collective action is difficult for domestic workers because they are isolated from one another. Government enforcement of applicable laws and regulations is a serious problem, particularly when workers are undocumented. Many of these workers lack entitlement to overtime or health benefits, unemployment or disability benefits, or Social Security when they retire.

How might a true "ethic of care" restructure the market for caretaking? What mix of organizing strategies, government subsidies, tax incentives, and statutory protections would be most helpful?

PUTTING THEORY INTO PRACTICE

4-10. The Cahn and McClain excerpt describes some of the gendered effects of the Covid-19 pandemic.[115] Some of them are the product of longstanding gender disparities in our society such as occupational segregation (discussed in Chapter 2) and the disproportionate caretaking burdens borne by women (discussed in Chapter 2 and in this chapter). What have you observed about the experiences of men versus women during the pandemic? What can or should be done to alleviate these gendered effects? Is it the government's responsibility to respond to them?

4-11. How much responsibility should private employers have to support employees with families? Should they provide paid leave? Flex-time and part-time options? Child-care assistance? Benefit plans with choices that include family-related assistance? Does it depend on the employer's labor market position? What

---

113. Full-time child-care workers in private households earned, on average, $482 per week. Bureau of Lab. Stats., Highlights of Women's Earnings in 2017, at 29 (Aug. 2018). Caretakers for the elderly are also disproportionately women of color and experience low wages and often unsafe and exploitative working conditions. See Peggie R. Smith, Aging and Caring in the Home: Regulating Paid Domesticity in the 21st Century, 92 Iowa L. Rev. 1835, 1848 (2007).

114. Shirley Lin, "And Ain't I a Woman?": Feminism, Immigrant Caregivers, and New Frontiers for Equality, 39 Harv. J.L. & Gender 67, 76 (2016).

115. See also Nicole Bateman & Martha Ross, Why Has Covid-19 Been Especially Harmful for Working Women?, Brookings (Oct. 2020).

problems do you foresee in passing such initiatives? Are any of them unfair to work-ers who do not have families?

4-12. What are the implications of difference theory for laws relating to wom-en's reproductive rights? Could the state be entitled or compelled, for example, to take greater control over the mother's risk-taking behavior during pregnancy, to express a stronger "ethic of care"?[116] Or would the "ethic of care" expand reproduc-tive rights by requiring access to contraception and abortion?

4-13. A program at the University of Michigan, funded in part by the National Science Foundation to address the acute shortage of female scientists, provides small grants to allow female scientists to hire

> . . . an extra set of hands in the lab or a substitute teacher in the classroom so they can spend more time at home without watching their careers stall. . . . Michigan has even paid for weekend day care so that female sci-entists have quiet time to write grants and journal articles. . . .
>
> [At Harvard, under a similar program,] the vast majority of the grants have gone to women with children. But [one male doctor] has turned his $25,000 fellowship over to the hospital to hire doctors to cover a portion of his work week in the emergency room so that he can attend a new clinical-research training program at Harvard . . . and spend more time with his 2-year-old daughter. . . . [The doctor] says he initially felt guilty about taking a fellowship designed for women. "I'm sensitive to the idea that women have it harder than men in making their academic and family careers work, and I didn't want to be competing for an award with women who deserve it," he says. But his wife, who is pregnant with their second child, is a lawyer with the Office of the Massachusetts General. "Her career is just as demanding and high-powered as mine," says [the doctor,] so he felt he qualified for the grant.[117]

Are government grants to assist scientists in managing the tough laboratory hours required of first-rate scientists a good policy? If so, does the acute underrep-resentation of female scientists justify giving priority to women?

4-14. How do you plan to cope with the challenges involved in fitting together your personal and professional commitments? Do you expect to work full time throughout your career? Do you plan to have children? If so, who will take care of them? What accommodations do you think are fair to expect from your employer? From your co-workers?

4-15. In a recent book on the division of domestic labor, Darcy Lockman finds that many professional women now of childbearing age who married fem-inist men find that traditional gender roles re-emerge when they have children. Part of the problem is that men compare themselves to their fathers and other men and see their "helping" as equal parenting. Mothers who don't always want to be the "default parent" when it comes to managing the household and assuming

---

116. The law regarding pregnant women and risk-taking behavior is covered in Chap-ter 5, Section B.

117. Robin Wilson, Family Science, Chron. Higher Educ., July 22, 2005, at A6, A7-A8.

inconvenient caretaking obligations often become angry or frustrated, and marriages suffer or don't survive.[118] The problem may be that the men are indeed doing more housework than they've observed other men do, but they often are not actually doing 50 percent. Additionally, women may have grown up with a socially constructed lesser tolerance for messiness or unfinished tasks that leads them to jump in and do more than their share of the work instead of demanding equal work. Have you observed similar patterns? How can they be addressed?

C. GENDER AND THE LEGAL SYSTEM

Women participate in the legal system in every respect — as parties, witnesses, lawyers, judges, and jurors. This section examines what difference women make in these various roles.

1. Women in Legal Education and the Legal Profession

For much of U.S. history, a long-held belief that women are unsuited to be lawyers prevailed, as reflected in the slow pace of admitting women to the legal academy. The University of Iowa and Washington University in St. Louis became the first two law schools to admit women in 1869. Most took much longer. Many law schools did not enroll women until the late 1920s and 1930s. Harvard remained all-male until 1950, and it was not until 1972 that all accredited law schools had eliminated explicit sex-based admissions policies. Until the 1960s, women constituted only about 3 percent of enrollment in law schools, less than 3 percent of the profession, and less than 1 percent of law professors.

With so few women in law school, the main theme in this era, and through the 1970s, was the classic formal equality story of exclusion. A variety of rationales, in addition to women's presumptive unsuitability for the practice of law, were cited to justify the status quo, including the distractibility and discomfort of men. Administrators worried about unchaperoned interactions in the library at Harvard; at Hastings, about the rustling of female skirts in the classroom; and at Columbia, about the "cranks and freaks" who would adversely affect the school's culture and competitive edge.[119] Other law school administrators used the lack of opportunities for women in the profession, and the anticipated insurmountable difficulty for women balancing the practice of law with marriage and family, to justify preserving precious law school seats for men. Dean Erwin Griswold of Harvard was notorious for inviting all the women students to dinner and asking them individually to explain

---

118. Darcy Lockman, All the Rage (2019).

119. For Harvard, see Deborah L. Rhode, Perspectives on Professional Women, 40 Stan. L. Rev. 1163, 1171 (1988); for Hastings, see Barbara Babcock, Woman Lawyer: The Trials of Clara Foltz 7-8 (2011); for Columbia, see Jerold Auerbach, Unequal Justice: Lawyers and Social Change in America 295 (1976).

why they were taking the place of a man.[120] With no accountability for discriminatory admissions policies, many law school administrators felt no compulsion to even explain their decisions. When a woman barred from applying to Columbia Law School in 1922 asked Dean Harlan Stone (later Chief Justice of the United States Supreme Court) why the school didn't admit women, his response was "[w]e don't because we don't."[121]

Discrimination on the basis of race, ethnicity, and religion was also pervasive.[122] Not until the mid-1960s were all members of the Association of American Law Schools able to report that they did not officially discriminate on the basis of race or ethnicity. Barriers to women of color were especially great because the few institutions that did not discriminate on the basis of race often did so on the basis of sex. Charlotte Ray, one of the first Black women to graduate from law school (Howard in 1873), gained admittance by using her initials rather than her first name on application papers. After an unsuccessful struggle to obtain legal work, she returned to her earlier career of teaching in public schools. Between 1875 and 1925, no more than twenty-five Black women were reported to be practicing law in the entire nation. By 1940, the number had only doubled.[123]

Pauli Murray, one of the first Black women civil rights scholars and activists, graduated first in her class at Howard in 1944. She found it shocking that men who had come to Howard partly because of its reputation as a center of civil rights litigation could so thoughtlessly discriminate against women. No matter how often she raised her hand, the professors rarely called on her.[124] When Harvard Law School rejected her for graduate studies, she requested a full review by the faculty and came as close as she ever did to publicly acknowledging gender identity as a closeted transgender individual. "Gentlemen," she wrote, "I would gladly change my sex to meet your requirements but since the way to such change has not been revealed to me, I have no recourse but to appeal to you to change your minds on this subject. And you tell me that one is as difficult as the other."[125] Murray ultimately became the first Black graduate to earn an advanced degree from Yale Law School but was still unable to secure a faculty appointment.[126]

As long as women remained at token levels, law schools did not have to reckon with whether or how they should change in response to the inclusion of women. Many simply ignored women's presence as much as possible, except for special issues or ceremonial occasions. For example, some professors observed Ladies' Days, on which they called only on women students for selected cases or hypothetical problems involving "women's concerns." Rape and needlework were favored topics.[127] Schools had no organizations for women law students, although

---

120. Julia Collins, Celebration 45: The Alumnae of Harvard Law Return to Cambridge, Harv. News Bull. (Feb. 25, 1999) (quoting Judith Hope).
121. Cynthia Fuchs Epstein, Women in Law 51 (1981) (quoting Stone).
122. Auerbach, supra note 119.
123. Geraldine Segal, Blacks in the Law 1, 4, 215, 240 (1983).
124. Rosalind Rosenberg, Jane Crow: The Life of Pauli Murray 139 (2017).
125. Id. at 138-39.
126. Id. at 283.
127. Collins, supra note 120.

associations were often available for wives of law students; activities included teas, bake sales, fashion shows, and speaker series with topics such as the importance of the well-informed wife (a woman "educated but not equal").[128]

Not until women began entering law school in significant numbers during the 1970s did the climate for women begin to improve considerably.[129] The women's rights and civil rights movements encouraged more women and people of color to apply to law school and to challenge discriminatory practices. During the Vietnam War, a reduction in the pool of qualified male law school applicants also helped to boost women's admission. By the mid-1980s, over a third of new entrants to law school were women.

Once women represented a substantial share of admitted law students, the leading narrative about women in legal education began to shift from one of exclusion to a question of difference. Do women bring a distinct set of aptitudes, learning styles, and interests to the study of law, and if so, how should law schools change in response? This question merged with another that formed the basis of a critique: is legal education itself, traditionally administered, quintessentially "male"? Some feminist scholars, often associated with difference theory, answered this question in the affirmative.[130] Studies of women's experiences in law schools in the 1980s, 1990s, and into the 2000s found that female students received lower grades than their male classmates, contrary to predictions based on test scores and college performance, and that they participated less in class, held fewer leadership positions, and received less mentoring. The findings showed especially pronounced disparities for lesbian and gay students and students of color.[131] Women law students also had higher rates of dissatisfaction, disengagement, and self-doubt than men.[132] Subsequent studies have shown more mixed results and some of these gaps have

---

128. Barbara Aronstein Black, Something to Remember, Something to Celebrate: Women at Columbia Law School, 102 Colum. L. Rev. 1451, 1454 (2002); Ruth Bader Ginsburg, Women at the Bar: A Generation of Change, 2 Puget Sound L. Rev. 1, 6 (1978).

129. Deborah L. Rhode, Midcourse Corrections: Women in Legal Education, 53 J. Legal Educ. 475, 479 (2003); see also Judith Richards Hope, Pinstripes and Pearls 155-62 (2004).

130. See, e.g., Carrie Menkel-Meadow, Feminist Legal Theory, Critical Legal Studies, and Legal Education or "The Fem-Crits Go to Law School," 38 J. Legal Educ. 61 (1988).

131. Some of the influential studies of the era include: Linda F. Wightman, Law School Admission Council Research Report Series, Women in Legal Education: A Comparison of the Law School Performance and Law School Experience of Women and Men 25 (1996); Lani Guinier et al., Becoming Gentlemen 41 (1997); Elizabeth Mertz et al., What Difference Does Difference Make: The Challenge for Legal Education, 48 J. Legal Educ. 1 (1998); Janice L. Austin et al., Results from a Survey: Gay, Lesbian, and Bisexual Students' Attitudes About Law School, 48 J. Legal Educ. 157 (1998).

132. Felice Batlan et al., Not Our Mother's Law School? A Third Wave Feminist Study of Women's Experiences in Law School, 39 U. Balt. L. F. 124, 131 (2009); Elizabeth Mertz, Inside the Law School Classroom: Toward a New Legal Realist Pedagogy, 60 Vand. L. Rev. 483, 509 (2007); Adam Neufield, Costs of an Outdated Pedagogy? Study on Gender at Harvard Law School, 13 J. Gender, Soc. Pol'y & L. 511, 516-17, 530-39 (2005); Claire G. Schwab, A Shifting Gender Divide: The Impact of Gender on Education at Columbia Law School in the New Millennium, 36 Colum. J.L. & Soc. Probs. 229, 325 (2003).

closed. For example, women have achieved equal representation in law reviews and judicial clerkships, although some studies have shown a persistent gap in the most prestigious judicial clerkships and continuing gaps for women of color in law review leadership.[133] Nevertheless, findings of gender gaps in law school performance and satisfaction sparked a critique that the traditional model of legal education does not work well for women or students of color.[134] That model is characterized by long-enduring methods such as the Socratic method, cold-calling, reading appellate cases, competition for grades and law review, and minimal client experience or experiential learning. Some feminist scholars have continued to call for jettisoning, or at least substantially revising, the traditional model to be more inclusive for women and students of color.[135]

Based on your experiences and observations, do you think women bring a "different voice" to legal education? Are women less prone to raise their hands before forming their thoughts? Less likely to dominate class time with idiosyncratic questions? Are they more collaborative in style and substance? Are they more respectful to faculty? Are any of those qualities generally shared with LGBTQ+ and students of color? Further, what changes to law schools have the inclusion of previously excluded groups wrought? Do you think discussions include a wider range of students since the early 1980s? Are students more welcoming of female and racial and sexual minority staff and faculty? Are faculty less harsh with students? Are there further changes law schools should make to better address the needs and interests of women? If so, what are they, and why do you think they have not yet done so?

The story of women in the legal profession also begins with exclusion. As noted in Chapter 1, the first woman attorney was not licensed to practice law until 1867. Among the justifications for excluding women was that women's proper role was in the "domestic sphere," not in the "occupations of civil life," for which their

---

133. Alice Shih, Yale Law Women, Yale Law School Faculty and Students Speak Up About Gender, Ten Years Later (2012), https://ylw.yale.edu/wp-content/uploads/2013/03/YLW-Speak-Up-Study.pdf (finding that men were responsible for 57 percent of class participation, a rate higher than in 2002, and a perception that women may be penalized socially for participating more than average); Lauren Graber, Are We There Yet? Progress Toward Gender-Neutral Legal Education, 33 B.C. J.L. & Soc. Just. 45, 68, 75 (2013) (Boston College female law students reported significantly less class participation than their male classmates, and men were nearly three times as likely as women to assert that they had never felt a loss of confidence in the classroom); for law reviews, see Ms. JD, Women on Law Review: A Gender Diversity Report (2012), and Adriane Kayoko Peralta, The Underrepresentation of Women of Color in Law Review Leadership Positions, 25 Berkeley La Raza L. J. 69 (2015). For women's underrepresentation in prestigious clerkships, see Dahlia Lithwick, Who Feeds the Supreme Court?, Slate (Sept. 14, 2015) (one-third of Supreme Court clerks are female); National Association of Law Placement: A Demographic Profile of Judicial Clerks — 2006-2016 (women constituted 46.6 percent of federal and 52.0 percent of state clerkships).

134. See, e.g., Kathryne M. Young, Understanding the Social and Cognitive Process in Law School that Creates Unhealthy Lawyers, 89 Fordham L. Rev. 2575, 2588-92 (2021) (surveying law students and documenting continuing racial and gender disparities in class participation that held constant whether the professor used cold-calling, panels, or volunteers).

135. See, e.g., Jamie R. Abrams, Legal Education's Curricular Tipping Point Toward Inclusive Socratic Teaching, 49 Hofstra L. Rev. 897 (2021).

"proper timidity and delicacy" made them unfit.[136] The rationales for exclusion also raise the question of difference. Matthew Hale Carpenter, in unsuccessfully defending the right of Myra Bradwell to become a member of the Illinois Bar, argued that while some cases may require the "rough qualities possessed by men, . . . [t]here are many causes in which the silver voice of a woman would accomplish more than the severity and sternness of man could achieve."[137] Whether or not you agree with this statement, do you think women bring special qualities to legal practice? Do women lawyers practice in a "different voice" that is more sensitive to values of care, compassion, and cooperation than prevailing legal norms?[138] Where would you look for evidence of this?

If women bring a "different voice" to the practice of law, where does it come from? Female litigators frequently report being told by judges and supervisors that they were too loud, shrill, or severe, or that they needed to smile more or look more feminine.[139] Writing about these differences, former public defender Lara Bazelon recounts how she learned to adopt a "more in sorrow than in anger" tone, and to behave in a "traditionally feminine and unthreatening manner."[140] To what extent do you suppose that women's distinctive voice is itself a reaction to the gendered world in which they find themselves?

Even if the qualities women bring to the practice of law are, at least in part, adaptive, might they be an advantage? Some think so. Lynn Hermle, a San Francisco litigator who has successfully defended clients in high-profile sex discrimination cases, puts it this way:

> Women typically grow up keenly conscious of how we appear to and make social connections with others. We are taught to want to be liked and accepted. We think about how we look and act and how we come across. This sensitivity can make women uniquely qualified to do well in front of jurors, who watch trial lawyers like hawks looking for field mice. . . . [Women also tend to have] keen emotional intelligence . . . [which enables them to be] particularly conscious of whether they are connecting and building credibility with a jury. . . . [T]his awareness allows a woman trial lawyer to determine how far to push an aggressive cross examination, especially one that which dismantles the credibility of a key witness or party. Obviously, an overly aggressive witness examination can backfire. Women trial lawyers are especially sensitive to where

---

136. Bradwell v. Illinois, 83 U.S. 130 (1872). For an excerpt of Justice Bradley's concurring opinion, see Chapter 1, Section A.

137. Id. at 137.

138. See Section A of this chapter. Two classics on this subject are Susan P. Sturm, From Gladiators to Problem-Solvers: Connecting Conversations About Women, the Academy, and the Legal Profession, 4 Duke J. Gender L. & Pol'y 119 (1997); Carrie Menkel-Meadow, Portia in a Different Voice: Speculations on Women's Lawyering Process, 1 Berkeley L.J. 39 (1985).

139. Lara Bazelon, What It Takes to Be a Trial Lawyer If You're Not a Man, Atlantic (Sept. 2018). This factor, as a cause of discrimination against women, is explored in Chapter 1, Section C.

140. Id.

to draw the line . . . [and to] get more leeway from a jury. . . . Women are less likely to be labeled as bullies or overly aggressive, especially if we've shown ourselves to have credibility and to have behaved respectfully to the judge.[141]

If Hermle is correct about these advantages, why is it, as she acknowledges, that "not many women lead high-profile jury trials and all-female teams are very rare"?[142] If she and Bazelon are correct about what works in the courtroom, is there a way for female litigators to be successful without reinforcing gender stereotypes?

Another setting in which gender differences have been extensively researched involves negotiating behavior. Over the past two decades, a large body of theoretical and empirical research has attempted to determine whether men and women have different negotiating styles and effectiveness. One finding is that gender appears to be mediated by other aspects of the negotiating context, including the relative social status, perceived power, and attitudes toward conflict of the participants.[143] It also matters whether negotiators are the same sex, whether they have negotiating experience or ongoing relationships, and whether they are acting for themselves or as representatives for someone else.[144]

Some research finds that women negotiators are more likely than men to disparage ethically questionable tactics, and are less likely to lower their ethical standards when doing so would benefit their economic outcomes.[145] Other research finds that female law students in the United States and United Kingdom are more likely to behave ethically and have a stronger sense of moral identity than their male classmates.[146] And female lawyers in the United States are less likely to receive disciplinary sanctions for ethical misconduct.[147] What do you make of these findings? If women achieved greater representation in leadership positions, might their influence help reorient practice in socially valuable directions?

More broadly, are the non-adversarial methods and problem-solving techniques that are associated (rightly or wrongly) with women simply better lawyering? Consider the following.

---

141. Lynne Hermle, I Defended Kleiner in the Ellen Pao Case—Here's Why We Need More Women Leading Trials, Bus. Insider (Sept. 12, 2017).

142. Id.

143. For the importance of status, see Emily T. Amanatullah & Catherine H. Tinsely, Ask and Ye Shall Receive? How Gender and Status Moderate Negotiation Success, 6 Negot. & Conflict Mgmt. Rsch. 253 (2013).

144. See Jessica A. Kennedy & Laura J. Kray, A Pawn in Someone Else's Game: The Cognitive, Motivational, and Paradigmatic Barriers to Women's Excelling in Negotiation, 35 Rsch. Org. Behav. 3, 6 (2015).

145. Id. at 16.

146. Aebra Coe, Female Law Students More Ethical Than Males, Study Says, Law 360 (Oct. 25, 2016).

147. Patricia Hatamyer & Kevin M. Simmons, Are Women More Ethical Lawyers? An Empirical Study, 31 Fla. St. U. L. Rev. 785, 799-803 (2004).

Andrea Kupfer Schneider

What's Sex Got to Do With It? Questioning Research on Gender & Negotiation

19 Nev. L.J. 919 (2019)

Negotiation scholars and teachers often talk about negotiation skills through the metaphor of tools in the toolbox. Teachers want to make sure that students have a variety of tools and we push our students to recognize the importance of each, even quoting the old cliché that "[i]f the only tool you have is a hammer, it is tempting to treat everything as if it were a nail."

[N]egotiation scholarship primarily studies the hammer, the skill of assertiveness in negotiation. In fact, the majority of empirical negotiation studies take this even further—studying only the hammer and imagining only a single opportunity to hit the nail on the head. Based on those studies, we make conclusions that if one chooses not to use the hammer at all or does not hold it as well as another, one is not a good builder. And negotiation scholars' advice is also too often focused only on this hammer—how to swing it harder, how to position your hands, the angle of the swing, and so forth. If we were teaching a class on building a home, we would recognize the need to ensure our construction crew had skills with other tools as well. Yet, the studies of negotiation skills fail to acknowledge this fact.

This gap is particularly notable when examining gender and negotiation. The vast majority of articles examining gender and negotiation focus on assertiveness—the hammer—and how women need to pick it up, swing harder, or hold it differently. Women's supposed lack of assertiveness has been used to explain the pay gap between the salaries of women and men along with a whole host of other inequities. This story falls short primarily because our research falls short. And when our research falls short—when we are only researching and emphasizing a part of the skills that are needed to be effective—this does a disservice to all negotiators.

In some of the most high profile and high stress negotiations, the recognition that more than assertiveness is needed was a hard won lesson. . . . Yet our empirical research—particularly on these other skills in negotiation—is lacking.

First, researchers focus on assertiveness, a typically masculine trait, and only one of several important negotiation skills. Therefore, we assume that both men and women need only to master that skill to the detriment of the mastery of any other negotiation skills. Second, assertiveness has become the only regularly tested negotiation skill as it is easily quantified. By failing to study the impact of any other skills—including skills that women might be better at than men—the practice to theory to practice cycle is hijacked by this narrow focus. Third, we tend to study negotiation in one-shot interactions with distributive outcomes. Far less often do we study the possibility of integrative outcomes. Even when we set up studies that focus on repeated interactions, they are often limited to prisoner's dilemma or dictator game scenarios—highly stylized and unrealistic structures. What this means is that while women are not recognized for the skills at which they might be inherently better, it also means that we are failing men by not highlighting opportunities for growth and improvement. . . .

There are (at least) three things that are wrong with research on women and negotiation. The first is that we study gender differences in negotiation and assume that these differences—as opposed to any other professional, cultural, age, or experiential difference—are determinative of differences in negotiation behavior. These stereotypes may or may not apply to any one of us in particular. Our behaviors in negotiation likely fall along a range from "masculine" to "feminine" that may or may not actually match our gender. If we examined negotiation behaviors using other lens—professional training, experience, family and culture, geography, or birth order—just to name a few, we would likely find similar ranges of behaviors. In other words, none of these studies show that gender is determinative of any single individual's skill sets. (And this is yet another whole area calling out for more research.)

A second lesson is that assertiveness is only one skill—out of at least five—in negotiation that makes one effective. We have studied one important skill, but it is only one of at least five, and there is no reason to think that results about this skill extend to the other four. Indeed, available research suggests the opposite. Since it has been relatively easy to study in the lab and in one-shot negotiations, that is what we study. (We only study the hammer and assume one swing.) And, as women have been historically socialized against being assertive (with resulting backlash if the appropriate boundaries are crossed), it is not surprising that women are then seen as less effective in those types of studies. And more recent studies even show the limit of assuming that women lack assertiveness. Nonetheless, if it is the only skill one studies, it appears to be the only one that counts. And this ignores the other skills—particularly social intuition, empathy, and ethicality—in which women appear to excel.

This leads to the third lesson—focusing solely on assertiveness is not only doing a disservice to women, it harms any negotiator who assumes that modulating their level of assertiveness is the only thing it takes in order to be effective. Both business and negotiation literature are consistent in noting that these other skills discussed in the article are exactly the types of skills the best leaders will possess. . . .

Only when we fix the research—only when we study more than the hammer—can we really trust that the lessons we draw are accurate and appropriate fixes for each of us individually.

PUTTING THEORY INTO PRACTICE

4-16. In 2019, after Paul, Weiss published a picture of its twelve new equity partners (all white, all but one male), the photo went viral and attracted the attention of the New York Times.[148] A letter to the editor following that article responded:

> Perhaps I am being naive, but why does diversity have to be the primary yardstick in our society for every decision involving the selection of human beings for elevated positions?

---

148. Noam Scheiber & John Eligon, Elite Law Firm's All-White Partner Class Stirs Debate on Diversity, N.Y. Times, Jan. 27, 2019, at A1.

There are times when ability should outweigh diversity. Medical care is one and our adversarial legal system is another. . . . Not everything in life needs to have diverse distribution of humanity.

In this case, Paul, Weiss already had an excellent record when it came to diversity, but it is a law firm in the business of winning cases for its clients. Paul, Weiss did not deserve this pubic shaming because in this one instance the two metrics of diversity and ability were not in sync. . . . Clients do not want their attorneys to fight the good fight [on social issues]; they want them to win. Putting diversity ahead of ability can be a self-defeating proposition for the firm—and the client.[149]

How would you respond?

4-17. Lelia Robinson, the first woman lawyer in Massachusetts, counseled her female colleagues: "Do not take sex into the practice. Don't be 'lady lawyers.' Simply be lawyers and recognize no distinction between yourselves and the other members of the bar."[150] If that was ever good advice, is it the right approach today? Why or why not?

4-18. Roe v. Wade was argued before the Supreme Court in 1971 and again in 1972 before the Court issued its ruling recognizing a constitutional right to terminate a pregnancy before a certain point. Sarah Weddington argued both times for the doctors who were challenging Texas's extreme anti-abortion law. Catherine Christopher Martin argues that Weddington initially relied on storytelling and contextual reasoning to persuade the Court that Texas's law was bad for women, especially poor and disadvantaged ones.[151] A year later, however, she shifted to focus primarily on rights. "Weddington was more successful," Martin argues, "arguing a rights-based approach to the men on the bench. The final opinion is defined by its rights-based analysis: the majority opinion carefully delineates the right of a woman to terminate a pregnancy, the fetus's lack of constitutional rights, and the moments at which the state's interest in protecting maternal health and protecting fetal life matures." Does it matter whether men and women reason differently (whether for biological or socially constructed reasons) if the decisionmakers are largely male? Does the addition of women to the Court change the value of rights-based reasoning? Do you agree with Martin's suggestion that some backlash against *Roe* might have been based "in the rejection of the notion of a woman having her own rights, separate and apart from her relationships to other people, particularly her potential child"? A brief filed in a 2016 abortion case included the personal abortion stories of more than 100 female lawyers.[152] Is that a good strategy? Chapter 5, Section B2 covers the overruling of Roe v. Wade. Could either strategy have prevented it?

4-19. In commenting on the lower class participation rates of women at Harvard Law School, an editorial in the student newspaper faulted women for "consciously choosing to let their male peers do most of the talking" and asserted that

149. Miles E. Kuttler, Letter to the Editor, N.Y. Times, Jan. 31, 2019, at A22.

150. Letter from Lelia J. Robinson [Sawtelle] to the Equity Club (Apr. 9, 1887), reprinted in Women Lawyers and the Origins of Professional Identity in America: The Letters of the Equity Club, 1887 to 1890, at 66 (Virginia G. Drachman, ed., 1993).

151. Catherine Martin Christopher, Nevertheless She Persisted: Comparing *Roe v. Wade*'s Two Oral Arguments, 49 Seton Hall L. Rev. 307 (2019).

152. Emma Green, The Power of Making Abortion Personal, Atlantic, (Jan. 8, 2016).

female students had a "duty" to speak up.[153] Another commentator, in response to arguments that the aggressive, competitive atmosphere of law school classrooms silences women, claimed that such assertions revive nineteenth-century stereotypes about women's inability to engage in the "hot strifes of the bar."[154] How would you respond? Is the problem that women don't speak up, or that they are less likely to think that every thought that crosses their mind is worth saying? To what extent is the kind of reticence being referred to a failing of women, and to what extent should it be viewed, instead, as a strength?

4-20. In response to a .05 GPA gender gap, researchers at Stanford Law School performed a natural experiment in which they studied the effects of smaller class size on grades. What they found is that although men do better than women in large lecture classes, women outperformed men in smaller classes that built in interactive engagement exercises and had a higher likelihood of written feedback on practice exams.[155] What conclusions would you draw from this research? Are there other reforms that might reduce the (diminishing) gender gap in law school grades? Should the Socratic method be scrapped? How different would a law school expressly designed for women be than law schools now?

4-21. Many have observed a generational divide in the approach to work-life balance. In an oversimplified version, Baby Boomers are said not to seek it, Gen-Xers fought hard for it, and Millennials seek to blend rather than balance, looking for ways to incorporate fun into work and prioritizing personal fulfillment, encompassing but not limited to family relationships, over income. If this captures some truth, what might be the effect on the legal profession as leadership passes from one generation to the next? Which approach might be most useful to women seeking to pursue demanding careers in law and raise children? To men? Are the answers different?

4-22. Chapter 1 noted a recent McKinsey study in which only 58 percent of women, as compared with 73 percent of men, expressed a desire to become a partner. To the extent the reason is women's wish to have a better work-family balance, is this a problem to be solved, or does it reflect a higher moral reasoning that men should try to emulate?

2.   Women Judges

The proportion of judges who are women has increased dramatically over the last two decades. With the appointment of Ketanji Brown Jackson to the U.S. Supreme Court, four out of the nine current justices are women. Thirty-five

153. The Study on Women's Experiences at Harvard Law School 1 (2004), discussed in "Women's Experience" Raises Concerns, Harv. L. Sch. Rec., Feb 26, 2004, at 1.

154. John O. McGinnis, At Law School, Unstrict Scrutiny, Wall St. J., July 27, 2005, at D10 (discussing Dan Subotnik, Toxic Diversity (2005)).

155. Daniel E. Ho & Mark G. Kelman, Does Class Size Affect the Gender Gap? A Natural Experiment in Law, 43 J. Legal Stud. 291 (2014).

percent of federal judges are women,[156] as are 36 percent of state court judges.[157] Women of color represent just over 8 percent of the federal judiciary, with Black women constituting 4 percent of sitting federal judges.[158] President Biden has made the appointment of female judges and women of color a priority. In his first six months, 77 percent of the individuals he nominated or announced his intent to nominate to the federal bench were women.[159] By the end of his first year in office, 24 percent of his judicial appointments were women of color,[160] and he has tripled the number of women on federal appeals courts.[161] However, as of May 2020, only 11 out of 1,387 federal judges identify themselves as LGBTQ+.[162]

Should this increase in women in the judiciary make a difference? Do female judges matter? The case for appointing more judges assumes that they do, but the empirical support for this assumption is limited. The studies show that having a woman judge helps plaintiffs in discrimination cases and other gender-related cases but not elsewhere.[163] Is this surprising? Rosemary Hunter writes:

> Why did we think women would transform institutions without simultaneously — or alternatively — being transformed by them? Why did we believe that women appointed to positions of power would be "representative" of women as a group, rather than being those who most resemble the traditional incumbents and are thus considered least likely to disturb the status quo? Why did we assume that women appointed to these positions would have the capacity to represent the whole, diverse, range of women's perspectives and experiences? And why did we imagine that individual women would want potentially to risk their newly-acquired status by taking a stand on behalf of other women, when it would be much safer for them

---

156. See American Constitution Society, Diversity of the Federal Bench: Current Statistics on the Gender and Racial Diversity of the Article III Courts, continuously updated at https://www.acslaw.org/judicial-nominations/diversity-of-the-federal-bench.

157. Nat'l Ass'n Women Judges, The American Bench 2022, available at https://www.nawj.org/statistics/2022-us-state-court-women-judges.

158. See Zoe Tillman, Biden's Supreme Court Promise Underscores a Reality: Black Women Rarely Get to the Federal Judiciary, BuzzFeed News (Jan. 28, 2022).

159. See Biden's Federal Judicial Picks are 77 Percent Women So Far, 19th News (July 7, 2021).

160. John Gramlich, Black Women Account for a Small Fraction of the Federal Judges Who Have Served to Date, Pew Rsch. Ctr. (Feb. 2, 2022).

161. See John Fritze, Not Just the Supreme Court: Biden Poised to Triple Number of Black Women on Federal Appeals Courts, USA Today, Feb. 22, 2022.

162. See Biden's Federal Judicial Picks, supra note 159.

163. See Susan Haire & Laura P. Moyer, Diversity Matters: Judicial Policy Making in the U.S. Courts of Appeals 53-54 (2015); Sally J. Kenney, Gender and Justice: Why Women in the Judiciary Really Matter 3 (2012); Christina L. Boyd et al., Untangling the Causal Effects of Sex on Judging, 54 Am. J. Pol. Sci. 389 (2010) (probability of judge deciding in favor of plaintiff in a discrimination case decreases about 10 percent when the judge is male, and increases when a woman serves on a panel with men).

to keep their heads down and attempt to gain some legitimacy amongst their skeptical peers and jealous subordinates?[164]

Is it likely that the large number of women of color appointed to the bench by President Biden will make more of a difference?

When controlled for ideology or partisanship, the effects of having female judges are less robust, which means what matters to judicial outcomes is not the gender of the judge but the judge's perspective on gender. That ideological perspective matters is already apparent in the replacement of Justice Ruth Bader Ginsburg, who was largely responsible for expanding the rights of women in numerous areas, by Justice Amy Coney Barrett, who voted with the majority to eliminate the constitutional right to abortion.[165]

The effect of gender attitudes was demonstrated in a 2018 controlled study in which 500 judges participated. The judges analyzed two mock court cases, one involving child custody and the other a claim by a woman that she was denied a promotion after taking six weeks of paid parental leave. The study found a strong relationship between the judges' gender attitudes and their view of the cases, with judges who hold conventional views of women's gender roles more likely to rule against the female plaintiff in the sex discrimination case, and in favor of the woman in the custody case. Notably, the study compared the judges' assessments to those of lay persons, finding that the association between belief in traditional gender roles and case outcomes was even stronger for judges than non-judges.[166]

In keeping with this emphasis on ideology and gender perspective in judging, rather than the gender of judges per se, one notable scholarly project has undertaken to examine how feminism might be brought to bear on judging. The Feminist Judgments Project brings together feminist legal scholars to rewrite judicial opinions in a wide variety of cases using feminist legal methods, including more contextual and less abstract reasoning, and greater attention to the impact of legal rules on women ("asking the woman question") and other previously excluded groups. The Project embraces the view that a judge's perspective shapes judicial decisionmaking, and that perspective is situated within a context of identity and experience. As project editors Kathryn Stanchi, Linda Berger, and Bridget Crawford explain:

> [A]ll legal actors—judges, juries, linguists, lawyers—engage in their decision making within a situated perspective that is informed by gender, race, class, religion, disability, nationality, language and sexual orientation. For judges, that (often unacknowledged) situated perspective of the decision

---

164. Rosemary Hunter, Can Feminist Judges Make a Difference?, 15 Int'l J. Leg. Pro. 7, 8 (2008).

165. See Alexandra Villarreal, Amy Coney Barrett: What Will She Mean for Women's Rights?, Guardian, Sept. 27, 2020; Sophie McBain, Amy Coney Barrett: The US Judge Poised to Undo Ginsburg's Legacy, New Statesman, Oct. 12, 2020; Margaret Talbot, Amy Coney Barrett's Long Game, New Yorker (Feb. 7, 2022).

166. Andrea Miller, Expertise Fails to Attenuate Gendered Biases in Judicial-Making, 10 Soc. Psych. & Personality Sci. 227 (2019).

maker may drive American jurisprudence as much as — if not more than — *stare decisis* does.[167]

The import of the project is to show both that feminist methods are possible within the constraints of judicial decisionmaking and that they make a difference. Do you think feminist methodology, or the gender of the judge, is more important in explaining the findings mentioned above, that female judges decide certain cases (employment discrimination and other gender-related cases) more favorably than male judges? What do you make of a study finding that judges with at least one daughter rule in "consistently more feminist fashion" than those who have only sons?[168]

Could the assumption that female judges make a difference be turned against women? In one of the first lawsuits alleging gender discrimination by a law firm, U.S. District Court Judge Constance Baker Motley denied a motion seeking her recusal on grounds that her sex and prior experience as a civil rights attorney would bias her in favor of the plaintiff.[169] In rejecting that motion, Judge Motley observed that if the "background or sex or race of each judge were, by definition, sufficient grounds for removal, no judge on this court could hear this case, or many others."[170] Does the motion make any more sense than one to recuse a male judge in such a case?

Consider a 2003 case in which an attorney requested recusal of a female judge in a case involving allegations that the defendant had groped a female nurse and used vulgar language. The attorney could not see how a female judge "would be fair because of the nature of the allegations."[171] Can you? Would a male judge necessarily be more "fair"? Then-President Trump complained about a case against Trump University being assigned to a judge whose parents had immigrated from Mexico because, he believed, the judge would be biased against him as a party because of his administration's immigration policies. Has a legitimate concern been raised in either case? Why or why not? To what extent do we want or expect judges to build on their experience of group membership in deciding cases?

This issue of when a person's background and experience renders them a better or worse judge arose in the confirmation hearings of Supreme Court Justice Sonia Sotomayor, when then Senator Jeff Sessions grilled her about comments she had made in a 2001 law student speech. She had said, "I would hope that a wise Latina woman with the richness of her experiences would more often than not reach a better conclusion than a white male who hasn't lived that life."[172] To put

---

167. Kathryn M. Stanchi et al., Introduction to the U.S. Feminist Judgments Project, in Feminist Judgments: Rewritten Opinions of the United States Supreme Court 4-5 (2016).

168. See Adam N. Glynn & Maya Sen, Identifying Judicial Empathy: Does Having Daughters Cause Judges to Rule for Women's Issues?, 59 Am. J. Pol. Sci. 37 (2015).

169. Blank v. Sullivan & Cromwell, 418 F. Supp. 1 (S.D.N.Y. 1975).

170. Id. at 4.

171. Lynn Hecht Schafran, Not from Central Casting: The Amazing Rise of Women in the American Judiciary, 36 U. Tol. L. Rev. 953, 959 (2005).

172. Derek Hawkins, "Wise Latina Woman": Jeff Sessions, Race, and His Grilling of Sonia Sotomayor, Wash. Post, Jan. 13, 2017 (quoting Sotomayor).

that claim in context, she had also said, "I willingly accept that we who judge must deny the differences resulting from experience and heritage but attempt, as the Supreme Court suggests, continuously to judge when those opinions, sympathies and prejudices are appropriate."[173] Senator Sessions, echoing concerns that others had expressed, claimed that Sotomayor had "evidenced a philosophy of law that suggests that a judge's background and experiences can and should—even should and naturally will—impact their decision, which I think goes against the American ideal and oath that a judge takes to be fair."[174] How should Sotomayor have responded? What is your view? Do white, male judges have experiences or characteristics that likely influence their judging? Are desirable judicial traits like "neutral" and "objective" masking a bias that favors those who have traditionally held power in this country?

More broadly, to what extent do we hope that judges will set their personal views aside to be disinterested decisionmakers? What does bias mean in this context? Is it coherent to claim both that women have a "different voice" and that they bring no identity-related characteristics and backgrounds to their own decisionmaking?

What is the best guarantee of a lack of bias in the courts—judges who are detached and objective, or those who are empathetic and understanding of other perspectives? In 2009, when a vacancy on the Court opened, President Obama announced his views on the qualities of the justice that he would appoint:

> I will seek somebody with a sharp and independent mind and a record of excellence and integrity. I will seek someone who understands that justice isn't about some abstract legal theory or footnote in a casebook. It is also about how our laws affect the daily realities of people's lives—whether they can make a living and care for their families; whether they feel safe in their homes and welcome in their own nation.
>
> I view that quality of empathy, of understanding and identifying with people's hopes and struggles as an essential ingredient for arriving at just decisions and outcomes.[175]

Commentators from the right were quick to condemn the President's statement. On Fox Forum, S. E. Cupp noted:

> The word empathy, according to its Greek derivation, means "physical affection, passion, and partiality." I thought Aristotle said the law is reason free from passion? And, if justice is blind, I'm fairly certain she's also impartial. But more importantly, who is on the receiving end of [empathy] by Obama's definition?[176]

---

173. Id.

174. Id. (quoting Sessions).

175. President Barack Obama, Remarks by the President on Justice David Souter (May 1, 2009).

176. S. E. Cupp, Obama's Wacky Supreme Court Vision, Fox Forum (May 2009).

Thomas Sowell claimed that the "very idea of the rule of law becomes meaningless when it is replaced by the empathies of judges."[177] Senator Orrin Hatch of Utah weighed in that empathy is a "code word for an *activist* judge."[178] John Kyl of Arizona, a member of the Senate Judiciary Committee, pledged to block any nominee who "takes into account human suffering and employs empathy from the bench."[179] By contrast, two-thirds of surveyed Americans assigned empathy the highest degree of importance in selecting a Supreme Court Justice, and those most knowledgeable about the Court were particularly likely to value empathy. The most commonly desired characteristic, endorsed by three-quarters of Americans, was that Justices "uphold the values of those who wrote the Constitution long ago." Are those positions always consistent, particularly on gender-related issues?[180]

What is the alternative to "empathy"? Is detachment possible? Desirable? Are empathy and objectivity compatible? Susan Bandes argues that empathy is both inevitable and essential to good judging; it enables judges to understand conflicting claims, but it does not dictate how they should be resolved. Thus, in her view, "it is misleading to discuss whether judges should exercise empathy . . . the questions are for whom they exercise it, how accurately they exercise it, how aware they are of their own limitations and blind spots, and what they do to correct for those blind spots."[181]

In the context of non-judicial conflict resolution, Susan Sturm and Howard Gadlin question the assumption that " 'detached neutrality' is the only or even the best way to achieve impartiality and reduce the expression of bias." They offer as an alternative the ideal of "multi-partiality," which they define as the ability to "critically analyz[e] a conflict from multiple vantage points—as a way to check the inevitable biases in decision making that have to be continually surfaced and corrected."[182] Are any of these models preferable for judicial decisionmaking?

Jerry Kang et al.

Implicit Bias in the Courtroom

59 UCLA L. Rev. 1124 (2012)

The problems of overt discrimination have received enormous attention from lawyers, judges, academics, and policymakers. While explicit sexism, racism, and other forms of bias persist, they have become less prominent and public over the

---

177. Thomas Sowell, "Empathy" vs. Law, Nat'l Rev. Online (May 5, 2009).

178. William Safire, On Language, N.Y. Times Mag., May 17, 2009, at 26.

179. Douglas O. Linder & Nancy Levit, The Good Lawyer: Seeking Quality in the Practice of Law 29 (2014) (quoting Kyl).

180. James L. Gibson, Expecting Justice and Hoping for Empathy, Pac. Standard (2010) (defining empathy as being able to understand how the law hurts or helps people).

181. Susan A. Bandes, Empathetic Judging and the Rule of Law, Cardozo L. Rev. de novo 133, 135-36 (2009).

182. Susan Sturm & Howard Gadlin, Conflict Resolution and Systemic Change, 3 J. Disp. Resol. 1, 4 (2007).

past century. But explicit bias and overt discrimination are only part of the problem. Also important, and likely more pervasive, are questions surrounding implicit bias—attitudes or stereotypes that affect our understanding, decisionmaking, and behavior, without our even realizing it.

How prevalent and significant are these implicit, unintentional biases? To answer these questions, people have historically relied on their gut instincts and personal experiences, which did not produce much consensus. Over the past two decades, however, social cognitive psychologists have discovered novel ways to measure the existence and impact of implicit biases—without relying on mere common sense. Using experimental methods in laboratory and field studies, researchers have provided convincing evidence that implicit biases exist, are pervasive, are large in magnitude, and have real-world effects. These fascinating discoveries, which have migrated from the science journals into the law reviews and even popular discourse, are now reshaping the law's fundamental understandings of discrimination and fairness. . . .

Even if we cannot remove the bias, perhaps we can alter decisionmaking processes so that these biases are less likely to translate into behavior. . . .

[M]ost judges view themselves as objective and especially talented at fair decisionmaking. For instance, Rachlinski et al. found in one survey that 97 percent of judges (thirty-five out of thirty-six) believed that they were in the top quartile in "avoid[ing] racial prejudice in decisionmaking" relative to other judges attending the same conference. . . .

Eric Uhlmann and Geoffrey Cohen have demonstrated that when a person believes himself to be objective, such belief licenses him to act on his biases. In one study, they had participants choose either the candidate profile labeled "Gary" or the candidate profile labeled "Lisa" for the job of factory manager. Both candidate profiles, comparable on all traits, unambiguously showed strong organization skills but weak interpersonal skills. Half the participants were primed to view themselves as objective. The other half were left alone as control.

Those in the control condition gave the male and female candidates statistically indistinguishable hiring evaluations. But those who were manipulated to think of themselves as objective evaluated the male candidate higher (M=5.06 versus 3.75, p=0.039, d=0.76). Interestingly, this was not due to a malleability of merit effect, in which the participants reweighted the importance of either organizational skills or interpersonal skills in order to favor the man. Instead, the discrimination was caused by straight-out disparate evaluation, in which the Gary profile was rated as more interpersonally skilled than the Lisa profile by those primed to think themselves objective. . . . In short, thinking oneself to be objective seems ironically to lead one to be less objective and more susceptible to biases. Judges should therefore remind themselves that they are human and fallible, notwithstanding their status, their education, and the robe.

But is such a suggestion based on wishful thinking? Is there any evidence that education and reminders can actually help? There is some suggestive evidence from Emily Pronin, who has carefully studied the bias blindspot—the belief that others are biased but we ourselves are not. In one study, Emily Pronin and Matthew Kugler had a control group of Princeton students read an article from Nature about environmental pollution. By contrast, the treatment group read an article allegedly published in

Science that described various nonconscious influences on attitudes and behaviors. After reading an article, the participants were asked about their own objectivity as compared to their university peers. Those in the control group revealed the predictable bias blindspot and thought that they suffered from less bias than their peers. By contrast, those in the treatment group did not believe that they were more objective than their peers; moreover, their more modest self-assessments differed from those of the more confident control group. These results suggest that learning about nonconscious thought processes can lead people to be more skeptical about their own objectivity. . . .

* * *

Does this analysis have any implications for gender differences in judging?

PUTTING THEORY INTO PRACTICE

4-23. During his confirmation hearings for appointment to the U.S. Supreme Court in 1991, then-Judge Clarence Thomas was accused of sexually harassing a woman, Anita Hill, with whom he had worked at the EEOC. Justice Thomas responded in a furious tirade, accusing his accusers of a "high-tech lynching." Was Thomas using his Blackness as a shield against claims of sexism? Is it ever appropriate to assume the accused's race makes the charge more or less likely?

What role might gender play in how nominees respond to the confirmation process? In 2018, then-Judge Brett Kavanaugh, when accused of attempted rape in his high school years at his confirmation hearings, similarly lashed out in anger, calling the hearings a "national disgrace."[183] During her confirmation hearings to the Supreme Court, then-Judge Ketanji Brown Jackson, the first Black woman ever nominated to the U.S. Supreme Court, was subjected to aggressively hostile interrogations by Republican Senators "featuring political dog-whistling . . . toxic partisanship, bitter attacks and nasty questioning full of innuendo."[184] Senators misstated her record, insulted her intelligence, and pontificated about matters that had no relevance to Judge Jackson's qualifications.[185] Judge Jackson stood her ground but she never lost her cool, exhibiting the professionalism, grace, and calm that her questioners lacked. Did Jackson's gender and race force her to remain composed when male judges could use anger to their advantage? Does difference theory help explain the contrast in the responses by Kavanaugh and Jackson? Or are the different responses simply indicative of the racist and sexist dynamics of the process?

---

183. See Michael S. Rosenwald, "A High-Tech Lynching": How Brett Kavanaugh Took a Page from the Clarence Thomas Playbook, Wash. Post, Sept. 27, 2018. The anger pervades his own personal account of the hearings. See Clarence Thomas, My Grandfather's Son: A Memoir (2021).

184. Editorial, The Respectful Supreme Court Hearing That Wasn't, N.Y. Times, Mar. 24, 2022.

185. Questions included: "Do you believe child predators are misunderstood? Do you agree with this book that is being taught with kids that the babies are racist? Can you define a woman?" Id.

One commentator wrote that "juxtaposition of Jackson's calm, confident, professionalism with the hostile, cynical and contemptuous questioning by senators such as Texas senator Ted Cruz is an object lesson for the entire world on the ongoing dynamics of systemic racism in the United States."[186] To what extent is it also an object lesson about systemic sexism? Is "righteous indignation" a gendered phenomenon?

4-24. In a 2018 Atlantic article, a 37-year-old African-American associate reported that she often has to bring a male attorney with her to court even if he knows little about the case because "that older white man at the table carries some kind of credibility" with judges.[187] Could you see yourself doing this? Would you also do this if the judge was a woman?

3. Juries and Gender

The jury system reflects a tension between the right to be judged by one's peers, and the right to an impartial tribunal. The peremptory strike is both a potential aid to achieving these goals and an instrument of bias. On balance, should litigants be able to take account of their experiences and instincts about gender in using their peremptory strikes? Or is this an example of the kind of gender bias that should be eliminated, if possible, from the criminal legal system?

J.E.B. v. Alabama ex rel. T.B.

511 U.S. 127 (1994)

Justice BLACKMUN delivered the opinion of the Court, in which STEVENS, O'CONNOR, SOUTER, and GINSBURG, JJ., joined.

I

On behalf of [the mother of a minor child], respondent State of Alabama filed a complaint for paternity and child support against petitioner J.E.B. in the District Court of Jackson County, Alabama. . . . The trial court assembled a panel of 36 potential jurors, 12 males and 24 females. After the court excused three jurors for cause, only 10 of the remaining 33 jurors were male. The State then used 9 of its 10 peremptory strikes to remove male jurors; petitioner used all but one of his strikes to remove female jurors. As a result, all the selected jurors were female.

Before the jury was empaneled, petitioner objected to the State's peremptory challenges on the ground that they were exercised against male jurors solely on the basis of gender, in violation of the Equal Protection Clause. . . . Petitioner argued

---

186. Steve Phillips, Ketanji Brown Jackson Hearing Reveals Republicans' Racist Fears, Guardian, Mar. 25, 2022.

187. Lara Bazelon, What It Takes to Be a Trial Lawyer If You're Not a Man, Atlantic (Sept. 2018) (quoting Kadisha Phelps).

that the logic and reasoning of Batson v. Kentucky, which prohibits peremptory strikes solely on the basis of race, similarly forbids intentional discrimination on the basis of gender. The court rejected petitioner's claim and empaneled the all-female jury. The jury found petitioner to be the father of the child and the court entered an order directing him to pay child support. . . .

. . . Today we reaffirm what, by now, should be axiomatic: Intentional discrimination on the basis of gender by state actors violates the Equal Protection Clause, particularly where, as here, the discrimination serves to ratify and perpetuate invidious, archaic, and overbroad stereotypes about the relative abilities of men and women.

II

Discrimination on the basis of gender in the exercise of peremptory challenges is a relatively recent phenomenon. Gender-based peremptory strikes were hardly practicable for most of our country's existence, since, until the 19th century, women were completely excluded from jury service. So well-entrenched was this exclusion of women that in 1880 this Court, while finding that the exclusion of African-American men from juries violated the Fourteenth Amendment, expressed no doubt that a State "may confine the selection [of jurors] to males." Strauder v. West Virginia [1880].

Many States continued to exclude women from jury service well into the present century, despite the fact that women attained suffrage upon ratification of the Nineteenth Amendment in 1920. States that did permit women to serve on juries often erected other barriers, such as registration requirements and automatic exemptions, designed to deter women from exercising their right to jury service. . . .

. . . In this country, supporters of the exclusion of women from juries tended to couch their objections in terms of the ostensible need to protect women from the ugliness and depravity of trials. Women were thought to be too fragile and virginal to withstand the polluted courtroom atmosphere. . . .

This Court in Ballard v. United States [1946], first questioned the fundamental fairness of denying women the right to serve on juries. Relying on its supervisory powers over the federal courts, it held that women may not be excluded from the venire in federal trials in States where women were eligible for jury service under local law. In response to the argument that women have no superior or unique perspective, such that defendants are denied a fair trial by virtue of their exclusion from jury panels, the Court explained:

> It is said . . . that an all male panel drawn from the various groups within a community will be as truly representative as if women were included. The thought is that the factors which tend to influence the action of women are the same as those which influence the action of men — personality, background, economic status — and not sex. Yet it is not enough to say that women when sitting as jurors neither act nor tend to act as a class. Men likewise do not act like a class. . . . The truth is that the two sexes are not fungible; a community made up exclusively of one is different from a community composed of both; the subtle interplay of influence one on

the other is among the imponderables. To insulate the courtroom from either may not in a given case make an iota of difference. Yet a flavor, a distinct quality is lost if either sex is excluded. . . .

Fifteen years later, however, the Court still was unwilling to translate its appreciation for the value of women's contribution to civic life into an enforceable right to equal treatment under state laws governing jury service. In Hoyt v. Florida [1961], the Court found it reasonable, "despite the enlightened emancipation of women," to exempt women from mandatory jury service by statute, allowing women to serve on juries only if they volunteered to serve. The Court justified the differential exemption policy on the ground that women, unlike men, occupied a unique position "as the center of home and family life." . . .

In 1975, the Court finally repudiated the reasoning of *Hoyt* and . . . struck down, under the Sixth Amendment, an affirmative registration statute nearly identical to the one . . . [upheld in 1961 in Hoyt v. Florida]. We explained: "Restricting jury service to only special groups or excluding identifiable segments playing major roles in the community cannot be squared with the constitutional concept of jury trial." The diverse and representative character of the jury must be maintained "'partly as assurance of a diffused impartiality and partly because sharing in the administration of justice is a phase of civic responsibility.'" [Taylor v. Louisiana (1975).]

III

Taylor relied on Sixth Amendment principles, but the opinion's approach is consistent with the heightened equal protection scrutiny afforded gender-based classifications. . . .

While the prejudicial attitudes toward women in this country have not been identical to those held toward racial minorities, the similarities between the experiences of racial minorities and women, in some contexts, "overpower those differences." . . .

Certainly, with respect to jury service, African-Americans and women share a history of total exclusion, a history which came to an end for women many years after the embarrassing chapter in our history came to an end for African-Americans. . . . Under our equal protection jurisprudence, gender-based classifications require "an exceedingly persuasive justification" in order to survive constitutional scrutiny. . . .

Far from proffering an exceptionally persuasive justification for its gender-based peremptory challenges, respondent maintains that its decision to strike virtually all the males from the jury in this case "may reasonably have been based upon the perception, supported by history, that men otherwise totally qualified to serve upon a jury might be more sympathetic and receptive to the arguments of a man alleged in a paternity action to be the father of an out-of-wedlock child, while women equally qualified to serve upon a jury might be more sympathetic and receptive to the arguments of the complaining witness who bore the child." . . .

We shall not accept as a defense to gender-based peremptory challenges "the very stereotype the law condemns." . . . Respondent's rationale, not unlike those regularly expressed for gender-based strikes, is reminiscent of the arguments advanced to justify the total exclusion of women from juries. Respondent offers virtually no support for the conclusion that gender alone is an accurate predictor of juror's attitudes; yet it urges this Court to condone the same stereotypes that justified the wholesale exclusion of women from juries and the ballot box. Respondent seems to assume that gross generalizations that would be deemed impermissible if made on the basis of race are somehow permissible when made on the basis of gender.

Discrimination in jury selection, whether based on race or on gender, causes harm to the litigants, the community, and the individual jurors who are wrongfully excluded from participation in the judicial process. The litigants are harmed by the risk that the prejudice which motivated the discriminatory selection of the jury will infect the entire proceedings. . . . The community is harmed by the State's participation in the perpetuation of invidious group stereotypes and the inevitable loss of confidence in our judicial system that state-sanctioned discrimination in the courtroom engenders.

When state actors exercise peremptory challenges in reliance on gender stereotypes, they ratify and reinforce prejudicial views of the relative abilities of men and women. Because these stereotypes have wreaked injustice in so many other spheres of our country's public life, active discrimination by litigants on the basis of gender during jury selection "invites cynicism respecting the jury's neutrality and its obligation to adhere to the law." . . . The potential for cynicism is particularly acute in cases where gender-related issues are prominent, such as cases involving rape, sexual harassment, or paternity. . . .

In recent cases we have emphasized that individual jurors themselves have a right to nondiscriminatory jury selection procedures. . . . Contrary to respondent's suggestion, this right extends to both men and women. . . . All persons, when granted the opportunity to serve on a jury, have the right not to be excluded summarily because of discriminatory and stereotypical presumptions that reflect and reinforce patterns of historical discrimination. Striking individual jurors on the assumption that they hold particular views simply because of their gender is "practically a brand upon them, affixed by law, an assertion of their inferiority." Strauder v. West Virginia [1880]. It denigrates the dignity of the excluded juror, and, for a woman, reinvokes a history of exclusion from political participation. The message it sends to all those in the courtroom, and all those who may later learn of the discriminatory act, is that certain individuals, for no reason other than gender, are presumed unqualified by state actors to decide important questions upon which reasonable persons could disagree.

IV

Our conclusion that litigants may not strike potential jurors solely on the basis of gender does not imply the elimination of all peremptory challenges. . . . Parties still may remove jurors whom they feel might be less acceptable than others on the panel; gender simply may not serve as a proxy for bias. Parties may also exercise their peremptory challenges to remove from the venire any group or class of individuals normally subject to "rational basis" review. . . . Even strikes based on characteristics that are disproportionately associated with one gender could be appropriate, absent a showing of pretext.

If conducted properly, voir dire can inform litigants about potential jurors, making reliance upon stereotypical and pejorative notions about a particular gender or race both unnecessary and unwise. Voir dire provides a means of discovering actual or implied bias and a firmer basis upon which the parties may exercise their peremptory challenges intelligently. . . .

V

Equal opportunity to participate in the fair administration of justice is fundamental to our democratic system. It not only furthers the goals of the jury system. It reaffirms the promise of equality under the law — that all citizens, regardless of race, ethnicity, or gender, have the chance to take part directly in our democracy. . . .

Justice O'CONNOR, concurring.

I agree with the Court that the Equal Protection Clause prohibits the government from excluding a person from jury service on account of that person's gender. . . . But today's important blow against gender discrimination is not costless. I write separately to discuss some of these costs, and to express my belief that today's holding should be limited to the government's use of gender-based peremptory strikes.

The principal value of the peremptory is that it helps produce fair and impartial juries. Moreover, "[t]he essential nature of the peremptory challenge is that it is one exercised without a reason stated, without inquiry and without being subject to the court's control." . . . Indeed, often a reason for it cannot be stated, for a trial lawyer's judgments about a juror's sympathies are sometimes based on experienced hunches and educated guesses, derived from a juror's responses at voir dire or a juror's "bare looks and gestures." That a trial lawyer's instinctive assessment of a juror's predisposition cannot meet the high standards of a challenge for cause does not mean that the lawyer's instinct is erroneous. . . . Our belief that experienced lawyers will often correctly intuit which jurors are likely to be the least sympathetic, and our understanding that the lawyer will often be unable to explain the intuition, are the very reason we cherish the peremptory challenge. But, as we add, layer by layer, additional constitutional restraints on the use of the peremptory, we force lawyers to articulate what we know is often inarticulable.

In so doing we . . . increase the possibility that biased jurors will be allowed onto the jury, because sometimes a lawyer will be unable to provide an acceptable gender-neutral explanation even though the lawyer is in fact correct that the juror is unsympathetic. Similarly, in jurisdictions where lawyers exercise their strikes in open court, lawyers may be deterred from using their peremptories, out of the fear that if they are unable to justify the strike the court will seat a juror who knows that the striking party thought him unfit. Because I believe the peremptory remains an important litigator's tool and a fundamental part of the process of selecting impartial juries, our increasing limitation of it gives me pause.

Nor is the value of the peremptory challenge to the litigant diminished when the peremptory is exercised in a gender-based manner. We know that like race, gender matters. A plethora of studies make clear that in rape cases, for example, female jurors are somewhat more likely to vote to convict than male jurors. . . . Moreover, though there have been no similarly definitive studies regarding, for example, sexual harassment, child custody, or spousal or child abuse, one need not be a sexist to share the intuition that in certain cases a person's gender and resulting life experience will be relevant to his or her view of the case. "Jurors are not expected to come into the jury box and leave behind all that their human experience has taught them." . . . Individuals are not expected to ignore as jurors what they know as men — or women.

Today's decision severely limits a litigant's ability to act on this intuition, for the import of our holding is that any correlation between a juror's gender and attitudes is irrelevant as a matter of constitutional law. But to say that gender makes no difference as a matter of law is not to say that gender makes no difference as a matter of fact. . . . Today's decision is a statement that, in an effort to eliminate the potential discriminatory use of the peremptory, . . . gender is now governed by the special rule of relevance formerly reserved for race. Though we gain much from this statement, we cannot ignore what we lose. In extending *Batson* to gender we have added an additional burden to the state and federal trial process, taken a step closer to eliminating the peremptory challenge, and diminished the ability of litigants to act on sometimes accurate gender-based assumptions about juror attitudes.

These concerns reinforce my conviction that today's decision should be limited to a prohibition on the government's use of gender-based peremptory challenges. The Equal Protection Clause prohibits only discrimination by state actors. . . .

Accordingly, I adhere to my position that the Equal Protection Clause does not limit the exercise of peremptory challenges by private civil litigants and criminal defendants. . . . This case itself presents no state action dilemma, for here the State of Alabama itself filed the paternity suit on behalf of petitioner. But what of the next case? Will we, in the name of fighting gender discrimination, hold that the battered wife — on trial for wounding her abusive husband — is a state actor? Will we preclude her from using her peremptory challenges to ensure that the jury of her peers contains as many women members as possible? I assume we will, but I hope we will not.

Justice KENNEDY, concurring in the judgment.
I am in full agreement with the Court.
The importance of individual rights to our analysis prompts a further observation concerning what I conceive to be the intended effect of today's decision. We do not prohibit racial and gender bias in jury selection only to encourage it in jury deliberations. . . .

In this regard, it is important to recognize that a juror sits not as a representative of a racial or sexual group but as an individual citizen. Nothing would be more pernicious to the jury system than for society to presume that persons of different backgrounds go to the jury room to voice prejudice. . . . The jury pool must be representative of the community, but that is a structural mechanism for preventing bias, not enfranchising it. . . . Thus, the Constitution guarantees a right only to an impartial jury, not to a jury composed of members of a particular race or gender. . . .

Justice SCALIA, with whom THE CHIEF JUSTICE and Justice THOMAS join, dissenting.
Today's opinion is an inspiring demonstration of how thoroughly up-to-date and right-thinking we Justices are in matters pertaining to the sexes (or as the

Court would have it, the genders), and how sternly we disapprove the male chauvinist attitudes of our predecessors. . . . The parties do not contest that discrimination on the basis of sex[1] is subject to what our cases call "heightened scrutiny". . . .

The core of the Court's reasoning is that peremptory challenges on the basis of any group characteristic subject to heightened scrutiny are inconsistent with the guarantee of the Equal Protection Clause. That conclusion can be reached only by focusing unrealistically upon individual exercises of the peremptory challenge, and ignoring the totality of the practice. Since all groups are subject to the peremptory challenge (and will be made the object of it, depending upon the nature of the particular case) it is hard to see how any group is denied equal protection. . . . That explains why peremptory challenges coexisted with the Equal Protection Clause for 120 years. This case is a perfect example of how the system as a whole is even-handed. While the only claim before the Court is petitioner's complaint that the prosecutor struck male jurors, for every man struck by the government petitioner's own lawyer struck a woman. To say that men were singled out for discriminatory treatment in this process is preposterous. The situation would be different if both sides systematically struck individuals of one group, so that the strikes evinced group-based animus and served as a proxy for segregated venire lists. . . . The pattern here, however, displays not a systemic sex-based animus but each side's desire to get a jury favorably disposed to its case. That is why the Court's characterization of respondent's argument as "reminiscent of the arguments advanced to justify the total exclusion of women from juries" is patently false. Women were categorically excluded from juries because of doubt that they were competent; women are stricken from juries by peremptory challenge because of doubt that they are well disposed to the striking party's case. . . . There is discrimination and dishonor in the former, and not in the latter—which explains the 106-year interlude between our holding that exclusion from juries on the basis of race was unconstitutional, Strauder v. West Virginia, and our holding that peremptory challenges on the basis of race were unconstitutional, Batson v. Kentucky.

Although the Court's legal reasoning in this case is largely obscured by anti-male-chauvinist oratory, to the extent such reasoning is discernible it invalidates much more than sex-based strikes. . . . [The Court's analysis] places all peremptory strikes based on any group characteristic at risk, since they can all be denominated "stereotypes." Perhaps, however (though I do not see why it should be so), only the stereotyping of groups entitled to heightened or strict scrutiny constitutes "the very stereotype the law condemns"—so that other stereotyping (e.g., wide-eyed blondes and football players are dumb) remains OK. Or perhaps when the Court refers to "impermissible stereotypes," it means the adjective to be limiting rather than

---

1. Throughout this opinion, I shall refer to the issue as sex discrimination rather than (as the Court does) gender discrimination. The word "gender" has acquired the new and useful connotation of cultural or attitudinal characteristics (as opposed to physical characteristics) distinctive to the sexes. That is to say, gender is to sex as feminine is to female and masculine to male. The present case does not involve peremptory strikes exercised on the basis of femininity or masculinity (as far as it appears, effeminate men did not survive the prosecution's peremptories). The case involves, therefore, sex discrimination plain and simple.

descriptive—so that we can expect to learn from the Court's peremptory/ stereo-typing jurisprudence in the future which stereotypes the Constitution frowns upon and which it does not. . . .

[M]ake no mistake about it: there really is no substitute for the peremptory. Voir dire (though it can be expected to expand as a consequence of today's decision) cannot fill the gap. The biases that go along with group characteristics tend to be biases that the juror himself does not perceive, so that it is no use asking about them. It is fruitless to inquire of a male juror whether he harbors any subliminal prejudice in favor of unwed fathers. . . .

In order, it seems to me, not to eliminate any real denial of equal protection, but simply to pay conspicuous obeisance to the equality of the sexes, the Court imperils a practice that has been considered an essential part of fair jury trial since the dawn of the common law. The Constitution of the United States neither requires nor permits this vandalizing of our people's traditions.

For these reasons, I dissent.

NOTE ON EQUALITY AND IMPARTIALITY IN THE JURY CONTEXT

As Justice O'Connor notes, there are some cases in which gender does make a difference. Does pretending otherwise improve the accuracy of the jury system? What exactly does impartiality mean in the context of the constitutional right to a jury of one's peers? Is it that a potential juror should have no views on any relevant subject? Or that jury perspectives in some sense should be drawn from a cross-section of the community, and "not arbitrarily skewed for or against any particular group or characteristic"? Should the goal be proportional representation on juries? Is there a tension between prohibiting gender-based peremptory strikes, which assumes that gender is or should be irrelevant to a juror's capacity to serve, and guaranteeing that jurors are selected from a fair cross-section of the community, which assumes that diversity in juror representation matters? Consider Marina Angel's discussion of teaching Susan Glaspell's short story, "A Jury of Her Peers," in which women interpret the facts surrounding a woman investigated for the murder of her husband very differently than the male officials conducting the investigation.[188] Angel uses the story, first produced as a play in 1916, to illustrate the contemporary importance of incorporating diverse gender perspectives into legal decision-making.

Although *J.E.B.* has met with considerable support in theory, it has proven more problematic in practice. Part of the difficulty, Charles Ogletree notes, is that while gender may be an imperfect proxy for relevant attitudes, it is not an entirely irrational one. The stereotypes that influence lawyers in jury selection may also be ones that "affect the behavior of men and women in the jury box."[189] Moreover,

---

188. Marina Angel, Teaching Susan Glaspell's A Jury of Her Peers and Trifles, 53 J. Legal Educ. 548 (2003); Marina Angel, Susan Glaspell's Trifles and A Jury of Her Peers: Woman Abuse in a Literary and Legal Context, 45 Buff. L. Rev. 779 (1997).

189. Charles Ogletree, Just Say No! A Proposal to Eliminate Racially Discriminatory Uses of Peremptory Challenges, 31 Am. Crim. L. Rev. 1099, 1104 (1994).

inventive lawyers can always summon nondiscriminatory reasons for a challenge, and most trial courts are reluctant to reject them as pretextual unless they are patently implausible or clearly incorporate impermissible stereotypes. According to the Supreme Court, *any* reason, no matter how "silly or superstitious," will be sufficient, as long as it is not demonstrably a pretext for discrimination.[190]

Appellate courts are reluctant to reverse lower court rulings justifying peremptory challenges, which often turn on factual determinations of credibility. Lawyers who feel ethically obligated to gain sympathetic hearings for their clients may be equally reluctant to acknowledge — even to themselves — the role that impermissible stereotypes play in their juror selections. Experienced litigators and jury consultants believe that identities such as race, sex, ethnicity, and religion routinely figure in juror selection.[191]

Given these evidentiary hurdles, it is perhaps unsurprising that claims of gender discrimination in peremptory challenges are relatively rare. A survey of cases in the first five years under *J.E.B* found only 127 reported complaints and 23 reversals in all state and federal systems. Clearly the ruling has not been as burdensome as critics predicted. But neither has it been as effective as supporters hoped. Surveyed cases include numerous examples of peremptories that have been sustained despite the stereotypes underlying them. Women have been struck for being "timid," "not assertive," "weak," "vacillating," overweight, feminist, and single mothers.[192] Other explanations that courts have accepted are that the potential juror seemed "odd" or "not very bright," "dyed her hair," was "over-educated," or looked like a drug dealer.[193]

In a 2016 case, Foster v. Chatman, the Supreme Court reversed a thirty-year-old murder conviction because the prosecutors relied on illegal race-based peremptory challenges.[194] With respect to one juror, the Court found the prosecutors' "neutral" explanations to be pretextual because they had "willingly accepted white jurors with the same traits" that rendered the Black juror "unattractive." Is this comparative analysis likely to succeed in challenging gender-based peremptories? Which traits and qualities are most likely to motivate the exclusion of female jurors today?

PUTTING THEORY INTO PRACTICE

4-25. In the trial of O.J. Simpson for murder of his battered white wife, jury consultants for both sides found that Black women were the group most likely to

---

190. Purkett v. Elem, 514 U.S. 765, 768 (1995).

191. See Leonard Post, A Loaded Box of Stereotypes, Nat'l L.J., Apr. 25, 2005, at A1, A18.

192. Susan Hightower, Sex and the Peremptory Strike: An Empirical Analysis of J.E.B. v. Alabama's First Five Years, 52 Stan. L. Rev. 895, 924-26 (2000).

193. Illegal Racial Discrimination in Jury Selection: A Continuing Legacy, Equal Justice Initiative 18, 23-25 (2010); Alexander Papachristou, Blind Goddess: A Reader on Race and Justice 142-49 (2011); Gilad Edelman, Why Is It So Easy for Prosecutors to Strike Black Jurors?, New Yorker (June 5, 2015).

194. Foster v. Chatman, 578 U.S. 488 (2016).

vote for acquittal; they were least likely to credit incriminating domestic violence evidence, or to respond favorably to Marcia Clark, a white woman who was the lead prosecutor.[195] If you had been one of the defense lawyers in the *Simpson* case, would you have tried to use your peremptory strikes to increase the representation of Black women on the jury?

4-26. How should courts deal with strikes based on an individual's sexual orientation or gender identity?[196] Should lawyers be entitled to ask jurors questions about conduct that might suggest non-heterosexual behavior or non-cisgender identity?

4-27. Consider a case in which the defendant was on trial for violating a restraining order that protected his battered wife. The prosecutor used her three peremptory challenges to strike the first three jurors (all male) on the panel who had indicated prior involvement with a protective order. The defendant was convicted and appealed, claiming gender bias in jury selection. The prosecutor admitted that she assumed that men involved in such a dispute would likely have been defendants rather than complainants. Does the defendant have grounds for appeal?[197]

4. *Women as Criminal Defendants*

At all stages of the criminal legal system, gender differences may have differential effects on women, especially women of color. This section addresses these differences specifically in the context of police interrogation and criminal sentencing.

Janet E. Ainsworth

In a Different Register: The Pragmatics of Powerlessness in Police Interrogation

103 Yale L.J. 259, 260, 286–87, 301-02 (1993)

Imagine that you are in police custody, about to be interrogated concerning a crime. Before the questioning begins, the interrogating officer tells you that you have the right to remain silent and to have an attorney present during questioning. If you decide to invoke your right to the presence of an attorney, you must be very careful about how you phrase your request. . . .

---

195. Albert W. Alschuler, How to Win the Trial of the Century: The Ethics of Lord Brougham and the O.J. Simpson Defense Team, 29 McGeorge L. Rev. 311, 312 (1998).

196. SmithKline Beecham Corp. v. Abbott Lab'ys, 740 F.3d 471, 484 (9th Cir. 2014) (striking down the use of peremptory challenges based on sexual orientation).

197. See State v. Jensen, 76 P.3d 188 (Utah Ct. App. 2003); Debora L. Threedy, Legal Archeology and Feminist Legal Theory: A Case Study of Gender and Domestic Violence, 29 Women's Rts. L. Rep. 171 (2008).

Whether any particular person undergoing police interrogation will adopt the mode of expression that I have called the female register is not a random matter. Rather, some distinct segments of the population — women, members of certain ethnic communities, and the socioeconomically powerless — are more likely than others to speak in this register. Thus, suspects who fall into any of these categories are less apt to use the mode of expression that will give them the highest degree of constitutional protection. . . .

Whether a speaker adopts one register of speech rather than another depends to some degree on the specific situation in which the speech occurs. Therefore, pragmatic analysis of any particular interaction must take into account the context of that interaction, including the power relations inherent in the situation. A communicative context in which the speaker is, or is made to feel, relatively powerless enhances that individual's tendency to adopt the mode of expression characteristic of the female register. . . .

In a majority of jurisdictions, the standard governing invocation of the right to counsel affords greater protection to suspects who speak in a direct and assertive manner. Implicit in the majority doctrine is the assumption that direct and assertive speech — a mode of expression more characteristic of men than women — is, or should be, the norm. This kind of gender bias, which tacitly treats prototypically male behavior and experience (confident, assertive, powerful) as a synonym for human behavior and experience, is especially pernicious because it is generally invisible and therefore immune to criticism. The androcentric nature of such legal doctrines can easily be mistaken for true gender neutrality. As this study demonstrates, the law's incorporation of a male normative standard may be invisible but it is not inconsequential. Those whose behavior fails to conform to these presumed norms of behavior encoded within legal doctrine are penalized.

The framers of the majority doctrine never asked the "woman question," and failed to shape legal standards to take into account the characteristic speech patterns of women. The insight derived from asking the woman question — that the underpinnings of legal doctrine unconsciously and unwittingly incorporate a bias favoring males — raises another question. If women were not considered in the framing and interpretation of legal doctrine, are there other groups whose perspective may likewise be missing from the law?

* * *

Historically, women appear to be underrepresented at many stages of the criminal legal system. A 2015 study found that women are 46 percent less likely to be held in jail prior to trial, get bail set in amounts that are about 54 percent lower than what men are required to pay, and are 58 percent less likely to be sentenced to prison.[198] Do these data undercut the Ainsworth critique, above, or hide its reality?

Ainsworth identifies five features of the "female" register: (1) use of hedge words, like "kind of," "I think," and maybe; (2) adding tag questions to the end of

---

198. See Natalie Goulette et al., From Initial Appearance to Sentencing: Do Female Defendants Experience Disparate Treatment?, 43 J. Crim. Just. 406 (2015).

a declarative sentence, such as "isn't it?" or "shouldn't I?"; (3) use of modal verbs, like "may," "might," and "could"; (4) avoiding the imperative grammatical mood (e.g., saying "Would you call my lawyer?" instead of "Call my lawyer."); and (5) use of a rising inflection in making a declarative sentence.[199] How might these language patterns affect women's outcomes with respect to other issues covered in this book, like employment, sexual assault, and education?

How should the law take into account that the powerless tend to speak in a less confident "register"? Ainsworth describes three standards that lower courts have used to assess the adequacy of invocation of the constitutional right to counsel during custodial interrogation:

> 1) the so-called threshold-of-clarity standard, under which an attempted invocation of the right to counsel must satisfy a certain threshold of clarity before it will be considered effective; 2) the per se invocation standard, under which any postwarning reference by the suspect to a desire for counsel is considered a per se invocation of the right to counsel, necessitating the cessation of police-initiated questioning; and 3) the clarification standard, under which an ambiguous or equivocal invocation of the right to counsel permits the police to continue the exchange in order to clarify the suspect's intent before proceeding with further questioning.[200]

In light of Ainsworth's critique, which standard seems most appropriate? Are there other measures that should also be taken to reduce the penalty for speaking in a "female register"?

Is "female register" the right term? To what extent might the term be overinclusive, capturing women who speak assertively? Can you propose a better term?

Although there are more men in prison than women, since 1980, the rate of growth for female imprisonment has been twice that of men.[201] As of 2020, there are 1.2 million women in prison or otherwise under the supervision of the criminal legal system.[202] Women of color are disproportionately represented. In 2019, the imprisonment rate for African American women was 1.7 times that of white women, and Latina women were 1.3 times more likely to be imprisoned than white women.[203]

Traditionally, judges considering the individual circumstances of defendants when determining punishment gave women more lenient sentences than men who committed similar crimes because they were often perceived as less dangerous and culpable (due to less violent behavior and criminal records), more open to rehabilitation, and more likely to have primary caretaking responsibilities that increased the costs of incarceration. Such factors, coupled with chivalrous or paternalistic views of primarily male judges, led to significant advantages for some women, and

---

199. Janet E. Ainsworth, In a Different Register: The Pragmatics of Powerlessness in Police Interrogation, 103 Yale L.J. 259, 276-82 (1993)

200. Id. at 301-02.

201. The Sentencing Project, Incarcerated Women and Girls (Nov. 24, 2020). Of all youth arrests, the percentage of girls has risen dramatically. Id.

202. Id.

203. Id.

for some crimes.[204] However, women who commit particularly egregious crimes have tended to receive even harsher sentences than men, presumably because they deviate so far from accepted notions of femininity.[205] This phenomenon operates particularly against African-American women, who are often viewed as more independent and less worthy of protection.[206]

During the 1980s, in a general effort to promote more consistency and proportionality in punishment, Congress passed the Sentencing Reform Act, which attempted to prescribe uniform sentences for similar conduct. The Federal Sentencing Commission established the Federal Sentencing Guidelines to shift the focus of punishment away from the characteristics of the defendant to the characteristics of the crime. The Guidelines prohibited consideration of traditional "individualizing" factors, except in "extraordinary" situations, and specified that family ties and responsibilities were not ordinarily relevant. Supreme Court decisions have determined that Federal Sentencing Guidelines cannot be mandatory, although they remain as advisory. States, which handle the vast majority of criminal cases, have their own guidelines.

The Federal Guidelines permit a downward adjustment for family circumstances only in truly exceptional circumstances. Being a single parent is not generally viewed as an exceptional circumstance. A primary concern is that greater discretion for family circumstances would reward women for their status as mothers or, alternatively, penalize women who do not have children. Pregnancy is also not a mitigating factor on the theory that giving a downward departure for that status would send "an obvious message to all female defendants that pregnancy is 'a way out.' "[207] Is this a reasonable approach?

Consider the fact that about two-thirds of incarcerated women are mothers, and the consequences for both them and their children are often tragic. Most states remove infants from imprisoned mothers almost immediately after birth, and these women do not have the opportunity to nurse or bond with their newborns. Many of these children land in foster care. Children of imprisoned parents are five to six times as likely as their peers to end up behind bars, and four times as likely to drop out of school.[208]

---

204. See Stephanie Bontrager et al., Gender and Sentencing: A Meta-Analysis of Contemporary Research, 16 J. Gender Race & Just. 249, 351-54, 360 (2013); Nancy Gertner, Women Offenders and the Sentencing Guidelines, 14 Yale J.L. & Feminism 291, 292 (2002); Amy Farrell et al., Intersections of Gender and Race in Federal Sentencing: Examining Court Contexts and the Effects of Representative Court Authorities, 14 J. Gender Race & Just. 85, 89-92 (2010); Carissa Byrne Hessick, Race and Gender as Explicit Sentencing Factors, 14 J. Gender Race & Just. 127, 139-40 (2010).

205. Ryan Elias Newby, Evil Women and Innocent Victims: The Effect of Gender on California Sentences for Domestic Homicide, 22 Hastings Women's L.J. 113, 119-20, 155, 156 (2011).

206. See Goulette et al., supra note 198.

207. United States v. Pozzy, 902 F.2d 133, 138-39 (1st Cir. 1990).

208. Ann Booker Loper & Elena Hontoria Tuerk, Parenting Programs for Incarcerated Parents: Current Research and Future Directions, 17 Crim. Just. Pol'y Rev. 407, 408 (2006).

Women in prison have multiple challenges in caring for themselves and their families. More than half experienced sexual abuse as adults or children, 60 percent struggle with substance abuse, and three-quarters have some symptoms of mental illness.[209] Mental and reproductive health care services for inmates are grossly inadequate.[210] Given that pregnancy is a sex-linked characteristic (cisgender men do not become pregnant), and women have disproportionate responsibility for children, does the current family circumstances approach further equality, or undermine it? What type of equality?

In 1994, President Nelson Mandela of the Republic of South Africa signed a Presidential Act providing an early release from prison for certain categories of prisoners, including "all mothers in prison on 10 May 1994, with minor children under the age of twelve (12) years." Fathers were not included. President Mandela explained that he was motivated predominantly by a concern for children who had been deprived of the nurturing and care that their mothers would ordinarily have provided.[211] Today, the law of South Africa requires that before a caregiver is sentenced to prison, the court must seriously consider the impact of imprisonment and, if possible, keep the offender out of prison through an alternative such as correctional supervision.[212] While this law is facially gender-neutral, another South African law provides for children to remain with their incarcerated mothers for two years.[213] Would this approach be constitutional in the United States?

A long prison sentence is more likely to interfere with the rights of women to procreate, given their finite period of reproduction. In addition, the risks of exposure to sexual violence are greater for female than for male prisoners.[214] Should either of these factors should be taken into account at sentencing?

Some evidence indicates that gender-neutral risk-assessment instruments that are used to determine the risks that offenders pose to society overestimate the risks of recidivism for female offenders. Should courts be required to correct for these biases?[215]

---

209. See sources cited in Carolyn Sufrin, Jailcare: Finding the Safety Net for Women Behind Bars 10 (2017).

210. For inadequate mental health and addiction treatment, see The Sentencing Project, To Build a Better Criminal Justice System (Marc Mauer and Kate Epstein, eds., 2012). For inadequate prenatal, contraception, and abortion services see Sufrin, supra note 209, at 10-14.

211. President of the Republic of South Africa v. Hugo, 1997 (4) SA 1 (CC).

212. See Ann Skelton, blog post, Children in Prison with Their Mothers—South Africa Leading the Way (Apr. 22, 2016).

213. Id.

214. Mirko Bagaric & Brienna Bagaric, Mitigating the Crime That Is the Over Imprisonment of Women: Why Orange Should Not Be the New Black, 41 Vt. L. Rev. 537, 563, 565, 567-71 (2017). Some evidence suggests that the risk of sexual abuse is three times higher for female than for male prisoners. Id. Although women constitute only 7 percent of the state prison population, they comprise 46 percent of sexual abuse victims. Christina Piecora, Female Inmates and Sexual Assault, Jurist (Sept. 15, 2014).

215. Jennifer Skeem & John Monahan, Gender, Risk Assessment and Sanctioning: The Cost of Treating Women Like Men, 40 Law & Hum. Behav. 580 (2016).

In the United States, one of the factors "not ordinarily relevant" to determining whether to depart from the Federal Sentencing Guidelines is a defendant's mental or emotional condition, although those factors may affect determinations of guilt, as in cases where the defense is insanity. In one well-publicized case, Andrea Yates, who suffered from severe postpartum depression, drowned her five children, ages six months to seven years, in the family bathtub. What facts would you need before deciding on guilt and sentencing in the Yates case? One commentator explains:

> The "baby blues," or "blues," occurs in fifty to seventy percent of women in the first six to eight weeks after birth; symptoms include crying, general depression, and fatigue. The "blues" does not impair a mother's judgment and is probably not a disorder or disease. Postpartum depression occurs in ten to twenty percent of women and may persist for one year. It is categorized as a type of reaction depression and involves feelings of hopelessness, inadequacy, anxiety, and moodiness. Although studies are few, the level of support that the mother receives from the father and family is more determinative of the depression than are demographic and biological factors. Postpartum psychosis occurs in one to two of every one thousand births and can lead to suicide or infanticide. It involves a major deviation from the normal processes of thinking, behavior, and emotion. Emotional reactions may be inappropriate to the circumstances, and actions may not be related to facts. For example, a mother may say that she sees the room upside down, express concern that a small pimple on her child's face is a misplaced testis, or fear that the hospital staff is part of a conspiracy to kill the baby. Anxiety can lead to panic attacks; a mother often has obsessive thoughts about harming the baby by putting it in the oven, drowning it, cutting off its body parts, or dropping it from an elevated surface. Hospitalization is necessary for the protection of both the mother and the child.[216]

Is compassion appropriate in the Andrea Yates case? Does it matter that postpartum depression is a female-specific defense? One study of twenty-four cases in which postpartum psychosis was offered as a defense found that eight women were acquitted and four were given probation, while ten were sentenced to between three and twenty years, and two received life sentences.[217] Are those disparities defensible? Yates was convicted for the murders of three of the children. A jury deliberated for forty minutes before sentencing her to life in prison instead of the death penalty. Her conviction was subsequently reversed. On retrial, she was found not guilty by reason of insanity and sentenced to an indefinite civil commitment.

Should sentencing be affected by a woman's involvement in a controlling relationship? The issue frequently arises in the context of drug conspiracies. A significant number of the female defendants involved in those conspiracies — sometimes called "women of circumstance" — are "wives, mothers, sisters, daughters,

---

216. Michele Connell, The Postpartum Psychosis Defense and Feminism: More or Less Justice for Women?, 63 Case W. Res. L. Rev. 143, 146-47 (2002).

217. Id. at 147-48.

girlfriends, and nieces, who become involved in crime because of fear, financial dependence or romantic attachment arising from relationships with male drug traffickers."[218] Many are "desperate, unsuspecting or coerced women who often have no prior criminal history and serve as the sole caretakers of young children," charged with conspiracy and subject to harsh sentencing laws.[219] Women may also suffer disproportionate sentences, either because they refuse to cooperate with the prosecution, out of loyalty or fear, or else because they do not know enough valuable information to obtain a reduced sentence. A "safety valve" in the federal Violent Crime Control and Drug Enforcement Act of 1994 provides relief to non-violent, low-level drug offenders who cooperate with the authorities, but this will not help women too fearful to cooperate or too uninformed to provide valuable evidence. Nor does it assist women facing state charges.[220]

Consider the case of Kemba Smith, a student at Hampton University with no prior criminal record. She became involved with a man eight years older, who was the ringleader of a cocaine enterprise. By the time Smith realized that her boyfriend was a drug dealer, he was abusing her, and she feared retaliation (he eventually killed his best friend for informing on him). Smith never handled any of the drugs, but she received a twenty-four-year prison sentence for conspiracy to distribute cocaine. President Clinton pardoned her after six years of incarceration and a mass media campaign.[221] What sentence would have been appropriate? Would women like Smith be more likely to engender sympathy from juries if they were white and upper-class, like Yates?

PUTTING THEORY INTO PRACTICE

4-28. A criminal defendant, charged with first-degree rape and indecent behavior with a juvenile, claimed this statement was his request for an attorney: "If y'all, this is how I feel, if y'all think I did it, I know that I didn't do it so why don't you just give me a lawyer dawg, cause this is not what's up." Should this constitute an invocation of counsel that warrants termination of a police interview?[222] Do you make any assumptions about the race or gender of the defendant? Should it matter?

4-29. A young woman, referred to at the time as "Miss America Bandit," was convicted of a string of bank robberies. At sentencing, the judge ordered a downward departure based on the defendant's domination by her boyfriend, even though there were no indications of physical abuse. The judge's comments during the sentencing hearing included: "men have exercised traditional control over

---

218. Shimica Gaskins, Note, "Women of Circumstance" — The Effects of Mandatory Minimum Sentencing on Women Minimally Involved in Drug Crimes, 41 Am. Crim. L. Rev. 1533, 1534 (2004).

219. Id. at 1536.

220. Id. at 1547.

221. See id. at 1535.

222. State v. Demesme, 228 So. 3d 1206, 1206 (La. 2017) (upholding denial of defendant's motion to suppress the statement obtained during the interview).

the activities of women, and I'm not going to ignore that, no matter how much flak I get from women's lib"; and "I think it's a fact of life that men can exercise a Svengali influence over women"; and "women are a soft touch, particularly if sex is involved."[223]

Is this judge taking the social reality of the defendant into consideration, or is he instead reasoning from his own understanding of gender differences? If the latter, should this be a legitimate consideration in sentencing or impermissible gender stereotyping?

4-30. In 2016, Brock Turner, a white Stanford University athlete, was convicted of rape of an incapacitated person (an unconscious, intoxicated woman), along with two related crimes, which together carried a maximum punishment of fourteen years and a minimum of two years in prison. On the recommendation of the probation office, Judge Aaron Persky sentenced him to six months in jail (which was reduced to three months with good behavior) and ordered him to register as a sex offender and participate in a sex offender rehabilitation program.[224] The judge, himself a former Stanford athlete, said that his decision to impose a lesser sentence than the six years recommended by the prosecutor reflected the defendant's lack of a prior criminal record or likely danger to others, his intoxication at the time of the incident, thirty-nine character letters from friends and family that indicated "a period of, essentially, good behavior," the "severe impact" of a prison sentence, and the adverse collateral consequences that the defendant had already suffered from the felony conviction and the publicity accompanying it.[225]

The Turner case attracted a firestorm of protest, exacerbated by a letter from Turner's father, who asserted that the verdict was a "steep price to pay for 20 minutes of action."[226] Although the defendant expressed regret for the incident, he blamed the campus drinking culture and "sexual promiscuity," and even claimed the victim seemed to enjoy the experience.[227] After the victim's statement went viral, activists launched a successful recall campaign against the judge. A review of the sentence showed no evidence of a pattern of bias by Persky. Was the recall justified? Do you think a female judge would have given the same or different sentence, or explained the sentence differently? Would a female judge have been as likely to

---

223. The case is United States v. Mast, No. CR-88-0720-AAH-1 (C.D. Cal. 1989), rev'd on other grounds, 925 F.2d 1472 (9th Cir. 1991); see also John Griffith, Woman Faces Counts in Bank Case, Oregonian, Feb. 4, 1992, at C8; Kim Murphy, "Soft Touch" Bandit Gets a Break from Judge on Term, L.A. Times, May 13, 1989.

224. Liam Stack, Light Sentence for Brock Turner in Stanford Rape Case Draws Outrage, N.Y. Times, June 6, 2016, at A15; Thomas Fuller, Court Papers Give Insight into Stanford Sex Assault, N.Y. Times, June 12, 2016, at A8.

225. Sam Levin, Stanford Sexual Assault: Read the Full Text of the Judge's Controversial Decision, Guardian (June 14, 2016).

226. For the funds raised, see Julia Ioffe, When the Punishment Feels Like a Crime, Huff. Post (June 1, 2018).

227. Emily Bazelon, Why the Stanford Rape Conviction Actually Represents Progress, N.Y. Times Mag., June 9, 2016; see also Abby Jackson, 39 Separate Letters Pleaded for a Lenient Sentence, Bus. Insider (June 15, 2016); Eliana Dockterman, On Campuses, "Party Culture" No Longer Excuses Rape, Time, June 27, 2016, at 21.

be recalled? In an era of mass incarceration, partly caused by excessively harsh sentences, how would you evaluate the trade-offs between ensuring appropriate sanctions and discouraging empathy and leniency by elected judges? Is this an example of feminist concerns being co-opted into the mass incarceration agenda?

4-31. Do you assume that when women become terrorists, it is because they are under the influence of the men in their lives? The evidence shows that women have long been voluntarily involved in terrorism and that female terrorists, for strategic reasons, are actually more successful and more deadly than male terrorists on a per-episode basis.[228] Being a parent is no guarantee to the contrary; one of the 2015 San Bernardino terrorists was the mother of a six-month-old infant.[229] And yet, the debates over asylum and immigration continue to assume that women and their children are the victims of terrorism, rather than potential perpetrators.[230] Do any of the five theories discussed above provide a helpful perspective in understanding women's participation in terrorism? Do any help explain the societal reactions to, and assumptions about, women and terrorism?

4-32. The issues raised in this section were traditionally referred to as issues relating to the "criminal justice system." Given the various biases and injustices currently embedded in that system, only some of which are referred to in this section, is it appropriate to continue to use the word "justice"? If not, is there a more satisfactory alternative?

4-33. Much of this chapter assumes, in one way or another, that women have characteristics that are substantially different from men's characteristics. Do you believe this is true? If not, why is the concept of women's differences so resilient? If so, why does the law, by and large, ignore those differences? Formal equality assumes that most differences are exaggerated and should not have the consequences society gives them and that acting on those differences, even if they are real, only serves to reinforce them. Substantive equality assumes that these differences must be taken into account to "level the playing field." Nonsubordination theory assumes that these differences are socially constructed to further male dominance. Difference theory assumes that women's characteristics may, in some cases at least, provide a better model for society than those of men. From among these assumptions, which do you think is most accurate? Which should the law adopt? Are the answers to these two questions necessarily the same? Why or why not?

---

228. Jayne Huckerby, When Women Become Terrorists, N.Y. Times, Jan. 21, 2015, at A27; Fionnuala Ní Aoláin, Situating Women in Counterterrorism Discourses: Undulating Masculinities and Luminal Femininities, 93 B.U. L. Rev. 1085, 1092 (2013).

229. Some thought this fact made the incident especially "twisted." See San Bernardino: The Most Twisted Terrorist Plot Yet, Daily Beast (Dec. 4, 2015).

230. See, e.g., UNHCR Appeals for Urgent Action to Address Deteriorating Humanitarian Situation in Calais (Sept. 26, 2014), http://www.unhcr.org/542563199.html.

CHAPTER 5
AUTONOMY

For women's rights advocates, equality is a critical value, but so, too, is autonomy. This chapter shifts the emphasis from women having what men have to women being able to stand on their own, make their own decisions, and pursue their own notion of a life well lived.

The concept of autonomy is woven deeply into Anglo-American liberal legal premises. The law governing contracts, torts, and crimes typically assumes that the individual is capable of formulating a specific "intent" to act, of exercising free "choice" or "consent," and of behaving as a "reasonable" person. Women's rights advocates make similar assumptions when they argue that women should have freedom to control their own lives and make their own sexual and reproductive choices.

Contemporary social theory has challenged the Enlightenment view of the self as autonomous and capable of acting independently of external influence. Today, individuals are more often understood as constituted through multiple sources of identity and as subject to social, institutional, and ideological forces that construct and constrain their desires, choices, and perceptions of reality. This more complex view reveals limitations in the traditional view of autonomy and underscores the need for pragmatic strategies that address the less visible constraints on people's options. From this vantage point, freedom is a relative concept rather than an absolute one, but the assumption remains that, in most matters, more is better than less.

Typically, autonomy is thought to reside in the individual person and means the right to be free from interference by others. The contemporary women's rights movement, however, has often considered relationships as the foundation of autonomy rights and has argued for concepts of autonomy that encompass not just freedom from coercion but also the freedom to flourish. This chapter considers both forms of autonomy in the context of an array of issues relating to sexual autonomy, reproductive rights, and economic security.

A.   SEX AND CONSENT

1.   "Statutory" Rape: The (Ir)relevance of Consent

One of the most difficult and contested issues in the law of rape is that of consent. The chapter begins with the law of statutory rape, which criminalizes sex with individuals below a certain age, who lack the legal capacity to consent to sex.

641

Michael M. v. Superior Court of Sonoma County

450 U.S. 464 (1981)

Justice REHNQUIST announced the judgment of the Court and delivered an opinion, in which THE CHIEF JUSTICE, JUSTICE STEWART, and JUSTICE POWELL joined.

The question presented in this case is whether California's "statutory rape" law . . . violates the Equal Protection Clause of the Fourteenth Amendment. § 261.5 defines unlawful sexual intercourse as "an act of sexual intercourse accomplished with a female not the wife of the perpetrator, where the female is under the age of 18 years." The statute thus makes men alone criminally liable for the act of sexual intercourse.

In July 1978, a complaint was filed in the Municipal Court of Sonoma County, Cal., alleging that petitioner, then a 17-year-old male, had had unlawful sexual intercourse with a female under the age of 18, in violation of § 261.5. The evidence, adduced at a preliminary hearing showed that at approximately midnight on June 3, 1978, petitioner and two friends approached Sharon, a 16-year-old female, and her sister as they waited at a bus stop. Petitioner and Sharon, who had already been drinking, moved away from the others and began to kiss. After being struck in the face for rebuffing petitioner's initial advances, Sharon submitted to sexual intercourse with petitioner. Prior to trial, petitioner sought to set aside the information on both state and federal constitutional grounds, asserting that § 261.5 unlawfully discriminated on the basis of gender. The trial court and the California Court of Appeal denied petitioner's request for relief and petitioner sought review in the Supreme Court of California. . . .

The justification for the statute offered by the State, and accepted by the Supreme Court of California, is that the legislature sought to prevent illegitimate teenage pregnancies. That finding, of course, is entitled to great deference. . . .

We are satisfied not only that the prevention of illegitimate pregnancy is at least one of the "purposes" of the statute, but also that the State has a strong interest in preventing such pregnancy. At the risk of stating the obvious, teenage pregnancies, which have increased dramatically over the last two decades, have significant social, medical, and economic consequences for both the mother and her child, and the State. Of particular concern to the State is that approximately half of all teenage pregnancies end in abortion. And of those children who are born, their illegitimacy makes them likely candidates to become wards of the State.

We need not be medical doctors to discern that young men and young women are not similarly situated with respect to the problems and the risks of sexual intercourse. Only women may become pregnant, and they suffer disproportionately the profound physical, emotional, and psychological consequences of sexual activity. The statute at issue here protects women from sexual intercourse at an age when those consequences are particularly severe.

The question thus boils down to whether a State may attack the problem of sexual intercourse and teenage pregnancy directly by prohibiting a male from having sexual intercourse with a minor female. We hold that such a statute is sufficiently related to the State's objectives to pass constitutional muster.

Because virtually all of the significant harmful and inescapably identifiable consequences of teenage pregnancy fall on the young female, a legislature acts well within its authority when it elects to punish only the participant who, by nature, suffers few of the consequences of his conduct. It is hardly unreasonable for a legislature acting to protect minor females to exclude them from punishment. Moreover, the risk of pregnancy itself constitutes a substantial deterrence to young females. No similar natural sanctions deter males. A criminal sanction imposed solely on males thus serves to roughly "equalize" the deterrents on the sexes.

We are unable to accept petitioner's contention that the statute is impermissibly under-inclusive and must, in order to pass judicial scrutiny, be *broadened* so as to hold the female as criminally liable as the male. It is argued that this statute is not *necessary* to deter teenage pregnancy because a gender-neutral statute, where both male and female would be subject to prosecution, would serve that goal equally well. The relevant inquiry, however, is not whether the statute is drawn as precisely as it might have been, but whether the line chosen by the California Legislature is within constitutional limitations.

In any event, we cannot say that a gender-neutral statute would be as effective as the statute California has chosen to enact. The State persuasively contends that a gender-neutral statute would frustrate its interest in effective enforcement. Its view is that a female is surely less likely to report violations of the statute if she herself would be subject to criminal prosecution. In an area already fraught with prosecutorial difficulties, we decline to hold that the Equal Protection Clause requires a legislature to enact a statute so broad that it may well be incapable of enforcement. . . .

There remains only petitioner's contention that the statute is unconstitutional as it is applied to him because he, like Sharon, was under 18 at the time of sexual intercourse. Petitioner argues that the statute is flawed because it presumes that as between two persons under 18, the male is the culpable aggressor. We find petitioner's contentions unpersuasive. Contrary to his assertions, the statute does not rest on the assumption that males are generally the aggressors. It is instead an attempt by a legislature to prevent illegitimate teenage pregnancy by providing an additional deterrent for men. The age of the man is irrelevant since young men are as capable as older men of inflicting the harm sought to be prevented.

In upholding the California statute we also recognize that this is not a case where a statute is being challenged on the grounds that it "invidiously discriminates" against females. To the contrary, the statute places a burden on males which is not shared by females. But we find nothing to suggest that men, because of past discrimination or peculiar disadvantages, are in need of the special solicitude of the courts. Nor is this a case where the gender classification is made "solely for . . . administrative convenience," . . . or rests on "the baggage of sexual stereotypes." . . . As we have held, the statute instead reasonably reflects the fact that the consequences of sexual intercourse and pregnancy fall more heavily on the female than on the male.

Accordingly, the judgment of the California Supreme Court is Affirmed.

Justice BLACKMUN, concurring in the judgment.

I think . . . that it is only fair, with respect to this particular petitioner, to point out that his partner, Sharon, appears not to have been an unwilling participant in

at least the initial stages of the intimacies that took place the night of June 3, 1978.*
Petitioner's and Sharon's nonacquaintance with each other before the incident;
their drinking; their withdrawal from the others of the group; their foreplay, in

---

* Sharon at the preliminary hearing testified as follows: "Q. [by the Deputy District
Attorney]. On June the 4th, at approximately midnight—midnight of June the 3rd, were
you in Rohnert Park?" A. [by Sharon]. Yes. "Q. Is that in Sonoma County?" A. Yes. "Q. Did
anything unusual happen to you that night in Rohnert Park?" A. Yes. "Q. Would you briefly
describe what happened that night? Did you see the defendant that night in Rohnert Park?"
A. Yes. "Q. Where did you first meet him?" A. At a bus stop. "Q. Was anyone with you?" A. My
sister. "Q. Was anyone with the defendant?" A. Yes. "Q. How many people were with the
defendant?" A. Two. "Q. Now, after you met the defendant, what happened?" A. We walked
down to the railroad tracks. "Q. What happened at the railroad tracks?" A. We were drinking
at the railroad tracks and we walked over to this bush and he started kissing me and stuff,
and I was kissing him back, too, at first. Then, I was telling him to stop—"Q. Yes." A.—and
I was telling him to slow down and stop. He said, "Okay, okay." But then he just kept doing it.
He just kept doing it and then my sister and two other guys came over to where we were and
my sister said—told me to get up and come home. And then I didn't—"Q. Yes." A.—and
then my sister and—"Q. All right." A.—David, one of the boys that were there, started walking home and we stayed there and then later—"Q. All right." A.—Bruce left Michael, you
know. "The Court: Michael being the defendant?" The Witness: Yeah. We was lying there and
we were kissing each other, and then he asked me if I wanted to walk him over to the park; so
we walked over to the park and we sat down on a bench and then he started kissing me again
and we were laying on the bench. And he told me to take my pants off. I said, "No," and I was
trying to get up and he hit me back down on the bench and then I just said to myself, "Forget it," and I let him do what he wanted to do and he took my pants off and he was telling me
to put my legs around him and stuff—

"Q. Did you have sexual intercourse with the defendant?" A. Yeah. "Q. He did put his
penis into your vagina?" A. Yes. "Q. You said that he hit you?" A. Yeah. "Q. How did he hit
you?" A. He slugged me in the face. "Q. With what did he slug you?" A. His fist. "Q. Where
abouts in the face?" A. On my chin. "Q. As a result of that, did you have any bruises or any
kind of an injury?" A. Yeah. "Q. What happened?" A. I had bruises. "The Court: Did he hit
you one time or did he hit you more than once?" The Witness: He hit me about two or
three times.

"Q. Now, during the course of that evening, did the defendant ask you your age?"
A. Yeah. "Q. And what did you tell him?" A. Sixteen. "Q. Did you tell him you were sixteen?"
A. Yes. "Q. Now, you said you had been drinking, is that correct?" A. Yes. "Q. Would you
describe your condition as a result of the drinking?" A. I was a little drunk.

CROSS-EXAMINATION "Q. Did you go off with Mr. M. away from the others?" A. Yeah.
"Q. Why did you do that?" A. I don't know. I guess I wanted to. "Q. Did you have any need to
go to the bathroom when you were there." A. Yes. "Q. And what did you do?" A. Me and my
sister walked down the railroad tracks to some bushes and went to the bathroom. "Q. Now,
you and Mr. M., as I understand it, went off into the bushes, is that correct?" A. Yes. "Q. Okay.
And what did you do when you and Mr. M. were there in the bushes?" A. We were kissing and
hugging. "Q. Were you sitting up?" A. We were laying down. "Q. You were lying down. This
was in the bushes?" A. Yes. "Q. How far away from the rest of them were you?" A. They were
just bushes right next to the railroad tracks. We just walked off into the bushes; not very far.

"Q. So your sister and the other two boys came over to where you were, you and Michael
were, is that right?" A. Yeah. "Q. What did they say to you, if you remember?" A. My sister didn't say anything. She said, "Come on, Sharon, let's go home." "Q. She asked you
to go home with her?" A. (Affirmative nod.) "Q. Did you go home with her?" A. No. "Q.

645

which she willingly participated and seems to have encouraged; and the closeness of their ages (a difference of only one year and 18 days) are factors that should make this case an unattractive one to prosecute at all, and especially to prosecute as a felony, rather than as a misdemeanor chargeable under § 261.5. But the State has chosen to prosecute in that manner, and the facts, I reluctantly conclude, may fit the crime.

Justice BRENNAN, with whom Justices WHITE and MARSHALL join, dissenting. . . .

[E]ven assuming that prevention of teenage pregnancy is an important governmental objective and that it is in fact an objective of § 261.5 . . . , California still has the burden of proving that there are fewer teenage pregnancies under its gender-based statutory rape law than there would be if the law were gender neutral. To meet this burden, the State must show that because its statutory rape law punishes only males, and not females, it more effectively deters minor females from having sexual intercourse.[5]

The plurality assumes that a gender-neutral statute would be less effective than § 261.5 in deterring sexual activity because a gender-neutral statute would create significant enforcement problems. . . . However, a State's bare assertion

---

You wanted to stay with Mr. M.?" A. I don't know. "Q. Was this before or after he hit you?" A. Before.

"Q. What happened in the five minutes that Bruce stayed there with you and Michael?" A. I don't remember. "Q. You don't remember at all?" A. (Negative head shake.) "Q. Did you have occasion at that time to kiss Bruce?" A. Yeah. "Q. You did? You were kissing Bruce at that time?" A. (Affirmative nod.) "Q. Was Bruce kissing you?" A. Yes. "Q. And were you standing up at this time?" A. No, we were sitting down.

"Q. Okay. So at this point in time you had left Mr. M. and you were hugging and kissing with Bruce, is that right?" A. Yeah. "Q. And you were sitting up." A. Yes. "Q. Was your sister still there then?" A. No. Yeah, she was at first. "Q. What was she doing?" A. She was standing up with Michael and David. "Q. Yes. Was she doing anything with Michael and David?" A. No, I don't think so. "Q. Whose idea was it for you and Bruce to kiss? Did you initiate that?" A. Yes. "Q. What happened after Bruce left?" A. Michael asked me if I wanted to go walk to the park. "Q. And what did you say?" A. I said, "Yes." "Q. And then what happened?" A. We walked to the park.

"Q. How long did it take you to get to the park?" A. About ten or fifteen minutes. "Q. And did you walk there?" A. Yes. "Q. Did Mr. M. ever mention his name?" A. Yes. . . .

5. Petitioner has not questioned the State's constitutional power to achieve its asserted objective by criminalizing consensual sexual activity. However, I note that our cases would not foreclose such a privacy challenge. The State is attempting to reduce the incidence of teenage pregnancy by imposing criminal sanctions on those who engage in consensual sexual activity with minor females. We have stressed, however, that "[i]f the right of privacy means anything, it is the right of the individual, married or single, to be free from unwarranted governmental intrusion into matters so fundamentally affecting a person as the decision whether to bear or beget a child." Eisenstadt v. Baird, [1972]. Minors, too, enjoy a right of privacy in connection with decisions affecting procreation. Carey v. Population Services International, [1977]. Thus, despite the suggestion of the plurality to the contrary . . . , it is not settled that a State may rely on a pregnancy-prevention justification to make consensual sexual intercourse among minors a criminal act.

that its gender-based statutory classification substantially furthers an important governmental interest is not enough to meet its burden of proof under Craig v. Boren. . . .

The State has not produced such evidence in this case. Moreover, there are at least two serious flaws in the State's assertion that law enforcement problems created by a gender-neutral statutory rape law would make such a statute less effective than a gender-based statute in deterring sexual activity.

First, the experience of other jurisdictions, and California itself, belies the plurality's conclusion that a gender-neutral statutory rape law "may well be incapable of enforcement." There are now at least 37 States that have enacted gender-neutral statutory rape laws. Although most of these laws protect young persons (of either sex) from the sexual exploitation of older individuals, the laws of Arizona, Florida, and Illinois permit prosecution of both minor females and minor males for engaging in mutual sexual conduct. California has introduced no evidence that those States have been handicapped by the enforcement problems the plurality finds so persuasive.[7] Surely, if those States could provide such evidence, we might expect that California would have introduced it.

In addition, the California Legislature in recent years has revised other sections of the Penal Code to make them gender-neutral. For example [other California criminal law statutes], prohibiting sodomy and oral copulation with a "person who is under 18 years of age," could cause two minor homosexuals to be subjected to criminal sanctions for engaging in mutually consensual conduct. Again, the State has introduced no evidence to explain why a gender-neutral statutory rape law would be any more difficult to enforce than those statutes.

The second flaw in the State's assertion is that even assuming that a gender-neutral statute would be more difficult to enforce, the State has still not shown that those enforcement problems would make such a statute less effective than a gender-based statute in deterring minor females from engaging in sexual intercourse. Common sense, however, suggests that a gender-neutral statutory rape law is potentially a greater deterrent of sexual activity than a gender-based law, for the simple reason that a gender-neutral law subjects both men and women to criminal sanctions and thus arguably has a deterrent effect on twice as many potential violators. Even if fewer persons were prosecuted under the gender-neutral law, as the State suggests, it would still be true that twice as many persons would be subject to arrest. The State's failure to prove that a gender-neutral law would be a less effective deterrent than a gender-based law, like the State's failure to prove that a gender-neutral law would be difficult to enforce, should have led this Court to invalidate § 261.5.

---

7. There is a logical reason for this. In contrast to laws governing forcible rape, statutory rape laws apply to consensual sexual activity. Force is not an element of the crime. Since a woman who consents to an act of sexual intercourse is unlikely to report her partner to the police — whether or not she is subject to criminal sanctions — enforcement would not be undermined if the statute were to be made gender neutral. . . .

III

Until very recently, no California court or commentator had suggested that the purpose of California's statutory rape law was to protect young women from the risk of pregnancy. Indeed, the historical development of § 261.5 demonstrates that the law was initially enacted on the premise that young women, in contrast to young men, were to be deemed legally incapable of consenting to an act of sexual intercourse.[9] Because their chastity was considered particularly precious, those young women were felt to be uniquely in need of the State's protection.[10] In contrast, young men were assumed to be capable of making such decisions for themselves; the law therefore did not offer them any special protection.

It is perhaps because the gender classification in California's statutory rape law was initially designed to further these outmoded sexual stereotypes, rather than to reduce the incidence of teenage pregnancies, that the State has been unable to demonstrate a substantial relationship between the classification and its newly asserted goal. . . .

I would hold that § 261.5 violates the Equal Protection Clause of the Fourteenth Amendment, and I would reverse the judgment of the California Supreme Court.

NOTES

1. **Consent and Statutory Rape.** Technically, consent is not an element of statutory rape. Yet the extent to which Sharon participated willingly seems important to the Justices. Note that Justice Rehnquist and Justice Blackmun reach the same conclusion in the case, but apparently based on different views about Sharon's level of consent. From Justice Rehnquist, all we know is that Sharon was "struck in the face" for "rebuffing" Michael's advances and that then she "submitted" to sexual intercourse. Under Justice Blackmun's detailed reading of the facts, Sharon's participation, "in at least the initial stages" of the incident was "not unwilling." Which rationale for statutory rape laws does each narrative support? In what sense, if any, did Sharon lack capacity? Was she taken advantage of because of her

---

9. California's statutory rape law had its origins in the Statutes of Westminster enacted during the reign of Edward I at the close of the 13th century. . . . The age of consent at that time was 12 years, reduced to 10 years in 1576. . . . This statute was part of the common law brought to the United States. Thus, when the first California penal statute was enacted, it contained a provision . . . that proscribed sexual intercourse with females under the age of 10. In 1889, the California statute was amended to make the age of consent 14. . . . In 1897, the age was advanced to 16. . . . In 1913 it was fixed at 18, where it now remains. . . .

Because females generally have not reached puberty by the age of 10, it is inconceivable that a statute designed to prevent pregnancy would be directed at acts of sexual intercourse with females under that age. . . .

10. Past decisions of the California courts confirm that the law was designed to protect the State's young females from their own uninformed decision making. . . . It was only in deciding *Michael M.* that the California Supreme Court decided for the first time in the 130-year history of the statute, that pregnancy prevention had become one of the purposes of the statute.

age? If Sharon was "willing," what does this say about the majority's justification for the sex-based statute—that the fear of pregnancy is an effective deterrent?

What does it mean for a teenage girl to "consent" to sex? Michelle Oberman explains the complexity of this question:

> [E]ven assuming that girls do experience sexual pleasure and desire, these are only two of a multiplicity of factors which induce their consent to sex.
>
> The stories girls tell about the "consensual" sex in which they engage reflect a poignant subtext of hope and pain. Girls express longing for emotional attachment, romance, and respect. At the same time, they suffer enormous insecurity and diminished self-image. These two factors are clearly interrelated—the worse girls feel about themselves, the more they look to males for ratification of the women that they are becoming. The importance of being attractive to males takes on a central role in many girls' lives. . . . Girls want boyfriends, relationships, or somebody who will hold them and tell them that they are wanted.
>
> Girls negotiate access to the fulfillment of these emotional needs by way of sex. A girl who wants males to find her attractive, who wants acceptance and popularity, might reasonably consent to sex with a popular boy, to multiple popular boys, or with any partner who can persuade her that she is attractive and desirable. Males recognize, and occasionally exploit, girls' insecurity. . . . Modern statutory rape law . . . classifies intercourse as either consensual sex or rape. However, from the girl's vantage point, her consent may have been so fraught with ambivalence that it was meaningless. . . .
>
> If girls' autonomy is to be taken seriously, the law must evaluate the sexual decisions they make, and formulate a legal response which enhances the likelihood that those decisions are autonomous ones.[1]

If Oberman is right, what would such a legal response look like? Are the considerations for boys concerning unwanted sex different than they are for girls?

2. **Statutory Rape Laws.**   The crime of statutory rape is defined by the state's age-of-consent laws. Under those laws, a person below a stated age does not have the legal capacity to consent to sex, and therefore sex with that person is considered rape. At one time, the legal age of sexual consent was 10 or younger. The nineteenth-century reformers who succeeded in persuading states to increase the statutory age were motivated both by a desire to protect young women from sexual exploitation and, in important respects, to control their sexuality.[2]

---

1. Michelle Oberman, Turning Girls into Women: Re-Evaluating Modern Statutory Rape Law, 85 J. Crim. L. & Criminology 15, 70 (1994) (criticizing statutory rape law reform for too readily crediting teenage girls' consent to sex, contrary to research on girls' adolescent development).

2. See J. Shoshanna Ehrlich, You Can Steal Her Virginity but Not Her Doll: The Nineteenth Century Campaign to Raise the Legal Age of Sexual Consent, 15 Cardozo J.L. &

The age of consent now is 16, 17, or 18, depending on the state.[3] However, many consent statutes apply special rules to minors who are close in age to one another. These "Romeo and Juliet" rules sometimes apply a lesser penalty to the criminal sexual act and sometimes render the activity lawful. In Texas, for example, the age of consent is 17, but consensual sex with a person who is at least 14 is permitted if the other party is no more than three years older.[4] A person under the age of 14 cannot lawfully engage in sexual activity, regardless of the other party's age. In its proposed revisions to the Model Penal Code, the American Law Institute would include a felony offense titled sexual assault of a minor or oral sex with a person younger than 16 if the actor is more than five years older. The seriousness of the offense (and the severity of the potential penalty) increases if the actor is more than 10 years older than the minor or if the minor is younger than 12.[5] If you were drafting such provisions, what line would you draw?

The statutory rape laws of all states are now gender-neutral. The move to neutrality appears to have had less to do with a recognition of female sexual autonomy than with a recognition of male vulnerability to sexual exploitation — recognition brought on, at least in part, by well-publicized cases involving the solicitation of sex from underage boys by priests, teachers, and coaches. (See Note 3, below.) Most countries with legal traditions similar to the United States, such as Great Britain, Canada, and Australia, also have adopted gender-neutral statutory rape laws.[6]

3. **Gender Neutrality and Differential Treatment of Offenders and Victims.** Although statutory rape laws are sex-neutral, many prosecutors, judges, and juries, as well as society generally, tend to view the crime differently when the victims are male, particularly when the offenders are female.[7] In justifying gender-specific language in the earlier version of the Model Penal Code, its commentators claimed that the "potential consequences of coerced intimacy [for males] do not seem so grave. For one thing there is no prospect of unwanted pregnancy. And however devalued virginity has become for the modern woman, it would be difficult to believe that its loss constitutes comparable injury to the male."[8] What assumptions about masculinity underlie this claim? Should the sex of the victim affect the penalties?

Gender 229, 231 (2009); see also Holly Brewer, By Birth or Consent: Children, Law, and the Anglo-American Revolution in Authority (2007).

3. Marci A. Hamilton, 50-State Age of Majority v. Age of Consent, SOL Reform (Feb. 8, 2015).

4. Tex. Penal Code § 21.11 (2022).

5. Model Penal Code: Sexual Assault and Related Offenses, § 213.8 (Am. L. Inst., Tentative Draft No. 6, 2022).

6. Philip N. S. Rumney, In Defense of Gender Neutrality Within Rape, 6 Seattle J. Soc. Just. 481, 486 (2007).

7. See John Burrow et al., No Man's Land: The Denial of Victimisation in Male Statutory Rape Cases, 26 J. Sexual Aggression 316 (2020).

8. Susan Estrich, Rape, 95 Yale L.J. 1087, 1150 (1986) (quoting Model Penal Code § 213.1 cmt. at 338 (Am. Law Inst. 1980)).

Double standards regarding statutory rape remain common. A widespread attitude is that underage heterosexual men welcome an overture by an adult of the opposite sex. Boys may often be reluctant to acknowledge sexual abuse by women because the culture conditions them to view such encounters as "getting lucky."[9] Moreover, male adolescents may fear that resistance will make them look like a "pussy," "bitch," "fag," or even just like "a girl" and that complaints will result in disbelief or ridicule. Does this mean they are not harmed by being "forced" into sex they did not want?[10]

The culture's persistent double standards concerning sexual victimization help explain the harsher sentences that male sex offenders normally receive.[11] However, in some cases female offenders are beginning to receive harsh treatment if it appears that they exploited an underage male. One of the most well-known cases was a Seattle grade-school teacher, Mary Kay Letourneau, who at age 35 had sex with her 13-year-old student, for which she received a 7.5-year prison sentence. All but six months of the sentence was suspended conditional upon her entering a sex-offender treatment program and refraining from contact with the boy. Shortly thereafter, her sentence was reinstated after she was found in his company. She had one child with the boy prior to sentencing and conceived another during her brief release. The couple married once the boy became of age and reunited after she served her prison sentence.[12] Should cases with female perpetrators and male victims be treated any differently from the more typical statutory rape of girls by adult men? Female sexual offenders have varying profiles. Some are teachers who claim to have fallen in love with young students and pursued them in the hope that they would return their affection. Others were victims of child sexual abuse or other intergenerational abuse.[13] Should such different background circumstances matter?

Another double standard may influence prosecution for underage sex between persons of the same sex. One study found that, controlling for age of victim and age difference, same-sex pairings were more likely to result in arrest than male-female pairings. For same-sex participants, being in a romantic relationship actually increased the likelihood of arrest—a factor that has the opposite effect of reducing the risk of arrest between male-female couples.[14] Although the effect was smaller, the same researchers found statutory rape incidents with white victims were more likely to result in arrest than for victims of other races and ethnicities.[15] The authors suggest that statutory rape law enforcement lends itself to such

---

9. Alisa Graham, Simply Sexual: The Discrepancy in Treatment Between Male and Female Sex Offenders, 7 Whittier J. Child. & Fam. Advoc. 145, 160 (2007).

10. For discussion of the harm, see Kay L. Levine, No Penis, No Problem, 33 Fordham Urb. L.J. 357, 404 (2006).

11. Graham, supra note 9, at 153.

12. Jennifer Joseph et al., Mary Kay Letourneau Fualaau, Vili Fualaau Detail Their Path from Teacher-Student Sex Scandal to Raising Teenagers, ABC News (Apr. 10, 2015).

13. Levine, supra note 10, at 395.

14. Mark Chaffin et al., Same-Sex and Race-Based Disparities in Statutory Rape Arrests, 31 J. Interpersonal Violence 26, 36, 41 (2016).

15. Id. at 37, 42.

extrajudicial biases because it marshals the criminal law to police behavior that is common (consensual, underage sex) and can only be selectively enforced.[16]

4. **The Political Valence of Underage Sex.** The visibility of underage sex as an issue has risen in recent years due to a number of highly publicized scandals involving politicians. New York Democratic Congressman Anthony Weiner, for example, served eighteen months in prison for sexting a 15-year-old.[17] Numerous Republicans have also been involved in scandals. In 2006, for example, Florida Congressman Mark Foley was forced to resign after it was revealed that he had sexually propositioned teenage congressional pages via email and text.[18] Former Speaker of the House of Representatives J. Dennis Hastert, a Republican and former wrestling coach, served a fifteen-month sentence for illegally structuring bank withdrawals he used to buy the silence of one of the four former student-athletes he sexually abused.[19] In 2017, allegations surfaced that Alabama Senate candidate Roy Moore, during his thirties while serving as an assistant district attorney, sought out relationships with teenage girls between ages 14 and 18, some involving sexual conduct short of intercourse.[20] Underage sex again became an issue when, during the confirmation hearings of Supreme Court nominee Ketanji Brown Jackson, Republican members of the Senate Judiciary Committee tried to smear her and her defenders as pedophiles because, as a trial judge, she sentenced an 18-year-old who, as a high-schooler, uploaded four videos to YouTube depicting prepubescent boys engaged in sex acts, to only three months.[21] It was an odd issue to emphasize, given the fact that Republicans had rushed to defend those within their ranks who had propositioned, or engaged in, underage sex. At Dennis Hastert's sentencing, more than forty letters of support for him were submitted, many of them from national and state Republican lawmakers.[22] Although support for Roy Moore from Republicans was not uniform, many defended him, including the Alabama state auditor, who analogized Moore's behavior to conduct described in the Bible, such as Joseph and Mary. "Mary was a teenager and Joseph was an adult carpenter. They became parents of Jesus. There's just nothing immoral or illegal here. Maybe just a little bit unusual."[23]

---

16. Id. at 27.

17. Michael Gold, Anthony Weiner Released from Prison After Serving 18 Months for Sexting Teenager, N.Y. Times, May 14, 2019.

18. Greg Allen, Rep. Foley Quits over E-Mails to Male Teen Pages, NPR (Sept. 30, 2006).

19. See Liam Stack, Dennis Hastert, Ex-House Speaker Who Admitted Sex Abuse, Leaves Prison, N.Y. Times, July 18, 2017.

20. Stephanie McCrummen et al., Woman Says Roy Moore Initiated Sexual Encounter When She Was 14, He Was 32, Wash. Post, Nov. 9, 2017.

21. See Aaron C. Davis & Spencer S. Hsu, The Child Pornography Case at the Center of Ketanji Brown Jackson's Hearing, Wash. Post, Mar. 24, 2022.

22. See Sophia Tesfaye, Republicans Rush to Defend Dennis Hastert, Plead Court for Leniency in Alleged Pedophile Hugh Money Case, Salon (Apr. 25, 2016).

23. Philip Wegmann, Alabama State Auditor Defends Roy Moore Against Sexual Allegations, Invokes Mary and Joseph, Wash. Exam'r, Nov. 9, 2017 (quoting Jim Ziegler); see also Charles Belhea, Roy Moore's Supporters Stand by Their Candidate, Despite Sexual-Assault Allegations, New Yorker (Nov. 9, 2017).

Is this just the usual political hypocrisy?[24] Or is there a gender ideology embedded in the public responses to these incidents that helps to explain how politicians might take a strong, moral position against pedophilia while defending the men engaged in it?

5. **Child Marriage.**   The organization Save the Children estimates that a girl 14 years old or younger is married every eleven seconds.[25] Unchained at Last, an organization that fights child marriage in the United States, estimates that there were about a quarter million child marriages in the United States between 2000 and 2010.[26] In many cases, these unions are a way to cover up rape, avoid an unwed pregnancy, or enable the immigration of a distant relative from abroad. Because domestic violence shelters typically do not accept survivors under age 18, many underage victims have nowhere safe to go and are treated as runaways if arrested.[27] In one all-too-typical Florida case, a judge approved the marriage of an 11-year-old Pentecostal girl to end the investigation of rape by church elders.[28]

The U.S. government deplores the practice of child marriage internationally, and several states have passed laws since 2016 to raise the minimum age for marriage or to narrow or eliminate exceptions to marital age requirements. However, the vast majority of states permit child marriage, at least in some circumstances. Only six states limit marriage to those 18 and older with no exceptions.[29] Six additional states set 18 as the age minimum but also allow emancipated minors to marry.[30] Among the remaining states, eight states set the floor at age 17, and twenty-three set it at age 16; four states set the floor at 14 or 15, and nine states do not have a specified minimum age. In most states that allow marriage under the age of 18, the law requires parental consent, judicial approval, or both; some also have special rules in the event of pregnancy.[31] Some states have rejected proposed legislation to curb child marriages.[32] Opponents of such measures claim that some child marriages are consensual, sanctioned by religious traditions, and a way to avoid out-of-wedlock births. How would you respond? Should the legality or availability of abortion play a role in determining marriage laws?

What is the relationship between statutory rape laws and child marriages? Many states permit marriage at an earlier age than they allow legal consent to sex,

---

24. See Jordan Weissman, So, Let's Talk About Republicans and Sex Crimes, Slate (Apr. 9, 2022).

25. Nicholas Kristof, At 13, She Married Her Rapist—Legally, N.Y. Times, June 2, 2018, at SR3.

26. Id.

27. Nicholas Kristof, It Was Forced on Me: Child Marriage in the U.S., N.Y. Times, May 27, 2017, at SR1.

28. Id.

29. The marriage age rules are explored in detail in Tahirih Just. Ctr., Understanding State Statutes on Minimum Marriage Age and Exceptions (Aug. 26, 2021). The six states that have an age floor of 18 with no exceptions are Delaware, New Jersey, Pennsylvania, Minnesota, Rhode Island, and New York.

30. Id. These states include Georgia, Indiana, Kentucky, Ohio, Texas, and Virginia.

31. Id.

32. Kristof, It Was Forced on Me, supra note 27.

which means sex with an underage spouse is a criminal act unless the statutory rape law contains a marriage exception. A variation on this is to allow underage pregnant teenagers to consent to marriage but not to sex. Might marital exemptions from statutory rape incentivize child marriages?[33] Should statutory rape laws adopt the same age limits as consent to marriage laws? Should men arrested for statutory rape be allowed to marry their pregnant partners in lieu of jail time?[34]

PUTTING THEORY INTO PRACTICE

5-1. A law in State X defines statutory rape as sexual intercourse with a child under the age of 16. Colleen, age 20, gives birth to a baby fathered by 16-year-old Shane, who at the time of conception was 15. Colleen was, for several years, Shane's babysitter, and Shane never complained to his parents about the sexual liaison with Colleen. Colleen is charged with statutory rape but pleads to the lesser crime of contributing to a child's misconduct. After the child's birth, Colleen applies for public assistance, whereupon the Department of Social Services petitions the court to order Shane to contribute to the child's financial support. The Parentage Act of State X, which mandates that parents provide support for their children, makes no exception for minors, and courts have held that society has a legitimate interest in holding parents rather than the state responsible for support.[35] Should Shane be liable for child support?

5-2. A former New York sportscaster who buys sex from a 14-year-old victim is initially charged with statutory rape and then allowed to plead guilty to endangering the welfare of a child.[36] Should prosecutors use statutory rape laws to curb demand for child prostitution, which otherwise exposes customers to only misdemeanor liability? (Prostitution and human trafficking are covered more extensively in Chapter 3, Section D.)

5-3. In a celebrated case involving students at a New Hampshire prep school, an 18-year-old senior competed with other male students over who could "score" with the most girls. Owen Labrie invited a 15-year-old girl to join him for a "senior salute," which could involve anything from kissing to sexual intercourse. The girl claimed that she had said no three times to intercourse but acknowledged on cross-examination that she lifted up her arms so that he could take her shirt off and raised her hips so he could pull off her shorts. She also explained that "I wanted to

---

33. See Kaya Van Roost et al., Child Marriage or Statutory Rape? A Comparison of Law and Practice Across the United States, 70 J. Adolescent Health S72 (2022); Tahirih Just. Ctr., The Alarming Disconnect Between Age-Based Sex Offenses and Minimum Marriage Age (Aug. 2020).

34. See Rumney, supra note 6, at 486.

35. Alia Beard Rau, Arizona Statutory Rape Victim Forced to Pay Child Support, Arizona Republic, Sept. 2, 2014. For other cases, see Michael R. Hudzik & Anthony E. Chiola, Statutory Rape and the Duty to Pay Child Support (When One Crime Is Not Enough), 27 D.C.B.A. Brief 26 (2015).

36. Laura Italiano, Former Sportscaster Marvell Scott Pleads Guilty in Child Prostitute Case, N.Y. Post, Aug. 16, 2011; see also Amanda Shapiro, Buyer Beware: Why Johns Should Be Charged with Statutory Rape for Buying Sex from a Child, 23 J.L. & Pol'y 449 (2014).

not cause a conflict" and "I felt like I was frozen." Labrie denied that sexual pene-tration took place but acknowledged that he was wearing a condom. He claimed, "I thought she was having a great time."[37] A jury acquitted him of aggravated feloni-ous assault, a charge that required proof of nonconsent, but convicted him of three charges of misdemeanor sexual assault (because the victim was under 16) and one misdemeanor count of endangering the welfare of a minor. He was sentenced to one year in jail, followed by five years of probation, and was required to register for life as a sex offender. Harvard revoked an offer of admission.[38] Was this an appro-priate result? How would the case have come out under the new Model Penal Code formulation? How should the schools have responded?

2.   *Rape and the Criminal Law*

According to data from the U.S. Centers for Disease Control and Prevention (CDC), one in four women and about one in twenty-six men have experienced completed or attempted rape in their lifetimes.[39] Nearly half of all non-Hispanic multiracial women (48 percent) experience completed or attempted rape during their lifetime. The most recent surveys show a rate of 43.7 percent for American Indian/Alaska Native women, 29 percent for African-American women, 20 percent for Hispanic women, 17.2 percent for Non-Hispanic Asian/Pacific Islander women, and 28 percent for white women.[40] Lesbian, gay, bisexual, and transgender individ-uals are particularly vulnerable, with rates of violent victimization, including rape and sexual assault, nearly four times higher than those of non-LGBTQ+ popula-tions.[41] Young people are disproportionately likely to be raped. More than four in five female rape survivors reported that they were first raped before age 25, and almost half were first raped as a minor (i.e., before age 18).[42]

---

37. Emily Bazelon, The St. Paul's Rape Case Shows Why Sexual-Assault Laws Must Change, N.Y. Times Mag., Aug. 26, 2015.

38. Jeannie Suk, St. Paul's School and a New Definition of Rape, New Yorker (Nov. 3, 2015); Todd S. Purdum, St. Paul's Before and After the Owen Labrie Rape Trial, Vanity Fair (Mar. 1, 2016). Although his sentence was initially suspended pending appeal, Labrie lost his appeal and ultimately served the full sentence. See Alyssa Dandrea, Still in Jail, Owen Labrie Loses Last Appeal in St. Paul's Sex Assault Case, Concord Monitor, June 7, 2019.

39. Ctrs. for Disease Control and Prevention (CDC), Fast Facts: Preventing Sexual Vio-lence (June 22, 2022); Nat'l Sexual Violence Res. Ctr. (NSVRC), Statistics, https://www.nsvrc.org/statistics.

40. Kathleen C. Basile et al., The National Intimate Partner and Sexual Violence Sur-vey: 2016/2017 Report on Sexual Violence 3 (June 2022) (NISVS).

41. See Andrew R. Flores et al., Victimization Rates and Traits of Sexual and Gender Minorities in the United States: Results from the National Crime Victimization Survey, 2017, 6 Scis. Advances (Oct. 2, 2020). Transgender people of color are particularly likely to be targeted. See Rose Gilroy et al., Transgender Rights and Issues, 22 Geo. J. Gender & L. 417, 449 (2021).

42. CDC, Fast Facts, supra note 39; NSVRC, supra note 39.

According to the Bureau of Justice Statistics, most rapes go unreported.[43] Survivors of rape suffer a wide range of related "emotional, relational, hedonic, and dignitary" injuries, including sexually transmitted infections, depression, anxiety, and post-traumatic stress disorder.[44] In 2018, rape was estimated to cost the nation about $127 billion annually, more than any other crime.[45]

An overwhelming percentage of rape assailants are male.[46] Explanations for rape of women by men fall along three main dimensions: individual, sociobiological, and cultural. At the individual level,

> many rapists are attracted to power; they want the feeling of domination, adventure, and status that comes from coercing sex. Other men are motivated by anger; rape serves to punish or avenge some wrong by a particular woman, women in general, or another perceived adversary. Most rapists blame their victims, and some stress situational influences such as peer pressure or drug and alcohol abuse. Exposure to family violence during childhood increases the probability that men will become sexually violent as adults.[47]

The sociobiological argument is that, at an evolutionary level, men having intercourse with a large number of fertile females increases the chance that their genetic line will continue. Sociobiologists propose that for men who have difficulty attracting willing partners, coercive sex is "adaptive" and likely to be favored by natural selection.[48] Is this explanation undermined by the substantial variation in rape across time and culture?

Cultural explanations stress the eroticization of male aggression in popular films, television, fiction, pornography, and video games. Such frameworks also underscore the role of male-dominated institutions such as the military, fraternities, and athletic teams in fostering attitudes that legitimate male sexual aggression. For instance, Katherine Baker argues, "Date rape happens, in large part, [because for some men], the greater the number of sexual encounters they have, the more they demonstrate their masculinity to other men. Their desire for sex exists completely apart from its consensual nature, and it is integrally linked to the cultural construct of masculinity."[49]

The traditional rape statute required that a man (1) had intercourse with a woman, not his wife, (2) against her will, (3) by force, and (4) without consent.

---

43. Rachel E. Morgan & Alexandra Thompson, Bureau of Just. Stats., Crime Victimization, 2020, at 8 (Table 5) (Oct. 2021).

44. See Katharine K. Baker, Why Rape Should Not (Always) Be a Crime, 100 Minn. L. Rev. 221, 228 (2015).

45. NSVRC, supra note 39.

46. See NISVS, 2015 Data Brief—Updated Release 2018 (98 percent of female and 93 percent of male rape survivors report that their assailants were male).

47. Deborah L. Rhode, What Women Want: An Agenda for the Women's Movement 120 (2014).

48. See Owen D. Jones & Timothy H. Goldsmith, Law and Behavioral Biology, 105 Colum. L. Rev. 405 (2005).

49. Katharine K. Baker, Sex, Rape, and Shame, 79 B.U. L. Rev. 663, 665 (1999).

There was also a requirement that the woman physically resisted (sometimes "to the utmost"). Starting in the 1960s, feminist movements succeeded in expanding the acts and actors that counted as rape, eliminating the resistance requirement, taking the focus off women's "provocative" behavior (usually through rape shield evidence rules), and diversifying what counts as force.[50] A major remaining issue is what constitutes the line between coercive and consensual sex. What makes this line so difficult?

Deborah Tuerkheimer

Incredible Women: Sexual Violence and the Credibility Discount

166 U. Pa. L. Rev. 3, 16-17, 20, 32-33, 35, 40 (2017)

I use the term [credibility discounting] to refer to an unwarranted failure to credit an assertion where this failure stems from prejudice. Abundant evidence exists that credibility discounts are meted out at every stage of the criminal process: by police officers, prosecutors, jurors, and judges. . . . Acknowledging the existence of the credibility discount is not the same as insisting that all rape allegations are true. The problem that I identify here is a profound disconnect between perceptions of falsity and actual falsity. Before we further probe this disconnect, ask yourself: what percentage of rape accusations reported to the police are false? In one survey of nearly nine hundred police officers, more than half of the respondents stated that ten to fifty percent of sexual assault complainants lie about being assaulted, while another ten percent of respondents asserted that the number of false reports is fifty-one to hundred percent. Another study found that more than half of the detectives interviewed believed that forty to eighty percent of sexual assault complaints are false. This openly manifested skepticism largely explains the unusually high unfounding rates that characterize the police treatment of rape allegations.

Research on false rape allegations suggests that such skepticism is unwarranted. Admittedly, studying the prevalence of false reports is difficult because of the methodological challenge of identifying ground truth—a difficulty that largely accounts for significant discrepancies in findings. As one researcher aptly summarized the problem, "significant adherence to rape myths by the public, media, jurors, and the criminal legal system makes it practically impossible to unravel the highly layered 'truth' about false rape allegations." One major limitation of the research is its frequent reliance on official law enforcement documents to classify an allegation as false. Equating a police determination that an accusation is "unfounded" with the falsity of that accusation results in the uncritical adoption of any and all credibility discounts meted out in the course of an investigation. Yet researchers often fail to note, much less to disentangle, this effect. Another common methodological flaw is to equate an accuser recanting with a false accusation. Since many factors may cause a truthful complainant to recant her allegation, a

---

50. See Cynthia Lee & Angela P. Harris, Criminal Law: Cases and Materials 437 (4th ed. 2019).

failure to independently assess the underlying accusation tends to result in findings of false reporting rates that are misleadingly high. In short, methodological shortcomings in this area are rampant.

[However, among studies] which require a reasonably sound basis to believe that an allegation is false before classifying it accordingly, we see false reporting rates of 4.5 percent, 5.9 percent, and 6.8 percent. These figures are significantly lower than those provided by law enforcement officers when asked to estimate the incidence of false reporting. Moreover, research suggests that the kinds of cases most likely to be considered false — namely, those involving non-strangers and those involving intoxication — are in fact least likely to be false. Relatedly, commonplace assumptions on the part of law enforcement officers regarding rape accusers' motivations are misguided; even in false reports, revenge, regret and guilt are not usually factors. . . .

On occasion, law enforcement officers make explicit their priors regarding the probability that a rape allegation is false. For instance, in March 2016, explaining his resistance to a law that would require the testing of sexual assault kits, an Idaho sheriff asserted that "the majority of our rapes that are called in, are actually consensual sex." Similarly, in late 2015, a police chief at a Georgia college noted that "[m]ost of these sexual assaults are women waking up the next morning with a guilt complex. That ain't rape, that's being stupid. When the dust settles, it was all consensual."

While it is rather unusual for law enforcement officers to publicly acknowledge and endeavor to legitimate systemic disbelief, studies indicate that skepticism of rape accusations is endemic. There is also abundant anecdotal evidence that police officers are discounting complainant credibility when responding to allegations of rape. Consider, as just one example, the case of Lara McLeod, who in 2011 was arrested for falsely reporting her rape before the charges were ultimately dropped. From the beginning, the detective who first interviewed McLeod appeared to doubt her claims. Later, internal police documents and recordings would "show how grievously the police botched their investigation from start to finish, allowing their beliefs about sexual assault to influence the way they pursued the case." In the end, with McLeod's alleged rapist still uncharged, the police chief admitted that the investigation had been "shortcutted" while taking pains to underscore that "women do lie about rape, so it was important for officers not to be too credulous." The chief added that "[i]t is not uncommon for people to make false, malicious, salacious allegations of sexual assault.". . . .

Another prevailing sentiment is that, under certain circumstances, sex — with or without consent — is inevitable. According to researchers, many police officers suggested that victims "ought to expect 'what they get' if they invite someone over or agree to go somewhere with them." As one investigator stated, "it might not be right, but it's what happens, you go over there, what do you think's gonna happen?" By placing blame on the victim, investigators directly shift responsibility away from the rapist. [Prosecutors and jurors share these views. One prosecutor noted] that, in non-stranger cases, "jurors typically have questions about her behavior at the time of the incident — why did she agree to go back to his room after the date, why did she agree to watch pornographic movies with him, and so on." . . .

State v. Jones

299 P.3d 219 (Idaho 2013)

J. JONES, Justice.

Russell G. Jones appealed his conviction by an Elmore County jury on two counts of rape. The case was initially heard by the Idaho Court of Appeals, which affirmed on one count and reversed on the second. Jones sought review, which we granted in order to consider the force and resistance necessary with respect to a charge of forcible rape.

I.

In the spring of 2008, Jones, Craig Carpenter, and the victim, A.S., were long-time friends. Carpenter and A.S. were engaged and had children together but, unbeknownst to Carpenter, Jones and A.S. had been sexually involved for approximately four years. On May 22, 2008, after spending the night together in Jackpot, Nevada, A.S. and Jones drove back to Idaho and decided they would end their affair. But despite this, they returned to A.S.'s apartment and engaged in consensual sex that morning.

Afterwards, A.S. went to the bathroom and then returned to the bedroom, where Jones was looking at pornographic material on the computer. Jones sat next to A.S. on the bed and started touching her, and she responded by telling him that "I thought we had decided that the time before was the last time and it wasn't going to happen anymore." A.S. stated that at that point:

> I was laying on my stomach on the bed, and [Jones] got behind me. And I wasn't sure what he was doing, and I got up on my elbows to see what he was doing, and he was undoing his pants. . . . I told him, no, that I wasn't going to do this, and I looked back down, and that's when he leaned forward, and I was pushed down, like this, to where I couldn't get up, and he started having sex with me.

A.S. clarified that when she stated she was pushed down "like this" she meant that Jones "leaned forward to where his body was pushing on [hers]" and that her "hands were underneath [her] and she couldn't turn around." Jones then moved A.S.'s underwear to the side and had intercourse with her, while she "kept yelling at him and pleading for him to stop and please quit," which he ignored. Jones apologized to A.S. afterwards, asked her if she was okay, and admitted that he "lost control." He stated that if A.S. "wanted to press charges that [she] could because he was out of line." After Jones eventually left, A.S. contacted the Boise State University Women's Center. She told a counselor that she had been raped and was advised to call the police, which she did not do. Thereafter, A.S. continued to be in contact with Jones and subsequently went to Jackpot with him again.

On May 27, Jones went to A.S.'s apartment to watch movies. He spent the night and remained there in the morning after Carpenter left for work and A.S.'s children went to school. At the time, A.S. was taking an antihistamine for a bee sting and a prescription anti-anxiety medication, both of which caused her to feel drowsy. As a result of her drowsiness she laid down on the living room couch and started to "drift off." Jones went into the living room, sat next to her, and started stroking her hair. A.S. testified that after he "grabbed a handful of hair and pulled" hard enough to hurt her, she was nonresponsive in hopes that "if [she] just laid there and didn't move he would leave [her] alone." She further stated that:

> After he was done pulling my hair, he left me alone for a little bit. And then he grabbed my chest and squeezed my breast really hard. . . . He apparently didn't get the reaction he wanted, and he moved down to my vaginal area. . . . He started touching me outside, and then he started putting his fingers inside me really hard.

Jones then proceeded to pull down A.S.'s pants and underwear, and "pushed [her] legs apart and started having sex with [her]." In response, A.S. "just froze," and testified that she was "paralyzed" with fear.

Afterwards, Jones and A.S. went to the bedroom and shared a cigarette. Jones helped A.S. into bed and once again started to have sexual intercourse with her. She testified that:

> [A]bout a little ways into it he stopped, and then he said, "Baby, I do have a problem." He said, "What am I doing?" . . . He got off me and pulled his clothes back on and put mine back on. And then he sat me back up and asked me if he could have sex with me. And I just kept saying over and over again, no, my kids are going to be home soon.

Eventually, Jones left the apartment.

A.S. drove to Carpenter's brother's house and told the brother's girlfriend that she had been raped. They took A.S. to the hospital where she told the staff that she had been sexually assaulted, but that she did not want to press charges. But law enforcement was contacted, and A.S. provided a statement to police while at the hospital.

On May 29, A.S. met with a detective, who arranged for A.S. to make a recorded call to Jones. A.S. confronted Jones regarding the incidents, and Jones is heard on tape apologizing for both incidents, conceding that he "continued" with sexual intercourse despite her protests in the first incident and her not responding during the second and admitting that after the first incident he sent her text messages[2] "promising [her] it wouldn't happen again." Additionally, A.S. is clearly heard saying, "You think this is okay to do to people who are unconscious? Apparently you've

---

2. The text messages sent by Jones to A.S. were written down by Detective Bob Chaney and admitted into evidence:

May 22 1116: I'm so sorry yet Another Fuck up I'm good at it I'm in ur Hands tell me what to do

May 22 1130: I lost control, seem to be doing that alot lately

May 22 1132: Its my fault neither can I

May 22 1134: That scared me what should I do

May 22 1137[:] Please don't hate me, I hate myself

May 22 1148[:] I Take Full Responsibility if u want 2 press charges I understand I took From someone I Love May 23 256[:] Im sorry I have not been better 2u I hate what ive become

done this to [M.C.][3] before, and now you did it to me." In response, Jones says that he was already on felony probation for domestic battery and that he would have to register as a sex offender based on these new accusations. Jones also admits, when asked to describe the bad things he did in the past, that he had "hurt [M.C.]" and had also committed driving under the influence (DUI) offenses. Toward the end of the tape, A.S. asks Jones to describe what he did to her—he states that: "I think that I pushed things too far and I guess it's rape. I did it. You obviously didn't want any part of it."

Based on the May 22 incident in the bedroom (Count I) and the May 28 incident on the couch (Count II), Jones was charged with two counts of forcible rape under I.C. § 18-6101(3). At trial, A.S. testified regarding the events of both days. She admitted she had never informed police that she and Jones were sexually involved during the four years prior to the incidents. She also admitted her statements to the police were incomplete—specifically, she did not reveal that she and Jones had had consensual sex earlier in the day on May 22. Moreover, although she had shared text messages from Jones that she thought were incriminating, she did not show officers text messages sent by her to Jones that indicated that she loved him (and that would have revealed their relationship). A.S. also admitted that even at the time of trial, she was still concealing her relationship with Jones from Carpenter.

During cross-examination, defense counsel focused on a letter that A.S. wrote, had notarized, and gave to the prosecution before trial. In it, she recanted her allegations of rape, asserted that Jones was wrongfully charged, and characterized the incidents as a misunderstanding between her and Jones. But A.S. subsequently sent another letter to the prosecutor that retracted her retraction—she maintained that counseling had induced a change of heart and that she indeed wished to go forward with the charges.

The State then presented the testimony of the nurse who examined A.S. after the second incident. The nurse stated that A.S. was "visibly frightened" during their interaction: crying, avoiding eye contact, and speaking very softly. During the examination, A.S. "had her knees to her chest, kind of holding herself" and afterwards she laid down and "just kind of curled up." The nurse further testified that she found no physical evidence of trauma consistent with rape—there was no bruising, scrapes, or scratches on A.S.'s body. . . .

The State then called its final witness, detective Bob Chaney, who met with A.S. following the incidents and who arranged the taped call to Jones. That tape was played in its entirety for the jury. Detective Chaney then testified that he read and copied several text messages from Jones to A.S., which were admitted into evidence, but that he did not inspect any messages sent from A.S. to Jones—including those in which she told Jones that she loved him. He was unaware that Jones and A.S. had been in a long-term consensual sexual relationship, and that the two had engaged in consensual intercourse on May 22, prior to the first incident. Chaney testified that the lab report he received following A.S.'s examination yielded no traces of semen.

---

3. M.C. was Jones' former girlfriend.

Jones moved for a directed verdict at the close of evidence, alleging that the State failed to prove: 1) that A.S. resisted sexual intercourse and 2) that her resistance was overcome by force. The district court denied the motion, and the jury convicted Jones of both counts of forcible rape. He was sentenced to concurrent 25-year sentences, with five years determinate for each. Jones appealed. . . .

III

B

There was sufficient evidence to convict Jones on Count I.

The first question before this Court is whether there is sufficient evidence that Jones forcibly raped A.S. on May 22. Resolving this brings up two broader issues: whether verbal resistance qualifies as resistance under Idaho's forcible rape statute and the amount of force required to overcome this resistance.

Jones argues that scant Idaho case law illuminates the meaning of "force" and "resistance" and that "unless and until the [L]egislature affirmatively modifies the common law" of forcible rape, this Court must adhere to the common law understanding that "some quantum of physical resistance is required." He claims that A.S.'s purely verbal resistance to Jones on May 22 would be insufficient to support a charge of forcible rape. Jones additionally contends that the "extrinsic force standard" should apply, i.e., that a charge of forcible rape requires more force than is inherent in the sexual act. He asserts there was no evidence that he used any force that exceeded what "was required to achieve penetration." As he puts it:

> [A.S.] was already lying outstretched in a prone position on her stomach on the bed immediately prior to the intercourse at issue. . . . Given her physical position, it was necessary for Mr. Jones to position himself on top of [A.S.] in order to accomplish penetration. Additionally, [A.S.] testified that her arms were already underneath her prior to the intercourse — Mr. Jones did not physically hold her arms down or place her arms where they were pinned underneath [A.S.'s] body. . . . Finally, the act of pulling aside [A.S.'s] underwear was also incidental to the act of penetration.

Jones thus posits that the State failed to provide evidence of resistance or force that would support a conviction for the forcible rape charge in Count I.

With regard to resistance, the State responds that this Court has not followed the common law standard of "resistance to the utmost" for "at least 105 years." It argues that in Idaho the resistance factor exists "simply to show two elements of the crime — the assailant's intent to use force in order to have carnal knowledge and the woman's nonconsent." Because A.S. said no and "was effectively prevented from further resistance by being pushed onto the bed with her arms pinned," the State contends that there was sufficient evidence of resistance. Further, with regard to force, the State argues against the extrinsic force standard. Its contention is that "the only 'quantum' of force required by the statute is that necessary to 'effect' the penetration over the victim's resistance." The State argues that that much force was present here. We will first address the resistance issue.

1. **Resistance. . . .**

The Idaho Code defines forcible rape as follows:

Rape is defined as the penetration, however slight, of the oral, anal or vaginal opening with the perpetrator's penis accomplished with a female under any one (1) of the following circumstances:

. . . .

(3) Where she resists but her resistance is overcome by force or violence.

The term "resistance" is not defined in the statute and there is no legislative history to provide guidance. Thus, we begin our review by considering the common law. "At common law, [a] state had to prove beyond a reasonable doubt that the woman resisted her assailant to the utmost of her physical capacity to prove that an act of sexual intercourse was rape." Thus, under the utmost-physical-resistance standard, "verbal resistance was simply inadequate to prove anything."

The utmost-resistance requirement, beyond producing some severely inequitable results at trial, proved to be nearly impossible to establish. Thus, the utmost-resistance standard has since been abandoned to varying degrees. Approximately thirty-two states, the Model Penal Code, the District of Columbia Code, and the Uniform Code of Military Justice have done away with the resistance requirement completely, allowing prosecutors to establish a rape without any resistance present. Six more states' criminal codes expressly state that physical resistance is not required for a rape conviction.

As the State notes, Idaho began its departure from the common law rule about 105 years ago. . . .

In Idaho, the rape victim is not required to resist to the utmost of the victim's ability. The importance of resistance by the victim is simply to show two elements of the crime—the assailant's intent to use force in order to have sexual intercourse and the victim's non-consent.

Given the plain language of Idaho's forcible rape statute and Idaho's well-established case law regarding resistance, we hold the statute does not require that rape victims resist to their utmost physical ability and that verbal resistance is sufficient resistance to substantiate a charge of forcible rape. For one thing, there is no language in I.C. § 18-6101(3) requiring "physical" resistance. The statute only requires "resistance." It does not differentiate between physical or verbal resistance. Furthermore, [our cases] have expressly rejected the common law utmost physical resistance standard. As a result, the English common law regarding forcible rape has not applied in Idaho for over a century. Therefore, in this State verbal resistance is sufficient for a charge of forcible rape. Whether the evidence establishes the element of resistance is a fact-sensitive determination based on the totality of the circumstances, including the victim's words and conduct.

Beyond this, allowing verbal resistance to support a charge of forcible rape is sound policy. Requiring physical resistance by a rape victim naturally "increases the likelihood of the attacker's use of violence."

The State highlights the inequity of requiring physical resistance in situations in which the victim is restrained and unable to physically resist, as was the case here. It argued that because "Jones applied sufficient force to effectively prevent physical resistance" by A.S., it would be a "miscarriage of justice" to then hold that forcible rape did not occur due to merely verbal resistance. We agree. As this Court [has] observed . . . an inquiry "into the kind, character, and nature of the fight put up by the woman, rather than the nature of the assault and evident and manifest purpose and intent of the assailant," is in effect, backwards. Based on the evidence before it, the jury certainly had sufficient basis to find that on May 22, A.S. resisted Jones' advances. She testified that she "kept yelling at him and pleading for him to stop and please quit, and he just kept ignoring her." When asked if she tried to "strike out," she responded that "[she] couldn't," because "[her] hands were pinned down, and Jones' weight was on [her] on the bed." In sum, A.S.'s verbal resistance, in the form of repeated pleas for Jones to stop, was sufficient evidence of resistance under I.C. § 18-6101(3).

2. Physical force or violence overcoming resistance.

The next issue before us is the meaning of "force or violence" overcoming resistance, for the purposes of I.C. § 18-6101(3). There are two primary approaches for addressing this issue: the extrinsic force standard, which defines "force" as anything beyond that which is inherent or incidental to the sexual act itself and the intrinsic force standard, which deems the force inherent in intercourse as sufficient to substantiate a charge of forcible rape.

The extrinsic force standard is the traditional view and "is still the most commonly adopted." The standard, as stated by the Washington Court of Appeals . . . is that:

The *force* to which reference is made in forcible compulsion "is not the force inherent in the act of penetration but the force used or threatened to overcome or prevent resistance by the female." . . . Where the degree of force exerted by the perpetrator is the distinguishing feature between second and third degree rape, to establish second degree rape the evidence must be sufficient to show that the force exerted was directed at overcoming the victim's resistance and was more than that which is normally required to achieve penetration.

The primary justification for the extrinsic force standard seems to be textual. That is, if a forcible rape statute by definition requires penetration, then for an additional requirement of force to be meaningful, it necessarily must mean some force beyond that inherent in penetration. . . .

The intrinsic force standard, on the other hand, represents the more modern trend. It provides that any amount of force — even that which is inherent in intercourse — can substantiate a charge of rape. The seminal case adopting this standard is *In re M.T.S.*, 129 N.J. 422, 609 A.2d 1266 (N.J. 1992). In *M.T.S.*, the Supreme Court of New Jersey considered "whether the element of 'physical force' is met simply by an act of non-consensual penetration involving no more force than necessary to accomplish" the act. There, the victim had been sleeping, and woke up to realize her clothes were removed, and that the assailant was on top of her, in the act of penetration. After examining the state's "reformed statute," which defined rape without reference to a victim's resistance or submission, the court there found that:

> The understanding of sexual assault as a criminal battery, albeit one with especially serious consequences, follows necessarily from the Legislature's decision to eliminate non-consent and resistance from the substantive definition of the offense. Under the new law, the victim no longer is required to resist and therefore need not have said or done anything in order for the sexual penetration to be unlawful. The alleged victim is not put on trial, and his or her responsive or defensive behavior is rendered immaterial. We are thus satisfied that an interpretation of the statutory crime of sexual assault to require physical force in addition to that entailed in an act of involuntary or unwanted sexual penetration would be fundamentally inconsistent with the legislative purpose to eliminate any consideration of whether the victim resisted or expressed non-consent.

Other jurisdictions, with similar statutes, have adopted the intrinsic force standard.

Based on the plain language of I.C. § 18-6101(3), we hold that the extrinsic force standard applies in Idaho. Section 18-6101(3) defines forcible rape as "penetration, however slight," "[w]here [a woman] resists but her resistance is overcome by force or violence." Were we to construe "force" as encompassing the act of penetration itself, it would effectively render the force element moot. Force would *always* be present and never have to be proven, so long as there was sexual intercourse. Generally speaking, "it is incumbent upon a court to give a statute an interpretation which will not render it a nullity." Thus, in order to give full effect to the complete text of the statute, we adopt the extrinsic force standard. Beyond this, the intrinsic force standard is typically instituted in jurisdictions where the legislature has stepped in to amend its rape statute. But in Idaho, the Legislature has not undertaken any such reform. We must work within the confines of the statute as written. Thus, we conclude that some force beyond that which is inherent in the sexual act is required for a charge of forcible rape.

Even with the extrinsic force standard, a jury had sufficient evidence before it to conclude beyond a reasonable doubt that Jones used force that overcame A.S.'s resistance. This is because Jones used more force than is inherent in the sexual act during the incident on May 22. As A.S. testified, Jones "leaned forward" and she "was pushed down . . . to where [she] couldn't get up"; he "leaned forward to where his body was pushing on [hers]," pinning her hands underneath her so she could not turn around; and he removed her underwear to the side. Jones argues that all these actions were merely incidental to the act of intercourse. But Jones' use of his body weight to trap A.S.'s hands under her, and effectively forestall any struggle, seems in particular less "incidental" to sex and far more like force employed to overcome her resistance. Thus, a jury could well have found beyond a reasonable doubt that Jones used force to overcome A.S.'s resistance during the incident on May 22. Because both the resistance and force elements were present for this incident, we hold that there is sufficient evidence to sustain a conviction for forcible rape, and accordingly affirm Count I.

C

Because A.S. neither physically nor verbally resisted sexual intercourse on May 28, there was insufficient evidence to convict Jones on Count II.

Jones contends that there was insufficient evidence to support a conviction for forcible rape on Count II, particularly that A.S. never even verbally communicated to him that she did not want to engage in sexual activity or that he used force or violence to overcome any resistance. The State counters that "A.S.'s resistance was in feigning sleep—passive resistance," and that this was enough to show A.S.'s lack of consent to intercourse during the May 28 incident. Jones replies that "the States' position that non-resistance is proof of resistance," is untenable, not in accord with the plain language of 18-6101(3), and would effectively render the explicit resistance requirement a nullity.

We hold that there is insufficient evidence to support a charge of forcible rape based on Count II. By her own admission, A.S. "didn't respond" physically, or even verbally, to Jones' advances on May 28—she "just froze." Idaho's forcible rape statute expressly requires resistance. Satisfying this element with inactivity strains the definition of resistance, essentially nullifying the resistance requirement. Though studies have shown that "freezing up" is indeed a legitimate, understandable reaction of victims of sexual assault,[6] this Court has no authority to jettison the resistance requirement—modifying this State's statutes is the Legislature's province alone. As the statute is plainly written, some quantum of resistance is required, and A.S. did not resist Jones' advances on May 28. There was insufficient evidence on the element of resistance to support the conviction of forcible rape on Count II so we need not consider the issue of force.

The conviction on Count II is accordingly reversed. . . .

We affirm Jones' conviction on Count I, and reverse his conviction on Count II.

Steven Schulhofer

Reforming the Law of Rape

35 Law & Inequality 335, 342-45 (2017)

In almost half the states, sexual penetration is not a crime unless there is *both* non-consent *and* some sort of force. *Penetration without consent is not, in itself, a crime.*

---

6. See People v. Barnes, 721 P.2d 110, 118-19 (Ca. 1986) ("For example, some studies have demonstrated that while some women respond to sexual assault with active resistance, others 'freeze.' . . . One researcher found that many women demonstrate 'psychological infantilism'—a frozen fright response—in the face of sexual assault. . . .The 'frozen fright' response resembles cooperative behavior. . . . Indeed, . . . the 'victim may smile, even initiate acts, and may appear relaxed and calm.' . . . Subjectively, however, she may be in a state of terror. [Also] the victim may make submissive signs to her assailant and engage in propitiating behavior in an effort to inhibit further aggression. . . .These findings belie the traditional notion that a woman who does not resist has consented. They suggest that lack of physical resistance may reflect a 'profound primal terror' rather than consent.").

This last point is emphasized for a reason; it is not a misprint. All people (or almost all people) know, as a matter of common decency, that no one is supposed to ignore a clear expression of non-consent. Today many students learn in high school, and nearly all college students learn in freshman orientation, that it is unacceptable to ignore a clear expression of non-consent. But that is not a criminal law requirement in almost half the states. In all these jurisdictions, some sort of force is required, *in addition* to non-consent, to make out a crime. . . .

In a majority of states, it is finally true that non-consent alone suffices. . . . This battle is not over, but the trend is clear. . . .

That leaves two important issues where the trend is *not* clear and where reform still faces formidable opposition. First, what counts as consent? What is the minimum requirement? And second, when that minimum requirement is met—for example, when you have explicit permission—what circumstances nullify that *apparent* consent? When does *yes* mean *yes*? These are the places where the key battles for reform are now being fought. . . .

Among states that treat absence of consent as sufficient (together with sexual penetration) to establish the offense, there is wide and consequential disagreement about what "consent" means. There are three options in play. The first option says that to prove unwillingness, there must be some verbal protest. The second option says we should assume *non*-consent unless there is clear affirmative permission. In the first option, silence and passivity always imply consent; in the second option, silence and passivity always mean *no* consent. In the third option, silence and passivity can imply *either* consent or non-consent, depending on all the circumstances.

In media accounts, the requirement of affirmative permission is often portrayed as a nightmare of fascist intervention in private life, as if all sex would be illegal in the absence of a written agreement—signed, sealed, and notarized. You would never know from the alarmist media hype that realistic standards of affirmative consent, signaled by words or conduct, are already the law in many states, including Minnesota and Wisconsin, where these standards seem to work perfectly well.

Equally important, it is crucial to explain why this is the *right* standard. This standard simply says that people do not want to be sexually penetrated unless and until they indicate (by words or actual conduct) that they do. Without that requirement, the law would, in effect, be assuming that people are always receptive to sexual intercourse (at any time, with any person) until they do something to revoke that permission.

That is hardly an accurate description of ordinary life. Moreover, when we consider the specific contexts in which sexual abuse typically occurs, the point is even clearer. Sexual interaction too often occurs when someone's ability to express unwillingness is impaired, whether by fright, intimidation, alcohol, or drugs. A standard that treats silence or passivity as equivalent to consent—a standard that requires people to communicate their *un*willingness—presents enormous dangers of sexual abuse.

NOTES

1. **Rape Law Reform.**   Rape law reform in this country has come in roughly three waves. The first began with revisions to the Model Penal Code (MPC) in

the 1950s, which in turn stimulated statutory reforms in many states. This reform refocused the crime from the conduct of the victim to the conduct of the defendant and included, among other things, the abolition of the common provision requiring the victim to offer the "utmost" or "reasonable" resistance. To increase the likelihood of convictions and to reduce the scope for idiosyncratic or biased judgments, the MPC also divided rape into three categories. First-degree felony rape was reserved for life-threatening conduct where the parties were strangers or where the defendant inflicted serious bodily harm. Life-threatening rape between acquaintances was a second-degree felony. Less serious abuses were grouped under a new third-degree felony of "gross sexual imposition." These alternatives continue to raise subtle questions about naming the crime. Does the decision to call such conduct something other than "rape" matter?

The next wave was a series of law reforms enacted from the 1970s through the 1990s to respond to critiques of rape law by women's advocates. The most prominent examples were rape shield statutes (discussed in Note 5 below), the elimination or relaxation of the marital rape exemption, alterations in the substantive requirements of force and nonconsent, and a broadening of the definition of rape specified for federal reporting requirements.[51] It also included the substitution of gender-neutral language for traditional formulations that assumed that only women could be raped, and only by men.

During this second wave of rape reform, women's rights advocates also centered attention on changing laws and practices to recognize that "no means no." At the time, that proposition was not uncontroversial. Some commentators invoked studies indicating that women sometimes protested when they wanted sex to avoid looking promiscuous. The conservative critic John Leo argued that "the mating game does not proceed by words alone."[52] From this view, the "demonization" of men that was assertedly common in feminists' writing on date rape seemed profoundly unjust. If women were unclear about their preferences, men should not pay the price. Other commentators worried that broadening definitions of rape would give women unreasonable control to define, after the fact, what is or is not acceptable consensual sex.[53]

These objections intensified during the third wave of rape reform, when activists sought to institutionalize requirements of affirmative consent and address deficiencies in the way that state statutes dealt with campus assaults.[54] This third wave of reform was reflected in a new overhaul of the MPC provisions on rape and includes further modifications to the consent requirement, discussed in Note 2, below. Current reform efforts have also focused on responses to sexual assault by educational institutions (see Section 3 of this chapter) and in the military (see Note 11, below).

---

51. See U.S. Dep't of Just., Attorney General Holder Announces Revisions to the Uniform Crime Reports Definition of Rape (Jan. 6, 2012).

52. John Leo, Two Steps Ahead of the Thought Police 247 (1994).

53. See Neil Gilbert, The Phantom Epidemic of Sexual Assault, 103 Pub. Int. 54 (Spring 1991).

54. For a critique of state statutes particularly regarding consent and intoxication, see David Dematteo et al., Sexual Assault on College Campuses: A 50 State Survey of Criminal Sexual Assault Statutes and Their Relevance to Campus Sexual Assault, 21 Psych. Pub. Pol'y & L. 227 (2015).

2. **Consent.**   Much of the contemporary debate on rape law has centered on how to define consent, or its absence. On one end of the spectrum is the traditional rule that a victim who did not offer the "utmost" or at least "reasonable" resistance must have consented. On the other end of the spectrum is the Schulhofer recommendation in the excerpt above, which makes anything less than affirmative permission equivalent to a lack of consent.[55] The requirement of physical resistance has been abandoned. Several states have explicit or de facto affirmative consent rules. Where do you think consent rules ought to be located on the continuum?

The American Law Institute's (ALI's) proposed revision to the MPC in Section 213(e) defines consent as follows:

> **(i)** "Consent" for purposes of Article 213 means a person's willingness to engage in a specific act of sexual penetration, oral sex, or sexual contact.
>
> **(ii)** Neither verbal nor physical resistance is required to establish that consent is lacking. Consent may be express or it may be inferred from behavior—both action and inaction—in the context of all the circumstances.
>
> **(iii)** Notwithstanding subsection (2)(e)(ii) of this Section, consent is ineffective when given by a person incompetent to consent or under circumstances precluding the free exercise of consent, as provided in [other sections].
>
> **(iv)** Consent may be revoked or withdrawn any time before or during the act of sexual penetration, oral sex, or sexual contact. A clear verbal refusal—such as "No," "Stop," or "Don't"—establishes the lack of consent or the revocation or withdrawal of previous consent. Lack of consent or revocation or withdrawal of consent may be overridden by subsequent consent given prior to the act of sexual penetration, oral sex, or sexual contact.[56]

This rule, which was approved by the ALI membership in May 2022 and was awaiting final adoption at the time this book went to print, would make "willingness," not resistance, the standard. It would also explicitly make even verbal resistance unnecessary, though verbal resistance will establish the lack of consent. It would still allow defendants to argue consent could be inferred from behavior. Do these rules strike you as being ahead of the curve, behind it, or exactly on track with current legal and social thinking about rape?

3. **Cultural Attitudes, "Rape Myths," and Law Enforcement Responses.**   Of all major felonies, rape is said to be the "least reported, least indicted, and least likely to end in a conviction."[57] One study finds that of 100 rapes committed, an estimated 5 to 20 are reported to police, 0.4 to 5.4 percent are prosecuted, 0.2 to

---

55. See also Stephen Schulhofer, Unwanted Sex: The Culture of Intimidation and the Failure of Law (2000) (proposing a crime of "nonviolent sexual misconduct" for invading a person's bodily integrity in the face of ambivalence, objection, or silence). For a more equivocal view on affirmative consent, see Jonathan Witmer-Rich, Unpacking Affirmative Consent: Not as Great as You Hope, Not as Bad as You Fear, 49 Tex. Tech L. Rev. 57 (2016).

56. Model Pen. Code, Sexual Assault and Related Offenses § 213.0(2)(e) (Am. L. Inst., Tentative Draft No. 6 (Apr. 2022).

57. Deborah L. Rhode, Rape on Campus and in the Military: An Agenda for Reform, 23 UCLA Women's L.J. 1, 2 (2016).

5.2 percent result in conviction, and 0.2 to 2.8 percent result in incarceration.[58] Major factors affecting the likelihood of conviction include the degree of acquaintance between the victim and accused, the appearance and reputation of the victim, the capacity of the victim to recall key details, the availability of physical evidence, and the presence and degree of intoxication.[59]

Low conviction rates are partly attributed to "myths" about rape shared by judges, juries, and law enforcement personnel. These myths include the following: (1) only certain women (i.e., those with "bad" reputations) are raped; (2) only certain men (i.e., psychopaths) rape; (3) women invite or deserve rape by their appearance and behavior; and (4) women fantasize about or fabricate rape, motivated by desire, revenge, blackmail, jealousy, guilt, or embarrassment.

Such myths result in the credibility discounting that Deborah Tuerkheimer described. As she and other researchers note, there is little factual basis for common assumptions such as the belief that false reports are common and men are commonly arrested and prosecuted as a result.[60] The persistence of such myths is of particular concern because they discourage reporting and responses to reports by law enforcement officials and also because endorsement of such beliefs is associated with greater proclivities to commit sexual violence and less willingness to offer support to victims.[61]

Consider the following examples:

- Defense counsel for Bill Cosby, who had been accused of rape or sexual misconduct by more than fifty women, chastised the complainant Andrea Constand for "cavorting around with a married man old enough to be her grandfather." She suggested that Constand and other accusers had made up their stories in a bid for money and fame, and called one of them a "failed starlet" and "aged-out model" who "sounds as though she slept with every man on the planet."[62]
- Camille Paglia argues that a "girl who lets herself get dead drunk at a fraternity party is a fool. A girl who goes upstairs alone with a brother at a fraternity party is an idiot. Feminists call this 'blaming the victim.' I call it common sense."[63]

---

58. Kimberly A. Lonsway & Joanne Archambault, The "Justice Gap" for Sexual Assault Cases: Future Directions for Research and Reform, 18 Violence Against Women 145, 157 (2012).

59. Claire R. Gravelin et al., Blaming the Victim of Acquaintance Rape: Individual, Situational, and Sociocultural Factors. 9 Frontiers Psychol. 2422 (2019); see also Tamara Rice Lave, The Prosecutor's Duty to "Imperfect" Rape Victims, 49 Tex. Tech L. Rev. 219, 231 (2016).

60. Dana A. Weisler, Confronting Myths About Sexual Assault: A Feminist Analysis of the False Report Literature, 66 Fam. Rels. 46, 49-54 (2017).

61. Id. at 47.

62. Michael R. Sisak et al., Bill Cosby's Lawyers Get Slammed by Advocates for Women, Lubbock Avalanche J. (Apr. 25, 2018) (quoting Kathleen Bliss).

63. Camille Paglia, Sex, Art, and American Culture 51 (1992).

Do either of these examples exemplify a "rape myth"? Can you offer any better examples? Is it fair to say that today's society constitutes a "rape culture"?[64]

Some experts suggest that rape myths persist because they are a self-protective way to deal with the unsettling disconnect between the profound harms of sexual assault and its frequency.[65] Katharine Baker suggests that three factors help account for our problems in reducing rape: (1) the criminal burden of proof often makes it too difficult to prove lack of consent; (2) constructions of the rapist as "profoundly deviant and distinctly criminal" do not correspond to the characteristics of many men accused of rape; and (3) rape reform efforts often assume that women lack agency, a view that women themselves resist. Baker suggests that civil approaches to rape, and in particular the federal Department of Education's efforts to use Title IX to curb sexual assault on college campuses (discussed in the next section of this chapter), may be more effective in reducing nonconsensual sex and in dislodging current sex norms than further efforts to tighten the criminal law.[66] Margo Kaplan supports a public health approach to rape, declaring, "Our justice system cannot prosecute offenses effectively absent a change in deeply entrenched social norms that normalize sexual aggression. Public health interventions, however, can help shift the norms that thwart criminal prosecution — norms that criminal law has long been ineffective in changing."[67] Is she right? Does a public education approach have advantages over a criminal approach to rape? Do "slutwalks," where women dress suggestively to challenge the idea that clothing provokes or justifies rape, contribute to the dismantling of rape culture?

4. **Rape and Scientific Evidence.**   Following a sexual assault, victims often agree to an exam that yields a "rape kit" — a collection of hair, semen, and skin cell samples. The DNA extracted from these kits can be checked against databases of DNA from violent criminals and a match can lead to successful prosecutions. Because serial offenders are thought to account for a significant percentage of rapes, kit evidence can be a crucial law enforcement tool. However, it is estimated that hundreds of thousands of kits remain untested due to lack of resources.[68] Public outcry has begun making addressing that backlog a priority, and federal and local governments, as well as nonprofit groups, have allocated additional funding to the effort. Some women's rights advocates argue for limiting the use of kits to

----

64. Courtney Fraser, From "Ladies First" to "Asking for It": Benevolent Sexism in the Maintenance of Rape Culture, 103 Calif. L. Rev. 141, 143 (2015).

65. Holly Boux, "If You Wouldn't Have Been There That Night, None of This Would Have Happened To You": Rape Myth Usage in the American Judiciary, 40 Women's Rts. L. Rep. 237, 248 (2019).

66. Katharine K. Baker, Why Rape Should Not (Always) Be a Crime, 100 Minn. L. Rev. 221, 223-24 (2015).

67. Margo Kaplan, Rape Beyond Crime, 66 Duke L.J. 1045, 1051 (2017).

68. The exact extent of the problem is unknown because many cities have failed to compile statistics or have destroyed untested kits, although organizations such as End the Backlog have begun to chart the problem and propose reforms. See https://www.endthe backlog.org. For an estimate of at least 200,000 untested kits as of mid-2019, see Barbara Bradley Hagerty, An Epidemic of Disbelief: What New Research Reveals About Sexual Predators, Why Police Fail to Catch Them, Atlantic (July 22, 2019).

cases of stranger rape as a way of minimizing backlog and trauma to the victim.[69] Such evidence is generally irrelevant in cases of acquaintance rape, where the issue is typically consent. How would you respond?

Notably, use of DNA evidence has also been a principal source of the reversal of rape convictions. See Note 6, below.

5. **Rape Shield Laws, Character Evidence, and Defendant's Rights.** All states have rape shield laws. Many of these laws prohibit admission of evidence of the complainant's prior sexual conduct subject to one or more legislated exceptions, such as where the evidence would show prior sexual conduct between the complainant and the accused; an alternative source of semen, pregnancy, or injury; bias or motive to fabricate; a pattern of prior sexual conduct (sometimes making prostitution relevant); a mistaken belief by the accused in the complainant's consent; and prior false accusations of sexual assault by the complainant.[70] Other states allow judicial discretion, or have a catchall provision allowing evidence where necessary to protect the defendant's constitutional rights. A few states determine the admissibility of a woman's sexual history based on the purpose for which the evidence is offered. For example, a rape shield statute might prohibit sexual history evidence offered to prove the complainant's consent to the challenged act of sexual intercourse, but permit it as admissible if offered to attack the complainant's credibility. The converse is the case in other jurisdictions.[71]

Rape shield statutes have drawn criticism from all sides. Civil libertarians and criminal defense counsel often claim that the protections compromise defendants' rights to a fair trial. As stated by one defense counsel:

> Now a public-policy decision designed to correct vestiges of Victorian-era morality has stacked the deck against every citizen accused of a sex crime. . . .
>
> Our justice system depends on the belief that a randomly drawn jury, culled only for prejudice and partiality, can detect truth and falsity. But if a jury is given a skewed presentation of the facts, or if important facts are withheld from a jury, we cannot expect it to do justice.
>
> Most rape cases that turn on whether a sex act was consensual . . . [will] ultimately come down to a "he said/she said" contest between the accused and the accuser. But how can a jury accurately judge the credibility of the two parties if the accused has been presented in the worst possible light while the accuser is enshrouded in a cloak of purity?[72]

---

69. Taylor Gamble, Thinking Outside the Box: Limiting the Collection of Rape Kit Evidence in Acquaintance Rape Trials, 20 Cardozo J.L. & Gender 743, 760-62 (2014). For a novel recent proposal, see Emily Hessenthaler, Promoting Expedited Progress: The Case for Federal Sexual Assault Kit Tracking Software, 98 U. Det. Mercy L. Rev. 261, 263 (2021).

70. For a survey of rules, see Victoria Brown et al., Rape & Sexual Assault, 21 Geo. J. Gender & L. 367, 407-20 (2020).

71. See id.

72. Barry Tarlow, Criminal Justice: Rape Suspects' Uphill Road, L.A. Times, Aug. 17, 2003, at M3.

By contrast, many women's advocates claim that the exemptions compromise complainants' rights to privacy and deter other victims from reporting the crime. The problem is particularly acute for prostitutes, who are frequently vulnerable to sexual assault.[73] Shield laws do not prevent police and prosecutors from considering sexual history, nor do they prevent non-governmental actors and the media from publicizing such behavior.[74] Some commentators have also argued that the message implicitly communicated by shield laws is that jurors should assume that the complainant is a "good girl" untarnished by too much or the wrong kind of sexual behavior. On this view, feminist reformers may have "reinscribed the very chastity requirement they hoped to abolish."[75] How would you respond?

In one Oregon case involving admission of social media evidence, a grand jury declined to authorize a prosecution for sexual assault after seeing the teen victim's MySpace page where she talked about drinking and "getting some," and posted provocative pictures of herself. Such a self-portrait was said to be inconsistent with her claim to the police that she would never willingly have had sex.[76] In a California sexual assault case, the appellate court ruled that it was reversible error to exclude social media evidence to impeach a rape survivor's testimony that she was a virgin.[77] Some commentators have criticized such decisions as inconsistent with the intent of shield laws, while others have maintained that social media postings are inherently public and should be admissible.[78] What is your view?

Despite rape shield laws, some complainants—especially those involving celebrity defendants—are exposed by the media and subject to vilification in the press. In a widely publicized case involving basketball player Kobe Bryant, for example, the complainant received so many threats that she refused to testify and the prosecutor dropped the case.[79] In a *New York Times* op-ed, Dahlia Lithwick offered this assessment of the Bryant prosecution:

> Enacted with the best of intentions, rape shield statutes don't work, particularly in high-profile cases. . . . There is a class of cases that are simply beyond the ability of the legal system to resolve, both because some truths are ultimately unknowable, and because it isn't "justice" when everyone emerges from a trial so damaged that it hardly matters who won.[80]

---

73. Lave, supra note 59, at 240.

74. Aya Gruber, Rape, Feminism, and the War on Crime, 84 Wash. L. Rev. 581, 646-47 (2009).

75. I. Bennett Capers, Real Women, Real Rape, 60 UCLA L. Rev. 826, 874 (2013).

76. Beth C. Boggs & Misty L. Edwards, Does What Happens on Facebook Stay on Facebook? Discovery, Admissibility, Ethics, and Social Media, 98 Ill. Bar J. 366, 367 (2010).

77. People v. Flynn, No. F062483, 2013 WL 6047625 (Cal. Ct. App. 2013).

78. See Kim Loewen, Rejecting the Purity Myth: Reforming Rape Shield Laws in the Age of Social Media, 22 UCLA Women's L.J. 151, 160 (2015).

79. She then filed a civil suit, which ultimately settled. Kirk Johnson, As Accuser Balks, Prosecutors Drop Bryant Rape Case, N.Y. Times, Sept. 2, 2004, at A1.

80. Dahlia Lithwick, The Shield That Failed, N.Y. Times, Aug. 8, 2004, at SR11.

Do you agree? Are there offsetting benefits to victims from media coverage if it encourages others to come forward, as was true in cases involving Bill Cosby, Larry Nassar, and Harvey Weinstein? Do those cases pose similar concerns about the rights of those accused, who may be tried in the media without due process safeguards?

A related issue has arisen in controversies over the admission of the defendant's prior sexual misconduct at trial. Prior bad acts are ordinarily not admissible in a criminal trial because they are thought to be overly prejudicial.[81] In 1994, Congress enacted Federal Rules of Evidence 413 and 415, which created an exception to the general ban on character evidence to allow admission of the defendant's prior sexual violence in federal cases, even if relevant only to the defendant's disposition or propensity to engage in such conduct. Advocates of the federal exception argue that the severity of sex crimes, the frequency of serial offenses, and the difficulties of proof suggest a particular need for such evidence.[82] In cases that hinge on credibility, prior acts can lend crucial credibility to a complainant's testimony and encourage victims to come forward.

A case in point involved the criminal trial of entertainer Bill Cosby. By 2018, some fifty women had accused him of sexual misconduct dating back decades, the vast majority barred by statutes of limitations.[83] He reached civil settlements with some, and the only one that proceeded to criminal trial initially ended with a hung jury. Defense attorneys presented the complaining witness as a gold-digging "con artist," and because Pennsylvania does not have an exception to bans on character evidence for sexual misconduct, the court permitted only one other alleged victim to testify.[84] On retrial, the court permitted five other accusers to testify to show a pattern of behavior, and the jury convicted Cosby on three counts of aggravated indecent assault.[85] The criminal verdict was overturned on the grounds that subjecting Cosby to trial after an agreement not to prosecute violated his right to due process.[86] Subsequently, a then-teenaged victim of Cosby was awarded $500,000 in damages against him in a civil trial.[87]

---

81. Fed. R. Evid. 413-415 (2022).

82. See 140 Cong. Rec. S12,990 (daily ed., Sept. 20, 1994) (statement of Senator Dole); Tamara Lave & Aviva A. Orenstein, Empirical Fallacies of Evidence Law: A Critical Look at the Admission of Prior Sex Crimes, 81 U. Cin. L. Rev. 795, 806-07 (2013).

83. Graham Bowley, Now That He's Been Convicted, What Comes Next?, N.Y. Times, Apr. 28, 2018, at A17.

84. Attorneys used the same defense in the retrial. Graham Bowley & Jon Hurdle, In Bill Cosby's Case, Who's the Con Artist? Both Sides Close by Pointing Fingers, N.Y. Times, Apr. 24, 2018, at A16.

85. Timothy Williams, Why Cosby Verdict Is Probably Less Breakthrough than Anomaly, N.Y. Times, Apr. 28, 2018, at A18. The admissibility of such evidence is subject to appeal. Sherry F. Colb, Bill Cosby and the Rule Against Character Evidence, Justia's Verdict (Jan. 15, 2016).

86. Maryclaire Dale & Alanna Durkin Richer, Explainer: Why Bill Cosby's Verdict Was Overturned, AP News (June 30, 2021); see also Commonwealth v. Cosby, 252 A.3d 1092 (Pa. 2021).

87. Graham Bowley et al., A Verdict in the Bill Cosby Civil Trial Has Been Reached. Here's What to Know, N.Y. Times, July 21, 2022.

How would you balance the rights of defendants and interests of survivors and potential victims? Would you support an approach that allows evidence of prior sexual misconduct to be admissible, but only if it demonstrates a reasonably recent common pattern of abuse, as was the case in Cosby's trial?[88] How would you evaluate related concerns about laws requiring registration of former sex offenders and limitations on where they can live and work?

6. **Rape and Race.**   American law and enforcement practices have long treated allegations of sexual assault differently based on the race of the victim and the assailant. At one time, rape of a non-white woman was not a crime.[89] By contrast, the rape of a white woman by a Black man was considered the most horrific sexual offense and provided the most common justification for lynching. Although most rapes, like most other crimes, are intraracial rather than interracial, rapes in which Black men are the perpetrators and white women the victims have historically been the most widely broadcast and received the most serious sanctions. Some early legal statutes required that Black men convicted of raping white women be castrated.[90]

Racial disparities have persisted into the twenty-first century. In one survey of cases involving no weapons, prosecutors were over four times as likely to file charges if the victim was white.[91] In explaining their decisions, prosecutors often claimed that jurors are less willing to convict in cases involving poor and minority victims.[92] According to 2016 FBI statistics, over 29 percent of those arrested for rape in this country are Black — more than double the percentage of Blacks in the population (12 percent) — and fully a third of men under the age of 18 arrested for rape are Black.[93] Blacks are also overrepresented in the number of cases in which criminal convictions have been overturned and defendants exonerated, and the numbers are especially high in rape cases. The Innocence Project, which supports the work of attorneys seeking to reverse criminal convictions based on proof of actual innocence, reports that there have been 375 exonerations nationwide based on DNA evidence. Sixty percent of the exonerees are Black,[94] and 75 percent of individuals exonerated from their rape convictions are Black or Latino.[95] These

---

88. Deborah L. Rhode, Character in Criminal Justice Proceedings: Rethinking Its Role in Rules Governing Evidence, Punishment, Prosecutors and Parole, 45 Am. J. Crim. L. 353, 364 (2019).

89. See, e.g., George v. State, 37 Miss. 316 (Miss. Err. & App. 1859).

90. See A. Leon Higginbotham, Jr., & Anne F. Jacobs, The "Law Only as an Enemy": The Legitimization of Racial Powerlessness Through the Colonial Laws of Virginia, 70 N.C. L. Rev. 969, 1055-60 (1992).

91. Cassia Spohn & David Holleran, Prosecuting Sexual Assault: A Comparison of Charging Decisions in Sexual Assault Cases Involving Strangers, Acquaintances, and Intimate Partners, 18 Just. Q. 651, 680 (2001).

92. See Corey Rayburn Yung, Rape Law Gatekeeping, 58 B.C. L. Rev. 205, 229-30 (2017).

93. U.S. Dep't of Just., FBI, 2016 Crime in the United States, Table 21: Arrests by Race and Ethnicity (2016).

94. See Innocence Project, DNA Exonerations in the United States (2020).

95. Brandon Garrett, Duke L. Forensics F., Race and DNA Exonerations (June 5, 2020). For a national registry of exonerations, see https://www.law.umich.edu/special/exoneration/Pages/about.aspx.

exonerations are replete with examples of police, prosecutors, or both, withholding evidence and victims misidentifying their rapists. Misidentifications are often reinforced by prosecutorial misconduct designed to keep the victim from backing down from her identification of a perpetrator and to resist any effort by the victim to retract that identification.

These issues are illustrated in the recent controversy over Alice Sebold's memoir, Lucky,[96] detailing the case in which a Black man, Anthony Broadwater, served sixteen years in prison and twenty-three years on probation for raping Sebold, when it was revealed in late 2021 that Sebold had misidentified Broadwater as her rapist. Sebold had initially picked a different Black man in the police lineup, and later acknowledged that the composite sketch made based on the information she provided was inaccurate; however she stuck with her identification, in part because of lies by a prosecutor that made her feel she was correct in identifying Broadwater.[97] In another high-profile case of misidentification and prosecutorial misconduct, Jennifer Thompson became increasingly certain that the Black man she identified, Ronald Cotton, was her rapist based on lies and encouragement from law enforcement personnel. When she finally realized he was not, she had to overcome enormous resistance from prosecutors to retract her identification and aid Cotton in his efforts to be exonerated.[98]

The pattern of targeting Black men as rapists has helped to construct Black men as oversexualized and highly dangerous, especially to white women. Indeed, the image of Black men lusting after white women has been central to the narrative of the "Bestial Black Man"[99] — an image that pushes and exacerbates general stereotypes about Black men as violent, irresponsible, and uncivilized.

It is, in part, out of racial sympathy with the injustices that many Black men have experienced in the criminal legal system, especially when it comes to rape, that Black women tend to view rape differently than their white counterparts. It is also because, for Black women, being raped historically meant something different than it did for white women. Both of these dimensions are captured in a classic explanation by Angela Harris in 1990 for how the experience of race is not simply an additive burden to being a woman, but a transformative one.

> [T]he paradigm experience of rape for black women has historically involved the white employer in the kitchen or bedroom as much as the

---

96. Alice Sebold, Lucky (1999).

97. See Karen Zraick & Alexandra Alter, Man Is Exonerated in Rape Case Described in Alice Sebold's Memoir, N.Y. Times, Dec. 1, 2021; Johanna Berkman, Why Didn't More of Us Question Alice Sebold's Memoir?, N.Y. Mag. (Dec. 10, 2021); Alexandra Alter & Karen Zraick, Alice Sebold Apologizes to Man Wrongly Convicted of Raping Her, N.Y. Times, Nov. 30, 2021.

98. Jennifer Thompson-Cannino et al., Picking Cotton: Our Memoir of Injustice and Redemption (2010).

99. See N. Jeremi Duru, The Central Park Five, the Scottsboro Boys, and the Myth of the Bestial Black Man, 25 Cardozo L. Rev. 1315, 1323-24 (2004). See also Scott W. Stern, The NAACP's Rape Docket and the Origins of Criminal Procedure, 24 U. Pa. J.L. & Soc. Change 241, 318-19 (2021) (describing the Black feminist critique of Susan Brownmiller's assertion that claims of white women's false accusations of rape against Black men are a "rape lie").

strange black man in the bushes. During slavery, the sexual abuse of black women by white men was commonplace. Even after emancipation, the majority of working black women were domestic servants for white families, a job which made them uniquely vulnerable to sexual harassment and rape.

Moreover, as a legal matter, the experience of rape did not even exist for black women. During slavery, the rape of a black woman by any men, white or black, was simply not a crime. Even after the Civil War, rape laws were seldom used to protect black women against either white or black men, since black women were considered promiscuous by nature. In contrast to the partial or at least formal protection white women had against sexual brutalization, black women frequently had no legal protection whatsoever. "Rape," in this sense, was something that only happened to white women; what happened to black women was simply life.

Finally, for black people, male and female, "rape" signified the terrorism of black men by white men, aided and abetted, passively (by silence) or actively (by "crying rape"), by white women. . . . [S]ocial activist Ida B. Wells . . . saw that both the law of rape and Southern miscegenation laws were part of a patriarchal system through which white men maintained their control over the bodies of all black people: "[W]hite men used their ownership of the body of the white female as a terrain on which to lynch the black male." Moreover, Wells argued, white women, protected by the patriarchal idealization of white womanhood, were able to remain silent, unhappily or not, as black men were murdered by mobs. . . .

[T]he experience of rape for black women includes not only a vulnerability to rape and a lack of legal protection radically different from that experienced by white women, but also a unique ambivalence. Black women have simultaneously acknowledged their own victimization and the victimization of black men by a system that has consistently ignored violence against women while perpetrating it against men.[100]

How might Harris' critique apply to rape law reform efforts? Given the historical role of race in constructing rape victims and perpetrators, is it possible for the law of rape to address the harms of rape without reinforcing racial harms?

Another issue disproportionately affecting women of color is police sexual violence, which is the second most reported form of police misconduct (after excessive force).[101] Can you think of a benign explanation for why women of color are more likely than whites to be the victims of police sexual violence? One possibility, which also contributes to the ambivalence of Black women toward the law of rape,

---

100. Angela P. Harris, Race and Essentialism in Feminist Legal Theory, 42 Stan. L. Rev. 581, 601 (1990).

101. Dara E. Purvis & Melissa Blanco, Police Sexual Violence: Police Brutality, #metoo, and Masculinities, 108 Calif. L. Rev. 1487, 1490-91 (2020); see also Andrea J. Ritchie, Invisible No More: Police Violence Against Black Women and Women of Color (2017).

is that women of color are less likely to be believed when they accuse someone of rape.[102]

   7. **The Rape Crisis Counselor Privilege.**   It is contested whether and to what extent a rape complainant should have the right to shield disclosures made to rape crisis counselors. Most states have enacted privilege statutes that protect such information, but the statutes vary in whether the privilege is absolute or whether a judge may decide in camera that the probative value of the evidence to the defendant outweighs the victim's interests in confidentiality.[103]

   There are several justifications for the privilege. Victims of sexual assault are likely to obtain more effective counseling if confidentiality can be assured. Without that assurance, the injuries of a sexual assault may be compounded by public disclosure of intimate details from therapeutic sessions.[104] Rape crisis centers are often the primary source of assistance for victims, and failure to protect confidential disclosures to counselors at these centers, whether or not they are licensed physicians, would compromise treatment and reporting. The hardships would be particularly great for individuals who cannot afford assistance from psychiatrists who can assert the privilege.[105]

   The justifications for allowing defendants access to therapeutic records are also significant. In some rape cases, the boundaries of consent and coercion are blurred at best, and subtle, even unintended, encouragement by rape counselors to define an interaction as rape may affect how a complainant later recalls the event. Other relevant details in therapeutic records may include the complainant's prior involvement with the accused and a history of mental health problems.

   Given the enormous costs to the defendant of an unjust conviction, is some relinquishment of the complainant's privacy interests reasonable? How would you strike the balance?

   8. **Marital Rape.**   Early common law assumed that a married woman gave her irrevocable consent to intercourse with her husband. This assumption followed from the law's treatment of married women as their husbands' property. When this rationale became outdated, other justifications emerged for the marital exemption from rape law. According to the initial Model Penal Code, courts should not intrude on the "privacy" of the family relationship; forced sex by a husband is not as harmful as other sexual assaults; and spousal rape would be too easy to charge, too hard to disprove, and too readily available for blackmail. In many countries in Africa and the Middle East, attitudes toward marital rape still mirror those that sustained traditional exemption in Anglo-American law and about 123 countries do not recognize the crime.[106]

---

102. Lisa A. Crooms, Speaking Partial Truths and Preserving Power: Deconstructing White Supremacy, Patriarchy, and the Rape Corroboration Rule in the Interest of Black Liberation, 40 How. L.J. 459, 465 (1997).

103. Recent scholarship points out that "state laws do not necessarily recognize an absolute privilege for communications with a therapist or other medical professional," let alone counselors. Lara Bazelon & Bruce A. Green, Victims' Rights from A Restorative Perspective, 17 Ohio St. J. Crim. L. 293, 318 (2020).

104. For concern about a potential virtual "second rape," see id. 302.

105. Id. at 318.

106. See World Health Org., Violence Against Women Prevalence Estimates, 2018 (Mar. 9, 2021).

By 1993, all jurisdictions in the United States had abolished the marital rape exemption by statute or judicial decision, although some continued to treat it differently from other types of rape.[107] A survey of the law in 2018 revealed fifteen states with different rules applied to marital rape than to other rapes.[108]

Is there a convincing justification for treating marital rape with greater leniency than other sexual assault? The traditional arguments for the exemption are that criminalizing nonconsensual marital sex undermines marital privacy, overstates victim harm, and provides a way for a "vindictive wife" to use fabricated claims to gain leverage in a divorce case.[109] On the other hand, is there any reason to believe that wives are prone to make false charges?[110] Or to believe that spouses suffer fewer adverse effects from marital rape than stranger rape? A few courts have specifically rejected the rationale that marital rape is less traumatic than stranger rape. Does it follow that the law should treat marital rape exactly the same as other forms of sexual assault?

9. **Rape of Men.** For centuries, the problem of male rape went largely unrecognized and some countries still do not recognize it as a crime.[111] In the United States, the frequency with which men are victimized by rape has traditionally been hard to assess. Until 2012, the federal Uniform Crime Reporting program, which collects crime statistics from across the country, gathered data only on rape that met this definition: "the carnal knowledge of a female forcibly and against her will."[112] The definition was revised beginning in 2013 to remove the term "forcible" and to define rape in a gender-neutral way: "Penetration, no matter how slight, of the vagina or anus with any body part or object, or oral penetration by a sex organ of another person, without the consent of the victim."[113] Many other survey instruments also excluded inmates of prisons and jails, where rape of men is prevalent.[114] The Prison Rape Elimination Act of 2003 "mandates data collection as a first step to a longer-term and clearly idealistic goal of preventing rape in prison."[115] As mentioned earlier, current data show that nearly a quarter of men have experienced some form of sexual violence in their lifetime. Roughly 7 percent have been forced to penetrate someone else, and 2.6 percent have experienced completed or attempted rape.[116]

---

107. Samantha Allen, Marital Rape Is Semi-Legal in 8 States, Daily Beast (June 9, 2015); Michelle J. Anderson, Marital Immunity, Intimate Relationships, and Improper Inferences: A New Law on Sexual Offenses by Intimates, 54 Hastings L.J. 1465, 1470-71, 1537-74 (2003).

108. See P. Robinson & T. Williams, Mapping American Criminal Law ch. 24 (2018); Wayne R. LaFave, 2 Substantive Criminal Law § 17.4(d) (3d ed. 2021).

109. Jill Elaine Hasday, Contest and Consent: A Legal History of Marital Rape, 88 Calif. L. Rev. 1373, 1486-89 (2000).

110. LaFave, supra note 108; Hasday, supra note 109, at 1489.

111. Megan Lutz-Priefert, A Call for a More Permanent International Definition of Rape, 6 Creighton Int'l & Comp. L.J. 85, 86 (2015).

112. FBI, Uniform Crime Report, Crime in the United States, 2018.

113. Id.

114. See I. Bennett Capers, Real Rape Too, 99 Calif. L. Rev. 1259, 1266-67 (2011).

115. Id. at 1267; 42 U.S.C. §§ 15601-09 (2018).

116. NISVS, supra note 40, at 3; see also Lara Stemple & Ilan H. Meyer, The Sexual Victimization of Men in America: New Data Challenge Old Assumptions, 104 Am. J. Pub. Health 19 (2014).

The lack of data both reflects and perpetuates inattention to male victims of sexual violence. Does stereotyping about rape victims or rape perpetrators also play a role? Kim Shayo Buchanan argues that the interdisciplinary body of knowledge on prison rape is "systematically biased" because "it tends to highlight forms of abuse that conform to conventional gender expectations, and to ignore or rationalize more common forms of abuse that defy conventional understandings of gender."[117] For example, she asserts that female inmates are more likely to be sexually assaulted by other female inmates than by male staff, and yet we focus "almost exclusively on sexual abuse perpetrated by men."[118] Do we discount reports of sexual violence when the alleged perpetrator is female?[119] Buchanan argues that "researchers, advocates, and officials who participate in prison rape discourse encounter counter-stereotypical facts, they tend to ignore them, or to rationalize them by invoking alternative stereotypes, such as notions of romance or of racialized sexual aggression, to reconcile the unexpected facts with the governing stereotype of masculine domination and feminine vulnerability."[120] Is this "stereotype reconciliation" unique to prison rape? Or is she describing a general phenomenon relating to stereotyped thinking and confirmation bias? (Recall the discussion of cognitive phenomena that perpetuate stereotyped thinking in Chapter 1.)

Incomplete or biased data collection is just one of the obstacles to understanding and addressing the rape of men. Men subject to sexual abuse are at increased risk for physical and psychological problems, as well as substance abuse, and many feel that their masculinity has been called into question.[121] Humiliation and self-blame, together with an absence of resources for men at rape crisis centers, discourage reporting of the offense. In military and prison contexts, men also worry about retaliation. And yet, there is little discussion among lawmakers, policymakers, or researchers about the problem. Bennett Capers explores the lack of focus on the rape of men:

> As a society, we rarely think of male-victim rape. On the few occasions that we do, we assume male rape victimization occurs only in prisons. This assumption is wrong. . . . As a society we have been largely indifferent to the prevalence of male rape victimization. In the prison context, we dismiss it as par for the course, as "just deserts," or, worse yet, as a rarely stated but widely known component of deterrence . . . Outside the prison context, our response is no better. We tell ourselves male rape victimization is "exceedingly rare" or perhaps something that happens only to gay men. In short, we render male rape victimization invisible. . . .

117. Kim Shayo Buchanan, Engendering Rape, 59 UCLA L. Rev. 1630, 1633-39 (2012).

118. Id. at 1633, 1639. The National Alliance to End Sexual Violence is an advocacy group dedicated to addressing sexual violence against male victims. See endsexualviolence. org.

119. See, e.g., Conor Friedersdorf, The Understudied Female Sexual Predator, Atlantic (Nov. 28, 2016).

120. Id. at 1642-43.

121. See generally Joke Depraetere et al., Big Boys Don't Cry: A Critical Interpretive Synthesis of Male Sexual Victimization, 21 Trauma Violence & Abuse 991 (2018).

As with rates of sexual victimization within prisons, the data regarding male-victim rape outside of prisons are also likely conservative. The reasons for underreporting among men outside of prisons are similar to the reasons for underreporting within the prison system: the taint of homophobia; the fear of appearing weak and hence not masculine; and definitional and perceptual issues. . . .

When we talk about male rape, for the most part, it is not because we care about male rape or its actual victims. It is because male is something we can use strategically. . . . There are two areas where talk about male-victim rape is surprisingly common. The first area is in self-defense and provocation cases asserting what has come to be known as the 'gay panic' defense. The second area is in "trash" talk from law enforce officers and prosecutors. Both kinds of talk are problematic . . . and unjust.[122]

Capers concludes this article with a series of questions: "What happens to rape talk when we broaden the discussion to include male sexual victimization? What happens to the law of rape when we reconceive rape so that it is no longer just a crime men perpetrate against women but rather a crime one person perpetrates against another? What happens when we unthink gender and reconceptualize rape as a nongendered crime? What are the benefits? What are the drawbacks? What are the risks? What are the rewards?"[123] How would you respond to these questions? How might focusing on men as rape victims change the debate about rape law reform efforts?

10. **Rape and Penalties.**   Measures such as long sentences for rapists, sex offender registries, and extreme forms of punishment such as chemical castration typically emerge from conservative "tough on crime" quarters. Some feminist advocates have supported stricter punishments for sexual offenses and expressed outrage over the leniency of some rape sentences in particular cases. The highly publicized case of the Stanford swimmer, Brock Turner, who was sentenced to six months in the county jail for sexually assaulting an unconscious woman, generated just such criticism, resulting in a successful petition to recall the judge. (See Problem 4-30 in Chapter 4.) At the same time, other feminists have expressed growing concern about overincarceration in a criminal legal system gone wild, and a particular concern that men of color are the ones who bear the brunt of heightened punishments.[124] (See discussion of overincarceration in Chapter 3, Section C.) A separate worry is that juries, and others involved in the criminal legal system, will be less likely to fully enforce the criminal law—particularly for acquaintance rape—if punishment is too severe.

To what extent is increasing the criminal punishment of rape likely to further the protection of women's sexual autonomy, and at what cost? How should the need to deter, and to express a strong societal message against, sexual assault be balanced

---

122. Capers, supra note 114, at 1261, 1263, 1273-74, 1278.

123. Id. at 1297.

124. Aya Gruber, The Feminist War on Crime (2020); India Thusi, Feminist Scripts for Punishment: The Feminist War on Crime, 134 Harv. L. Rev. 2449 (2021).

against the recognition that the criminal legal system is deeply flawed, apprehends and convicts many innocent people, and disproportionately impacts people of color and poor people?

11. **Rape and the Military.** Rape is a significant problem in the United States armed services, where nearly one in four women report experiencing sexual assault.[125] Only about 20 percent of women and 7 percent of men filed an official report of the assault, and of those who did, 52 percent experienced professional or social retaliation.[126]

Despite efforts to step up enforcement, the numbers are not improving substantially. Reported assaults spiked in 2018 and reflected the highest rate since 2006, when Pentagon data became available.[127] An anonymous Defense Department survey found that the number of unreported sexual assaults at military academies rose nearly 50 percent between 2016 and 2018, even as the number of reported cases rose only slightly.[128] The problem is compounded by a structure that gives commanding officers the power to determine whether to institute charges and what sanctions to impose. According to statistics provided to Congress, commanders reduced as many as a third of sexual abuse punishments.[129] Less than one-third of perpetrators in substantiated charges receive legal or administrative sanctions.[130] In two cases, Air Force generals set aside jury convictions for sexual assault, in one instance reasoning that the defendant could not be guilty because he was a "doting father and husband."[131]

Some commentators believe that the most promising response to these persistent problems is to create an independent prosecutor to handle sex abuse cases in the military. Other countries that have taken sexual assault cases out of the chain of command have witnessed substantial improvement.[132] Yet proposals to remove responsibility from commanders have been opposed by the military and blocked in Congress.[133] Other researchers point to the need to change socialization processes

---

125. Melinda Wenner Moyer, "A Poison in the System:" The Epidemic of Military Sexual Assault, N.Y. Times Mag., Oct. 11, 2021.

126. Rand Corp., Sexual Assault and Sexual Harassment in the U.S. Military xx (Andrew R. Morral et al., eds., 2015).

127. W. J. Hennigan, More than 500 Sexual Assaults Happen in a Single Year at Some Military Installations: Report, Time (Feb. 4, 2019).

128. Dep't of Def., Annual Report on Sexual Harassment and Violence at the Military Service Academies, Academic Program Year 2017-2018 18 (Jan. 2019); Helene Cooper, Unreported Sexual Assaults Surge at Military Academies, Pentagon Finds, N.Y. Times, Feb. 1, 2019, at A21.

129. Tom Vanden Brook & Gregg Zoroya, Why the Military Hasn't Stopped Sexual Abuse, USA Today, May 16, 2013, at 1A.

130. Carl Andrew Castro et al., Sexual Assault in the Military, 17 Current Psychiatry Reps. 54 (2015).

131. Vanden Brook & Zoroya, supra note 129, at 1A.

132. Pending Legislation Regarding Sexual Assaults in the Military: Hearings Before the S. Comm. on Armed Servs., 113th Cong. 320, at 91 (2014).

133. Leo Shane III, Military Sexual Assault Reform Plan Fails Again, Mil. Times, June 18, 2015.

within military culture that exalt hypermasculinity and discount harms arising from assault.[134]

What do you think accounts for the pervasiveness of rape in the military?[135] How might it be more effectively addressed?

12. **Rape and War.** Women have long been targets of mass rape during wartime.[136] Accounts of brutalization are common in the literature of ancient Greece and Rome. The Old Testament similarly chronicles the invasion of Canaan by Hebrew tribes, whose spoils of war included "sheep, cattle, asses, and thirty-two thousand girls who had had no intercourse with a man."

In the United States, initial prohibitions on rape in wartime appeared in the 1863 military code for the Union Army, which drew on early humanitarian law protecting non-combatants. At the international level, Article 46 of the Hague Convention of 1907 outlawed rape during occupations, and the Geneva Convention of 1929, which governed treatment of prisoners of war, guaranteed female prisoners all the regard "due their sex." These prohibitions did little to deter massive rapes during World War II. The most notorious cases involved Japanese soldiers' "comfort facilities" or brothels, staffed by "comfort women." Most of these women were disfavored minorities, such as Koreans and Filipinos who were abducted or otherwise coerced into sexual slavery. An estimated 200,000 women were involved, often listed in official military documents as "military supplies"; almost three-quarters died from their treatment.[137] Although the International Military Tribunal of the Far East gathered evidence on these abuses, its charter did not include sexual offenses and its proceedings (the Tokyo Trials) largely ignored them except when they were coupled with other offenses.[138] In Germany, rape was subsumed under crimes against humanity but was not included in a single indictment. The Allies who ran the Nuremberg Tribunal also ignored atrocities committed by their own soldiers, including an estimated rape of some 100,000 to 800,000 women in the Soviet capture of Berlin.

After World War II, international law began to include explicit prohibitions on rape during wartime. Article 27 of the 1949 Geneva Conventions, and subsequent Protocols of 1977 protect women against rape, enforced prostitution, or any form of indecent assault. The 1998 Rome Statute, which defines the jurisdiction

---

134. Elisabeth Jean Wood & Nathaniel Toppelberg, The Persistence of Sexual Assault Within the U.S. Military, 54 J. Peace Rsch. 620, 629-30 (2017).

135. Valerie A. Stander & Cynthia J. Thomsen, Sexual Harassment and Assault in the U.S. Military: A Review of Policy and Research Trends, 181 Mil. Med., 22 (2016) (discussing factors such as military lifestyle, demographics, and culture).

136. For an overview, see Sexual Violence in Conflict Zones: From the Ancient World to the Era of Human Rights (Elizabeth D. Heineman ed., 2011). For an exploration of modern use of sexual brutality in war, see Elisabeth Jean Wood, Rape as a Practice of War: Toward a Typology of Political Violence, 46 Pol. & Soc'y 513 (2018).

137. Shellie K. Park, Broken Silence: Redressing the Mass Rape and Sexual Enslavement of Asian Women by the Japanese Government in an Appropriate Forum, 3 Asian-Pac. L. & Pol'y J. 2, 28 (2002).

138. Kelly D. Askin, A Decade of the Development of Gender Crimes in International Courts and Tribunals: 1993 to 2003, 11 Hum. Rts. Brief 16 (2004).

of the International Criminal Court (ICC), defines "rape, sexual slavery, enforced prostitution, forced pregnancy, enforced sterilization, or any other form of sexual violence of comparable gravity" as crimes against humanity, war crimes, and potentially part of genocide. The international community first began to prosecute rape as a human rights violation largely in response to the atrocities committed in Rwanda and Yugoslavia in the early 1990s. In Rwanda, an estimated 250,000 to 535,000 Tutsi women were raped, and some 200,000 murdered.[139] Estimates of the number of rapes that occurred during the Yugoslavian conflict range from 20,000 to 50,000. What made these rapes distinctive was their role in ethnic cleansing. For example, Muslim and Croatian women were raped in order to make women tainted and therefore unmarriageable within their cultures, as well as to produce Serbian babies. Many women were murdered after rape or held in camps where they were raped repeatedly, often until they died.[140]

Following these atrocities, for the first time an international tribunal recognized rape as a tool of genocide and a crime against humanity and indicted a former head of government, Slobodan Milosevic, for mass rapes constituting such a crime.[141] Although the United States is not currently a signatory to the Rome Statute, U.S. courts have provided civil relief to victims of wartime rape under the Alien Tort Claims Act. In 1995, for example, the Second Circuit Court of Appeals held that Radovan Karadzic, leader of the Bosnian-Serb territory, could be held accountable for rape as an act of genocide and other war crimes committed during the Yugoslav conflict. A jury subsequently awarded the plaintiffs $745 million in compensatory and punitive damages.[142]

Despite these efforts, rape remains common in armed conflict. According to organizations such as Amnesty International, more women have been raped in the Democratic Republic of the Congo (DRC) than in any other conflict. Some estimates have put the number at about 2 million, with one woman raped per minute.[143] Armed bands of soldiers have developed a "signature" form of rape: local defense forces (known as Mai Mai) use branches or bayonets. Almost none of the perpetrators have been punished, and the gynecologist who won a 2018 Nobel Prize for his treatment of the survivors narrowly escaped an assassination

139. Jennifer M. Hentz, The Impact of HIV on the Rape Crisis in the African Great Lakes Region, 12 Hum. Rts. Brief 12, 13 (2005).

140. Lynda E. Boose, Crossing the River Drina: Bosnian Rape Camps, Turkish Impalement, and Serb Cultural Memory, 28 Signs 71, 73-74 (2002).

141. See Adrienne Kalosieh, Consent to Genocide?: The ICTY's Improper Use of the Consent Paradigm to Prosecute Genocidal Rape in FOCA, 24 Women's Rts. L. Rep. 121, 129 (2003).

142. Kadic v. Karadzic, 70 F.3d 232 (2d Cir. 1995). Efforts to obtain reparations on behalf of Korean comfort women led to an agreement by Japan to contribute $8.8 million through a "Reconciliation and Healing Foundation," but the foundation was dissolved and effectively nullified in 2018. See Dasl Yoon, South Korea Dissolves Group Central to WWII-Era Sex-Slaves Pact with Japan, Wall St. J., Nov. 21, 2018.

143. Jeffrey Gettleman, Congo Study Sets Estimates for Rapes Much Higher, N.Y. Times, May 12, 2011, at A4; see also the study on which Gettleman's article is based: Amber Peterman et al., Estimates and Determinants of Sexual Violence Against Women in the Democratic Republic of Congo, 101 Am. J. Pub. Health 1060 (June 2011).

attempt.[144] Rohingya women and girls have suffered similar brutalities in Myanmar as part of an effort of ethnic cleansing against the Muslim minority.[145] In war-torn Syria, thousands of men, women, and children have been sexually assaulted, and in Liberia, 92 percent of surveyed women had experienced sexual violence.[146] Most recently, Russian soldiers have been accused of a still unquantified number of rapes as part of their 2022 invasion and occupation of Ukraine. As the war rages on, prosecutions have already begun.[147]

Sexual assaults in war tend to be more brutal and more public than in other contexts: gang rapes account for an estimated three-quarters of rapes in war, compared with less than one-quarter in peacetime.[148] Can you explain why? Susan Brownmiller argues that in war, the body of a raped woman "becomes a ceremonial battlefield . . . a message passed between men."[149] What message is that?

PUTTING THEORY INTO PRACTICE

5-4. On Tuesday, Raven had consensual sex with Scott and Jean. On Wednesday, Raven had sex with Scott and Ororo. On Thursday, Raven went to the police to charge Scott with rape. In your opinion, should rape shield rules prevent Scott from admitting evidence that Tuesday's sex was consensual as well? Why or why not? Are there other facts you would want to know to decide the admissibility of Scott's proffered evidence?

5-5. A single mother of three young children who can't make ends meet has unwanted sex with her landlord in order to persuade him not to evict her.[150] Should he be guilty of a crime? What additional facts would be relevant to your analysis?

5-6. In the 2018 Senate confirmation hearings of Supreme Court Justice Brett Kavanaugh, the most contested issue involved testimony by Professor Christine Blasey Ford that Kavanaugh had sexually assaulted her during a party when both were in high school. Other evidence submitted to the Senate Judiciary Committee included claims of heavy drinking and other sexual misconduct by Kavanaugh during his high school and college years. Kavanaugh denied the allegations and suggested that they were part of an "orchestrated political hit."[151] In response to

---

144. The Nobel Committee Shines a Spotlight on Rape in Conflict, Economist (Oct. 11, 2018).

145. Human Rts. Watch, "All of My Body Was Pain": Sexual Violence Against Rohingya Women and Girls in Burma (Nov. 16, 2017); Kristen Gelineau, Rohingya Methodically Raped by Myanmar's Armed Forces, AP News (Dec. 11, 2017).

146. Stephanie Nebehay, Thousands of Women, Men, Children Raped in Syria's War: U.N. Report, Reuters (Mar. 15, 2018); U.N. Office of the High Comm'r of Human Rights, Rape: Weapon of War (2016).

147. Deborah Amos, Ukraine's First War Rape Case Is Underway — But Prosecutions Are Rare, NPR (July 15, 2022).

148. Nobel Committee, supra note 144.

149. Susan Brownmiller, Against Our Will: Men, Women and Rape 35 (1976).

150. For a discussion of this and other hypotheticals, see Stephen Schulhofer, Taking Sexual Autonomy Seriously, 11 Law & Phil. 35 (1992).

151. Brett Kavanaugh, Senate Confirmation Hearing (Sept. 27, 2018).

questions about his drinking behavior, Kavanaugh responded in what many characterized as belligerent and vitriolic tones.[152]

In an open letter to the Senate, women law professors opposing Kavanaugh's nomination wrote: "Judge Kavanaugh has shown that he is unable to respect women in positions of power, manifests bias with respect to gender and political affiliation, does not meet basic standards of professionalism, and lacks independence, impartiality, and judicial temperament."[153] Would you have signed the letter? Suppose the Senate or the Trump administration had directed the FBI to conduct a full investigation into Justice Kavanagh's background and it had revealed significant evidence corroborating allegations of sexual misconduct while in high school. Should that have been enough to deny his confirmation? What if, as subsequent reporting indicated, Kavanaugh matured in his attitudes and behaviors and developed an excellent record in mentoring and hiring certain types of women lawyers?[154]

3. Campus Rape and Title IX

As is true with acquaintance rape generally, law enforcement officials are often unwilling to pursue campus rape charges due to difficulties of proof and a sense that the complainant was at least partly responsible.[155] The inadequacy of the criminal law in addressing campus sexual assault prompted advocates to turn to civil remedies, especially Title IX of the Education Amendments of 1972.[156] Title IX's application to peer sexual harassment (discussed in Chapter 3) opened the door to using the statute to pressure colleges to step up their efforts to address sexual assault. Like other forms of sexual harassment, campus sexual assault touches on themes of gender subordination. But because it involves sexual encounters between

---

152. See, e.g., Deborah L. Rhode, The Public Deserves Better, Politico (Oct. 4, 2018); Open Letter to the Senate by Women Law Professors, N.Y. Times, Oct. 3, 2018; Allyson Chiu, Brett Kavanaugh Likes Beer, but Not Questions About His Drinking Habits, Wash. Post, Sept. 28, 2018.

153. Open letter by Women Law Professors, supra note 152.

154. Robin Pogrebin & Kate Kelly, The Education of Brett Kavanaugh: An Investigation (2019).

155. Nancy Chi Cantalupo, Burying Our Heads in the Sand: Lack of Knowledge, Knowledge Avoidance, and the Persistent Problem of Campus Peer Sexual Violence, 43 Loy. U. Chi. L.J. 205, 239 (2011) (reporting study findings that only 7 percent of police investigations of campus sexual assault result in arrest and a mere 4 percent in conviction).

156. 20 U.S.C. § 1681 et seq. (2018). In addition to Title IX, two other federal statutes address campus sexual assault. The Clery Act requires universities that participate in federal financial aid programs to report annual statistics on crime, including sexual assault and rape, on or near their campuses, and to develop prevention policies. 20 U.S.C. § 1092 (2018). The Campus Sexual Violence Elimination Act, passed as part of the reauthorization of the Violence Against Women Act in 2013, requires campuses to offer victims assistance in reporting sexual violence and certain accommodations, such as changes in living arrangements and no-contact orders, establish standards for disciplinary procedures governing sexual assault, and provide prevention and awareness programming. 20 U.S.C. § 1092(f) (2018).

adults, it also raises issues of sexual autonomy. The touchstone of the alleged wrong is a lack of consent, and a major issue in campus rape allegations is how to distinguish coercive from consensual sex. This difficulty is often compounded by drugs and alcohol and a social context in which ambiguous and inconsistent understandings may coexist. Unlike criminal law, Title IX imposes legal obligations and grants recourse against educational institutions and not the alleged assailant. The statute has provided an avenue for rape victims to sue their universities for damages, as in the following case.

Doe v. Union College

2020 WL 1063063 (N.D. N.Y. Mar. 5, 2020)

Gary L. Sharpe, Senior District Judge:

Plaintiff, a Union College student who is identified by the pseudonym Jane Doe, commenced this action on March 1, 2019 against defendants Union College . . . and Alpha Chapter of Theta Delta Chi International Fraternity at Union College (hereinafter "TD Chi"). . . .

Before the court is University defendants' motion[] to dismiss [Doe's Title IX complaint].

On or about September 3, 2017, plaintiff, having arrived early to campus for a pre-orientation leadership program, attended a party at the all-male fraternity TD Chi. According to plaintiff, "TD Chi's parties are known by the entire College community to pose a significant risk to female students of sexual assault, harassment, and sexual violence," and Union "permitted and condoned its all-male fraternities, including and especially TD Chi, to foster a social environment rampant with sexual violence and harassment towards women."

Prior to arriving at the party, "[p]laintiff drank one or two shots of straight vodka," and "approximately two full cups of beer" while at the party. At some point, plaintiff asked a male, "Assaulter Roe," (hereinafter "Roe"), a senior student at Union, where the bathroom was located. After "escort[ing]" plaintiff to the bathroom and waiting for her, the two began a conversation. They then decided to go to Roe's apartment, where they smoked marijuana on Roe's terrace. "Plaintiff immediately felt the effects of the marijuana," which "hit her hard and very quickly, unlike anything she had ever known before."

After smoking on the terrace, Roe "led [p]laintiff back to his bedroom," where she felt "confused, dizzy and uncoordinated" so she laid down on the bed. Roe joined her on the bed, and "began to touch her breasts and put his hands down her pants." "[L]ack[ing] the ability and coordination" to push him away, and despite repeatedly telling him "No," Roe proceeded to take his clothes off and rape plaintiff.

The following day, plaintiff spoke with Kelley, Union's Title IX Coordinator. Plaintiff reported to Kelley that she had been sexually assaulted the night prior, and identified Roe as her rapist. In response, Kelley instructed plaintiff to contact the College's Wicker Wellness Center. Kelley did not take any further steps to investigate plaintiff's complaint or to report it to the proper authorities.

On or about January 16, 2018, after suffering "debilitating anxiety and depression," and "living in fear of her rapist being on the same campus," plaintiff decided to meet, for the second time, with the Title IX Office. Accompanied by her mother, plaintiff met with Kelley and Williams, the director of campus safety. This second time around, plaintiff was provided with the policy, and Kelley explained the process of filing a Title IX complaint and the potential avenues for relief available to plaintiff.

Following the meeting, University defendants issued a "No Contact Order" between plaintiff and Roe. Thereafter, plaintiff submitted her written statement regarding her Title IX complaint to University defendants. A few days later, after allegedly having been given an opportunity to review plaintiff's statement first, Roe submitted his own written statement in rebuttal.

Kelley then assigned two investigators to investigate plaintiff's Title IX complaint. The investigators "intentionally" chose not to interview plaintiff first, and, instead, interviewed pertinent witnesses and Roe prior to speaking with plaintiff. On or about February 23, 2018, the investigators gave Williams their final investigative report. Plaintiff alleges that the report contained misrepresentations of the nature and chronology of the investigation.

"On or about April 24, 2018, [p]laintiff attended a pre-decision conference, . . . during which time she met with the [h]earing [p]anel." The panel members consisted of the associate dean of students, two faculty members, the director of residential life, and a sophomore student. Neither counsel to the college nor Kelly were present at the conference.

Plaintiff alleges that University defendants failed to provide her with a copy of the "vital and necessary" materials for her participation in the conference. Despite informing the panel that she had not been provided with these materials, she was questioned for one and one-half hours, during which time the panelists repeatedly referenced the materials.

Thereafter, Roe attended his pre-decision conference, where he "was provided with the complete hearing packet of documents at the start of the conference." He was also given the opportunity to submit additional documentation and to make an impact statement.

On or about May 22, 2018, plaintiff was informed that University defendants found Roe "not responsible" by a vote of 3-2. In so holding, "the panel relied upon inaccurate sources which had previously been amended and corrected, and misquoted statements in the [r]eport and conference transcripts." Plaintiff alleges that these were errors that she had corrected in her responses to the report and to her hearing transcript, but "had obviously not been incorporated into those documents nor substantively considered by University [d]efendants." The panel also allegedly improperly failed to take into consideration her level of incapacitation.

On or about May 31, 2018, plaintiff appealed the unfavorable decision, which was ultimately denied.

Plaintiff contends that approximately three years prior to the assault, in September 2015, the U.S. Department of Education Office for Civil Rights (OCR) opened an investigation, which is currently ongoing, into a complaint that was filed against Union College for its alleged mishandling of a complaint of sexual assault. Additionally, University defendants have received multiple reports from women regarding experiences of sexual assault, which the University defendants have "refused to look into." University defendants "ha[ve], and continue[] to have, a policy of covering up complaints and instances of sexual misconduct on campus.". . .

Title IX provides that "[n]o person in the United States shall, on the basis of sex, be excluded from participation in, be denied the benefits of, or be subjected to discrimination under any education program or activity receiving Federal financial assistance." 20 U.S.C. § 1681 (a).

Plaintiff appears to allege Title IX liability premised on University defendants' deliberate indifference based on both Union's official policy in her first cause of action, and on University defendants' response to plaintiff's allegations regarding the assault in her second cause of action. The court addresses plaintiff's second cause of action first.

Title IX provides a private right of action against a federally-funded education institution based on peer sexual harassment "where the funding recipient acts with deliberate indifference to known acts of harassment in its programs or activities." Davis v. Monroe Cnty. Bd. of Educ. (1999). To allege a Title IX claim arising from harassment, a plaintiff must allege three elements: (1) "sexual harassment . . . that is so severe, pervasive, and objectively offensive that it "deprived the plaintiff of "access to the educational opportunities or benefits provided by the school"; (2) the school had "actual knowledge" of the harassment; and (3) the school was "deliberately indifferent to the harassment."

A defendant acts with deliberate indifference both when its response to known harassment "is clearly unreasonable in light of the known circumstances, and when remedial action only follows after a lengthy and unjustified delay." "Deliberate indifference must, at a minimum, cause students to undergo harassment or make them liable or vulnerable to it." Davis. "Only actual notice by an 'appropriate person' who can rectify a violation of Title IX can support a claim under Title IX."

Plaintiff alleges that University defendants violated Title IX by responding with deliberate indifference to her reports of sexual misconduct. University defendants seek dismissal, arguing that plaintiff fails to allege that she was intentionally discriminated against on the basis of her sex, and that, in any event, she has not sufficiently alleged that Union failed to comply with the policy to promptly and efficiently investigate her complaint.

To the extent that University defendants argue that plaintiff fails to allege that any actions taken by them were motivated by plaintiff's gender, the court agrees. "Because Title IX prohibits subjecting a person to discrimination on account of sex, it is understood to bar the imposition of university discipline where gender is a motivating factor in the decision to discipline." Thus, "Title IX claims require evidence of intentional discrimination" which requires a showing that "the defendant discriminated against [a plaintiff] because of [his or her] sex; that the discrimination was intentional; and that the discrimination was a 'substantial' or 'motivating factor' for the defendant's actions."

Here, although plaintiff labels her second cause of action "*Gender Discrimination* in violation of Title IX: Deliberate Indifference to Plaintiff's Rape as against the University Defendants," plaintiff has failed to adequately allege intentional gender discrimination on behalf of University defendants based upon her gender. As such, any gender discrimination claim in violation of Title IX is dismissed.

However, to the extent that University defendants allege that plaintiff fails to sufficiently allege that Union is liable for deliberate indifference by failing to properly respond to her sexual harassment, the court disagrees. Here, the complaint contains allegations that, taken together, support a plausible claim that University defendants were deliberately indifferent to her Title IX complaint.

For instance, plaintiff alleges that, in September 2017, Kelley, a "mandatory reporter," merely instructed plaintiff to contact the College's Wicker Wellness Center, but, in January 2018, when accompanied by her mother, Kelley met with plaintiff and assisted her in understanding how she could file a formal Title IX complaint with Union. In response, University defendants argue that they were not deliberately indifferent to plaintiff's complaint because an investigation was commenced in January after plaintiff filed a complaint of sexual misconduct with the Title IX office. However, this does not explain why the same action taken in January — assisting plaintiff in understanding how to file a formal Title IX complaint and providing her with a copy of the policy — was not taken in September, when plaintiff first went to Kelley.

Further, after plaintiff submitted a written statement regarding her Title IX complaint, Roe was notified, and allegedly was given an opportunity to review plaintiff's statement prior to submitting his own. This is in direct contravention of the policy, which states, in relevant part: "The Respondent will not be allowed to see the Complainant's Statement until after the Respondent has filed [his or her] statement in response to the original Complaint Form."

Additionally, during her conference, the panel allegedly failed to provide plaintiff with necessary hearing materials — which were provided to Roe — even after she made the panel aware of the fact that she did not have these materials. University defendants provide no response to this allegation. Plaintiff also alleges that she was not provided an opportunity to submit an impact statement at this time, even though Roe was.

Viewing these facts in the light most favorable to the plaintiff, the complaint contains sufficient allegations that University defendants acted with deliberate indifference in responding to plaintiff's sexual assault.

In addition to her Title IX claims arising out of University defendants' alleged deliberate indifference in responding to her allegations, plaintiff claims that University defendants were deliberately indifferent to a culture of sexual hostility and violence against women by instituting policies and permitting practices, which subjected her to a sexually hostile education environment. According to plaintiff, these policies and practices were the proximate cause of the sexual harassment she endured.

To successfully claim that University defendants violated Title IX through a policy of deliberate indifference, plaintiff must establish that the school was "on *actual notice* that their *specific policies* and *responses* to sexual assault were deficient, and their subsequent failure to remedy these policies was the proximate cause of her sexual assault." "[S]omething more than general knowledge of assaults campus-wide (i.e., some greater specificity) is required to satisfy the actual knowledge requirement."

Plaintiff argues that University defendants were on notice that Union's policies were deliberately indifferent to sexual violence against women, they failed to remedy these policies, and plaintiff was harmed and subjected to further harassment as a consequence. University defendants maintain that dismissal is necessary because plaintiff's allegations are broad and speculative, and fail to establish that Union's policies or procedures caused plaintiff's sexual assault.

In Simpson v. Univ. of Colorado Boulder, 500 F.3d 1170 (10th Cir. 2007), the court held that a "funding recipient can be said to have intentionally acted in clear violation of Title IX, when the violation is caused by official policy, which may be a policy of deliberate indifference to providing adequate training or guidance that is obviously necessary for implementation of a specific program or policy of the recipient." In *Simpson*, it was alleged that the university's football coach had "general knowledge of the serious risk of sexual harassment and assault during college-football recruiting efforts," he "knew that such assaults had indeed occurred," but he "nevertheless maintained an unsupervised player-host program to show high-school recruits a 'good time.'" The court found those allegations to be adequate for a jury to infer that the inadequacy of the policy, and the risk of an assault, was "so obvious" as to amount to deliberate indifference.

Here, unlike *Simpson*, plaintiff's allegations fail to allege sufficient facts to support a plausible inference that University defendants "actively created and/or condoned and/or were deliberately indifferent to a culture of sexual hostility and violence against women." And, to the extent that plaintiff alleges that the OCR is currently investigating Union, she does not allege that the OCR has made any conclusions regarding University defendants' policy, let alone that University defendants agreed to undertake specific remedial measures but then failed to do so. As such, plaintiff's claim of Title IX liability premised on an official policy is dismissed. . . .

[I]t is hereby . . . ordered that University defendants' motion to dismiss is granted . . . as to plaintiff's claims of a hostile education environment . . . and denied as to plaintiff's claims of deliberate indifference to her complaints of sexual misconduct. . . .

NOTES

1. **The Extent of the Problem.**   Estimates of the number of women who experience rape or sexual assault during their undergraduate years range from one in four to one in five. However, the absence of consistent definitions in nationally representative samples makes precise estimates difficult.[157] Rates are substantially lower for men and slightly higher for gender non-conforming students.[158] Prevalence rates also vary by race. One influential survey of undergraduates found that

---

157. RAINN, Campus Sexual Violence: Statistics, https://www.rainn.org/statistics/campus-sexual-violence (26.4 percent of female undergraduates); Christopher Krebs et al., Bureau of Just. Stats., Campus Climate Survey Validation Study: Final Technical Report, Bureau of Justice Statistics (Jan. 2016) (about 20 percent).

158. RAAIN, supra note 157 (6.8 percent of undergraduate men experience rape or sexual assault; 23.1 percent of transgender, genderqueer, and gender non-conforming college students have been sexually assaulted).

25 percent of Native American women, 23 percent of Latina women, 23 percent of white women, 22 percent of multiracial women, 21 percent of Pacific Islander women, 18 percent of Black women, and 12 percent of Asian American women reported having experienced campus sexual assault.[159]

There is a strong consensus that campus sexual assault is vastly underreported. Only about 12 to 20 percent of campus rapes are reported to the police or campus law enforcement.[160] A large-scale study at Columbia University found that nearly half of students had experienced unwanted sexual contact, but only 2 percent of these students made a formal report to the university.[161] Women of color are particularly reluctant to trust campus reporting systems and may have greater reason to fear that their reports will be disbelieved or not taken seriously.[162]

The consequences for survivors are severe and include high rates of post-traumatic stress disorder, depression, and drug or alcohol abuse, which, in turn, are linked to higher dropout rates and impaired educational performance.[163]

2. The Law in the Courts. As the court made clear in Doe v. Union College, proof that the university acted with a discriminatory motive is not necessary; the university's culpability is established by its deliberate indifference to actual notice of an alleged assault. Although such cases are highly fact-specific, the court's decision is fairly representative of successful cases: the plaintiff reported a sexual assault to university officials and can identify specific instances of the university's failure to respond seriously and fairly to the allegations.[164] The actual notice and deliberate indifference standard sets a high bar, however, and courts often find that the facts fall short.[165] Some courts have additionally required plaintiffs to prove that the defendant's deliberate indifference "caused" further harassment to the plaintiff.[166] Applying this standard, courts have found that the university's refusal to discipline and remove the assailant, thereby forcing the complainant to share the campus with her assailant, is not enough to support liability absent subsequent harassment

---

159. Jessica C. Harris, Women of Color Undergraduate Students' Experiences with Campus Sexual Assault: An Intersectional Analysis, 44 Rev. Higher Educ. 1, 3 (2020).

160. White House Council on Women and Girls, Rape and Sexual Assault: A Renewed Call to Action (Jan. 2014) (12 percent); Sofi Sinozich & Lynn Langton, U.S. Dep't of Justice, Bureau of Just. Stats., Rape and Sexual Assault Victimization Among College-Age Females, 1995-2013 (Dec. 2014) (20 percent).

161. Jennifer S. Hirsch et al., Sexual Health Initiative to Foster Transformation, Final Report 3 (Mar. 2019).

162. See Harris, supra note 159, at 6-7.

163. White House Council, supra note 160, at 14.

164. See, e.g., Reed v. S. Ill. Univ., No. 3:18-CV-1968-GCS, 2020 U.S. Dist. LEXIS 101359 (S.D. Ill. 2020); Doe v. Sarah Lawrence Coll., 453 F. Supp. 3d 653 (S.D.N.Y. 2020).

165. See, e.g., Shank v. Carleton Coll., 993 F.3d 567 (8th Cir. 2021); Doe v. Board of Regents, No. 1:20-CV-00172 JAR, 2022 U.S. Dist. LEXIS 81680 (E.D. Mo. 2022); Emily O. v. Regents of the Univ of Cal., 2021 U.S. Dist. LEXIS 78082 (C.D. Cal. 2021).

166. See, e.g., Doe v. Univ. of Ky., 959 F.3d 246 (6th Cir. 2020); Kollaritsch v. Mich. State Univ. Bd. of Trs., 944 F.3d 613 (6th Cir. 2019); K.T. v. Culver-Stockton Coll., 865 F.3d 1054 (8th Cir. 2017).

or abuse, even if deliberate indifference is established.[167] Does this approach place too little value on sexual autonomy and the harms to victims that result from universities' indifferent and ineffective responses to sexual assault?[168]

Doe defeated the university's motion to dismiss her claim of deliberate indifference to her sexual assault (the more typical claim in campus assault cases) but lost her claim that the university's deliberate indifference to a culture of sexual assault put her at heightened risk of assault. Why did the court side with the university on the latter claim? Plaintiffs sometimes prevail on claims alleging systemic failures to mitigate known risk of sexual assault, but such cases have involved particularly egregious facts, including the *Simpson* case discussed in *Doe.* There, the Tenth Circuit recognized a Title IX claim arising out of the athletic department's football recruiting program. The "gist of the complaint was that CU sanctioned, supported, even funded, a program (showing recruits a 'good time') that, without proper control, would encourage young men to engage in opprobrious acts."[169] The court held that the university "had general knowledge of the serious risk of sexual harassment and assault during college-football recruiting efforts" and displayed "deliberate indifference to providing adequate training or guidance that is obviously necessary for implementation" of the recruiting program. Although claims like this often fail, this theory was used successfully in cases against the University of Tennessee and Baylor University.[170] How far should this theory extend — should universities be liable for their failure to provide adequate sexual assault training to students, thereby creating a heightened risk of assault?[171] Given that no university could credibly deny awareness that sexual assault is a problem on college campuses, would this turn deliberate indifference into a negligence standard? How far should Title IX go in requiring universities to protect students' sexual autonomy?

3. **Federal Administrative Enforcement.** A separate enforcement path lies in the U.S. Department of Education's Office for Civil Rights (OCR). OCR may initiate an investigation proactively or in response to a complaint filed with the agency. OCR has statutory authority to terminate federal funding to noncompliant educational institutions, a sanction that the agency has never used. Rather, in practice, OCR requires schools it finds to be in violation of Title IX to enter into agreements promising to take specified actions to achieve compliance.

As evident in the *Doe* case, OCR enforcement is independent of litigation. It neither preempts, nor is a prerequisite to, a private lawsuit brought by a sexual

---

167. See, e.g., Doe v. Board of Regents, 20-cv-856-wmc, 2022 U.S. Dist. LEXIS 127531 (W.D. Wisc. July 19, 2022).

168. See Emily Suski, Institutional Betrayals as Sex Discrimination, 107 Iowa L. Rev. 1685 (2022).

169. Simpson v. Univ. of Colo., 500 F.3d 1170 (10th Cir. 2007).

170. See Doe v. Baylor Univ., 336 F. Supp. 3d 763 (W.D. Tex. 2018); Doe v. Univ. of Tenn., 186 F. Supp. 3d 788 (M.D. Tenn. 2016); Erin E. Buzuvis, Title IX and Official Policy Liability: Maximizing the Law's Potential to Hold Educational Institutions Accountable for Their Responses to Sexual Misconduct, 73 Okla. L. Rev. 35 (2020).

171. See Karasek v. Regents of the Univ. of Cal., 534 F. Supp. 3d 1136 (N.D. Cal. 2021) (alleged systemic failure to educate students about sexual assault and consent stated a "heightened risk" claim under Title IX).

assault victim. Courts are not bound by OCR findings, and violating the standards OCR uses to determine compliance will not necessarily make a school liable in litigation. Nor is OCR bound by the legal standards courts use in civil damages actions. That is because the Supreme Court, in crafting the actual notice and deliberate indifference standard in *Davis* (discussed in Chapter 3) limited its ruling to private lawsuits for damages. Because OCR's administrative enforcement scheme has a different remedy (termination of federal funds) and enforcement procedure, OCR is not bound by the same Title IX standards as courts.

OCR's rules for determining Title IX compliance in addressing campus sexual assault have vacillated wildly with changes in presidential administrations.[172] In 2001, soon after the *Davis* decision, OCR revised its official guidance to clarify that it would follow a tougher standard than courts by requiring schools to respond to sexual assault upon actual *or* constructive notice with prompt, corrective action.[173] The document established additional principles, including that schools may not merely defer to the criminal legal process and are obliged to independently investigate assault allegations in a fair and equitable process. Despite such strong statements, little concrete action was taken by OCR in the next decade to enforce these principles.

Responding to alarming data and pressure from Title IX activists, the Obama administration made addressing campus sexual assault more of a priority.[174] In 2011, OCR issued a new "Dear Colleague" letter (DCL) clarifying the requirements it would impose on schools and promising tougher enforcement.[175] Some of the more controversial elements of the DCL included directing schools to apply a preponderance of the evidence standard instead of a heightened "clear and convincing" standard for resolving contested allegations, discouraging cross-examination, and disapproving of mediation in sexual assault cases (the rationales for these changes are discussed below). By 2016, 159 postsecondary institutions were under investigation by OCR for their handling of sexual assault.[176]

Pushback was swift and fierce. Critics argued that the pressure to respond to OCR's new wave of enforcement was causing universities to shortchange the rights of the accused. At some institutions, the Title IX enforcement office acted as investigator, prosecutor, judge, and jury, prompting due process concerns, including by

---

172. For discussion and defense of OCR's role in detailing Title IX policy on campus sexual assault, see Samuel R. Bagenstos, This Is What Democracy Looks Like: Title IX and the Legitimacy of the Administrative State, 118 Mich. L. Rev. 1053 (2020).

173. Off. for Civ. Rts., U.S. Dep't of Educ., Revised Sexual Harassment Guidance: Harassment of Students by School Employees, Other Students, or Third Parties (2001).

174. For a history of the evolution of OCR's approach to sexual assault and the feminist activism to behind it, see Karen M. Tani, An Administrative Right to Be Free from Sexual Violence? Title IX Enforcement in Historical and Institutional Perspective, 66 Duke L.J. 1847 (2016).

175. Off. for Civ. Rts., Dep't of Educ., Dear Colleague Letter (Apr. 4, 2011).

176. Tyler Kingkade, Federal Campus Rape Investigations Near 200, and Finally Get More Funding, Huff. Post (Jan. 5, 2016).

a small but vocal group of Harvard faculty.[177] New advocacy groups represented the interests of students disciplined for sexual assault, who argued that men accused of sexual assault were the new victims.[178]

The critics found a receptive audience in the Trump administration, which withdrew the 2011 DCL and initiated a formal rule-making process to issue new Title IX regulations.[179] Women's rights groups sued the Department, alleging a chilling effect on reporting and discrimination against complainants, but failed to secure judicial relief.[180] In 2018, the Department proposed a lengthy and detailed set of new regulations specific to sexual harassment and assault procedures, which were finalized in 2020.[181] The major changes include requiring institutions of higher education to allow cross-examination of both parties in sexual misconduct hearings (even if cross-examination is not done in other student conduct hearings), and requiring schools to use the same standard of proof for student sexual assault that they apply to all faculty misconduct, even if it is the clear and convincing evidence standard (and even if other student conduct charges, including other types of harassment, are resolved under the preponderance standard). The regulations also hold OCR to the judicial standard of actual notice and deliberate indifference and restrict Title IX authority over off-campus assaults, even if the aftermath creates a hostile environment on campus.

The new regulations have generated fierce opposition from women's groups and many in the higher education community. Critics of allowing cross-examination argue it will exacerbate complainants' trauma and further discourage reporting.[182] Similarly, use of the clear and convincing proof standard reinforces skepticism of complainants and tilts the scales toward the accused, making it harder for institutions to discipline assailants and prevent assaults.[183] Other provisions, such as the new approach to off-campus assault and lowering the standard for institutional response, tie OCR's hands and turn Title IX enforcement into a paper tiger.[184]

---

177. Judith Shulevitz, Accused College Rapists Have Rights Too, New Republic (Oct. 11, 2014); Elizabeth Bartholet et al., Rethink Harvard's Sexual Harassment Policy, Bos. Globe, Oct. 14, 2014.

178. Robin Wilson, Presumed Guilty, Chron. Higher Educ. (Sept. 1, 2014); Ariel Kaminer, A New Factor in Campus Sexual Assault Cases, N.Y. Times, Nov. 19, 2014, at A22.

179. For critique and discussion of the politics behind this, see Nancy Chi Cantalupo, Dog Whistles and Beachheads: The Trump Administration, Sexual Violence, and Student Discipline in Education, 54 Wake Forest L. Rev. 303 (2019).

180. Survjustice, Inc. v. DeVos, No. 3:18-cv-00535, 2019 U.S. Dist. LEXIS 54616 (N.D. Ca. Mar. 29, 2019).

181. Nondiscrimination on the Basis of Sex in Education Programs or Activities Receiving Federal Financial Assistance, 85 Fed. Reg. 30026 (May 19, 2020) (final rules); Nondiscrimination on the Basis of Sex in Education Programs or Activities Receiving Federal Financial Assistance, 83 Fed. Reg. 61,462 (proposed Nov. 29, 2018).

182. See Naomi Mann, Classrooms into Courtrooms, 59 Houston L. Rev. 363 (2021).

183. See Deborah L. Brake, Fighting the Rape Culture Wars Through the Preponderance of the Evidence Standard, 78 Mont. L. Rev. 109 (2017).

184. Joanna L. Grossman & Deborah L. Brake, A Sharp Backward Turn: Department of Education Proposes to Undermine Protections for Students Against Sexual Harassment and Assault, Justia's Verdict (Nov. 27, 2018).

The Biden administration came in vowing to undo the Trump administration's changes to Title IX rules. However, unlike the Dear Colleague Letters previously used by OCR to issue guidance on sexual assault, final regulations cannot be rescinded by a presidential directive. Revising regulations requires a formal rulemaking process with a lengthy public comment period. In June 2022, the Biden administration announced new proposed regulations that, if adopted, would reverse many of the Trump administration's changes and largely restore the previous principles.[185] These include restoring Title IX coverage for off-campus conduct that creates a hostile environment; restoring the actual or constructive notice and prompt corrective action standard for OCR; and permitting but not requiring a hearing with questioning by advisors (including cross-examination). The proposed rules also endorse the position taken by the American Law Institute (ALI), permitting use of a clear and convincing evidence standard only by the relatively small number of schools that apply that standard to other student misconduct and discrimination cases; those schools that apply the preponderance standard to such matters, as most do, must also use it to resolve sexual misconduct complaints.[186] The public comment period extended through September 2022, with the final process of reviewing and finalizing the regulations likely extending into the following year.

What about this issue might explain the back-and-forth between administrations? Is there a system that is equally fair to both the victim and the accused?

4. **Affirmative Consent.** College student conduct codes need not track the criminal law; they may define and prohibit a broader range of sexual misconduct. Like rape law reformers, campus activists have pushed to require affirmative consent. Antioch was the first college to do so in the early 1990s, and was ridiculed by Saturday Night Live.[187] Affirmative consent has since become more common, with many colleges and universities requiring some indication of affirmative consent, either verbal or nonverbal, and a number of states, including New York and California, requiring publicly funded universities to adopt such policies.[188] The California statute defines "affirmative consent" as "affirmative, conscious and voluntary agreement to engage in sexual activity. . . . Lack of protest or resistance does not mean consent, nor does silence mean consent. Affirmative consent must be ongoing throughout a sexual activity and can be revoked at any time."[189] A few campuses have gone further and required that the consent be "enthusiastic."[190] Do such rules

---

185. Nondiscrimination on the Basis of Sex in Education Programs or Activities Receiving Federal Financial Assistance, 87 Fed. Reg. 41390 (proposed July 12, 2022).

186. Id. at 41486. For the full set of principles endorsed by the ALI, see American Law Institute, Black Letter of Student Sexual Misconduct: Procedural Frameworks for Colleges and Universities, Tentative Draft No. 1 (Apr. 2022) (approved by the ALI membership May 2022).

187. Is It Date Rape?, Saturday Night Live, NBC (Oct. 2, 1993).

188. See Vanessa Grigoriadis, Blurred Lines: Rethinking Sex, Power and Consent on Campus 119 (2017); Cal. Educ. Code, § 67386 (2022); N.Y. CLS Educ. § 6441 (2022).

189. Cal. Educ. Code § 67386 (2022).

190. Jeannie Suk Gersen, St. Paul's School and a New Definition of Rape, New Yorker (Nov. 3, 2015).

promote sexual autonomy by ensuring unambiguous consent, or do they interfere with it by prescribing rules for expressing consent?

Affirmative consent policies have their critics, who warn of an overreaching sex bureaucracy and unfairness to men who do not get clear signals of what women want.[191] Laura Kipnis argues that "campuses are using consent standards to remedy sexual ambivalences or awkward sexual experiences and to adjudicate relationship disputes post break-ups."[192] Shifting the burden on accused students to prove that they obtained affirmative consent before having sex may also raise due process problems.[193]

Even if affirmative consent policies are optimal in theory, are they workable in practice? In one survey at Columbia University, students reported that the affirmative consent standard at the school rarely figured into their sexual experiences.[194] In an another study of male college students, most endorsed the "yes means yes" standard, but when asked to describe their most recent sexual encounter, even those who claimed to follow that standard often had not.[195]

Is even affirmative consent not good enough? Some commentators have pointed out that consent is not the same thing as sex that is wanted, highlighting a problem sometimes referred to as "gray rape," "bad sex," or "regret sex." Students may consent to unwanted sex for any number of reasons, including peer pressure; a desire to attract, retain, or not antagonize a partner; and a wish not to appear a "tease."[196] In a widely circulated essay, Veronica Rukh described a situation that she later called "rape-ish":

> before I even had a chance to decide . . . we were making out. In my state of extreme intoxication, my mind was racing in search of a decision. This was exciting. This was fun. But this was also really, really weird and ultimately not a road I wanted to go down . . . It wasn't until he grabbed a condom that I really knew how I felt. I was not okay with this. I didn't want to have sex with him. But I did . . . At the time I didn't know why. Maybe I didn't want to feel like I'd led him on. Maybe I didn't want to disappoint him. Maybe I just didn't want to deal with the . . . verbal tug of war that so often happens before sleeping with someone. It was easier to just do it.[197]

191. Jacob Gersen & Jeannie Suk, The Sex Bureaucracy, 104 Calif. L. Rev. 881, 931 (2016).

192. Laura Kipnis, Unwanted Advances: Sexual Paranoia Comes to Campus 17 (2017); Gersen & Suk, supra note 191, at 931.

193. See, e.g., Mock v. Univ. of Tenn., No. 14-1687-II (Ch. Ct. Davidson Cnty. Tenn., Aug. 4, 2015).

194. Jia Tolentino, Safer Spaces, New Yorker 39 (Sept. 19, 2018).

195. Peggy Orenstein, It's Not That Men Don't Know What Consent Is, N.Y. Times, Feb. 24, 2019, at SR4 (describing research by Nicole Bedera).

196. Robin West, Consensual Sexual Dysphoria: A Challenge for Campus Life, 66 J. Legal Educ. 804, 807 (2017); Joan Howarth, Shame Agent, 66 J. Legal Educ. 717, 731 (2017).

197. Kipnis, supra note 192, at 198.

Should these facts fail an affirmative consent standard? Should they fail an enthusiastic consent standard? How can or should campus codes attempt to deal with such situations?

5. **The Rights of Students Accused of Sexual Assault.** Critics of tougher Title IX enforcement contend that universities have gone too far in punishing unsuspecting men for incidents like the one Rukh described. They claim that victims' shame, anger, and embarrassment lead to sanctions against men who thought that they were engaging in consensual activity.[198] Since the Obama administration's stepped-up enforcement, hundreds of cases have been brought by men suing their universities for due process violations and even for sex discrimination under Title IX.[199] The complaints have alleged shoddy investigations; inadequate opportunities to review charges, present evidence, and question witnesses; and biased adjudication.[200] Some of the early cases succeeded on due process grounds, but typically lost under Title IX, with courts explaining that bias toward complainants (even if it exists) is not the same thing as bias against men.[201] More recently, however, the tide may be turning, as more courts have drawn plausible inferences of sex discrimination from what they view as unfair procedures toward students accused of sexual misconduct.[202] Courts have cited refusals to allow the male accused student to cross-examine the complainant, an over-eagerness to credit a female complainant's testimony, a statistical pattern of finding male students responsible, and indications of outside pressure to crack down on sexual assault, as facts that, in some combination, may support an inference of anti-male bias.[203] Other courts have declined to infer gender bias against males from procedural irregularities and allegations of unfair treatment.[204] What factual basis should courts require to support a claim of sex discrimination against male students accused of sexual assault in campus disciplinary proceedings? Is providing due process and protecting the rights of accused

---

198. Kathryn Joyce, The Takedown of Title IX, N.Y. Times Mag., Dec. 9, 2017, at 69.

199. Grigoriadis, supra note 188, at 138-39.

200. Emily Yoffe, The College Rape Overcorrection, Slate: DoubleX (Dec. 7, 2014); Kipnis, supra note 192. For rebuttal of these narratives, see Kelly Allison Behre, Deconstructing the Disciplined Student Narrative and Its Impact on Campus Sexual Assault Policy, 61 Ariz. L. Rev. 885, 923-24 (2019).

201. See Erin E. Buzuvis, Title IX and Procedural Fairness: Why Disciplined-Student Litigation Does Not Undermine the Role of Title IX in Campus Sexual Assault, 78 Mont. L. Rev. 71 (2017); Bethany Corbin, Riding the Wave or Drowning?: An Analysis of Gender Bias and Twombly/Iqbal in Title IX Accused Student Lawsuits, 85 Fordham L. Rev. 2665 (2017).

202. See Dana Bolger et al., A Tale of Two Title IX's: Title IX Reverse Discrimination Law and Its Trans-Substantive Implications for Civil Rights, 55 U.C. Davis 743 (2021); Sarah L. Swan, Discriminatory Dualism in Process: Title IX, Reverse Title IX, and Campus Sexual Assault, 73 Okla. L. Rev. 69 (2020).

203. See, e.g., Doe v. Regents of Univ. of Minn., 999 F.3d 571 (8th Cir. 2020); Doe v. Univ. of Ark.-Fayetteville, 974 F.3d 858 (8th Cir. 2020); Doe v. Baum, 903 F.3d 575 (6th Cir. 2018); Doe v. Miami Univ., 882 F.3d 579 (6th Cir. 2018).

204. See, e.g., Doe v. Univ. of Chic., No. 20 CV 7293, 2021 U.S. Dist. LEXIS 116182 (N.D. Ill. 2021); Doe v. Williams Coll., 530 F. Supp. 3d 92 (D. Mass. 2021); Z.J. v. Vanderbilt Univ., 355 F. Supp. 3d 646 (M.D. Tenn. 2018).

students incompatible with protecting the sexual autonomy of students who are assaulted?[205]

Another concern is potential bias against men of color accused of sexual assault. Although data on the racial demographics of students disciplined for sexual misconduct is lacking, some commentators have raised concerns that the same stereotypes about Black men that have entrenched racial bias in the criminal enforcement of rape law (discussed in Section A2 of this chapter) will manifest in student disciplinary processes.[206] Others argue that this critique itself deploys sexual and racial stereotypes about Black men and ignores the experiences of, and biases against, women of color alleging sexual assault.[207] How can advocates for racial and gender justice craft legal strategies for addressing campus sexual assault that avoid pitting Black men against Black women?[208]

6. **Athletes and Sexual Assault.** Many cases of campus sexual assault involve athletes.[209] In one college town, the failure to prosecute campus rape cases was so egregious that the Department of Justice launched an investigation and negotiated an agreement providing for independent oversight of university campus assault procedures.[210] Women's reluctance to accuse popular athletes and colleges' reluctance to discipline them can further entrench cultures of entitlement and abuse.[211]

---

205. See Alexandra Brodsky, A Rising Tide: Learning About Fair Disciplinary Process from Title IX, 66 J. Legal Educ. 822 (2016).

206. See Ben Trachtenberg, How University Title IX Enforcement and Other Discipline Processes (Probably) Discriminate Against Minority Students, 107 Nev. L. J. 18 (2017); Janet Halley, Trading the Megaphone for the Gavel in Title IX Enforcement, 128 Harv. L. Rev. F. 103 (2015).

207. See Nancy Chi Cantalupo, And Even More of Us Are Brave: Intersectionality and Sexual Harassment of Women Students of Color, 42 Harv. J. L. & Gender 1 (2019); Antuan M. Johnson, Title IX Narratives, Intersectionality, and Male-Biased Conceptions of Racism, 9 Geo. J. L. & Mod. Critical Race Persps. 57 (2017).

208. See Brake, Fighting the Rape Culture Wars, supra note 183, at 137-39, 144-49 (discussing the ways racial and sexual stereotypes hurt the credibility of women of color who are assaulted and the racial politics of the pushback against Title IX).

209. Athletes are found responsible for sexual assault at a rate three times that of the general student body, with football players overrepresented among them. See Kenny Jacoby, College Athletes More Likely to Be Disciplined for Sex Assault, USA Today, Dec. 12, 2019. For a discussion of the sports culture that contributes to the problem and early cases involving athletes, see Grigoriadis, supra note 188, at 193-99 (2017); Deborah Brake, Sport and Masculinity: The Promise and Limits of Title IX, in Masculinities and Law: A Multidimensional Approach (2011). For more recent examples of sexual assault allegations involving athletes, see Molly Henson-Clancy, LSU Routinely Mishandled Sexual Misconduct Claims Against Football Players, Report Finds, Wash. Post, Mar. 5, 2021; Doe v. Brown Univ. 233 A.3d 389 (R.I. 2021) (alleged sexual assault by three football players).

210. Jon Krakauer, Missoula: Rape and the Justice System in a College Town 340 (2015).

211. Todd W. Crosset, Athletes, Sexual Assault, and Universities' Failure to Address Rape-Prone Subcultures on Campus, in The Crisis of Campus Sexual Violence: Cultural Perspectives on Prevention and Response 74, 76, 79 (Sara Corrigen Wooten & Roland W. Mitchell eds., 2015).

Not all accusations of sexual abuse by athletes have been verified, however, and some worry that athletes are prime targets for attention-seeking claims. This concern gained force when Duke University lacrosse players who hired a young African-American woman to perform as a stripper at a party were later accused by the woman of raping her. The case sparked a firestorm of national media attention, but the charges against the athletes were eventually dropped, and the prosecutor was disbarred, when inconsistencies in the victim's account and other exculpatory evidence came to light that had not been shared with the defendants or the court.[212] Some male athletes found responsible for sexual assault have sued their universities, alleging that they were victims of stereotypes against male athletes.[213] Is it possible to acknowledge the problems with male athletic culture and sexual assault without stereotyping male athletes?

The insular culture of sport can also heighten the vulnerability of athletes to sexual assault. A particularly egregious example came to light when more than 160 women came forward claiming they had been sexually abused by Michigan State University (MSU) gymnastics team doctor Larry Nassar.[214] Nassar was finally tried, convicted, and sentenced to life in prison, but many earlier reports fell on deaf ears and it took the FBI over a year to take action.[215] The Department of Education found MSU in violation of both Title IX and the Clery Act, fining the university $4.5 million, and MSU settled a civil lawsuit brought by Nassar's victims for a record $500 million.[216] Congress responded to the Nassar scandal by passing the Safe Sport Act, which places broad mandatory reporting obligations on coaches and other persons involved in Olympic sports and other sports organizations, and established the Center for Safe Sport, which mandates abuse prevention strategies and education.[217]

Men are also victims of sexual abuse in athletic settings. When Penn State assistant football coach Jerry Sandusky's longtime sexual abuse of boys finally came to light, long after an eyewitness account of the abuse was disclosed to head coach Joe Paterno, Paterno famously stated, "To be frank with you, I don't know that it would have done any good [to hear more details], because I never heard of rape . . . and a man."[218] This sentiment, widely shared in the sports community, has contributed to the invisibility of the sexual abuse of male athletes. For decades, male wrestlers

---

212. See Bennett L. Gershman & Joel Cohen, No Gatekeeper of Justice, Nat'l L.J., Feb. 19, 2007, at A22; Race to Injustice: Lessons Learned from the Duke Lacrosse Rape Case (Michael L. Siegel, ed., 2009).

213. See, e.g., John Does 1-2; John Does 4-11 v. Regents of the Univ. of Minn., 999 F.3d 571 (8th Cir. 2021).

214. Carla Correa & Meghan Louttit, More Than 160 Women Say Larry Nassar Sexually Abused Them: Here Are His Accusers in Their Own Words, N.Y. Times, Jan. 24, 2018.

215. See Dan Barry et al., Molested as F.B.I. Case Plodded for a Year, N.Y. Times, Feb. 4, 2018, at A1.

216. Erica L. Green, Education Department Hits Michigan State with Record Fine Over Nassar Scandal, N.Y. Times, Sept. 5, 2019; Mitch Smith & Anemona Hartocollis, Michigan State's 500 Million for Nassar Victims Dwarfs Other Settlements, N.Y. Times, May 16, 2018.

217. See Carmen Rios Safer Sports, Safer Girls, Ms. Mag. (Mar. 12, 2018).

218. Sally Jenkins, Joe Paterno's First Interview Since the Penn State-Sandusky Scandal, Wash. Post, Jan. 14, 2014.

at Ohio State University were sexually abused by their team doctor, who later committed suicide in 2015.[219] Many of the former wrestlers were finally empowered to speak out after witnessing the courage of Nassar's (female) victims, even as they acknowledged struggling as men to come to terms with expectations about masculinity and the presumed ability of men, especially wrestlers, to protect themselves from such abuse.

What accounts for such longstanding, systemic failures to acknowledge and end sexual abuse of athletes? What policies should be put in place to better prevent and detect such abuse?

7. **Substance Abuse.** *Doe* is typical of many campus rape cases in that both parties had been drinking or taking drugs when the sexual encounter occurred.[220] In the Columbia University study mentioned above, two-thirds of the students' experiences of nonconsensual sexual activity involved alcohol or drug use.[221] How should intoxication affect how universities handle these cases? Must the accused student have been aware that his partner was too intoxicated to consent in order to be found responsible? What if he was too intoxicated to tell? Should culpability depend on who was more drunk? Given the known linkage between alcohol and sexual assault, under what circumstances, if any, should colleges have a duty to curb alcohol consumption to protect students from the risk of sexual assault?[222]

Regardless of any legal duty, should colleges do more to crack down on drinking that contributes to sexual assault? Some research suggests that it is not drinking itself that increases the likelihood of sexual assault, but rather drinking in connection with party subcultures that endorse rape myths and normalize sexual aggression.[223] It is well known that alcohol is "often used to create a gray area, a realm of plausible deniability where no one supposedly has to take responsibility for what he (or she) wanted to do."[224] Another problem is that national rules governing most sororities forbid the use of alcohol on sorority premises, thereby enabling fraternities to have a monopoly on hosting parties with alcohol.[225] Would you support changing these rules, to give sororities the flexibility to permit alcohol? Alternatively, should colleges consider banning alcohol on campus entirely?[226] Such prohibitions have proven difficult to enforce and may only encourage students to drink

---

219. Catie Edmondson & Marc Tracy, For Wrestlers, #MeToo Stirs Buried Beast, N.Y. Times, Aug. 2, 2018, at A1.

220. Christopher P. Krebs et al., The Campus Sexual Assault Study, Nat'l Inst. of Justice vii, xviii (2007); Aaron White & Ralph Hingson, The Burden of Alcohol Use: Excessive Alcohol Consumption and Related Consequences Among College Students, 35 Alcohol Rsch.: Current Revs. 201, 212 (2013).

221. Hirsch et al., supra note 161, at 3.

222. See Helfman v. Northeastern Univ., 149 N.E. 3d 758 (2020).

223. Kaitlin M. Boyle & Lisa Slattery Walker, The Neutralization and Denial of Sexual Violence in College Party Subcultures, 37 Deviant Behav. 1392, 1403 (2016); Maggie Koerth Baker, Science Says Toxic Masculinity — More Than Alcohol — Leads to Sexual Assault, FiveThirtyEight (Sept. 26, 2018).

224. Caroline Knapp, Drinking: A Love Story (1996).

225. Brake, supra note 183, at 29.

226. No Kegs, No Liquor: College Crackdown Targets Drinking and Sexual Assault, N.Y. Times, Oct. 29, 2015, at A14.

elsewhere. Some activists worry that too much emphasis on alcohol puts the focus on victims who drink rather than on perpetrators who rape.[227] Where campuses have rules prohibiting alcohol use, advocates for survivors have urged colleges to grant sexual assault complainants amnesty for violating these rules in order to encourage the reporting of sexual assaults. Brett Sokolow, President of the National Center for Higher Education Risk Management, disagrees with this approach, arguing that it is unfair when both students involved in a sexual assault were intoxicated and in violation of campus rules, but only the accused is subject to sanctions. In his view, this is creating "Title IX plaintiffs."[228] How would you respond?

8. **Restorative Justice Approaches.**   Both the case law and OCR enforcement have focused on internal dispute resolution processes for resolving sexual assault complaints, which culminate in a finding by the institution that the accused student either is or is not responsible for the alleged conduct. Might non-adversarial restorative justice procedures have advantages over adversarial processes, at least where both parties voluntarily opt for them?[229] These initiatives require offenders to accept responsibility for their conduct and make reparations. The theory is that through direct dialogue with victims, students who have engaged in wrongful conduct gain a greater understanding of the consequences of their actions, which can lead to genuine remorse, empathy, and reconciliation; lower the risk of repeat offenses; and give victims a greater sense of justice and closure.[230] What benefits or risks do you foresee with such an approach? Does it matter that the parties are part of an educational institution, or should that be irrelevant?

9. **Prevention Strategies.**   Some campus prevention programs have proven effective in increasing knowledge and decreasing rape-supportive attitudes, but the jury is still out on whether they actually reduce sexual violence.[231] Targeted interventions such as bystander intervention, education about consent, and risk reduction and self-defense strategies for women, appear to have promise.[232] One course taken by female first-year college students in Canada emphasizing healthy relationships and self-defense dramatically reduced the risk of rape and attempted rape for

---

227. Robin Wilson, Why Campuses Can't Talk About Alcohol When It Comes to Sexual Assault, Chron. Higher Educ. (Sept. 4, 2014).

228. Yoffe, supra note 200, at 1 (quoting Sokolow, Sex and Booze).

229. See Madison Orcutt et al., Restorative Justice Approaches to the Informal Resolution of Student Sexual Misconduct, 45 J. Coll. & U. L. 1 (2020); Donna Coker, Crime Logic, Campus Sexual Assault, and Restorative Justice, 49 Tex. Tech. L. Rev. 147 (2017).

230. See Amy B. Cyphert, The Devil Is in the Details: Exploring Restorative Justice as an Option for Campus Sexual Assault Responses Under Title IX, 96 Denv. L. Rev. 51 (2018).

231. See Roberta E. Gibbons & Julie Evans, Nat'l Online Resource Ctr. on Violence Against Women, The Evaluation of Campus-Based Gender Violence Prevention Programming: What We Know About Program Effectiveness and Implications for Practitioners (Jan. 2013); Sarah DeGue et al., A Systematic Review of Primary Prevention Strategies for Sexual Violence Perpetration, 19 Aggression & Violent Behav. 346 (2014).

232. Eilene Zimmerman, Campuses Struggle with Approaches for Preventing Sexual Assault, N.Y. Times, June 22, 2016, at F2; Caitlin B. Henriksen et al., Mandatory Bystander Intervention Training, in Crisis of Campus Sexual Violence: Critical Perspectives on Prevention and Response 176 (Sara Carrigan Wooten & Roland W. Mitchell, eds., 2016).

women who completed the course.[233] Critics worry that this approach does not actually decrease the number of assaults, but simply protects certain women (those who use the strategies taught in class) from experiencing them.[234] Researchers in the Columbia University study mentioned above recommend a holistic public health approach that educates students on "a broad range of topics, going beyond consent to include positive and healthy social and sexual relationships, sex education, sexual refusal skills, and bystander training."[235] Another approach would target high-risk groups for committing sexual assault, such as fraternities, whose members are more likely than non-members to endorse sexual aggression and engage in sexual assault.[236] Some schools have sought to shut down fraternities and all-male clubs altogether.[237] Others have sought to enlist them in rape prevention campaigns, by providing peer education programs and bystander intervention training, and by penalizing or suspending fraternities that fall short.[238]

Which of these strategies seem most likely to be effective? What role can sororities play? How would you evaluate the rape prevention efforts on your college campus? Is college too late for such efforts?[239]

PUTTING THEORY INTO PRACTICE

5-7. In a 2014 case at Yale, a young woman drinking with friends exchanged text messages with a former sexual partner in which she told him that she was getting drunk and stated "don't let me try to seduce you. . . . Sex is awesome . . . and I might try to get it from you. But I shouldn't. I don't think." The two engaged in sex and she later charged him with assault, claiming she was too intoxicated to do anything other than "capitulate." An adjudicative panel found that while "alcohol may have reduced [her] inhibitions," her actions "taken as a whole, do not indicate that she lacked the ability to make or act on considered decisions."[240] Is the standard applied by the panel appropriate? If not, what should the standard be?

5-8. In responding to concerns about the adequacy of procedural protections for students accused of sexual assault, Guardian columnist Jessica Valenti wrote: "on the one side, there are the 20 percent of college women who can expect to be victimized by rapists and would-be rapists; on the other side is a bunch of adult men (and a few women) worrying themselves to death that a few college-aged men might have to find a new college to attend."[241] Does that trivialize the harm of

---

233. Charlene Y. Senn et al., Efficacy of a Sexual Assault Resistance Program for University Women, 372 New Eng. J. Med. 2326 (2015).

234. Grigoriadis, supra note 188, at 219.

235. Hirsch et al., supra note 161, at 3.

236. Grigoriadis, supra note 188, at 231.

237. Alexandra Robbins, A Frat Boy and a Gentleman, N.Y. Times, Jan. 27, 2019, at SR5.

238. Id.

239. Serena Patel, Gender Respect Education: A Proposal to Combat Commercial Sexual Exploitation, 23 Am. U. J. Gender Soc. Pol'y & L. 393, 406-10 (2015).

240. Robin Wilson, Colleges Wrestle with How to Define Rape, Chron. Higher Educ. (Jan. 16, 2015).

241. Zoë Heller, Rape on the Campus, N.Y. Rev. Books (Feb. 5, 2015) (quoting Valenti).

being labeled a rapist and forced to apply to another school with a record of sexual misconduct? Or does it capture legitimate frustration with the longstanding failure to protect students from assault? How fair and adequate are your school's sexual assault procedures?

5-9. In a widely publicized case involving Columbia University, a male student who was found not responsible for sexual misconduct sued the university for sex discrimination and intentional infliction of emotional distress. He claimed that the administration had allowed his accuser to launch a prolonged campaign to harass him and that it would never have let a male student target a female student in the same way that he had been targeted. Among other things, the university had allowed the complaining witness to carry a mattress everywhere she went while on campus, including the graduation ceremony, and had given her academic credit and logistical support for her "Mattress Performance (Carry That Weight)," which doubled as her senior thesis project. The university art gallery also displayed an exhibit that featured prints of a couple having sex that included an obscenity and an inked-over New York Times article about the accused student.[242] The university ultimately settled the case out of court.[243] How would you evaluate its conduct?

5-10. According to a female Swarthmore student, a male friend with whom she had been sexually involved fell asleep on her bed. Because the two had decided, she thought mutually, just to be friends, she climbed in next to him. When he began taking off her clothes, she "basically said, 'No, I don't want to have sex with you.' And then he said, 'Okay, that's fine,' and stopped. . . . And then he started again a few minutes later, taking off my panties, taking off his boxers. I just kind of laid there and didn't do anything—I had already said no. I was just tired and wanted to go to bed. I let him finish. I pulled my panties back on and went to sleep." She told a drug and alcohol counselor about the incident, who responded that the student was "such a good guy" that she must be mistaken. Three months later she complained to a dean. Both students graduated, and she never learned the outcome of any investigation.[244] If the facts were as she stated them, what if any sanctions should have been imposed on the male student? How would you respond to a sexual trauma counselor who told a student under similar circumstances that "[y]ou should probably expect something when you sleep in bed with a guy"?[245]

5-11. In 2019, three women brought a class action lawsuit against Yale University after being groped at off-campus fraternity parties. They alleged that "fraternities elevate men to social gatekeepers and relegate women and nonbinary students to sexual objects." The prior month, after a year-long review of campus culture, the Dean of Yale College stated: "I condemn the culture described in these accounts; it runs counter to our community values of making everyone feel welcome, respected and safe. I also offer some plain advice about events like these: don't go to them." He added that Yale "plays no formal role in the organizations not affiliated with the university, including Greek organizations." The lawsuit countered that fraternities

---

242. Emily Bazelon, Have We Learned Anything from the Columbia Rape Case?, N.Y. Times Mag., May 29, 2015.

243. Tolentino, supra note 194, at 36.

244. Simon Van Zuylen-Wood, Rape Happens Here, Phila. Mag. (Apr. 24, 2014).

245. Olivia Ortiz, A Four-Year Struggle, Chi. Maroon (June 3, 2014).

"act as extensions of Yale," by providing party spaces, and that the university allows them to use the Yale name and campus facilities for recruitment.[246] Should a university that takes these steps to sever ties with fraternities be held responsible for the environments created at fraternity parties?

5-12. Callisto Campus is a third-party reporting system used at a small number of colleges. It permits students who have experienced sexual harassment or assault to save time-stamped written records of a sexual assault, to agree to report it only if another victim names the same perpetrator, or to report it directly to campus administrators. What are the advantages of this technology over a traditional reporting system? Should colleges be required to make this alternative available in order to comply with Title IX?

4. *Religious Practices and Sexual Autonomy*

How should the law respond when religious practices constrain women's physical health and sexual autonomy? One site of tension concerns the practice of female genital mutilation (FGM) or, as it is more sympathetically referred to, female genital surgeries (FGS), female genital cutting (FGC), or — the term used by some activists within Muslim communities and, now, the U.S. Citizenship and Immigration Services — female genital surgeries/cutting (FGS/C). Is any one of these terms more neutral than the others? More respectful? Are there dangers of wrapping the entire range of practices into just one term?

In Re Kasinga

U.S. Dep't of Justice Board of Immigration Appeals File A73 476 695 (1996)

The applicant is a 19-year-old native and citizen of Togo. . . . She is a member of the Tchamba-Kunsuntu Tribe of northern Togo. She testified that young women of her tribe normally undergo ["female genital mutilation," abbreviated throughout as FGM] at age 15. However, she did not because she initially was protected from FGM by her influential, but now deceased, father.

The applicant stated that upon her father's death in 1993, under tribal custom, her aunt . . . became the primary authority figure in the family. [The mother was driven from the family home and her whereabouts are unknown.]

The applicant further testified that her aunt forced her into a polygamous marriage in October 1994, when she was 17. The husband selected by her aunt was 45 years old. . . . [U]nder tribal custom, her aunt and her husband planned to force her to submit to FGM before the marriage was consummated. . . . [She fled to Ghana, and then the United States, and is now in detention by the Immigration and Naturalization Service.]

---

246. McNeil v. Yale University, No. 3:19-cdv00209-VAB, 2019 WL 5783597 (D. Conn. July 18, 2019); Anemona Hartocollis, Women Sue Yale Over a Fraternity Culture They Say Enables Harassment, N.Y. Times, Feb. 12, 2019, at A15.

The applicant testified that the Togolese police and the Government of Togo were aware of FGM and would take no steps to protect her from the practice. She further testified that her aunt had reported her to the Togolese police. Upon return, she would be taken back to her husband by the police and forced to undergo FGM. . . .

[T]he form of FGM practiced by her tribe . . . is of an extreme type involving cutting the genitalia with knives, extensive bleeding, and a 40-day recovery period. . . . FGM in its extreme form is a practice in which portions of the female genitalia are cut away. In some cases, the vagina is sutured partially closed. This practice clearly inflicts harm or suffering upon the girl or woman who undergoes it.

FGM is extremely painful and at least temporarily incapacitating. It permanently disfigures the female genitalia. FGM exposes the girl or woman to the risk of serious, potentially life-threatening complications. These include . . . bleeding, infection, urine retention, stress, shock, psychological trauma, and damage to the urethra and anus. It can result in permanent loss of genital sensation and can adversely affect sexual and erotic functions.

[Section 101(a)(42)(A) of the Immigration and Nationality Act] defines a "refugee" eligible for asylum as any person "who is outside any country of such person's nationality . . . and who is unable or unwilling to return to, and is unable or unwilling to avail himself or herself of the protection of, that country because of . . . a well-founded fear of persecution on account of race, religion, nationality, membership in a particular social group, or political opinion." We agree . . . that this level of harm can constitute "persecution" . . .

In accordance with [precedent], the particular social group is defined by common characteristics that members of the group either cannot change, or should not be required to change because such characteristics are fundamental their individual identities. The characteristics of being a "young woman" and a "member of the Tchamba-Kunsuntu Tribe" cannot be changed. The characteristic of having intact genitalia is one that is so fundamental to the individual identity of a young woman that she should not be required to change it. . . .

Record materials state that FGM "has been used to control women's sexuality." It also is characterized as a form of "sexual oppression" that is "based on the manipulation of women's sexuality in order to assure male dominance and exploitation. . . .

We therefore find that the persecution the applicant fears in Togo [is] "on account of" her status as a member of the defined group.

L. Amede Obiora

Bridges and Barricades: Rethinking Polemics and Intransigence in the Campaign Against Female Circumcision

47 Case W. Res. L. Rev. 275, 288-90, 295-99, 316-17, 329 (1997)

Genital scarification and reconstruction are time-honored and worldwide practices. As extant cultural traditions, the practices are particularly prevalent in Africa where they are reported to occur in about twenty-six countries; the exact number of women affected is unknown, but it is estimated between 80 and 110 million. Within the African context, the age at which it is performed varies between localities and it is possible to distinguish at least four major forms of incidence. The ritualized marking of female genitalia begins with the mildest forms of the procedures, where the clitoris is barely nicked or pricked to shed a few drops of blood. This procedure is innocuous and has a strictly symbolic connation.

The next range of surgeries extend to the removal of the clitoral prepuce, hood, or outer skin. This is the form that ritual Muslims refer to as sunna, and medical data indicates that it poses minimal health risks if scientifically performed and monitored. Sunna is most comparable to male circumcision and there is some suggestion that it may serve the purpose of hygiene and cleanliness. A more radical form of female genital surgeries is known as excision or clitoridectomy. In this procedure, the clitoral glans and some of the nympha or labia minora, the narrow lip-like enclosures of the genital anatomy, are severed. The most extreme form of the surgeries is called infibulation, and it has been identified as the form that presents the most significant health risks and hazards. The procedure entails scrapping the labia majora, the two rounded folds of tissue that contour the external boundaries of the vulva, and stitching the remaining raw edges together in a manner that ensures that only a tiny opening will be left after the surgery heals. . . .

"Western-biased themes of bodily 'integrity' and tightly bounded individuality tend to confuse and distort the issue. . . .

Female circumcision is embedded in an intricate web of habits, attitudes, and values, along with having both functional and symbolic connotations. In Africa, the practice is validated and undergirded by a wide spectrum of principles, in addition to temporal and spiritual beliefs. Recurring themes such as sexuality and fertility express preeminent indigenous values like solidarity among women, public recognition of lifecycle change, and procreation for social continuity. Some of these themes are not peculiar to cultures that practice circumcision. Adherence to rites of passage, for example, is an abiding phenomenon in the West.

[Obiora surveys a number of different symbolic meanings for female circumcision in different tribes, including circumcision as a test of courage; as a symbolic linking with tribal history; as a means of making the body symbolically fertile; as a sacrifice to a fertility deity; as a rite of purification; as a means of sex differentiation; as an aesthetic practice; as a symbol of individual identity; as a kind of cosmetic surgery akin to ear piercing; as a contraceptive device; as a means of inaugurating a girl into sexual womanhood; and finally as a way to discourage premarital sex.] . . .

Instead of being subject to a monolithic regime of patriarchs, it may well be that African women resort to female circumcision to recreate notions of womanhood adept for their peculiar conditions of existence. . . .

The regrettable focus on determinism explains the inclination of some radical feminists to discount or marginalize the perspectives of African women . . .

Through the years in Africa, outside interventionists, whether colonialist or missionary (and now feminist), continue to presume that it is their duty as the "advanced" to elevate and enlighten the "backward." . . . Not surprisingly, their campaigns, often couched in terms of virtual monopoly on good judgment, are perceived as unduly ethnocentric and presumptuous. . . . Moreover, they tend to pre-judge and alienate the only forces — women, the "victims" and perpetrators — capable of facilitating or subverting meaningful change.

NOTES

1. **Women's Autonomy, or Cultural Imperialism?** What do you make of the Obiora critique of Westerners who criticize the various female genital surgeries discussed in the readings above? Are Western feminists who advocate for reform of societies whose cultures and religions "oppress" women being arrogant? Imperialist? Essentialist? Are these different ways of saying that feminists are ignoring intersectionality concerns?

Is it wrong to criticize these practices because they are associated with a different culture or different religion? Is it possible for feminists to advocate for better treatment of women globally without being culturally insensitive, or without accounting for the wide variety of women's circumstances and commitments?

Some scholars have noted that there are dissenters within the Muslim culture who are already challenging FGS/C.[247] Is that a reason for Westerners to back off their criticism and allow these women their agency, or is it, instead, a reason to join encourage these dissenters by making their own (Western) voices known?[248]

Cyra Akila Choudhury compares the complex struggles of women in non-Western cultures to the struggles of non-white feminists within the West. She observes that both "postcolonial and critical race feminists have resisted attacks based on culture by white feminists" while also having "to articulate the fight for change against dominant cultural norms within their communities."[249] She suggests further that the best strategy among feminists in these struggles is "a politics of solidarity — one in which feminists come together to engage in unflinching critique from positions of equality rather than civilizational superiority."[250] Similarly, Helen Stacy argues that legal prohibitions are most likely to be successful when they work in tandem with broader social movements. So, for example, laws against footbinding in China were not effective until anti-footbinding societies enlisted parents to take an oath that they would not bind their daughter's feet or allow their sons to marry a woman who had been subjected to the practice.[251] Is this the answer — both resisting communities and finding alliances within them? What do you think this means in practice? Does it recognize intersectionality concerns?

2. **The Legal Regulation of FGS/C.** UNICEF estimates that more than 200 million girls and women alive today have had some form of FGS/C.[252] Its elimination, despite the critiques of Obiora and others,[253] has become a near consensus

---

247. See, e.g., Madhavi Sunder, Piercing the Veil, 112 Yale L.J. 1399 (2003). As an example, see Islamic Relief Worldwide, Women in Somalia Warn Against the Dangers of Female Genital Mutilation/Cutting (Nov. 27, 2020).

248. Sunder, supra note 247.

249. Cyra Akila Choudhury, Beyond Culture: Human Rights Universalisms Versus Religious and Cultural Relativism in the Activism for Gender Justice, 30 Berkeley J. Gender L. & Just. 226, 230 (2015).

250. Id. at 230-31.

251. Helen M. Stacy, Human Rights and the Human Rights System, 28 Law & Soc. Inquiry 110, 177 (2009).

252. UNICEF Data, Female Genital Mutilation (FGM) (May 2022).

253. See, e.g., Leti Volpp, Framing Cultural Difference: Immigrant Women and Discourses of Tradition, 22 differences: A J. of Feminist Cultural Stud. 90 (2011) ("anxiety

goal, globally. On February 6, 2003, the first lady of Nigeria, Mrs. Stella Obasanjo, declared "Zero Tolerance to FGM" in Africa during a conference organized by the Inter-African Committee on Traditional Practices Affecting the Health of Women and Children. This day has since been observed around the world, with February 6, 2030, set as the target date for the complete elimination of FGM.

In 1996, the United States became the second country in the world to ban a wide range of FGS/C practices.[254] U.S. directors of international financial institutions are required to oppose non-humanitarian loans to countries where the procedures are commonly practiced if local governments have not undertaken educational measures to combat the practice.[255] Federal legislation also makes it illegal to "knowingly circumcise[], excise[] or infibulate[] the whole or any part of the labia majora or labia minora or clitoris of another person who has not attained the age of 18 years."[256] The maximum sentence is five years. The statute explicitly rejects the possibility of a cultural defense: "No account shall be taken of the effect on the person on whom the operation is to be performed or any belief on the part of that person, or any other person, that the operation is required as a matter of custom or ritual."[257] Is this the right policy?

In re Kasinga was the first case in which fear of female genital mutilation was recognized as a form of prosecution for purposes of U.S. asylum laws, as well as the first situation in which asylum was based on gender. Other cases followed.[258] Numerous international conventions, declarations, and statements ban or oppose FGS/C practices, and at least eighty-four countries in the world have domestic legislation that either specifically prohibits them or allows them to be prosecuted through other laws, such as the criminal or penal code, child protections laws, violence against women laws, or domestic violence laws.[259] Meanwhile, experts note a shift in some Muslim communities away from infibulation practices to sunna circumcision.[260] Does this shift disprove the criticisms of those like Obiora who spoke out against Western feminist advocacy against FGS/C, or is it a vindication of those criticisms?

Despite the growing consensus against FGS/C, occasional voices continue to be raised questioning whether a total ban on the practices is warranted. An international, interdisciplinary group of scholars and medical personnel, for example, write that "Western-centric implications . . . unequally distribute the right to dispose of one's body according to race and ethnicity. Indeed, the prohibition only concerns the customary genital cutting practices in African and South-Asian countries

---

about forms of gender subordination practiced in immigrant communities can function as a proxy for xenophobia").

254. Federal Prohibition of Female Genital Mutilation Act, 18 U.S.C. § 116 (2018).

255. 22 U.S.C. § 262k-2 (2018).

256. 18 U.S.C. § 116 (2018).

257. Id.

258. See, e.g., Bah v. Mukasey, 529 F.3d 99 (2d Cir. 2008).

259. See World Bank, Compendium of International and National Legal Frameworks on Female Genital Mutilation (6th ed. 2022) (country-by-country listing)

260. See, e.g., R. Elise B. Johansen, Discourses of Change: The Shift from Infibulation to Sunna Circumcision Among Somali and Sudanese, PLoS ONE (June 17, 2022).

but does not apply to female genital surgeries, which are increasingly desired and practiced on white adult women and under-age girls worldwide."[261] Does this critique necessarily follow from intersectional analysis? Are critics of FGS/C ignoring differences between women?

For further exploration of the tensions between religious practices and women's equality, see the discussion of veiling in Chapter 1, and the discussion of religious exemptions to the contraceptive mandate in Section B1 of this chapter.

PUTTING THEORY INTO PRACTICE

5-13. In 1996, a group of Somali immigrants living in Seattle sought to persuade a hospital to perform largely symbolic circumcisions on their daughters, a procedure that involved simply pricking the clitoral hood and that was less intrusive than male circumcision. The parents presented this as an alternative to sending their daughters to Africa for a more extreme procedure. The hospital initially agreed but changed course when it was inundated with complaints.[262] What would you have advised? Should such a procedure be banned given that circumcision is now performed on a majority of male newborns?[263]

5-14. In several different immigrant groups in the United States, parents are expected to arrange for their daughters' marriages. A survey of agencies throughout the world that had encountered forced marriage cases reported multiple forms of fraud, force, or coercion to make girls (some as young as 13) enter or stay in a forced marriage. Tactics included emotional blackmail, isolation, social ostracism, economic threats, and threats of physical violence and loss of immigration status.[264] Over half of the cases involved Muslim families.[265] In response to the problem of forced marriages, the United Kingdom established a "Forced Marriage Unit" and national helpline, passed a law creating a special "forced marriage protective order" in family court, made changes to the visa sponsorship process, and conducted overseas "rescue" operations as well as extensive community education, outreach, and training. The number of forced marriages declined as a result of these measures, but according to a government report, in 2017 there were almost 1,200 cases of forced marriage in the United Kingdom. More than a quarter involved victims younger than 18, and 15 percent were younger than 15. Twenty-one percent of victims were male.[266]

---

261. See, e.g., Sarah O'Neill et al., Rethinking the Anti-FGM Zero-Tolerance Policy: From Intellectual Concerns to Empirical Challenges, 12 Current Sexual Health Reports 266 (2020).

262. See Doriane Lambelet Coleman, The Seattle Compromise: Multicultural Sensitivity and Americanization, 47 Duke L.J. 717 (1998).

263. Child Trends Databank, Infant Male Circumcision (Jan. 2014) (58 percent in 2010, down from 63 percent in 2001).

264. See Tahirih Just. Ctr., Forced Marriages in Immigrant Communities in the United States 8 (Sept. 2011).

265. Id. at 11.

266. See Nadia Khomami, More Than 1,000 Cases of Forced Marriage in U.K, Reports Says, Guardian (May 10, 2018).

Should forced marriages be banned in the United States or regulated in some manner, or should they be tolerated in the name of religious liberty and the avoidance of imperialist judgment against other cultures?

5-15. The city council in a U.S. coastal city has passed an ordinance that provides: "A woman wearing a burkini may not be present on any public beach in the city. A woman who is apprehended wearing a burkini on a public beach is subject to a fine of up to $250 and, upon a second offense, up to 30 days in jail." Burkinis are full-body swimsuits that cover a woman's entire body except the face, hands, and feet. A burkini is light enough for swimming, but modest enough to allow Muslim women whose religious beliefs prohibit a public display of their bodies to enjoy the beach.

One city councilman defended the policy by saying that "burkinis are not respectful of good morals" and a "dangerous symbol of Islamic extremism." Another councilman stated that the ordinance is aimed at "ostentatious clothing that makes reference to an allegiance to terrorist movements who are at war with us." "It is a matter of public order," he went on. "Burkinis are a provocation on our public beaches. Anti-Muslim feelings run high, here, and if we allow these radical outfits, someone is going to get hurt. This ordinance is for the women's own good." To date, two women have been apprehended under the ordinance.

Should this ordinance be upheld if challenged?[267] Why or why not?

5. Sex Work and Human Trafficking

Sex work, traditionally known as prostitution,[268] involves the exchange of sexual services for financial compensation. Although it has been a common practice across time and culture, in the United States, it remained relatively invisible until the antebellum period. With industrialization, urbanization, and Western migration, markets for sex increased and provoked significant challenge. The first major initiatives, variously characterized as "moral reform" and "social purity" campaigns, began in the 1830s and resurfaced in the late nineteenth and early twentieth centuries. At the outset, the leaders were mainly male clergy and philanthropists, but women's organizations soon joined the crusade. Their goals were to reform prostitutes and to discourage men from employing or recruiting them. These efforts led to expanded criminal prohibitions and enforcement strategies. While accurate figures on the total amount of prostitution in the United States are unavailable, most studies indicate that about 10 to 20 percent of American men acknowledge having purchased sex at some point in their lives.[269]

---

267. Such ordinances have been enacted in France. See Jayne Huckerby, France's Burkini Bans Put Muslim Women in Danger, Time (Aug. 24, 2016).

268. The term sex work is generally preferred by those involved in the occupation because it carries less stigma and will be used here except where prostitute is more legally or historically accurate.

269. See Michael Shively et al., A National Overview of Prostitution and Sex Trafficking Demand Reduction Efforts, Final Report to the Department of Justice 7 (2012).

When sex work is coerced, it is a subset of the broad range of crimes known as human trafficking, which also includes forced labor, sex tourism, debt bondage, involuntary servitude, child marriage, and rape.[270] After drugs, trafficking is the largest criminal enterprise globally, with annual profits estimated at close to $150 billion.[271] Globally, the most recent United Nations data show that 50 percent of victims of human trafficking are trafficked for sex, 38 percent for forced labor, and the remainder for a variety of coercive practices, including forced marriage and organ removal.[272] Half of victims of human trafficking are adult women and one third are children. In low-income countries, most child victims are forced into labor, whereas in high-income countries, they are far more likely to be forced into sex.[273]

No one defends human trafficking, the victims of which either did not consent or, because of age or incapacity, are unable to consent. The only question is about the most effective and sensible ways to control it. In contrast, there is some debate, examined below, about whether people ought to be able to buy and sell non-coercive sex — a debate infused with the question whether the sale of sex can ever be, in fact, non-coercive. There is a growing consensus among human rights and civil rights advocates in favor of decriminalizing prostitution. Ironically, as explained below, this movement has been hampered by global efforts to control human trafficking. As you consider measures to prevent coercive sex throughout this section, you should reflect on what impact these measures are likely to have on the sale of non-coercive sex, if you think such a thing exists.

---

270. The definition of trafficking in the 2000 United Nations Convention Against Transnational Organized Crime; Protocol to Prevent, Suppress, and Punish Trafficking in Persons, Especially Women and Children includes "the recruitment, transportation, transfer, harboring or receipt of persons, by means of the threat or use of force or other forms of coercion, of abduction, of fraud, of deception, of the abuse of power or of a position of vulnerability or of the giving or receiving of payments or benefits to achieve the consent of a person having control over another person, for the purposes of exploitation." Exploitation includes "the prostitution of others or other forms of sexual exploitation, forced labor or services, slavery, or practices similar to slavery, servitude, or the removal of organs." Protocol to Prevent, Suppress, and Punish Trafficking in Persons, Especially Women and Children, Supplementing the United Nations Convention Against Transnational Organized Crime, Dec. 12, 2000, 2237 U.N.T.S. 319.

The United States has adopted a similar, although somewhat narrower, definition in the Victims of Trafficking and Violence Protection Act of 2000. It prohibits: "(A) sex trafficking in which a commercial sex act is induced by force, fraud, or coercion, or in which the person induced to perform such an act has not attained 18 years of age; or (B) the recruitment, harboring, transportation, provision, or obtaining a person for labor or services, through the use of force, fraud, or coercion for the purpose of subjection to involuntary servitude, peonage, debt bondage, or slavery." Victims of Trafficking and Violence Protection Act of 2000, 22 U.S.C. § 7101 (2018).

271. Aryn Baker, The Survivor, Time (Jan. 28, 2019), at 38; Ann Wagner & Rachel Wagley McCann, Prostitutes or Prey? The Evolution of Congressional Intent in Combatting Sex Trafficking, 54 Harv. J. on Legis. 1, 24 (2017).

272. U.N. Off. on Drugs and Crime, Global Report on Trafficking in Persons 2020 (hereinafter 2020 U.N. Report on Trafficking in Persons), at 10.

273. Id. at 9-10.

Legal approaches to sex work across the globe fall into four main categories:

- Criminalization, i.e., prohibition of buying and selling sexual services and related practices such as pimping, pandering, and solicitation;
- Regulation, i.e., removal of penalties from activities that meet state-imposed requirements, such as zoning restrictions, licensing regulations, health requirements, and health exams;
- Partial decriminalization, i.e., removal of penalties from the sex worker's sale of sex, but not from its purchase (the client) or the other related activities (e.g., the pimp); or
- Full decriminalization, i.e., removal of penalties from all consensual sexual activities and related commercial practices.

Today, the legal status of sex work varies widely around the world. Most countries either prohibit or regulate the sale of sex, but the scope of permissible behavior, the severity of penalties, and the practices of enforcement agencies differ considerably.

In the United States, every state but Nevada prohibits buying or selling sexual intercourse for money or offering to do so. Every state but Nevada also makes it a crime to knowingly encourage or compel a person to sell sex for money (pandering) or to receive "something of value" knowing that it was earned through an act of prostitution (pimping).[274] Most jurisdictions classify first-time offenses as misdemeanors, but typically punish repeat behavior as a felony. Some states have harsher penalties for the customer and a smaller number have harsher penalties for the seller.[275]

Nevada permits prostitution in counties with populations under 700,000 persons, subject to highly restrictive licensing conditions. Sex workers must be registered and fingerprinted by the police, must submit to frequent testing for sexually transmitted diseases, and must work in brothels where they typically have little control over their hours or customers.[276] To prevent pimping, some counties require that brothel owners and managers be female.[277] Is this constitutional? Does it violate Title VII?

In many countries, particularly those in Asia, South America, and the Mideast, prostitution remains a criminal offense. The prohibitions in some traditional societies are quite severe. In other nations, a de facto regulatory system has evolved despite formal prohibitions. Through de facto or de jure licensing structures, a growing number of Asian and European countries are also developing sex tourism industries. Restrictions range from fairly laissez-faire approaches to tightly controlled zoning systems for licensed brothels. Most European countries follow the "Nordic model" or partial decriminalization, which prohibits the purchase but not the sale of sex. New Zealand has fully decriminalized prostitution.

Consider the following perspectives on sex work and their policy implications.

---

274. Melissa Farley, Prostitution and Trafficking in Nevada: Making the Connections (2007).

275. ProCon.org, U.S. Federal and State Prostitution Laws (2018).

276. See Michelle Rindels, Indy Explains: How Prostitution Laws Work in Nevada, Nev. Indep., May 27, 2018.

277. Natalia Benitez et al., Prostitution and Sex Work, 19 Geo. J. Gender & L. 331 (2018).

Dorchen Leidholdt

Prostitution: A Violation of Women's Human Rights

1 Cardozo Women's L.J. 133, 135-38 (1993)

Prostitution is not about women making money. It is about other people — usually men — making money off women's bodies. Pimps, brothel owners, club owners, hotel chains, travel agencies, pornographers, organized crime syndicates, and governments are the real economic beneficiaries of the sex trade in women. . . .

Prostitution is not about individuals. It is an institution of male dominance, and it is also a global industry in which the prostituting of women is constantly being packaged in new ways, using new forms of technology, tapping new markets: sex-tourism, mail-order bride selling, sex entertainment, sex immigration, dial-a-porn, computer pornography.

Just as prostitution isn't about individuals, it isn't about choice. Instead, prostitution is about the absence of meaningful choices; about having alternative routes to survival cut off or being in a situation where you don't have options to begin with. . . . [T]he majority of women in prostitution in the country—most studies estimate 60 to 70 percent—have histories of sexual abuse in childhood. . . . Add to this the reality that the population targeted by pimps and traffickers is teenagers. It becomes clear that the majority of prostitutes are socialized into "sex work" in childhood and adolescence when consent is meaningless and choice an illusion.

Then there are the related factors of poverty, lack of education, and homelessness. . . .

Choice vanishes when, in order to endure the prostitution, women become addicted to alcohol or drugs, or become prostitutes to support their addiction. In the Portland, Oregon, study, 85 percent of the women were drug or alcohol abusers.

Nor is choice present when a woman is so traumatized by having stranger after stranger use her body as a seminal spittoon that she accepts prostitution as her destiny.

Just as prostitution is not about choice, it's not about work. Or if it is, it is work in the same way that slavery or bonded labor is work—work that violates human dignity and every other human right. What other kind of work has as job training years of being sexually abused in childhood? What other job has as its working conditions: rape . . . beatings . . . and premature death and murder?

Is Sex Work Decriminalization the Answer? What the Research Tells Us

ACLU Research Brief (Oct. 2020)

[R]esearch overwhelmingly suggests that criminalization of sex work, including criminalization of buying but not of selling, sex known as the "end-demand" or "Nordic" model, increases the risk of violence and threatens the safety of sex workers. . . .

In criminalized contexts, sex workers face violence from clients, related both to the context of interactions and the actual and perceived lack of police protection. For example, 22 percent of the 250 female sex workers surveyed in Baltimore, Maryland reported physical or sexual violence by a client in the past three months. Research suggests a strong association between rushing negotiation and experiences with client-perpetrated violence; when sex work is illegal workers may be not able to as effectively screen clients or negotiate fees or activities. The lack of time or conditions to agree upon a fee in advance can increase the risk of disagreements and violence or aggressive escalation by the client during or after the fact. . . .

Research in Canada and Norway shows that . . . [e]ven when clients are the stated target of police, sex workers remain at a heightened risk of violence. . . . Research suggests that decriminalizing or legalizing sex work for both the buyer and seller may better help to protect sex workers from client violence. After the Netherlands legalized prostitution through specific regulations and only in specifically designated public areas known as "tippelzones," they saw a 30 to 40 percent decrease in sex crimes citywide, and research indicated a long-term decrease in sexual abuse and crimes involving drugs if licensing was introduced from the state in the tippelzone.

Limited research on loosening restrictions surrounding sex-related work in the U.S. suggests that sex workers may be safer under less restrictions. For instance, during the period of inadvertent decriminalization of "indoor prostitution" in Rhode Island from 1980 to 2009, there was a 30 percent decrease in reported rape offenses against sex workers post-criminalization. Several studies of conditions under legalized sex work, including legalized brothels in Nevada, indicate that legalization entails higher regulation and scrutiny, resulting in a decreased risk of violence due to greater oversight, regulated negotiation systems, greater peer support from social networks, and more positive relations with law enforcement. . . .

Research shows that in heavily policed, criminalized contexts, including end-demand models, sex workers are often physically or sexually coerced by police through threat of detention, violence (including rape), or extortion. . . . [A] recent study examining the impact of police and client violence on sex workers in Baltimore, Maryland found that 70 percent of sex workers in the same had been incarcerated, with an average of 15 instances of imprisonment within their lives. . . .

Although legalization — the scenario which removes criminal penalties for some sex work, provided the participants comply with relevant regulations — may help to reduce violence from clients . . . , it may also maintain a level of police surveillance and contact with negative consequences to sex workers. . . .

Due to historical discrimination by and mistrust of the police and the risk of being arrested when sex work is criminalized, sex workers report crimes to police at low rates. In a study of sex workers in Sacramento Valley, California, most sex workers indicated that they did not report violence to the police because of fear that law enforcement would blame the sex workers themselves, a fear that sex workers surveyed in Chicago and New York City also predominantly reported. Furthermore, in a Baltimore study, police officers themselves expressed the view that violence was an inevitable consequence of sex work and not worth addressing in a serious manner. . . .

The empirical research points to a negative relationship between criminalization of sex work and physical and mental health. . . . [The research] demonstrates that criminalization can negatively impact HIV/STI prevention and increase risk of transmission by limiting sex workers' screening and negotiation abilities, such as for condom use. . . . Based on a systemic review of 87 studies from several continents, researchers developed an HIV transmission model and concluded that, . . . through decrease in sexual violence, police harassment, and unsafe work environments, . . . decriminalization could result in the prevention of over one-third of projected HIV transmissions among female sex workers between 2014-2024. . . . Sex workers in Northern Ireland reported an increase in requests for unsafe sex practices following a change from legalized prostitution to an end-demand model. . . . Another study noted that following a period of decriminalization in Rhode Island, incidences of gonorrhea decreased by over 40 percent. . . .

International research suggests that criminalization, including criminalization of the buyer only, reduces access to needed health services, as a result of stigma and discrimination, and reduces the ability to access valuable peer education about HIV/STI prevention and condom distribution, thereby increasing sexual health risks. [It also shows] a positive relationship between decriminalization or legalization and greater access to health services, such as STI testing, screenings, emergency services, and affordable health care. . . .

[R]esearch points to a negative relationship between criminalization of sex work and financial security, and suggests decriminalization can lead to more stable and higher income. . . .[278]

NOTES

1. **Sex Work and Its Relationship to Sex, Race, Class, Gender Identity, and Immigrant Status.**   From the beginning of the campaign against prostitution in the United States, race and class mattered. Class, race, and ethnic prejudice underpinned many of the early "anti-vice" campaigns. Moral reformers were particularly concerned by the prospect of husbands of white women consorting with lower-class immigrants and women of color.

Criminal laws enacted to prohibit prostitution, although generally sex-neutral in form, have tended to be sex-biased in practice. Hard numbers are unavailable, but sources as recent as 2015 and 2016 report that about nine out of every ten arrests for sex work in the United States were of sellers, not buyers,[279] and that fewer than 1 percent of prostitution-related arrests are for pimping.[280] Moreover, female sex workers are prosecuted at far higher rates than males.[281]

---

278. This report is available at https://www.aclu.org/sites/default/files/field_docum ent/aclu_sex_work_decrim_research_brief_new.pdf.

279. Simon Hedlin, Can Prostitution Law Reform Curb Sex Trafficking? Theory and Evidence on Scale Substitution, and Replacement Effects, 50 U. Mich. J. L. Reform 329, 333 (2016).

280. John Elrod, Filling the Gap: Refining Sex Trafficking Legislation to Address the Problem of Pimping, 68 Vand. L. Rev. 961, 979 (2015).

281. Benitez et al., supra note 277, at 360; Danielle Augustson & Alyssa George, Prostitution and Sex Work, 16 Geo. J. Gender & L. 229, 255, 258 (2015).

Criminalization takes a special toll on LGBTQ+ workers who are already subject to particular stigma and discrimination.[282] LGBTQ+ individuals make up 40 percent of the homeless youth, even though they are only about 7 percent of the youth population.[283] Studies in New York and Chicago show that many LGBTQ+ youth resort to survival sex after being kicked out of their homes for their gender non-conformity.[284] Non-heterosexual orientation is positively associated with rushing negotiations with clients, and with having to use physical means of self-defense.[285] One study of sex workers in Baltimore found that transgender women were eight times more likely to have HIV than cisgender women, as well as higher rates of depression, mental health issues, and problems with substantive abuse.[286] LGBTQ+ women are also more likely to be profiled as sex workers. In the largest U.S. survey of transgender people, approximately three in ten Black transgender women and multiracial transgender women reported that a police officer has assumed they were sex workers. All the transgender respondents of one survey of 305 LGBTQ+ people in the Jackson Heights neighborhood of New York City reported being profiled as sex workers, stopped and searched, often verbally or physically abused, and even arrested on account of possessing condoms as evidence of prostitution, although none were working as sex workers at the time.[287]

Women of color are also both disproportionately vulnerable to the circumstances that cause many individuals to turn to sex work, and disproportionately arrested and prosecuted for sex work crimes.[288] For example, Black youth make up 63 percent of minors arrested for prostitution-related offenses in the United States.[289] Black and LatinX individuals accounted for 91 percent of arrests for "loitering for the purposes of prostitution" in New York in 2018.[290] In California, Black women are arrested for prostitution at fourteen times their percentage of the population.[291]

Immigrant women are also differentially affected. The first restrictive federal immigration law, the Page Act of 1875, prohibited the immigration of Chinese women on the ground they might promote prostitution or other immoral activities.[292] This view continues in today's vigorous enforcement efforts by the U.S. Department of Homeland Security against Asian migrant women working in massage parlors where sex work may also take place.[293] Because prostitution-related

---

282. Benitez et al., supra note 277, at 335.

283. Nina Luo, Data for Progress, Decriminalizing Survival: Policy Platform and Polling on the Decriminalization of Sex Work 10 (Jan. 2020).

284. ACLU Research Brief, supra note 278, at 12.

285. Id.

286. Id.

287. Id.

288. See Cheryl Nelson-Butler, A Critical Race Feminist Perspective on Prostitution & Sex Trafficking in America, 27 Yale J.L. & Feminism 95, 132 (2015).

289. Jasmine Sankofa, Black Girls and the (Im)possibilities of a Victim Trope, 62 UCLA L. Rev. 1645 (2015).

290. Luo, supra note 283, at 9.

291. Id. (citing study).

292. See Kerry Abrams, Polygamy, Prostitution, and the Federalization of Immigration Law, 105 Colum. L. Rev. 641, 643 (2005).

293. Luo, supra note 283, at 11.

charges are considered to be crimes of "moral turpitude," even an arrest without a formal charge or conviction can trigger immigration consequences, including deportation or disqualification from citizenship or visas reserved for trafficking survivors or survivors of violence.[294]

2. **The Autonomy of Sex Workers.** At issue in debates over sex work are fundamental issues about the meaning of consent and the nature of sexual expression. Among the most divisive issues are the extent to which individuals who sell sexual services make genuinely free choices to do so, and the extent to which commercial sex is work like any other legal industry.

What complicates the debate is the diversity of stories among workers and the inadequate or conflicting data concerning their experiences. As one worker put it, "[s]ome [women] feel they are victims. Some *are* victims. And then there are others who say that they made that choice and celebrate that choice."[295] Rachel Moran falls into the first category. She began to sell sex at age 14, after she became a ward of the state because her father had committed suicide and her mother had a severe mental illness. She took to the streets where she had no skills and no other options when her older boyfriend pressured her into prostitution. She later entered a brothel and began using drugs to dull the pain. In her view, consent is never truly present in sex work; it always constitutes a human rights abuse.[296]

By contrast, other sex workers claim that the first time they felt powerful was the first time they turned a trick.[297] Some individuals "choose to do sex work because it offers better pay and more flexible working conditions," or because it allows them to "explore and express their sexuality."[298] According to one sex worker:

[B]eing able to earn [a substantial income] is a blessing. . . . I have no regret for my experiences. Prostitution brought me social life, money, sex and entertainment. . . . I was alone in college, on welfare with a son. He wanted football clothes. He got them.[299]

Another woman agreed:

I've always considered my place in sex work really privileged because I've always worked indoors and I've always been really in control of my work. I really love what I do. It's an amazing income and it's putting me through college. . . . [But as a woman of color,] I've been busted over and over again more so than the peers that I work with, who are mainly educated and white.[300]

---

294. Id.

295. Sex Trade Workers and Feminists: Myths and Illusions, in Good Girls/Bad Girls: Feminists and Sex Trade Workers Face to Face 202 (Laurie Bell ed., 1987).

296. Rachel Moran, Buying Sex Should Not Be Legal, N.Y. Times, Aug. 28, 2015, at A19.

297. Gail McPherson, The Whore Stigma: Female Disorder and Male Unworthiness, 37 Soc. Text 39, 54 (1993).

298. Open Society Foundation, Understanding Sex Work in an Open Society (2015).

299. Anonymous, Prostitution: A Narrative by a Former "Call Girl," 1 Mich. J. Gender & L. 105, at 105 (1993).

300. Hannah Alsgaard, Introduction: Symposium, Uncovered: The Policing of Sex Work, 26 Berkeley J. Gender L. & Justice, 198, 200 (2011) (quoting Luette Chavez).

One sex worker who had previously worked in a male-dominated occupation servicing telephone lines recalled that "I came home exhausted every day plus I was harassed by guys on the job. Working as a prostitute in a massage parlor is far less draining and I still get that kick of being an assertive woman."[301] The prominent Hollywood Madame, Heidi Fleiss, "wouldn't recommend prostitution as a career because it doesn't have great long-term prospects." But in the short term, the money can help someone finish school, start a business, or do something else "positive with her life."[302]

Cristina Schultz Warthen worked as an escort while attending Stanford Law School. Her Internet site featured topless photos and listed rates ranging from $1,250 for two hours to $3,000 for six hours. According to one posting on the site, "I have paid off 100 percent of my student loans and I have tried to send a positive message to SF escorts re: assumptions about the nature and social status of women in the business."[303] In another posting, Warthen states, "During my education, I was continually taught to question paradigms and assumptions. I never understood, however, why this questioning had to stop when it bumped up against accepted social and sexual norms. I never understood why you had to be a down-to-earth educated chaste career-girl or a sexual, sensual adventuress or temptress."[304] She eventually pled guilty to tax evasion and agreed to pay $243,000 and serve a year of home detention and three years of probation.[305] Was this an appropriate result? If Warthen eventually applies to the bar, could she ever satisfy the standard requiring applicants to demonstrate "good moral character"?

Research on male sex workers reflects a similar diversity of experience. Although some are young, impoverished, addicted, and abused, others appear to freely choose their work and appear to suffer few ill effects.[306]Even for well-compensated sex workers, however, many feminists, such as Dorchen Leidholdt in the reading above, question whether prostitution represents the kind of free, informed, individual choice that is worthy of respect. Many studies show that over 80 percent of sex workers wish they could get out of the business.[307] Forty percent of sex workers start as teenage runaways or trafficked children.[308] As Catharine MacKinnon notes, "[i]f prostitution is a free choice, why are the women with the

---

301. McPherson, supra note 297, at 57.

302. Heidi Fleiss, as told to Nadya Labi, In Defense of Prostitution, Legal Affairs (Sept./Oct. 2003).

303. Dan Reed, Stanford Law Grad, U.S. Clash over Cache of Cash, San Jose Mercury News, Oct. 6, 2004, at B1.

304. John Roemer, Degree of Flexibility: Stanford Law Grad Turned Escort Says Her Legal Training Taught Her to Question Assumptions, S.F. Daily J., Oct. 25, 2004, at A1; Howard Mintz, Stanford Law School Grad Pleads Guilty to Running Escort Service, San Jose Mercury News, Jan. 26, 2009.

305. Mintz, supra note 304; She Works Hard for the Money, Playboy 49 (Feb. 1, 2005).

306. Thayne D. Stoddard, Male Prostitution and Equal Protection: An Enforcement Dilemma, 21 Duke J. Gender L. & Pol'y 227, 233-35 (2013).

307. Laws.com, The Prostitution Statistics You Have to Know (Dec. 23, 2019), https://sex-crimes.laws.com/prostitution/prostitution-statistics.

308. Id.

fewest choices the ones most often found doing it?"[309] In her view, "[u]nderstood as a practice of sexual exploitation, prostitution cannot be made safe."[310] According to some sociologists, when prostitutes give favorable accounts of their experience, they are engaging in "neutralizing techniques":

> Sociologists use the term to describe the way in which socially despised and marginalized groups survive their marginal condition. Such techniques may be employed because the only alternative available may be the painful one of self-contempt. The idea that prostitution is freely chosen is such a technique.[311]

By contrast, defenders of sex work are offended by the dismissal of their own perceptions as false consciousness. As members of one Canadian organization of sex workers put it:

> When you are a prostitute that says, "Well, I don't agree with the way you're interpreting my life, I don't feel oppressed or I don't feel exploited in the way that you're saying," they say things like "she's too blinded to her own oppression to see her experience for what it really is, and it really is the patriarchy." They find it necessary to interpret prostitutes' experience of their lives and then feed it back to the prostitutes to tell them what's really happening, whereas they wouldn't dare be so condescending or patronizing with any other group of women.[312]

Defenders of sex work also question the ideal of romantic sex that seems to underpin the aversion to it.

> We need to reflect on whether romantic love is really the only valid foundation for sexual interaction; to question the view that "legitimate" sexual intimacy must be tied to spiritual connection. All too many of us seem to have swallowed wholesale this ideology: we abhor . . . "impersonal" sex; we yearn for intimate "pillow talk"; we disdain the prostitute for engaging in sex without "real connection." (Which of us hasn't engaged in sex without connection? It wasn't prostitutes who told their daughters to "close your eyes and think . . . [of the Empire]."[313]

---

309. Catharine MacKinnon, Prostitution and Civil Rights, 1 Mich. J. Gender & L. 13, 27-28 (1996).

310. Catharine MacKinnon, Trafficking, Prostitution, and Inequality, 46 Harv. Civ. Rights-Civ. Lib. L. Rev. 271, 299 (2011). While this view has led MacKinnon to oppose the movement to decriminalize sex work altogether, she considers the Nordic model of partial decriminalization, under which buyers of sex are penalized but not the sellers, to be "sex equality in inspiration and effect." Id. at 301.

311. Sheila Jeffreys, The Idea of Prostitution 137 (1997).

312. Realistic Feminists: An Interview with Valerie Scott, Peggy Miller, and Ryan Hotchkiss of the Canadian Organization for the Rights of Prostitutes, in Good Girls/Bad Girls, at 204, 213 (Laurie Bell ed., 1987). For similar views among sex workers, see Emily Bazelon, Oppression or Profession?, N.Y. Times Mag., May 8, 2016, at 35-43.

313. Carlin Meyer, Decriminalizing Prostitution: Liberation or Dehumanization?, 1 Cardozo Women's L.J. 105, 117 (1993).

Is the ideal of romantic love itself gendered? The limited available evidence suggests that women tend to "shy away from straightforward cash for sex transactions" and prefer at least the illusion of affection and romance.[314] Does a romantic façade make the transaction any more, or less, exploitative?

3. **Reforming the Law Relating to Sex Work.**   Current legal policies toward sex work are expensive and largely ineffective deterrents. Thousands are spent prosecuting woman offenders, who typically return almost immediately to the streets. A Texas study found that it costs over four times as much to incarcerate prostitutes as to fund their participation in rehabilitative programs.[315] Although some evidence suggests that most sex workers would like to quit, a variety of forces make exit difficult: lack of education and employment skills, the stigma of an arrest record, substance abuse and mental health problems, and control by pimps.[316]

Most women's rights advocates and sex workers agree on two points relating to the law of sex work: criminal penalties for workers are not appropriate, and more strategies are necessary to ensure the safety of sex workers. From this perspective, many feminists point out that the best way for society to minimize the harms associated with prostitution is to maximize women's other employment choices, increase their access to social services, and reduce the safety risks and social stigma associated with consensual commercial sex.

Most women's rights advocates and sex workers are also united in opposing regulation as an alternative to decriminalization. While regulation may sound good in theory, sex workers generally object to the highly restrictive conditions imposed by licensing structures and to the large share of profits taken by brothel owners (typically 50 percent). Counties in Nevada exclude women with criminal records or sexually transmitted diseases, brothels limit women's mobility and choices, and licensing structures permanently stigmatize women as sex workers. As a result, despite the relatively safe working conditions and substantial incomes available, licensed brothels are an unattractive option for most sex workers,[317] and all but a small percentage operate outside of licensed establishments.[318]

Other countries offer a less stigmatized model. In Windsor, Canada, city authorities sought to create a safe "adult entertainment destination" while respecting escorts' "right to self-determination in their work." Sex work is licensed, advertised, and "normalized," and workers are given information about health, safety,

---

314. Mireya Navarro, The West Gets Wilder, N.Y. Times, Jan. 8, 2006, at S2 (quoting Amalia Cazebas).

315. Kim Wilks, Tex. Criminal Justice Coal., Effective Approaches for Reducing Prostitution in Texas: Proactive and Cost-Efficient Strategies to Help People Leave the Streets (2013).

316. C. Aaron McNeece & Elizabeth Mayfield Arnold, Program Closure: The Impact on Participants in a Program for Female Prostitutes, 12 Rsch. Soc. Work Prac. 159, 168 (2002) (reporting that 90 percent of interviewees expressed desire to leave). For other research, see Shively et al., supra note 269, at 14; MacKinnon, Trafficking, supra note 310, at 271, 290.

317. Brynn N.H. Jacobson, Addressing the Tension Between the Dual Identities of the American Prostitute: Criminal and Victim; How Problem-Solving Courts Can Help, 37 Seattle U. L. Rev. 1023, 1043 (2014).

318. See Sylvia Law, Commercial Sex: Beyond Decriminalization, 73 S. Cal. L. Rev. 523, 560 (2000); Augustson & George, supra note 281, at 245.

social services, and financial planning.[319] In Germany, which has the highest per capita rate of sex workers in any European country, the occupation is heavily regulated and heavily taxed. The goal was to allow workers the right to enter into enforceable employment contracts, and register for health insurance, pension plans, and other benefits.[320] However, few individuals have taken advantage of those rights and high levels of sex tourism have spawned difficulties in preventing solicitation and trafficking.[321] The experience in the Netherlands is similar. Brothels are legal, as is street prostitution in certain zones, and sex workers have access to pensions, social security benefits, and state-organized health care. However, illegal prostitution and trafficking remain problems, and many workers are unwilling to take advantage of benefits that would stigmatize them as prostitutes.[322]

The partial decriminalization approach that prohibits the purchase, but not sale of sex (the Nordic model) has been embraced by a growing number of European countries. In 2014, the European Parliament endorsed it as the recommended approach, and the strategy has spread to other countries as well, including Iceland and South Korea.[323] Sweden, which pioneered the approach, mandates fines or prison up to six months for customers, and also provides social assistance such as shelters, education, and job training to sellers seeking to leave sex work.[324] The approach is credited with reducing the frequency of street prostitution and trafficking and enjoys the support of about four-fifths of the public.[325] Although arrests are infrequent, sex workers oppose this approach on the grounds that it makes their lives less safe by forcing them underground to protect patrons. As The ACLU Research Brief, excerpted above, explains, when sex work is underground,

---

319. Eleanor Maticka-Tyndale et al., Making a Place for Escort Work: A Case Study, 42 J. Sex. Rsch. 1, 2, 7-8 (2005).

320. Ashleigh M. Kline, The Fallacy of Free Will in Prostitution: Encouraging Prostitution Reform to Prevent the Repeated Victimization of Vulnerable Persons, 25 Mich. State Int'l L. Rev. 665, 683 (2017); Nisha Lilia Diu, Welcome to Paradise: Inside the World of Legalised Prostitution, Telegraph (2013).

321. Kline, supra note 320, at 683-86.

322. Jacobson, supra note 317, at 1039; Janet Halley et al., From the International to the Local in Feminist Legal Responses to Rape, Prostitution/Sex Work, and Sex Trafficking: Four Studies in Contemporary Governance Feminism, 29 Harv. J.L. & Gender 335, 398 (2006); MacKinnon, Trafficking, supra note 310, at 304-06.

323. Resolution on Sexual Exploitation and Prostitution and Its Impact on Gender Equality, Eur. Parl. Doc. 2013/2103(INI) 0162 (2014).

324. Roger Mathews, Prostitution, Politics, and Policy, 113 (2008); Sweden Unveils Tougher Penalties for Buying Sex, The Local: Sweden's News in English (Jan. 27, 2011); Ahulamit Almog & Ariel Bendor, Views on Prostitution, 30 Hastings Women's L.J. 3, 16 (2019).

325. Melissa Farley, Prostitution, Trafficking and Cultural Amnesia: What We Must Not Know in Order to Keep the Business of Sexual Exploitation Running Smoothly, 18 Yale J. L. & Feminism 109, 138 (2006); Kline, supra note 320, at 688; Gunilla S. Ekberg, The Swedish Law That Prohibits the Purchase of Sexual Services, 10 Violence Against Women 1187, 1189-93 (2004); Sheila Jeffreys, The Industrial Vagina: The Global Sex Trade 203 (2009). Street prostitution has reportedly declined by 50 percent since the law's passage. Sweden's Law a Success: Report, The Local: Sweden's News in English (July 3, 2010).

workers are more vulnerable to violence and are less able to insist on condoms and to seek health and safety services.[326]

The model that seems to have attracted the most support from sex workers and human rights organizations is that of decriminalization. The ACLU Research Brief, excerpted above, relies on dozens of studies and metadata showing that sex workers are, on average, safer, better paid, and healthier, both physically and in terms of their mental health, than sex workers under other legal regimes. New Zealand follows this model, coupled with support services for sex workers. There, a comprehensive, independent review found that five years after passage of the decriminalization law, the number of sex workers had not increased, that these workers felt more able to report incidents of violence and abuse, and that their working conditions and access to health services had improved.[327] Whether that model is easily replicable, particularly in countries more accessible to traffickers and sex tourism, is open to debate. Spain, which has also decriminalized sex work, has seen a spike in sex tourism and many workers feel unable to claim basic labor rights.[328] Many sex workers there argue that what they need is unionization, and an Association of Sex Professionalism is fighting for that right.[329] In a few countries, including the Netherlands, workers are establishing their own cooperatives, which give them control over working conditions, and they are planning to provide education and pensions.[330]

The U.S. public traditionally opposed decriminalization, but a 2020 survey found that 51 percent of respondents believe that sex work should be decriminalized, as compared to 38 percent who oppose decriminalization and 13 percent who are unsure. Two-thirds of respondents between 18 and 44 favor decriminalization.[331] Earlier ballot initiatives to decriminalize sex work were unsuccessful. A 2008 initiative to legalize prostitution in San Francisco was defeated by a 58 to 42 percent margin, and a 2004 Berkeley, California, proposal to make prostitution the city's lowest law enforcement priority (along with marijuana possession) lost by a two-to-one margin. Voters and city leaders have often opposed such measures because they would insulate pimps, not just prostitutes, from prosecution and increase risks of public nuisance.[332] Have things changed since these defeats? Could a partial

---

326. See Rachel Marshall, Sex Workers and Human Rights: A Critical Analysis of Laws Regarding Sex Work, 23 Wm & Mary J. Women & L. 47, 62-63 (2016); Aziza Ahmed, Feminism, Power, and Sex Work in the Context of HIV/AIDS: Consequences for Women's Health, 34 Harv. J.L. & Gender 225, 255 (2011); Bazelon, Oppression or Profession, supra note 312, at 40.

327. Open Society Foundation, Laws and Policies Affecting Sex Work 5 (2012).

328. Meaghan Beatly, The Other Women, Nation, Jan. 7, 2019, at 19.

329. Id. at 19-21.

330. Gisela Williams, A Dutch Effort to Form a Prostitute Cooperative Is Met with Hope and Skepticism, N.Y. Times, Aug. 14, 2017, at A8.

331. Zack Budryk, Poll: Majority Favors Decriminalizing Sex Work, The Hill, Jan. 30, 2020.

332. See Johnny California, Measure K in California Defeated—Prostitution Laws Still Enforced (Nov. 6, 2008); see Melissa Hope Ditmore, Prostitution and Sex Work 115 (2010).

decriminalization approach along the lines of the Nordic model be made politically palatable in the United States?[333]

Some municipalities have attempted to crack down on customers by launching sting operations targeted at buyers rather than sellers; publishing the names and photos of those convicted; impounding vehicles or taking away the driving licenses of those convicted of solicitation from their cars; posting Internet videos of men soliciting prostitutes; and requiring attendance at "John schools," which educate participants on the harms and risks of prostitution. Such schools have been effective in significantly reducing recidivism.[334] In surveys in England, Scotland, and the United States, men agreed that being placed on a sex offender registry would be the most effective deterrent to their purchase of sex. Other effective deterrents would be prison time and public exposure.[335] Which of these approaches seem most desirable? What about the objection made in the ACLU Research Brief that even targeting the customers rather than the sex workers themselves pushes the business of sex work underground, where it is less safe for women?

More politically acceptable are diversion programs pioneered by problem-solving courts, such as Hartford, Connecticut's Community Court and New York City's Midtown Community Court. These programs allow sellers who plead guilty to prostitution to avoid incarceration if they participate in individualized treatment plans. Such plans include social services designed to address underlying problems, such as substance abuse or lack of education and employment skills. As an added incentive for participation, commentators urge that successful completion of the program should expunge prostitution-related crimes.[336] These initiatives have substantially reduced recidivism rates, as have some similar efforts targeted at rehabilitating juvenile offenders.[337] Why do you think more communities have not adopted such approaches? Do you accept the premise that sex workers need treatment?

4. **Human Trafficking.** A significant part of the current global trafficking industry involves deception, kidnapping, or outright purchase of women and girls for work in the sex trade. Some women or their families are duped by advertisements or agents promising jobs such as waitresses, au pairs, sales clerks, actresses, and exotic dancers. Other women voluntarily accompany a new husband or a

---

333. In 2019, Massachusetts representative Ayanna Pressley introduced a resolution in Congress, as part of a wider effort to reduce incarceration and promote race and gender inequalities, to decriminalize sex work between consenting adults. See H. Res. 702, 116th Cong., 1st Sess. (introduced Nov. 14, 2019).

334. Shively et al., supra note 269, at iv-vi, 24-83; Ann Mathieson et al., Prostitution Policy: Legalization, Decriminalization, and the Nordic Model, 14 Seattle J. Soc. Just. 367, 415 (2015); Edrina Nazaradeh, There Is No Such Thing as a Child Prostitute: Why Decriminalization Is Only the First Step in California, 45 Pepp. L. Rev. 189, 234 (2018).

335. Allow States and Victims to Fight Online Sex Trafficking (SESTA-FOSTA) Act of 2017, Pub. L. No. 115-164, 132 Stat. 1253 (2018) (codified as amended at 18 U.S.C. §§ 1591, 1595, 2421A and 47 U.S.C. § 230); Melissa Farley et al., Men Who Buy Sex: Who They Buy and What They Know 26 (2009).

336. Jacobson, supra note 317, at 1051.

337. Christina Hoag, New Laws Treat Teen Prostitutes as Abuse Victims, AP & ABC News (Apr. 18, 2009); Bernice Yeung, Throw Away Girls, Cal. Law., Nov. 2003, at 59.

boyfriend to another region or country where they are sold into bondage.[338] Some, such as massage parlor workers, are recruited by traffickers who arrange jobs, housing, and student and travel visas. These traffickers expect recipients to remain in sex work until they pay off their five-figure debts for that assistance.[339] Women and children are also drugged or kidnapped and smuggled across state lines. Many are then sold into child marriages or to brothels and kept against their will by a variety of methods. Typically, they are taken to a city or foreign country where they lack marketable skills and familiarity with the language and legal culture. Their passports and other forms of identification are confiscated, and they are threatened with assault, murder, or prosecution by local authorities if they try to escape. Some are told that if they do manage to leave, their family members will suffer retaliation. Female refugees displaced by war or disasters may also be forced to resort to "survival sex."[340] Other traffickers employ what psychologists term a "trauma bond," which alternates affection with violence and neglect.[341] Technology has facilitated the recruitment and sale of sex workers, and the majority of underage victims have been advertised or sold online.[342]

Once women have been forced into the sex trade, the social stigma that they encounter further restricts their employment and marriage options; many will be ostracized if they return to their original communities.[343] Children who are abused or orphaned as a result of HIV and armed conflict may also end up in brothels.[344]

Some women are promised freedom after they have earned enough to repay their travel, purchase price, room and board, and interest on these debts. Often, however, such promises are not kept, or the costs remain prohibitive. Women who refuse to work may be raped, physically assaulted, denied food, or forcibly restrained from leaving houses of prostitution.[345] Some workers have ten- to eighteen-hour shifts in squalid conditions with no choice of customers and little birth control or health care. The rising rate of sexually transmitted disease, coupled with longstanding beliefs about the value of intercourse with virgins, has heightened demand for ever-younger partners of both sexes, and purchase of preteens and adolescents has become increasingly common. A representative account appears in a State Department Trafficking Report:

> Neary grew up in rural Cambodia. Her parents died when she was a child, and, in an effort to give her a better life, her sister married her off when she was 17. Three months later, she and her husband went to visit a fishing

338. The Human Trafficking Legal Ctr., Human Trafficking and Domestic Violence Fact Sheet 2-3 (2018).

339. Nicholas Kulish et al., Behind Illicit Massage Parlors, a Vast Crime Web, N.Y. Times, Mar. 3, 2019, at A1.

340. Gaiutra Bahadur, Survival Sex, Ms. Mag., Summer 2008, at 28-29.

341. Aryn Baker, supra note 271, at 41.

342. Wagner & McCann, supra note 271, at 24. For the role of technology, see 2020 U.N. Report on Trafficking in Persons, supra note 272, at 38-39.

343. See U.S. Dep't of State, Trafficking in Persons Report 20 (June 2019).

344. Julia O'Connell Davidson, Children in the Global Sex Trade (2005).

345. Id. at 8-9 (reporting rates of rape between 60 and 75 percent, and rates of physical assault between 70 and 95 percent).

village. Her husband rented a room in what Neary thought was a guest house. But when she woke the next morning, her husband was gone. The owner of the house told her she had been sold by her husband for $300 and that she was actually in a brothel.

For five years, Neary was raped by five to seven men every day. In addition to brutal physical abuse, Neary was infected with HIV and contracted AIDS. The brothel threw her out when she became sick, and she eventually found her way to a local shelter. She died of HIV/AIDS at the age of 23.[346]

A recent account of domestic trafficking profiles Jae, a 17-year-old New York woman who was lured to North Dakota by an online boyfriend. He told her that she could double the salary she earned as a McDonald's cashier, and when she followed him, he began beating her and forcing her to have sex with his drug dealer. After breaking up with the boyfriend, she fell in with a pimp and ended up posting ads on Backpage to meet his quota of tricks.[347]

Trafficking also supports the rapidly increasing sex tourism industry. Estimates suggest Americans and Canadians account for about a quarter of a rapidly expanding market.[348] A growing number of companies offer "sex tours" to countries such as Thailand and the Philippines, where purchasers have ready access to bars and brothels. In Cambodia, where nearly half the countries' 30,000 to 40,000 sex workers are under 15, scantily dressed girls purchased from impoverished families parade with numbers around their neck in front of potential buyers.[349] Children who fail to please are often beaten and starved and suffer devastating consequences, including trauma, disease, drug addiction, unwanted pregnancy, and social ostracism.[350]

Such activities reflect racist as well as sexist dynamics. Male tourists can convince themselves that women and children from other races and nationalities are hyper-sexed exotic "others" who willingly cater to sexual fantasies and benefit economically from doing so. Children are particularly attractive because they are easily exploited and relatively cheap. In rationalizing his sexual transactions with 14- and 15-year-old girls in Mexico and Colombia, one retired schoolteacher noted: "If they don't have sex with me, they may not have enough food. If someone has a problem with me doing this, let UNICEF feed them. I've never paid more than $20 to these young women, and that allows them to eat for a week."[351] Similar rationalizations, along with the other revenue and corruption generated by sex tourism and lack of enforcement resources, encourage officials in many impoverished countries to

346. Id. at 6.

347. Aryn Baker, supra note 271, at 38-41.

348. Linda Miller, Child Sex Tourism and Its Relationship to Global Human Trafficking, 12 U. St. Thomas J. L & Pub. Pol'y 1 (2017).

349. Kelly Master, Exposing the Child Sex Trafficking Epidemic in Cambodia, Relevant (June 5, 2017).

350. Raven Washington, Treating the International Child Sex Tourism Industry as a Crime Against Humanity, 24 Sw. J. Int'l L. 361, 379 (2018).

351. Fed. Bureau of Investigation, 76 FBI Law Enforcement Bulletin 1, 16-21 (2007).

tolerate child prostitution.[352] The problem is compounded by the reluctance of victims to cooperate with prosecutions out of fear of prosecution or retaliation.[353]

The U.S. State Department, as well as many experts in the field, has advocated a four-pronged approach to human trafficking: prevention, punishment, protection, and partnership. Prevention approaches focus on challenging the cultural devaluation of women, expanding their education and employment opportunities, providing services for victims, reducing poverty in the countries that supply the global trade, and distributing better information to vulnerable groups about the strategies of traffickers and the legal remedies available.[354] Partnerships among governments and non-governmental organizations are crucial in that effort.

Anti-trafficking legislation has dramatically increased, and in 2015, Congress passed the Justice for Victims of Trafficking Act. It expanded support for trafficking prosecution and services and restitution for victims, as well as enhanced penalties for offenders.[355] Some experts have criticized these approaches as well intentioned in principle but ineffective in practice. Inadequate resources have been available for prevention and protective strategies, and customers have been subject to minimal sanctions.[356] In 2018, federal prosecutors initiated only 171 cases involving human trafficking, and a housing program for victims has been canceled.[357] The inadequacy of resources, training, and penalties is partly responsible for making the global sex trade an expanding vehicle for international crime. In many foreign countries, enforcement of anti-trafficking laws remains grossly inadequate due to lack of funding, corruption of police and immigration officials, and governmental ambivalence about curtailing profitable sex tourism activities.[358]

The Trafficking Victims Protection Act (TVPA) of 2000, reauthorized several times since, attempts to respond to these problems by increasing the maximum penalties for trafficking to twenty years, providing a civil damages remedy for victims, increasing assistance to international law enforcement efforts, and giving the president discretionary power to impose sanctions on nations that fail to meet minimum standards for enforcement of anti-trafficking prohibitions. In addition, the TVPA establishes an annual Trafficking in Persons (TIP) Report, published by the State Department, that separates countries into Tier 1 countries, which meet the minimum standards set by the U.S. government for eliminating trafficking; Tier 2 countries, which do not comply with the minimum standards but are making

352. Kathy Steinman, Sex Tourism and the Child: Latin America's and the United States' Failure to Prosecute Sex Tourists, 13 Hastings Women's L.J. 53, 65 (2002). Washington, supra note 350, at 366-69.

353. Washington, supra note 350, at 369.

354. U.S. Dep't of State, Trafficking in Persons Report, supra note 343, at 3

355. Pub. L. 114-22, 129 Stat. 227. In a one-year period between October 2014 and October 2015, 236 trafficking bills were enacted. Rebecca Beitsch, More States Separate Prostitution, Sex Trafficking, PEW Charitable Trusts Research and Analysis (Oct. 21, 2015).

356. Heather C. Gregorio, More than "Johns," Less Than Traffickers: In Search of Just and Proportional Sanctions for Buyers of Sex with Trafficking Victims, 90 N.Y.U. L. Rev. 626 (2015); Wagner & McCann, supra note 271, at 57.

357. Nicholas Kristof, More Jeffrey Epsteins Are Out There, N.Y. Times, Sept. 15, 2019.

358. For the low number of trafficking convictions, see 2020 U.N. Report on Trafficking in Persons, supra note 272, at 13, 52.

"significant efforts to bring themselves into compliance"; and Tier 3 countries, which do not comply with the minimum standards and are not making "significant efforts to bring themselves into compliance." The United States will not provide "nonhumanitarian, nontrade-related foreign assistance" to Tier 3 countries and will also direct the International Monetary Fund to vote against "any loan or other utilization of the funds of the respective institution to that country." The 2022 reauthorization bill expands and strengthens some of the original provisions.[359]

To combat child sexual tourism, Congress in 2003 passed the Prosecutorial Remedies and Other Tools to End the Exploitation of Children Today (PROTECT) Act and the Trafficking Victims Reauthorization Act, which increase penalties to a maximum of thirty years of imprisonment for engaging in child sexual trafficking. It also provides a private right of action for trafficking victims to sue for actual and punitive damages.[360] However, enforcement has been minimal,[361] which has led some commentators to advocate more reliance on other strategies, such as civil suits against sex tourists, consumer protests, and adoption of voluntary codes of conduct by hotels and travel agencies.[362]

The 2000 Trafficking Act also addresses the third area in which increased efforts are necessary: protection of victims. Traditionally, the targets of trafficking have been subject to immediate deportation, which deters reporting and cooperation with enforcement efforts. Under the Act, some 5000 T visas as well as social services are available each year for women who are assisting investigators and who would "suffer extreme hardship" if deported. However, that remedy remains underutilized because many victims are unable to provide usable information to law enforcement or fear that they or their families will be subject to retaliation if they cooperate.[363]

Sanctions for well-financed traffickers have also been inadequate, as the recent notorious case of financier Jeffrey Epstein demonstrates. In 2008, in response to efforts by a high-powered defense team and Epstein's personal connections, he was allowed to plead to state charges of solicitation of a prostitution from a minor, instead of well-documented federal trafficking charges. He served thirteen months in jail but was allowed to leave it for twelve hours a day, six days a week, to work in his Florida offices.[364] Charges were brought again in 2019, based on evidence of

---

359. See Press Release, Menendez, Risch, Kaine, Rubio Introduce International Trafficking Victims Protection Reauthorization Act (TVPRA) of 2022 (May 10, 2022).

360. 8 U.S.C. § 2255(a) (2018).

361. As of 2018, federal prosecutors had brought only sixty-eight criminal cases under the PROTECT ACT for sexual abuse of children overseas. Victims had filed only eleven cases. The Human Trafficking Legal Ctr. U.S. Legal Remedies for Minor Victims of Sex Tourism and Sex Trafficking 3, 5 (2018).

362. David Lee Mundy, Using Transnational Tort to Combat Sex Trafficking and Sex Tourism, 9 Regent J. Int'l L. 247 (2013); Vincent Bevins, Brazil Targets Sex Tourism Before the World Cup, L.A. Times, Apr. 26, 2014.

363. Lise Olsen, Sex Trafficking Victims Live in Visa Limbo, Hous. Chron., Nov. 24, 2008; Jayrashri Srikantiah, Perfect Victims and Real Survivors: The Iconic Victim in Domestic Human Trafficking Law, 87 B.U. L. Rev. 157, 178-80 (2007).

364. Mike Baker, Denied Full Justice, Epstein's Accusers Urge Investigators to Keep Digging, N.Y. Times, Aug. 10, 2019, at A20.

a widespread conspiracy spanning several countries that involved sexual abuse of many trafficked women and underage girls. Epstein committed suicide in prison before a complete investigation revealed the full scope of his activities and the identities of all accomplices.[365] However, his female accomplice, Ghislaine Maxwell, was sentenced in 2022 to twenty years in prison for her part in soliciting minors in the conspiracy.[366]

At the international level, the United Nations Protocol to Prevent, Suppress, and Punish Trafficking in Persons, Especially Women and Children (supplementing the United Nations Convention Against Transnational Organized Crime) directs signatory nations to consider implementing measures to assist victims, such as medical, psychological, and counseling services, and employment, education, and training opportunities. To that end, the United States has pledged financial assistance to groups that work against trafficking and provide assistance to its victims. However, there has been controversy over policies targeting funds only to domestic and international groups that oppose prostitution.

One dispute involved the "anti-prostitution pledge," a requirement that organizations receiving funding for HIV/AIDS prevention must have a policy opposing prostitution.[367] Advocates of the pledge, including a coalition of feminists and religious organizations, stressed the harms to women from prostitution and trafficking. Critics charged that it would prevent grants to HIV initiatives involving sex workers, whose support is critical to reducing incidence of the disease.[368] In 2013, the Supreme Court held that the requirement violated the First Amendment as applied to U.S. organizations by requiring them to "pledge allegiance to the Government's policy of eradicating prostitution."[369]

5. **Technology, Sex Work, and Sex Trafficking.** Any efforts to reform the law relating to sex work would have to take into account the role of technology in allowing more individuals to purchase phone sex, Internet sex, and escort services from the privacy of their homes or hotel rooms.[370] Use of online technologies allow customers to more easily evade arrest by avoiding street encounters and accessing tips about sting operations.[371] It also creates new opportunities for online harassment, threats, and privacy breaches.[372] Yet research suggests that Internet-based sex work is significantly less risky for sex workers than work obtained out in the streets, and enables more of them to avoid reliance on pimps.[373] Those who work

---

365. Id.

366. Benjamin Weiser et al., Maxwell Sentenced to 20 Years in Prison for Aiding Epstein's Abuse, N.Y. Times, June 28, 2022.

367. The pledge was added as an amendment to the United States Leadership Against HIV/AIDs, Tuberculosis, and Malaria Act of 2003, 22 U.S.C. § 7601, 1117 Stat. 711, at 733-34 (2018).

368. Ahmed, supra note 326, at 242-45.

369. Agency for Int'l Dev v. All. for Open Soc'y Int'l, 570 U.S. 205 (2013). The funding ban still applies to foreign organizations. See Bazelon, supra note 312, at 40.

370. Benitez et al., supra note 277, at 332.

371. Id. at 18-19.

372. Id. at 6 (citing studies).

373. Id. at 5 (citing a systematic review of twenty-eight studies from multiple countries showing that sex workers in outdoor environments experienced higher levels of violence

in high-end escort services, especially, incur fewer risks of either arrest or physical abuse, and often make substantial sums. Details of such services emerged in 2007, with the arrest of the "D.C. Madam," and in 2008, with the forced resignation of New York Governor Eliot Spitzer, who patronized the Emperor's Club, an escort service charging between $1,000 and $5,000 an hour.[374]

The same technologies that have facilitated sex work as an occupation, however, have also facilitated coercive sex markets. In recognition of the role of technology in sex trafficking, in 2018, Congress passed SESTA-FOSTA, a combination of two bills, the Stop Enabling Sex Traffickers Act and the Fight Online Sex Trafficking Act. This law prohibits digital platforms from intentionally or knowingly facilitating prostitution and sex trafficking. Within a year, six sites known to be regularly used for sex work shut down in the United States.[375]

The impact of this legislation on sex work in the United States has forced a debate over the relationship between voluntary sex work and sex trafficking from a regulatory standpoint. Laws enacted to regulate one necessarily affect the other, often with unintended consequences. Thus, for example, individuals choosing to engage in sex work complain that the recent laws restricting online adult ads, while arguably beneficial in reducing sex trafficking, make it harder for sex workers to attract and vet customers before meetings, and forces them onto the streets and into more dangerous encounters.[376] This concern is backed up by recent data from 185 cities, which found that the use of the Erotic Services section (ERS) of Craigslist is correlated with lower rates of female homicides, higher screening, and more efficient transactions, and that limiting access to these forums displaced workers to less safe, less public areas, reduced the negotiating power of sex workers, and increased their clients' insistence on unprotected sex.[377] In response to the concern, legislation was introduced in March 2022 to study these effects.[378]

One report cites a lack of consensus in the literature about the relationship between legalization or decriminalization of sex work and human trafficking.[379] Some research links harsher prostitution laws to a reduction in sex trafficking, but the hybrid end-demand model of decriminalization is also associated with a decrease in trafficking rates, and other research from the European Union suggests that decriminalization does not necessarily increase trafficking.[380]

---

than those working in indoor environments) (citing study); see also Scott R. Peppet, Prostitution 3.0?, 98 Iowa L. Rev. 1989 (2013).

374. Eric Lipton, Woman in Escort Case Plans to Name Names in Defense, N.Y. Times, Apr. 29, 2007, at A20; Stefano Eposito et al., "I Offer an Authentic Experience": Prostitute Says Going Rate Here Is Only $700 to $800 an Hour, Sex Workers Outreach Project Chicago (Mar. 16, 2008).

375. Heidi Vogt & John McKinnon, New Law Targets Sex Trafficking. I Could Also Hit Online Dating, Wall St. J., May 30, 2018.

376. Timothy Williams, Backpage's Sex Ads Are Gone. Child Trafficking? Hardly, N.Y. Times, Mar. 11, 2017, at A16.

377. Id. at 14 (citing studies).

378. The bill is called the SESTA/FOSTA Examination of Secondary Effects for Sex Workers Study Act, available at https://www.govinfo.gov/app/details/BILLS-117hr6928ih.

379. ACLU Research Brief, supra note 278, at 13.

380. Id. at 13-14 (citing studies).

6. **Juvenile Sex Work.**   Another issue involves whether to treat juvenile prostitutes as victims or offenders. The U.S. legal system is not consistent in how it treats them. Minors are considered incapable of consenting to sex under statutory rape law but are typically prosecuted for commercial sex under prostitution law. State criminal prohibitions on juvenile prostitution are also inconsistent with federal anti-trafficking laws treating minors as victims and giving them a safe harbor from incarceration.[381] To deal with these inconsistencies, the majority of states have passed safe harbor legislation that removes or reduces criminal penalties for minors involved in prostitution-related offenses and provides them with specialized services.[382] Other jurisdictions have rebuttable presumptions that prevent prosecution unless the state can prove that minors entered prostitution "completely on their own."[383] A minority of states also allow for expungement of victims' offenses that are related to trafficking.[384]

However, only ten states fully immunize child sex workers from criminal prosecution.[385] Opponents of full immunity argue that it removes incentives for minors to testify against pimps and traffickers and ensures that the minors will be placed in facilities and support programs that will keep them off the streets and provide necessary treatment. Critics worry that without the threat of prosecution of minors, they will be even more attractive targets for pimps and traffickers.[386] By contrast, supporters of full immunity argue that criminalizing minors is unjust and counterproductive, and it deflects attention from targeting the real criminals—pimps, johns, and traffickers. Criminalization creates an adversarial relationship between law enforcement and victims and increases their trauma and sense of vulnerability.[387] Many juvenile placements lack appropriate services and their punitive response to behavioral issues often exacerbates problems and ensures high recidivism.[388] An alternative strategy, pioneered in Alberta, Canada, provides that minors involved in sex work will not be criminally charged but can be designated children in need of protection if they are unwilling to access support programs that will adequately protect them from future exploitation. These children can then be placed

---

381. Britta S. Loftus, Coordinating U.S. Law on Immigration and Human Trafficking: Lifting the Lamp to Victims, 43 Colum. Hum. Rts. L. Rev. 143, 186, 210 (2011).

382. Nazaradeh, supra note 334, at 203, n. 95.

383. Wagner & McCann, supra note 271, at 95.

384. Id.

385. Nazaradeh, supra note 334, at 205. See also Nicholas R. Larche, Victimized by the State: How Legislative Inaction Has Led to the Revictimization and Stigmatization of Victims of Sex Trafficking, 38 Seton Hall Legis. J. 281, 295 (2014).

386. Nazaradeh, supra note 334, at 208-09; Tessa Dysart, Child, Victim, or Prostitute? Justice Through Immunity for Prostituted Children, 21 Duke J. Gender L. & Pol'y 255, 256, 281 (2014).

387. Nazaradeh, supra note 334, at 210-11.

388. Id. at 212; Jeremy L. Thompson & Chanelle Artiles, Dismantling the Sexual Abuse to Prison Pipeline: Texas's Approach, 41 T. Marshall L. Rev. 239, 265 (2016); Child Welfare Information Gateway, Child Welfare and Human Trafficking 11 (2015).

in safe houses for a relatively short period where they receive specialized services and a plan for future placement and support.[389] What is your view? If appropriate facilities and services are not in place or too many minors refuse to participate, how should law enforcement respond?

PUTTING THEORY INTO PRACTICE

5-16. In 2015, The Erotic Service Providers Legal, Education and Research Project filed suit in federal district court challenging California's anti-prostitution law on the ground that it deprives individuals of the fundamental right to engage in consensual private sexual activity.[390] Plaintiffs were three sex workers and a disabled man who wished to purchase sexual services. What arguments would you make in support of the plaintiffs? What arguments would you make in opposition? In your ideal world, would there be no exchange of sex for money, or would such exchanges carry no legal penalties or social stigma?

5-17. Before its closure in 2014, the Shady Lady Ranch brothel, two-and-a-half hours northwest of Las Vegas, challenged Nevada laws restricting prostitution to women and offered male sex workers to female customers. In what respect, if any, does the brothel's decision to cater to female customers' demand for male sex workers reflect progress for women?

5-18. In a highly publicized marketing event, a 22-year-old University of California-San Diego graduate auctioned her virginity on the website of the Moonlight Bunny Ranch, a brothel in Carson City, Nevada.[391] She reportedly received over 10,000 bids, the highest of which was $3.8 million.[392] Critics argued that she degraded herself and women generally, while others saw it as an instance of female autonomy and choice. What is your view?

5-19. OnlyFans is a website where content creators post intimate selfies, softcore porn, or hard-core porn for paid subscribers, who can also request (and pay for) personalized content or specific images or videos.[393] The site, founded in London in 2016, now has 1.5 million creators and 150 million users. The site collects 20 percent as a fee, and the creators keep the rest. Some argue that this model gives some creators the ability to make more money than if they performed for an online pornography company and also more control over the type of content they

389. The Protection of Children Involved in Prostitution Act, discussed in Alberta Children's Services, Protection of Children Involved in Prostitution: Protective Safe House Review (2004). The program has had modest success in enhancing victim well-being.

390. Erotic Service Providers Legal Education & Research Project v. Gascon, No. 15-1007 (N.D. Cal. 2015).

391. Natalie Dylan, Why I'm Selling My Virginity, Daily Beast (Jan. 23, 2009).

392. The winning bidder, who paid a $250,000 deposit, later withdrew from the deal, allegedly because his wife objected. Cynthia Fagan, "Deflower Deal" Guy Pulls Out, N.Y. Post, May 30, 2009.

393. See https://onlyfans.com/how.

choose to do.[394] Does this mitigate some of the feminist concerns raised by traditional sex work or pornography? Which ones? Or is it just a technologically more advanced version of the world's oldest profession?

5-20. The World Association of Introduction Agencies recognizes some 2,700 matchmaking agencies worldwide and about 400 to 500 operating in the United States; an estimated 14,000 women enter the country annually after meeting men on mail-order bride websites.[395] Many mail-order bride agencies provide a fantasy for American men who have been, as many agencies put it, "unlucky in love." The women are typically portrayed as exotic, dutiful, accommodating, and "untainted by feminism."[396] A website listing for Brides 4U describes Asian brides as "attractive physically, very feminine, petite and slender, . . . gentle and polite, . . . charming and attentive to their partner, . . . and respecting [of] traditions." Latin brides are described as having "exotic beauty, refreshingly sunny disposition[s] . . . and traditional upbringings where old fashioned values and family virtues remain a vital way of life." Cherry Blossoms portrays Filipinos who are "subservient and docile."[397] The website of Chance for Love maintains: "The Russian woman has not been exposed to the world of rampant feminism that asserts its rights in America. She is the weaker gender and knows it."[398] Another website, GoodWife.com, features images of scantily clad homemakers in sexually provocative poses while cooking and cleaning. The site explains:

> We, as men, are more and more wanting to step back from the types of women we meet now. With many women taking on the "me first" feminist agenda and the man having to take a back seat to her desire for power and control, many men are turned off by this and look back to having a more traditional woman as our partner.[399]

What problems would you foresee from such arrangements, and what legal regulations would help to address them?

---

394. Tiarra Rogers, Liberation and Ownership under OnlyFans (unpublished paper, 2021).

395. Christina L. Pollard, Here Come Many More Mail-Order Brides: Why IMBRA Fails Women Escaping the Russian Federation, 46 Cap. U. L. Rev. 609, 631 (2018); Victoria I. Kusel, Gender Disparity, Domestic Abuse, and the Mail-Order Bride Industry, 7 Albany Gov't L. Rev. 166, 167 (2014).

396. Pollard, supra note 395, at 632, 657 (quoting websites and congressional testimony).

397. Beverly Encarguez Perez, Woman Warrior Meets Mail-Order Bride: Finding an Asian American Voice in the Women's Movement, 18 Berkeley Women's L.J. 211, 221 (2003).

398. David Crary, Protecting Mail-Order Brides, Ariz. Rep., July 6, 2003, at A2.

399. Jane Kim, Trafficked: Domestic Violence, Exploitation in Marriage, and the Foreign-Bride Industry, 51 Va. J. Int'l L. 443, 470-71 (2011) (quoting GoodWife.com).

B. PREGNANCY AND AUTONOMY

1. Control of Conception and Other Aspects of Women's Health

Woman's role in reproduction has always been a factor in limiting her life choices and opportunities. Thus, contraception, pregnancy, abortion, and other reproductive issues have been central to controversial debates about women's autonomy.

Women's reproductive choices were not broadly regulated in the United States until the nineteenth century. The momentum for legal control of women's options came largely from moral reformers and physicians who, in response to the increased demand by women for contraception and abortion, wanted to assert technical, ethical, and social superiority over their competitors, particularly midwives. In 1873, Congress passed the Comstock Law, which prohibited dissemination of information about abortion and contraception. While the early efforts to overturn this regulation asserted women's right to control their own bodies, feminist pioneers such as Margaret Sanger also used eugenic arguments in favor of birth control. Reflecting this mix of motivations, throughout the early twentieth-century fertility control emerged as a right for the privileged and a duty for the poor.

Social, legal, and technological developments in the second half of the twentieth century created new challenges and questions. The birth control pill was first approved for use in 1960, and the number of women relying on it for contraception greatly increased with the passage in 1970 of Title X, a law that led to the creation of federally supported family planning clinics. That greatly increased access to contraception for poor women.[400] At the same time, more liberal sexual mores, opportunities for women in paid employment, economic pressure within families to control fertility, and the availability of oral contraception helped liberalize public attitudes and practices. Despite these social and cultural changes, many state laws banning contraception remained on the books.[401] And today, there is a re-emergence of opposition to birth control, at least some types and in some contexts. In light of these new threats, consider as you read these materials what the best theoretical foundation is for securing the right to access to contraception, as well as whether the state has any obligations toward individuals who lack the resources to meaningfully exercise it.

---

400. Public Health Service Act of 1970 Tit. X, Pub. L. 91-572 (1970).

401. Deborah L. Rhode, Justice and Gender 202-07 (1989). For a comprehensive history of the regulation of contraception, see Linda Gordon, Woman's Body, Woman's Right: Birth Control in America (rev. ed. 1990); see also Priscilla J. Smith, Contraceptive Comstockery: Reasoning from Immorality to Illness in the Twenty-First Century, 47 Conn. L. Rev. 971 (2015).

Griswold v. Connecticut

381 U.S. 479 (1965)

Mr. Justice Douglas delivered the opinion of the Court.

[Appellants, Planned Parenthood personnel who prescribed contraceptives for "married persons," were charged as accessories to the violation of the Connecticut statute prohibiting the use of contraceptives. The Court first held that they had standing to assert their patients' privacy rights.]

[W]e are met with a wide range of questions that implicate the Due Process Clause of the Fourteenth Amendment. . . . We do not sit as a super-legislature to determine the wisdom, need, and propriety of laws that touch economic problems, business affairs, or social conditions. This law, however, operates directly on an intimate relation of husband and wife and their physician's role in one aspect of that relation.

The association of people is not mentioned in the Constitution nor in the Bill of Rights. The right to educate a child in a school of the parents' choice — whether public or private or parochial — is also not mentioned. Nor is the right to study any particular subject or any foreign language. Yet the First Amendment has been construed to include certain of those rights. . . . In other words, the First Amendment has a penumbra where privacy is protected from governmental intrusion. . . .

The foregoing cases suggest that specific guarantees in the Bill of Rights have penumbras, formed by emanations from those guarantees that help give them life and substance. Various guarantees create zones of privacy. The right of association contained in the penumbra of the First Amendment is one, as we have seen. The Third Amendment in its prohibitions against the quartering of soldiers "in any house" in time of peace without the consent of the owner is another facet of that privacy. The Fourth Amendment explicitly affirms the "right of the people to be secure in their persons, houses, papers, and effects, against unreasonable searches and seizures." The Fifth Amendment in its Self-Incrimination Clause enables the citizen to create a zone of privacy which government may not force him to surrender to his detriment. The Ninth Amendment provides: "The enumeration in the constitution, of certain rights, shall not be construed to deny or disparage others retained by the people." . . . We have had many controversies over these penumbral rights of "privacy and repose." These cases bear witness that the right of privacy which presses for recognition here is a legitimate one.

The present case, then, concerns a relationship lying within the zone of privacy which, in forbidding the use of contraceptives rather than regulating their manufacture or sale, seeks to achieve its goals by . . . having a maximum destructive impact upon that relationship. Such a law cannot stand in light of the familiar principle, so often applied by the Court, that a "governmental purpose to control or prevent activities constitutionally subject to state regulation may not be achieved by means which sweep unnecessarily broadly and thereby invade the area of protected freedoms." NAACP v. Alabama [ex rel. Flowers, 377 U.S. 288, 1964]. Would we allow the police to search the sacred precincts of marital bedrooms for telltale signs of the use of contraceptives? The very idea is repulsive to the notions of privacy surrounding the marriage relationship.

We deal with a right of privacy older than the Bill of Rights—older than our political parties, older than our school system. Marriage is a coming together for better or worse, hopefully enduring, and intimate to the degree of being sacred. It is an association that promotes a way of life, not causes; a harmony in living, not political faiths; a bilateral loyalty, not commercial or social projects. Yet it is an association for as noble a purpose as any involved in our prior decisions.

Reversed.

Mr. Justice GOLDBERG, whom THE CHIEF JUSTICE and Mr. Justice BRENNAN join, concurring. . . .

[I]t should be said of the Court's holding today that it in no way interferes with a State's proper regulation of sexual promiscuity or misconduct. As my Brother Harlan so well stated in his dissenting opinion in Poe v. Ullman [1961]:

> Adultery, homosexuality and the like are sexual intimacies which the State forbids . . . but the intimacy of husband and wife is necessarily an essential and accepted feature of the institution of marriage, an institution which the State not only must allow, but which always and in every age it has fostered and protected. It is one thing when the State exerts its power either to forbid extra-marital sexuality . . . or to say who may marry, but it is quite another when, having acknowledged a marriage and the intimacies inherent in it, it undertakes to regulate by means of the criminal law the details of that intimacy.

In sum, I believe that the right of privacy in the marital relation is fundamental and basic—a personal right "retained by the people" within the meaning of the Ninth Amendment.

Burwell v. Hobby Lobby Stores, Inc.

573 U.S. 682 (2014)

Justice ALITO delivered the opinion of the Court.

We must decide in these cases whether the Religious Freedom Restoration Act of 1993 (RFRA) permits the United States Department of Health and Human Services (HHS) to demand that three closely held corporations provide health-insurance coverage for methods of contraception that violate the sincerely held religious beliefs of the companies' owners. We hold that the regulations that impose this obligation violate RFRA, which prohibits the Federal Government from taking any action that substantially burdens the exercise of religion unless that action constitutes the least restrictive means of serving a compelling government interest. . . .

I

Congress enacted RFRA in 1993 in order to provide very broad protection for religious liberty. RFRA's enactment came three years after this Court's decision in *Employment Div., Dept. of Human Resources of Ore. v. Smith*, which largely repudiated the method of analyzing free-exercise claims that had been used in cases like

Sherbert v. Verner, and *Wisconsin v. Yoder.* In determining whether challenged government actions violated the Free Exercise Clause of the First Amendment, those decisions used a balancing test that took into account whether the challenged action imposed a substantial burden on the practice of religion, and if it did, whether it was needed to serve a compelling government interest. . . .

In *Smith,* however, the Court rejected "the balancing test set forth in *Sherbert.*" . . .

This Court . . . observ[ed] that use of the *Sherbert* test whenever a person objected on religious grounds to the enforcement of a generally applicable law "would open the prospect of constitutionally required religious exemptions from civic obligations of almost every conceivable kind." The Court therefore held that, under the First Amendment, "neutral, generally applicable laws may be applied to religious practices even when not supported by a compelling governmental interest." *City of Boerne v. Flores.*

Congress responded to *Smith* by enacting RFRA. "[L]aws [that are] 'neutral' toward religion," Congress found, "may burden religious exercise as surely as laws intended to interfere with religious exercise." In order to ensure broad protection for religious liberty, RFRA provides that "Government shall not substantially burden a person's exercise of religion even if the burden results from a rule of general applicability." If the Government substantially burdens a person's exercise of religion, under the Act that person is entitled to an exemption from the rule unless the Government "demonstrates that application of the burden to the person — (1) is in furtherance of a compelling governmental interest; and (2) is the least restrictive means of furthering that compelling governmental interest."

As enacted in 1993, RFRA applied to both the Federal Government and the States, but the constitutional authority invoked for regulating federal and state agencies differed. As applied to a federal agency, RFRA is based on the enumerated power that supports the particular agency's work, but in attempting to regulate the States and their subdivisions, Congress relied on its power under Section 5 of the Fourteenth Amendment to enforce the First Amendment. In *City of Boerne,* however, we held that Congress had overstepped its Section 5 authority because "[t]he stringent test RFRA demands" "far exceed[ed] any pattern or practice of unconstitutional conduct under the Free Exercise Clause as interpreted in *Smith.*"

Following our decision in *City of Boerne,* Congress passed the Religious Land Use and Institutionalized Persons Act of 2000 (RLUIPA). That statute, enacted under Congress's Commerce and Spending Clause powers, imposes the same general test as RFRA but on a more limited category of governmental actions. And, what is most relevant for present purposes, RLUIPA amended RFRA's definition of the "exercise of religion." Before RLUIPA, RFRA's definition made reference to the First Amendment. In RLUIPA, in an obvious effort to effect a complete separation from First Amendment case law, Congress deleted the reference to the First Amendment and defined the "exercise of religion" to include "any exercise of religion, whether or not compelled by, or central to, a system of religious belief." And Congress mandated that this concept "be construed in favor of a broad protection of religious exercise, to the maximum extent permitted by the terms of this chapter and the Constitution."

At issue in these cases are HHS regulations promulgated under the Patient Protection and Affordable Care Act of 2010 (ACA). ACA generally requires employers with 50 or more full-time employees to offer "a group health plan or group health insurance coverage" that provides "minimum essential coverage." Any covered employer that does not provide such coverage must pay a substantial price. Specifically, if a covered employer provides group health insurance but its plan fails to comply with ACA's group-health-plan requirements, the employer may be required to pay $100 per day for each affected "individual." And if the employer decides to stop providing health insurance altogether and at least one full-time employee enrolls in a health plan and qualifies for a subsidy on one of the government-run ACA exchanges, the employer must pay $2,000 per year for each of its full-time employees.

Unless an exception applies, ACA requires an employer's group health plan or group-health-insurance coverage to furnish "preventive care and screenings" for women without "any cost sharing requirements." Congress itself, however, did not specify what types of preventive care must be covered. Instead, Congress authorized the Health Resources and Services Administration (HRSA), a component of HHS, to make that important and sensitive decision. The HRSA in turn consulted the Institute of Medicine, a nonprofit group of volunteer advisers, in determining which preventive services to require.

In August 2011 . . . the HRSA promulgated the Women's Preventive Services Guidelines. The Guidelines provide that nonexempt employers are generally required to provide "coverage, without cost sharing" for "[a]ll Food and Drug Administration [(FDA)] approved contraceptive methods, sterilization procedures, and patient education and counseling." Although many of the required, FDA-approved methods of contraception work by preventing the fertilization of an egg, four of those methods (those specifically at issue in these cases) may have the effect of preventing an already fertilized egg from developing any further by inhibiting its attachment to the uterus.

HHS also authorized the HRSA to establish exemptions from the contraceptive mandate for "religious employers." That category encompasses "churches, their integrated auxiliaries, and conventions or associations of churches," as well as "the exclusively religious activities of any religious order." In its Guidelines, HRSA exempted these organizations from the requirement to cover contraceptive services. In addition, HHS has effectively exempted certain religious nonprofit organizations, described under HHS regulations as "eligible organizations," from the contraceptive mandate. An "eligible organization" means a nonprofit organization that "holds itself out as a religious organization" and "opposes providing coverage for some or all of any contraceptive services required to be covered . . . on account of religious objections." To qualify for this accommodation, an employer must certify that it is such an organization. . . .

In addition to these exemptions for religious organizations, ACA exempts a great many employers from most of its coverage requirements. Employers providing "grandfathered health plans"—those that existed prior to March 23, 2010, and that have not made specified changes after that date—need not comply with many of the Act's requirements, including the contraceptive mandate. And employers with fewer than 50 employees are not required to provide health insurance at all. . . .

II

Norman and Elizabeth Hahn and their three sons are devout members of the Mennonite Church, a Christian denomination. The Mennonite Church opposes abortion and believes that "[t]he fetus in its earliest stages . . . shares humanity with those who conceived it."

Fifty years ago, Norman Hahn started a wood-working business in his garage, and since then, this company, Conestoga Wood Specialties, has grown and now has 950 employees. Conestoga is organized under Pennsylvania law as a for-profit corporation. The Hahns exercise sole ownership of the closely held business; they control its board of directors and hold all of its voting shares. One of the Hahn sons serves as the president and CEO.

The Hahns believe that they are required to run their business "in accordance with their religious beliefs and moral principles."

As explained in Conestoga's board-adopted "Statement on the Sanctity of Human Life," the Hahns believe that "human life begins at conception." It is therefore "against [their] moral conviction to be involved in the termination of human life" after conception, which they believe is a "sin against God to which they are held accountable." The Hahns have accordingly excluded from the group-health-insurance plan they offer to their employees certain contraceptive methods that they consider to be abortifacients.

The Hahns and Conestoga sued HHS and other federal officials and agencies under RFRA and the Free Exercise Clause of the First Amendment, seeking to enjoin application of ACA's contraceptive mandate insofar as it requires them to provide health-insurance coverage for four FDA-approved contraceptives that may operate after the fertilization of an egg. These include two forms of emergency contraception commonly called "morning after" pills and two types of intrauterine devices. . . .

David and Barbara Green and their three children are Christians who own and operate two family businesses. Forty-five years ago, David Green started an arts-and-crafts store that has grown into a nationwide chain called Hobby Lobby. There are now 500 Hobby Lobby stores, and the company has more than 13,000 employees. Hobby Lobby is organized as a for-profit corporation under Oklahoma law. . . .

David serves as the CEO of Hobby Lobby, and his three children serve as the president, vice president, and vice CEO. . . . They specifically object to the same four contraceptive methods as the Hahns and, like the Hahns, they have no objection to the other 16 FDA-approved methods of birth control. . . .

III . . .

The first question that we must address is whether this provision applies to regulations that govern the activities of for-profit corporations like Hobby Lobby, Conestoga, and Mardel.HHS contends that neither these companies nor their owners can even be heard under RFRA. According to HHS, the companies cannot sue because they seek to make a profit for their owners, and the owners cannot be heard because the regulations, at least as a formal matter, apply only to the companies and not to the owners as individuals. HHS's argument would have dramatic consequences. . . .

RFRA applies to "a person's" exercise of religion, and RFRA itself does not define the term "person." We therefore look to the Dictionary Act, which we must consult "[i]n determining the meaning of any Act of Congress, unless the context indicates otherwise."

Under the Dictionary Act, "the wor[d] 'person' . . . include[s] corporations, companies, associations, firms, partnerships, societies, and joint stock companies, as well as individuals." . . .

We see nothing in RFRA that suggests a congressional intent to depart from the Dictionary Act definition, and HHS makes little effort to argue otherwise. We have entertained RFRA and free-exercise claims brought by nonprofit corporations, and HHS concedes that a nonprofit corporation can be a "person" within the meaning of RFRA. . . .

The principal argument advanced by HHS and the principal dissent regarding RFRA protection for Hobby Lobby, Conestoga, and Mardel focuses not on the statutory term "person," but on the phrase "exercise of religion." According to HHS and the dissent, these corporations are not protected by RFRA because they cannot exercise religion. Neither HHS nor the dissent, however, provides any persuasive explanation for this conclusion.

Is it because of the corporate form? The corporate form alone cannot provide the explanation because, as we have pointed out, HHS concedes that nonprofit corporations can be protected by RFRA. The dissent suggests that nonprofit corporations are special because furthering their religious "autonomy . . . often furthers individual religious freedom as well." But this principle applies equally to for-profit corporations: Furthering their religious freedom also "furthers individual religious freedom." In these cases, for example, allowing Hobby Lobby, Conestoga, and Mardel to assert RFRA claims protects the religious liberty of the Greens and the Hahns.

If the corporate form is not enough, what about the profit-making objective? In *Braunfeld*, we entertained the free-exercise claims of individuals who were attempting to make a profit as retail merchants, and the Court never even hinted that this objective precluded their claims. . . . Business practices that are compelled or limited by the tenets of a religious doctrine fall comfortably within that definition. Thus, a law that "operates so as to make the practice of . . . religious beliefs more expensive" in the context of business activities imposes a burden on the exercise of religion.

If, as *Braunfeld* recognized, a sole proprietorship that seeks to make a profit may assert a free-exercise claim, why can't Hobby Lobby, Conestoga, and Mardel do the same?

Some lower court judges have suggested that RFRA does not protect for-profit corporations because the purpose of such corporations is simply to make money. This argument flies in the face of modern corporate law. . . . While it is certainly true that a central objective of for-profit corporations is to make money, modern corporate law does not require for-profit corporations to pursue profit at the expense of everything else, and many do not do so. For-profit corporations, with ownership approval, support a wide variety of charitable causes, and it is not at all uncommon for such corporations to further humanitarian and other altruistic objectives. . . .

HHS would draw a sharp line between nonprofit corporations (which, HHS concedes, are protected by RFRA) and for-profit corporations (which HHS would leave unprotected), but the actual picture is less clear-cut. Not all corporations that decline to organize as nonprofits do so in order to maximize profit. For example, organizations with religious and charitable aims might organize as for-profit corporations because of the potential advantages of that corporate form, such as the freedom to participate in lobbying for legislation or campaigning for political candidates who promote their religious or charitable goals. . . .

In any event, the objectives that may properly be pursued by the companies in these cases are governed by the laws of the States in which they were incorporated — Pennsylvania and Oklahoma — and the laws of those States permit for-profit corporations to pursue "any lawful purpose" or "act," including the pursuit of profit in conformity with the owners' religious principles. . . .

Finally, HHS contends that Congress could not have wanted RFRA to apply to for-profit corporations because it is difficult as a practical matter to ascertain the sincere "beliefs" of a corporation. . . .

These cases, however, do not involve publicly traded corporations, and it seems unlikely that the sort of corporate giants to which HHS refers will often assert RFRA claims. HHS has not pointed to any example of a publicly traded corporation asserting RFRA rights, and numerous practical restraints would likely prevent that from occurring. . . . The companies in the cases before us are closely held corporations, each owned and controlled by members of a single family, and no one has disputed the sincerity of their religious beliefs.[28.] . . .

For all these reasons, we hold that a federal regulation's restriction on the activities of a for-profit closely held corporation must comply with RFRA.

IV

[W]e must next ask whether the HHS contraceptive mandate "substantially burden[s]" the exercise of religion. We have little trouble concluding that it does.

As we have noted, the Hahns and Greens have a sincere religious belief that life begins at conception. They therefore object on religious grounds to providing health insurance that covers methods of birth control that . . . may result in the destruction of an embryo. By requiring the Hahns and Greens and their companies to arrange for such coverage, the HHS mandate demands that they engage in conduct that seriously violates their religious beliefs.

If the Hahns and Greens and their companies do not yield to this demand, the economic consequences will be severe. If the companies continue to offer group health plans that do not cover the contraceptives at issue, they will be taxed $100 per day for each affected individual. For Hobby Lobby, the bill could amount to $1.3 million per day or about $475 million per year. . . .

28.. To qualify for RFRA's protection, an asserted belief must be "sincere"; a corporation's pretextual assertion of a religious belief in order to obtain an exemption for financial reasons would fail.

Although these totals are high, *amici* supporting HHS have suggested that the $2,000 per-employee penalty is actually less than the average cost of providing health insurance. . . .

[I]t is far from clear that the net cost to the companies of providing insurance is more than the cost of dropping their insurance plans and paying the ACA penalty. Health insurance is a benefit that employees value. If the companies simply eliminated that benefit and forced employees to purchase their own insurance on the exchanges, without offering additional compensation, it is predictable that the companies would face a competitive disadvantage in retaining and attracting skilled workers. . . .

In sum, we refuse to sustain the challenged regulations on the ground—never maintained by the Government—that dropping insurance coverage eliminates the substantial burden that the HHS mandate imposes. We doubt that the Congress that enacted RFRA—or, for that matter, ACA—would have believed it a tolerable result to put family-run businesses to the choice of violating their sincerely held religious beliefs or making all of their employees lose their existing healthcare plans.

In taking the position that the HHS mandate does not impose a substantial burden on the exercise of religion, HHS's main argument (echoed by the principal dissent) is basically that the connection between what the objecting parties must do (provide health-insurance coverage for four methods of contraception that may operate after the fertilization of an egg) and the end that they find to be morally wrong (destruction of an embryo) is simply too attenuated. HHS and the dissent note that providing the coverage would not itself result in the destruction of an embryo; that would occur only if an employee chose to take advantage of the coverage and to use one of the four methods at issue.

This argument dodges the question that RFRA presents (whether the HHS mandate imposes a substantial burden on the ability of the objecting parties to conduct business in accordance with *their religious beliefs*) and instead addresses a very different question that the federal courts have no business addressing (whether the religious belief asserted in a RFRA case is reasonable). The Hahns and Greens believe that providing the coverage demanded by the HHS regulations is connected to the destruction of an embryo in a way that is sufficient to make it immoral for them to provide the coverage. This belief implicates a difficult and important question of religion and moral philosophy, namely, the circumstances under which it is wrong for a person to perform an act that is innocent in itself but that has the effect of enabling or facilitating the commission of an immoral act by another. Arrogating the authority to provide a binding national answer to this religious and philosophical question, HHS and the principal dissent in effect tell the plaintiffs that their beliefs are flawed. For good reason, we have repeatedly refused to take such a step. . . .

[T]he Hahns and Greens and their companies sincerely believe that providing the insurance coverage demanded by the HHS regulations lies on the forbidden side of the line, and it is not for us to say that their religious beliefs are mistaken or insubstantial. Instead, our "narrow function . . . in this context is to determine" whether the line drawn reflects "an honest conviction," and there is no dispute that it does. . . .

V . . .

HHS asserts that the contraceptive mandate serves a variety of important interests, but many of these are couched in very broad terms, such as promoting "public health" and "gender equality." RFRA, however, contemplates a "more focused" inquiry: It "requires the Government to demonstrate that the compelling interest test is satisfied through application of the challenged law 'to the person' — the particular claimant whose sincere exercise of religion is being substantially burdened." This requires us to "loo[k] beyond broadly formulated interests" and to "scrutiniz[e] the asserted harm of granting specific exemptions to particular religious claimants" — in other words, to look to the marginal interest in enforcing the contraceptive mandate in these cases.

In addition to asserting these very broadly framed interests, HHS maintains that the mandate serves a compelling interest in ensuring that all women have access to all FDA-approved contraceptives without cost sharing. Under our cases, women (and men) have a constitutional right to obtain contraceptives, and HHS tells us that "[s]tudies have demonstrated that even moderate copayments for preventive services can deter patients from receiving those services." . . .

We find it unnecessary to adjudicate this issue. We will assume that the interest in guaranteeing cost-free access to the four challenged contraceptive methods is compelling within the meaning of RFRA, and we will proceed to consider the final prong of the RFRA test, *i.e.*, whether HHS has shown that the contraceptive mandate is "the least restrictive means of furthering that compelling governmental interest."

The least-restrictive-means standard is exceptionally demanding, and it is not satisfied here. HHS has not shown that it lacks other means of achieving its desired goal without imposing a substantial burden on the exercise of religion by the objecting parties in these cases. . . .

The most straightforward way of doing this would be for the Government to assume the cost of providing the four contraceptives at issue to any women who are unable to obtain them under their health-insurance policies due to their employers' religious objections. This would certainly be less restrictive of the plaintiffs' religious liberty, and HHS has not shown, that this is not a viable alternative. . . . It seems likely, however, that the cost of providing the forms of contraceptives at issue in these cases (if not all FDA-approved contraceptives) would be minor when compared with the overall cost of ACA. . . .

In the end, however, we need not rely on the option of a new, government-funded program in order to conclude that the HHS regulations fail the least-restrictive-means test. HHS itself has demonstrated that it has at its disposal an approach that is less restrictive than requiring employers to fund contraceptive methods that violate their religious beliefs. As we explained above, HHS has already established an accommodation for nonprofit organizations with religious objections. Under that accommodation, the organization can self-certify that it opposes providing coverage for particular contraceptive services. If the organization makes such a certification, the organization's insurance issuer or third-party administrator must "[e]xpressly exclude contraceptive coverage from the group health insurance coverage provided in connection with the group health plan" and "[p]rovide separate payments for any contraceptive services required to be covered" without imposing "any cost-sharing requirements . . . on the eligible organization, the group health plan, or plan participants or beneficiaries."

We do not decide today whether an approach of this type complies with RFRA for purposes of all religious claims. At a minimum, however, it does not impinge on the plaintiffs' religious belief that providing insurance coverage for the contraceptives at issue here violates their religion, and it serves HHS's stated interests equally well.

The principal dissent identifies no reason why this accommodation would fail to protect the asserted needs of women as effectively as the contraceptive mandate, and there is none. . . .

HHS and the principal dissent argue that a ruling in favor of the objecting parties in these cases will lead to a flood of religious objections regarding a wide variety of medical procedures and drugs, such as vaccinations and blood transfusions, but HHS has made no effort to substantiate this prediction. HHS points to no evidence that insurance plans in existence prior to the enactment of ACA excluded coverage for such items. Nor has HHS provided evidence that any significant number of employers sought exemption, on religious grounds, from any of ACA's coverage requirements other than the contraceptive mandate. . . .

In any event, our decision in these cases is concerned solely with the contraceptive mandate. Our decision should not be understood to hold that an insurance-coverage mandate must necessarily fall if it conflicts with an employer's religious beliefs. Other coverage requirements, such as immunizations, may be supported by different interests (for example, the need to combat the spread of infectious diseases) and may involve different arguments about the least restrictive means of providing them. . . .

The contraceptive mandate, as applied to closely held corporations, violates RFRA. Our decision on that statutory question makes it unnecessary to reach the First Amendment claim raised by Conestoga and the Hahns. . . .

Justice GINSBURG, with whom Justice SOTOMAYOR joins, and with whom Justice BREYER and Justice KAGAN join as to all but Part III-C-1, dissenting.

I

"The ability of women to participate equally in the economic and social life of the Nation has been facilitated by their ability to control their reproductive lives." Planned Parenthood of Southeastern Pa. v. Casey. Congress acted on that understanding when, as part of a nationwide insurance program intended to be comprehensive, it called for coverage of preventive care responsive to women's needs. Carrying out Congress' direction, the Department of Health and Human Services (HHS), in consultation with public health experts, promulgated regulations requiring group health plans to cover all forms of contraception approved by the Food and Drug Administration (FDA). The genesis of this coverage should enlighten the Court's resolution of these cases.

The Affordable Care Act (ACA), in its initial form, specified three categories of preventive care that health plans must cover at no added cost to the plan participant or beneficiary. Particular services were to be recommended by the U.S.

Preventive Services Task Force, an independent panel of experts. The scheme had a large gap, however; it left out preventive services that "many women's health advocates and medical professionals believe are critically important." 155 Cong. Rec. 28841 (2009) (statement of Sen. Boxer). To correct this oversight, Senator Barbara Mikulski introduced the Women's Health Amendment, which added to the ACA's minimum coverage requirements a new category of preventive services specific to women's health.

Women paid significantly more than men for preventive care, the amendment's proponents noted; in fact, cost barriers operated to block many women from obtaining needed care at all. And increased access to contraceptive services, the sponsors comprehended, would yield important public health gains.

As altered by the Women's Health Amendment's passage, the ACA requires new insurance plans to include coverage without cost sharing of "such additional preventive care and screenings . . . as provided for in comprehensive guidelines supported by the Health Resources and Services Administration [(HRSA)]," a unit of HHS. Thus charged, the HRSA developed recommendations in consultation with the Institute of Medicine (IOM). The IOM convened a group of independent experts, including "specialists in disease prevention [and] women's health"; those experts prepared a report evaluating the efficacy of a number of preventive services. Consistent with the findings of "[n]umerous health professional associations" and other organizations, the IOM experts determined that preventive coverage should include the "full range" of FDA-approved contraceptive methods.

In making that recommendation, the IOM's report expressed concerns similar to those voiced by congressional proponents of the Women's Health Amendment. The report noted the disproportionate burden women carried for comprehensive health services and the adverse health consequences of excluding contraception from preventive care available to employees without cost sharing.

In line with the IOM's suggestions, the HRSA adopted guidelines recommending coverage of "[a]ll [FDA-]approved contraceptive methods, sterilization procedures, and patient education and counseling for all women with reproductive capacity." Thereafter, HHS, the Department of Labor, and the Department of Treasury promulgated regulations requiring group health plans to include coverage of the contraceptive services recommended in the HRSA guidelines . . . This opinion refers to these regulations as the contraceptive coverage requirement.

While the Women's Health Amendment succeeded, a countermove proved unavailing. The Senate voted down the so-called "conscience amendment," which would have enabled any employer or insurance provider to deny coverage based on its asserted "religious beliefs or moral convictions." That amendment, Senator Mikulski observed, would have "pu[t] the personal opinion of employers and insurers over the practice of medicine." Congress left health care decisions—including the choice among contraceptive methods—in the hands of women, with the aid of their health care providers. . . .

III . . .

[T]he Court sees RFRA as a bold initiative departing from, rather than restoring, pre-*Smith* jurisprudence. To support its conception of RFRA as a measure detached from this Court's decisions, one that sets a new course, the Court points first to [RLUIPA], which altered RFRA's definition of the term "exercise of religion." . . . That definitional change, according to the Court, reflects "an obvious effort to effect a complete separation from First Amendment case law."

The Court's reading is not plausible. RLUIPA's alteration clarifies that courts should not question the centrality of a particular religious exercise. But the amendment in no way suggests that Congress meant to expand the class of entities qualified to mount religious accommodation claims, nor does it relieve courts of the obligation to inquire whether a government action substantially burdens a religious exercise.

Next, the Court highlights RFRA's requirement that the government, if its action substantially burdens a person's religious observance, must demonstrate that it chose the least restrictive means for furthering a compelling interest. "[B]y imposing a least-restrictive-means test," the Court suggests, RFRA "went beyond what was required by our pre-*Smith* decisions." But as RFRA's statements of purpose and legislative history make clear, Congress intended only to restore, not to scrap or alter, the balancing test as this Court had applied it pre-*Smith*. . . .

With RFRA's restorative purpose in mind, I turn to the Act's application to the instant lawsuits. That task, in view of the positions taken by the Court, requires consideration of several questions, each potentially dispositive of Hobby Lobby's and Conestoga's claims: Do for-profit corporations rank among "person[s]" who "exercise . . . religion"? Assuming that they do, does the contraceptive coverage requirement "substantially burden" their religious exercise? If so, is the requirement "in furtherance of a compelling government interest"? And last, does the requirement represent the least restrictive means for furthering that interest? . . .

RFRA's compelling interest test, as noted, applies to government actions that "substantially burden *a person's exercise of religion*." . . . There is . . . no support for the notion that free exercise rights pertain to for-profit corporations.

Until this litigation, no decision of this Court recognized a for-profit corporation's qualification for a religious exemption from a generally applicable law, whether under the Free Exercise Clause or RFRA. The absence of such precedent is just what one would expect, for the exercise of religion is characteristic of natural persons, not artificial legal entities. . . .

The First Amendment's free exercise protections, the Court has indeed recognized, shelter churches and other nonprofit religion-based organizations. "For many individuals, religious activity derives meaning in large measure from participation in a larger religious community," and "furtherance of the autonomy of religious organizations often furthers individual religious freedom as well." The Court's "special solicitude to the rights of religious organizations," *Hosanna-Tabor Evangelical Lutheran Church and School v. EEOC*, however, is just that. No such solicitude is traditional for commercial organizations. Indeed, until today, religious exemptions had never been extended to any entity operating in "the commercial, profit-making world."

The reason why is hardly obscure. Religious organizations exist to foster the interests of persons subscribing to the same religious faith. Not so of for-profit corporations. Workers who sustain the operations of those corporations commonly are not drawn from one religious community. Indeed, by law, no religion-based criterion can restrict the work force of for-profit corporations. The distinction between a community made up of believers in the same religion and one embracing persons of diverse beliefs, clear as it is, constantly escapes the Court's attention. . . .

The Court's determination that RFRA extends to for-profit corporations is bound to have untoward effects. Although the Court attempts to cabin its language to closely held corporations, its logic extends to corporations of any size, public or private. Little doubt that RFRA claims will proliferate, for the Court's expansive notion of corporate personhood — combined with its other errors in construing RFRA — invites for-profit entities to seek religion-based exemptions from regulations they deem offensive to their faith.

Even if Hobby Lobby and Conestoga were deemed RFRA "person[s]," to gain an exemption, they must demonstrate that the contraceptive coverage requirement "substantially burden[s] [their] exercise of religion." Congress no doubt meant the modifier "substantially" to carry weight. In the original draft of RFRA, the word "burden" appeared unmodified. . . .

The Court barely pauses to inquire whether any burden imposed by the contraceptive coverage requirement is substantial. . . . I agree with the Court that the Green and Hahn families' religious convictions regarding contraception are sincerely held. But those beliefs, however deeply held, do not suffice to sustain a RFRA claim. RFRA, properly understood, distinguishes between "factual allegations that [plaintiffs'] beliefs are sincere and of a religious nature," which a court must accept as true, and the "legal conclusion . . . that [plaintiffs'] religious exercise is substantially burdened," an inquiry the court must undertake. . . .

Undertaking the inquiry that the Court forgoes, I would conclude that the connection between the families' religious objections and the contraceptive coverage requirement is too attenuated to rank as substantial. The requirement carries no command that Hobby Lobby or Conestoga purchase or provide the contraceptives they find objectionable. Instead, it calls on the companies covered by the requirement to direct money into undifferentiated funds that finance a wide variety of benefits under comprehensive health plans. . . .

Importantly, the decisions whether to claim benefits under the plans are made not by Hobby Lobby or Conestoga, but by the covered employees and dependents, in consultation with their health care providers. . . . Any decision to use contraceptives made by a woman covered under Hobby Lobby's or Conestoga's plan will not be propelled by the Government, it will be the woman's autonomous choice, informed by the physician she consults.

Even if one were to conclude that Hobby Lobby and Conestoga meet the substantial burden requirement, the Government has shown that the contraceptive coverage for which the ACA provides furthers compelling interests in public health and women's well being. Those interests are concrete, specific, and demonstrated by a wealth of empirical evidence. To recapitulate, the mandated contraception coverage enables women to avoid the health problems unintended pregnancies may visit on them and their children. The coverage helps safeguard the health of women for whom pregnancy may be hazardous, even life threatening. And the mandate secures benefits wholly unrelated to pregnancy, preventing certain cancers, menstrual disorders, and pelvic pain.

That Hobby Lobby and Conestoga resist coverage for only 4 of the 20 FDA-approved contraceptives does not lessen these compelling interests. Notably, the corporations exclude intrauterine devices (IUDs), devices significantly more effective, and significantly more expensive than other contraceptive methods. Moreover, the Court's reasoning appears to permit commercial enterprises like Hobby Lobby and Conestoga to exclude from their group health plans all forms of contraceptives. . . .

Perhaps the gravity of the interests at stake has led the Court to assume, for purposes of its RFRA analysis, that the compelling interest criterion is met in these cases. It bears note in this regard that the cost of an IUD is nearly equivalent to a month's full-time pay for workers earning the minimum wage; that almost one-third of women would change their contraceptive method if costs were not a factor; and that only one-fourth of women who request an IUD actually have one inserted after finding out how expensive it would be. . . .

The Court ultimately acknowledges a critical point: RFRA's application "*must* take adequate account of the burdens a requested accommodation may impose on nonbeneficiaries." No tradition, and no prior decision under RFRA, allows a religion-based exemption when the accommodation would be harmful to others — here, the very persons the contraceptive coverage requirement was designed to protect.

After assuming the existence of compelling government interests, the Court holds that the contraceptive coverage requirement fails to satisfy RFRA's least restrictive means test. But the Government has shown that there is no less restrictive, equally effective means that would both (1) satisfy the challengers' religious objections to providing insurance coverage for certain contraceptives (which they believe cause abortions); and (2) carry out the objective of the ACA's contraceptive coverage requirement, to ensure that women employees receive, at no cost to them, the preventive care needed to safeguard their health and well being. A "least restrictive means" cannot require employees to relinquish benefits accorded them by federal law in order to ensure that their commercial employers can adhere unreservedly to their religious tenets.

Then let the government pay (rather than the employees who do not share their employer's faith), the Court suggests. "The most straightforward [alternative]," the Court asserts, "would be for the Government to assume the cost of providing . . . contraceptives . . . to any women who are unable to obtain them under their health-insurance policies due to their employers' religious objections." The ACA, however, requires coverage of preventive services through the existing employer-based system of health insurance "so that [employees] face minimal logistical and administrative obstacles." Impeding women's receipt of benefits "by requiring them to take steps to learn about, and to sign up for, a new [government funded and administered] health benefit" was scarcely what Congress contemplated. . . .

And where is the stopping point to the "let the government pay" alternative? Suppose an employer's sincerely held religious belief is offended by health coverage of vaccines, or paying the minimum wage, or according women equal pay for substantially similar work? Does it rank as a less restrictive alternative to require the government to provide the money or benefit to which the employer has a religion-based objection? . . .

IV

Among the pathmarking pre-*Smith* decisions RFRA preserved is *United States v. Lee*. Lee, a sole proprietor engaged in farming and carpentry, was a member of the Old Order Amish. He sincerely believed that withholding Social Security taxes from his employees or paying the employer's share of such taxes would violate the Amish faith. This Court held that, although the obligations imposed by the Social Security system conflicted with Lee's religious beliefs, the burden was not unconstitutional. The Government urges that *Lee* should control the challenges brought by Hobby Lobby and Conestoga. In contrast, today's Court dismisses *Lee* as a tax case. Indeed, it was a tax case and the Court in *Lee* homed in on "[t]he difficulty in attempting to accommodate religious beliefs in the area of taxation."

But the *Lee* Court made two key points one cannot confine to tax cases. "When followers of a particular sect enter into commercial activity as a matter of choice," the Court observed, "the limits they accept on their own conduct as a matter of conscience and faith are not to be superimposed on statutory schemes which are binding on others in that activity." The statutory scheme of employer-based comprehensive health coverage involved in these cases is surely binding on others engaged in the same trade or business as the corporate challengers here, Hobby Lobby and Conestoga. Further, the Court recognized in *Lee* that allowing a religion-based exemption to a commercial employer would "operat[e] to impose the employer's religious faith on the employees." No doubt the Greens and Hahns and all who share their beliefs may decline to acquire for themselves the contraceptives in question. But that choice may not be imposed on employees who hold other beliefs. Working for Hobby Lobby or Conestoga, in other words, should not deprive employees of the preventive care available to workers at the shop next door, at least in the absence of directions from the Legislature or Administration to do so. . . .

Would the exemption the Court holds RFRA demands for employers with religiously grounded objections to the use of certain contraceptives extend to employers with religiously grounded objections to blood transfusions (Jehovah's Witnesses); antidepressants (Scientologists); medications derived from pigs, including anesthesia, intravenous fluids, and pills coated with gelatin (certain Muslims, Jews, and Hindus); and vaccinations (Christian Scientists, among others)?

The Court, however, sees nothing to worry about. Today's cases, the Court concludes, are "concerned solely with the contraceptive mandate. . . ." But the Court has assumed, for RFRA purposes, that the interest in women's health and well being is compelling and has come up with no means adequate to serve that interest, the one motivating Congress to adopt the Women's Health Amendment.

There is an overriding interest, I believe, in keeping the courts "out of the business of evaluating the relative merits of differing religious claims," *Lee* (Stevens, J., concurring in judgment), or the sincerity with which an asserted religious belief is held. Indeed, approving some religious claims while deeming others unworthy of accommodation could be "perceived as favoring one religion over another," the very "risk the Establishment Clause was designed to preclude." The Court, I fear, has ventured into a minefield, by its immoderate reading of RFRA. I would confine religious exemptions under that Act to organizations formed "for a religious purpose," "engage[d] primarily in carrying out that religious purpose," and not "engaged . . . substantially in the exchange of goods or services for money beyond nominal amounts."

NOTES

1. **The Constitutional Right to Contraception.** The Court in *Griswold* based the right to contraception squarely on the special status of marriage in this society. In Eisenstadt v. Baird, the Court extended *Griswold* to prevent Massachusetts from barring distribution of contraceptives to unmarried persons. In so ruling, the Court reasoned that "the goals of deterring premarital sex and regulating the distribution of potentially harmful articles cannot reasonably be regarded as legislative aims of [the contraception law]" since it would be irrational to make an unwanted child the "punishment for fornication." In the Court's view: "If the right of privacy means anything, it is the right of the individual, married or single, to be free from unwarranted governmental intrusion into matters so fundamentally affecting a person as the decision whether to bear or beget a child."[402] In striking down a Texas statute prohibiting same-sex sodomy in Lawrence v. Texas, the Supreme Court cited *Eisenstadt* and *Carey* for the proposition that the liberty interest protected sexual decisions by unmarried persons, but stopped short of declaring a fundamental right to all sexual activity between consenting adults.[403]

With liberty as the core constitutional value underlying the right to privacy, individual autonomy is at the center of the right. It seems obvious that female contraception allows women to maintain greater control over their reproductive lives. Do you think liberty is a more promising framework than equality for grounding women's right to exercise reproductive control? Or a more limited one?

How far should this right to use contraception extend? Should it apply to minors? Although, in Carey v. Population Serv. Int'l, the Court invalidated a New York law that, among other things, restricted the sale of contraceptives to minors younger than 16, it sidestepped the question whether minors have a constitutional right of access to contraception.[404] Without firm constitutional protection, minors are at the mercy of state legislators. Twenty-three states and the District of Columbia permit minors to consent to contraceptive services on their own behalf, and another twenty-four states permit them to consent in at least some circumstances, such as when the minor is already a parent or is married. In the four states with no statute, minors need parental consent as they would for any other medical procedure or prescription unless they seek services with a provider federally funded by Title X, which requires that services be provided regardless of age.[405]

---

402. 405 U.S. 438, 453 (1972).
403. 539 U.S. 558 (2003).
404. 431 U.S. 678 (1977).
405. Guttmacher Inst., Minors' Access to Contraceptive Services (Aug. 2022).

For many decades, *Griswold* was deemed sacrosanct, even though many scholars at one time questioned its grounding as a matter of constitutional interpretation.[406] A controversial nominee to a seat on the U.S. Supreme Court, Robert Bork, was not confirmed by the Senate in 1987 largely because of his opposition to the ruling.[407] Nevertheless, with the 2012 campaign for the Republican nomination for president emerged a growing conservatism about issues dealing with reproductive autonomy, which was on display in the *Hobby Lobby* case. That backlash only intensified after Donald Trump won the 2016 presidential election. Several federal judges confirmed since the 2016 election have been unwilling to say that *Griswold* was decided correctly, and, as discussed below in the materials on abortion, Justice Clarence Thomas has explicitly called for *Griswold* to be overruled. Will constitutional protection for contraception survive? Why or why not?

2. **Access to Contraception.**   Even with constitutional protection for the right to use prescription contraception, individual access is widely variable based on factors like income, insurance coverage, and the availability of local providers. The modern battle over contraception has been about how accessible contraceptives should be and who should pay for them. Somewhat surprisingly, it has also become a highly political issue.

In the decades after *Griswold*, the battles over contraception began to revolve largely around funding and the issue of "contraceptive equity." An important site of controversy has been over coverage by employer-based health insurance plans. As late as the year 2000, most employer-based insurance plans did not cover prescription contraceptives (which are used only by people with female reproductive organs).[408] This changed due to the widespread adoption of state-mandated benefit laws, beginning with Maryland in 1998.[409] But even as coverage became widespread, the plans imposed costs through co-payments or deductibles that made contraception unaffordable for many women.

Efforts to pass a federal contraceptive equity bill were unsuccessful until the Affordable Care Act was signed into law in 2010 and the HHS regulations at issue in Burwell v. Hobby Lobby Stores were enacted. The mandate was based on a comprehensive study of health care needs and access in the United States, which was conducted by the nonpartisan, congressionally chartered group, the Institute of Medicine (IOM).[410] IOM focused on health outcomes and access, ultimately concluding that contraception is an "essential health benefit" and that the largest

---

406. See, e.g., Robert P. George & David L. Tubbs, The Bad Decision That Started It All, Nat'l Rev., July 18, 2005, at 39-40.

407. See Mark Gitenstein, Matters of Principle: An Insider's Account of American's Rejection of Robert Bork's Nomination to the Supreme Court (1992).

408. Lawsuits challenging the exclusion of prescription contraceptives from employer-based insurance plans as unlawful discrimination are discussed in Chapter 2, Section B.

409. See Joanna L. Grossman, Expanding the Core: Pregnancy Discrimination Law as It Approaches Full Term, 52 Idaho L. Rev. 825, 833 (2016). On current mandates, see Guttmacher Inst., Insurance Coverage of Contraceptives (Aug. 1, 2022).

410. 77 Fed. Reg. 8725–26 (2022).

barrier to access is cost.[411] The Women's Preventative Services Guidelines, which require "coverage, without cost sharing" for all FDA-approved contraceptive methods, sterilization procedures, and patient education and counseling, reflect the consensus of the medical profession that women's health depends on access to contraception. Although there are still gaps in coverage, the impact of this mandate has been enormous. The proportion of women paying for prescription oral contraceptives dropped from 20 percent to less than 4 percent. In total, more than 55 million women can obtain birth control at no cost. In 2013 alone, after the mandate took effect, women saved $1.4 billion in costs for oral contraceptives.[412] What arguments justify the shifting of this cost from women to everyone covered by an insurance plan? Are those arguments any less compelling when an employer claims a religious objection to covering contraceptives?

Even after the U.S. Supreme Court upheld these regulations against a RFRA challenge in *Hobby Lobby* because of the religious exemption provided in the regulations, RFRA challenges continued. In Zubik v. Burwell, a number of non-church employers, including a Roman Catholic-supported home for low-income elderly and several religiously based colleges, claimed that the requirement that they submit notice of the exemption to their insurer itself impermissibly requires their involvement in the provision of contraception, in violation of their religious liberty. The Supreme Court ultimately declined to rule on the merits, opting instead to vacate and remand for lower courts to consider the feasibility of providing contraceptive coverage to women without the notice to which the challengers objected.[413] The contraceptive mandate was then weakened substantially by the Trump administration, which issued an order permitting any insurer to omit contraceptive coverage for religious or moral reasons.[414] The Supreme Court upheld the validity of the order in Little Sisters of the Poor Saints Peter and Paul Home v. Pennsylvania.[415] Justice Ruth Bader Ginsburg dissented, castigating the majority for casting "totally aside countervailing rights and interests in its zeal to secure religious rights to the nth degree" notwithstanding Congress' desire "to afford gainfully employed women comprehensive, seamless, no-cost insurance coverage for preventive care protective of their health and well-being."[416] The expansive religious exemption

---

411. This is also true for adolescents. See David Eisenberg et al., Cost as a Barrier to Long-Acting Reversible Contraceptive (LARC) Use in Adolescents, 52 J. Adolescent Health 59 (2013).

412. Gaylynn Burroughs, Not Going Back: The Affordable Care Act and Medicaid, Ms. Mag., Dec. 27, 2016; see also Ashley H. Snyder et al., The Impact of the Affordable Care Act on Contraceptive Use and Costs Among Privately Insured Women, 28 Women's Health Issues 219 (2018); Jennifer Hickey, Insuring Contraceptive Equity, 17 N.W. J. L. & Soc. Pol'y 61 (2022).

413. Zubik v. Burwell, 578 U.S. 403 (2016).

414. See Religious Exemptions and Accommodations for Coverage of Certain Preventive Services Under the Affordable Care Act, 83 FR 57536-01 (effective Jan. 14, 2019); Moral Exemptions and Accommodations for Coverage of Certain Preventive Services Under the Affordable Care Act, 83 FR 57592 (effective Jan. 14, 2019).

415. 140 S. Ct. 2367, 2400 (2020).

416. Id. at 2403-04.

was estimated to result in the loss by 125,000 women of childbearing age of contraceptive coverage they previously enjoyed.

The expansion of religious exemptions to the contraceptive mandate was part of a broader set of initiatives undertaken by the Trump administration to reduce access to preventative sexual and reproductive health services domestically and abroad. The Trump administration first reinstated the "global gag rule," which prevents entities that receive U.S. foreign aid from mentioning or referring patients for abortion.[417] Although ostensibly targeted at abortion, this rule, which has been used during every Republican presidential administration since Ronald Reagan, significantly curtails access to contraceptive and other sexual health services as well because clinics cannot afford to stay open without the funding and providers curtail services to avoid running afoul of the rule.[418] The global gag rule also increases the rate of abortion in some regions because of the effect on contraceptive access.[419] The Trump administration also cut funding to the Teen Pregnancy Prevention Program and introduced a domestic gag rule.[420] President Biden rescinded both the global and domestic gag rules and expanded Title X support for family planning in other ways. For example, the new rule requires providers to be gender-inclusive and expands anti-discrimination protections to cover sexual orientation, gender identity, and sex characteristics. It also provides for greater use of telehealth services and expands the type of health-care providers that can operate Title X clinics beyond just physicians.[421]

A growing number of states permit pharmacists to prescribe nonpermanent birth control, such as oral contraceptives. If large drug store chains begin providing this service, access to contraceptives would greatly expand.[422] Many experts believe that there is no medical reason why temporary contraceptives should not be accessible without a prescription, like many drugs with similar risk profiles.[423] In 2022, the FDA received its first application for an over-the-counter birth control pill.[424] Should this be a policy priority?

3. **Religion and Women's Reproductive Autonomy.** *Hobby Lobby* involves a longstanding, and perhaps increasing, tension between religion and women's rights. It raises a similar issue to those involved in the public accommodations

---

417. See Presidential Memorandum Regarding the Mexico City Policy (Jan. 23, 2017).

418. See, e.g., Sophie Cousins, US Global Gag Rule Is Having "Chilling Effect" on Sexual Health Service, 363 BMJ 4886 (Nov. 2018).

419. See Yana Rodgers, The Global Gag Rule and Women's Reproductive Health (2019).

420. On the history of the domestic gag rule, see Nat'l Family Planning & Reproductive Health Ass'n, Domestic Gag Rule: Challenges for Title X Patients and Providers (June 2017).

421. Dep't Health & Human Servs., Ensuring Access to Equitable, Affordable, Client-Centered, Quality Family Planning Services, 42 C.F.R. Part 59 (effective Nov. 8, 2021). See also Ruth Dawson, Guttmacher Inst., After Years of Havoc, the Biden-Harris Title X Rule Is Now in Effect: What You Need to Know (Dec. 14, 2021).

422. Lauren Yong, One-Stop Shopping, Ms. Mag., Spring 2018, at 10.

423. See Ibis Reproductive Health, Moving the Birth Control Pill Over the Counter in the United States (July 2015).

424. Alice Miranda Ollstein, FDA Weighs First-Ever Application for Over-the-Counter Birth Control Pills in the Wake of *Roe*'s Fall, Politico (July 11, 2022).

cases discussed in Chapter 1, Section D (religious objections to providing goods and services for gay weddings), and, in the employment context, to the ministerial exception under Title VII addressed in Chapter 1. Are you satisfied with the way the majority weighed religious freedom against advancement of women's health and the economic consequences of lessening women's ability to control reproduction?[425] Is there a limit to the protection for religious freedom when the Court defers not only to the business owners' statements about their religious beliefs but also to their beliefs about whether particular methods qualify as "abortifacients"? Priscilla Smith argues that the plaintiffs' beliefs about when pregnancy occurs (upon fertilization of an egg) and whether contraceptive devices can prevent implantation of an embryo in the uterine wall are contrary to scientific consensus and reminiscent of the arguments made in defense of Comstock laws.[426] Is there room under the *Hobby Lobby* decision for a debate about the scientific truth underlying the claimed "belief"?

Consider Elizabeth Sepper's perspective on *Hobby Lobby*:

> The Supreme Court could have treated *Hobby Lobby* as implicating women's status in society. As feminists have long recognized, without control over their reproductive health, women can pursue their professional and educational ambitions only with great difficulty. Empirical studies confirm that access to contraception contributes to higher educational attainment and more financially desirable jobs for women, in turn reducing the gender pay gap. Women themselves experience the use of contraception as enabling them "to take better care of themselves or their families, support themselves financially, complete their education, or get or keep a job."
>
> The fact that only women bear children and (due to the limits of today's technology) use prescription contraceptives is biological, but the imposition of financial burdens on reproductive control is social. By allowing employers to exclude contraceptives from insurance plans, society, not biology, has subjected women to inequality. With the women's preventive services mandate, Congress responded to this inequality.
>
> The courts instead treated gender equality as extraneous to the federal contraceptive mandate.[427]

Do you agree with her critique? The evidence is strong that the ability to control the number and timing of pregnancies is central to the ability of women to control

425. See generally Kara Loewentheil, The Satanic Temple, Scott Walker, and Contraception: A Partial Account of Hobby Lobby's Implications for State Law, 9 Harv. L. & Pol'y Rev. 89 (2015); Mark L. Rienzi, Contraceptive Access and Religious Liberty: Can We Afford to Protect Both?, in The Contested Place of Religion in Family Law 88, 89 (Robin Fretwell Wilson ed., 2018).

426. Priscilla J. Smith, Contraceptive Comstockery: Reasoning from Immorality to Illness in the Twenty-First Century, 47 Conn. L. Rev. 971 (2015).

427. Elizabeth Sepper, Gendering Corporate Conscience, 38 Harv. J.L. & Gender 193, 208-09 (2015).

their lives and achieve equality in other dimensions.[428] Should the government be obligated to provide it? Under what theory of equality?

4. **Men and Contraception.**   Historian Linda Gordon underlines the class and gender ideologies of birth control, explaining how men, particularly those of lower socioeconomic status, tend to associate masculinity with sexual images of virility — an identity that is undercut by the use of contraception "because it introduces calculation and negotiation with women into sexual relations." Among the prosperous, masculinity is associated to a greater extent with earning power, responsibility, children's high achievement, and other goals that tend to be served by contraceptive use. Race and ethnicity are further complicating factors. At various times and circumstances, racial and ethnic pride might stimulate fertility, or it might stimulate greater use of contraception. Recent research finds that one in eight sexually active high school girls has experienced reproductive coercion, in which a male partner sabotages his sexual partner's contraceptive use, deliberately damages a condom or removes it during sex, or otherwise pressures his partner to become pregnant against her wishes.[429] The problem appears to be especially pronounced for Black and Latina women.[430] Race and ethnicity also affect the availability of competing opportunities to motherhood and thus the motivation to reproduce.[431] To what extent does women's reproductive control require changing the dominant understanding of masculinity?

Most methods of contraception are used by women, but male condom use has increased dramatically. Roughly 8 percent of women of reproductive age (15-49) rely on their partners' use of condoms, 18 percent of women rely on female sterilization, 14 percent use birth control pills, 6 percent rely on male sterilization, and 11 percent use injectable contraceptives, vaginal rings, or IUDs.[432] The remaining 43 percent rely on various levels of abstinence or do not use any form of contraception. In the wake of reduced access to abortion in some states, there are reports of increased demand for vasectomies.[433]

Significantly, of course, female contraceptive alternatives do not protect against AIDS and other sexually transmitted diseases. However, the ACA

---

428. See, e.g., Adam Sonfield et al., The Social and Economic Benefits of Women's Ability to Determine Whether and When to Have Children, Guttmacher Inst. 7-14 (Mar. 2019); Claudia Goldin & Lawrence F. Katz, The Power of the Pill: Oral Contraceptives and Women's Career and Marriage Decisions, 110 J. Pol. Econ. 730 (2002).

429. Amber L. Hill et al., Reproductive Coercion and Relationship Abuse Among Adolescents and Young Women Seeking Care at School Health Centers, 134 Obstetrics & Gynecology 351, 353 (2019); Deborah L. Brake & Joanna L. Grossman, Reproducing Inequality Under Title IX, 43 Harv. J.L. & Gender 171, 183-84 (2020).

430. Hill et al., supra note 429, at 353. See also Alexandra Brodsky, Rape-Adjacent: Imagining Legal Responses to Nonconsensual Condom Removal, 32 Colum. J. Gender & L. 183 (2017); Rachel Camp, Coercing Pregnancy, 21 Wm. & Mary J. Women & L. 275 (2015).

431. Gordon, supra note 401, at 480-81, xix-xxi.

432. See Guttmacher Inst., Contraceptive Use in the United States (May 2021); Kimberly Daniels et al., U.S. Dep't Health & Human Servs., Current Contraceptive Status Among Women Aged 15-44: United States, 2011-2013 (Dec. 2014).

433. See Meena Venkataramanan, Men Rush to Get Vasectomies After *Roe* Ruling, Wash. Post, June 29, 2022.

contraceptive mandate requires insurance coverage without cost only for female methods of contraception; it does not cover contraceptive methods used by men, such as condoms. Greer Donley argues that this gap in ACA coverage promotes a stereotypical view that birth control is a "woman's problem" and reinforces gender inequity by encouraging women to bear the risks and side effects of contraception and by associating blame for unwanted pregnancy with women.[434] Do you agree? Would mandating coverage of all forms of male and female birth control advance women's reproductive autonomy? Would it likely change attitudes about gender, sex, and pregnancy?

5. **Emergency Contraception and Conscience Laws.** The "morning after pill" is a form of emergency contraception that is most effective when taken twelve to twenty-four hours after intercourse and can be effective up to seventy-two hours afterward. Emergency contraception works by several methods: suppressing ovulation, preventing fertilization, disrupting transport of a fertilized egg, or preventing its implantation in the uterus. Of the 3 million unintended pregnancies that occur in the United States each year, estimates suggest that access to emergency contraception could prevent 1.5 million pregnancies, of which, half now end in abortion.[435]

In 1999, the FDA approved the "morning-after pill" by prescription as a form of emergency birth control but resisted the decision to make it available on an over-the-counter basis. An enormous controversy ensued. Unfettered over-the-counter access was finally approved for women 18 and older in August 2006, and, in 2013, for women of all ages.[436]

As the morning-after pill was working its way through the regulatory process, a related controversy was playing out in pharmacies and religious hospitals. Forty-five states and the federal government have "conscience laws" that enable institutions and individuals to refuse to provide abortion, contraception, or sterilization services that are "contrary to [their] religious beliefs or moral principles."[437] Since 2005, a provision known as the Weldon Amendment has been included in annual federal spending bills; it prohibits federal funding for any federal, state, or local agency that discriminates against any "health care entity" that does not provide or offer referrals or insurance coverage for abortions.[438] Accordingly, Catholic hospitals follow the U.S. Conference of Catholic Bishops' Ethical and Religious Directives for Catholic Health Care Services, which prohibit all forms of contraceptive services and counseling, medical and surgical abortions, sterilizations, and even

---

434. Greer Donley, Contraceptive Equity: Curing the Sex Discrimination in the ACA's Mandate, 71 Alabama L. Rev. 499 (2019).

435. Deana Pisoni, Ninth Annual Review of Gender and Sexuality Law: Health Law Chapter: Access to Contraceptives, 9 Geo. J. Gender & L. 1125, 1131 (2008).

436. See Gardiner Harris, F.D.A. Easing Access to "Morning After" Pill, N.Y. Times, Apr. 22, 2009, at A14; Michael D. Shear & Pam Belluck, U.S. Drops Bid to Limit Sales of Morning-After Pill, N.Y. Times, June 10, 2013, at A1.

437. See, e.g., 42 U.S.C. § 300a-7(c)(B) (2018); Guttmacher Inst., Refusing to Provide Health Services (Aug. 1, 2022).

438. Guttmacher Inst., The Weldon Amendment: Interfering with Abortion Coverage and Care (July 2021).

emergency contraception to victims of rape.[439] Some hospitals prohibit affiliated doctors from performing similar medical procedures elsewhere. The impact of these restrictions has increased with the trend of religiously affiliated health care facilities merging with non-sectarian institutions.[440]

Efforts to enact federal legislation that would require hospitals to provide access to a full range of reproductive services have uniformly failed. A number of states, however, require all hospitals to provide either information about emergency contraception, a referral for the morning-after pill, or on-site emergency contraception treatment, which means that "conscience clauses" apply only to procedures such as abortion, sterilization, and artificial insemination, and not to emergency contraception.[441] Should states require hospitals to provide all lawful medical procedures?

In recent years, controversies have centered on the right of pharmacists to refuse to fill prescriptions for the morning-after pill. Pharmacists who believe that life begins at conception consider emergency contraception to be similar to abortion because it may prevent implantation of an embryo. (This is similar to the argument of the defendants in *Hobby Lobby*, who argued that four of the contraceptives covered by the HHS mandate are "abortifacients.") The FDA classifies the morning-after pill as a contraceptive, based on the view of medical experts that it is not abortifacient because it does not disrupt or destroy an implanted embryo. In small communities, pharmacists' refusals to fill prescriptions or make referrals have undermined access to this medication. Six states have laws permitting pharmacists' refusals on ethical or religious grounds, and many more have considered adopting such laws.[442]

Both sides in the debate claim the moral high ground. Pharmacists argue that customer's "convenience should not trump another person's moral conscience." Neither, they contend, should pharmacists be forced to say "I don't kill people myself but let me tell you about the guy down the street who does."[443] Women's rights advocates like Ellen Goodman respond that "the pharmacist's license does not include the right to dispense morality."[444] Should state law or pharmacy boards dictate policy in this area? Or should we let the market decide?

In response to the rollback of abortion rights by the Supreme Court, the Biden administration issued guidance for pharmacists that included, among

---

439. See U.S. Conference of Catholic Bishops, Ethical and Religious Directives for Catholic Health Care Services (5th ed. Nov. 17, 2009); see also Sandhya Somashekhar, A Pregnant Woman Wanted Her Tubes Tied, Her Catholic Hospital Said No., Wash. Post, Sept. 13, 2015 (describing 2015 Michigan case in which Catholic hospital refused a tubal ligation to a woman with a brain tumor).

440. See Katie Hafner, As Catholic Hospitals Expand, So Do Limits on Some Procedures, N.Y. Times, Aug. 10, 2018, at A1.

441. For an overview, see Guttmacher Inst., Rights vs. Responsibilities: Professional Standards and Provider Refusals (2005).

442. Guttmacher Inst., Refusing to Provide Health Services (Aug. 1, 2022).

443. Sheila G. Liaugminas, Pharmacists Battling Lawsuits over Conscience Issues, Nat'l Cath. Reg., Feb. 13-19, 2005, at 1; Editorial, Prescription Politics Hard to Swallow, Balt. Sun, Apr. 22, 2005, at 13A.

444. Ellen Goodman, Pharmacists and Morality, Bos. Globe, Apr. 14, 2005, at A14.

other things, a warning that the refusal to dispense mifepristone, one of the two drugs typically used to induce a medication abortion, to a patient experiencing a first-trimester miscarriage may violate the ACA's ban on sex discrimination.[445] Do you agree? How much, if any, discretion should pharmacists and health-care providers have to refuse services based on their individual moral or religious beliefs?

6. **Beyond the Right to Contraception: The Reproductive Justice Movement.** Both *Griswold* and *Hobby Lobby* involved restrictions on access to contraception. The right *not* to bear a child lies at the center of the reproductive rights movement and at the center of the legal framework for protecting reproductive autonomy. But for some women, the right to *have* a child has been infringed as well, through, for example, forced sterilization. The reproductive justice (RJ) movement, which was begun by a group of Black women who had gathered at a conference in Chicago in 1994 to discuss the Clinton administration's effort to deemphasize reproductive health care as a political strategy, argues for meaningful access to sexual and reproductive health services rather than simply the lack of government interference with choice. The RJ movement draws on both autonomy and critical race feminism in asking how constructions of race, gender, and class converge to impede reproductive control. As explained by Loretta Ross, one of the movement's founders, and Rickie Solinger:

> Reproductive justice is . . . a political movement that splices *reproductive rights* with *social justice* to achieve *reproductive justice*. The definition of reproductive justice goes beyond the pro-choice/pro-life debate and has three primary principles: (1) the right *not* to have a child; (2) the right to *have* a child; and (3) the right to *parent* children in safe and healthy environments. In addition, reproductive justice demands sexual autonomy and gender freedom for every human being.
>
> At the heart of reproductive justice is this claim: all fertile persons and persons who reproduce and become parents require a safe and dignified context for these most fundamental human experiences. Achieving this goal depends on access to specific, community-based resources including high-quality health care, housing and education, a living wage, a healthy environment, and a safety net for times when these resources fail. Safe and dignified fertility management, childbirth, and parenting are impossible without these resources. . . .

While still supporting autonomy-based rights to prevent pregnancy, the reproductive justice movement widens the lens to focus on access to contraception for marginalized communities as well as other dimensions of reproductive control such as surrogacy, coercive sterilization, welfare caps, the prosecution of pregnant women, access to prenatal care for incarcerated women, and the treatment of

---

445. U.S. Dep't Health & Human Servs., Guidance to Nation's Retail Pharmacies: Obligations Under Federal Civil Rights Laws to Ensure Access to Comprehensive Reproductive Health Care Services, https://www.hhs.gov/sites/default/files/pharmacies-guidance.pdf.

pregnant immigrant women.[446] Is autonomy an adequate frame for this broader approach? What preconditions and resources are necessary for a person to make autonomous reproductive decisions?

In 2009, Colorado began offering free long-acting birth control (LARC), such as intrauterine devices and implants, to teenagers and poor women, and then studied the impact of the program. After just four years, the teen birth rate dropped by 40 percent and the abortion rate by 42 percent. Unplanned births among unmarried women under 25 who have not finished high school also declined.[447] Economist Isabel Sawhill argues that single parenthood is the primary driver of inequality, and that LARCs can be used to combat it.[448] Others criticize policies that provide incentives for LARC use because of the history of and potential for coercion.[449] Would you support a program like this in your state? Why or why not? Is there any cost to women's autonomy in this program?

7. **Access to Treatment for Infertility.**   One impediment to the exercise of reproductive autonomy to bear a child is infertility. The CDC estimates that as many as 7 million women suffer some degree of infertility.[450] With advances in reproductive technology, women have many more options for treating infertility. Roughly 10 percent of women ages 18-49 have sought medical help for infertility.[451] Assisted reproductive technology can be an effective way to overcome infertility, but it is expensive and financially out of reach for many women, making insurance coverage a necessity. Moreover, although the public perception of infertility is often focused on women who have postponed childrearing in order to pursue higher education or careers, infertility is disproportionately experienced by women of color and women of lower socioeconomic status.[452] One of the tenets of the reproductive justice movement is that all people have a right to become parents if they so choose. Should the government facilitate access to and subsidize treatment for infertility?

---

446. See Lisa C. Ikemoto, Reproductive Rights and Justice: A Multiple Feminist Theories Account, in Research Handbook on Feminist Jurisprudence 249 (Robin West & Cynthia Bowman eds., 2019).

447. Sabrina Tavernise, Colorado's Effort Against Teenage Pregnancies Is a Startling Success, N.Y. Times, July 5, 2015, at A1; Lisa M. Goldthwaite et al., Adverse Birth Outcomes in Colorado: Assessing the Impact of a Statewide Initiative to Prevent Unintended Pregnancy, 105 Am. J. Pub. Health 60 (2015).

448. Isabel Sawhill, Generation Unbound: Drifting into Sex and Parenthood Without Marriage (2014).

449. Guttmacher Inst., Powerful Contraception, Complicated Programs: Preventing Coercive Promotion of Long-Acting Reversible Contraceptives, 24 Guttmacher Pol'y Rev. (May 10, 2021).

450. Anjani Chandra et al., Nat'l Health Stats. Rep., Infertility Service Use in the United States: Data from the National Survey of Family Growth, 1982-2010, at 1 (Jan. 2014).

451. Gabriela Weigel et al., Kaiser Family Found., Coverage and Use of Fertility Services in the U.S. (Sept. 15, 2020).

452. See Madeline Curtis, Inconceivable: How Barriers to Infertility Treatment for Low-Income Women Amount to Reproductive Oppression, 25 Geo. J. on Poverty L. & Pol'y 323 (2018).

Many health insurance providers in the United States extend benefits for fertility treatment only after proof of medical infertility, usually defined as one year of unprotected heterosexual intercourse without achieving a pregnancy. Should insurance companies be forced to cover treatment for LGBT patients who might have what is generally called "social infertility," or the inability to achieve pregnancy because of the lack of heterosexual sex?[453]

8. **Gender Bias in Health Care.** Health concerns about female contraception are part of a broader set of issues related to gender bias in health care. Some of these complaints concern the failure to provide adequate warnings and instructions for contraceptives, and to provide research and treatment for women with conditions such as heart disease, renal disease, and lung cancer, for which men receive better health care.[454]

One representative study found that emergency rooms incorrectly sent home a disproportionate number of women and Black patients despite warning signs of heart attacks.[455] Other problems concern the overuse of certain invasive procedures or restrictive instructions. Such biases may be related to the fact that, for decades, women were disproportionately excluded from medical research and drug test trials.[456] To rectify such exclusions the NIH Revitalization Act of 1993 required the National Institutes of Health of the Department of Health and Human Services to ensure that women and minorities were among the subjects of clinical research.

Concerns about the lack of attention to women's health have been fueled by the discovery of numerous drugs and other products that, as in the case of some contraceptives, have turned out to be medically unsafe for women. Examples have included the Dalkon Shield contraceptive; DES, a synthetic estrogen hormone prescribed for miscarriages, later linked to cancer and birth defects; and Bendectin, an anti-nausea medication prescribed for morning sickness but later found to cause birth defects. Concerns have also been raised about silicone breast implants. In the 1990s, the makers of the implants spent more than $6 billion settling about 370,000 claims for arthritic and autoimmune disorders claimed to have resulted from the rupture and leakage of silicone from the implants. During this time, the FDA withdrew approval of the implants except for "urgent need" patients who had had mastectomies, at which point saline implants dominated the market. Subsequently, in 2006, a new type of silicone implant was approved, with the requirement of ten

453. See Stephanie Fairyington, Should Same-Sex Couples Receive Fertility Benefits?, N.Y. Times, Nov. 2, 2015; Rose Holden Vacanti Gilroy, The Law of Assisted Reproductive Technologies: Imposing Heteronormative Family Structures onto Queer Families, 31 Tul. J.L. & Sexuality 27, 33-35 (2022); Marie-Amélie George, Queering Reproductive Justice, 54 U. Rich. L. Rev. 671 (2020).

454. See Mary Crossley, Infected Judgment: Legal Responses to Physician Bias, 48 Vill. L. Rev. 195, 225, 227-29 (2003) (citing studies); Sandra C. Gan et al., Treatment of Acute Myocardial Infarction Among Men and Women, 343 New Eng. J. Med. 8 (July 2000).

455. See, e.g., Maya Dusenbery, Is Medicine's Gender Bias Killing Young Women?, Pac. Std., Mar. 23, 2015.

456. Crossley, supra note 454, at 224 (citing studies).

years of follow-up study.[457] In 2010, half of the almost 300,000 breast augmentation procedures performed in the United States made use of silicone implants.[458] Based on five years of post-approval studies, the FDA determined that silicone implants "have a reasonable assurance of safety and effectiveness when used as labeled" and "despite frequent local complications and adverse outcomes, the benefits and risks . . . are sufficiently well understood for women to make informed decisions about their use."[459] In 2019, a particular type of implant was recalled worldwide after proof of its link to a rare cancer.[460] The FDA had refused to ban the implant a few months before the recall, even though it had been banned by thirty-eight other countries, including most of Europe.[461] In 2022, the FDA issued a new warning that breast implants of all types are linked to a few types of rare cancer.[462] What is the right balance between regulating to protect women's safety and allowing them the autonomy to choose which risks to bear?

One women's health care controversy centers on whether states should require or promote vaccination of school-age girls with Gardasil, a vaccine designed to protect against four strands of the human papilloma virus (HPV). HPV is the most common sexually transmitted disease, with which 79 million people are currently infected.[463] It is responsible for almost all cervical cancers, as well as a significant percentage of cancers of the vulva, vagina, penis, anus, mouth, and throat, and 90 percent of genital warts. There are about 12,000 new cervical cancer cases every year and about 4,000 deaths from the disease. Black and Hispanic women have disproportionately high rates of cervical cancer and face worse outcomes.[464] In 2006, the FDA approved Gardasil for females ages 9 to 26.[465] Conservative groups like the Family Research Council have opposed the vaccine because female adolescents could see it as "license to engage in premarital sex."[466] Such opposition has helped block proposed legislation in about half of the states to require vaccination, as well

---

457. See FDA Approves Silicone Gel-Filled Breast Implants After In-Depth Evaluation (Nov. 17, 2006). On the history of breast implants, see Florence Williams, Breasts: A Natural and Unnatural History (2012).

458. See Food & Drug Admin, FDA Update on the Safety of Silicone Gel-Filled Breast Implants at 3 (June 2011).

459. Id. at 34.

460. Denise Grady, Breast Implants Linked to Rare Cancer Are Recalled Worldwide, N.Y. Times, July 24, 2019, at A20.

461. Denise Grady & Roni Caryn Rabin, FDA Won't Ban Sales of Textured Breast Implants Linked to Cancer, N.Y. Times, May 2, 2019, at A17.

462. See Roni Caryn Rabin, Breast Implants May Be Linked to Additional Cancers, FDA Warns, N.Y. Times, Sept. 8, 2022.

463. See Ctr. for Disease Control and Prevention (CDC), Genital HPV Infection—Fact Sheet (Aug. 20, 2019.

464. See Ctr. for Disease Control & Prevention, Cervical Cancer Rates by Race & Ethnicity (Aug. 2, 2019).

465. See Letter from Norman W. Baylor, Dep't of Health & Human Serv., to Patrick Brill-Edwards, M.D., Worldwide Regulatory Affairs (June 8, 2006).

466. Nancy Gibbs, Defusing the War over the "Promiscuity" Vaccine, Time, June 21, 2006 (quoting Bridget Maher).

as efforts to require its coverage in insurance policies.[467] New evidence shows that the rate of HPV infection in girls has decreased by 64 percent since the introduction of the vaccine.[468] Australia is on the verge of eliminating cervical cancer as a result of a school-based vaccination program and an expansion of adult screening for HPV.[469] Are these data points a sufficient counter to the moral opposition?

In 2009, the FDA approved Gardasil for use in boys 9 through 26 years of age.[470] In 2011, an advisory committee of the FDA recommended that all boys of the requisite ages receive the vaccine. In support of the recommendation, the committee stated: "HPV vaccination of males offers an opportunity to decrease the burden of HPV related disease in both males and females. In addition to providing direct benefit to boys by preventing future genital warts or anal cancer there is also the potential that vaccinating boys will reduce the spread of HPV from males to females and reduce some of the HPV-related burden that women suffer from."[471] As a legislator, would you support a mandate for both boys and girls to receive the vaccine?

9. **Sterilization.** Sterilization is currently the second-most widely used birth control technique. Sterilization has an unbecoming history, due to its compulsory application to poor, minority, and mentally disabled women. In a 1927 case rejecting a constitutional challenge to forced sterilization of persons involuntarily committed to an asylum, Justice Oliver Wendell Holmes infamously declared: "Three generations of imbeciles is enough."[472] The view of the Supreme Court toward compulsory sterilization ultimately changed,[473] but some states continue to authorize sterilization for certain offenses such as child sexual abuse.[474]

Sterilization for poor and minority women as a condition of receiving welfare has led to federal and state regulations designed to prevent such coercion. However, as forced sterilization laws tightened, it became more difficult for parents and guardians to obtain the procedure for developmentally disabled women whose best interests—including their autonomy—might benefit from sterilization. Attention then shifted to how sterilization standards should be calibrated not only to protect women, but also enable them to live richer, sexually active lives. Some jurisdictions such as Connecticut attempt to accommodate these competing concerns by allowing courts to authorize sterilization if presented with clear and convincing evidence

---

467. See Henry J. Kaiser Family Found., The HPV Vaccine: Access and Use in the U.S. (July 12, 2021).

468. Jan Hoffman, HPV Sharply Reduced in Teenage Girls Following Vaccine, Study Says, N.Y. Times, Feb. 22, 2016, at A14.

469. Livia Albeck-Ripka, In Australia, Cervical Cancer Could Soon Be Eliminated, N.Y. Times, Oct. 3, 2018.

470. See Letter from Wellington Son, M.D., Dep't of Health & Human Serv., to Patrick Brill-Edwards, Merck & Co., Inc. (Oct. 16, 2009).

471. CDC, Online Newsroom Press Briefing Transcript (Oct. 25, 2011).

472. Buck v. Bell, 274 U.S. 200, 207 (1927).

473. See Skinner v. Oklahoma, 316 U.S. 535 (1942).

474. See, e.g., Cal. Penal Code § 645 (2022) (authorizing hormone suppression treatment for parolees convicted of certain sexual offenses); Wash. Rev. Code § 9.92.100 (2022) (authorizing sterilization for persons convicted of sex with female under age 10).

that it is in the best interests of the individual or that the individual would choose it for herself if able.[475] Is this a good balance?

10. **Menstrual Equity.**   Since 2015, a new movement for "menstrual equity" has emerged.[476] In her 2017 book, Periods Gone Public, Jennifer Weiss-Wolf defines menstrual equity as follows: "In order to have a fully equitable and participatory society, we must have laws and policies that ensure menstrual products are safe and affordable and available to those who need them. The ability to access these items affects a person's freedom to work and study, to be healthy, and to participate in daily life with basic dignity."[477] She describes the underlying problems and the movement in these terms:

> Globally, the disparate impact of menstruation on women's well-being is significant, though not widely known. On any given day, there are eight hundred million people on the planet who are menstruating, of whom at least five hundred million lack adequate resources—basic supplies, facilities, information, support—for managing their periods. Stigma, often rooted in misogyny, is part of the cause. So too is disproportionate poverty among women and girls. The result is denial of key opportunities for equality—educational, economic, and social.
>
>   The United States is not immune to this problem—quite the contrary. It is only recently that we've begun to publicly understand and reflect in our laws that many populations here also struggle with compromised menstrual access and the burden of shame:
>
> - For the nearly one in five American teenagers who live in poverty, lack of menstrual products and support can lead to compromised health, lost classroom time, and even disciplinary intervention.
> - Those experiencing homelessness report isolation and/or infection caused by using tampons and pads for longer than recommended or by improvising with items such as paper bags or newspapers.
> - Incarcerated individuals and those held in detention or correction systems lack agency to manage menstruation and often must beg or bargain for basic hygiene needs, which still may be denied, part of a degrading and dehumanizing power imbalance.[478]

Is Weiss-Wolf right to conclude that menstrual equity is a core component of gender equality and individual dignity? How does the menstrual equity movement mirror the strengths and weaknesses of substantive equality theory? Is autonomy or equality a better frame for advancing access to products and support for menstruation? Advocates have fought for laws to provide free menstrual products in

---

475. Conn. Gen. Stat. § 45a-699(b) (2022).

476. See Bridget J. Crawford et al., The Ground on Which We All Stand: A Conversation About Menstrual Equity Law and Activism, 26 Mich. J. Gender & L. 341 (2019).

477. Jennifer Weiss-Wolf, Periods Gone Public xvi (2017).

478. Jennifer Weiss-Wolf, The ERA Campaign and Menstrual Equity, 43 Harbinger 168, 168-69 (May 17, 2019).

public schools, prisons, and shelters; to eliminate sales tax on menstrual products; to allow coverage by health care spending accounts; and to force better labeling about product ingredients.[479] They have succeeded in getting several states to eliminate sales tax for menstrual products.[480]

Some have suggested that the menstrual equity movement is overly focused on the provision of products to the detriment of focusing on the stigma and discrimination, harassment, and oppression of those who menstruate.[481] A recent report found that many girls are forced to miss school during their periods because they don't have access to menstrual products or suffer teasing about them.[482] One study shows that menstruating women are viewed as less competent than non-menstruating persons, and another shows that boys who are not taught about menstruation often harass girls and as young men try to regulate women's menstrual hygiene.[483] This strand of the menstrual equity movement has commonalities with non-subordination theory. What are strengths and weaknesses of the arguments for menstrual equity? Some object to the term "feminine hygiene" products and referring to only women and girls in relation to menstruation because it excludes transmen or non-binary individuals who menstruate. Should gender-neutral terms be used in this context?[484]

A New York Congressman got into a public fight with the office that controls the purse strings after he was refused reimbursement for $37 spent on tampons for female employees and visitors to his office. He thanked Paul Ryan for providing toilet paper, but asked why not tampons?

In 2022, Scotland became the first country to mandate that all menstrual products be provided by the government free of charge.[485] Although relatively new, the menstrual equity movement has raised social awareness about the impact of

---

479. Karen Zraick, It's Not Just the Tampon Tax, Why Periods Are Political, N.Y. Times, July 22, 2018; see also Bridget J. Crawford & Emily Gold Waldman, The Unconstitutional Tampon Tax, 53 U. Rich. L. Rev. 439 (2019); Holly Seibeold & Gianna Fienberg, Free to Bleed: Virginia House Bill 83 and the Dignity of Menstruating Inmates, 22 Rich. Pub. Int. L. Rev. 69 (2019); Abigail Durkin, Profitable Menstruation: How the Cost of Feminine Hygiene Products Is a Battle Against Reproductive Justice, 18 Geo. J. Gender & L. 131 (2017).

480. See taxfreeperiod.com.

481. Chris Bobel, Menstrual Pads Can't Fix Prejudice, N.Y. Times, Mar. 31, 2018, at SR6; Margaret E. Johnson, Menstrual Justice, 53 U.C. Davis L. Rev. 1 (2019).

482. Siri Tellier & Maria Hyttel, Menstrual Health Management in Eastern and Southern Africa (May 2018).

483. Inga T. Winkler & Virginia Roaf, Taking the Bloody Linen Out of the Closet: Menstrual Hygiene as a Priority for Achieving Gender Equity, 21 Cardozo J. L. & Gender 1, 4 (2014) (citing Tomi-Ann Roberts et al., "Feminine Protection": The Effects of Menstruation on Attitudes Towards Women, 26 Psychol. Women Q. 131, 131 (2002)); Johnson, supra note 481 (citing Katherine R. Allen et al., More Than Just a Punctuation Mark: How Boys and Young Men Learn About Menstruation, 32 J. Fam. Issues 129, 132-33, 136, 143-45, 146, 148 (2011)).

484. A coloring book, The Adventures of Toni the Tampon, seeks to introduce the idea that some men menstruate.

485. Remy Tumin, Scotland Makes Period Products Free, N.Y. Times, Aug. 15, 2022.

menstruation and society's treatment of it and has achieved remarkable legislative successes with bipartisan support. Why do you think that is? Are there lessons to be learned that could be useful in addressing other women's health and reproductive rights issues?

PUTTING THEORY INTO PRACTICE

5-21. The Women's Health and Cancer Rights Act of 1998 was passed to require that insurance plans that include coverage for mastectomy also cover reconstruction of the removed breast and also of the other breast in order to produce a symmetrical appearance. Is this entitlement best viewed as a gender equality issue? An autonomy issue? Does it serve to reinforce the concept of women as sexual objects? Or does it expand their life choices in a positive way?

5-22. You are appointed the guardian ad litem for Beth, an 18-year-old woman who has the mental function of an 8-year-old. Beth is able to work in a sheltered workshop setting and to take care of her own basic physical needs, but she is not able to cook, drive, read, balance a checkbook, or follow complicated instructions. She would like to move from her parents' home to a supervised group-home setting with people her own age. Her parents are agreeable to the move, as long as she has a tubal ligation first so that, if she becomes sexually active, she cannot become pregnant. Because she is incompetent, state law requires a judicial order authorizing the procedure. Your role is to make a recommendation to the court about whether the procedure is in Beth's best interests.

What will you recommend to the court? What additional evidence, if any, would you need to gather to support your recommendation?

5-23. Should pharmacists who morally oppose abortion be protected from adverse employment action if they refuse to dispense prescription drugs used for conditions unrelated to pregnancy but which might have an adverse effect on a developing fetus (e.g., methotrexate used to treat rheumatoid arthritis)?

5-24. In *Hobby Lobby*, the majority made clear that only a sincere religious belief could be the basis for an exemption from the contraceptive coverage mandate. Would it be appropriate in litigation to ask business owners who are seeking the exemption whether they have ever personally used contraception? How else might the sincerity of a claimed religious belief be tested?

5-25. There are nearly 50,000 new HIV infections a year, over 20 percent of them in people under the age of 24. An antiretroviral medication, Truvada, originally approved to treat HIV, has been found to *prevent* HIV infection.[486] What strategies, if any, would you favor to obtain wider use of this drug? Should information about it be provided in sex education classes? Should it be available to teenagers without the consent of their parents? Should it be *required* for children in high-risk families?

---

486. For results of her appeal, see Patel v. State, 60 N.E. 3d 1041 (Ind. Ct. App. 2016). See Jason Potter Burda, PREP and Our Youth: Implications in Law and Policy, 30 Colum. J. Gender & L. 295, 296 (2016).

Should employers be able to refuse insurance coverage for HPV vaccines and HIV prevention drugs based on a claim that they violate their religious beliefs "by making them complicit in facilitating homosexual behavior, drug use, and sexual activity outside of marriage between one man and one woman?"[487]

2. Abortion

Access to abortion has been the most contested site for women's claims to reproductive autonomy. As noted in the prior section, the legal regulation of abortion began in earnest in the nineteenth century. Physicians advocated the criminalization of abortion using arguments that related not only to protecting potential life, but also to ensuring women's performance of marital and maternal obligations, preserving the ethnic character of the nation, and maintaining the social order.[488] By the 1960s, about 1 million abortions were being performed annually, most of them illegally. Because of their illegality, many abortions were performed under unsafe conditions by unskilled practitioners. Between 1,000 and 10,000 individuals, who were disproportionately poor and minority women, died each year from botched abortions. These human costs were a catalyst of reform activity that culminated in the Supreme Court's opinion in Roe v. Wade, which recognized a constitutional right to terminate a pregnancy before viability or at any point if necessary to preserve the pregnant person's life or health.[489] *Roe* was reaffirmed and applied many times over the course of almost five decades. Yet, in 2022, in Dobbs v. Jackson Women's Health Organization, the Supreme Court overruled *Roe* and all the subsequent cases that recognized a constitutional right to seek an abortion.[490] Drastically changing the landscape for abortion access, this ruling raises many questions about the implications for women's equality and reproductive autonomy.

While attitudes about abortion were changing in the 1960s and about one-third of states liberalized their statutes, at the time of the Roe v. Wade decision in 1973, half the states still prohibited termination of pregnancy except where necessary to preserve maternal life.[491]

Roe v. Wade

410 U.S. 113 (1973)

Justice BLACKMUN delivered the opinion of the Court. . . .

---

487. See Braidwood Mgmt. v. Becerra, No. 4:20-cv-00283-O, 2022 WL 4091215 (Sept. 7, 2022).

488. Reva Siegel, Reasoning from the Body: A Historical Perspective on Abortion Regulation and Questions of Equal Protection, 44 Stan. L. Rev. 261, 279 (1992).

489. Deborah L. Rhode, Justice and Gender 207 (1989).

490. 142 S. Ct. 2228 (2022).

491. Rhode, supra note 489, at 208.

[Texas law makes] it a crime to "procure an abortion," as therein defined, or to attempt one, except with respect to "an abortion procured or attempted by medical advice for the purpose of saving the life of the mother." Similar statutes are in existence in a majority of the States. . . .

Three reasons have been advanced to explain historically the enactment of criminal abortion laws in the 19th century and to justify their continued existence.

It has been argued occasionally that these laws were the product of a Victorian social concern to discourage illicit sexual conduct. Texas, however, does not advance this justification in the present case. . . .

A second reason is concerned with abortion as a medical procedure. When most criminal abortion laws were first enacted, the procedure was a hazardous one for the woman. . . . Modern medical techniques have altered this situation. . . .

The third reason is the State's interest—some phrase it in terms of duty—in protecting prenatal life. Some of the argument for this justification rests on the theory that a new human life is present from the moment of conception. The State's interest and general obligation to protect life then extends, it is argued, to prenatal life. . . .

The Constitution does not explicitly mention any right of privacy. In a line of decisions, however going back perhaps as far as [1891], the Court has recognized that a right of personal privacy, or a guarantee of certain areas or zones of privacy, does exist under the Constitution. In varying contexts, the Court or individual Justices have, indeed, found at least the roots of that right in the First Amendment . . . ; in the Fourth and Fifth Amendments . . . ; in the penumbras of the Bill of Rights . . . ; or in the concept of liberty guaranteed by the first section of the Fourteenth Amendment. . . . These decisions make it clear that only personal rights that can be deemed "fundamental" or "implicit in the concept of ordered liberty," . . . are included in this guarantee of personal privacy. They also make it clear that the right has some extension to activities relating to marriage, Loving v. Virginia [1967]; procreation, Skinner v. Oklahoma [1942]; contraception, Eisenstadt v. Baird [1972]; family relationships, Prince v. Massachusetts [1944]; and child rearing and education, Pierce v. Society of Sisters [1925], Meyer v. Nebraska [1923].

This right of privacy, whether it be founded in the Fourteenth Amendment's concept of personal liberty and restrictions upon state action, as we feel it is, or, as the District Court determined, in the Ninth Amendment's reservation of rights to the people, is broad enough to encompass a woman's decision whether or not to terminate her pregnancy. The detriment that the State would impose upon the pregnant woman by denying this choice altogether is apparent. Specific and direct harm medically diagnosable even in early pregnancy may be involved. Maternity, or additional offspring, may force upon the woman a distressful life and future. Psychological harm may be imminent. Mental and physical health may be taxed by child care. There is also the distress, for all concerned, associated with the unwanted child, and there is the problem of bringing a child into a family already unable, psychologically and otherwise, to care for it. In other cases, as in this one, the additional difficulties and continuing stigma of unwed motherhood may be involved. All these are factors the woman and her responsible physician necessarily will consider in consultation. . . .

We, therefore, conclude that the right of personal privacy includes the abortion decision, but that this right is not unqualified and must be considered against important state interests in regulation . . .

The appellee and certain *amici* argue that the fetus is a "person" within the language and meaning of the Fourteenth Amendment. In support of this, they outline at length and in detail the well-known facts of fetal development. If this suggestion of personhood is established, the appellant's case, of course, collapses, for the fetus' right to life would then be guaranteed specifically by the Amendment. . . .

The Constitution does not define "person" in so many words. Section 1 of the Fourteenth Amendment contains three references to "person." . . . None indicates, with any assurance, that it has any possible pre-natal application.

All this, together with our observation . . . that throughout the major portion of the 19th century prevailing legal abortion practices were far freer than they are today, persuades us that the word "person," as used in the Fourteenth Amendment, does not include the unborn. . . .

. . . We need not resolve the difficult question of when life begins. When those trained in the respective disciplines of medicine, philosophy, and theology are unable to arrive at any consensus, the judiciary, in the development of man's knowledge, is not in a position to speculate as to the answer. . . .

[W]e do not agree that, by adopting one theory of life, Texas may override the rights of the pregnant woman that are at stake. [The State does, however,] does have an important and legitimate interest in preserving and protecting the health of the pregnant woman, whether she be a resident of the State or a nonresident who seeks medical consultation and treatment there, and [it] has still *another* important and legitimate interest in protecting the potentiality of human life. These interests are separate and distinct. Each grows in substantiality as the woman approaches term and, at a point during pregnancy, each becomes "compelling."

With respect to the State's important and legitimate interest in the health of the mother, the "compelling" point, in the light of present medical knowledge, is at approximately the end of the first trimester. This is so because of the now-established medical fact . . . that until the end of the first trimester mortality in abortion may be less than mortality in normal childbirth. It follows that, from and after this point, a State may regulate the abortion procedure to the extent that the regulation reasonably relates to the preservation and protection of maternal health. Examples of permissible state regulation in this area are requirements as to the qualifications of the person who is to perform the abortion[,] . . . the facility in which the procedure is to be performed, and the like.

This means, on the other hand, that, for the period of pregnancy prior to this "compelling" point, the attending physician, in consultation with his patient, is free to determine, without regulation by the State, that, in his medical judgment, the patient's pregnancy should be terminated. If that decision is reached, the judgment may be effectuated by an abortion free of interference by the State.

With respect to the State's important and legitimate interest in potential life, the "compelling" point is at viability. This is so because the fetus then presumably has the capability of meaningful life outside the mother's womb. State regulation protective of fetal life after viability thus has both logical and biological justifications. If the State is interested in protecting fetal life after viability, it may go so far as to proscribe abortion during that period, except when it is necessary to preserve the life or health of the mother.

Measured against these standards, [Texas law], in restricting legal abortions to those "procured or attempted by medical advice for the purpose of saving the life of the mother," sweeps too broadly. The statute makes no distinction between abortions performed early in pregnancy and those performed later, and it limits to a single reason, "saving" the mother's life, the legal justification for the procedure. The statute, therefore, cannot survive the constitutional attack made upon it here. . . .

[dissent omitted]

Planned Parenthood of Southeastern Pennsylvania v. Casey

505 U.S. 833 (1992)

Justice O'CONNOR, Justice KENNEDY, and Justice SOUTER announced the judgment of the Court and delivered the opinion of the Court [with Justice BLACKMUN and Justice STEVENS joining in certain parts of the opinion].

I

Liberty finds no refuge in a jurisprudence of doubt. Yet 19 years after our holding that the Constitution protects a woman's right to terminate her pregnancy in its early stages, Roe v. Wade [1973], that definition of liberty is still questioned. Joining the respondents as amicus curiae, the United States, as it has done in five other cases in the last decade, again asks us to overrule *Roe*. . . .

II . . .

[T]he reservations any of us may have in reaffirming the central holding of *Roe* are outweighed by the explication of individual liberty we have given combined with the force of *stare decisis*. . . .

. . . [F]or two decades of economic and social developments, people have organized intimate relationships and made choices that define their views of themselves and their places in society, in reliance on the availability of abortion in the event that contraception should fail. The ability of women to participate equally in the economic and social life of the Nation has been facilitated by their ability to control their reproductive lives. The Constitution serves human values, and while the effect of reliance on *Roe* cannot be exactly measured, neither can the certain cost of overruling *Roe* for people who have ordered their thinking and living around that case be dismissed. . . .

IV . . .

The trimester framework no doubt was erected to ensure that the woman's right to choose not become so subordinate to the State's interest in promoting fetal life that her choice exists in theory but not in fact. We do not agree, however, that the trimester approach is necessary to accomplish this objective. A framework of this rigidity was unnecessary and in its later interpretation sometimes contradicted the State's permissible exercise of its powers.

Though the woman has a right to choose to terminate or continue her pregnancy before viability, it does not at all follow that the State is prohibited from taking steps to ensure that this choice is thoughtful and informed. Even in the earliest stages of pregnancy, the State may enact rules and regulations designed to encourage her to know that there are philosophic and social arguments of great weight that can be brought to bear in favor of continuing the pregnancy to full term and that there are procedures and institutions to allow adoption of unwanted children as well as a certain degree of state assistance if the mother chooses to raise the child herself. "[T]he Constitution does not forbid a State or city, pursuant to democratic processes, from expressing a preference for 'normal childbirth.'" . . . It follows that States are free to enact laws to provide a reasonable framework for a woman to make a decision that has such profound and lasting meaning. This, too, we find consistent with *Roe*'s central premises, and indeed the inevitable consequence of our holding that the State has an interest in protecting the life of the unborn. . . .

Numerous forms of state regulation might have the incidental effect of increasing the cost or decreasing the availability of medical care, whether for abortion or any other medical procedure. The fact that a law which serves a valid purpose, one not designed to strike at the right itself, has the incidental effect of making it more difficult or more expensive to procure an abortion cannot be enough to invalidate it. Only where state regulation imposes an undue burden on a woman's ability to make this decision does the power of the State reach into the heart of the liberty protected by the Due Process Clause. . . .

A finding of an undue burden is a shorthand for the conclusion that a state regulation has the purpose or effect of placing a substantial obstacle in the path of a woman seeking an abortion of a nonviable fetus. A statute with this purpose is invalid because the means chosen by the State to further the interest in potential life must be calculated to inform the woman's free choice, not hinder it. . . .

Some guiding principles should emerge. What is at stake is the woman's right to make the ultimate decision, not a right to be insulated from all others in doing so. Regulations which do no more than create a structural mechanism by which the State, or the parent or guardian of a minor, may express profound respect for the life of the unborn are permitted, if they are not a substantial obstacle to the woman's exercise of the right to choose. . . . Unless it has that effect on her right of choice, a state measure designed to persuade her to choose childbirth over abortion will be upheld if reasonably related to that goal. Regulations designed to foster the health of a woman seeking an abortion are valid if they do not constitute an undue burden. . . .

These principles control our assessment of the Pennsylvania [Abortion Control Act of 1982], and we now turn to the issue of the validity of its challenged provisions.

V . . .

Except in a medical emergency, the statute requires that at least 24 hours before performing an abortion a physician inform the woman of the nature of the procedure, the health risks of the abortion and of childbirth, and the "probable gestational age of the unborn child." The physician or a qualified nonphysician must inform the woman of the availability of printed materials published by the State describing the fetus and providing information about medical assistance for childbirth, information about child support from the father, and a list of agencies which provide adoption and other services as alternatives to abortion. An abortion may not be performed unless the woman certifies in writing that she has been informed of the availability of these printed materials and has been provided them if she chooses to view them. . . .

To the extent [two prior Supreme Court cases] find a constitutional violation when the government requires, as it does here, the giving of truthful, nonmisleading information about the nature of the procedure, the attendant health risks and those of childbirth, and the "probable gestational age" of the fetus, those cases go too far, are inconsistent with *Roe*'s acknowledgment of an important interest in potential life, and are overruled. . . . It cannot be questioned that psychological well-being is a facet of health. Nor can it be doubted that most women considering an abortion would deem the impact on the fetus relevant, if not dispositive, to the decision. In attempting to ensure that a woman apprehend the full consequences of her decision, the State furthers the legitimate purpose of reducing the risk that a woman may elect an abortion, only to discover later, with devastating psychological consequences, that her decision was not fully informed. If the information the State requires to be made available to the woman is truthful and not misleading, the requirement may be permissible.

We also see no reason why the State may not require doctors to inform a woman seeking an abortion of the availability of materials relating to the consequences to the fetus, even when those consequences have no direct relation to her health. An example illustrates the point. We would think it constitutional for the State to require that in order for there to be informed consent to a kidney transplant operation the recipient must be supplied with information about risks to the donor as well as risks to himself or herself. . . .

The idea that important decisions will be more informed and deliberate if they follow some period of reflection does not strike us as unreasonable, particularly where the statute directs that important information become part of the background of the decision. The statute, as construed by the Court of Appeals, permits avoidance of the waiting period in the event of a medical emergency and the record evidence shows that in the vast majority of cases, a 24-hour delay does not create any appreciable health risk. In theory, at least, the waiting period is a reasonable measure to implement the State's interest in protecting the life of the unborn, a measure that does not amount to an undue burden.

Whether the mandatory 24-hour waiting period is nonetheless invalid because in practice it is a substantial obstacle to a woman's choice to terminate her pregnancy is a closer question. The findings of fact by the District Court indicate that because of the distances many women must travel to reach an abortion provider, the practical effect will often be a delay of much more than a day because the waiting period requires that a woman seeking an abortion make at least two visits to the doctor. The District Court also found that in many instances this will increase the exposure of women seeking abortions to "the harassment and hostility of anti-abortion protestors demonstrating outside a clinic." . . . As a result, the District

Court found that for those women who have the fewest financial resources, those who must travel long distances, and those who have difficulty explaining their whereabouts to husbands, employers, or others, the 24-hour waiting period will be "particularly burdensome."

These findings are troubling in some respects, but they do not demonstrate that the waiting period constitutes an undue burden. We do not doubt that, as the District Court held, the waiting period has the effect of "increasing the cost and risk of delay of abortions," but the District Court did not conclude that the increased costs and potential delays amount to substantial obstacles. . . .

[One provision] of Pennsylvania's abortion law provides, except in cases of medical emergency, that no physician shall perform an abortion on a married woman without receiving a signed statement from the woman that she has notified her spouse that she is about to undergo an abortion. The woman has the option of providing an alternative signed statement certifying that her husband is not the man who impregnated her; that her husband could not be located; that the pregnancy is the result of spousal sexual assault which she has reported; or that the woman believes that notifying her husband will cause him or someone else to inflict bodily injury upon her. A physician who performs an abortion on a married woman without receiving the appropriate signed statement will have his or her license revoked, and is liable to the husband for damages.

[The District Court found that the reasons some women do not consult their husbands about the decision to obtain an abortion include domestic violence, sexual abuse, rape, and sexual mutilation.] . . .

[T]he District Court's findings reinforce what common sense would suggest. In well-functioning marriages, spouses discuss important intimate decisions such as whether to bear a child. But there are millions of women in this country who are the victims of regular physical and psychological abuse at the hands of their husbands. Should these women become pregnant, they may have very good reasons for not wishing to inform their husbands of their decision to obtain an abortion. Many may have justifiable fears of physical abuse, but may be no less fearful of the consequences of reporting prior abuse to the Commonwealth of Pennsylvania. Many may have a reasonable fear that notifying their husbands will provoke further instances of child abuse; these women are not exempt from [the] notification requirement. Many may fear devastating forms of psychological abuse from their husbands, including verbal harassment, threats of future violence, the destruction of possessions, physical confinement to the home, the withdrawal of financial support, or the disclosure of the abortion to family and friends. These methods of psychological abuse may act as even more of a deterrent to notification than the possibility of physical violence, but women who are the victims of the abuse are not exempt from [the] notification requirement. And many women who are pregnant as a result of sexual assaults by their husbands will be unable to avail themselves of the exception for spousal sexual assault, because the exception requires that the woman have notified law enforcement authorities within 90 days of the assault, and her husband will be notified of her report once an investigation begins. If anything in this field is certain, it is that victims of spousal sexual assault are extremely reluctant to report the abuse to the government; hence, a great many spousal rape victims will not be exempt from the notification requirement. . . .

The spousal notification requirement is thus likely to prevent a significant number of women from obtaining an abortion. It does not merely make abortions a little more difficult or expensive to obtain; for many women, it will impose a substantial obstacle. We must not blind ourselves to the fact that the significant number of women who fear for their safety and the safety of their children are likely to be deterred from procuring an abortion as surely as if the Commonwealth had outlawed abortion in all cases. . . .

This conclusion is in no way inconsistent with our decisions upholding parental notification or consent requirements. . . . Those enactments, and our judgment that they are constitutional, are based on the quite reasonable assumption that minors will benefit from consultation with their parents and that children will often not realize that their parents have their best interests at heart. We cannot adopt a parallel assumption about adult women.

We recognize that a husband has a "deep and proper concern and interest . . . in his wife's pregnancy and in the growth and development of the fetus she is carrying." . . . With regard to the children he has fathered and raised, the Court has recognized his "cognizable and substantial" interest in their custody. . . . If this case concerned a State's ability to require the mother to notify the father before taking some action with respect to a living child raised by both, therefore, it would be reasonable to conclude as a general matter that the father's interest in the welfare of the child and the mother's interest are equal.

Before birth, however, the issue takes on a very different cast. It is an inescapable biological fact that state regulation with respect to the child a woman is carrying will have a far greater impact on the mother's liberty than on the father's. The effect of state regulation on a woman's protected liberty is doubly deserving of scrutiny in such a case, as the State has touched not only upon the private sphere of the family but upon the very bodily integrity of the pregnant woman. . . . The Court has held that "when the wife and the husband disagree on this decision, the view of only one of the two marriage partners can prevail. Inasmuch as it is the woman who physically bears the child and who is the more directly and immediately affected by the pregnancy, as between the two, the balance weighs in her favor." . . .

Women do not lose their constitutionally protected liberty when they marry. The Constitution protects all individuals, male or female, married or unmarried, from the abuse of governmental power, even where that power is employed for the supposed benefit of a member of the individual's family. These considerations confirm our conclusion that [the spousal notification provision] is invalid.

[The Court also upheld a provision requiring consent to an abortion, except in a medical emergency, for an unemancipated minor under 18, unless the court determines that she is mature and capable of giving informed consent, or that an abortion would be in her best interests.]

Justice BLACKMUN, concurring in part, concurring in the judgment in part, and dissenting in part. . . .

State restrictions on abortion violate a woman's right of privacy. . . .

A State's restrictions on a woman's right to terminate her pregnancy also implicate constitutional guarantees of gender equality. State restrictions on abortion compel women to continue pregnancies they otherwise might terminate. By restricting the right to terminate pregnancies, the State conscripts women's bodies into its service, forcing women to continue their pregnancies, suffer the pains of childbirth, and in most instances, provide years of maternal care. The State does not compensate women for their services; instead, it assumes that they owe this duty as a matter of course. This assumption—that women can simply be forced to accept the "natural" status and incidents of motherhood—appears to rest upon a conception of women's role that has triggered the protection of the Equal Protection Clause. See, e.g., Mississippi Univ. for Women v. Hogan [1982]; Craig v. Boren [1976]. The joint opinion recognizes that these assumptions about women's place in society "are no longer consistent with our understanding of the family, the individual, or the Constitution." . . .

Justice SCALIA, with whom THE CHIEF JUSTICE, JUSTICE WHITE, and Justice THOMAS join, concurring in the judgment in part and dissenting in part. . . .

The States may, if they wish, permit abortion-on-demand, but the Constitution does not require them to do so. The permissibility of abortion, and the limitations upon it, are to be resolved like most important questions in our democracy: by citizens trying to persuade one another and then voting. . . .

That is, quite simply, the issue in this case: not whether the power of a woman to abort her unborn child is a "liberty" in the absolute sense; or even whether it is a liberty of great importance to many women. Of course it is both. The issue is whether it is a liberty protected by the Constitution of the United States. I am sure it is not. I reach that conclusion not because of anything so exalted as my views concerning the "concept of existence, of meaning, of the universe, and of the mystery of human life." . . . Rather, I reach it for the same reason I reach the conclusion that bigamy is not constitutionally protected—because of two simple facts: (1) the Constitution says absolutely nothing about it, and (2) the longstanding traditions of American society have permitted it to be legally proscribed. . . .

In truth, I am as distressed as the Court is . . . about the "political pressure" directed to the Court: the marches, the mail, the protests aimed at inducing us to change our opinions. How upsetting it is, that so many of our citizens (good people, not lawless ones, on both sides of this abortion issue, and on various sides of other issues as well) think that we Justices should properly take into account their views, as though we were engaged not in ascertaining an objective law but in determining some kind of social consensus. The Court would profit, I think, from giving less attention to the fact of this distressing phenomenon, and more attention to the *cause* of it. That cause permeates today's opinion: a new mode of constitutional adjudication that relies not upon text and traditional practice to determine the law, but upon what the Court calls "reasoned judgment," . . . which turns out to be nothing but philosophical predilection and moral intuition. . . .

As long as this Court thought (and the people thought) that we Justices were doing essentially lawyers' work up here—reading text and discerning our society's traditional understanding of that text—the public pretty much left us alone. Texts and traditions are facts to study, not convictions to demonstrate about. But if in reality our process of constitutional adjudication consists primarily of making *value judgments* . . . then a free and intelligent people's attitude towards us can be expected to be (*ought* to be) quite different. The people know that their value judgments are quite as good as those taught in any law school—maybe better. If, indeed, the "liberties" protected by the Constitution are, as the Court says, undefined and unbounded, than the people *should* demonstrate, to protest that we do not implement their values instead of *ours*. . . .

We should get out of this area, where we have no right to be, and where we do neither ourselves nor the country any good by remaining.

Reva Siegel

Reasoning from the Body: A Historical Perspective on Abortion Regulation and Questions of Equal Protection

44 Stan. L. Rev. 261, 267, 361-63, 370 (1992)

Social forces play a powerful part in shaping the process of reproduction. Social forces define the circumstances under which a woman conceives a child, including how voluntary her participation in intercourse may be. Social forces determine whether a woman has access to methods of preventing and terminating a pregnancy, and whether it is acceptable for her to use them. Social forces determine the quality of health care available to a woman during pregnancy, and they determine whether a pregnant woman will be able to support herself throughout the term of gestation, or instead will be forced to depend on others for support. Social relations determine who cares for a child once it is born, and what resources, rewards, and penalties attend the work of gestating and nurturing human life. . . .

[T]oday, as in the nineteenth century, legislators enacting restrictions on abortion may act from judgments about the sexual and maternal conduct of the women they are regulating, and not merely from a concern about the welfare of the unborn. Legislators may condemn abortion because they assume that any pregnant woman who does not wish to be pregnant has committed some sexual indiscretion properly punishable by compelling pregnancy itself. Popular support for excusing women who are victims of rape or incest from the proscriptions of criminal abortion laws demonstrates that attitudes about abortion do indeed rest on normative judgments about women's sexual conduct. Opinion polls like Louisiana's suggest that the public assumes a woman can be coerced into continuing a pregnancy because the pregnancy is her sexual "fault."

Along distinct, but related lines, legislators may view abortion as repellant because it betrays a lack of maternal solicitude in women, or otherwise violates expectations of appropriately nurturing female conduct. If legislators assume that women are "child-rearers," they will take for granted the work women give to motherhood and ignore what it takes from them, and so will view women's efforts to avoid some two decades of life-consuming work as an act of casual expedience or unseemly egoism. Thus, they will condemn women for seeking abortion "on demand," or as a mere "convenience," judging women to be unnaturally egocentric because they do not give their lives over to the work of bearing and nurturing children—that is, because they fail to act like mothers, like normal women should. . . .

Even if state actors have adopted restrictions on abortion out of a genuine and single-minded concern for the welfare of the unborn, archaic or stereotypical assumptions about women may nonetheless deeply bias their deliberations, making fetal life-saving by compelled pregnancy seem reasonable where otherwise it would not. A legislature's attitudes about women may cause it to underestimate or disregard the burdens it would impose on them by compelling pregnancy. A latent assumption that motherhood is women's "normal" condition can easily render state actors oblivious to the life-consuming consequences of forcing women to perform its work—just as a latent assumption that motherhood is women's "deserved" condition will cause indifference to the burdens the legislation will inflict. In short, a legislature may not decide that it is reasonable to save unborn life by compelling pregnancy, "but for" the archaic or stereotypic assumptions about women it holds. If restrictions on abortion are adopted in these circumstances, they offend constitutional guarantees of equal protection. . . .

[S]tate action restricting abortion injures women. . . . First, restrictions on abortion do not merely force women to bear children; powerful gender norms in this society ensure that almost all women who are forced to bear children will raise them as well, a result that legislatures adopting restrictions on abortion both desire and expect. Second, the work legislatures would force women to perform defines women's social status along predictable, gender-delineated lines. Women who perform the socially essential labor of bearing and rearing children face diverse forms of stigmatization and injury, none of which is ordained by the physiology of gestation, and all of which is the doing of the society that would force women to bear children. Third, when states adopt restrictions on abortion, they compel women to become mothers, while in no respect altering the conditions that make the institution of motherhood a principal cause of women's subordinate social status. When the gender-based impositions of abortion-restrictive regulation are considered in light of the forms of gender bias that may animate it, it is clear abortion-restrictive regulation is and remains caste legislation which subordinates women in ways that offend constitutional guarantees of equal protection. . . .

Robin West

The Supreme Court 1989 Term, Foreword: Taking Freedom Seriously

104 Harv. L. Rev. 43, 82-85 (1990)

From a postdemocratic liberal perspective, support for reproductive freedom—like all freedom—should rest on the demonstrated capacity of pregnant women to decide whether to carry a fetus to term or to abort responsibly. Correlatively, support for expanded reproductive freedom should rest on the claim that only by accepting the responsibility to make these judgments do women manifest their freedom to pursue their authentically chosen and desired life goals. . . . [W]hat a rights-focused liberalism obscures is that the meaningful distinction between murder and abortion is not in the nominal and question-begging difference between a "fetus" and a "baby," but rather in the moral quality of the underlying decision that liberal legalism insulates from scrutiny. Unlike the homicidal decision to take another's life, the decision to abort is more often than not a morally responsible decision. The abortion decision typically rests not on a desire to destroy fetal life but on a responsible and moral desire to ensure that a new life will be borne only if it will be nurtured and loved. . . .

[While there are risks to basing reproductive freedom on responsibility, a] failure to rest reproductive freedom on a theory of responsibilities may ensure the complete erosion of the right. . . . The Court's manifest ambivalence over the constitutional status of the right to privacy that undergirds reproductive freedom has compromised the persuasiveness of the appeal to rights and constitutional authority that has to date characterized the pro-choice movement. Pro-choice groups consequently must turn their attention away from courts and to the legislatures and the public who will increasingly be responsible for either protecting or obliterating this individual liberty. As the audience of the "pro-choice/pro-life" debate shifts away from courts and to legislatures, it may be prudent—whether or not philosophically wise—to focus attention on reproductive responsibility as well as on reproductive rights. If the premise of the rights-based argument—a Court willing to guard the individual liberty protected by the right against even well-intended state infringement—ceases to exist, the argument must change. Liberals and feminists must develop alternative, public-regarding arguments supporting those rights and the liberty they protect that transcend the circular and increasingly false insistence that they simply exist.

Minimally, a responsibility-based argument for reproductive freedom that would justify rather than supplant the rights-based claim of Roe v. Wade would more accurately correspond to the experience of women. Women need the freedom to make reproductive decisions not merely to vindicate a right to be left alone but often to strengthen their ties to others: to plan responsibly and have a family for which they can provide, to pursue professional or work commitments made to the outside world, or to continue supporting their families or communities. At other times the decision to abort is necessitated not by a murderous urge to end life, but by the harsh reality of a financially irresponsible partner, a society indifferent to the care of children, and a workplace incapable of accommodating or supporting the needs of working parents. At many other times the need to abort follows directly from a violent sexual assault. When made for any of these reasons, the decision to abort is not one made in an egoistic private vacuum. Whatever the reason, the decision to abort is almost invariably made within a web of interlocking, competing, and often irreconcilable responsibilities and commitments.

By focusing on the moral quality of reproductive decisions rather than insulating them from understanding, liberals could redirect societal attention toward this web of shared responsibilities and societal failures. We might then begin to recognize that we have a collective responsibility to address the variable causes that result in unwanted pregnancies, from the pervasive acceptance of sexual violence in our culture to our collective refusal to provide meaningful material assistance for the nurturing of children and families. Whatever the fate of Roe, widespread understanding of the moral nature of the abortion decision, the profound sense of responsibility that often accompanies it, and the societal failure to assume responsibility for the causes and effects of unwanted pregnancy, childbirth, and motherhood would strengthen, not weaken, the case for abortion rights and the freedoms those rights ought to protect. Without a Court willing to protect those rights in the face of societal opposition, however, that understanding may be necessary to the liberty's very existence.

Loretta J. Ross & Rickie Solinger

Reproductive Justice: An Introduction

121-22 (2017)

In the decades following *Roe*, mainstream reproductive rights and feminist organizations did not effectively predict or object to the limits of the *Roe* decision, especially the ways its dependence on a negative right did not protect women who needed guaranteed access to information and services, not official neglect. The mainstream liberal women's movement celebrated choice as the defining achievement of modern women. . . . [O]ver time, choice was typically portrayed as the modern woman's personal key to the ownership and control of her own body. . . . But "choice" turned out to be a flimflam mantra more suited to describing a commercial transaction (as in "Italian Beef, the Better Choice") than to providing the foundation for female dignity or the signal condition of modern womanhood for all. *Roe v. Wade* and its legalization of choice had guaranteed nothing to women who could not pay for reproductive options. These women remained dangerously vulnerable. After *Roe*, many poor women of color suffered coerced sterilization, were denied public assistance if they had one "too many" children, and were targeted for other methods of population control. The anti-civil rights, anti-welfare political culture depended, after *Roe*, on the symbol of the hyperfertile woman of color as toxic reproducer, as a female unfit for rights or choices. . . . [T]he major reproductive rights organizations did not devote themselves to repudiating racialized and class-biased attitudes about fertility and legitimate motherhood or promoting strategies for making sure that access to contraception and abortion achieved the status of rights for all.

Rachel Rebouché

Reproducing Rights: The Intersection of Reproductive Justice and Human Rights

7 UC Irvine L. Rev. 579, 591-95 (2017)

WHAT'S WRONG WITH REPRODUCTIVE RIGHTS?

Reproductive justice, as distinguished from reproductive rights, has gained significant momentum. In increasing numbers, U.S. nonprofit groups have dropped "pro-choice" from their materials and incorporated "reproductive justice" into their organizations' names. Reproductive justice "[f]rom its inception" has been "globally conscious," and reproductive justice advocates draw from feminist ideas to support "indigenous movements of women, who are best able to develop solutions that fit their culture and situation."

Most commentators describe the origin of reproductive justice as beginning with the leaders of nonprofit groups advocating for women of color, such as the SisterSong Women of Color Collective. Advocates attended the [1994 International Conference on Population and Development, or ICPD] where they were inspired by the human rights movement and the ICPD's focus on poverty, gender equality, and the empowerment of women. However, they believed that their communities were not represented in the remarks of government delegates. In the United States, mainstream reproductive rights organizations overlooked or undermined the experiences of marginalized populations of women.

Thus, a foundation of reproductive justice is critical race theory, and the movement "focuses on the intersectionality of oppression". . . .

[T]he reproductive justice movement is explicitly critical of rights, though not necessarily *human* rights. . . . Most materials on reproductive justice emphasize that the conventional rhetoric around abortion rights "fits best the situation of relatively privileged women in Western, industrialized nations" because a rights framework "requires that a woman know that she has reproductive rights, that her nation and her community acknowledge those rights, and that she is able to exercise them." A privacy right is only valuable to those who can exercise privacy and autonomy vis-à-vis the state. That is often not possible for those particularly vulnerable to state power, such as women subject to racial discrimination, receiving state assistance, or new to a country.

[R]eproductive justice supports an expansive agenda for reproductive health. . . . Reproductive justice advocates contend that concentrating on abortion law diverts attention from a range of other reproductive experiences. For example, reproductive justice advocates have lobbied for better treatment of incarcerated, pregnant women (such as removing shackles during labor). Reproductive justice initiatives address reproductive issues across the life span, including pre- and post-birth healthcare; the availability of sexual education, contraceptives, and reproductive technologies; and affordable childcare. [R]eproductive justice emphasizes the linkages between present discrimination and the legacies of forcibly controlling the fertility of women of color and low-income women. Reproductive justice activists lament that mainstream reproductive rights organizations have not concentrated on the racial and income disparities that perpetuate racial injustice and continue to plague the delivery of reproductive healthcare. Abortion rights victories, though important, are therefore not sufficient. . . . As Lindsay Wiley writes, "Access to healthcare—not merely as a matter of the 'right to choose' contraception or abortion, but as a matter of the general affordability, availability, and cultural appropriateness of a wide range of health services for women and families—is a priority issue for the movement."[112.] Constitutional litigation can create a reliance on courts, lawmakers, and lawyers. Yet courts may not have the tools to implement remedies for systemic social or structural problems, and they do not make political and policy decisions that affect directly the delivery of health services.

This is not to suggest that the reproductive justice movement has abandoned abortion advocacy. But rather than focusing on litigating privacy rights, reproductive

---

112.. 112. Lindsay F. Wiley, Health Law as Social Justice, 24 Cornell J.L. & Pub. Pol'y 47, 61 (2014).

justice prioritizes community engagement with vulnerable populations of women, and focuses on the experiences of those living under abortion laws. Accordingly, a fourth commitment, related to affordable and accessible healthcare, is the insistence that advocacy must address the various avenues by which women meet their reproductive health needs. This entails, according to writings on reproductive justice, sustained community engagement and research into how law shapes women's health.

Dobbs v. Jackson Women's Health Organization

142 S. Ct. 2228 (2022)

Justice ALITO delivered the opinion of the Court.

Abortion presents a profound moral issue on which Americans hold sharply conflicting views. Some believe fervently that a human person comes into being at conception and that abortion ends an innocent life. Others feel just as strongly that any regulation of abortion invades a woman's right to control her own body and prevents women from achieving full equality. Still others in a third group think that abortion should be allowed under some but not all circumstances, and those within this group hold a variety of views about the particular restrictions that should be imposed.

For the first 185 years after the adoption of the Constitution, each State was permitted to address this issue in accordance with the views of its citizens. Then, in 1973, this Court decided *Roe v. Wade*. Even though the Constitution makes no mention of abortion, the Court held that it confers a broad right to obtain one. It did not claim that American law or the common law had ever recognized such a right, and its survey of history ranged from the constitutionally irrelevant (*e.g.*, its discussion of abortion in antiquity) to the plainly incorrect (*e.g.*, its assertion that abortion was probably never a crime under the common law). After cataloging a wealth of other information having no bearing on the meaning of the Constitution, the opinion concluded with a numbered set of rules much like those that might be found in a statute enacted by a legislature.

Under this scheme, each trimester of pregnancy was regulated differently, but the most critical line was drawn at roughly the end of the second trimester, which, at the time, corresponded to the point at which a fetus was thought to achieve "viability," *i.e.*, the ability to survive outside the womb. Although the Court acknowledged that States had a legitimate interest in protecting "potential life," it found that this interest could not justify any restriction on pre-viability abortions. The Court did not explain the basis for this line, and even abortion supporters have found it hard to defend *Roe*'s reasoning. . . .

At the time of *Roe*, 30 States still prohibited abortion at all stages. In the years prior to that decision, about a third of the States had liberalized their laws, but *Roe* abruptly ended that political process. It imposed the same highly restrictive regime on the entire Nation, and it effectively struck down the abortion laws of every single State. . . .

Eventually, in *Planned Parenthood of Southeastern Pa. v. Casey*, the [controlling joint opinion] concluded that *stare decisis*, which calls for prior decisions to be followed in most instances, required adherence to what it called *Roe*'s "central holding"—that a State may not constitutionally protect fetal life before "viability"—even if that holding was wrong. Anything less, the opinion claimed, would undermine respect for this Court and the rule of law.

Paradoxically, the judgment in *Casey* did a fair amount of overruling. . . . *Casey* threw out *Roe*'s trimester scheme and substituted a new rule of uncertain origin under which States were forbidden to adopt any regulation that imposed an "undue burden" on a woman's right to have an abortion. The decision provided no clear guidance about the difference between a "due" and an "undue" burden. But the three Justices who authored the controlling opinion "call[ed] the contending sides of a national controversy to end their national division" by treating the Court's decision as the final settlement of the question of the constitutional right to abortion.

As has become increasingly apparent in the intervening years, *Casey* did not achieve that goal. . . .

We hold that *Roe* and *Casey* must be overruled. The Constitution makes no reference to abortion, and no such right is implicitly protected by any constitutional provision, including the one on which the defenders of *Roe* and *Casey* now chiefly rely—the Due Process Clause of the Fourteenth Amendment. That provision has been held to guarantee some rights that are not mentioned in the Constitution, but any such right must be "deeply rooted in this Nation's history and tradition" and "implicit in the concept of ordered liberty." *Washington v. Glucksberg* (1997).

The right to abortion does not fall within this category. Until the latter part of the 20th century, such a right was entirely unknown in American law. Indeed, when the Fourteenth Amendment was adopted, three quarters of the States made abortion a crime at all stages of pregnancy. . . . *Roe*'s defenders characterize the abortion right as similar to the rights recognized in past decisions involving matters such as intimate sexual relations, contraception, and marriage, but abortion is fundamentally different, as both *Roe* and *Casey* acknowledged, because it destroys what those decisions called "fetal life" and what the law now before us describes as an "unborn human being."

Stare decisis, the doctrine on which *Casey*'s controlling opinion was based, does not compel unending adherence to *Roe*'s abuse of judicial authority. *Roe* was egregiously wrong from the start. Its reasoning was exceptionally weak, and the decision has had damaging consequences. And far from bringing about a national settlement of the abortion issue, *Roe* and *Casey* have enflamed debate and deepened division.

It is time to heed the Constitution and return the issue of abortion to the people's elected representatives. . . . That is what the Constitution and the rule of law demand.

I

The law at issue in this case, Mississippi's Gestational Age Act contains this central provision: "Except in a medical emergency or in the case of a severe fetal abnormality, a person shall not intentionally or knowingly perform . . . or induce an abortion of an unborn human being if the probable gestational age of the unborn human being has been determined to be greater than fifteen (15) weeks." . . .

Respondents are an abortion clinic, Jackson Women's Health Organization, and one of its doctors. [When respondents sued to block enforcement of this law, the District Court entered summary judgment in their favor, and the Court of Appeals affirmed.]

We granted certiorari to resolve the question whether "all pre-viability prohibitions on elective abortions are unconstitutional." . . .

II

We begin by considering the critical question whether the Constitution, properly understood, confers a right to obtain an abortion. . . . [W]e address that question in three steps. First, we explain the standard that our cases have used in determining whether the Fourteenth Amendment's reference to "liberty" protects a particular right. Second, we examine whether the right at issue in this case is rooted in our Nation's history and tradition and whether it is an essential component of what we have described as "ordered liberty." Finally, we consider whether a right to obtain an abortion is part of a broader entrenched right that is supported by other precedents. . . .

The Constitution makes no express reference to a right to obtain an abortion, and therefore those who claim that it protects such a right must show that the right is somehow implicit in the constitutional text.

Roe, however, was remarkably loose in its treatment of the constitutional text. It held that the abortion right, which is not mentioned in the Constitution, is part of a right to privacy, which is also not mentioned. . . .

Roe expressed the "feel[ing]" that the Fourteenth Amendment was the provision that did the work, but its message seemed to be that the abortion right could be found *somewhere* in the Constitution and that specifying its exact location was not of paramount importance. The *Casey* Court did not defend this unfocused analysis and instead grounded its decision solely on the theory that the right to obtain an abortion is part of the "liberty" protected by the Fourteenth Amendment's Due Process Clause.

We discuss this theory in depth below, but before doing so, we briefly address one additional constitutional provision that some of respondents' *amici* have now offered as yet another potential home for the abortion right: the Fourteenth Amendment's Equal Protection Clause. Neither *Roe* nor *Casey* saw fit to invoke this theory, and it is squarely foreclosed by our precedents, which establish that a State's regulation of abortion is not a sex-based classification and is thus not subject to the "heightened scrutiny" that applies to such classifications. The regulation of a medical procedure that only one sex can undergo does not trigger heightened constitutional scrutiny unless the regulation is a "mere pretex[t] designed to effect an invidious discrimination against members of one sex or the other." *Geduldig v. Aiello* (1974). And as the Court has stated, the "goal of preventing abortion" does not constitute "invidiously discriminatory animus" against women. *Bray v. Alexandria Women's Health Clinic* (1993). Accordingly, laws regulating or prohibiting abortion are not subject to heightened scrutiny. Rather, they are governed by the same standard of review as other health and safety measures. . . .

With this new theory addressed, we turn to *Casey*'s bold assertion that the abortion right is an aspect of the "liberty" protected by the Due Process Clause of the Fourteenth Amendment.

The underlying theory on which this argument rests — that the Fourteenth Amendment's Due Process Clause provides substantive, as well as procedural, protection for "liberty" — has long been controversial. But our decisions have held that the Due Process Clause protects two categories of substantive rights.

The first consists of rights guaranteed by the first eight Amendments. Those Amendments originally applied only to the Federal Government, but this Court has held that the Due Process Clause of the Fourteenth Amendment "incorporates" the great majority of those rights and thus makes them equally applicable to the States. The second category — which is the one in question here — comprises a select list of fundamental rights that are not mentioned anywhere in the Constitution.

In deciding whether a right falls into either of these categories, the Court has long asked whether the right is "deeply rooted in [our] history and tradition" and whether it is essential to our Nation's "scheme of ordered liberty." And in conducting this inquiry, we have engaged in a careful analysis of the history of the right at issue. . . .

Historical inquiries of this nature are essential whenever we are asked to recognize a new component of the "liberty" protected by the Due Process Clause because the term "liberty" alone provides little guidance. "Liberty" is a capacious term. * * * As the Court cautioned in *Glucksberg*, "[w]e must . . . exercise the utmost care whenever we are asked to break new ground in this field, lest the liberty protected by the Due Process Clause be subtly transformed into the policy preferences of the Members of this Court." In interpreting what is meant by the Fourteenth Amendment's reference to "liberty," we must guard against the natural human tendency to confuse what that Amendment protects with our own ardent views about the liberty that Americans should enjoy. . . . When we engage in that inquiry in the present case, the clear answer is that the Fourteenth Amendment does not protect the right to an abortion.

Until the latter part of the 20th century, there was no support in American law for a constitutional right to obtain an abortion. No state constitutional provision had recognized such a right. Until a few years before *Roe* was handed down, no federal or state court had recognized such a right. . . .

Not only was there no support for such a constitutional right until shortly before *Roe*, but abortion had long been a *crime* in every single State. At common law, abortion was criminal in at least some stages of pregnancy and was regarded as unlawful and could have very serious consequences at all stages. American law followed the common law until a wave of statutory restrictions in the 1800s expanded criminal liability for abortions. By the time of the adoption of the Fourteenth Amendment, three-quarters of the States had made abortion a crime at any stage of pregnancy, and the remaining States would soon follow. *Roe* either ignored or misstated this history, and *Casey* declined to reconsider *Roe*'s faulty historical analysis. It is therefore important to set the record straight.

We begin with the common law, under which abortion was a crime at least after "quickening" — *i.e.*, the first felt movement of the fetus in the womb, which usually occurs between the 16th and 18th week of pregnancy.

The "eminent common-law authorities (Blackstone, Coke, Hale, and the like)," *all* describe abortion after quickening as criminal. . . .

Although a pre-quickening abortion was not itself considered homicide, it does not follow that abortion was *permissible* at common law — much less that abortion was a legal *right*. . . . In sum, although common-law authorities differed on the severity of punishment for abortions committed at different points in pregnancy, none endorsed the practice.

In this country, the historical record is similar. The "most important early American edition of Blackstone's Commentaries" reported Blackstone's statement that abortion of a quick child was at least "a heinous misdemeanor." . . . Manuals for justices of the peace printed in the Colonies in the 18th century typically restated the common-law rule on abortion, and some manuals repeated Hale's and Blackstone's statements that anyone who prescribed medication "unlawfully to destroy the child" would be guilty of murder if the woman died. . . . The few cases available from the early colonial period corroborate that abortion was a crime. . . . The original ground for drawing a distinction between pre- and post-quickening abortions is not entirely clear, but some have attributed the rule to the difficulty of proving that a pre-quickening fetus was alive. At that time, there were no scientific methods for detecting pregnancy in its early stages. . . .

[T]he original ground for the quickening rule is of little importance for present purposes because the rule was abandoned in the 19th century. During that period, treatise writers and commentators criticized the quickening distinction as "neither in accordance with the result of medical experience, nor with the principles of the common law." In 1803, the British Parliament made abortion a crime at all stages of pregnancy and authorized the imposition of severe punishment. . . . In this country during the 19th century, the vast majority of the States enacted statutes criminalizing abortion at all stages of pregnancy. By 1868, the year when the Fourteenth Amendment was ratified, three-quarters of the States, 28 out of 37, had enacted statutes making abortion a crime even if it was performed before quickening. Of the nine States that had not yet criminalized abortion at all stages, all but one did so by 1910. . . .

This overwhelming consensus endured until the day *Roe* was decided. At that time, also by the *Roe* Court's own count, a substantial majority — 30 States — still prohibited abortion at all stages except to save the life of the mother. And though *Roe* discerned a "trend toward liberalization" in about "one-third of the States," those States still criminalized some abortions and regulated them more stringently than *Roe* would allow. In short, the "Court's opinion in *Roe* itself convincingly refutes the notion that the abortion liberty is deeply rooted in the history or tradition of our people." The inescapable conclusion is that a right to abortion is not deeply rooted in the Nation's history and traditions. On the contrary, an unbroken tradition of prohibiting abortion on pain of criminal punishment persisted from the earliest days of the common law until 1973. . . .

Instead of seriously pressing the argument that the abortion right itself has deep roots, supporters of *Roe* and *Casey* contend that the abortion right is an integral part of a broader entrenched right. *Roe* termed this a right to privacy and *Casey* described it as the freedom to make "intimate and personal choices" that are "central to personal dignity and autonomy." . . . Ordered liberty sets limits and defines the boundary between competing interests. These attempts to justify abortion through appeals to a broader right to autonomy and to define one's "concept of existence" prove too much. Those criteria, at a high level of generality, could license fundamental rights to illicit drug use, prostitution, and the like. None of these rights has any claim to being deeply rooted in history.

What sharply distinguishes the abortion right from the rights recognized in the cases on which *Roe* and *Casey* rely is something that both those decisions acknowledged: Abortion destroys what those decisions call "potential life" and what the law at issue in this case regards as the life of an "unborn human being." None of the other decisions cited by *Roe* and *Casey* involved the critical moral question posed by abortion. They are therefore inapposite. They do not support the right to obtain an abortion, and by the same token, our conclusion that the Constitution does not confer such a right does not undermine them in any way.

In drawing this critical distinction between the abortion right and other rights, it is not necessary to dispute *Casey*'s claim (which we accept for the sake of argument) that "the specific practices of States at the time of the adoption of the Fourteenth Amendment" do not "mar[k] the outer limits of the substantive sphere of liberty which the Fourteenth Amendment protects." . . . Defenders of *Roe* and *Casey* do not claim that any new scientific learning calls for a different answer to the underlying moral question, but they do contend that changes in society require the recognition of a constitutional right to obtain an abortion. Without the availability of abortion, they maintain, people will be inhibited from exercising their freedom to choose the types of relationships they desire, and women will be unable to compete with men in the workplace and in other endeavors.

Americans who believe that abortion should be restricted press countervailing arguments about modern developments. They note that attitudes about the pregnancy of unmarried women have changed drastically; that federal and state laws ban discrimination on the basis of pregnancy; that leave for pregnancy and childbirth are now guaranteed by law in many cases; that the costs of medical care associated with pregnancy are covered by insurance or government assistance; that States have increasingly adopted "safe haven" laws, which generally allow women to drop off babies anonymously; and that a woman who puts her newborn up for adoption today has little reason to fear that the baby will not find a suitable home. They also claim that many people now have a new appreciation of fetal life and that when prospective parents who want to have a child view a sonogram, they typically have no doubt that what they see is their daughter or son.

Both sides make important policy arguments, but supporters of *Roe* and *Casey* must show that this Court has the authority to weigh those arguments and decide how abortion may be regulated in the States. They have failed to make that showing, and we thus return the power to weigh those arguments to the people and their elected representatives. . . .

The most striking feature of the dissent is the absence of any serious discussion of the legitimacy of the States' interest in protecting fetal life. . . . The dissent has much to say about the effects of pregnancy on women, the burdens of motherhood, and the difficulties faced by poor women. These are important concerns. However, the dissent evinces no similar regard for a State's interest in protecting prenatal life. . . .

Our opinion is not based on any view about if and when prenatal life is entitled to any of the rights enjoyed after birth. The dissent, by contrast, would impose on the people a particular theory about when the rights of personhood begin. According to the dissent, the Constitution *requires* the States to regard a fetus as lacking even the most basic human right — to live — at least until an arbitrary point in a pregnancy has passed. Nothing in the Constitution or in our Nation's legal traditions authorizes the Court to adopt that "'theory of life.'"

III

We next consider whether the doctrine of *stare decisis* counsels continued acceptance of *Roe* and *Casey*. *Stare decisis* plays an important role in our case law, and we have explained that it serves many valuable ends. . . .

We have long recognized, however, that *stare decisis* is "not an inexorable command," and it "is at its weakest when we interpret the Constitution" . . . [because] we place a high value on having the matter "settled right." In addition, when one of our constitutional decisions goes astray, the country is usually stuck with the bad decision unless we correct our own mistake. An erroneous constitutional decision can be fixed by amending the Constitution, but our Constitution is notoriously hard to amend. . . .

In this case, five factors weigh strongly in favor of overruling *Roe* and *Casey*. . . .

The nature of the Court's error. An erroneous interpretation of the Constitution is always important, but some are more damaging than others. The infamous decision in *Plessy v. Ferguson*, was one such decision. . . . It was "egregiously wrong" on the day it was decided, and as the Solicitor General agreed at oral argument, it should have been overruled at the earliest opportunity. *Roe* was also egregiously wrong and deeply damaging. . . . [W]ielding nothing but "raw judicial power," the Court usurped the power to address a question of profound moral and social importance that the Constitution unequivocally leaves for the people. *Casey* described itself as calling both sides of the national controversy to resolve their debate, but in doing so, *Casey* necessarily declared a winning side. Those on the losing side — those who sought to advance the State's interest in fetal life — could no longer seek to persuade their elected representatives to adopt policies consistent with their views. The Court short-circuited the democratic process by closing it to the large number of Americans who dissented in any respect from *Roe*. . . .

The quality of the reasoning. Under our precedents, the quality of the reasoning in a prior case has an important bearing on whether it should be reconsidered. . . . The weaknesses in *Roe*'s reasoning are well-known. Without any grounding in the constitutional text, history, or precedent, it imposed on the entire country a detailed set of rules much like those that one might expect to find in a statute or regulation. . . . This elaborate scheme was the Court's own brainchild. . . .

An even more glaring deficiency was *Roe*'s failure to justify the critical distinction it drew between pre- and post-viability abortions. . . . The most obvious problem with any such argument is that viability is heavily dependent on factors that have nothing to do with the characteristics of a fetus. One is the state of neonatal care at a particular point in time. Due to the development of new equipment and improved practices, the viability line has changed over the years. . . . Viability also depends on the "quality of the available medical facilities." . . . [V]iability is not really a hard-and-fast line. A physician determining a particular fetus's odds of surviving outside the womb must consider "a number of variables," including "gestational age," "fetal weight," a woman's "general health and nutrition," the "quality of the available medical facilities," and other factors. . . .

The *Casey* plurality, while reaffirming *Roe*'s central holding, pointedly refrained from endorsing most of its reasoning. It revised the textual basis for the abortion right, silently abandoned *Roe*'s erroneous historical narrative, and jettisoned the trimester framework. But it replaced that scheme with an arbitrary "undue burden" test and relied on an exceptional version of *stare decisis* that, as explained below, this Court had never before applied and has never invoked since. . . .

Workability. Our precedents counsel that another important consideration in deciding whether a precedent should be overruled is whether the rule it imposes is workable — that is, whether it can be understood and applied in a consistent and predictable manner. *Casey*'s "undue burden" test has scored poorly on the workability scale. . . . [This test calls] on courts to examine a law's effect on women, but a regulation may have a very different impact on different women for a variety of reasons, including their places of residence, financial resources, family situations, work and personal obligations, knowledge about fetal development and abortion, psychological and emotional disposition and condition, and the firmness of their desire to obtain abortions. In order to determine whether a regulation presents a substantial obstacle to women, a court needs to know which set of women it should have in mind and how many of the women in this set must find that an obstacle is "substantial." . . .

Effect on other areas of law. *Roe* and *Casey* have led to the distortion of many important but unrelated legal doctrines, and that effect provides further support for overruling those decisions. . . . The Court's abortion cases have diluted the strict standard for facial constitutional challenges. They have ignored the Court's third-party standing doctrine. They have disregarded standard *res judicata* principles. They have flouted the ordinary rules on the severability of unconstitutional provisions, as well as the rule that statutes should be read where possible to avoid unconstitutionality. And they have distorted First Amendment doctrines. . . .

Reliance interests. We last consider whether overruling *Roe* and *Casey* will upend substantial reliance interests. Traditional reliance interests arise "where advance planning of great precision is most obviously a necessity." In *Casey*, the controlling opinion conceded that those traditional reliance interests were not implicated because getting an abortion is generally "unplanned activity," and "reproductive planning could take virtually immediate account of any sudden restoration of state authority to ban abortions." For these reasons, we agree with the *Casey* plurality that conventional, concrete reliance interests are not present here. . . . [T]he controlling opinion in *Casey* perceived a more intangible form of reliance. It wrote that "people [had] organized intimate relationships and made choices that define their views of themselves and their places in society . . . in reliance on the availability of abortion in the event that contraception should fail" and that "[t]he ability of women to participate equally in the economic and social life of the Nation has been facilitated by their ability to control their reproductive lives." But this Court is ill-equipped to assess "generalized assertions about the national psyche." *Casey*'s notion of reliance thus finds little support in our cases, which instead emphasize very concrete reliance interests, like those that develop in "cases involving property and contract rights." . . .

Our decision returns the issue of abortion to those legislative bodies, and it allows women on both sides of the abortion issue to seek to affect the legislative process by influencing public opinion, lobbying legislators, voting, and running for office. Women are not without electoral or political power. It is noteworthy that the percentage of women who register to vote and cast ballots is consistently higher than the percentage of men who do so. In the last election in November 2020, women, who make up around 51.5 percent of the population of Mississippi, constituted 55.5 percent of the voters who cast ballots. . . .

And to ensure that our decision is not misunderstood or mischaracterized, we emphasize that our decision concerns the constitutional right to abortion and no other right. Nothing in this opinion should be understood to cast doubt on precedents that do not concern abortion. . . .

Neither [*Roe* nor *Casey*] has ended debate over the issue of a constitutional right to obtain an abortion. . . . We do not pretend to know how our political system or society will respond to today's decision overruling *Roe* and *Casey*. And even if we could foresee what will happen, we would have no authority to let that knowledge influence our decision. We can only do our job, which is to interpret the law, apply longstanding principles of *stare decisis*, and decide this case accordingly. We therefore hold that the Constitution does not confer a right to abortion. *Roe* and *Casey* must be overruled, and the authority to regulate abortion must be returned to the people and their elected representatives. . . .

VI

We must now decide what standard will govern if state abortion regulations undergo constitutional challenge and whether the law before us satisfies the appropriate standard. Under our precedents, rational-basis review is the appropriate standard for such challenges. . . . It follows that the States may regulate abortion for legitimate reasons, and when such regulations are challenged under the Constitution, courts cannot "substitute their social and economic beliefs for the judgment of legislative bodies." A law regulating abortion, like other health and welfare laws, is entitled to a "strong presumption of validity." It must be sustained if there is a rational basis on which the legislature could have thought that it would serve legitimate state interests. These legitimate interests include respect for and preservation of prenatal life at all stages of development; the protection of maternal health and safety; the elimination of particularly gruesome or barbaric medical procedures; the preservation of the integrity of the medical profession; the mitigation of fetal pain; and the prevention of discrimination on the basis of race, sex, or disability.

These legitimate interests justify Mississippi's Gestational Age Act. . . .

Justice THOMAS, concurring.

I join the opinion of the Court because it correctly holds that there is no constitutional right to abortion. . . .

I write separately to emphasize a . . . more fundamental reason why there is no abortion guarantee lurking in the Due Process Clause. . . . [T[he Due Process

Clause at most guarantees *process*. It does not, as the Court's substantive due process cases suppose, "forbi[d] the government to infringe certain 'fundamental' liberty interests *at all*, no matter what process is provided." . . .

The resolution of this case is thus straightforward. Because the Due Process Clause does not secure *any* substantive rights, it does not secure a right to abortion. . . . [I]n future cases, we should reconsider all of this Court's substantive due process precedents, including *Griswold*, *Lawrence*, and *Obergefell*. Because any substantive due process decision is "demonstrably erroneous," we have a duty to "correct the error" established in those precedents. After overruling these demonstrably erroneous decisions, the question would remain whether other constitutional provisions guarantee the myriad rights that our substantive due process cases have generated. . . . For example, we could consider whether any of the rights announced in this Court's substantive due process cases are "privileges or immunities of citizens of the United States" protected by the Fourteenth Amendment. . . .

"[S]ubstantive due process exalts judges at the expense of the People from whom they derive their authority." Nowhere is this exaltation of judicial policymaking clearer than this Court's abortion jurisprudence. . . . That 50 years have passed since *Roe* and abortion advocates still cannot coherently articulate the right (or rights) at stake proves the obvious: The right to abortion is ultimately a policy goal in desperate search of a constitutional justification.

[S]ubstantive due process distorts other areas of constitutional law. For example, once this Court identifies a "fundamental" right for one class of individuals, it invokes the Equal Protection Clause to demand exacting scrutiny of statutes that deny the right to others. . . . Substantive due process is the core inspiration for many of the Court's constitutionally unmoored policy judgments.

[S]ubstantive due process is often wielded to "disastrous ends." For instance, in *Dred Scott v. Sandford* (1857), the Court invoked a species of substantive due process to announce that Congress was powerless to emancipate slaves brought into the federal territories. . . . Now today, the Court rightly overrules *Roe* and *Casey* — two of this Court's "most notoriously incorrect" substantive due process decisions — after more than 63 million abortions have been performed. The harm caused by this Court's forays into substantive due process remains immeasurable. . . .

Justice KAVANAUGH, concurring. . . .

On the question of abortion, the Constitution is . . . neither pro-life nor pro-choice. The Constitution is neutral and leaves the issue for the people and their elected representatives to resolve through the democratic process in the States or Congress — like the numerous other difficult questions of American social and economic policy that the Constitution does not address. . . .

Instead of adhering to the Constitution's neutrality, the Court in *Roe* took sides on the issue and unilaterally decreed that abortion was legal throughout the United States up to the point of viability (about 24 weeks of pregnancy). The Court's decision today properly returns the Court to a position of neutrality and restores the people's authority to address the issue of abortion through the processes of democratic self-government established by the Constitution. . . .

To be clear, then, the Court's decision today *does not outlaw* abortion throughout the United States. On the contrary, the Court's decision properly leaves the question of abortion for the people and their elected representatives in the democratic process. Through that democratic process, the people and their representatives may decide to allow or limit abortion. . . .

In arguing for a *constitutional* right to abortion that would override the people's choices in the democratic process, the plaintiff Jackson Women's Health Organization and its *amici* emphasize that the Constitution does not freeze the American people's rights as of 1791 or 1868. I fully agree. To begin, I agree that constitutional rights apply to situations that were unforeseen in 1791 or 1868 — such as applying the First Amendment to the Internet or the Fourth Amendment to cars. Moreover, the Constitution authorizes the creation of new rights — state and federal, statutory and constitutional. But when it comes to creating new rights, the Constitution directs the people to the various processes of democratic self-government contemplated by the Constitution — state legislation, state constitutional amendments, federal legislation, and federal constitutional amendments. The Constitution does not grant the nine unelected Members of this Court the unilateral authority to rewrite the Constitution to create new rights and liberties based on our own moral or policy views. . . .

Chief Justice ROBERTS, concurring in the judgment. . . .

I would take a more measured course. I agree with the Court that the viability line established by *Roe* and *Casey* should be discarded under a straightforward *stare decisis* analysis. That line never made any sense. Our abortion precedents describe the right at issue as a woman's right to choose to terminate her pregnancy. That right should therefore extend far enough to ensure a reasonable opportunity to choose, but need not extend any further — certainly not all the way to viability. Mississippi's law allows a woman three months to obtain an abortion, well beyond the point at which it is considered "late" to discover a pregnancy. I see no sound basis for questioning the adequacy of that opportunity.

But that is all I would say, out of adherence to a simple yet fundamental principle of judicial restraint: If it is not necessary to decide more to dispose of a case, then it is necessary *not* to decide more. . . .

This Court's jurisprudence since *Casey*, moreover, has "eroded" the "underpinnings" of the viability line, such as they were. The viability line is a relic of a time when we recognized only two state interests warranting regulation of abortion: maternal health and protection of "potential life." That changed with *Gonzales v. Carhart* (2007). There, we recognized a broader array of interests, such as drawing "a bright line that clearly distinguishes abortion and infanticide," maintaining societal ethics, and preserving the integrity of the medical profession. The viability line has nothing to do with advancing such permissible goals. . . . It is indeed "telling that other countries almost uniformly eschew" a viability line. Only a handful of countries, among them China and North Korea, permit elective abortions after twenty weeks; the rest have coalesced around a 12-week line. The Court rightly rejects the arbitrary viability rule today. . . .

Our established practice is instead not to "formulate a rule of constitutional law broader than is required by the precise facts to which it is to be applied."

Overruling the subsidiary rule is sufficient to resolve this case in Mississippi's favor. The law at issue allows abortions up through fifteen weeks, providing an adequate opportunity to exercise the right *Roe* protects. By the time a pregnant woman has reached that point, her pregnancy is well into the second trimester. Pregnancy tests are now inexpensive and accurate, and a woman ordinarily discovers she is pregnant by six weeks of gestation. Given all this, it is no surprise that the vast majority of abortions happen in the first trimester. Presumably most of the remainder would also take place earlier if later abortions were not a legal option. Ample evidence thus suggests that a 15-week ban provides sufficient time, absent rare circumstances, for a woman "to decide for herself " whether to terminate her pregnancy. . . .

Both the Court's opinion and the dissent display a relentless freedom from doubt on the legal issue that I cannot share. I am not sure, for example, that a ban on terminating a pregnancy from the moment of conception must be treated the same under the Constitution as a ban after fifteen weeks. . . . I would decide the question we granted review to answer — whether the previously recognized abortion right bars all abortion restrictions prior to viability, such that a ban on abortions after fifteen weeks of pregnancy is necessarily unlawful. The answer to that question is no, and there is no need to go further to decide this case. I therefore concur only in the judgment.

Justice BREYER, Justice SOTOMAYOR, and Justice KAGAN, dissenting.

For half a century, *Roe v. Wade* and *Planned Parenthood of Southeastern Pa. v. Casey* have protected the liberty and equality of women. . . . Respecting a woman as an autonomous being, and granting her full equality, meant giving her substantial choice over this most personal and most consequential of all life decisions.

Roe and *Casey* . . . recognized that "the State has legitimate interests from the outset of the pregnancy in protecting" the "life of the fetus that may become a child." So the Court struck a balance, as it often does when values and goals compete. It held that the State could prohibit abortions after fetal viability, so long as the ban contained exceptions to safeguard a woman's life or health. It held that even before viability, the State could regulate the abortion procedure in multiple and meaningful ways. But until the viability line was crossed, the Court held, a State could not impose a "substantial obstacle" on a woman's "right to elect the procedure" as she (not the government) thought proper, in light of all the circumstances and complexities of her own life.

Today, the Court discards that balance. It says that from the very moment of fertilization, a woman has no rights to speak of. A State can force her to bring a pregnancy to term, even at the steepest personal and familial costs. An abortion restriction, the majority holds, is permissible whenever rational, the lowest level of scrutiny known to the law. And because, as the Court has often stated, protecting fetal life is rational, States will feel free to enact all manner of restrictions. The Mississippi law at issue here bars abortions after the 15th week of pregnancy. Under the majority's ruling, though, another State's law could do so after ten weeks, or five or three or one — or, again, from the moment of fertilization. States have already passed such laws, in anticipation of today's ruling. More will follow. Some States have enacted laws extending to all forms of abortion procedure, including taking medication in one's own home. They have passed laws without any exceptions for when the woman is the victim of rape or incest. Under those laws, a woman will have to bear her rapist's child or a young girl her father's — no matter if doing so will destroy her life. So too, after today's ruling, some States may compel women to carry to term a fetus with severe physical anomalies — for example, one afflicted with Tay-Sachs disease, sure to die within a few years of birth. States may even argue that a prohibition on abortion need make no provision for protecting a woman from risk of death or physical harm. Across a vast array of circumstances, a State will be able to impose its moral choice on a woman and coerce her to give birth to a child.

Enforcement of all these draconian restrictions will also be left largely to the States' devices. A State can of course impose criminal penalties on abortion providers, including lengthy prison sentences. But some States will not stop there. Perhaps, in the wake of today's decision, a state law will criminalize the woman's conduct too, incarcerating or fining her for daring to seek or obtain an abortion. And as Texas has recently shown, a State can turn neighbor against neighbor, enlisting fellow citizens in the effort to root out anyone who tries to get an abortion, or to assist another in doing so.

The majority tries to hide the geographically expansive effects of its holding. Today's decision, the majority says, permits "each State" to address abortion as it pleases. That is cold comfort, of course, for the poor woman who cannot get the money to fly to a distant State for a procedure. Above all others, women lacking financial resources will suffer from today's decision. In any event, interstate restrictions will also soon be in the offing. After this decision, some States may block women from traveling out of State to obtain abortions, or even from receiving abortion medications from out of State. Some may criminalize efforts, including the provision of information or funding, to help women gain access to other States' abortion services. Most threatening of all, no language in today's decision stops the Federal Government from prohibiting abortions nationwide, once again from the moment of conception and without exceptions for rape or incest. If that happens, "the views of [an individual State's] citizens" will not matter. The challenge for a woman will be to finance a trip not to "New York [or] California" but to Toronto.

Whatever the exact scope of the coming laws, one result of today's decision is certain: the curtailment of women's rights, and of their status as free and equal citizens. Yesterday, the Constitution guaranteed that a woman confronted with an unplanned pregnancy could (within reasonable limits) make her own decision about whether to bear a child, with all the life-transforming consequences that act involves. And in thus safeguarding each woman's reproductive freedom, [as the Court noted in *Casey*,] the Constitution also protected "[t]he ability of women to participate equally in [this Nation's] economic and social life." But no longer. As of today, this Court holds, a State can always force a woman to give birth, prohibiting even the earliest abortions. A State can thus transform what, when freely undertaken, is a wonder into what, when forced, may be a nightmare. Some women, especially women of means, will find ways around the State's assertion of power. Others — those without money or childcare or the ability to take time off from work — will not be so fortunate. Maybe they will try an unsafe method of abortion, and come to physical harm, or even die. Maybe they will undergo pregnancy and have a child, but at significant personal or familial cost. At the least, they will incur the cost of losing control of their lives. The Constitution will, today's majority holds, provide no shield, despite its guarantees of liberty and equality for all.

One piece of evidence on that score seems especially salient: The majority's cavalier approach to overturning this Court's precedents. . . . The majority has no good reason for the upheaval in law and society it sets off. *Roe* and *Casey* have been the law of the land for decades, shaping women's expectations of their choices when an unplanned pregnancy occurs. Women have relied on the availability of abortion both in structuring their relationships and in planning their lives. The legal framework *Roe* and *Casey* developed to balance the competing interests in this sphere has proved workable in courts across the country. No recent developments, in either law or fact, have eroded or cast doubt on those precedents. Nothing, in short, has changed. Indeed, the Court in *Casey* already found all of that to be true. *Casey* is a precedent about precedent. It reviewed the same arguments made here in support of overruling *Roe*, and it found that doing so was not warranted. The Court reverses course today for one reason and one reason only: because the composition of this Court has changed. *Stare decisis*, this Court has often said, "contributes to the actual and perceived integrity of the judicial process" by ensuring that decisions are "founded in the law rather than in the proclivities of individuals." Today, the proclivities of individuals rule. The Court departs from its obligation to faithfully and impartially apply the law. We dissent. . . .

Roe and *Casey* were from the beginning, and are even more now, embedded in core constitutional concepts of individual freedom, and of the equal rights of citizens to decide on the shape of their lives. Those legal concepts, one might even say, have gone far toward defining what it means to be an American. For in this Nation, we do not believe that a government controlling all private choices is compatible with a free people. So we do not (as the majority insists today) place everything within "the reach of majorities and [government] officials." We believe in a Constitution that puts some issues off limits to majority rule. Even in the face of public opposition, we uphold the right of individuals — yes, including women — to make their own choices and chart their own futures. Or at least, we did once.

Some half-century ago, *Roe* struck down a state law making it a crime to perform an abortion unless its purpose was to save a woman's life. . . . The Court explained that a long line of precedents, "founded in the Fourteenth Amendment's concept of personal liberty," protected individual decisionmaking related to "marriage, procreation, contraception, family relationships, and child rearing and education." For the same reasons, the Court held, the Constitution must protect "a woman's decision whether or not to terminate her pregnancy." The Court recognized the myriad ways bearing a child can alter the "life and future" of a woman and other members of her family. A State could not, "by adopting one theory of life," override all "rights of the pregnant woman." At the same time, though, the Court recognized "valid interest[s]" of the State "in regulating the abortion decision." The Court noted in particular "important interests" in "protecting potential life," "maintaining medical standards," and "safeguarding [the] health" of the woman. . . . The Court therefore struck a balance, turning on the stage of the pregnancy at which the abortion would occur. . . .

Then, in *Casey*, the Court considered the matter anew, and again upheld *Roe*'s core precepts. . . .

Central to that conclusion was a full-throated restatement of a woman's right to choose. . . . So too, *Casey* reasoned, the liberty clause protects the decision of a woman confronting an unplanned pregnancy. Her decision about abortion was central, in the same way, to her capacity to chart her life's course. . . .

We make one initial point about this analysis in light of the majority's insistence that *Roe* and *Casey*, and we in defending them, are dismissive of a "State's interest in protecting prenatal life." Nothing could get those decisions more wrong. . . . The strength of those state interests is exactly why the Court allowed greater restrictions on the abortion right than on other rights deriving from the Fourteenth Amendment. But what *Roe* and *Casey* also recognized — which today's majority does not — is that a woman's freedom and equality are likewise involved. That fact — the presence of countervailing interests — is what made the abortion question hard, and what necessitated balancing. . . .

The majority makes this change based on a single question: Did the reproductive right recognized in *Roe* and *Casey* exist in "1868, the year when the Fourteenth Amendment was ratified"? . . . The majority's core legal postulate, then, is that we in the 21st century must read the Fourteenth Amendment just as its ratifiers did. . . . Or said more particularly: If those people did not understand reproductive rights as part of the guarantee of liberty conferred in the Fourteenth Amendment, then those rights do not exist. . . .

Those responsible for the original Constitution, including the Fourteenth Amendment, did not perceive women as equals, and did not recognize women's rights. When the majority says that we must read our foundational charter as viewed at the time of ratification (except that we may also check it against the Dark Ages), it consigns women to second-class citizenship. . . . A woman's place in society had changed, and constitutional law had changed along with it. The relegation of women to inferior status in either the public sphere or the family was "no longer consistent with our understanding" of the Constitution. Now, "[t]he Constitution protects all individuals, male or female," from "the abuse of governmental power" or "unjustified state interference." So how is it that, as *Casey* said, our Constitution, read now, grants rights to women, though it did not in 1868? . . . The answer is that this Court has rejected the majority's pinched view of how to read our Constitution. [I]n the words of the great Chief Justice John Marshall, our Constitution is "intended to endure for ages to come," and must adapt itself to a future "seen dimly," if at all. That is indeed why our Constitution is written as it is. The Framers . . . understood that the world changes. So they did not define rights by reference to the specific practices existing at the time. Instead, the Framers defined rights in general terms, to permit future evolution in their scope and meaning. And over the course of our history, this Court has taken up the Framers' invitation. It has kept true to the Framers' principles by applying them in new ways, responsive to new societal understandings and conditions.

Nowhere has that approach been more prevalent than in construing the majestic but open-ended words of the Fourteenth Amendment — the guarantees of "liberty" and "equality" for all. And nowhere has that approach produced prouder moments, for this country and the Court. . . . The Fourteenth Amendment's ratifiers did not think it gave black and white people a right to marry each other. To the contrary, contemporaneous practice deemed that act quite as unprotected as abortion. Yet the Court in *Loving v. Virginia* (1967), read the Fourteenth Amendment to embrace the Lovings' union. If, *Obergefell* explained, "rights were defined by who exercised them in the past, then received practices could serve as their own continued justification" — even when they conflict with "liberty" and "equality" as later and more broadly understood. The Constitution does not freeze for all time the original view of what those rights guarantee, or how they apply. . . .

It was settled at the time of *Roe*, settled at the time of *Casey*, and settled yesterday that the Constitution places limits on a State's power to assert control over an individual's body and most personal decisionmaking. A multitude of decisions supporting that principle led to *Roe*'s recognition and *Casey*'s reaffirmation of the right to choose; and *Roe* and *Casey* in turn supported additional protections for intimate and familial relations. The majority has embarrassingly little to say about those precedents. It (literally) rattles them off in a single paragraph; and it implies that they have nothing to do with each other, or with the right to terminate an early pregnancy. But that is flat wrong. The Court's precedents about bodily autonomy, sexual and familial relations, and procreation are all interwoven — all part of the fabric of our constitutional law, and because that is so, of our lives. Especially women's lives, where they safeguard a right to self-determination.

And eliminating that right, we need to say before further describing our precedents, is not taking a "neutral" position, as Justice Kavanaugh tries to argue. His idea is that neutrality lies in giving the abortion issue to the States, where some can go one way and some another. But would he say that the Court is being "scrupulously neutral" if it allowed New York and California to ban all the guns they want? [W]hen it comes to rights, the Court does not act "neutrally" when it leaves everything up to the States. Rather, the Court acts neutrally when it protects the right against all comers. And to apply that point to the case here: When the Court decimates a right women have held for 50 years, the Court is not being "scrupulously neutral." It is instead taking sides: against women who wish to exercise the right, and for States (like Mississippi) that want to bar them from doing so. Justice Kavanaugh cannot obscure that point by appropriating the rhetoric of even-handedness. His position just is what it is: A brook-no-compromise refusal to recognize a woman's right to choose, from the first day of a pregnancy. And that position, as we will now show, cannot be squared with this Court's longstanding view that women indeed have rights (whatever the state of the world in 1868) to make the most personal and consequential decisions about their bodies and their lives. . . .

Consider first, then, the line of this Court's cases protecting "bodily integrity." "No right," in this Court's time-honored view, "is held more sacred, or is more carefully guarded," than "the right of every individual to the possession and control of his own person." *Casey* recognized the "doctrinal affinity" between those precedents and *Roe*. And that doctrinal affinity is born of a factual likeness. There are few greater incursions on a body than forcing a woman to complete a pregnancy and give birth. For every woman, those experiences involve all manner of physical changes, medical treatments (including the possibility of a cesarean section), and medical risk. Just as one example, an American woman is 14 times more likely to die by carrying a pregnancy to term than by having an abortion. . . .

So too, *Roe* and *Casey* fit neatly into a long line of decisions protecting from government intrusion a wealth of private choices about family matters, child rearing, intimate relationships, and procreation. Those cases safeguard particular choices about whom to marry; whom to have sex with; what family members to live with; how to raise children — and crucially, whether and when to have children. In varied cases, the Court explained that those choices — "the most intimate and personal" a person can make — reflect fundamental aspects of personal identity; they define the very "attributes of personhood." And they inevitably shape the nature and future course of a person's life (and often the lives of those closest to her). So, the Court held, those choices belong to the individual, and not the government. That is the essence of what liberty requires.

And liberty may require it, this Court has repeatedly said, even when those living in 1868 would not have recognized the claim — because they would not have seen the person making it as a full-fledged member of the community. Throughout our history, the sphere of protected liberty has expanded, bringing in individuals formerly excluded. In that way, the constitutional values of liberty and equality go hand in hand; they do not inhabit the hermetically sealed containers the majority portrays. . . . *Casey* similarly recognized the need to extend the constitutional sphere of liberty to a previously excluded group. The Court then understood, as the majority today does not, that the men who ratified the Fourteenth Amendment and wrote the state laws of the time did not view women as full and equal citizens. A woman then, *Casey* wrote, "had no legal existence separate from her husband." Women were seen only "as the center of home and family life," without "full and independent legal status under the Constitution." But that could not be true any longer: The State could not now insist on the historically dominant "vision of the woman's role." And equal citizenship, *Casey* realized, was inescapably connected to reproductive rights. "The ability of women to participate equally" in the "life of the Nation" — in all its economic, social, political, and legal aspects — "has been facilitated by their ability to control their reproductive lives." Without the ability to decide whether and when to have children, women could not — in the way men took for granted — determine how they would live their lives, and how they would contribute to the society around them. . . .

Faced with all these connections between *Roe/Casey* and judicial decisions recognizing other constitutional rights, the majority tells everyone not to worry. It can (so it says) neatly extract the right to choose from the constitutional edifice without affecting any associated rights . . . The first problem with the majority's account comes from Justice Thomas's concurrence — which makes clear he is not with the program. . . . According to the majority, no liberty interest is present — because (and only because) the law offered no protection to the woman's choice in the 19th century. But here is the rub. The law also did not then (and would not for ages) protect a wealth of other things. It did not protect the rights recognized in *Lawrence* and *Obergefell* to same-sex intimacy and marriage. It did not protect the right recognized in *Loving* to marry across racial lines. It did not protect the right recognized in *Griswold* to contraceptive use. For that matter, it did not protect the right recognized in *Skinner v. Oklahoma* (1942), not to be sterilized without consent. So if the majority is right in its legal analysis, all those decisions were wrong, and all those matters properly belong to the States too — whatever the particular state interests involved. . . .

[T]oday's decision, taken on its own, is catastrophic enough. As a matter of constitutional method, the majority's commitment to replicate in 2022 every view about the meaning of liberty held in 1868 has precious little to recommend it. Our law in this constitutional sphere, as in most, has for decades upon decades proceeded differently. It has considered fundamental constitutional principles, the whole course of the Nation's history and traditions, and the step-by-step evolution of the Court's precedents. It is disciplined but not static. It relies on accumulated judgments, not just the sentiments of one long-ago generation of men (who themselves believed, and drafted the Constitution to reflect, that the world progresses). And by doing so, it includes those excluded from that olden conversation, rather than perpetuating its bounds.

As a matter of constitutional substance, the majority's opinion has all the flaws its method would suggest. Because laws in 1868 deprived women of any control over their bodies, the majority approves States doing so today. Because those laws prevented women from charting the course of their own lives, the majority says States can do the same again. Because in 1868, the government could tell a pregnant woman — even in the first days of her pregnancy — that she could do nothing but bear a child, it can once more impose that command. Today's decision strips women of agency over what even the majority agrees is a contested and contestable moral issue. It forces her to carry out the State's will, whatever the circumstances and whatever the harm it will wreak on her and her family. In the Fourteenth Amendment's terms, it takes away her liberty. Even before we get to *stare decisis*, we dissent.

By overruling *Roe, Casey,* and more than 20 cases reaffirming or applying the constitutional right to abortion, the majority abandons *stare decisis*, a principle central to the rule of law. . . . The majority today lists some 30 of our cases as overruling precedent, and argues that they support overruling *Roe* and *Casey*. But none does. . . . The Court found, for example, (1) a change in legal doctrine that undermined or made obsolete the earlier decision; (2) a factual change that had the same effect; or (3) an absence of reliance because the earlier decision was less than a decade old. (The majority is wrong when it says that we insist on a test of changed law or fact alone, although that is present in most of the cases. None of those factors apply here: Nothing — and in particular, no significant legal or factual change — supports overturning a half-century of settled law giving women control over their reproductive lives. First, for all the reasons we have given, *Roe* and *Casey* were correct. . . . However divisive, a right is not at the people's mercy. . . .

Contrary to the majority's view, there is nothing unworkable about *Casey*'s "undue burden" standard. . . . General standards, like the undue burden standard, are ubiquitous in the law, and particularly in constitutional adjudication. . . . Of course, it has provoked some disagreement among judges. *Casey* knew it would: That much "is to be expected in the application of any legal standard which must accommodate life's complexity." . . . As for lower courts, there is now a one-year-old, one-to-one Circuit split about how the undue burden standard applies to state laws that ban abortions for certain reasons, like fetal abnormality. . . . To borrow an old saying that might apply here: Not one or even a couple of swallows can make the majority's summer.

Anyone concerned about workability should consider the majority's substitute standard. . . . Must a state law allow abortions when necessary to protect a woman's life and health? And if so, exactly when? How much risk to a woman's life can a State force her to incur, before the Fourteenth Amendment's protection of life kicks in? Suppose a patient with pulmonary hypertension has a 30-to-50 percent risk of dying with ongoing pregnancy; is that enough? And short of death, how much illness or injury can the State require her to accept, consistent with the Amendment's protection of liberty and equality? Further, the Court may face questions about the application of abortion regulations to medical care most people view as quite different from abortion. What about the morning-after pill? IUDs? In vitro fertilization? And how about the use of dilation and evacuation or medication for miscarriage management?

Finally, the majority's ruling today invites a host of questions about interstate conflicts. Can a State bar women from traveling to another State to obtain an abortion? Can a State prohibit advertising out-of-state abortions or helping women get to out-of-state providers? Can a State interfere with the mailing of drugs used for medication abortions? The Constitution protects travel and speech and interstate commerce, so today's ruling will give rise to a host of new constitutional questions. Far from removing the Court from the abortion issue, the majority puts the Court at the center of the coming "interjurisdictional abortion wars." In short, the majority does not save judges from unwieldy tests or extricate them from the sphere of controversy. To the contrary, it discards a known, workable, and predictable standard in favor of something novel and probably far more complicated. It forces the Court to wade further into hotly contested issues, including moral and philosophical ones, that the majority criticizes *Roe* and *Casey* for addressing. . . .

Subsequent legal developments have only reinforced *Roe* and *Casey*. . . .

Moreover, no subsequent factual developments have undermined *Roe* and *Casey*. Women continue to experience unplanned pregnancies and unexpected developments in pregnancies. Pregnancies continue to have enormous physical, social, and economic consequences. Even an uncomplicated pregnancy imposes significant strain on the body, unavoidably involving significant physiological change and excruciating pain. For some women, pregnancy and childbirth can mean life-altering physical ailments or even death. Today, as noted earlier, the risks of carrying a pregnancy to term dwarf those of having an abortion. Experts estimate that a ban on abortions increases maternal mortality by 21 percent, with white women facing a 13 percent increase in maternal mortality while black women face a 33 percent increase. Pregnancy and childbirth may also impose large-scale financial costs. The majority briefly refers to arguments about changes in laws relating to healthcare coverage, pregnancy discrimination, and family leave. Many women, however, still do not have adequate healthcare coverage before and after pregnancy; and, even when insurance coverage is available, healthcare services may be far away. Women also continue to face pregnancy discrimination that interferes with their ability to earn a living. Paid family leave remains inaccessible to many who need it most. . . .

Mississippi's own record illustrates how little facts on the ground have changed since *Roe* and *Casey*, notwithstanding the majority's supposed "modern developments." Sixty-two percent of pregnancies in Mississippi are unplanned, yet

Mississippi does not require insurance to cover contraceptives and prohibits educators from demonstrating proper contraceptive use. The State neither bans pregnancy discrimination nor requires provision of paid parental leave. . . . The only notable change we can see since *Roe* and *Casey* cuts in favor of adhering to precedent: It is that American abortion law has become more and more aligned with other nations. . . .

Roe and *Casey* continue to reflect, not diverge from, broad trends in American society. It is, of course, true that many Americans, including many women, opposed those decisions when issued and do so now as well. Yet the fact remains: *Roe* and *Casey* were the product of a profound and ongoing change in women's roles in the latter part of the 20th century. Only a dozen years before *Roe*, the Court described women as "the center of home and family life," with "special responsibilities" that precluded their full legal status under the Constitution. By 1973, when the Court decided *Roe*, fundamental social change was underway regarding the place of women — and the law had begun to follow. By 1992, when the Court decided *Casey*, the traditional view of a woman's role as only a wife and mother was "no longer consistent with our understanding of the family, the individual, or the Constitution." Under that charter, *Casey* understood, women must take their place as full and equal citizens. And for that to happen, women must have control over their reproductive decisions. Nothing since *Casey* — no changed law, no changed fact — has undermined that promise. . . .

The reasons for retaining *Roe* and *Casey* gain further strength from the overwhelming reliance interests those decisions have created. The Court adheres to precedent not just for institutional reasons, but because it recognizes that stability in the law is "an essential thread in the mantle of protection that the law affords the individual." . . . *Casey* understood that to deny individuals' reliance on *Roe* was to "refuse to face the fact[s]." Today the majority refuses to face the facts. "The most striking feature of the [majority] is the absence of any serious discussion" of how its ruling will affect women. By characterizing *Casey*'s reliance arguments as "generalized assertions about the national psyche," it reveals how little it knows or cares about women's lives or about the suffering its decision will cause.

In *Casey*, the Court observed that for two decades individuals "have organized intimate relationships and made" significant life choices "in reliance on the availability of abortion in the event that contraception should fail." Over another 30 years, that reliance has solidified. For half a century now, in *Casey*'s words, "[t]he ability of women to participate equally in the economic and social life of the Nation has been facilitated by their ability to control their reproductive lives." Indeed, all women now of childbearing age have grown up expecting that they would be able to avail themselves of *Roe*'s and *Casey*'s protections.

The disruption of overturning *Roe* and *Casey* will therefore be profound. Abortion is a common medical procedure and a familiar experience in women's lives. About 18 percent of pregnancies in this country end in abortion, and about one quarter of American women will have an abortion before the age of 45. Those numbers reflect the predictable and life-changing effects of carrying a pregnancy, giving birth, and becoming a parent. As *Casey* understood, people today rely on their ability to control and time pregnancies when making countless life decisions: where to live, whether and how to invest in education or careers, how to allocate financial resources, and how to approach intimate and family relationships. Women may count on abortion access for when contraception fails. They may count on abortion access for when contraception cannot be used, for example, if they were raped. They may count on abortion for when something changes in the midst of a pregnancy, whether it involves family or financial circumstances, unanticipated medical complications, or heartbreaking fetal diagnoses. Taking away the right to abortion, as the majority does today, destroys all those individual plans and expectations. In so doing, it diminishes women's opportunities to participate fully and equally in the Nation's political, social, and economic life. . . .

The majority proclaims that " 'reproductive planning could take virtually immediate account of any sudden restoration of state authority to ban abortions.' " Even the most effective contraceptives fail, and effective contraceptives are not universally accessible. Not all sexual activity is consensual and not all contraceptive choices are made by the party who risks pregnancy. The Mississippi law at issue here, for example, has no exception for rape or incest, even for underage women. Finally, the majority ignores, as explained above, that some women decide to have an abortion because their circumstances change during a pregnancy. Human bodies care little for hopes and plans. Events can occur after conception, from unexpected medical risks to changes in family circumstances, which profoundly alter what it means to carry a pregnancy to term. In all these situations, women have expected that they will get to decide, perhaps in consultation with their families or doctors but free from state interference, whether to continue a pregnancy. For those who will now have to undergo that pregnancy, the loss of *Roe* and *Casey* could be disastrous.

That is especially so for women without money. When we "count[] the cost of [*Roe*'s] repudiation" on women who once relied on that decision, it is not hard to see where the greatest burden will fall. In States that bar abortion, women of means will still be able to travel to obtain the services they need. It is women who cannot afford to do so who will suffer most. These are the women most likely to seek abortion care in the first place. Women living below the federal poverty line experience unintended pregnancies at rates five times higher than higher income women do, and nearly half of women who seek abortion care live in households below the poverty line. . . .

Finally, the expectation of reproductive control is integral to many women's identity and their place in the Nation. That expectation helps define a woman as an "equal citizen[]," with all the rights, privileges, and obligations that status entails. It reflects that she is an autonomous person, and that society and the law recognize her as such. . . . Withdrawing a woman's right to choose whether to continue a pregnancy does not mean that no choice is being made. It means that a majority of today's Court has wrenched this choice from women and given it to the States. To allow a State to exert control over one of "the most intimate and personal choices" a woman may make is not only to affect the course of her life, monumental as those effects might be. It is to alter her "views of [herself]" and her understanding of her "place[] in society" as someone with the recognized dignity and authority to make these choices. Women have relied on *Roe* and *Casey* in this way for 50 years. Many have never known anything else. When *Roe* and *Casey* disappear, the loss of power, control, and dignity will be immense. . . .

After today, young women will come of age with fewer rights than their mothers and grandmothers had. The majority accomplishes that result without so much as considering how women have relied on the right to choose or what it means to take that right away. The majority's refusal even to consider the life-altering consequences of reversing *Roe* and *Casey* is a stunning indictment of its decision. . . .

With sorrow — for this Court, but more, for the many millions of American women who have today lost a fundamental constitutional protection — we dissent.

NOTES

1. **Articulating the Right to Abortion.**   Few, if any, Supreme Court cases have received as much criticism as Roe v. Wade. As noted in *Dobbs*, critics pointed to the lack of a constitutional basis for the right,[492] as well as the failure of *Roe*'s trimester system to fully acknowledge the state's interest in protecting fetal life.[493] Scholars favoring a right to abortion disagreed over the most appropriate and stable grounds for the right, in part as a response to these criticisms, and the strategic calculation that if the right was to survive, it might need a better articulated basis than *Roe* gave it.

Reva Siegel, for example, argued that, while the privacy rationale was adequate, an equality framework would better capture the important social dimensions of women's reproductive choice. Equality arguments figured in Justice Blackmun's concurring opinion in *Casey*, but even when the right to abortion was protected, those arguments have never been fully accepted by the Court. Note how Justice Alito disposes of the equality argument — concluding that discrimination based on the sex-unique characteristic of pregnancy is not discrimination based on sex, under Geduldig v. Aiello (a case discussed in Chapter 2). But does this response speak to Siegel's analysis, which is based on what an unwanted pregnancy can do to limit women's opportunities and status within society? Is Siegel's analysis really a formal equality analysis, or is it something else — like substantive equality, or nonsubordination theory?

What are the consequences of viewing the right to abortion as fundamentally a problem of equality and unequal power rather than privacy? The first speaks primarily to the uneven consequences a woman may experience as a result of an unwanted pregnancy, the second to a woman's right to make decisions affecting her own body without interference from the state. Aren't both grounds necessary to fully capture the case for leaving the abortion up to the pregnant woman?

Now that *Dobbs* rejected both privacy and equality rationales, what arguments should abortion advocates advance to the states or Congress, in whose hands the law now rests? In addition to these rationales, what about the responsibility-based theory advanced by Robin West? The rationale offers no additional constitutional hook, but

---

492. A classic critique by a scholar who supported abortion as a matter of policy but thought it had no constitutional basis is John Hart Ely, The Wages of Crying Wolf, 82 Yale L.J. 920 (1973).

493. See, e.g., Patrick Lee & Robert P. George, The Wrong of Abortion, in Abortion, in Contemporary Debates in Applied Ethics 13 (Andrew Cohen & Christopher Heath Wellman, eds., 2005).

some have long found the rhetoric to be more appealing than choice, and more likely to persuade politicians and the public upon whom, after *Dobbs*, the right to abortion now depends. As Marjorie M. Shultz put it decades ago, the "uncritical embrace of extreme autonomy rhetoric and *exclusively* woman-regarding positions . . . undermine[s] our persuasiveness, [renders] us vulnerable on grounds of principle, and [damages] our aspirations for a humane and responsible world." Shultz also raised concerns that, on principle, an unrestricted autonomy-based right would affect other legal principles in an undesirable way, such as undercutting the responsibility of doctors and employers to take reasonable measures to protect the safety of a fetus.[494] Linguist and political analyst George Lakoff argued that proponents of women's rights should avoid terms like "choice," which are too consumer-oriented, and even "abortion," which sounds negative. They should instead, he argued, focus on personal freedom from government interference and the lack of support for contraception and sex education.[495] William Saletan went further: "What we need is an explicit pro-choice war on the abortion rate." Activists should concede, he argued, that abortion is wrong but focus on reducing its necessity while avoiding dragging the criminal law into "personal tragedies."[496]

Is this just terminology? Are these suggestions likely to make any difference, going forward?

Commentators like Linda McClain have cautioned against responsibility-based theories for the abortion right, whether strategic or principled, on the ground that such theories will trigger too much second-guessing of women's decisions without adequate societal or governmental commitment to family support and reproductive health. It will also, she argued, leave women vulnerable to charges of irresponsibility, as even the most compelling cases of constraint can be framed, in the right hands, as instances of mere "convenience."[497]

Moral philosopher Judith Jarvis Thomson famously based the right to choose an abortion by analogy to the alternative of conscripting a person's body for the benefit of another:

> You wake up in the morning and find yourself back to back in bed with an unconscious violinist. A famous unconscious violinist. He has been found to have a fatal kidney ailment, and the Society of Music Lovers has canvassed all the available medical records and found that you alone have the right blood type to help. They have therefore kidnapped you, and last night the violinist's circulatory system was plugged into yours, so that your kidneys can be used to extract poisons from his blood as well as your own.

---

494. Marjorie Schultz, Abortion and the Maternal-Fetal Conflict: Broadening Our Concerns, 1 S. Cal. Rev. L. & Women's Stud. 79, 81 (1992).

495. George Lakoff, The Foreign Language of Choice, Alternet, reviewed in Katha Pollitt, If the Frame Fits, Nation, July 11, 2005.

496. William Saletan, Three Decades After *Roe*, an Abortion War We Can All Support, N.Y. Times, Jan. 22, 2006, at E17.

497. Linda C. McClain, The Poverty of Privacy?, 3 Colum. J. Gender & L. 119, 173 (1992); see also Pamela S. Karlan & Daniel R. Ortiz, In a Diffident Voice: Relational Feminism, Abortion Rights, and the Feminist Legal Agenda, 87 Nw. U. L. Rev. 858 (1993) (expressing concern over relational feminism in the abortion context).

The director of the hospital now tells you, "Look, we're sorry the Society of Music Lovers did this to you—we would never have permitted it if we had known. But still, they did it, and the violinist is now plugged into you. To unplug you would be to kill him. But never mind, it's only for nine months. By then he will have recovered from his ailment, and can safely be unplugged from you."[498]

Is this analogy persuasive?

Coming full circle, Katha Pollitt argued that "the only way feminists will regain ground in the abortion wars is to let go of language framing abortion as an icky but necessary evil, and instead push for a more positive view of abortion as a 'good thing for society,' precisely because it allows women 'to commit to education and work and dreams without having at the back of the mind . . . that maybe it's all provisional because at any moment an accidental pregnancy could derail them for life.'"[499]

Pre-*Dobbs*, the "Shout Your Abortion" campaign turned to social media to destigmatize abortion and use individual stories to educate people about the varied reasons women choose to terminate pregnancies.[500] Survey data have shown that among women who choose to have an abortion, 40 percent of surveyed women say they cannot afford a child; half say that having a baby would interfere with work, school, or the ability to care for dependents; and one-third say they do not want to be a single parent or are having problems with their husband or partner.[501] Physical and mental health issues are also often cited. Does Justice Alito recognize these reasons? Which ones, if any, do you think should be sufficient? An amicus brief submitted to the U.S. Supreme Court in Whole Woman's Health v. Cole presents the stories of 113 lawyers who claimed that without having had an abortion, their ability to pursue a professional career would have been substantially compromised, or completely thwarted.[502] Are these stories relevant to the debate? If so, how about the brief on behalf of 3,348 women who claim to have been injured, physically or psychologically, by an abortion procedure?[503]

---

498. Judith Jarvis Thomson, A Defense of Abortion, 1 Phil. & Pub. Aff. 47, 48-49 (1971).

499. Katha Pollitt, Pro: Reclaiming Abortion Rights (2014).

500. Caitlin Gibson, How #ShoutYourAbortion Is Transforming the Reproductive Rights Conversation, Wash. Post, Nov. 15, 2015; Carey Dunne, Tired of Hiding: Five Doctors Who Provide Abortions Come Out, Guardian (Aug. 6, 2019); Noel León, Nat'l Women's L. Ctr., Diagnosing Discrimination (2018) (on the stigma abortion providers face).

501. Lawrence B. Finer et al., Reasons U.S. Women Have Abortions: Quantitative and Qualitative Perspectives, 37 Persps. on Sexual and Reprod. Health 110, 113 (2005); see also M. Antonia Biggs et al., 13 BMC Women's Health 29 (2013). Sixty-nine percent of women who get an abortion are at or below the poverty level. See Rickie Solinger, Reproductive Politics: What Everyone Needs to Know 75 (2013).

502. Brief of Janice MacAvoy et al., Whole Woman's Health v. Cole, filed Jan. 4, 2016. For another brief on behalf of actress Amy Brenneman and other women who tell their reasons for obtaining an abortion, see Brief for Kate Banfield et al. as Amici Curiae Supporting Petitioners, Whole Woman's Health v. Cole, filed on Dec. 30, 2015.

503. See Brief of 3,384 Women Injured by Abortion & the Justice Foundation Supporting Respondents, Whole Woman's Health v. Cole (Dec. 10, 2015).

2. **Abortion Bans after *Dobbs*.** In anticipation of and in response to the ruling in *Dobbs*, several states enacted criminal bans on abortion. Though these bans vary somewhat in the particulars, most of them ban abortion at every stage of gestation unless necessary to save the life of the pregnant patient. In Texas, for example, the law now makes it a felony punishable by life in prison to provide a medical or surgical abortion to another person at any point after fertilization; the only exception is when the pregnancy has created or exacerbated a physical condition that threatens the life of the woman or exposes her to serious risk of major bodily impairment.[504] As of September 2022, eleven states, largely concentrated in the South, had abortion bans in effect.[505] On the opposite end of the political spectrum, several states, including New York, California, and Colorado, took steps to solidify protection for abortion rights in their statutes or constitutions.[506] Although the bans might not raise substantive due process issues after *Dobbs*, they raise other legal issues such as whether one state can prevent its citizens from traveling out of state for an abortion; whether states can restrict the use of the drugs necessary for a medication abortion when the FDA has deemed them safe and effective; and whether the medical emergency exceptions are unconstitutionally vague because they give doctors insufficient notice about whether medical care provided in the case of miscarriage, stillbirth, or a threat to the pregnant person's life might subject them to criminal prosecution. Although the majority in *Dobbs* suggested that its ruling would settle the abortion issue, the myriad legal questions and political controversies that arose its wake are likely to keep abortion as a front-burner for years to come.

In The New Abortion Battleground, David Cohen, Greer Donley, and Rachel Rebouché highlight some of the looming conflicts spurred by returning the issue of abortion to the states:

> The Supreme Court's decision to overturn *Roe v. Wade* will usher in a new era of abortion law and access. Borders and jurisdiction will become the central focus of the abortion battle. What had been, until now, a uniform national right has become a state-by-state patchwork. In a post-*Roe* country, states will attempt to impose their local abortion policies as widely as possible, even across state lines, and will battle one another over these choices; at the same time, the federal government may intervene to thwart state attempts to control abortion law. In other words, the interjurisdictional abortion wars are coming. . . .
>
> Antiabortion jurists and advocates have long forecasted that abortion law will become simpler if *Roe* is overturned. This claim has been a central part of their efforts . . . [arguing that *Roe*] created an unworkably complex legal framework. . . . [T]he opposite is true: overturning *Roe* and *Casey* will create a complicated world of novel interjurisdictional legal

504. Human Life Protection Act of 2021, 87th Leg., H.B. 1280 (effective Aug. 25, 2022).

505. The abortion landscape is changing rapidly. Several sites provide real-time updates on the state of abortion law, including the Center for Reproductive Rights, at https://reproductiverights.org/maps/abortion-laws-by-state.

506. Id.

conflicts over abortion. Instead of creating stability and certainty, it will lead to profound confusion because advocates on both sides of the abortion controversy will not stop at state borders in their efforts to apply their policies as broadly as possible. . . . [Anti-abortion states will] not only pass laws that criminalize in-state abortion, but also attempt to impose civil and criminal liability for those who travel out of state for abortion care or those who provide that care for their citizens or help them get it. . . . [A]bortion-supportive states will seek the opposite and, in an effort to expand abortion access as broadly as possible, pass laws that protect their providers and residents from legal sanctions after helping out-of-state residents obtain care. . . .

Roe's demise is just one part of the story behind the seismic shift in abortion law; the other is that abortion *practice* has changed in ways that make borders less relevant. The rise of telehealth for medication abortion — abortion completed solely with medication during the first ten weeks of pregnancy — allows abortion provision to occur across state and country lines. Virtual clinics, offering remote medication abortion through telehealth, have begun to operate in greater numbers, and brick-and-mortar clinics have expanded their practice into virtual care as well. . . .

Additional interjurisdictional conflicts will also arise because the federal government could play a more pronounced role in abortion regulation, by deploying strategies to protect or limit abortion nationally.[507]

3. ***Stare Decisis*, Reliance, and Autonomy.**   Part of *Casey*'s rationale for preserving *Roe* was that women had come to rely upon the right to choose abortion. What is the nature of the reliance recognized in *Casey*? One possibility is that people were accustomed to relying on abortion as a backup if they fail to use other forms of contraception or those methods fail. Can this be what the three Justices of the lead opinion in *Casey* had in mind? An alternative view is that women have come to see themselves as having some control and autonomy in personal decisionmaking, which *Roe* had come to symbolize, and it is this autonomy that enables them to plan their lives in long-range terms. Is this what the plurality of Justices had in mind? If so, this reasoning is specifically rejected by Justice Rehnquist in his *Casey* dissent, which is joined by four other Justices:

The joint opinion . . . turns to what can only be described as an unconventional — and unconvincing — notion of reliance, a view based on the surmise that the availability of abortion since *Roe* has led to "two decades of economic and social developments that would be undercut if the error of *Roe* were recognized." . . . The joint opinion's assertion of this fact is undeveloped and totally conclusory. In fact, one cannot be sure to what economic and social developments the opinion is referring. Surely it

---

507. David S. Cohen, Greer Donley & Rachel Rebouché, The New Abortion Battleground, 123 Colum. L. Rev. (forthcoming 2023).

is dubious to suggest that women have reached their "places in society" in reliance upon *Roe*, rather than as a result of their determination to obtain higher education and compete with men in the job market, and of society's increasing recognition of their ability to fill positions that were previously thought to be reserved only for men.[508]

How does Justice Alito's opinion in *Dobbs*, which was issued thirty years after the opinion in *Casey*, treat the issue of reliance? What different assumptions about individual autonomy and choice do the authors of the two opinions make?

4. **Public Opinion on Abortion**. Abortion is fairly widely accepted, at least in some circumstances. In a 2019 Quinnipiac University poll, 65 percent of respondents said that they agree with Roe v. Wade, and only 8 percent say that abortion should be illegal in all cases.[509] When respondents are asked about first-trimester abortion, support is even stronger.[510] Eighty-nine percent of abortions occur in the first twelve weeks of pregnancy.[511] Support for abortion is at an all-time high.[512] Post-*Dobbs*, support for legal abortion remains strong. A majority of voters in Mississippi, the state whose law was upheld in *Dobbs*, say they disagree with the ruling.[513] In Texas, which has banned abortion in virtually all cases, only 15 percent of voters agree with such a strict approach.[514] Many were surprised when voters in Kansas, a "reliably Republican state," resoundingly voted against (59-41) a referendum that would have permitted the legislature to pass restrictive abortion laws despite a ruling from the Kansas Supreme Court that abortion is protected under the state's constitution.[515] Polls suggest that support for abortion has grown since *Dobbs* and become more politically salient.[516]

---

508. Planned Parenthood v. Casey, 505 U.S. at 956, 957 (1992) (Rehnquist, C.J., dissenting); Carrie Dan, NBC/WSJ Poll: Support for Roe v. Wade Hits New High, NBC News (July 23, 2018).

509. Quinnipiac Univ., U.S. Voter Support for Abortion Is High, Quinnipiac University National Poll Finds; 94 Percent Back Universal Gun Background Checks (May 22, 2019). This poll and others with comparable findings can be found at Abortion & Birth Control, Polling Report (July 2019).

510. Lydia Saad, Trimesters Still Key to U.S. Abortion Views, Gallup (June 13, 2018); Ariana Eunjung Cha, "Late-Term" Abortions Challenge Both Sides, Wash. Post, Feb. 7, 2019.

511. Guttmacher Inst., Induced Abortion in the United States (Sept. 2019).

512. Rachel Frazin, Poll: 77 Percent Say Supreme Court Should Uphold Roe v. Wade, The Hill (June 7, 2019); Pew Rsch. Ctr., Public Opinion on Abortion (Oct. 15, 2018).

513. Ashton Pittman, Poll: Most Mississippi Voters Oppose Dobbs Ruling, Want Some Abortion Access (July 18, 2022) (51 percent disagree with ruling and support "some form of legal abortion").

514. Reese Oxner, 78% of Texas Voters Think Abortion Should Be Allowed in Some Form, Tex. Trib., May 4, 2022.

515. Nate Cohn, Kansas Result Suggests 4 Out of 5 States Would Back Abortion Rights in Similar Vote, N.Y. Times, Aug. 4, 2022.

516. Catherine Lucey, Support for Legalized Abortion Grows Since Dobbs Ruling, Wall St. J., Sept. 3, 2022; Elaine Kamarck, Can the Abortion Issue Save Democrats in the 2022 Midterm Elections, Brookings (Aug. 24, 2022).

Polling evidence also shows that many people consider themselves both pro-choice and pro-life.[517] They believe that the decision to have an abortion should be a personal choice between a person who is pregnant and health-care providers, but at the same time they disapprove of abortion because of, say, the sex of the fetus or when the woman should have been able to control the circumstances leading to the pregnancy.[518]

What are the implications of these polls? To what extent should public opinion control the abortion issue?

5. **Fetal Personhood?**   At one time it seemed possible, as the majority in *Roe* maintained, that legal issues about abortion could be decided without having to resolve the "difficult question of when life begins." The stated goal of the anti-abortion movement, however, is the recognition of fetal personhood and a national ban on abortion.[519] Its efforts in recent years to enact legislation or pass constitutional amendments providing that life begins at conception reflect this goal. At least twenty states have considered measures declaring that personhood begins at conception. In 2020, Georgia passed an anti-abortion law that included a "personhood" clause, which defines the term "natural person" to include "any unborn child with a detectable human heartbeat." This law had been blocked because it ran afoul of *Roe/Casey*, but the Eleventh Circuit ruled a few weeks after *Dobbs* that it could now take effect.[520] Among other consequences, the state now allows an embryo or fetus to be claimed as a dependent that comes with a $3,000 tax exemption beginning around the sixth week of gestation.[521]

What are the implications of the personhood provision? Does it mean that abortion must be banned in all cases? Can embryos be created for purposes of in vitro fertilization if they might not be used? Would any miscarriage necessitate a state murder investigation? How would it affect frozen embryos? Would a pregnant woman be able to declare her fetus as a dependent for tax purposes? Would she be entitled to welfare benefits immediately upon becoming pregnant? Could the federal government deport a pregnant non-citizen if the embryo or fetus is already deemed a natural person and entitled to birthright citizenship?

6. **Informed Consent for Abortion After *Dobbs*.** In the wake of *Casey*, many states passed restrictions on abortion, which pro-choice advocates consistently opposed.[522] Many of these regulations were packaged as "informed consent" requirements and included things like mandatory counseling with prescribed content, waiting periods, mandatory ultrasounds, and, in some cases, the distribution of medical misinformation. As states move to ban abortion in the wake of *Dobbs*,

---

517. For a graphic presentation of the evidence, see Pub. Religion Research Inst., Pro-Choice/Pro/Life: Overlapping Identities (Jan. 25, 2013).

518. See Karlyn Bowman & Jennifer Marsico, Opinions About Abortion Haven't Changed Since *Roe v. Wade*, Atlantic (Jan. 22, 2014).

519. Kate Zernike, Is a Fetus a Person? An Anti-Abortion Strategy Says Yes, N.Y. Times, Aug. 30, 2022, at A1.

520. Sistersong Women of Color Reproductive Justice Collective v. Governor of Georgia, No. 20-13024, 2022 WL 2824904 (July 20, 2022).

521. Ava Sassani, Georgia Abortion Law Says a Fetus Is Tax Deductible, N.Y. Times, Aug. 4, 2022.

522. See generally Guttmacher Inst., An Overview of Abortion Laws (Nov. 13, 2019).

these restrictions will play less of a role. Might informed consent rules like these nonetheless persist in states allowing abortion? Should they? Is there a justification for any special rules for abortion that do not apply to other forms of health care?

7. **Spousal Notice and Consent Provisions.** *Casey* held that Pennsylvania's spousal consent provision was unconstitutional but it was never repealed. Could it now be enforced? Is there any basis for challenging the constitutionality of such a law after *Dobbs*? Does it violate equal protection principles to allow a woman's husband to veto her decision to terminate a pregnancy? In states that allow abortion, should men have a right to participate in the abortion decision? In a widely circulated New York Times op-ed piece, Dalton Conley argues that "if we want to make fathers relevant, they need rights too. If a father is willing to legally commit to raising a child with no help from the mother, he should be able to obtain an injunction against the abortion of the fetus he helped create."[523] Similarly, Glenn Sacks objects to the "anti-male double standards" that require men to be responsible for child support if the woman carries an unplanned pregnancy to term, but gives them "no say" in that decision or the decision to terminate the pregnancy.[524]

How would you respond?

8. **Parental Consent and Notification Requirements.** *Casey* upheld provisions requiring minors to have parental consent before obtaining an abortion, as long as the state made available a bypass procedure permitting exemptions from the consent requirement. This gave rise to parental consent laws that established and regulated the judicial bypass procedure. Under then-binding Supreme Court precedents, states that wished to require parental notification or consent had to allow the pregnant minor to bypass the requirement by proving to a judge that she was mature and well-informed enough to make the decision on her own or, if not, that it was still in her best interests to obtain an abortion without notifying or attempting to obtain her parents' consent.[525] At the peak, thirty-seven states required parental involvement in a minor's decision to have an abortion.

Initially, it seemed that most minors who pursued a bypass procedure obtained judicial permission to obtain an abortion.[526] As time went on, however, research involving interviews of professionals from every state with a bypass provision documented numerous difficulties faced by minors in pursuing bypass petitions, including their inability to obtain helpful and reliable information, pay the costs, and find a judge who will hear the petition. Minors who are in state custody face additional problems, including confusion about who is authorized to provide consent. Once

---

523. Dalton Conley, A Man's Right to Choose, N.Y. Times, Dec. 1, 2005, at A35.

524. Glenn Sacks, Alito and the Rights of Men, L.A. Times, Nov. 1, 2005, at B11.

525. The most recent U.S. Supreme Court decision on the subject is Ayotte v. Planned Parenthood of N. New England, 546 U.S. 320 (2006) (striking down parental notification law because it did not make an exception for a medical emergency). For a regularly updated state-by-state survey of parental consent laws, see Guttmacher Inst., Parental Involvement in Minors' Abortions (Aug. 1, 2022).

526. A ten-year study in Massachusetts cited by a state appellate judge in 1997 showed that all bypass petitions but thirteen were granted, and of these thirteen, all but one were reversed on appeal; in the one remaining case, the parents eventually gave consent. See Am. Acad. of Pediatrics v. Lungren, 940 P.3d 797, 836, n.12 (Cal. 1997) (Kennard, J., dissenting).

a petition is before the court, abuse of judicial discretion is also a problem. Some judges grill the minors on their sex lives or deliver stern lectures on the need for parental consultation.[527] More recent studies have found that bypass procedures cause the pregnant teens to feel humiliated and ashamed, cause delays in accessing abortion care, and disproportionately affect minors who identify as racial or ethnic minorities.[528] Do any of these findings affect your view of whether parental consent should be required?

After *Dobbs*, there will be relatively few states that both allow abortion and require parental consent, so it is unclear whether the judicial bypass rules will survive. Should they? Should minors have the same rights as adults in this context, or should their parents be involved? If parental consent is required, does the judicial bypass standard make sense? In one recent Florida case, a pregnant minor was denied a judicial bypass order because her high school GPA was too low, evidence in the court's view that she was not mature enough to make the decision on her own.[529] Is it rational to require a minor who is not mature enough to decide to terminate a pregnancy to give birth and either consent to adoption or raise a child instead?

9. **Abortion "Regret."**   One of the few pre-*Dobbs* cases to uphold a restriction on pre-viability abortions came in *Gonzalez v. Carhart*.[530] In that 2007 case, the Supreme Court upheld the Federal Partial-Birth Abortion Ban Act against a constitutional challenge. The law prohibited doctors from using one of the two standard methods of terminating a pregnancy after the first trimester, known medically as "intact dilation and evacuation." Justice Kennedy grounded the majority opinion in concern about potential emotional harm to women who undergo this method of abortion. As he wrote:

> The Act proscribes a method of abortion in which a fetus is killed just inches before completion of the birth process. Congress stated as follows: "Implicitly approving such a brutal and inhumane procedure by choosing not to prohibit it will further coarsen society to the humanity of not only newborns, but all vulnerable and innocent human life, making it increasingly difficult to protect such life." . . .
>
> The Act's ban on abortions that involve partial delivery of a living fetus furthers the Government's objectives. No one would dispute that, for many, D&E is a procedure itself laden with the power to devalue human life. . . .

---

527. See Rachel Rebouché, Parental Involvement Law and New Governance, 34 Harv. J.L. & Gender 175, 188-96 (2011).

528. See Elizabeth Janiak et al., Massachusetts' Parental Consent Law and Procedural Timing Among Adolescents Undergoing Abortion, 133 Obstetrics & Gynecology 978 (2019); Kate Coleman-Minihan et al., Judicial Bypass Study Finds Process to Be Punishing, 64 J. Adolescent Health 20 (2019).

529. Ann Branigin, How Hard Is It to Get a Court-Approved Abortion?, Wash. Post, Jan. 27, 2022.

530. 550 U.S. 124 (2007).

Respect for human life finds an ultimate expression in the bond of love the mother has for her child. The Act recognizes this reality as well. Whether to have an abortion requires a difficult and painful moral decision. . . . While we find no reliable data to measure the phenomenon, it seems unexceptionable to conclude some women come to regret their choice to abort the infant life they once created and sustained. . . . Severe depression and loss of esteem can follow. . . .

In a decision so fraught with emotional consequence some doctors may prefer not to disclose precise details of the means that will be used, confining themselves to the required statement of risks the procedure entails. From one standpoint this ought not to be surprising. Any number of patients facing imminent surgical procedures would prefer not to hear all details, lest the usual anxiety preceding invasive medical procedures become the more intense. This is likely the case with the abortion procedures here in issue. . . .

It is, however, precisely this lack of information concerning the way in which the fetus will be killed that is of legitimate concern to the State. . . . The State has an interest in ensuring so grave a choice is well informed. It is self-evident that a mother who comes to regret her choice to abort must struggle with grief more anguished and sorrow more profound when she learns, only after the event, what she once did not know: that she allowed a doctor to pierce the skull and vacuum the fast-developing brain of her unborn child, a child assuming the human form.[531]

In dissent, Justice Ginsburg offered this response:

[T]he Court invokes an antiabortion shibboleth for which it concededly has no reliable evidence: Women who have abortions come to regret their choices, and consequently suffer from "[s]evere depression and loss of esteem." . . . Because of women's fragile emotional state and because of the "bond of love the mother has for her child," the Court worries, doctors may withhold information about the nature of the intact D&E procedure. . . . The solution the Court approves, then, is *not* to require doctors to inform women, accurately and adequately, of the different procedures and their attendant risks. . . . Instead, the Court deprives women of the right to make an autonomous choice, even at the expense of their safety. This way of thinking reflects ancient notions about women's place in the family and under the Constitution — ideas that have long since been discredited. . . .

Criticism of the gender paternalism reflected in the *Carhart* decision has been extensive. Some criticisms focused on how "abortion regret" arguments, in the name of women's welfare, exploit and magnify the stigma associated with having an

---

531. Id. at 156-60.

abortion.[532] Others refuted the genuineness of the position. Reva Siegel, for example, documented the growing use of claims about post-abortion syndrome ("PAS") as no more than a cynical strategy to broaden support for the anti-abortion movement. In the course of her argument, Siegel quoted David Reardon, an anti-abortion activist:

> While committed pro-lifers may be more comfortable with traditional "defend the baby" arguments, we must recognize that many in our society are too morally immature to understand this argument. They must be led to it. And the best way to lead them to it is by first helping them to see that abortion does not help women, but only makes their lives worse.[533]

No reputable studies have found a causal link between abortion and women's depression or suicidal tendencies?[534] Is it true, as Justice Ginsburg states, that abortion-regret arguments are based on paternalistic stereotypes and anti-woman rhetoric? Jeannie Suk argues that the invocation of post-abortion syndrome exploits the emphasis on women's victimization used by legal reformers to secure more protection for women in other areas, such as sexual violence and harassment.[535] As she observes, a "consistent method of reasoning about women is visible from *Roe*, through *Casey*, and finally to *Carhart*: that of inferring from potential psychological harm the state's interest in protecting women from said harm. Whether the source is maternity, male violence, or abortion, women's psychological trauma is a distinct in which the state is interested." Is this plausible? Predictable?

What research, if any, would affect your views on whether, and to what extent, abortion harms women? In 2009, one set of researchers concluded that, compared to women who had never had an abortion, women who had had an abortion were at increased risk of severe anxiety, mood, and substance abuse disorders.[536] Subsequent research using the same data but controlling for prior mental health difficulties and experience of violence found no such association with anxiety and mood disorders, although it did find an association with substance abuse, which the researchers attributed to the likelihood they had been unable to control for other relevant risk factors.[537] Another study in 2016 found that women who showed

---

532. On abortion stigma, see Anuradha Kumar et al., Conceptualising Abortion Stigma, 11 Culture, Health & Sexuality 625 (2009).

533. Reva B. Siegel, Dignity and the Politics of Protection: Abortion Restrictions Under *Casey/Carhart*, 117 Yale L.J. 1695, 1718-19 (2008) (quoting David Reardon, Politically Correct vs. Politically Smart: Why Politicians Should be Both Pro-Woman and Pro-Life, 2 Post-Abortion Rev. 3 (Fall 1994)).

534. Caroline Maia Corbin, Abortion Distortions, 71 Wash. & Lee L. Rev. 1175, 1179-81 (2014).

535. Jeannie Suk, The Trajectory of Trauma: Bodies and Minds of Abortion Discourse, 110 Colum. L. Rev. 1193 (2010).

536. See Priscilla K. Coleman et al., Induced Abortion and Anxiety, Mood, and Substance Abuse Disorders: Isolating the Effects of Abortion in the National Comorbidity Survey, 43 J. Psychiatric Rsch. 770 (2009).

537. See Julia R. Steinberg & Lawrence B. Finer, Examining the Association of Abortion History and Current Mental Health: A Reanalysis of the National Comorbidity Survey Using a Common-Risk-Factors Model, 72 Soc. Sci. & Med. 72 (2011).

up at an abortion facility but were denied because it was too late in pregnancy were at greater risk of adverse psychological outcomes than women who successfully obtained an abortion, at least in the immediately subsequent years; it found no basis for restricting access to abortion based on potential psychological effects.[538] That study also found that women who are denied abortion access are four times as likely to end up living below the poverty level as women who are successful in their desire to terminate a pregnancy.[539] What explains, then, the Court's rationale that restricting certain types of abortion is for women's own good? Does it reflect a stereotypical way of thinking about how women make decisions versus how men make decisions?

10. **Funding and Reproductive Rights.** Underfunding of family planning programs has long restricted poor women's reproductive choices and increased the necessity for, and thus the number of, abortions. Nearly half of pregnancies are unintended, and 42 percent of these end in abortion (up from 40 percent in 2008). Black women are more than twice as likely to have unintended pregnancies as non-Hispanic white women, and poor women are more than five times as likely as women at the highest income level.[540] Women of color are more likely to be on Medicaid.[541] Two-thirds of the 1.5 million unplanned births in 2010 were paid for by public insurance programs, primarily Medicaid, as compared to 38 percent of planned births.[542]

Federal funding legislation, known as the Hyde Amendment, limits federal reimbursement for abortions to very narrow exceptions, such as when necessary to save the life of the mother or to end pregnancies resulting from rape or incest. The restriction applies to funding provided through the Department of Health and Human Services and primarily affects Medicaid. In a 1980 decision, the Supreme Court upheld this legislation on the ground that it does not impose an unconstitutional condition on women's exercise of their fundamental right to an abortion, but simply leaves them in the same place they would be absent any federal funding program.[543] Consider this perspective from the reproductive justice movement:

> When a low-income person makes a decision to have an abortion, her federal health insurance, Medicaid, will not pay for it. So to pay for the abortion she may have to make the brutal decision to use money meant to pay for basic necessities, such as heat and water and rent and food for herself

---

538. M. Antonia Biggs et al., Women's Mental Health and Well-Being Five Years After Receiving or Being Denied an Abortion: A Prospective, Longitudinal Cohort Study, 74 JAMA Psychiatry 169 (2017).

539. See Diane Greene Foster et al., Socioeconomic Outcomes of Women Who Receive and Women Who Are Denied Wanted Abortions, 108 Am. J. Pub. Health 407 (2018).

540. See Guttmacher Inst., Unintended Pregnancy in the United States (Jan. 2019).

541. See Alina Salganicoff et al., Kaiser Family Found., The Hyde Amendment and Coverage for Abortion Services (July 30, 2019).

542. Adam Sonfield & Kathryn Kost, Public Costs from Unintended Pregnancies and the Role of Public Insurance Programs in Paying for Pregnancy-Related Care: National and State Estimates for 2010 (Feb. 2015).

543. Harris v. McRae, 448 U.S. 297 (1980).

and her children. And the time it takes to raise money for an abortion often means that this person will have an abortion later in her pregnancy, when the procedure becomes less medically routine and more expensive. The officials who make law and policy do not compute the ways that her poverty and the state's refusal to provide comprehensive health care rob the woman of dignity and physical safety and are likely to deepen her poverty and lack of options.[544]

Does the reproductive justice framework, discussed in the prior section of this chapter, require government funding for abortion? Although deemed constitutional and more than four decades old, the Hyde Amendment became a political issue again in the 2020 election cycle.[545] Would you support its repeal? Why or why not? Does the ruling in *Dobbs* make it more or less pressing?

Before *Dobbs*, a majority of states provided their own funding to make abortion accessible to poor women, but a majority also restricted the ability of private health insurance plans to cover abortion.[546] What explains this apparent inconsistency? Now that states are free to ban or greatly restrict access to abortion, the average cost of abortion will increase significantly due to the travel and other costs associated with interstate travel. Some states that have moved to protect abortion rights after *Dobbs* have also allocated money that will help not only their own residents obtain abortion care but out-of-state patients who travel to obtain care as well.[547] Should the federal government provide funding?

11. **Sex Education and Teen Pregnancy.**   The federal government in recent decades has provided various funding programs to support pregnancy prevention for teenagers. For much of this period, the funds have been available only for programs premised on abstinence as the sole prevention strategy. Thus, qualifying programs have been required to teach that abstaining from sex "is the only certain way to avoid out-of-wedlock pregnancy, sexually transmitted diseases, and other associated health problems," that a "mutually faithful monogamous relationship in context of marriage is the expected standard of human sexual activity," and that "sexual activity outside of marriage is likely to have harmful physical and psychological effects."[548] The Obama administration encouraged evidence-supported sex education curriculums that were shown in "at least one rigorous evaluation to be effective at changing some sexual behavior, such as reducing pregnancy rates or rates of sexual activity." Under the Trump administration, however, the Department

---

544. Loretta J. Ross & Rickie Solinger, Reproductive Justice: An Introduction 135-36 (2017).

545. Maggie Astor, What Is the Hyde Amendment? A Look at Its Impact as Biden Reverses His Stance, N.Y. Times, June 7, 2019, at A12; Julian Shen-Berro, The Hyde Amendment: How a 43-Year-Old Provision Became a 2020 Issue, Huff. Post (June 6, 2019).

546. Guttmacher Inst., State Funding of Abortion Under Medicaid (Aug. 1, 2022); Guttmacher Inst., Regulating Insurance Coverage of Abortion (July 1, 2022).

547. Casey Parks, States Pour Millions Into Abortion Access, Wash. Post, May 13, 2022.

548. 42 U.S.C. § 710(b)(2) (2018). For a history of the federal programs, see Sexuality Information & Educ. Council of the U.S., Abstinence Only Until Marriage Funding (July 2018).

of Health and Human Services reverted to supporting only programs that emphasize abstinence or "sexual risk avoidance."[549]

The political popularity of abstinence-only programs has not been matched by any demonstration of effectiveness. The vast majority of abstinence-only curricula include factual inaccuracies and distortions, and none have been found to delay sexual activity.[550] A large-scale analysis from researchers from the University of Georgia showed that states that prescribe abstinence-only sex education programs in public schools have significantly higher teenage pregnancy and birth rates than states with more comprehensive sex education programs.[551] A study showed that students who take virginity pledges — a common feature of abstinence-only programs — delayed sexual activity slightly, but when they did have sex, they used condoms less frequently and were less likely to be tested for sexually transmitted infections (STIs).[552] Students who take part in abstinence-only programs are also more likely to believe, incorrectly, that condoms do not protect against STIs.[553]

Critics of abstinence-only programs generally do not object to approaches that encourage teens to resist unwanted sex but believe that teens should also have accurate information about sexual activity and birth control. Some critics also argue that abstinence-only initiatives violate minors' constitutional rights concerning health and procreation decisions, and that the religious message included in some federally-funded programs violates the First Amendment Establishment Clause. One federal court struck down a Louisiana program on that ground.[554]

12. **Abortion Laws and the First Amendment.** Even after *Dobbs*, some constitutional issues remain in the abortion context, including whether counseling requirements amount to compelled disclosures of a government viewpoint, contrary to the First Amendment,[555] or whether doctors should be forced to make certain statements to patients, even ones they believe are not backed by medical science.

In National Institute of Family and Life Advocates v. Becerra, the Supreme Court considered the constitutionality of a California law (the FACT Act) that compelled licensed women's health centers to inform women that the state provides

---

549. Pam Belluck, Trump Administration Pushes Abstinence in Teen Pregnancy Programs, N.Y. Times, Apr. 23, 2018, at A17; Jesseca Boyer, New Name, Same Harm: Rebranding of Federal Abstinence-Only Programs, 21 Guttmacher Pol'y Rev. (2018).

550. See generally John Santelli et al., Abstinence-Only Until Marriage: An Updated Review of U.S. Policies and Programs and Their Impact, 61 J. Adolescent Health 273 (2017).

551. See Kathrin F. Stanger-Hall & David W. Hall, Abstinence-Only Education and Teen Pregnancy Rates: Why We Need Comprehensive Sex Education in the U.S., 6 PLoS ONE 1371 (2011).

552. See John S. Santelli et al., Abstinence-Only-Until-Marriage: An Updated Review of U.S. Policies and Programs and Their Impact, 61 J. Adolescent Health 273 (2017).

553. Julie F. Kay, What's Not Being Said About Sex and Who It's Hurting (Mar. 27, 2008).

554. ACLU of Louisiana v. Foster, No. Civ. A. 02-1440, 2002 WL 1733651 (E.D. La. July 24, 2002).

555. See Caroline Mala Corbin, Compelled Disclosures, 65 Ala. L. Rev. 1277 (2014) (arguing yes).

free or low-cost services, including abortions, and give them a phone number and compelled unlicensed clinics to disclose that they are not authorized to provide medical services.[556] The law was designed to regulate crisis pregnancy centers (CPCs), organizations that "offer a limited range of free pregnancy options, counseling, and other services," but "aim to discourage and prevent women from seeking abortions."[557] CPCs have become a powerful tool in the anti-abortion arsenal; with more than 3,500 in operation across the country, they greatly outnumber abortion clinics. Not all CPCs operate in the same manner, but reports show they often rely on deception, shame, or confusion to get "abortion-minded" women through the door.[558] California responded to these reports with a law designed to make sure women had accurate information about their options. In an opinion written by Justice Clarence Thomas, the majority held that the law violated the First Amendment:

> [N]either California nor the Ninth Circuit has identified a persuasive reason for treating professional speech as a unique category that is exempt from ordinary First Amendment principles. We do not foreclose the possibility that some such reason exists. We need not do so because the licensed notice cannot survive even intermediate scrutiny. California asserts a single interest to justify the licensed notice: providing low-income women with information about state-sponsored services. Assuming that this is a substantial state interest, the licensed notice is not sufficiently drawn to achieve it.
>
> If California's goal is to educate low-income women about the services it provides, then the licensed notice is "wildly underinclusive." The notice applies only to clinics that have a "primary purpose" of "providing family planning or pregnancy-related services" and that provide two of six categories of specific services. Other clinics that have another primary purpose, or that provide only one category of those services, also serve low-income women and could educate them about the State's services. . . . But most of those clinics are excluded from the licensed notice requirement without explanation. Such "[u]nderinclusiveness raises serious doubts about whether the government is in fact pursuing the interest it invokes, rather than disfavoring a particular speaker or viewpoint." *Entertainment Merchants Assn.*, 564 U.S., at 802 . . .
>
> California could inform low-income women about its services "without burdening a speaker with unwanted speech." Most obviously, it could

---

556. 138 S. Ct. 2361 (2018); California Reproductive Freedom, Accountability, Comprehensive Care, and Transparency Act (FACT Act) requires clinics that primarily serve pregnant women to provide certain notices. Cal. Health & Safety Code § 123470 et seq. (2019).

557. *Becerra*, 138 S. Ct. at 2368 (citing Watters et al., Pregnancy Resource Centers: Ensuring Access and Accuracy of Information 4 (2011)).

558. See, e.g., NARAL, Crisis Pregnancy Center Lie: The Insidious Threat to Reproductive Freedom (2017); see also Helen Norton, Pregnancy and the First Amendment, 87 Fordham L. Rev. 2417 (2019); see also Montoya et al., The Problems with Crisis Pregnancy Centers: Reviewing the Literature and Identifying New Directions for Future Research, 14 Int'l J. Women's Health 757 (2022).

inform the women itself with a public-information campaign. California could even post the information on public property near crisis pregnancy centers. California argues that it has already tried an advertising campaign, and that many women who are eligible for publicly-funded healthcare have not enrolled. But California has identified no evidence to that effect. And regardless, a "tepid response" does not prove that an advertising campaign is not a sufficient alternative. . . .

We next address the unlicensed notice. . . . Our precedents require disclosures to remedy a harm that is "potentially real not purely hypothetical," and to extend "no broader than reasonably necessary." Otherwise, they risk "chilling" protected speech." Importantly, California has the burden to prove that the unlicensed notice is neither unjustified nor unduly burdensome. It has not met its burden.

We need not decide what type of state interest is sufficient to sustain a disclosure requirement like the unlicensed notice. California has not demonstrated any justification for the unlicensed notice that is more than "purely hypothetical." The only justification that the California Legislature put forward was ensuring that "pregnant women in California know when they are getting medical care from licensed professionals." . . . Indeed, California points to nothing suggesting that pregnant women do not already know that the covered facilities are staffed by unlicensed medical professionals. At this preliminary stage of the litigation, we agree that petitioners are likely to prevail on the question whether California has proved a justification for the unlicensed notice. . . .

The application of the unlicensed notice to advertisements demonstrates just how burdensome it is. The notice applies to all "print and digital advertising materials" by an unlicensed covered facility. These materials must include a government-drafted statement that "[t]his facility is not licensed as a medical facility by the State of California and has no licensed medical provider who provides or directly supervises the provision of services." An unlicensed facility must call attention to the notice, instead of its own message, by some method such as larger text or contrasting type or color. This scripted language must be posted in English and as many other languages as California chooses to require. As California conceded at oral argument, a billboard for an unlicensed facility that says "Choose Life" would have to surround that two-word statement with a 29-word statement from the government, in as many as 13 different languages. In this way, the unlicensed notice drowns out the facility's own message. More likely, the "detail required" by the unlicensed notice "effectively rules out" the possibility of having such a billboard in the first place. . . .

We express no view on the legality of a similar disclosure requirement that is better supported or less burdensome.

In a dissenting opinion, Justice Stephen Breyer argued that the law should have been evaluated under the Court's abortion precedents, rather than under First Amendment doctrine, an argument mooted by the later decision in *Dobbs*. Should states be permitted to regulate crisis pregnancy centers? In what ways?

Is the majority's application of the First Amendment in this context likely to promote or impair women's autonomy? To what extent does the ruling demonstrate Catharine MacKinnon's thesis that neutral principles of freedom and autonomy, including the First Amendment, invisibly further the subordination of women?

13. **Self-Induced Abortions and Abortion Rates.**   More restrictive abortion laws do not necessarily mean fewer abortions. Data show that in states where abortions are hardest to get because of the inaccessibility of services, there are more live births, but not as many as pregnancy rates would predict, probably because some of the pregnancies are terminated through self-induced abortions.[559]

The most common self-induced abortions today are medication abortions, which use drugs designed for that purpose. The FDA has approved a two-drug regimen (mifepristone and misopristol) for medication abortion up to seventy days of gestation.[560] The first drug (one pill) blocks progesterone, which is necessary for a pregnancy to progress; the second drug (four pills, taken twenty-four to forty-eight hours later), which is also used in the case of incomplete miscarriage, causes cramping and bleeding that empties the contents of the uterus. Over half of clinic abortions before eight weeks of gestation are done this way; the remainder involve a surgical procedure. Medication abortion is more than 97 percent effective and has fewer complications than commonly used drugs such as Tylenol and Viagra.[561] The cost of such abortions is about half that of surgical abortions, and the process can be managed privately without delays or the trauma imposed by current restrictions and harassment of clinic patients.

Medication abortions have been proven safe, even when done outside of a clinic.[562] The development of this protocol has greatly increased the ability of individuals to undergo self-managed abortion. It is used more in states with restrictive abortion laws than in other states, as evidenced by the fact that Google searches for advice on self-abortion are higher in states where clinic abortions are harder to obtain.[563] The state with the most Google searches for self-induced abortion is Mississippi, which had only one clinic that performed abortions before *Dobbs* (and now has none). A study of Google search trends showed a record-high number of searches mentioning "abortion pill" or "abortion medications" (350,000) during

---

559. It is difficult to measure the prevalence of self-managed abortion. For different approaches, see Lauren Ralph et al., Prevalence of Self-Managed Abortion Among Women of Reproductive Age in the United States, 3 JAMA Network Open e2029245 (2020); Gilda Sedgh & Sarah C. Keogh, Novel Approaches to Estimating Abortion Incidence, 16 Reproductive Health 44 (2019).

560. FDA, Mifeprex Information, https://www.fda.gov/drugs/postmarket-drug-safety-information-patients-and-providers/mifeprex-mifepristone-information; see also Kaiser Family Foundation, The Availability and Use of Medication Abortion (Apr. 6, 2022).

561. Farhad Manjoo, Abortion Pills Should Be Everywhere, N.Y. Times, Aug. 3, 2019, at SR4.

562. Abigail R.A. Aiken, Safety and Effectiveness of Self-Managed Medication Abortion Provided Using Online Telemedicine in the United States: A Population Based Study, 10 Lancet 100200 (June 1, 2022).

563. Guttmacher Inst., Many Young Women in the United States Turn to Google for Information on Self-Abortion (Feb. 26, 2018).

the week when the draft opinion in *Dobbs* was leaked to the media.[564] Even when abortion is legally available, some women may decide to manage their own abortions. A study in Texas showed that while most women prefer a clinic abortion, "poverty, limited resources, and local facility closures limited women's ability to obtain abortion care in a clinic setting and were key factors in deciding to attempt abortion self-induction."[565]

Comparisons to other countries show that abortion rates are lower in countries where it is legal. For example, in Western Europe, where abortions are broadly available, the abortion rate is 12 per 1,000 women, whereas in Latin America, where abortion laws are more restrictive, the rate is 32 per 1,000 women.[566] Abortions are also safer where they are legal because the methods used and sanitary conditions are better. Women who are driven to seek illegal abortions do so at a later gestational age, which has higher risks. In South Africa, the annual number of abortion-related deaths fell by 91 percent after the liberalization of the abortion law. Worldwide, although abortion rates declined significantly between 1995 and 2003, they have now leveled off at 35 per 1,000 women between ages 15 and 44.[567]

In the United States, there was a long-term decline in abortions starting thirty years ago; but the number started to rise again in 2017.[568] About half of abortion patients have family incomes below the federal poverty level.[569] Women in the highest income group had an abortion rate less than half the national rate, and the greatest decline occurred among adolescent women, due to greater reliance on long-acting contraception.[570] At current rates, about one in four U.S. women is expected to have an abortion during her reproductive years, but an increasing number may rely on a nonsurgical methods.[571]

14. **Who Should Decide?** *Roe* and *Casey* imposed limits on the power of states to restrict abortion by recognizing a constitutional right to terminate a pre-viability pregnancy. *Dobbs* eliminated that right and returned the decisionmaking power to the legislative branch of the state and federal governments. What should be the right balance between judicial and legislative power in regulating reproductive decisions? Justice Ginsburg had criticized the majority decision in *Roe* for going too far when the "legislatures all over the United States were moving on this question. The law was in a state of flux," and the Court "bit off more than it could chew." It would have been enough to invalidate the extremely restrictive Texas statute and leave the rest to legislative developments. In her view, that would have avoided the

564. Mary Kekatos, Spike in Google Searches for Abortion Pills May Lead to Rise in Unsafe Abortions, ABC News (June 29, 2022).

565. Tex. Pol'y Eval. Proj., Texas Women's Experiences Attempting Self-Induced Abortion in the Face of Dwindling Options (Nov. 17, 2015).

566. Guttmacher Inst., Abortion in Latin America and the Caribbean (Mar. 2018).

567. See Guttmacher Inst., Unintended Pregnancy and Induced Abortion Worldwide (Mar. 2022).

568. Guttmacher Inst., Long-Term Decline in US Abortions Reverses (June 2022).

569. Rachel K. Jones & Jenn Jerman, Population Group Abortion Rates and Lifetime Incidence of Abortion: United States, 2008-2014, 107 Am. J. Pub. Health 1904 (2017).

570. Id. at 1907.

571. Id. at 1908.

backlash against "unelected judges" making such fundamental decisions.[572] Some scholars disagree that this approach would have been preferable. They rely on evidence indicating that a majority of the public in the 1970s supported giving women the right to choose but some legislatures were moving in the direction of less, not greater, recognition of that right.[573] How do you think control over reproductive decisions should be allocated among courts, legislatures, and women?

In *Dobbs*, Justice Alito wrote in the majority opinion that *Casey* had left judges with "an unwieldy and inappropriate task" of evaluating the constitutionality of abortion laws. Kavanaugh wrote separately to emphasize that the Court should be "neutral" on abortion:

> On the question of abortion, the Constitution is therefore neither pro-life nor pro-choice. The Constitution is neutral and leaves the issue for the people and their elected representatives to resolve through the democratic process in the States or Congress — like the numerous other difficult questions of American social and economic policy that the Constitution does not address.[574]

The dissent noted that although the majority says it is permitting "each State" to decide how to regulate abortion, "[t]hat is cold comfort, of course, for the poor woman who cannot get the money to fly to a distant State for a procedure."[575] A few months after *Dobbs*, GOP Senator Lindsey Graham introduced a bill to ban abortions nationwide after fifteen weeks.[576] Would such a bill be constitutional after *Dobbs*? How would you respond to such a bill?

15. **Anti-Abortion Activism.**   Anti-abortion advocates have long sought to dissuade women from obtaining an abortion through clinic pickets and protest activities. After the Supreme Court found civil rights statutes inapplicable to protect clinic access, Congress passed the Freedom of Access to Clinic Entrances Act (FACE).[577] FACE allows for civil remedies and/or criminal penalties against anyone who "by force or threat of force or by physical obstruction, intentionally injures, intimidates or interferes with or attempts to injure, . . . or intimidate such person

---

572. Adam Liptak, Gay Vows, Repeated from State to State, N.Y. Times, Apr. 12, 2009, at SR1 (quoting Justice Ginsburg).

573. Samantha Luks & Michael Salamone, Abortion, in Public Opinion and Constitutional Controversy 81 (Nathaniel Persily et al., eds., 2008); see also Linda Greenhouse & Reva B. Siegel, Before (and After) Roe v. Wade: New Questions About Backlash, 120 Yale L.J. 100 (2011) (arguing that the polarization of debates about abortion was due not to Roe v. Wade, but instead to a party realignment caused when Republicans campaigning for Richard Nixon in 1972 took an anti-abortion stance in order to draw Catholics and social conservatives away from the Democratic Party).

574. 142 S. Ct. 2228, 2305 (2022) (Kavanaugh, J., concurring).

575. Id. at 2318 (Breyer, J., Sotomayor, J., & Kagan, J., dissenting).

576. Amy B. Wang & Caroline Kitchener, Graham to Introduce Bill that Would Restrict Abortions Nationwide, Wash. Post, Sept. 13, 2022.

577. See, e.g., Bray v. Alexandria Women's Health Clinic, 506 U.S. 263 (1993) (holding that Section 1985 of the Civil Rights Statutes did not provide a federal cause of action to stop demonstrations at abortion clinics based on a violation of the civil rights of women). For FACE, see 18 U.S.C. § 248(a)(1) (2018).

from, obtaining or providing reproductive health services." Violators are subject to one year in prison or up to $10,000 in fines, or both, for the first violation, and up to three years in prison and up to $25,000 in fines for the second. If bodily injury or death results, other penalties are possible. The Act also authorizes a private right of action in favor of physicians, clinic staff, and patients who are injured by conduct proscribed by the Act. Critics of FACE have argued that it violates the First Amendment, the Eighth Amendment, the Tenth Amendment, and the Religious Freedom Restoration Act, but the Act has survived numerous constitutional attacks at the federal appellate level.

State laws also provide some protection for health care providers and for women seeking abortions. These include general trespass laws and actions for tortious interference with business, false imprisonment, and intentional infliction of emotional distress. Thirteen states and the District of Columbia prohibit certain specified actions. For example, some state laws provide specific protections such as "bubble zones" around clinics, within which protesters may not approach clinic workers and clients, or prohibit excessive noise outside a clinic, possess or have access to a weapon during a demonstration at a medical facility, threaten or intimidate staff, or block the entrance to a clinic.[578] Some of these restrictions have been upheld, while others have been struck down.[579] Should these laws survive despite the elimination of constitutional protection for abortion?

Targeted harassment of clinic doctors and staff has substantially increased since 2010. A 2014 survey of 242 providers conducted by the Feminist Majority Foundation found that nearly 70 percent of abortion providers said they had experienced frequent harassment and that there had been a 25 percent increase in threats and targeted intimidation tactics between 2010 and 2014. "The overwhelming majority of clinics (88%) reported experiencing some type of anti-abortion activity in the first half of 2018, with 62% of providers experiencing activity at least once a week."[580]

Since 1993, at least eleven people have been killed in attacks on abortion clinics in the United States. In November 2015, three people were killed when a gunman opened fire with an assault-style rifle at a facility in Colorado Springs, mumbling "no more baby parts" in an interview after his arrest.[581] Another murder involved a Wichita doctor, George Tiller, in his church sanctuary. An Operation Rescue "Tiller Watch" web page had featured vitriolic postings, and pro-life leaders

578. See Guttmacher Inst., Protecting Access to Clinics (Nov. 1, 2014).

579. See, e.g., Madsen v. Women's Health Center, 512 U.S. 753 (1994); Schenck v. Pro-Choice Network of W. New York, 519 U.S. 357 (1997); Hill v. Colorado, 530 U.S. 703 (2000); McCullen v. Coakley, 573 U.S. 464 (2014); see also Scheidler v. NOW, 547 U.S. 9 (2006).

580. Erin Gistaro, Feminist Majority Foundation, Almost Half of U.S. Abortion Clinics Experience Severe Violence, Threats of Severe Violence, and/or Severe Harassment According to New Feminist Majority Foundation Survey (Jan. 16, 2019); see also Nat'l Abortion Fed'n, 2018 Violence and Disruption Statistics.

581. Liam Stack, A Brief History of Deadly Attacks on Abortion Providers, N.Y. Times, Nov. 29, 2015.

had denounced Tiller as "a baby killer" and "mass murderer."[582] The doctor who attempted to take Dr. Tiller's place has faced harassment and a number of threats, including a letter from an anti-abortion activist who befriended the killer of Dr. Tiller, warning the doctor to check under her car for explosives before turning the key.[583] Is this type of violence likely to increase or decrease now that the Supreme Court has overruled Roe v. Wade?[584]

PUTTING THEORY INTO PRACTICE

5-26. California passed a law requiring public universities to provide access to privately funded medication abortion, beginning in 2023. Studies show that about 500 students at these universities now seek medication abortions every month, many have to travel significant distances, and primary care doctors and nurse practitioners could safely provide such services.[585] If you were a legislator, would you have supported the bill? What objections might you anticipate?

5-27. A pregnant woman went to the emergency room after her water broke at eighteen weeks.[586] Doctors told her that her pregnancy was no longer viable but they could still detect fetal cardiac activity. Under Texas's abortion ban, doctors cannot terminate a pregnancy unless it threatens the life of the pregnant patient or imposes a risk that the patient will suffer substantial impairment of a major bodily function. The penalty for performing an unlawful abortion is a prison sentence from five years to life, and a civil penalty of $100,000. The risks of remaining pregnant while awaiting a miscarriage include infection, hemorrhage, and death. If you were the lawyer for the hospital, how would you advise the doctor in this situation?

5-28. After the ruling in *Dobbs*, the Idaho legislature began debating a strict abortion ban. The Republican legislators debated but ultimately declined to include an exception for abortions necessary to save the life of the pregnant person. Is this constitutional after *Dobbs*?

5-29. Research shows consistently that, even in the United States, most families prefer boys to girls, especially as first or only children.[587] A number of states now make it illegal to intentionally perform an abortion when that abortion is sought

---

582. The Tiller Watch page was taken down after his murder. See George Tiller Killed: Abortion Doctor Shot at Church, Huff. Post (July 1, 2009).

583. Jenny Deam, Doctor Struggles to Fill Role of Slain Kansas Abortion Provider, L.A. Times, Mar. 5, 2012.

584. Vera Bergengruen, Armed Demonstrators and Far-Right Groups Are Escalating Tensions at Abortion Protests, Time (July 8, 2022).

585. Cal. S.B. 24, 2019-20 Leg. Sess. (Cal. 2019); Victoria Colliver, California Is Poised to Require Medication Abortion on State College Campuses, Politico (Aug. 8, 2018).

586. Carrie Feibel, Because of Texas Abortion Law, Her Wanted Pregnancy Became a Medical Nightmare, Tex. Trib., Aug. 3, 2022.

587. See Frank Newport, Americans Prefer Boys to Girls, Just as They Did in 1941 (June 23, 2011). The evidence for male favoritism is stronger in China and India. See Jeff Jacoby, Choosing to Eliminate Unwanted Daughters, Bos. Globe, Apr. 6, 2008.

solely on account of the sex of the unborn child.[588] Are those laws enforceable, or wise? What about laws to prohibit sex selection in in-vitro fertilization?

5-30. When diagnosed before birth, genetic abnormalities prompt couples to have an abortion 90 percent of the time. A number of states now ban the abortion of fetuses with severe genetic abnormalities.[589] If you were a state legislator, where would you stand on whether abortions should be allowed on this ground?

5-31. Some Jewish women object to politicians' use of biblical language in support of abortion bans or restrictions because Judaism does not endorse the view that fetuses have souls, nor does it condemn abortion. Should Jewish women be entitled to access to abortion as a matter of religious freedom?[590]

5-32. A Michigan father defended against a paternity suit in which he was ordered to pay $500 per month in child support on the grounds that the law on which it was based constitutes sex discrimination. The father, represented by the National Center for Men, argued that he had been deprived of the right to avoid parenthood. He claimed that the mother had falsely assured him that she was unable to get pregnant due to a medical condition and that she was using birth control just in case. The state also denied him any right to determine whether the pregnancy would be carried to term.[591] Should his defense to a child support action be accepted?

5-33. Two weeks before her sentencing hearing on a forgery conviction in a jurisdiction allowing abortions, Yuriko wrote to the judge telling him that she was pregnant and wished to have an abortion. The judge offered her a deal: If she agreed to bring the fetus to term, he would give her probation instead of a prison sentence.[592] Should this kind of plea bargain be permissible?

3. Pregnancy and Contractual Autonomy

This section addresses what legal rules should govern women who are willing to bear children for someone else, as a surrogate, or through other arrangements arising from non-traditional methods of reproduction. In this area, the law has struggled to keep up with medical technology and evolving social practice. This new frontier presents crucial challenges for women's autonomy and public policy.

---

588. See, e.g., N.D. Cent. Code § 14-02.1-04.1 (2022); N.C. Gen. Stat. § 90-21.121 (2022).

589. N.D. Cent. Code 14-02.1-04.1 (2022).

590. Lindsay Schnell, Jews, Outraged by Restrictive Abortion Laws, Are Invoking the Hebrew Bible in the Debate, USA Today, July 24, 2019. See also Rebecca Todd Peters, Trust Women: A Progressive Christian Argument for Reproductive Justice (2018).

591. Dubay v. Wells, 506 F.3d 422 (6th Cir. 2007).

592. The facts were taken from Cleveland Bar Ass'n v. Clearly, 754 N.E.2d 235 (Ohio 2001), described and critiqued in April L. Cherry, The Detention, Confinement, and Incarceration of Pregnant Women for the Benefit of Fetal Health, 16 Colum. J. Gender & L. 147 (2007).

In re Baby M

537 A.2d 1227 (N.J. 1988)

Wilentz, C.J.

In this matter the Court is asked to determine the validity of a contract that purports to provide a new way of bringing children into a family. For a fee of $10,000, a woman agrees to be artificially inseminated with the semen of another woman's husband; she is to conceive a child, carry it to term, and after its birth surrender it to the natural father and his wife. The intent of the contract is that the child's natural mother will thereafter be forever separated from her child. The wife is to adopt the child, and she and the natural father are to be regarded as its parents for all purposes. The contract providing for this is called a "surrogacy contract," the natural mother inappropriately called the "surrogate mother."

We invalidate the surrogacy contract because it conflicts with the law and public policy of this State. While we recognize the depth of the yearning of infertile couples to have their own children, we find the payment of money to a "surrogate" mother illegal, perhaps criminal, and potentially degrading to women. Although in this case we grant custody to the natural father, the evidence having clearly proved such custody to be in the best interests of the infant, we void both the termination of the surrogate mother's parental rights and the adoption of the child by the wife/stepparent. We thus restore the "surrogate" as the mother of the child. We remand the issue of the natural mother's visitation rights to the trial court. . . .

We find no offense to our present laws where a woman voluntarily and without payment agrees to act as a "surrogate" mother, provided that she is not subject to a binding agreement to surrender her child. . . .

I. FACTS

In February 1985, William Stern and Mary Beth Whitehead entered into a surrogacy contract. It recited that Stern's wife, Elizabeth, was infertile, that they wanted a child, and that Mrs. Whitehead was willing to provide that child as the mother with Mr. Stern as the father.

The contract provided that through artificial insemination using Mr. Stern's sperm, Mrs. Whitehead would become pregnant, carry the child to term, bear it, deliver it to the Sterns, and thereafter do whatever was necessary to terminate her maternal rights so that Mrs. Stern could thereafter adopt the child. Mrs. Whitehead's husband, Richard, was also a party to the contract; Mrs. Stern was not. Mr. Whitehead promised to do all acts necessary to rebut the presumption of paternity under the Parentage Act. Although Mrs. Stern was not a party to the surrogacy agreement, the contract gave her sole custody of the child in the event of Mr. Stern's death. . . .

Mr. Stern, on his part, agreed to attempt the artificial insemination and to pay Mrs. Whitehead $10,000 after the child's birth, on its delivery to him. In a separate contract, Mr. Stern agreed to pay $7,500 to the Infertility Center of New York ("ICNY"). The Center's advertising campaigns solicit surrogate mothers and encourage infertile couples to consider surrogacy. ICNY arranged for the surrogacy contract by bringing the parties together, explaining the process to them, furnishing the contractual form, and providing legal counsel.

The history of the parties' involvement in this arrangement suggests their good faith. William and Elizabeth Stern were married in July 1974, having met at the University of Michigan, where both were Ph.D. candidates. Due to financial considerations and Mrs. Stern's pursuit of a medical degree and residency, they decided to defer starting a family until 1981. Before then, however, Mrs. Stern learned that she might have multiple sclerosis and that the disease in some cases renders pregnancy a serious health risk. Her anxiety appears to have exceeded the actual risk, which current medical authorities assess as minimal. Nonetheless that anxiety was evidently quite real, Mrs. Stern fearing that pregnancy might precipitate blindness, paraplegia, or other forms of debilitation. Based on the perceived risk, the Sterns decided to forego having their own children. The decision had special significance for Mr. Stern. Most of his family had been destroyed in the Holocaust. As the family's only survivor, he very much wanted to continue his bloodline.

Initially the Sterns considered adoption but were discouraged by the substantial delay apparently involved and by the potential problem they saw arising from their age and their differing religious backgrounds. They were most eager for some other means to start a family.

The paths of Mrs. Whitehead and the Sterns to surrogacy were similar. Both responded to advertising by ICNY. . . . Mrs. Whitehead's response apparently resulted from her sympathy with family members and others who could have no children (she stated that she wanted to give another couple the "gift of life"); she also wanted the $10,000 to help her family.

Both parties, undoubtedly because of their own self-interest, were less sensitive to the implications of the transaction than they might otherwise have been. Mrs. Whitehead, for instance, appears not to have been concerned about whether the Sterns would make good parents for her child; the Sterns, on their part, while conscious of the obvious possibility that surrendering the child might cause grief to Mrs. Whitehead, overcame their qualms because of their desire for a child. At any rate, both the Sterns and Mrs. Whitehead were committed to the arrangement; both thought it right and constructive. . . .

On February 6, 1985, Mr. Stern and Mr. and Mrs. Whitehead executed the surrogate parenting agreement. After several artificial inseminations over a period of months, Mrs. Whitehead became pregnant. The pregnancy was uneventful and on March 27, 1986, Baby M was born. . . .

Mrs. Whitehead realized, almost from the moment of birth, that she could not part with this child. She had felt a bond with it even during pregnancy. . . . She apparently broke into tears and indicated that she did not know if she could give up the child. . . .

Nonetheless, Mrs. Whitehead was, for the moment, true to her word. Despite powerful inclinations to the contrary, she turned her child over to the Sterns on March 30 at the Whiteheads' home.

The Sterns were thrilled with their new child. They had planned extensively for its arrival, far beyond the practical furnishing of a room for her. It was a time of joyful celebration — not just for them but for their friends as well. The Sterns looked forward to raising their daughter, whom they named Melissa. . . .

Later in the evening of March 30, Mrs. Whitehead became deeply disturbed, disconsolate, stricken with unbearable sadness. She had to have her child. She could not eat, sleep, or concentrate on anything other than her need for her baby. The next day she went to the Sterns' home and told them how much she was suffering.

The depth of Mrs. Whitehead's despair surprised and frightened the Sterns. She told them that she could not live without her baby, that she must have her, even if only for one week, that thereafter she would surrender her child. The Sterns, concerned that Mrs. Whitehead might indeed commit suicide, not wanting under any circumstances to risk that, and in any event believing that Mrs. Whitehead would keep her word, turned the child over to her. . . .

The struggle over Baby M began when it became apparent that Mrs. Whitehead could not return the child to Mr. Stern. Due to Mrs. Whitehead's refusal to relinquish the baby, Mr. Stern filed a complaint seeking enforcement of the surrogacy contract. . . .

The Whiteheads immediately fled to Florida with Baby M. They stayed initially with Mrs. Whitehead's parents, where one of Mrs. Whitehead's children had been living. For the next three months, the Whiteheads and Melissa lived at roughly twenty different hotels, motels, and homes in order to avoid apprehension. From time to time Mrs. Whitehead would call Mr. Stern to discuss the matter; the conversations, recorded by Mr. Stern on advice of counsel, show an escalating dispute about rights, morality, and power, accompanied by threats of Mrs. Whitehead to kill herself, to kill the child, and falsely to accuse Mr. Stern of sexually molesting Mrs. Whitehead's other daughter.

Eventually the Sterns discovered where the Whiteheads were staying, commenced supplementary proceedings in Florida, and obtained an order requiring the Whiteheads to turn over the child. Police in Florida enforced the order, forcibly removing the child from her grandparents' home. She was soon thereafter brought to New Jersey and turned over to the Sterns. . . .

The trial took thirty-two days over a period of more than two months. . . . [The trial court] held that the surrogacy contract was valid; ordered that Mrs. Whitehead's parental rights be terminated and that sole custody of the child be granted to Mr. Stern; and, after hearing brief testimony from Mrs. Stern, immediately entered an order allowing the adoption of Melissa by Mrs. Stern, all in accordance with the surrogacy contract. . . .

II. INVALIDITY AND UNENFORCEABILITY OF SURROGACY CONTRACT

. . . A. Conflict with Statutory Provisions

The surrogacy contract conflicts with: (1) laws prohibiting the use of money in connection with adoptions; (2) laws requiring proof of parental unfitness or abandonment before termination of parental rights is ordered or an adoption is granted; and (3) laws that make surrender of custody and consent to adoption revocable in private placement adoptions.

(1) Our law prohibits paying or accepting money in connection with any placement of a child for adoption. Violation is a high misdemeanor. Excepted

are fees of an approved agency (which must be a non-profit entity) and certain expenses in connection with childbirth.

Considerable care was taken in this case to structure the surrogacy arrangement so as not to violate this prohibition. . . . Nevertheless, it seems clear that the money was paid and accepted in connection with an adoption. . . .

Mr. Stern knew he was paying for the adoption of a child; Mrs. Whitehead knew she was accepting money so that a child might be adopted; the Infertility Center knew that it was being paid for assisting in the adoption of a child. The actions of all three worked to frustrate the goals of the statute. . . .

The evils inherent in baby-bartering are loathsome for a myriad of reasons. The child is sold without regard for whether the purchasers will be suitable parents. The natural mother does not receive the benefit of counseling and guidance to assist her in making a decision that may affect her for a lifetime. In fact, the monetary incentive to sell her child may, depending on her financial circumstances, make her decision less voluntary. Furthermore, the adoptive parents may not be fully informed of the natural parents' medical history. . . .

(2) The termination of Mrs. Whitehead's parental rights, called for by the surrogacy contract and actually ordered by the court, fails to comply with the stringent requirements of New Jersey law. . . .

In order to terminate parental rights under the private placement adoption statute, there must be a finding of "intentional abandonment or a very substantial neglect of parental duties without a reasonable expectation of a reversal of that conduct in the future." . . .

In this case a termination of parental rights was obtained not by proving the statutory prerequisites but by claiming the benefit of contractual provisions. . . . [A] contractual agreement to abandon one's parental rights, or not to contest a termination action, will not be enforced in our courts. . . .

(3) The provision in the surrogacy contract stating that Mary Beth Whitehead agrees to "surrender custody . . . and terminate all parental rights" contains no clause giving her a right to rescind. It is intended to be an irrevocable consent to surrender the child for adoption—in other words, an irrevocable commitment by Mrs. Whitehead to turn Baby M over to the Sterns and thereafter to allow termination of her parental rights. . . .

Such a provision, however, making irrevocable the natural mother's consent to surrender custody of her child in a private placement adoption, clearly conflicts with New Jersey law. . . .

The[] strict prerequisites to irrevocability constitute a recognition of the most serious consequences that flow from such consents: termination of parental rights, the permanent separation of parent from child, and the ultimate adoption of the child. Because of those consequences, the Legislature severely limited the circumstances under which such consent would be irrevocable. The legislative goal is furthered by regulations requiring approved agencies, prior to accepting irrevocable consents, to provide advice and counseling to women, making it more likely that they fully understand and appreciate the consequences of their acts. . . .

The provision in the surrogacy contract whereby the mother irrevocably agrees to surrender custody of her child and to terminate her parental rights conflicts with the settled interpretation of New Jersey statutory law. . . .

B. Public Policy Considerations

The surrogacy contract's invalidity . . . is further underlined when its goals and means are measured against New Jersey's public policy. The contract's basic premise, that the natural parents can decide in advance of birth which one is to have custody of the child, bears no relationship to the settled law that the child's best interests shall determine custody. . . .

The surrogacy contract guarantees permanent separation of the child from one of its natural parents. Our policy, however, has long been that to the extent possible, children should remain with and be brought up by both of their natural parents. . . . This is not simply some theoretical ideal that in practice has no meaning. The impact of failure to follow that policy is nowhere better shown than in the results of this surrogacy contract. A child, instead of starting off its life with as much peace and security as possible, finds itself immediately in a tug-of-war between contending mother and father.

The surrogacy contract violates the policy of this State that the rights of natural parents are equal concerning their child, the father's right no greater than the mother's. . . . The whole purpose and effect of the surrogacy contract was to give the father the exclusive right to the child by destroying the rights of the mother.

The policies expressed in our comprehensive laws governing consent to the surrender of a child stand in stark contrast to the surrogacy contract and what it implies. Here there is no counseling, independent or otherwise, of the natural mother, no evaluation, no warning. . . .

Under the contract, the natural mother is irrevocably committed before she knows the strength of her bond with her child. She never makes a totally voluntary, informed decision, for quite clearly any decision prior to the baby's birth is, in the most important sense, uninformed, and any decision after that, compelled by a preexisting contractual commitment, the threat of a lawsuit, and the inducement of a $10,000 payment, is less than totally voluntary. . . .

Although the interest of the natural father and adoptive mother is certainly the predominant interest, realistically the *only* interest served, even they are left with less than what public policy requires. They know little about the natural mother, her genetic makeup, and her psychological and medical history. Moreover, not even a superficial attempt is made to determine their awareness of their responsibilities as parents.

Worst of all, however, is the contract's total disregard of the best interests of the child. There is not the slightest suggestion that any inquiry will be made at any time to determine the fitness of the Sterns as custodial parents, of Mrs. Stern as an adoptive parent, their superiority to Mrs. Whitehead, or the effect on the child of not living with her natural mother.

This is the sale of a child, or, at the very least, the sale of a mother's right to her child, the only mitigating factor being that one of the purchasers is the father. Almost every evil that prompted the prohibition on the payment of money in connection with adoptions exists here. . . .

The main difference [between adoption and surrogacy], that the unwanted pregnancy is unintended while the situation of the surrogate mother is voluntary and intended, is really not significant. Initially, it produces stronger reactions of sympathy for the mother whose pregnancy was unwanted than for the surrogate mother, who "went into this with her eyes wide open." On reflection, however, it appears that the essential evil is the same, taking advantage of a woman's circumstances (the unwanted pregnancy or the need for money) in order to take away her child, the difference being one of degree.

In the scheme contemplated by the surrogacy contract in this case, a middle man, propelled by profit, promotes the sale. Whatever idealism may have motivated any of the participants, the profit motive predominates, permeates, and ultimately governs the transaction. The demand for children is great and the supply small. The availability of contraception, abortion, and the greater willingness of single mothers to bring up their children has led to a shortage of babies offered for adoption. . . .

Intimated, but disputed, is the assertion that surrogacy will be used for the benefit of the rich at the expense of the poor. In response it is noted that the Sterns are not rich and the Whiteheads not poor. Nevertheless, it is clear to us that it is unlikely that surrogate mothers will be as proportionately numerous among those women in the top 20 percent income bracket as among those in the bottom twenty percent. Put differently, we doubt that infertile couples in the low-income bracket will find upper income surrogates. . . .

The long-term effects of surrogacy contracts are not known, but feared — the impact on the child who learns her life was bought, that she is the offspring of someone who gave birth to her only to obtain money; the impact on the natural mother as the full weight of her isolation is felt along with the full reality of the sale of her body and her child; the impact on the natural father and adoptive mother once they realize the consequences of their conduct. . . .

The surrogacy contract is based on, principles that are directly contrary to the objectives of our laws. It guarantees the separation of a child from its mother; it looks to adoption regardless of suitability; it totally ignores the child; it takes the child from the mother regardless of her wishes and her maternal fitness; and it does all of this, it accomplishes all of its goals, through the use of money.

Beyond that is the potential degradation of some women that may result from this arrangement. In many cases, of course, surrogacy may bring satisfaction, not only to the infertile couple, but to the surrogate mother herself. The fact, however, that many women may not perceive surrogacy negatively but rather see it as an opportunity does not diminish its potential for devastation to other women. . . .

IV. CONSTITUTIONAL ISSUES

Both parties argue that the Constitutions — state and federal — mandate approval of their basic claims. . . . The right asserted by the Sterns is the right of procreation; that asserted by Mary Beth Whitehead is the right to the companionship of her child. We find that the right of procreation does not extend as far as claimed by the Sterns. As for the right asserted by Mrs. Whitehead, since we uphold it on other grounds . . . , we need not decide that constitutional issue. . . .

V. CUSTODY . . .

Our reading of the record persuades us that the trial court's decision awarding custody to the Sterns (technically to Mr. Stern) should be affirmed. . . .

Our custody conclusion is based on strongly persuasive testimony contrasting both the family life of the Whiteheads and the Sterns and the personalities and characters of the individuals. The stability of the Whitehead family life was doubtful at the time of trial. Their finances were in serious trouble. . . . Mr. Whitehead's employment, though relatively steady, was always at risk because of his alcoholism, a condition that he seems not to have been able to confront effectively. Mrs. Whitehead had not worked for quite some time, her last two employments having been part-time. . . . Certain of the experts noted that Mrs. Whitehead perceived herself as omnipotent and omniscient concerning her children. She knew what they were thinking, what they wanted, and she spoke for them. As to Melissa, Mrs. Whitehead expressed the view that she alone knew what that child's cries and sounds meant. Her inconsistent stories about various things engendered grave doubts about her ability to explain honestly and sensitively to Baby M — and at the right time — the nature of her origin. . . . In short, while love and affection there would be, Baby M's life with the Whiteheads promised to be too closely controlled by Mrs. Whitehead. The prospects for wholesome, independent psychological growth and development would be at serious risk.

The Sterns have no other children, but all indications are that their household and their personalities promise a much more likely foundation for Melissa to grow and thrive. There *is* a track record of sorts — during the one-and-a-half years of custody Baby M has done very well, and the relationship between both Mr. and Mrs. Stern and the baby has become very strong. The household is stable, and likely to remain so. Their finances are more than adequate, their circle of friends supportive, and their marriage happy. Most important, they are loving, giving, nurturing, and open-minded people. They have demonstrated the wish and ability to nurture and protect Melissa, yet at the same time to encourage her independence. . . . All in all, Melissa's future appears solid, happy, and promising with them. . . .

VI. VISITATION

The trial court's decision to terminate Mrs. Whitehead's parental rights precluded it from making any determination on visitation. . . . We therefore remand the visitation issue to the trial court for an abbreviated hearing. . . .

We also note the following for the trial court's consideration: First, this is not a divorce case where visitation is almost invariably granted to the non-custodial spouse. . . . Mrs. Whitehead spent the first four months of this child's life as her mother and has regularly visited the child since then. Second, she is not only the natural mother, but also the legal mother, and is not to be penalized one iota because of the surrogacy contract. Mrs. Whitehead, as the mother (indeed, as a mother who nurtured her child for its first four months — unquestionably a relevant consideration), is entitled to have her own interest in visitation considered. . . .

CONCLUSION

This case affords some insight into a new reproductive arrangement: the artificial insemination of a surrogate mother. . . .

We have found that our present laws do not permit the surrogacy contract used in this case. . . .

[T]he Legislature remains free to deal with this most sensitive issue as it sees fit, subject only to constitutional constraints.

If the Legislature decides to address surrogacy, consideration of this case will highlight many of its potential harms. . . . Legislative consideration of surrogacy may also provide the opportunity to begin to focus on the overall implications of the new reproductive biotechnology — *in vitro* fertilization, preservation of sperm and eggs, embryo implantation and the like. The problem is how to enjoy the benefits of the technology — especially for infertile couples — while minimizing the risk of abuse. The problem can be addressed only when society decides what its values and objectives are in this troubling, yet promising, area. . . .

NOTES

1. **Gestational Surrogacy.** In *Baby M*, Mary Beth Whitehead was the child's genetic mother as well as the surrogate carrier — an arrangement now referred to as "traditional surrogacy." The New Jersey Supreme Court determined that her rights could not be terminated on the basis of a contract signed before the birth of the child. Thus, custody of the child was adjudicated between her and the child's biological father under the customary test applied in custody disputes between biological parents — i.e., the best interests of the child.

When the genetic and gestational functions are separated, the issue of parentage becomes more complicated. With "gestational surrogacy," the surrogate provides the womb, but not the egg. With sperm and egg provided either by the intended parents or donors, conception is achieved through *in vitro* fertilization. Today, almost all surrogacy arrangements are done this way. In Johnson v. Calvert, the gestational mother asserted parental rights against the intended parents, who were also both the genetic parents of the child.[593] The California Supreme Court interpreted the state's version of the Uniform Parentage Act to permit a finding of parenthood on either genetic or gestational grounds, concluding that "when the two means do not coincide in one woman, she who intended to procreate the child — that is, she who intended to bring about the birth of a child that she intended to raise as her own — is the natural mother under California law."[594]

Matters can become even more complicated when neither claimant is the genetic mother. In one egg donor case, a Pennsylvania court voided a surrogacy contract and declared that the legal mother of triplets was the gestational surrogate, not the contracting couple. The court determined that the egg donor was comparable to a sperm donor.[595] Celebrity talk-show host Sherri Shepard attempted to avoid her responsibilities for a child carried by a surrogate because she and her husband parted ways during the pregnancy. The child was not related genetically to Sherri or to the surrogate; an egg donor was used instead. Her ex-husband, the biological father, is raising the child as a single father and sought child support from Shepard, who sought to invalidate the agreement as against public policy.

---

593. 851 P.2d 776 (Cal. 1993).

594. Id. at 500.

595. J.F. v. D.B., 66 Pa. D. & C. 4th 1 (Pa. Ct. Comm. Pl. 2004).

A Pennsylvania trial court held that the surrogacy agreement was enforceable, tying Shepard to a child who was brought into this world because of her actions but whom she has never met and to whom she is not genetically related.[596] Does her ex ante intent make her more of a mother than the gestational carrier?

The vast majority of surrogacy contracts are honored by both parties whether or not they are legally enforceable, but the law develops through the cases in which there are conflicts between the intended parents and the surrogate. In the absence of controlling statutory authority, state court rulings have produced mixed results. The rulings reflect two primary approaches: (1) an intent-based approach, which seeks to fulfill the intentions of the parties (*Calvert*); or (2) the genetic contribution test, which looks to the genetic tie between parent and child.[597] The Wisconsin Supreme Court has held that surrogacy agreements are enforceable under conventional contract law as long as enforcement is not contrary to the child's best interests.[598] Is that a good compromise, or does it defeat the purpose of a pre-conception surrogacy agreement to invite a substantive review of the choices the parties made by contract?

Several cases involving gay and lesbian parents and non-traditional reproductive procedures have recognized the parental status of two people of the same sex.[599] Issues involving gay and lesbian parents are explored more fully in Chapter 2, Section D.

2. **The Prevalence and Regulation of Surrogacy.** The *Baby M* ruling thrust the surrogacy issue into the public eye. In the year after the ruling, legislatures all over the country considered bills to permit, prohibit, or regulate surrogacy. Most did not become law, but some states, including New York, banned surrogacy.[600]

In the intervening decades, the demand for surrogacy has increased dramatically. Exact numbers are hard to get, but worldwide it is estimated that approximately 7 million children have been born through some means of assisted reproductive technology.[601] The American Society for Reproductive Medicine estimates that the number of surrogate births increased from a few hundred in 2005 to a few thousand in 2013.[602] The Centers for Disease Control, which tracks in vitro fertilization data, reports that gestational carrier cycles resulted in the birth of 18,400

---

596. In re Baby S., 128 A.3d 296 (Pa. 2015).

597. On competing approaches, see Browne C. Lewis, Three Lies and a Truth: Adjudicating Maternity in Surrogacy Disputes, 49 U. Louisville L. Rev. 371 (2011).

598. In re the Paternity of F.T.R., 833 N.W.2d 634 (Wis. 2013).

599. See, e.g., K.M. v. E.G., 117 P.3d 673 (Cal. 2005); Carvin v. Britain, 122 P.3d 161 (Wash. 2005).

600. N.Y. Dom. Rel. § 123 (repealed 2021). Other states that still ban paid surrogacy include Arizona, Indiana, Louisiana, Michigan, Nebraska, North Dakota, and Utah. On *Baby M*'s influence, see Elizabeth S. Scott, Surrogacy and the Politics of Commodification, 72 L. Contemp. Prob. 109 (2009). On the role of brokers, see Carol Sanger, Developing Markets in Baby-Making: In the Matter of Baby M, 29 Harv. J.L. & Gender (2007).

601. Emily Galpern, Assisted Reproductive Technologies: Overview and Perspective Using a Reproductive Justice Framework (Dec. 2007).

602. Suzanne Rico, Surrogacy: Joyful, Frightening, Always Risky, Atlantic (Apr. 2013); Sara Rimer, No Stork Involved, but Mom and Dad Had Help, N.Y. Times, July 12, 2009, at A1.

babies between 1999 and 2013; the percentage of total IVF cycles that involved a gestational carrier rose from 2.1 percent in 2010 to 5.4 percent in 2019.[603]

A number of models for regulating surrogacy have been proposed. The Uniform Status of Children of Assisted Conception Act (1988) gave jurisdictions a choice about whether to allow surrogacy arrangements.[604] This Act was withdrawn and superseded in 2002 by the amended Uniform Parentage Act (UPA), which has become very influential across the country. Section 8 of the UPA, which provides for enforceable agreements using either traditional or gestational surrogacy, is "bracketed," again to allow for omission of the surrogacy provisions without undermining the other provisions of the Act. The UPA was revised again in 2017, with revisions to the surrogacy provision designed to be more consistent with surrogacy practice.

Section 8 of the UPA imposes some restrictions on valid gestational agreements. For example, a married gestational mother's husband must be a party to the agreement, and the gestational agreement cannot "limit the right of the gestational mother to make decisions to safeguard her health or that of the embryos or fetus." To serve as a surrogate, a woman must be at least 21, have given birth to at least one child, complete a physical and mental health evaluation, and have independent legal representation. The intended parents must also complete physical and mental health evaluations and have independent legal representation. With genetic surrogacy only, the UPA allows the surrogate to withdraw her consent to the agreement until seventy-two hours after birth. Does that distinction make sense? Why or why not?

Some state legislatures have adopted laws that permit, but regulate, surrogacy. These laws tend to be more restrictive than the UPA provision. The Illinois Gestational Surrogacy Act, enacted in 2004, only allows for gestational surrogacy. The act requires that a gestational surrogate be at least 21 years old, have given birth already at least once, receive mental and physical health evaluations, and receive independent legal advice. The surrogate must be allowed to choose her own doctor, but the intended parents can insist on behavioral changes that protect fetal health, such as giving up smoking and undergoing prenatal testing. The intended parents must prove infertility or a documented medical reason for resorting to surrogacy. At least one of them must provide a gamete used to conceive any resulting child.[605] New Jersey legalized gestational surrogacy in 2018, after a long legislative battle, and New York reversed its longstanding criminal ban on surrogacy in 2021.[606] California, which has allowed surrogacy by judicial decision since 1993,

---

603. Nat'l Ctr. for Chronic Disease Prevention and Health Promotion, Div. of Reprod. Health, ART and Gestational Carriers, CDC (Aug. 5, 2016); Ctrs. for Disease Control and Prevention, 2019 Assisted Reproductive Technology: Fertility Clinic and National Summary Report.

604. Nat'l Conf. Commr's State Law, Uniform Status of Children of Assisted Conception Act (1988).

605. 750 Ill. Comp. Stat. § 47/1 et seq. (2022); see also Fla. Stat. § 745.15 (2022); N.H. Rev. Stat. §§ 168-B:1 (2022); Nev. Rev. Stat. § 126.045 (2022); Va. Code § 20-159 (2022).

606. See New Jersey Gestational Carrier Agreement Act, N.J.S.A. 9:17-60 et seq. (2022); N.Y. Fam. Ct. § 581-401 (2022).

adopted a surrogacy-enabling statute in 2015.[607] This statute does not impose as many restrictions on surrogacy as the Illinois statute, focusing instead on the formality of the agreement and disclosures about the payment of medical expenses. Is one approach preferable? Which concerns about surrogacy does Illinois's more restrictive law try to answer? Does it do so effectively?

The legal landscape for surrogacy remains a patchwork. A handful of jurisdictions expressly disallow surrogacy by statute.[608] Another group of states have no statute on surrogacy, but have favorable court rulings on the enforceability of surrogacy arrangements.[609] Another group of states allow surrogacy under some but not all circumstances.[610] Some states, such as Virginia, require that the surrogate mother be married and already have a child.[611] Other jurisdictions require prior court approval of the arrangement.[612] Some statutes require proof of the intended mother's infertility or other medical need.[613] The most common restrictions are prohibitions or limits on what can be paid. At least four states require the intended parents to be married.[614] Before the Obergefell v. Hodges ruling, discussed in Chapter 2, Section D, the marriage requirement meant that gay couples could not avail themselves of surrogacy as a path to parenthood. Now, however, surrogacy is available to any couple that chooses to marry. Is the elimination of marriage's gender requirement likely to have repercussions for parentage law generally or surrogacy in particular? Does the use of surrogacy by gay male couples raise the same concerns about exploitation of women that some see with hiring one woman to carry a baby for another?

Due to the wide variation in state law on surrogacy, there is considerable uncertainty among parties when they are from different jurisdictions. A case in point involved a man from Ohio and his fiancée from Texas, who entered into a surrogacy contract with a Pennsylvania woman through an Indiana-based agency. After the biological mother gave birth to triplets, a Pennsylvania court voided the contract and gave custody to the mother. An Ohio court contradicted that decision and identified the Texas woman as the legal mother. When the triplets were 2 years old, a Pennsylvania appellate court overturned the trial court decision and ordered the children to be placed with their biological father.[615] Could any of the underlying state policies be as important as stability in the life of the affected children? In another case, the surrogate fled to Michigan, where surrogacy agreements are

---

607. Cal. Fam. Code § 7962 (2022).

608. See, e.g., Ind. Stat. § 31-21-1-1 (2022); Mich. Comp. Laws § 722.851-861 (2022) (same). See Jenna Casolo et al., Assisted Reproductive Technologies, 20 Geo. J. Gender & L. 313 (2019).

609. See, e.g., P.M. v. T.B., 907 N.W.2d 522 (Iowa 2018).

610. See, e.g., La. Rev. Stat. § 9:2713 (2022) (prohibiting traditional and compensated surrogacy but permitting altruistic gestational surrogacy).

611. Va. Code § 20-158 (2022).

612. Utah Code § 78b-15-801-809 (2022).

613. See, e.g., N.H. Rev. Stat. § 168-B:17 (2022) (paid surrogacy permitted if intended mother has demonstrated medical need).

614. Fla. Stat. § 742.15 (2022); Tenn. Code Ann. § 36-1-102(50) (2022); Tex. Fam. Code § 160.754 (2022); Utah Code §§ 78b-15-801 (2022).

615. Theresa Glennon, Inaction Causes Harm, Nat'l L.J. July 24, 2006, at 31.

unenforceable, to avoid turning over a child with significant birth defects to the intended parents, who indicated they would place the child for adoption.[616] Do these stories justify federal intervention or a unified approach to surrogacy?

The world community reflects similar divisions in legal approaches, with all pre-conception arrangements prohibited in most Middle Eastern countries, China, Denmark, Norway, Switzerland, Costa Rica, and Germany, and only unpaid surrogacy allowed in Korea and Australia. In Great Britain, surrogacy agreements are unenforceable, and it is illegal to advertise for or broker surrogacy arrangements.[617] Surrogacy has increasingly become a feature of "reproductive tourism," in which couples from countries like the United States and England hire surrogate carriers in places like India, where it can be done more cheaply and without legal regulation.[618] Surrogacy in the United States can cost between $40,000 and $100,000, of which about $25,000 is paid to the surrogate. India was a hub for international surrogacy because the cost was a fraction of that in the United States — between $5,000 and $12,000 in India. But India enacted a law banning transnational surrogacy in 2015 and then all commercial surrogacy in 2018.[619] In 2021, India passed a law to allow "altruistic surrogacy" (payment of expenses only) for couples who have been married at least five years, are medically unable to produce a child, and have no surviving children; the surrogate must be a relative of the couple.[620] Despite the higher price in the United States, it has become one of the leading destinations for international surrogacy because of the perception that the law supports enforcement of paid surrogacy contracts, at least in particular states.[621] International surrogacy arrangements, however, have led to conflicts about parentage, citizenship, and other matters when the surrogate and the intended parents come from countries with conflicting laws.[622] The lack of personal contact between intended parents and surrogates may also open the door to greater fraud.[623] Does international surrogacy also heighten concerns about the potential exploitation of women (see Note 4)? Is

---

616. Elizabeth Cohen, Surrogate Offered $10,000 to Abort Baby, CNN Health, Mar. 6, 2013; see also Tamar Lewin, Surrogates and Couples Face a Maze of Laws, State by State, N.Y. Times, Sept. 18, 2014, at A1.

617. See Jill Elaine Hasday, Intimacy and Economic Exchange, 119 Harv. L. Rev. 491 (2005); Margaret Foster Riley, with Richard A. Merrill, Regulating Reproductive Genetics: A Review of American Bioethics Commissions and Comparison to the British Human Fertilization and Embryology Authority, 6 Colum. Sci. & Tech. L. Rev. 1, 4 (2005).

618. See Debora Spar, Reproductive Tourism and the Regulatory Map, 352 New Eng. J. Med. 531-33 (2005); Debora Spar, The Baby Business: How Money, Science, and Politics Drive the Commerce of Conception (2006).

619. Saptarshi Ray, India Bans Commercial Surrogacy to Stop "Rent a Womb" Exploitation of Vulnerable Women, Telegraph, Dec. 20, 2018.

620. Id.

621. See Tamar Lewin, Coming to U.S. for Baby, and Womb to Carry It: Foreign Couples Heading to America for Surrogate Pregnancies, N.Y. Times, July 5, 2014, at A1.

622. See Hague Conference on Private Int'l Law, A Study of Legal Parentage and the Issues Arising from International Surrogacy Arrangements (Mar. 2014).

623. See, e.g., Alan Zarembo, Scam Targeted Surrogates as Well as Couples, L.A. Times, Aug. 13, 2011.

it a coincidence that India has one-third of the world's poorest people and operated as a "surrogacy hub"?

3. **Decisional Autonomy and Regret.**   One justification for the court's ruling in *Baby M* was a concern that women may irrevocably consent to relinquishing a child without fully understanding and appreciating the consequences of their acts. When providing guidance to the lower court on visitation for Mrs. Whitehead, the court offered this view:

> It seems to us that given her predicament, Mrs. Whitehead was rather harshly judged — both by the trial court and by some of the experts. She was guilty of a breach of contract, and indeed, she did break a very important promise, but we think it is expecting something well beyond normal human capabilities to suggest that this mother should have parted with her newly born infant without a struggle. Other than survival, what stronger force is there?

Is this accurate, condescending, or both? What assumptions about women's ability to make decisions, particularly those involving reproduction, underlie the court's view? Do similar ones underlie the U.S. Supreme Court's ruling in Gonzales v. Carhart, noted in the prior section, that Congress can constitutionally prohibit a particular method of abortion in part to save "a mother who comes to regret her choice to abort" from "grief more anguished and sorrow more profound" when she learns later how the abortion was performed?[624] Are empirical studies, which tend to show that most surrogates are happy with the experience and would do it again, relevant to the legal questions about surrogacy?

In Johnson v. Calvert, the California Supreme Court had a different perspective than the New Jersey Supreme Court about the surrogate mother's decisional autonomy:

> The argument that a woman cannot knowingly and intelligently agree to gestate and deliver a baby for intending parents carries overtones of the reasoning that for centuries prevented woman from attaining equal economic rights and professional status under the law. To resurrect this view is both to foreclose a personal and economic choice on the part of the surrogate mother, and to deny intending parents what may be their only means of procreating a child of their own genes.[625]

In a subsequent California case involving another surrogate who was not the genetic mother, it was the intended father who changed his mind; he no longer wished to be either married or a father. In that case, as well, the court held that the party's original intent should be controlling and that the father would remain responsible for child support.[626]

Some commentators have criticized approaches that give gestational carriers fewer rights to change their minds than those surrogates who are also genetic

---

624. 550 U.S. 124, 159-60 (2007).
625. Id. at 503.
626. In re Marriage of Buzzanca, 72 Cal. Rptr. 2d 280 (Ct. App. 1998).

mothers. The concern is that this both devalues the care invested during gestation and also encourages more couples to undergo egg extraction, a prolonged and difficult process that results in more high-risk pregnancies, so that the surrogate will only have a gestational and not genetic relationship to the infant.[627] If these are valid concerns, what follows? Could the act of gestation create strong emotional ties for which surrogacy law needs to account? A pregnant surrogate in California filed suit to invalidate an agreement she had made to bear triplets for a single man in Georgia. In her complaint, she refers to herself as a mother "as a matter of biologic fact" and cites studies on the physiologic and emotional aspects of pregnancy.[628] Should any of this be relevant to a legal dispute over the enforceability of the contract?

Throughout the materials in reproductive autonomy, we have seen different perspectives on the nature of decisionmaking during pregnancy, which turn in part on assumptions about whether a woman develops a bond with the baby she is carrying before it is born. Is the purported attachment to an embryo or fetus simply something courts use to justify an outcome they otherwise seek to reach? Or can we develop a unified approach to understanding the relationship between adults and embryos or fetuses? Professors Greer Donley and Jill Wieber Lens propose a subjective understanding in order to reconcile seeming tensions between, for example, abortion advocacy, which has relied on the denial of fetal personhood, and the fact that many who experience stillbirth and miscarriage grieve those losses much like a parent who loses a living child.[629] In their view, the law can and should recognize that "fetal value is created by, and dependent on, the individual pregnant person — some pregnant people feel attached to their fetus, attributing various levels of "personhood" to it at different points in pregnancy." The law could both recognize a right to abortion and issue birth certificates for a stillborn baby because in these different contexts, the pregnant person's perception of the fetus is different. Does this framing seem useful? Does it assuage concerns about rights creep, where recognizing fetal value in the context of loss could have collateral consequences for abortion? Would it have changed the outcome in *Baby M.* or Johnson v. Calvert?

4. **Critical Takes on Surrogacy.** Feminist scholars have divided over the issue of surrogacy. When the trial court in *Baby M* ordered the surrogacy agreement enforced (a ruling later overturned), Betty Friedan saw "frightening implications for women" and a "terrifying denial of what should be basic rights for women."[630] The principal feminist defense of surrogate contracts credits the surrogate's expression of intent that her role will be limited to gestation and legitimates the contracting father's intent to play an equal parental role. According to Marjorie Shultz:

---

627. Jennifer Hendricks, Essentially a Mother, 13 Wm & Mary J. Women & L. 429, 477 (2007).

628. C.M. v. M.C., 213 Cal. Rptr. 3d 351 (Ct. App. 2017) (upholding surrogacy agreement against statutory and constitutional challenges).

629. Greer Donley & Jill Wieber Lens, Abortion, Pregnancy Loss, and Subjective Fetal Personhood, 75 Vanderbilt L. Rev. (forthcoming 2022).

630. James Barron, Views on Surrogacy Harden After *Baby M* Ruling, N.Y. Times, Apr. 2, 1987, at A1.

Rules that would determine legal parenthood on the basis of individual intentions about procreation and parenting—at least in the context of reproductive technology—would recognize, encourage and reinforce men's choices to nurture children. By adopting a sex-neutral criterion such as intention, the law would partially offset the biological disadvantages men experience in accessing child-nurturing opportunities. The result would parallel recent legal efforts to offset the burdens that childbearing imposes on women who seek equal access to market employment.[631]

How might considerations of the racial implications of surrogacy affect this analysis? Consider Anita Allen's concern:

> Minority women increasingly will be sought to serve as "mother machines" for embryos of middle and upper-class clients. It's a new, virulent form of racial and class discrimination. Within a decade, thousands of poor and minority women will be used as a "breeder class" for those who can afford $30,000 to $40,000 to avoid the inconvenience and danger of pregnancy.[632]

April Cherry and Dorothy Roberts also worry that such reproductive technologies reinforce racial hierarchy, particularly in light of current estimates of the cost of the procedure, ranging from $30,000 to $70,000.[633] Patricia Williams wrote that surrogacy agreements, with their "heavy-worded legalities" remind her of the terms used to force her enslaved ancestor to carry a child for her slaveholder. "My great-great-grandmother's powerlessness came about as the result of a contract to which she was not a party; Mary Beth Whitehead's powerlessness came about as a result of a contract that she signed at a discrete point of time — yet which, over time, enslaved her."[634] How should the policymakers respond to these concerns?

Of what significance to the debate over surrogacy arrangements are the economic pressures that might lead a surrogate to offer her services? Toward which legal approach does recognition of these pressures lead? Margaret Radin is concerned about the "commodification of personhood" that surrogacy represents.[635] Gloria Steinem, in a debate over a bill to legalize surrogacy in New York, argued that commercial surrogacy means that "women in economic need become commercialized vessels for rent, and the fetuses they carry become the property of others. . . . The bill ignores the socio-economic and racial inequalities of the reproductive commercial surrogacy industry, and puts disenfranchised women at the

---

631. Marjorie Maguire Shultz, Reproductive Technology and Intent-Based Parenthood: An Opportunity for Gender Neutrality, 1990 Wis. L. Rev. 297, 302-03.

632. Anita L. Allen, The Black Surrogate Mother, 8 Harv. Blackletter J. 17, 30 (1991).

633. April L. Cherry, Nurturing the Service of White Culture: Racial Subordination, Gestational Surrogacy, and the Ideology of Motherhood, 10 Tex. J. Women & L. 83 (2001); Dorothy E. Roberts, Race and the New Reproduction, 47 Hastings L.J. 935 (1996). For costs, see Alex Kuczynski, Her Body, My Baby, N.Y. Times Mag., Nov. 30, 2008, at 45.

634. Patricia J. Williams, The Alchemy of Race and Rights 225-26 (1992).

635. Margaret Jane Radin, Market Inalienability, 100 Harv. L. Rev. 1849, 1885 (1987).

financial and emotional mercy of wealthier and more privileged individuals."[636] By contrast, Judge Richard Posner takes an economic efficiency approach in arguing that the financial constraints that push a woman toward becoming a surrogate are no different and no more objectionable than the considerations that motivate all kinds of decisionmaking throughout the economy.[637] This is essentially the framework applied by one court:

> Although common sense suggests that women of lesser means serve as surrogate mothers more often than do wealthy women, there has been no proof that surrogacy contracts exploit poor women to any greater degree than economic necessity in general exploits them by inducing them to accept lower-paid or otherwise undesirable employment.[638]

Who is right? Can women give meaningful consent to act as surrogates without any future parental rights, or are these arrangements inherently exploitative? Consider the words of one woman, who served as a surrogate for a gay male couple, in an essay entitled "Mutual Exploitation":

> The obvious assumption is the possibility of exploitation by the intended parents towards the surrogate. However, the reverse is just as easily possible and likely much more prevalent than people realize. In fact, the process may work best when there is mutual exploitation, to a degree. . . . [T]he experience was absolutely ideal. I had amazing people doting on me constantly, and I had the enjoyable pregnancy I had previously missed. It was a spiritual experience to be able to help create a life for two people who so desired a child, and I got to play the nurturing role. . . . On top of all this, I was compensated, and after it all, my life went back to being my life. So I can say, with absolute certainty, that any construed exploitation done "against" me was equally matched.[639]

Critics of surrogate contracts like Nancy Ehrenreich have emphasized how surrogacy arrangements support ideological messages about having a child "of one's own" that have reinforced male dominance and women's sense of obligation to bear children:

> Given the discourse surrounding this issue, which treats infertility as a human tragedy of immense proportions and child rearing as an inviolable right, enforcing such contracts would seem to suggest that it is absolutely essential for women to become mothers by whatever means possible.[640]

---

636. Vivian Wang, Surrogate Pregnancy Battle Pits Progressives Against Feminists, N.Y. Times, June 12, 2019, at A17.

637. Richard Posner, The Ethics and Economics of Enforcing Contracts of Surrogate Motherhood, 5 J. Contemp. Health L. & Pol'y 21, 26 (1989).

638. Johnson v. Calvert, 19 Cal. Rptr. 494, 503 (Cal. 1993).

639. Beth Jones, Mutual Exploitation: A Response, in Pregnant Man? A Conversation, 22 Yale J.L. & Feminism 207, 257 (2010).

640. Nancy Ehrenreich, Surrogacy as Resistance? The Misplaced Focus on Choice in the Surrogacy and Abortion Funding Contexts, 41 DePaul L. Rev. 1369, 1376 (1992).

Do you agree? Is there another way to read women's desire for surrogacy arrangements? What about men's desire? Is the intended father acting out of a male chauvinist vanity in "wanting a child that is 'his,' or is he expressing a male commitment to nurturing a child?"[641]

Lori B. Andrews, who has vigorously defended surrogacy contracts, is concerned about the implications of assuming that women cannot make responsible reproductive decisions. If gestation gives rise to "special rights" for surrogates to change their minds, could it not also justify "special responsibilities," such as a woman's responsibility to have a cesarean section if doctors believe it would be beneficial to the child? Andrews concludes:

> Some feminists have criticized surrogacy as turning participating women, albeit with their consent, into reproductive vessels. I see the danger of the anti-surrogacy arguments as potentially turning *all* women into reproductive vessels, without their consent, by providing government oversight for women's decisions and creating a disparate legal category for gestation.[642]

What is your view? What regulations do you believe should govern surrogacy arrangements?

5. **Reproductive Choices in the Surrogacy Context.**   A recurring conflict in surrogacy cases—at least those that make national news—is whether a provision in the contract allowing the intended parents to make the decision whether to terminate a pregnancy can be enforced. It is common for surrogacy contracts to provide that the gestational surrogate must terminate the pregnancy (or reduce the number of fetuses being carried, a practice known as "selective reduction") upon request of the intended parents. While a few statutes specifically prohibit this type of clause, most states have no rules regarding the scope or content or surrogacy agreements.[643] In states that allow legal abortions after *Dobbs*, can this provision be enforced? Consider the implications of either specific performance—a court order that a woman must have an abortion—or damages for breach of contract. Would either be appropriate and/or lawful in this context? Deborah Forman writes:

> Although contracts often contain abortion and selective reduction provisions such as these, practitioners routinely describe these as unenforceable, even while advocating their inclusion in the contract. A closer look reveals a somewhat more nuanced perspective: consensus that specific performance of such provisions would never occur but disagreement about whether a surrogate could be liable in damages for breach of contract. Scholars have been a bit more willing to challenge conventional wisdom on the specific performance point, but they by and large echo the

---

641. Shultz, supra note 631, at 353.

642. Lori Andrews, Surrogate Motherhood: The Challenge for Feminists, 16 Law, Med. & Health Care 72, 78 (1988).

643. See, e.g., Utah Code § 78B-15-808(2) & (3) (2022) ("A gestational agreement may not limit the right of the gestational mother to make decisions to safeguard her health or that of the embryo or fetus.").

practitioner perspective—that provisions relating to abortion are either unenforceable altogether or at best subject to a suit for damages.[644]

If the conventional wisdom is correct, why do lawyers continue to include termination clauses in surrogacy contracts? What purpose do they serve? Does a statute prohibiting this type of clause answer any of the concerns about surrogacy described in the preceding materials?

6. Frozen "Pre-embryos": Balancing Wanted and Unwanted Parenthood. As many as a million embryos lie in frozen storage, with little clear law on how to resolve disputes that arise about their use.[645] There is no guarantee that an embryo will result in a live birth—only about a third of all in vitro fertilization cycles do—but, for many, it is the pathway to parenthood.[646] In one Tennessee case, Davis v. Davis, a couple had planned on using frozen embryos to start a family, but divorced before a pregnancy had been achieved. At divorce, the wife sought custody of the embryos for possible future implantation and the husband sought authority to prevent implantation. The trial court declared that the embryos were "human beings" and awarded custody to the wife on the grounds that such action was the most likely to protect their best interests. The Tennessee Court of Appeals reversed, concluding that the parties shared an equal interest in the embryos, that the husband had a constitutionally protected right not to beget a child where no pregnancy had yet taken place, and that there was no compelling state interest to justify implantation against the will of either party.

On appeal to the state supreme court, the wife changed her position, deciding that rather than use the embryos to become pregnant herself, she wanted to donate them to a childless couple. The court rejected the approaches of both the trial court and the court of appeals, holding that "preembryos are not, strictly speaking, either 'persons' or 'property,' but occupy an interim category that entitles them to special respect because of their potential for human life." The court stated that, if possible, a contest over pre-embryos should be resolved according to prior agreement. Where no such agreement exists, each party's constitutional privacy interests require that their individual positions, burdens, and interests be weighed against those of the other party, with the court's choosing the disposition that avoids the most harm. In *Davis*, the court balanced the interests as follows:

> Beginning with the burden imposed on Junior Davis, we note that the consequences are obvious. Any disposition which results in the gestation of the preembryos would impose unwanted parenthood on him, with all of its possible financial and psychological consequences. The impact that this unwanted parenthood would have on Junior Davis can only be

---

644. Deborah L. Forman, Abortion Clauses in Surrogacy Contracts: Insights from a Case Study, 49 Fam. L.Q. 29, 34-35 (2015).

645. See Tamar Lewin, Industry's Growth Leads to Leftover Embryos, and Painful Choices, N.Y. Times, June 17, 2015, at A1.

646. Ctrs. for Disease Control and Prevention, 2019 Assisted Reproductive Technology: ART Success Rates.

understood by considering his particular circumstances, as revealed in the record.

Junior Davis testified that he was the fifth youngest of six children. When he was five years old, his parents divorced, his mother had a nervous break-down, and he and three of his brothers went to live at a home for boys run by the Lutheran Church. Another brother was taken in by an aunt, and his sister stayed with her mother. From that day forward, he had monthly visits with his mother but saw his father only three more times before he died in 1976. Junior Davis testified that, as a boy, he had severe problems caused by separation from his parents. He said that it was especially hard to leave his mother after each monthly visit. He clearly feels that he has suffered because of his lack of opportunity to establish a relationship with his parents and particularly because of the absence of his father.

In light of his boyhood experiences, Junior Davis is vehemently opposed to fathering a child that would not live with both parents. Regardless of whether he or Mary Sue had custody, he feels that the child's bond with the non-custodial parent would not be satisfactory. He testified very clearly that his concern was for the psychological obstacles a child in such a situation would face, as well as the burdens it would impose on him. Likewise, he is opposed to donation because the recipient couple might divorce, leaving the child (which he definitely would consider his own) in a single-parent setting.

Balanced against Junior Davis's interest in avoiding parenthood is Mary Sue Davis's interest in donating the preembryos to another couple for implantation. Refusal to permit donation of the preembryos would impose on her the burden of knowing that the lengthy IVF procedures she underwent were futile, and that the preembryos to which she contributed genetic material would never become children. While this is not an insubstantial emotional burden, we can only conclude that Mary Sue Davis's interest in donation is not as significant as the interest Junior Davis has in avoiding parenthood. If she were allowed to donate these preembryos, he would face a lifetime of either wondering about his parental status or knowing about his parental status but having no control over it. He testified quite clearly that if the preembryos were brought to term he would fight for custody of his child or children. Donation, if a child came of it, would rob him twice — his procreational autonomy would be defeated and his relationship with his offspring would be prohibited.

The case would be closer if Mary Sue Davis were seeking to use the preembryos herself, but only if she could not achieve parenthood by any other reasonable means. We recognize the trauma that Mary Sue has already experienced and the additional discomfort to which she would be subjected if she opts to attempt IVF again. Still, she would have a reasonable opportunity, through IVF, to try once again to achieve parenthood in all its aspects—genetic, gestation, bearing, and rearing.

Further, we note that if Mary Sue Davis were unable to undergo another round of IVF, or opted not to try, she could still achieve the child-rearing aspects of parenthood through adoption. The fact that she and Junior Davis pursued adoption indicates that, at least at one time, she was willing to forego genetic parenthood and would have been satisfied by the child-rearing aspects of parenthood alone.[647]

Is this analysis consistent with the principle of equality? Is it an application of the "ethic of care"? Pragmatism? Stereotyped thinking? Resistance to stereotypes?

Mary Sue Davis was unable to conceive children through the usual means because, after six painful tubal pregnancies, both of her fallopian tubes were inoperative. Each of the six IVF attempts involved a month of subcutaneous injections and five anesthetizations for the aspiration procedure. Should this painful series of treatments have been considered in the balancing of interests?

Is it clear to you why Junior Davis' strong feelings—about not fathering children he could not raise himself in a nuclear family—weighed more heavily than Mary Sue Davis' wish to succeed in her efforts to produce one or more children for herself or for others? The court stated that "[o]rdinarily, the party wishing to avoid procreation should prevail, assuming that the other party has a reasonable possibility of achieving parenthood by means other than use of the preembryos in question."[648] The court seemed to suggest that further IVF procedures or adoption would offer reasonable possibilities for Mary Sue Davis to achieve parenthood. How should courts balance a person's last chance at parenthood versus another person's strong desire to avoid it? Does it matter whether the party seeking to use the embryos is male or female? Does the Supreme Court's ruling in *Dobbs* weaken a person's interest in avoiding parenthood?[649] Some commentators have criticized rulings that deny a party a last chance at parenthood, arguing that there is no convincing evidence of psychological harm from involuntary genetic parenthood, and that whatever interest individuals have in avoiding genetic parenthood should be waivable in advance.[650] Is a person's interest in biological parenthood strong enough that it should outweigh an agreement to the contrary?

Most states do not address the proper resolution of embryo disputes by statute. Although the law is still emerging in this area, the trend among courts hearing these disputes has been to favor the right not to procreate over the right to procreate, as the court did in *Davis*. But when the frozen embryo represents a party's last chance to conceive a biological child, courts have split on the right approach. In 2015, a judge in California upheld a consent form a couple signed shortly after they married, which provided that any embryos stored at a fertility clinic would be destroyed if the couple divorced. After the couple divorced, the wife sought to void the agreement. Although these embryos were the last chance for the 46-year-old wife,

---

647. Davis v. Davis, 842 S.W.2d 588, 597 (Tenn. 1992).

648. Id. at 604; see also J.B. v. M.B., 783 A.2d 707, 717 (N.J. 2001) (refusing to allow husband to have pre-embryos for use by a surrogate over his soon-to-be ex-wife's objection because he was fertile and had other opportunities to procreate).

649. 142 S. Ct. 2228 (2022).

650. Glenn Cohen, The Constitution and the Rights Not to Procreate, 60 Stan. L. Rev. 1135 (2008). For other commentary, see Jessica Berg, Owning Persons: The Application of Property Theory to Embryos and Fetuses, 40 Wake Forest L. Rev. 159, 161 (2005).

who was a cancer survivor, to become a biological parent, the judge sided with her ex-husband, ordering the embryos be discarded, because he "should be free from court compelled fatherhood and the attendant uncertainties it would bring."[651]

Would the judge in the California case have reached the same conclusion if the parties had not agreed in advance to the destruction of the embryos? That was the situation in a Pennsylvania case decided three years earlier. In Reber v. Reiss, the court applied the same balancing test used in *Davis*, because the parties had not entered into an agreement prior to creating the pre-embryos about their disposition in the event of divorce or disagreement. The court concluded that the wife's interest in biological parenthood outweighed the husband's interest in non-parenthood, particularly because the pre-embryos in dispute were her "only opportunity to achieve biological parenthood and her best chance to achieve parenthood at all."[652] An Iowa court rejected both standard approaches (contract or balancing test) in favor of a rule requiring "contemporaneous mutual consent" before use implantation of any pre-embryo.[653] Several courts have held that a pre-procedure agreement to destroy embryos in the event of one party's death or divorce is enforceable and consistent with public policy.[654]

A few states have enacted statutes addressing the status or use of cryopreserved pre-embryos. For example, Florida requires couples and IVF programs to agree in advance about the disposition of pre-embryos in the event of a divorce or the death of a spouse.[655] Louisiana requires the treatment of pre-embryos as "juridical persons" and prohibits the destruction of pre-embryos or their use for research purposes.[656] How would you resolve the competing concerns? Restrictions on the use and discarding of embryos are likely to increase now that there is no recognized right of abortion under the federal constitution. Some states may pass laws to require that embryos be treated as full persons. Does this possibility affect men and women equally?

PUTTING THEORY INTO PRACTICE

5-34. Facebook and Apple now offer to pay for female employees to freeze their eggs.[657] Is this good for working women? Or is it just a way to influence women to subordinate their reproductive choices to someone else (i.e., their employers)?

---

651. See Findley v. Lee, No. FDI-13-780539 (Cal. Super. Ct. Nov. 18, 2015); Maura Dolan, Divorced Couple's Frozen Embryos Must Be "Thawed and Discarded," Judge Rules, L.A. Times, Nov. 18, 2015.
652. 42 A.3d 1131, 1142 (Pa. Super. Ct. 2012); see also Szafranski v. Dunston 34 N.E.3d 1132 (Ill. App. 2015).
653. In re Marriage of Witten, 672 N.W.2d 768, 783 (Iowa 2003); see also Casolo et al., supra note 608.
654. Kass v. Kass, 696 N.E.2d 174 (N.Y. 1998); Roman v. Roman, 193 S.W.3d 40 (Tex. App. 2006); In re Marriage of Dahl & Angle, 194 P.3d 834 (Or. Ct. App. 2008).
655. Fla. Stat. § 742.17 (2022).
656. La. Rev. Stat. § 9:121 et seq. (2022).
657. Sarah Buhr, Facebook and Apple Offer to Pay for Female Employees to Freeze Their Eggs (Oct. 14, 2014).

5-35. One surrogate learned from ultrasound tests that the fetus she was carrying suffered from multiple birth defects that would require multiple surgeries upon birth and leave the child with only a 25 percent chance of having a "normal life." The intended parents already had three special-needs children and wanted to spare another child from suffering. The contract required an abortion under such circumstances. The gestational carrier states that she has always been against abortion and refuses to terminate the pregnancy.[658] Who should prevail? How does the Supreme Court's ruling in *Dobbs* factor into the enforceability question? What if the state where the surrogate lives has banned abortion in the wake of *Dobbs*?

5-36. Mari Smith underwent two rounds of egg stimulation and created and preserved twelve embryos for use by a surrogate. She had no medical need for assisted reproduction but did not want to be out of work for any lengthy period of time for fear of losing her clientele. Moreover, after watching a friend give birth, she exclaimed: "I don't want to go through that if I don't have to."[659] A week later she wired money to a broker to start searching for a surrogate. Does a case like this affect your views on surrogacy? Why or why not?

5-37. Patricia Williams has argued that "to try to criminalize surrogacy is a bit like trying to criminalize contraception or abortion, in that it comes too close to criminalizing sexuality, libido, intimacy . . ."[660] Is that an apt comparison? Why or why not? Now that states have the constitutional authority to criminalize abortion (but not contraception), can surrogacy be distinguished?

5-38. In several documented cases, fertility clinics have mixed up pre-embryos, implanting an embryo belonging to one couple into an unrelated woman. What should be done in these cases? Does the genetic mother have a superior claim to motherhood over the gestational mother, or vice versa? How might it affect your analysis if the race of the baby differs from the race of woman who gives birth?

5-39. Every year since 2002, Congress has authorized the spending of between $1 million and $2 million to promote the donation of frozen embryos to recipients who intend to use the embryos to bear and raise a child. Is this a good policy?

5-40. Dr. Eleanora Porcu, who helped to develop the technology for freezing of eggs (or oocyte cryopreservation), saw the possibility of freezing unfertilized eggs as a way of sidestepping the Roman Catholic Church's ban on freezing embryos, which the Church deems immoral. However, she is opposed to giving healthy women the opportunity to freeze their eggs just so that they can postpone childbearing for their own convenience. This practice is harmful to feminism, she says, because "[i]t means that we're accepting a mentality of efficiency in which pregnancy and motherhood are marginalized." "We've demonstrated that we are able to do everything like men. . . . Now we have to do the second revolution, which

---

658. The problem is described in Forman, supra note 644. See also Brittney Kern, "You Are Obligated to Terminate This Pregnancy Immediately": The Contractual Obligations of a Surrogate to Abort Her Pregnancy, 36 Women's Rts. L. Rep. 344 (2015).

659. Sarah Elizabeth Richards, Birth Rights: Inside the Social Surrogacy Debate, Elle, Apr. 17, 2014.

660. Patricia J. Williams, Womb Wars: Fetal Factories, Virgin Vessels and Our Misguided Surrogacy Debate, Nation (Feb. 24, 2014).

is not to become dependent on a technology that involves surgical intervention. We have to be free to be pregnant when we are fertile and young."[661] Do you agree?

5-41. Would enactment of a "personhood amendment," discussed in the previous section, have an effect on surrogacy? On the regulation of cryopreserved pre-embryos or embryos?

4.   The Pregnant Woman and Fetus as Adversaries

Another way pregnant women are policed is through surveillance, prosecution, and punishment for using drugs or engaging in other behaviors that are potentially detrimental to the fetus.

Ferguson v. City of Charleston

532 U.S. 67 (2001)

Justice STEVENS delivered the opinion of the Court.

In this case, we must decide whether a state hospital's performance of a diagnostic test to obtain evidence of a patient's criminal conduct for law enforcement purposes is an unreasonable search if the patient has not consented to the procedure. More narrowly, the question is whether the interest in using the threat of criminal sanctions to deter pregnant women from using cocaine can justify a departure from the general rule that an official nonconsensual search is unconstitutional if not authorized by a valid warrant.

I

In the fall of 1988, staff members at the public hospital operated in the city of Charleston by the Medical University of South Carolina (MUSC) became concerned about an apparent increase in the use of cocaine by patients who were receiving prenatal treatment. In response to this perceived increase, as of April 1989, MUSC began to order drug screens to be performed on urine samples from maternity patients who were suspected of using cocaine. If a patient tested positive, she was then referred by MUSC staff to the county substance abuse commission for counseling and treatment. However, despite the referrals, the incidence of cocaine use among the patients at MUSC did not appear to change.

Some four months later, Nurse Shirley Brown, the case manager for the MUSC obstetrics department, heard a news broadcast reporting that the police in Greenville, South Carolina, were arresting pregnant users of cocaine on the theory that such use harmed the fetus and was therefore child abuse. Nurse Brown discussed the story with MUSC's general counsel, Joseph C. Good, Jr., who then contacted

---

661. Rachel Lehmann-Haupt, Why I Froze My Eggs, Newsweek 50-51 (May 11 & 18, 2009).

Charleston Solicitor Charles Condon in order to offer MUSC's cooperation in prosecuting mothers whose children tested positive for drugs at birth.

After receiving Good's letter, Solicitor Condon took the first steps in developing the policy at issue in this case. He organized the initial meetings, decided who would participate, and issued the invitations, in which he described his plan to prosecute women who tested positive for cocaine while pregnant. The task force that Condon formed included representatives of MUSC, the police, the County Substance Abuse Commission and the Department of Social Services. Their deliberations led to MUSC's adoption of a 12-page document entitled "POLICY M-7," dealing with the subject of "Management of Drug Abuse During Pregnancy."

The first three pages of Policy M-7 set forth the procedure to be followed by the hospital staff to "identify/assist pregnant patients suspected of drug abuse." The first section, entitled the "Identification of Drug Abusers," provided that a patient should be tested for cocaine through a urine drug screen if she met one or more of nine criteria. It also stated that a chain of custody should be followed when obtaining and testing urine samples, presumably to make sure that the results could be used in subsequent criminal proceedings. The policy also provided for education and referral to a substance abuse clinic for patients who tested positive. Most important, it added the threat of law enforcement intervention that "provided the necessary 'leverage' to make the policy effective." That threat was, as respondents candidly acknowledge, essential to the program's success in getting women into treatment and keeping them there.

The threat of law enforcement involvement was set forth in two protocols, the first dealing with the identification of drug use during pregnancy, and the second with identification of drug use after labor. Under the latter protocol, the police were to be notified without delay and the patient promptly arrested. Under the former, after the initial positive drug test, the police were to be notified (and the patient arrested) . . . [unless she consented] to substance abuse treatment.

The last six pages of the policy contained forms for the patients to sign, as well as procedures for the police to follow when a patient was arrested. The policy also prescribed in detail the precise offenses with which a woman could be charged, depending on the stage of her pregnancy. If the pregnancy was 27 weeks or less, the patient was to be charged with simple possession. If it was 28 weeks or more, she was to be charged with possession and distribution to a person under the age of 18—in this case, the fetus. If she delivered "while testing positive for illegal drugs," she was also to be charged with unlawful neglect of a child. Under the policy, the police were instructed to interrogate the arrestee in order "to ascertain the identity of the subject who provided illegal drugs to the suspect." Other than the provisions describing the substance abuse treatment to be offered to women who tested positive, the policy made no mention of any change in the prenatal care of such patients, nor did it prescribe any special treatment for the newborns.

II

Petitioners are 10 women who received obstetrical care at MUSC and who were arrested after testing positive for cocaine. . . .

Petitioners' complaint challenged the validity of the policy under various theories, including the claim that warrantless and nonconsensual drug tests conducted for criminal investigatory purposes were unconstitutional searches. Respondents advanced two principal defenses to the constitutional claim: (1) that, as a matter of fact, petitioners had consented to the searches; and (2) that, as a matter of law, the searches were reasonable, even absent consent, because they were justified by special non-law-enforcement purposes. The District Court rejected the second defense because the searches in question "were not done by the medical university for independent purposes. [Instead,] the police came in and there was an agreement reached that the positive screens would be shared with the police." [The Fourth Circuit Court of Appeals reversed on the grounds that the searches were reasonable under the "special needs" exception.]

We granted certiorari . . . to review the appellate court's holding on the "special needs" issue.

III

Because MUSC is a state hospital, the members of its staff are government actors, subject to the strictures of the Fourth Amendment. . . . Moreover, the urine tests conducted by those staff members were indisputably searches within the meaning of the Fourth Amendment. . . . Neither the District Court nor the Court of Appeals concluded that any of the nine criteria used to identify the women to be searched provided either probable cause to believe that they were using cocaine, or even the basis for a reasonable suspicion of such use. Rather, the District Court and the Court of Appeals viewed the case as one involving MUSC's right to conduct searches without warrants or probable cause. . . . The reasonable expectation of privacy enjoyed by the typical patient undergoing diagnostic tests in a hospital is that the results of those tests will not be shared with nonmedical personnel without her consent. . . . In none of our prior cases was there any intrusion upon that kind of expectation.

The critical difference between those [previous] four drug-testing cases and this one, however, lies in the nature of the "special need" asserted as justification for the warrantless searches. In each of those earlier cases, the "special need" that was advanced as a justification for the absence of a warrant or individualized suspicion was one divorced from the State's general interest in law enforcement. . . . In this case, however, the central and indispensable feature of the policy from its inception was the use of law enforcement to coerce the patients into substance abuse treatment. This fact distinguishes this case from circumstances in which physicians or psychologists, in the course of ordinary medical procedures aimed at helping the patient herself, come across information that under rules of law or ethics is subject to reporting requirements, which no one has challenged here. . . .

Respondents argue in essence that their ultimate purpose — namely, protecting the health of both mother and child — is a beneficent one. . . . While the ultimate goal of the program may well have been to get the women in question into substance abuse treatment and off of drugs, the immediate objective of the searches was to generate evidence for law enforcement purposes in order to reach that goal. The threat of law enforcement may ultimately have been intended as a means to an end, but the direct and primary purpose of MUSC's policy was to ensure the use of those means. In our opinion, this distinction is critical. Because law enforcement involvement always serves some broader social purpose or objective, under respondents' view, virtually any nonconsensual suspicionless search could be immunized under the special needs doctrine by defining the search solely in terms of its ultimate, rather than immediate, purpose. Such an approach is inconsistent with the Fourth Amendment. Given the primary purpose of the Charleston program, which was to use the threat of arrest and prosecution in order to force women into treatment, and given the extensive involvement of law enforcement officials at every stage of the policy, this case simply does not fit within the closely guarded category of "special needs."

Accordingly, the judgment of the Court of Appeals is reversed, and the case is remanded for further proceedings consistent with this opinion.

Dissenting opinion by Justice SCALIA, with whom THE CHIEF JUSTICE and Justice THOMAS join as to Part II.

There is always an unappealing aspect to the use of doctors and nurses, ministers of mercy, to obtain incriminating evidence against the supposed objects of their ministration — although here, it is correctly pointed out, the doctors and nurses were ministering not just to the mothers but also to the children whom their cooperation with the police was meant to protect. But whatever may be the correct social judgment concerning the desirability of what occurred here, that is not the issue in the present case. The Constitution does not resolve all difficult social questions, but leaves the vast majority of them to resolution by debate and the democratic process — which would produce a decision by the citizens of Charleston, through their elected representatives, to forbid or permit the police action at issue here. The question before us is a narrower one: whether, whatever the desirability of this police conduct, it violates the Fourth Amendment's prohibition of unreasonable searches and seizures. In my view, it plainly does not.

I . . .

Until today, we have never held — or even suggested — that material which a person voluntarily entrusts to someone else cannot be given by that person to the police, and used for whatever evidence it may contain. Without so much as discussing the point, the Court today opens a hole in our Fourth Amendment jurisprudence, the size and shape of which is entirely indeterminate. . . .

II . . .

The conclusion of the Court that the special-needs doctrine is inapplicable rests upon its contention that respondents "undertook to obtain [drug] evidence from their patients" not for any medical purpose, but "for the specific purpose of incriminating those patients." In other words, the purported medical rationale was merely a pretext; there was no special need. . . . This contention contradicts the District Court's finding of fact that the goal of the testing policy "was not to arrest patients but to facilitate their treatment and protect both the mother and unborn child." . . . This finding is binding upon us unless clearly erroneous. . . .

The cocaine tests started in April 1989, neither at police suggestion nor with police involvement. Expectant mothers who tested positive were referred by hospital staff for substance-abuse treatment—an obvious health benefit to both mother and child. . . . And, since "infants whose mothers abuse cocaine during pregnancy are born with a wide variety of physical and neurological abnormali-ties," . . . which require medical attention, . . . the tests were of additional medical benefit in predicting needed postnatal treatment for the child. Thus, in their origin—before the police were in any way involved—the tests had an imme-diate, not merely an "ultimate" . . . purpose of improving maternal and infant health. . . .

[I]t is not the function of this Court—at least not in Fourth Amendment cases—to weigh petitioners' privacy interest against the State's interest in meet-ing the crisis of "crack babies" that developed in the late 1980's. I cannot refrain from observing, however, that the outcome of a wise weighing of those interests is by no means clear. The initial goal of the doctors and nurses who conducted cocaine-testing in this case was to refer pregnant drug addicts to treatment cen-ters, and to prepare for necessary treatment of their possibly affected children. When the doctors and nurses agreed to the program providing test results to the police, they did so because (in addition to the fact that child abuse was required by law to be reported) they wanted to use the sanction of arrest as a strong incentive for their addicted patients to undertake drug-addiction treatment. And the police themselves used it for that benign purpose, as is shown by the fact that only 30 of 253 women testing positive for cocaine were ever arrested, and only 2 of those prosecuted. . . . It would not be unreasonable to conclude that today's judgment, authorizing the assessment of damages against the county solicitor and individual doctors and nurses who participated in the program, proves once again that no good deed goes unpunished.

NOTES

1. **Drug Testing of Welfare Recipients.**   The 1996 welfare reform act (TANF), discussed in Section C, below, included a provision making clear that states would not be prohibited by federal law from sanctioning welfare applicants who tested positive for controlled substances.[662] As of 2017, fifteen states had laws requiring drug testing or screening for all public assistance applicants or recipients, and another twenty were considering such requirements.[663] Benefits can be denied if a drug test is negative, or if the recipient refuses to be tested, although in some states recipients can receive benefits, especially if they enroll in a drug treatment plan.[664]

Even though federal welfare law authorizes drug testing or screening for applicants, several courts have blocked state laws that impose random or universal drug testing as a violation of the Fourth Amendment. In 2014, in Lebron v. Secre-tary, Florida Dep't of Children and Families, the Eleventh Circuit Court of Appeals

---

662. 21 U.S.C. § 862 (b) (1996).

663. Nat'l Conference of State Legislatures, Drug Testing for Welfare Recipients and Public Assistance (Mar. 24, 2017).

664. For the range of state approaches, see id. See also Arthur Delaney, States Continue Welfare Drug Tests Despite Underwhelming Results, Huff. Post (Oct. 8, 2015).

enjoined Florida's system of mandatory drug tests for all TANF applicants.[665] According to the Governor, the measure was a valid means of saving revenue and ensuring that benefits accomplish their intended purpose. "Welfare is for the benefit of children, and the money should go to the benefit of children," he stated. "This makes all the sense in the world."[666] However, the court found that the state had made no showing of a special need for mandatory, suspicionless testing sufficient to suspend normal Fourth Amendment search and seizure protections. Nor was consent to the tests by beneficiaries freely and voluntarily given.

Relevant to the court's analysis in *Lebron* was a study finding a lower rate of drug use among TANF applicants than in the Florida population generally.[667] National studies similarly find that the rate of drug use among TANF recipients in different states ranges from .07 to 2.14 percent, compared with 9 percent among the general public.[668] After the Eleventh Circuit decision, states that maintained testing programs have generally tested only those who have been identified by a preliminary questionnaire as raising reasonable suspicion of drug use.[669]

Is the denial of welfare benefits for not agreeing to a drug test, or passing it, permissible after *Ferguson*? Even if it does not violate the Fourth Amendment, is it unlawfully discriminatory? What if there are not adequate drug treatment facilities? See Note 5, below.

2. **Criminal Prosecutions of Drug-Using Pregnant Women.** According to the Department of Health and Human Services, about 8.3 percent of pregnant women in 2020 used illicit drugs, the most common of which was marijuana.[670] Drug use by a pregnant woman can enhance certain serious risks to the fetus, including preterm labor, low birth weight, growth retardation, smaller head circumference, impaired motor development, greater difficulty with tasks that require visual attention and focus, and higher incidences of depression, anxiety, attention-deficit disorders, and delinquent and aggressive behaviors.

The long-term damage from prenatal, illicit drug use, especially cocaine, does not appear to be as serious as was once thought and is sometimes less severe than the effects of legal substances like tobacco and alcohol. A study based on 4,419 cocaine-exposed children showed that IQ scores averaged only about four points lower than those of unexposed children, and that children outgrow some of the

---

665. 772 F.3d 1352 (11th Cir. 2014).

666. Michael C. Bender, Drug Test Law Faces Challenge, St. Petersburg Times, Sept. 8, 2011, at A1 (quoting Rick Scott).

667. *Lebron*; see also Victoria Palacio, CLASP, Drug Testing SNAP Applicants Is Ineffective and Perpetuates Stereotypes (July 2017); David H. Carpenter, Cong. Rsch. Serv., Constitutional Analysis of Suspicionless Drug Testing Requirements for the Receipt of Governmental Benefits (Mar. 6, 2015).

668. Bryce Covert & Josh Israel, States Spend Millions to Drug Test the Poor, Turn Up Few Positive Results, Think Progress (Apr. 20, 2017).

669. See Guttmacher Inst., State Laws and Policies: Substance Use During Pregnancy (Aug. 1, 2022) (identifying eight states where health-care providers are required to test for prenatal exposure if drug use is suspected).

670. SAMHSA, 2020 Nat'l Survey on Drug Use and Health: Women, at 28 (July 2022).

effects in terms of brain and body size.[671] New research suggests that *in utero* exposure to methamphetamine is a growing problem and may pose similar or even greater dangers than cocaine.[672]

Other research suggests a causal connection between paternal use of toxic substances, such as smoking, excessive alcohol, and drugs, and adverse fetal health outcomes. Yet fathers are rarely blamed for the consequences of their substance abuse.[673] Should the role of male-mediated fetal harm be taken into account in establishing causality of fetal harm attributed to the mother?[674]

According to a study by ProPublica, prosecutors in at least forty-five states have charged pregnant women who use drugs under various criminal statutes prohibiting delivery of a controlled substance to a minor, child abuse or endangerment, and homicide.[675] Early on, many of the charges were rejected on appeal, on the grounds that the statutes under which charges were brought were not intended to apply to unborn children as victims.[676] With the enactment of more specific statutes, however, charges are more often upheld. In 2014, Tennessee became the first state to expressly criminalize drug use by a pregnant woman.[677] According to Amnesty International, about 700 women have been charged under "fetal assault" laws in Tennessee, Alabama, and South Carolina alone, with hundreds more charged in other states.[678] One county in Alabama has been keeping pregnant women who are charged with a drug offense in jail until they complete a drug-treatment program, regardless of whether they have been determined to need such treatment, and indefinitely if they do not qualify for available programs.[679]

Race and class are factors in who are affected by these laws. First, the effects of substance abuse can interact with other risk factors and cultural biases. For example,

671. Susan Okie, The Epidemic That Wasn't, N.Y. Times, Jan. 27, 2009, at D1.

672. Deepika Sankaran et al., Methamphetamine: Burden, Mechanism and Impact on Pregnancy, the Fetus, and Newborn, 42 J. Perinatology 293 (2022); Lindsay K. Admon et al., Amphetamine- and Opioid-Affected Births: Incidence, Outcomes, and Costs, United States, 2004-2015, J. Public Health (Dec. 19, 2018); Tricia E. Wright et al., Methamphetamines and Pregnancy Outcomes, 9 J. Addict. Med. 111 (2015); Sabrina D. Diaz, et al., Effects of Prenatal Methamphetamine Exposure on Behavioral and Cognitive Findings at 7.5 Years of Age, 164 Pediatrics 6 (2014).

673. Cynthia Daniels & Christin L. Munsch, Pregnancy Criminalization, Reproductive Asymmetry, and Race: An Experimental Study, 13 Feminist Criminology 560, 562-63 (2018).

674. Id. at 565-66, 577.

675. Leticia Miranda et al., ProPublica, How States Handle Drug Use During Pregnancy (Sept. 30, 2015); Editorial Bd., The Mothers Society Condemns, N.Y. Times, Jan 20, 2019; see also Lynn M. Paltrow & Jeanne Flavin, Arrests of and Forced Interventions on Pregnant Women in the United States, 1973-2005, 38 J. Health Pol., Pol'y & L. 299, 309 (2013).

676. See, e.g., Cochran v. Commonwealth, 315 S.W.3d 325, 329 (Ky. 2010) (citing legislative concern about discouraging pregnant alcohol or substance abusers from seeking prenatal care and drug treatment); McKnight v. State, 661 S.E.2d 354 (S.C. 2008).

677. Tenn. Code § 39-13-107 (2022).

678. Amnesty Int'l, Criminalizing Pregnancy: Policing Pregnant Women Who Use Drugs in the USA, at 8 (2017).

679. Marisa Lati, Pregnant Women Were Jailed over Drug Use to Protect Fetuses, Wash. Post, Sept. 8, 2022.

research shows that among women who drink at the same rate, children born to low-income women have a 70.9 percent rate of fetal alcohol syndrome, compared to a 4.5 percent rate for those of upper income women. Better nutrition is the difference.[680]

Race and class also affect how service providers and other law enforcement actors respond to drug use by pregnant women. Twenty-five states require health-care professionals to report suspected prenatal drug abuse,[681] and one study found that despite similar rates of substance abuse, Black women are ten times more likely than white women to be reported to government authorities.[682] Racial stereotypes about pregnant women and mothers likely affect these reports. One analysis of evening news programs found that "White women who use drugs during pregnancy tend to be portrayed as psychologically addicted, guilt-ridden, and treatment-seeking. In contrast, poor Black women tend to be portrayed as mindlessly addicted, intentionally causing harm to their fetuses, and unwilling to seek treatment."[683]

Whatever the reason, it is clear that a disproportionate number of these defendants in fetal assault cases are women of color.[684] In the largest systematic study of criminal cases related to pregnancy, researchers analyzed 413 arrests and forced interventions over thirty years and found that 71 percent of cases were brought against low-income women who qualified for indigent defense, and 52 percent of the cases were brought against African-American women.[685] (Updated research found 1,331 additional cases between 2006 and 2020, suggesting that the total number of cases is increasing.[686])

Some courts have ordered female offenders with a history of substance abuse to avoid becoming pregnant, as a term of probation. Such a probationary condition has generally been overturned because it is not reasonably related to the crime committed (which often has nothing to do with childrearing) or to the goal of rehabilitation. Some trial courts have ordered women who have been convicted of child abuse not to become pregnant as a condition of probation. A judge in Texas imposed such a condition on a 20-year-old mother with no criminal history, who had been convicted of failing to protect her toddler from abuse by the child's

---

680. Dorothy E. Roberts, Race and the New Reproduction, 47 Hastings L.J. 935, 953-54 (1996).

681. Guttmacher Inst., supra note 669.

682. Roberts, supra note 680, at 947-48; see also Emma Ketteringham et al., Healthy Mothers, Healthy Babies, 20 CUNY L. Rev. 77 n. 53 (2016); Sarah C. M. Roberts et al., Does Adopting a Prenatal Substance Use Protocol Reduce Racial Disparities in CPS Reporting Related to Maternal Drug Use? 35 J. Perinatology 146 (2015).

683. Daniels & Munsch, supra note 673, at 564.

684. Paltrow & Flavin, supra note 675, at 311 (noting that of 368 defendants in such cases for whom race was available, 59 percent were women of color, and 52 percent were African American).

685. Amnesty Int'l, Criminalizing Pregnancy 10 (2017).

686. Nat'l Advocates for Pregnant Women, Arrests and Other Deprivations of Liberty of Pregnant Women, 1973-2020; Lynn Paltrow, Constitutional Rights for the "Unborn" Would Force Women to Forego Theirs, Ms. Mag. (Apr. 15, 2021); Nat'l Advocates for Pregnant Women, Confronting Pregnancy Criminalization: A Practical Guide for Healthcare Providers, Lawyers, Medical Examiners, Child Welfare Workers, and Policymakers (June 2022).

father; she was on probation for ten years.[687] Many of these cases, too, have been overturned on appeal.[688]

3. Criminalization of Pregnancy?   The news in recent years has been filled with stories of pregnant women arrested or prosecuted for conduct other than use of illegal drugs. To what should extent should the conduct of pregnant women be regulated?

Thirty-eight states have laws that make fetal homicide a crime, and twenty-nine of those apply to the earliest stages of pregnancy, defined variously as "conception," "fertilization," or "post-fertilization."[689] In addition, the federal Unborn Victims of Violence Act can be used to treat fetuses as victims of crimes, including at the hands of the women gestating them.[690] Are these laws good policy?

A Utah law enacted in 2010 makes it criminal homicide for a woman to engage in conduct that intentionally or knowingly causes a miscarriage. This law has become a model for legislation in other states.[691] Is it a reasonable statute?[692] In one Indiana case, a despondent pregnant woman who was thirty-three weeks pregnant swallowed rat poison in an effort to end her life after her boyfriend abandoned her. Although the woman lived, the baby, who was delivered by emergency C-section, did not. She was convicted of murder, and the conviction was upheld by the Indiana Court of Appeals.[693] Is a murder prosecution reasonable under these circumstances?[694]

In the 2-1 decision, the dissenting judge suggested that holding the woman's actions covered by Indiana's feticide statute could result in the criminalization of pregnant women who smoke, drink, or take over-the-counter cold remedies and sleep aids. The majority responded that the statute requires the intention to terminate a pregnancy.[695] Is this a satisfactory limiting principle?

According to the Department of Health and Human Services, 10.4 percent of pregnant women use alcohol during pregnancy, and 8.4 percent use tobacco(down from 14 percent in 2017) — almost twice as many the number of

---

687. Steven Kreytak, Travis Judge Tells Woman to Stop Having Kids, Austin American Statesman, Sept. 12, 2008.

688. See, e.g., Trammell v. State, 751 N.E.2d 283 (Ind. Ct. App. 2001) (no-pregnancy condition excessively infringes on defendant's privacy rights and serves no rehabilitative purpose).

689. Nat'l Conf. of State Legislatures, State Laws on Fetal Homicide and Penalty-Enhancement for Crimes Against Pregnant Women (May 1, 2018).

690. 18 U.S.C. § 1841 (2018).

691. See H.B. 402 59th Leg. Gen. Sess. (Utah 2010).

692. See Lynn M. Paltrow & Farah Diaz-Tello, Caution: Pregnancy May Be Hazardous to Your Liberty, Huff. Post (Mar. 2, 2010) (arguing "no," and citing a number of other state law examples).

693. See Shuai v. State, 966 N.E.2d 619 (Ind. Ct. App. 2012).

694. For the argument that such prosecutions "fly in the face of medical and public health recommendations regarding the most effective and appropriate ways to respond to suicide attempts and drug-dependency disorders," see Lynn Paltrow, Is Locking Up Pregnant Women the New Cure for State Financial Woes and Mental Health Problems?, RH Reality Check (Mar. 30, 2011).

695. Id.

pregnant women who use illicit drugs (8.3 percent).[696] Some unknown number of other pregnant women drive too fast, fail to use seatbelts, or work extended hours against the advice of their doctors. Which of these behaviors, if any, deserve legal penalties?

Jennifer Jorgensen was pregnant and not wearing a seatbelt when she was in a car accident. She consented to an emergency cesarean section at thirty-four weeks of gestation because the fetus was showing signs of distress but the baby died six days later from injuries caused by the accident. She was charged with manslaughter for the baby's death, as well as for the deaths of two people in the car she hit. She was alleged to have been speeding and under the influence of a prescription drug and alcohol. A jury found her not guilty on all counts except for manslaughter in connection with the death of her child. On appeal, however, the state's highest court held that the criminal law was not intended "to hold pregnant women criminally responsible for conduct with respect to themselves and their unborn fetuses unless such conduct is done intentionally."[697] What might have led the jury to convict Jorgensen for manslaughter of her child, but not of the two strangers killed in the same accident?

A pregnant woman in Alabama miscarried after being shot by another woman during a fight. The pregnant woman was arrested and charged in the death of the fetus for starting the fight that ultimately resulted in her miscarriage.[698] The charges were dropped, but the arrest revealed the slippery slope from laws designed to protect fetuses from exposure to drugs to greater surveillance and criminalization of pregnancy in general. A New York Times article in 2018 gave numerous examples of pregnant women who faced criminal charges for falling down the stairs, throwing out a miscarried fetus, failing a drug test after eating a poppy seed bagel, or even simply for miscarrying.[699] These cases are sometimes brought under child abuse laws and sometimes under fetal homicide laws.

Some pregnant women have been charged for risky conduct, even if it did not cause harm to the fetus. One woman, for example, twice took a half a Valium to manage stress late in her pregnancy. Her baby was born healthy but she was nonetheless arrested and charged with "knowingly, recklessly, or intentionally" exposing her baby to a controlled substance in the womb — a felony punishable by up to ten years in prison.[700] Is this reasonable?

Should a pregnant woman who is in an abusive relationship and does not leave her batterer be prosecuted under a child abuse statute? Her abuser is subject to additional penalties. Federal legislation criminalizes harm caused to a "child *in utero*" during the course of other specified offenses. Should a man who assaults his

---

696. See SAMHSA, supra note 670, at 28.

697. People v. Jorgensen, 41 N.E.3d 778, 780 (N.Y. 2015).

698. Sarah Mervosh, Alabama Woman Who Was Shot While Pregnant Is Charged in Fetus's Death, N.Y. Times, June 27, 2019, at A17.

699. Editorial Bd., When Prosecutors Jail a Mother for a Miscarriage, N.Y. Times, Dec. 28, 2018.

700. See Debra DeBruin & Mary Faith Marshall, Coercive Interventions in Pregnancy: Law and Ethics, 23 J. Health Care L. & Pol'y 187, 194-95 (2021).

pregnant partner be guilty of a separate crime under federal law if he causes injury to the fetus?

4. **Civil Alternatives to Criminal Prosecution.** As of August 2022, twenty-four states consider substance abuse during pregnancy to be a form of child abuse, and three consider it grounds for civil commitment.[701] Some courts have interpreted their state statutes strictly. In a 2013 case, for example, the New Jersey Supreme Court held that a court cannot make a finding of abuse or neglect based on an expectant mother's drug use during pregnancy unless there is evidence of actual or imminent harm when the baby is born, and a positive drug test at birth is insufficient evidence of such harm. With respect to an entry on the baby's medical record, which noted "the presence of the following cocaine metabolite(s) . . . Benzoylecgonine = 88 ng/g" in the baby's meconium, the court wrote:

> Neither the hospital records nor any other document explains what benzoylecgonine is or discloses the meaning of the level reported in this case. On its own, the one entry does not tell us whether the mother is an addict or used an illegal substance on a single occasion. The notation does not reveal the severity or extent of the mother's substance abuse or . . . the degree of future harm posed to the child . . . Judges at the trial and appellate level cannot fill in missing information on their own or take judicial notice of harm. Instead, the fact-sensitive nature of abuse and neglect cases turns on particularized evidence.[702]

Would the individualized, evidence-based inquiry called for by this court be an improvement to the other laws and proposed laws discussed in this section? Does a more generalized approach offer sufficient benefits to offset the possible harm of overreaching?

If drug abuse during pregnancy constitutes child neglect, what governmental responses are most appropriate? Removal of the child from the parent and in some cases termination of parental rights are the most likely options. In Montana, before an effort was made to steer pregnant women with substance abuse issues into treatment programs (see Note 5, below), two-thirds of foster care cases were tied to drug abuse by mothers.[703] Is either foster care or termination of parental rights a good option for the child?

5. **Alternative, Non-Punitive Approaches.** Every leading medical organization, including the American Medical Association and the American College of Obstetricians and Gynecologists, has concluded that the best response to substance abuse

---

701. Guttmacher Inst., supra note 669. For examples, see, e.g., Fla. Stat. § 415.503(9) (g)(1) (2022); 705 Ill. Comp. Stat. § 405/2-18(2)(c)(d) (2022); Nev. Rev. Stat. § 432B.330(1) (b) (2022).

702. New Jersey Dep't of Children & Families, Div. of Youth & Family Servs. v. A.L, 59 A.3d 576 (N.J. 2013).

703. Emma Coleman, Ctr. for Child Health Pol'y, Many States Prosecute Pregnant Women for Drug Use. New Research Says That's a Bad Idea (Dec. 5, 2019).

during pregnancy is education and treatment rather than punishment.[704] Among the research supporting this position is a 2019 study showing that the odds of a child being born with Neonatal Abstinence Syndrome (NAS) are significantly higher in states that take the harsher, punitive policies.[705] This is because when women are afraid to visit the doctor out of fear of punitive measures, they do not obtain adequate prenatal care, which can lead to complications like premature birth.[706] "The only time drug withdrawal is harmful," one report author stated, "is when it isn't diagnosed immediately after birth."[707] Women who opt out of the health care system also forego opportunities for drug treatment that may benefit both themselves and their newborns.[708]

Several of the pregnant addicts facing well-publicized prosecutions for criminal child abuse had sought treatment but found either that waiting lists were long or that the programs available would not accept pregnant women. In New York City, at one time, 87 percent of drug treatment programs rejected pregnant Medicaid patients addicted to crack cocaine.[709] In response to this problem, nineteen states have either created or funded drug treatment programs specifically targeted to those who are pregnant, and seventeen states and the District of Columbia provide pregnant people with priority access to state-funded drug treatment programs.[710] Ten states prohibit publicly funded treatment programs from discriminating against pregnant women.[711] In Montana, the law now provides that pregnant women who seek addiction treatment are protected from prosecution.[712] Is this a good idea?

To address the funding shortages in treatment programs, Congress in 2018 passed the Alcohol, Drug Abuse, and Mental Health Administration Reorganization Act, which expands block grants provided to states for drug treatment programs,

---

704. Am. Medical Ass'n, Policy Statement H-420.969, Legal Interventions During Pregnancy (modified 2018); Am. Medical Ass'n, Policy Statement H-420.950, Substance Use Disorders During Pregnancy (modified 2019); Am. College Obstetricians & Gynecologists, Committee Opinion 473, Substance Abuse Reporting and Pregnancy: The Role of the Obstetrician-Gynecologist (2011, reaff'd 2014); see also Linda C. Fentiman, The New "Fetal Protection": The Wrong Answer to the Crisis of Inadequate Health Care for Women and Children, 84 Denv. U. L. Rev. 537, 594-97 (2006).

705. See Laura J. Faherty, Association of Punitive and Reporting State Policies Related to Substance Use in Pregnancy With Rates of Neonatal Abstinence Syndrome, JAMA Network Open (Nov. 13, 2019).

706. Coleman, supra note 703; Anna North, These Policies Were Supposed to Stop Pregnant Women from Drinking. A New Study Says They're Hurting Babies, Vox (May 8, 2019); Meenakshi S. Subbaraman & Sarah C. M. Roberts, Costs Associated with Alcohol Use During Pregnancy: Results from 1972-2015 Vital Statistics, 14 PLoS ONE (May 8, 2019); see also Criminalizing Pregnancy, supra note 685.

707. Coleman, supra note 703.

708. Id.

709. Rachel Roth, Making Women Pay: The Hidden Costs of Fetal Rights 140 (2000).

710. Guttmacher Inst., supra note 669.

711. Id.

712. Coleman, supra note 703.

including money targeted at addressing the particular needs of pregnant, drug-addicted women.[713]

Should treatment be forced on pregnant women with drug problems? In Kentucky and Arizona, the mother of a child born with NAS must enroll in drug treatment within ninety days and keep a regular schedule of postnatal care or else face termination of her parental rights.[714] Is this a reasonable approach?

6. **Abortion Bans and Pregnancy Loss.** Even before the Supreme Court eliminated federal constitutional protection for abortion in *Dobbs*, there were many reports of wrongful arrests of people for feticide who in fact had suffered a miscarriage (loss before twenty weeks of gestation) or stillbirth (loss at or after twenty weeks).[715] Among known pregnancies, 10 to 20 percent end in miscarriage, and .06 percent end in stillbirth.[716] One-third of American women will experience an unintentional loss of a known pregnancy at some point.[717] How will police, prosecutors, and courts determine whether fetal demise was intended or unintended? In one recent case, a woman in Nebraska was charged with helping her 17-year-old daughter have a medication abortion after the state's gestational age limit of twenty weeks; the daughter was also arrested.[718] Before *Dobbs*, the prosecutor had never charged anyone for illegally performing an unlawful abortion. Law enforcement subpoenaed Facebook messages between the woman and her daughter in which they discussed the acquisition of medication abortion pills and plans to dispose of the fetus. How might prosecutions like this affect the behavior of individual people who are pregnant or the way in which health-care providers treat them? Medical providers routinely ask female patients for the date of their last menstrual period, regardless of whether it bears any relation to the care being sought. Should people who menstruate hesitate to provide this information to avoid surveillance for pregnancy and abortion? In states that adopt fetal personhood laws, will widespread pregnancy surveillance be justified or even required as a matter of child welfare?

The ruling in *Dobbs* has also stoked fears that rogue prosecutors will be emboldened to arrest and charge women for self-managed abortion or pregnancy loss, even when they have done nothing that violates applicable law. For example, a prosecutor in Texas obtained an indictment against Lizelle Herrera for an alleged "self-induced abortion."[719] She was arrested, thrown in jail, and subjected to a $500,000 bond. Texas law, however, does not criminalize any conduct that a

---

713. Pub. L. No. 102-321, 106 Stat. 323 (codified as amended in scattered sections of 42 U.S.C.A. §§ 201-300 (Supp. 2018).

714. See Coleman, supra note 703.

715. See, e.g., Kassie McClung & Brianna Bailey, She Was Charged with Manslaughter After a Miscarriage, Cases Like Hers Are Becoming More Common in Oklahoma, Frontier (Jan. 7, 2022).

716. CDC, Stillbirth (2022); Mayo Clinic, Miscarriage (2022).

717. Nat'l Advocates for Pregnant Women, Pregnancies and Pregnancy Outcomes in the United States (Sept. 2021).

718. A Nebraska Woman Is Charged with Helping Her Daughter Have an Abortion, NPR (Aug. 10, 2022).

719. Carrie N. Baker, Texas Woman Lizelle Herrera's Arrest Foreshadows Post-*Roe* Future, Ms. Mag. (Apr. 16, 2022).

pregnant person takes to end her own pregnancy; both the murder and assault laws have explicit exceptions for such conduct.[720] Herrera was released with an apology after a weekend in jail, but in addition to harm she likely experienced, the prosecutor's actions have a chilling effect on others who might want to undertake a self-managed abortion. If/When/How released preliminary findings in August 2022 of a study about criminal consequences for self-managed abortion, concluding that "police and prosecutors overstep the authority conferred by criminal statutes, and find ways to punish people even where there is no authorizing statute. As 'trigger bans' are being deployed across the country, this portends an increase in criminalization driven more by stigma than the letter of the law."[721]

Some states have taken steps to ensure that individuals are not prosecuted or punished for self-managed abortion or pregnancy losses. Colorado, for example, passed the Reproductive Health Equity Act in 2022, which provides that a public entity shall not "[d]eprive, through prosecution, punishment, or other means, an individual of the individual's right to act or refrain from acting during the individual's own pregnancy based on the potential, actual, or perceived impact on the pregnancy, the pregnancy's outcomes, or on the pregnant individual's health."[722] Illinois, New York, and Rhode Island have repealed their fetal homicide laws.[723] Would you support repeal of a state's fetal homicide law? Why or why not?

PUTTING THEORY INTO PRACTICE

5-42. A nonprofit organization founded as Children Requiring a Caring Kommunity (C.R.A.C.K.), later renamed Project Prevention, was established to provide "effective prevention measures to reduce the tragedy of numerous drug-affected pregnancies." The Project offers $300 to drug-abusing females who promise to be sterilized or to receive long-term birth control. As of May 2022, 7,833 people had taken advantage of the offer. Of those whose race is noted, 31 percent are Black or Hispanic.[724] Is Project Prevention a good approach? Is its approach more or less defensible than court-mandated probation conditions?

5-43. National Advocates for Pregnant Women issued a report that identifies dozens of cases across the country in which a court has determined that a "prospective father's failure to control his pregnant partner constitutes civil child abuse or neglect."[725] In some cases, men have lost access to their children temporarily or

---

720. Tex. Stat. § 19.06 (2022).

721. Laura Huss et al., If/When/How, Self-Care, Criminalized: August 2022 Preliminary Findings (2022).

722. Colo. Rev. Stat. § 25-6-404 (2022).

723. Pew Rsch. Ctr., More States Shield Against Rogue Abortion Prosecutions (May 4, 2022).

724. See Project Prevention, http://www.projectprevention.org/statistics; see also Lynn Paltrow, Why Caring Communities Must Oppose C.R.A.C.K./Project Prevention: How C.R.A.C.K. Promotes Dangerous Propaganda and Undermines the Health and Well Being of Children and Families, 5 J.L. Soc'y 11, 13-15 (2003).

725. Nat'l Advocates for Pregnant Women, Harming Fathers: How the Family Court System Forces Men to Regulate Pregnancy (2022).

permanently because they failed to get their pregnant partner off drugs. The report quotes one father as follows: "How am I supposed to force her to stop? I have been supportive and sent her to get help. I don't own her; she is not a pet. I cannot force her. Even if I was married to her, I could not force her to stop using drugs." What arguments would you use to defend or oppose this practice?

5-44. To be eligible for Medicaid-subsidized prenatal care in New York, a pregnant woman is compelled by law to be interviewed by a battery of professionals, including nurses, health educators, financial officers, HIV counselors, and social workers. The questions include personal details about any past and current romantic relationships, experience with domestic violence, use of alcohol and drugs, mental illness, eating habits, earning capacity, and the earning capacity of any boyfriends.[726] Is this appropriate? Are poor, pregnant women entitled to any privacy with respect to their personal relationships and habits, or is this divulging of information a reasonable quid pro quo for public assistance?

5-45. A 28-year-old woman from Salt Lake City failed to follow medical advice to have a cesarean section. As a result, one of her twins was stillborn, although he could have been saved if the mother had undergone the procedure. She was arrested for first-degree criminal homicide and child endangerment. What defenses could be raised on her behalf? Should her conduct be criminalized? The woman later pled guilty to two counts of child endangerment and the homicide charge was dropped.[727] Is this an appropriate outcome? Should the failure of a mother to consent to a medically recommended cesarean section be a relevant factor to consider in a subsequent abuse and neglect action on behalf of the child, even if the vaginal birth was successful?[728]

5-46. Loretta Ross and Rickie Solinger, reproductive justice activists and scholars, argue that feticide and chemical endangerment laws "define drug users as illegitimate mothers. These laws that punish vulnerable women ignore the context in which many fertile women live, a context structurally distorted by racism, systemic poverty, and inadequate health care."[729] In a related vein, Lynn Paltrow, executive director of the National Advocates for Pregnant Women, argues that the "biggest threats to life — born and unborn — do not come from mommies — but rather [from] poverty, barriers to health care, persistent racism, and environmental

---

726. For details about the New York State Prenatal Assistance Program, see Khiara M. Bridges, Privacy Rights and Public Families, 34 Harv. J.L. & Gender 113 (2011). For discussion of the larger issue of what conditions the state may place on public assistance, see Dorothy Roberts, The Only Good Poor Woman: Unconstitutional Conditions and Welfare, 72 Denv. U.L. Rev. 931 (1995).

727. See Monica K. Miller, Refusal to Undergo a Cesarean Section: A Woman's Right or a Criminal Act?, 15 Health Matrix 383 (2005).

728. See New Jersey Div. of Youth & Family Servs. v. V.M., 974 A.2d 448 (N.J. Super. Ct. App. Div. 2009) (yes), discussed critically in Jessica L. Waters, In Whose Best Interest? New Jersey Division of Youth and Family Services v. V.M. and B.G. and the New Wave of Court-Controlled Pregnancies, 34 Harv. J.L. & Gender 81 (2011).

729. Loretta J. Ross & Rickie Solinger, Reproductive Justice: An Introduction 219 (2017).

hazards."[730] How could the law better take account of the structural inequalities these authors describe?

C. WOMEN AND POVERTY

According to U.S. Census Bureau data, 56 percent of the 38.1 million people living in poverty in the United States are women. In 2018, almost 12.9 percent of women lived in poverty, as compared with 10.6 percent of men. Over 30 percent of children live in poverty. Women of color are disproportionately represented among the poor. Latinas make up 18.1 percent of the population, but 27.1 percent of women in poverty. Black women represent 12.8 percent of the population, but 22.3 percent of women in poverty. Just under 23 percent of women with disabilities live in poverty. Poverty rates among LGBTQ+ women are also disproportionately high, and almost 30 percent of transgender people live in poverty.[731]

The causes of these disparities are no great mystery. Many of the phenomena explored in this book contribute, including the fact that women, especially women of color and women with disabilities, are more likely to be segregated in low-wage positions or contingent work; are paid less than men for the same work; are more likely to have childrearing responsibilities, often without either private or public support or work-family policies that account for the extra load; and are more often the victims of domestic violence. These factors build on one another. Without adequate employment, women may not have the health insurance necessary to prevent the financial shock of unexpected medical expenses, or the savings that might help them weather other financial shocks, such as job loss during the pandemic.[732] With low credit scores, which are increasingly relied on for access to economic citizenship, the poor are caught in a cycle of high interest rates, large required down payments, and reduced access to rentals, cell phone plans, and employment.[733] Surprisingly, given that they have less money to steal, they are also more vulnerable to identity theft.[734]

---

730. Jessica Mason Pieklo, Murder Charge Dismissed in Mississippi Stillbirth Case, RH Reality Check, Apr. 4, 2014.

731. Robin Bleiweis et al., Fact Sheet, The Basic Facts About Women in Poverty (Aug. 3, 2020) (collecting data). The federal government set the poverty line in 2018 at $13,064 annual income for a single person younger than 65, and $25,465 for a family of two adults and two children. Id.

732. Nicole Bateman & Martha Ross, Why Has COVID-19 Been Especially Harmful for Working Women, Brookings (Oct. 2020); Nichant Yonzan et al., The Impact of COVID-19 on Poverty and Inequality: Evidence from Phone Surveys, World Bank Blogs (Jan. 18, 2022). See also Talha Burki, The Indirect Impact of COVID-19 on Women, 20 Lancet Infect. Dis. 904 (2020) (although mortality rates worldwide from COVID-19 are higher for men, women are more likely to bear the brunt of the social and economic consequences of the pandemic).

733. See Pamela Foohey & Sara Sternberg Greene, Credit Scoring Duality, 86 L. & Contemp. Probs. (forthcoming 2022).

734. See Sara S. Greene, Stealing (Identity) from the Poor, 106 Minn. L. Rev. 59 (2021).

1. *Welfare and Welfare Reform*

Welfare began in the United States as part of state "mothers' pensions" programs for destitute families. Use of the term "pension" implied that the payment was a substitute for money that the women's husbands might otherwise receive in paid employment. Implicit in these early programs was the understanding that child-rearing is work and that a mother's devotion to the care of her children is important.[735] The initial purpose was to relieve impoverishment caused by mothers having been widowed or abandoned by their husbands — i.e., "worthy" mothers. From the very beginning, the programs excluded Black women, immigrants, and unwed mothers, either through the failure to establish programs in locations where these populations were concentrated or through discriminatory eligibility requirements, including residency and moral character requirements. In 1931, the first national survey of mothers' pensions, broken down by race, found that only 3 percent of recipients were Black.[736]

In 1935, the federal Aid to Families with Dependent Children (AFDC) program was established, and with the civil rights movement of the 1960s came successful legal challenges to welfare criteria that excluded racial and ethnic minorities. As a result, an increasing proportion of welfare recipients were never married, non-Caucasian, and adolescent. With this demographic transformation came a shift in the image of women on welfare from "worthy," to lazy, promiscuous, and socially irresponsible. Accordingly, attention began to focus less on child welfare and more on mothers' sexual and reproductive practices.

In 1996, the adoption of the Personal Responsibility and Work Opportunity Reconciliation Act of 1996 (PRWORA) shifted national welfare policy again.[737] Rather than a potentially long-term public entitlement of support for poor, single-parent families, the Temporary Assistance for Needy Families (TANF) program instituted time-limited benefits with lifetime caps and work requirements, distributed through a shrinking state block grant program. Reflecting the moral judgments that accompanied women on welfare, PRWORA provisions also undertook to promote marriage and two-parent families, to discourage out-of-wedlock pregnancies, and to encourage women on welfare to give up their children for adoption.

---

735. See Jill Duerr Berrick, From Mother's Duty to Personal Responsibility: The Evolution of AFDC, 7 Hastings Women's L.J. 257, 258-59 (1996); Bridgette Baldwin, Stratification of the Welfare Poor: Intersections of Gender, Race & "Worthiness" in Poverty Discourse and Policy, 6 Modern American 4, 4-5 (2010).

736. See Linda Gordon, Pitied but Not Entitled: Single Mothers and the History of Welfare 48 (1994). General sources on women and welfare include Mimi Abramovitz, Regulating the Lives of Women: Social Welfare Policy from Colonial Times to the Present (1988); Jill Quadagno, The Color of Welfare: How Racism Undermined the War on Poverty (1994); Dorothy E. Roberts, Welfare and the Problem of Black Citizenship, 105 Yale L.J. 1563 (1996).

737. Personal Responsibility and Work Opportunity Reconciliation Act of 1996, Pub. L. No. 104-93, 110 Stat. 2105 (1996) (codified in scattered sections of 42 U.S.C.).

Sara Sternberg Greene

The Bootstrap Trap

67 Duke L.J. 233, 235-41 (2017)

In 1996, public benefits law was transformed, fundamentally altering the safety net for poor parents in the United States. Congress passed the Personal Responsibility and Work Opportunity Reconciliation Act (PRWORA) of 1996, which ended a sixty-year-old program that had entitled qualifying families to cash assistance. Despite debate about the specifics of the PRWORA, there was widespread, bipartisan agreement that change was needed because the existing welfare program's structure unintentionally disincentivized work and promoted dependency. President Bill Clinton said when he announced the welfare reform bill, "Today the Congress will vote on legislation that gives us a chance . . . to transform a broken system that traps too many people in a cycle of dependence to one that emphasizes work and independence, to give people on welfare a chance to draw a paycheck, not a welfare check." Indeed, one of the four stated statutory goals of the PRWORA was to "end the dependence of needy parents on government benefits by promoting job preparation, work, and marriage."

The new program designed to meet this and other statutory goals, Temporary Assistance for Needy Families (TANF), imposed lifetime limits on receiving aid, subjected able-bodied participants to work requirements, incentivized states to cut welfare rolls, and transformed welfare into a block grant program that gave states wide flexibility in how they spend welfare funds. By 2016, the number of welfare recipients had fallen to only 2.7 million from a peak of 14.2 million recipients in 1994, a drop of 81 percent. Now, twenty years after welfare was reformed, the public safety net is by many accounts dead.

The idea behind TANF was that parents would work and, if their income was below a specified level, their earnings would be supplemented by the Earned Income Tax Credit (EITC). Thus, a robust cash assistance program for people who were not working would no longer be needed. When President Clinton signed the welfare reform bill into law, he said "The best antipoverty program is still a job." He promised that welfare reform would "reward the work of millions of working poor Americans by realizing the principle that if you work forty hours a week and you've got a child in the house, you will no longer be in poverty."

But whether or not parents found [jobs], periods of financial distress were common, and parents were left to find alternative forms of support. For many parents, this alternative support was credit. Just as welfare was reformed and the public safety net diminished, credit cards were becoming newly available to low-income families. Changes in state usury laws allowed lenders to extend credit to riskier borrowers while utilizing higher interest rates to make up for the increased risk. Credit card companies then began targeting low-income consumers, who just a decade before, would not have qualified for credit cards.

Credit has become a lifeline for poor families, but many of them also find themselves in an enduring cycle of unmanageable debt. These cycles of debt can wreak havoc on credit histories and scores. And though credit histories were once tools used primarily by the financial industry to decide whether and how much money to loan consumers, they have taken on a new importance. In 2017, an increasing number of industries use credit histories to aid in their decisions about whether to grant access to a wide range of economic resources: rental housing, insurance, utilities, and jobs. A low credit score and flawed report can mean restricted access to institutions necessary for economic stability, and thus, the collateral consequences of bad credit are profound. . . .

[In-depth, semistructured interviews of low-income families in this study reveal] a previously undetected conflict in what remains of the safety net: the conflict between the goal of self-sufficiency and the risks that adhere when low-income families realize that goal. The post-welfare reform public safety net promotes and even requires one type of behavior — self-sufficiency — but the new private safety net, which encompasses the credit reporting and scoring systems and accompanying regulations, is a danger to those who are both financially unstable and attempting to be self-sufficient. Those families that best adhere to the very behavior encouraged by the public safety net, then, end up at particular risk for long-term economic hardship. . . .

The tension in the existing safety net ultimately leads to the conclusion that a new public safety net program is needed. From a public policy perspective, the existing safety net penalizes the very behavior many policymakers across the political spectrum say that they want to encourage and incentivize. And from an equality standpoint, the current safety networks to exacerbate poverty and inequality, rather than to reduce it. . . .

NOTES

1. **The Impact of Welfare Reform.**   The impact of welfare reform has been substantial. In 2020, only about 2.1 million Americans were receiving TANF, compared with 14 million who were receiving AFDC in 1993.[738] This represents a fraction of American families living in poverty. In 2019, only 23 percent of families with children living in poverty received TANF assistance,[739] which is so inadequate, and the burdens so substantial and hard to understand, that many potential recipients do not bother applying.[740] In 2020, the national median monthly TANF assistance for a family of three was $492, which is 27 percent of the poverty line. The total TANF budget has not increased with inflation, and grants are worth 40 percent less than they were in 1996.[741]

One of the reasons so many fewer people are receiving welfare, and in amounts so much lower in inflation-adjusted dollars, is that states can use TANF block grants

---

738. Kimberly Amadeo, What Is a Welfare Program: Welfare Programs Explained, Balance (Oct. 21, 2021). For earlier comparisons, see Thomas Gabe, Cong. Rsch. Serv., Welfare, Work and Poverty Status of Female-Headed Families with Children: 1987-2013 (2014).

739. Amadeo, supra note 738.

740. Pam Fessler, 20 Years Since Welfare's Overhaul, Results Are Mixed, NPR (Aug. 22, 2016).

741. Ctr. on Budget & Pol'y Priorities, Policy Basics: Temporary Assistance for Needy Families (Mar. 1, 2022).

for many purposes other than cash assistance to the needy, and often choose to do so. Today, states spend only about one-quarter of their combined federal TANF funds and the state funds they are required to spend under federal law on basic assistance to meet the essential needs of families with children. Another quarter is spent on child care for low-income families and other activities to connect TANF families to work.[742] A large and growing share of state and federal TANF funds is spent on other services, such as pre-K, or expanding the state Earned Income Tax Credit, or other underfunded programs such as the child protective services system, including foster care.[743] Some use the grants to finance college scholarships or to plug holes in state budgets.[744] On the use of such funds to discourage teen pregnancy and promote marriage, see Note 2, below.

As a result of these factors, TANF benefits vary widely by state. The maximum benefit for a family of three in Arkansas is $204, which is 11 percent of the poverty line. The comparable benefit amount in New Hampshire is $1,098.[745] The racial dimension is also striking. Fifty-two percent of Black children live in the sixteen states with benefit levels below 20 percent of the poverty line, as compared to 41 percent of Latinx children, and 37 percent of white children.[746] Individuals who cannot survive on the benefits they receive often resort to off-the-books jobs where their income is unreported. If detected, such violations of welfare rules can subject them to substantial penalties, including extended or permanent bans from further assistance.[747]

Kathryn Edin and Luke Shaefer offer case histories of the hardships among the poorest of the poor, those living on $2.00 in cash income, who account for one-fifth of families living below the poverty line. Modonna Harris, one such woman, lost her cashier's job and was unable to find other work. She and her 15-year-old daughter lived in a homeless shelter and received meals from the shelter and other nonprofits during the week. They struggled with food shortages on weekends. Chicago had so many people on the waiting list for housing assistance that it was accepting no new applicants. She had not applied for TANF because she didn't know anyone getting benefits and she had assumed that government officials "just weren't giving it anymore." When prompted to apply, she showed up at the government office only a half-hour before it opened and already there were too many applicants for staff to schedule her an appointment.[748]

As the Greene excerpt explains, the credit options available to those in poverty are often what sentences them to a lifetime cycle of dependency from which they

742. See Liz Schott et al., Ctr.on Budget and Policy Priorities, How States Use Federal and State Funds Under the TANF Block Grant (Oct. 15, 2015).

743. Id.

744. See Clyde Haberman, 20 Years Later, Welfare Overhaul Resonates for Families and Candidates, N.Y. Times, May 1, 2016.

745. See Ctr. on Budget & Pol'y Priorities, Policy Basics, supra note 741.

746. Id.

747. Kaaryn S. Gustafson, Public Assistance and the Criminalization of Poverty 67-69, 141, 143, 160 (2011).

748. Kathryn J. Edin & H. Luke Shaefer, $2.00 a Day: Living on Almost Nothing in America 6-9, 33 (2015).

cannot escape. Greene proposes a new program, which she calls Financial Services for Family Stability, to which states could direct some of their TANF block grants. The goal of the program would be to "support clients in finding a solution to their debt problems and to develop client skills to allow them to have better control over their money."[749] Money advisors would be trained in all aspects of debt and money management and in skills relating to supporting people through times of crisis, including how to be compassionate, caring, and non-judgmental.[750] Is this a positive example of the ethic of care? Greene proposes that advisers would help clients learn to plan and budget, and also to objectively assess available financial options, including credit alternatives, and whether the for-profit option for higher education they may be considering makes sense for them.[751] Greene argues that one of the benefits of the program is that it is consistent with a self-sufficiency narrative.[752] Is that a virtue? Or does such a narrative reinforce the ideologies of poverty that cause them to be blamed for their own economic circumstances? For further examination of this question, see Section 3, below.

The federal American Rescue Plan, signed into law in March 2022, provides for $1 billion in pandemic-related funds, some of which states may use to provide additional non-recurrent short-term benefits to families with children through September 2022.[753] How would you propose such funds be prioritized?

2. **Welfare Reform and the Promotion of Marriage.** One set of programs that have replaced a portion of the support families used to receive for basic assistance are those that are presumed to reduce out-of-wedlock pregnancies or to promote marriage. In the former category, two-thirds of states use TANF funds for abstinence and/or other teen-pregnancy prevention programs, visiting nurse services, and after-school programs. To promote marriage, almost half the states have undertaken a number of healthy marriage initiatives that include parenting skills training, premarital and marriage counseling, and initiatives to promote responsible fatherhood.[754]

In 2002, the federal government funded A Healthy Marriage Initiative, designed to promote stable marriages and responsible fatherhood. Activities include marriage education programs, public service announcements, and courses in relationship skills for adults and adolescents.[755] Bonuses were given to states that met targets in reducing out-of-wedlock births and abortions.[756] The program was discontinued but supporters have continued to argue that incentives should be

---

749. Sara Sternberg Greene, The Bootstrap Trap, 67 Duke L.J. 233, 299-304 (2016).

750. Id. at 300.

751. Id.

752. Id. at 299.

753. See Barbara Sprunt, Here's What's in the American Rescue Plan, NPR (Mar. 11, 2021).

754. See Schott et al., supra note 742.

755. See Julia M. Fisher, Marriage Promotion Policies and the Working Poor: A Match Made in Heaven?, 25 B.C. Third World L.J. 475, 485 n.71 (2005).

756. Id. See Marnie Eisenstadt, Birth Figures Deliver Bonus: State Receives $25 Million in Federal Money as Out-of-Wedlock Births Decline, Post-Standard (Syracuse N.Y.), Oct. 14, 2004, at A8.

given for marriage because, as leaders such as Marco Rubio have argued, marriage is "the greatest tool" for lifting people out of poverty.[757]

Advocates of these programs point to statistics showing that children who grow up with both of their biological parents are more successful across a broad range of outcomes than children who grow up with only one parent, including higher educational attainment, better behavioral outcomes, and better mental health. However, it is not clear to what extent these positive outcomes are due to pre-existing characteristics of the parents who choose to marry (and not to divorce) rather than to marriage itself.[758]

Critics of the "healthy marriage" approach to welfare reform charge that, even if marriage is a legitimate government goal, marriage alone is not sufficient to lift couples out of poverty and promotion programs are ineffective in promoting it. Researchers have generally found no consistent correlation between state expenditures on marriage programs and marriage or divorce rates.[759] One review of a federal program, Building Strong Families, which gave counseling and support to unwed couples with children, revealed no positive impact on whether the couples got married or remained involved, or whether fathers supported their children.[760] Critics also argue that the marriage promotion approach reflects an unduly narrow definition of healthy families, and that the money would be better spent on programs that are critically underfunded, such as child care. Marriage promotion is particularly problematic for Black and Latino families, given the ways in which incarceration and joblessness have narrowed the pool of eligible men, and the extended family patterns that are common in these racial groups.[761] The underlying assumption of marriage promotion tends to pathologize caretaking patterns that are highly constructive for many individuals, particularly low-income women of color. Research on these women finds that many see marriage as a luxury but children as a necessity, a chief source of identity and meaning.[762]

The Center for Law and Social Policy proposes "Marriage Plus" as an alternative, which would include not only marriage counseling and relationship training, but pregnancy prevention, mental health support, greater child-care services, reform of the child support system, and employment training and placement.[763] Is this an improvement?

---

757. Bryce Covert, Nearly a Billion Dollars Spent on Marriage Promotion Programs Have Achieved Next to Nothing, Think Progress (Feb. 11, 2014).

758. Kimberly A. Yuracko, The Meaning of Marriage: Does Marriage Make People Good or Do Good People Marry?, 42 San Diego L. Rev. 889 (2005); Jennifer M. Randles, Marriage Promotion Policy and Family Inequality, 6 Soc. Compass 671, 673 (2012).

759. Id.

760. Id.; see also Randles, supra note 758, at 674.

761. Angela Onwuachi-Willig, The Return of the Ring: Welfare Reform's Marriage Cure as the Revival of Post-Bellum Control, 93 Calif. L. Rev. 1647, 1690 (2005); Randles, supra note 758, at 676.

762. Randles, supra note 758, at 677 (citing studies).

763. For the Marriage Plus proposal, see Theodora Ooms et al., Beyond Marriage Licenses: Efforts in States to Strengthen Marriage and Two-Parent Families, Ctr. for Law & Social Pol'y (Apr. 2004).

Is marriage promotion a legitimate governmental objective? Is it a better use of federal funds than, say, child-care subsidies? What data might you need to answer that question?

2.   *Gender and Evictions*

The risk of eviction for female renters is almost 8 percent higher than that for male renters. When race and income levels are taken into account, studies show that the gap is much larger. A study drawing on millions of court records of eviction cases between 2012 and 2016 over thirty-nine states concluded that Blacks are almost 60 percent more likely to be evicted than whites, and 36 percent more Black women are evicted than Black men.[764] In high-poverty Black neighborhoods, other research shows that women are twice as likely to be evicted as men.[765]

What explains these gaps? The Milwaukee study, led by sociologist Matthew Desmond, who was awarded the Pulitzer Prize for his work on the subject,[766] linked the disparities to some familiar factors: women's low wages, their disproportionate responsibility for children, and the risks of intervention by child protective services.

> Although women in high-poverty black neighborhoods are more likely to work than men, their wages are often lower than the wages of working men from these neighborhoods. Children can also pose a challenge to single mothers beyond the cost of larger rental units to accommodate them. Children can result in landlords coming under increased state scrutiny. Children might test positive for lead poisoning, for example, and the Environmental Protection Agency will step in. Child protective services may be alerted if the home is unsafe or unsanitary. Overcrowded children are also hard on apartments. Calls to the police to report domestic violence could also provoke the ire of landlords and lead to eviction if a male abuser was not on the lease. Thus, women often choose between reporting unsafe or unhealthy conditions and facing evictions, or keeping quiet about their situations and living in deteriorated housing or with abusive partners.[767]

The study also identified a less obvious explanation: the interactions between mostly male landlords and female renters.

---

764. Peter Hepburn et al., Racial and Gender Disparities among Evicted Americans, 7 Socio. Sci. 649, 655-56 (2020). The gap is almost 10 percent among Latinx renters. Id. at 656.

765. See Matthew Desmond, MacArthur Foundation, Poor Black Women Are Evicted at Alarming Rates, Setting Off a Chain of Hardship 2 (Policy Research Brief 2014).

766. His foundational work is Matthew Desmond, Evicted: Poverty and Profit in the American City (2016).

767. Desmond, Poor Black Women, supra note 765, at 2.

As the fieldwork shows, the interaction between predominantly male landlords and female tenants is also a culprit and often turns on gender dynamics. Men who fell behind in rent, for example, often went directly to the landlord. When Jerry was served an eviction notice, he promptly balled up and threw it in the face of his landlord. The two commenced yelling at each other until Jerry stomped back to his trailer. Meanwhile, Larraine, who had also been served notice, recoiled from conflict. "I couldn't deal with it. I was terrified by it, just terrified," she told the researcher.

After Jerry calmed down, he returned and offered to work off his rent by cleaning up the trailer park and doing some maintenance work, something men often offer to do, the researchers found. The landlord accepted his offer. The outcome for Larraine was different. After avoiding her landlord, she would eventually come up with the rent, borrowing from her brother. But by that time, her landlord had had enough. He felt that Larraine had taken advantage of him. In keeping with women's generally nonconfrontational approach, Larraine, like many other women renters facing eviction, engaged in "ducking and dodging" landlords often put it.[768]

Is this a downside of women's "different voice"? See Chapter 4. Is there a solution?

The consequences of eviction can be devastating. They include not only the loss of the renter's home and having to find another place to live, usually worse than before, or having no housing at all, either of which can be highly and even permanently detrimental to the physical and mental health of the family, especially children. It also often means losing a job, one's credit, and often most if not all of the renter's possessions. These losses are all cumulative, and often irreversible. Many landlords will not rent to persons who have been evicted, and an eviction can disqualify a person from affordable housing programs.[769] Serial evictions are not unusual in high-poverty neighborhoods. The Milwaukee study showed that, on average, one in every seven Black renters who was filed against for eviction was repeatedly filed against.[770] Likewise, without a safe place to call home, it may become impossible to find a job, replace possessions (including clothes for work), or improve a ruined credit rating. As Desmond reports, eviction is not just a temporary setback or a brief detour but can throw the renter and her family onto an entirely different path, from which there is virtually no turning back. In this sense, he argues, eviction is not just a condition of poverty, but a cause of it.[771]

In a report for the MacArthur Foundation, Desmond assesses the gender gap in this way: "Poor black men may be locked up, but poor black women are locked out. Both phenomena work together to propagate economic disadvantage in the

---

768. Id.

769. Desmond, Evicted, supra note 766.

770. Hepburn et al., supra note 764, at 656. That figure is almost 50 percent higher than for white renters.

771. Desmond, Evicted, supra note 766. See also Matthew Desmond, Eviction and the Reproduction of Poverty, 118 Amer. J. Socio. 88 (2012).

inner city."[772] Can the eviction problem be fixed without also addressing the racism and sexism that underlies it?

3. *Ideologies of Poverty*

According to data from the Organisation for Economic Co-operation and Development (OECD), the United States has the highest relative poverty rate among OECD peers with similar gross domestic products.[773] The United States has one of the lowest rates of social expenditure on the poor, spending a smaller percentage of its economy on cash transfer programs to help the needy than twenty-six other developed countries.[774] This is widely viewed as a function, at least in part, of an ideology that assumes that the people who are poor simply do not try hard enough.

Heavily influential in this view of poverty is the work of Charles Murray, especially his 1984 book, Losing Ground. Murray argued that poverty programs, instead of lifting the poor out of poverty, further entrench them by eliminating the incentive to work. According to Murray, the culture of dependency not only undermines the ability of the poor to support themselves; it also weakens family structures and fosters illegitimacy.[775] Along the same lines, George Gilder argued that poverty programs create moral hazard. According to Gilder, it is work, family, and faith, not handouts, that enable families to achieve economic security.[776] Critical to Gilder's ideology is the importance of gender roles in motivating men to support their families. According to Gilder, when women abandon traditional, biology-created gender roles, they do so at the expense of children who need their care, and men, whose sexual energies and aggressions can be expected to lead them toward various dangerous, antisocial pursuits, if they are not steered in the right direction by marriage.[777] Today, these views tend to be supplemented by the political claim that improving economic supports for the poor creates a slippery slope that leads to socialism.[778]

The view that people who work hard enough can get ahead continues to inform debates over the government's role in reducing poverty. In a recent poll, 60 percent of people (and almost 80 percent of Republicans, and 45 percent of Democrats) said that most people who want to get ahead can make it if they're willing to work hard.[779] Forty percent of people (74 percent of Republicans and

---

772. Desmond, Poor Black Women, supra note 765.

773. Annie Lowrey, How America Treats Its Own Children, Atlantic (Jun. 21, 2018).

774. See id.; Jorgan Weissman, How Poor Are America's Poor, Really?, Slate (Jan. 5, 2015).

775. Charles Murray, Losing Ground: American Social Policy, 1950-1980 (1984).

776. See George Gilder, Wealth and Poverty (1993).

777. George Gilder, Men and Marriage 15-16 (1986).

778. See Jonathan Chait, The One Argument Conservatives Have Made Against Every New Social Program, Intelligencer, April 9, 2021.

779. Pew Rsch. Ctr., In a Politically Polarized Era, Sharp Divides in Both Partisan Coalitions, 3. Views of the Economic System and Social Safety Net (Dec. 17, 2019).

25 percent of Democrats) think that poor people have it easy because they can get government benefits without doing anything in return.[780]

What is the appropriate response to such views? Consider the following.

Barbara Ehrenreich

Time to Wake Up: Stop Blaming Poverty on the Poor

The Shriver Report: A Woman's Nation Pushes Back from the Brink 40 (Olivia Morgan & Karen Skelton eds., 2014)

Poverty is not a character failing or a lack of motivation. Poverty is a shortage of money. For most women in poverty, in both good times and bad, the shortage of money arises largely from inadequate wages. When I worked on my book *Nickel and Dimed: On (Not) Getting by in America*, I took jobs as a waitress, nursing-home aide, hotel housekeeper, Wal-Mart associate, and a maid with a house-cleaning service. I did not choose these jobs because they were low-paying. I chose them because these are the entry-level jobs most readily available to women. What I discovered is that in many ways, these jobs are a trap: They pay so little that you cannot accumulate even a couple of hundred dollars to help you make the transition to a better-paying job. They often give you no control over your work schedule, making it impossible to arrange for child care or take a second job. . . . To be poor—especially with children to support and care for—is a perpetual high wire act. . . .

Instead of treating low-wage mothers as the struggling heroines they are, our political culture still tends to view them as miscreants and contributors to the "cycle of poverty." . . . Sadly, this has become the means by which the wealthiest country in the world manages to remain complacent in the face of alarmingly high levels of poverty: by continuing to blame poverty not on the economy or inadequate social supports, but on the poor themselves.

It's time to revive the notion of a collective national responsibility to the poorest among us, who are disproportionately women and especially women of color.

Ann Cammett

Deadbeat Dads & Welfare Queens: How Metaphor Shapes Poverty Law

34 B.C. J.L. & Soc. Jus. 233, 233-38, 265 (2014)

According to political scientist Martin Gilens, exhaustive studies examining Americans' attitudes on race and their views on welfare spending have demonstrated that "perceptions of blacks continue to play the dominant role in shaping the public's attitudes toward welfare." Therefore, although the majority of public assistance recipients are White, welfare's association with Blacks in the public

---

780. Id.

imagination continues to drive policy around poverty issues as a whole. The rhetorical discourse about self-sufficiency, personal responsibility, and deservedness has laid the groundwork for the transformation or, more accurately, the evisceration of the social safety net. . . .

[Traditionally], the social construction of poor Black single mothers deemed them the agents of their own misfortune due to their unmarried status—assumed to indicate loose morals, hypersexuality, and presumed laziness—framed as reliance on public assistance rather than work. For example, stigmatizing metaphors such as the "Welfare Queen" were built on longstanding race and gender stereotypes and widely held beliefs. . . .

[A] related phenomenon [is] the . . . intersection of the Welfare Queen as "race code" for undeserving beneficiaries of welfare . . . with aggressive child support enforcement. This change in policy was designed to transfer the burden of financial support from the government to non-resident fathers. If the Welfare Queen is a public identity, her corollary is the "Deadbeat Dad." The political backlash over expanded access to assistance for Black mothers evolved in tandem with the identification of Deadbeat Dads as the engines of child poverty, even when fathers were poor themselves. This concept of a "broken" family, another ubiquitous metaphor, headed by a poor single mother in need of rehabilitation and an "absent" father, is another powerful cultural narrative informing the social construction of poor Black families. . . .

The use of tropes like the Welfare Queen and the Deadbeat Dad have shifted the focus of policy debates surrounding poverty programs from helping those in difficult economic situations to punishing those perceived to be at the heart of economic problems.

Camille Gear Rich

Reclaiming the Welfare Queen: Feminist and Critical Race Theory Alternatives to Existing Anti-Poverty Discourse

25 S. Cal. Interdisc. L.J. 257, 260-61 (2016)

Introduced in the 1980s by Ronald Reagan in a campaign speech, the original welfare queen was the criminal mastermind, alleged baby thief, and accused murderer Linda Taylor who, when she was not committing major crimes, committed welfare fraud by collecting public assistance checks under multiple names in various states. But the welfare queen construct that ultimately emerged placed less emphasis on technical fraud and more emphasis on the welfare queen's alleged sense of entitlement and irrepressible procreative instincts. Specially, the welfare queen archetype is typically represented as a woman whose irresponsible choice to have children out of wedlock has caused her to turn to the state for financial support. Fiscally and sexually irresponsible, she is a threat to social order precisely because she rejects the importance of the nuclear family as a bedrock social institution. The welfare queen is also represented as indolent, as she finds ways to indefinitely extend her right to demand support from the state and to maximize the dollars the state confers. She is an immediate threat because she imposes a financial burden on the state to support her children. She is also seen as a future threat because she fails to transmit the values of restraint, respect for law and order, and fiscal responsibility to her children. As a consequence, the welfare queen promises to birth both a new generation of welfare dependents that will look to the state for financial assistance and a new generation of criminals that must be incarcerated lest they inflict further social and financial damage.

NOTES

1. **The Work/Welfare Debate.** Federal TANF law requires states to meet work participation rate targets or face a penalty. These targets mean that half of families receiving TANF assistance must work at least thirty hours a week. In two-parent families, 90 percent must be engaged in work, generally for thirty-five hours a week. Many states do not consider college attendance as meeting work requirements; the number of recipients enrolled in college has dropped since reform.[781] States are required to reduce or take away benefits when a family member refuses to meet the state's work requirements without "good cause." Most states take away the entire family's benefit if a parent fails to meet the work requirements.[782]

Most Americans support such requirements. In one poll, 87 percent agreed that it is appropriate to require people to seek work or participate in a training program "if they are able to do so."[783] However, a comprehensive review of the consequences of adding such requirements by the Brookings Institute concludes that very few recipients choose not to work. The vast majority who do not meet the work requirements are employed, but do not meet the twenty-hour mandate because of health difficulties, high unemployment, or unstable jobs and working conditions.[784] Imposing burdensome and time-consuming requirements would also deter applicants and increase the risks and consequences of erroneous denials.[785]

Is work the best route for women's autonomy? Equal access to job opportunities, along with equal pay, access to reproductive services, and the elimination of gender violence and harassment, have all been important parts of the feminist agenda. Should that remain the emphasis?

Consider the following:

[T]raditional welfare strategies can be detrimental to women. . . . Joint property approaches [whereby individual men pay their partners for

781. Noah Zatz, What Welfare Requires from Work, 54 UCLA L. Rev. 373, 415 (2006) (citing state definitions); Juliette Terzieff, Welfare Clock Should Stop for College Moms, Women's eNews (Apr. 20, 2006).

782. See Ctr. on Budget & Pol'y Priorities, Policy Basics, supra note 741.

783. Id.; Emily Badger & Margot Sanger-Katz, Who's Able-Bodied Anyway?, N.Y. Times, Feb. 4, 2019.

784. Lauren Bauer et al., Brookings, Work Requirements and Safety Net Programs at 2, 17 (2018); Elizabeth G. Patterson, Work Expectations and the Able-Bodied Adult: Myths and Realities in Food Stamp Reform, 8 Wake Forest J. L. & Pol'y 363, 400-02 (2018).

785. Bauer et al., supra note 784, at 2, 17; see also Pam Fessler, More Than 750,000 Could Lose Food Stamps Under Trump Administration Proposal, NPR (Apr. 1, 2019).

taking care of the house and children] rely on individual breadwinners to fund household labor, while welfare strategies rely on the state. State funding is advantageous for women, because it frees them from serving individual men and sheds class bias by funding household work at a uniform level regardless of the earnings of the family members who support it. Nonetheless, by paying women to stay home with their children rather than providing real support for parents (especially single parents) to work at paid jobs, welfare strategies still encourage women to invest in homemaking and caregiving to the exclusion of their job skills—which may harm women and their families in the long run. . . .

I realize that work alone is no panacea. It is the platform on which equal citizenship should be built, not the entire edifice. Still, the importance of work to the future cannot be overemphasized; abandoning work as a political and cultural ideal would be a serious mistake. People need more than money or property: We need life projects. We need goals and activities to which we can commit our hearts, minds, and bodies. We need to struggle with our capacities and our limits, in sustained ways in stable settings. We need to work alongside others in pursuit of common goals. We need to feel that we are contributing to something larger than ourselves and our own families. Most of us even need something that requires regular rhythms and structure and provides a mechanism for deferring gratification. We need to feel that we are earning our keep—that we have a source of wherewithal that is our own. We also need public recognition for our labors. It is difficult to imagine any single activity that can fulfill all these purposes for the vast majority of people other than working. We have seen what happens to people when they don't have work to give life structure and meaning, and it is not exemplary. There is a reason why democratic societies have organized themselves as employment societies. Paid work is the only institution that can be sufficiently widely distributed to provide a stable foundation for a democratic order. It is also one of the few arenas—perhaps the only one—in which diverse groups of people can come together and develop respect for each other through shared experience. Can we think of a society anywhere in the world we would want to emulate in which most people do not work for a living? . . .[786]

Should welfare programs be pushed in the direction of ensuring that women have work? If so, what policy recommendations would follow?

Martha Fineman, a leading champion of improved state support for women with children, has a different emphasis. Rejecting the implication that dependency is bad for women, Fineman argues that it should be embraced as endemic to the human condition.

In popular and political discourse, the idea of "subsidy" is viewed as an equally negative companion to dependence, the opposite of the ideal of self-sufficiency. But a subsidy is nothing more than the process of allocating

---

786. Vicki Schultz, Life's Work, 100 Colum. L. Rev. 1881, 1914-15 (2000).

collective resources to some persons or endeavors rather than other persons or endeavors because a social judgment is made that they are in some way "entitled" or the subsidy is justified. . . .

. . . We all live subsidized lives. Sometimes the benefits we receive are public and financial, such as in governmental direct transfer programs to certain individuals like farmers or sugar growers. Public subsidies can also be indirect, such as the benefits given in tax policy. Private economic subsidy systems work in the forms of foundations, religions, and charities. But, a subsidy can also be non-monetary, such as the subsidy provided by the uncompensated labor of others in caring for us and our dependency needs. . . .

The interesting question in our subsidy shaped society . . . has to be why only some subsidies are differentiated and stigmatized while others are hidden. In substantial part, subsidies are hidden when they are not called subsidy (or welfare, or the dole), but termed "investments," "incentives," or "earned" when they are supplied by government, and called "gifts," "charity," or the product of familial "love" when they are contributions of caretaking labor. . . .

As a result of such discussion, the very terms of independence and self-sufficiency might well be redefined or re-imagined in the public mind. Independence is not the same as being unattached. Independence from subsidy and support is not attainable, nor is it desirable — we want and need the contexts that sustain us. A different understanding of independence is needed and attainable. Independence is gained when an individual has the basic resources that enable her or him to act consistent with the tasks and expectations imposed by the society. This form of independence should be every citizen's birthright, but independence in this sense can only be achieved when individual choices are relatively unconstrained by inequalities, particularly those inequalities that arise from poverty.[787]

What is your view? Can the views of Fineman and Schultz be reconciled? Does an emphasis on women's dependency lead to policies that undermine their autonomy? Does an emphasis on autonomy undermine the policies necessary for women's well-being? Consider this further analysis by Fineman:

Rejection of the idea that there is some collective responsibility for dependency is not surprising in a society such as ours. American political ideology offers an iconic construct of the autonomous individual and trusts the abstraction of an efficiency-seeking market as an ordering mechanism. We have an historic and highly romanticized affair with the ideals of the private and the individual, as contrasted with the public and the collective, as the appropriate units of focus in determining social good. . . .

The theory of dependency I set forth develops a claim of "right" or entitlement to support and accommodation from the state and its institutions on the part of caretakers — those who care for dependents. Their

---

787. Martha Albertson Fineman, Cracking the Foundational Myths: Independence, Autonomy, and Self-Sufficiency, 8 Am. U. J. Gender Soc. Pol'y & Law 13, 22-23, 25-26 (2000).

labor should be treated as equally productive even if unwaged, and should be measured by its societal value, not by economic or market indicators. The fact that dependency work has been un- or under-valued in the market is an argument *for* governmental intervention and restructuring to mandate adjustment and market accommodation, as well as more direct reparations.[788]

Some welfare reform advocates have argued that if even some form of anti-shirking provision is politically necessary, it should be a more tailored approach than the current law, penalizing only those who refuse available jobs or training, and expanding hardship exemptions for those whose health, illiteracy, language skills, or job market make work requirements unrealistic.[789] Would you expect both Fineman and Schultz to support this approach?

2. **Income Inequality.** Inequality in the United States has never been greater. The top 1 percent of earners earn about forty times more than the bottom 90 percent of earners — the highest gap among the G7 nations.[790] Women make up only 27 percent of the top 10 percent of earners, and less than 17 percent of the top 1 percent.[791] Global patterns for women are even worse. The number of individuals with fortunes worth at least $1 billion more than doubled between 2010 and 2018, and only 256 women ranked among the world's 2,208 billionaires.[792]

Income inequality is not the same thing as poverty. Poverty means that basic, minimum standards of adequate food, shelter, education, and other basic needs are not met. These standards change over time, and relate to choices society makes about how much is enough. Debates about solutions to poverty are typically framed in terms of charity, or how much the well-to-do should feel obligated toward their fellow citizens who do not have enough. Economic inequality, by contrast, refers to relative economic circumstances, and to the reality that the reason some people have too little is because some people have too much. Framed this way, debates over solutions to economic inequality tend to focus not on what voluntary support for the poor is warranted, but on what is owed by people who have been favored under existing systems of privilege to those who have not.[793]

Is economic inequality the natural and inevitable product of a market system in which people differ in how hard they work, how talented they are, and how much risk they assume?[794] That is the view associated with those who believe in

---

788. Martha Albertson Fineman, The Autonomy Myth: A Theory of Dependency xiii-xv (2004); see also Clare Huntington, Failure to Flourish: How Law Undermines Family Relationships (2014); Maxine Eichner, The Free-Market Family: How the Market Crushed the American Dream (and How It Can Be Restored) (2019).

789. Patterson, supra note 784, at 405-06.

790. Income World Population Review, Income Inequality by Country 2022. See also Inst. for Pol'y Stud., Income Inequality (Feb. 20, 2019).

791. Inst. for Pol'y Stud., supra note 790.

792. Id.; Patterson, supra note 784, at 405-06.

793. Katharine T. Bartlett, Feminism and Economic Inequality, 35 Minn. J. L. & Inq. 265, 284-86 (2017).

794. See Igor Bobic, Rand Paul: Of Course Income Inequality Is Linked to How Hard You Work, HuffPost Politics (Aug. 11, 2015).

neoliberalism, or market libertarianism. Market libertarianism holds that "society collectively benefits from unregulated markets because they are the most efficient means through which equilibrium is established between what people, pursuing their own preferences, are willing to pay for what other people, pursuing their own self-interest, are willing to sell."[795]

French economist Thomas Piketty argues that it is market libertarian ideologies, not how hard people work, or natural economic or technological forces, that explain the economic inequality gap.[796] Feminist scholars have applied market critiques in a variety of contexts to show the relationship between market ideologies and economic inequality. June Carbone and Naomi Cahn, for example, explain how marriage markets both reflect and exacerbate pervasive economic inequalities.[797] Deborah Dinner shows how market libertarianism infiltrated the interpretation of Title VII, causing courts to apply the anti-stereotyping principle in a way that reinforced the economic inequalities that foreclose opportunities to individuals on a class basis. Focusing on the anti-stereotyping principle as a problem of inaccuracy and thus inefficiency, Dinner claims, sidetracked advocates and lawmakers from structural reforms of the workplace that would raise working-class wages, accommodate the needs of pregnant women and parents with children, and otherwise treat workers with greater fairness.[798]

How complete an explanation for economic inequality is the ideology of market libertarianism? Consider the following:

> An alternative way to theorize economic inequality is as a product of race and/or gender subordination. . . . Although these race and gender critiques powerfully show how both racism and sexism stack the deck against women and minorities, they describe the effects of subordination rather than explain its means of operation and success. Sex and race critiques prove what motivates — explicitly or implicitly — those who exercise power in society, and predict which particular people occupy the lowest rungs in social relations. This evidence alone, however, does not show how racism and sexism have been normalized, nor how these systems cover their tracks as systems. A fuller economic theory would show not only how power is distributed along race and gender lines, but also how those who benefit under that distribution of power get away with it. . . .
>
> As "feminism has unmasked maleness as a form of power that is both omnipotent and nonexistent, an unreal thing with very real consequences," so a robust critique of market libertarianism unmasks a system

---

795. See Bartlett, supra note 793, at 276-77.

796. See Thomas Piketty, Capital and Ideology (2020); Thomas Piketty, Capital in the 21st Century (2013).

797. June Carbone & Naomi Cahn, Marriage Markets: How Inequality Is Remaking the American Family (2014).

798. See Deborah Dinner, Beyond "Best Practices": Employment Discrimination Law in the Neoliberal Era, 92 Ind. L.J. 1059 (2017); Deborah Dinner, The Costs of Reproduction: History and the Legal Construction of Sex Equality, 46 Harv. C.R.-C.L. L. Rev. 415 (2011).

that is advanced as free and best for us all and reveals that system as a man-made, exercise of power, with the very real and unjust consequence of wealth concentration in the hands of the few at the expense of the rest. The systems of subordination work together. So should their critiques.[799]

Is this the right way to describe the relationship between critiques of market libertarianism, and gender and race critiques? How else might it be described?

PUTTING THEORY INTO PRACTICE

5-47. A 2017 survey by the Federal Reserve system found that 40 percent of adults would not be able to cover an unexpected $400 in emergency expenses, and the proportions were even higher for people of color, controlling for their education level.[800] Imagine you are one of these adults. What choices do you have in dealing with such an emergency?

5-48. Your state legislature is considering a measure to give low-income individuals and couples who periodically attend parenting classes an annual tax deduction (or cash benefits if they do not pay taxes). Would you support the proposal? Should schools be required to offer marriage relationship skills and fatherhood classes? How about giving poor couples an annual cash "bonus" for staying married?

5-49. You are a single mother with two children under age 5. You have a minimum wage job at a local grocery store. It does not provide health benefits. Prepare a budget based on living expenses in your locality. Could you manage without welfare assistance? If not, what benefits would be most critical? With welfare assistance, could you meet basic subsistence needs?

5-50. In a new book, Dorothy Roberts argues that the child welfare system in the United States should be abolished.[801] As she wrote in a related blog post,

> Imagine if there were an arm of the state that sent government agents to invade Black people's homes, kept them under intense and indefinite surveillance, regulated their daily lives, and forcibly separated their families, often permanently. The left would put toppling this regime high on its agenda, right? This racist structure exists in the United States today, and yet the left pays little attention to it. The child welfare system — the assemblage of public and private child protection agencies, foster care, and preventive services — is a crucial part of the carceral machinery in Black communities. . . .
>
> The child welfare system is a powerful state policing apparatus that functions to regulate poor and working-class families — especially those that

---

799. Bartlett, supra note 793, at 275-76, 287 (citing Catharine A. MacKinnon, Toward a Feminist Theory of the State 125 (1989)).

800. Bd. of Governors of the Fed. Reserve Sys., Report on the Economic Well-being of U.S. Households in 2017, 21-22 (2018).

801. Dorothy Roberts, Torn Apart: How the Child Welfare System Destroys Black Families — and How Abolition Can Build a Safer World (2022).

are Black, Latinx, and Indigenous — by wielding the threat of taking their children from them. . . . In cities across the nation, CPS surveillance is concentrated in impoverished Black neighborhoods, where all parents are ruled by the agencies' threatening presence. Fifty-three percent of Black children in America will experience a CPS investigation at some point before their eighteenth birthday. During CPS investigations, caseworkers may inspect every corner of the home, interrogate family members about intimate details of their lives, strip-search children to look for evidence, and collect confidential information from schools, healthcare providers, and social service programs. If caseworkers detect a problem, like drug use, inadequate medical care, or insecure housing, they will coerce families into an onerous regimen of supervision that rarely addresses their needs. More disruptive still is the forcible family separation that often follows CPS investigations. . . . Most of the money spent on child welfare services goes to keeping children away from their families. . . .

Today's child welfare system still revolves around an ideology that confuses poverty with child neglect and attributes the suffering caused by structural inequities to parental pathologies. It then prescribes useless therapeutic remedies in place of radical social change. The abolition of family policing should be at the top of the left's agenda. . . . As with prison abolition, the aim is not to reform the child protection system; the aim is to replace it with a society that attends to children's welfare in a radically different way. With a common vision for meeting human needs and ensuring safety, we can build a world where caging people and tearing families apart are unimaginable.[802]

Do you agree? Why or why not?

5-51. The right to counsel in criminal cases is secured by Gideon v. Wainright. Two scholars have noted that this right has disproportionately offered protection for men, who more often engage with the criminal legal system. They also note that women are more likely to face compulsory and highly punitive encounters with the justice system in civil courts — particularly in the context of family law, eviction, and debt collection — and argue that *Gideon* should be extended to those cases.[803] Do you agree, particularly in the case of eviction?

5-52. Consider the issue of women's poverty through each of the theoretical frameworks presented in this book. What contributions, if any, does the framework make toward better understanding why women are disproportionately poor, and what should be done about it?

---

802. Dorothy Roberts, Abolish Family Policing, Too, Dissent (Summer 2021).

803. See Kathryn A. Sabbeth & Jessica K. Steinberg, The Gender of Gideon, 69 UCLA L. Rev. (forthcoming 2022); see also Gideon v. Wainwright, 372 U.S. 335 (1963).

Principal cases are indicated by italics.

A

A-B, In the Matter of, 526
A.C. v. Metropolitan Sch. Dist. of
    Martinsville, 334
ACLU v. Gonzales, 558
ACLU of La. v. Foster, 813
Adarand Constructors,
    Inc. v. Pena, 233
AFSCME v. Washington, 98
Ainsworth v. Ainsworth, 424
Alamo Rent-A-Car; EEOC v., 173
Aldrich v. Randolph Cent.
    Sch. Dist., 92
A.M. v. Indianapolis Pub. Schs., 358
American Acad. of Pediatrics
    v. Lungren, 807
American Booksellers Ass'n v. Hudnut,
    548, 555
American Library Ass'n; United States
    v., 558
American Nurses Ass'n v. Illinois, 98
A.N.A. v. Breckinridge Cnty. Bd. of
    Educ., 328
Anderson v. Fogelqvist, 241
Anthony; United States v., 40
A-R-C-G, In the Matter of, 525, 526
Arizona Governing Comm. for Tax
    Deferred Annuity & Deferred Comp.
    Plans v. Norris, 302
Arlene's Flowers, Inc.; State v., 214
Arlington Heights v. Metropolitan
    Housing Dev. Corp., 76
Arneault v. Arneault, 400
Arnold v. Barbers Hill Indep. Sch.
    Dist., 330
Ashcroft v. ACLU, 558
Ashcroft v. Free Speech Coalition, 558
Associated Gen. Contractors of Ohio, Inc.
    v. Drabnik, 233
AT&T Corp. v. Hulteen, 251
Attorney Gen. v. Mass. Interscholastic
    Athletic Ass'n, Inc., 351
Austin; People v., 562
Ayanna v. Dechert, LLP, 285, 289, 293

Ayotte v. Planned Parenthood of N. New
    England, 807

B

Baby M, In re, 822, 829, 830, 834, 835
Back v. Hastings on Hudson Union Free Sch.
    Dist., 285, 293, 294
Backus v. Baptist Med. Ctr., 260
Baehr v. Lewin, 384
Bah v. Mukasey, 708
Bair v. Shippensburg Univ., 491
Baker v. California Land Title Co., 155
Baker v. Nelson, 384
Baker v. State, 385
Ballard v. United States, 568, 623
Balliro, In re, 527
Balow v. Michigan State Univ., 368, 372
Barnes; People v., 665
Baskerville v. Culligan Int'l Co., 453
Batson v. Kentucky, 623
Bauer v. Lynch, 198
Baum; Doe v., 697
Baylor Univ.; Doe v., 692
Beattie v. Line Mountain Sch. Dist., 350
Beltran; People v., 544
Berndsen v. North Dakota Univ. Sys., 373
Berry v. Great Am. Dream, Inc., 199
Berry; People v., 528, *529,* 532
Bethel Sch. Dist. v. Fraser, 491
Biediger v. Quinnipiac Univ., 372,
    373, 375
Black, In re Marriage of, 421
Blackburn Coll.; Doe v., 488
Blank v. Sullivan & Cromwell, 617
Blew v. Verta, 422
Bloomberg L.P.; EEOC v., 591
Board of Dirs. of Rotary Int'l v. Rotary Club of
    Duarte, 200, 207, 208
Board of Educ. for Sch. Dist. of Phila.;
    United States v., 173
Board of Regents; Doe v., 691, 692
Board of Visitors of VMI; Doe v., 322
Bobb v. Municipal Court, 59
Boerne, City of v. Flores, 736

X

X option for gender identification, 15, 16

Y

Yale University, 702, 703–704
Yates, Andrea, 636, 637
Young, Iris Marion, 274
Young Women's Leadership School, 328

YouTube, 564
Yugoslavia, rape convictions in, 683
Yuracko, Kimberly, 191–192

Z

Zero Tolerance to FGM, 708
Zola, Warren K., 355–357
Zoning regulation of adult entertainment
    businesses, 712